The British Fighter since 1912

The Royal Air Force's solo aerobatic Tornado F 3 demonstrator for 1991, being flown by Flight Lieutenant Archie Neill and Flight Lieutenant Jim Brown of No 25 (Fighter) Squadron. The aeroplane is liveried in a stylised adaptation of this Squadron's black and silver colours to commemorate the 75th Anniversary of its formation in September 1915. In 1992 No 25 Squadron was formally adopted by the town of Folkestone in Kent, thereby recalling the long period between the World Wars when it was based at nearby Hawkinge. For a short time No 25 Squadron was the RAF's sole fighter squadron based in Britain. (Photo: Geoff Lee)

The British Fighter since 1912

Francis K Mason

PUTNAM

ALSO BY FRANCIS MASON IN THE
PUTNAM SERIES

Hawker Aircraft since 1920

First published in Great Britain in 1992 by
Putnam Aeronautical Books, an imprint of
Conway Maritime Press Ltd,
101 Fleet Street,
London EC4Y 1DE

British Library Cataloguing-in Publication Data
Mason, Francis K. (Francis Kenneth), 1928—
The British Fighter since 1912
I.   Title
623.74640941

ISBN 0 85177 852 6

Book designed and typeset by the Author in
Ehrhardt and Rockwell with Apple®
Macintosh® SE, using MicrosoftWord©,
Aldus PageMaker© and MacDraft©.
Acknowledgement is made to C A Mason.
Printed and bound in Great Britain by
Butler & Tanner Ltd, Frome

CONTENTS

INTRODUCTION

It is perhaps a sad moral reflection that, of all flying machines, the fighter aeroplane has throughout its 80-year history come to constitute in the public's mind the pinnacle of the aircraft designer's skill, the front-runner of flying spectacle and the ambition of the Service fledgling pilot. Speed and agility of the fighter, demonstrated by professional pilots at countless displays down the years, have nurtured this appeal, nowhere more dramatically than in Britain. Not surprisingly such an attitude is fiercely countered, even ridiculed by the devotees of other types of aircraft, often with justification (for who does not stand in awe of the supersonic Concorde?), yet it must be said that, for all the tenets of Douhet's doctrine that the bomber is the air force's *raison d'être*, the fighter has in most aspects of design been in the forefront of technology, for the demands for speed, acceleration, altitude and strength in the fighter have, in their achievement, pushed the limits of technical knowledge and ingenuity ever forward.

Britain has always been exceptionally fortunate in being able to call upon men of outstanding talents throughout those eighty years, both in producing and flying her aircraft and, if there is one quality that is common to both professions, it must be individualism. Men like Barnwell, Camm, Carter, de Havilland, Folland and Mitchell have left their indelible stamp on their creations no less than the flying men such as Bader, Ball, Beamont, Bedford, Bishop, Braham, Bulman, Cunningham, Duke, Johnson, Lucas, McCudden, Mannock, Saint, Sayer and Tuck—to mention but a handful of our legendary pilots. All were ready when their country called. All were supreme individualists, ready to back their own judgement, ability and experience, and were encouraged to do so in a society that applauded — and sometimes rewarded — a winner.

Yet it was Camm who once remarked that all military aircraft possess four dimensions; span, length, height and politics. And this has never been more appropriate than in the fighter aeroplane. When Trenchard was waging his battles in Whitehall to secure the survival of the Royal Air Force after the First World War, the fighter became a casualty, by default. Trenchard was a bomber man in the best Douhet tradition, so much so that 'security of base', the fourth principle of war, was permitted to lapse for almost a decade. The 'ten year rule' dominated not only the annual military appropriations but Air Force politics as well. Yet, when Trenchard left the Air Staff at the beginning of 1930, Sir John Salmond strived to restore a balance to the RAF's inventory by encouraging advances in fighter design — just ten years before the pivotal Battle of Britain. Well might the cynical politician, ignorant of the terrible risks undertaken, proclaim that the whole philosophy of the ten year rule had been fully justified.

Nevertheless, justifiable or not, the lesson of Trenchard's neglect (some would say, an unavoidable neglect) was to be stark in its reality, and is no less relevant half a century later. Britain had allowed her air defences to mark time, so much so that from an unchallenged position of great strength and efficiency at the Armistice of 1918, her Air Force was being overtaken in technology and manpower at an alarming rate fifteen years later, and it would be a further seven years before her defences could be strengthened sufficiently to withstand an assault. Central to that transformation were, of course, the creation of an exceptionally efficient air defence system, over which presided arguably the greatest-ever fighter commander, Hugh Dowding, the designers Mitchell and Camm, and the immortal Few.

The Battle of Britain occurred only a quarter century after the first true fighting aeroplane flew. As will be seen in this book, Britain produced over 200 different types of fighter during those 25 years, aircraft whose maximum speed crept up from less than 90 miles per hour to over 300, their ceiling from around 12,000 to well over 30,000 feet. In the next 50 years fewer than 70 different fighters have been produced in Britain, yet their performance has advanced from 300 to 1,300 miles per hour, their ceiling to well over 60,000 feet. More sobering is the fact that a fighting aeroplane in 1913 would have cost roughly the same as a fairly expensive private motor car; in 1990 the cost of a Tornado is comparable with that of a well-equipped hospital. At the dawn of air combat the aircraft designer sought to achieve flight stability in his wood-and-fabric creation; the fast jets of today, constructed of exotic materials such as titanium, aluminium/lithium alloys and carbon-fibre reinforced plastics are intentionally unstable in the interests of agility — such is the power of their control systems and the strength of their airframes. During the Kaiser's War, the pilot and observer/gunners could not abandon their aeroplanes *in extremis*, for the parachute was not in general use. Today the ejection seat is an integral part of every high performance military aircraft, and is designed to save the crew in almost any conceivable emergency and in any condition of flight. In fighter armament, fowling pieces firing buckshot, and carbines, have been replaced in turn by machine guns, large calibre cannon, and rocket projectiles; today the fighter may be armed with an active missile and fired at a target 'beyond visual range' with a better than average chance of destroying that target.

Such is the speed of technological advance as the twentieth century approaches its close that for any nation, bearing international responsibilities, to allow its air defences to become weakened by some nebulous 'peace dividend' — itself a euphemism for a sort of ten-year rule, and a sop to ideological pacifism — is to abrogate those responsibilities at a stroke. Let the lessons of the

Battle of Britain, Korea, Suez, the Falkland Islands and the Gulf War be seen in the context of the Geddes Axe, the ten year rule of the 1920s, the Socialists' cancellation of supersonic research in 1946, the 1957 Defence White Paper, the defence cuts of the mid-1960s, the run-down of the Fleet Air Arm in the 1970s, and the supposed peace dividend following the disintegration of the Communist Bloc.

Central to this nation's defence responsibility is its continuing ability to protect its cities and key installations in the metropolitan area as well as being capable, at short notice, to provide effective defence of overseas dependencies and to fulfil treaty obligations for collective security. To do so, its air force must possess equipment — not least a fighter force — and highly trained personnel equal to any potential aggressor. Without that ability, the hallmarks of civilised democracy, the Welfare State, a benevolent Monarchy, freedom of expression and a respected, domestic rule of law, are as nothing in a world beset around by international terrorism, political blackmail and proliferating dictatorships.

Any historical commentary on a relatively modern military subject is bound, almost by definition, to be constrained to some extent by secrecy, be it motivated by national security, commercial or professional safeguards, or personal considerations. Historical and technical research is a continuing process, alleviated from time to time by the rediscovery of lost records and by the regular expiry of the 30- and 50-year security restrictions under the Official Secrets Acts. Official records, so often interpreted after superficial examination as gospel, are frequently exposed as little more than partisan projection of 'fact' for lay consumption under the pretext of necessary propaganda. The subject of this book represents nothing less than a minefield, involving the many political sacred cows of successive governments, the highest endeavours of professional men and the economic strength and prestige of commercial manufacturers. Every so often a part of the minefield is swept, disclosing the nature of gaps in the historian's knowledge. One by one the anomalies of fact and assumption are explained.

Many years ago Putnam embarked on a series of books, each devoted to an aspect of aviation history compiled by specialists in their field, and together this series has come to represent a unique reference source for students of aviation history. It has to be said, however, that some of these works were completed at a time when the subject aircraft companies were still active as independent manufacturers within the industry. Since their publication the nature of this industry has undergone fundamental change; and old allegiances have become blurred by the worship of a corporate image. True, the spectre of nationalization was real but shortlived, yet the dogma of 'history is bunk' took its toll, and priceless records were, at best, severely thinned out or, worse, consigned to a convenient skip. It is to be hoped that the present and future captains of industry will recognise that in their custody lie the records of past endeavour, and that from those endeavours one may learn the lessons, salutory and otherwise, for the benefit of the future.

Nevertheless, serious research *is* a continuing activity, made easier by such agencies, vital to our heritage, as the Public Records Office, the Air Historical Branch and the Royal Air Force Museum, and it is from their archives that a growing knowledge of our recent aviation history can be ascertained.

Acknowledgements

Among the former Putnam titles was a book similarly titled to the present work, written by the late Peter Lewis over twenty years ago, and I must acknowledge that his work represented the inspiration for this book, although my approach to and treatment of the subject is rather closer to the established 'Putnam formula'; I have, moreover, been fortunate to benefit from the fruits of continuing research, both by other historians and myself, since Mr Lewis' book was last published.

I therefore express my indebtedness to the works of the late Charlie Andrews, the late Chris Barnes, J M Bruce, G R Duval, Robert Fairclough, the late A J Jackson, Derek James, the late H F King, Peter London, Eric Morgan, Harald Penrose, Stephen Ransom, the late Oliver Tapper, the late H A Taylor, Owen Thetford and Kenneth Wixey.

For their considerable assistance by unearthing records, I would especially thank R H Searle, Chief Librarian at the Royal Aerospace Establishment, Farnborough, to Peter Murton, Peter Elliott, Anna McIlwaine, Andrew Renwick and Ben Travers at the Royal Air Force Museum, and Flt Lt Rod Smith and Terry Heffernan, formerly in charge of records at the Aeroplane and Armament Experimental Establishment, Boscombe Down, and the long-suffering staff at the Public Records Office, Kew. I have been afforded unstinted help and encouragement by Harry Holmes of British Aerospace (Manchester), John Coombes of British Aerospace (Kingston), David Kamiya of British Aerospace (Preston), Darryl Cott of British Aerospace (Hatfield), Jim Colman of Boulton & Paul PLC, Norwich, Del Holyland of Martin-Baker Aircraft Co Ltd, Dave Birch of the Rolls-Royce Heritage Trust, Jack Titley of Rolls-Royce Ltd, Derby, and John Hutchinson of Rolls-Royce (Bristol) PLC. At Vickers PLC, Brian Wexham went to great trouble to ensure that I was able to select the best photographs still available from the Company's archives.

I have tried, where possible, to acknowledge the source of each photograph individually, which appears in this book, either to the owner of the original copyright or, where copyright has clearly lapsed under the terms of the 1989 Copyright Act, or has been reassigned, for the loan of a print. I must, however, express my sincere appreciation to Roger Jackson, Jack Bruce, Eric Morgan and Ray Sturtivant, new and old friends who have clearly gone out of their way to make easier my job of assembling a large collection of historic photographs, many of which are extremely rare, some even unique. To Roger, who has painstakingly administered his late father's superb collection of photographs, as well as those of Chris Barnes and Charlie Andrews, and went to great trouble to look out pictures of inestimable value for my use, I offer my unqualified gratitude. Jack, Eric and Ray were particularly generous with their loans, especially as there was no knowing whether they would need the pictures to illustrate their own literary works.

To John Stroud, a much respected historian in his own right who has for so many years been Editor of the entire Putnam series (which, by the way, also includes a whole range of authoritative books on commercial and foreign aviation), I can only express my admiration and thanks for undertaking the daunting task of reading, checking and advising on the proofs of this work. I know my fellow Authors will join me in recognising John as the guiding light in our literary efforts.

Finally I should acknowledge the use of many of the general arrangement drawings originally executed (often by meticulous reference to the manufacturers' originals, now alas dispersed to the four winds) by the late L E Bradford for the Putnam books; these drawings contributed to the reputation, authority and

welcome uniformity of the series in its early days, and in this respect I am also grateful to the Authors for their permission to reproduce these drawings. Having done my best to execute drawings of 'post-Bradford' aircraft, I have come to realise the magnitude of his achievement and the accuracy of his work.

The Putnam Series relevant to this book

Aircraft of the Royal Air Force — Owen Thetford
Armstrong Whitworth Aircraft since 1913 — Oliver Tapper
Avro Aircraft since 1908 — A J Jackson
Blackburn Aircraft since 1910 — A J Jackson
Bristol Aircraft since 1910 — C H Barnes
British Aeroplanes, 1914-1918 — J M Bruce
British Aircraft, 1809-1914 — Peter Lewis
British Aviation: The Pioneer Years — Harald Penrose
British Aviation: The Great War and Armistice — Harald Penrose
British Flying Boats and Amphibians, 1909-1952 — G R Duval
British Naval Aircraft since 1912 — Owen Thetford
De Havilland Aircraft since 1915 — A J Jackson
English Electric Aircraft and their Predecessors — Stephen Ransom and Robert Fairclough
Fairey Aircraft since 1915 — H A Taylor
Gloster Aircraft since 1917 — Derek N James
Handley Page Aircraft since 1907 — C H Barnes
Hawker Aircraft since 1920 — Francis K Mason
Parnall Aircraft since 1914 — Kenneth E Wixey
Saunders and Saro Aircraft since 1917 — Peter London
Shorts Aircraft since 1900 — C H Barnes
Sopwith Aircraft, 1912-1920 — H F King
Supermarine Aircraft since 1914 — C F Andrews and E B Morgan
Vickers Aircraft since 1908 — C F Andrews and E B Morgan
Westland Aircraft since 1915 — Derek N James

Clarification of Convention and Style

In an effort to conform to correct contemporary styles of usage, recourse has been made to Ministry and Company Instructions as a guide.

1. Mr Noel Pemberton Billing used no hyphen in his own name, but inserted the hyphen in the name of his Company, Pemberton-Billing Ltd, and therefore also in references to the Company's aircraft.
2. Prior to about August 1917 a comma was inserted in the name of the Company Sir W G Armstrong, Whitworth & Co Ltd; thereafter, as Sir W G Armstrong Whitworth Aircraft Ltd, it was omitted.
3. Suffix letters used in the designations of sub-variants of aircraft produced by the Royal Aircraft Factory were inconsistent in contemporary usage, being both capital and lower case letters. Following an internal memorandum, said to

have been issued in 1917, capital suffix letters were adopted (eg, B.E.2C, S.E.5A, etc), including retrospective references, and for uniformity are used throughout this work. The Author is aware of continuing controversy with regard to this matter.
4. An Air Ministry Instruction, confirmed by the SBAC, issued in December 1947, required the Mark numbers of aircraft and Service engines, equipment, etc, to change universally from Roman to Arabic characters with effect from 1 January 1948; this Instruction was not retrospective. Thus Mark XX and Mark 20 are both correct, depending on the date reference is made.
5. Although the American term 'Radar' was not adopted in Britain until about 1942 (the initials RDF having been employed in Britain prior to that date), the word 'Radar' is used throughout this book according to common practice.

1. THE FIRST WORLD WAR AND THE ORIGINS OF AIR COMBAT

Among the great pioneers of British aviation, Geoffrey de Havilland was pre-eminent as a designer-constructor-pilot, and it is by no means fanciful to attribute to him the origins of the fighting aeroplane in Britain. His first design had been built at Fulham and taken to Crux Easton in Hampshire for testing. Powered by a 45 hp Iris four-cylinder engine and flown by de Havilland himself, the aircraft crashed on its first flight early in April 1910, fortunately without injuring the pilot. This was followed by a second design, the de Havilland No 2, also powered by the Iris engine; it was first flown on 10 September the same year at Newbury, Berkshire, and on this machine the intrepid pilot set about teaching himself to fly!

Beset by financial strictures, de Havilland obtained the appointment as assistant designer and test pilot with the Army Balloon Factory at Farnborough in December 1910, taking with him the No 2 aircraft, which the War Office purchased for £400 and promptly designated it the F.E.1 (Farman Experimental, owing to a superficial resemblance to the current Farman configuration). After being flown by de Havilland at Farnborough in January 1911, the F.E.1 suffered an accident, but was rebuilt and appeared once more in September, now being re-designated the F.E.2; it featured a two-seat nacelle with dual controls, and in 1912 tests were made mounting a Maxim machine gun in the front of the nacelle.

While it might be said that the Royal Aircraft Factory cut its teeth on the F.E.2 , other designers had been moving towards military aircraft. Claude Grahame-White had produced several aeroplanes since 1910 and they had become familiar sights at Hendon and flying meetings in the hands of private owners. His Type 6 Military Biplane, designed by John North, followed the familiar pusher formula and featured a Colt machine gun in the nose of the nacelle.

As Hendon catered for the public appetite with numerous air meetings, Brooklands had become the focal point for aircraft development among the private manufacturers and flying schools. Among the former were T O M Sopwith, A V Roe, Howard Wright, Flanders, Vickers and Martin and Handasyde; a dozen flying schools had, by 4 August

1914, trained no fewer than 318 pilots.

T O M Sopwith, himself a famous sporting pilot, had assembled a small staff at Brooklands and in 1912 delivered his first product, the Tractor Biplane, to the RNAS. The proceeds of this sale were used to acquire premises in Kingston-upon-Thames, establishing workshops and a tiny design section. In 1913 the Sopwith Aviation Company was formed, and among the early aircraft that emerged from these shops was the Tabloid, a little tractor biplane with an 80 hp Gnome; the prototype, modified as a seaplane, won the 1914 Schneider Trophy contest at 86.75 mph. Both the Tabloid and the Schneider seaplane won contracts, the latter remaining in service throughout the First World War.

The British and Colonial Aeroplane Company, whose aircraft bore the name 'Bristol' as a trademark until 1920 when B & CAC went into liquidation, had produced aeroplanes for military purposes since 1911, principally of the so-called boxkite configuration. An abortive digression into marine aircraft was followed by an attractive single-seat, tractor biplane which came to be known as the Bristol Scout A, and this was followed by a family of related scouts, two Scout Bs accompanying No 5 Squadron, RFC, to France in September 1914.

The other fighting aircraft manufacturer to undertake production of combat designs was Vickers Ltd, long known for its manufacture of armaments. The company's first five aircraft (produced during 1911) were all what were known as 'school machines'; the Vickers No 6 was entered for the 1912 Military Trials but without success. Later that year, in response to an Admiralty contract for a gun-carrying aircraft, work began on a series of designs that came to be known as the Gunbus family. All were of the pusher biplane layout. The first five aircraft, E.F.B. 1 to 5 (Experimental Fighting Biplanes) were variations on a common theme, and E.F.B. 5 became the prototype of the definitive F.B.5 Gunbus — of which more than 200 were produced, including 50 in France.

Despite these efforts to produce gun-armed fighting aeroplanes during the 18 months before the outbreak of war in August 1914, no such aircraft had reached operational use, although trials with a handful of aircraft had been made by the

RFC and RNAS with Maxim and Lewis guns.

On the outbreak of war the RFC possessed a total of 63 aeroplanes, while 50 landplanes and seaplanes — as well as six airships — equipped the RNAS. Only seven RFC Squadrons had been formed, and of these, Nos 2, 3, 4 and 5 Squadrons flew to France during the first six weeks of war, taking with them a heterogeneous collection of aircraft.

The increasing activity by enemy airships, as much over Britain as over the French Channel ports and the British Expeditionary Force in France, spurred efforts to arm RFC and RNAS scouts sent up on 'anti-Zeppelin' patrols towards the end of 1914.

It was the appearance of the German Fokker monoplane over the Western Front that focussed the War Office's need to equip the RFC with aircraft capable of meeting the enemy scouts on equal terms. The Fokker monoplane was itself not exceptional in terms of performance (with a speed not significantly different from that of the Sopwith Tabloid); its tactical strength lay in its ability to fire a machine gun through its propeller without its bullets striking the blades. This enabled the pilot to fly directly at his adversary, aim his gun and fire while continuing to manœuvre so as to hold his sights on the target. The French had also addressed the problem and had produced a similar system of firing forward, but in this instance the propeller was fitted with deflector plates which protected the blades from damage while allowing a high proportion of bullets to pass through the propeller arc.

The fact that no reliable interrupter gear had yet been developed for British aircraft resulted in the perpetuation of the 'gunbus' pusher, an archaic design that might otherwise have been allowed to disappear much sooner than was the case. The other alternative was to fit a gun or guns on the upper wing or on the sides of the fuselage of tractor biplanes, using flexible mountings, and this expedient was undertaken (unofficially) by individual pilots—with limited success.

By mid-1915 the number of RFC squadrons in France had grown to nine, but in the main their aircraft consisted of B.E.2Cs, Tabloids and a handful of Bristol Scout Cs.

In Britain, while the B.E.2C had entered production at Farnborough, Geoffrey de Havilland had been appointed chief designer with the Aircraft Manufacturing Company (Airco) at Hendon in June 1914. His first design in his new post reverted to the gunbus formula, being a two-seat reconnaissance biplane armed with a machine gun in the nacelle's nose. Encouraged by this aircraft, the D.H.1, de Havilland embarked on a smaller, single-seat derivative, the D.H.2. This little aeroplane, regarded as the first successful British operational fighter, was surprisingly agile for its configuration, with the result that orders totalling around 450 aircraft were placed, and these served with nine RFC squadrons. Armed with a single gun, the D.H.2 did much to blunt the Fokker 'scourge', though by the time it reached the Front in February 1916 the threat was already diminishing.

The age of air combat had arrived. The first steps had been taken to establish the parameters of the dogfighter: high speed, agility, good rate of climb,

effective armament and strength of construction. With a number of unorthodox exceptions, this was the accepted pattern of design aims in a long line of distinguished fighting scouts that emanated from the factories in Britain during the last two years of the First World War, with the Sopwith Pup, Triplane, Camel and Snipe, the S.E.5 and 5A and the Bristol F.2B Fighter matching and eventually overcoming the best that Germany could produce.

With the aircraft industry, built on such famous names as Bristol, Vickers, Sopwith, Avro, Shorts, Fairey, Blackburn, and Handley Page, not forgetting the Royal Aircraft Factory, others arrived on the scene to exploit the traditional skills in wooden and metal construction, with young designers attracted by the widening vistas of aviation. Companies like Martinsyde, Beardmore, Boulton & Paul, Pemberton-Billing and many others, all contributed to the air combat scene. Fighter armament advanced from the single cavalry carbine of the Bristol

Scout to multiple Vickers and Lewis rifle-calibre machine guns and, in due course, to the successful development of the Vickers, Scarff-Dibovski, Ross and Sopwith-Kauper gun synchronizing gear to permit firing through the propeller.

In engine design Britain was slower to achieve reliability than continental manufacturers, and during the first half of the War engines of predominantly French origin (Anzani, Clerget, Gnome, Le Rhône and Renault) featured in a majority of British fighting aeroplanes. Later Rolls-Royce, Bentley, Beardmore, Wolseley and Napier engines started to demonstrate their power and reliability, and inevitably supplanted the foreign designs, although by no means exclusively.

Thus, by the Armistice in November 1918, the Royal Air Force (then only seven months old after its creation on 1 April that year) was the most powerful air service in the world. In every sphere of military aviation, by no means least in fighters, British aircraft were supreme.

Royal Aircraft Factory F.E.2

Origins of the Royal Aircraft Factory's F.E.2 lay in Geoffrey de Havilland's second aeroplane, which was bought by the Factory on his appointment as designer and pilot at Farnborough at the end of 1910. It was initially named the F.E.1 (Farman Experimental, on account of its resemblance to contemporary Farman biplanes), but after a crash it was re-built in September 1911 with a 50hp Gnome engine and re-designated the F.E.2. It was again re-built, this time with a 70hp Renault, in 1913, but crashed the following year. In the meantime de Havilland had prepared a new design, ostensibly based on the F.E.2 yet bearing little resemblance to the previous aeroplane, being a three-bay pusher biplane in which an observer-gunner occupied the front cockpit, with the pilot's cockpit behind and raised about eighteen inches. This version, the F.E. 2A, appeared early in 1915 and was designed as a fighting aircraft from the outset, so the designation was accordingly changed to Fighting Experimental. A dozen aircraft were ordered for the RFC to be powered by the 100hp Green,

A late production F.E.2B night fighter, B487, built by Ransomes, Sims & Jefferies of Ipswich with a 160hp Beardmore. (Photo: Ransomes, Sims & Jefferies Ltd).

but this was found to be unsatisfactory owing to poor power-weight ratio and the next version, the F.E.2B, was modified to take the 120hp Beardmore driving a two-blade propeller, the top half of the engine being uncowled.

The F.E.2B was ordered into production at the Factory and four sub-contractors, and the first aircraft was handed over to the RFC in May, being delivered to No 6 Squadron at Abeele in France, commanded by Maj G S Shepherd. The first aircraft was flown to France by Capt Louis Arbon Strange (later Lt-Col, DSO, OBE, MC, AFC*) on 15 May. Within three months the 'Fokker scourge'

was being experienced by the Allied air forces on the Western Front, and more fighter squadrons were hurriedly formed with F.E.2Bs, namely Nos 20, 22 and 25, and these moved to France early in 1916. Armed with a single Lewis gun in the bow position, the F.E.2B began to make its presence felt even though, unlike the Fokker monoplane, it lacked a synchronized front gun. In fact both the F.E.2B and the single-seat D.H.2 (the latter also arriving in France in growing numbers) possessed surprising agility. The famous German pilot, Max Immelmann, fell to the aircraft of 2/Lieut G R McCubbin and Corp J H Waller of No

The prototype F.E.2D, 7995, showing the 200hp Rolls-Royce Mk I driving a four-blade propeller, and stack-type exhaust pipes; note the nosewheel-type main undercarriage and the low-sided pilot's cockpit — characteristic of early F.E.2Ds. (Photo: The Bristol Aeroplane Co Ltd.)

25 Squadron on 18 June 1916. During the great Battles of the Somme F.E.2Bs gave valuable service both in air combat and in gun attacks against enemy ground forces.

A total of 1,939 F.E.2Bs was built, and served on 32 RFC squadrons. A new version, the F.E.2C night fighter, was produced in which the cockpits of the two crew members were transposed, the pilot occupying the front cockpit to facilitate night landing. However, only two examples were built, of which one served with No 25 Squadron in 1916.

Although a change to the 160hp Beardmore in later F.E.2Bs had improved the aircraft's speed at sea level from 80 mph to 91 mph, it was considered inadequate to meet the new German fighting scouts that were coming into service in 1916. A further engine change, to the 250hp Rolls-Royce Mk I or III engine — later named the Eagle — in a somewhat cleaner cowling, characterized the F.E.2D which arrived in service in June. Unfortunately the first aircraft to land in France was delivered intact to the Germans when the pilot accidentally landed at Lille, mistaking it for St Omer.

The more powerful Rolls-Royce gave little improvement at low altitude but, owing to less power loss as height increased, bestowed a gain of about 10 mph at 5,000 feet. Be that as it may, the Germans were already one step ahead with their Fokker D II, soon to be joined by the D III with a speed of 100 mph — and twin front guns.

Moreover, with the arrival of the long awaited gun synchronizing gear in Brit-ain and France, a new generation of front-gun tractor biplane scouts was on the threshold of service, so that the days of the pusher biplane fighter were, by the autumn of 1916, already numbered. As the F.E.2D began joining or replacing the F.E.2B in service it became immediately clear that the Germans had, by examination of the captured aircraft, identified the F.E.2D's weak spot — an absence of rearward defence — and, as losses to enemy tractor scouts increased, a second Lewis gun on a telescopic mounting was added between the cockpits capable of firing aft over the top wing. To do so the observer had to stand on his seat, exposing almost the whole of his body to the slipstream. Nevertheless there occurred a number of combats in which the old pusher fighters gave good account of themselves, as exemplified by a fight on 6 July 1917, between six F.E. 2Ds of No 20 Squadron and about forty enemy fighters; the British pilots forced down five German aircraft, one of which was flown by the redoubtable Manfred von Richthofen, who was wounded.

The suitability of the F.E.2 for night flying prompted the RFC to adapt the 2D for night bombing, the value of which was becoming apparent by early 1917. Henceforth, therefore, this re-

Type: Single pusher engine, two-seat, three-bay fighting scout biplane.
Manufacturers: The Royal Aircraft Factory, Farnborough, Hants; Boulton & Paul Ltd, Norwich, Norfolk; Richard Garrett & Sons, Leiston, Suffolk; Ransomes, Sims & Jefferies, Ipswich, Suffolk; G & J Weir Ltd, Glasgow; Alex Stephen & Sons, Glasgow.
Powerplant: (F.E.2A) 100hp Green; (F.E.2B) 120 or 160hp Beardmore; (F.E.2C) 160hp Beardmore; (F.E.2D) 250hp Rolls-Royce (Eagle) Mk I or III. For other experimental installations, see text.
Dimensions: Span, 47ft 9in; length, 32ft 3in; height, 12ft 7½in; wing area, 494 sq ft.
Weights: (F.E.2D) Tare, 2,509lb; all-up, 3,469lb.
Performance: (F.E.2D) Max speed, 94 mph at 5,000ft; climb to 5,000ft, 11 min; service ceiling, 17,500ft; endurance, 3¼ hours.
Armament (late F.E.2Bs and F.E.2D fighters): One bracket-mounted 0.303in Lewis machine gun in front of observer's cockpit, and one Lewis gun mounted between cockpits.
Prototypes: F.E.2 (Renault), No 604; F.E.2A, No 2864; F.E.2D, No 7995.
Summary of Production: (F.E.2B), 51 by Royal Aircraft Factory; 250 by Boulton & Paul; 436 by Weir; 250 by Ransomes; 60 by Garrett; 150 by Stephens; 740 by unknown manufacturers. (F.E.2D), 85 by Royal Aircraft Factory; 300 by Boulton & Paul.
Summary of RAF Service: F.E.2Bs served with Nos 6, 11, 12, 16, 18, 20, 23, 24, 28, 33, 36, 51, 58, 64, 83, 90, 100, 101, 102, 116, 118, 131, 133, 148, 149, 166, 191, 192, 199, 200 and 246 Squadrons of the RFC and RAF. F.E.2Ds served with Nos 20, 25, 33, 51, 57, 83, 101, 102, 148, 149 and 192 Squadrons.

An F.E.2B, built by G & J Weir Ltd, and experimentally modified as a night fighter with two Lewis guns attached to a searchlight, power for which was provided by a wind-driven generator under the nose. Note the four lights under each wing — presumably added to facilitate night landing — and the Holt flare brackets. The 120hp Beardmore engine drives a two-blade propeller. The speed of this aircraft must have been severely reduced by all these accoutrements! (Photo: The Bristol Aeroplane Co Ltd.)

sponsibility was increasingly assumed by the F.E.2D squadrons in France. At home, F.E.2Bs and 2Ds were issued to Home Defence squadrons, starting at the end of 1916, in the rôle of anti-Zeppelin night fighters, but usually proved unable to reach the height normally flown by the enemy airships. Several interceptions were thwarted by the F.E.'s inability to climb much above about 14,000 feet. A number of experi-ments was undertaken to improve the fighters' armament, including the mount-ing of a one-pounder quick-firing gun, twin Lewis guns coupled to a searchlight on the nose, and of 0.45in Maxim guns. As a means of reducing weight and drag, Nos 36 and 51 (Home Defence) Squad-rons converted their F.E.2Ds to single-seaters by fairing over the front cockpit and arming their aircraft with either one or two fixed Lewis guns in the nose.

In the course of constant attempts to wring more speed from the old biplane, trial installations of the 284hp Rolls-Royce Eagle III, 200 hp RAF 3A and 230hp BHP engines were examined, the latter aircraft being the F.E.2H. None was adopted for service, and the F.E.2B and 2D soldiered on right up to the Armistice, aircraft that were regarded with affection, but whose passing was not mourned.

Royal Aircraft Factory B.S.1

Designed by Geoffrey de Havilland in 1912 at the Royal Aircraft Factory, the B.S.1 (c.f. Blériot Scout, indicating a tractor aeroplane) was the first single-seat high-speed scout to be built as such anywhere in the world. It was an ex-traordinarily advanced concept and an attractive little biplane with well-stag-gered wings. In some respects it clearly owed its design to experience gained in the B.E.2 (Blériot Experimental) — itself a derivative of the classic Blériot tractor monoplane.

Unlike, however, the customary rec-tangular-section fuselage, the B.S.1 featured a circular-section wooden monocoque structure blending into a 100hp two-row ten-cylinder Gnome engine. Streamlined flying wires, or Raf-wires, were employed and cut-outs in the upper and lower wings provided the pilot with a good field of vision.

De Havilland first flew the B.S.1 during March 1913, but later the same month the aircraft crashed from a flat spin and was damaged, the pilot suffer-ing a broken jaw. The aeroplane was repaired and, in an attempt to improve directional control, the rudder was en-larged and fins added above and below the rear fuselage. A new engine, the 80hp Gnome, was fitted together with a propeller of reduced pitch; the aircraft was re-designated the B.S.2, and shortly afterwards the S.E.2 (Santos Experi-mental). Before its accident, the B.S.1's performance had been measured, re-turning a speed of 91.4 mph, a climb of 900 feet per minute, and an endurance of three hours.

The first aeroplane in the world to be designed and built from the start as a single-engine, single-seat fighting scout, the R.A.F. B.S.1 at Farnborough in 1913. (Photo: Royal Aerospace Establishment, Neg. No 71197)

Type: Single-engine, single-seat tractor biplane scout.
Manufacturer: The Royal Aircraft Factory, Farnborough, Hants.
Powerplant: 100hp Gnome ten-cylinder two-row air-cooled engine.
Structure: Wooden monocoque fuselage of circular section; two-spar wings of spruce and ash construction with fabric covering.
Dimensions: Wing span, 27ft 6in; length, 22ft. 0in.
Weight: All-up, approx. 1,200lb.
Performance: Max speed, 91mph at sea level; initial climb, 900ft/min; endurance, three hours.
Armament: None.
Prototype: One (first flown by Geoffrey de Havilland in March 1913). No production.

Royal Aircraft Factory F.E.3/A.E.1

Built at the Royal Aircraft Factory early in 1913, the F.E.3 (Fighting Experi-mental) was an interesting two-bay two-seat pusher biplane designed as a gun-carrier. The principal feature of note was the absence of the customary pairs of tail booms to support the empennage, their place being taken by a single tubular boom around which the hollow propeller shaft rotated. Torsional rigid-ity of the tail unit was achieved by plentiful bracing wires, tensioned be-tween the wings and sternpost, and between the landing skids and tailplane.

Power was provided by a French 80hp Chenu engine (of somewhat un-reliable reputation that had recently powered Coventry Ordnance and Mar-tin Handasyde sporting aircraft) which drove the pusher propeller by means of a shaft under the nacelle to a chain drive at the rear.

After brief flying trials in the hands of

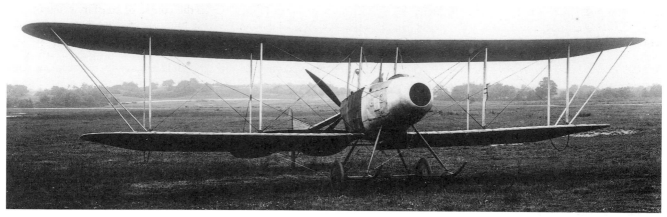

The Royal Aircraft Factory's F.E.3 at Farnborough in 1913. (Photo: Royal Aerospace Establishment Neg No 82 dated 1 June 1913)

de Havilland and other Farnborough pilots the aircraft was fitted with a single 1½-pdr Coventry Ordnance quick-firing gun which fired through the engine cooling intake, but only ground firing tests were performed during the summer of 1913.

The aircraft was also referred to as the A.E.1 (Armoured Experimental), but was not proceeded with, and saw no service.

Type: Single pusher engine, two-seat, two-bay biplane.
Manufacturer: Royal Aircraft Factory, Farnborough, Hants.
Powerplant: One 80hp Chenu engine with shaft and chain drive to four-blade pusher propeller mounted on hollow shaft through which passed the single tail support boom.
Structure: Mixed wood and metal nacelle structure with metal and fabric covering; twin-spar wooden three-bay wing structure with moderate stagger and fabric covering. Single tubular tail support boom.
Dimensions: Span, 48ft; length, 33ft; wing area, 480 sq ft.
Weight Loaded: 2,100lb.
Performance: Max speed, 75 mph at sea level; initial climb, 350 ft/min; ceiling, 5,000ft.
Armament: Ground trials with 37mm 1½-pdr COW gun in nose of nacelle.
Prototype: One. No production.

Vickers E.F.B.1 Destroyer

One of the earliest fighting aeroplane requirements, if not the first, issued by the Admiralty after the creation of the Naval Wing of the RFC in 1912, was for a gun-carrying machine whose armament was intended to be used for offensive as distinct from purely defensive purposes. Thus, by implication owing to the inability to fire forward through a tractor propeller, this dictated the pusher biplane configuration.

Vickers, Sons & Maxim Ltd had produced aeroplanes since January 1911, almost all monoplanes, but late the following year Major Archibald Reith Low and George H Challenger set about the design of the first of the famous Gunbus series, the E.F.B.1 (Experimental Fighting Biplane); it was also named the Destroyer, and earned a contract for Vickers early in 1913.

Employing two pairs of steel tail booms attached at their forward ends to the rear spar of the mainplanes and

The E.F.B.1 Destroyer on Vickers' stand at the 1913 Olympia Aero Show. Generous tailplane and elevator areas were characteristic of all the Gunbus designs. (Photo: *'Flight'*)

converging to meet at the sternpost, the two-seat aircraft featured generous wing stagger, and the forward raking of the interplane struts was matched by the rake of the tail boom struts, thereby lending the aircraft an air of aggression. The internal structure was of steel tube throughout, the wings being fabric-covered and the nacelle clad in duralumin sheet.

A 60/80hp Wolseley eight-cylinder vee air-cooled engine drove a Vickers-Levasseur two-blade propeller with scimitar-shaped blades. The front cockpit was occupied by the observer who was provided with a 0.303in Vickers-Maxim gun, mounted so as to traverse through 60-degree lateral and vertical arcs.

The E.F.B.1 was displayed at the

1913 Olympia Aero Show, but unfortunately crashed soon afterwards — possibly on its first flight — almost certainly owing to longitudinal instability.

Type: Single pusher engine, two-seat fighting biplane.
Manufacturer: Vickers Ltd, Erith, Kent.
Powerplant: One 60/80hp Wolseley eight-cylinder air-cooled engine driving a four-blade Vickers-Levasseur pusher propeller.
Structure: Fabric-covered, all-metal twin-spar wings with two pairs of steel tubular tail booms. Duralumin sheet-clad, steel-frame nacelle. Skid-and-wheel undercarriage.
Dimensions: Span, 40ft 0in; length, 27ft 6in; height, 11ft 11in; wing area, 380 sq ft.
Weights: Tare, 1,760lb; all-up, 2,660lb.
Performance: Max speed, 70 mph at sea level; initial climb, 450 ft/min; endurance, 4½ hr.
Armament: One 0.303in Vickers-Maxim machine gun in nose of nacelle.
Prototype: One. No production.

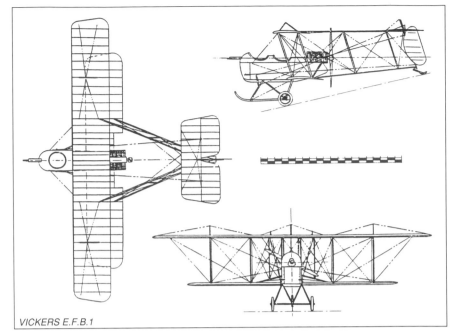

VICKERS E.F.B.1

Grahame-White Type 6

An almost exact contemporary of the Royal Aircraft Factory's F.E.3, the Grahame-White Type 6 gun-carrier was designed by John Dudley North, the 19-year-old graduate of the Aeronautical Syndicate who joined Claude Grahame-White at Hendon in 1912. Like the F.E.3, North's Type 6 also used a tail boom which passed through the pusher propeller shaft.

However the design differed in several important respects. Careful to avoid a lack of torsional rigidity in the tail unit (which was to lead to the F.E.3 being grounded), North retained two conventional steel tubular tail booms below the propeller shaft boom, thereby obtaining a triangular section structure that could be cross-braced to provide greater strength. Like the F.E.2, the engine, this time a 90hp Austro-Daimler, was located in the front of the nacelle — completely enclosed — but in this instance the engine's crankshaft itself was extended aft, below the cockpits, to chain reduction sprockets at the rear of the nacelle. The observer-gunner's cockpit was located in the centre of the nacelle, with the pilot's cockpit immediately behind him.

A 30-calibre Colt machine gun on a flexible mounting, capable of traversing

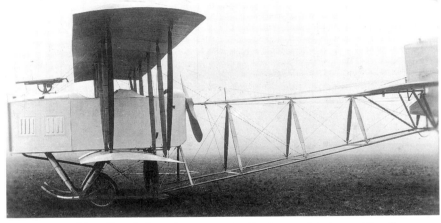

The Grahame-White Type 6. Scarcely apparent in this photograph is the exceptionally narrow-track undercarriage, the landing wheels being located inboard of the skids.

90 degrees either side and 50 degrees in azimuth, was positioned in front of the gunner's position.

Grahame-White was clearly competing against Farnborough's F.E.2 and F.E.3, as well as Vickers' Gunbus, for Admiralty orders, and his Type 6 duly appeared at the 1913 Olympia Aero Show. When, however, the Farn-borough pilots criticised the suspect tail support structure of the F.E.3, interest centred on the Vickers E.F.B. series. North accordingly abandoned the unorthodox tail boom arrangement and in his next gun-carrier essay, the Type 11, adopted the conventional four-boom layout.

Type: Single pusher engine, two-seat, fighting biplane.
Manufacturer: The Grahame-White Aviation Co Ltd, Hendon, Middlesex.
Powerplant: One 90hp Austro-Daimler water-cooled in-line engine driving two-blade pusher propeller.
Structure: Predominantly steel tubular structure with fabric-covered parallel-chord unstaggered wings; three-boom tail support structure. Skid-and-wheel undercarriage.
Dimensions: Span, 42ft 6in; length, 33ft 9in.
Weights: Tare, 2,200lb; all-up, 2,950lb.
Performance: Max speed, 70 mph at sea level; initial climb, 340 ft/min; endurance, 2¾ hr.
Armament: One 30-calibre Colt machine gun on nose of nacelle.
Prototype: One. No production and no Service number allotted.

Vickers E.F.B.2

Even before the Vickers E.F.B.1 was lost early in its flight trials, Archibald Low was at work on a new design in a further attempt to meet the Admiralty's requirement for a gun carrier. Not satisfied with the new Wolseley engine, he now turned to the Gnome *monosoupape* nine-cylinder rotary, claimed by its manufacturers to develop 100hp. This aeroplane, the E.F.B.2, featured wings of slightly reduced span and overhang, and without stagger, the interplane struts, tail boom struts and stern post all being vertical. The large tailplane was now almost semi-circular in plan, and the single central landing skid gave place to a pair of skids located immediately inboard of the wheels.

An unusual feature was the inclusion of a pair of huge celluloid windows on each side of the nacelle, while the decking immediately forward of each cockpit coaming was also transparent. A trunnion-mounted Vickers-Maxim machine gun, with limited arcs of fire, was incorporated in the extreme nose — but in such a position that prevented accurate aiming.

From all accounts the E.F.B.2 was pleasant to fly, being flown frequently during the second half of 1913 at Brooklands by Capt Herbert F Wood, Vickers' technical adviser, and by Harold Barnwell, the company's chief pilot. It was clear, however, that the Gnome *monosoupape* was not giving anything like its widely advertised power, and the E.F.B.2's performance was disappointing, failing even to match that of the earlier aircraft. Nevertheless, the aeroplane went a long way in encouraging Low to persevere with the Gunbus formula, backed strongly by Capt Wood.

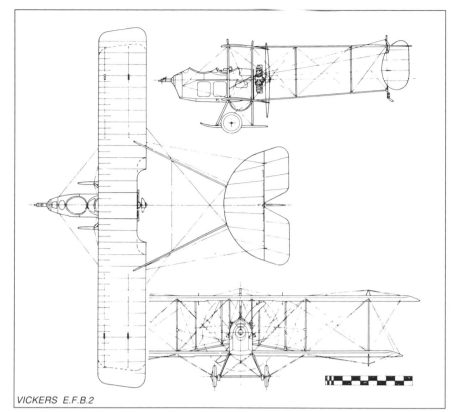

VICKERS E.F.B.2

Type: Single pusher engine, two-seat fighting biplane.

Manufacturer: Vickers Ltd (Aviation Dept), Knightsbridge, London.

Powerplant: One 80hp Gnome *monosoupape* nine-cylinder air-cooled rotary engine driving two-blade pusher propeller.

Structure: Predominantly steel-tubular construction with fabric-covered wings and tail, and duralumin-covered nacelle; twin skid-and-wheel undercarriage.

Dimensions: Span, 38ft 7in; length, 29ft 2in; height, 9ft 7in; wing area, 380 sq ft.

Weights: Tare, 1,050 lb; all-up, 1,760lb.

Performance: Max speed, 60 mph at sea level; initial climb, 200 ft/min; endurance, 2¼ hr.

Armament: Single trunnion-mounted 0.303in Vickers-Maxim machine gun in extreme nose of nacelle.

Prototype: One. No production.

The Vickers E.F.B.2 at Brooklands in 1913. (Photo: Vickers Ltd., via Eric Morgan)

Sopwith Tabloid

The arrival on the aviation scene of the diminutive Sopwith Tabloid towards the end of 1913 was widely regarded as the most momentous event of the year. Originally conceived as a conveniently-proportioned two-seat sporting biplane, which Harry Hawker could take with him to visit his home in Australia, the design was schemed up in chalk on the floor of a skating rink — then T O M Sopwith's 'factory' in Canbury Park Road, Kingston-upon-Thames — by Sopwith, Hawker, Sigrist and others; it was then formalised by R J Ashfield, the company's chief draughtsman. Construction of the aircraft, known then as the

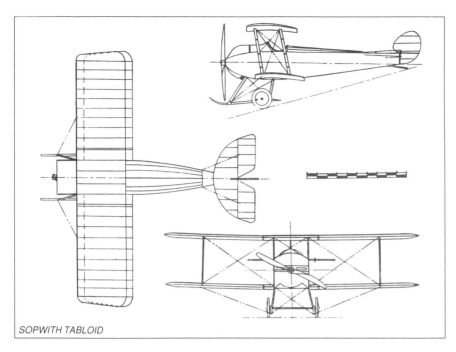

SOPWITH TABLOID

S.S., was completed in great secrecy within two months, and first flown by Hawker in November 1913 at Brooklands.

Powered by an 80hp Gnome the aeroplane, now named the Tabloid, was a tractor biplane with a single cockpit in which pilot and passenger sat side-by-side. Most unusual for its day, it possessed single-bay wings while the rudder, hinged on the stern post, was without a fixed fin. Lateral control was by means of wing warping, the wings being without ailerons. The engine was almost entirely enclosed, a pair of small slots in the front of the cowling sufficing for cooling purposes.

Delivered to Farnborough by Hawker, the Tabloid underwent official trials on 29 October, demonstrating that with pilot and passenger and with full fuel, it possessed a top speed of 90 mph, a stalling speed of 36 mph and an initial climb rate of 1,200 ft/min. Early in 1914 Hawker set off for Australia taking with him the Tabloid prototype, returning with it in June.

In the meantime the aircraft went into limited production for the RFC and RNAS as a single-seat scout; a fin was added forward of the rudder hingeline, and a cut-out was incorporated in the upper wing above the cockpit.

One of the early production Tabloids was modified with twin-float undercarriage and, powered by a 100hp Gnome *monosoupape* rotary, was entered for the second Schneider Trophy race at Monaco flown by Howard Pixton on 20 April 1914. Not only did the Tabloid win the race but eclipsed every other contestant, returning an average speed of 85.5 mph, compared with 51 mph of the second place finisher. Pixton went on to establish a new world speed record for seaplanes at 92 mph. (The further history of the Tabloid seaplanes is recorded under the Sopwith Schneider, see page 26).

By June 1914 five Tabloids had been produced for the RNAS, and production continued until about May 1915, with a total of between 40 and 50 being completed. The aircraft did not carry a gun armament as standard, although several experiments were performed mounting a single Lewis gun. One RNAS Tabloid was fitted with a Lewis gun to fire forward through the propeller, the blades being protected by deflector plates.

After the outbreak of war four Tabloids of the RFC went to France in August, at least two of which flew scouting patrols with Nos 3 and 4

Above: *An early production Sopwith Tabloid, No 326.*

Right: *A Tabloid with the Military Wing, Farnborough.* (Photos: Royal Aerospace Establishment, Farnborough)

Squadrons. Later two aircraft joined the RNAS Eastchurch Squadron at Antwerp, but these were equipped to carry 20lb bombs; indeed, on 8 October, flown by Sqn Cdr Spenser Grey and Flt Lt R L G Marix, they attacked targets in Germany, the latter pilot hitting the airship shed at Düsseldorf and destroying the new German Zeppelin Z IX. Four RNAS Tabloids were shipped out to the Dardanelles early in 1915, but by May the type was being withdrawn from operational service.

Type: Single-engine, single-seat, single-bay biplane scout.
Manufacturer: The Sopwith Aviation Co Ltd, Kingston-upon-Thames, Surrey.
Powerplant: One 80hp Gnome nine-cylinder air-cooled rotary engine driving two-blade propeller.
Structure: All-wood construction; wire-braced box-girder fuselage with curved stringer-formed top decking; two-spar single-bay wings without ailerons. Twin wheel-and-skid undercarriage.
Dimensions: Span, 25ft 6in; length, 20ft 4in; height, 8ft 5in; wing area, 241.3 sq ft.
Weights: Tare, 730lb; all-up, 1,120lb.
Performance: Max speed, 92 mph at sea level; initial climb, 1,200 ft/min; endurance, 3½ hr.
Prototype and Production: One prototype and between 40 and 50 production examples.
Summary of Service: Served with Nos 3, 4 and 7 Squadrons, RFC, and Nos 1 and 3 Squadrons, RNAS; also aboard HM Seaplane Carrier *Ark Royal*, and at RNAS Great Yarmouth.

Sopwith Gun Bus

While it is well known that the Tabloid was the first scout to be produced by the Sopwith Aviation Company, and was later to be followed by a series of such aircraft for which the name Sopwith became synonymous, it should be said that the company had produced a wide range of other types of aircraft. One of these was a fairly large single-engine twin-float pusher seaplane powered by a 100hp Anzani radial engine for the Greek Naval Air Service in 1913.

This aeroplane proved satisfactory to the extent that a follow-up order was placed in March 1914 by that Service for six further examples to be built as landplanes, and to be armed with a single Lewis gun on the nose. These aircraft became known as the Sopwith Gun Buses, but were not ready for delivery to Greece when war broke out with Germany, and all were taken on charge by the British Admiralty. Apart from the wheel-and-skid undercarriage, the original four-bay Gun Bus biplanes also differed from the earlier Greek Seaplane in being powered by a 100hp Gnome *monosoupape* and the contours of the nacelle's nose were altered to provide a reasonable field of fire for the gunner. A four-wheel undercarriage was fitted.

Later thirty further Sopwith Gun Buses were ordered by the Admiralty under sub-contract with Robey & Co Ltd of Lincoln, but of these only seventeen were delivered fully assembled, the others being supplied for spares. These aircraft were powered by 150hp Sunbeam engines whose size and weight required an enlarged nacelle and stronger undercarriage, and the lower wing, in-

A Robey-built Sopwith Gun Bus, probably the first such aircraft, No. 3833, before installation of the nose Lewis gun and alterations to the nose contours; note the twin wheel-and-skid under-carriage, and the radiator immediately aft of the pilot's cockpit. (Photo: A J Jackson Collection)

stead of being attached directly to the bottom of the nacelle, was now a continuous structure which passed below the nacelle and was secured by struts

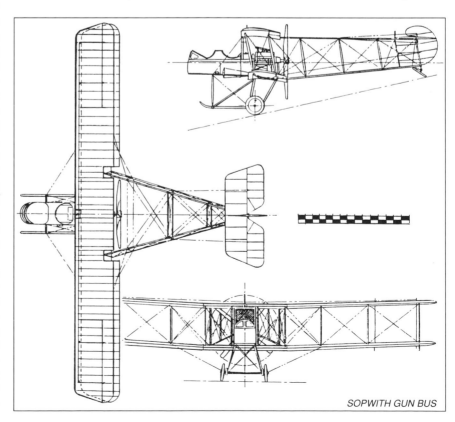

SOPWITH GUN BUS

attached to the wingspars; the number of landing wheels was reduced to two, and the aircraft was fitted with an enlarged, balanced rudder.

It is believed that only one Sopwith Gun Bus joined an operational unit, the Squadron commanded by Cdr Charles Rumney Samson RN (later Air Cdre, CMG, DSO, AFC, RAF) at Dunkerque early in 1915. Others were used by the RNAS for training at Hendon.

Type: Single pusher engine, two-seat four-bay biplane gun-carrier.
Manufacturers: The Sopwith Aviation Co Ltd, Kingston-upon-Thames, Surrey; Robey & Co Ltd, Lincoln.
Powerplant: One 100hp Gnome *monosoupape* engine driving pusher propeller (first six aircraft); one 150hp Sunbeam engine (remaining seventeen aircraft).
Structure: All-wood construction with ply and fabric covering; two-spar four-bay wings.
Dimensions (Sunbeam aircraft): Span; 50ft; length, 32ft 6in; wing area, 474 sq ft.
Performance: Max speed, 80 mph at sea level.
Production: 23 aircraft, Nos 801–806 (Gnome engines); Nos 3833–3862 (Sunbeam engines, of which only 3833–3849 were delivered assembled; remainder delivered for spares).
Summary of Service: One aircraft believed to have served with RNAS Squadron at Dunkerque; also used for training at Hendon.

Vickers E.F.B.3

Third and last of Archibald Low's Gunbus designs for Vickers was the E.F.B.3 (or Vickers Type 18B), displayed at the Fifth Olympia Aero Show on 16 March 1914. Convinced that with only minor improvements in the E.F.B.2 his new design would secure a production order from the War Office (for the Admiralty appeared to be showing preference for Sopwith and Short gun carriers), Low determined to improve the efficiency of the upper wing by eliminating the trailing edge cut-out. This necessitated moving the engine aft by about nine inches to allow clearance for the propeller; in order to counteract the shift of c.g., this in turn required moving the crew correspondingly forward.

The transparent panels in the sides of the E.F.B.2's nacelle were discarded as largely superfluous; steel structural components were used throughout (except for wing and tail surfaces); and the ailerons on top and bottom wings were interconnected by steel struts, replacing wing warping.

Other features of the E.F.B.2 were retained, including the trunnion-mounted front gun and identical tailplane and rudder; yet, despite the alterations to the nacelle, the E.F.B.3 was marginally shorter and lighter than its predecessor. It was therefore difficult to reconcile that the speed performance was not noticeably better. In the course of flight trials a new vertical tail surface was fitted, comprising a fixed triangular fin forward of the sternpost and a revised rudder.

Notwithstanding the Admiralty's interest elsewhere, twelve production E.F.B.3s were ordered, but before they were completed they were taken over by the War Office, and an extensive redesign undertaken — which emerged as

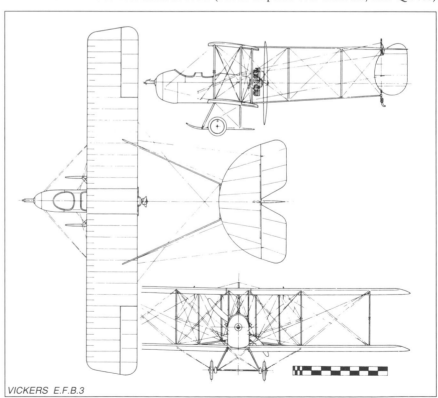

The Vickers E.F.B.3 at Brooklands in 1914. (Photo: Imperial War Museum, Ref: Q67488)

VICKERS E.F.B.3

the E.F.B.5. Although the unofficial name Gunbus had been in use for some months in the Vickers works, it was now formally adopted, despite the fact that Sopwith (also using the Brooklands flying field) was using the same name for that company's similar aircraft.

Type: Single pusher engine, two-seat, two-bay fighting biplane.
Manufacturer: Vickers Ltd (Aviation Dept), Knightsbridge, London.
Powerplant: One 100hp Gnome *monosoupape* nine-cylinder air-cooled rotary engine driving two-blade pusher propeller.

Structure: All-steel structure with metal-clad nacelle; fabric-covered wings and tail surfaces. Twin wheel-and-skid landing gear.

Dimensions: Span, 37ft 4in; length, 27ft 6in; height, 9ft 9in; wing area, 385 sq ft.

Weights: Tare, 1,050lb; all-up, 1,680lb.

Performance: Max speed, 60 mph at sea level; climb, 300 ft/min: range, 300 miles.

Armament: One 0.303in Vickers machine gun on trunnion mounting in the nose of the nacelle.

Prototype and Production: One prototype

which circumstantial evidence suggests later became the prototype E.F.B.5, with serial number 32; twelve aircraft, Nos. 861-872, were ordered by the Admiralty, but taken over by the War Office before completion, probably as F.B.5s.

R.A.F. S.E.2/2A

It has already been stated that the Royal Aircraft Factory's B.S.1, having crashed in March 1913, was rebuilt as the B.S.2, and that this machine was shortly to be re-designated the S.E.2, these initials denoting Scout Experimental.

The revision of the B.S.1 had centred largely upon the vertical tail surfaces, as its failure to recover from the spin from which it crashed pointed to a serious lack of directional control, a characteristic confirmed by those pilots who had flown it. Small fixed dorsal and ventral fins were added, and these certainly improved the aeroplane's handling, serving to prompt a further rebuild in which more extensive changes were made.

The new configuration, termed the S.E.2A and allotted the Army number 609, featured much enlarged dorsal and ventral fins and a revised rudder whose contours blended smoothly into the fins. A tailskid was now added in place of the strengthened lower segment of the rudder on which the S.E.2 had rested while on the ground. The wooden monocoque fuselage of the B.S.1 and S.E.2 was replaced aft of the cockpit by a structure of longerons, stringers and frame spacers covered with fabric. The engine cowling was given longer chord with a smaller diameter front aperture, and a large spinner was added to the propeller. All wing and undercarriage struts were replaced by members of improved section, the bracing wires were changed to Raf-wires and the landing skids improved (the latter were later removed altogether). Responsibility for these extensive alterations was entrusted to a design section leader at Farnborough named Henry Phillip Folland.

The S.E.2A was taken on charge by No 5 Squadron RFC, commanded by Maj J F A Higgins (later Air Marshal Sir John, KCB, KBE, DSO, AFC, RAF) at Farnborough in January 1914, and soon afterwards joined No 3 Squadron at Netheravon. Later, in October that year, it flew out to France for operations over

The sole S.E.2, seen here at Farnborough, later served with the RFC in France.

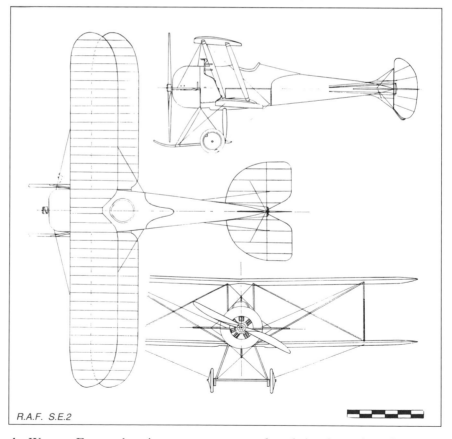

R.A.F. S.E.2

the Western Front, where its armament was said to vary from the pilot's 0.45in Service revolver to a pair of army rifles mounted on the sides of the fuselage to fire outside the propeller arc.

It is perhaps of interest to note that,

apart from being faster than almost all other aircraft in France, the S.E.2A was faster than the Sopwith Tabloid at the time its seaplane version won the Schneider Trophy race, and that it achieved this performance with an 80hp Gnome.

Type: Single-engine, single-seat, single-bay scout biplane.
Manufacturer: The Royal Aircraft Factory, Farnborough, Hants.
Powerplant: One 80hp Gnome engine driving two-blade propeller.
Structure: All-wood construction. Wooden monocoque rear fuselage of the S.E.2 replaced by built-up wooden structure covered by fabric in the S.E.2A. Twin wheel-and-skid undercarriage.
Dimensions: Span, 27ft 6in; length, 22ft. *All-up Weight:* 1,200lb. *Performance:* (S.E.2) Max speed, 80 mph; (S.E.2A) 96 mph at sea level.
Armament: Two 0.303in fixed rifles mounted on the sides of the fuselage firing forward and angled outwards to avoid the propeller blades.
Prototype: One only, No. 609; this later served with Nos 3 and 5 Squadrons RFC between January 1914 and March 1915.

Bristol
Scout A and B

Formed in February 1910 by Sir George White, the British and Colonial Aeroplane Co Ltd had been engaged in aircraft manufacture since the first appearance in the spring of that year of the Boxkite, an adaptation of the Henry Farman biplane with 50hp Gnome engine. As a result of wide-ranging recruitment at home and abroad the company acquired the services of a number of distinguished aircraft designers, among them Frank Sowter Barnwell and the Romanian Henri Coanda, who joined the company in December 1911 and January 1912 respectively. Three semi-autonomous design offices were established, and Coanda was given charge of general design policy, at the same time pursuing his own advanced ideas on biplanes and monoplanes. His only pusher biplane design was the two-seat P.B.8, intended as a trainer and powered by an 80hp Gnome; this was never flown as the War Office requisitioned its engine on the outbreak of war. Another of Coanda's designs, begun in 1913, was a single-seat monoplane, the S.B.5, intended for the Italian government; this also was never flown, and work had only started on the fuselage before the project

The Bristol Scout A in its original guise with small wings, uncovered wheel spokes and semi-enclosed engine cowling; standing in front is Harry Busteed. (Photo: T L Fuller, Amesbury)

was abandoned.

With the increasing interest being shown in single-seat military scouts, Frank Barnwell was given permission to re-design the S.B.5 as a scout biplane, with wings and tailplane very similar in plan to those of the P.B.8, and using much of the unfinished fuselage of the S.B.5.

This little aeroplane, affectionately known as the 'Baby Biplane', but increasingly as the Bristol Scout, was the forerunner of a long-lived class of Bristol designs. Powered by an 80hp Gnome, the Scout featured the same ailerons and wing stagger as the P.B.8 and incorporated a balanced rudder and two-wheeled V-strut undercarriage. A measure of its simplicity of structure and size may be judged by its all-up weight of no more

than 957lb with pilot and fuel for three hours' flight.

Accorded the Bristol sequence number 206, the Scout was flown at Larkhill in February 1914 by Harry Busteed, and in a very short time proved capable of a speed of 95 mph. It then appeared the following month at the Olympia Show where its small size caused something of a sensation.

In April the Scout returned to Filton to be fitted with slightly larger wings which improved the handling qualities and reduced the landing speed without significantly affecting the top speed; the engine cowling was also improved. Busteed then flew the aircraft to Farnborough where, on 14 May, it underwent an AID performance test, returning a speed range from 40 to 97.5 mph.

Thereafter No 206 was flown in a number of sporting events and, purchased by the 22-year-old Lord John Carbery (later Carberry), it was unfortunately lost in the English Channel when it ran out of fuel on the return flight of the London—Paris—London air race on 11 July — but not before the pilot and aeroplane had established an unofficial British air speed record of 100.5 mph. Carbery had fitted an 80hp Le Rhône in place of the Gnome.

The modified Scout A at Brooklands with enlarged wings and improved engine cowling. (Photo: Author's Collection)

The next two Scouts, which differed from No 206 principally in the engine cowling (and were referred to as the Scout B, while the earlier machine became the Scout A in retrospect), were requisitioned by the War Office at the outbreak of war and delivered to Farnborough during the latter half of August.

Type: Single-engine, single-seat, single-bay scout biplane.
Manufacturer: The British and Colonial Aeroplane Co Ltd, Filton, Bristol.
Powerplant: Scout A. One 80hp Gnome, and later 80hp Le Rhône engine driving two-blade wooden propeller. Scout B. One 80hp Gnome engine.
Structure: Predominantly light-gauge steel tubular construction with fabric covering; simple V-strut twin-wheel undercarriage.
Dimensions: Scout A. Span, 22ft 0in (later 24ft 7in); length, 19ft 9in; height, 8ft 6in; wing area, 161 sq ft (later 198 sq ft). Scout B. Span, 24ft 7in; length, 20ft 8in; height, 8ft 6in; wing area 198 sq ft.
Weights: Scout A. Tare, 617lb (later 750lb); all-up, 957lb (later 1,100lb). Scout B. Tare, 750lb; all-up, 1,100lb.
Performance: Scout A. Max speed, 95 mph (later 100 mph); initial climb, 800 ft/min; endurance, 3 hr (later 5 hr). Scout B. Max speed, 100 mph; initial climb, 1,000 ft/min; endurance, 2½ hr.
Armament: Initially none, but Scout B No 633 later fitted with two 0.303in rifles mounted on sides of nose to fire outside the propeller.

Prototypes and Service: One Scout A, 'No 206' (first flown by Harry Busteed on 23 February 1914 at Larkhill). Two Scout Bs, 633 and 634 (first flown in August 1914), served with Nos 3 and 5 Squadrons, RFC.

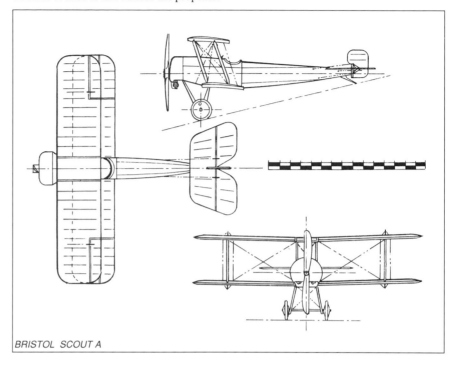

BRISTOL SCOUT A

Avro Type 508

One of several companies which tried their hand at gun-carrier biplanes in the two years before the War was A V Roe & Co Ltd, a manufacturer that had made long strides since its founder, the pioneering pilot-designer Alliott Verdon Roe, had taken his first faltering steps into the air on 8 June 1908 at Brooklands. By the time the Avro 508 was produced in December 1913 the company had already launched the Type 504 — the most widely used trainer flown in Britain during the First World War.

The Type 508 was a two-seat, three-bay pusher biplane whose square-section nacelle was constructed of ash longerons and spruce struts and was fabric-covered; it accommodated an observer-gunner in the nose and the pilot amidships, forward of the fuel tank. At the rear, carried on steel tubular bearers, the 80hp Gnome rotary drove a two-blade pusher propeller. Ailerons were fitted on both upper and lower wings.

The aircraft was exhibited in an incomplete state at Belle Vue Gardens, Manchester, on New Year's Day, 1914, and the following month appeared in its finished state on the Avro stand at the Olympia Aero Show in London.

The Avro 508 won no production order, probably on account of being somewhat underpowered. Indeed it is not known for certain whether the single example was ever flown.

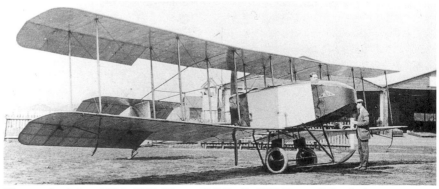

The completed Avro 508 in 1914. (Photo: G S Leslie/J M Bruce Collection)

Type: Single pusher engine, two-seat three-bay gun carrier biplane.
Manufacturer: A V Roe & Co Ltd, Miles Platting, Manchester, and Brooklands, Surrey
Powerplant: One 80hp Gnome rotary air-cooled engine driving two-blade pusher propeller.
Structure: Wings and nacelle constructed in wood with fabric covering; steel tubular engine bearers. Twin-wheel and single-skid undercarriage.
Dimensions: Span, 44ft 0in; length, 26ft 9in; height, 10ft 0in; wing area, 468 sq ft.
Weights: Tare, 1,000lb; all-up, 1,680lb.
Performance: Max speed, 65 mph at sea level; endurance, 4½ hr.
Armament: Provision intended for a single machine gun on nose of nacelle.
Prototype: One (possibly not flown); no production.

Short S.81 Gun Carrier

It would be anomalous to omit an entry in this work covering the Short S.81 Gun Carrier, although it is difficult to imagine this large seaplane as a fighter in any accepted sense. It was in fact the last variation in a series of single-engine pusher biplanes which had started life in 1910 as the S.27 Type, and progressed by way of such aircraft as the S.33, S.38, S.62 and S.80, and which had appeared in either land- or seaplane guise. The S.80 had been produced with both wheel and float undercarriage, and the S.81 was an immediate derivative ordered specifically to undergo air gunnery trials with a 1½-pounder Vickers shell-firing gun.

Unlike most other companies' single-engine pusher biplanes, the Short S.81's tail booms did not converge to a single sternpost and rudder, but were rigged in parallel both in plan and elevation, each terminating in a sternpost and each supporting a balanced rudder without fixed fin, as well as a cylindrical tail float. The relatively short main floats were rubber sprung (an innovation introduced by Oswald Short) and small cylindrical stabilizing floats were mounted under the lower wingtips.

Power was provided by a 160hp Gnome two-row engine driving a four-blade pusher propeller, the top wing centre-section being cut away to provide blade clearance. The reinforced nacelle itself

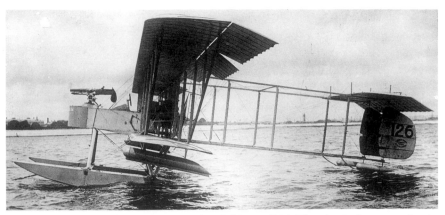

The Short S.81 Gun Carrier, 126, moored at Calshot in 1914. The wingtip floats were found to be necessary as the weight of the gun so raised the aircraft's c.g. that when turning during taxying there was a risk of striking the water with a wingtip. (Photo: A J Jackson Collection)

was shortened to no more than five feet and mounted the 1½-pounder gun on a superstructure in the nose; the gunner's cockpit was located on the port side of the gun's breech.

Designed by Arthur Camden Pratt, the sole Short S.81, Admiralty No 126, was first flown in about April 1914 at Calshot where Lieut R H Clark-Hill RN flew the gunnery trials. It is said that, when the Vickers gun was fired, the recoil was so severe that the aircraft

stalled and dropped 500 feet. Needless to say, the trials were not considered to be a success, and the gun was then passed to the RFC. Further trials with another gun, the recoilless six-pounder Davis, were flown at RNAS Great Yarmouth in March and April 1915. However, with experiments imminent to develop gun synchronizing mechanisms, the gun-carrying pushers' days were numbered, and the Short S.81 disappeared from the scene.

Type: Single pusher engine, two-seat, twin-float, three-bay biplane gun carrier.
Manufacturer: Short Bros, Eastchurch, Isle of Sheppey, Kent.
Powerplant: One 160hp Gnome two-row engine driving four-blade pusher propeller.
Structure: Light-gauge steel tubular construction with fabric and duralumin covering; twin main float undercarriage with twin wingtip stabilizing floats and twin tail floats. Ailerons on upper wings only.
Dimensions: Span, 67ft 0in; wing area, 540 sq ft.
Weights: Tare, 2,200lb; all-up: 3,600lb.
Performance: Max speed, 60 mph at sea level.
Armament: One 1½-pdr Vickers gun with special mounting on nose of nacelle.
Prototype: One, No. 126 (first flown in about April 1914 at Calshot). No production.

Vickers F.B.5 Gunbus

Although the evolution of the initial production version of the Vickers F.B.5 Gunbus has been shown to have followed a natural progression by means of the E.F.B. series of experimental designs, a number of complicating design considerations were necessarily introduced as the reality of production approached. Not unnaturally the manufacturers were at pains in overcoming these complications not to compromise the aircraft's excellent handling characteristics which had, after all, attracted both the Admiralty and War Office.

To begin with the gun mountings that had appeared in the E.F.B.2 and 3 were clearly unsatisfactory and tended to suggest that Vickers' own machine gun was not suitable for this class of gun carrier owing to the untidy belt-fed arrangement and the difficulty of aiming the trunnion-mounted gun. Accordingly a new experimental design appeared (the E.F.B.4) in which a drum-fed Lewis gun was to be mounted on a spigot immediately forward of the gunner's cockpit. While this was regarded as an acceptable compromise, diehard opponents pointed to the necessity to change drums frequently owing to their 97-round capacity. It also led to substantial redesign of the Gunbus nose, and required the gunner to stand exposed while aiming and firing the gun.

Other production considerations had to be faced, and extensive changes in the wing and tail planforms were adopted in the interests of simpler and quicker manufacture. The wing chord was increased and given square tips, while the familiar semi-circular tailplane was replaced by a huge rectangular surface; the rudder was also increased in area.

As already stated, a production order for twelve E.F.B.3s had been placed by the Admiralty in 1914, but these were taken over by the War Office at the outbreak of war, and the original E.F.B.3 is believed to have undergone progressive modification to become the E.F.B.5, or prototype F.B.5, but retained the curved tailplane leading edge.

Convinced that war was imminent, and that the Gunbus would be de-

A production Vickers F.B.5 Gunbus. Note the spigot mounting on the nose for a Lewis gun. (Photo: Vickers Ltd., Neg No 43)

manded in substantial numbers, Major Wood recommended that Vickers should begin manufacturing fifty production aircraft without waiting for Service contracts. These were in due course covered by three orders, covering 46 aircraft for the RFC, and two orders covering four Admiralty aircraft. Two of the latter were delivered early in 1915 with 150hp Smith engines.

The Gunbus first flew against the Germans when, on Christmas Day 1914, a German seaplane flew up the Thames Estuary towards London. An F.B.5 took off from Joyce Green but failed to engage, partly due to a faltering engine. The first of the Vickers aircraft to go to France arrived on 5 February 1915 but, such was the infancy of military aviation, squadrons were not yet specialists in any recognised air fighting rôle, and each possessed a variety of different aircraft, and none was initially wholly equipped

with F.B.5s. Those that did possess examples in those early months in France were Nos 5 and 16 Squadrons.

At home, however, the RFC had begun to recognise the need to establish squadrons equipped with aircraft armed with an in-built gun, capable of defending itself without recourse to hand-held small arms. The Gunbus, relatively simple to fly, fairly manœuvrable, and available in fast growing numbers, was an obvious choice to equip the first specialist fighting scout squadron and, on 11 July, No 11 Squadron (commanded by Maj George William Patrick Dawes, later DSO, AFC) arrived in France with a full complement of F.B.5s.

Despite its very modest performance, and the appearance of the early Fokker monoplanes — with their synchronized front gun — the Gunbus acquitted itself well, particularly against enemy aircraft of its own vintage. It was on 7 November

1915 that 2/Lieut Gilbert Stuart Martin Insall of No 11 Squadron won the Victoria Cross for an action involving the destruction of an Aviatik. Having forced the enemy aircraft down he then dropped an incendiary bomb on it. His own aircraft was then damaged by ground fire and was forced to land in the French lines. The following night, despite coming under enemy artillery fire, Insall and his observer repaired the Gunbus and at first light flew it back to their own airfield.

With the increasing ascendancy of German fighting scouts late in 1915, the Gunbus became hopelessly outclassed, but the F.B.5 soldiered on for a further six months until replaced by new Allied fighters. No 11 Squadron received its first Nieuport 13s in March 1916, but did not give up its F.B.5s until July. All told, Gunbuses equipped eight RFC squadrons, of which Nos 2, 5, 7, 11, 16 and 18 flew them in France.

A variant of the Gunbus was the F.B.5A, of which four examples were produced. These possessed armoured nacelles and were powered by 110hp Clerget engines but, being as yet relatively untried, these engines gave trouble and this version was not pursued further.

Unfortunately no accurate figures for total production of the Gunbus have been traced, and it is believed that the

Another view of an F.B.5. The fuel tank, immediately aft of the pilot's cockpit is clearly visible. (Photo: Vickers Ltd, Neg No 143)

number was around 210; rather higher figures, sometimes quoted, are thought to have been confused by inclusion of aircraft withdrawn from France to join training squadrons, and therefore duplicated.

Type: Single pusher engine, two-seat, two-bay fighting biplane.

Manufacturer: Vickers Ltd (Aviation Dept), Knightsbridge, London.

Powerplant: One 100hp Gnome *monosoupape* engine driving two-blade pusher propeller; also 110hp Clerget (F.B.5A); 150hp Smith Static.

Structure: Steel tubular structure with fabric covering; twin wheel and twin skid undercarriage.

Dimensions: Span, 36ft 6in; length, 27ft 2in; height, 11ft 0in; wing area, 382 sq ft.

Weights: Tare, 1,220lb; all-up, 2,050lb.

Performance: Max speed, 73 mph at sea level; climb to 5,000ft, 16 min; endurance, 4½ hr.

Armament: One 0.303in Lewis machine gun on spigot mounting in front of observer's cockpit.

Prototype and Production: One prototype, No 32. Known production aircraft: Nos 648, 664, 681 (3); Nos 861-872 (12); 1534-1535 (2); 1615-1651 (36); 2338-2347 (10); 2865-2868 (4); 2870-2883 (14); 3595-3606 (12); 4736 (1); 5074-5075, 5078-5079, 5083-5084, 5454-5503 (56, built by Darracq), 5618-5623

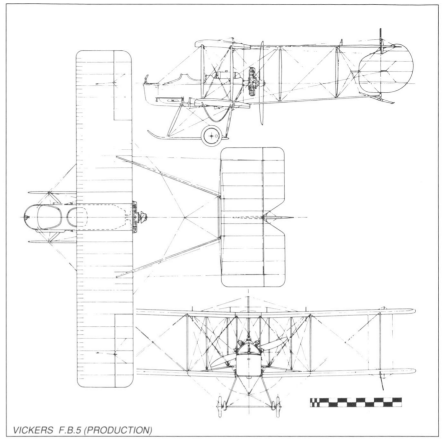

VICKERS F.B.5 (PRODUCTION)

(6); 5649-5692 (44); 5729 (1), 7510-7519 (10, possibly not all completed).

Summary of Service: F.B.5s served with Nos. 2, 5, 7, 10 (Reserve), 11, 16, 18 and 24 Squadrons, RFC; No 1 Squadron, RNAS. One aircraft to the Middle East in 1917.

Sopwith Schneider and Baby

When it became obvious that the various gun carrier seaplanes, especially those designed for the large Davis and COW guns (such as the Short S.81 and the so-called North Sea Scout) would be of little value in air-to-air combat, the Admiralty turned logically to the aeroplane that had won the 1914 Schneider Trophy contest — the Sopwith Tabloid modified with floats — and ordered it into production in November 1914.

Early aircraft retained the old wing warping and triangular fin of the racing version, as well as the parallel-sided engine cowling with tapering curve on the upper panel. Most aircraft were armed with a single Lewis gun mounted at a shallow angle to fire through the wing centre section and above the propeller arc. Later examples introduced

An early Sopwith Schneider at Calshot in 1915. Note the triangular fin, the absence of ailerons and the upward-firing Lewis gun fitted in an aperture in the top wing. (Photo: G.S. Leslie/J.M. Bruce Collection)

ailerons and an enlarged, curved fin, and one aircraft was flown with improved Linton Hope floats.

These aircraft were appropriately named Sopwith Schneiders, and a total of about 136 examples was produced. They entered service early in 1915 and served on many of the seaplane stations

around the coasts of Britain on antiairship and submarine patrols.

Schneiders also served at sea, being carried by ships of the Home Fleet. One was flown off the seaplane carrier HMS *Campania* on 6 August 1915 by Flt Lt W L Welsh using a two-wheeled dolly which dropped into the sea after take-

A Sopwith Baby armed for anti-Zeppelin patrols with Le Prieur rockets attached to the interplane struts; note also the bomb racks under the fuselage, aft of the main float struts. (Photo: G S Leslie/J M Bruce Collection)

off; while the ship steamed into wind at 17 knots, the Schneider's take-off run was 113 feet. Schneiders also served in the Aegean, at the Dardanelles, in the Eastern Mediterranean and Red Sea.

The Sopwith Baby

In the quest for better performance with the addition of more equipment (the Schneider was also fitted with provision to carry a 65lb bomb), the 110hp Clerget replaced the Gnome in September 1915 and, with this engine, the aircraft became known as the Sopwith Baby. A new cowling was introduced which, being horseshoe-shaped when seen from the front, left the lower one-third of the engine exposed. The Baby also featured a synchronized Lewis gun on the nose decking, firing through the propeller, although some aircraft retained the upward-firing gun of the Schneider. A total of 286 Babies was built, many of them by the Blackburn Aeroplane & Motor Co Ltd of Leeds.

The Schneider was a genuine fighter though it seems unlikely that it would have withstood more than about 2g in combat; it was a generally popular aeroplane and saw considerable service both in home waters and in the Near and Middle East where it was frequently adapted to carry a pair of 65lb bombs — principally for anti-submarine work.

Inevitably, with this constant increase in equipment (as well as sea anchor, homing pigeon, and emergency rations, as well as spare drums for the Lewis gun), yet more power was demanded, and a further engine change resulted in the 130hp Clerget being fitted, this version being built by Blackburn and by the Fairey Aviation Co Ltd (see Fairey Hamble Baby, page 88); it also underwent experimental modification by the RNAS at Port Victoria (see under Port Victoria P.V.2/2bis, page 64).

Sopwith Babies remained in service right up to the Armistice, and a number was supplied to the Royal Norwegian Naval Air Service with interchangeable wheel, ski and float undercarriage, while both Schneiders and Babies were also supplied to the US Navy.

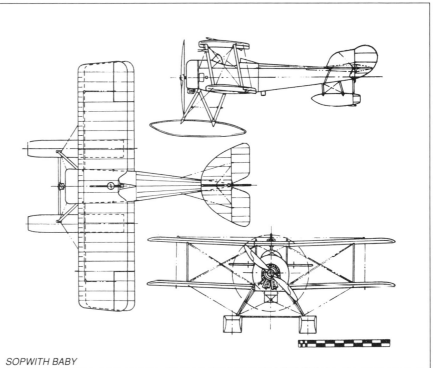

SOPWITH BABY

Type: Single-engine, single-seat, single-bay fighting scout twin-float biplane.

Manufacturers: Sopwith Aviation Co Ltd, Kingston-upon-Thames, Surrey; Blackburn Aeroplane & Motor Co Ltd, Leeds, Yorkshire.

Powerplant: One 100hp Gnome *monosoupape* engine driving two-blade propeller; 100hp Clerget; 130hp Clerget.

Structure: All-wood construction with two-spar, two-bay wings, fabric and ply covered; twin main float and single tail float undercarriage; wing warping later replaced by ailerons.

Dimensions: Span, 25ft 8in; length 22ft 10in (23ft 0in with 130hp Clerget); height, 10ft 0in; wing area, 240 sq ft.

Weights (130hp Clerget): Tare, 1,226lb; all-up, 1,715lb.

Performance (130hp Clerget): Max speed, 100 mph at sea level; climb to 10,000ft, 35 min; endurance, 2¼ hr.

Armament: One 0.303in Lewis free-firing machine gun angled upwards to fire through wing above propeller; superseded by a synchronized Lewis gun on fuselage nose; Schneider could carry one 65lb bomb; Baby could carry two. Ranken darts used for anti-airship attacks.

Production: No prototypes. Schneider production (all Sopwith), 1436-1447 (12), 1556-1579 (24) and 3707-3806 (100). Baby production, 8118-8217 (100, Sopwith); N300, N1010-N1039, N1060-N1069, N1100-N1129, N1410-N1449, N2060-N2134 (186, Blackburn).

Summary of Service: Served at RNAS Calshot, Dundee, Dunkerque, Felixstowe, Fishguard, Great Yarmouth, Killingholme, Scapa Flow, and Westgate; and aboard carriers, light cruisers and other ships in home waters, the Mediterranean, Aegean and Middle East.

Bristol S.S.A.

The Bristol S.S.A. armoured scout. (Photo: Claude Breguet, via Jean Deveaux)

At Filton, while Barnwell was producing the Scout No 206, Henri Coanda embarked on a new single-seat tractor biplane at the request of the French firm of Breguet, it being intended for production in France. Known formally as the S.S.A. (or Single-Seat Armoured), this aircraft was required to feature armoured protection for the pilot, engine and fuel tank, a requirement met by enclosing all within a single monocoque component of sheet steel, the pilot's seat being formed by the shape of the rear bulkhead.

An 80hp Clerget rotary engine was contained within a steel cowling with a large hemispherical spinner pierced with radial slots to permit entry of cooling air to the engine. The staggered wings were placed well forward to balance the weight of the armoured 'bath', while the tail unit was carried on an exceptionally slender rear fuselage. The undercarriage was also novel in consisting of castoring mainwheels to assist cross-wind landing, while the landing skids extended aft from the wheels, thereby dispensing of the need to provide a tailskid. The tail surfaces were similar to those of the Scout A.

First flown by Sidney Sippé at Larkhill on 8 May 1914 (given the company sequence number 219) suffered a heavy landing on arrival at Farnborough. After repair it was flown by Harry Busteed at Filton on 26 June, but crashed on landing when an undercarriage bracing wire failed. The pilot was slightly injured, although the aircraft itself was severely damaged.

The French authorities however agreed to accept delivery of it at Breguet's factory, where it was to be rebuilt, and Bristol took no further part in the S.S.A.'s development.

Type: Single-engine, single-seat, single-bay armoured scout biplane.
Manufacturer: The British and Colonial Aeroplane Co Ltd, Filton, Bristol.
Powerplant: One 80hp Clerget rotary engine driving two-blade propeller.
Structure: Steel monocoque front fuselage accommodating pilot, engine, fuel and oil tanks; steel tubular frame structure in wings, rear fuselage and tail, all fabric-covered. Twin castoring mainwheels.
Dimensions: Span, 27ft 4in; length, 19ft 9in; wing area 200 sq ft.
Weights: Tare, 913lb; all-up, 1,200lb.
Performance: Max speed, 106 mph at sea level; endurance, 3 hr.
Armament: None.
Prototype: One (sequence No 219; first flown by Sidney Sippé at Larkhill on 8 May 1914); no production.

Avro Type 511 Arrowscout

The Avro 511 at Hendon on 23 May 1914 carrying the racing number 14 for the Aerial Derby race around London (which was cancelled owing to bad weather). It was to have been flown by Fred Raynham, seen here in the cockpit. (Photo: via J M Bruce)

Displaying numerous obvious Avro design characteristics, the Avro Type 511 was one of three aeroplanes displayed by the company at the Olympia Aero Show in March 1914. It was a small aircraft designed to undertake fast scouting duties in the event of war, and for this reason the Type 511 gained its unofficial name of Arrowscout.

Designed by H E Broadsmith, the company's assistant designer, the 511 featured staggered, swept-back wings with single broad-chord interplane struts. Power was provided by an 80hp Gnome *monosoupape* in a close-fitting circular cowling and was intended to bestow a top speed of between 95 and 100mph, but this was not achieved in practice. At the other end of the scale, the landing speed of 35mph was achieved by the use of two small interconnected flaps under the lower wings—an innovation whose efficiency was demonstrated many years before it was almost universally adopted.

In other respects — the compound-circular balanced rudder without fin, ailerons on upper and lower wings and landing wheels with central skid — the 511 was unremarkable.

The Type 511 is believed to have been first flown by Fred Raynham during April 1914, but little further flying was done before the swept wings were replaced by unswept surfaces and the aircraft re-designated the Type 514; in this form it was first flown by Raynham during July. With the outbreak of war in the following month work on the aircraft was discontinued.

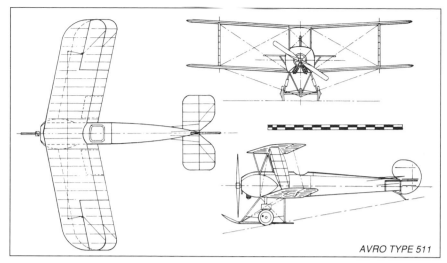

AVRO TYPE 511

Type: Single-engine, single-seat single-bay scout biplane.
Manufacturer: A V Roe & Co Ltd, Clifton Street, Miles Platting, Manchester; and Brooklands Aerodrome, Byfleet, Surrey.
Powerplant: One 80hp Gnome *monosoupape* seven-cylinder rotary engine.
Structure: Box-girder fuselage with four ash longerons with spruce cross struts; sparless swept wings of cellular construction. All fabric covered.
Dimensions: Span, 26ft 0in; length, 22ft 4in; height, 9ft 4in; wing area, 235 sq ft.
Weights: Tare, 675lb; all-up, 1,165lb.
Performance: Max. speed, about 90mph; landing speed, 35mph.
Armament: None fitted
Prototype: One (first flight, probably April 1914). No production.

R.A.F. B.E.2

Originally designed by Major Frederick Michael Green and Geoffrey de Havilland in 1911, the B.E.1 (Blériot Experimental) two-seat tractor biplane demonstrated considerable evidence of advanced structural and aerodynamic thought, and its general configuration could be traced throughout its immediate successor, the B.E.2 which, in numerous sub-variants, continued to serve until the final year of the War. The prototype B.E.2 was flown by de Havilland himself at the Military Trials of 1912 and, although inelligible to compete, was shown to be superior in all respects to the Cody biplane which was declared the winner. The B.E.2, B.E.2A and B.E.2B were all unequivocally reconnaissance aircraft, being without provision for any sort of armament. Powered by the 70hp Renault, a total of 44 aircraft accompanied the RFC squadrons to France in 1914.

The next version, the B.E.2C — the most famous of all B.E.s — bore the fruits of research by Edward Teshmaker Busk, the Assistant Engineer Physicist at the Royal Aircraft Factory who, by

The prototype B.E.2C at Farnborough on 2 July 1914. (Photo: The Royal Aerospace Establishment, Farnborough, Neg. No 408)

studying the flying characteristics of a B.E.2A, prepared the first practical data on the stability and controllability of aeroplanes to become available in Britain. Retaining the fuselage, engine installation and undercarriage of the B.E.2B, the prototype B.E.2C first appeared in June 1914, having wings of considerable stagger; ailerons replaced wing warping, and a fixed fin was added forward of the rudder.

Certainly the stability and control of the B.E.2 had been transformed, and its steadiness in the air seemed to recommend its value as a reconnaissance machine, the rôle assumed at that time to be the *raison d'être* of the military aeroplane. On this account, production

orders totalling 144 aircraft had been placed by the Admiralty with commercial sub-contractors before the end of 1914, as well as orders for 146 aircraft placed with the British & Colonial Aeroplane Co Ltd by the War Office. The first Squadron wholly equipped with B.E.2Cs was No 8, and this arrived in France in mid-April 1915. Early aircraft retained the 70hp Renault engine that powered the previous B.E. series, but at about this time production B.E.2Cs began appearing with the Royal Aircraft Factory's own engine, the RAF 1A, and this had a number of different exhaust manifolds, the best known being a pair of vertical stacks attached to the leading edge of the upper wing. At the

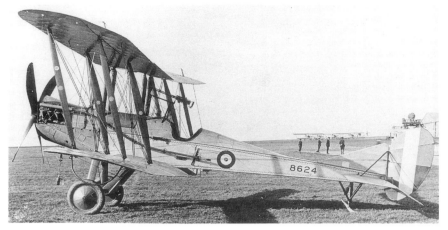

Left: *A B.E.2C, No 8624, of the RNAS, probably at Cranwell, modified as a single-seat fighter and armed with a single Lewis gun over the pilot's cockpit. Equipped with Holt flares under the lower wings, this was probably flown as a night fighter.* (Photo: G Quick). Below: *A Bristol-built B.E. 2E night fighter, No 7216, equipped to carry Le Prieur rockets on the interplane struts; the mounting for a Lewis gun may be discerned above the pilot's cockpit, although the gun is not fitted, Note the larger fin fitted on the B.E.2E.* (Photo: Via C Bowyer)

same time the B.E.2C's landing gear underwent change, the twin skids being omitted; a pair of steel tube spreader bars were introduced at the apex of the V-struts, between which passed the wheel axle. Rather later, oleo struts replaced the front tubular V-struts. The wheel axle was not attached rigidly to the spreader bars and springing was achieved by binding the spreader bars with lengths of rubber cord.

It was in the late summer of 1915 that the B.E.2C entered the most tragic phase of its history, for this was the moment when the Germans introduced their Fokker monoplane scouts, armed with a mechanically synchronized front gun, an innovation that not only revolutionized but generally simplified offensive air combat tactics.

No 8 Squadron in particular, which had assumed the rôle of long-range reconnaissance well behind the German lines, now suffered heavy losses under the guns of the enemy scouts, as did the growing number of squadrons equipped with B.E.2Cs. Although pilots took matters into their own hands and attempted to mount Lewis guns on make-shift structures for their defence, these only served to further reduce the B.E.'s already modest performance.

In truth the one characteristic that had commended the B.E.2C to its crews had been its steady, leisurely flying gait, so much so that, if attacked by an enemy scout, it possessed no agility with which to escape destruction. By September 1915 Nos 2, 4, 6, 7, 8, 9, 10, 12, 13, 15 and 16 Squadrons (more than half the total) were equipped with B.E.2Cs in France, and all were to suffer very heavy casualties.

The only remedy available, if the RFC was to continue to perform its allotted reconnaissance rôle, was to provide fighting escorts, but it was to be several months before suitable escort fighters could be brought into service. In the meantime the 'Fokker scourge' continued unabated.

Type: Single-engine, two-seat, two-bay reconnaissance biplane; also anti-airship night interceptor.

Manufacturers: The Royal Aircraft Factory, Farnborough, Hants (B.E.2C prototype only). Barclay, Curle & Co Ltd, Glasgow; William Beardmore & Co Ltd, Dalmuir, Dunbartonshire; The Blackburn Aeroplane & Motor Co Ltd, Leeds; The British & Colonial Aeroplane Co Ltd, Bristol; The Daimler Co Ltd, Coventry; William Denny & Bros, Dumbarton; The Eastbourne Aviation Co Ltd, Eastbourne; The Grahame-White Aviation Co Ltd, Hendon, London, Handley Page Ltd, London; Hewlett & Blondeau Ltd, Clapham, London; Martinsyde Ltd, Brooklands, Surrey; Napier & Miller Ltd, Old Kirkpatrick, Renfrewshire; Ruston, Proctor & Co Ltd, Lincoln; Vickers Ltd (Aviation Dept), Knightsbridge, London; The Vulcan Motor & Engineering Co (1906) Ltd, Southport, Lancs; G & J Weir Ltd, Glasgow; Wolseley Motors Ltd, Birmingham.

Powerplant: 70hp Renault; 90hp RAF 1A; 105hp RAF 1B; 105hp RAF 1D; 90hp Curtiss OX-5; 150hp Hispano-Suiza.

Structure: Steel tubular construction with ply, metal sheet and fabric covering; cable bracing, later Raf-wire bracing. Two-bay, twin-spar wings with steel tubular interplane struts with wooden fairings. Early aircraft with twin-skid, twin-wheel undercarriage, later replaced by plain V-strut, twin-wheel unit without skids; some aircraft with oleo struts as forward member of V-strut structure.

Dimensions: Span, 37ft 0in; length, 27ft 3in; height, 11ft 1½in; wing area, 371 sq ft.

Weights (RAF 1A engine): Tare, 1,370lb; all-up, 2,142lb.

Performance (RAF 1A engine): Max speed, 77 mph at sea level; climb to 10,000ft, 45 min 15 sec; service ceiling, 10,000ft; endurance, 3¼ hr.

Armament: Varied from none to four Lewis guns, sometimes including a rearward-firing gun on the pilot's cockpit; anti-airship aircraft were usually armed with single or twin Lewis guns on spigot or flexible mountings, and individual aircraft had provision for canisters of Ranken darts, or up to ten Le Prieur rockets on the interplane struts.

Production: The best estimate available of the total number of B.E.2Cs built is 1,310, of which about 330 were delivered initially to the RNAS (some were transferred to the RFC).

Summary of Service: B.E.2Cs served with Nos 2, 4, 5, 6, 7, 8, 10, 12, 15, 16 and 21 Squadrons, RFC, on the Western Front, and Nos 19 (Reserve), 33, 36, 39, 50, 51, 75 and 141 Squadrons, Home Defence.

Increasingly the B.E.2Cs had also been employed as bombers, both with the RNAS and the RFC, but weighed down with bombs, however small, they were no less vulnerable to enemy scouts than the reconnaissance aircraft. In home skies, however, they came to be used with mounting success in the anti-airship rôle, the first being the destruction of the Schütte-Lanz SL.11, shot down by Lieut W Leefe Robinson over Cuffley, Hertfordshire, on the night of 2/3 September 1916, for which he was awarded the Victoria Cross; on the night of the 24th of that month 2/Lieut Frederick Sowrey shot down Zeppelin L32 over Billericay, Essex. Both pilots belonged to No 39 (Home Defence) Squadron. Three other Zeppelins also fell to B.E.2C pilots.

It was the steadiness as a potential gun platform, as well as the ease with which it could be flown at night, that rendered the B.E.2C a suitable aircraft to counter the German airships, and in this rôle the aircraft appeared with a variety of weapons, and most Home Defence B.E.2Cs were armed with either single or twin Lewis guns, firing incendiary ammunition from flexible mountings. Some of the RNAS aircraft were flown as single-seat night fighters, the observer's front cockpit being faired over. Other examples were experimentally flown with Le Prieur rockets mounted on the outer pairs of interplane struts, but in general the addition of such external accoutrements simply deprived the aircraft of the last vestiges of useful speed. B.E.2Cs served widely overseas, and several were employed as single-seat fighters in the Middle East, but with marked lack of success.

Many attempts were made to improve the B.E.2C's speed performance, and the experimental installation of the 150hp Hispano Suiza engine early in 1916 certainly bestowed a useful speed of 95 mph at sea level; the increased weight of the engine by some 400lb, however, severely affected the handling of the aircraft, and the few examples were, perhaps surprisingly, confined to training duties.

The persistence with which the War Office continued to order production of the B.E.2C (as well as the later B.E.2D and B.E.2E, neither of which proved any better as fighting aircraft), fuelled the growing accusations that illogical preference was being afforded for aircraft designed at the State-owned Royal Aircraft Factory — even though every production B.E.2 was manufactured by private sub-contractors.

The accompanying data refers to the B.E.2C.

Pemberton-Billing P.B. 9

Noel Pemberton Billing, the colourful aviation pioneer who had developed a fully-equipped aerodrome in Essex *before* any manned aeroplane had achieved sustained, powered flight in Britain — and had himself later gained his Royal Aero Club pilot's Certificate after only four hours' tuition, started the design of marine aircraft in September 1913 in a small factory he acquired at Woolston, Southampton; as evidence of his faith in these aircraft he adopted the word 'Supermarine' as his telegraphic address. The Pemberton-Billing P.B.1 flying boat was shown at Olympia in March 1914.

As soon as the War started in August that year he turned his attention to the design of a small single-seat tractor scout and completed the work in a single day. Simplicity of manufacture was the keynote of this aircraft, termed the P.B.9, its 50hp Gnome rotary being mounted within ply panels which avoided the use of compound curves, while the wings featured no dihedral and no stagger. Construction of the aircraft was completed within one week, giving rise to the nickname 'Seven Day Bus'. There were no centre section struts, the in-

The Pemberton-Billing P.B. 9 (Photo: J M Bruce)

board pairs of interplane struts being attached to upper and lower wings close to the fuselage, so that the aircraft was, in effect, a one-and-a-half-bay biplane.

The P.B.9 was first flown in August by Victor Mahl (who had tuned Howard Pixton's winning Sopwith Tabloid for the 1914 Schneider Trophy race, and had only learned to fly at Brooklands in May that year). The aircraft was almost certainly fairly tricky to fly, and was probably never fitted with any armament. It was not selected for purchase by the Services, but was later used by the RNAS for training at Hendon, being allocated the naval serial number 1267.

Type: Single-engine, single-seat biplane scout.

Manufacturer: Pemberton-Billing Ltd., Woolston, Southampton

Powerplant: One 50hp Gnome seven-cylinder rotary driving 8ft diameter wooden propeller.

Structure: All-wood box structure with ash longerons, covered with ply and fabric. Wings of twin ash spar construction built as single components, the lower wing spars passing beneath the fuselage.

Dimensions: Span, 26ft 6in; length, 20ft 0in; wing area, 205 sq ft.

Weight: Tare, 560lb.

Performance: Max speed, 78 mph at sea level; initial rate of climb, 500 ft/min; range, approx 150 miles.

Armament: None fitted.

Prototype: One (first flown by Victor Mahl in August 1914); later allocated No 1267 (naval). No production.

R.A.F. S.E.4 and 4A

The sole S.E.4 as first flown with the tripod undercarriage. The I-shaped wing struts are clearly shown. (Photo: Royal Aerospace Establishment, Neg No 399 dated 17 June 1914)

Designed by Henry Folland, the S.E.4 was intended quite simply to be the fastest aeroplane in the world. First flown by Norman Spratt in June 1914 — only two months after the Sopwith Tabloid seaplane had won the Schneider Trophy at 86 mph and demonstrated a top speed of around 100 — the S.E.4 achieved a speed of 135 mph, faster by a considerable margin than any other aeroplane then flying.

Power was provided by the 160hp Gnome fourteen-cylinder two-row rotary, totally enclosed in a smooth-contoured cowling fronted by a large spinner which, after trouble due to engine overheating, had an intake cut in the nose to allow more airflow to pass through to the engine. The fuselage was reminiscent of the S.E.2A but was covered overall with ply. The wings were similar to those of the earlier aircraft but rigged without stagger, and featured single cabane and interplane struts on each side; full-span ailerons-cum-flaps replaced the former wing warping.

The most unusual feature was the undercarriage which initially comprised a transverse half-elliptic leaf spring attached to the apex of an inverted tripod, the landing wheels being attached to the extremities of the spring. This proved unsatisfactory owing to a tendency of the aircraft to roll while taxying and, after initial flight trials, it was replaced by a conventional pair of V-struts.

Although no armament was ever fitted, there is no doubt but that the aircraft attracted interest as a potential fighting scout, and it was flown on occasion by Maj J M Salmond (later Marshal of the Royal Air Force Sir John,

GCB, CMG, CVO, DSO), who reported favourably on it.

The big Gnome, however, continued to give trouble, and the landing speed (at 52 mph) was considered too high for Service pilots. The engine was replaced by a 100hp Gnome *monosoupape* and, not surprisingly, the speed performance decreased to mediocrity. Development of the S.E.4 was finally abandoned when it was badly damaged following a wheel collapse while landing.

The S.E.4A

Only superficially related to the S.E.4, the S.E.4A was said to be an attempt to suit the former aircraft to quantity production and, in so doing, almost all the S.E.4's novel features disappeared, other than the ailerons-cum-flaps. It is true that the S.E.4A flew initially with a huge open-nosed spinner, but engine overheating ensued nonetheless and a conventional cowling without spinner was substituted. It may be of interest to remark that the outline and structure of the S.E.4's tail unit was to reappear almost unaltered in the design of the much more illustrious S.E.5 which

started in 1916.

Four examples were produced in 1915, being flown frequently by Maj Frank Goodden, who by then had been appointed the Factory's Chief Test Pilot. Provision was made to mount a Lewis gun above the upper wing, and at least one S.E.4 was based at Joyce Green on Home Defence duties at the end of that year. However, the aeroplane's performance was not outstanding and failed to arouse further official interest.

Type: Single-engine, single-seat, single-bay tractor biplane.

Manufacturer: The Royal Aircraft Factory, Farnborough, Hants.

Powerplant: S.E.4. 160hp Gnome; 100hp Gnome *monosoupape*. S.E.4A. 80hp Gnome; 80hp Le Rhône.

Structure: Composite wood and steel construction with ply and fabric covering. S.E.4 with single interplane and cabane struts; twin interplane and cabane struts on S.E.4A.

Dimensions: S.E.4. Span, 27ft 6in; length, 21ft 4in; height, 9ft 0in (with tripod undercarriage); wing area, 188 sq ft. S.E.4A. Span, 27ft 5 1/10 in; length, 20ft 10in; height, 9ft 5in.

Performance: S.E.4 (160hp Gnome). Max speed, 135 mph at sea level; initial rate of climb, over 1,600 ft/min. (100hp Gnome). Max speed, 92 mph at sea level. S.E.4A. Max speed, approx 90 mph at sea level.

Armament: S.E.4. None. S.E.4A. Provision for single Lewis gun on upper wing.

Prototype and Production: One S.E.4, No. 628. Four S.E.4As.

The S.E.4 with conventional V-strut undercarriage. The early wartime attempt at camouflage is interesting. (Photo: Royal Aerospace Establishment, Neg. No 489, dated 12 August 1914)

Bristol Scout C and D

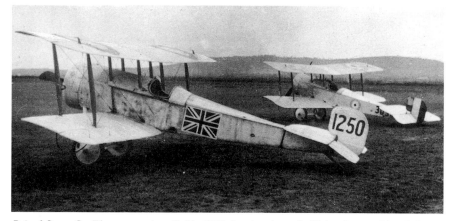

Bristol Scout Cs. The nearest aircraft, No 1250, bearing the early Union flag marking, is known to have served with the RNAS at Redcar early in 1915. (Photo: RAF Museum, Neg No P001030.

The development of Barnwell's Bristol Scout continued without interruption after the two Scout Bs had been requisitioned by the War Office on the outbreak of war (see page 23). Soon afterwards the War Office and Admiralty expressed growing enthusiasm for the new class of Scout aircraft and placed orders with several manufacturers, notably with Sopwith for the Tabloid. On 5 November 1914 Bristol received an order from the War Office for twelve improved Scouts (the Scout C), but two days later the Admiralty ordered twenty-four, and claimed priority of delivery. A rather one-sided compromise was reached as the Admiralty received the first example on 16 February 1915, while the following twelve Scout Cs were delivered to the RFC between 23 April and 13 June that year. By the end of the summer a total of 161 Scout Cs had been ordered, of which the RFC received 87 and the RNAS 74.

Produced at Brislington, Bristol, the Scout C differed externally from the B in dispensing with external engine cowling stiffeners, but all early aircraft retained the 80hp Gnome engines; however, War Office aircraft from the twenty-third onwards were powered by 80hp Le Rhônes, while the Admiralty insisted on continuing with Gnomes owing to their better reliability. Production continued until February 1916 but, despite the number built, Scouts never fully equipped any Squadron, instead being distributed among a dozen units at home and in France.

When, in 1916, shortage of 80hp Gnomes arose, a small number of Scout Cs was completed with 80hp and 110hp Clerget rotaries; with the latter engine the Scout C had a top speed of 109 mph at 3,000 feet (compared with 92 mph when powered by the standard Gnome).

It was, nevertheless, in a Gnome-powered Scout C of No 6 Squadron that Capt Lanoe G Hawker DSO, RFC, won the Victoria Cross on 25 June 1915. Armed only with a single-shot Martini carbine, mounted to fire to starboard of the propeller, he succeeded in forcing down three German two-seaters, all armed with machine guns. Armament carried by other Scouts at this time included a 0.45in Martini carbine firing incendiary ammunition and, occasionally, a Lewis machine gun.

The RNAS undertook numerous anti-Zeppelin patrols using Scout Cs, and on 3 November 1915 Flight-Lt H F Towler RN made the first deck take-off from HMS *Vindex*, formerly an Isle of Man steamer which had been fitted with a small flight deck forward. On 2 August the following year Flight-Lt C T Freeman RN, also flying from *Vindex*, took off to attack one of a pair of Zeppelins; although he succeeded in hitting his target with a Ranken dart, the airship turned back and made good its escape.

More spectacular were the experiments involving the mounting of a Bristol Scout C, No 3028, on the upper wing of Sqn Cdr John Cyril Porte's prototype Baby, No 9800, a large three-engine flying-boat — the object being to carry anti-Zeppelin fighters further from the coast so as to have a better chance of engaging the German airships. Flown by Porte himself on 17 May 1916, the flying-boat took off and the Bristol Scout, flown by Flight-Lt M J Day RN of HMS *Vindex*, separated successfully at 1,000 feet over Harwich. Although completely successful, the idea was not taken up as new fighting scouts were about to come into service with more chance of success and using more conventional methods of attack.

Meanwhile Barnwell had left Bristol for service with the RFC, but returned in August 1915 to prepare a further improvement in the Scout, based on reports of the Type C by the Services. The principal change was intended to be adoption of the 100hp Gnome *monosoupape*, which required a slightly enlarged engine cowling, but which bestowed a top speed of about 110 mph at sea level. In the event, of the 160 Scout Ds produced, only the first 60 delivered to the RNAS were powered by the big engine, which was found to suffer from severe engine vibration (causing the centre section fuel tank to leak), so that

A Bristol Scout D, No 7052, from the first production batch of aircraft powered by the 80hp Le Rhône. (Photo: RAF Museum, Neg No P020227)

A Bristol Scout D of the second Le Rhône-powered batch, built for the RFC. A number of these aeroplanes were fitted by the Service with an external Vickers gun, as shown here, equipped with either Challenger or Scarff-Dibovski interrupter gear. (Photo: RAF Museum, Neg No 022216)

the remaining 20 Admiralty aircraft reverted to 80hp Gnomes. The great majority of the RFC aircraft were fitted with 80hp Le Rhônes — which still returned a respectable speed of 100 mph at sea level.

The Scout D also introduced rafwires in place of twisted-strand cables, and the underwing skids were moved closer to the wingtips. A few RFC Scout Ds were delivered to France early in 1916 armed with a single Vickers machine gun equipped with Vickers-Challenger interrupter gear, enabling it to fire through the propeller arc, while some of the RNAS examples were similarly armed, but with Scarff-Dibovski interrupter gear. Many Scout Ds went further afield; they were flown operationally by Nos 14, 67 (Australian) and 111 Squadrons in Palestine, with Nos 30 and 63 in Mesopotamia, and with No 47 Squadron in Macedonia.

The wartime Bristol Scouts were very popular little aeroplanes among their pilots, with crisp and light handling qualities; they were only robbed of a prominent place in the annals of the RFC by their lack of a synchronized gun until too late to be capable of matching opponents possessed of much superior performance.

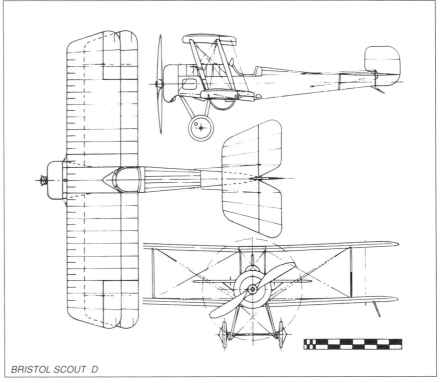

BRISTOL SCOUT D

Type: Single-engine, single-seat, single-bay biplane scout.

Manufacturer: The British & Colonial Aeroplane Co Ltd, Filton and Brislington, Bristol.

Powerplant: Scout C. 80hp Gnome; 80hp Le Rhône; 80hp Clerget; 110hp Clerget. Scout D. 80hp Le Rhône; 100hp Gnome *monosoupape*; 80hp Gnome.

Dimensions: Scout C and D. Span, 24ft 7in; length, 20ft 8in; height, 8ft 6in; wing area, 198 sq ft.

Weights: Scout C (80hp Le Rhône). Tare, 757lb; all-up, 1,195lb. Scout D (100hp Gnome *monosoupape*). Tare, 760lb; all-up, 1,250lb.

Performance: Scout C (80hp Le Rhône). Max speed, 92.7 mph at sea level; initial rate of climb, 1,000 ft/min; service ceiling, 15,500ft; endurance, 2½ hr. Scout D (100hp Gnome *monosoupape*). Max speed, 110 mph at sea level; initial rate of climb, 1,100 ft/min; service ceiling, 13,500 ft; endurance, 2 hr.

Armament: Varied greatly from no fixed armament to a wide range of single weapons, either fixed to fire above or on either side of the propeller (including Lewis machine gun, service rifle, cavalry carbine, 0.45in Martini-Henry rifle or shot gun firing chain shot) or Vickers machine gun on nose decking to fire forward through propeller arc by means of

various types of interrupter gear.

Prototypes and Production. No prototypes. Scout C production: 161 aircraft (Nos 1243-1266 and 3013-3062, 74 for the Admiralty; Nos 1602-1613, 4662-4699 and 5291-5327, 87 for the War Office. Scout D production: 160 aircraft (Nos 7028-7057 and A1742-A1791, 80 for the War Office; Nos 8951-9000 and N5390-N5419, 80 for the Admiralty).

Summary of Service: Scout C and D served in small numbers with Nos. 1, 2, 3, 4, 5, 6, 7, 8, 9, 10, 11, 12, 13, 15, 16, 18, 21, 24 and 25 Squadrons, RFC, in France, and Nos 14, 30, 47, 63, 67 (Australian) and 111 Squadrons, RFC, in Near and Middle East. Also many RNAS Stations at home, in France and the Mediterranean, as well as HM Seaplane Carrier *Vindex.*

Armstrong Whitworth F.K.1

The Aeroplane Department of the heavy engineering enterprise, Sir W G Armstrong, Whitworth & Co Ltd, came into being at the beginning of 1914, its first works manager and aircraft designer being the Dutch-born Frederick Koolhoven. A qualified pilot himself, who had already acquired design experience working on Deperdussin monoplanes, Koolhoven's first aircraft for Armstrong Whitworth was a small single-bay unstaggered biplane designated the F.K.1.

Of exceptional simplicity in the interests of possible future production orders as a military scout, the F.K.1 was intended to be powered by an 80hp Gnome rotary; however, as this engine was not immediately available, recourse was made to the 50hp version, with the result that the aircraft was substantially underpowered. Although the tail unit included a fixed fin forward of the rudder hingepost, there was initially no tailplane, a balanced elevator being fitted.

The F.K.1 was first flown by Koolhoven himself in September 1914. He was clearly dissatisfied with the longitu-

The Armstrong Whitworth F.K.1 in its original form with parallel-chord ailerons and no tailplane. (Photo: C H Brooks)

dinal and lateral control, and the ailerons were replaced by much enlarged surfaces with inverse taper, and a fixed tailplane was added.

Although no reliable design and performance figures appear to have survived, the aircraft was obviously inferior to such contemporary aircraft as the Sopwith Tabloid and Bristol Scout, and its development was not pursued.

Type: Single-engine, single-seat, single-bay tractor biplane.
Manufacturer: Sir W G Armstrong, Whitworth & Co Ltd, Newcastle-upon-Tyne.
Powerplant: One 50hp Gnome rotary engine driving two-blade propeller.
Structure: Steel and wood composite construction; square-section box-girder fuselage, fabric covered. Twin-wheel, single-skid undercarriage.
Performance: Max speed, 75 mph at sea level; landing speed, 30 mph.
Armament: None.
Prototype: One (first flown by Frederick Koolhoven in September 1914). No production.

Grahame-White Type 11

Among the so-called gun-carrier pusher biplanes exhibited at the 1914 Olympia Aero Show was John North's Grahame-White Type 11 — which acquired the company's uncompromising name Warplane. With proportions somewhat similar to those of the Vickers E.F.B.3, the Type 11 was similarly powered by a 100hp Gnome *monosoupape* which drove a very large four-blade pusher propeller; however by introducing chain drive the propeller was well clear of the wing's trailing edge, without the need to incorporate a cut-out.

The Grahame-White Type 11 'Warplane' on display at Olympia on 16 March 1914. Behind it on the left is one of Grahame-White's famous pre-War 'Charabancs'. (Photo: G S Leslie/ J M Bruce Collection)

The two-spar, two-bay wings were of parallel chord with slight sweep-back on leading and trailing edges, and were rigged without stagger; ailerons were fitted to both upper and lower wings. The undercarriage, with twin wheels, featured three struts on each side but dispensed with skids.

Observers at the Olympia Show

expressed some surprise at the short tail moment, the leading edge of the dorsal fin and tailplane being only some six feet from the wing trailing edge, and also at the fact that the fin and much of the elevator were almost clear of the slipstream. Nevertheless the Type 11 attracted much acclaim, largely it is suspected on account of the superb crafts-

manship evident in its manufacture.

Unfortunately, the misgivings voiced at Olympia were confirmed when the French pilot, Louis Noel, first flew the Warplane at Hendon in May, and reported very poor longitudinal stability and control. Despite a speed roughly comparable with that of the Vickers E.F.B. series, these flawed handling properties discouraged North from pursuing the gun carrier pusher biplane formula any further.

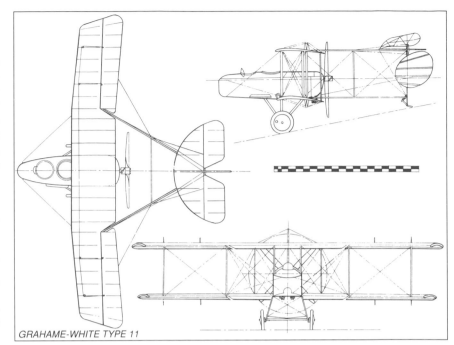

GRAHAME-WHITE TYPE 11

Type: Single pusher engine, two-seat, two-bay gun carrier biplane.
Manufacturer: The Grahame-White Aviation Co Ltd, Hendon, Middlesex.
Powerplant: One 100hp Gnome *monosoupape* engine driving four-blade pusher propeller.
Dimensions: Span: 37ft 0in.
Weights: Tare, 1,000lb; all-up, 1,550lb.
Performance: Max speed, 80 mph at sea level.

Armament: Intended to make provision to mount a Lewis machine gun on the front cockpit.

Prototype: One (first flown by Louis Noel at Hendon in May 1914). No production.

Martinsyde S.1

The Martinsyde S.1 with the initial four-wheel undercarriage. (Photo: A J Jackson Collection)

The association that grew up between H P Martin and George Handasyde before the First World War resulted in the establishment of Martinsyde Ltd at Brooklands, a company which achieved distinction with a series of attractive monoplanes. With the appearance of the outstanding Sopwith Tabloid at Brooklands, however, it was not long before Martinsyde joined the growing number of companies determined to compete for military orders for small tractor biplane scouts.

Superficially resembling the Tabloid, particularly in the engine cowling, the first single-seat scout was the Martinsyde S.1, powered by an 80hp Gnome; it differed, however, in the undercarriage design which incorporated two mainwheels and a pair of skids in front of which were added two smaller, balancing wheels. Later this unwieldy arrangement was discarded in favour of conventional V-struts on each side and plain twin-wheel undercarriage, also dispensing with the skids.

On account of its ability to mount a Lewis gun on the upper wing from the outset, the S.1 quickly earned production orders, and the first of about sixty Service aircraft appeared towards the end of 1914, all being produced by the parent company. Fewer than a dozen joined RFC squadrons on the Western Front, and one of these gave rise to a famous incident. Capt Louis Strange was flying an S.1 of No 6 Squadron and, finding that the ammunition drum on the Lewis gun had jammed, stood up in his cockpit to gain a firmer grip on the drum so to release it — holding the control column between his knees. The aircraft began to climb steeply, stalled and entered an inverted spin and, not having the benefit of seat straps, Strange was thrown out of the cockpit, still retaining his hold on the drum. Fortu-

nately this, which only moments earlier he had been trying to free, remained jammed, and after losing about 5,000 feet the aircraft righted itself and the pilot managed to struggle back into his cockpit.

Four S.1s were shipped to the Middle East Brigade in 1915, equipping one Flight of No 30 Squadron in Mesopotamia. More than forty were supplied to training units in Britain that year and the S.1 was withdrawn from operational use in France during the summer of 1915, but a small number was shipped out to Mudros in the Aegean in 1918 to equip No 144 Squadron. Several other examples were tested at the Royal Aircraft Factory with early front gun interruptor equipment.

Type: Single-engine, single-seat, single-bay tractor biplane scout.

Manufacturer: Martinsyde Ltd., Brooklands, Surrey.

Powerplant: One 80hp Gnome engine driving two-blade propeller.

Structure: All-wood with fabric covering; ailerons on upper and lower wings.

Dimensions: Span, 27ft 8in; length, 21ft 0in; wing area, 208 sq ft.

Performance: Max speed, 87 mph.

Armament: One 0.303in Lewis machine gun on upper wing, firing above propeller.

Prototype and Production: One prototype, believed to be No 710. 61 production examples: Nos 724, 741, 743, 748-749, 2448-2455, 2820-2831, 4229-4252 and 5442-5453 (some of these may not have been completed).

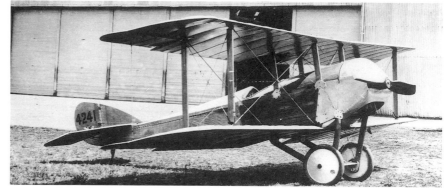

The Martinsyde S.1 with the later two-wheel undercarriage. (Photo: A J Jackson Collection)

Summary of Service: S.1s served in small numbers on each of the following: Nos. 1, 2, 4, 6, 9, 10, 14, 16, 23, 24, 30, 67 and 144 Squadrons, RFC.

R.A.F. F.E.6

Relatively little is known of the F.E.6, other than it was a two-bay, single-engine pusher biplane which was built in the second half of 1914 by the Royal Aircraft Factory, and was powered by a 120hp Austro-Daimler driving a four-blade propeller. It followed the unusual configuration of the F.E.3 (see page 14) in that the tail unit was carried on a single steel boom which extended aft through the propeller shaft.

From the accompanying sketch, taken from a Factory drawing, the F.E.6 can be seen to possess no wing stagger and

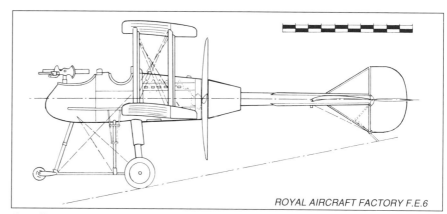

ROYAL AIRCRAFT FACTORY F.E.6

that ailerons were fitted to the upper and lower wings. The mainwheels of the undercarriage appear to have been carried on oleo struts and there was a small auxiliary nosewheel. The gun armament may have been a 6-pounder Davis recoilless weapon. Whether the aircraft was built and flown exactly to this design is not known.

Sopwith Two-Seat Scout

The Sopwith Two-Seat Scout was directly related to the Sopwith Admiralty Type 807, a seaplane which was in turn developed from the aircraft prepared for the 1914 Round-Britain contest. In appearance it might be described as a 'stretched' Sopwith Tabloid, with lengthened fuselage to accommodate a pair of widely separated cockpits, and two-bay wings; it was powered by a 100hp Gnome *monosoupape* engine, cowled in a manner reminiscent of the Tabloid. The wings were rigged without stagger, and

A Sopwith Two-Seat Scout, No 1064. (Photo: G S Leslie/J M Bruce Collection)

ailerons were fitted to both upper and lower wings.

The aircraft attracted the attention of the Admiralty who placed an order for

24 examples, their intended rôle being that of anti-Zeppelin patrol. However, with a two-man crew and a heterogeneous choice of hand-held weapons, its ceiling was limited to no more than 3,000 feet, and it is impossible to imagine just how these aircraft could intercept the airship raiders. The armament carried ranged from a Service rifle firing Hales grenades, and a shot-gun firing chain-shot, to a signal pistol with two rounds; others carried a Mauser rifle firing incendiary ammunition.

The Two-Seat Scouts were flown by the RNAS at Hendon, Killingholme and Great Yarmouth on anti-airship patrols, quickly earning the nickname 'Spinning Jenny'. Pilots overworked their engines in fruitless attempts to climb above 3,000 feet, resulting in frequent engine failures and a subsequent tendency to spin. As spin recovery was not yet included in flying training syllabuses, these gyrations were usually fatal. It is believed that all surviving Two-Seat Scouts had been withdrawn from service by the end of 1915 — without having engaged so much as a single enemy airship.

Type: Single-engine, two-seat, two-bay biplane scout.
Manufacturer: The Sopwith Aviation Co Ltd, Kingston-upon-Thames, Surrey.
Powerplant: One 100hp Gnome *monosoupape* engine driving two-blade propeller.
Dimensions: Span, 36ft 0in.
Performance: Max speed, 69 mph at sea level; climb to 3,000ft, 20 min; ceiling, 3,000ft; endurance, 3½ hr.
Armament: Choice of weapons included a Service rifle firing Hales grenades, a shot-gun firing chain-shot or a Mauser rifle firing incendiary ammunition; some aircraft had provision to carry small bombs.
Production: No prototype. 24 production aircraft, Nos. 1051-1074.
Summary of Service: Aircraft served on RNAS Stations at Hendon, Killingholme and Great Yarmouth.

Grahame-White Type 13

Both Vickers and Grahame-White tried their hands at two-seat tractor scouts in 1914, the Vickers aircraft appearing at the Olympia Show that year, powered by a 100hp Gnome *monosoupape*; this was not, however, sufficiently promising to warrant diverting work away from the Gunbus series, which Harold Barnwell considered most likely to attract substantial production orders, and the Vickers Two-Seat Scout was abandoned that summer.

The Grahame-White two-seat scout, the Type 13, was — like the Sopwith 'Spinning Jenny' — developed from a seaplane intended for the 1914 Round-Britain race (which was cancelled); but in this instance, however, the aircraft had been fitted with floats that were too short so that, when the pilot opened the throttle prior to its first flight, the aircraft nosed over. It was recovered from the water and re-built with wheel undercarriage.

The manufacturers clearly believed that the little Type 13 possessed adequate performance to attract the Admiralty or the War Office in the rôle of reconnaissance scout. The wings were heavily staggered and employed N-type interplane struts, which were fairly unusual for the period, while the forward cabane struts were raked sharply back. The undercarriage evidently gave trouble as it was modified to incorporate

The Grahame-White Type 13 two-seat scout as it appeared immediately after re-building with wheel undercarriage and before this was changed to incorporate V-struts. (Photo: G S Leslie/J M Bruce Collection)

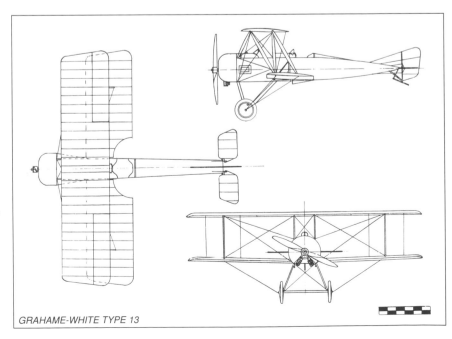

GRAHAME-WHITE TYPE 13

plain V-struts with their apex on the extremities of the axle spreader bar. Ailerons were fitted to the top wing only, and there was no fixed tailplane.

The pilot occupied the rear cockpit which was located well aft of the upper wing's trailing edge, there being no cut-out in this wing. However, a gesture to the pilot's field of vision was made by providing large triangular transparent panels in the sides of the box-section fuselage, and transparent panels in the lower wing roots; large cut-outs were also provided in the trailing edge roots of the lower wings. On the other hand the observer's cockpit was positioned directly below the upper wing centre-section and, although it was over the lower wing's leading edge, the observer's downwards view was restricted by large

convex fairings on either side of the fuselage aft of the engine.

Power was provided by the familiar Gnome *monosoupape* engine which bestowed a top speed of 85 mph; fuel sufficient for an endurance of 5½ hours could be carried. The strut and bracing arrangement seems to have been unnecessarily complex and would undoubtedly have led to difficulties in service; in

any case the Service authorities decided against adoption of the aircraft for the reconnaissance rôle, probably on account of the distance and difficulty of communication between pilot's and observer's cockpits.

The sole example of the Type 13 is believed to have been flown as a trainer by the RNAS who shared the aerodrome at Hendon with Grahame-White.

Type: Single-engine, two-seat, single-bay tractor biplane scout.
Manufacturer: The Grahame-White Aviation Co Ltd, Hendon, Middlesex.
Powerplant: One 100hp Gnome *monosoupape* engine driving two-blade propeller.
Dimensions: Span, 27ft 10in; length, 26ft 6in.
Weights: Tare, 1,040lb; all-up, 1,800lb.
Performance: Max speed, 85 mph at sea level; endurance, 5½ hr.
Armament: None.
Prototype: One (probably flown in about October 1914, and used by the RNAS at Hendon). No production.

Airco D.H.1

In June 1914 Geoffrey de Havilland, one of Britain's pioneer designer/pilots and originator of the Royal Aircraft Factory's B.E. series at Farnborough, joined the Aircraft Manufacturing Company (Airco) at Hendon and at once embarked on a pusher biplane intended for air fighting and reconnaissance.

Benefitting from his experience at Farnborough, de Havilland's first Airco design, the D.H.1 almost inevitably featured the pusher engine configuration owing to the absence of any reliable gun interrupter gear. The two-man crew comprised a gunner/observer in the nose of the nacelle and the pilot situated amidships. Power was intended to be provided by a 120hp Beardmore at the outset, but no example was available and the D.H.1 was fitted with a 70hp Renault. With this engine the prototype was first flown by de Havilland himself at Hendon in January 1915 and, despite its limited power, returned a fairly good performance by current standards. The two-bay wings, of two-spar construction, were provided with generous gap but without stagger, and the tail unit, comprising tailplane, elevator, fin and rudder, was carried on two pairs of wooden booms which converged in plan to meet on the rudder hinge line — though there was no stern post as such. As originally completed the prototype,

Upper Photo: *The prototype D.H.1 with 70hp Renault engine with the original air brake aerofoils immediately aft of the pilot's cockpit.* (Photo: Flight, Neg No 0192) Lower Photo: *No 4606, the D.H.1A prototype with 120hp Beardmore engine complete with large radiator directly behind the pilot's head; note the observer's cut-down cockpit and gravity fuel tank under the upper wing.* (Photo: The Royal Aeronautical Society)

probably un-numbered, featured a pair of air brakes each consisting of a three-feet aerofoil hinged to the fuselage im-

mediately aft of the front centre section struts; these were found to be unsatisfactory and were quickly discarded.

The D.H.1 was ordered into limited production, but by the time the first examples began to appear the Beardmore engine was becoming available and was first fitted in aircraft No 4606, this version being designated the D.H.1A. By that time, however, Airco had become heavily involved with development of the more important D.H.2 single-seat fighter, and the majority of production D.H.1As came to be built by Savages Ltd of King's Lynn, Norfolk. On all production aircraft the coaming of the front cockpit was cut down much lower so as to improve the arc of fire for the Lewis gun.

A total of seventy-two production D.H.1s and 1As was produced; only six were sent overseas, these joining the Middle East Brigade and No 14 Squadron at Ismailia in 1916. At home, twenty-four aircraft served with Home Defence squadrons, and forty-three were delivered to training units (including No 35 Reserve Squadron and No 199 Training Squadron). The survivors were finally withdrawn from RAF charge at the time of the Armistice in 1918.

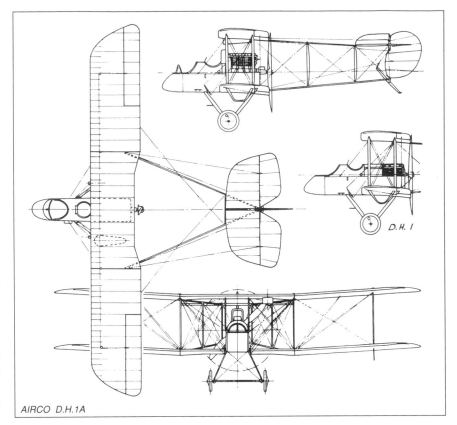

AIRCO D.H.1A

Type: Single-engine, two-seat reconnaissance and fighting scout with pusher engine.

Manufacturers: The Aircraft Manufacturing Co Ltd, Hendon, London (prototypes and early production aircraft); Savages Ltd., King's Lynn, Norfolk (production D.H.1As)

Powerplant: (D.H.1) One 70hp Renault liquid-cooled in-line engine. (D.H.1A) One 120hp Beardmore liquid-cooled in-line engine. Two-blade propellers.

Structure: Fabric-covered wooden construction with two-bay, two-spar wings with upper and lower ailerons. Wooden tail booms.

Dimensions: Span, 41ft 0in; length (D.H.1), 28ft 11⅝in; (D.H.1A) 28ft 11¼in; height (D.H.1), 11ft 4in; (D.H.1A) 11ft 2in; wing area, 426.25 sq ft.

Weights: (D.H.1) tare, 1,356lb; all-up, 2,044lb. (D.H.1A), tare, 1,610lb; all-up, 2,340lb.

Performance: (D.H.1) max speed, 80 mph at sea level; climb to 3,500ft, 11 min 15 sec. (D.H.2) max speed, 90 mph at sea level; climb to 5,000ft, 10 min 25 sec; service ceiling, 13,500ft.

Armament: One 0.303in Lewis gun on pillar mounting in front cockpit.

Prototypes: One D.H.1 (probably un-numbered, flown by Geoffrey de Havilland at Hendon in January 1915), and one D.H.1A (No 4606, converted from D.H.1)

Production: Total of 72 production D.H.1s and 1As between Nos 4600-4648 and A1611-A1660.

Summary of Service: 24 aircraft to Home Defence squadrons, 43 to Home Training Units and 6 to the Middle East (see text).

Airco D.H.2

The steadily-increasing tempo of air combat during the early months of 1915, particularly over the Western Front, progressing from the use of hand-held small arms to the inclusion of synchronized automatic weapons fixed to the aircraft to fire forward through the tractor propellers of purpose-built fighters — with the appearance of the German E-series monoplanes — concentrated the attention of British designers on the need to develop a reliable gun interruptor mechanism.

Until, however, such equipment arrived, recourse was made to the established 'gun bus' formula that had been pursued with some success by such manufacturers as the Royal Aircraft Factory, Vickers, Sopwith, and by Geoffrey de Havilland himself with his two-seat D.H.1 and 1A. Realising that in many respects these aircraft were too large and cumbersome to engage in nimble dogfighting, he set about designing a single-seat derivative, much reduced in size and weight. His D.H.2 has come to be recognised as the first British fighter aircraft to be designed specifically with the aerial dogfight as its *raison d'être*.

With a span of only 28ft 3in (compared to the D.H.1's 41 feet), the 100hp Gnome *monosoupape* rotary-powered D.H.2 prototype completed its initial flight trials in July 1915. When the aircraft was first flown the idea of fixing the gun in the nose to fire forward along the aircraft's line of flight had not been

Right: *The prototype Airco D.H.2, No 4732, powered by a 100hp Gnome monosoupape engine driving a two-blade propeller; the fuel tank was located immediately behind the pilot in the fuselage* (Photo: A J Jackson Collection)

Below: *A production D.H.2, No 7851, with 110hp Le Rhône driving a four-blade propeller. Earlier aircraft were fitted with their fuel tank under the port upper wing, unlike this example whose tank is above the starboard wing.* (Photo: G S Leslie/J M Bruce Collection)

accepted by the War Office; instead, two flexible brackets were provided on either side of the cockpit, and the pilot was required to transfer his gun from bracket to bracket — *and* control his aircraft in combat at the same time. This was despite the fact that a French pilot, Roland Garros in a Moranc Type L scout, had already demonstrated in combat the superiority of a fixed centre-line gun. In due course a single central gun mounting was provided for the D.H.2

Be that as it may, it was not until 7 February 1916 that the first RFC Squadron, No 24 commanded by Major Lanoe George Hawker VC, arrived in France, followed by Nos 29 and 32 some weeks later. The first German aircraft fell to the guns of a No 24 Squadron D.H.2 on 2 April.

A total of 400 D.H.2s was produced by Airco, of which 266 were sent to France during 1916, 32 to the Middle East and 100 equipped training units in Britain; the other two flew with Home Defence units.

The D.H.2 was to a large extent responsible for the final eclipse of the 'Fokker scourge' and was heavily engaged during the Battle of the Somme. No 24 Squadron alone fought no fewer than 774 combats, in the course of which

its pilots destroyed 44 enemy machines. Major Hawker himself was shot down and killed after a marathon combat with the legendary Manfred von Richthofen on 23 November 1916. No 32 Squadron's commanding officer, Maj L W B Rees, had won the Victoria Cross for

single-handedly attacking an enemy formation of ten enemy two-seaters on 1 July.

At first regarded by its pilots as a tricky aeroplane to fly, mainly on account of its very sensitive controls and the difficulty of spin recovery, the D.H.2 soon came to be greatly appreciated for its tough structure and manœuvrability, and as experience and training improved. Once the central gun mounting had been adopted, pilots could concentrate on flying their fighters directly at their targets. Nevertheless, when the gun interruptor gear had been developed successfully, conventional tractor scouts quickly replaced the old pusher biplanes, and the D.H.2 gradually disappeared from front line service early in 1917.

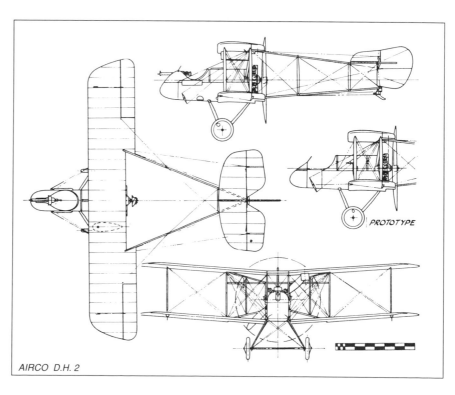

AIRCO D.H. 2

Type: Single-engine, single-seat fighting scout biplane with pusher engine.
Manufacturer: The Aircraft Manufacturing Co Ltd., Hendon, London
Powerplant: One 100hp Gnome *monosoupape* air-cooled rotary engine; a few aircraft with 110hp Le Rhône rotary engine; two blade propellers.
Structure: Fabric-covered wooden construction with two-bay, two-spar wings; steel tubular booms supporting tail unit.
Dimensions: Span, 28ft 3in; length, 25ft 2½in; height, 9ft 6½in; wing area, 249 sq ft.
Weights (Gnome): Tare, 943lb; all-up, 1,441lb.
Performance (Gnome): Max speed, 93 mph at sea level; climb to 5,000ft, 8 min 25 sec; service ceiling, 14,000ft; endurance, 2¾ hr.
Armament: One 0.303in Lewis machine gun on offset pillar mounts on either side of the nose, or a single central mounting.
Prototype: One, 4732 (first flown by Geoffrey de Havilland, probably in July 1915).
Production: Total of 451 ordered, but only 400 delivered (from 5916-6015, 7842-7941, 8725, A2533-A2632, A4764-A4813, A4988-A5087).
Summary of Service: Served with Nos 24, 29 and 32 Sqns, Western Front; Nos 5, 11 and 18 Sqns, Palestine; No 111 Sqn. and 'X' Flt, Macedonia; 'A' Flt, No 47 Sqn.; RNAS Composite Fighting Sqn.; No 10 Reserve Squadron, Joyce Green.

A.D. Sparrow

The Sparrow No 1536 at Chingford in 1915.   (Photo: National Aviation Museum, Canada)

Following the creation of the Naval Wing in 1912, the Admiralty established an Air Department whose purpose was to deal with all matters relating to naval aviation. The popular but eccentric Harris Booth, late of the National Physical Laboratory, was given charge of all technical considerations and, in due course, headed an aircraft design section whose products were to be contracted out for manufacture by private companies.

One of Booth's first designs was the A.D. Sparrow, or Scout, of 1915, an extraordinary-looking pusher biplane intended for anti-Zeppelin fighting, and to be armed with a two-pounder Davis recoilless, quick-firing gun; and it was the installation of this weapon that dictated the design of the nacelle. The A.D. Sparrow was a single-bay, heavily-staggered biplane, powered by an 80hp Gnome rotary engine; the tail booms were rigged parallel in plan and elevation and carried an enormous 21ft-span tailplane and elevator with widely-spaced twin fins and rudders. In order to provide ground clearance for the propeller, the nacelle was attached to the upper wings and, with large wing gap, the lower wing was a continuous structure placed five feet below the nacelle. A twin wheel-and-skid undercarriage of exceptionally narrow track was fitted, stability on the ground being achieved by the tail skids at the base of the tail fins.

Almost certainly owing to the esteem in which Booth was held, four examples of the Sparrow were ordered — two from the Blackburn Aeroplane & Motor Co of Leeds, and two from Hewlett & Blondeau Ltd. It is said that all four were built and delivered to the RNAS at Chingford, Essex, but, being somewhat overweight and underpowered, were found to be difficult to control in the air and were soon abandoned. As far as is known, the Davis gun was never fitted.

Type: Single pusher engine, single-seat, single-bay biplane scout.
Manufacturers: The Blackburn Aeroplane & Motor Co Ltd, Leeds; Hewlett & Blondeau Ltd, Leagrave, Bedfordshire.
Powerplant: One 80hp Gnome rotary engine driving two-blade propeller.
Structure: Predominantly wood with fabric covering; twin wheel-and-skid undercarriage.
Dimensions (Approx only): Span, 33ft 5in; length, 22ft 9in; height, 10ft 3in.
Weights and Performance: Not known.
Armament: Intended to be armed with one 2-pdr Davis recoilless, quick-firing gun in the nose of the nacelle.
Prototypes: Four, Nos 1452-1453 (Hewletts), and 1536-1537 (Blackburn). No production.

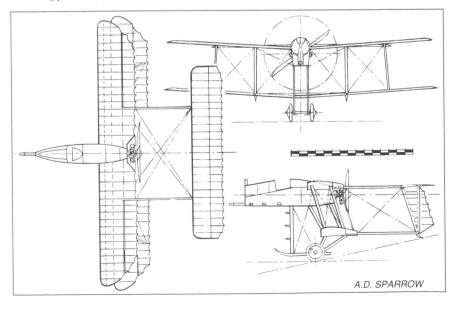

A.D. SPARROW

Above and right: *The Vickers F.B.7 in 1915; the picture on the right shows the handed propellers.* (Photos: J M Bruce, above, and via E B Morgan, right).

Vickers F.B. 7

Designed under contract to Vickers Ltd by R L Howard Flanders (founder of a pioneering aircraft company which carried his name at Brooklands) and generally regarded as the first British twin-engine 'fighter', the Vickers F.B.7 was more accurately a gun-carrier, in the same context as the earlier Gunbus series. It was of most ungainly appearance, possessing large wing gap without stagger, but with considerable top wing overhang. This, and the mounting of rotary engines within the wing gap, resulted in a veritable maze of struts and bracing wires.

Designed to mount a one-pounder Vickers gun on the observer's nose cockpit, the fuselage was of rectangular section at the forward end, fairing to inverted triangular section aft of the pilot's cockpit below the trailing edge of the upper wing. The twin-wheel undercarriage possessed very wide track and a central skid. Twin kingposts extended above the upper wings in the plane of the outer interplane struts, supporting cable-bracing for the outer sections of the wing. There was no dihedral on upper and lower wing except on the overhang sections of the upper wing. Ailerons were only fitted on the upper wings and there was no fixed tail fin foward of the balanced rudder.

The prototype F.B.7 was powered by uncowled 100hp Gnome *monosoupape* handed rotaries, but these were enclosed in cowled nacelles soon after its first flight in August 1915. When, however, the War Office ordered a dozen aircraft it was found that these engines were in short supply and the production version, termed the F.B.7A, was to be powered by a pair of 80hp Renault V-eight engines — permitting a small reduction in the number of struts. Only one F.B.7A, which also featured a re-designed fuselage with the pilot's cockpit moved forward of the wings, was completed, only to be discovered that the aircraft had suffered a substantial loss of performance due to the reduction in available power. Vickers, therefore, sought and obtained cancellation of the production contract.

Type: Twin-engine, two-seat, two-bay tractor biplane gun-carrier.
Manufacturer: Vickers Ltd (Aviation Department), Knightsbridge, London.
Powerplant: F.B.7. Two 100hp Gnome *monosoupape* handed rotary engines. F.B.7A. Two 80hp Renault V-eight engines.
Structure: Steel tubular construction throughout with ply and fabric covering.
Dimensions: Span, 59ft 6in; length, 36ft 0in; wing area, 640 sq ft.
Weights: (F.B.7). Tare, 2,136lb; all-up, 3,196lb.
Performance: (F.B.7). Max speed, 75 mph at 5,000ft; climb to 5,000ft, 18 min; endurance, 2½ hr.
Armament: Single one-pounder Vickers quick-firing gun in nose.
Prototypes: One F.B.7 (flown in August 1915); one F.B.7A, No 5717. No production.

Vickers E.S.1 and E.S.2

Harold Barnwell's E.S.1 was, like the F.B.7, first flown in August 1915 and, on account of its remarkable perform-ance, became popularly known as the Barnwell Bullet. In appearance it was very advanced for its day, being a single-bay, unstaggered biplane with fully-cowled 100hp Gnome *monosoupape* engine. The wooden fuselage was of circular section almost as far aft as the tailplane, and its speed performance (117 mph at sea level) was largely attrib-utable to careful attention to detail design. Wings and tailplane were of rectangular planform, and the fin was gracefully curved to blend with a rounded rudder.

Such was the extraordinary perform-ance demonstrated by the E.S.1 that the War Office sent the only example, No 7509, to France for operational trials

Left: *The sole Vickers E.S.1, No 7509, showing the attempt to fully cowl a rotary engine.* (Photo: via E B Morgan).

Below: *The second E.S.2, No 7760. This view well illustrates the bulky fuselage and the aperture in the upper wing between the cabane struts, introduced to improve the pilot's upward field of vision. Note also the rounded wingtips.* (Photo: G S Leslie/J M Bruce Collection)

with line pilots, although it was in fact unarmed. Unfortunately the E.S.1 met with outspoken criticism from Service pilots who complained that the bulky fuselage and upper wing severely restricted the view from the cockpit. Moreover, being fully cowled, the engine frequently overheated and the aircraft narrowly escaped being consumed by fire. It was eventually written off by Capt P H L Playfair (later Air Marshal Sir Patrick, KBE, CB, CVO, MC).

Encouraged to pursue the design, Vickers had already produced the E.S.2 (sometimes referred to as the E.S.1 Mark II), and this flew in September 1915 with a 110hp Clerget in a shorter chord cowling. Most obvious changes, however, were embodied in the wings which now featured rounded tips of slightly greater span, and an enlarged trailing edge cut-out as well as an aperture in the centre section between the spars to improve the pilot's field of vision.

Later the Clerget was replaced by a Le Rhône of similar power, and this returned a speed similar to that of the E.S.1 — despite the inclusion of armament in the later aircraft. This comprised a fixed Vickers machine gun mounted on the port upper longeron forward of the cockpit and recessed into the nose decking to fire forward through the propeller by means of the new Vickers-Challenger interrupter gear.

Although the fuselage section was of marginally smaller diameter, the E.S.2 still met with opposition from pilots for its lack of downward visibility, and the E.S.2 (of which two examples were produced) was abandoned. Their value nevertheless lay in the experience they afforded Vickers in the development of later tractor scouts which, from early 1916, began to replace the old pusher Gunbus formula in service.

Type: Single-engine, single-seat, single-bay biplane scout.
Manufacturer: Vickers Ltd (Aviation Department), Knightsbridge, London.
Powerplant: E.S.1. 100hp Gnome *monosoupape* engine. E.S.2. 110hp Clerget; 110hp Le Rhône.
Structure: Predominantly wooden construction with fabric covering. Ailerons on upper and lower wings; twin-wheel undercarriage without skid.
Dimensions: E.S.1. Span, 24ft 4½in; length, 20ft 3in; height, 8ft 0in; wing area, 215 sq ft. E.S.2 (Clerget). Span, 24ft 5½in; length, 20ft 3in; height, 8ft 2in; wing area, 215 sq ft.
Weights: E.S.1. Tare, 843lb; all-up, 1,295lb. E.S.2 (Clerget). Tare, 981lb; all-up, 1,502lb.
Performance: E.S.1. Max speed, 117 mph at sea level; climb to 5,000ft, 6 min 40 sec; service ceiling, 15,500ft; endurance, 3 hr. E.S.2 (Clerget). Max speed, 112 mph at sea level; climb to 5,000ft, 6 min 25 sec; endurance, 2 hr.
Armament: E.S.1, none. E.S.2, one fixed 0.303in Vickers machine gun in the nose with Vickers-Challenger interrupter gear.
Prototypes: E.S.1, one, No 7509 (first flown in August 1915). E.S.2, two, Nos 7759 and 7760 (first flown in September 1915). No production.

Martinsyde G.100 and G.102 Elephant

Built during the summer of 1915, the Martinsyde G.100 was designed largely by A A Fletcher and, from the outset, was intended as a long-range escort single-seat fighter. It was a well-proportioned two-bay tractor biplane with moderate stagger and was fitted with ailerons on upper and lower wings. Power was provided by a 120hp Beardmore straight-six water-cooled engine which, in the prototype No 4735, drove a three-blade propeller — an unusual feature for its day.

Probably flown by F P Raynham at the end of August, the prototype was followed by 100 production aircraft in two batches, the three-blade propeller having been replaced by the more customary two-blade type. Although G.100s were distributed among several squadrons, which employed them as escorts for their own bombing machines, only No 27 came to be fully equipped with

A production Martinsyde G.102, A3948, with the Lewis gun on the upper wing; just visible is the spigot mounting for another Lewis gun on the port side of the cockpit's rear coaming. (Photo: J W R Taylor)

the type, arriving in France on 1 March 1916. And it was about this time that the sobriquet 'Elephant' gained popularity — presumably on account of the aeroplane's unusually large proportions for a single-seater — so much so that this animal was portrayed in No 27 Squadron's Badge (which has remained in use to this day).

Indeed, with a fuel load sufficient to sustain a 5½-hour endurance, the power and load-carrying capacity of the Elephant quickly recommended it for use as a bombing aircraft, although it continued to be used in offensive fighting patrols. The first bombing attack was carried out by six Elephants of No 27 Squadron against Bapaume on 1 July 1916, the day on which the Somme offensive was launched.

Normal gun armament of the Elephant in the air fighting rôle was a single Lewis gun above the upper wing centre-section; to this was frequently added a second Lewis gun immediately aft of the pilot's cockpit, firing rearwards; it is difficult to imagine how the pilot, while controlling his aircraft in combat, could contrive to aim and fire this gun with the slightest accuracy.

Soon after the G.100s first arrived in France, a more powerful version, the

G.102, appeared, powered by the 160hp Beardmore engine. Although of poorer reliability, this engine increased the Elephant's speed by about 7 mph. This version remained in service for the rest of the War, principally with home-based training units, but also in the Middle East.

Type: Single-engine, single-seat, two-bay biplane escort fighter (also extensively used as a bomber).

Manufacturer: Martinsyde Ltd, Brooklands, Surrey.

Powerplant: G.100. One 120hp Beardmore straight six-cylinder water-cooled in-line engine driving two-blade propeller. G.102. 160hp Beardmore.

Dimensions: Span, 38ft 0in; length, 26ft 6in (G.102, 27ft 0in); height, 9ft 8in; wing area, 410 sq ft.

Weights: G.100. Tare, 1,759lb; all-up, 2,424lb. G.102. Tare, 1,793lb; all-up, 2,458lb.

Performance: G.100. Max speed, 96 mph at sea level; climb to 10,000ft, 19 min; service ceiling, 14,000ft; endurance, 5½ hr. G.102. Max speed, 103 mph at sea level; climb to 10,000ft, 15 min 55 sec; service ceiling, 16,000ft; endurance, 4½ hr.

Armament: One 0.303in Lewis machine gun mounted above the upper wing centre section to fire above the propeller arc, and one Lewis gun mounted aft of the cockpit to fire rearwards.

Prototype: One G.100, No 4735 (probably first flown by F P Raynham in August 1915 at Brooklands).

Production: G.100, 100 aircraft (Nos 7258-7307 and 7459-7508); G.102, 171 aircraft (A1561-A1610, A3935-A4004 and A6250-A6300).

Summary of Service: Martinsyde Elephants served with Nos 18, 20, 21, 23, 25 and 27 Squadrons, RFC, in France, with Nos 51, 63 and 110 Squadrons based in Britain, and with Nos 30, 67, 72 and 142 Squadrons in the Middle East).

Pemberton-Billing P.B.23 and P.B.25

In the seven months following the first flight of the P.B.9 in August 1914, Noel Pemberton Billing undertook the design of a further dozen aircraft, none of whose manufacture has been confirmed, although one of these may have been the P.B. Boxkite (said to have been allocated

the number 1374, and powered by a 50hp Gnome rotary engine). His P.B.23, a single-engine pusher biplane scout, was almost certainly inspired by Geoffrey de Havilland's Airco D.H.2, which predated it by more than two months.

However, whereas the D.H.2's nacelle was mounted directly on the lower wing, the P.B.23 featured a well-streamlined, metal-clad nacelle strut-mounted

The sole Pemberton-Billing P.B.23 with 80hp Le Rhone engine, metal-clad nacelle and pronounced dihedral on the lower wing; the aircraft was affectionately known as 'Sparklet' or 'Push-Proj'; the Lewis gun can just be seen projecting from the front of the nacelle. (Photo: P T Capon).

The first production Pemberton-Billing P.B.25 Scout, No 9001, with 110hp Clerget engine, swept wings and fabric-covered nacelle. (Photo: G S Leslie / J M Bruce Collection)

in the wing gap, with two pairs of plain struts being attached to the upper longerons and the upper wing, and pairs of plain struts to the lower longerons and the lower wing spars. Twin fins and rudders were located inboard on the wide-span tailplane, the entire empennage being carried on four booms which extended aft from the rear spars of the upper and lower mainplanes. The P.B.23 featured parallel-chord unswept wings, the lower wings having pronounced dihedral, but the upper wing being flat. A single, fixed forward Lewis machine gun was located low down in the nacelle's extreme nose and could, with difficulty, be re-armed from the cockpit.

The 80hp Le Rhône, fitted initially, was obviously underpowered when the P.B.23 first flew in September 1915, and it was proposed to fit a 100hp Gnome *monosoupape*. The aircraft failed to impress the War Office, but the Admiralty ordered twenty examples of a modified version (allocated the serial numbers 9001-9020). In fact this version, which emerged as the P.B.25, only

superficially resembled the earlier aircraft. The nacelle was lengthened and constructed entirely of wood with fabris covering. Both wings were swept back eleven degrees, and the lower wing's dihedral much reduced; the lower fuselage/wing mountings now comprised a pair of N-struts. The vertical tail surfaces were increased in area.

The first 'production' P.B.25, 9001 (officially termed the Scout) was fitted with an uncowled 110hp Clerget rotary engine driving a two-blade propeller,

but 9002 was powered by the 100hp Gnome driving a four-blade propeller, and with the latter the aircraft returned a performance about ten per cent better than that of the D.H.2. Be that as it may, the Airco aircraft had already been selected for production and its continued delivery to the RFC squadrons in France was a matter of considerable urgency, so that the P.B.25 does not appear to have reached any operational unit. Moreover, the Scout quickly gained a bad reputation for being particularly difficult to handle during take-off and landing. Examples are known to have flown with the RNAS at Hendon and Eastchurch, but reliable confirmation that all twenty aircraft ordered were completed cannot be gained.

The accompanying data refers to the Pemberton-Billing P.B.25.

Type: Single-engine, single-seat, single-bay pusher biplane scout.
Manufacturer: Pemberton-Billing Ltd., Woolston, Southampton.
Powerplant: One 100hp Gnome *monosoupape* nine-cylinder rotary engine; one 110hp Clerget nine-cylinder rotary engine.
Structure: All-wooden construction, fabric-covered.
Dimensions: Span, 33ft 0in; length, 42ft 1in; height, 10ft 5in; wing area, 277sq ft.
Weights: Tare, 1,080lb; all-up, 1,576lb.
Performance: Max speed, 99mph at sea level; climb to 6,000ft, 8 min 30 sec; range, approx 200miles.
Armament: One 0.303in Lewis machine gun on nose of nacelle immediately forward of cockpit.
Production: Twenty aircraft ordered (9001-9020), but completion of all aircraft has been questioned.

R.A.F. F.E.8

Designed under the leadership of the Royal Aircraft Factory's chief draughtsman, John Kenworthy, the F.E.8 was born shortly before the appearance of a successful British gun interrupter gear and was therefore, of necessity, a pusher biplane scout. Generally regarded as possessing more pleasing lines than the business-like Airco D.H.2, the F.E.'s performance was extraordinarily similar; like the D.H.2, production of the F.E.8 was spurred by the growing number of German fighting scouts over the

The first prototype R.A.F. F.E.8 at Farnborough in November 1915 shortly before its crash, showing its general similarity with the D.H.2; note the position of the remotely-controlled Lewis gun in the nose. (Photo: Royal Aerospace Establishment, No 975 dated 11 November 1915)

Western Front.

The prototype F.E.8, possibly allotted the number 7456, was first flown in

about October 1915, but crashed the following month; a second prototype, possibly 7457, was hurriedly constructed

Another view of the F.E.8 prototype here showing the unstaggered, parallel-chord wings, and the large spinner on the four-blade propeller. (Photo: Royal Aerospace Establishment, No. 973 dated 11 November 1915)

and rushed to France, where it was favourably commented upon — prompting the immediate raising of production sub-contracts with private manufacturers, namely the Darracq company and Vickers.

However, delays in establishing these production lines resulted in the F.E.8 not reaching fighter squadrons in France until June 1916, the first being two aircraft with No 29 Squadron at Abeele, commanded by Maj E L Conran. The first to be fully equipped with F.E.8s was No 40 Squadron which, commanded by Maj Robert Loraine (one of the original RFC pilots, and later Lt-Col, DSO, MC), arrived at St Omer in August.

It was in the late summer of 1916 that reports filtered back to the Factory that the F.E.8 was suffering a spate of spinning accidents, and that the aircraft was attracting an ill-reputation in this respect, being referred to as the 'spinning incinerator'. It was quickly established that, although pusher aircraft tended to spin more readily from the stall, the F.E.8 possessed spinning characteristics not significantly different from other aircraft. The indefatigable Factory pilot, Maj Frank Goodden, deliberately spun an F.E.8 three times in each direction from no more than 3,500 feet, and recovered by applying the customary control movements. The fact was that RFC pilots were still not, in 1916, being instructed in spin recovery as a matter of routine during their flying training.

Nevertheless the F.E.8s clearly became outclassed in air combat within three months of their first arrival over the Western Front. Yet they continued in service, even though casualties increased sharply. No 40 Squadron was to suffer a disaster when, on 9 March 1917, nine F.E.8s were attacked by *Jasta 11*, led by Manfred von Richthofen. In a fight that lasted half an hour, eight of the British machines were forced down or destroyed, and the last aircraft crashed on landing.

The F.E.8 was ultimately withdrawn from operational service in July that year, when No 41 Squadron disposed of its aircraft in favour of Airco D.H.5s.

Type: Single pusher engine, single-seat, two-bay biplane scout.

Manufacturers: The Royal Aircraft Factory, Farnborough, Hants; The Darracq Motor Engineering Co Ltd, Fulham, London; Vickers Ltd (Aviation Department), Knightsbridge, London.

Powerplant: 100hp Gnome *monosoupape* rotary engine driving four-blade propeller (as standard); also 110hp Le Rhône and 110hp Clerget.

Dimensions: Span, 31ft 6in; length, 23ft 8in; height, 9ft 2in; wing area, 218 sq ft.

Weights: Tare, 895lb; all-up, 1,346lb.

Performance: Max speed, 94 mph at sea level; climb to 10,000ft, 17 min 30 sec; service ceiling, 14,500ft; endurance, 2½ hr.

Armament: Prototype armed with remotely controlled 0.303in Lewis machine gun mounted low in the extreme nose of the nacelle. Production aircraft armed with spigot-mounted Lewis gun level with the pilot's eyes.

Prototypes: Two; possibly Nos 7456 and 7457, built by the Royal Aircraft Factory, and first flown in about October 1915.

Production: 295 (245 by Darracq: Nos 6378-6477, A41-A65 and A4869-A4987; 50 by Vickers, Nos 7595-7644). Two aircraft, 3689 and 3690, were apparently allocated to the Admiralty but were probably not built.

Summary of Service: F.E.8s served with Nos 5, 29, 40 and 41 Squadrons, RFC, in France, and with various home-based training units.

Vickers F.B.8

Whereas Vickers' F.B.7 had been designed by Howard Flanders, the company's second essay in twin-engine fighter design was undertaken by Reginald Kirshaw ('Rex') Pierson during the autumn of 1915, and the single example was flown that November. Compared to the F.B.7, Pierson's aircraft was of extraordinarily compact design, its wing span being over 20 feet shorter and its all-up

The Vickers F.B.8 at Brooklands late in 1915. As well as the oil slinger rings round the Gnome engines, a pair of vertical shields on the sides of the gunner's cockpit contributed some protection from the hot castor oil sprayed by the rotary engines. (Photo: via E B Morgan)

weight some 500lb less. Powered by the same 100hp Gnome *monosoupape* handed rotaries as the earlier aircraft, the F.B.8 was accordingly about 20 mph faster; these engines were encircled by oil slinger rings.

The wings of the F.B.8, being of only slightly unequal span, featured no significant overhang, so that untidy kingpost-supported bracing was superfluous and the strut arrangement was altogether tidier; ailerons were fitted to both upper and lower wings. The undercarriage and tail unit, however, remained much the same. The big one-pounder Vickers gun was discarded in favour of a Lewis gun on a spigot mounting forward of the observer-gunner's bow position.

It is perhaps strange, however, that Pierson persisted in locating the pilot's cockpit in the same position as in the original F.B.7 (under the trailing edge of the upper wing); the earlier design had been criticised on account of the distance between the two crew members, and communication between them would have been almost impossible during operational flying, and was much reduced in the F.B.7A.

Other than this assumed flaw, the F.B.8 was an ingenious and promising design which might have attracted official interest had not the introduction into single-engine tractor scouts of front gun interrupter gears not been imminent. Even so, as will be evident, Vickers persisted with pusher designs employing free-firing bow guns for some years. Pierson, on the other hand, was to call on his experience with the F.B.8 to produce his famous, much larger F.B.27

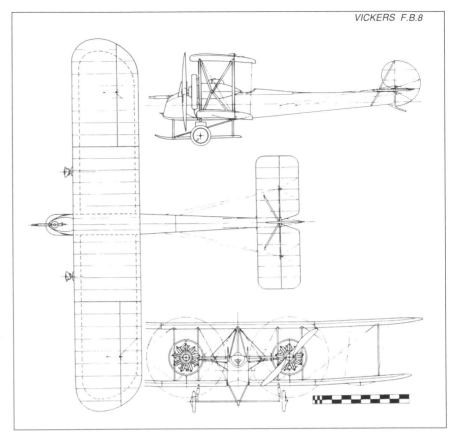

VICKERS F.B.8

Vimy heavy bomber just two years later — an aircraft that bore more than a superficial resemblance to his twin-engine fighter.

Type: Twin engine, two-seat, two-bay tractor biplane gun carrier.
Manufacturer: Vickers Ltd (Aviation Department), Knightsbridge, London.
Powerplant: Two 100hp Gnome *monosoupape* nine-cylinder handed rotary engines driving two-blade propellers.
Structure: Steel tubular construction throughout with ply and fabric covering.
Dimensions: Span, 38ft 4in; length, 28ft 2in; wing area, 468 sq ft.
Weights: Tare, 1,840lb; all-up, 2,700lb.
Performance: Max speed, 98 mph at sea level; climb to 5,000ft, 10 min; ceiling, 14,000ft; endurance, 3 hr.
Armament: One 0.303in Lewis gun on nose spigot mounting.
Prototype: One (flown in November 1915). No production.

Sopwith 1½-Strutter

This quaintly-named aircraft earned its place in early British military aviation history as the first RFC and RNAS fighter to be provided with a machine gun synchronized to fire through a tractor propeller for, owing to the previous lack of a reliable synchronizing gear, British fighting scouts had employed free-firing guns mounted in the nose of a nacelle with a pusher engine in the rear. Moreover, because it was now possible to accommodate a gunner in addition to the pilot, the 1½-Strutter

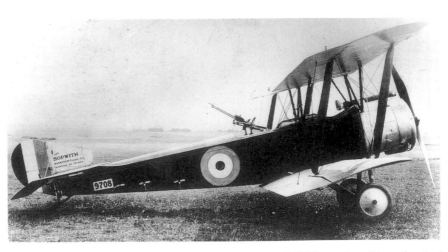

An early Sopwith-built 1½-Strutter, No 9708, of No 3 Wing, RNAS, complete with synchronized Vickers gun and Lewis gun on Scarff ring. (Photo: G S Leslie/J M Bruce Collection)

Another view of a 1½-Strutter two-seater of the the RNAS; note the exceptionally tidy engine cowling with the synchronized Vickers gun mounted above it. (Photo: G S Leslie/J M Bruce Collection)

became the first British operational two-seat fighting scout and thereby created a design formula that was to survive in the RFC and RAF for more than a quarter century. The 1½-Strutter is thought to have owed its name to the arrangement of the centreplane struts which, being attached to the top fuselage longerons, did not extend the full depth of the interplane gap. In service with the RNAS the aircraft was officially termed the Sopwith Type 9700 and in the RFC the Sopwith Two-Seater.

The structure of the 1½-Strutter followed conventional Sopwith practice, the wire-braced wooden box members of the fuselage being fabric-covered aft of the gunner's cockpit, and forward by plywood sheet. The pilot was situated directly below the top wing centre section with a single Vickers machine gun mounted centrally on the nose and engine cowling. The observer's position was some four feet aft of the pilot, the intervening space being occupied by the main fuel tank. Several front gun synchronizing systems appeared in 1½-Strutters, including Vickers-Challenger, Scarff-Dibovski, Ross and Sopwith-Kauper, and either Nieuport or Scarff ring mountings were used for the Lewis gun on the observer's cockpit. An unusual feature at the time was the provision of an adjustable tailplane whose incidence could be controlled by a wheel in the cockpit.

The 1½-Strutter was originally ordered by the Admiralty both as a two-seat fighter and as a light bomber, and the first prototype, No. 3686, was first flown in mid-December 1915 by Harry Hawker. The early orders for 150 aircraft were placed with Sopwith for the RNAS, of which the last 35 were single-seat bombers, the remainder two-seat fighters. Other orders were placed for the RFC with Sopwith, Fairey, Vickers and Ruston, Proctor for about 600 two-seat fighters. However, shortly before the Battle of the Somme, it was reported that the RFC was desperately short of fighting aircraft in France, with a result that the Admiralty agreed to transfer a total of 77 1½-Strutters to the RFC, all of them two-seat fighters.

The 1½-Strutter evidently impressed its pilots from the outset, the attractively compact aircraft being powered initially by a 110hp Clerget rotary, which bestowed a speed of 107 mph at sea level. Production aircraft from the Sopwith and Ruston, Proctor factories began appearing in April 1916, the Admiralty's bombers being delivered that month to No 5 Wing, RNAS at Coudekerque in France, and the RFC's fighters joining Nos 45 and 70 Squadrons at Gosport and Farnborough respectively, also in April. Such was the shortage of fighters on the Somme front that No 70 Squadron began flying its 1½-Strutters to France in May, and the first of the ex-RNAS transfers joined the Squadron's 'C' Flight and followed in July. These were the only RFC 1½-Strutter squadrons to see action over the Western Front during 1916, delivery of new aircraft being slow to accelerate, and No 45 Squadron did not in fact complete its establishment until the last day of September. The RNAS, in addition to its transfer of 1½-Strutters to the RFC, also 'lent' one Flight of 'Naval Eight', the famous No 8 (Naval) Squadron which also flew the aircraft for a short period.

Although increasingly outclassed by the newly-arrived Albatros D Is, armed with a pair of Spandau front guns and possessing a top speed of 109 mph, the 1½-Strutter acquitted itself well, largely

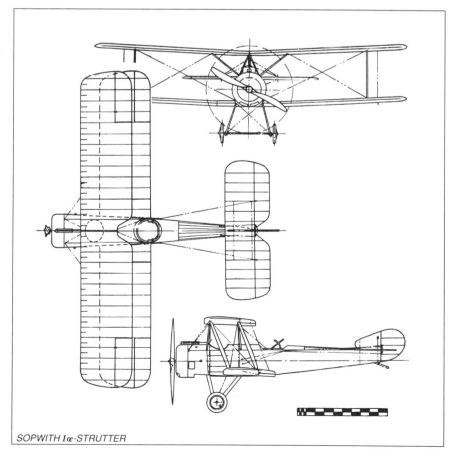

SOPWITH 1½-STRUTTER

A single-seat 1½-Strutter, B762, equipped to be flown from the rear cockpit, and with the front cockpit faired over. Twin Lewis guns are mounted over the pilot's windscreen, and no Vickers gun is fitted. Note the head fairing behind the cockpit. The aircraft had been rebuilt by No 1 (Southern) Aircraft Repair Depot, South Farnborough, for a Home Defence Squadron. (Photo: R.A.F. Museum, Neg. No P04632)

on account of its own front gun which, in the early weeks, appeared to take the Germans unawares. Nevertheless, it was by no means as nimble as the German single-seaters, and casualties began to mount on the two Squadrons. Towards the end of October No 45 Squadron lost three of its aircraft in a single day.

Only one other Squadron, No 43 (later famous as 'The Fighting Cocks'), flew 1½-Strutters in France, arriving in January 1917. By then the aircraft were being delivered with 130hp Clerget engines, but the additional power did little to improve the aircraft's performance significantly. No 43 Squadron flew its aircraft with distinction in trench attacks during the Battles of Arras and Messines.

The heavy casualties suffered by the RFC in France during 'Bloody April' served to emphasise the desperate need to introduce new fighting scouts into service to counter the new Albatros and Fokkers which had begun to dominate the skies over France. The 1½-Strutter started to be replaced in France from July 1917, although three other Home Defence Squadrons of the RFC (Nos. 37, 44 and 78) began receiving the aircraft in the same month, but most had

disappeared from operational service by the end of that year, replaced by Sopwith Camel single-seaters. Only No 78 Squadron retained 1½-Strutters, at Suttons Farm, until July 1918.

Various figures have been quoted for the total production of Sopwith 1½-Strutters, and the number most usually quoted by generally reliable sources is 1,534; it is also stated that as many as 4,500 examples were built under licence in France by Lioré et Olivier and Hanriot, of which 514 were purchased for the American Expeditionary Force. At least three squadrons of the Belgian air force flew 1½-Strutters, and some aircraft reached Russia. Shortly before the Armistice twenty aircraft were supplied to Romania, and other examples flew in Latvia and Japan.

Type: Single-engine, single- or two-seat biplane fighter or light bomber.
Manufacturers: The Sopwith Aviation Co Ltd, Kingston-upon-Thames; The Fairey Aviation Co Ltd, Hayes; Hooper & Co Ltd, Chelsea, London; Mann, Egerton & Co Ltd, Norwich; Morgan & Co, Leighton Buzzard; Ruston, Proctor & Co Ltd, Lincoln; Vickers Ltd, Crayford; Wells Aviation Co Ltd, Chelsea, London; Westland Aircraft Works, Yeovil; F. Lioré et Olivier, Levallois-Perret, France; Hanriot et Cie, Billancourt, France.
Powerplant: One 110hp Clerget 9Z or 130hp Clerget 9Bc nine-cylinder rotary engine (also 80hp Le Rhône 9C, 110hp Le Rhône 9J, 130hp Le Rhône Jby, and 135hp Clerget 9Ba)
Structure: All-wooden construction with fabric and plywood covering.
Dimensions: Span, 33ft 6in; length, 25ft 3in; height, 10ft 3in; wing area, 346sq ft.
Weights (two-seat fighter): Tare, 1,305lb; all-up, 2,150lb.
Performance (two-seat fighter, Clerget 9Bc): Maximum speed, 107mph at sea level; climb to 10,000ft, 17 min 48 sec; service ceiling, 15,500ft; range, approx. 230 miles.
Armament (two-seater): One fixed, synchronized forward-firing 0.303in Vickers machine gun on nose, and one free 0.303in Lewis machine gun on Nieuport or Scarff mounting on rear cockpit.
Prototype: One, No. 3686 (first flown by Harry Hawker in December 1915)
Production (fighters only; approx. figures): Sopwith, 161; Fairey, 100; Hooper, 100; Mann, Egerton, 55; Morgan, 150; Ruston, Proctor, 350; Vickers, 150; Wells, 100; Westland, 50. Overseas (all versions), figure of 4,500 quoted.
Summary of Service (fighters only): Nos 37, 43, 44, 45, 70 and 78 Squadrons, RFC and RAF; Nos 5 and 8 (Naval) Squadrons, RNAS. (Also thirteen *Escadrilles* of *l'Armée de l'Air*, three squadrons of the Belgian Flying Corps, and 88th, 90th and 99th Aero Squadrons of the US Air Service).

Vickers E.F.B.6 and F.B.9

The efforts to extend the successful F.B.5 Gunbus formula, as has been shown, brought forth the twin-engine F.B.7 and F.B.8, which appeared too late to warrant further work on them. Another design, the Vickers E.F.B.6, was less radical in that it retained the basic F.B.5 single pusher engine format.

The sole Vickers E.F.B.6 at Brooklands. (Photo: J M Bruce)

Right: *An early F.B.9 showing the improved nacelle nose shape and enlarged tailplane; compare with the late production F.B.5 pictured at the bottom of page 25. (Photo: Vickers PLC).*

Below: *A production F.B.9 with the improved nose profile; this aircraft, almost certainly destined for, or serving with a training unit, is equipped with dual controls, as evidenced by the linked elevator control arms on the side of the nacelle; no provision is made to mount a gun on the front cockpit. Note the absence of landing skids on these F.B.9s. (Photo: Vickers PLC)*

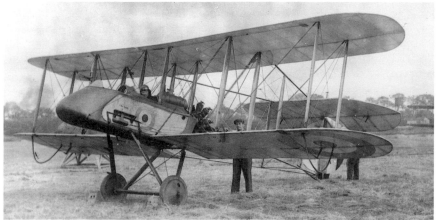

It did however adopt the upper wing's greatly increased span with large overhang that characterised Flanders' F.B.7, in an effort to increase the F.B.5's load-carrying ability. Like the F.B.7, however, this aeroplane was blighted by the plethora of struts and bracing wires necessary for this wing configuration, and its poor performance on only a single engine resulted in the aircraft's further development being abandoned.

Instead efforts focussed on generally cleaning up the F.B.5 itself, and in December 1915 the prototype F.B.9 was first flown. This retained the 100hp Gnome *monosoupape* rotary but featured smaller wings with rounded tips; the landing skids were omitted and the nacelle nose was redesigned to appear as a D-shape in side elevation. Raf-wires replaced the former twisted-strand cables for interplane bracing; and the spigot mounting for the nose Lewis gun was replaced by a Vickers ring to permit the gun to traverse.

The nose profile underwent further improvement, the bottom line of the nacelle being lengthened to make possible an improved aerodynamic shape. Thus modified the F.B.9 possessed a maximum speed of 82.6 mph at sea level — an increase of about a dozen miles per hour over the F.B.5. At least one F.B.9 with the improved nose profile was powered by a 110hp Le Rhône engine.

Although Vickers had high hopes for this new Gunbus, and orders were placed for about 119 production aircraft, there is little doubt that from the outset the War Office was more interested in the F.B.9 as a trainer than as an operational gun carrier. That alone was ample testimony to its excellent handling qualities, but the truth was that the Gunbus was already being rendered obsolete by the arrival of the synchronized front gun. It is possible, though doubtful, that a few F.B.9s were sent to France, and it is unlikely that any were flown operationally. On the other hand, fifty were distributed among home-based training units, including No 6 Reserve Squadron at Catterick, and No 10 Reserve Squadron at Joyce Green.

The accompanying data refer to the production F.B.9.

Type: Single pusher engine, single-seat, two-bay biplane gun carrier.
Manufacturer: Vickers Ltd, Knightsbridge, London; aircraft built at Weybridge, Surrey.
Powerplant: One 100hp Gnome *monosoupape* engine driving two-blade pusher propeller (as standard); also 110hp Le Rhône engine.
Dimensions: Span, 33ft 9in; length, 28ft 5½in; height, 11ft 6in; wing area, 340 sq ft.
Weights: Tare, 1,029lb; all-up, 1,892lb.
Performance: Max speed, 82.6 mph at sea level; climb to 10,000ft, 51 min; endurance, 5 hr.
Armament: One 0.303in Lewis machine gun on Vickers or Scarff ring mounting on front cockpit.
Prototype and Production: One prototype (first flown in December 1915). Approximately 119 production aircraft (Nos 5271-5290, 7812-7835, A1411-A1460 and A8601-A8625)
Summary of Service: No evidence has been traced to suggest that F.B.9s flew operationally. Fifty aircraft were distributed among such units as Nos 6 and 10 Reserve Squadrons, and No 187 Training Squadron in the United Kingdom.

Robey Peters
Tractor Scout

Very little is known about the designs of J A Peters, produced while he was working with Robey & Co Ltd of Lincoln, a company which had undertaken sub-contract manufacture of Sopwith Gun Bus aircraft early in 1915. Three such designs came to be built, of which two were single-seat scouts, one a tractor and the other a pusher biplane. The latter is said to have suffered an accident during its first flight.

Nor is it known whether the little tractor scout was even completed, although the accompanying photograph shows it awaiting installation of its engine — said to have been an 80hp Clerget — and covering of the airframe. Construction appears to have been of wood throughout, and one assumes it would have been fabric covered overall. There is slight stagger on the wings, and ailerons are fitted to upper and lower flying surfaces. A balanced rudder, without fin, is apparent, and all bracing is of twisted-strand cabling.

The position of the pilot's cockpit is interesting in that it is located directly below mid-chord of the upper wing, so that the trailing edge cut-out would have been of little value in extending the

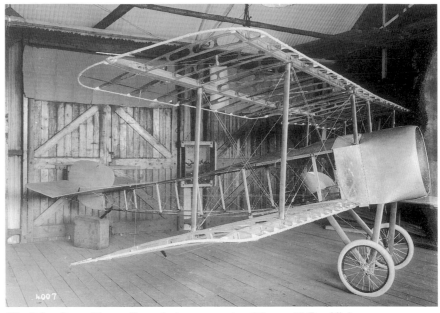

The Robey Peters Tractor Scout during construction. (Photo: N Franklin)

pilot's field of vision, while the cabane struts and bracing wires, close on either side, would appear to constitute an almost impenetrable maze to negotiate for entry and exit from the cockpit.

There is no evidence in the photograph as to whether any gun armament was intended to be mounted, as the pilot is situated too far forward to operate a gun on the upper wing, unless it was proposed to mount an upward-firing Lewis gun projecting through the wing centre section. It is not even known

whether the cowling shown in the photograph represented the ultimate shape and position of the engine cowling; if so, it would seem that the c.g. limits would have been exceptionally constricted, for it is not known what position was intended for the fuel tank.

From the general design configuration, outlined above, it seems likely that Peters would have been engaged in the design of this aircraft early in 1915, and that the accompanying photograph was taken during the summer of that year.

Avro Type 521

This single-bay derivative of the famous Avro 504 was intended to be a two-seat fighter. It was designed late in 1915 and embodied features from several 504 sub-variants, including the straight upper longerons of the 504 prototype, the short-span ailerons and tail unit of the 504A, the cabane struts peculiar to the 504E and the V-strut undercarriage of the 504G.

The wing span was reduced from the 504's 36ft to about 27ft 6in, and generous cut-outs were provided in upper and lower wings, as were ailerons. Power was provided by a 110hp Clerget rotary in cowlings reminiscent of the 504.

Mr J M Bruce has speculated that the Type 521 was evolved by way of a naval version of the 504, which may or may

The Avro Type 521 prototype at Farnborough in 1916 during evaluation. (Photo: Royal Aerospace Establishment)

not have been completed; however, he points out that, not being intended for the RNAS, the 521 was fitted with a balanced rudder without fixed tailfin.

The prototype was flown early in

1916 at Trafford Park, Manchester, by Fred Raynham, who complained that it was longitudinally unstable and 'unpleasant to fly'; it was however sent to the Royal Aircraft Factory for evaluation in mid-February.

In due course a production order followed for 25 aircraft, intended for the RFC, but it seems that few, if any, were delivered, and that the Type 521 which is known to have crashed at Gosport in 1917 was in all likelihood the prototype.

Type: Single-engine, two-seat, single-bay scout biplane.
Manufacturer: A V Roe & Co Ltd, Miles Platting, Manchester.
Powerplant: One 110hp Clerget rotary engine driving two-blade propeller.
Structure: All-wood construction with fabric covering.
Dimensions: Span, approx 27ft 6in.
Prototype and Production: One prototype, No 1811 (first flown by F P Raynham in January or February 1916), 25 production aircraft ordered, Nos 7520-7544, but it is not known how many, if any, were completed.

Sopwith Pup

As far as any aeroplane of the First World War could be described as a 'pilot's aeroplane', the delightful little Sopwith Scout — universally known as the Pup, other than in official documents — certainly deserved that description. It is said that the design of the Pup was motivated by the ascendancy of German fighting scouts during the latter half of 1915 and the urgency to give the British flying services an aeroplane that could meet the enemy on equal terms. This urgency clearly dictated the utmost simplicity of design and manufacture, and at least one happy circumstance contributed to the tactical excellence of the Pup in service: the long-awaited availability of front gun interrupter gear, so that almost all Pups were armed with a single forward-firing Vickers gun equipped with Sopwith-Kauper mechanical synchronizing gear.

It is difficult to conceive a simpler airframe structure than that of the Pup. The fuselage comprised a box girder made up from ash longerons and spruce spacers, the whole structure wire-braced and surmounted by curved decking formed by stringers. Aft of the front fireproof bulkhead, structure rigidity was achieved by diagonal ash struts. The

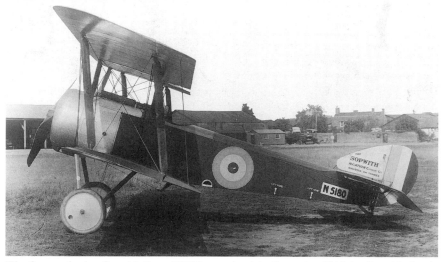

The first production Sopwith Pup, N5180, completed in September 1916 by Sopwith for the Admiralty; it was later flown by the Special Duty Flight, RNAS, 'A' Squadron, at Furnes. (Photo: The Sopwith Aviation Co Ltd)

equal span, single-bay wings were moderately staggered and the cabane struts were splayed outwards to provide a broad centre section which was generously cut away over the pilot's cockpit. The wing structure was built up on twin spars of spindled spruce with spruce ribs and ash riblets; steel tube was employed in the wingtips and fin, rudder and elevator, as well as the tailplane spar on which the elevator was hinged. The V-struts of the undercarriage were of plain steel tube, and the split wheel axles were sprung by rubber cord, the latter arrangement being patented by T O M

Sopwith himself. Relatively small ailerons were fitted on upper and lower wings. At first glance the Pup might appear to be a diminutive offspring of the Sopwith 1½-Strutter — and it was this that may have caused the name Pup to become common usage.

The prototype Pup, No 3691, was passed by Sopwith's experimental department on 9 February 1916 and was first flown by Harry Hawker at Brooklands almost certainly before the end of that month. Numerous influential visitors from the War Office and Admiralty visited Brooklands to watch the Pup on test, and it was evident that large production orders would be forthcoming. Sopwith was, however, already heavily engaged in producing 1½-Strutters, and it was necessary to initiate considerable sub-contract manufacture, three companies, William Beardmore, Standard Motors and Whitehead Aircraft, being contracted to contribute the lion's share of Pup production. Meanwhile Sopwith produced five more prototypes, all powered by 80hp Clergets.

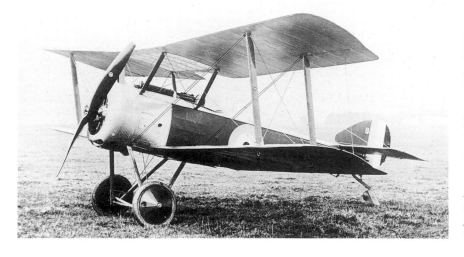

An RFC Pup. Note the large transparent panel in the broad upper wing centre section — made possible by the splayed-out cabane struts. (Photo: G S Leslie/J M Bruce Collection)

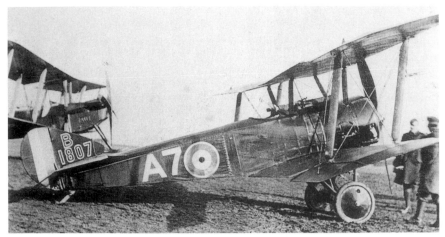

A Standard-built Sopwith Pup, B1807, possibly with an RFC Squadron in France. (Photo: Stuart Leslie)

Sopwith was, however, primarily an Admiralty contractor, and all six Pup prototypes were delivered to Admiralty charge; and it was for the RNAS that the first production order was placed, for 20 Pups built by Sopwith (N5180–N5199) and powered by 80hp Le Rhône engines. With this modest power the Pup possessed a sea level maximum speed of 111.5 mph, and maintained a top speed of over 100 mph up to around 12,000 feet — a performance not previously matched by any fully-loaded British scout.

The first production Pups began appearing in September 1916 and by the end of that month were being flown by No 1 Wing, RNAS, and had gained their first victories over enemy aircraft. (One of the prototypes had been sent out to France in May for operational trials with Naval 'A' Fighting Squadron.)

While Sopwith-built Pups were being delivered to the RNAS in a steadily growing trickle, those destined for the RFC (produced initially by Beardmore) were even slower to materialise, although the first to be delivered arrived on No 54 Squadron, commanded by Maj Kelham Kirk Horn MC, at Castle Bromwich, also in September.

It was a measure of the administrative constraints imposed by the War Office and Admiralty that, despite the heavy aircraft losses suffered by the RFC in the Battle of the Somme during the summer of 1916, there were no means to allow Sopwith to supply Pups to the War Office. Instead, when Sir Douglas Haig appealed to the War Office for reinforcements, the Admiralty — with Cabinet approval — decided to form a new RNAS Pup unit, No 8 (Naval) Squadron on 25 October, under Sqn Cdr G R Bromet (later Air Vice-Marshal Sir Geoffrey, KBE, CB, DSO, RAF), a Squadron that was to gain immortality

with a succession of Sopwith aircraft during the next two years; although only one Flight was initially equipped with Pups, it was soon shown that these aircraft were so much better than the Nieuport Scouts and the 1½-Strutters, and Pups quickly re-equipped the whole Squadron. Within a month the Pups had shot down twenty enemy aircraft, and in February and March 1917 two more units, Nos 3 and 9 (Naval) Squadrons had been equipped with Sopwith-built Pups. During the period immediately before the Battle of Arras, which opened on 9 April, No 3 Squadron, based at Marieux under Sqn Cdr Redford Henry Mulock (later Air Cdre, CBE, DSO, RAF), destroyed so many enemy aircraft that

the Germans began deliberately to avoid combat with the Pups — at a time when other Allied aircraft were suffering catastrophic losses.

Meanwhile No 54 Squadron had completed its working up with Pups and had moved to France on Christmas Eve 1916, and by April the only other two RFC Squadrons to fly these aircraft in France, Nos 46 and 66, had also re-equipped. The latter Squadron in particular, commanded by Maj (later Air Vice-Marshal, OBE, MC, AFC, RAF) Owen Tudor Boyd, was very heavily engaged during the Battles of Arras and Messines. No 54 Squadron's Capt (later Gp Capt) William Victor Strugnell won two Military Crosses when, over a period of three months, he destroyed seven enemy aircraft, the first during the Battle of Arras.

The numerous combat successes by this handful of Pup squadrons during 'Bloody April' demonstrated all to clearly that the system of aircraft supply from the factories needed radical overhaul, and that had the Sopwith Pup not taken eight months to begin to emerge from the production lines in 1916, the RFC would have been adequately equipped to

Type: Single-engine, single-seat, single-bay biplane scout.

Manufacturers: The Sopwith Aviation Co Ltd, Kingston-upon-Thames, Surrey; William Beardmore & Co Ltd, Dalmuir, Dunbartonshire; The Standard Motor Co Ltd, Coventry; Whitehead Aircraft Ltd, Richmond, Surrey.

Powerplant: One 80hp Le Rhône; 80hp Gnome; 80hp Clerget; 100hp Gnome *monosoupape* engine.

Structure: Wooden box-girder fuselage with ash longerons and spruce spacers, wire-braced and fabric-covered; two-spar staggered wings with spindled spruce spars, spruce ribs and ash riblets; steel tubular wingtips and tail unit with fabric covering.

Dimensions: Span, 26ft 6in; length, 19ft 3¾in; height, 9ft 5in; wing area, 254 sq ft.

Weights: (Le Rhône) Tare, 787lb; all-up, 1,225 lb. (Gnome *monosoupape*) Tare, 856lb; all-up, 1,297lb.

Performance: (Le Rhône) Max speed, 111.5 mph at sea level; climb to 10,000ft, 14 min; service ceiling, 17,500ft; endurance, 3 hr. (Gnome *monosoupape*) Max speed, 110 mph at sea level; climb to 10,000ft, 12 min 25 sec; service ceiling, 18,500ft; endurance, 1¾ hr.

Armament: One 0.303in Vickers machine gun with Sopwith-Kauper synchronizing gear to fire through propeller arc. Some Pups armed with eight Le Prieur rockets in addition to gun; other aircraft fitted with single Lewis gun, but not synchronized.

Prototypes: Six. No 3691 (first flown by Harry Hawker at Brooklands, probably during February 1916); Nos 9496, 9497 and 9898-9900, all built by Sopwith.

Production: Total, 1,770. (Beardmore, Nos 9901-9950 and N6430-N6459; Standard, A626-A675, A7301-A7350, B1701-B1850, B5901-B6150 and C201-C550; Whitehead, A6150-A6249, B2151-B2250, B5251-B5400, B7481-B7580, C1451-C1550, C3707-C3776 and D4011-D4210; Sopwith, N5180-N51199, N6160-N6209 and N6460-N6479)

Summary of Service: Pups served with Nos 46, 54 and 66 Squadrons, RFC, in France; Nos. 46, 61 and 112 Squadrons, RFC, Home Defence; No 66 Squadron, RFC, Italy; with CFS, Upavon, and numerous other training units. Naval Pups served with Nos 3, 4, 8, 9 and 12 (Naval) Squadrons, RNAS; Special Duty Flight; No 1 (Naval) Wing, RNAS; aboard HM Carriers *Argus, Campania, Furious* and *Manxman*; HM Light Cruisers *Caledon, Cassandra, Cordelia, Dublin* and *Yarmouth*; and HM Battle Cruiser *Repulse*. Also numerous training untis and Stations at home and overseas.

Another Standard Pup, A674, of No. 66 Squadron, seen at Filton, Bristol, in March 1917. (Photo: Bristol Aeroplane Co Ltd.)

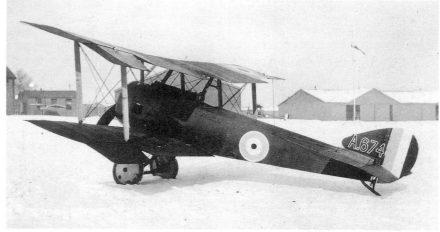

meet the emergency that threatened in France in the spring of 1917.

By the autumn of that year the Pups' single Vickers gun was no longer able to match the new, more heavily armed German scouts, and it was replaced in France by the Sopwith Camel. At home, however, Pups had begun delivery to a number of Home Defence squadrons in order to counter the German bombing attacks which, made by Gotha G IVs, had begun on 25 May 1917 against southeast England.

Alas, through no fault of the aircraft or their pilots but rather because of the lack of a suitable raid warning system, scarcely any success was achieved against the raiders. However the Pup was found to be admirably suitable for night flying and, beginning in December 1917, as the Germans embarked on night raiding with their bombers, they began equipping special night training Squadrons in Britain, namely Nos 187, 188 and 189.

Such were the excellent handling qualities of the Pup that it was a natural instrument for countless experiments, the majority of which were conducted with the naval aircraft. Trials with flotation bags under the lower wings led to

their fitting to a number of Pups which operated over the sea; lying flat underneath the lower wings during normal flight, they would inflate if the aircraft was forced to alight on the water, thereby enabling the Pup to remain afloat for several hours.

Pups performed many of the early trials aboard ships at sea. In June 1917 Flt Cdr F J Rutland flew a Pup from a twenty-foot platform on the fo'c'sle of the light cruiser HMS *Yarmouth* which was sailing at 20 knots into wind, an experiment that led to the fitting of similar platforms aboard HM Cruisers *Caledon, Cassandra, Cordelia* and *Dublin.* And it was Flt Sub-Lt B A Smart who won a DSO when, on 21 August

that year, he took off from HMS *Yarmouth* off the Danish coast to shoot down the Zeppelin L.23 before alighting on the sea beside another British cruiser.

The Pup also made the pioneering landings on the deck of a ship at sea. The first aircraft carrier to be equipped with a fairly large flight deck was HMS *Furious,* whose 228-foot deck was located forward of her superstructure. Sqn Cdr E H Dunning made two successful landings on 2 August 1917 by sideslipping round the superstructure to arrive low over the deck so slowly that naval personnel could grab toggles under the wings to pull the Pup on to the deck. Tragically the Pup suffered a burst tyre on the third landing; it lurched overboard and Dunning lost his life.

Later an after-deck was added to HMS *Furious* to enable aircraft to land more conventionally. However there was nothing to prevent aircraft from slewing sideways and damaging their undercarriage, and some Pups were fitted with skids in place of wheels, as well as rudimentary arrester hooks.

In the RFC many of the Home Defence Pups were powered by 100hp Gnome *monosoupape* engines, and these served to improve performance at altitude. A pilot who had already won the Military Medal while flying D.H.2s with No 29 Squadron, was flying as an instructor at Joyce Green in mid-1917 and flew a *monosoupape* aircraft against the raiding Gothas on several occasions. His name was Lieut James Thomas Byford McCudden. A year later, flying the S.E.5 with No 56 Squadron, he raised his victory tally to 57 enemy aircraft destroyed, and in so doing added the Victoria Cross, two DSOs and two MCs to his gallantry decorations. He is on record as having paid unqualified tribute to the little Pup, 'which could turn twice to an Albatros' once. . .'

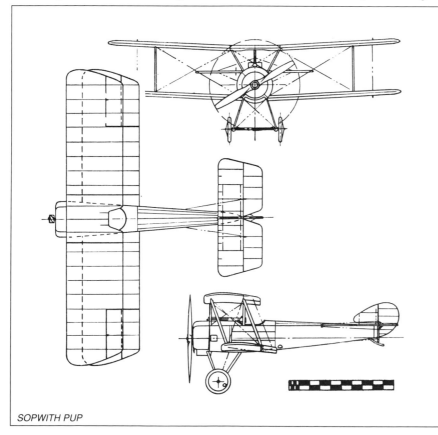

SOPWITH PUP

R.A.F. B.E.12

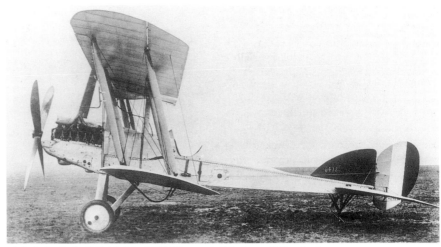

A Daimler-built B.E.12, No 6478 (Photo: A J Jackson Collection)

It is believed that the Royal Aircraft Factory's B.E.12 was first flown at about the same time as the Sopwith Pup. No two fighters, conceived to counter the same threat, can have been more different, yet well illustrate the different approaches to the supply of military aircraft by Government and commercial industry. Whereas the Sopwith Pup was an inspired design born of independent thought, the B.E.12 was evolved, for reasons of expediency, from an existing design of barely adequate mediocrity.

To meet urgent demands from the RFC in France for a single-seat fighter to meet the threat posed by the new German scouts, the Royal Aircraft Factory simply adapted the B.E.2C, producing a prototype by modifying a Bristol-built aircraft (No 1697) by installing a 150hp RAF 4A engine, changing to single-bay wings and deleting the front cockpit. Sub-contracted production was put in hand at the Coventry Ordnance Works, Daimler and Standard Motors, all in Coventry.

By the beginning of July 1916 a single B.E.12 had been delivered to No 10 Squadron at Chocques in France, and the first Squadron, fully equipped with the aircraft, was No 19 which arrived at Fienvilliers on 1 August under the command of Maj R M Rodwell. No 21 Squadron re-equipped with B.E.12s later the same month. It soon became apparent that by simply increasing the engine power and adopting single-bay wings did not transform the B.E.2C into an effective fighter, and in the following month it was — at the insistence of

General Trenchard himself—withdrawn from the fighter rôle in France and transferred to bombing. Losses had become prohibitive.

Meanwhile the Factory had attempted to improve the B.E.12's manoeuvrability by fitting a top wing similar to that of the B.E.2E, but adding extended ailerons on the top wing only, with enormous horn balances. This aircraft, No 6511, was termed the B.E.12A, but after trouble was experienced during flight tests, the aircraft reverted to standard ailerons on

upper and lower wings; the aircraft's designation was temporarily changed to B.E.12Ae, but soon reverted to B.E.12A. Needless to say, after the previous experiences, B.E.12As were not issued to RFC squadrons in France, although a small number was sent to Palestine in 1917 for use by No 67 (Australian) Squadron until early the following year.

Both B.E.12s and 12As were issued to Home Defence squadrons at the end of 1916, and on the night of 16/17 June 1917 Lieut L P Watkins of No 37

Above: *A single-bay B.E.12A, A6303, which was unusual in having strut-linked ailerons instead of the customary cables; note also the large overhang of the upper wings.* (Photo: Real Photographs Co.)

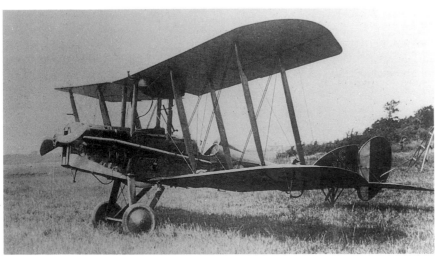

Left: *An Hispano-Suiza powered Daimler-built B.E.12B, C3114, of a Home Defence unit based at Gosport; this version reverted to two-bay wings.* (Photo: C A Nepean Bishop)

Squadron, flying B.E.12 No 6610, shot down Zeppelin L48 from 14,000 feet over Theberton, Suffolk.

The B.E.12B was a version specially developed in 1917 as a night fighter and was powered by a 200hp Hispano-Suiza engine. Its armament comprised a pair of Lewis guns side-by-side on a special mounting above the upper wing centre-section; the starboard gun was fitted with a Hutton illuminated sight and, for firing directly ahead (over the propeller), a plain ring and bead sight was attached to the starboard cabane struts. For upward firing and changing the ammunition drums, the guns pivoted downwards so as to be within reach of the cockpit. The engine and exhaust system were similar to those on the S.E.5A — by then being developed by the Factory.

A total of thirty-six B.E.12Bs was issued to Home Defence Squadrons.

Type: Single-engine, single-seat, single-bay biplane scout.
Manufacturers: The Royal Aircraft Factory, Farnborough, Hants; The Coventry Ordnance Works Ltd, Coventry; The Daimler Co Ltd, Coventry; The Standard Motor Co Ltd, Coventry.
Powerplant: B.E.12 and 12A. One 150hp RAF 4A engine. B.E.12B. 200hp Hispano-Suiza.
Structure: Wooden construction with fabric covering; plain V-strut, twin-wheel undercarriage without skids.
Dimensions: Span (B.E.12 and 12B), 37ft 0in; length, 27ft 3in; height (B.E.12), 11ft 1½in; wing area, 371 sq ft.
Weights: (B.E.12A) Tare, 1,610 lb; all-up, 2,327lb.
Performance: B.E.12A. Max speed, 100 mph at sea level; climb to 10,000ft, 24 min 15 sec; service ceiling, approx 12,000ft.
Armament: B.E.12. Either one synchronized 0.303in Vickers machine gun or one fixed Lewis gun on each side of the fuselage on Strange mountings. B.E.12B. Twin Lewis guns mounted on upper wing centre section to fire above the propeller arc.
Prototypes: One B.E.12 prototype, No 1697, modified (probably first flown in February 1916). One B.E.12A prototype, No 6511.
Production: 600, according to known serial numbers. (50 by Standard, Nos 6136-6185; 50 by Coventry Ordnance, A562-A611; and 500 by Daimler, Nos 6478-6677, A4006-A4055, A6301-A6350 and C3081-C3280).
Summary of Service: B.E.12s served with Nos 10, 19 and 21 Squadrons, RFC, in France; Nos 17, 47 and 150 Squadrons, RFC, in Macedonia; Nos 36, 37, 50, 51, 76 and 76 (Home Defence) Squadrons, RFC. B.E.12As served with No 67 (Australian) Squadron in Palestine, and Nos 50, 76 and 112 (Home Defence) Squadrons, RFC. B.E.12Bs served with Nos 50, 51, 76 and 77 (Home Defence) Squadrons, RFC.

Bristol Type 6 T.T.A.

In September 1915, at much the same time that Rex Pierson at Vickers began work on his twin-engine F.B.8 gun carrier, Frank Barnwell started the design of an aircraft of similar concept. The Bristol designer, however, went further in attempting to provide what was intended to be a more effective armament by including a gun for rearward defence.

His Type 6 twin-tractor aircraft (T.T., later to be termed the T.T.A.) was a very large three-bay biplane, scheduled to be powered by two 150hp RAF 4A engines; by the time the prototype began to take shape, however, all available engines of this type had been earmarked for the B.E.12, and Bristol had to make do with a pair of 120hp Beardmore engines. The crew consisted of a gunner in the nose, provided with a pair of free Lewis guns, and the pilot whose cockpit was behind the wings; a single rearward-firing free Lewis gun was to be fitted aft of the rear cockpit. Very large ailerons, each pair with two interconnecting struts, were fitted to upper and lower wings, while the tail unit was, in effect, an enlarged version of that on the Bristol Scout, being without a fixed fin. Fuel was carried in three main fuselage tanks and one behind each engine, with pressure

The Bristol T.T.A. before its delivery to Upavon for evaluation; it is said that the figure on the extreme left is Captain C A Hooper. (Photo: Bristol Aeroplane Co Ltd., Neg No ET294)

feed being provided by a wind-driven pump.

Two aircraft, Nos 7750 and 7751, were ordered at a price, less engines, of £2,000 apiece, and the first was flown by Captain C A Hooper, RFC, on 26 April, being followed by the second on 27 May. One was flown for evaluation at Upavon, but came in for criticism on several counts, including the pilot's very poor field of vision, the impossibility of communication between the two crew members and the general sluggishness of the controls.

However, like so many aspiring fighter aircraft designed before the end of 1915, the T.T.A. was overtaken by events with the arrival of the synchronized front gun, and further work on its development was abandoned.

Type: Twin-engine, two-seat, three-bay biplane gun carrier.
Manufacturer: The British & Colonial Aeroplane Co Ltd, Filton, Bristol.
Powerplant: Two 120hp Beardmore engines driving two-blade propellers.
Dimensions: Span, 53ft 6in; length, 39ft 2in; height, 12ft 6in; wing area, 817 sq ft.
Weights: Tare, 3,820lb; all-up, 5,100lb.
Performance: Max speed, 86.7 mph at sea level; climb to 6,000ft, 17 min 15 sec; service ceiling, 9,500ft.
Armament: Two free-firing Lewis machine guns on nose cockpit, and a single rearward-firing Lewis gun on rear cockpit. (No armament fitted for trials.)
Prototypes: Two, Nos 7750 and 7751 (first flown by Capt C A Hooper RFC on 26 April 1916). No production.

Bristol Type 8 S.2A

The first prototype S.2A, 7836, with 110hp Clerget engine. (Photo: Bristol Aeroplane Co Ltd.)

Once the Bristol Type 6 T.T.A. had passed out of the design stage, Frank Barnwell turned his attention to another original idea to overcome the lack of a reliable synchronized front gun, this time producing what was in effect a two-seat development of the Scout D, but instead of pursuing the customary tandem cockpit layout, which would be expected to require lengthening the fuselage by several feet, he adopted side-by-side accommodation of the crew in a single cockpit. While the pilot could concentrate on controlling the aircraft, his gunner could load, aim and fire the armament.

Two prototypes, Nos 7836 and 7837, were produced to meet an Admiralty requirement for a two-seater, and the first was flown at Filton in May 1916. Powered by a 110hp Clerget rotary, it featured the tail unit of the Scout D as well as similar wings, though with reduced rake at their tips. The centre section of the upper wing was somewhat wider than on the Scout owing to the increased fuselage width, while the cabane struts were angled outwards, but without stagger; because the lower wing was

mounted slightly further aft, stagger was maintained on the interplane struts. The broader fuselage also allowed for a wider track undercarriage.

As neither prototype was ever fitted with armament, it is not known what gun mounting was intended, although it seems probable that the gun would have been fitted on top of the wing to fire over the propeller.

The S.2A was not adopted for production, despite a moderately good performance, having been overshadowed by the Sopwith Pup with synchronized front gun. Trouble had been experienced with the Clerget engine in the first prototype, possibly due to inadequate cooling, and the second prototype was later flown at Gosport with the Gnome *monosoupape* engine.

Type: Single-engine, two-seat, single-bay biplane scout.
Manufacturer: The British & Colonial Aeroplane Co Ltd, Filton, Bristol.
Powerplant: One 110hp Clerget engine; also 100hp Gnome *monosoupape* engine.
Dimensions: Span, 28ft 2in; length, 21ft 3in; height, 10ft 0in.
Weights: All-up, 1,400lb.
Performance: Max speed, 95 mph at sea level; endurance, 3 hr.
Armament: Probably a single Lewis machine gun mounted above the wing centre section.
Prototypes: Two, Nos 7836 and 7837 (first flown in May 1916). No production.

Pemberton-Billing P.B.29E

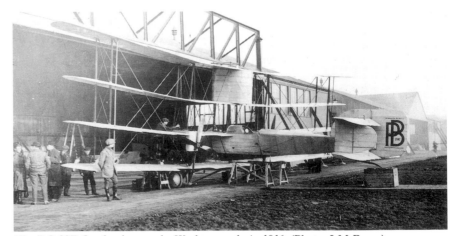

The P.B.29E Quadruplane at the Woolston works in 1916. (Photo: J M Bruce)

If the problem of acquiring a synchronized front gun for fighting scouts was being surmounted at the turn of 1915, another difficulty was not. German airship raids over southern England had occupied the minds of several aircraft designers for some months, not to mention the acute embarrassment caused to the War Office and Admiralty, for the difficulties posed by locating, attacking and destroying the huge and almost silent intruders at night seemed insuperable. Warning of their approach was seldom forthcoming, so that by the time intercepting aircraft could take-off — always assuming that a pilot, trained or experienced in night flying was available — the airship would most likely have

travelled on to another area.

Pemberton-Billing, always a man to brush aside orthodoxy, conceived the idea of the patrol fighter capable of remaining aloft throughout the hours of darkness. It would, on account of the considerable fuel load necessary, be a relatively large aeroplane. In the late

autumn of 1915 he therefore completed the design of a radical aircraft, the P.B.29E, to demonstrate his ideas.

The large twin-engine quadruplane featured high aspect ratio two-bay wings; the second wing mounted two 90hp Austro-Daimler engines in underslung nacelles driving pusher propellers, this wing being attached to the upper longerons of the fuselage. The fuselage accommodated pilot and observer, as well as the fuel tanks, while the bottom wing was a continuous structure which passed below the fuselage. A third crew member, the gunner, occupied a position in a nacelle in the gap between the two upper wings and was provided with a Lewis gun with all-round field of fire above the aircraft. Outboard of the engines all four wings were swept back about ten degrees.

Aft of the cockpit the rear fuselage was faired to a triangular cross section and carried a biplane tail unit with twin fins and rudders. The main units of the undercarriage were mounted directly below the engines so as to provide very wide track for ease of landing at night.

The aircraft, which, as far as is known, was not allocated any serial number, was first flown at Chingford, Essex, on Sunday 16 January 1916, the only apparently surviving evidence of this fact being that Pemberton Billing himself referred to the flight having taken place on that day in a Parliamentary bye-election speech he gave in the Mile End constituency which he was contesting. The P.B.29E, known in the Woolston works as the Night Fighter, had taken only seven weeks to build, but was destroyed in a flying accident several weeks later, not however before it had been flown by several naval pilots. However, Noel Pemberton Billing's thoughts had already turned irrevocably towards politics and he determined to sell his company, thereby effectively ending his direct participation in the production of aircraft.

Type: Twin-engine, three-crew anti-airship patrol/interceptor quadruplane.
Manufacturer: Pemberton-Billing Ltd., Woolston, Southampton.
Powerplant: Two 90hp Austro-Daimler six-cylinder water-cooled in-line pusher engines driving four-blade propellers.
Structure: All-wood construction with fabric covering; two-spar, two-bay quadruplane wings and biplane tail with twin fins and rudders.
Dimensions, weights and performance: Not known (designed for up to 10 hours' endurance)
Armament: One 0.303in Lewis gun in free mounting on gunner's cockpit in nacelle occupying centre section gap between the two upper wings.
Prototype: One, probably first flown on 16 January 1916 at Chingford, Essex. No production.

Supermarine Night Hawk

It is necessary and perhaps logical at this point to diverge from the strict chronological sequence of events to continue the saga of Pemberton Billings' anti-Zeppelin quadruplane because, although the P.B.29E had been destroyed early in 1916, the Admiralty had shown sufficient interest in the large, long-endurance gun carrier to warrant further development. The fact that this development continued for another year before a new aircraft appeared is in itself irrelevant, and the appearance of other companies' aircraft in the meantime — conceived along similar lines — serves to emphasize Pemberton Billings' particular flair for original thought.

The departure of Noel Pemberton Billing to the House of Commons and the subsequent formation of the Supermarine Aviation Works Ltd at Woolston under Hubert Scott-Paine were accompanied by the continuation of the theme demonstrated by the P.B.29E anti-airship patrol fighter. The new aircraft, initially referred to as the P.B.31E and whose design drawings bore the signature of one Reginald J Mitchell, was renamed the Supermarine Night Hawk and pursued the general configuration of the P.B.29E.

The Supermarine Night Hawk, 1388, at Woolston in 1917.   (Photo: Real Photographs Co.)

The quadruplane wings and biplane tail were retained, although the overall strength factor was substantially increased and three-bay wings introduced. The pusher Austro-Daimlers were replaced by 100hp Anzani tractors driving four-blade handed propellers. The fuselage, now of square section from nose to tail, occupied the whole of the centre wing gap and the upper gun nacelle now extended from the centre fuselage upwards to the level of the top wing's upper surface. The primary offensive weapon, a 1½-pounder Davis gun was installed at the front of this superstructure in a traversing mounting, and a Lewis gun, for defence, was mounted on a Scarff ring at the rear of the superstructure; a second Lewis, also on a Scarff ring, was located in the nose of the fuselage. The pilots' cockpit was situated in the fuselage below the wing trailing edge, being enclosed and surrounded by extensive glazing; dual controls were provided. A novel feature was the provision of a rest bunk to enable crew members to relax in turn during lengthy flights. Another was the installation of a small searchlight, mounted on gimbals in the extreme nose and intended to illuminate targets as well as to assist night landings; power for the searchlight was to be provided by a small auxiliary engine carried in the aircraft.

To enable the Night Hawk to remain airborne for up to about eighteen hours, over 2,000lb of fuel could be carried in nine tanks in the fuselage, all fuel leads being armoured against battle damage.

Despite being generally underpowered, the Anzani engines proved capable of bestowing the maximum required speed of 75mph, although the normal patrol speed would in all likelihood have been between 55 and 60mph; the landing speed was 35 mph.

Although it was Pemberton-Billing who had enlisted the Admiralty's support for the Night Hawk before his eventual election as Member for East Herts, the aircraft was not completed until after his departure and was therefore generally referred to as a product of Supermarine. It was allocated the naval serial number 1388, and was test flown by Clifford B Prodger at Eastchurch, beginning in February 1917. A second example, 1389, was cancelled, but no reason was ever given for the cancellation and it has been assumed that the increasing success being achieved by relatively conventional interceptors led the Admiralty to lose interest in Pemberton-Billings' radical idea. Be that as it may, the idea of locating a gunner in a separate nacelle, with all-round field of fire clear of the propeller arc, had sparked widespread interest among the fighter designers, and a number of single-engine aircraft appeared in the latter war years displaying variations on the same theme.

Type: Twin-engine, four-crew anti-airship patrol interceptor.
Manufacturer: The Supermarine Aviation Works Ltd, Woolston, Southampton.
Powerplant: Two 100hp Anzani nine-cylinder air-cooled radial tractor engines driving four-blade handed wooden propellers.
Structure: All-wood construction with fabric and ply covering; three-bay quadruplane wings with approx. ten degrees of sweepback on the outer sections. Inverse tapered ailerons on all wings. Four-mainwheel undercarriage.
Dimensions: Span (top wing), 60ft 0in; length, 37ft 0in; height, 17ft 8½in; wing area, 962 sq ft.
Weights: Tare, 3,677lb; all-up, 6,146lb.
Performance: Max speed, 75mph at 1,000ft; landing speed, 35 mph; time to 10,000ft, 60min; normal endurance, 9hr; maximum endurance, 18hr.
Armament: One 1½-pounder Davis gun on traversing mounting in the nose of the gunner's superstructure, and one 0.303in Lewis machine gun on Scarff ring at the rear; one Lewis gun on Scarff ring in the fuselage nose.
Prototypes: One, No 1388, first flown by Clifford B Prodger at Eastchurch in February 1917. Second prototype, 1389, cancelled. No production.

Sopwith Triplane (Clerget)

The Pup had not even reached the RNAS or RFC squadrons when the Sopwith Triplane made its first flight in the hands of Harry Hawker at the beginning of June 1916. That the Pup's design represented the basis of the Triplane almost goes without saying, yet there were two intermediate stages in the process of thought. In the early spring of that year Herbert Smith had started the design of a somewhat grotesque-looking triplane escort fighter with very high aspect ratio wings, the top wing supporting a nacelle in which the gunner's cockpit was situated; the aircraft was to be powered by a 250hp Rolls-Royce Mk I engine (see Sopwith L.R.T.Tr., page 78). Smith's next design was a triplane fighter derived from the 1½-Strutter, this aircraft being scheduled for the 150hp water-cooled Hispano-Suiza engine (see page 103). Neither of these engines was yet readily available and so the airframes were held temporarily in abeyance.

Smith now turned to the Pup, seeing in the application of triplane wings, possessing the same, or smaller chord than those of the L.R.T.Tr., considerable potential for further improvement

The first prototype Sopwith Triplane, N500, at RNAS Chingford for Admiralty trials and before being given its Service paint scheme. The pilot in the cockpit is said to be Flight-Lt L E Hardstaff, Admiralty Test Pilot. (Photo: G S Leslie / J M Bruce Collection).

in performance and handling. The fuselage aft of the cockpit remained almost identical to that of the Pup, though stressed for a larger engine, but the tail surfaces were later reduced in area, the tip rake of the tailplane and elevators being reversed.

The Triplane wings, however, were radical and ingenious. By limiting the chord to no more than 3ft 3in, compared to the Pup's 5ft 3in, the wing area was in fact reduced from 254 to 231 sq ft — with exactly the same span; at the same time, with ailerons on all six wings, their total area was increased from 22 to 34 sq ft, thereby retaining the crisp handling with no extra stick load. The pilot's field of view was improved by the reduced wing chord and by the location of the centre wing in line chordwise with the pilot's eye level. The I-type interplane and cabane struts were the subject of Patent No 127,858, held by Fred Sigrist, and were rigged to give a total stagger of 36 inches between top and bottom wings, compared with 18 inches between the Pup's two wings. This arrangement of struts permitted fewer bracing wires to

Left: *The Triplanes, N5387 '15' and N5425 '16' of No 1 (Naval) Squadron.* Below: *N5493 and N6290 of No 8 (Naval) Squadron. The former aircraft was flown by the Australian pilot, Capt Robert Alexander Little, DSO*, DSC*, the highest-scoring pilot from that country. His score of 47 victories is believed to have been achieved solely while flying Pups and Triplanes with Naval Eight. He was killed on 27 May 1918, while on leave in England, when he took off to attack a Gotha at night; he was blinded by a searchlight as he closed with the raider and crashed.* (Photos: J M Bruce)

be used, with only a single landing wire and a doubled flying wire necessary on each side. Power for the Triplane was provided initially by the 110hp Clerget engine, although the 130hp version was introduced into at least one production batch before the end of 1916. Most aircraft also retained the single synchronized Vickers gun of the Pup.

The prototype Triplane, N500, was sent to France in June for operational trials with Naval 'A' Fighting Squadron at Furnes (and was ordered off against a suspected enemy aircraft within fifteen minutes of refuelling). This aircraft was representative of the proposed initial production version, but the second prototype, N504, was powered by the 130hp Clerget and carried twin Vickers guns.

The first production order was placed by the Admiralty in August, followed by orders from the War Office for 100 aircraft to be built by Sopwith, and 166 by Clayton & Shuttleworth of Lincoln. In due course, however, owing to the critical shortage of RFC fighters in France, it was agreed that in return for Spad S.7s which were held by the Admiralty, the War Office would relinquish their orders for Triplanes in favour of the RNAS. In the event none of the original 266 RFC Triplanes were built. Instead, the Admiralty placed orders totalling 145 aircraft with Sopwith and Clayton & Shuttleworth, as well as 25 from Oakleys of Ilford (of which only three were completed).

Once again the artificial bureaucracy that concealed petty jealousies between the Admiralty and War Office robbed the fighting men of the weapons that would have stood them in good stead when the air war took such a disastrous turn in the spring of 1917.

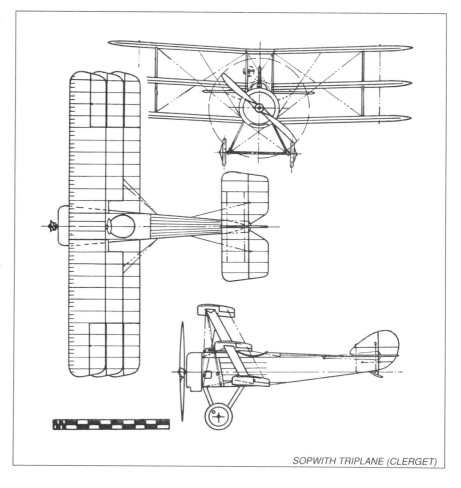

SOPWITH TRIPLANE (CLERGET)

As it was, the RNAS put their relatively small number of Triplanes to excellent use. Production had got underway at Sopwith and Clayton in the late autumn of 1916, and the first deliveries were being made to the RNAS at the turn of the year. By the end of February No 1 (Naval) Squadron at Chipilly, under the command of Sqn Cdr F K Haskins (later Air Cdre, DSC, RAF) had received seventeen Triplanes; then it was the turn of 'Naval Eight' at Auchel, who gave up their Pups in exchange for Triplanes in March, and No 10 (Naval) Squadron in May.

It was a Canadian pilot on Naval Ten who was to become the greatest fighting exponent of the Triplane in the person of Flight Sub-Lt Raymond Collishaw (later Air Vice-Marshal, CB, DSO*, OBE, DSC, DFC, RAF). Given command of 'B' Flight, Collishaw generated an extraordinary *esprit* by his example, and his pilots — all Canadians and superb pilots in their own right — had their Triplanes painted black overall and given names such as *Black Prince*, *Black Death*, *Black Sheep* and *Black Maria* (Collishaw's aircraft), and so on. In air combats during June, Collishaw alone shot down no fewer than sixteen German aircraft, of which thirteen were single-seat fighters; apart from Collishaw himself, four other pilots of

'Black Flight' between them destroyed 54 German aircraft. Their flight commander would, by the end of the War become the third highest-scoring British Commonwealth fighter pilot, with a score of 60 victories; he also served with great distinction in the Second World War.

As already stated, a few Triplanes were fitted with the 130hp Clerget, an additional power that gave the little fighter a top speed of 117 mph, and six of the aircraft built by Clayton & Shuttleworth (N533-N538) were armed with twin Vickers guns. A total of six Triplanes

was loaned to France, but these were returned to the RNAS when the shortage of fighters became acute early in 1917; even the original prototype was pressed into service with Naval One, while the second served with Naval Eight.

The Triplane's swansong was during the third Battle of Ypres in August 1917. By the end of the month Naval Ten was being re-equipped with the Sopwith Camel, and by Christmas the Triplane had been withdrawn from operational service.

Type: Single-engine, single-seat, single-bay triplane scout.

Manufacturers: The Sopwith Aviation Co Ltd, Kingston-upon-Thames, Surrey; Clayton & Shuttleworth Ltd, Lincoln; Oakley Ltd, Ilford, Essex

Powerplant: One 110hp or 130hp Clerget rotary engine driving two-blade propeller.

Structure: All-wooden wire-braced box-girder fuselage with fabric covering; triplane, single-bay, two-spar wings with single interplane and cabane I-struts.

Dimensions: Span, 26ft 6in; length, 18ft 10in; height, 10ft 6in; wing area, 231 sq ft.

Weights: (130hp Clerget) Tare, 1,101lb; all-up, 1,541lb.

Performance: (130hp Clerget) Max speed, 117 mph at sea level, 104 mph at 13,000ft; climb to 10,000ft, 11 min 50 sec; service ceiling, 20,500ft; endurance, 2¾ hr.

Armament: Either one or two synchronized 0.303in Vickers machine guns on nose top decking with Sopwith-Kauper interrupter gear.

Prototypes: Two, N500 and N504 (N500 first flown by Harry Hawker at Brooklands early in June 1916); both built by Sopwith.

Production: Total of 145 (95 by Sopwith: N5420-N5494 and N6290-N6309; 47 by Clayton & Shuttleworth: N524, N533-N538 and N5350-N5389; three by Oakley, N5910-N5912).

Summary of Service: Triplanes served with Nos 1, 8, 9, 10 and 12 (Naval) Squadrons, RNAS, on the Western Front; also with 'E' Squadron, RNAS, in Macedonia; with No 2 (Naval) Wing, RNAS, at Mudros in the Aegean; and at RNAS Manston and Port Victoria. A small number was loaned or supplied to France, the USA and Russia.

Deployment of British Fighter Squadrons — July 1916

Home Bases		
No 19 Squadron	B.E.12	Filton
No 28 Squadron	F.E.2B	Gosport
No 36 Squadron	Bristol Scout and B.E.12	Cramlington
No 38 Squadron	B.E.12	Castle Bromwich
No 40 Squadron	F.E.8	Gosport
No 41 Squadron	D.H.2	Gosport
No 45 Squadron*	Sopwith 1½-Strutter	Thetford
No 47 Squadron	B.E.12	Beverley
No 48 Squadron	B.E.12	Rendcombe
No 50 Squadron	B.E.12A and B.E.12B	Dover
No 51 Squadron	B.E.12B	Thetford
No 66 Squadron	B.E.12B	Netheravon
France		
No 1 Squadron	(Nieuport 12 and Morane Parasol)	Bailleul
No 3 Squadron	(Morane Parasol)	La Houssoye
No 11 Squadron	F.E.2B	Bertangles
No 15 Squadron	Bristol Scout	Marieux
No 18 Squadron	F.E.2B	Bruay
No 20 Squadron	F.E.2D	Clairmarais
No 22 Squadron	F.E.2B	Bertangles
No 23 Squadron	F.E.2B	Izel-le-Hameau
No 24 Squadron	D.H.2	Bertangles
No 25 Squadron	F.E.2B	Auchel
No 27 Squadron	Martinsyde G.100	Fienvillers
No 29 Squadron	D.H.2	Abeele
No 32 Squadron	D.H.2	Treizennes
No 60 Squadron	(Morane Parasol)	Vert Galand
No 70 Squadron	Sopwith 1½-Strutter	Fienvillers
RFC in the Balkans		
No 17 Squadron*	Bristol Scout and D.H.2	Mikra Bay, Greece
RNAS in France		
No 1 (Naval) Squadron	Bristol Scout C (and Nieuport)	Furnes
No 3 (Naval) Squadron	Bristol Scout (and Nieuport)	St Pol

* One Flight only

2. AFTER THE SOMME

The Battle of the Somme of July 1916, fought almost exactly half-way through the First World War, can be seen in retrospect to have occurred at a watershed in the fortunes of the British aircraft industry and the two flying Services. Those of the Royal Flying Corps suffered a considerable setback in heavy casualties, relative to the numbers involved, over the terrible ground battle, and it quickly emerged that the aircraft whose job it was to support the soldiers on the ground had been hopelessly inadequate for their tasks — bombing and reconnaissance — and the aircraft needed to protect them from enemy fighting scouts were simply no match for them, although the D.H.2 had successfully countered the superiority of the Fokker monoplanes that had ruled the skies in the previous year.

Moreover, considerable antagonism had arisen between the private aircraft manufacturers and the Royal Aircraft Factory, largely due to a suspicion that the Factory's designs were favoured as a matter of principle, rather than quality, compared to those of the commercial companies, which were bound by the terms of the Excess Profits Act. The Factory existed as a kind of laboratory, preparing designs of new aircraft, undertaking research and building prototypes which, if considered suitable for service, were then sub-contracted for quantity production elsewhere; these sub-contractors frequently possessed little or no experience in building aircraft, taking an unconscionable time to get production into full swing. There were even accusations that the Factory plagiarised commercial designs which were submitted for official scrutiny. The established companies of the aircraft industry not only had to support their own design staffs and experimental departments, but re-invest any profits earned to expand their plant and premises.

The Society of British Aircraft Constructors (SBAC) had been formed on 29 March to express the views of the aircraft companies with one voice to the Treasury and central provisioning departments. To begin with, however, membership of the Society was viewed with scepticism, if not suspicion, feeling that it could be viewed by politicians and senior members of the Services as some sort of profit-seeking trade union. The growling and grumbling that surfaced in Parliament, expressing these accusations under protection of privilege, resulted in two commissions of enquiry, the one held into the relationship that existed between the RFC and the Royal Aircraft Factory, and the other — quite unrelated — into the affairs of the Factory itself.

Neither enquiry brought about any immediate remedies, although an unfortunate casualty was Lieut-Col Mervyn O'Gorman, Superintendent of the Factory, who was replaced and moved sideways to become Consulting Engineer in aeronautics at the War Office. Widely regarded as the father of British aeronautical technical development in its early days, O'Gorman had indeed superintended the development and manufacture of every conceivable type of component that went to make up an aircraft, be it a balloon, aeroplane or airship.

In future it was intended that the Factory would be headed by a Superintendent rather more qualified in administrative than technical affairs, though he should be conversant with the basics of aeronautics, with subordinate Heads of Design and Production. A civilian Controller of Aircraft Supplies was to be appointed as an intermediary between the Factory and commercial contractors. Independent evaluation of aircraft designed to meet military needs would continue to be undertaken by the RFC Testing Squadron, then attached to the Central Flying School at Upavon, but this would in due course be moved to Martlesham Heath in Suffolk and given the status of an autonomous Establishment within the Service.

If the RFC enquiry brought about no significant changes in its procurement of aircraft and equipment, it did represent a forum at which views on the system's weaknesses could be aired. An incidental consequence was the progressive ending of each Service's 'favoured franchise' which committed specific commercial companies to produce aircraft exclusively for either the RNAS or RFC. Indeed each Service would prepare formal operational requirements for future equipment, and both Admiralty and War Office would make these available for general tender — which would inevitably embrace the Factory.

No such enquiry was conducted into the affairs of the Air Department at the Admiralty, and this led to a deepening suspicion that the War Office had somehow succeeded in gaining authority to claim priority for equipment acquisition. Already the suggestion had been mooted in Parliament for the creation of an independent Air Ministry, but in an orchestrated clamour by the Generals and Admirals this had been effectively vetoed in the belief that the Services would lose all authority to state their requirements. Indeed, the Admiralty had already set up an experimental Scaplane Test Flight on the Isle of Grain (Port Victoria), responsible to its own Air Department which, it was intended, would assume for the RNAS the same responsibilities as the Factory had for the RFC.

Returning to the affairs of the Factory, criticism had been growing for months that its products had been, almost without exception, inferior to those designed by independent manufacturers, yet appeared to have been selected for service in preference. While this was strenuously denied by those employed at the Factory, it could hardly be denied that Farnborough had yet to come up with anything to compare with aircraft like the Bristol Scout and Sopwith Pup.

There had been no serious suggestion that the Factory should be closed and, although men like Geoffrey de Havilland had left to join independent manufacturers, others such as Henry Folland were beginning to make reputations for themselves, while on the research side brilliant men like Henry Tizard were setting standards by which aircraft — from any source — would come to be measured.

On the engine side, French designs, the majority subject of licence production in Britain, had hitherto dominated the scene, but by 1916 British engine companies were pursuing indigenous designs led, it must be said, by the Factory with its RAF 1A and 4A. Rolls-Royce had produced its first aero engine, which would become famous as the Eagle — arguably the finest engine to appear during the whole War. A former naval engineering officer, Wilfred Owen Bentley, had been doing valuable work to overcome inherent weaknesses in the rotary, and within a year would be producing engines of his own design.

As would be expected, an increase in power output was of the utmost importance for the advance in aircraft performance, and already licence production of the 150hp Hispano-Suiza had begun in Britain in the spring of 1916; it would be this engine that would power the finest fighting scouts produced by the Factory, the S.E.5, followed by the 200hp version in the S.E.5A, designed largely by Henry Folland.

Among the commercial manufacturers, Sopwith, Bristol and Vickers had become firmly established with fighters that were already in series production, while encouragement was lent to other firms, previously only engaged in subcontract work, to support their own design teams and to tender their own design proposals. A score of such designs came to be built, and some earned limited production runs; among these were companies like Parnall, a firm well-established in woodworking and which had, since the beginning of the War, been building Avro 504 trainers. After a shaky start, the company produced the Panther naval fighter, which was rewarded by a modest production contract for the Royal Navy, as well as export

orders. Companies like Beardmore, Blackburn, Grahame-White, Armstrong Whitworth and Airco continued to thrive, not only upon the occasional production order but from the purchase of prototypes, many of which contributed significantly to the advance of aeronautical knowledge.

At the front line, air combat was by now established as demanding much more than the rudimentary skills in flying. Indeed, the flying training syllabus for Service pilots had become divided into 'pure' and 'applied' flying. For the fighter pilot this demanded that the ability to merely fly his aeroplane had to be instinctive before he could be trained to fight. By mid-1917 men of exceptional talents in the air were arriving on the Squadrons in France, men who were to become household names. The first, and probably the best known to the British public, was Albert Ball; a 20-year-old when he joined his first squadron in 1916 on artillery spotting duties, he soon arrived on a fighter squadron where he began flying a Nieuport Scout. By the following year he was a flight commander on No 56 Squadron, flying S.E.5s, but after just one month he was killed in action. Ball was a loner, the archetypal fighter pilot who amassed a score of 44 enemy aircraft destroyed and was awarded a posthumous Victoria Cross to add to his three DSOs and the MC.

In the last year of the War, as British pilots and fighters established parity with, and ultimately superiority over their German counterparts with such aircraft as the Camel, S.E.5A, Bristol

F.2B Fighter and eventually the Snipe, another series of events much closer to home was to have far-reaching results. The onset of daylight bombing raids in 1917 over London and southeast England by a handful of Gotha bombers, which the British defences seemed powerless to prevent, created such a furore of public indignation that the Government was forced straightway to set up a commission of enquiry, headed by the veteran South African, General Jan Smuts PC, CH. As the German raiders changed tactics and donned the cloak of darkness for their activities with the approach of winter, Smuts' committee announced its proposals, which included the amalgamation of the RFC and RNAS under the aegis of an independent Air Ministry. And so, on 1 April 1918, was created the Royal Air Force.

At once it was appreciated by the Cabinet, if no one else, that in the age of the large bomber, Britain, her cities, industries and people were at an enemy's mercy, and that, by bringing weapons of destruction to bear on the civilian population, pressures, hitherto unimagined, could force the nation to submit — while her army and navy remained unbeaten. No other circumstance was ever to have a more profound effect upon the concept and development of the fighter. Gone for ever was the euphemism 'fighting scout', customarily regarded as the epitome of the nimble dogfighter. Henceforth the uncompromising term 'interceptor' implied exactly the aircraft which the RFC had lacked in 1917 — but would not be wanting in the RAF in 1940.

Port Victoria
P.V.2 / P.V.2bis

Aircraft whose designation carried the prefix Port Victoria were those produced by an RNAS unit situated on the Isle of Grain on the northern banks of the Medway estuary in Kent. Originally commissioned as the Royal Naval Aeroplane Repair Depot early in 1915, the

The P.V.2, N.1, with Linton Hope floats. (Photo: Imperial War Museum, Neg. No. MH 2876)

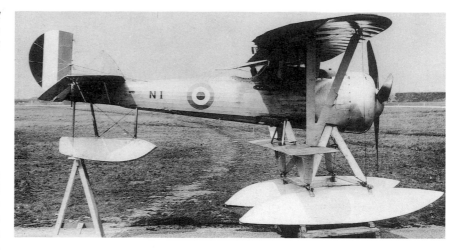

The P.V.2bis, N1, with the upper wing raised above the fuselage and a new centresection inserted. (Photo: Imperial War Museum, Neg No MH 2875)

name Port Victoria was adopted to distinguish it from the nearby RNAS seaplane base. It later became the Marine Experimental Depot, of which one component came into being as the Experimental Construction Depot under the command of Lt J W Seddon RN.

The first aircraft produced, the P.V.1, was a development of the Sopwith Baby, fitted with high-lift wings to enable it to be flown safely while mounting external bombs and other military equipment. The first original design to be undertaken was the P.V.2, a small twin-float anti-Zeppelin seaplane fighter, intended to be armed with a Davis two-pounder gun. Initially completed with angular pontoon floats, the aircraft, N.1, was a sesquiplane, the lower wing being of short span and chord, and the upper wing of broad chord and span. When viewed from ahead, the interplane and float struts formed a 'W', the interplane struts being angled sharply outwards. Power was provided by a 100hp Gnome *monosoupape* driving a four-blade propeller. The upper wing, in two halves, was attached to the top fuselage longerons providing an excellent field of fire for the Davis gun and uninterrupted upward field of vision for the pilot.

However, by the time N.1 was completed, the Davis gun had been abandoned, and the aircraft was converted into a straightforward fighting scout by mounting two Lewis guns on the upper wings. It was quickly found that these wings created a blind area for the pilot during alighting and the seaplane was rebuilt with a continuous upper wing raised twelve inches above the fuselage, and at this time Linton Hope floats replaced the earlier pontoons. In this form N.1 was re-designated the P.V.2bis and first flown early in 1917 and, although not ordered into production, it proved popular among its pilots and contributed much valuable information for the development of later aircraft from Port Victoria.

Type: Single-engine, single-seat, twin-float sesquiplane fighting scout seaplane.
Manufacturer: RNAS Experimental Construction Depot, Port Victoria, Isle of Grain, Kent.
Powerplant: One 100hp Gnome *monosoupape* air-cooled nine-cylinder rotary engine driving four-blade propeller.
Structure: Wire-braced wooden box-girder fuselage formed to circular section and fabric-covered; fabric-covered two-spar wings with faired steel tube interplane and float struts.
Dimensions: Span (P.V.2), 27ft 0in; (P.V.2bis), 29ft 0in; length, 22ft 0in; height (P.V.2), 8ft 4in; (P.V.2bis), 9ft 4in; wing area (P.V.2), 168 sq ft; (P.V.2bis), 180 sq ft.
Weights (P.V.2bis): Tare, 1,211 lb; all-up, 1,702 lb.
Performance (P.V.2bis): Max speed, 93 mph at sea level; climb to 3,000 ft, 6 min; service ceiling, 10,000 ft.
Armament: Intended to mount one Davis two-pounder gun above fuselage with ten rounds of ammunition; changed to proposal to mount two Lewis guns above the wing centre section to fire above the propeller.
Prototype: One, N.1 (first flown at the Isle of Grain as P.V.2 in June 1916, and as P.V.2bis early in 1917). No production.

Vickers F.B.12

Design of the F.B.12 was begun early in 1916 as an attempt to extend the Gunbus formula into the single-seat scout class, presumably to provide a replacement for the 'first generation' D.H.2s and F.E.8s. However, by the time it was flown in June that year, both the Sopwith Pup and Triplane had appeared and demonstrated a considerable advance in performance.

The F.B.12, A7351, with short span wings, after it had been fitted with a Gnome monosoupape engine; note the fixed Lewis gun in the nose. (Photo: Vickers Ltd, Neg No. 35)

The prototype Vickers F.B.12C, A7352, show-
ing the flat-sided nacelle and in its final form
during 1917 with a 100hp Anzani radial
engine. (Photo: Vickers Ltd, Neg No 134)

If in fact the engine originally intended for the F.B.12, the 150hp Hart nine-cylinder radial, had been available in time, the Vickers aircraft would probably have matched the Pup's performance, but as it was not, an 80hp Le Rhône was substituted and bestowed a maximum speed of only 95 mph. When it first appeared the aircraft featured short wings with elliptical tips and a circular-section nacelle located in the centre of the wing gap. Armament comprised a single Lewis gun protruding from the upper part of the nose. In this form the engine was soon changed to a 100hp Gnome *monosoupape* and this increased the speed by about five miles per hour.

A production order was raised for 50 aircraft, including the prototype, and the design underwent much modification before the second example appeared. The wings were lengthened to feature square-raked tips and the nacelle was altered to near-rectangular section, the engine being changed once again, this time to a 100hp Le Rhône; these changes, one imagines, were introduced to facilitate production, but had increased the drag and the aircraft, now termed the F.B.12C, could still only manage about 100 mph, although the rate of climb was improved. Finally a 100hp Anzani engine was installed, but again without significant improvement.

With no advance in performance evident, the F.B.12C's production was halted after only seventeen aircraft had been completed. As far as is known, none entered operational service, although it is believed that the Gnome-powered prototype underwent trials in France in December 1916, and an F.B.12C flew with a Home Defence unit the following year.

Type: Single pusher engine, single-seat, two-bay biplane scout.
Manufacturer: Vickers Ltd (Aviation Department), Knightsbridge, London.
Powerplant: F.B.12. 80hp Le Rhône; 100hp Gnome *monosoupape*. F.B.12C. 110hp Le Rhône; 100hp Anzani.
Dimensions: F.B.12. Span, 26ft 0in; length, 21ft 6in; height, 8ft 7in; wing area, 204 sq ft. F.B.12C. Span, 29ft 9in; length, 21ft 10in; height, 8ft 7in; wing area, 237 sq ft.
Weights: F.B.12 (80hp Le Rhône). Tare, 845lb; all-up, 1,275lb. F.B.12C (100hp Le Rhône). Tare, 927lb; all-up, 1,400lb.
Performance: F.B.12 (80hp Le Rhône). Max speed, 95 mph at sea level; climb to 5,000ft, 9 min 50 sec; service ceiling, 11,500ft. F.B.12C (100hp Le Rhône). Max speed, 100 mph at sea level; climb to 5,000ft, 6 min 55 sec; service ceiling, 14,500ft.
Armament: One 0.303in Lewis machine gun in nose of nacelle.
Prototype: One F.B.12, A7351 (first flown, June 1916).
Production: F.B.12C. 17 aircraft completed (A7352-A7368).
Summary of Service: A7351 underwent trials in France in December 1916; and at least one aircraft flew with a Home Defence unit in 1917.

Grahame-White Type 20

One of the lesser-known contenders for consideration as a single-seat scout was the Grahame-White Type 20 single-bay biplane which is believed to have flown in mid-1916.

Characterized by unusually thick, staggered wings with large gap, the Type 20 was of all-wood construction, the slim fuselage being formed to circular section. The tail unit comprised a fixed fin and balanced rudder, but no tailplane was fitted forward of the balanced elevator. Ailerons were fitted on

The Grahame-White Type 20 scout. (Photo: G S Leslie / J M Bruce Collection)

both upper and lower wings, hinged to the rear spars. The twin V-strut twin-wheel undercarriage was raked forward, presumably so as to dispense with a landing skid.

Power was provided by an 80hp

Clerget 7Z seven-cylinder rotary engine within a narrow-chord oil-sling ring, this engine being licence-built by Gwynnes Ltd of Hammersmith. Also considered as an alternative to this engine was the 80hp Le Rhône.

With a top speed probably between 80 and 90 mph (without armament fitted), it is unlikely that this little aeroplane excited much serious attention at the War Office or Admiralty and, as far as is known, underwent no official trials; its development, therefore, was probably very shortlived.

Vickers F.B.11

This large single-engine aeroplane was one of three strange-looking aircraft built to meet a War Office requirement for a long-range escort fighter, with a suggested secondary rôle as an anti-Zeppelin patrol fighter, the others being the Sopwith L.R.T.Tr and the Armstrong Whitworth F.K.12 (see pages 78 and 81). High speed performance was not a prerequisite as it was intended that the aircraft should closely accompany bombing aircraft and provide them with all-round gun protection without breaking formation. The need to fire directly forward was therefore of less significance than all-round protection.

The interpretation of the operational requirement by the three contending manufacturers differed considerably, Howard Flanders at Vickers opting for a single-bay unstaggered biplane, to be powered by one of the new 250hp Rolls-Royce water-cooled in-line engines. Pilot and one gunner were situated in closely-spaced tandem cockpits under the trailing edge of the upper wing, and a second gunner occupied a well-shaped nacelle extending forward from the upper surface of the top wing and supported by a pair of raked struts attached to the fuselage nose. Twin wheels and central skid comprised the undercarriage and, for entry to his cockpit, the nacelle gunner had to ascend a veritable flight of steps up the front port skid strut, up the side of the engine cowling, and on upwards by means of the port front nacelle strut.

Two F.B.11s were ordered and the first was completed some time in July

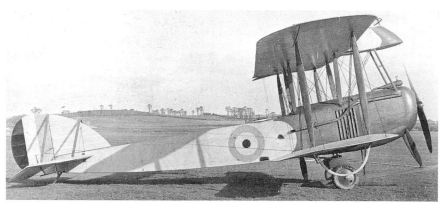

The Vickers F.B.11 late in 1916. (Photo: G.S. Leslie)

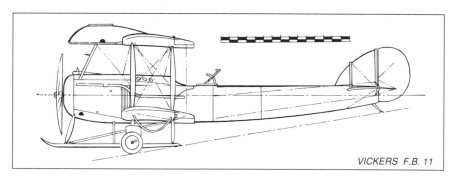

VICKERS F.B. 11

1916, several weeks before the Rolls-Royce engine could be delivered, and the first flight of the aircraft, A4814, was considerably delayed until the early autumn. By that time the idea of large escort fighters had been abandoned as bombers of the calibre of the Airco D.H.4 — capable of putting up an effective self-defence — were coming into prospect.

Type: Single-engine, three-seat, single-bay biplane escort gun carrier.
Manufacturer: Vickers Ltd (Aviation Department), Knightsbridge, London.
Powerplant: One 250hp Rolls-Royce Vee-twelve water-cooled in-line engine driving two-blade propeller.
Dimensions: Span, 51ft 0in; length, 44ft 6in; height, 15ft 8⅛in; wing area, 846 sq ft.
Weights: Tare, 3,340lb; all-up, 4,934lb.
Performance: Max speed, 98 mph at sea level; climb to 5,000ft, 16 min 30 sec; endurance, 4½ hr.
Armament: One 0.303in Lewis machine gun on Scarff ring on gunner's cockpit aft of the pilot's cockpit, and one Lewis gun on nacelle gunner's cockpit with all-round field of fire.
Prototypes: Two, A4814 and A4815 (first flight by A4814 in late September or early October 1916). No production.

Parnall Scout

The Parnall Scout of 1916 was one of those aircraft which themselves came to naught yet, being somewhat adventurous in approach, contributed more than a modicum to the growing fund of knowledge about design parameters. Parnall & Sons of Bristol, an established firm formerly engaged in general woodworking, had for some time been manufacturing Avro 504s and Fairey Hamble Babies, and the high quality of workmanship evident in those aircraft had prompted the Admiralty to encourage the company to embark on designs of its own.

Designed by A Camden Pratt, the

One of only two known photographs of the completed Parnall Scout, shown here in the Eastville shops. Just visible above the wing centre section is what appears to be the Davis gun mounting. (Photo: G Wansbrough-White)

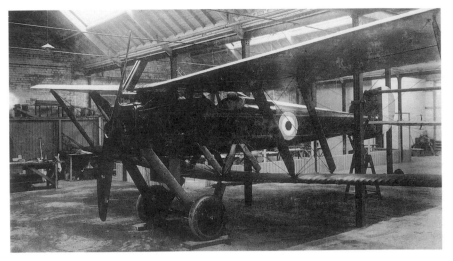

company's first aircraft was a relatively big, single-engine biplane intended for the RNAS as a night fighter which, in 1916, would have been a euphemism for an 'anti-Zeppelin' aircraft. However, unlike other such aircraft, it was intended to possess high performance and great strength. To these ends a water-cooled 250hp Sunbeam in-line engine was selected as powerplant and an extremely strong structure designed. The two-bay wings of unequal span were rigged with considerable stagger, the upper wing being located fairly close to the fuselage to afford the pilot a good upward field of vision; the lower wing was also a continuous structure, located below the fuselage. The sturdy undercarriage, comprising twin V-struts, was positioned well forward to cater for the big engine.

Whether the Scout ever flew is not known. It was delivered to Upavon for its official tests — and such tests occasionally included an aircraft's maiden flight — but on measurement of its weight and c.g. range it was immediately decided that the safety factor was dangerously deficient. As far as is known, all work on the aircraft stopped forthwith. It was subsequently burned to make space available for other work at the factory.

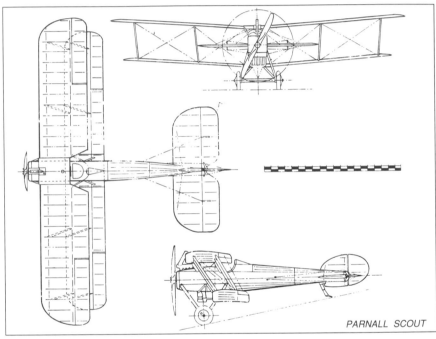

PARNALL SCOUT

Type: Single-engine, single-seat, two-bay biplane night fighter.
Manufacturer: Parnall & Son, Eastville, Bristol.
Powerplant: One 250hp Sunbeam water-cooled in-line engine driving two-blade propeller.
Dimensions: Span, 44ft 0in.
Performance: Design max speed, 113.5 mph at sea level.
Armament: Intended to fit a two-pounder Davis recoilless gun, inclined to fire upwards at about 45 degrees immediately forward of the cockpit.
Prototype: One, N505 (probably completed in July 1916, but it is not known whether it was flown). No production.

Whitehead Scout

Another company better known for its sub-contract manufacture of other firms' designs than its own was Whitehead Aircraft Co Ltd of Townshend Road, Richmond, Surrey. No fewer than 720 Sopwith Pups had been ordered from this relatively modest manufacturer during 1916, yet this considerable workload did not deter the company from venturing to design a single-seat scout of its own that year.

It was perhaps surprising that the Whitehead Scout did not reflect its manufacturer's familiarity with the highly successful Pup, but the two aircraft could hardly have been more different; indeed, it appears to have owed more to the unsuccessful Vickers E.S.2, which it closely resembled with its circular-section fuselage, gracefully curved fin and rudder and rounded wingtips.

Thus it was a not unattractive little aeroplane, powered by an 80hp Le Rhône, with slightly staggered, parallel chord, single-bay wings. The cockpit, however, was located at the point of the fuselage's greatest girth so that the pilot could have had scarcely any downward field of vision owing to the width of the side fairings; he was nevertheless provided with a generous cutout in the upper wing trailing edge. The engine cowling featured four external stiffening ribs with oil drainage apertures at the bottom; it is likely that engine overheating would have resulted from the limited frontal cooling air aperture.

Although no pictures have been located which show the sole example of the Whitehead fitted with armament, there seems no reason to suggest that a synchronized Vickers gun could not have been fitted, nor that a more powerful engine would not have been introduced in due course. The aircraft was not, however, selected for production, and was probably rejected on the same grounds as the Vickers E.S.2 — inadequate field of vision from the cockpit.

Close-up view of the Whitehead Scout which well illustrates the width of the fuselage 'shoulders' on either side of the cockpit. (Photo: J M Bruce)

Sage Type 2

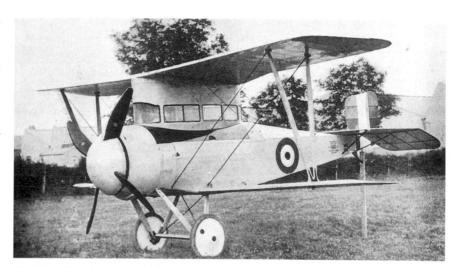

The Sage Type 2 at the RNAS Station, Cranwell, in 1916. (Photo: J M Bruce)

Another long-established woodworking company which entered the aircraft industry by means of sub-contract manufacture was Frederick Sage of Peterborough. After engaging in airship component production for the Admiralty, followed by contracts to produce Short 184 seaplanes in 1915, Sage secured the services of Eric Cecil Gordon England, one of Britain's pioneer airmen (Royal Aero Club Certificate No 68), who was appointed head of the company's aeronautical department. In January 1916 he was joined by Clifford Wilfrid Tinson, formerly of Bristols and the Admiralty's Air Department, to become Chief Designer; he took over the design of a new two-seat fighter, the Sage Type 2 (the Type 1 had been an unbuilt bomber project).

The Sage 2 represented a novel approach to a familiar problem, that of mounting a gun to fire directly forward past a tractor propeller. It has been shown that, apart from the ultimate solution provided by gun interrupter gear, several companies had pursued designs that incorporated gunners' nacelles which tended to be fairly large and imposed substantial drag. Tinson's design incorporated an enclosed cabin, accommodating both pilot and gunner, its superstructure occupying the entire depth of the wing gap between fuselage and upper wing, so that the gunner could stand with his head and shoulders above the wing. In the absence of a gun ring, he was provided with two spigots on which could be mounted a Lewis gun with arcs of fire both forward and aft.

With a wing span of only 22 feet, the Type 2 was an extraordinarily compact and clean design and, added to the fact that it was powered by a beautifully cowled 100hp Gnome *monosoupape*, its performance was outstanding for an armed two-seater. Construction was very simple, the fuselage being a wooden box-girder, faired by formers and stringers with curved upper decking; the wing

Type: Single-engine, two-seat, single-bay biplane fighter.
Manufacturer: Frederick Sage & Co Ltd, Peterborough.
Powerplant: One 100hp Gnome *monosoupape* engine driving four-blade propeller.
Structure: All-wooden construction with ply and fabric covering.
Dimensions: Span, 22ft 2½in; length, 21ft 1⅝in; height, 9ft 6in; wing area, 168 sq ft.
Weights: Tare, 890lb; all-up, 1,546lb.
Performance: Max speed, 112 mph at sea level; climb to 10,000ft, 6 min 30 sec; service ceiling, 16,000ft; endurance, 2½ hr.
Armament: One 0.303in Lewis machine gun on fore or aft spigot mountings on upper wing fired by gunner standing in cabane superstructure.
Prototype: One, not allotted serial number (first flown 10 August 1916; crashed 20 September 1916). No production.

gap was fairly large, and the only wing struts were a pair of V interplane members. The cabin superstructure replaced the customary cabane struts and was of excellent aerodynamic cross-section. Tinson's former association with Frank Barnwell was evident in the Sage's balanced rudder, which was identical to that of the Bristol Scout; as on the Scout, there was no fixed vertical fin.

First flown on 10 August 1916, the Sage at once demonstrated its remarkable performance by recording a maximum speed of 112 mph at sea level, but its flying was shortlived. During a test flight at Cranwell on 20 September, its sternpost failed, and in an attempted landing the aircraft struck a tree and was destroyed. Although by then the front gun interrupter gear had been accepted as reliable in service, the Sage would have represented an excellent two-seat escort fighter; however, the Admiralty had no such requirement, and further development was abandoned.

Vickers F.B.14

The Vickers F.B.14 was variously referred to as a reconnaissance fighter and a general purpose aircraft. It was a large single-engine, single-bay, two-seat biplane with two crew members in tandem cockpits. Whereas former reconnaissance aircraft had perpetually suffered heavy losses over the Western Front, the F.B.14 was an attempt to provide an aircraft with a speed to match that of enemy scouts. Accordingly, it was intended to fit a 230hp Beardmore-Halford-Pullinger (BHP) engine, but no such engine was available at the time Vickers had completed the first airframe in July 1916 and had to be content with a 160hp Beardmore. Although this naturally reduced the performance of the F.B.14, the War Office placed an order for 150 aircraft, and later increased the figure to 250. Trouble was being experienced with the Beardmore engine, and those airframes which were completed were delivered straight into store to await resolution of the engine problems. A 120hp Beardmore was tried, but such was the further reduction in performance, that this experiment was hurriedly abandoned.

Typical of Howard Flanders' designs, the F.B.14 featured an upper wing larger than the lower, the interplane

The single-bay Vickers F.B.14A with 150hp Lorraine-Dietrich engine. (Photo: Vickers Ltd, Neg. No 6316 J)

struts being splayed outwards. The pilot's cockpit was located directly beneath the upper wing but was provided with large transparent panels in the wing centre section and in the lower wing roots. A synchronized Vickers gun was mounted in the centre of the nose decking, and the gunner's cockpit, with a Scarff ring and Lewis gun, were located just aft of a cutout in the upper wing's trailing edge. Ailerons were fitted to upper and lower wings, and a long, curved fin blended with the unbalanced rudder.

In view of the continuing powerplant difficulties an F.B.14 was set aside to be fitted with a 150hp Lorraine-Dietrich V-eight, liquid-cooled in-line engine. This aircraft was re-styled the F.B.14A.

At roughly the same time another F.B.14 (ordered separately) was specially produced to accommodate the big V-twelve 250hp Rolls-Royce Mark IV (later termed the Eagle IV), driving a four-blade propeller. This aircraft, the F.B.14D, C4547, was also given enlarged, two-bay wings, and certainly proved on test at Martlesham in March 1917 to have a significantly better performance, but by then the Bristol Fighter was demonstrating a similar performance — with better to come — and it was not considered worthwhile to pursue the Vickers aircraft. One further experimental version was the F.B.14F powered by a 150hp RAF 4A engine, also driving a four-blade propeller, and this aircraft, A8391, reverted to single-bay wings rigged with increased stagger.

As far as it known very few of the F.B.14s held in store were completed. The F.B.14D, once its trials at Martlesham were completed, was sent to Orfordness for armament experiments, and while there was flown against the Gotha bombers which attacked London in daylight on 17 July 1917, but was

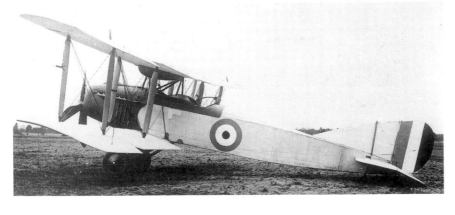

Left: *The F.B.14D, C4547, with 250hp Rolls-Royce Mark IV engine.* (Photo: Vickers Ltd, Neg No 138)

unable to bring its experimental gun-sights to bear on a target. About half-a-dozen Beardmore-powered F.B.14s were issued to Home Defence units, but apparently these were not flown operationally, and unsubstantiated records suggest that some may have been sent to the Middle East for service in Mesopotamia; none has been traced as being held on charge by squadrons in that theatre.

Except where stated, the accompanying table of leading particulars refers to the F.B.14 with the 160hp Beardmore.

Type: Single-engine, two-seat, single-bay fighter-reconnaissance biplane.
Manufacturer: Vickers Ltd (Aviation Department), Knightsbridge, London.
Powerplant: F.B.14. 160hp Beardmore; 120hp Beardmore. F.B.14A. 150hp Lorraine-Dietrich. F.B.14D. 250hp Rolls-Royce Mark IV. F.B.14F. 150hp RAF 4A.
Dimensions: Span, 39ft 6in; length, 28ft 5in; height, 10ft 0in; wing area, 427 sq ft.
Weight: Tare, 1,662lb; all-up, 2,603lb.
Performance: Max speed, 99.5 mph at sea level; climb to 10,000ft, 40 min 50 sec; service ceiling, 10,000ft; endurance, 3¾ hr.
Armament: One synchronized 0.303in Vickers machine gun on fuselage nose decking, and one 0.303in Lewis gun on Scarff ring on gunner's rear cockpit.
Prototypes: One F.B.14, A678 (first flown in August 1916); one F.B.14A; one F.B.14D, C4547; one F.B.14F, A8391.
Production: Out of a total of 252 aircraft ordered, only 100 are believed to have been built, and roughly half of these were completed with engines. (A679-A727, A3505, A8341-A8490).
Summary of Service: Either six or seven F.B.14s were issued to Home Defence squadrons.

Vickers F.B.19

It will be recalled that the Vickers E.S.1 and E.S.2 single-seaters of 1915 (see Page 44) had been criticised and probably rejected for service on account of the very poor field of view from the cockpit caused by the circular section of the fuselage. In other respects the aircraft had been commended in the context of standards existing at that time, and Vickers had been sufficiently encouraged to persist with the basic design. The outcome was the F.B.19, which appeared in August 1916 with an almost flat-sided fuselage aft of the carefully faired circular-section nose.

The single-bay wings were of equal span, and when the aircraft first appeared there was no stagger; it was powered by a 100hp Gnome *monosoupape*. As well as a cutout in the trailing edge of the upper wing, there was a large clear-view aperture between the spars of the wing centre section.

Armament comprised a single Vickers gun located in a channel set into the port side of the forward fuselage below the upper longeron, firing through a small aperture in the front of the engine cowling and equipped with Vickers-Challenger interrupter gear.

When a much-modified version of the F.B.19 appeared soon afterwards with modified wings rigged with considerable stagger, it was termed the Mark II and the original aircraft became the Mark I retrospectively. Despite a very modest performance the Mark II, which inherited the unofficial name Bullet from the earlier E.S. aircraft, was ordered into limited production, with either 110hp

This photograph of an F.B.19 Mk II well illustrates the efforts made to improve the pilot's field of view from the cockpit. (Photo: Vickers Ltd, Neg No 89)

Clerget or Le Rhône engines. Six examples were sent to France for operational trials late in 1916, but were not popular and were soon returned home. One aircraft reached No 14 Squadron in the Middle East in May 1917 and another was issued to No 47 in Greece during June, while No 30 in Mesopotamia flew a third. No 111 Squadron included five amongst its assortment of fighters in Palestine during 1918. The only other Squadron to fly F.B.19s was No 141 which received two at Biggin Hill, also in 1918. It is said that a few were shipped to Russia in 1916 and it seems that these can only have been Mark Is, but no reliable records survive to confirm this, nor the number sent.

The accompanying dimensions, weights and performance data refer to the F.B.19 Mark II with 110hp Le Rhône engine.

Type: Single-engine, single-seat, single-bay biplane fighting scout.
Manufacturer: Vickers Ltd (Aviation Department), Knightsbridge, London.
Powerplant: Mark I. 100hp Gnome *monosoupape* engine; 110hp Le Rhône. Mark II. 110hp Clerget; 110hp Le Rhône.
Dimensions: Span, 24ft 0in; length, 18ft 2in; height, 8ft 3in; wing area, 215 sq ft.
Weights: Tare, 892lb; all-up, 1,478lb.
Performance: Max speed, 98 mph at sea level; climb to 10,000ft, 14 min 50 sec; service ceiling, 15,000ft; endurance, 3¼ hr.
Armament: Single 0.303in Vickers machine gun mounted in trough on port side of nose to fire through the propeller arc, synchronized by Vickers-Challenger gear.
Prototypes: Two Mark Is, A1968 and A1969 (first flown in August 1916).
Production: Records suggest that as many as thirty-six F.B.19s were issued to the RFC, although contract cover has only been confirmed for fourteen (two Mark Is, A2120 and A2992, and twelve Mark IIs, A5225-A5236).
Summary of Service: Surviving records show that single Mark IIs served with No 14 Squadron (Middle East), No 30 (Mesopotamia) and No 47 (Greece); No 111 Squadron received five in Palestine in August 1917, and No 141 Squadron flew two at Biggin Hill in 1918. Some were issued to home-based training units in 1918.

Bristol M.1 Monoplanes

All credit is due to Frank Barnwell at Bristol for his defiance in the face of ill-informed prejudice by venturing into the realm of monoplane design. Ever since the summary ban imposed by the War Office following a number of crashes involving monoplanes in 1912, reluctance by the military authorities to accept such aircraft had discouraged designers and manufacturers from flying in the face of such misplaced prejudice. Even when the Germans introduced their successful series of *Eindekker* scouts in 1915, the War Office remained trenchantly unconvinced.

Barnwell's M.1 design, started early in 1916, was lent urgency by the increasing casualties over the Western Front even though, with the arrival of such fighters as the Airco D.H.2, the air fighting was becoming less one-sided. The first example, known as the M.1A and built as a private venture, was first flown without armament at Filton on 14 July by the great free-lance test pilot, Fred Raynham, and at once demonstrated a marked performance superiority over current biplane scouts, returning a maximum speed of 132 mph at sea level on a 110hp Clerget engine.

The new monoplane's fuselage retained the wooden box-girder of the Bristol biplane scouts, but faired throughout its length to circular section with formers and stringers. The two-spar wings were attached at their main spar ends to the upper longerons, being externally cable-braced below to the bottom longerons and above to a pair of hooped tubular members which formed a cabane under which the cockpit was located; this cabane thus provided some

The exceptionally clean lines of the Bristol M.1A prototype, A5138, are evident in this photograph taken in July 1916 at the time of its first flight. (Photo: The Bristol Aeroplane Co Ltd.)

protection for the pilot in the event of the aircraft overturning while landing. The wings, rigged with two degrees of dihedral but zero incidence, were of distinctive planform, possessing elliptical leading edge and straight trailing edge with rounded tips. The tailplane and elevator were scarcely altered from those of the Scout biplanes, but a fixed fin was introduced forward of the unbalanced rudder. A large hemispherical spinner with a small aperture in the nose was fitted over the two-blade propeller, having been shown on some Scout Ds to result in a marked reduction in drag — although care had to be taken to avoid engine overheating.

The prototype underwent AID evaluation in July, confirming the initial performance measurements, and these led to the purchase of the first aircraft (which became A5138) and an order for

Type: Single-engine, single-seat, shoulder-wing monoplane fighting scout.

Manufacturer: The British & Colonial Aeroplane Co Ltd, Filton and Brislington, Bristol.

Powerplant: M.1A. One 110hp Clerget engine. M.1B. 110hp Clerget; 150hp Bentley A.R.1. M.1C. 110hp Le Rhône.

Structure: Wooden box-girder formed to circular section; two-spar wings attached to upper longerons and cable-braced to lower longerons and cabane members over cockpit.

Dimensions: Span, 30ft 9in; length, 20ft 3in (M.1A), 20ft 5½in (M.1C); height (M.1C), 7ft 9½in; wing area, 163 sq ft.

Weights: M.1C. Tare, 896lb; all-up, 1,348lb.

Performance: M1C. Max speed, 130 mph at sea level; 111.5 mph at 10,000ft.; climb to 10,000ft, 10 min 25 sec; service ceiling, 20,000ft; endurance, 1¾ hr.

Armament: M.1A, nil. M.1B and M.1C. One 0.303in Vickers machine gun with either Constantinesco CC or Sopwith-Kauper interrupter gear.

Prototypes: One M.1A, A5138 (first flown by Fred Raynham on 14 July 1916); four M.1Bs, A5139-A5142.

Production: Total of 125 M.1Cs, C4901-C5025.

Summary of Service: M.1Bs and M.1Cs flew with Nos 14, 72, 111 and 150 Squadrons (the last-named Squadron being formed from 'A' Flights of Nos 17 and 47 Squadrons). All these Squadrons served either in Macedonia or the Middle East.

Despite retaining its Vickers gun, this Bristol M.1C is said to have been serving with the Wireless Experimental Establishment at Biggin Hill late in, or shortly after, the War. (Photo: RAF Museum, Neg No P021463)

four further prototypes (A5139–A5142), modified to include a synchronized Vickers gun with Constantinesco CC interrupter gear, mounted on the port upper longeron. This version, the M.1B, featured a cutout panel in the starboard wing root for downward vision, and the cabane hoops were discarded in favour of four straight tubular members arranged pyramidally. The 110hp Clerget engine was retained, although one of the M.1Bs was tested with a 150hp Bentley A.R.1 engine in March 1917.

Despite being eagerly awaited by RFC squadrons on the Western Front, a production contract was delayed, due it was said to War Office apprehension at the Bristol's high landing speed — 49 mph; this may have stemmed from the rumour that a senior officer crashed one of the prototypes, having misjudged his landing speed.

When production M.1Cs (with 110hp Le Rhône engine, cutouts in both wing roots and a centrally mounted Vickers gun with Sopwith-Kauper interrupter gear) appeared, it transpired that none was scheduled for France. A total of 125 aircraft was built and, apart from a small number used for training on Salisbury Plain and at Hounslow, Marske and Montrose, these only served with squadrons in the Balkans and the Middle East. First was No 14 Squadron in Palestine at Deir-el-Belah in May 1917, followed

in August by No 111 Squadron on the same aerodrome; M.1Cs were issued to 'A' Flights of Nos 17 and 47 Squadrons at Mikra Bay in Salonika for operations against the Turks and Bulgars, and these Flights merged to form No 150 Squadron in January 1918. The only other Squadron was No 72 which received the monoplanes at Basra in March 1918.

The last to be declared obsolete were those of No 150 Squadron when it was disbanded in September 1919.

After the Armistice an M.1B and several M.1Cs were repurchased by Bristol, reconditioned and sold to civilian owners who flew them in sporting events for several years.

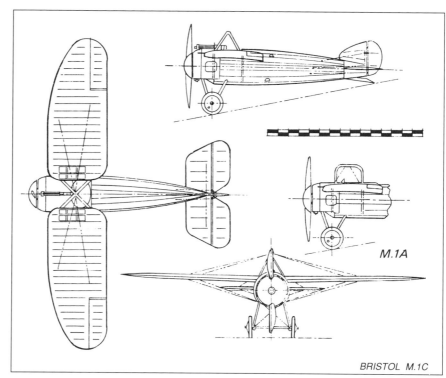

M.1A

BRISTOL M.1C

Airco D.H.5

The first appearance in operational service of de Havilland's D.H.5 as late as May 1917 was a curious anachronism that tended to emphasise the mediocrity of this, the only essay into tractor scout design by Airco. De Havilland's pre-occupation with the D.H.3 and D.H.4 bombers for much of 1916, and the survival of his D.H.2 in service throughout that year together served to sidetrack the designer away from fully exploiting the arrival of the first British gun interruptor equipment until the summer. Even so, the configuration of the D.H.5 was unorthodox owing to de Havilland's determination to perpetuate the excellent field of vision for the pilot that had been a feature of the D.H.2 pusher.

To achieve this the D.H.5 was rigged with a pronounced backward stagger of

The unarmed prototype Airco D.H.5, A5172, with flat-sided fuselage and horn-balanced rudder. The position of the pilot's cockpit is well illustrated. (Photo: de Havilland Aircraft Co Ltd.)

27 inches on the wings, enabling the pilot's cockpit to be located directly below the leading edge of the upper wing. Unfortunately this peculiar feature led to some unsavoury handling characteristics, particularly at low air-

speeds. Powered by a 110hp Le Rhône rotary, the aircraft first appeared in prototype form as A5172 in the early autumn of 1916, the fuselage in effect being a wooden box girder with flat sides and with rounded top decking formed

A production D.H.5, B371, built by the British Caudron Co Ltd, with the five-gallon gravity fuel tank on the starboard upper mainplane. The inscription on the side of the fuselage reads 'Presented by the Solanki — Princes, Chiefs & Nobles', showing this to be one of many aircraft subscribed by the British Empire. (Photo: J M Bruce)

by frames and stringers; both wings and fuselage were internally crossbraced with wire stays. The main fuel tank was located immediately behind the pilot, with a small gravity tank above the upper wing. Although the prototype flew with a small horn-balanced rudder (of a shape characterised in de Havilland's designs for the next twenty years), production aircraft possessed slightly larger, but unbalanced rudders; these aircraft also differed from the prototype in having the fuselage faired to octagonal cross-section.

At least 550 D.H.5s were built by Airco and three sub-contractors, and the first entered operational service with No. 24 Squadron in May 1917, straightway attracting criticism on account of their dismal performance at altitude, being inferior to the new two-seat Bristol F.2B Fighter and the nine-month-old Sopwith Pup. It was also discovered that elevator control rapidly diminished as speeds approached the stall.

Accordingly the D.H.5 came to be employed increasingly as a ground-strafing fighter and, despite its armament of only one Vickers machine gun, proved to be well suited to this hazardous rôle — largely on account of the pilot's excellent field of vision. Aircraft of No 41 Squadron were used to good effect during the Battle of Ypres in August, and for the Battle of Cambrai in November D.H.5s of Nos 64 and 68 Squadrons were also equipped to carry up to four 20lb Cooper bombs.

Cambrai was effectively the D.H.5's swansong and, during the next three months, all were replaced by S.E.5As in operational service. Nor did they survive long among the training units.

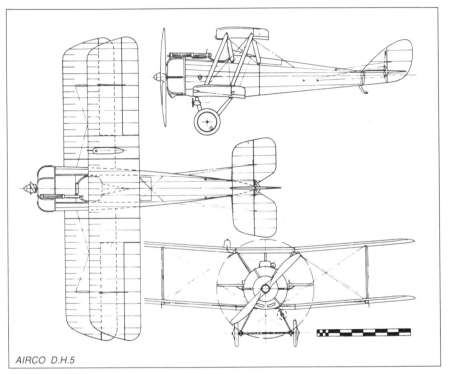

AIRCO D.H.5

Type: Single-engine, single-seat tractor biplane fighting scout; also ground attack fighter.

Manufacturers: The Aircraft Manufacturing Co Ltd, Hendon, London; Darracq Motor Engineering Co Ltd, Fulham, London; British Caudron Co Ltd, Cricklewood, London; March, Jones & Cribb Ltd., Leeds.

Powerplant: One 110hp Le Rhône nine-cylinder air-cooled rotary engine; some aircraft with one 110hp Clerget air-cooled rotary engine.

Structure: Fabric-covered all-wood box girder fuselage faired to octagonal section; single-bay two-spar wings rigged with 27 inches of backward stagger.

Dimensions: Span, 25ft 8in; length, 22ft 0in; height, 9ft 1½in; wing area, 212 sq ft.

Weights: Tare, 1,010lb; all-up, 1,492lb.

Performance: Max speed, 109 mph at sea level; climb to 10,000ft, 12 min 25 sec; service ceiling, 16,000ft; endurance, 2¾ hr.

Armament: One 0.303in Vickers machine gun with Constantinesco CC interrupter gear on top of nose, offset to port; provision later made to carry up to four 20lb Cooper bombs.

Prototype: One, A5172 (first flown by Geoffrey de Havilland in the autumn of 1915).

Production: Approx. 550 aircraft from A9163-A9361 (Airco); A9363-A9562 (Darracq); B331-B380 (British Caudron); and B4901-B5000 (Marsh, Jones & Cribb); one aircraft, B7775, rebuilt by No. 1 (Southern) Aeroplane Repair Depot.

Summary of Service: Served with Nos. 24, 32, 41, 64 and 68 (Australian) Squadrons; also with Schools of Aerial Fighting.

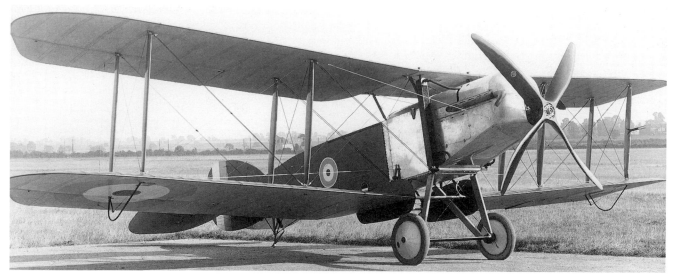

Bristol F.2A

The first Bristol F.2A prototype, A3303, at about the time of its first flight on 9 September 1916, powered by a 190hp Rolls-Royce Falcon I with vertical radiators on the sides of the nose. This aircraft featured wing-root endplates and wingtips reminiscent of the B.E.2, of which Bristol had produced so many. (Photo: The Bristol Aeroplane Co Ltd.)

In March 1916 Frank Barnwell began the design of a new two-seat fighter embodying many of the lessons learned from the Royal Aircraft Factory's B.E.2 (of which Bristol had produced several hundreds). Intended to use the 120hp Beardmore engine, this design was referred to as the R.2A, and was a fairly large two-bay biplane with wings of equal span; the pilot's cockpit was located under a large trailing edge cutout, and his observer/gunner was situated close behind with a Lewis gun on a Scarff ring. A single synchronized Lewis gun was mounted forward on the upper starboard longeron. It was realised that the R.2A would be somewhat underpowered and in May the design was altered to introduce a 150hp Hispano-Suiza, and to feature wings of unequal span and part-Warren girder interplane struts; this was the R.2B.

Two months later Bristol was offered one of the new 190hp Rolls-Royce vee-twelve water-cooled engines (soon to be named the Falcon I), and Barnwell undertook a fresh re-design, the F.2A, based largely on the R.2s and returning to the equal-span two-bay wings of the original design, but retaining the sprung tail skid of the R.2B. The front Lewis gun was changed to a Vickers and re-positioned in the centre of the nose where it was located in a tunnel through the front fuel tank; fifty gallons of fuel were carried in two tanks, sufficient for 3¼ hours' flying.

The fuselage box girder structure was strengthened and an adjustable-incidence tailplane incorporated, permitting the aircraft to be flown 'hands-off' over a wide speed range. The rear fuselage was given more pronounced taper in side elevation, thereby slightly increasing the observer/gunner's rearward field of fire. Wireless equipment was to be provided as a standard fitting. One of the characteristic features of the F.2 family that would become familiar for many years was the continuous lower wing structure which was located about ten inches below the fuselage, being 'carried' by struts attached to the lower fuselage longerons. The centre section of this wing was an open structure with steel carry-through spars without fabric covering. The wings, with top and bottom ailerons, were rigged with 17.1 inches of stagger.

The first prototype, A3303, was flown on 9 September at Filton by Capt C A Hooper, and went on to Upavon for Service evaluation on the 21st. It was soon found that the Falcon's vertical radiators, mounted on the sides of the nose, obscured the pilot's field of view during landing and a new nose configuration was designed to incorporate a single annular radiator within the engine cowling.

A second prototype, A3304, was flown on 25 October, this aeroplane being fitted with a 150hp Hispano-Suiza — also with front annular radiator. This was the version intended for production, but all Hispano-Suizas were now required for the Royal Aircraft Factory's S.E.5, and an order was issued for fifty F.2As, to be powered by Rolls-Royce Falcon Is. The production version also featured blunt wingtips, a feature that was to remain unchanged in all subsequent F.2s.

These F.2As began delivery to the RFC in February 1917 and were issued to No 48 Squadron at Rendcombe, Gloucestershire, where a special training unit was formed for the Bristols' crews. No 48, commanded by Maj A Vere Bettington (later Gp Capt, CMG, RAF) flew to Bertangles in France on 8 March, moving on to Bellevue soon after. The Squadron's début in action on 5 April ended in disaster when six F.2As, led by Capt W Leefe Robinson VC, ran into five Albatros D IIIs, led by

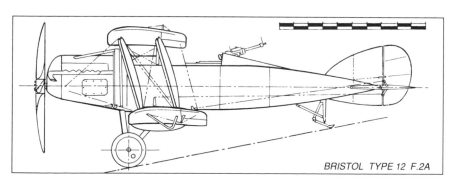

BRISTOL TYPE 12 F.2A

Manfred von Richthofen. Four of the Bristols were shot down, two of them by the enemy leader. Further casualties were suffered in the days following until it became apparent to the British pilots that the F.2A was being flown incorrectly in combat, and that relying wholly on the rear gun was to exploit only a small part of the fighter's potential. Gradually the pilots began to fly their aircraft as if they were single-seaters, using the front gun *offensively*, and relying on the rear gun primarily for defence. Thereafter the Bristol's true value was fully appreciated and, when the F.2B arrived soon after, the RFC found that it had a superb general purpose fighter (see page 85).

[There was to be a curiously analogous combat twenty-three years later, when Boulton Paul Defiant two-seat turret fighters of No 141 Squadron, fighting their first combat in the Battle of Britain, encountered enemy Messerschmitt single-seaters over the English Channel. Once again the British pilots fought their fighters as gun platforms for their rear gunners and once more suffered catastrophic losses, six out of nine Defiants being destroyed. After the incident, however, there was to be no recourse to front gun armament — the Defiant had none.]

Type: Single-engine, two-seat, two-bay biplane general purpose fighter.
Manufacturer: The British & Colonial Aeroplane Co Ltd, Filton and Brislington, Bristol.
Powerplant: First prototype and production F.2As. One 190hp Rolls-Royce Falcon I 12-cylinder water-cooled in-line engine. Second prototype. 150hp Hispano-Suiza.
Structure: Wooden structure with duralumin, ply and fabric covering, reinforced locally with steel tubular members.
Dimensions: Span, 39ft 3in; length, 25ft 10in; height, 9ft 6in; wing area, 389 sq ft.
Weights: Falcon I. Tare, 1,700lb; all-up, 2,700lb.
Performance: Falcon I. Max speed, 110 mph at sea level; climb to 10,000ft, 14 min 30 sec; service ceiling, 16,000ft; endurance, 3¼ hr.
Armament: One 0.303in Vickers machine gun in nose with Constantinesco CC interrupter gear, and one Lewis gun on Scarff ring in rear cockpit.
Prototypes: Two, A3303 (first flown on 9 September 1916 by Capt CA Hooper at Filton), and A3304.
Production: 50 aircraft (A3305-A3354).
Summary of Service: Bristol F.2As served with No 48 Squadron, RFC, in France, and at a training unit at Rendcombe.

Armstrong, Whitworth F.K.10

Possibly originally undertaken as a design exercise to investigate the potential of the quadruplane configuration, Frederick Koolhoven's F.K.10 attracted the interest of the Services as a possible fighter. A prototype was built during the late summer of 1916, emerging as a lanky two-seater powered by a 110hp Clerget engine and featuring a slim, angular fuselage in which the pilot's cockpit was located forward of the wings, and an observer's cockpit aft of them. The wings, of only 3ft 7in chord, spanned 27ft 10in, and were rigged with a total stagger of 4ft 3in. The tail comprised a rather crude horn-balanced rudder with fixed fin below the fuselage, fixed tailplane and unbalanced elevator. The undercarriage consisted of single faired struts on each side, with the spreader bar heavily cable-braced between its extremities and the lower longerons. Single interplane and cabane I-struts were employed, and the second from top wing possessed no centre section so as to leave the crew's field of view less obstructed. Ailerons were fitted on all wings. A single synchronized Vickers gun was provided for the pilot and was mounted on the aircraft's centreline over the engine cowling, the observer's cockpit being

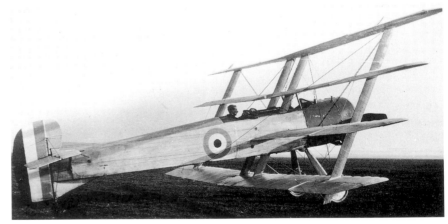

Upper photo: *The first prototype F.K.10 with slim fuselage and no fixed fin above.* (Photo: via J M Bruce). Lower photo: *A Phoenix Dynamo-built F.K.10, N511, with deeper fuselage and Scarff ring on the rear cockpit.* (Photo: G S Leslie)

equipped with a mounting for a Lewis gun.

A total of three prototypes is believed to have been built by Armstrong Whitworth, after which the War Office ordered five production aircraft from Angus Sanderson of Newcastle, and the Admiralty ordered three from the Phoenix Dynamo company of Bradford, though it is not known whether all were built. Most were fitted with 130hp Clergets.

The production F.K.10s were rather more elegantly styled than the original prototype, with larger fuselage section and tidied-up tail surfaces. One of the RFC machines was flown by the Training Unit at Gosport, and the first RNAS aircraft, N511, underwent its Service trials at Boroughbridge in April 1917; another of the naval aircraft was completed as a bomber with racks for light bombs.

Type: Single-engine, two-seat, single-bay quadruplane fighter.

Manufacturers: Sir W G Armstrong, Whitworth & Co Ltd, Newcastle-upon-Tyne; The Phoenix Dynamo Manufacturing Co Ltd, Bradford; Angus Sanderson & Co, Newcastle-upon-Tyne.

Powerplant: One 110hp Clerget engine; also 130hp Clerget; 110hp Le Rhône.

Dimensions: Span, 27ft 10in; length, 22ft 3in; height, 11ft 6in; wing area, 390.4 sq ft.

Weights: (130hp Clerget). Tare, 1,236lb; all-up, 2,019lb.

Performance: (130hp Clerget). Max speed, approx 90 mph at sea level; climb to 10,000ft, 37 min 10 sec; service ceiling, 10,000ft; endurance, 2½ hr.

Armament: One synchronized 0.303in Vickers machine gun on nose, and one 0.303in Lewis gun on rear cockpit mounting.

Prototypes: Believed three, A5212-A5214 (built by Armstrong, Whitworth).

Production: Total of eight ordered (B3996-B4000 for RFC, built by Angus Sanderson; N511, N512 and N514 built by Phoenix Dynamo).

Summary of Service: Single examples flown by the RFC at Gosport, and by the RNAS at Manston, both probably in 1917.

Wight Quadruplane Scout

Towards the end of 1916 the Isle of Wight company, J Samuel White & Co, was engaged in work on a diminutive quadruplane single-seat scout, occasionally referred to as the Wight Type 4. Originally designed by Howard Wright (who had already left the company) the aircraft was powered by a 110hp Clerget rotary in a narrow-chord 'oil sling' cowling and, in its initial form featured wings of two different spans, the lowest being the shortest. Wing chord was only 2ft 9in, and tiny ailerons of some nine inches chord were fitted on the three upper wings. The undercarriage comprised single struts well raked outwards and wheels slotted into the lower wings' leading edge; this arrangement, however, demanded an exceptionally long mounting for the tailskid in order to provide ground clearance for the lower wing's trailing edge.

In order to employ an uninterrupted rectangular elevator, the horn-balanced rudder was hinged high on a fixed, triangular fin. As originally designed, the Scout featured twin parallel tubular interplane struts, but lack of side area resulted in these being crudely faired together by the simple expedient of wrapping them with fabric to create a single broad-chord surface; the struts in the lowest wing gap were not so treated. In all likelihood the aircraft was not flown in this somewhat dangerous configuration.

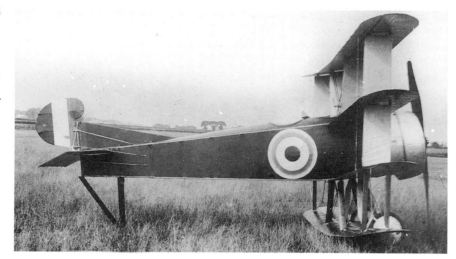

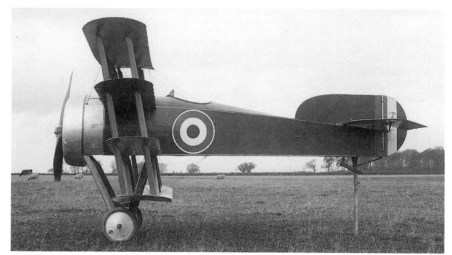

Upper photo: *The Wight Quadruplane on its long tailskid mounting, as it originally appeared with high-set rudder, small fin, wrapped wing struts and short undercarriage.* Lower photo: *After rebuilding with modified tail, wings, and lengthened undercarriage with conventional tailskid. The lack of forward view for the pilot is readily apparent.* (Photos: A J Jackson Collection)

Early in 1917 a complete rebuild of the aircraft was begun. A much altered tail unit was designed, employing a split elevator with cutout, thereby allowing an unbalanced rudder to be fitted, together with a much enlarged fin. The fuselage was less tapered in side elevation, resulting in a longer sternpost. A more conventional undercarriage was substituted with twin V-struts, the aft members passing through the lower wing to anchor on the lower longerons, allowing the wheels to be located well below the leading edge of the lower wing and thus permitting a conventionally-mounted tailskid.

Wing and aileron chords were increased so that the spars and interplane struts could be moved further apart and, with the increased side area of fuselage and tail, there was no need to fair the struts with fabric. A third and final configuration featured wings moved slightly further aft with progressively shorter spans from top to bottom, and with similar outward rake on the interplane struts; ailerons were only fitted on the two top wings.

Indeed the Scout appeared as a much safer-looking aeroplane, and Marcus Manton went ahead with flight tests. At some time towards the end of 1917 the prototype was purchased by the Admi-

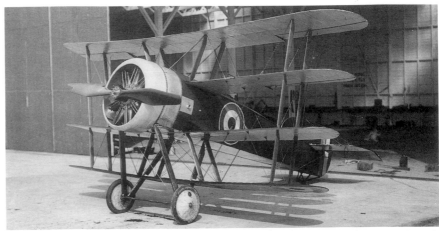

The Quadruplane Scout, N549, in its final form with wings reducing equally in span from the top and raked interplane struts, and ailerons on the top two wings only. (Photo: A J Jackson Collection)

ralty, allotted the naval number N546, and evaluated at Martlesham. Manton stated that N546 ultimately crashed into a cemetary.

It is inconceivable that, despite its innovatory approach, the Quadruplane was ever seriously considered as a realistic operational fighter.

Type: Single-engine, single-seat, single-bay quadruplane scout.
Manufacturer: J Samuel White & Co, Cowes, Isle of Wight.
Powerplant: One 110hp Clerget rotary engine driving two-blade propeller.
Dimensions: Span, approx 19ft.
Prototype: One, N546.

Sopwith L.R.T.Tr.

Designed at a time when the RFC was still seeking a long-range escort fighter capable of firing a gun directly forward without perpetuating the old Gunbus formula, the Sopwith L.R.T.Tr. was certainly the weirdest-looking aircraft to emerge from that company's shops during the War. Accorded the nickname 'The Egg Box' by those at Sopwith, the aircraft (whose initials are thought to have stood for Long-Range Tractor Triplane) featured heavily-staggered, three-bay wings of equal span and chord with I-type interplane and cabane struts similar to those on the Sopwith Triplane scout.

The top wing carried a large streamlined nacelle in the nose of which was situated a gunner's cockpit intended to have been provided with a pillar mounting for a Lewis gun. The pilot's cockpit was located beneath the trailing edge of the upper wing, and immediately aft of this was a second gunner's cockpit, also with a Lewis gun for rearward defence.

The fuselage was a very robust struc-

The Sopwith long-range triplane escort fighter. The nacelle gunner mounted to his cockpit by means of a step on the front chassis strut, two steps on the engine cowling and a final stirrup step under the nacelle. (Photo: A J Jackson Collection).

ture built up around a deep, wooden box-girder with rounded top decking. Power was provided by a single 250hp Rolls-Royce Mark I (Eagle I) water-cooled vee-twelve in-line engine with its radiator in the extreme front. The undercarriage with twin V-struts and mainwheels was located almost directly below the aircraft's c.g. and was supplemented by a chassis extending forward with two balancing wheels. The aircraft

could therefore rest tail-up on the balancing wheels or tail-down on the tailskid, depending on the number of crew and quantity of fuel carried.

It is likely that the big Rolls-Royce engine bestowed a useful maximum speed, but by the time the triplane was flown, towards the end of 1916, the RFC's requirement had lapsed owing to the imminent arrival in service of the Bristol Fighters.

Type: Single-engine, three-seat, three-bay triplane fighter.

Manufacturer: The Sopwith Aviation Company Ltd, Kingston-upon-Thames, Surrey.

Powerplant: One 250hp Rolls-Royce Mark I (Eagle I) in-line engine driving two-blade propeller.

Dimensions: Span, 53ft; length, 38ft.

Performance: Max speed, approx107 mph

Armament: One 0.303in Lewis machine gun on gunner's position in nose of wing-mounted nacelle, and another on the rear gunner's cockpit in the fuselage amidships.

Prototype: One. No production.

Left: *The Sopwith L.R.T.Tr. resting on its tailskid.* (Photo: G S L / J M B Collection)

Blackburn Triplane

At a time when it must have seemed that British aircraft designers were prepared to go to any lengths to create the oddest conceivable fighters in their search for a solution of the forward-firing gun requirement, even the Blackburn Triplane appears anachronistic, to say the least.

It will be recalled that the eccentric Harris Booth, while at the Admiralty's Air Department, had designed a peculiar pusher biplane, known as the A.D. Sparrow scout (see page 42), and that two such aircraft were built by the Blackburn company of Leeds. In 1916 Booth left the Air Department and immediately joined Blackburn, where he set about the design of a pusher triplane which one can only conjecture as being loosely based on his original Sparrow concept with which he seems to have been obsessed.

Retaining the Sparrow's parallel tail booms, its huge tailplane and tailskids at the base of the rudders, the nacelle was arguably of improved shape, through which the spars of the centre wing passed. A wider-track undercarriage was provided and, initially, a 110hp Clerget rotary was selected. All flying surface trailing edges were formed with wire — which imposed an archaic appearance of scalloped edges when the fabric tautened under the effects of dope. Booth even proposed retaining the two-pounder Davis recoilless gun although it is

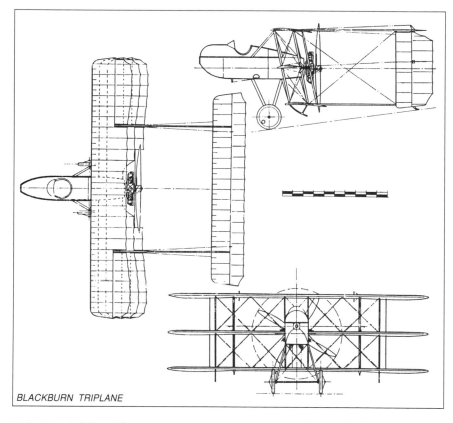

BLACKBURN TRIPLANE

The Blackburn Triplane with its original 110hp Clerget engine and four-blade propeller. (Photo: J M Bruce)

difficult to reconcile this weapon with the aircraft's rôle as a scout.

The aircraft was completed towards the end of 1916 when it was despatched to Eastchurch, having undergone an engine change to the 100hp Gnome *monosoupape*. On 20 February 1917 the Triplane was accepted by the Admiralty as N502, but one month later it was struck off charge as serving no useful purpose. It had been claimed that the aircraft possessed a maximum speed of 115 mph with the *monosoupape* engine, but this must be discounted as most improbable.

Type: Single pusher engine, single-seat, single-bay triplane scout.
Manufacturer: Blackburn Aeroplane & Motor Co Ltd, Leeds.
Powerplant: One 110hp Clerget engine driving four-blade propeller; later one 100hp Gnome *monosoupape* with two-blade propeller.
Dimensions: Span, 24ft 0in; length, 21ft 5⁵⁄₁₆in; height, 8ft 6in; wing area, 221 sq ft.
Weights: (100hp Gnome). Tare, 1,011lb; all-up, 1,500lb.
Performance: (100hp Gnome). Max speed, probably approx 95 mph; endurance, 3 hr.
Armament: Intended as one 2-pdr Davis recoilless gun in nose of nacelle.
Prototype: One, N502.

Vickers F.B.16

The Vickers F.B.16 was designed by Rex Pierson as a private venture in the first place principally to demonstrate the Vickers-sponsored 150hp Hart radial engine which, it will be recalled, had not been ready in time for the F.B.12. The new engine gave its name to Pierson's design and the Hart Scout originally appeared as a single-bay biplane, its fairly heavily staggered wings being of unequal span and chord with rounded tips. The engine was neatly cowled, but evidently suffered from overheating as the cowling was soon removed. The fin and rudder also underwent alteration, the fin being reduced in area and the rudder shape changed to present a smoothly curved upper line, while the fuselage aft of the cockpit was reduced in depth in favour of a small headrest fairing.

The Hart engine gave almost continuous trouble and it was removed from the F.B.16 which, early in the autumn of 1916, was redesigned and re-emerged as the F.B.16A in December, now powered by a 150hp Hispano-Suiza driving a two-blade propeller. This installation, which featured a frontal radiator, allowed a narrower fuselage which was

The Vickers F.B.16A with 150hp Hispano-Suiza, with very small gap between the nose decking and the upper wing. (Photo: Vickers Ltd, Neg No 135)

now flat sided with curved top and bottom fairings. The unequal-span wings were retained but were given raked tips. Armament comprised a synchronized Vickers gun and a Lewis gun on a sliding mounting above the upper wing centre-section.

After the first F.B.16A was destroyed in a fatal accident, a second machine, A8963, was built and sent to Martlesham for Service trials during which it returned a top speed of 120 mph at 6,500 feet; it was not, however, recommended for production owing, it is believed, to an official preference for the S.E.5. Nevertheless, its development continued and A8963 reappeared as the

F.B.16D in the summer of 1917 with a 200hp Hispano-Suiza, returning to Martlesham in July where its speed at 10,000 feet was recorded as 135 mph. The F.B.16D became a favourite mount of Capt J T B McCudden MC who used to visit Joyce Green when on leave from France.

Once more the F.B.16 underwent extensive redesign, much larger two-bay wings being fitted; the fuselage was also lengthened to allow the installation of a 275hp Lorraine-Dietrich vee-eight liquid-cooled engine, also with a frontal radiator. Although this variant, the F.B.16E, had a top speed of about 144 mph at sea level, this performance was bettered by the final variant, the F.B.16H, powered by a 300hp Hispano-Suiza, which had a maximum speed of 147 mph and could reach 10,000ft in 7 minutes 50 seconds.

These were some of the highest speeds yet confirmed by a fully-armed fighter at that time (mid-1918), but they were achieved using foreign engines, and the

This photo of the F.B.16D shows the small aperture in the spinner through which the engine-mounted Lewis gun fired; the aircraft is believed to have been painted red overall. (Photo: Vickers Ltd, Neg No 103)

The F.B.16E in the Darracq works awaiting its 200hp Lorraine-Dietrich engine. (Photo: Vickers Ltd, Neg No 95)

Service policy was moving slowly in favour of British designs; in any case, fighters of comparable performance, such as the Sopwith Snipe and Dolphin, were already approaching production status, and the Vickers work, perhaps unjustly, remained purely experimental.

Type: Single-engine, single-seat, single- and two-bay biplane scout.
Manufacturer: Vickers Ltd (Aviation Department), Knightsbridge, London.
Powerplant: F.B.16. One 150hp Hart radial engine. F.B.16A. 150hp Hispano-Suiza. F.B.16D. 200hp Hispano-Suiza. F.B.16E. 275hp Lorraine-Dietrich. F.B.16H. 300hp Hispano-Suiza.
Dimensions: F.B.16A. Span, 25ft 0in; length, 19ft 0in; height, 7ft 10in; wing area, 199 sq ft. F.B.16D. Span, 25ft 0in; length, 19ft 6in; wing area, 207 sq ft. F.B.16E. Span, 31ft 0in; length, 21ft 0in; wing area, 272 sq ft.
Weights: F.B.16D. Tare, 1,376lb; all-up, 1,875lb. F.B.16E. Tare, 1,495lb; all-up, 2,200lb.
Performance: F.B.16D. Max speed, 140 mph at sea level; climb to 10,000ft, 10 min 25 sec; service ceiling, 18,500ft. F.B.16E. Max speed, 144 mph at sea level; climb to 10,000ft, 7 min 50 sec; service ceiling, 24,000ft.
Armament: F.B.16D. One 0.303in Lewis gun mounted between cylinder banks of engine and firing through propeller shaft, and a Lewis gun on sliding mounting above upper wing centre section. F.B.16E. Two synchronized Vickers guns in cowling above engine and a Lewis gun on sliding mounting above upper wing.
Prototypes: One prototype served as F.B.16 and F.B.16A; a second F.B.16A, A8963, also served as prototype F.B.16D, E and H.

Armstrong, Whitworth F.K.12

The second version of the Armstrong, Whitworth F.K.12 escort fighter, No 7838, with enlarged fuselage and underslung gunners' nacelles. (Photo: Real Photographs Co.)

If the products of Sopwith and Vickers, in the search for an escort fighter, had appeared quaint, that of Frederick Koolhoven at Armstrong, Whitworth was nothing less than incongruous. Both the L.R.T.Tr and the F.B.11 had employed single nacelles in which to accommodate additional gunners, both selecting the top wing as a logical position from which to gain the widest field of fire. Koolhoven decided on two nacelles, and placed them at the front of the central wing of a large single-bay triplane, powered by a single 250hp Rolls-Royce Mark I.

When the F.K.12 first appeared towards the end of 1916, the central wing — with by far the greater span — was located well forward on the fuselage, so that the engine only just extended beyond the leading edge; the top and bottom wings were much smaller structures, carried on struts above and below the fuselage and rigged without stagger. The gunners' nacelles were long structures mounted above the central wing, extending forward of the propeller. The undercarriage comprised a pair of mainwheels mounted on a single strut extending from beneath the engine and attached to the leading edge of the lower wing, and a small, sprung auxiliary wheel under each lower wingtip. A rear skid was carried on long pyramidal struts extending downwards from the fuselage immediately to the rear of the lower wing.

The first configuration was not considered successful and was followed by a no less extraordinary aircraft which was probably newly built, rather than an adaptation of the first. This retained the same arrangement of 'short-long-short' wings as previously but with a much deeper fuselage occupying the entire gap between the two lower wings. These two-bay wings were set further aft on the fuselage so that the engine extended further forward. The twin gunners' nacelles, now mounted beneath the central wing, were much shorter so the gunners's cockpits were behind and outboard of the propeller. (They were incidentally no more than two feet from the open ends of the big Rolls-Royce engine's exhaust manifolds.)

The undercarriage now comprised two pairs of landing wheels mounted on heavy vertical members attached to the sides of the fuselage and were thus of very narrow track; a conventional tailskid was attached under the rear fuselage, and the wingtip balancing wheels were discarded in favour of hooped skids.

The aircraft, No 7838, was flown by Lieut-Cdr Peter Legh, but no reliable records of the flight trials of the aircraft have been traced. A total of four F.K.12 prototypes was ordered by the War Office, but it is thought likely that the two aircraft described here were the only examples completed.

Type: Single-engine, three-seat, two-bay triplane escort fighter.
Manufacturer: Sir W G Armstrong, Whitworth & Co Ltd, Newcastle-upon-Tyne.
Powerplant: One 250hp Rolls-Royce Mk I twelve-cylinder liquid-cooled in-line engine driving four-blade propeller.
Armament: Two 0.303in Lewis machine guns on rocking-post mountings in nacelles carried on central wing.
Prototypes: Four ordered, Nos 7838-7841. It is not known how many were completed.

Port Victoria P.V.4

Shortly after Port Victoria embarked on its P.V.2 anti-Zeppelin seaplane, work started on a two-seat pusher landplane fighter powered by a 110hp Le Rhône rotary. This aircraft was not built, and may have been designated the P.V.3. The design was, however, considered so favourably that Port Victoria was officially instructed to commence a twin-float derivative which became the P.V.4. Pursuing the P.V.2's sesqui-plane wing layout with upper wing attached to the crew nacelle's top longerons, the resulting design was exceptionally compact, the gunner being located in the extreme nose with a Scarff ring-mounted Lewis gun forward of the pilot's cockpit. The tail unit was carried on two pairs of converging booms attached to upper and lower mainplanes. Linton Hope floats were fitted from the outset.

The main problem lay in the official choice of the 150hp Smith 'Static' radial engine. The P.V.4's airframe was completed during the autumn of 1916, but the Smith engine was never delivered and, in order to meet the stipulated maximum speed of 92 mph, only such engines as the 150hp Hispano-Suiza or 190hp Rolls-Royce Falcon would have sufficed — but neither could be fitted in the P.V.4. In the event recourse had to

Designed largely by Capt William Higley Sayers RNAS, the P.V.4 was delayed by the non-delivery of the American-designed Smith Static engine. (Photo: Imperial War Museum)

be made to a 110hp Clerget and, not surprisingly, the top speed performance fell far short of the target. Moreover, use of the Clerget moved the aircraft's centre of gravity too far aft, and when the tailplane was rigged to counterbalance this, all longitudinal control was lost below 63 mph.

By that time, however, pusher fighters were regarded as *de trop* with the arrival of reliable gun interrupter gears, so it was not thought worthwhile to undertake the necessary redesign of the P.V.4's tail unit, and its further development was therefore abandoned.

Type: Single pusher engine, two-seat twin-float sesquiplane fighting scout seaplane.
Manufacturer: RNAS Experimental Construction Depot, Port Victoria, Isle of Grain, Kent.
Powerplant: One 110hp Clerget 9Z nine-cylinder air-cooled rotary engine driving four-blade pusher propeller.
Structure: Wire-braced wooden box-girder central nacelle formed to near-circular section with wooden two-spar sesquiplane wings. Twin Linton Hope main floats and tail float.
Dimensions: Span, 32ft 0in; *Weight:* all-up: 2,400lb.
Performance: Max speed, 80.5 mph at sea level.
Armament: One 0.303in Lewis machine gun on Scarff ring in nose of nacelle.
Prototype: One, N.8 (first flown at the Isle of Grain in mid-1917). No production.

R.A.F. F.E.4

Outline sketches of the Royal Aircraft Factory's F.E.4 had been prepared soon after the outbreak of War when it seemed possible that large gun-carrying aircraft might be demanded by the military. It was not until well into 1915 that detail design was taken over by S J

Waters and Henry Folland, the purpose of the aircraft being loosely described as being 'ground attack', for which it was required to carry a 1½-pounder Coventry Ordnance Works quick-firing gun.

Two aircraft were built during 1916; they were very large biplanes, powered by two pusher engines, and normally carried a crew of three, two seated in tandem in a nose cockpit with the pilot in front, and a Lewis gunner aft of the wings. The two-bay wings were of

unequal span, that of the upper wing being no less than 75 feet, and a daring innovation was the absence of cabane struts, the engines being mounted within the wing gap clear of the lower wing and outboard of the inner interplane struts. A sturdy twin mainwheel undercarriage of wide track was included with large oleo struts below the engines, and without cross-axle, and a pair of auxiliary nosewheels was fitted in the extreme nose. Another unusual feature was the upper outer section of each wing which could be folded downwards for ease of stowage. The tail comprised biplane surfaces, a central fin and three rudders.

The first F.E.4 appeared with a pair of RAF 5 engines (in effect RAF 4As adapted as pushers) which incorporated miniature four-blade fans in front and driven from the crankshafts to assist engine cooling. The second aircraft was powered by two 250hp Rolls-Royce Eagle Is, their crankcases enclosed in sheet-metal cowlings. While the first example, No 7993, was sent to the Central Flying School, the second embarked on a series of engine trial installations, the Eagles being replaced in turn by two 200hp RAF 3As, 150hp RAF 4As and 170hp RAF 4Bs. It is interesting to note that, when powered by the RAF 3As, the aircraft was also fitted with a gunner's cockpit fairing above the upper wing.

The F.E.4 was already obsolete when it first flew, and it is difficult to see how effective the COW gun could ever have been, fired as it was from the rear seat in thc nose cockpit. Although production was planned to be undertaken by The Daimler Company, these arrangements were abandoned.

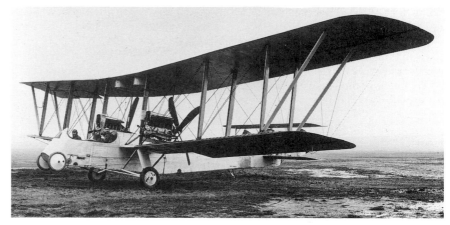

The first F.E.4, No 7993, powered by a pair of 150hp RAF 5 pusher engines; note the gravity tanks, one for each engine under the wing centre section.(Photo: Royal Aerospace Establishment)

Type: Twin pusher engine, three-seat, two-bay biplane ground attack fighter.
Manufacturer: The Royal Aircraft Factory, Farnborough, Hampshire.
Powerplant: Two 150hp RAF 5 in-line engines driving four-blade pusher propellers; also two 250hp Rolls-Royce Eagle I; two 200hp RAF 3A; two 150hp RAF 4A; two 170hp RAF 4B.
Dimensions: Span, 75ft 2in; length, 38ft 2½ in; height, 16ft 9in; wing area, 1,032 sq ft.
Weights: (RAF 5). Tare, 3,754lb; all-up, 5,988lb.
Performance: (RAF 5). Max speed, 84.3 mph at sea level; climb to 10,000ft, 30 min 5 sec; ceiling, 12,000ft.
Armament: One 1½-pounder COW gun in the rear of the nose cockpit; two Lewis machine guns on the sides of the nose cockpit, and a third Lewis gun with a movable mounting in a gunner's cockpit amidships.
Prototypes: Two, Nos 7993 and 7994. No production.
Summary of Service: One aircraft, No 7993, with the Central Flying School.

Wight Baby

The established manufacturer of naval aircraft, J Samuel White of East Cowes in the Isle of Wight, was fortunate to possess the services of Howard Wright, a successful designer of long experience. In 1916 he produced a twin-float single-seat scout, much on the lines of the Sopwith Baby, though somewhat larger and heavier.

Of simple, if not crude, design the Wight aircraft was a single-bay biplane with single-acting ailerons on the top wing only; the wings were of unequal span and chord with double-camber, and the tail surfaces were of generous

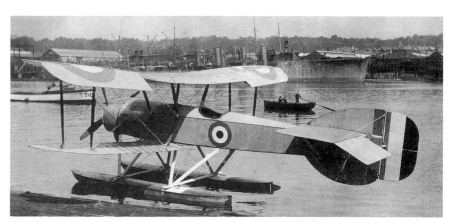

The first prototype Wight Baby, No 9097, at Cowes before the floats were re-positioned further apart. (Photo: A J Jackson Collection)

proportions with a large rectangular tailplane and elevator. Being without stagger or cutout, the upper wing obscured much of the pilot's field of view. However, the 100hp Gnome *monosoupape* engine, driving a four-blade propeller,

Type: Single-engine, single-seat, single-bay, twin-float biplane scout.
Manufacturer: J Samuel White & Co, East Cowes, Isle of Wight.
Powerplant: One 100hp Gnome *monosoupape* engine driving four-blade propeller.
Structure: Wooden box-girder fuselage with fabric and ply covering; two-spar, folding, double-camber, single-bay wings with unequal span and chord; twin three-step wooden floats.
Dimensions: Span, 30ft 8in; length, 26ft 8in; height, 9ft 1in; wing area, 297 sq ft.
Weights: Tare, 1,277lb; all-up, 1,864lb.
Performance: Max speed, approx 90 mph at sea level; climb to 6,500ft, 20 min 30 sec; service ceiling, 9,300ft; endurance, 2½ hr.
Armament: None fitted.
Prototypes: Three, Nos 9097, 9098 and 9100. No production.

bestowed a fairly respectable top speed of about 90 mph at sea level.

The floats were much longer than those of the Sopwith Baby and therefore obviated the need for a tail float; partway through the Wight's trials these floats were re-fitted further apart to improve stability on the water.

In 1917 one of the three Baby prototypes was flown at Felixstowe, and afterwards underwent Service trials at the Isle of Grain. By then, however, the aircraft's performance had been thoroughly eclipsed by other in-service naval scouts and it was not developed further.

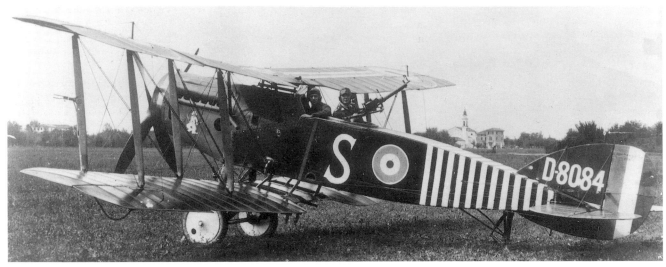

A Bristol F.2B Fighter of No 139 Squadron, D8084 'S', at Villaverla on the Italian Front in 1918; formed from 'Z' Flight of No 34 Squadron, No 139 Squadron destroyed 27 enemy aircraft in only four months. (Photo: The Bristol Aeroplane Co Ltd.)

Bristol F.2B Fighter

The first Bristol F.2 with alterations recommended by the AID during the F.2A trials (see page 75) was flown on 25 October 1916. These modifications included the covering of the lower wing centre section below the fuselage, and the angling downwards of the upper longerons from the rear of the front cockpit forward in order to improve the pilot's view while landing. The first 150 F.2Bs, from a contract for 200 (A7101-A7300), retained the 190hp Rolls-Royce Falcon I of the earlier F.2A, but from A7251 onwards the 220hp Falcon II was fitted.

The next order for 250 aircraft introduced the definitive Falcon III of 275hp, and this engine remained standard for the Fighter for the remainder of the War and beyond — although several alternative engines were adopted when pressure on Falcon production increased sharply in 1918.

The Bristol F.2B Fighter was one of a handful of truly great British fighters of the War, alongside such aircraft as the S.E.5A, and Sopwith Pup and Camel. The shock defeat of No 48 Squadron, with its heavy losses of F.2As, might have had serious repercussions had the War Office concluded that the British fighters suffered a fundamental design flaw, and decided to cancel the large production contracts which had by then been negotiated. Fortunately it was the line pilots themselves who took matters into their own hands, changing tactics by employing the Fighter's front gun offensively.

By the time No 11 Squadron, commanded by Maj Cuthbert Trelawder Maclean (later Air Vice-Marshal, CB, DSO, MC, RAF), arrived in No 13 Wing at La Bellevue, the new tactics were paying off handsomely. On 20 June the Squadron drew first blood when an Albatros D III attacked a Bristol head-on, but was met and destroyed by a short burst from the British fighter's front gun. The pilot of the F.2B was Lt Andrew Edward McKeever, a Canadian from Ontario who was to become the finest exponent of the two-seat fighter. This was his first victory, and by the end of the year (when he was posted to England as an instructor) he had destroyed a total of thirty enemy aircraft, of which eight fell to the gun of his observer, Sergeant L F Powell. McKeever was to be awarded the DSO and two MCs (and Powell the DCM), only to die on Christmas Day 1919 from injuries suffered in a car accident.

Such was the esteem in which the

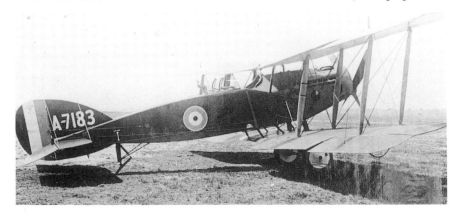

The second F.2B to be fitted with a Rolls-Royce Falcon III engine, A7183 from the first production batch built by The British & Colonial Aeroplane Company. This aircraft was used primarily for engine testing. (Photo: Author's Collection)

Bristol Fighter was now held that in July 1917 the War Office decided to standardize the aircraft on all fighter- and corps-reconnaissance squadrons of the RFC, replacing the B.E.2 and B.E.12 and, in due couse, the R.E.8 — a process that lasted well into the post-War years. On 2 September the parent company received an order for a further 800 F.2Bs (which it could meet as the B.E.2 production at Filton was coming to an end), and the following month orders for a further 800 were placed with three manufacturing sub-contractors.

Meanwhile No 20 Squadron (Maj E H Johnston) at St Marie-Capelle, and No 22 Squadron (Maj L W Learmont DSO, MC) at Boisdinghem had received F.2Bs, replacing F.E.2s, and in September No 39 Squadron at Woodford, Essex, changed to F.2Bs for Home Defence duties. The same month a small number of Bristol Fighters joined the newly-formed No 111 Squadron in Palestine, joining Bristol Scouts, D.H.2s and Nieuports.

As the numbers of F.2Bs in France continued to grow, it became increasingly noticeable that German pilots were deliberately avoiding combat with them unless they possessed overwhelming numerical superiority. Even so, there were Bristol pilots who seemed undaunted by unfavourable odds. On 30 November 1917 McKeever and Powell encountered two German reconnaissance two-seaters escorted by seven Albatros single-seaters, and shot down both the former and two of the latter before making good their escape.

In 1918 the pace of production was further increased, with a total of 2,867 aircraft completed by Bristol and four sub-contractors (the latter producing 1,000 aircraft between them). Inevitably it was not long before Rolls-Royce reported that it would be unable to keep pace with engine demand, as production of both the Eagle and Falcon was already running at capacity, while the very large 600hp Condor would soon enter production. This situation had been foreseen some months earlier, but continuing indecision by the War Office had already led to delays in the delivery of

engines. A number of alternative engines had been specified, including the 200hp Sunbeam Arab and the 200hp Hispano-Suiza, the latter being intended for aircraft built by the National Aircraft Factory No 3 at Aintree, Liverpool. The available Falcons were intended to be confined to aircraft built by Bristol, with Arabs suggested as suitable alternatives should airframe production outstrip engine availability. In the event only a tiny number of Bristol-built F.2Bs was completed with the Sunbeam engine.

These alternative engines underwent official tests in F.2Bs early in 1918, the Hispano-Suiza in B1201 during January, and the Arab in B1204 in March. The performance in both was most unsatisfactory and bestowed a much inferior performance compared with those aircraft with Falcons. Moreover, production of the 200hp Hispano-Suiza had encountered problems, and the reduced numbers available were reserved for the S.E.5A, with the result that the Hispano-powered F.2B was abandoned, and the NAF No 3-built aircraft were completed with Falcons.

Choice of the Arab had also been unfortunate. The engine had been ordered in considerable numbers as early as 1916, largely on the strength of design figures submitted before it had undergone rigorous testing. In January 1917 the engine had been ordered in quantity from the Auston Motor Company and from Willys-Overland in Canada. When the trials were completed in May that year, the engine was found to have serious cylinder and crankcase design faults, so that final drawings could not be issued until December. Production plans had called for 1,800 engines to be delivered by the end of 1917, but only 81 had been completed. Furthermore, when installed in the Bristol Fighter, it is said that engine life was an average of only four hours due to excessive vibration causing crankshaft failure.

Because of the much-reduced performance of the Arab engine, it was decided to confine it to F.2Bs entering service with Corps Reconnaissance squadrons in April 1918, and to issue Falcon-powered aircraft to the Fighter and Fighter-Reconnaissance squadrons. This was rescinded after the creation of the Air Ministry on 2 January 1918, and it transpired that Arab-powered aircraft were only used as replacements for second-line units.

By mid-1918 fifteen squadrons had been equipped with F.2B Fighters. Of these, Nos 11, 48 and 62 were flying primarily fighter patrols, including escort duties, over the Western Front; Nos 20, 22 and 88 Squadrons were performing fighter-reconnaissance duties in France; No 12 was engaged in Corps Reconnaissance (what would later be termed army co-operation), and would be joined by No 9 Squadron in July. Nos 33, 36, 39, 75, 140 and 141 Squadrons were based on airfields in England for home defence against German bombers and airships, and would be joined by No 76 Squadron soon after. Further afield No 34 Squadron was engaged in fighter-reconnaissance on the Italian Front, being joined by No 139 in July. In Palestine No 67 Squadron was flying fighter patrols in aircraft that had formerly been used by No 111 Squadron. One other Squadron, No 35, would begin to equip with Bristol F.2Bs in France, replacing Armstrong Whitworth F.K.8s for army co-operations duties, but was not fully operational before the Armistice in November.

Before going on to summarise the Bristol Fighter's peacetime activities, it is necessary to mention some of the numerous experiments undertaken with the aircraft as it underwent a continuous programme of development. Engines which were flown experimentally in the aircraft included the 230hp Siddeley Puma (and a 290hp high-compression

An F.2B of a Home Defence Squadron in 1918; this aircraft is inscribed 'Presented by Maharajah Bahadur Sir Rameswar Singh of Darbhanga, No. 2 "The Lord Chelmsford"'. (Photo: Author's Collection)

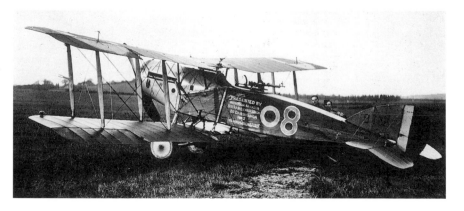

J6586 was the first Bristol Fighter Mark II, which made its first flight in December 1920; it underwent trials at Martlesham Heath with the tropical radiator in 1921 and was converted to a dual-control trainer in 1924. (Photo: R C Sturtivant)

version), 200hp Wolseley Viper, 300hp Hispano-Suiza and 200hp RAF 4D; single-bay wings were flown on several test aircraft, and three-bay high aspect ratio wings were also flown, both types in 1923.

Although strictly outside the scope of this work, extensive plans were laid to build Bristol Fighters in the United States of America (on the recommendation of General Pershing), and with them to equip American forces, as that country had entered the War with scarcely a respectable modern military aeroplane. Unfortunately these plans were long delayed, partly due to an attempt to fit the unsuitable American Liberty 12 engine in the aircraft; various other American engines were tried, including the Liberty 8, Wright H, Curtiss D-12 and a 350hp Packard, but none produced any significant improvement over Frank Barnwell's original design. In all, some 68 aircraft (including prototypes) were produced in America.

Post-War Service

The Armistice of November 1918 ended any immediate threat of air attack on Britain, and brought about enormous reductions in her air force, so much so that home-based interceptor fighter squadrons almost entirely disappeared in the post-War cutbacks. The Bristol Fighter, of which the new Royal Air Force possessed no fewer than 1,583 at the end of the War, had shown itself to be an excellent reconnaissance fighter, well suited to the rôle of army co-operation.

As the RAF assumed the rôle of air policing, under international mandate in the Middle East, squadrons equipped with D.H.9s and Bristol F.2Bs were sent out to, or re-formed at numerous foreign stations, many of them with very rudi-

mentary landing strips. The majority of wartime F.2B squadrons remained in being only until 1919 or 1920, the exception being No 20 which, without even returning to Britain from the continent after the Armistice, was posted direct to India for service on the North West Frontier, continuing to fly Bristol Fighters until March 1932 — the longest term of service by an F.2B Squadron.

It had already been discovered that

operating the Falcon-powered fighters in the harsh conditions of heat and dust in the Middle East during the War had resulted in very low serviceability among the aircraft, their engines frequently overheating and quickly wearing out. The Royal Aircraft Establishment (formerly the Factory) at Farnborough undertook a programme of trials to find means by which these problems might be overcome. Early remedies included the simple expedient of cutting extra louvres in the engine cowling to allow unrestricted airflow through the frontal radiator; radiator shutters were removed and, eventually, tropical radiators with coarse matrices were introduced; aircraft thus built or modified became Bristol Fighter Mark IIs, and also carried desert survival equipment.

Type: Single-engine, two-seat, two-bay biplane army co-operation reconnaissance fighter.

Manufacturers (in Britain): The British & Colonial Aeroplane Co Ltd (Bristol Aeroplane Co Ltd), Filton and Brislington, Bristol; Sir W G Armstrong, Whitworth & Co Ltd, Newcastle-upon-Tyne; The Gloucestershire Aircraft Co Ltd, Cheltenham; Harris & Sheldon Ltd, Birmingham; Marshall & Sons, Gainsborough; National Aircraft Factory No 3, Aintree, Liverpool; Angus Sanderson & Co, Newcastle-upon-Tyne; The Standard Motor Co Ltd, Coventry; The Austin Motor Co (1914) Ltd, Birmingham.

Air Ministry Specification: Spec 21/21 covered post-War re-building and reconditioning of wartime aircraft.

Powerplant: One 190hp Rolls-Royce Falcon I twelve-cylinder liquid-cooled in-line engine; 220hp Falcon II; 275hp Falcon III; 200hp Sunbeam Arab; 200hp Hispano-Suiza; 300hp Hispano-Suiza; 230hp Siddeley Puma; 290hp Siddeley Puma (high compression); 200hp RAF 4D; 200hp Wolseley W4A Viper; 290hp Liberty 8; 400hp Liberty 12.

Structure: All-wooden construction with ply and fabric covering.

Dimensions: (Falcon) Span, 39ft 3in; length, 25ft 10in; height, 9ft 9in; wing area, 405.6 sq ft.

Weights: (Falcon III) Tare, 1,934lb; all-up, 2,779lb.

Performance: (Falcon III) Max speed, 126 mph at sea level, 105 mph at 15,000 ft; climb to 10,000ft, 11min 15 sec; service ceiling, 20,000ft; endurance, 3 hr.

Armament: One fixed, synchronized 0.303in Vickers machine gun mounted centrally beneath nose cowling with Constantinesco CC interrupter gear, and one or two Lewis guns on rear cockpit Scarff ring; later aircraft could carry up to twelve 20lb Cooper fragmentation bombs under the lower wings.

Prototypes: See Bristol F.2A (page 75)

Production: (in Britain) Total of 5,329 built. (Bristol, 3,451: A7101-A7300, B1101-B1350, C751-C1050, C4601-C4900, D7801-D8100, E2151-E2650, E5253-E5308, F4271-F4970, H1240-H1707, J6586-J6800 (Mk II), J7617-J7699 (Mk II), J8242-J8291 (Mk III), J8429-J8458 (Mk III); Gloster, 550: C9836-C9985, E9507-E9656, H834-H1083; Austins, four known: H6055-H6058; Armstrong, Whitworth, 250: E1901-E2150; Harris & Sheldon, 100: F5074-F5173; Marshalls, 150: D2626-D2775; NAF No 3, 500: D2126-D2625; Angus Sanderson, 250: E2651-E2900; Standard Motors, 74: E5179-E5252.)

Summary of RFC and RAF Service: Bristol F.2Bs equipped Nos 9, 11, 12, 20, 22, 48, 62 and 88 Squadrons, and also served with Nos 4, 10, 12, 15, 16 and 35 Squadrons, Western Front; Nos 33, 36, 39, 76, 140 and 141 Squadrons, Home Defence; equipped No 67 Squadron (later No 1 Squadron, Australian Flying Corps) and flew with No 111 Squadron in Palestine; Nos 34 and 139 Squadrons, Italian Front. Post-War, F.2Bs equipped Nos 2, 4, 13, 16 and 24 Squadrons at home; Nos 100 and 105 Squadrons in Ireland, 1918-1922; No 8 Squadron, Belgium, 1918-1920; Nos 5, 20, 28, 31 and 114 Squadrons in India; Nos 6, 14 and 208 Squadrons in Middle East.

In due course aircraft engaged in operations, particularly on the North West Frontier of India, were required to carry up to twelve 20-pound Cooper fragmentation bombs, and this in turn demanded local strengthening of the airframe; these aircraft were termed Mark IIIs. In 1926 further design changes introduced Handley Page slots on the upper wings, revised upper fin and an enlarged, horn-balanced rudder and further strengthening of the undercarriage, aircraft with these modifications being Mark IVs. And all the while the Rolls-Royce Falcon III remained the standard engine.

At home a total of four army co-operation Squadrons (Nos 2, 4, 13 and 16) continued flying F.2Bs until the late nineteen-twenties, and No 24 Squadron flew them on communications duties. Nos 5, 20, 28 and 31 were equipped with successive versions in India and on the North West Frontier until the early nineteen-thirties, as Nos 6, 14 and 208 served on various stations throughout the Middle East (Nos 4 and 208 Squadrons were also engaged in the brief activities in Turkey during and after the Chanak crisis of 1922, and No 2 was sent to China for several weeks in 1927 to protect the international settlement at Shanghai).

The 'Brisfit' was a very popular aeroplane among its crews throughout its long service, largely thanks to its excellent Rolls-Royce Falcon engine; it was a sturdy aircraft, capable of withstanding considerable combat damage in war, and rough field conditions before the age of metalled runways.

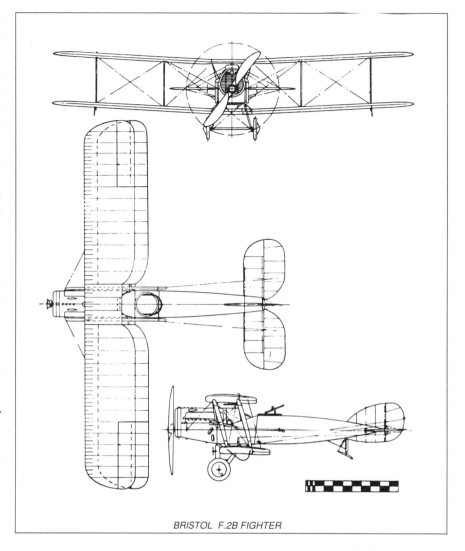

BRISTOL F.2B FIGHTER

The beautifully restored Bristol F.2B, painted as D8096, is maintained in flying condition by the Shuttleworth Trust at Old Warden, Bedfordshire; it is here shown at Filton. (Photo: The Bristol Aeroplane Co Ltd.)

Fairey F.2

The Fairey F.2, a twin-engine biplane with a span of 77 feet, was described by its makers as a long-range fighter intended for the RNAS, although no record appears to have survived describing precisely what its exact operational use was intended to be, although it may reasonably be conjectured to have been as a gun-carrying escort aircraft, also capable of carrying a small load of bombs.

As the first Fairey-designed aircraft to be built (the company having produced a small number of Short seaplanes in 1915), the F.2 was a three-seat, three-bay biplane, rigged without stagger and with considerable wing overhang braced from kingposts above the outboard interplane struts. Of all-wood, fabric-covered construction, it was intended to be powered by two 200hp Brotherhood tractor engines in the first two aircraft, followed by two aircraft with 190hp Rolls-Royce Falcons arranged as pushers; in the event, only one aircraft was completed, in the autumn of 1916, and this was powered by Falcons installed as tractors. It is believed that construction

The sole Fairey F.2, No 3704, with cowled Rolls-Royce Falcon I engines; the maximum speed of over 90 mph was fairly creditable for such a large aircraft, though any sort of fighter-like agility is extremely unlikely. (Photo: G S Leslie/J M Bruce Collection)

of the other three aircraft was started but not proceeded with, owing to the non-availability of the Brotherhood engines. In any event, the sole completed aircraft was not flown until about May 1917.

The F.2 carried a pilot and two gunners, the latter being provided with Lewis guns on Scarff rings in the nose and amidships; the pilot's cockpit was located just forward of the wing leading edges. A monoplane tail unit was incorporated carrying twin fins and unbalanced rudders. The undercarriage comprised a robust structure of ten struts, arranged W-fashion in end elevation, mounting four wheels in tandem pairs.

As was mandatory on all large naval aircraft, the wings were made to fold so as to enable the big aeroplane to be hangared.

Type: Twin-engine, three-seat, three-bay biplane long-range fighter.
Manufacturer: The Fairey Aviation Co Ltd, Hayes, Middlesex.
Powerplant: Two 190hp Rolls-Royce Falcon I 12-cylinder water-cooled engines driving four-blade tractor propellers.
Structure: All-wood, wire-braced construction with fabric covering.
Dimensions: Span, 77ft 0in; length, 40ft 6½in; height, 13ft 5⅝in; wing area, 718.4 sq ft.
Weight: All-up, 4,880lb.
Performance: Max speed, 92.5 mph at sea level; climb to 5,000ft, 6 min; endurance, 3½ hr.
Armament: Two 0.303in Lewis machine guns on Scarff rings in nose and midships cockpits; aircraft capable of carrying small bombs.
Prototypes: Four ordered, Nos 3702-3705; only one, No 3704, completed in late autumn 1916 (believed first flown in May 1917). No production.

Fairey Hamble Baby

The task of enabling the Sopwith Baby fighter seaplane to carry a small bomb load and still retain some vestige of worthwhile performance occupied the attention of several design teams, not least those at Port Victoria, Fairey Aviation and the Blackburn company. The most significant contribution, not only with regard to the Baby itself but to aircraft design in general, was made by Richard Fairey. He introduced to the Baby the principle of increasing wing camber by means of wing flaps for take-off, thereby increasing lift — an idea pioneered by A W Judge and A A Holle at the Varioplane company. Fairey, however, went one stage further by introducing differential control of the flaps for use as conventional ailerons as well. The Fairey Patent Camber Gear was the first such use in the world of flaps-cum-ailerons, and the principle remains in use in numerous modern aircraft.

The Sopwith Baby underwent considerable redesign at Fairey, although the original fuselage remained almost unaltered. A Sopwith-built Baby, No 8134, was tested at Hayes and Hamble with the new wings which were in-

A Fairey-built Hamble Baby. The tailplane span of these aircraft was over a foot greater than that of Sopwith-built aircraft. (Photo: A J Jackson collection)

creased in span and given rounded tips, the new flaps being hinged along the entire trailing edges of both wings.

Production Fairey-built Babies incorporated vertical tail surfaces of more angular shape, as well as an enlarged tail float

Type: Single-engine, single-seat, single-bay float-equipped biplane bombing scout.
Manufacturers: The Fairey Aviation Co Ltd, Hayes, Middlesex, and Hamble Point, Hampshire.
Powerplant: One 110hp or 130hp Clerget rotary engine driving two-blade propeller.
Dimensions: Span, 27ft 9¼in; length, 23ft 4in; height, 9ft 6in; wing area, 246 sq ft.
Weights (110hp Clerget): Tare, 1,386lb; all-up, 1,946lb.
Performance: Max speed, 92 mph at sea level; climb to 2,000ft, 5 min 30 sec; service ceiling, 7,500ft; endurance, 2 hr.
Armament: One synchronized 0.303in Lewis machine gun on upper nose decking.
Prototype: Total of 180. (Fairey: N1320-N1339 and N1450-N1479; Parnall: N1190-N1219 and N1960-N2059).
Summary of Service: Hamble Babies served with the RNAS and RAF (after April 1918) at Calshot, Cattewater and Fishguard, and aboard HM Seaplane Carrier *Empress*; also at Santa Maria di Leuca (Italy), Suda Bay (Crete), Lemnos (Aegean), Port Said and Alexandria.

and Fairey-designed main floats.

A total of 180 Fairey Hamble Babies was ordered from Fairey and Parnall & Sons, the latter company producing 130, these aircraft retaining the original Sopwith floats and tail unit; the first 30 Parnall and the first 20 Fairey examples were powered by 110hp Clerget rotaries, and the remainder by the 130hp version.

A further variation involved the last 74 Parnall-built Babies, known as Baby Converts, which were completed as landplanes; these retained the original float mounting struts, to which were attached twin landing skids and wheels.

Hamble Babies served with the RNAS and RAF at home and overseas, undertaking anti-submarine patrols in the Aegean, and bombing operations against Turkish installations in the Levant.

R.A.F. F.E.9

One of Farnborough's truly ill-conceived designs was the F.E.9 two-seat reconnaissance fighter, possibly intended as a replacement for the elderly F.E.2B, and which was designed in 1916, and probably flown shortly before the end of that year. Powered by a 200hp Hispano-Suiza, priority supplies of which were reserved for the Factory, the F.E.9 was a pusher biplane originally flown with single-bay wings of greatly differing span and with heavily horn-balanced ailerons on the upper wing only. The crew nacelle extended well forward and was located high up in the wing gap so as to afford the gunner in the nose a good all-round field of fire with a Scarff ring-mounted Lewis gun; a second Lewis gun could be spigot-mounted between the cockpits. The engine radiator occupied the whole depth of space betwen the nacelle and the upper wing. The tail booms converged in side elevation and supported the tail, being attached to the tailplane's rear spar; the fin and unbalanced rudder were of roughly equal area.

A total of 27 F.E.9s was scheduled for production, though the number eventually built, quoted from various sources, differed between three and eight. Apart from coming too late on the scene to be of any realistic value in service, the

The first F.E.9, A4818, with single-bay wings and displaying the heavily overbalanced ailerons. (Photo: The Royal Aerospace Establishment, Neg No 2397, dated 15 May 1917)

F.E.9 suffered inevitably from greatly overbalanced ailerons, which tended to turn the aircraft on to its back during a steep turn. The horn balances were progressively reduced, but the only result was to reduce the rudder's effect in turn.

Second and third prototypes appeared in the late spring of 1917 with two-bay wings, at about the time the first aircraft was undergoing flight trials with various aileron and rudder shapes, in the hands of Capt G T R Hill MC (brother of Roderic Hill, and later to become well known as Professor Geoffrey Hill).

One of the F.E.9s was issued to a Home Defence squadron later in 1917, but evidently failed to impress anyone.

Type: Single pusher engine, two-seat, single- and two-bay biplane reconnaissance fighter.
Manufacturer: The Royal Aircraft Factory, Farnborough, Hampshire.
Powerplant: One 200hp Hispano-Suiza water-cooled in-line engine driving four-blade pusher propeller.
Dimensions: Span, 37ft 9½in; length, 28ft 3in; height, 9ft 9in; wing area, 365 sq ft.
Weight: All-up, 2,480lb.
Performance: Max speed, 105 mph at sea level; climb to 5,000ft, 8 min 25 sec; absolute ceiling, 15,500ft.
Armament: One 0.303in Lewis machine gun with Scarff ring on nose cockpit; provision for a second Lewis gun on a spigot mounting between the cockpits.
Prototypes: Three, A4818-A4820. A further 24 aircraft were scheduled for production but few, if any, were completed.

Sopwith Camel

The Camel was born of both necessity and circumstance. The need inevitably arose for a fighting scout that was faster and more heavily armed than the Pup and Triplane, without sacrificing those aeroplanes' excellent handling qualities; it was needed quickly, so that production must be capable of building up rapidly. Compared with the engines available a year earlier, the choice of reliable powerplant was, late in 1916, much wider when Herbert Smith began working on the Camel — even though it seemed likely that rotaries of French origin would continue to dominate the stage for the immediate future. Gun synchronization gears had been made more reliable, with the Constantinesco hydraulic system rather better than the Sopwith-Kauper mechanical gear, although, for perhaps obvious reasons, Smith chose to incorporate the latter in the Camel.

It was therefore logical that the Camel design should not diverge too far from that of the Pup, yet be capable of accommodating a larger, more powerful engine as well as a pair of front guns in an airframe of similar overall size. It seems that after T O M Sopwith had sanctioned the building of four prototypes, the Admiralty stepped in with an

A Sopwith-built F.1 Camel with 150hp B.R.1 rotary engine, B6230, of No. 9 (Naval) Squadron at Bray Dunes, France, the first squadron to be equipped with the fighter in June 1917. (Photo: A J Jackson Collection)

order for two more — though it is not clear whether all the 'private venture' aircraft came to be completed. As originally designed the Camel was to have featured about 2½ degrees of dihedral on both upper and lower wings but, for ease of manufacture it was decided to make the top wing flat; Smith therefore arbitrarily doubled the dihedral of the lower wing to compensate — thereby creating the Camel's characteristic 'pinched wing' appearance from the front.

The first prototype, referred to as the F.1, was cleared by the company's experimental department on 22 December 1916, and may have been flown by Harry Hawker on that date. The aircraft was powered by a 110hp Clerget 9Z rotary and featured a flat, constant-chord upper wing, built as a single component and with short ailerons on upper and lower wings. A second prototype, the F.1/1, had tapered wings with broad-chord I-form interplane struts. The third aircraft to fly was the F.1/3, and no firm evidence appears to have come to light to confirm the completion of an F.1/2, but this may have been used for structural tests.

The two Admiralty prototypes, N517 and N518, followed, and the latter underwent trials with the first 150hp Admiralty Rotary No 1, designed by W O Bentley who employed aluminium for the air-cooled cylinders; the engine was soon to be renamed the Bentley Rotary or B.R.1 and, when tests at Martlesham Heath in N518 showed a performance much the same as the original F.1 prototype, this engine was selected to power the majority of RNAS Camels.

The Bentley entered production quickly and by the time Sopwith received the first order for 50 production Camels from the Admiralty a small number of these engines was becoming available, the other aircraft being fitted with 130hp Clerget 9Bs. As the Sopwith order was soon increased to 500 aircraft, contracts were issued to Ruston, Proctor for 250, to Boulton & Paul for 100, to Clayton & Shuttleworth for 100 and to Portholme for 50 aircraft. Production aircraft differed from the prototypes in having their top wings built in three sections for ease of rigging, and featured a cut-out panel in the centresection to increase the pilot's field of view; the ailerons were also lengthened.

Sopwith began delivery of Camels to the RNAS on 4 May 1917, the first being issued in June to No 4 (Naval) Squadron at Bray Dunes in France, commanded by Sqn Cdr B L Huskisson RN. From the outset the Camel was found to be a tricky aeroplane to fly, particularly among pilots thoroughly accustomed to the almost viceless qualities of the Pup and Triplane. The concentration of major weight components — engine, propeller, guns, fuel and pilot — in an extraordinarily compact envelope — coupled with the fierce gyroscopic couple of the rotary engine imposed a sharp tendency to drop the

nose in a right-hand turn, whereas to the left the nose came up; and if the turn was tightened without coarse use of rudder the Camel would snap into a spin in the other direction. Yet, in practised hands, the stubby little aircraft was a magnificent dogfighter, its powerful elevator and sensitive ailerons bestowing a degree of manœuvrability unmatched by contemporary German scouts — except the Fokker Dr I triplane.

No 4 (Naval) Squadron took less than a fortnight to come to terms with the Camel's idiosyncracies and, during a patrol along the Belgian coast on the lookout for German bombers on 4 July, came upon a formation of sixteen Gothas, and drove down two. Within a month Nos 3, 6 and 9 (Naval) Squadrons had been fully re-equipped; 'Naval Eight' was the next to exchange its beloved Triplanes.

Meanwhile, in the RFC, No 70 at Liettres became the first Camel Squadron in July and was fully equipped in time to support the Ypres offensive which opened on the 31st. No 73 Squadron, newly formed on 1 July under Maj H F A Gordon, received the new fighters at home and, at the end of the year, moved to France.

Moreover, in August, Camels started re-equipping Home Defence units as No 44 Squadron, commanded at Hainault Farm by Maj Gilbert Ware Murlis-Green (later Gp Capt, DSO, MC, RAF) began the tricky job of flying the aircraft at night. On the night of 3/4 September Murlis-Green, Capt C J Q Brand (later Air Vice-Marshal Sir Quintin, KBE, DSO, MC, DFC, RAF) and Lt C C Banks took off

A standard F.1 Camel built by Boulton & Paul, B9175, and flown by No 44 Squadron as a night fighter during the late summer of 1917; the twin Vickers gun armament was later discarded as unsuitable for night fighting. (Photo: A J Jackson Collection)

at night to attack a formation of Gothas over southeast England, but without scoring. Nevertheless, the work done by No 44 proved that the Camel *could* be flown effectively at night, and helped to bring order to the haphazard system of night defence over England; the use of the Camel by No 44, and in particular by Murlis-Green and Brand, led directly to the development of the Camel as a dedicated night fighter, as will be shown below.

By the end of 1917 Camels were being flown operationally by nine RFC and six RNAS squadrons in France, two RFC squadrons in Italy, and No 44 at home; night flying training on Camels was also being undertaken by Nos 80, 81 and 89 Squadrons in Britain. Some 3,450 aircraft had been ordered, and the fighter was being produced at nine factories. Production contracts placed with Hooper & Co, Marsh, Jones & Cribb, and Portholme specified a change to the 110hp Le Rhône, an engine that entailed a switch to the Constantinesco hydraulic interrupter gear — although the speed performance was slightly inferior to that of the Clerget-powered Camel.

These very large orders would clearly place strain on the supply of Clerget and Le Rhône engines, even though the production of Bentleys was accelerating quickly, and it was decided to investigate a possible change to the 100hp Gnome *monosoupape*. Despite the lower power of this engine, the Camel's performance held up remarkably well; yet relatively few Gnome-powered aircraft were produced, and none is thought to have reached an operational unit. In

December 1917 a Camel was flown at Martlesham fitted with the 150hp version of the *monosoupape* engine, which featured an unusual switch in the cockpit enabling the pilot to cut out two, four, six or eight of the nine cylinders. An eye witness has recalled seeing the aircraft approaching, low down and flying on only one cylinder, when the pilot suddenly selected all nine cylinders to the accompaniment of a great blast of flame. However, the 150hp Gnome *monosoupape* engine was not adopted for service.

Returning to the special problems posed by night fighting in Camels, it was quickly discovered by the No 44 Squadron pilots that firing the two Vickers guns produced such a muzzle flash that all night vision was momentarily destroyed, the guns being located immediately in front of the pilot's face. Fairly extensive changes were made in developing the Camel as a night fighter, and included removal of the Vickers and substituting a pair of Lewis guns on a special double Foster mounting on the upper wing centre section; the pilot's cockpit was repositioned about twelve inches further aft to enable him to aim and reload the guns, and the fuel tank was moved from its customary position behind the pilot to the front fuselage to compensate for the aft movement of the

cockpit. Navigation lights and Holt flare brackets were added to the wings. Some armament variations appeared on the night fighter squadrons, a few Camel pilots preferring to retain one of the Vickers in place of one of the Lewis guns. Most of the night fighters were painted overall with dark green dope, the national and squadron insignia being partly or completely obscured.

From the earliest days of the Camel's service in France the aircraft had been employed as a ground attack aircraft, often carrying light bombs under the fuselage, in addition to its more accustomed rôle in air-to-air combat, and had frequently suffered heavy losses from ground fire (as did all close support aircraft). Sopwith was accordingly asked to produce a version of the Camel especially for the 'trench fighting' rôle, and in February came up with the T.F.1. An F.1 Camel, B9278 with standard 110hp Le Rhône installed, was prepared featuring armoured protection for the front fuselage, together with a pair of downward-firing Lewis guns between the undercarriage struts in addition to a Lewis gun above the upper wing centre section. The T.F.1 Camel was not put into production, but provided valuable information which led to development of the T.F.2 Salamander — a heavily armed trench fighter that was just reaching France at the time of the Armistice (see page 135).

The air fighting in France during 1918 was some of the bitterest of the entire War. Early in the year the strength of RFC squadrons was increased from eighteen to twenty-four aircraft, and by the opening of the final great German

A characteristically drab, full-standard F.1 Camel night fighter of No 51 Squadron, almost certainly at Marham, Norfolk, in 1918. The Squadron was then ostensibly a Home Defence night fighter unit, but was also engaged in crew training. (Photo: Imperial War Museum)

offensive, on 21 March, seven Camel squadrons had achieved the planned establishment. The following day twelve aircraft of No 73 and twelve from No 80 Squadron shot down six German aircraft in the course of a single patrol; on the 24th, Capt J L Trollope MC* of No 43 Squadron alone destroyed six aircraft in a single day, a feat repeated by Capt H W Woollett DSO, MC* of the same Squadron on 12 April.

On 21 April Camels of No 209 Squadron (formerly 'Naval Nine') were engaged in one of the most famous air combats of the War. On the morning of that day three Flights of Camels left Bertangles for a patrol in strength over the Somme, but one became separated in a fight with Albatros two-seaters. The two remaining Flights, led by the Canadian, Capt A R Brown, continued to

their patrol area, in due course becoming involved in a fight with fifteen Fokker Dr I triplanes. Seeing a scarlet-painted enemy scout about to attack one of his novice pilots, Brown went for the enemy fighter and, with a single burst, shot it down near Corbie. Later it was discovered that the pilot, Baron Manfred von Richthofen, victor of 80 air combats, had died in his cockpit. Later it was suggested that von Richthofen had been killed by small arms fire from the ground, but this has been discounted as a means of denying that this great fighter pilot had been defeated in air combat. All the supportable evidence indicates that Brown — himself an experienced pilot — was the true victor.

Camels also fought with considerable success with two squadrons of the United States Air Service in France shortly

before the end of the War. Although the 17th Aero Squadron lost six aircraft in a fight on 1 July, this and the 148th Squadron between them destroyed eleven German aircraft on 24 September — out of a total of eighteen shot down on the British Front.

Many famous names featured among Camel pilots, including men like Lt-Col Raymond Collishaw DSO, DSC, DFC, Maj D R MacLaren DSO, MC, DFC, Maj W G Barker VC, DSO, MC, and Capt H W Woollett DSO MC* — each of whom shot down more than fifty enemy aircraft during the War.

Lesser-known operations undertaken by the Camel night fighter squadrons were the night offensive patrols — in a later war to be known as intruder operations. No 151 Squadron, flying from Vignacourt during the last months of the War, bombed German airfields at night, as well as destroying sixteen bombers in the vicinity of their bases without loss to themselves.

Four Camel Squadrons, Nos 28, 66, 139 and 225, fought on the Italian Front during 1918, although the last-named

A standard Beardmore-built 2F.1 Camel destined for the RNAS. The double-patch stencil on the side of the fuselage aft of the cockpit indicates the position of the rear fuselage detachment line. Note the Lewis gun mounting required to draw the gun down for re-arming. (Photo: A J Jackson Collection)

was employed to fly escort for bombers crossing the Adriatic to attack targets in Albania. The only Victoria Cross to be won by a Camel pilot was awarded to Lt Alan Jerrard of No 66 Squadron in Italy, three of whose Camels were attacking an Austrian airfield when they were confronted by nineteen enemy fighters. Jerrard fought the enemy alone, shooting down two and enabling his two fellow pilots to escape safely; his aircraft was badly damaged and he was forced to land and surrender.

At sea Camels took over much of the work pioneered by the Pup. The 2F.1 Camel was specially developed for work from ships and was flown in prototype form (as N5) as early as March 1917. This version was distinguishable in having a fuselage built in two parts (the joint being just aft of the cockpit), the object of which was to enable the rear section to be detached for storage aboard ship. The joint necessitated a pair of external rocking levers to enable the elevator control cables to be disconnected. The wing span was reduced by about a foot, and the cabane struts, instead of being faired, were plain steel tubes.

As with the RFC's night fighters, the 2F.1 Camels were armed with an upward-firing Lewis gun, while a single Vickers was usually retained. Their principal task with the Home Fleet was to attack German airships and seaplanes at large over the North Sea, and they achieved a fair degree of success.

Another memorable series of trials involved Camel take-offs from towed lighters. The first attempt was made on 30 May 1918 by the redoubtable Col Charles Rumney Samson (later Air Cdre, CMG, DSO, AFC, RAF) who was to fly a Camel from a lighter being towed by HM Destroyer *Truculent* off the coast at Orfordness. Because the lighter was not fitted with a flight deck, the Camel was equipped with skids instead of wheels, and these skids engaged in channels running the full length of the vessel. Unfortunately, as the fighter began its take-off, the skids jumped out of the channels, and the Camel fell over the side and was smashed to pieces as the

The Sopwith 2F.1 Camel prototype, N5, armed with one Vickers and one Lewis gun and equipped to carry up to eight Le Prieur anti-airship rockets on the interplane struts. The photograph is said to have been taken at Martlesham Heath in 1918. (Photo: A J Jackson Collection)

Type: Single-engine, single-seat, single-bay biplane fighting scout, night interceptor and trench fighter.

Manufacturers: The Sopwith Aviation Co Ltd, Kingston-upon-Thames, Surrey; William Beardmore & Co Ltd, Dalmuir, Dunbartonshire; Boulton & Paul Ltd, Norwich; British Caudron Co, Cricklewood, London; Clayton & Shuttleworth Ltd, Lincoln; The Fairey Aviation Co Ltd, Hayes, Middlesex; Hooper & Co Ltd, London SW1; March, Jones & Cribb Ltd, Leeds; Nieuport & General Aircraft Co Ltd, Cricklewood, London; Portholme Aerodrome Ltd, Huntingdon; Ruston, Proctor & Co Ltd, Lincoln.

Powerplant: One 110hp Clerget 9Z nine-cylinder rotary engine driving two-blade propeller; 130hp Clerget 9B (140hp Clerget 9Bf); 110hp Le Rhône 9J; 150hp B.R.1; 100hp Gnome *monosoupape*; 150hp Gnome *monosoupape*; 180hp Le Rhône.

Structure: All-wooden structure, wire-braced and fabric-covered; ailerons fitted to upper and lower mainplanes.

Dimensions: (F.1 Camel) Span, 28ft 0in; length (Clerget), 18ft 9in; height (Clerget), 8ft 6in; wing area, 231 sq ft.

Weights: (130hp Clerget) Tare, 929lb; all-up, 1,453lb. (2F.1) Tare, 956lb; all-up, 1,523lb.

Performance: (F.1 Camel, 130hp Clerget) Max speed, 117 mph at sea level, 113 mph at 10,000ft; climb to 10,000ft, 10 min 35 sec; service ceiling, 19,000ft; endurance, 2½ hr. (F.1 Camel, 150hp B.R.1) Max speed, 125 mph at sea level; 121 mph at 10,000ft; climb to 10,000ft, 8 min 10 sec; service ceiling, 22,000ft; endurance, 2½ hr.

Armament: Standard armament was two 0.303in synchronized Vickers machine guns on top of fuselage forward of cockpit. Sopwith-Kauper mechanical, or Constantinesco hydraulic interrupter gear. Many Camels carried up to four 25lb bombs under the fuselage. Home Defence Camels were armed with two Lewis machine guns on a double Foster mounting above the upper wing centre section, firing above the propeller. 2.F1 Camels were usually armed with one synchronized Vickers gun on nose and one Lewis gun on Admiralty mounting above the upper wing.

Prototypes: Four (but possibly six). F.1/1 and F.1/3 prototypes un-numbered; two Admiralty prototypes, N517 and N518. (First flight, possibly 22 December 1916, made by Harry Hawker at Brooklands). N5 was prototype 2F.1.

Production: Generally stated to be a total of 5,695, plus about 230 2F.1s, but at least 100 were cancelled. (Sopwith, 500: N6330-N6379, B3571-B3950, B6201-B6450, and probably F8496-F8595; Boulton & Paul, 1,625: B5151-B5250, B9131-B9330, C1601-C1700, C3281-C3380, D6401-D6700, D9131-D9530, F1301-F1550, F1883-F1957, F6301-F6500, F8646-F8695 and H2646-H2745; British Caudron, 100: C6701-C6800; Clayton & Shuttleworth, 600: B5651-B5750, B7181-B7280, D3326-D3425, D9581-D9680, E4374-E4423, F3096-F3145 and F4974-F5073*; Hooper, 375: B5401-B5450, C1551-C1600, F2083-F2182, H734-H833 night fighters, and H7343-H7412*; Marsh, Jones & Cribb, 175: C8301-C8400 and F5174-F5248; Nieuport & General, 300: C1-C200, F3196-F3245 and F3918-F3967; Portholme Aerodrome, 250: B4601-B4650, B7131-B7180, D9531-D9580, E5129-E5178 and F1958-F2007; Ruston, Proctor, 1,575: B2301-B2550, B5551-B5650, B7281-B7480, C8201-C8300, D1776-D1975, D8101-D8250, E1401-E1600, E7137-E7336, F2008-F2082 and F3968-F4067. 2F.1s: William Beardmore, 200: N6600-N6649, N6750-N6699, N6800-N6949 and N7100-N7149; Hooper, 30: N8130-N8159) *Some of these aircraft probably cancelled). The manufacturer of another small batch around N8204 is not known.

Summary of Service: Sopwith Camels served with Nos 3, 43, 46, 54, 65, 70, 71 (becoming No 4 Squadron, Australian Flying Corps), 73, 80, 151 and 152 Squadrons, RFC and RAF, in France; with Nos 1, 3, 4, 8, 9, 10 and 13 (Naval) Squadrons, RNAS in France (becoming Nos. 201, 203, 204, 208, 209, 210 and 213 Squadrons, RAF, after 1 April 1918); with Nos 28, 66, 139 and 225 Squadrons, RAF, in Italy; with Nos 17 and 150 Squadrons, RAF, in Greece; with Nos 220 and 222 Squadrons, RAF, in the Aegean; with No 47 Squadron in Russia; and with Nos 37, 50, 51, 61, 75, 78, 81, 89, 94, 112, 143, 155, 187, 188, 189, 198, 230, 233 and 274 Squadrons, RAF, in the United Kingdom.

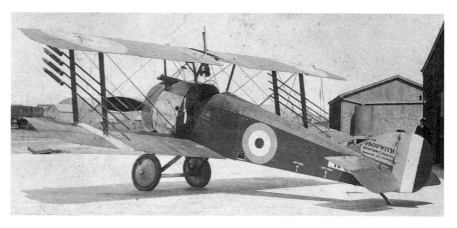

lighter passed over it. Samson miraculously fought his way out of the wreckage and was rescued unhurt.

Later a short deck was fitted to the lighter and the first successful take-off, using a normal wheel undercarriage, was accomplished by Lt S C Culley RN on 31 July. Towed lighters with Camels were used operationally, and, during a foray by the Harwich Force towards the Heligoland Bight on 11 August 1918, Culley took off from a lighter, climbed to 18,000 feet and shot down the Zeppelin L53 — despite one of his guns jamming. This was the last German airship to be shot down during the War. Two others had recently been destroyed by carrier-borne Camels when, on 19 July, seven aircraft, each carrying a pair of 50lb bombs, had taken off from HMS *Furious* and hit the German airship sheds at Tondern, destroying the Zeppelins L54 and L60; only two of the Camels returned safely to *Furious*, flown by Captains F W Dickson and Bernard Arthur Smart DSO* (the pilot who had shot down a Zeppelin while flying a Pup on 22 August 1917, see page 55).

One other interesting experiment of 1918 involved naval Camels, that of providing British airships with their own fighter protection. While the 2F.1 Camels N6622 and N6814 of No 212 Squadron were being prepared at Felixstowe, the airship R.23 was being fitted with a horizontal surface beneath its keel, under which the upper wing of the Camel would rest, retained in place by a quick-release hook which engaged with the fighter's top wing centre section structure. A preliminary drop was made without pilot and with the Camel's controls locked, and this was followed by a live drop by Lt R E Key DFC of No

212 Squadron who started his engine successfully, dropped away without trouble, and flew round the R.23 before landing at the airship station at Pulham. Similar trials, employing other fighter aircraft, continued until 1925 when they were finally abandoned.

Camels remained in service for eighteen months after the War, but were eventually discarded by the RAF, largely in favour of the Sopwith Snipe.

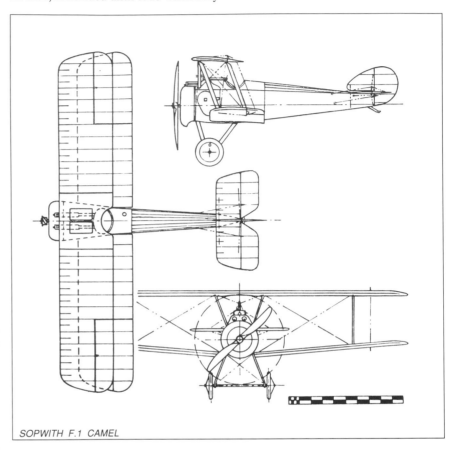

SOPWITH F.1 CAMEL

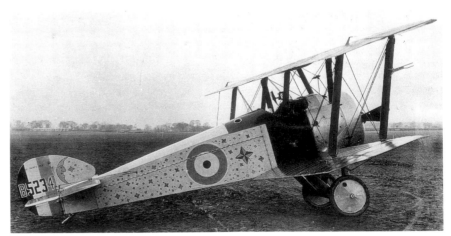

An unarmed Boulton & Paul-built F.1 Camel, B5234, in a distinctly unofficial livery, possibly photographed after the War, suggesting that it was the personal transport of a senior officer. (Photo: R C Sturtivant)

A standard Royal Aircraft Factory-built S.E.5A, B4897, at Farnborough, showing the strengthened undercarriage that was introduced in 1917. (Photo: The Royal Aerospace Establishment, Neg No 2097, dated 17 November 1917)

R.A.F.
S.E.5 and S.E.5A

Genesis of the Royal Aircraft Factory's excellent S.E.5 design lay entirely in the Hispano-Suiza engine, designed by the Swiss engineer Marc Birkigt, a 150hp V-eight liquid-cooled in-line engine of which the War Office ordered fifty examples from France, as well as negotiating a manufacturing licence, in mid-1915. Being thus a Service-sponsored engine, it was not unnatural that the Royal Aircraft Factory should be instructed to produce a suitable fighter design, for its power-weight ratio of about 0.33 bhp/lb compared favourably with most fighter engines extant, such as the 110hp Clerget which returned a figure of 0.28 bhp/lb. Leading the project at Farnborough was the chief engineer, Maj F M Green, with Henry Folland, assisted by John Kenworthy, being responsible for the principal design; Maj Frank Goodden, the Factory's chief pilot, was also closely involved.

The design was entirely new, although it has been suggested that some of its inspiration lay in the Martinsyde RG, for the compact front fuselage was superficially reminiscent of that aeroplane; the remainder of the aircraft was a natural progression from the S.E.4A.

Fundamental to the design was that it should be relatively simple to fly, yet represent a worthwhile advance in performance, armament and agility over fighters such as the D.H.2 which, it should be remembered, was still in service at the end of 1916. For ease of manufacture, the structure was simple and straightforward with wings of parallel chord, a wooden box-girder fuselage, and tail surfaces little changed from the S.E.4A. The single-bay, staggered wings were built around two spruce spars with internal wire bracing, and with ailerons on upper and lower wings.

A large car-type radiator was located immediately forward of the engine, and the fuel tank was mounted on the top longerons directly behind; the tank was initially cowled by an extension of the top engine cowling panel, but the panel was omitted on production aircraft. Early aircraft also featured a small gravity fuel tank above the upper wing, offset to port of the centreline.

After long delays, the fifty Hispano-Suiza engines, ordered the previous year, began delivery in August 1916, and manufacture of three prototype S.E.5s started the following month. These aircraft possessed sharply raked wingtips and short exhaust manifolds each with a single central outlet.

In the morning of 22 November Frank Goodden flew the first prototype S.E.5, A4561, at Farnborough, and

The first prototype S.E.5, as it first appeared with heavily raked wingtips and single-exit exhaust manifolds. A photograph taken less than a week after the first flight. (Photo: The Royal Aerospace Establishment, Neg No 1915, dated 28 November 1916)

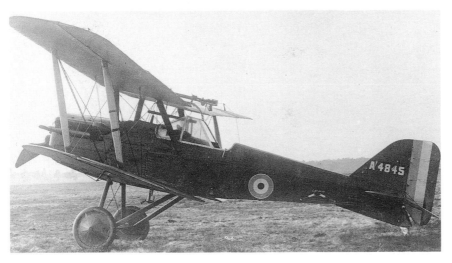

The first production Factory-built S.E.5, A4845, displaying the unpopular canopy over the pilot's cockpit; the engine is also fitted with a single-exit exhaust manifold, though in this instance the exit is at the front of the branch pipe. Note the original style of single-tube undercarriage V-struts. (Photo: T Heffernan)

expressed delight with the new fighter, a view not shared by Capt Albert Ball DSO, who flew the aircraft a day or so later. The second prototype, A4562, was flown on 4 December and soon afterwards went to France for brief operational trials with No 60 Squadron (giving rise to some incorrect impressions that 'the S.E.5 equipped the Squadron from January 1917 onwards'). The judgement was more reasoned than that of Ball, speaking of the S.E.5 as being comparable with the Nieuport 17 and Spad

VII, though more stable and simpler to fly. It was, the report stated, likely to be much steadier in gun firing.

On 28 January the first S.E.5 prototype crashed near Farnborough, killing the Factory's popular chief pilot, Frank Goodden. The official findings were convoluted, suggesting that the propeller had 'burst', and that the ensuing vibration had caused the wing structure to fail. In fact it seems most likely that wing structure collapse occurred in the first instance during aerobatics. Be that

as it may, the design was modified to incorporate strengthened rear spars, shortened wings with reduced rake, and strengthened strut/spar joints. The result was an immensely strong airframe that became a hallmark of the S.E.

A preliminary order for 24 S.E.5s had already been received by the Factory, these aircraft being fitted — for the most part — with the imported Hispano engines. However, these aircraft had progressed too far to include the new wing changes. They were issued to No 56 Squadron at London Colney, near St Albans, commanded by Maj R G Blomfield, and used for training before being changed for the strengthened aircraft which were taken to France the following month. Among those pilots who joined the Squadron during the training period was Capt Albert Ball, posted in as a flight commander; he had not yet become reconciled with the S.E.5, and obtained permission to continue flying a Nieuport.

Early production S.E.5s featured semi-enclosed cockpits intended to give protection from the slipstream for the pilot while attempting to load the Lewis gun, or clear stoppages on the Vickers; it was, however, much disliked by the pilots, and was replaced by a small rigid windscreen which became a standard fitting.

Meanwhile licence production of the Hispano-Suiza engine had been undertaken by the Wolseley Motors company, but this had got off to a slow start. The Air Board had sanctioned the purchase of 8,000 engines from the Mayen company in France although, once again,

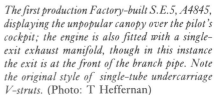

Above: One of the last S.E.5As to be produced, F8990 'R' of No 74 Squadron was built by Vickers Ltd. The photograph was probably taken during 1919. (Photo: RAF Museum, Neg No P013091)

Right: Another famous fighter Squadron with S.E.5As was No 111, two of whose aircraft, identified by the zig-zag markings, are shown at an aerodrome in Palestine at the time of the Allenby offensive. B139, in the foreground is a Martinsyde-built aircraft, carrying four 20lb Cooper bombs. (Photo: RAF Museum Neg No P01102)

No 85 Squadron was commanded by two successive holders of the Victoria Cross, Bishop and Mannock — the two highest-scoring RAF fighter pilots of all time. The S.E.5A shown here (another very late production aircraft) displays No 85's distinctive hexagon marking, a device still carried by the Squadron half a century later. (Photo: A J Jackson Collection)

these would not start arriving in Britain until late in 1917 (and were to be found to have poorly manufactured components). A geared version of the 150hp Hispano-Suiza had been developed which produced a nominal 200 bhp; this was tested in the third S.E.5 prototype, A4563, early in 1917, and underwent operational trials with Nos 56 and 84 Squadrons in France. It was readily distinguishable by the higher propeller line and a slightly deeper fuselage forward of the cockpit, the aircraft being re-termed the S.E.5A.

The S.E.5A became the subject of all production contracts placed from March 1917 onwards, and featured a number of other refinements, such as the addition of a streamlined headrest fairing behind the cockpit (although a number of pilots had this removed as they considered it to restrict their rearward vision).

Nor were the early Wolseley-built engines satisfactory, and weaknesses in components led to fairly frequent engine failures. By the time these had been rectified, production of Hispano-Suiza engines was running some six months behind schedule, as were examples of a high-compression version of the 150hp engine, developed by Wolseley and named the Viper.

A Vickers-built S.E.5A, F5609, serving with the Central Flying School, possible shortly after the War. (Photo: RAF Museum, Neg No P04734)

Despite these difficulties, S.E.5As began re-equipping No 56 Squadron in June, and No 60 Squadron the following month, the majority of their aircraft being produced by Martinsyde at Brooklands. In August No 84 Squadron at Lilbourne in Northamptonshire, commanded by Maj William Sholto Douglas (later Marshal of the Royal Air Force Lord Douglas of Kirtleside, GCB, MC, DFC), received the S.E.5A and moved to France in September. By the end of the year Nos 24, 32, 40, 41, 56, 60 and 84 Squadrons had been re-equipped and were serving in France, a most disappointing number bearing in mind that almost 3,000 aircraft had been on order for almost six months, and only 828 had been delivered. Altogether sixteen squadrons had been expected to be flying the

S.E.5A by December 1917.

Added to the engine troubles were problems with the gun interrupter gear (although the Constantinesco equipment was elsewhere considered to be reliable); it was found that the hydraulic system of the interrupter was incompatible with some batches of the Wolseley-built Hispanos — a weakness not finally overcome until February 1918. Nevertheless, by the spring of that year the S.E.5A was generally considered to be over its troubles and to be the best British fighter of the day. It was faster, though less manoeuvrable than the Sopwith Camel, and capable of withstanding considerable damage in combat. Some of the best-known pilots of the RFC and RAF of the First World War flew the aircraft. Maj Edward

('Mick') Mannock VC, DSO**, MC*, scored 54 of his 73 victories while flying S.E.5As with Nos 40, 70 and 85 Squadrons; Lt-Col W A Bishop VC, DSO*, MC, DFC, shot down 27 enemy aircraft out of his total score of 72 victories while with Nos 60 and 85 Squadrons. Other high-scoring S.E.5A pilots included Maj J T B McCudden VC, DSO*, MC*, DFC, Capt A W Beauchamp-Proctor VC, DSO, MC*, DFC, Capt G E H McElroy MC**, DFC*, Capt J I T Jones DSO, MC, DFC*, MM, and Lieut A P F Rhys Davids DSO, MC*.

The S.E.5A had undergone a number of improvements, including the strengthening of the undercarriage; the forward member of the V-struts, previously a single tubular member, was now doubled, the two steel tubes being faired over with ply or sheet metal. Increasing numbers of aircraft were fitted with direct-drive Wolseley Viper engines but, being heavier than the Hispano, were generally disliked. A geared development, the Adder, also appeared, but this was even heavier.

S.E.5As were issued to Home Defence units but were regarded as unsuitable as interceptors owing to the length of time needed to warm up their engines before take-off. After the first German daylight raids over southeast England in June 1917, No 56 Squadron was ordered back from France (in spite of objections by Trenchard) to Bekesbourne in Kent. After having kicked its heels for a fortnight, without so much as seeing a German raider, the Squadron returned to France. Four other Home Defence Squadrons became operational on S.E.5As, but all had been replaced with Camels by the end of the War.

S.E.5As did not fight on the Italian Front, but three Squadrons, Nos 17, 47 and 150, flew the aircraft in Macedonia. In Palestine, Nos 111 and 145 Squadrons' S.E.s were heavily engaged during General Allenby's final offensive through Palestine in the late summer of 1918, both in the ground attack rôle (using 20lb Cooper bombs) and in patrols over the enemy aerodromes to discourage German pilots from taking off. No 72 Squadron served in Mesopotamia until February 1919 when its duties were taken over by No 30, also flying S.E.5As.

Like the Camel, the S.E.5A did not survive long in the peacetime RAF, the last squadron aircraft being withdrawn from Nos 56 and 81 in January 1920. Small numbers served in Canada and Australia.

It had been planned to build 1,000

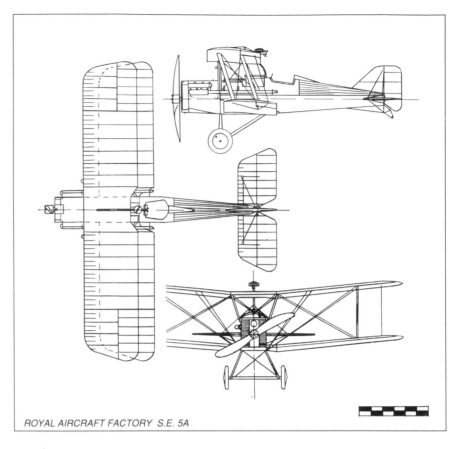

ROYAL AIRCRAFT FACTORY S.E. 5A

Type: Single-engine, single-seat, single-bay biplane fighting scout.

Manufacturers: The Royal Aircraft Factory, Farnborough, Hampshire; The Austin Motor Co Ltd, Birmingham; The Air Navigation Co Ltd, Addlestone; Martinsyde Ltd, Brooklands; Vickers Ltd, Crayford and Weybridge, Surrey; Wolseley Motors Ltd, Birmingham.

Powerplant: S.E.5: 150hp Hispano-Suiza; also 200hp Wolseley W.4A Viper. S.E.5A: 200hp Hispano-Suiza; 220hp Hispano-Suiza; 240hp Hispano-Suiza; 200hp Wolseley W.4A Viper; 200hp Wolseley W.4B Viper.

Structure: Wooden box-girder, wire-braced and fabric-covered; twin spruce spar wings, fabric-covered and with ailerons on upper and lower wings; variable incidence tailplane.

Dimensions: Span, 28ft 0in (early S.E.5s), 26ft 7½in (late S.E.5s and S.E.5As); length, 21ft 4in (S.E.5), 20ft 11in (S.E.5A); height, 9ft 5in (S.E.5), 9ft 6in (S.E.5A); wing area, 249 sq ft (early S.E.5s), 244 sq ft (late S.E.5s and S.E.5As).

Weights: S.E.5A (200hp Hispano-Suiza). Tare, 1,400lb; all-up, 1,953lb.

Performance: S.E.5A (200hp Hispano-Suiza). Max speed, approx 135 at sea level; climb to 10,000ft, 10 min 20 sec; service ceiling, 22,000ft; endurance: 3 hr.

Armament: One fixed, synchronized 0.303in Vickers machine gun with Constantinesco interrupter gear on nose, offset to port, with 400 rounds; and one Lewis gun on Foster mounting above upper wing centre section with four 97-round drums. Four 20lb Cooper bombs could be carried on racks under the fuselage.

Prototypes: Three S.E.5 prototypes, A4561-A4563 (first flown by Maj Frank Goodden on 22 November 1916 at Farnborough). One S.E.5B, A8947 (a modified S.E.5).

Production: 48 S.E.5s (excluding prototypes; all built by Royal Aircraft Factory: A4845-A4868 and A8898-A8947); 5,180 S.E.5As built in Britain (Royal Aircraft Factory, 200: B4851-B4900, C1051-C1150 and D7001-D7050; Martinsyde, 500: B1-B200, D3911-D4010, E3154-E3253 and F5249-F5348; Vickers, 2,165: B501-B700, C5301-C5450, C9486-C9635, D201-D450, D3426-D3575, D5951-D6200, D8431-D8580, E1251-E1400, E3904-E4103, F551-F615, F5449-F5698 and F8946-F9145; Austin, 1,550: B8231-B8580*, C8661-C9310, E5637-E5936, F7951-F8200; Air Navigation Co, 336: C1751-C1950, E5937-E6036 and H674-H710 approx; Wolseley, 400: C6351-C6500, D6851-D7000 and F851-F950. *Some of these aircraft may not have been completed.)

Summary of RFC and RAF Service: S.E.5s served with Nos 56 and 60 Squadrons in France. S.E.5As served with Nos 1, 24, 29, 32, 40, 41, 56, 60, 64, 68, 74, 84, 85 and 92 Squadrons in France; S.E.5As served with Nos 17, 47 and 150 Squadrons in Greece; S.E.5As served with Nos 30, 72, 111 and 145 Squadrons in the Middle East; and S.E.5As served with Nos 50, 61, 81, 87, 93, 94 and 143 Squadrons in the United Kingdom (not all operationally).

aircraft in America for the Air Service, and a contract to that effect had been agreed with the Curtiss company; this was cancelled at the end of the War, and only one Curtiss-built example was completed. 57 others, known as S.E.5Es, were however built from components shipped out from Britain in 1922-23 and these served as advanced trainers.

One other version appeared in Britain as the S.E.5B, a much-modified S.E.5A, A8947. In this a Viper engine, with a much cleaned-up mounting and cowling, was fitted, together with sesquiplane wings and outward-raked interplane struts. The car-type radiator was replaced by a chin-mounted unit and the propeller fitted with a large spinner. To

provide a performance comparison, the larger wings were afterwards replaced by standard components while retaining the improved engine installation (in a version known as the S.E.5C) but, although this returned the best performance figures of any S.E.5 variant, it appeared much too late to warrant putting it into production.

Martinsyde R.G.

Following the transfer of the Martinsyde G.100/102 Elephant from its intended rôle of fighter to bomber, George Handasyde remained determined to pursue a similar but smaller fighter design, the R.G. (=Revised G-Type), and he, working with A A ('Tony') Fletcher, came up with a single-bay biplane of exceptionally clean lines and compact configuration, powered initially by a 190hp Rolls-Royce Falcon I engine driving a four-blade propeller. It is likely that the first prototype, probably A318, was flown in January 1917.

When first officially tested at Farnborough in February this aircraft returned a top speed of 130 mph at sea level, and an ability to reach 10,000 feet in 10 minutes 20 seconds (compared with 125 mph and 14 minutes 10 seconds of the Factory's own S.E.5 prototype which underwent the same tests during the following month.

However, it had already been decided to go ahead with production of both the S.E.5 and the Sopwith Camel and, even though Handasyde acquired a 275hp Falcon III for the R.G., this was doomed by circumstances also; despite returning

The attractive Martinsyde R.G. at Brooklands in 1917; its similarity with the S.E.5A (which ironically came to be built in quantity by Martinsyde) is striking, even though it avoided use of the recalcitrant Hispano-Suiza engine. (Photo: G S Leslie / J M Bruce Collection)

a speed of 136 mph during its official tests in June, it had by then been decreed

that all Falcon IIIs would be reserved for Bristol F.2B Fighters.

Type: Single-engine, single-seat, single-bay biplane scout.
Manufacturer: Martinsyde Ltd., Brooklands, Surrey.
Powerplant: One 190hp Rolls-Royce Falcon I (later 275hp Falcon III) 12-cylinder water-cooled in-line engine driving four-blade propeller.
Dimensions: Span, 32ft 0in; length, (Falcon I) 25ft 8in, (Falcon III) 25ft 10in; height, 9ft 10in; wing area, 310 sq ft.
Weights: (Falcon III) Tare, 1,740lb; all-up, 2,261lb.
Performance: (Falcon III) Max speed, 136 mph at sea level; climb to 10,000ft, 7 min 20 sec; service ceiling, 23,500ft; endurance, 2 hr.
Armament: Two fixed, synchronized 0.303in Vickers machine guns on nose decking.
Prototypes: Believed three, possibly A318-A320 (believed first flown in January 1917). No production.

Nestler Scout

A relatively little known and short-lived single-seat scout was designed by the Frenchman M Boudot for the small company of F C Nestler Ltd of Westminster, London, during 1916, a firm that had been on the fringe of the aircraft industry since before the War, when it negotiated the British franchise in foreign aeroplanes.

The Nestler Scout was a small aircraft for the 100hp Gnome *monosoupape* engine fitted and, no doubt, was fast on this account. Though unremarkable, it was a well-proportioned single-bay biplane with moderately staggered wings with ailerons fitted top and bottom. There was no fixed fin, and the rudder was not unlike that of the Avro 504. The fuselage appears to have been the customary fabric-covered wooden box-girder with curved upper decking, and the wings were evidently built in two halves, being

joined on the centreline of the aircraft without centre section.

The aircraft was accepted by the Air Board for preliminary trials and a freelance pilot engaged for the purpose in January. This was J B Fitzsimmons, an ex-RFC pilot who had been invalided from the Service. It is said that the Nestler was an agile aeroplane and Fitzsimmons evidently found little trouble in its handling. However on 26 March the pilot was engaging in some low level aerobatics in a high wind when the fabric began stripping from the wings; the aircraft crashed into a hangar and Fitzsimmons was killed.

The Scout was totally wrecked and no attempt was made to continue work on the design. Boudot later joined the Grahame-White company on the design staff.

The Nestler Scout early in 1917, possibly in a shed at Hendon where it underwent flight trials. (Photo: A J Jackson Collection)

Short S.364 (Scout No 3)

Although Short Bros Ltd was better known for the company's large torpedo-carrying seaplanes during the First World War, both Horace and Oswald Short became interested in producing designs intended to meet the Air Department's Specification N.2A for a two-seat float-equipped scout. What came to be known as Experimental Scout No 1, N36, was designed by Horace in 1916 and was in some respects a scaled-down adaptation of the large Type 310A seaplane. Launched at Rochester on 2 January 1917, the aircraft failed to get airborne in its initial form and, although the fuselage was lengthened to increase the elevator moment and the aircraft was flown by Ronald Kemp three weeks later, it was clear that the design would not interest the Admiralty. (Horace Short was to die on 6 April after a short illness, and his younger brother Oswald took over responsibility for leading the company's design staff.)

A more realistic approach had, however, already be adopted by Oswald, producing a somewhat more compact two-bay biplane with unstaggered wings of equal span. This was referred to by its company sequence number S.364 (and also as Scout No 3) and, with a 200hp Sunbeam Afridi engine, was first flown by John Lankester Parker on 27 March. It was however found to be underpowered and in due course the engine was replaced by a 260hp Sunbeam Maori.

The Short S.364 at Rochester with the enlarged floats, but still powered by the 200hp Sunbeam Afridi engine. (Photo: Imperial War Museum, Neg No MH2872)

The fuselage was a box-girder structure with rounded top decking. The twin main floats had been found to be too narrow for safety on the water and were replaced by wider and deeper floats; small cylindrical wing floats were attached under the lower wings directly below the outboard interplane struts. The wings were of an experimental Admiralty aerofoil design, BRI.31, intended to give moderate lift but low drag. No forward gun was envisaged, the armament consisting solely of a Lewis gun on the observer's cockpit with a Scarff ring.

Although the Admiralty expressed polite interest in the S.364, which had,

after all, been designed to the N.2A Specification, the aircraft — as with most Short seaplanes — was expensive, the airframe being costed at £1,200 and the Maori engine at almost £1,400. By contrast, the Sopwith Pup in its shipborne version, cost £770, plus just under £700 for the 100hp Gnome, apart from being armed with a front gun and possessing a top speed some 20 mph greater than the S.364. Of course the two aircraft were in no way comparable, yet it was the Pup's ability to operate from a fairly wide range of vessels with a wheel undercarriage that rendered the N.2A Specification largely superfluous.

Type: Single-engine, two-seat, twin-float, two-bay biplane scout seaplane.
Manufacturer: Short Bros Ltd, Rochester, Kent.
Powerplant: One 200hp Sunbeam Afridi liquid-cooled in-line engine; later replaced by 260hp Sunbeam Maori twelve-cylinder in-line engine.
Dimensions: Span, 39ft 0in; length, 28ft 0in; wing area, 375 sq ft.
Armament: One 0.303in Lewis machine gun with Scarff ring on rear cockpit; provision to carry two 65lb bombs.
Prototype: One (first flown by John Lankester Parker on 27 March 1917); no production.

Vickers F.B.24

Harold Barnwell's F.B.24 was, like some products of other commercial manufacturers, dogged by official refusal to make available Hispano-Suiza engines for production aircraft on the grounds that delayed production of the engine resulted in all those available being reserved for the S.E.5. When originally projected in the late autumn of 1916, the F.B.24 had been intended to have a 150hp Hart radial engine, but this had met with general disapproval in the F.B.16, and its use was evidently abandoned. Vickers did, however, manage to acquire a 200hp Hispano-Suiza engine for prototype use, and the first aircraft thus powered, the F.B.24B, is said to have been flown at the end of March 1917.

The F.B.26B was a well-proportioned two-bay biplane, intended as a reconnaissance fighter, the wings being of unequal span; the top wing was built in two halves which joined on the aircraft's centre-line, without centre section. The pilot, being situated directly below the upper wing (with two small clear panels in it), possessed a very poor field of view, while the observer, armed with a Lewis gun on Scarff ring, was located in line with the wing trailing edge which, although cut away, severely restricted the gun's field of fire.

The performance with the Hispano engine was modest, and it was generally felt that the F.B.24B was underpowered. The next variant to be built, the F.B.24C, was therefore powered by the 275hp Lorraine-Dietrich 8Bd, and both front and side radiator versions were flown; the long curved tail fin, fitted previously, was shortened. This version returned a top speed in the

The Vickers F.B.24C with 275hp Lorraine-Dietrich 8Bd V-8 engine with frontal radiator and modified fin and rudder. It is difficult to see how exactly the pilot gained entry to his cockpit, let alone abandoned it in any emergency, with the centre section struts immediately fore and aft. (Photo: Vickers Ltd, Neg No 52)

region of 133 mph at sea level.

On account of the criticism of the crew's poor location, the last two versions built, the F.B.24E and the 24G were re-designed with the top wings attached to the upper fuselage longerons, so that both pilot and observer/gunner had unrestricted view all round above the wings. On both aircraft the lower wing was located clear of the underside of the fuselage, the wing shape and interplane struts remaining much the same as on the F.B.24C, and also retaining the shortened tail fin. However, whereas the F.B.24E was

powered by the 200hp Hispano-Suiza, the F.B.24G was fitted with a 375hp Lorraine-Dietrich 13 V-12 engine; the latter was an ungainly-looking aeroplane with lengthened, unstaggered wings and enlarged tailplane, bulky engine installation and ailerons apparently fitted only on the upper wing. Untidy radiators were attached to the sides of the fuselage. Maximum speed was said to be about 140 mph at sea level.

Although not looked upon with much favour by British authorities, the F.B.24G is said to have been produced by Darracq in France after the War.

Type: Single-engine, two-seat, two-bay biplane reconnaissance fighter.
Manufacturer: Vickers Ltd (Aviation Department), Knightsbridge, London.
Powerplant: F.B.24B and F.B.24E, 200hp Hispano-Suiza. F.B.24C, 275hp Lorraine-Dietrich 8Bd. F.B.24G, 375hp Lorraine-Dietrich 13.
Dimensions: F.B.24C. Span, 37ft 6in; length, 26ft 6in; wing area, 384 sq ft. F.B.24G. Span, 38ft 3in; length, 30ft 0in; wing area, 450 sq ft.
Weights: F.B.24C. Tare, 1,709lb; all-up, 2,650lb. F.B.24G. Tare, 2,332lb; all-up, 3,680lb.
Performance: F.B.24C. Max speed, approx 133 mph at sea level; climb to 10,000ft, 11 min; service ceiling, 23,000ft; endurance, 3 hr.
Armament: All versions up to and including F.B.24E armed with one synchronized 0.303in Vickers machine gun on nose, and one Scarff ring-mounted Lewis gun on rear cockpit. The F.B.24G may have been armed with twin synchronized Vickers guns.
Prototypes: Number built not known (first flight by F.B.24B believed to have taken place in March 1917). No production in Britain.

Beardmore W.B.III

The well-known engineering and shipbuilding firm of William Beardmore & Co Ltd of Dalmuir, Dunbartonshire, became involved in aero-engine manufacture shortly before the outbreak of war in 1914 when it obtained a licence to produce Austro-Daimler engines. Soon

afterwards the company received sub-contracts to produce the B.E.2C and, rather later, the Sopwith Pup. When, in 1916, major sub-contractors were encouraged to originate designs of their own, Lieut G Tilghman Richards was appointed Chief Designer in Beardmore's aviation department.

After two designs, the W.B.I (a bomber) and the W.B.II (a reconnaissance aircraft) had failed to receive quantity orders, Beardmore undertook

extensive modification of the Sopwith Pup to improve its application to operations aboard ship, principally by reducing its dimensions for storage by introducing folding wings. To do this the Pup's wings were re-arranged to eliminate stagger, four additional interplane struts were added close to the fuselage to retain rigidity on the wing-fold chord line and to maintain the truss with the wings folded. The fuselage was lengthened by about twelve inches so as to

A standard late production Beardmore W.B.III (S.B.3D). Obvious differences between this and the Sopwith Pup include the absence of wing stagger, the extra interplane struts close to the fuselage adjacent to the wing-fold line, the lengthened fuselage aft of the cockpit and the lenthened tailskid to allow ground clearance with the wings folded. (Photo: J M Bruce Collection)

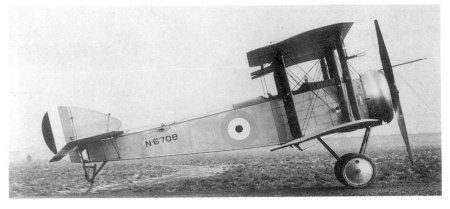

avoid interference between the tailplane and the outboard interplane struts, and folding skids were introduced under the lower wings.

The prototype W.B.III was in fact produced by modifying a Beardmore-built Pup (9950), originally intended for the Admiralty. Also included was provision to fold the undercarriage into the fuselage beneath the cockpit to reduce storage height; an alternative arrangement was provided to enable the entire undercarriage to be jettisoned in the event of an emergency ditching on water.

A total of one hundred W.B.IIIs was ordered under the Service designation S.B.3, the S.B.3D being said to denote 'dropping' undercarriage, and S.B.3F (for 'folding' undercarriage). S.B.3s served aboard HMS *Furious*, *Nairana* and *Pegasus*, and at the time of the Armistice fifty-five were on RAF charge, the remainder in store. It is said that a small number was supplied to Japan.

Type: Single-engine, single-seat shipboard interceptor scout biplane.
Manufacturer: William Beardmore & Co Ltd, Dalmuir, Dunbartonshire.
Powerplant: One 80hp Le Rhône air-cooled rotary engine, or one 80hp Clerget air-cooled rotary engine.
Construction: Wooden construction throughout with ash longerons and diagonal spacers, spruce wing spars and ribs, and birch riblets. Front of fuselage covered with aluminium sheet, and ply in area of cockpit; remainder fabric-covered.
Dimensions: Span, 25ft 0in; length, 20ft 2¼in; height, 8ft 1¼in; wing area, 243 sq ft.
Weights: Tare, 890lb; all-up, 1,289lb.
Performance: Max speed, 103mph at sea level; climb to 5,000ft, 9 min; service ceiling, 12,400 ft; endurance, 2¾ hr.
Armament: One 0.303in Lewis machine gun mounted over the wing centre section to starboard, angled slightly upwards to fire over the propeller.
Prototype: One, 9950 (converted Pup, first flown January 1917)
Production: One hundred aircraft (N6100—N6129 and N6680—N6749)
Summary of Service: Known to have served aboard ships of the Grand Fleet and aboard HM Carriers *Furious*, *Nairana* and *Pegasus* during 1918-19.

Grahame-White Type 21

Clearly representing an attempt to refine the Type 20 (see page 66), the Grahame-White Type 21 appeared early in April 1917, powered by an 80hp Le Rhône engine driving a four-blade propeller. Most readily visible change was the use of I-form interplane and cabane struts with prominent spacer fairings at their extremities.

In almost every respect, however, the design differed in detail; the fuselage, instead of being formed to almost circular section, was a plain, flat-sided, wooden box-girder, only faired with rounded top decking; the fin and rudder were enlarged , although the latter was now no longer balanced; the front pair of undercarriage struts was mounted fur-

The attractive, but anachronistic Grahame-White Type 21. (Photo: J M Bruce Collection)

ther forward — directly behind the engine, and a small, faired headrest was incorporated immediately aft of the cockpit. The previous design's large wing gap was retained, as was the unusually large number of bracing wires.

In all likelihood the wings were of reduced thickness, for the Type 21 returned a speed of 107 mph at sea level, a not unreasonable performance on only 80 horsepower, although there is no evidence that any armament was ever carried.

There appeared to be little inherently disagreeable about the Type 21, except that it flew about a year later than other scouts of similar capabilities; and, apart from a possible training rôle, it could have contributed little to meeting the needs of the fighting Services.

Sopwith Hispano Triplane

First of the Sopwith Hispano Triplanes, N509, with direct-drive 150hp Hispano-Suiza engine, at Manston, probably in the late summer of 1917. (Photo: Harald Penrose)

Further evidence of the inconvenience caused by the delays in introducing the Hispano-Suiza engine into production in Britain was afforded by the late appearance of Sopwith's triplane powered by this engine. Although the design was undertaken at roughly the same time as that of the Clerget-powered Triplane (see page 60), it has frequently been assumed that the two scouts were closely related; in fact, whereas the Clerget Triplane was related to the Pup, the Hispano aircraft was more closely associated with the earlier 1½-Strutter (see page 48).

Indeed the only feature, apart from the triplane configuration itself, common to the two designs was the use of broad-chord I-form interplane and cabane struts. The Hispano-powered triplane employed wings of 4ft 3in chord, compared with 3ft 3in on the Clerget aircraft. The fuselage, tail and undercarriage of the former were little changed from those of the 1½-Strutter.

It seems that the first prototype airframe (N509) of the Hispano Triplane was completed in about December 1916, and that the 150hp Hispano-Suiza direct-drive engine was not delivered to Brooklands until March 1917; surviving records suggest that Harry Hawker first flew the aircraft in late April or early May. The engine installation was of more pleasing appearance than that of, for instance, the S.E.5, though not necessarily more efficient, being of almost circular section. It was later found necessary to provide exit louvres in the rear

of the cowling to permit better through-flow of cooling air from the frontal radiator. The exhaust system comprised a four-branch collector manifold leading into a four-foot straight exit pipe on each side, extending aft almost as far as the cockpit coaming.

A second prototype, N510, with a 200hp Hispano-Suiza geared-drive engine, was completed later. Unfortunately, due to the delays in receiving

their engines, the two triplanes were, by the time they were ready to fly, already being eclipsed by the Camel, S.E.5A, and Bristol F.2B Fighter. Moreover, the new triplanes were only armed with single synchronized front guns. After official trials, however, they were both taken on Admiralty charge, only to be written off in accidents later in 1917, N509 at Manston and N510 at Eastchurch.

Type: Single-engine, single-seat, single-bay triplane scout.
Manufacturer: The Sopwith Aviation Co Ltd, Kingston-upon-Thames, Surrey.
Powerplant: One 150hp Hispano-Suiza direct-drive in-line engine driving two-blade propeller; second aircraft with 200hp Hispano-Suiza geared engine.
Structure: All-wood box-girder with wire bracing and fabric covering; single-bay, two-spar triplane wings with I-form struts; ailerons on all wings.
Dimensions: Span, 28ft 6in; length, 23ft 2in; wing area, 340 sq ft.
Performance: Max speed, 120 mph at sea level; climb to 10,000ft, 9 min.
Armament: One synchronized 0.303in Vickers machine gun on fuselage top decking immediately forward of the cockpit, firing through the propeller arc.
Prototypes: Two; N509 (probably flown in late April or early May 1917 by Harry Hawker) and N510. No production

Sopwith Dolphin

Yet another fighter aircraft, designed with the Hispano-Suiza engine in mind, was the Sopwith 5F.1 Dolphin. Designed by Herbert Smith, the Dolphin

The first Dolphin prototype as it originally appeared with frontal radiator, unbalanced rudder and fabric-covered rear decking almost up to the cockpit. (Photo: Imperial War Museum, Neg No Q66093)

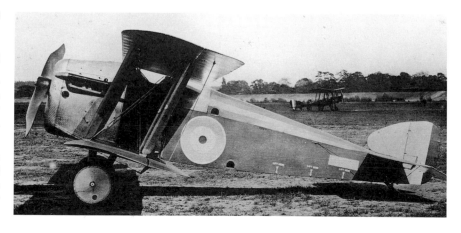

was almost certainly conceived as the result of promise being shown by the Factory's S.E.5, yet features of other, less prominent aircraft clearly influenced the Sopwith product, not least the back-staggered D.H.5 with the magnificent field of view for the pilot. Like the Camel, designed by R J Ashfield, and whose fierce manœuvrability was largely attributable to the concentration of all principal masses within a compact space, Smith placed propeller, engine, radiators, pilot, fuel, guns and ammunition in the front 8ft 9in of the fuselage; before long, two further guns would be added within this space. . .

One of the novel ideas in vogue at Sopwith was a small design sub-department whose job was to accelerate the manufacture of promising prototype aircraft at the behest of Ashfield and Smith. And thereby two or three Dolphin prototypes were put in hand very quickly. The first was almost certainly flown early in June 1917, powered by one of the few 150hp Hispano-Suiza geared engines released for prototype work. Though by no means a satisfactory aircraft as it stood, this prototype showed such promise, returning a speed of around 136 mph at sea level and

providing a superb tactical field of view for the pilot, that on 29 June the War Office provisioning department awarded Sopwith a contract for no fewer then 500 production aircraft — the largest single order yet received by the company — worth over half a million pounds, a staggering sum for a 'private sector' aircraft manufacturer at the time.

The Dolphin featured the simple wooden box-girder fuselage, wire-braced and with rounded top decking, and a tail unit not unlike that of the Camel, with unbalanced rudder. The two-bay, two-spar wings were back-staggered twelve

inches, and constructed with spindled spruce spars with spruce interplane struts. The upper wing structure was discontinued at the roots, but steel tubular carry-through members formed part of a tubular superstructure which surrounded the cockpit, with the pilot's head projecting above, thereby allowing an unrestricted field of view in the upper hemisphere. Because the front fuselage was very deep, the wing gap was maintained at a constant 4ft 3in. The nose cowling was also exceptionally deep, in part on account of the frontal car-type radiator and also to the front Vickers guns being buried in the top decking.

The prototype went to France for operational trials on 13 June as at least two further prototypes were nearing completion at Brooklands. These early trials showed that the deep frontal radiator was unsatisfactory, and was discarded in favour of a pair of vertical radiator matrices mounted on the fuse-

Above: *A full-standard Sopwith Dolphin night fighter serving with No 1 Training Squadron, armed with twin front Vickers and twin flexible Lewis machine guns.* (Photo: RAF Museum, Neg No P016297)

Left: *Dolphins of No 87 Squadron. Although the photograph is of indifferent quality, just visible are the Lewis guns mounted on the lower wing of D3775.* (Photo: RAF Museum, Neg No P011343)

lage sides adjacent to the cockpit. A horn-balanced rudder replaced the initial unbalanced unit, although this temporarily resulted in a smaller fin. The repositioning of the radiator allowed much cleaner nose contours, thereby giving the pilot a better (though not ideal) view both forwards and downwards, as well as exposing the front halves of the gun barrels. The second prototype also featured fairly generous cutouts in the lower wing roots to extend the pilot's view downwards.

At least two of the Dolphin prototypes were in France for Service trials in June, one of which appears to have been forced down behind the enemy lines during July, as a Dolphin featured in the periodic list, issued by the Germans, of Allied aircraft which had fallen into their hands.

The series of modifications showed considerable promise and provided the basis for a standard of preparation in the production aircraft. Further re-styling of the nose immediately forward of the cockpit resulted in improved view for the pilot and the lower wing root cutouts were abandoned. The fin and rudder were tidied up, the rudder horn balance being faired into an enlarged fin, allowing a smooth curve over the upper line. The upper decking of the fuselage aft of the cockpit, previously fabric-covered, was changed to ply for a length of about four feet to allow for hatch access to the wireless bay behind the cockpit. In this form the Dolphin underwent final Service trials at Martlesham Heath in August 1917, returning a performance slightly better than the original evaluation.

Production Dolphins began appearing in October, albeit slowly owing to the continuing shortage of reliable Hispano engines. These aircraft featured a pair of Lewis guns mounted on the front carry-through wing member directly in front of the pilot's face (incidentally making the Dolphin the most heavily armed single-seat fighter to enter service thus far). However, these additional Lewis guns were unpopular as, in the fierce manœuvring of combat, the Lewis guns tended to swing about and had a habit of striking the pilot in the face. In due course, individual pilots expressed their own ideas in the matter of armament, usually discarding one or both the Lewis guns.

Because of sub-standard manufacture of the Hispano-Suiza engines (the reduction gears were inconsistently case-hardened, leading to disintegration), it was decided to start by re-equipping home-based squadrons, the first being No 87 at Hounslow in December, commanded by Capt C W J Darwin, followed immediately by No 79 at Beaulieu in Hampshire, commanded by Maj M W Noel; these two Squadrons moved to France early in 1918, by which time No 87 Squadron had decided to mount the two Lewis guns on the Dolphin's lower wings, firing outside the propeller arc — even though this meant that the guns could not be reloaded after a single 97-round drum had been fired by each.

In January 1918 Dolphins started delivery to No 141 Squadron, a night fighter Home Defence unit formed for the specific defence of London under the 24-year-old Maj Philip Babington MC, AFC (later Air Marshal Sir Philip,

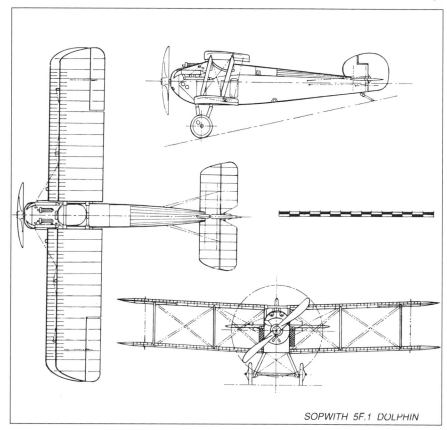

SOPWITH 5F.1 DOLPHIN

Type: Single-engine, single-seat, two-bay biplane fighter.
Manufacturers: The Sopwith Aviation Co Ltd, Kingston-upon-Thames, Surrey; The Darracq Motor Engineering Co Ltd, Fulham, London; Hooper & Co Ltd, London SW.1
Powerplant: Mark I: One 200hp Hispano-Suiza geared engine. Mark II: 300hp Hispano-Suiza direct-drive engine. Mark III: 200hp Hispano-Suiza direct-drive engine.
Structure: Wire-braced box-girder fuselage with spruce longerons and spacers. Twin spindled-spruce spars in back-staggered two-bay wings with steel tubular carry-through centre section structure in upper wing; cockpit located beneath this superstructure.
Dimensions: Span, 32ft 6in; length, 22ft 3in; height, 8ft 6in; wing area, 263.25 sq ft.
Weights: Tare, 1,410lb; all-up, 1,959lb.
Performance: Max speed, 136 mph at sea level, 114 mph at 15,000ft; climb to 10,000ft, 12 min 5 sec; service ceiling, 20,000ft.
Armament: Two synchronized 0.303in Vickers machine guns on top decking of nose with Constantinesco hydraulic interrupter gear; either one or two Lewis machine guns usually mounted on forward carry-through wing spar member. Provision to carry up to four 25lb bombs.
Prototypes: Believed to be three (the first probably flown at the beginning of June 1917). One prototype Mark II was D3615 (a modified Mark I).
Production: Total of 2,074 aircraft completed, excluding initial prototypes (Sopwith, 1,400: C3777-C4276, D3576-D3775, E4424-E4623 and E4629-E5128; Darracq, 365: C8001-C8200, F7034-F7133 and J151-J215; Hooper, 309: D5201-D5400 and J1-J109).
Summary of Service: Dolphins served operationally with Nos 19, 23, 79 and 87 Squadrons, RFC and RAF, in France; with No 141 Squadron, RFC, on Home Defence duties between January and March 1918; served non-operationally with Nos 81 and 123 Squadrons (these Squadrons became Nos 1 and 2 Squadrons, Canadian Air Force, respectively); and with Nos 90 and 91 Squadrons, RAF, non-operationally in the United Kingdom.

KCB, MC, AFC, RAF). To this Squadron fell the task of flying the Dolphin at night, and in this the aircraft was hopelessly unsuitable. Landing a Dolphin at any time was tricky enough, but judging height at night was found to be well-nigh impossible, and the aircraft quickly earned the sobriquet 'Blockbuster': if, as the result of a misjudged landing approach, the Dolphin overturned, the pilot, whose head projected above the upper wing, was in danger of being decapitated, or at least burned alive if the fuel tank immediately behind him ruptured. This hazard was to some extent reduced in February when Dolphins appeared with crash pylons of various designs above the wings or cockpit. So congested and confined was the Dolphin's cockpit that no Service pilot could ever express confidence that the aircraft had been designed with the safety and comfort of the pilot uppermost in mind.

Moreover, as with the S.E.5A, the length of time needed to warm up the Hispano engine rendered the Dolphin unsuitable for the intercepter rôle, and it was quickly replaced by the Bristol F.2B Fighter with Home Defence squadrons.

The first Squadron to re-equip with Dolphins in France during January 1918 was No 19 at Sainte Marie Capelle under Lt-Col William Douglas Stock Sanday DSO, MC. By the time the great German offensive opened on 21 March Nos 19, 23 and 79 Squadrons were operational in France, with No 87 arriving the following month. No 87 Squadron was to undertake offensive patrols during the final Allied push during September and October. In a combat typical of this period, Dolphins of No 19, escorting D.H.9 bombers of No 98 Squadron, were attacked by a large formation of enemy fighters; the British aircraft shot down ten of the enemy, but five Dolphins and four D.H.s were lost.

It had been intended to retain Dolphins in service as standardized equipment in the peacetime RAF but, although the quality and supply of the Hispano engine seemed to be under control at last, British engines seemed to be the logical choice. Two late variants of the Dolphin were the Mark II with the 300hp direct-drive Hispano-Suiza (and a maximum speed of about 146 mph at sea level), and the Mark III with 200hp direct-drive Hispano-Suiza. Of these, the Mark II was certainly the most promising, as demonstrated by the prototype, D3615, and was almost certainly the fastest fighter in 1918; moreover, being without the suspect reduction gears, the Hispano had become an altogether more reliable engine.

Nevertheless, it must be said that the previous delays and troubles besetting the Hispano-Suiza engines resulted in an extraordinary waste of money and effort on aircraft such as the Sopwith Dolphin, for almost three-quarters of all those built — over 2,000 of them — never left the storage depots, where they were awaiting their engines, before being scrapped.

Martinsyde F.1

Designed early in 1917, possibly by Tony Fletcher shortly before he left Martinsyde Ltd, the F.1 was the first of a new series of fighters which culminated in the Buzzard. It was clearly influenced by the Bristol F.2 Fighter, even to the extent of placing the fuselage in the wing gap and clear of the lower wing. It was a two-bay biplane, and in effect a scaled-up derivative of the successful G.100/102 Elephant, the airframe being strengthened to accommodate the new Rolls-Royce Mark III (Eagle III).

The broad-chord wings were rigged with slight stagger, and ailerons were fitted to upper and lower wings. The upper wing was clear of the top decking of the fuselage by some nine inches, while the lower wings were left uncovered below the fuselage, as on the Bristol F.2A; however, unlike the Bristol, the F.1's wings remained uncovered — resulting in unnecessary end drag.

The F.1 was officially declared to be a fighter, and it certainly possessed a fairly respectable performance for such a big single-engine aircraft. Nevertheless, a feature of the F.1, which drew puzzled comments from Martlesham

The Martinsyde F.1, A3933, the nature and proposed location of whose armament remains something of an enigma. (Photo: J M Bruce Collection)

following its trials in July 1917, was the location of the crew, the observer's cockpit being directly below the upper wing (with entry to it only possible through a large aperture in the wing's centre section); the pilot's cockpit was about five feet aft of the observer, well clear of the wing trailing edge and with precious little view forward. No armament was fitted in the prototype, A3933, and no logical suggestion indicated exactly what gun armament was proposed.

With the Bristol Fighter becoming firmly established in production, it was hardly surprising that development of the F.1 was not pursued further, and it is not known if the planned second prototype was even completed.

Type: Single-engine, two-seat, two-bay biplane fighter.
Manufacturer: Martinsyde Ltd, Brooklands, Surrey.
Powerplant: One 250hp Rolls-Royce Mark III (Eagle III) engine driving four-blade propeller.
Dimensions: Span: 44ft 6in; length, 29ft 1in; height, 8ft 6in; wing area, 467 sq ft.
Weights: Tare, 2,198lb; all-up, 3,260lb.
Performance: Max speed, approx 112 mph at sea level; climb to 10,000ft, 13 min 40 sec; service ceiling, 16,500ft; endurance, 3¾ hr.
Armament: None fitted in prototype.
Prototypes: Two ordered, A3933 and A3934 (A3933 flown in May 1917). No production.

Martinsyde F.2

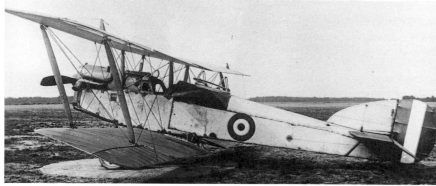

The *Martinsyde F.2* at Brooklands in 1917; just visible are the cutouts in the pilot's cockpit coaming, made to improve the view for landing. (Photo: P Jarrett)

The Martinsyde F.2 was produced almost simultaneously with the F.1, but was designed under the direction of E Bouillon, newly appointed chief designer of the company. Owing some obvious family resemblance to the previous Martinsyde fighters, the F.2 diverged from the widely influential Bristol F.2 Fighter in being a single-bay biplane and with the lower wing close up to the fuselage — although the rear spar was not directly attached to the lower longerons.

Unfortunately the aircraft's future was compromised from the start by the choice of a 200hp Hispano-Suiza engine, which would have had to be replaced in the event of a production order. The wings were well staggered and the top wing, unlike the F.1, was located well above the fuselage, and this time the pilot sat forward of the observer/gunner. However, when the aircraft underwent its trials in May 1917, it was criticised on account of the view from the pilot's cockpit, and in order to rectify this small cutouts were made in the side coamings in the front of the cockpit.

The dominance of the Bristol Fighter, sealed the fate of the Martinsyde F.2 which otherwise returned a fairly creditable performance. At least its conventional armament of a synchronized Vickers gun and a Scarff ring-mounted Lewis evoked no adverse comments.

Type: Single-engine, two-seat, single-bay biplane reconnaissance fighter.
Manufacturer: Martinsyde Ltd, Brooklands, Surrey.
Powerplant: One 200hp Hispano-Suiza engine driving two-blade propeller.
Dimensions: Span: 32ft 0in; length, 25ft 0in; height, 8ft 2in; wing area, 334 sq ft.
Weights: Tare, 1,547lb; all-up, 2,355lb.
Performance: Max speed, 120 mph at sea level; climb to 10,000ft, 13 min 30 sec; service ceiling, 17,000ft; endurance, 2½ hr.
Armament: One synchronized 0.303in Vickers machine gun mounted on nose, forward of pilot's cockpit and to port of aircraft's centreline, and one Lewis gun with Scarff ring on rear cockpit.
Prototype: Believed one only. (Assumed to have flown in May 1917 at Brooklands). No production.

Vickers F.B.25

The *Vickers F.B.25*, almost certainly at Joyce Green. As originally designed with a nose-mounted searchlight, the nacelle was some three feet longer, with an auxiliary nosewheel to prevent the aircraft from nosing over when landing. (Photo: via E B Morgan)

The resolute persistence with which Vickers continued to build derivatives of the outmoded Gunbus formula, two years after it had been shown to be thoroughly out of place in the presence of dedicated dogfighters, never fails to astonish historians, particularly when one remembers that the company had already demonstrated its ability to build promising tractor scouts in the course of those two years.

It can be argued that the Gunbus was always justified by the nature of its armament, and in the F.B.25 this was to consist of the experimental Vickers Crayford rocket gun. The aircraft was a two-bay staggered biplane, powered by a 150hp direct-drive Hispano-Suiza engine. The nacelle was fairly short, but sufficiently broad-beamed to accommodate the pilot and gunner almost side-by-side, — the gunner's position to starboard and staggered slightly forward

Type: Single pusher engine, two-seat, two-bay biplane night fighter.
Manufacturer: Vickers Ltd (Aviation Department), Knightsbridge, London.
Powerplant: One 150hp Hispano-Suiza direct-drive engine driving two-blade pusher propeller.
Dimensions: Span, 41ft 6in; length, 28ft 1in; height, 10ft 10in; wing area, 500 sq ft.
Weights: Tare, 1,608lb; all-up, 2,454lb.
Performance: Max speed, 91 mph at sea level, 84.5 mph at 10,000 ft; climb to 10,000ft, 27 min 10 sec; service ceiling, 11,500ft; endurance, 4½ hr.
Armament: One Vickers Crayford rocket gun in nose of nacelle.
Prototype: One (believed first flown in June 1917).

of the pilot. The upper wing possessed no centre section, the two halves meeting on the aircraft's centreline; the lower wing, however, included a separate centre section, to which the V-struts of the landing gear were attached.

Being proposed as an anti-airship night fighter, the F.B.25 was intended to include a ten-inch searchlight in the extreme nose, but all available evidence suggests that this was never fitted.

The sole example underwent trials at Martlesham Heath in late June or early July 1917 but crashed, possibly while landing in a strong wind (the report on the trials stated that, owing to poor controls, the aircraft proved to be 'almost unmanageable in a wind over 20 mph'. The serial number of this aircraft is not known, although a document, traced recently, refers to it as No '13, and it has been suggested that this may indicate A9813 (formerly a cancelled number intended for a Sopwith Triplane).

Vickers
F.B.26 Vampire

The Vickers F.B.26 Vampire Mk I, B1484, at Joyce Green in the configuration in which it underwent Service trials in July 1917 with the Eeman gun installation. (Photo: P T H Green Collection)

Another new Vickers pusher aircraft flown in 1917 was the single-seat F.B.26 (later named the Vampire), an altogether smaller aircraft than the F.B.25. It was originally designed as a day-fighting scout with a pair of Lewis guns in the extreme nose, and was powered by a 200hp Hispano-Suiza engine. As initially flown, the upper wing was, in characteristic Vickers fashion, devoid of centre section and the two halves were attached together on the aircraft's centreline. The Hispano was at first installed with its car-type radiator at the rear of the engine; this however gave inadequate cooling and after an equally ineffective trial with a pair of radiators mounted transversely under the upper wing rear spar, these radiators were mounted vertically on the sides of the fuselage — and this arrangement sufficed. Various other changes were made to the wings (including the addition of a centre section) and tail unit and a four-blade propeller was substituted.

An Eeman triple-Lewis gun mounting was incorporated in the nose, and the revised prototype, now numbered B1484, underwent official trials at Martlesham Heath in July, returning a speed of 124 mph at sea level and demonstrating a service ceiling of 20,500 feet. Being fitted with flare brackets, it seems clear that the aircraft was then being considered in the rôle of anti-airship night fighter, and its demonstrated performance would seem to have been consistent with this rôle, while an excellent field of vision was afforded the pilot. Shortly after the aircraft returned to Joyce Green, the entire Eeman gun installation was raised almost a foot, probably to facili-

tate re-loading the guns in flight, but the new location severely reduced the pilot's field of view and it was quickly discarded.

B1484 was to be destroyed in an accident on 25 August when it crashed from a spin shortly after taking off from Joyce Green, killing the famous pilot Harold Barnwell. A second aircraft, B1486, was built, probably during the autumn of 1917, also as a night fighter with the triple-gun Eeman installation. It was taken on charge by No 39 (Home Defence) Squadron at Woodford in October, and passed on to No 141 Squadron in February 1918, then at Biggin Hill; it was not much appreciated on account of poor flying qualities and the usual problem with the Hispano of lengthy warming up before take-off.

At least one other example, B1485, was built in 1918, this time powered by a 230hp Bentley B.R.2 rotary engine. This was intended as a trench fighter and featured 500 pounds of armour protection in the nacelle. The year 1918 also brought the official naming of military aircraft, Vickers aircraft being required to bear names beginning with 'V'; thus the Bentley-powered F.B.26A became the Vampire Mk II, and, in retrospect, the Hispano-powered F.B.26, the Vampire Mk I. By the time the Vampire Mk II underwent its Service trials by the RAF, however, the Sopwith Salamander had been ordered into production as the principal British trench fighter, and the Vickers aircraft was abandoned.

Type: Single pusher engine, single-seat, single-bay biplane night fighter (Vampire Mk I) and trench fighter (Vampire Mk II).

Manufacturer: Vickers Ltd (Aviation Department), Knightsbridge, London.

Powerplant: Vampire Mk I. 200hp Hispano-Suiza; Vampire Mk II, 230hp Bentley B.R.2 rotary engine.

Dimensions: Span, 31ft 6in; length (Vampire Mk I), 23ft 5in; height, 9ft 5in; wing area, 267 sq ft.

Weights: Vampire Mk I. Tare, 1,407lb; all-up, 2,030lb.

Performance: Vampire Mk I. Max speed, approx 124 mph at sea level; climb to 10,000ft, 9 min 54 sec; service ceiling, 20,500ft; endurance, 3 hr.

Armament: Originally two 0.303in Lewis machine guns in extreme nose, increased to three in Eeman mounting; Vampire Mk II had two Lewis guns in the nose.

Prototypes: Total of six ordered, B1484-B1489; B1484 and B1486 were Vampire Mk Is, and B1485 a Vampire Mk II. B1487-B1489 probably not built. No production.

Port Victoria P.V.5 and P.V.5A

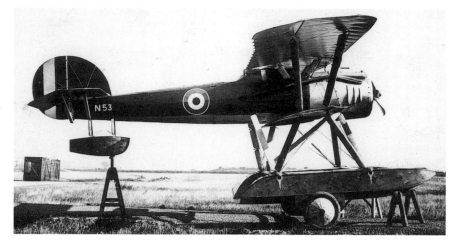

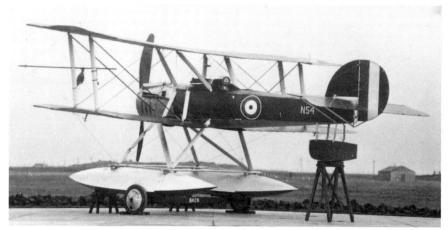

Upper photo: *The P.V.5, N53, showing the unusual annular cowling for the 150hp Hispano-Suiza engine, somewhat reminiscent of the Sopwith Hispano Triplane.* (Photo: Imperial War Museum, Neg No Q67579). *Lower photo: The P.V.5A, N54, with equal-span wings and Linton Hope floats at the time of its official trials in April 1918.* (Photo: G S Leslie /J M Bruce Collection)

At the beginning of 1917 the system of British aircraft procurement and supply came under scrutiny with a reorganization of the Air Board. This, among other things, led to the transfer of aircraft supply to the Ministry of Munitions, and the Admiralty's Experimental Construction Depot at Port Victoria hovered on the brink of extinction. At that time, two new aircraft were nearing completion, ordered by the Air Department to meet the need for a single-seat fighting scout seaplane, capable also of light bombing duties.

These aircraft, which differed markedly from each other, were the P.V.5 and P.V.5A; both had been designed for the 150hp Smith Static and were awaiting this engine when the Depot's future was threatened. In due course, owing to the non-delivery of the Smith engine, it was decided to go ahead with the P.V.5 with a 150hp Hispano-Suiza, but to abandon the P.V.5A. The former aircraft, N53, was an attractive twin-float sesquiplane, clearly based on the P.V.2, with the main floats and high-lift wings braced together with struts appearing as a 'W' when seen from the front. The engine was neatly enclosed in an unusual annular cowling with the faired valve covers just breaking the external contours. Although designed for Linton Hope floats, N53 was completed with flat-bottom pontoons, canted outwards so as to force water spray away from the propeller and engine radiator, and to provide some measure of shock absorption. A single synchronized Vickers gun was mounted immediately forward of the cockpit, and a pair of 65lb bombs could be carried in the fuselage.

It is said that the P.V.5 was first flown in July 1917, but did not undergo official trials until September. It proved very popular among its pilots, being manœuvrable and pleasant to fly. Climb and ceiling were, however, disappointing and the maximum speed was lower than specified in the Admiralty requirement.

Soon after these trials had been completed, it was decided to resurrect the P.V.5A — conventional by comparison with the P.V.5 in being a single-bay biplane with wings of equal span. The aircraft, N54, was completed around the end of 1917 with Linton Hope floats, and powered by a 200hp Hispano-Suiza. Completing its official trials in April 1918, it returned a much better performance than its predecessor, albeit sacrificing its pleasant flying qualities.

Not surprisingly, however, as almost eighteen months had elapsed since the issue of the original requirement, the Sopwith Baby, Pup and Camel had demonstrated their ability to meet almost all the Admiralty's shipborne aircraft scouting requirements, and any further need for the P.V.5s had disappeared.

Type: Single-engine, single-seat, twin-float sesquiplane (P.V.5) and single-bay biplane (P.V.5A) fighting scout/light bomber.

Manufacturer: RNAS Experimental Construction Depot, Port Victoria, Isle of Grain.

Powerplant: P.V.5. One 150hp Hispano-Suiza engine; P.V.5A. 200hp Hipano-Suiza.

Dimensions: P.V.5. Span, 32ft 0in; length, 25ft 6in; height, 9ft 9in; wing area, 245 sq ft. P.V.5A. Span, 33ft 1in; length, 26ft 9in; height, 13ft 1in; wing area, 309 sq ft.

Weights: P.V.5. Tare, 1,788lb; all-up, 2,456lb. P.V.5A. Tare, 1,974lb; all-up (no bombs), 2,518lb.

Performance: P.V.5. Max speed, 94.5 mph at sea level; climb to 6,500ft, 20 min 15 sec; service ceiling, 9,900ft. P.V.5A. Max speed, 102.5 mph at sea level; climb to 6,500ft, 9 min; service ceiling, 13,700ft.

Armament: Both aircraft armed with one synchronized 0.303in Vickers machine gun forward of cockpit on top decking. P.V.5 could carry two 65lb bombs.

Prototype: P.V.5, N53 (believed first flown in July 1917); P.V.5A, N54. No production.

Sopwith Bee

The diminutive Sopwith Bee at Brooklands in 1916. (Photo: A J Jackson Collection)

Sometime in mid-1916 the Sopwith factory found time and space to build a tiny biplane for the personal use of Harry Hawker as both a runabout and an aerobatic mount. Of extreme simplicity, the Sopwith Bee was powered by a 50hp Gnome seven-cylinder rotary engine, and its single-bay wings incorporated wing-warping for lateral control; the rudder was horn balanced.

In common with current Sopwith fighting scouts, every effort was made to concentrate the components of greatest mass in the smallest possible space around the aircraft's c.g., with the result that the cockpit was close up behind the engine and situated directly beneath the wing centre section; this required the provision of an enormous cutout in the upper wing, and in all probability the pilot's head protruded above the upper surface. A standard Pup undercarriage was fitted.

It was quite possible that the Admiralty's requirement for a very small scout, capable of operating from Torpedo-Boat Destroyers (and the appearance of the P.V.7 and P.V.8, see below) that prompted Sopwith to test the Bee in this context, and a single synchronized Vickers machine gun was fitted. However, no records of this venture appear to have survived, and no further development was undertaken.

Type: Single-engine, single-seat, single-bay aerobatic biplane, adapted as a fighting scout.

Manufacturer: The Sopwith Aviation Co Ltd, Brooklands, Surrey.

Powerplant: One 50hp Gnome seven-cylinder rotary engine driving two-blade propeller.

Dimensions: Span, 16ft 3in; length, 14ft 3in.

Armament: Later fitted with one synchronized 0.303in Vickers machine gun.

Port Victoria P.V.7 and P.V.8

Early in 1916 the Admiralty directed the Experimental Construction Depot at Port Victoria and the Experimental Flight at Eastchurch to examine the feasibility of producing a small scout capable of taking off from a very short platform aboard a Torpedo-Boat Destroyer, specifying the use of a geared 45hp ABC Gnat engine.

Both agencies produced independent designs, Capt W H Sayers RFC producing the P.V.7 at Port Victoria; at East-

church, Lieut G H Millar RNVR devised a rather different sort of aircraft. However, when Sqn Cdr H R Busteed moved from Eastchurch to assume command of Port Victoria, he took with him both

Millar and his design, which was then designated the P.V.8. To differentiate between their design origins, the P.V.7 came to be called the Grain Kitten, and the P.V.8 the Eastchurch Kitten.

Above: *The P.V.7 Grain Kitten, N539, whose good looks belied poor flying qualities.* (Photo: A J J Jackson Collection)

Left: *The Eastchurch Kitten, N540, after the addition of a fixed tailplane; note the ailerons on upper and lower wings. The Lewis gun could not be fired at the angle shown here as it was not synchronized.* (Photo: G S Leslie / J M Bruce Collection)

The P.V.7 was unquestionably the more attractive of the two, with sesquiplane wings, outward canted and paired interplane struts, gracefully tapering fuselage in plan and low aspect ratio ailerons on the top wing only. There was a spigot-mounted Lewis gun above the wing. However, tested first on 22 June 1917, the P.V.7 proved difficult to handle on the ground, and tail-heavy in the air; moreover the sesquiplane layout, with high-lift wings, was shown to be unsuitable for the tiny aeroplane.

By contrast, the aesthetically less-pleasing Eastchurch Kitten was much more successful. It featured heavily staggered single-bay wings of equal span employing I-form interplane and cabane struts from a crashed Sopwith Triplane, and when first flown on 7 September, it featured a balanced elevator without fixed tailplane. The pilot, Harry Busteed himself, reported severe longitudinal instability, with the result that a fixed tailplane was added, and much of the elevator horn balance was removed. To provide some shock absorption during landing, very big landing wheels with large-section tyres were fitted.

As with almost all Port Victoria's aircraft, the engines promised for the two Kittens never materialised, and both aircraft had to be modified to take the direct-drive 35hp version of the ABC Gnat. This engine, designed by Granville Bradshaw, was an ingenious horizontally-opposed twin-cylinder air-cooled engine weighing 115lb dry. Yet, despite the obvious success of the P.V.8, and the ease with which it could be flown, interest in the idea was short-lived.

Type: Single-engine, single-seat, single-bay lightweight biplane scout.
Manufacturer: RNAS Experimental Construction Depot, Port Victoria, Isle of Grain.
Powerplant: One direct-drive 35hp ABC Gnat horizontally-opposed two-cylinder air-cooled engine.
Dimensions: P.V.7. Span, 18ft 0in; length, 14ft 11in; height, 5ft 3in; wing area, 85 sq ft. P.V.8. Span, 18ft 0in; length, 15ft 7½in; height, 5ft 5in; wing area, 106 sq ft.
Armament: Both aircraft equipped to carry one 0.303in Lewis gun above wing centre section.
Prototypes: P.V.7, N539 (first flown by H R Busteed on 22 June 1917). P.V.8, 540 (first flown by Busteed on 7 September 1917). No production.

Austin-Ball A.F.B.1

Captain Albert Ball was still only nineteen years of age in April 1916, while flying B.E.2Cs on reconnaissance flights over the Western Front with No 13 Squadron, RFC. In a letter, written that month to his parents he tells of his idea for an aircraft 'better than the Fokker'. Several months later, while on leave in England, Ball met representatives of the Austin Motor Company, who in turn approached the Air Board to seek an order to build two examples of Ball's aircraft. It was, however, Ball himself who secured the order by going straight to Maj-Gen Sefton Brancker, Director of Air Organisation.

It is a quirk of irony that, when Ball expressed his first ideas for his fighter, he had not yet been in combat, yet by the time the Austin-Ball A.F.B.1 was ready for flight in July 1917, the young pilot had been dead for two months — killed on active service on 7 May after gaining a total of 44 air victories and being awarded the Victoria Cross, three DSOs and the MC, all before his 21st birthday.

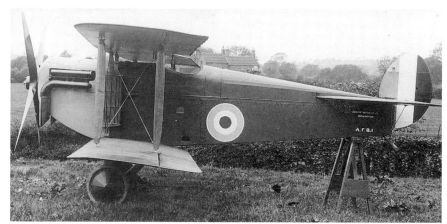

The Austin-Ball A.F.B.1. It has often been incorrectly suggested that the aircraft possessed anhedral on the wings, probably stemming from an optical illusion created by the small sweepback on the parallel-chord surfaces. (Photo: A J Jackson Collection)

Ball's aircraft reflected his particular style of combat, a fast single-seater and an upward-firing gun with which to rake an enemy aircraft from below. It was a portly, single-bay biplane, powered by the 200hp Hispano-Suiza, and armed with one Lewis gun firing through the hollow propeller shaft and another on a Foster mounting on the upper wing. A well-shaped nose cowling was made possible by mounting the engine radiators on the fuselage sides, while the deep fuselage allowed the top wing to be located close to the fuselage — thereby providing the pilot with an excellent field of view over the wing, and at the same time retaining a good wing gap. The only significant criticism levelled at the design concerned the absence of a fixed tail fin, a deficiency that was evidenced by poor lateral control, although the rudder was balanced.

When first tested at Martlesham Heath in July 1917, the un-numbered A.F.B.1

Type: Single-engine, single-seat, single-bay biplane fighting scout.
Manufacturer: The Austin Motor Co (1914) Ltd, Birmingham.
Powerplant: One 200hp Hispano-Suiza engine driving four-blade propeller.
Dimensions: Span, 30ft 0in; length, 21ft 6in; height, 9ft 3in; wing area, 290 sq ft.
Weights: Tare, 1,525lb; all-up, 2,077lb.
Performance: Max speed, 138 mph at sea level; climb to 10,000ft, 8 min 55 sec; service ceiling, 22,000ft; endurance, 2¼ hr.
Armament: One 0.303in Lewis machine gun firing through hollow propeller shaft, and one Lewis gun on Foster mounting on upper wing centre section.
Prototype: Two A.F.B.1s were ordered, but it is believed that the second was not completed. No production.

returned the excellent top speed of 138 mph at sea level, and could reach 10,000 feet in under nine minutes. While this performance was at least comparable with that of the the the S.E.5A, and superior to the Camel, the forward armament of a hub-firing Lewis gun — though radi-

cal by 1916 standards — was not favoured in an era of twin synchronized Vickers. Nevertheless, there was more irony in the fact that Ball never became fully reconciled with the S.E.5 (preferring the nimble Nieuport), yet his aircraft was clearly conceived along similar

lines. Moreover there is some circumstantial evidence to suggest that it was in recognition of Austin's perseverence with the A.F.B.1 that the company was awarded a huge production contract — for over 800 *S.E.5As*!

Avro Type 530

It might be contended that the secret of success enjoyed by the Bristol F.2B Fighter was due to two circumstances, namely that it had already been developed into an aircraft for which there was a demand before any would-be competitor, and that it avoided using the Hispano-Suiza engine. Almost every one of those other challengers, as has been shown, favoured the Hispano engine and, as a result, were defeated by the prior claims on its faltering supply on behalf of the S.E.5.

The Avro 530 was just one more such aircraft which fell victim of the short supply of Hispano engines. The aircraft was directly comparable with the Bristol Fighter and was, if anything, slightly superior in some aspects of performance. Built at Avro's works in Manchester and first flown at Hamble in Hampshire in July 1917, it featured a 200hp Hispano-Suiza engine with a frontal radiator, all enclosed in an annular cowling; cooling airflow to the radiator passed through a large spinner which itself improved the shape of the nose. The deep fuselage was a wire-braced wooden box-girder, fabric-covered and formed to improved aerodynamic shape by secondary stringers. The wooden, two-bay, two-spar wings of RAF 14 section were also fabric-covered and not only included ailerons, but also underwing trailing-edge flaps on upper and lower wings for landing — the latter being operated by a handwheel in the pilot's cockpit.

Unfortunately the fuselage was so deep that, in placing the upper wing in line with the pilot's eye level — so as to achieve the best possible field of view upwards and downwards — the wing scarcely cleared the upper decking of the front fuselage; this was further aggravated by fairing over the single forward-firing synchronized Vickers gun. Careful attention to detail elsewhere in-

The Avro 530 with 200hp Hispano-Suiza engine. (Photo: British Aerospace plc, Manchester)

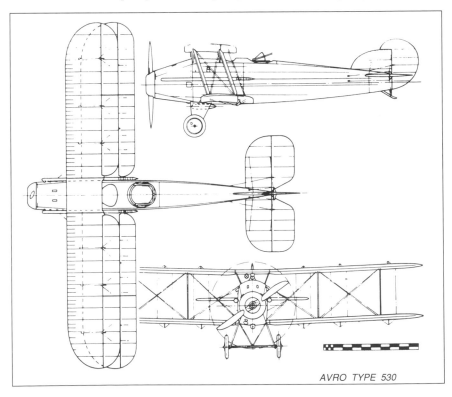

AVRO TYPE 530

Type: Single-engine, two-seat, two-bay biplane fighter.

Manufacturer: A V Roe & Co Ltd, Manchester.

Powerplant: One 200hp Hispano-Suiza engine driving two-blade propeller; later one 200hp Sunbeam Arab engine.

Dimensions: Span, 36ft 0in; length, 28ft 6in; height, 9ft 7in; wing area, 325.5 sq ft.

Weights: Tare, 1,695lb; all-up, 2,500lb.

Performance: Max speed, 114 mph at sea level; climb to 10,000ft, 15 min; service ceiling, 18,000ft; endurance, 4 hr.

Armament: One synchronized 0.303in Vickers machine gun faired on nose, forward of the pilot's cockpit; one Lewis gun with Scarff ring on the rear cockpit.

Prototype: One, first flown in July 1917. No production.

cluded fairing the undercarriage V-struts together to provide a single aerodynamic member on each side.

Only one example of the Type 530 was completed, and it became immediately obvious that the aircraft possessed no future while fitted with the Hispano-Suiza engine, even though the engine for which the Avro was designed was the 300hp version. The sole prototype was therefore extensively modified to incorporate the 200hp Sunbeam Arab eight-cylinder water-cooled in-line engine. The landing flaps were removed in favour of lengthened ailerons, and the fairings were removed from the undercarriage V-struts.

However, by the time these changes had been made, production of the well-established Bristol Fighter — a much-liked aircraft among its crews — had accelerated to an impressive rate, and there could therefore be no question of introducing a new aircraft with untried operational qualities.

R.A.F. N.E.1

Conceived with the same purpose in mind as the slightly earlier Vickers F.B.25 (see page 107), the Royal Aircraft Factory's lanky N.E.1 (Night Experimental) made little pretence at elegance. Intended initially as a night anti-airship fighter, it was a three-bay biplane powered by a 200hp Hispano-Suiza engine driving a four-blade pusher propeller in the best Gunbus tradition. The tailbooms, parallel in plan, converged in side elevation to the mainspar of the tailplane, to which was hinged a heavily horn-balanced elevator. A semi-circular fixed fin was mounted symmetrically and centrally on the tailplane and forward of an unbalanced rudder.

The nacelle was located within the wing gap, clear of the lower wing, but the space between nacelle and upper wing was occupied by the engine's radiator. The divided undercarriage was of very wide track to assist night landing, the oleo struts being anchored directly below the inboard interplane struts.

The starkly functional nacelle mounted a ten-inch searchlight in the extreme nose, and would be operated by the pilot who occupied the front of the cockpit, with the gunner behind him. The principal armament was proposed as being either the Coventry Ordnance Works

The N.E.1, B3971, at Farnborough in its original configuration, but without any armament mounted. (Photo: Royal Aerospace Establishment, Neg No 2736, dated 19 September 1917)

quick-firing gun or the Vickers Crayford rocket gun, supplemented by either one or two spigot-mounted Lewis guns. An unusual piece of equipment was a radio telephony installation.

A total of six N.E.1s was built, and the first, B3971, is believed to have flown in mid-September 1917. Despite its cumbersome gait, it was found to be simple to fly and land, though its speed was far from outstanding. The aircraft under-went official trials in November that year.

A number of design variations appeared in subsequent examples. The fin shape was revised on at least one aircraft, and the searchlight was omitted from others in which the bow position was occupied by the gunner, with the pilot aft. All aircraft were confined to experimental flying, with the last pair being completed in 1918.

Type: Single pusher engine, two-seat, three-bay biplane night fighter.
Manufacturer: The Royal Aircraft Factory, Farnborough, Hampshire.
Powerplant: One 200hp Hispano-Suiza engine driving four-blade pusher propeller.
Dimensions: Span, 47ft 10in; length, 30ft 2in; height, 9ft 2in; wing area, 555.1 sq ft.
Weights: Tare, 2,071lb; all-up, 2,946lb.
Performance: Max speed, 95 mph at 10,000ft; climb to 10,000ft, 16 min 10 sec; service ceiling, 17,500ft; endurance, 2¾ hr.
Armament: One Vickers Crayford rocket gun or one Coventry Ordnance Works quick-firing gun; either one or two spigot-mounted Lewis guns.
Prototypes: Six, B3971-B3976. First flight by B3971 believed to have been in mid-September 1917. No production.

Mann, Egerton H.1 and H.2

The Norwich car manufacturer, Mann, Egerton & Co, entered the aircraft industry in 1915 and became engaged in building Short Type 184 patrol sea-planes on sub-contract, going on to produce a small number of an improved version of this aircraft, known as the Mann, Egerton Type B. Other sub-contracted aircraft followed, including the French Spad S.VII, and in 1917 the company embarked on an aircraft entirely of its own origin, designed by J W Carr and intended to approximate to the Admiralty requirement for a naval land or ship-based single-seat scout, set out in Specification N.1A — to which the Beardmore W.B.IV was also being designed. An important aspect of this requirement was the aircraft's ability to remain afloat for a specified period after an enforced alighting on the water.

This aeroplane was the Mann, Egerton H.1, a compact two-bay, equal-span biplane powered by a 200hp Hispano-Suiza engine and with the facility of wing-folding for shipboard stowage. To

Left: *The Mann, Egerton H.1, N44, displaying its large buoyancy chambers under the fuselage and wingtips.* Below: *The H.2, N45. Small biplanes of the First World War, equipped with folding wings, seldom featured any stagger owing to the difficulty of maintaining rigidity of structure on asymmetric lines of fold, not to mention the complexity of tensioning of control runs to the ailerons.* (Photos: G S Leslie / J M Bruce Collection)

enable the aircraft to ditch in greater safety, the undercarriage was jettisonable and, to remain afloat, a large external buoyancy chamber was attached below the engine cowling, extending aft beyond the trailing edge of the lower wings. In addition, there were floats under the lower wingtips.

The only prototype H.1, N44, was flown in late September or early October by Clifford B Prodger, followed almost immediately by its official trials. All went well to begin with, it being pleasant to fly and manœuvrable, and even declared suitable for night flying. Unfortunately it failed the flotation test.

A second aircraft, the H.2 (N45) was immediately put in hand, fundamentally the same as N44 but without external buoyancy chambers; instead, internal inflatable air bags were provided, which could be trimmed by hand pump. The engine exhaust pipes were shortened considerably, and the rudder was increased in area and horn balanced.

The discarding of the external impedimenta allowed a significant all-round increase in performance. The H.2 was officially tested in December and flew at the Isle of Grain, but no production order was awarded.

Type: Single-engine, single-seat, two-bay land-based or shipborne biplane scout.
Manufacturer: Mann, Egerton & Co Ltd, Norwich, Norfolk.
Powerplant: One 200hp Hispano-Suiza engine driving two-blade propeller.
Dimensions: Span, 30ft 9in; length, 21ft 11in; height, 8ft 11½ in; wing area, 310 sq ft.
Weights: H.1. Tare, 1,838lb; all-up, 2,404lb. H.2. Tare, 1,760lb; all-up, 2,326lb.
Performance: H.1. Max speed, 100 mph at 6,500ft; climb to 10,000ft, 18 min; service ceiling, 12,800ft; H.2. Max speed, 113 mph at 6,500ft; climb to 10,000ft, 12 min 30 sec; service ceiling, 16,800ft.
Armament: One synchronized 0.303in Vickers machine gun on fuselage, forward of cockpit, offset to port; one Lewis gun above upper wing centre section.
Prototypes: One H.1, N44, and one H.2, N45. N44 was first flown in late September or early October 1917. No production.

Robey Peters Three-Seater

It will be recalled that the Lincoln company of Robey & Co had produced a pair of single-seat scouts to the design of J A Peters during 1915 (see page 52), but that neither had succeeded in attracting significant official attention. A year later the company was encouraged to offer prototypes, under Admiralty sponsorship, of an anti-airship fighter armed with the Davis 2-pounder recoilless quick-firing gun.

This time Peters evolved a large three-bay, three-seat tractor biplane,

The Robey-Peters Three-Seater. Although the field of view provided for the two gunners could hardly have been better, that from the pilot's cockpit left much to be desired. (Photo: Ministry of Defence, Royal Aerospace Establishment, Farnborough)

powered by a 250hp Rolls-Royce (Eagle) engine driving a two-blade propeller. The fuselage was located more or less centrally within the wing gap, and two gunners' nacelles were attached, under-slung beneath the upper wing, it being intended to provide a Davis gun on each. A very sturdy, but rather narrow-track undercarriage, with central skid, was braced to the front fuselage and through the lower wing to the lower fuselage longerons. A well-proportioned, curved fin and balanced rudder lent a facade of elegance to the big aeroplane.

Perhaps the least attractive feature of the design — particularly for the pilot — was the location of his cockpit, only two feet forward of the tail fin. As if to acknowledge the exceptionally poor field of view from this position, large transparent panels were provided in the sides of the cockpit. No windscreen was fitted; instead a spine fairing (of the same contours as the faired headrest) was continued forward of the cockpit. The only explanation for the curious location

of the pilot's cockpit so far aft seems to be that of weight distribution.

Of the two prototypes ordered, the first (believed to be No 9498) was not ready for flight until fairly late in 1917 owing to a low priority for delivery of the Rolls-Royce engine. However, there came anti-climax when the machine crashed on its maiden flight, and the

venture was abandoned — presumably without completion of the second prototype.

Peters left Robey shortly afterwards and the following year became chief designer for The Alliance Aeroplane Company of Luton; in 1919 he produced an aircraft intended for the Atlantic Flight competition.

Type: Single-engine, three-seat, three-bay biplane fighter.
Manufacturer: Robey & Co Ltd, Lincoln.
Powerplant: One 250hp Rolls-Royce (Eagle) engine driving two-blade propeller.
Dimensions: Span, 54ft 6in; length, 29ft 6in.
Armament: Two two-pounder Davis recoilless guns intended for gunners' nacelles on upper wing. Probably never fitted.
Prototypes: Two, Nos 9498 and 9499. Only 9498 believed completed.

Alcock A.1

Flight-Lieut John W Alcock (later to be knighted for his epic first non-stop flight across the Atlantic) was serving with No 2 Wing, RNAS, at Mudros in the Aegean during the summer of 1917 when he built a small biplane scout, variously referred to as the Alcock A.1 and 'Sopwith Mouse'. Many of the design calculations were performed by Cdr Constantine of the Greek Navy at Mudros.

Alcock's fighter employed numerous components from crashed aircraft, including the fuselage, undercarriage and most of the lower wing from a Sopwith Triplane, and the upper wing of a Pup, into which was inserted a new centre section with cutout. A 100hp Gnome *monosoupape* engine drove a two-blade propeller, and the two-bay wings were rigged without effective stagger, the interplane struts converging downwards owing to the considerable difference in the two wing chords. It is not known whether the vertical tail surfaces (dorsal and ventral fins, and unbalanced rudder) were newly constructed or salvaged components, but the tailplane and elevator bear a similarity to those of the Pup.

The fuselage was located roughly in the centre of the wing gap, clear of the lower wing, with the new centre section

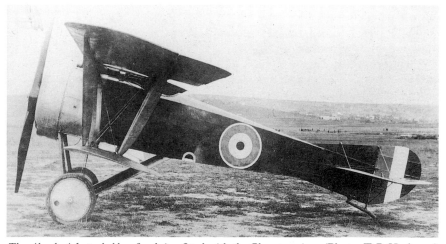

The Alcock A.1, probably after being fitted with the Clerget engine. (Photo: T R Hackman)

of the upper wing level with the pilot's horizontal line of sight. Twin synchronized Vickers guns were mounted forward of the cockpit.

Contrary to the account in the official history (*The War in the Air, Vol. 5*), Alcock did not fly his aircraft, being shot down in a Handley Page O/400 and

captured by the Turks on 30 September 1917, before its completion. Nevertheless it was subsequently flown, probably on 15 October by Wing Capt Francis Rowland Scarlett (later Air Vice-Marshal, CB, DSO, RAF), and was later destroyed when it was struck on the ground by a D.H.4 at Mudros.

Type: Single-engine, single-seat, two-bay biplane fighting scout.
Manufacturer: Flight-Lieut J W Alcock, RNAS, and personnel of No 2 Wing, RNAS, Mudros.
Powerplant: One 100hp Gnome *monosoupape* engine driving two-blade propeller; later fitted with 110hp Clerget engine.
Armament: Two synchronized 0.303in Vickers machine guns.

The Author is indebted to Mr J M Bruce for permission to reproduce the above material, which represents the result of research among former members of No 2 Wing, RNAS. The official history also incorrectly states that the Alcock A.1 was powered by a captured Benz engine.

Bristol M.R.1

In mid-1916 the British & Colonial

Aeroplane Co was asked by the War Office to examine the possibility of producing an all-metal version of the Bristol F.2A that would be more suitable for service in the Middle East than

the contemporary wooden aircraft.

A preliminary scheme was prepared by Frank Barnwell in July that year, and this was later passed to W T Reid to develop into reality. Though by no

A Bristol Type 13 M.R.1, fitted with the metal wings and carrying the spurious number A58623 at the time of ground tests in 1918. (Photo: A J Jackson Collection)

means the first metal aeroplane in Britain or elsewhere, much of Reid's work was of a truly pioneering nature, and the final design incorporated numerous innovative features that became the subject of patents held jointly by Reid and his employers.

Two prototypes were ordered, but the first, A5177, was not completed until October 1917, and was delivered initially with wooden wings. A5177 superficially resembled the Bristol F.2A, particularly as the lower wing section, located below the fuselage, was an open structure. Power was provided by a 150hp Hispano-Suiza mounted on steel tubular bearers bolted to the front of all four longerons. The fuselage was constructed in four sections, each a wire-braced steel tubular box girder, bolted together and covered with aluminium sheet. No attempt was made to include double-curvature sheeting, but local strengthening was achieved by riveting sections of corrugated aluminium on the inside of the skin, thereby maintaining a smooth external finish. The steel wings, built by the Steel Wing company of Cheltenham, were fabric covered (as were the tail surfaces), and the interplane and cabane struts were of steel

tube, hot rolled to slim elongated section; Raf-wires were widely employed.

At one time it was intended to fit wings constructed on the Mayrow principle with composite steel and duralumin sub-structure and, although such wings were subjected to static tests, it is unlikely that they were flown on an M.R.1.

First flown by Capt Barnwell, A5177 was delivered to representatives of the Air Board on 23 October, but the steel wings were not completed until 1918,

when the first set appeared on the second prototype, A5178, followed later on A5177. A5178 was also fitted with a 180hp Wolseley Viper engine.

Apart from the obvious lessons learned in the design of predominantly metal aeroplanes, the two M.R.1s provided a great deal of information about the specialised tools and manufacturing techniques essential for any largescale switch to metal aircraft — a field in which their manufacturers would in due course take a leading part.

Type: Experimental single-engine, two-seat, two-bay biplane fighter.
Manufacturer: The British & Colonial Aeroplane Co Ltd, Brislington, Bristol.
Powerplant: One 150hp Hispano-Suiza engine driving two-blade propeller; also 180hp Wolseley Viper engine.
Structure: All-metal construction. Fuselage of steel tubular box-girder construction with aluminium semi-monocoque sheet covering. Two-spar wings using rolled high-tensile steel strip with fabric covering.
Dimensions: Span, 42ft 2in; length, 27ft 0in; height, 10ft 3in; wing area, 458 sq ft.
Weights: Tare, 1,700lb; all-up, 2,810lb.
Performance: Max speed, 110 mph at sea level; climb to 10,000ft, 20 min.
Armament: One synchronized 0.303in Vickers machine gun mounted to fire through tunnel in the top engine cowling; one Lewis gun with Scarff ring on rear cockpit amidships.
Prototypes: Two, A5177 and A5178 (first flight by A5177 in October 1917). One of these aircraft carried a spurious number, A58623, during ground tests in 1918. No production.

Beardmore W.B.IV

Encouraged no doubt by the Admiralty's ready acceptance of radical features in his W.B.III (see page 101), Tilghman Richards of William Beardmore pursued another naval fighter of even more unusual ingenuity — this time in a two-bay biplane of the Company's own design, intended to meet Specification N.1A. In order to achieve stability while floating on the sea, following an emergency ditching, not only was the undercarriage capable of being jettisoned but the engine, a 200hp Hispano-Suiza, was located behind the pilot and on the aircraft's centre of gravity, driving the tractor propeller by an extension shaft which passed between the pilot's feet. The radiator was placed behind the engine, mounted between

The Beardmore W.B.IV, N38, with its midships engine location, aft of the pilot's cockpit. (Photo: The Science Museum, London)

the rear interplane struts.

The pilot was afforded an excellent all-round field of view, his cockpit being raised high in the nose of the aircraft, forward of the wings, and was watertight below the coaming. The fuselage was

unusual in itself in being entirely plywood-clad, and another innovation was the provision of a large flotation chamber faired into the underside of the nose and projecting on each side to form a large lateral buoyancy surface. When the

W.B.IV first appeared, it also featured floats faired under each lower wingtip. For shipboard stowage the wings could be folded back.

Three W.B.IVs were ordered by the Admiralty, but only one, N38, came to be built. Flown late in 1917, this sole example was delivered to the RNAS Isle of Grain station for trials which may have included ditching tests without the wing floats fitted. At all events the aircraft was damaged while alighting on the water, the nose buoyancy chamber being damaged with the result that N38 sank.

Many contemporary observers considered the W.B.IV to have been one of the most advanced aircraft produced during the First World War with regard to its innovative, yet practical features.

It was, after all, the first British aircraft in which the engine drove a tractor propeller by means of an extension shaft — pre-dating aircraft such as the Westland F.7/30 by at least fifteen years. Its top speed of only 110 mph was, however, considered disappointing by the standards set by contemporary scouts and no production was ordered.

Type: Single-engine, single-seat, two-bay shipborne fighting scout biplane.
Manufacturer: William Beardmore & Co Ltd, Dalmuir, Dunbartonshire.
Admiralty Specification: N.1A (of 1917)
Powerplant: One 200hp Hispano-Suiza water-cooled in-line engine driving two-blade propeller through an extension shaft.
Construction: All-wood construction with ply-covered fuselage. Jettisonable undercarriage and folding wings. Buoyancy chamber incorporated under the front fuselage.
Dimensions: Span, 35ft 10in; length, 26ft 6in; height, 9ft 10½in; wing area, 350 sq ft.
Weights: Tare, 2,055lb; all-up, 2,595lb.
Performance: Max speed, 110 mph at sea level; climb to 5,000ft, 7 min; service ceiling, 14,000ft; endurance, 2½ hr.
Armament: One fixed, synchronized 0.303in Vickers machine gun in port side of nose with breech inside cockpit; and one 0.303in Lewis gun on tripod mounting above the pilot's windscreen.
Prototypes: Three ordered (N38—N40) but only N38 completed and flown (1917).

Westland N.1B

Origins of the Westland Aircraft Works at Yeovil lay firmly in the production of naval aircraft. For two years, since the company's formation in 1915, the factory had been building Short 184 and 166 seaplanes, as well as Sopwith 1½-Strutters under the management of Robert Arthur Bruce (late of Sopwith), and in 1917 he and Arthur Davenport embarked on the design of a small fighter seaplane, intended to meet the Admiralty requirement N.1B.

Two prototype seaplanes were produced, N16 and N17. They were two-bay biplanes, powered by 150hp Bentley B.R.1 rotary engines. There was provision for wing folding for shipboard stowage, and the floats were interchangeable with landing wheels.

N16 was completed in October 1917 with a pair of short Sopwith floats, to which was added a tail float, mounted on struts beneath the rear fuselage; a small water rudder was hinged to an extension rod from the flying rudder directly above. Camber-changing flaps were carried below the trailing edges of upper and lower wings. Armament comprised a synchronized Vickers gun enclosed in a fairing on the nose decking, and a free-firing Lewis gun was mounted above the upper wing centre section. Racks for two 65lb bombs could be attached below the fuselage.

The second aircraft, N17, differed principally in the float arrangement.

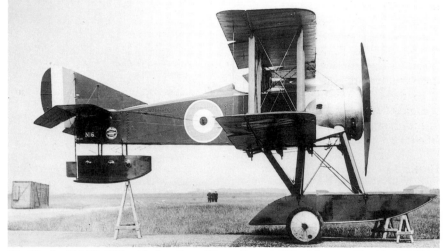
The Westland N.1B, N16, with short floats. (Photo: Imperial War Museum Neg No MH2886)

Much longer Westland-designed floats were fitted, with adequate length to obviate the need for a tail float. Other changes included the omission of the wing flaps and removal of the fairing over the Vickers gun. N17 was also fitted with the Sopwith floats for a short period to provide a basis for comparison.

Flown on test by Cdr J W Seddon at the Isle of Grain, the Westland sea-planes performed well, and certainly showed themselves superior to the Sopwith Baby. However, with the ability of the Sopwith Pup (to be followed by the Camel) to operate from very short platforms aboard ship and with a wheel undercarriage, the Admiralty was beginning to express less interest in seaplane scouts, and Westland was unlucky not to receive a production contract.

Type: Single-engine, single-seat, twin-float, two-bay biplane scout.
Manufacturer: The Westland Aircraft Works, Yeovil, Somerset.
Admiralty Specification: N.1B of 1917.
Powerplant: One 150hp Bentley B.R.1 rotary engine driving two-blade propeller.
Structure: Wooden construction throughout, with fabric covering.
Dimensions: Span, 31ft 3½in; length, 25ft 5½in; height, 11ft 2in; wing area, 278 sq ft.
Weights: Tare, 1,504ln; all-up, 1,978lb.
Performance: Max speed, 108 mph at sea level; climb to 10,000ft, 28 min 40 sec.
Armament: One synchronized 0.303in Vickers machine gun on nose, and one Lewis gun above centre section of upper wing.
Prototypes: Two, N16 and N17 (first flown in October 1917). No production.

Martinsyde F.3

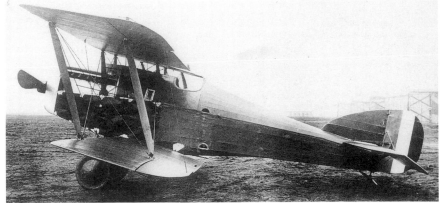

The attractive Martinsyde F.3, showing the neatly faired fuselage below the cockpit evolved to cover the lower wing's rear spar attachment. (Photo: G Kinsey)

Realising that to persevere with the two-seat fighter would likely lead nowhere, with official determination to introduce the Bristol F.2B Fighter into widespread production, George Handasyde returned to the single-seater and, in the F.3, produced what was widely regarded as an outstanding aircraft. Once more, however, he was to be frustrated by the absence of the right engine at the right time.

The F.3 has been described as having the appearance of a 'cleaned-up' S.E.5A, with fastidious attention paid to minor details. The single-bay wings possessed considerable stagger (24 inches), a feature that placed the lower rear spar rather far aft under the lower longerons; yet by careful fairing, Handasyde avoided an untidy 'step' in the under fuselage contours. The twin Vickers guns were concealed within the upper nose decking and, by and large, the pilot was provided with a good field of view.

Six F.3s were ordered during the late summer of 1917 and the first, B1490, flew in November with a non-standard Rolls-Royce Falcon which developed 285hp and which was installed without radiator shutters. The aircraft was officially tested the same month, being reported on with some enthusiasm and returning a top speed of 142 mph level.

Early in 1918, a standard Falcon III was installed in the F.3 and tested in May; this time radiator shutters were included and the performance was found to have suffered slightly — although one assumes that the pilot had more control of engine temperatures. Nevertheless, with production of Rolls-Royce engines by then stretched to the limit, there was no likelihood of the F.3 being ordered into production. Accordingly the design underwent changes to accommodate the 300hp Hispano-Suiza engine, and the aircraft emerged as the F.4 Buzzard (see page 137).

Type: Single-engine, single-seat, single-bay biplane fighter.
Manufacturer: Martinsyde Ltd, Brooklands, Surrey.
Powerplant: One 285hp Rolls-Royce Falcon experimental; later 275hp Rolls-Royce Falcon III.
Dimensions: Span, 32ft 10in; length, 25ft 8in; height, 8ft 8in; wing area, 320 sq ft.
Weights: Tare, 1,790lb; all-up, 2,325lb.
Performance: Max speed, 142 mph at sea level; climb to 10,000ft, 6 min 50 sec; service ceiling, 24,000ft.
Armament: Two synchronized 0.303in Vickers machine guns in upper nose decking.
Prototypes: Six, B1490-B1495. B1490 first flown in November 1917.
Summary of Service: Four F.3s recorded as having been delivered to Home Defence units in 1918.

Sopwith Snipe

The opinion, frequently expressed, that the Sopwith Snipe was 'the best British fighter' to be produced during the First World War, needs careful qualification. It was certainly the most highly developed Sopwith fighter to reach combat status before the Armistice. It did not, however, possess the best performance among British fighters in service at that time, although it inherited the superb manoeuvrability of the Camel, the aircraft it was designed to replace. Moreover that manoeuvrability was achieved with more tolerance of control mishandling than was the case in the Camel.

The extravagant claims for the Snipe were probably to some extent made on account of the isolated instances of outstanding combat success — not least that in which Maj W G Barker won the Victoria Cross only fifteen days before the Armistice. Furthermore, the fact that the decision to adopt the Snipe as the RAF's standard single-seat fighter during the years immediately following the coming of peace suggested that it

The second 7F.1 Snipe prototype, B9963, with single-bay wings and 250hp Bentley B.R.2 rotary engine. (Photo: J M Bruce Collection)

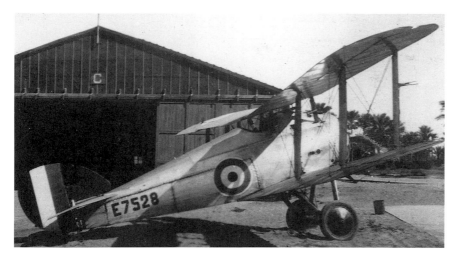

Snipe E7528 of No 25 (Fighter) Squadron deployed to San Stephano in Italy during the Chanak Crisis in 1922. (Photo: RAF Museum, Neg No P004052)

was the best available. The reasoning that lay behind this decision was that relatively large numbers of Snipes had been stockpiled during the last six months of the War, and that many of the planned manufacturers wished to opt out of the aircraft industry on the coming of peace. Sopwith itself occupied extensive factory space in Kingston and was apparently well staffed to continue with aircraft production in the long term. (It could not be foreseen that, within two years of the War's end, T O M Sopwith would face crippling tax demands on War Profits and be forced into voluntary liquidation, nor that his pilot and close colleague, Harry Hawker, would step in to save the Canbury Park Road offices and shops with the formation of the H G Hawker Engineering Company. Although Hawker was to lose his life in the same year that his company was formed, that company was to return to the aircraft industry through the revenue earned from repairing and rebuilding Snipes for the RAF in the early 1920s.)

Be that as it may, the Snipe was an excellent and highly adaptable fighter which shouldered a difficult task during the RAF's transition from war to peace. It should not be forgotten that an extremely high proportion of the RAF's fighter pilots had served on at least one of Sopwith's wartime aircraft, and many of these pilots had hopes of being granted commisions in the Service after the War.

The Snipe's origin lay in the Air Board's decision to proceed with sup-

port for an enlarged version of W O Bentley's B.R.1 rotary, which had been successfully matched with the Camel. Bentley's new engine, which retained the aluminium alloy cylinders with steel liners, was increased in bore and stroke, so that its capacity increased from 17.3 to 24.95 litres, in turn producing a power increase to 250hp; more important, the power/weight ratio was considerably improved, rising from 0.375 to 0.526 bhp/lb in the new B.R.2.

The B.R.2 was first bench run in October 1917, and the first of six Sopwith prototypes, B9962, was flown the following month, albeit with a B.R.1 engine. The new aircraft, referred to by Sopwith as the 7F.1 Snipe, was designed to the Air Board's Specification A.1A, and originally featured single-bay wings and a flat-sided fuselage, as well as a fin and rudder similar to those on the Camel. With a narrow upper wing centre section, the cabane struts were rigged almost vertically. Within a month the first B.R.2 had been delivered and was fitted in the first prototype, which then underwent its preliminary official trials at Martlesham in December.

The second prototype retained the single-bay wings, but the centre section was increased in width; the cabane struts were lengthened and angled slightly outwards from the fuselage. The tail was redesigned with a parallel chord fin and horn-balanced rudder, this shape being retained on the other prototypes and the early production aircraft. The third prototype introduced two-bay wings, this feature being adopted on all subsequent Snipes.

One of the attractive attributes of the Snipe was its comparatively low cost for, compared with the S.E.5A with 200hp Hispano-Suiza engine at a total of £2,067 and the Martinsyde Buzzard at £2,205, the Snipe's total airframe and engine cost was £1,826, and in March 1918 — when the Snipe was officially declared superior to the other contenders to Specification A.1A — a total of 1,700 Snipes was ordered from Sopwith and six other manufacturers, to be followed soon after by orders for 800 more. Of these, and other Snipes ordered before the end of the War, a total of 2,172 came to be built.

Production of the Snipe was slow to accelerate, principally due to the number of B.R.1 engines still on order, and manufacture was undertaken by Gwynne's Ltd, Hammersmith, and The Humber Motor Co Ltd, Coventry. Indeed, when the first of the Sopwith-built Snipes began delivery to the RAF, the Service was in no position to introduce the new fighter into widespread use immediately, and growing numbers of fully equipped aircraft began assembling at aircraft parks in Britain.

Snipes of No 32 Squadron, at Lympne in 1924. E6268 carried an early version of the Squadron's unofficial badge on its fin as well as No 32's blue and white stripe down the fuselage. (Photo: RAF Museum, Neg No P019363)

Such was the ferocity of the German offensive that opened on the Western Front in April 1918 that it was as much as the new RAF could manage to ensure the existing fighter squadrons in France were kept up to strength with their established fighters and with pilots, and it was not until August that No 43 Squadron, commanded by Sqn Ldr C C Miles MC at Fienvillers began receiving Snipes, joining Camels. The next was No 201, which received at least one Snipe during October in France. This aircraft was being flown on the 27th of that month by Maj William George Barker DSO* MC** (attached temporarily to the Squadron) when he attacked and shot down a German two-seater from 21,000 feet over the Forêt de Mormal. Almost immediately he was attacked by a Fokker D VII and wounded, and was then surrounded by a formation of about fifteen enemy aircraft. Although again wounded, Barker shot one of these down, and forced down two others. He then fainted, and the Snipe fell out of control. Regaining consciousness, he found himself in the midst of another large German formation and, although his left elbow was shattered by a bullet, he shot down another enemy fighter. Now down to 12,000 feet and with smoke coming from his aircraft, Barker decided to ram a D VII, but at the last moment shot it down from a range of about three yards. He dived away and, shaking off yet another enemy formation, just managed to re-cross the lines at a few feet before crashing. Barker survived his wounds to be awarded the Victoria Cross for one of the most remarkable air combats ever fought.

The only other Snipe unit to see combat during the War was No 4 Squadron, Australian Flying Corps. Its aircraft took part in attacks on the German airfield at Rebaix on 30 October and on Enghien on 9 November.

Meanwhile the Snipe had undergone further development. A long-range version, the 7F.1A, intended as an escort fighter for the bombers of the Independent Force, had been produced by fitting an enlarged (50-gallon) fuel tank beneath the pilot's seat in addition to those forward and aft of the cockpit. These long-range Snipes were being delivered to the RAF when the War ended.

Another interesting version was pro-

Type: Single-engine, single-seat, two-bay biplane fighter.
Manufacturers: The Sopwith Aviation Co Ltd, Kingston-upon-Thames, Surrey; Boulton & Paul Ltd, Norwich; Coventry Ordnance Works Ltd, Coventry; March, Jones & Cribb Ltd, Leeds; The Kingsbury Aviation Co, Kingsbury; D Napier & Son Ltd, Acton, London; Nieuport & General Aircraft Ltd, Cricklewood, London; Portholme Aerodrome Ltd, Huntingdon; and Ruston, Proctor & Co Ltd, Lincoln.
Air Board Specification: A.1A of 1917.
Powerplant: Prototype. One 150hp Bentley B.R.1 rotary. Standard. One 250hp Bentley B.R.2 rotary. Experimental: One 320hp ABC Dragonfly I radial engine.
Structure: All-wooden construction with fabric, ply and sheet metal covering.
Dimensions: Standard production. Span, 31ft 1in; length, 19ft 9in; height, 8ft 9in; wing area, 271 sq ft.
Weights: Tare, 1,312lb; all-up, 2,020lb.
Performance: Standard production. Max speed, 125 mph at sea level, 121 mph at 10,000ft; climb to 10,000ft, 9 min 25 sec; service ceiling, 20,000ft; endurance, 3 hr.
Armament: Two synchronized 0.303in Vickers machine guns on the fuselage forward of the cockpit; up to four 25lb bombs could be carried on racks under the fuselage.
Prototypes: Six, B9962-B9967 (B9962 first flown in November 1917 at Brooklands).
Production: 2,172, excluding prototypes (Sopwith, 683: E7987-E8286, F2333-F2532, F7001-F7030, H4865-H4917 and J3617-J3716; Boulton & Paul, 425: E6137-E6536 and J451-J475; Coventry Ordnance Works, 150: E6537-E6686; Napier, 150: E6787-E6936; Nieuport & General, 100: E6937-E7036; Ruston, Proctor, 524: E7337-E7836 and H351-H374; Portholme, 100: E8307-E8406; March, Jones & Cribb, 10: J681-J690; Kingsbury, 30: J6493-J6522).
Summary of Service: Wartime: Snipes served with Nos 43 and 201 Squadrons, RAF, and No 4 Squadron, Australian Flying Corps in France. Post-War: Snipes served with Nos 43, 45, 70, 80, 201 and 208 Squadrons, RAF, in France, Belgium and Germany between November 1918 and February 1920; with Nos 3, 19, 23, 25, 29, 32, 37, 41, 43, 56, 78, 81, 111 and 143 Squadrons, RAF, in the United Kingdom between November 1918 and May 1926; and with Nos. 1, 3, 25 and 56 Squadrons, RAF, in Turkey, the Middle East and India between January 1920 and November 1926.

duced by fitting one of the first examples of the 320hp ABC Dragonfly engine in the last Snipe prototype, B9967, as early as April 1918. Several other aircraft, including E7990 and F7017, were similarly powered, and one underwent trials at Martlesham Heath in October that year, returning a speed of 156 mph at sea level. E7990 became the prototype Sopwith Dragon (see page 144).

It seems likely that, with hundreds of Snipes at the Aircraft Parks during the last half of 1918, it was intended that the fighter would supersede the Pup, Camel and Beardmore W.B.III with the Royal Navy, and several were with the Grand Fleet at the time of the Armistice; these aircraft were fitted with a hydrovane forward of the undercarriage so as to reduce the risk of overturning in the event of ditching.

Post-War Service

The process of introducing Snipes into service with the RAF continued after

A Nieuport & General-built Snipe of No 56 (Fighter) Squadron with night flying equipment. (Photo: A J Jackson Collection)

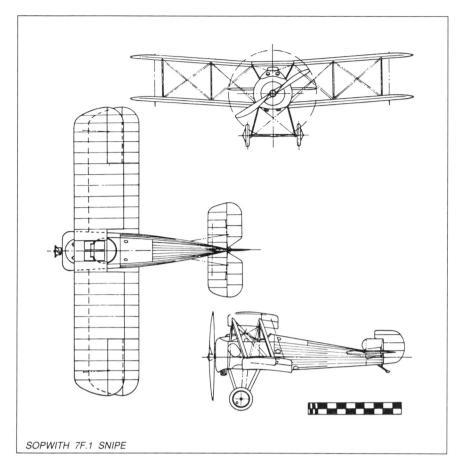

SOPWITH 7F.1 SNIPE

squadrons in the RAF had grown to ten (Nos 3, 17,19, 25, 29, 32, 41, 56 and 111 at home, and No 1 in Iraq).

The Snipe continued in service with four Squadrons until 1926, the last being withdrawn from No 1 when that Squadron disbanded at Hinaidi on 1 November that year.

Immediately following the end of the War large numbers of brand-new Snipes were scrapped. Three years later it became all too obvious that this action had been precipitate, and the inevitable attrition among the remaining aircraft gave rise to the possibility that some squadrons would have to be prematurely disbanded owing to a growing shortage of aircraft. At the instigation of Air Marshal Sir John Salmond KCB, CMG, CVO, DSO, in 1921 commanding the Inland Area, a halt was called to the deliberate destruction of aircraft (whether in store or damaged in accidents) so that a continuing programme of salvaging and re-building could be undertaken by the Service and at the manufacturers. In due course more than 200 Snipes, which would otherwise have been scrapped, were returned to operational service.

With the arrival of new aircraft, such as the Gloster Grebe and Gamecock in the mid-1920s, no one mourned the passing of the Snipe, stalwart fighter though it had undoubtedly been. With it passed into history the old rotary engine — a relic of the earliest days of aviation — now confined to a dwindling number of Avro 504K trainers. To many members of the British public, the Snipe introduced the spectacle of formation aerobatics, which originated at the 1921 Hendon Pageant when Sqn Ldr Christopher Draper led a display by Snipes of the Central Flying School. It fell to No 17 Squadron to give the farewell display by Snipes in 1926.

the Armistice, Nos 45 and 208 Squadrons in France receiving their first aircraft in November 1918. In England, No 78 (Home Defence) Squadron received a few aircraft, but they did not fully replace the Squadron's Camels before it was disbanded the following year. Snipes also joined No 81 (Home Defence) Squadron in November for a few weeks. Nos 70 and 80 Squadrons re-equipped with Snipes on the continent during December. These Squadrons, as well as Nos 37 and 143 (Home Defence) Squadrons, flew Snipes for only a few months after the War.

Early in 1920, however, the long term re-equipping with Snipes began in earnest, both at home and overseas. In January that year No 1 Squadron (Sqn Ldr, later Gp Capt John Benjamin Graham MC, AFC) re-formed at Risalpur in India with Snipes which it retained until November 1926, after having moved to Iraq in May 1921. Also in January 1920 No 56 Squadron (Sqn Ldr Duncan William Grinnell-Milne MC, DFC) re-

formed at Aboukir in Egypt with Snipes, returning to England with them later.

No 25 Squadron (Sqn Ldr Sir Norman Roderick Alexander Leslie BT, CBE) received Snipes at Hawkinge in February 1920 and held the distinction for many months of being the only home-based fighter squadron in the Royal Air Force; it was to keep its Snipes until September 1924, having taken them to Turkey for a year in September 1922 during the Chanak crisis.

No 3 Squadron re-formed with Snipes at Bangalore in India on 1 April 1920 and, by April 1924 the list of Snipe

E8132 was one of the first production batch of Snipes built by Sopwith and is shown here wearing the wartime markings of No 208 Squadron which was based in Germany after the Armistice. (Photo: RAF Museum)

Port Victoria P.V.9

At about the time that the Port Victoria Kittens were nearing completion in 1917, the Experimental Construction Depot at Port Victoria received instructions to design a single-seat scout seaplane, retaining the best features of the P.V.2 (see page 64), but with improved performance, as a possible replacement for the Sopwith Baby.

Given a free hand, there is little doubt but that Cdr Seddon's design staff could have come up with an outstanding design. Unfortunately, instead of being permitted to use a high-lift wing section, the Admiralty insisted on the RAF 15 aerofoil, with the result that climb performance and ceiling were to suffer.

The P.V.9 was an attractive aeroplane although, on account of the unsuitable wings, it was bigger than originally intended. It was, like the P.V.2, a sesquiplane and retained the earlier seaplane's 'W' arrangement of interplane and float struts. The fuselage was again located within the gap, and very close to upper and lower wings, thereby providing the pilot with an excellent field of view. An innovative feature was the location of the fuel tanks within the sides of the fuselage forward of the cockpit, but outside the fuselage primary structure so that the cockpit could occupy the unrestricted width of the primary box girder. A single synchronized Vickers gun was mounted on the nose decking,

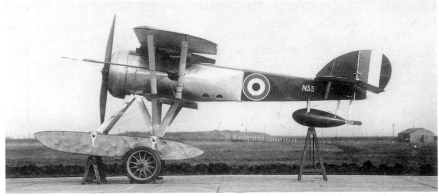

The Port Victoria P.V.9 prototype, N55; the presence of the long pressure boom on the interplane struts suggests that the photograph was taken at the time of its official tests. (Photo: J M Bruce)

and a free-firing Lewis gun was provided on top of the upper wing centre-section forward of a generous cutout in the upper wing trailing edge. The undercarriage consisted of twin pontoon-type main floats and a streamlined, circular-section tail float.

The P.V.9 was originally intended to be powered by a 110hp Clerget, but instead was fitted with a 150hp Bentley B.R.1 rotary. The single prototype, N55, first flew in December 1917 but, owing to recurring trouble with this engine,

was not officially tested until May. Unfortunately the aircraft underwent its trials with an unsuitable propeller, with the result that the performance returned did not accurately reflect the P.V.9's real potential. That, however, was immaterial — as were the complimentary remarks about the aircraft in general — as the proposed rôle of the aircraft had long since been rendered superfluous by the capabilities of the Sopwith Pup and Camel; therefore there was no further need for the P.V.9's development.

Type: Single-engine, single-seat, twin-float, single-bay sesquiplane scout.
Manufacturer: RNAS Experimental Construction Depot, Port Victoria, Isle of Grain.
Powerplant: One 150hp Bentley B.R.1 rotary engine driving two-blade propeller.
Dimensions: Span, 30ft 11in; length, 25ft 2in; height, 9ft 0in; wing area, 227 sq ft.
Weights: Tare, 1,404lb; all-up, 1,965lb.
Performance: Max speed, 110.5 mph at 2,000ft; climb to 10,000ft, 27 min 20 sec; service ceiling, 11,500ft.
Armament: One synchronized 0.303in Vickers machine gun on fuselage forward of the cockpit, and one Lewis gun on upper wing centre section.
Prototype: One, N55 (first flown in December 1917). No production.

Sopwith Hippo

When design of the Sopwith 3F.2 Hippo two-seat fighter began in the summer of 1917 it was perfectly obvious that, unless some unforeseen circumstance rendered the Bristol F.2B Fighter fatally flawed in service, no new design stood any chance of being accepted for production within the Bristol's operational category. On account of new Defence Regulations, introduced in 1917, which

forbade the construction of any aeroplane without sanction from the Air Board or Admiralty (to avoid waste of strategic materials), it was necessary to obtain a licence to go ahead with the construction of the Hippo, and Licence No 16 was issued for two such prototypes, X10 and X11.

The purpose, therefore, of the Hippo

was to further exploit the concept of attaching the upper and lower wings of a biplane to the top and bottom of a deep fuselage, and locating the pilot and gunner immediately forward and aft of the top wing respectively. Central to this configuration, intended to provide uninterrupted fields of view for the crew in the upper hemisphere, was the rigging

The second Sopwith 3F.1 Hippo, X11 at Brooklands with increased wing dihedral, smooth contoured fin and rudder, Scarff ring on rear cockpit and rear fuselage of reduced depth. (Photo: Real Photographs Co, Neg No 1683)

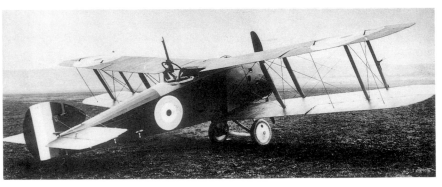

of the wings with considerable back stagger — a configuration formerly approached by the single-seat Sopwith Dolphin (see page 103). In order to avoid using an engine that was in heavy demand, the Hippo employed the big eleven-cylinder 200hp Clerget 11EB rotary.

The first prototype, which may have been X10, was probably flown in December 1917 and featured only three degrees of dihedral on the wings and short, horn-balanced ailerons, a small angular fin and rudder and a rocking-post mounting for the rear Lewis gun. The second example, known to be X11, followed soon after and differed in numerous respects. The dihedral was increased to five degrees (increasing the illusion from some aspects that the wings were swept forward); lengthened, unbalanced ailerons were included, and the fin and rudder enlarged to give a combined outline similar to that of the Camel. A Scarff ring was fitted on the rear cockpit, and the rear fuselage top decking was reduced in depth.

The Hippo underwent official trials in January but, not surprisingly — owing to the relatively low power output of the Clerget engine — it was not accepted for production, and a second licence for a third Hippo, X18, was withdrawn the following month.

Type: Single-engine, two-seat, two-bay biplane fighter.
Manufacturer: The Sopwith Aviation Co Ltd, Kingston-upon-Thames and Brooklands, Surrey.
Powerplant: One 200hp Clerget 11EB eleven-cylinder rotary engine driving two-blade propeller.
Dimensions: Span, 38ft 9in; length, 24ft 6in; height, 9ft 4in; wing area, 340 sq ft.
Weights: Tare, 1,481lb; all-up, 2,590lb.
Performance: Max speed, 115.5 mph at 10,000ft; climb to 10,000ft, 13 min 25 sec; service ceiling, 17,000ft.
Armament: Two synchronized 0.303in Vickers machine guns in nose, forward of pilot's cockpit, and either one or two double-yoked Lewis guns on rear cockpit.
Prototypes: Two, X10 and X11 (first flown at Brooklands, probably in December 1917). A third prototype, X18, was cancelled. No production.

Boulton & Paul P.3 Bobolink

Established since 1873 as a wood-working firm, Boulton & Paul of Norwich entered the aircraft industry during the First World War and quickly created for itself an excellent reputation for its production of aircraft such as the Sopwith Camel, under the management of Geoffrey ffiske. In August 1917, Boulton & Paul secured the services of John North (late of the Austin Motor Co) as its chief designer, and straightway determined to submit designs of its own. North's first aircraft, known by the company as the Hawk — but later changed to Bobolink, when Boulton & Paul were required to give names of birds to their fighters, beginning with 'Bo. . .' — was extremely unfortunate not to be rewarded by a production order.

Taking the bull by the horns, North entered the design competition held under the Specification A.1A, which called for a single-seat fighter to replace the Sopwith Camel. Like the ultimate winner, the Sopwith Snipe, the Bobolink was powered by the Bentley B.R.2 rotary and featured two-bay wings and twin synchronized Vickers guns. Like the Snipe, six prototypes, C8652-C8657, were ordered. A number of ingenious features were included in the design, not least of which were the fuel tanks: the fuel was carried in two tanks behind the

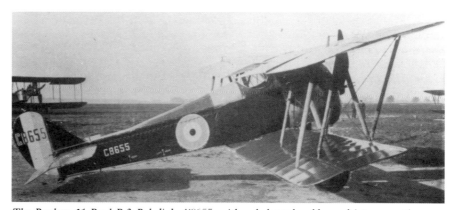
The Boulton & Paul P.3 Bobolink, C8655, with unbalanced rudder and interconnecting strut between the upper and lower ailerons. (Photo: G S Leslie / J M Bruce Collection)

pilot, side-by-side and separated by a sheet of armour; in the event of fire in one tank, it could be jettisoned to reduce the risk of the aircraft being totally destroyed. 'N'-type interplane struts were employed to simplify rigging of the wings, which were of very light weight (each lower mainplane weighed only 29 pounds).

The Bobolink was probably first flown in January 1918, and underwent its official trials in March. It proved to be lighter than the Snipe and slightly faster, but was criticised on account of poor ground handling, resulting from its very narrow track undercarriage. There is some evidence that handling problems in the air may have delayed the Bobolink's trials, and that this may have told against the aircraft; the decision in favour of the Snipe was announced *before* the report on John North's entry was completed. Some photographs show the Bobolink with a somewhat overbalanced rudder, suggesting a hurried cure for a lack of directional control.

Type: Single-engine, single-seat, two-bay biplane fighter.
Manufacturer: Boulton & Paul Ltd, Norwich, Norfolk.
Powerplant: One 250hp Bentley B.R.2 rotary engine driving two-blade propeller.
Dimensions: Span, 29ft 0in; length, 20ft 0in; height, 8ft 4in; wing area, 266 sq ft.
Weights: Tare, 1,226lb; all-up, 1,992lb.
Performance: Max speed, 125 mph at 10,000ft; climb to 10,000ft, 9 min 20 sec; service ceiling, 19,500 ft; endurance, 3¼ hr.
Armament: Two synchronized 0.303in Vickers machine guns in the fuselage nose forward of the cockpit.
Prototype: Six, C8652-C8657. (Some records suggest that C8652-C8654 were referred to as P.5 Hawks; only C8655 is known to have been built.)

Blackburn N.1B

The Admiralty's requirement, set out in Specification N.1B, calling for a long-range escort fighter capable of accompanying the large patrol flying boats, prompted the Blackburn Aeroplane company to produce a design to compete with the Supermarine N.1B Baby, which would make its first flight in February 1918. Another contender, which had flown but proved unsuccessful with a speed of only 93 mph, was the Norman Thompson N.1B two-seat flying-boat.

The Blackburn N.1B, designed by Harris Booth — not hitherto renowned for beauty of design — was a remarkably elegant little biplane flying-boat with a span of only 34ft 10in. The hull was designed by Major Linton Hope, with the slightly staggered wings placed above the hull, and the 200hp Hispano-Suiza pusher engine located close up under the upper wing centre section. The pilot's cockpit was situated forward of the wings with a single Lewis gun in front and offset to starboard, and the gracefully upward-curving rear hull section supporting a biplane tail with twin fins and rudders. Wingtip balancing floats were fitted directly below the interplane struts.

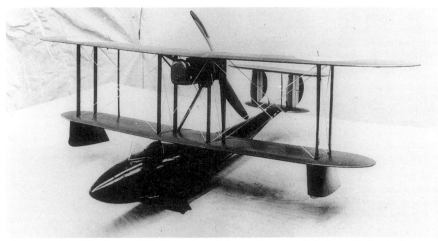

A model of the Blackburn N.1B flying-boat fighter. (Photo: A J Jackson Collection)

For all the promise shown by the Blackburn design, the Admiralty requirements were changed before the first prototype was completed, and only the hull of N56 had been finished when work on the N.1B was halted. (This hull was incorporated in a post-War aircraft, the Blackburn Pellet, and entered for the 1923 Schneider Trophy race; the aircraft was however destroyed in an accident before the race.)

The accompanying data are design figures only.

Type: Single pusher engine, single-seat biplane flying-boat escort fighter.
Manufacturer: The Blackburn Aeroplane & Motor Co Ltd, Leeds.
Powerplant: One 200hp Hispano-Suiza engine driving two-blade pusher propeller.
Dimensions: Span, 34ft 10in; length, 28ft 3½in.
Weights: Tare, 1,721lb; all-up, 2,390lb.
Performance: Max speed, 114 mph at sea level; climb to 10,000ft, 18 min; ceiling, 16,000ft; endurance, 3 hr.
Armament: One 0.303in Lewis gun forward of pilot's cockpit, offset to starboard.
Prototypes: Three ordered, N56–N58; only N56 partly completed.

Supermarine N.1B Baby

Because progress on the Blackburn N.1B was slow (see above), the Supermarine contender to the same specification was completed and tested before the official requirement was allowed to lapse. Designed by F J Hargreaves, the Baby was of very similar general configuration to that of the Blackburn, but featured a monoplane tail with single tailplane and elevator placed above a single fin and rudder. The hull, also built in mahogany on the Linton-Hope principle, possessed a straight top line, its cross-section being almost circular with a skirted planing bottom. As originally flown, ailerons were only fitted to the upper wings, but were later repeated on the lower wings as well. A small triangular fin was added above the tailplane.

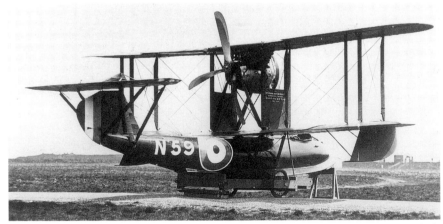

The Supermarine Baby, N59, after being fitted with ailerons on the lower wings, and with the auxiliary fin above the tailplane. (Photo: G S Leslie / J M Bruce Collection)

The engine installation, a 200hp Hispano-Suiza pusher engine mounted close under the upper wing centre section, comprised a partly cowled nacelle with flat car-type radiator in front. The front inboard interplane struts were duplicated and located on either side of the wing fold line, thereby maintaining structural rigidity with the wings folded.

First flown in February 1918 by Flight-Lt Goodwin, the Supermarine Baby, N59, well exceeded the performance demanded, returning a sea level top speed of 117 mph; no armament was carried on test, although ballast carried suggested that allowance was being made

Type: Single pusher engine, single-seat, single-bay biplane flying-boat fighter.

Manufacturer: The Supermarine Aviation Works Ltd, Woolston, Southampton.

Air Department Specification: N.1B of 1917.

Powerplant: One 200hp Hispano-Suiza engine driving four-blade pusher propeller; later one 200hp Sunbeam Arab engine.

Dimensions: Span, 30ft 5⅞in; length, 26ft 3½in; height, 10ft 7in; wing area, 309 sq ft.

Weights: Tare, 1,699 lb; all-up, 2,326lb.

Performance: Max speed, 117 mph at sea level; climb to 10,000ft, 25 min 10 sec; endurance, 3 hr.

Armament: None carried on test, but allowance probably made for a single Vickers machine gun.

Prototypes: Three, N59-N61. Only N59 completed, and first flown in February 1918.

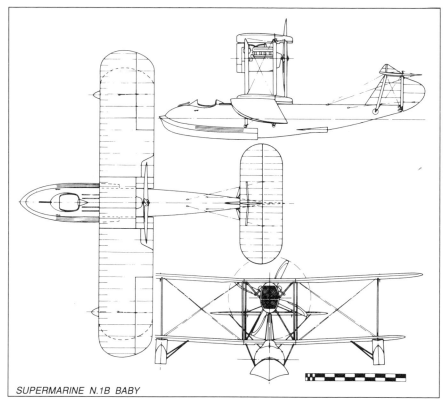

SUPERMARINE N.1B BABY

for a single Vickers gun.

As already stated, the Air Department's N.1B requirement was abandoned in its original terms, and Supermarine therefore went ahead on its own with development of the Baby, installing a 200hp Sunbeam Arab in place of the Hispano engine. The second and third aircraft, N60 and N61, were not built, but would have also been Arab-powered. N59 underwent official trials in August 1918 with the Arab and, al-though rather heavier than with the Hispano engine, produced much the same performance figures.

B.A.T. F.K.22 and F.K.23 Bantam

In 1917 Samuel Waring (later Lord Waring of Foots Cray) founded the British Aerial Transport company (B.A.T.) of Willesden, London, and secured the services of Frederick Kool-hoven — late of Armstrong, Whitworth — as chief designer; he brought with him Bob Noorduyn, also of Dutch descent, as his chief draughtsman. Accordingly the aircraft which came to be produced by the new company continued to bear the initials applied to those designed by Koolhoven for his previous employer.

These new designs were all to be radical by accepted British standards, but nonetheless represented a realistic approach to fighter design. All the fighters were to be of wooden monocoque construction with split-axle undercarriage, and all but the last wartime design (the Basilisk) were to be characterized by the upper wing being located on top of

The B.A.T. F.K.22 Bantam, B9947, showing well the flat top wing and the cockpit aperture. (Photo: A J J Jackson Collection)

and attached directly to the top of the fuselage. All were to be high perform-ance aircraft.

The first Koolhoven design for B.A.T. was the F.K.22, an aircraft intended for the 120hp ABC Mosquito, but this engine failed to advance beyond bench testing, so the airframe was altered to take the 170hp ABC Wasp, but this also failed to come up to early expectations, the aircraft being temporarily referred to as the Bantam Mk I. In the end the F.K.22, B9945, underwent trials in February 1918 at Martlesham Heath powered by a 100hp Gnome *mono-soupape* rotary, being designated the B.A.T. F.K. 22 Bantam Mk II.

The Bantam's fuselage was a true monocoque structure with three-ply birch sheet wrapped round ash formers to provide a near-elliptical cross-section; the tail fin was built integrally with the fuselage. Each wing was constructed in three sections, only the outer sections having dihedral. Both centre sections were attached directly to the fuselage,

Left: *The B.A.T. F.K.22 Bantam Mk II with 100hp Gnome* monosoupape *rotary engine; note the wide-track undercarriage in relation to the aircraft's span.* (Photo: C.A. Nepean Bishop)

Below: *The first production F.K.23 Bantam Mk I with 170hp ABC Wasp engine; the port Vickers gun port is just visible in the lower segment of the engine cowling. F1653 first flew in March 1918 and was taken on charge by the RAE on 13 August 1920, but crashed near Aldershot on 10 January 1922.* (Photo: Royal Aerospace Establishment, Farnborough).

the top wing incorporating a large circular aperture so the pilot's head protruded above the upper surface. Ailerons were fitted on upper and lower wings, and wooden interplane struts were employed.

Despite the earlier reference to the Bantam Mk I, this was correctly applied to an entirely new design, which Koolhoven referred to as the F.K.23. It was smaller than the F.K.22, but the same basic form of monocoque construction was applied although the upper wing was now built as a single structure and possessed no dihedral. The lower wing was still made in three sections, with dihedral on the outer sections, and with no stagger.

Because the aircraft's centre of gravity was fairly far aft and the fuselage relatively short, the tail control surfaces possessed a short moment, a deficiency that became all too obvious during spin recovery; the Bantam's spin was vicious and rotation accelerated quickly, so that coarse and powerful use of the controls was essential. One or two aircraft were lost from spins and Maj Christopher Draper, a noted exponent of the Bantam, was fortunate to escape without injury when he spun a Bantam into the ground — thanks to the great strength of the fuselage structure.

The Bantam Mk I was very fast and highly manœuvrable, and earned a small production order for twelve aircraft, to be powered by the 170hp ABC Wasp I. It underwent some re-design, the rudder being increased in area to assist spin recovery, steel tubular interplane struts fitted and dihedral introduced to the upper wing. Wasp I- and II-powered Bantams were submitted for evaluation in October 1918 and March 1920 under the new Air Ministry Specification se-

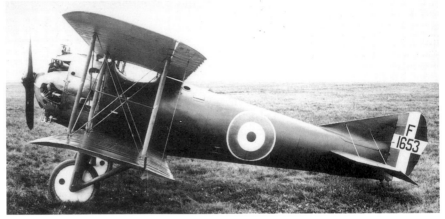

ries No 1A (later termed the Directorate of Research Type 1) and produced a sparkling performance; the latter version returned a maximum speed of 150 mph at sea level, and a time to 10,000 feet of just under seven minutes.

The Wasp was never popular in the RAF and, as there appeared to be sufficient Snipes in storage for demands of the foreseeable future, there was no call to increase the production order. Of the twelve production aircraft built, eight were eventually sold to private

owners, and one (F1660) was sent to America for tests and evaluation; two of the civil aircraft finished up in Holland. The last two aircraft of the production order (F1663 and F1664) were held in storage until 1920, when they were assembled as J6579 and J6580 with Wasp II engines for various tests at the RAE and A & AEE; after the engine failed in J6580, a 200hp Armstrong Siddeley Lynx was fitted, but both aircraft were finally struck off charge in January 1922.

Type: Single-engine, single-seat, two-bay biplane fighter.
Manufacturer: The British Aerial Transport Co Ltd, Willesden, London.
Air Ministry Specification: No 1A of 1918.
Powerplant: Bantam Mk I. 170hp ABC Wasp I; 200hp ABC Wasp II; Bantam Mk II. 100hp Gnome *monosoupape*; 100hp Le Rhône.
Dimensions: Production Bantam I. Span, 25ft 0in; length, 18ft 5in; height, 6ft 9in; wing area, 185 sq ft.
Weights: Production Bantam I. Tare, 833lb; all-up, 1,321lb.
Performance: Production Bantam I (Wasp I). Max speed, 128 mph at sea level; climb to 10,000ft, 9 min; service ceiling, 20,000ft.
Armament: Two synchronized 0.303in Vickers machine guns mounted low down on the sides of the nose.
Prototypes: Six B.A.T.22s ordered, B9944-B9949; only B9944 and B9947 confirmed as being completed.
Production: Twelve B.A.T.23s ordered, F1653-F1664; F1663 and F1664 became J6579 and J6580 respectively.

Avro Type 504 Night Fighters

It is of course well known that the Avro 504 was the most widely-used British training aircraft of the First World War, no fewer than 8,340 examples being produced during the War itself (and many others afterwards). Scarcely recalled is the fact that specially converted versions were used as early as 1915 on anti-Zeppelin patrols. On 15 May that year Flt Sub-Lt Mulock, flying an Avro, intercepted LZ38, but was unable to attack it with his two grenades and two incendiary bombs before the enemy airship climbed away from the fighter.

Following such early efforts as these, it was decided to convert the Avro 504 to a single-seater for the anti-Zeppelin rôle, fitting an extra fuel tank in place of the front cockpit, and arming it with a Lewis gun mounted to fire upwards through a cutout in the upper wing centre section. With an endurance of no less than eight hours, this version was termed the Avro 504C, with a low aspect ratio fin for the RNAS, and the 504D, without fin for the RFC. These aircraft were powered by 80hp Gnome rotaries.

Of much greater significance was the decision, taken early in the winter of 1916-17, to equip Home Defence squadrons with the Avro 504J and K, again modified as single-seaters, but now armed with a Lewis gun on a Foster mounting above the wing; the gravity fuel tank was moved from the centre of the wing to the port side. Power was provided by either a 100hp Gnome *monosoupape* engine or a 110hp Le Rhône, and these aircraft could reach an altitude of 18,000 feet; they were specifically introduced to replace the RFC's aging B.E.2Cs, whose

An RNAS Avro 504C night fighter with upwards-firing Lewis gun. (Photo: J M Bruce)

ceiling was little more than 12,000 feet. One other motive for this decision was to enable the night fighter pilots, who would soon be flying the tricky Camel at night, to gain experience with a rotary-powered tractor fighter. In the event, no

fewer than 226 Avro 504J and K night fighters were still flying with the Home Defence units, including five squadrons, at the time of the Armistice.

The accompanying data table refers to the Avro 504K night fighter of 1918.

Type: Single-engine, single-seat, two-bay biplane night fighter.
Manufacturers: A V Roe & Co Ltd, Manchester and Hamble, Hampshire; The Grahame-White Aviation Co Ltd, Hendon, London; The Humber Motor Co Ltd, Coventry.
Powerplant: One 100hp Gnome *monosoupape* engine; 110hp Le Rhône; 130hp Clerget.
Dimensions: Span, 36ft 0in; length, 29ft 5in; height, 10ft 5in; wing area, 330 sq ft.
Weights: (Mono-Gnome). Tare, 1,100lb; all-up, 1,800lb.
Performance: (Mono-Gnome). Max speed, 94 mph at sea level; climb to 10,000ft, 15 min 30 sec; absolute ceiling, 18,200ft; endurance, 3½ hr.
Armament: One 0.303in Lewis gun with Foster mounting on upper wing centre section.
Production: Total of 274 Avro 504Js and Ks issued to Home Defence units during 1918.
Summary of Service: Avro 504Js and Ks served with Nos 33, 36, 51, 75, 77, 90, 92 and 155 (Home Defence) Squadrons, RFC and RAF, during 1918, and with Nos 186, 187, 188, 189, 190 and 198 (Night Fighter Training) Squadrons.

A Humber-built Avro 504K single-seat night fighter of a Home Defence unit, with Lewis gun on Foster mounting. (Photo: Ranald MacDonald Esq, OBE)

Beardmore W.B.V

Designed and built at the same time as the W.B.IV, which it resembled more than superficially, the Beardmore W.B.V

shipborne single-seat fighter also approximated to the naval requirements set out in Admiralty Specification N.1A, but additionally made provision to mount a French 37mm quick-firing Canon Puteaux — called for in an Appendix to the Specification.

In the W.B.V the 200hp Hispano-Suiza engine was located conventionally in the nose of the aircraft with the barrel of the cannon lying in the vee between the cylinder banks; the gun's muzzle projected forward into the hollow propeller shaft, and the breech extended aft

The second Beardmore W.B.V, N42, with a single Lewis gun in place of the 37mm cannon. (Photo: Science Museum, London)

into the pilot's cockpit forward of the control column.

Increased wing chord and slightly greater fin area in the tail was provided, but the large nose buoyancy chamber of the W.B.IV was omitted, the latter being to some extent offset by the provision of inflatable flotation bags which, when not inflated, lay flush along the underside of the lower wing leading edge. Folding wings and jettisonable undercarriage were included, as on the W.B.IV.

Once more three prototypes, N41 — N43, were ordered and at least two were completed. However, during flight trials by RNAS pilots, it was considered extremely dangerous to attempt to load the Puteaux gun behind the control column while in flight — possibly in combat conditions. The naval pilots are said to have refused to expose themselves to such obvious risks, and the shell-firing gun was removed, being replaced by a Vickers and Lewis gun, as on the W.B. IV. Now bereft of its *raison d'être* there was clearly no need to pursue further trials, and the W.B.V's further development was halted. Its marginally improved performance had, after all, only been achieved by deleting the large nose buoyancy chamber.

Type: Single-engine, single-seat two-bay shipborne fighting scout biplane.
Manufacturer: William Beardmore & Co Ltd., Dalmuir, Dunbartonshire.
Admiralty Specification: N.1A and Appendix.
Powerplant: One 200hp Hispano-Suiza liquid-cooled engine driving two-blade propeller.
Construction: As Beardmore W.B.IV but without nose buoyancy chamber; engine mounted conventionally in the nose.
Dimensions: Span, 35ft 10in; length, 26ft 7in; height, 11ft 10in; wing area, 394 sq ft.
Weights: Tare, 1,860lb; all-up, 2,500lb.
Performance: Max speed, 112 mph at sea level; climb to 5,000 ft, 6 min; service ceiling, 14,000 ft; endurance, 2½ hr.
Armament: Initially armed with single 37mm Canon Puteaux firing through the propeller shaft; after removal it was replaced by a fixed 0.303in Vickers gun in the nose and a Lewis gun mounted to fire upwards through a cutout in the upper wing centre section.
Prototypes: Three (N41-N43), of which N41 and N42 are known to have been completed (in 1917). No production.

Austin A.F.T.3 Osprey

It has been shown that, in 1917, the Austin Motor Company was already making positive efforts to contribute aircraft of its own origination, even though the Austin-Ball A.F.B.1 (see page 111) was not strictly the company's own design. The issue that year by the War Office of an official Specification, A.1A, for a successor to the Sopwith Camel was an added spur to perseverance.

Before John North left Austin to join Boulton & Paul, he had schemed up the design of a small triplane fighter, much on the lines of the Sopwith Clerget Triplane, but intended for the new Bentley B.R.2 rotary engine. John Kenworthy now left the Royal Aircraft Factory — where he had been engaged in the design of the S.E.5 — to join Austin as chief designer, and took over responsibility for the new triplane, termed the A.F.T.3 (and later named the Osprey).

Despite it being officially notified as a contender to meet an Air Board requirement, Kenworthy discovered that Austin was required to obtain a licence to build prototypes under the new Regulations, and this may conceivably reflect the Air Board's belief that the triplane configuration would no longer be adequate to meet the new operational requirement. Such prejudice may have been justifiable, having regard to the relatively high performance already being demonstrated by conventional biplanes, but certainly suggests that the Austin aeroplane was compromised from the start.

Nevertheless, Licence No 17 was issued for the manufacture of three prototypes, X15-X17. The Osprey was an attractive little aircraft, being flown early in 1918 and submitted for evalu-

The Austin A.F.T.3 Osprey, X15, probably at the time of its official trials in March 1918. (Photo: The Royal Aeronautical Society)

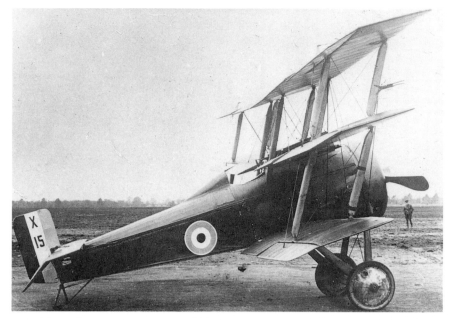

ation in March (by which time the Sopwith Snipe had already been adjudged the successful contender under Specification A.1A). Built very much on the lines of the Sopwith Clerget Triplane, with wooden box-girder fuselage, the Austin was a smaller aircraft, although its wing gaps were deeper and the wing chord greater. Considerable thought had been given to simplicity of construction and ease of maintenance, all six ailerons being interchangeable, as were the interplane struts. An interesting undercarriage feature (obviously 'borrowed' from Austin cars) was the attachment of a leaf-spring to the centre of the spreader bar, extending outwards to the bottom of the V-struts and attached to the half-axles at its extremities, which were bound with elastic chord.

The rudder was a small angular, balanced surface, but no fixed fin was fitted, and the tailplane was adjustable in flight. The armament comprised twin synchronized Vickers guns on the nose decking and, as originally called for in Specification A.1A, provision had been made to mount a Lewis gun on the steel tubular carry-through members of the centre wing.

After the announcement of the Sopwith Snipe's success, Austin stopped work on the Osprey, and the other two prototypes remained unbuilt after the withdrawal of the Licence.

Type: Single-engine, single-seat, two-bay triplane fighter.
Manufacturer: The Austin Motor Co (1914) Ltd, Birmingham.
Powerplant: One 230hp Bentley B.R.2 rotary engine driving two-blade propeller.
Dimensions: Span, 23ft 0in; length, 17ft 7in; height, 10ft 8in; wing area, 233 sq ft.
Weights: Tare, 1,106lb; all-up, 1,888lb.
Performance: Max speed, 118.5 mph at 10,000ft; climb to 10,000ft, 10 min 20 sec; service ceiling, 19,000ft.
Armament: Two synchronized 0.303in Vickers machine guns on fuselage decking forward of cockpit; provision originally made for one Lewis gun on centre wing carry-through structure.
Prototypes: Three ordered, X15-X17, under Licence No 17; X16 and X17 not completed.

Bristol Type 21 Scout F and F.1

Throughout 1917 Capt Frank Barnwell had been engaged in advancing his basic Bristol Scout concept, but inevitably had to turn his attention away from the rotary engine when it became generally accepted as having reached the realistic limit of its power. The Scout E was schemed up to accommodate a proposed 200hp ten-cylinder water-cooled radial known as the 'Cruciform', but when this failed to materialise, Barnwell altered his design to take the much sought-after 200hp Hispano-Suiza in-line engine. The new design was designated the Scout F.

When, however, a contract for six prototypes was raised, on 4 June 1917, it was made clear that the Hispano engine

The first Bristol Scout F, B3989, with the unpopular Sunbeam Arab engine; the humped fairing over the engine covers the water header tank. (Photo: A J Jackson Collection)

would not be available (owing to prior claims for the S.E.5A), and that the 200hp Sunbeam Arab should be used instead. Installation of this engine itself presented little trouble, and Barnwell, by placing the water header tank over the engine, managed to achieve a very clean cowling. His locating of the radiator within a tunnel fairing between the

undercarriage V-struts proved exceptionally neat, and became an established position for this cumbersome component of water-cooled engines. Another unusual feature, though not unique at the time, were the N-type interplane struts which obviated the need for incidence cable bracing.

Although the first Scout F prototype,

The only Bristol Scout F.1 built, B3991, with the Cosmos Mercury radial engine; note that ailerons are only fitted on the upper wing. (Photo: The Bristol Aeroplane Co Ltd.)

B3989, was completed in November 1917, it was not flown until March the following year, mainly because of troubles being experienced by the Arab engine, early examples displaying severe vibration which seemingly defied cure. While efforts were being made to rectify these problems, numerous improvements were made in the cockpit and armament installation on the Scout. However, despite putting up an excellent performance during trials (138 mph at sea level, and climb to 10,000 feet in 9 minutes 20 seconds), the manufacturer decided to cast around for yet another engine and to abandon the existing design. Only two Scout Fs were completed, the second being flown at the Central Flying School.

It is likely that Barnwell was already aware of the engine designs of Alfred Hubert Roy (later Sir Roy) Fedden and L F G Butler at the Bristol company of Brazil Straker. These two engines, the two-row, fourteen-cylinder Mercury and the single-row, seven-cylinder Jupiter radials, were to become subjects of fairly large production orders after the Brazil Straker company was bought by the Cosmos Engineering Company. Attracted by the Mercury's high power output and low overall diameter, Barnwell decided on this engine for his revised Scout F.1, B3991. Indeed, the Mercury had only been bench run in about February 1918. When installed in the F.1, extreme care was taken to keep drag to an absolute minimum by enclosing it in a compound curved cowling, through which only the cylinder heads protruded. The Scout F.1 was officially tested in September 1918 and produced a top speed of 145 mph at sea level.

Unfortunately, with the signing of the Armistice, the order for 200 Cosmos Mercury engines was cancelled, and further development of the Scout F.1 also came to an end and, although one further prototype, B3992, only awaited an engine, it too was dismantled — although the wings underwent structural strength tests at Farnborough in 1919.

Type: Single-engine, single-seat, single-bay biplane fighter.
Manufacturer: The British & Colonial Aeroplane Co Ltd, Filton, Bristol.
Powerplant: Scout F. One 220hp Sunbeam Arab II water-cooled in-line engine. Scout F.1. One 347hp Cosmos Mercury fourteen-cylinder air-cooled radial engine.
Dimensions: Span, 29ft 7½ in; length, (Scout F) 20ft 10in, (Scout F.1) 20ft 0in; height, 8ft 4in; wing area, 260 sq ft.
Weights: Scout F. Tare, 1,436lb; all-up, 2,210lb.
Performance: Scout F. Max speed, 138 mph at sea level; climb to 10,000ft, 9 min 20 sec; service ceiling, 21,000ft. Scout F.1. Max speed, 145 mph at sea level; climb to 10,000ft, 5 min 25 sec.
Armament: Twin synchronized 0.303in Vickers machine guns on upper nose decking.
Prototypes: Six prototypes ordered, B3989-B3994. B3989 and B3990 were built as Scout Fs; B3991 was begun as a Scout F but completed as Scout F.1; B3992-B3994 were not completed. No production.

Nieuport B.N.1

The manufacturer Nieuport & General Aircraft Co Ltd of Cricklewood had been formed before the War with the purpose of producing French Nieuport aircraft under licence in Britain. During 1917 the company was contracted to build several hundred Sopwith Camels, and at this time, in a quest to follow up with aircraft of its own design, secured the services of Henry Folland as its chief designer, one of a growing number of experienced designers and engineers who were becoming disenchanted with conditions at the Royal Aircraft Factory.

Folland's first design essay with Nieuport was the B.N.1, yet another contender for selection as the Camel's replacement under the Air Board's

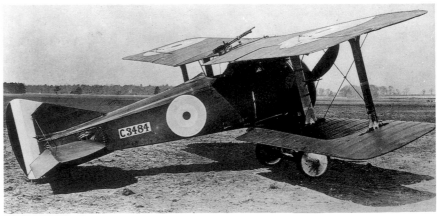

The Nieuport B.N.1, C3484, at Martlesham Heath in March 1918. This aircraft lacked ailerons on the lower wings. (Photo: J M Bruce Collection)

Specification A.1A. The aircraft bore the unmistakable stamp of Folland's design influence, with features such as the I-form interplane struts and the ventral tail fin, reminiscent of the S.E.4.

The B.N.1 was, however, an unstaggered, two-bay biplane powered by one of the first half-dozen Bentley B.R.2 rotaries to become available, and armed with two synchronized Vickers guns and a free Lewis gun on the upper wing. A large conical spinner was originally fitted over the propeller, but this was soon discarded.

Three prototypes, C3484-C3486, were ordered, and the first B.N.1 was completed and flown in February 1918. It arrived at Martlesham Heath at the beginning of March to take part in the competitive evaluation under Specification A.1A (also officially attended by the Sopwith Snipe, Austin Osprey and Boulton & Paul Bobolink). Unfortunately, on 10 March, the Nieuport caught fire in the air near Sutton Bridge, and was totally destroyed. As it was too late to complete a replacement aircraft for the trials, Nieuport was obliged to withdraw.

There is no doubt that the B.N.1 was superior in most aspects of performance to the Snipe, and the only record of a speed measurement that appears to have survived shows that it possessed a maximum speed of 127 mph at 15,000 feet (compared with 110 mph by the Snipe at that height), while its absolute ceiling of 26,000 feet contrasted with about 21,500 feet of the Snipe. As stated previously, it was the Sopwith Snipe which was declared the winner.

One of the other B.N.1 prototypes underwent structural strength tests, and the third was scrapped without being completed.

Type: Single-engine, single-seat, two-bay biplane fighter.
Manufacturer: The Nieuport & General Aircraft Co Ltd, Cricklewood, London.
Air Board Specification: A.1A of 1917.
Powerplant: One 230hp Bentley B.R.2 rotary engine driving two-blade propeller.
Dimensions: Span, 28ft 0in; length, 18ft 6in; height, 9ft 0in; wing area, 260 sq ft.
Weight: All-up, 2,030lb.
Performance: Max speed, 127 mph at 15,000ft; climb to 15,000ft, 16 min; absolute ceiling, 26,000ft; endurance, 3 hr.
Armament: Twin synchronized 0.303in Vickers machine guns on the nose forward of the cockpit, and one Lewis gun on sliding mounting above the upper wing centre section to fire over the propeller. (The Lewis gun was probably removed for the official tests.)
Prototypes: Three ordered, C3484-C3486; only C3484 was completed and flown (first flight, February 1918). No production.

Sopwith 2FR.2 Bulldog

Design of the Sopwith FR.2 started in August 1917, soon after the licensing regulations came into effect, and the Sopwith company was issued with Licence No 2 to build four prototypes, X2-X5. The aircraft was intended as an ultimate replacement for the Bristol F.2B Fighter and, as the designation implied, was to be a reconnaissance fighter. As originally designed, the private venture two-seat FR.2 was to be powered by the 200hp Hispano-Suiza but, as the delivery of these engines fell further and further behind schedule, Herbert Smith changed the design to take the eleven-cylinder 200hp Clerget rotary, and this was re-termed the 2FR.2 Bulldog Mk I.

The first prototype, assumed to be X2 (though the aircraft may not have carried the number), appeared early in 1918 with single-bay wings. The pilot's cockpit was located squarely beneath the upper wing centre section which featured a large central aperture through which the pilot's head protruded; immediately forward of this cockpit, in a prominent hump, were mounted the twin Vickers guns with most of their barrel length exposed. The observer-gunner's large cockpit was situated below and aft of the upper wing's trailing edge and was provided with a pair of

The second Sopwith Bulldog, as yet unmarked as X3, at Brooklands with the horn-balanced ailerons. (Photo: The Imperial War Museum, Neg No Q.66099)

Lewis guns, the forward weapon on a telescopic mounting, the other gun in the rear of the cockpit on a swinging pillar to protect the aircraft's tail. The upper and lower wings were fitted with plain ailerons, and the fin and rudder were similar to those fitted on the modified Sopwith Dolphin.

The single-bay wings were quickly found to be much too small, and a

Type: Single-engine, two-seat, single- and two-bay biplane reconnaissance fighters.
Manufacturer: The Sopwith Aviation Co Ltd, Kingston-upon-Thames and Brooklands, Surrey.
Powerplant: Mark I. One 200hp Clerget eleven-cylinder rotary engine. Mark II. One 360hp ABC Dragonfly IA nine-cylinder air-cooled radial engine.
Dimensions: Two-bay wings. Span, 33ft 9in; length (Mark I), 23ft 0in; height, 8ft 9in; wing area, 335 sq ft.
Weights: Mark I, two-bay wings. Tare, 1,441lb; all-up, 2,495lb.
Performance: Mark I, two-bay wings. Max speed, 109 mph at 10,000ft; climb to 10,000ft, 15 min 35 sec (Mk II, 9 min 28 sec); service ceiling, 15,000ft.
Armament: Two synchronized 0.303in Vickers machine guns on the nose, forward of the pilot's cockpit, with 1,200 rounds of ammunition; two Lewis guns on the rear cockpit.
Prototypes: Four ordered, X2-X5. X2 was single-bay Bulldog Mk I; X3 was two-bay Bulldog Mk I; X4 was Bulldog Mk II. X5 was probably not completed. No subsequent production.

second aircraft (later marked X3) was quickly produced with much enlarged two-bay wings, being initially fitted with horn-balanced ailerons. In due course these were changed to plain ailerons, and in this form X3 underwent official trials in May 1918. However, its performance was generally disappointing, even though the aircraft was applauded on several counts, not least the crew members' field of view. With a top speed of only 109 mph at 10,000 feet and a service ceiling of no more than 15,000 feet, the Bulldog fell short of the Bristol Fighter — which it was intended to replace.

The third prototype, X4 (designated the Bulldog Mk II) with the 360hp ABC Dragonfly IA nine-cylinder radial engine, and which started its official trials the following month, was compromised from the start by its engine. No armament was fitted and the rear cockpit reduced in size with a close coaming; the secondary structure was removed from the wing centre section, the carry-through members being plain steel tubes attached to the inner ends of the wing spars. In other respects X4 was similar to X3, but neither was awarded a production contract, and it is believed that X5 was not completed.

Avro Type 531 Spider

Among the manufacturers who were prompted to produce 'home defence' fighters at the time of the Gotha raids on England in 1917-18 was A V Roe which designed and built the Type 531 as a privately financed project. It was hoped that this ingenious little single-seat biplane would be selected to replace the Avro 504 K 'night fighters' then serving with the Home Defence squadrons.

Employing numerous components of the 504 for ease and speed of manufacture, the Type 531 featured entirely new wings, the lower wing being much shorter and narrower than the upper, the two wings being interbraced by a triangulated system of six faired steel tubular struts without any flying or landing wires; this system, it was argued, would simplify the tedious and time-consuming rigging of the aircraft in the field. To afford the best possible field of vision for the pilot, the cockpit was located directly beneath a large cutout in the centre section of the very broad chord upper wing.

When first flown, the aircraft (dubbed the Spider on account of its Warren girder strut arrangement) was powered by a 110hp Le Rhône rotary engine, but this was soon replaced by a 130hp Clerget. It was flown in mock combat with contemporary in-service scouts (including the Camel and SE.5A) and

The Avro 531 Spider at Hamble in 1918. (Photo: British Aerospace plc, Neg No A10/6)

proved more than a match by reason of its excellent manœuvrability — this despite the Avro's traditional lack of a fixed vertical tail fin. However, it was quickly pointed out that the Spider's agility was to some extent achieved by its reversion to a single gun armament. The adoption of the single front gun had been supported by the argument that it was more desirable to possess more ammunition for a single gun than less for two, particularly for night fighting. Plans were afoot to fit 150hp Bentley B.R.1 or 170hp ABC Wasp engines, but by mid-1918 the German air attacks on England had petered out, while new aircraft — such as the Sopwith Snipe — were approaching Service entry. Two serial numbers were allotted to Spiders, but neither was taken on Service charge, and it is thought that only one example was completed.

Type: Single-engine, single-seat fighting scout biplane

Manufacturers: A V Roe & Co Ltd, Clifton Street, Miles Platting, Manchester

Powerplant: One 110hp Le Rhône 9-cylinder rotary engine; one 130hp Clerget 9-cylinder rotary engine.

Structure: Fuselage of spruce longerons and frames; twin spar wings with steel Warren girder interplane bracing. All fabric-covered.

Dimensions: Span, 28ft 6in; length, 20ft 6in; height, 7ft 10in; wing area, 189 sq ft.

Weights (Clerget): Empty, 1,148lb; loaded, 1,734lb.

Performance (Clerget): Max speed, 120 mph at sea level; climb to 5,000ft, 4.0 min; service ceiling, 19,000ft.

Armament: One fixed synchronized 0.303in Vickers machine gun with 800 rounds.

Prototype: One (probably B3952, first flown in April 1918). No production.

Austin Greyhound

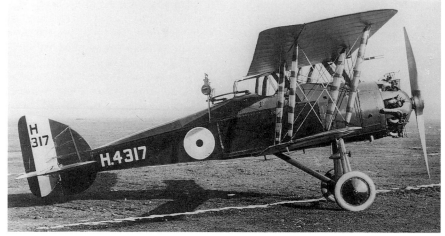

Compromised by its Dragonfly engine, the Austin Greyhound, whose first prototype is shown here, might well otherwise have been selected to replace the Bristol Fighter. (Photo: R C Sturtivant)

As the Austin Osprey was undergoing its flight trials in March 1918, the design of Austin's last wartime military product was submitted to the Air Board on news that a new Specification was about to be issued for a Bristol Fighter replacement. The new design was the handsome Greyhound, a two-seat, two-bay biplane of strictly conventional appearance and construction. Unlike the privately-funded Sopwith Bulldog, the Greyhound was officially sponsored from the start and was therefore among the first aircraft to be allotted the new 320hp ABC Dragonfly I, a nine-cylinder air-cooled engine on which many hopes were to be pinned. In due course the new Air Ministry's Specification Type III was issued and the Greyhound seemed a promising contender for acceptance.

Designed by John Kenworthy, the Greyhound featured a flat-sided and fairly deep fuselage, the pilot and observer/gunner enjoying an excellent field of view, this being partly afforded by a lower wing of narrow chord. The wings, rigged with moderate stagger, were of unequal span and chord, and carried ailerons top and bottom. The tail comprised fixed ventral and dorsal fins, with the tailskid integral with a triangular segment below the rudder — reminiscent of the S.E.5A. The rudder's horn balance was faired to provide an unbroken outline with the dorsal fin.

Although quickly completed during the summer of 1918, under a contract signed on 18 May, the first of three prototypes was held up by prolonged engine trials, and it was the second aircraft, H4318, which underwent official evaluation at Martlesham Heath in January 1919. H4317 followed on 15 May that year, and remained with the A & AEE until September 1920. The third aircraft made its maiden flight in February 1920, the same month that H4318 was delivered to the RAE (the Factory at Farnborough having been renamed an Establishment to avoid confusion with the new RAF), but was damaged and written off after a landing accident on 29 August 1921.

Despite an enormous amount of work on it, the Dragonfly engine never truly succeeded in overcoming its fundamental mechanical weaknesses and brought about the abandonment of numerous promising aircraft, among them the attractive Greyhound. It might have proved possible to substitute another engine had such a decision been taken early on, but after the Armistice aircraft production contracts were being severely cut back, and the design staff at Austin was, in any case, quickly shrinking.

Type: Single-engine, two-seat, two-bay biplane fighter.
Manufacturer: The Austin Motor Co (1914) Ltd, Birmingham.
Air Ministry Specification: Type III of 1918.
Powerplant: One 320hp ABC Dragonfly I nine-cylinder air-cooled radial engine driving two-blade propeller.
Structure: All-wooden construction with fabric, ply and aluminium sheet covering.
Dimensions: Span, 39ft 0in; length, 26ft 8½in; height, 10ft 4in; wing area, 400 sq ft.
Weights: Tare, 1,838lb; all-up, 3,032lb.
Performance: Max speed, 134 mph at sea level, 126 mph at 10,000ft; climb to 10,000ft, 10 min 50 sec; service ceiling, 22,000ft; endurance, 3 hr.
Armament: Two synchronized 0.303in Vickers Mk I machine guns in nose, and one Lewis gun with Scarff ring on rear cockpit.
Prototypes: Three, H4317-H4319; all built, but no subsequent production.

Westland Wagtail

Designed under the leadership of Robert Bruce and Arthur Davenport, the Westland Wagtail was a private venture essay in the light fighter concept, undertaken during the winter of 1917-18 and shortly afterwards submitted to meet

The third Westland Wagtail prototype, C4293, with the abbreviated fin; just visible are the enormous wing centre section cutouts above the cockpit. (Photo: J M Bruce Collection)

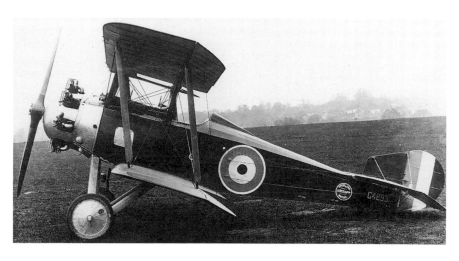

the new Type IA Specification which called for an aircraft to be powered by a 180hp engine, and returning better performance and handling than the Sopwith Camel — which at that time was expected to be phased out of service in 1919.

Almost simultaneously the new 170hp ABC Wasp I seven-cylinder radial engine appeared and, from the outset, attracted considerable interest among aircraft designers on account of its relatively high power/weight ratio of 0.59 bhp/lb. The Wagtail was accordingly designed for this engine. Its structure was strictly orthodox with wooden box-girder fuselage with spruce longerons and curved upper decking provided by fairings and stringers. Twin ash spars and spruce ribs of RAF 15 section provided the structure of the moderately staggered wings, with upper and lower ailerons. The cockpit was located approximately above the mid-chord line of the lower wing, while the upper wing was generously cut away both between the main spars and on the trailing edge. Twin synchronized Vickers guns were mounted, widely separated, on the nose.

Six prototype Wagtails, C4290-C4295, were ordered by the Air Board in February, principally to conduct engine trials with the new Wasp engine (which was already encountering serious mechanical faults). The fuselage of the first airframe was employed for structural tests — possibly at Farnborough. This order was reduced to three flying prototypes, C4291-C4293, late in March, this despite the fact that all five remaining airframes were well advanced.

First flight of the Wagtail C4291 was made by Capt F Alexander RFC in April 1918, after which the aspect ratio of the fin was reduced, and this modification was introduced on the other two prototypes. The second Wagtail also flew before the end of April, but was extensively damaged when its Bessoneaux hangar was burned down in the famous fire caused when an employee endeavoured to prove that it was possible to extinguish a lighted cigarette by dropping it into a tin of petrol. C4293 was delivered to Martlesham Heath on 8 May for trials, but was damaged in a landing accident there; hurriedly repaired, it was flown to Farnborough for investigation into the engine problems.

A fortnight later, however, work was suspended on Wasp-powered aircraft while the manufacturers undertook a redesign of the copper-finned cylinders and of the valve gear.

The second Wagtail, C4292, was rebuilt and fitted with a 200hp Wasp II (with steel-finned cylinders), only to be struck off charge at Martlesham Heath in February 1920. Later that year, two further Wagtails, J6581 and J6582, were ordered and, although these used many components of the two cancelled airframes (C4294 and C4295), the new prototypes differed somewhat from the earlier

aircraft. Both were fitted with Wasp II engines at Farnborough in March 1921, before having 150hp Armstrong Siddeley Lynx seven-cylinder radial engines installed. Because of this engine's greater weight, a nose bay was removed, thereby shortening the nose but maintaining the aircraft's centre of gravity within limits. A revised fin replaced the former truncated surface, and a strengthened undercarriage was fitted. In this form J6581 was first flown on 15 September 1921, and was followed by J6582 on 7 October. Both aircraft were grounded and struck off charge in August 1922.

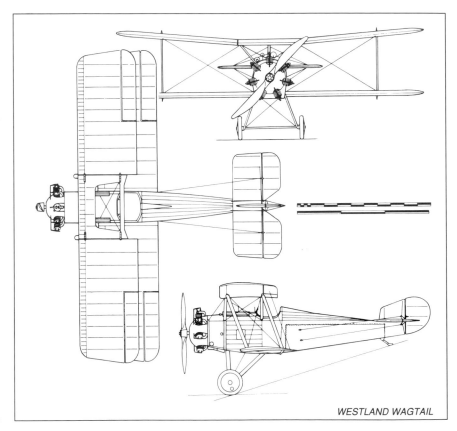

WESTLAND WAGTAIL

Type: Single-engine, single-seat, single-bay biplane light fighter.
Manufacturer: The Westland Aircraft Works, Yeovil, Somerset.
Air Ministry Specification: RAF IA of 1918 (later D of R Type I)
Powerplant: One 170hp ABC Wasp I seven-cylinder air-cooled radial engine driving two-blade propeller; later 200hp Wasp II, and 150hp Armstrong Siddeley Lynx.
Structure: All-wood primary construction with fabric covering; steel elevator and rudder.
Dimensions: Span, 23ft 2in; length, 18ft 11in; height, 8ft 0in; wing area, 190 sq ft.
Weights: (Wasp I). Tare, 746lb; all-up, 1,330lb.
Performance: (Wasp I). Max speed, approx 130 mph at sea level, 125 mph at 10,000ft; climb to 10,000ft, 7 min 30 sec; service ceiling, 20,500ft; endurance, 2½ hr.
Armament: Two synchronized 0.303in Vickers Mk I machine guns on nose with 1,000 rounds of ammunition.
Prototypes: Six ordered, C4290-C4295; C4290 used for ground tests; C4291-C4293 built and flown (C4291 first flown by Capt F Alexander in April 1918); C4294 and C4295 cancelled, but their components were used in two further prototypes, J6581 and J6582 (first flown with Lynx engines on 15 September 1921).

Sopwith T.F.2 Salamander

The Sopwith T.F.2 Salamander prototype, E5429, at Brooklands (Photo: Author's Collection)

The early formative years of British military aviation were spent largely in developing the aeroplane as a battlefield support element, that is to say a vehicle for reconnaissance over the Western Front in France. It is true that the RNAS contrived some outstanding bombing operations in those early years, sometimes achieving results out of all proportion to the efforts expended, what would in later years be termed strategic operations. In the mid-War years the aeroplane came to be used as a *weapon* against enemy forces in the field: fighting scouts would be armed with a gun or guns as well as light bombs, yet retain their ability to defend themselves on equal terms against enemy fighters. Such an aeroplane was the F.1 Camel.

The Camel also came to be developed into what was known as a 'trench fighter', an aircraft whose principal rôle was to attack battlefield targets, and which carried armour protection against small arms fire from the ground.

That the T.F.1 Camel was regarded as no more than an interim expedient is, however, emphasised by the fact that, when the first example was sent to France for operational trials on 7 March 1918, a purpose-designed trench fighter, the T.F.2 Salamander, was already coming into being.

In January that year Sopwith had been asked to produce an aircraft to meet BEF Specification No 2, with performance superior to that of the T.F.1 Camel. It was therefore not unnatural that the new aircraft would be related to the Snipe rather than the Camel, and this is borne out by the speed with which new prototypes were built. Assembly of the first three of six prototypes (E5429-E5434) began at the end of January; the first was delivered to Brooklands for final assembly on 26 April, made its maiden flight the next day, and was flown to France on 9 May for operational trials — by which time three other prototypes had been flown. At the end of June, when the third aircraft, E5431, underwent Service evalu-

ation, an order for 500 aircraft was placed with Sopwith; later orders for 600 Salamanders, placed with other manufacturers were either reduced or cancelled at the end of the War.

Like the Snipe, the Salamander was powered by a 230hp Bentley B.R.2 rotary and featured two-bay wings. The same plain ailerons and small tail surfaces as those on early Snipes were fitted, although these underwent modifications in step with the Snipe. Unlike the Snipe, however, the Salamander featured a flat-sided fuselage, while the entire front fuselage was constructed in armour plate, weighing no less than 650 pounds. Armament remained the nose-mounted pair of Vickers guns, but with ammunition increased from 1,500 to 2,000 rounds. (Various other armament schemes were flown experimentally, and at least one Salamander was armed with

a battery of eight Lewis guns, all mounted to fire downwards.)

Production of Salamanders was accelerating rapidly when the Armistice was signed, but only two were in France at that time. One of these had been delivered to No 86 Squadron at Phalempin, a squadron that had been declared a 'trench fighting unit'; a week later this order was rescinded. Two other Squadrons in England, Nos 95 at Wyton and 157 at Upper Heyford, had also been declared as ground attack squadrons, and between them took five Salamanders on charge before further deliveries were suspended.

A total of 210 Salamanders had been delivered into storage when production at Sopwith and Glendower was halted in 1919. One production aircraft, F6533, was sent to the United States for evaluation at McCook Field.

Type: Single-engine, single-seat, two-bay biplane trench fighter.

Manufacturers: The Sopwith Aviation Co Ltd, Kingston-upon-Thames, Surrey; The Glendower Aircraft Co Ltd, London.

Specification: British Expeditionary Force Specification No 2 of 1917.

Powerplant: One 230hp Bentley B.R.2 rotary engine driving two-blade propeller.

Dimensions: (Production) Span, 31ft 2⅝in; length, 19ft 6in; height, 9ft 4in; wing area, 272 sq. ft.

Weights: (Production) Tare, 1,844lb; all-up, 2,512lb.

Performance: (Production) Max speed, 125 mph at sea level; climb to 10,000ft, 17 min 5 sec; service ceiling, 13,000ft; endurance, 1½ hr.

Armament: Standard armament was two synchronized 0.303in Vickers machine guns on nose with 1,000 rounds per gun.

Prototype: Six, E5429-E5434 (E5429 was first flown on 27 April 1918)

Production: Total of 1,100 Salamanders ordered. (Sopwith, 500, F6501-F7000; Glendower, 100, J5892-J5991; Palladium Autocars, 100, J5992-J6091; No 3 National Aircraft Factory, 400: J6092-J6491). Only 210 aircraft were completed (Sopwith, 160: F6501-F6660; Glendower, 50: J5892-J5941); remainder cancelled.

Summary of Service: Salamanders were delivered to No 86 Squadron in France, and to Nos 95 and 157 Squadrons in the United Kingdom, but these units did not become operational on them.

R.A.F. A.E.3 Farnborough Ram

A Farnborough Ram Mk II with Bentley BR.2 rotary engine (Photo: R H Lines)

The Royal Aircraft Factory's A.E.3, whose initials are believed to have signified Armed (or Armoured) Experimental, was a derivative of the N.E.1 night fighter (see page 113), but developed for the rôle of trench strafing in answer to a B.E.F. requirement. It retained the same or similar unstaggered, three-bay wings, tail booms and undercarriage of the N.E.3, but featured a crew nacelle constructed of quarter-inch armour plate.

It is unlikely that the A.E.3 was designed to the same B.E.F. Specification as the Sopwith Salamander trench fighter for, whereas the latter's armament was appropriate for a trench fighter capable of both air-to-air and air-to-ground combat, the A.E.3 was intended to pour a stream of fire into enemy trenches as it flew relatively slowly, straight and level overhead. For this purpose it was armed in the nose of the nacelle with double-yoked Lewis guns which could be depressed, as well as a third Lewis gun on a telescopic mounting between the cockpits, capable of firing aft and abeam for self-defence.

Three aircraft were ordered, and the first flew at the beginning of April 1918, and all three were flying by June. During this period the Factory at Farnborough was renamed an Establishment (becoming the RAE), and a ruling issued whereby aircraft designed by the former Factory should be referred to as Farnborough products. Thus named the

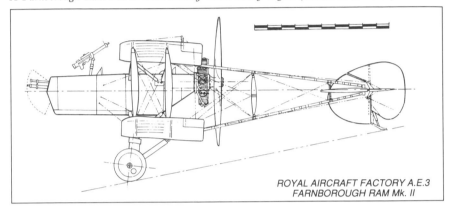

ROYAL AIRCRAFT FACTORY A.E.3
FARNBOROUGH RAM Mk. II

Ram, the A.E.3 was therefore the only Factory aircraft bestowed with an official name.

The Ram Mk I was powered by a 200hp Sunbeam Arab eight-cylinder in-line engine, and the Mk II a 230hp Bentley B.R.2 rotary. A Mark III was proposed with a B.R.1 engine and wings of greater chord, but it is assumed that this was not built.

Type: Single pusher engine, two-seat, three-bay biplane trench fighter.
Manufacturer: The Royal Aircraft Factory (Establishment), Farnborough, Hampshire.
Specification: British Expeditionary Force Requirement of 1917.
Powerplant: Mk I, 200hp Sunbeam Arab; Mk II, 230hp Bentley B.R.2 rotary engine.
Dimensions: Span, 47ft 10½in; length, 27ft 8½in; height, 10ft 0in.
Performance: Max speed, 95 mph at sea level.
Armament: Two Lewis guns in extreme nose of nacelle and one Lewis gun on telescopic mounting offset to port between cockpits.
Prototypes: Three, B8781-B8783, all built; first flown in April 1918. No production.

Sopwith 8F.1 Snail

Origins of the Sopwith Snail go back to October 1917 when Herbert Smith was managing the design of a small fighter, to be powered by the new ABC Wasp radial engine and intended for submission to meet the Air Board Specification A.1A. As originally designed, this aero-

Paradoxically the Snail Mk II, C4284, was the first to fly. The unusual appearance of the centre section struts was caused by the mounting of the guns on the upper longerons, resulting in the forward struts being anchored to the lower longerons. (Photo: J M Bruce)

plane, the 8F.1, was to be constructed on strictly conventional lines, that is wooden box-girder fuselage, faired to oval section, although Smith called on a number of successful features from recent Sopwith designs — concentration of principal masses in the nose of the Camel, the benefits of back-staggered

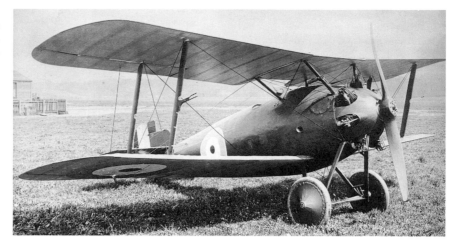

The monocoque Sopwith Snail Mk I, C4288, with conventionally back-staggered wings. The excellent aerodynamic form of the fuselage is readily apparent in this photograph taken at Brooklands. (Photo: J M Bruce)

wings and forward location of the cockpit prominent among them. Indeed the 8F.1 was smaller than the Camel, though not strictly a light fighter in the accepted sense.

Six 8F.1 prototypes, C4284–C4289, were ordered on 31 October, but on 23 November the Air Board asked that the last two aircraft be designed around a monocoque fuselage. As the first of the monocoque aircraft began to take shape early in 1918, it earned the company nickname Snail, presumably on account of its shell-like fuselage, and this name was adopted officially when the new regulations regarding the naming of aircraft were issued. Thus the monocoque aircraft logically became the Snail Mark I, and the fabric-covered prototype the Mark II.

It was the Mk II which appeared first in April, being easily identifiable by the back stagger on the wings; the top wing was so rigged as to lie directly over the cockpit with the result that a large cutout was necessary in order for the pilot's head to protrude above the upper surface. The Mark I was completed before the end of the same month and featured normal forward-staggered wings which resulted in the cockpit being below the wing's trailing edge, which was also cut away.

Both aircraft featured an exceptionally neat installation of the two Vickers guns low in the sides of the nose and almost totally enclosed within the fuselage. The monocoque fuselage was built up with ply skin over circular formers with wooden stringers.

Although the aircraft both returned fairly good performance figures, their handling was severely criticised as demonstrating the vicissitudes of the Camel to an extreme, but with added difficulties at low speeds. Be that as it may, once again the general unreliability of the Wasp engine brought about the end of Snail development, and only one example of each version was completed.

Type: Single-engine, single-seat, single-bay biplane fighter.
Manufacturer: The Sopwith Aviation Co Ltd, Kingston-upon-Thames and Brooklands, Surrey.
Air Board Specification: A.1A of 1917.
Powerplant: One 170hp ABC Wasp seven-cylinder radial engine.
Structure: Mk I. Wooden monocoque fuselage. Mk II. Wooden box-girder fuselage with fabric covering.
Dimensions: Span, 25ft 9in; length, 18ft 8in; height, 8ft 3in; wing area, 250 sq ft.
Weight: All-up, 1,478lb.
Performance: Max speed, 127 mph at sea level; climb to 10,000ft, 7 min 58 sec.
Armament: Two synchronized 0.303in Vickers machine guns in the sides of the nose.
Prototypes: Six ordered, C4284–C4289; only C4284 (Mk II, first flown, April 1918) and C4288 (Mk I, first flown, May 1918) completed; the other aircraft cancelled. No production.

Martinsyde F.4 Buzzard

The prototype Martinsyde F.4 Buzzard was, in effect, the F.3 example experimentally fitted with a 300hp Hispano Suiza engine, selected on account of the heavy demand for the Rolls-Royce Falcon III by the Bristol Fighter during 1918. The 18.5 litres engine, which by then was beginning to acquire a much improved reputation for reliability, despite its problems of sub-standard manufacture in the previous year, was a bored-out version of the 200hp engine, perpetuating the 90-degree Vee-eight water-cooled in-line design, and return-

ing a power-weight ratio of 0.50 bhp/lb.

The F.3 thus modified was re-termed the F.4 Buzzard, according to the new ruling that single-seat fighters should be named after birds of prey. The only other modification of note made to the F.3 was the re-positioning of the cockpit ten inches further aft, thereby improving the pilot's view, particularly downwards. The prototype was tested at Martlesham Heath in June, recording performance figures markedly superior to those of the production Snipe — 10 per cent better speed, 38 per cent faster climb and 35 per cent greater ceiling. (A junior draughtsman, employed in preparing production drawings of the F.4 at this time was a young man named Sydney Camm.)

On the strength of these excellent

figures, Martinsyde was awarded a production order for 150 machines, and it was being said that the Buzzard would enter widespread service with the RAF in 1919. During July and August Martinsyde's order was increased to 450, and 1,000 further aircraft were ordered from Boulton & Paul, Hooper, and Standard Motors. Three examples of a special long-range version, the Buzzard Mk IA, were also ordered from Martinsyde (H6540–H6542).

Production got underway very quickly at Brooklands, but, with the signing of the Armistice, all the 'shadow' contracts were cancelled outright. Martinsyde was instructed to complete only those aircraft on which work had started, with the result that a total of 338 Buzzards was built, of which 57 had reached the

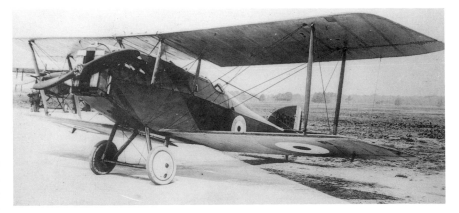

Standard production Martinsyde F.4 Buzzard, D4256, probably at Martlesham Heath in May 1919. (Photo: Imperial War Museum)

RAF; none was ever to reach an operational squadron, although at least five were flown by the Central Flying School for several months.

The decision not to adopt the Buzzard as front line equipment in the peacetime Royal Air Force in preference to the Snipe has been frequently called into question by historians down the years, in view of the Martinsyde's obvious superiority in performance. In support of the decision, however, it should be emphasised that the Buzzard was over 25 per cent more costly to produce than the Snipe (a powerful deciding factor in the atmosphere of post-War austerity), and that almost 200 more Snipes had been built and were in storage at Aircraft Parks. The Snipe had, moreover, reached operational squadrons — albeit few of them — and a host of aspiring peacetime pilots had been weaned on Sopwith fighters.

True, the Sopwith company was to go into voluntary liquidation in 1920, but Martinsyde was to follow suit only one year later.

Nevertheless, Buzzards underwent a good deal of post-War development and experiment. Several examples acquired Falcon III engines, a two-seat reconnaissance version was produced, and a floatplane appeared. The three long-range Buzzard IAs, referred to above and intended to be the precursors of an escort fighter for the RAF's Independent Force of bombers, were subjected to lengthy trials both at Martlesham Heath and Farnborough, H6541 not being struck off charge by the RAE until July 1923.

Many of the War-surplus Buzzards were re-purchased by Martinsyde, only to be sequestrated in 1921 by Aircraft Disposals Co Ltd when the manufacturers closed down. Four of these 'Tinsides' were supplied to the Irish Air Corps, and another was presented to Japan, where subsequent indigenous designs displayed unmistakable Martinsyde influence.

Type: Single-engine, single-seat, single-bay biplane fighter.
Manufacturer: Martinsyde Ltd, Brooklands, Surrey.
Powerplant: One 300hp Hispano-Suiza Vee-eight water-cooled in-line engine driving two-blade Lang propeller.
Structure: Cable-braced wooden box-girder fuselage with fabric, ply and duralumin sheet covering; unequal-span two-bay two-spar wooden wings rigged with moderate stagger.
Dimensions: Span, 32ft 5⅝in; length, 25ft 5⅝in; height, 10ft 4in; wing area, 320 sq ft.
Weights: Tare, 1,811lb; all-up, 2,398lb;
Performance: Max speed, 146 mph at sea level, 139.5 mph at 15,000ft; climb to 10,000ft, 6 min 40 sec; service ceiling, 26,000ft; endurance, 2½ hr.
Armament: Two synchronized 0.303in Vickers machine guns mounted within the nose cowling; provision made to carry light bombs up to total weight of about 220lb.
Prototype: One Martinsyde F.3 modified.
Production: A total of 338 Buzzards was built from a total of 1,453 ordered (Martinsyde, 453: D4211-D4360 and H6540-H6542 (Mk IAs); and H7613-H7912 of which 178 were completed; Boulton & Paul, 500, all cancelled: H8763-H9112 and J1992-J2141; Hooper Ltd, 200, all cancelled: J3342-J3541; and The Standard Motor Co, Ltd, 300, all cancelled: J5592-J5891).
Summary of Service: Eleven Buzzards are recorded as having been flown by RAF Station detachments and flights during 1919 and 1920, five by the Central Flying School and two by the RAF Communications Wing).

Armstrong, Whitworth F.M.4 Armadillo

Variously described elsewhere as 'pugnacious' and 'far from elegant', the F.M.4 Armadillo was surely nothing short of ugly, and was possibly the brainchild of Frederick Koolhoven, who had left Armstrong, Whitworth to join the British Aerial Transport company following the failure of his F.K.10 and 12, his place being taken as chief designer by Fred Murphy.

Subject of Licence No 18, two prototypes (X19 and X20) of this small two-bay biplane were authorized, and X19

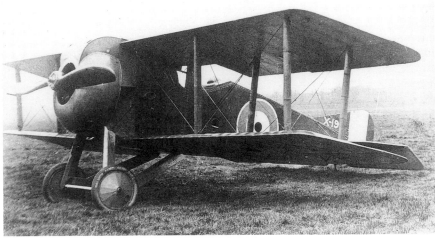

The first Armstrong, Whitworth F.M.4 Armadillo, X19; when it first appeared the undercarriage V-struts were much slimmer; in this photograph they appear to have been strengthened considerably. (Photo: G S Leslie)

appeared in September 1918. Rigged with scarcely any stagger, the wings were of fairly broad chord, and the upper wing — without conventional centre section — was attached to the top shoulders of the square-section fuselage. This was in keeping with Koolhoven's latest preoccupation, that of setting the upper wing level with the pilot's eyes.

The fuselage was a plain wooden box girder with flat ply sheet covering the sides, but without any attempt to provide any rounded decking. The engine was a 230hp Bentley B.R.2 rotary with a cowling that completely enveloped the cylinders, and included a fairly small aperture for cooling air entry. A most incongruous feature was a humped fairing, curving up from the front of the cowling to the top line of the upper wing, inside which were mounted the aircraft's twin Vickers guns.

The reasoning behind this wing layout was obviously to provide the pilot with an excellent field of view forward and above, but the bulk of the nose and the lower wings severely restricted the pilot's view of the ground, especially when landing, despite cutouts in the wings, and the aircraft was severely criticised on this account — not to mention many others.

It is difficult to understand what lay behind the production of this machine so late in the War for, with over one hundred horsepower more that the Le Rhône Camel of the previous year available, the speed performance of the Armadillo showed scarcely any advance. It is not known whether the second example was completed.

Type: Single-engine, single-seat, two-bay biplane fighter.
Manufacturer: Sir W G Armstrong, Whitworth & Co Ltd, Newcastle-upon-Tyne.
Powerplant: One 230hp Bentley B.R.2 rotary engine.
Dimensions: Span, 27ft 9in; length, 18ft 10in; height, 7ft 10in; wing area, 232 sq ft.
Weights: Tare, 1,250lb; all-up, 1,860lb.
Performance: Max speed, 125 mph at sea level; climb to 10,000ft, 6 min 30 sec; ceiling, 24,000ft.
Armament: Two synchronized 0.303in Vickers machine guns under fairing over the nose.
Prototypes: Two; X19 and X20 authorised under Licence No 18. X19 flown in September 1918; X20 may not have been completed. No production.

Sopwith Buffalo

The appalling carnage that had prevailed on the Western Front during the long years of territorial stalemate brought forth the realisation that the effective use of the aeroplane against battlefield targets could well represent the vital extra dimension needed to break the deadlock between the opposing armies. The greatest obstacle to this use was the huge numbers of soldiers packed into the trenches, who could put up a veritable curtain of small-arms fire against marauding aeroplanes — an obstacle that was to persist in air warfare as recently as 1991.

Thus were born the 'trench fighters', the armoured fighters such as the T.F.1 Camel and the T.F.2 Salamander. To this strictly offensive rôle was soon added what became known as the 'contact patrol' fighter, in effect representing a return to the original purpose of the military aeroplane, that of tactical reconnaissance. In later years this specialist aircraft would become known simply as the reconnaissance fighter.

In September 1918 appeared the Sopwith Buffalo, designed with this rôle in mind. Unlike the Salamander, which was strictly a single-seat ground attack fighter, the Buffalo carried an observer/gunner, and was therefore one step closer to the Bristol Fighter.

Powered by a 230hp Bentley B.R.2 rotary engine, the Buffalo was of fairly

The second Buffalo trench fighter, H5893, showing the fuselage side armour extended aft beyond the gunner's cockpit together with the rear Scarff gun ring. (Photo: Sopwith Aviation Co Ltd)

orthodox configuration with two-bay, forward-staggered wings, and flying surfaces of typical Sopwith outline; plain ailerons were fitted on all wings. The first of two officially-sponsored prototypes, ordered in July 1918, H5892, was heavily armoured aft as far as the rear of the gunner's cockpit, and featured rather crude-looking fairings to provide the transition from the engine's circular section to the flat-sided centre and rear fuselage.

The second aircraft appeared late in October with the side armour extended further aft of the rear cockpit, cutaway trailing edge of the lower wing roots, and with much tidier side fairings. The second example also carried a Scarff ring for the Lewis gun on the gunner's cockpit in place of the rocking-pillar

Type: Single-engine, two-seat, two-bay biplane contact patrol fighter.
Manufacturer: The Sopwith Aviation Co Ltd, Kingston-upon-Thames and Brooklands, Surrey.
Powerplant: One 230hp Bentley B.R.2 rotary engine driving two-blade Lang propeller.
Dimensions: Span, 34ft 6in; length, 23ft 3½ in; height, 9ft 6in; wing area, 326 sq ft.
Weights: Tare, 2,178lb; all-up, 3,071lb.
Performance: Max speed, 114 mph at 1,000ft; climb to 3,000ft, 4 min 55 sec; service ceiling, 9,000ft.
Armament: One synchronized 0.303in Vickers machine gun on nose decking, and one Lewis gun on rear cockpit (with Scarff ring on second aircraft).
Prototypes: Two, H5892 and H5893 (H5892 first flown on 19 September 1918, and H5893 in October 1918). No production.

mounting of the first aircraft. To support the weight of armour while on the ground, the undercarriage was considerably strengthened, as were the inboard wing sections. Not surprisingly the Sopwith Buffalo was not as fast nor manoeuvrable as its elder kin.

The first prototype was sent to France and arrived at Marquise on 20 October 1918 for operational trials, but these had not been completed when the Armistice was signed. The second prototype underwent official trials during November and December at Martlesham Heath but, with rapidly dwindling operational responsibilities, the RAF did not adopt the aircraft for service.

B.A.T. F.K.25 Basilisk

It is to be assumed that by the time Frederick Koolhoven arrived at his final wartime fighter design, the F.K.25 Basilisk, he had become disenchanted with his habit of attaching the top wing directly to the top of the fuselage, for in this aircraft the upper wing was built in two halves and joined on the aircraft's centreline; the wing was located well clear of the fuselage, being braced to it by a single, central N-strut.

The engine was once again the 320hp ABC Dragonfly — alas, still uncured of its self-destructive tendencies — and therein, of course, lay the ultimate fate of the aircraft. Apart from this fatal shortcoming, the Basilisk was a rugged, high performance fighter.

Three prototypes were ordered, and the first of these, F2906, was flown in September. Its two Vickers guns were mounted on the upper decking of the nose, but were soon to be covered by a large tapered fairing which extended aft to form the front coaming of the cockpit; the sides of the cockpit were cut fairly low so that, in conjunction with the cutaway lower wing root trailing edge, the pilot's field of view downwards was extremely good. The fin and horn-balanced rudder were of continuous

The ill-fated B.A.T. Basilisk prototype, F2906. (Photo: G S Leslie/ J M Bruce Collection)

contour of attractive shape, but early tests demanded a slight increase in rudder area. Plain ailerons were fitted on all four wings, although these were replaced by extended horn-balanced ailerons on the second aircraft.

The first Basilisk prototype was lost in a tragic accident early in May 1919, which cost the life of Flight-Cdr Peter Legh RN — the first post-War death of a test pilot. In an attempt on the world's altitude record while flying from Hendon, the Basilisk's engine caught fire and the aircraft crashed. This accident was cited as the cause of the death of the pilot, who might otherwise have survived had the aircraft been fitted with a metal-asbestos firewall forward of the cockpit, this statement leading to the mandatory introduction of such a firewall on every military and civilian aircraft thereafter.

All three Baslisks came to be built, the remaining two spending much of their time at Martlesham Heath between July 1919 and September 1920, when they were grounded on account of their recalcitrant Dragonfly engines.

Type: Single-engine, single-seat, two-bay biplane fighter.
Manufacturer: The British Aerial Transport Co Ltd, Willesden, London.
Powerplant: One 320hp ABC Dragonfly seven-cylinder radial engine.
Dimensions: Span, 25ft 4in; length, 20ft 5in; height, 8ft 2in; wing area, 212 sq ft.
Weights: Tare, 1,454lb; all-up, 2,182lb.
Performance: Max speed, 142.5 mph at 6,500ft; climb to 10,000ft, 8 min 25 sec; service ceiling, 22,500ft; endurance, 3¼ hr.
Armament: Two synchronized 0.303in Vickers machine guns on upper nose decking.
Prototypes: Three, F2906-F2908. (F2906 first flown in September 1918). No production.

Sopwith Swallow

The little Sopwith Swallow monoplane fighter was a direct development of the Scooter, a company venture which appeared in June 1918 and employed a Camel fuselage with a parasol wing mounted above but very close to the fuselage, braced with Raf-wires to a pyramidal cabane above the wing and to the lower longerons below. Powered by a 130hp Clerget, it was frequently flown

Although the Swallow was first delivered to Martlesham Heath, as shown here, in October 1918, its official tests were not completed until the following May. (Photo: J Kinsey)

by Harry Hawker for personal transport and as an aerobatic mount.

The Swallow flew in October, again using a Camel fuselage but retaining the twin Vickers guns and powered by a 110hp Le Rhône. The wing was located rather higher above the fuselage to enable the pilot to attend to his guns.

Only one Swallow was built, B9276, and this underwent official trials in May 1919, but displayed no improvement over the Camel. That the Swallow was in any way influenced by the appearance in the summer of 1918 of the German Fokker D VIII parasol monoplane is unlikely, yet the dimensions and weights were extraordinarily similar. However, employing a cantilever wing and the minimum of attachment struts, the German aeroplane was some 15 mph faster on the same nominal power.

Type: Single-engine, single-seat, parasol monoplane fighter.
Manufacturer: The Sopwith Aviation Co Ltd, Brooklands, Surrey.
Powerplant: One 110hp Le Rhône rotary engine driving two-blade propeller.
Dimensions: Span, 28ft 10in; length, 18ft 9in; wing area, 162 sq ft.
Weights: Tare, 889lb; all-up, 1,420lb.
Performance: Max speed, approx 122 mph at sea level; climb to 10,000ft, 9 min 55 sec; ceiling, 18,500ft.
Armament: Two synchronized 0.303in Vickers machine guns on upper decking of nose.
Prototype: One, B9276; first flown in October 1918.

Deployment of British Fighter Squadrons at the Armistice — 11 November 1918

Home Bases

No 33 Squadron	Avro 504K (NF)	Kirton Lindsey
No 36 Squadron	Bristol F.2B Fighter	Usworth
No 37 Squadron	Sopwith Camel	Stow Maries
No 44 Squadron	Sopwith Camel	Hainault Farm
No 50 Squadron	Sopwith Camel	Bekesbourne
No 51 Squadron	Sopwith Camel	Marham
No 61 Squadron	Sopwith Camel	Rochford
No 75 Squadron	Bristol F.2B Fighter	North Weald
No 76 Squadron	Bristol F.2B Fighter	Ripon
No 77 Squadron	Avro 504K (NF)	Penstone
No 78 Squadron	Sopwith Camel	Sutton Farm
No 90 Squadron	Avro 504K (NF)	Buckminster
No 91 Squadron	Sopwith Dolphin	Kenley
No 112 Squadron	Sopwith Camel	Throwley
No 123 Squadron*	Sopwith Dolphin	Upper Heyford
No 138 Squadron	Bristol F.2B Fighter	Chingford
No 141 Squadron	Bristol F.2B Fighter	Biggin Hill
No 143 Squadron	Sopwith Camel	Detling
No 155 Squadron	Sopwith Camel	Feltham
No 157 Squadron*	Sopwith Salamander	Upper Heyford
No 213 Squadron	Sopwith Camel	Scopwick
No 230 Squadron**	Sopwith Camel	Bentley
No 233 Squadron**	Sopwith Camel	Dover

France

No 1 Squadron	S.E.5A	Bouvincourt
No 3 Squadron	Sopwith Camel	Inchy
No 11 Squadron	Bristol F.2B Fighter	Bettoncourt
No 12 Squadron	Bristol F.2B Fighter	Estourmel
No 19 Squadron	Sopwith Dolphin	Abscon
No 20 Squadron	Bristol F.2B Fighter	Clary
No 22 Squadron	Bristol F.2B Fighter	Aniche
No 23 Squadron	Sopwith Dolphin	Bertry East
No 32 Squadron	S.E.5A	La Brayelle
No 35 Squadron	Bristol F.2B Fighter	La Grand Fayt
No 40 Squadron	S.E.5A	Aniche
No 41 Squadron	S.E.5A	Halluin
No 43 Squadron	Sopwith Snipe	Bouvincourt
No 45 Squadron	Sopwith Camel	Bettoncourt
No 46 Squadron	Sopwith Camel	Busigny
No 48 Squadron	Bristol F.2B Fighter	Reckem
No 54 Squadron	Sopwith Camel	Merchin
No 56 Squadron	S.E.5A	La Targette
No 60 Squadron	S.E.5A	Quievy
No 62 Squadron	Bristol F.2B Fighter	Villers-les-Cagnicourt
No 64 Squadron	S.E.5A	Aniche
No 68 Squadron	S.E.5A	Baizieux
No 70 Squadron	Sopwith Camel	Menin
No 73 Squadron	Sopwith Camel	Malencourt
No 74 Squadron	S.E.5A	Cuerne
No 80 Squadron	Sopwith Camel	Flaumont
No 84 Squadron	S.E.5A	Bertry
No 85 Squadron	S.E.5A	Phalempin
No 87 Squadron	Sopwith Dolphin	Boussières
No 88 Squadron	Bristol F.2B Fighter	Bersée
No 92 Squadron	S.E.5A	Bertry
No 94 Squadron	S.E.5A	Senlis
No 151 Squadron	Sopwith Camel	Bancourt
No 152 Squadron	Sopwith Camel	Carvin
No 201 Squadron	Sopwith Camel/Snipe	La Targette
No 203 Squadron	Sopwith Camel	Bruille
No 204 Squadron	Sopwith Camel	Heule
No 208 Squadron	Sopwith Camel/Snipe	Maretz
No 209 Squadron	Sopwith Camel	Izel-le-Hameau
No 210 Squadron	Sopwith Camel	Boussières

Belgium

No 24 Squadron	S.E.5A	Bisseghem
No 29 Squadron	S.E.5A	Marcke
No 39 Squadron	Bristol F.2B Fighter	Bavichove
No 65 Squadron	Sopwith Camel	Bisseghem
No 79 Squadron	Sopwith Dolphin	Nivelles

Mediteraanean

No 28 Squadron	Sopwith Camel	Sarcedo, Italy
No 66 Squadron	Sopwith Camel	San Pietro, Italy
No 150 Squadron	S.E.5A	Kirec, Macedonia
No 220 Squadron	Sopwith Camel	Imbros, Aegean
No 222 Squadron	Sopwith Camel	Thasos, Aegean
No 225 Squadron	Sopwith Camel	Aliminni, Italy

Middle East

No 72 Squadron	Bristol M.1C/SE.5A	Basra, Mesopotamia
No 111 Squadron	S.E.5A	Qantara, Egypt
No 145 Squadron	S.E.5A	Ramleh, Palestine

*   Squadron non-operational
** One Flight only equipped with fighters

3. POST-WAR AUSTERITY

When the War ended, Britain possessed the largest and most powerful air force in the world by a wide margin, a position of leadership she was only to occupy once more, and then only briefly. By the time the warring leaders signed the peace document in 1919, however, the Royal Air Force was already in decline, as first the nation's economists and later the politicians counted the cost of war. Indeed, only four years after the guns fell silent, a Conservative leader went so far as to suggest the dissolution of the RAF.

It is well known how Trenchard fought successfully for the survival of the Royal Air Force by well-judged deployment of his slender resources overseas and, by so doing, was able to demonstrate how an air force could discharge responsibilities, traditionally undertaken by ground forces, much more 'cost effectively'. Moreover Trenchard had to wage a war of his own against the predatory admirals and generals in Whitehall, all bickering to justify their inflated claims on the slender defence funds.

But Trenchard was single-mindedly a bomber protagonist, who saw little value in the fighter aeroplane, except possibly to escort his bomber formations. He had, after all, commanded the RAF's Independent Force in 1918, potentially a powerful weapon that, given time, would have imposed the will of the Allies on Germany by systematically striking towns and cities far from the Western Front. When one considers the volatile nature of the German nation, teetering on the brink of revolution late in 1918, such an air offensive might have had catastrophic results for the Central Powers. At the time of the Armistice Trenchard's bombers were just beginning to flex their muscles.

Thus it was that the RAF's famous fighter squadrons were disbanded or transferred to other rôles until, in 1922, only one, No 25 with Snipes, remained in Britain — and even that squadron only survived because its commanding officer enjoyed influence in high places. As already explained, the Sopwith Snipe and the Bristol F.2B Fighter had been selected to serve as standard equipment

of the RAF's peacetime fighter arm; indeed, these wartime workhorses continued to serve until 1926 and 1932 respectively.

As the production of other wartime fighters was terminated by contract cancellation, and war profit tax legislation threatened famous companies with ruin, fighter manufacturers such as Sopwith and Martinsyde disappeared for ever. Others sought survival in different spheres of aircraft manufacture.

Not that the Air Ministry was encouraged to seek new fighters. With a Chief of the Air Staff pre-occupied with other matters, the intrastructure no longer existed that could think in terms of new requirements when fighter squadrons scarcely featured in the post-War establishment. There is was little more that the requirements department could do than simply leave the outstanding Specifications 'on the table'. What had started as a series of Air Board Requirements in 1917, to be joined by the somewhat nebulous British Expeditionary Force Requirements, were consolidated in 1918 as RAF Type Requirements. Some of the latter remained unchanged, while others were re-drafted at the time of the Armistice by the Department (or Directorate) of Research in an effort to consolidate a single standard formula for future aircraft requirements in each category.

By 1920 a new system of requirements was being introduced, although once again some existing Specifications were allowed to remain unchanged. Perhaps predictably, the 1920 Specifications included few new fighter requirements, and none attracted serious consideration simply because few companies could risk the financial outlay for prototypes which were unlikely to be rewarded by production contracts. In any case the few fighter manufacturers of any former substance had either parted with their senior designers or were scratching an existence by rebuilding or repairing aircraft like the Snipe, Bristol Fighter or de Havilland D.H.9A.

Moreover, examination of the early post-War Specifications discloses a lack of understanding at the Air Ministry of the parlous state of affairs that now

existed in the aircraft industry. Engine production had fallen to a mere shadow of the wartime output, and several of the promising late-wartime engines were proving to be failures. The faltering growth of commercial aviation and multi-engine bombers claimed much of the remaining output. Just as serious was a growing estrangement between Service and Industry as each became introspectively pre-occupied with its future survival. The extraordinarily close relationship, which came into being between the manufacturers and Service, had all but disappeared in 1919 as the Geddes axe was wielded so indiscriminately

Slowly, however, not only the aircraft industry but the Royal Air Force itself began to emerge from the post-War doldrums. Men who had proved their prowess in the War — designers like Henry Folland, Geoffrey de Havilland, Frank Barnwell and W G Carter, great airmen like Sir John Salmond, not forgetting the practical scientists such as Henry Tizard, and the leaders of industry of the calibre of T O M Sopwith, Richard Fairey, Henry Royce and many others — now applied their various talents to reconstructing British aviation according to the financial resources available, and a start was made to repair the ties between the Royal Air Force (through the Air Ministry) and the industry (by such establishments as those at Farnborough and Martlesham Heath).

By the end of 1923 the number of home-based fighter squadrons had grown to nine (of which six were equipped with Snipes), and a total of eight fighter Specifications were being tendered to by six manufacturers; from these would come the Armstrong Whitworth Siskin, Gloucestershire Grebe and the Hawker Woodcock.

Even though the Sopwith company had gone into liquidation in 1920, a new company had been formed almost immediately as the Australian pilot and friend of T O M Sopwith, Harry Hawker, agreed to purchase the former Sopwith premises in Kingston; an attempt to produce motor cars and motor cycles proved unnecessary when contracts were received to recondition Snipes for the RAF. Soon after the formation of the

Hawker Engineering Company, Hawker was killed in a flying accident, leaving Sopwith as Chairman.

Another manufacturer that survived was the Gloucestershire Aircraft Company, then of Cheltenham. By securing the services of Henry Folland and adapt-ing the wartime Nieuport Nighthawk fighter by a series of aerodynamic improvements, the company built a sound basis on which to flourish. For the next fifty years the two companies, Hawker and Gloster, were to become the most prolific producers of fighter aircraft.

Indeed it has been the unequalled achievement of Hawker that there has never been a time since 1913 that Kingston-designed aeroplanes have been absent from Britain's air forces. Rolls-Royce can lay claim to a similar record with its superlative engines.

Westland Weasel

First flown at about the time of the Armistice, the Westland Weasel was one of almost a dozen aircraft whose future — or, more accurately, the lack of it — was compromised by the failure of Granville Bradshaw's ABC Dragonfly engine.

The two-seat, two-bay Weasel bi-plane was designed by Robert Bruce and Arthur Davenport during the summer of 1918 in response to the RAF Type IIIA Specification which called for a successor to the Bristol F.2B Fighter which was expected, under wartime conditions, to be due for replacement during 1919-20. Like the Wagtail, the Weasel possessed no dihedral on the lower wings, but pronounced dihedral on the upper planes. The pilot's cockpit was located below the rear spar of the upper wing, necessitating an inter-spar aperture in the wing centresection above his head for upward view; being well staggered, the lower wing was sufficiently far aft to give the pilot a good view forward and downwards for landing. Generous trailing-edge cutouts were provided on both upper and lower wings which were both fitted with ailerons. The tailplane incidence was adjustable in flight.

Choice of the Dragonfly engine — recommended, it should be said, by the Air Ministry — proved unfortunate, to say the least. Not only was it found to be almost ten per cent heavier than forecast by the manufacturer, but was thirteen per cent down on power. The cylinder finning proved wholly inadequate for cooling, resulting in constant overheating. More serious was the frequent failure of crankshafts (presumably due to fatigue) as it was discovered that the engine's designed running speed coincided with the crankshaft's critical vibration frequency in torsion.

Three prototype Weasels were ordered on 3 May 1918, and F2912 was flown in November by Capt Stuart

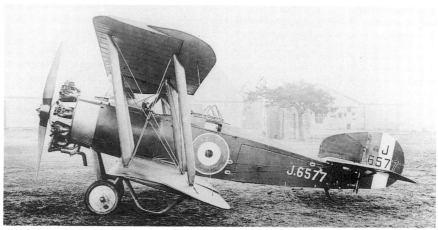

The fourth and final Westland Weasel, the Mk II, J6577, with horn-balanced ailerons, enlarged fin and muffs on engine exhaust pipes. (Photo: Air Ministry, dated 20 August 1923; see text)

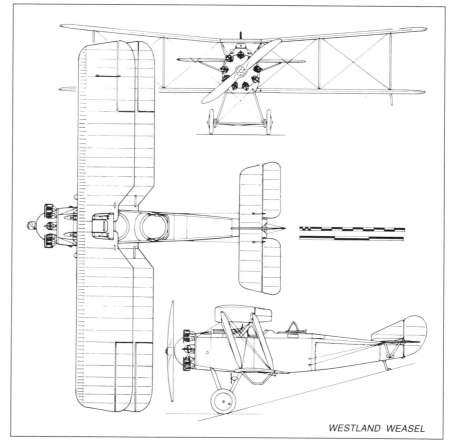

WESTLAND WEASEL

Keep. Little or no further flying was done during the next four or five months while alterations were made in the forward fuselage to take account of the unexpectedly heavy engine. F2913 flew in June and F2914 in September.

The first Weasel underwent preliminary trials at Martlesham Heath in May to establish its handling characteristics with the revised c.g., but was destroyed during November in a forced landing following an engine fire; the pilot, Flt Lt

Augustus Henry Orlebar AFC was un-hurt. (Some records suggest that the aircraft was fitted with an Armstrong Siddeley Lynx engine at the time).

After discontinuation of the Dragon-fly engine's development, all efforts to suit the Weasel for an active Service rôle were abandoned late in 1919. Instead, the two remaining original prototypes were confined to the development of other engines. F2913 was fitted with a Bristol Jupiter IV radial engine in 1921, and continued flying at the RAE until January 1924, being written off charge in October that year.

F2914 also had a long and varied life, suffering but surviving a number of forced landings. In 1920 its fin and rudder were redesigned to incorporate a horn-balanced rudder; beginning in November it underwent some further alteration and emerged in January 1922, powered by a 350hp Armstrong Siddeley Jaguar II two-row radial engine, appearing in this form in the New Types Park at the RAF Hendon Pageant on 24 June, and again at the 1923 Display. A

Jaguar III was fitted in November 1923, and F2914 continued flying at Farnborough until 9 April 1925.

A fourth Weasel prototype had been ordered from Westland on 29 August 1919 under the designation Mark II, designed to the new D of R Type 2 Specification. Powered at the outset by a 450hp Cosmos Jupiter II radial, this aircraft, J6577, first flew in March 1920, but in July appeared at Martlesham with a Jaguar II engine. A year later this was replaced by a 436hp Jupiter IV. J6577 differed from the earlier prototypes in being fitted with horn-balanced ailerons.

The fate of this aeroplane is something of a mystery. After appearing in the New Types Park at Hendon in June 1922, it is said that J6577 crashed near Martlesham Heath following a fire in the air, and was burned out. Several records, however, show that this aircraft was flying at Martlesham in 1923, and the accompanying Air Ministry photo-graph is date-stamped 20 August 1923; moreover the aircraft as depicted appears to be fitted with heat-exchanger muffs on the exhaust pipes of the type developed by Bristol early in 1923.

The data table refers to the Weasel Mk I with Dragonfly engine.

Type: Single-engine, single-seat, two-bay biplane fighter.
Manufacturer: The Westland Aircraft Works, Yeovil, Somerset.
Air Ministry Specifications: RAF Type IIIA of 1918, and D of R Type 2 of 1919.
Powerplant: One 320hp ABC Dragonfly I; also 350hp Armstrong Siddeley Jaguar II, 450hp Cosmos Jupiter II, 436hp Bristol Jupiter IV, and possibly Armstrong Siddeley Lynx.
Dimensions: Span, 35ft 6in; length, 24ft 10in; height, 10ft 1in; wing area, 368 sq ft.
Weights: Tare, 1,867lb; all-up, 3,071lb.
Performance: Max speed 130.5 mph at sea level; climb to 10,000ft, 10 min; ceiling, 20,700ft.
Armament: Two synchronized 0.303in Vickers machine guns on front fuselage decking, and one Lewis gun with Scarff ring on rear cockpit.
Prototypes: Four, F2912-F2914 (Mk Is) and J6577 (Mk II). No production.

Sopwith Dragon

As previously told (see page 120), the final Sopwith Snipe prototype, B9967, was fitted experimentally with a 320hp ABC Dragonfly I engine, and appeared in the spring of 1918 (possibly, as suggested by J M Bruce, as an insurance against any failure of the Nieuport Nighthawk). In this respect it may be contended, though not strictly accu-rately, that B9967 was therefore re-garded as the Dragon prototype.

Be that as it may, the performance attained by the Dragonfly Snipe was such as to encourage Sopwith to perse-vere and, in September 1918, a contract was received to build a prototype pow-ered by a new version of the Dragonfly, the 360hp Mark IA. This aircraft, E7990, another modified Snipe, first flew in January 1919, and certainly confirmed an excellent performance. Fitted with plain ailerons and the smooth-contoured fin and rudder, this aircraft attained a top speed of 150 mph at sea level, and a service ceiling of 25,000 feet with full ammunition and fuel.

A production order, signed with Sopwith on 16 October 1918 for 300

A production Sopwith Dragon, said to be J3909, with horn-balanced upper ailerons and heating muffs round the exhaust pipes. (Photo: Royal Aerospace Establishment, Farnborough)

Snipes (J3617-J3916), was altered on 21 November to cover a similar number of Dragons. Of these the airframes of about 200 aircraft were completed and deliv-ered into storage to await engines. A few, possibly no more than half a dozen, were

taken out of storage at random to have their Dragonfly IA engines fitted. One, J3628, was shipped to America for evalu-ation, and at least two others were at Farnborough during 1919-20 for engine trials. None reached an RAF squadron.

Type: Single-engine, single-seat, two-bay biplane fighter.
Manufacturer: The Sopwith Aviation Co Ltd, Kingston and Brooklands, Surrey.
Powerplant: One 360hp ABC Dragonfly IA nine-cylinder radial engine.
Dimensions: Span, 31ft 1in; length, 21ft 9in; height, 9ft 6in; wing area, 271 sq ft.
Weights: Tare, 1,405lb; all-up, 2,132lb.
Performance: Max speed, 150 mph at sea level; climb to 10,000ft, 7 min 30 sec; service ceiling, 25,000ft.
Armament: Two synchronized 0.303in Vickers machine guns on upper nose decking.
Prototype: One, E7990 (first flown in January 1919).
Production: Small number of aircraft completed from stored airframes (minimum of six known examples).

Sopwith Snark

Although ostensibly designed to RAF Specification Type 1 of 1918, the Sopwith Snark appears to have been a sincere though experimental attempt to carry aloft a much larger forward-firing armament than had hitherto been the norm, and to obtain the necessary lift from a relatively compact airframe Herbert Smith returned once more to the triplane formula.

Bearing in mind that design of the Snark started at roughly the same time that No 87 Squadron began flying its Dolphins with Lewis guns mounted under their lower wings, it is not inconceivable that this idea was in some way associated with the decision taken to fit Lewis guns beneath the lower wings of the new triplane, and four such guns were thus included — in addition to the customary pair of synchronized Vickers guns.

The Snark, of which three prototypes were produced, displayed several interesting features, not least being the monocoque fuselage. The rigging of the wings was unusual in that the stagger was much greater between the centre and lower wings than above, giving the appearance of 'bent' interplane struts; the centre section pedestal struts mounting the centre wing on the upper longerons were rigged vertically in front and side elevations, but those attached to the top wing were raked forwards and outwards. The centre wing featured a small trailing-edge cutout above the cockpit, that in the top wing being much more generous.

The airframe of the first prototype was completed in October 1918, but awaited its engine, originally intended to be a 320hp Dragonfly I. However the decision to redesign much of this engine

The first Sopwith Snark prototype, F4068. This photograph was taken in September 1918, before the airframe had been cleared for flight and with a non-flight engine installed; it was to be another ten months before a Dragonfly engine, acceptable for flight, was finally installed. Note the early form of engine cowling; on the final prototype this was improved by the addition of a spinner. Ailerons were fitted on all six wings. (Photo: The Sopwith Aviation Co Ltd, Neg No S1079, dated September 1918)

led to a delay, and the extensively modified 360hp Mark IA was not forthcoming until the following March. A further engine change delayed the first flight until July, by which time the other two prototypes had also been completed. The last aircraft, F4070, displayed a much cleaned-up engine cowling, with a large spinner enclosing the propeller hub.

Despite the triplane configuration the Snark possessed a creditable top speed of 130 mph at sea level when flown at Martlesham Heath on official trials in 1921, though it is not clear whether guns or ballast were being carried. It was generally liked by its pilots although its manœuvrability could not match that of the little Sopwith Triplane of 1916. The inevitable problems of the Dragonfly engine proved to be little more than academic as the Snark was never seriously considered as likely Service equipment.

Type: Single-engine, single-seat, single-bay experimental triplane fighter.
Manufacturer: The Sopwith Aviation Co Ltd, Kingston and Brooklands, Surrey.
Air Ministry Specification: RAF Type I of 1918.
Powerplant: One 360hp ABC Dragonfly IA nine-cylinder radial engine.
Dimensions: Span, 26ft 6in; length, 20ft 9in; height, 10ft 1in; wing area, 322 sq ft.
Weight: All-up, 2,283lb.
Performance: Max speed, 130 mph at sea level.
Armament: Two synchronized 0.303in Vickers machine guns in nose cowling, and four free-firing Lewis guns under the lower wings, each with one 97-round drum.
Prototypes: Three, F4068-F4070 (first flight by F4068, July 1919). No production.

Bristol Badger

The Bristol designation F.2C came to be used, after the appearance in service of the famous F.2B Fighter in 1917, for a proposed replacement, the design of which began in November that year. Originally this project was intended to be fitted with either a Bentley B.R.2 rotary engine or a 260hp Salmson

water-cooled radial engine.

The promise held out by the powerful new ABC Dragonfly, however, attracted the attention of Frank Barnwell, who then embarked on an entirely new design with this engine — though still retaining the F.2C designation.

Named the Type 23 Badger (to conform to Technical Department Instruction No 538 of 1918 which required multi-seat fighters to be named after mammals), the new aircraft was a two-

seat, single-bay, staggered biplane of fabric-covered, wooden box-girder construction, with the N-type interplane struts which had been a feature of the Bristol Scout F. Ailerons were fitted to the upper wing only and — again reverting to the Scouts — no fixed tail fin was included.

Three prototypes, F3495-F3497, were ordered on 14 May but, in view of troubles and delays being experienced with the Dragonfly engine, design work

The Bristol Type 23 F.2C Badger Mark II prototype, F3496, with the Cosmos Jupiter I radial engine; the fixed tail fin has been added, the Vickers gun armament omitted and the rear cockpit faired over. (Photo: The Bristol Aeroplane Co Ltd, Neg No 67)

continued slowly during 1918. Ironically, the first prototype was damaged in a crash landing during take-off for its first flight on 4 February 1919, the accident being caused by an air lock in the fuel feed. The pilot, Cyril Uwins, was unhurt.

This aircraft, the Badger Mk I, was repaired and given an improved, more pointed engine cowling, and the opportunity was taken to fit a slightly enlarged rudder. The work only occupied ten days, and F3495 was handed over to the Air Board on 15 February; it subsequently underwent prolonged performance and handling trials at Martlesham Heath, remaining there until September 1920.

Meanwhile the second prototype, the Badger Mk II F3496, had been scheduled for the 400hp Cosmos Jupiter I nine-cylinder radial engine, but the bench tests delayed delivery so that its first flight was not accomplished until 24 May 1919. Production of the Jupiter, which would have recovered the heavy cost of development for its manufacturers, had been cancelled after the Armistice, foreshadowing virtual ruin for Cosmos Engineering Co Ltd. Believing that the Jupiter engine held considerable promise, the British & Colonial Aeroplane company began negotiating the acquisition of all assets of the Cosmos company — under some pressure from the British Government. A preliminary order was then placed for six experimental engines for test purposes, two of these being intended for flight in the Badger.

No trouble was experienced with the Jupiter in F3496 during trials. The aircraft, however, had been criticised on

account of inadequate lateral and directional control, and it was decided to fit a conventional fixed fin. This prototype was handed over to Air Ministry charge in June and was delivered to Martlesham in October, but is believed to have crashed the same month after being fitted with a Dragonfly IA engine. . .

Owing to the handling deficiencies of the second Badger, the third of the original prototypes was delayed pending wind-tunnel tests, and was first flown in February 1920. Another Badger had been completed in 1919 for aerodynamic tests, powered by an Armstrong Siddeley Puma engine, but in fact only the wings and undercarriage were of Badger design. Locally referred to as the Badger X (for experimental) the aircraft was entered on the Civil Register as K110, but had already crashed on 22 May that year.

If one accepts that this was indeed the fourth Badger, a fifth had been designed to conform to RAF Type II Specification of 1918 — later re-designated the D of R Type II. A single prototype, J6492, was ordered on 19 November 1918 as a Badger Mk II, to be powered by a 500hp

Cosmos Jupiter II. This aeroplane featured new control surfaces including a horn-balanced rudder integral with the outline of the fin, and ailerons with 'park-bench' balances; the latter, designed by Leslie Frise (Barnwell's assistant), were in effect a combination of aerodynamic and mass balances, strut-mounted on but angled forward of the control surface. They were to be developed later into the patented Frise balanced ailerons.

J6492 was flown in March 1920 and taken on charge by the Air Ministry immediately. It was straightway loaned to its manufacturer to continue flight testing of the Jupiter engine, paying several visits to Martlesham Heath and Farnborough before being struck off charge at the RAE in October 1923.

For all its delays and setbacks, the Badger was an important aircraft, and the work it did provided a great amount of data which enabled the Air Ministry to begin drafting realistic fighter requirements from 1922 onwards. The Jupiter, whose development and progressive improvement continued for a further ten years (and remained in RAF

Type: Single-engine, two-seat, single-bay experimental biplane fighter.

Manufacturer: The British & Colonial Aeroplane Co Ltd, Filton, Bristol (later The Bristol Aeroplane Co Ltd.)

Air Ministry Specification: RAF Type II (later D of R Type II).

Powerplant: Badger Mk I. One 320hp A.B.C. Dragonfly I. Badger Mk II. 450hp Cosmos Jupiter I; 500hp Cosmos Jupiter II.

Dimensions: Span, 36ft 9in; length, 23ft 8in; height, 9ft 1in; wing area, 357.2 sq ft.

Weights: Tare, 1,948lb; all-up, 3,152lb.

Performance: Max speed, 135 mph at sea level (Mk II, 142 mph at sea level); climb to 10,000ft, 11 min 0 sec; service ceiling, 20,600ft.

Armament: Two synchronized 0.303in Vickers machine guns in nose, and one Lewis gun with Scarff ring on rear cockpit.

Prototypes: Four ordered, F3495-F3497 (Mk I, F3495, first flown 4 February 1919; Mk II, F3496, 24 May 1919); J6492 (flown in March 1920). No production.

service until the eve of the Second World War), may be seen as the first truly successful static radial replacement for the old rotary engine. The industry was fortunate indeed that Roy Fedden — the originator of the Cosmos Jupiter — remained as Chief Engineer with the Bristol engine company for the next 22 years.

Sopwith Snapper

Last of the Sopwith fighters to fly was the Snapper, enigmatically referred to in some old company records as the R.M.1. Its design started during the spring of 1918, soon after the issue of RAF Specification No I, and seems to have been motivated as an attempt to produce the smallest viable fighter powered by the new 320hp ABC Dragonfly I radial engine, and carrying a normal armament of twin Vickers guns. As originally conceived, the Snapper was intended to have a wooden monocoque fuselage but, in the interests of ease and speed of production, this was abandoned in June 1918, and another start was made, reverting to the time-honoured wooden box-girder structure. The delay was further compounded by a three-month wait while delivery of the more powerful Dragonfly IA was arranged.

The first of three prototypes, F7031-F7033, finally appeared in April 1919. It was a single-bay staggered biplane with the cockpit set well back and with wing trailing-edge cutouts and ailerons on upper and lower wings. The familiar crankcase cowling enclosed much of the Dragonfly engine and was neatly faired into the flat-sided centre and rear fuselage section.

By placing the cockpit well aft, it was possible to mount the front guns, semi-buried in the front decking without need of a humped nose. The now-familiar near-rectangular fin with semi-circular leading edge appeared once again with horn-balanced rudder hinged on the sternpost.

F7031 was first flown at Brooklands in May 1919, and was soon followed by the other two aircraft which featured a re-contoured crankcase cowling which matched the outline of a large spinner with central aperture. One of these aircraft was temporarily admitted to the British Civil Register as K149/G-EAFJ in June for entry by Harry Hawker in that year's Aerial Derby, but its participation was officially forbidden on the grounds that its engine was still on the Secret List; this was not strictly correct, and a more likely reason was that the Dragonfly IA engine had only been cleared for short flying hours and, in any case, was still technically the property of the Air Ministry.

The first prototype underwent Martlesham trials in September 1919, returning the excellent speed of 140 mph at sea level and 133 mph at 15,000 feet. There is some circumstantial evidence to suggest that the aircraft may have encountered symptoms of wing flutter at this time — though hardly severe enough to endanger the aircraft. Little was known of this phenomenon at that time. The aircraft was returned to Sopwith for some modifications to the wings during October and November, but the nature of these has not been traced. In December the aircraft returned to Martlesham where, it is said, two-bay wings were fitted. The other two Snappers were delivered to the RAE for trials on the Dragonfly engines, and their ultimate fate is not known.

Type: Single-engine, single-seat, single-bay biplane fighter.
Manufacturer: The Sopwith Aviation Co Ltd, Kingston and Brooklands, Surrey.
Air Ministry Specification: RAF Type I Specification of 1918.
Powerplant: One 360hp ABC Dragonfly IA seven-cylinder radial engine.
Dimensions: Span, 28ft 0in; length, 20ft 7in; height, 10ft 0in; wing area, 292 sq ft.
Weights: Tare, 1,462lb; all-up, 2,190lb.
Performance: Max speed, 140 mph at sea level; climb to 10,000ft, 7 min 50 sec; service ceiling, 23,000ft.
Armament: Two synchronized 0.303in Vickers machine guns semi-buried in nose upper decking.
Prototypes: Three, F7031-F7033. (F7031 first flown, May 1919). No production.

A Sopwith Snapper, almost certainly the first aircraft, F7031, at Martlesham Heath in September 1919 with revised cowling and armament installed. (Photo: G S Leslie/ J M Bruce Collection)

Armstrong, Whitworth Ara

Unlike previous Armstrong Whitworth fighter aircraft the Ara, designed by Fred Murphy, was of orthodox configuration, although one or two features were unusual, and these tended to reflect a sense of awkwardness of gait.

Its design began in the summer of 1918 and followed what was to become a familiar path, ending in oblivion. No doubt persuaded that the rotary engine had reached the limit of its power potential, and perhaps disappointed by the modest performance of the Bentley-powered Armadillo, Murphy turned almost inevitably to the ABC Dragonfly, and produced a two-bay biplane of moderate stagger and small ailerons on upper and lower wings. The outboard pairs of interplane struts were located very close to the wingtips.

Reminiscent of the Armadillo's flat-

The first Ara prototype, F4971. It is not known when, or even whether this fighter was ever presented for Service evaluation at Martlesham Heath. (Photo: via K M Molson)

sided fuselage, the Ara's box girder was scarcely tapered towards the tail, but was at least provided with a curved top decking; the relative thickness of the rear fuselage in side elevation served to accentuate the small area of the fin and rudder. The upper wing was mounted clear of the fuselage and sufficiently close to be in line with the pilot's eye level.

Perhaps Murphy's most noteworthy design feature was the pointed crankcase cowling of the Dragonfly, a highly practical and, it is assumed, efficient attempt to limit the drag of the untidy radial engine; while other Dragonfly-powered aircraft appeared with blunt cowlings, with little or no attempt to improve the shape of the propeller hub, Murphy achieved from the outset a near perfect solution.

The first prototype Ara, F4971, was completed in the spring of 1919, and was followed by a second aircraft on which the wing gap was increased so that not only was the upper wing raised slightly further above the fuselage but the lower

wing was positioned about six inches below it.

Victim of the Dragonfly's frustrating problems, the Ara passed into obscurity towards the end of 1919 following the

closure of its manufacturer's aviation department, despite an outstanding performance. No record of its handling qualities appears to have survived.

Type: Single-engine, single-seat, two-bay experimental biplane fighter.
Manufacturer: Sir W G Armstrong, Whitworth Co Ltd, Newcastle-upon-Tyne.
Powerplant: One 320hp ABC Dragonfly I nine-cylinder radial engine.
Dimensions: Span, 27ft 5in; length, 20ft 3in; height, 7ft 10in; wing area, 257 sq ft.
Weights: Tare, 1,320lb; all-up, 1,930lb.
Performance: Max speed, 150 mph at sea level; climb to 10,000ft, 4 min 30 sec; ceiling, 28,000ft; endurance, 3¼ hr.
Armament: Two synchronized 0.303in Vickers machine guns mounted within the lower segments of the nose cowling.
Prototypes: Three, F4971-F4973 (first flown in mid-1919). No production.

Siddeley S.R.2 Siskin

The following two aircraft, the Siddeley Siskin and the Nieuport Nighthawk, were the only aircraft, originally powered by the infamous ABC Dragonfly radial engine, to occupy a significant place in the history of British aviation, even though the original aircraft subsequently underwent a fair degree of alteration by foster parent companies.

The Siddeley-Deasy Motor Car Company of Coventry, apart from undertaking the manufacture of other companies' designs during the First World War, began to build aircraft of in-house design during 1917, after Maj F M Green, J Lloyd and S D Heron (formerly of the Royal Aircraft Factory) joined the firm in senior design appointments. After designing a modified ver-

sion of the R.E.8 (taken from the production line and re-designated the R.T.1, but which was not put into production), Maj Green began detailed work on a design which he had sketched out while still at Farnborough, where he had intended using the 300hp RAF 8 fourteen-cylinder two-row radial engine, then under early development.

However, by the time the new aircraft design had begun to take shape early in 1918, aircraft designers were becoming enamoured with the potential offered by

the ABC Dragonfly single-row radial which was claimed to possess an exceptionally good power/weight ratio. Green accordingly adopted this engine and tendered his design to Air Board Specification A.1A (which became RAF Specification Type I in April 1918). Based on the promised power/weight ratio of 0.53 bhp/lb, the aircraft was expected to achieve a top sea level speed of around 160 mph. In the event the Dragonfly never exceeded a figure of more than 0.445 bhp/lb. Nevertheless,

A Siddeley Siskin prototype with the Dragonfly engine; note the slim, unfaired interplane struts. (Photo: J M Bruce Collection)

Siddeley-Deasy received a contract in May to produce six prototypes, C4541-C4546. Owing to delayed delivery of the first engine cleared for flight, the first Siskin to fly (the third prototype, C4543) was not taken aloft until May 1919, and even then the engine was developing no more than about 270 hp.

The S.R.2 Siskin (named in accordance with TDI 506A and 538) was an attractive aeroplane, displaying much of the S.E.5's character, though with interesting new features, not least of which was the undercarriage; this comprised single oleo struts for each wheel, each end of the axle being attached to the apices of paired V-struts by radius struts. The engine cowling was also novel, with each cylinder aligned to lie in a fluted channel in the crankcase cowling, this arrangement being intended to ensure the best possible cooling air flow through the cylinder fins. Like the S.E.5 and other Factory aircraft, the Siskin possessed tail fins above and below the rear fuselage. Despite the disappointing engine power, the Siskin returned a maximum speed of 145 mph at 6,500

feet when C4543 visited Martlesham Heath in July 1919.

By March 1920 the first five Siskin prototypes had flown, all with Dragonfly engines, even though it had already been decided to seek an alternative engine. Such an engine was near at hand. This was a development of the RAF 8 fourteen-cylinder engine referred to above. On leaving the Factory to join Siddeley-Deasy, S D Heron had sought and gained permission to continue its design development in his new appointment. Considerable progress was made before differences of opinion arose over cylinder design and Heron left the

company to take up a design appointment in America. His departure resulted in a run-down in effort on the new engine, now named the Jaguar, until S M Viale took over the design late in 1919. By mid-1920 the engine was bench running and showing some promise, and an early Jaguar I, rated at 325 hp, was flown in the first Siskin prototype, C4541, on 20 March 1921.

By then a much improved version of the aircraft, the Armstrong Whitworth Siskin III had been ordered in prototype form and a whole new chapter in the Siskin's life was about to open (see page 163).

Type: Single-engine, single-seat, single-bay biplane fighter.
Manufacturer: The Siddeley-Deasy Motor Car Co Ltd, Coventry.
Specification: Air Board Specification A.1A (later RAF Type I).
Powerplant: One 320hp ABC Dragonfly I; later 325hp Siddeley Jaguar I.
Structure: Fabric and ply covered wooden box-girder construction.
Dimensions: Span, 27ft 6in; length, 21ft 3in; height, 9ft 9in; wing area, 247 sq ft.
Weights: Tare, 1,463lb; all-up, 2,181lb.
Performance: Max speed, 145 mph at 6,500ft; climb to 10,000ft, 7 min 50 sec; service ceiling, 23,800ft.
Armament: Two synchronized 0.303in Vickers machine guns on upper nose decking.
Prototypes: Six ordered, C4541-C4546 (first flight, May 1919, by C4543). No confirmation can be traced that C4546 was completed.

Nieuport Nighthawk

It has been said that the Nieuport Nighthawk fighter marked both the beginning and end of the Dragonfly engine saga, and its inclusion in this work at this point may be seen in the latter context as well as representing the transition from the wartime fighter genre to that of an austerity which characterized the beginnings of RAF re-equipment in peacetime. As already explained, aircraft such as the Sopwith Snipe and Bristol F.2B Fighter provided the main equipment of the fighter squadrons for half a dozen years after the Armistice — and the RAF could count itself fortunate that aircraft of such adequacy were available at all.

It will be recalled that in October 1917 the Air Board, in deciding upon a new fighter engine to power the proposed Camel replacement, selected the Bentley rotary. Five months later the Sopwith Snipe was announced as being the new fighter, and both aircraft and engine were ordered into largescale production. That these decisions were correct, despite severe criticism at the time, was to

The third Nieuport Nighthawk prototype, apparently at Martlesham Heath in the second half of 1919 during performance trials; no armament is fitted. (Photo: J M Bruce Collection)

be confirmed by subsequent events. A few days after the decision was taken to order the Bentley, the Air Board became aware of the ABC Dragonfly radial which promised to develop 40 per cent more power at a weight increase of only 26 per cent; not for a further ten months would these figures be seen to be wildly optimistic, while almost two years would pass before the extent of the Dragonfly's design weaknesses were fully appreciated.

In the meantime the Air Board (and

later the Air Ministry) raised two fighter Specifications in which it was implicit that the aircraft should be powered by the Dragonfly engine — and the aircraft designers needed no second bidding. The Nieuport Nighthawk was designed by Henry Folland, who called on his experience with both the S.E.5 and Nieuport B.N.1 to produce an exceptionally neat two-bay biplane, yet keeping an eye on the need for ease of manufacture. To this end he employed numerous S.E.5 components, and the tail assembly was virtually unchanged from that of the B.N.1.

While the performance of the Dragonfly was still far from being confirmed, Nieuport received an order for three Nighthawk prototypes (F2909-F2911) on 25 April 1918 to Air Board Specification A.1(C) — which was shortly to be consolidated within the new RAF Type I Specification. As a measure of the misplaced faith in the Dragonfly engine demonstrated by the Air Ministry that summer, it should be stated that orders totalling 11,050 engines (as a cost of almost £12m) were placed with thirteen manufacturers, far exceeding any previous order placed for an aircraft or aero engine.

Long before flight-cleared engines were delivered for the Nighthawk prototypes, the Air Ministry placed an order for 150 production aircraft on 28 August 1918 with Nieuport (England) Ltd, and there is no doubt that considerable progress had been made with airframe component manufacture by the date of the Armistice.

Records of the delivery dates of the first few flight-cleared Dragonfly I engines to Nieuport are convoluted, but it seems that the first example(s) may have arrived sometime in January or February, and it is said that a flight by the first prototype may have been made in April. (Doubt must be cast on this as it seems that flight clearance of all Dragonflies may have been temporarily withdrawn that month while bench-running engine temperatures were examined.) It is, however, known that F2911 was flying by the end of May, and that this aircraft was delivered to Martlesham Heath in June, remaining there for seven months, during which it flew less than a dozen hours.

In September that year the entire Dragonfly development and production programe was cancelled, contractors being required only to complete engines already more than half completed. In the event some 1,147 Dragonfly Is and IAs were delivered, the majority into storage; for the most part these had been produced by Vickers Ltd in its Crayford works.

The total number of production Nieuport Nighthawks completed (excluding the prototypes) was 70, plus 54 airframe spares without engines. Of these at least seven were delivered to the RAE at Farnborough for various engine tests — between them surviving more than a dozen forced landings — while about six underwent various trials at the A & AEE at Martlesham; one was used by the Marine Aircraft Experimental Establishment (MAEE) on the Isle of Grain for flotation tests before going on to Farnborough. Thirteen were taken over by the Gloucestershire Aircraft Company, as well as an unknown number of airframes from storage, and rebuilt as Mars VI/Nighthawks or Mars X/Nightjars (see page 152). Some of the above, including at least three of the RAE aircraft, had their Dragonfly engines removed and replaced by Bristol Jupiter engines as part of the long and successful development of this engine. As far as can be discovered, the last Nieuport Nighthawk to remain flying was J2405, an original Dragonfly aircraft delivered to the RAE in January 1920; it took part in the Jupiter development, as well as tests with Fairey metal propellers before meeting its end in a forced landing on 30 September 1930.

Type: Single-engine, single-seat, two-bay biplane fighter.
Manufacturers: Nieuport (England) Ltd, Cricklewood; The Nieuport and General Aircraft Co Ltd, Cricklewood; The Gloucestershire Aircraft Co Ltd, Cheltenham, Glos.
Specification: Air Board Specification A.1(C) of 1917, later RAF Type I of 1918.
Powerplant: One 320hp ABC Dragonfly I; also Bristol Jupiter II.
Dimensions: Span, 28ft 0in; length, 18ft 6in; height, 9ft 6in; wing area, 276 sq ft.
Weights: Tare, 1,500lb; all-up, 2,218lb.
Performance: Max speed, 151 mph at sea level, 134 mph at 15,000ft; climb to 10,000ft, 7 min 10 sec; service ceiling, 24,500ft; endurance, 3 hr.
Armament: Two synchronized 0.303in Vickers machine guns on upper nose decking.
Prototypes: Three, F2909-F2911 (F2909 may have been first flown in April 1919).
Production: A total of 286 Nieuport Nighthawks was ordered: H8513-H8662, J2392-J2462, J6801-J6848 and J6925-J6941; of these, 70 were completed with Dragonfly I or IA engines, and 54 airframes were assembled without engines or guns. The remainder were cancelled.

Fairey Pintail

RAF Type 19 Specification was issued in 1919 setting out requirements for a naval amphibian reconnaissance fighter capable of being flown from a land airfield, an aircraft carrier or from water. Some emphasis was placed on the reconnaissance aspect and it was implicit that an observer should be carried. Two tenders were awarded prototype contracts: Parnall for the Possum, and Fairey for the Pintail. However, in the single-float Possum the emphasis on the reconnaissance rôle seems to have been pursued to the effective exclusion of the fighter capability, but the Fairey Pintail two-bay biplane was certainly a neat, compact and orthodox design capable of air combat, featuring twin floats and an upper wing located in line with the pilot's eye level. The tail unit was unusual in that the tailplane lay across the top of the rear fuselage with the rudder almost entirely below the chord line of the tailplane. The aircraft was

The third Pintail, the Mark III, N135, showing the lengths gone to by the designer to ensure an unrestricted upward field of view for the crew. Note the small auxiliary fins below the tailplane. (Photo: Air Ministry D of R, RTP Neg No 381, dated 8 June 1923)

designed by F Duncanson.

The first of three prototypes, N133, the Pintail Mk I, flown by Lt-Col Vincent Mitchell in April 1921, featured wheels that retracted between the floats, but this arrangement was not found to be practical owing to the somewhat narrow wheel track that resulted. The Mark II, N134, was flown by Capt Norman Macmillan in the following year with a slightly lengthened fuselage and wheels located outboard of the floats. N135, the Mark III was similar to the Mk II, but its wheels, which were not retractable, were located within the floats so that about six inches of tyre was exposed below the float step.

The Pintail was not adopted by the Service, although three examples, similar to the Mark III, were sold to the Imperial Japanese Navy in November 1924. These aircraft featured an increased wing gap so that the upper wing was located well above the fuselage.

In its official trials, though attracting criticism in some respects, the Pintail was applauded for its superlative field of vision in the upper hemisphere for both pilot and observer. However, possessing little wing stagger, the lower wing severely restricted the pilot's view when landing or alighting on the water.

Type: Single-engine, two-seat, two-bay, twin-float, naval fighter-reconnaissance amphibian biplane.
Specification: RAF Type 19 Specification of 1919.
Powerplant: One 475hp Napier Lion twelve-cylinder broad-arrow water-cooled in-line engine.
Dimensions: Span, 40ft 0in; length, 32ft 3in; height, 11ft 0in; wing area, 400sq ft.
Weight: All-up, 4,700lb.
Performance: Max speed, 125 mph at sea level.
Armament: One synchronized 0.303in Vickers machine gun on nose, and one Lewis gun with Scarff ring on rear cockpit.
Prototypes: Three. N133 (Mk I, first flown by Lt-Col Vincent Mitchell in April 1921), N134 (Mk II) and N135 (Mk III).
Production: Three Mark IVs for the Imperial Japanese Navy. No production for the British Services.

Supermarine Sea King II

Another fighter amphibian, called for by the Air Ministry soon after the War, was loosely defined in the D of R Type 6 Specification, drafted in 1920 and issued in June 1921. In this the emphasis was placed upon the aircraft's ability to operate from the deck of an aircraft carrier, but also in a secondary function from water. In the event the Fairey Flycatcher was to be selected, having shown that it could be flown as a landplane, floatplane and an amphibian (see page 154). Supermarine, on the other hand, had already produced a small single-seat flying-boat, the Sea Lion I, which was entered for the 1919 Schneider Trophy race, being powered by a 160hp Beardmore straight-six water-cooled in-line engine.

Although the Sea Lion I sank during the race meeting, it was salvaged and, after a number of alterations, attracted considerable attention, labelled as a fighter, at the Olympia Aero Show in July 1920. Various alternative engines were being suggested and in due course a much modified version, powered by the 300hp Hispano-Suiza engine driving a four-blade pusher propeller, was designed by Reginald J Mitchell as the Sea King Mk II, and was first flown in January 1922.

This was an unstaggered single-bay biplane with equal-span wings. The hull was constructed on the Linton-Hope principle with mahogany planking attached to elm frames; the fin and rudder were mounted wholly above the hull with a braced tailplane partway up the fin. Boat-style wingtip floats were at-

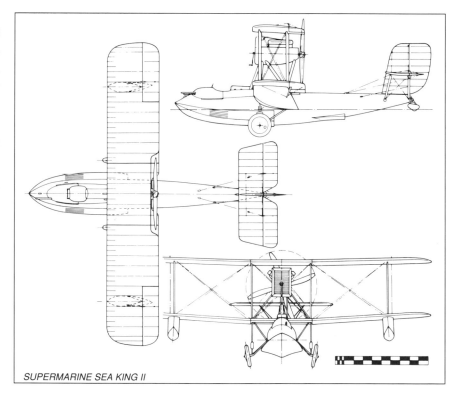

SUPERMARINE SEA KING II

Type: Single pusher engine, single-seat, single-bay biplane amphibian flying-boat fighter.
Manufacturer: Supermarine Aviation Works Ltd, Southampton.
Powerplant: One 300hp Hispano-Suiza engine driving four-blade pusher propeller.
Structure: Hull of mahogany planking attached to elm frames and covered with doped fabric; two-spar, two-bay wings of wooden construction.
Dimensions: Span, 32ft 0in; length, 26ft 9in; height, 11ft 7in.
Weights: Tare, 2,115lb; all-up, 2,850lb.
Performance: Max speed, 125 mph at sea level; climb to 10,000ft, 12 min; endurance, 2 hr.
Armament: Provision for one Lewis gun on bows, offset to port.
Prototype: One private venture aircraft, G-EBAH (first flown in January 1922).

tached below the lower wings and the landing wheels were anchored to the sides of the hull, retracting outwards and upwards. A single Lewis gun could be mounted on the bows, offset to port.

Those who flew the Sea King II declared it to be very manœuvrable and it possessed an aerobatic capability equal to any contemporary landplane fighter (c.f. *Supermarine Aircraft since 1914*, C F Andrews and E B Morgan, p.56), and although it won no support from the Air Ministry it was further developed into the Sea Lion II and entered for the 1922 Schneider Trophy race at Naples. Flown by Henri Biard, the little British flying-boat won the race at a speed of 145.7 mph.

The Supermarine Sea King II outside the Woolston Works. (Photo: E B Morgan)

Gloucestershire Mars VI Nighthawk

In the years immediately following the Armistice of 1918 the Air Ministry possessed neither the will nor financial means to order new military aircraft for the fledgling RAF, preferring instead to improve and develop existing designs. One of these was the Nieuport Nighthawk, a product of H P Folland following his departure from the Royal Aircraft Factory during the War. The Nighthawk had entered production before the War's end and had been built by the Gloucestershire Aircraft Company, but without reaching operational service. Folland, who left Sir Samuel Waring's Group after the Armistice, joined Gloucestershire and set about a series of Nighthawk derivatives under the generic name Mars, the first of which was the Bamel racer; this was followed by the Sparrowhawk I, II and III (Mars II, III and IV) fleet fighters, sold to the Imperial Japanese Navy. The fifth derivative was the Mars VI Nighthawk which differed little from the original Nieuport aircraft save from the choice of engine, retaining wooden construction throughout and employing ash longerons and wing spars with wire-braced spruce struts and ribs.

The original 320hp ABC Dragonfly I engine was replaced initially by the 325hp Armstrong Siddeley Jaguar II 14-cylinder two-row radial, and the first Mars VI Nighthawk, H8534, was deliv-

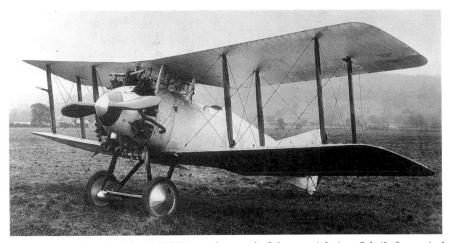

The Gloucestershire Nighthawk J6926 was the second of three special aircraft built for tropical trials to evaluate the Jaguar II and Jupiter III engines; this aircraft, fitted with a 385hp Bristol Jupiter II, seen here at Hucclecote, later underwent Service trials with Nos 1 and 8 Squadrons in Iraq during 1923-24. (Photo: via Derek James)

ered to the RAE in November 1920 before going on to the A & AEE on 21 May the following year for preliminary performance tests. Official trials started at Farnborough on 14 July 1922, and H8534 was joined by J6925 and J6926 (both with Jaguar engines) and J6927 (with a 385hp Jupiter III) for compara-

Type: Single-engine, single-seat fighter biplane.

Manufacturer: Conversion by Gloucestershire Aircraft Co Ltd, Cheltenham

Air Ministry Specification: D of R Type I (1920)

Powerplant: One 325hp Armstrong Siddeley Jaguar II fourteen-cylinder air-cooled radial, one 325hp Bristol Jupiter III or 398hp Jupiter IV nine-cylinder radial.

Structure: Wire-braced ash and spruce construction with fabric covering overall.

Dimensions: Span, 28 ft 0 in; length, 18 ft 0 in; height, 9 ft 0 in; wing area, 270 sq ft.

Weights: (Jaguar) Tare, 1,816 lb; all-up, 2,217 lb. (Jupiter) Tare, 1,818 lb; all-up, 2,270lb.

Performance: (Jaguar) Max speed, 150 mph at sea level; climb to 20,000 ft, 24 min; service ceiling, 23,000 ft. (Jupiter) Max speed, 150 mph at sea level; climb to 20,000 ft, 16.5 min; service ceiling, 26,000 ft.

Armament: Two synchronized 0.303in Vickers machine guns on top decking of nose, with 1,000 rounds of ammunition.

Prototypes and Production: First aircraft completed, H8534 (first flown, c.November 1920); at least 31 aircraft flown and possibly about 90 further aircraft completed but stored. Three aircraft flown by Nos 1, 8 and 55 Squadrons, RAF.

tive trials. A total of over 100 conversions was completed by Gloster, but as far as can be discovered only six were taken on charge by the RAF (H8532, H8524 and H8544; and J6925-J6927). H8544 was shipped to the Middle East, arriving at the Air Depot, Hinaidi, Iraq, in 1923, and underwent brief handling trials with No 1 (Fighter) Squadron. All three of the J-serial Nighthawks flew with No 1 Squadron, J6925 being badly damaged on 19 July 1924 before being rebuilt by the Air Depot and issued in turn to Nos 8 and 55 Squadrons as JR6925. No 8 Squadron flew these three aircraft, and undertook a 100hr test on the Jupiter-engined J6927 under tropical conditions.

Of the remaining Nighthawks whose conversions were completed, 25 were bought by the Greek government and delivered in 1923, some of them remaining in operational service until 1938.

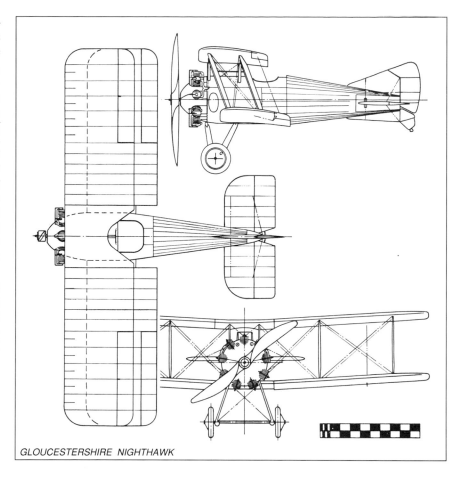

GLOUCESTERSHIRE NIGHTHAWK

Gloucestershire Mars X Nightjar

By 1921 the Air Ministry was beginning to consider the pressing need to provide the RAF with a deck-landing fleet fighter to replace the Sopwith Camel, and set about drafting a Specification for a purpose-designed naval interceptor (which would eventually emerge as the Fairey Flycatcher). As an interim measure, however, the Air Ministry fell back on the established expedient of adapting existing surplus airframes to meet the requirement in the short term. Folland at Gloucestershire Aircraft accordingly set about a further adaptation - the last as it transpired - of the surplus Nieuport Nighthawk airframes which came to be known as the Mars X Nightjar.

While the basic airframe structure of the Nighthawk remained unchanged, the naval fighter featured an entirely new wide-track, long-stroke undercarriage which incorporated 'jaws' at the extremities of the wheel spreader bar to

The Gloucestershire Mars X Nightjar, H8539, during its period of flight trials at Farnborough in June 1922; this aeroplane later served with No 203 Squadron and No 401 Flight in 1923. Note the wide-track undercarriage with arrester jaws on the spreader bar, and the external mounting of the Vickers gun. (Photo: Air Ministry (RAE), Neg No MH3273)

engage the fore-and-aft arrester cables then in vogue aboard British aircraft carriers. Also adopted as a matter of economy was the 230hp Bentley B.R.2 rotary engine of which plentiful surplus stocks remained, in place of the wholly discredited ABC Dragonfly. The customary twin-Vickers armament was retained but the guns were carried

externally on the shoulders of the front fuselage.

The first Nightjar to be converted, H8535, was delivered to the A & AEE in May 1921 for performance trials, and then to the RAE in December. On 16 January 1922 it undertook deck landing trials aboard HM Carrier *Argus*, but on returning to Martlesham on 8 May that year it was damaged and not flown again.

The following month, however, the first of nine Nightjars, H8536, was delivered to No 203 Squadron at Leuchars where they replaced Camels; two other aircraft were employed by a deck landing training flight on the station. Six Nightjars were embarked in HMS *Argus* in September 1922 which sailed to the Dardanelles during the Chanak crisis. No 203 Squadron was re-designated No 402 Flight on 1st April 1923 with the creation of the Fleet Air Arm and

handed over its remaining Nightjars to Nos 401, 403 and 404 Flights which continued to work at sea with HM Carriers *Argus*, *Eagle*, *Furious* and *Hermes*. As far as can be discovered, the last aircraft in

service was J6932 which crashed from a spin while landing at Leuchars on 12 September 1924. By then, however, the Flycatcher had already joined Nos 401-406 Flights of the new Fleet Air Arm.

Type: Single-engine, single-seat, two bay naval biplane interceptor.

Manufacturer: Gloucestershire Aircraft Co Ltd, Cheltenham.

Powerplant: One 230hp Bentley B.R.2 nine-cylinder air-cooled rotary engine.

Structure: Wire-braced ash and spruce box-girder construction with fabric covering.

Dimensions: Span, 28ft 0in; length, 18ft 4in; height, 9ft 8in; wing area, 270 sq ft.

Weights: Tare, 1,765lb; all-up, 2,165lb.

Performance: Max speed, 120 mph at sea level; climb to 15,000ft, 23 min; service ceiling, 19,000ft.

Armament: Two nose-mounted synchronized 0.303in Vickers Mk I machine guns with 500 rounds per gun.

Production and Summary of Service: Total of 19 aircraft converted (H8535-H8540, J6930-J6941, and J6972), plus three (H8541-H8542 and H8545) possibly not completed. Served with No 203 Squadron, RAF, and Nos 401-406 Flights, FAA.

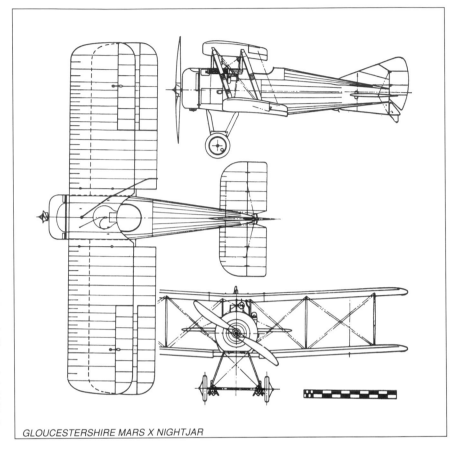

GLOUCESTERSHIRE MARS X NIGHTJAR

Fairey Flycatcher

One of the problems facing the Directorate of Research at the Air Ministry in the half-dozen years following the Armistice in formulating fighter requirements was to establish 'the threat' in the absence of a potential enemy within striking distance of Britain. To over-estimate the likely performance of a potential enemy aircraft would be to demand a fighter possessing a performance either beyond the power available from existing engines, or beyond a realistic cost, bearing in mind the time

and research necessary to advance to that performance. Accordingly, advances in performance demands tended to be fairly modest, but at the same time aircraft designers were encouraged to

put forward (and if necessary patent) ideas whereby the *flexibility* of aircraft operation might be increased.

Thus it was that when the Directorate drafted its Type 6 Specification in

The first Fairey Flycatcher prototype, N163, at Martlesham Heath with an Armstrong Siddeley Jaguar engine but without brackets for the Vickers guns on the sides of the fuselage. (Photo: Air Ministry)

Right: *A standard production Flycatcher fitted with the alternative twin-float undercarriage; note the retention of the Fairey oleo struts at the rear float attachment points.* (Photo: G S Leslie/J M Bruce Collection).

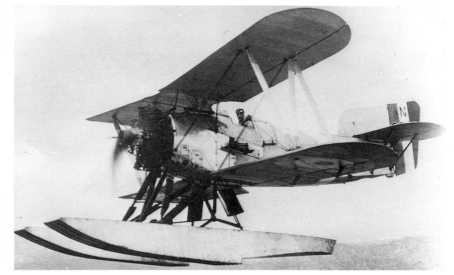

Below: *A wheel-equipped Flycatcher flying from a carrier deck with an unidentified Fleet Air Arm Flight. Just visible are the starboard Vickers machine gun on the side of the fuselage and the arrester jaws on the undercarriage spreader bar.* (Photo: Harold B Bennett)

1920, it had in mind an aircraft capable of attaining a sea level speed of perhaps about 140 mph, capable of operating with a wheel undercarriage primarily from an aircraft carrier, but also capable of alighting on the water. Because Supermarine had already produced a small single-seat flying-boat amphibian, this aeroplane — with suitable alterations — came to be regarded as a realistic contender to the Type 6 Specification. Nor could such an approach to the requirement be lightly written off; after all, the Sea King II was developed very simply into the Sea Lion II, which won the 1923 Schneider Trophy contest at 145.7 mph.

There is no doubt, however, that the Air Ministry regarded the single-seat flying-boat fighter as too unorthodox an approach, and issued in 1922 a new version of the Type 6 Specification, now termed 6/22, implicit in which was that the performance of the fighter should not be fundamentally compromised by its ability to alight on water. In other words the aircraft should be designed for deck operation, but possess a degree of component interchangeability to enable it, if necessary, to operate from water. This effectively ruled out the Supermarine flying-boat amphibian concept. Specification 6/22, moreover, stipulated the use of either the Armstrong Siddeley Jaguar or Bristol Jupiter engines.

Both Fairey and Parnall submitted design tenders, the Fairey Flycatcher and the Parnall Plover (see page 157). Three prototypes of each were ordered and the first Flycatcher, N163, was flown by Lt-Col Vincent Nicholl in November 1922, powered by a 400hp Armstrong Siddeley Jaguar III two-row fourteen-cylinder radial engine. Designed by F Duncanson, it was a stocky little single-bay biplane with a wing span of only 29 feet. One of the important features of the Jaguar engine was its small diameter and this served to accentuate the stubby appearance of the nose which, on account of the weight of the engine, was relatively short. The undercarriage was ingenious and, from all accounts, efficient; it embodied the same 'oleo-cum-radius arm' principle as the Siddeley S.R.2 Siskin's, though geometrically reversed, the side V-struts being located in front of the wheels, whose Fairey oleo-pneumatic struts were attached directly below the front wing spar. Hydraulic wheel brakes were also included.

Only the upper wing was rigged with dihedral, the lower wing being flat, while the heavy stagger contributed good downward visibility from the cockpit. Faired interplane N-struts were located well inboard from the wingtips (giving rise later to fairly frequent suggestions of wing flutter). Outstanding manœuvrability was bestowed by generous tail control surfaces (even though none was balanced), and a short landing run of only 50 yards was made possible by the full-span Fairey camber-changing trailing-edge flaps and the wheel brakes.

Folding wings were not included, yet the span of only 29 feet was small enough to enable the Flycatcher to use carrier lifts without difficulty. In this respect, another design feature — that of no airframe component exceeding a length of 13ft 6in — contributed to the ease of dismantling and storage in a confined space.

Many anecdotes helped to generate the Flycatcher's popularity: the aircraft was on occasion flown out of the below-deck hangar over the bows of an aircraft carrier, and the crackling sound of its propeller blade tips as it pulled out of a dive was remembered for many years by those who watched Flycatchers at the flying displays of the 1920s. (Captain Norman Macmillan flew the Flycatcher in 1925 on the first official diving tests ever called for by the Air Ministry to determine an aircraft's terminal velocity.)

The first prototype was re-engined with a Bristol Jupiter IV in 1923, and the second aircraft was flown that year with interchangeable wheel and float under-

Delightful flying study of a Flycatcher. Note the mounting bracket for the starboard Vickers gun below the cockpit sill. (Photo: G S Leslie/ J M Bruce Collection)

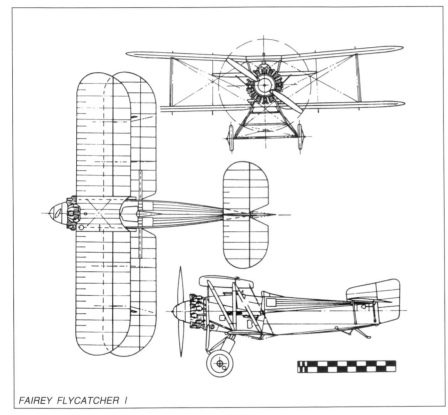

FAIREY FLYCATCHER I

Type: Single-engine, single-seat, single-bay shipborne biplane fighter.

Manufacturer: The Fairey Aviation Co Ltd, Hayes, Middlesex.

Air Ministry Specifications: Mk I: 6/22 (formerly D of R Type 6); Mk II: N.21/26.

Powerplant: One 400hp Armstrong Siddeley Jaguar IV two-row fourteen-cylinder air-cooled radial engine driving two-blade propeller.

Dimensions: Span, 29ft 0in; length, 23ft 0in; height, 12ft 0in; wing area, 288 sq ft.

Weights: Tare, 2,038lb; all-up, 3,028lb.

Performance: Max speed, 133 mph at sea level; service ceiling, 19,000ft; range 310 miles.

Armament: Either two synchronized 0.303in, or one 0.303in and one 0.50in Vickers machine guns on sides of fuselage below cockpit sills.

Prototypes: Three, N163-N165 (N163 first flown by Lt-Col Vincent Nicholl in November 1922). Mk II, N216 (first flown in October 1926).

Production: Total (excluding four prototypes), 193, all Mk Is: N9611-N9619, N9655-N9680, N9697, N9902-N9965, J7455-J7496 (re-numbered as N9854-N9895), S1060-S1073, S1273-S1297, S1409-S1419 and S1590.

Summary of Service: Flycatchers served with No 401 Flt (2-24 to 4-33), No 402 Flt (4-23 to 10-32), No 403 Flt (7-24 to 4-35), No 404 Flt (1924 to 11-32), No 405 Flt (7-24 to 4-33), No 406 Flt (5-24 to 6-34), No 407 Flt (9-27 to 11-32) and No 408 Flt (3-29 to 11-31), Fleet Air Arm; served aboard HM Carriers *Argus, Courageous, Eagle, Furious, Glorious* and *Hermes*, and with 2nd, 4th and 5th Cruiser Squadrons from January 1933.

carriage. The third Flycatcher, N165, with Jupiter engine, was fitted with amphibian floats, the wheels being located in their undersides immediately forward of the step.

An initial batch of nine production Flycatchers, based on the second prototype, N164, was ordered in January 1923 for Service comparison with the Parnall Plover. Shortly afterwards an order was placed for 26 further aircraft, and production continued until 1931. A total of 193 Flycatcher Mk Is was built, and for twelve years served as the Fleet Air Arm's principal shipboard fighter.

The first Flycatchers joined the Fleet Air Arm in April 1923 when six aircraft of the first batch were delivered to No 402 Flight at Leuchars for HMS *Eagle*, remaining with this unit until October 1932. During 1924 Flycatchers equipped Nos 401, 403, 404, 405 and 406 Flights, replacing all former carrier-based and catapult fighters in service. Later, Flycatchers also equipped Nos 407 and 408 Flights, and served aboard HM Carriers *Argus, Courageous, Eagle, Furious, Glorious* and *Hermes* as well as with the 2nd, 4th and 5th Cruiser Squadrons. The last aircraft, floatplanes of No 403 Flight with the 5th Cruiser Squadron, were withdrawn from service in 1935 when they were replaced by Hawker Osprey IIIs.

Flycatcher Mk II

An opportunity to tender for a Flycatcher replacement arose early in 1927 when Specification N.21/26 was issued for a carrier-borne single-seat fighter with a speed of not less than 160 mph. Designed by Marcel Lobelle, who had been appointed Chief Designer at the Fairey Aviation company in 1925, the Flycatcher Mk II, N216, bore scarcely any resemblance to the Mark I.

Whereas the previous version had been of mixed wood and metal construction, N216 was a fabric-covered all-metal structure with sheet duralumin covering on the front fuselage aft as far as the trailing edge of the lower wing. A conventional V-strut undercarriage was fitted, Fairey oleo struts constituting the forward members.

N216 was flown in October 1926 and came to be fitted with both the 480hp Bristol Mercury IIA and the much heavier 540hp Armstrong Siddeley Jaguar VIII. During official trials N216 achieved a maximum speed of 164 mph at 10,000 feet. Other aircraft tendered to this Specification included the Gloster Gnatsnapper, Hawker Hoopoe, Armstrong Whitworth Starling and Vickers Type 123/141.

It was, however, the arrival of a new in-line Rolls-Royce engine, the F.XI, that eventually convinced the Air Ministry that a major break from the traditional, bulky radial engine in fighters

The sole Flycatcher Mk II, N216. The main differences from the Mk I are readily apparent, including re-designed fin and rudder, the reversion to paired interplane struts, aileron interconnecting struts, and V-strut undercarriage. The Vickers gun armament was to have been located in the upper decking of the nose. N216 is shown here with the Jaguar VIII engine. (Photo: via R C B Ashworth)

was on the horizon, and no production contract was issued for any contender to Specification N.21/26. And thus it came about that the Flycatcher Mk I remained

in service for seven more years.

The data table opposite refers to the Flycatcher Mk I.

Parnall Plover

After the failure of the Parnall anti-Zeppelin Scout of 1916 and the departure of Camden Pratt, the post of chief designer at Parnall was taken over by Harold Bolas, an extraordinarily inventive engineer who had participated in the general exodus from the Royal Aircraft Factory in 1917. His powers of ingenuity had found expression in the Parnall Panther, a naval reconnaissance/gun spotting aircraft which embraced a host of original ideas, not least a fuselage which folded sideways aft of the cockpit for shipboard stowage. The company was fortunate to survive the post-War contract cancellations, especially when its production order for 300 Panthers was reduced by half, and then given to Bristols.

The original company of Parnall & Sons had been taken over by W & T Avery Ltd of Smethwick, who promptly closed the company after the loss of the Panther contract, and left the industry; whereupon George Parnall established a new company, George Parnall & Co Ltd at the Coliseum Works, Bristol, retaining the services of Bolas as the chief designer.

First of Bolas' new designs to be built was the Plover, submitted for tender to Specification 6/22, and rival to the Fairey Flycatcher. No doubt restrained

Often said to have only been fitted with the Armstrong Siddeley Jaguar, the third Parnall Plover prototype, N162, is shown here with the Bristol Jupiter radial at Martlesham Heath in August 1923; it is likely that no guns were fitted at this time, although the cartridge and link chutes forward of the rear centre section struts are clearly visible. (Photo: Air Ministry, RTP Neg No 499)

by George Parnall, the chief designer produced a strictly orthodox and attractive little single-bay biplane, intended at the outset for the Bristol Jupiter radial engine. As stated in the above entry for the Flycatcher, 6/22 required the aircraft to be primarily capable of deck operation, with a secondary ability to operate from water so that, when prototypes were ordered, provision was made for wheel and float undercarriages to be interchangeable.

Three prototypes, N160-N162, were called for, the first being flown before

the end of 1922 with a Bristol Jupiter engine; N161 was the amphibian version, also with a Jupiter, and N162 was flown with the Jupiter and Armstrong Siddeley Jaguar engines in turn. Ironically the Plover was a much more attractive aeroplane than the Flycatcher, yet failed to attract a significant production order. Three more development aircraft were ordered, N9608-N9610, the first two being equipped with wheels and the third with floats. These were followed by seven Jupiter-powered production aircraft (N9702-N9708), and six of these were distributed between Nos 403, 404 and 405 Fleet Fighter Flights of the RAF between April 1923 and July 1924.

Despite possessing dimensions, weights and performance almost identical to the Flycatcher, as well as employing the Fairey camber-changing full-span flaps, the Plover was found to be far less popular than the Fairey aircraft in the air, as well as being an awkward aeroplane to rig quickly and accurately.

One Plover, N9705, was de-militarized and, as G-EBON, transferred to the Civil Aircraft Register in mid-1926. Entered for the King's Cup Race on 9 July that year, and flown by Sqn Ldr Sir Christopher Quintin Brand, it retired with a broken fuel feed. It was to be written off after an accident in January 1929.

The development Plover N9608, shown here, also participated in Service trials with No 404 Fleet Fighter Flight in 1923. (Photo: via R C B Ashworth)

Type: Single-engine, single-seat, single-bay biplane shipborne fighter.

Manufacturer: George Parnall & Co Ltd, Coliseum Works, Bristol.

Air Ministry Specification: 6/22

Powerplant: One 436hp Bristol Jupiter III nine-cylinder radial engine; also Armstrong Siddeley Jaguar fourteen-cylinder two-row radial engine.

Dimensions: Span, 29ft 0in; length, 23ft 0in.

Weights: Tare, 2,035lb; all-up, 3,020lb.

Performance: Max speed, 131 mph at 10,000ft; ceiling 18,800ft.

Armament: Two synchronized 0.303in Vickers Mk I machine guns mounted in upper part of nose with 600 rounds per gun.

Prototypes: N160-N162 (N160 first flown in about November 1922).

Production: Total of 10: N9608-N9610 (for development); N9702-N9708 (for Service evaluation and trials).

Service: Six Plovers served with Nos 403, 404 and 405 Fleet Fighter Flights, RAF, for Service evaluation during 1923-24.

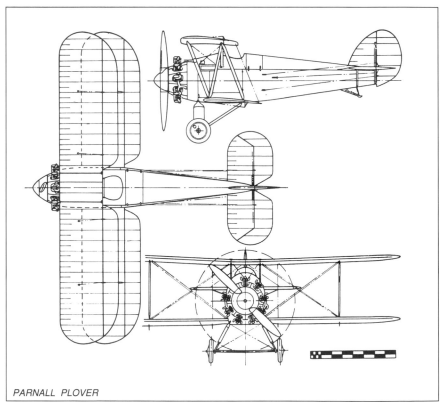

PARNALL PLOVER

Bristol Type 52 and 53 Bullfinch

Shortly after the Bristol Aeroplane company took over the Jupiter engine from the defunct Cosmos company in July 1920, Frank Barnwell embarked on the design of a parasol monoplane single-seat fighter to be powered by this engine, capable of being converted relatively simply to a two-seat biplane. This ingenious design gained support from the Air Ministry, who recognised the potential economies that could stem from the combination of interceptor fighter and fighter-reconnaissance aircraft in a single basic design — in effect aimed at meeting both D of R Specification Types 1 and 2. Accordingly a new Specification, 2/21, was drafted around Barnwell's proposals, and three prototypes, J6901-J6903, were ordered on 21 June 1921.

Construction of the fuselage was of box-girder form with carbon steel tubular components, sweated into machined end sockets to form a tie-rod braced structure; aluminium and steel sheet covered the fuselage forward of the cockpit, but for ease of maintenance the rear fuselage was of fabric-covered square section without rounded decking. A pair of side-by-side tailskids were faired to provide what were in effect twin ventral tail fins, the single balanced oval-shaped rudder being hinged above the rear fuselage without dorsal fin. The wing, of

The Bullfinch Mk II, J6903, transformed into a two-seat biplane; the entire undercarriage was moved aft by about 12 inches to compensate for the longer rear fuselage. (Photo: via R C Sturtivant)

equally radical configuration, was constructed of wood in two halves, being bolted together on the aircraft's centre-line over cabane struts. Each half-wing increased in thickness from the centre-line to semi-span, and reduced from this point to the wing tip, the underwing struts attaching on the chordline of maximum thickness. The undercarriage comprised a pair of V-struts, the forward members being telescopic with coil springs and oleo shock-absorbers.

The name Bullfinch was agreed in March 1922 (after the Air Ministry had refused to accept Pegasus), and the first Bristol Type 52 MFA, J6901 (the single-seat monoplane version) was ready for flight on 6 November that year; and the second aircraft, J6902, also a Type 52, made its maiden flight the following May.

The first Type 53 MFB Bullfinch, J6903, flew initially as a monoplane in April, but during the latter half of 1923 was modified to become a two-seat biplane. This was simply achieved by inserting a self-contained 37-inch long, square-section fuselage bay immediately aft of the single-seater's cockpit; accommodating the observer/gunner's cockpit with Lewis gun on Scarff ring; this additional bay carried a parallel-chord cantilever, fabric-covered two-spar wing directly below, thereby creating a biplane with no less that 6ft 6in wing stagger. J6903, the Bullfinch Mk II, was first flown in this configuration on 17 March 1924.

J6901 underwent performance trials at Martlesham Heath, beginning on 7 April 1924, but was struck off charge in September. J6902 spent much of its life with the RAE (but attended the 1924 Hendon Display as New Type No 3, and underwent Service trials with No 13 Squadron at Martlesham in 1925). The Bullfinch Mk II spent two months at the A & AEE from July 1924 before going on to Farnborough, where it made its final flight on 16 June the following year.

The Bullfinch proved an interesting experiment, but nothing more. It failed to achieve a worthwhile performance, and the two-seater finished up significantly overweight so that, even without armament fitted, its maximum speed was scarcely better than a five-year-old, fully-equipped, Bristol F.2B Fighter.

Type: Single-engine, single- and two-seat parasol monoplane and cantilever biplane fighter.

Manufacturer: The Bristol Aeroplane Co Ltd, Filton, Bristol.

Air Ministry Specifications: D of R Types 1 and 2, and 2/21.

Powerplant: One 425hp Bristol Jupiter III nine-cylinder air-cooled radial engine driving two-blade propeller.

Dimensions: Span, 38ft 5in; length, 24ft 5in (Type 52), 27ft 6in (Type 53); height, 10ft 9in; wing area, 267 sq ft (Type 52), 391 sq ft (Type 53).

Weights: Type 52, tare, 2,175lb; all-up 3,205lb. Type 53, tare, 2,495lb; all-up, 4,088lb.

Performance: Type 52. Max speed, 135 mph at 15,000ft; service ceiling, 22,000ft. Type 53. Max speed, 120 mph at 15,000ft; service ceiling, 18,000ft.

Armament: Type 52. Provision for two synchronized 0.303in Vickers machine guns in nose. Type 53. As Type 52 plus Lewis gun with Scarff ring on rear cockpit.

Prototypes: Type 52, two, J6901 and J6902; Type 53, one, J6903. No production.

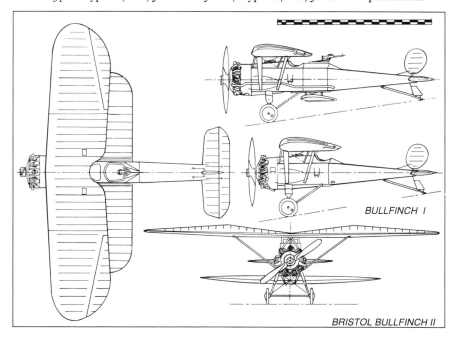

BULLFINCH I

BRISTOL BULLFINCH II

Short Springbok

Ever since early 1918, when the War's end was still out of sight, the Air Ministry had been anxious to introduce a replacement for the Bristol F.2B Fighter. However, widespread cancellation of production contracts at the end of the War resulted in the decision to keep the 'Brisfit' in service for the time being, while leaving open the requirement for an eventual replacement.

In due course, as RAF commitments became focused in the harsh environments of the Middle East and the North-West Frontier of India, it was felt that the wood and fabric airframes of in-service aircraft would quickly deteriorate, and would demand replacement sooner rather than later. Short Brothers had already submitted a projected development of the all-metal single-engine Silver Streak commercial passenger/cargo aircraft, but this had been cancelled as part of the swingeing post-Armistice austerity policies of the Geddes Committee; this project was now, late in 1922, reinstated under Specification 19/21.

Two prototypes, J6974 and J6975, of the new Short all-metal two-seat fighter, named the S.3 Springbok, were ordered in December, and the first was flown at the A & AEE on 19 April 1923 by John Lankester Parker. Powered by a 425hp Bristol Jupiter IV radial, the new aircraft, intended ultimately to carry two synchronized Vickers front guns and a Lewis gun on the rear cockpit, broke entirely new ground among British fighters, possessing twin steel wing spars with duralumin-plate ribs with sheet aluminium covering. The fuselage was a monocoque duralumin shell riveted to L-section oval frames with longitudinal stiffners between the frames.

Although the Springbok clearly led the way towards an all-metal Service fighter, there were not only the customary sceptics, but also the realists who pointed to the lack of trained sheet-metal tradesmen in the RAF, and when the prototype Springboks showed signs of skin splitting while at Martlesham Heath the RAF was powerless to make repairs. J6974 was returned to Shorts for the wings to be re-covered with doped fabric; the second aircraft was repaired by skinning with thicker sheet in areas prone to splitting.

J6975, however, was destroyed on 30 November 1923 when it spun and crashed near Martlesham soon after take-off, killing the pilot. The cause was diagnosed as rudder blanking during spinning, and a new wing design was prepared, leading to the Springbok Mk II, of which six examples (later reduced to three) were ordered in 1924.

The Springbok II was also powered by the Jupiter IV, but the wing arrangement was completely changed. The lower wing, of much reduced chord, instead of passing below the fuselage, as on the Mk I, was now attached to stubs at the bottom of the fuselage. The latter now featured raised frames to carry the upper wing roots and, by thus raising the cockpit, improved the pilot's view. Slight

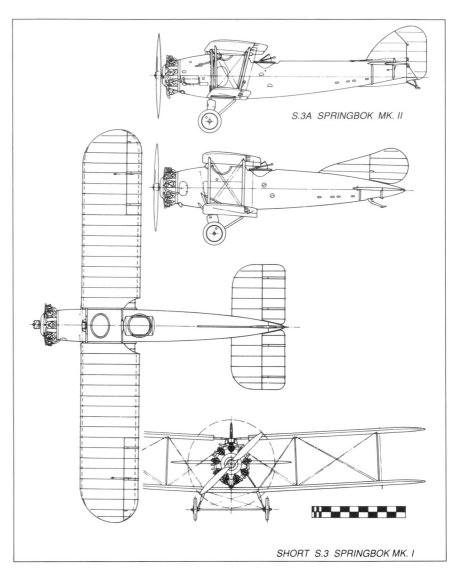

S.3A SPRINGBOK MK. II

SHORT S.3 SPRINGBOK MK. I

Type: Single-engine, two-seat, two-bay biplane fighter.
Manufacturer: Short Bros Ltd, Rochester, Kent.
Air Ministry Specifications: D of R Type 3A, later 19/21.
Powerplant: One 425hp Bristol Jupiter IV nine-cylinder radial engine.
Dimensions: Span, 42ft 0in; length, 26ft 11in (Mk I), 29ft 6in (Mk II); wing area, 463 sq ft (Mk I), 460 sq ft (Mk II).
Weights: All-up, 4,080lb (Mk I), 4,270lb (Mk II).
Performance: Max speed at sea level, 121 mph (Mk I), 123 mph (Mk II)
Armament: Provision for two synchronized 0.303in Vickers machine guns in nose and one Lewis gun with Scarff ring on rear cockpit.
Prototypes: Mk I, two, J6974 and J6975 (J6974 first flown by John Parker on 19 April 1923); Mk II, three, J7295-J7207 (first flight by J7295, 25 March 1925); three other Mk IIs, J7298-J7300, cancelled. No production.

sweepback was incorporated on both upper and lower wings. The tail surfaces were also re-designed, the tailplane being raised to the top of the rear fuselage, while the fin and horn-balanced rudder were of reduced aspect ratio; and finally the front oleo strut of the landing gear was raked forwards, instead of backwards.

The first Springbok II, J7295, was flown at Grain by Parker on 25 March 1925 and, after several brief trials at Martlesham, appeared in the New Types Park (as No 3) at the 1925 Hendon Display in June that year. It was returned to Rochester in 1926 where it was re-built as the Short S.3B Chamois.

Both the second and third Springbok IIs underwent trials at Martlesham during the second half of 1925, before disappearing into obscurity. The three cancelled aircraft, J7298-J7300, had been proposed as improved Marks III-V respectively, but the nature of these improvement is not known.

The sad truth was that the all-metal monocoque Springbok was about half a decade ahead of its time and, although the concept had been fostered by the Air Ministry in Whitehall, the Service in the field was not equipped to exploit it.

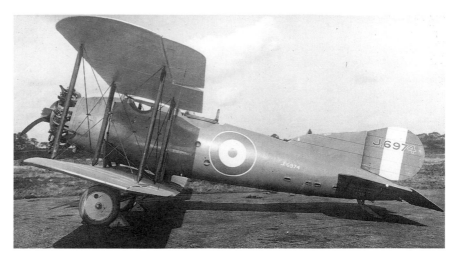

The first Springbok Mk I, J6974, showing the absence of wing stagger and the location of the fuselage within the wing gap. The slots cut in the rear fuselage monocoque are hand grips for ground handling. The aircraft was painted blue-grey overall. (Photo: via R C B Ashworth)

Gloucestershire (Gloster) Grebe

After the Sopwith Snipe, the Gloucestershire Grebe was the second fighter to be produced in quantity after the Armistice and adopted for service with the RAF, first joining No 111 (Fighter) Squadron in October 1923. This claim, however, must be qualified as will be shown in due course.

The origins of the Grebe lay in the two-seat experimental trainer, the Grouse (itself a modified Sparrowhawk), in which H P Folland had devised an ingenious combination of the Gloster II.L.B. aerofoil sections. In the Grouse the upper wing of H.L.B.1 high-lift section was rigged at a higher angle of incidence than that of the lower; the latter, of H.L.B.2 medium-lift properties, gave better lift for take-off and at low flying speeds but, because of its thinner section, produced less drag at higher speeds. When powered by a seven-cylinder

The prototype Grebe, J6969, wearing the racing number '14' for the 1923 King's Cup race, during which it was forced to retire with a broken landing wire. (Photo Imperial Museum)

Armstrong Siddeley Lynx engine developing only 185hp, the two-seat Grouse returned a maximum speed of 128mph — compared with the Sopwith Snipe single-seater's 120mph from a 230hp Bentley rotary.

This successful demonstration of Folland's design ideas encouraged the Air Ministry to order three single-seat examples of the Grouse, Specification 3/23 calling for use of the 350hp Armstrong Siddeley Jaguar III fourteen-cylinder two-row radial. Initially referred to as the Nighthawk (Thick Winged), the first aircraft, J6969, was flown in May 1923, and delivered to the A & AEE at Martlesham Heath the following month, appearing as 'No 14' in the New Types Park at the Hendon Air Pageant on 30 June. During the

A Gloster Grebe of No 25 (Fighter) Squadron, whose pilots were acknowledged to be the finest exponents of this little fighter. Note the anti-flutter V-struts added outboard of the interplane struts. (Photo: RAF Museum, Neg No P018533)

course of instrument tests at the RAE its maximum speed was measured at 152 mph at sea level. Now re-named the Grebe Mark I, a total of four Jaguar III-powered prototypes was built (including a Company-owned demonstrator, G-EBHA), and, following a favourable handling report from the A & AEE, a production order for a dozen aircraft was drafted. However, a new Specification, 37/23, had been issued calling for a further improvement with the introduction of the 400hp Jaguar IV, and the first example of this, the Grebe Mark II, J7283 was flown in August, seven months before the contract was eventually signed. Indeed six aircraft joined one flight of No 111 (Fighter) Squadron at Duxford when it was re-formed on 1 October — in all likelihood the only occasion in the RAF's history that fighters joined a front line squadron before contract cover for their manufacture had even been agreed.

Construction of the Grebe was of wood throughout, with ash longerons, spruce struts and stringers and ply formers, the fuselage being fabric-covered. The single-bay wings with spruce spars and girder ribs were braced by metal tie rods, the upper wings being joined on the aircraft centreline. Twin tanks in the upper wing supplied fuel to the engine by gravity feed. The fin and rudder were reminiscent of those on the SE.5 — although at least one Grebe was modified to feature the Gamecock's vertical surfaces.

The Grebe was popular among Service pilots, and in October 1924 it joined No 25 (Fighter) Squadron, commanded by Sqn Ldr Arthur Hicks Peck DSO MC, at Hawkinge, the first to be fully equipped with the aircraft (in the meantime, however, No 41 Squadron had re-equipped with Siskin IIIs). No 25 was followed by Nos 19, 29, 32 and 56 Squadrons. The aircraft was highly

manoeuvrable but, when flown towards its stress limits during aerobatics, it proved tricky to handle, being prone to tail instability and wing flutter. The latter was largely the result of considerable over-hang outboard of the interplane struts and it was in an attempt to remedy this that additional V interplane struts were later added under the outer sections of the upper wing—but with a slight performance penalty. No. 25 Squadron was widely regarded as the leading exponent of the Grebe's flying abilities, and gave a memorable display of air drill and synchronised aerobatics at the 1925 Hendon Air Pageant.

Grebes were employed in an interesting range of trials, one aircraft being armed with a single 0.5in Vickers machine gun for comparison with another with a 0.5in Colt. Grebes J7385 and J7400 were modified for launching trials from the airship R.33, the first such

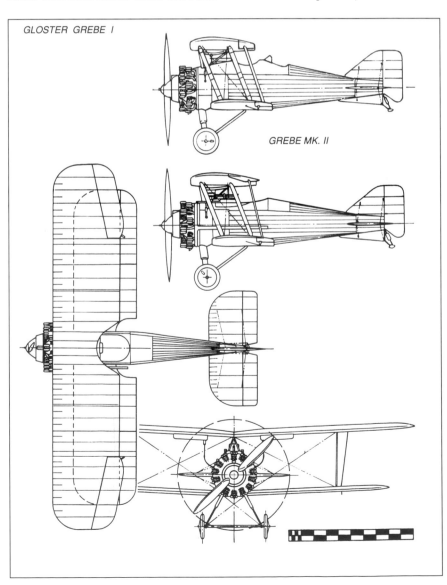

GLOSTER GREBE I

GREBE MK. II

A Gloster Grebe II at Martlesham Heath fitted with the additional interplane V-struts, introduced in an attempt to alleviate the wing flutter to which the aircraft was so prone. This Grebe is also fitted with non-standard low-pressure tyres. (Photo: via Derek N James)

successful launch being achieved on 21 October 1926 by Fg Off Robert Linton Ragg (later Air Marshal, CB, CBE, AFC) of the RAE. The company-owned demonstration Grebe, G-EBHA, was flown with a Jupiter VI driving a Hele-Shaw Beacham variable-pitch propeller, the latter being found to offer significant improvements in climb performance.

Three ex-RAF Grebes, J7381, J7394 and J7400, were supplied to New Zealand in 1928 (one of them as a two-seat trainer), and two of them remained in service for ten years. In the RAF No 25 Squadron continued to fly Grebes longer than the other squadrons, disposing of its last aircraft in June 1929 in favour of Siskin IIIAs. A total of 108 Grebe fighters had been produced for the Service, in addition to 21 dual control two-seaters (termed Grebe Mark IIIDC).

Type: Single-seat, single-engine, single-bay biplane interceptor.

Manufacturer: Gloucestershire Aircraft Co Ltd., Cheltenham and Gloucester.

Air Ministry Specifications: 2/23 for Grebe I prototypes; 37/23 for Grebe II production.

Powerplant: One 400hp Armstrong Siddeley Jaguar IV fourteen-cylinder two-row air-cooled radial engine driving two-blade wooden fixed-pitch Watts propeller.

Structure: All-wood construction with fabric covering

Dimensions: Span, 29ft 4in; length, 20ft 3in; height, 9ft 3in; wing area, 254 sq ft.

Weights: Tare, 1,695lb; all-up, 2,538lb.

Performance: Max speed, 162 mph at sea level; climb to 20,000ft, 24 min; service ceiling, 23,500ft; normal range, approx. 310 miles.

Armament: Two fixed, synchronized 0.303in Vickers Mk. I machine guns in the top decking of the fuselage nose with 600 rounds per gun.

Prototypes and Production: Four prototypes (J6969, first flown May 1923; J6970 and J6971; G-EBHA, company-owned). 108 Mark II fighters (J7283-J7294, J7357-J7402, J7406-J7417, J7568-J7584, J7586-J7603, J7784-J7786); 21 Mark IIIDC trainers (J7519-J7538, J7585).

Summary of Service: Served with Nos 19, 25, 29, 32, 56 and 111 (Fighter) Squadrons, RAF.

Armstrong Whitworth Siskin

Despite the failure of the ABC Dragonfly, and unlike so many other aircraft which had accompanied this engine into obscurity, the Siddley S.R.2 Siskin had showed sufficient promise for Major F M Green to persevere with the design, and early in 1920 the original prototype was re-engined with an early Armstrong Siddeley Jaguar fourteen-cylinder radial engine, then developing about 320hp. At the same time, in response to an Air Ministry suggestion, he drew up outline proposals to redesign the entire aircraft, employing an all-steel structure.

The former wooden box-girder in the fuselage was to be replaced by a similar structure fabricated in high tensile steel tubular members, with rounded decking formers and stringers in light alloy. The wooden wing spars gave place to twin

The second 'hand-built' pre-production Siskin III, J6982, illustrating the sesquiplane wing arrangement with V-form interplane struts. (Photo: Air Ministry [A & AEE])

steel tubular components, although the aircraft retained its fabric covering. The successful undercarriage design featuring radius rods from rear-mounted V-struts was retained, as was the small ventral tail fin. Power was to be provided by a 325hp Jaguar III engine, and a single prototype, J6583, was ordered on 31 May 1920.

Before this aircraft was completed, however, Armstrong Whitworth decided to investigate the possibility of continu-

An early Siskin III, J7148, which was employed for trials with various cowlings and spinners in attempts to reduce the drag of the Jaguar engine. The picture was taken at Martlesham Heath in June 1924. (Photo: Air Ministry [A & AEE])

ing the wooden Siskin in unarmed two-seater configuration as a private venture, believing that such an aircraft could well appeal to foreign air forces, as well as civilian sporting pilots. Moreover it was being suggested at the Air Ministry that there would in due course be a requirement for an advanced trainer capable of bridging the training gap between the *ab initio* stage and that of the operational fighter. A single two-seat Siskin Mk II, G-EBEU, was therefore flown in 1922 to demonstrate the feasibility of the proposal, and was flown by Frank Courtney in the first King's Cup race on 8 September 1922, but retired; the following year the same pilot and aeroplane won the race at a speed of 149 mph. A second Mark II, G-EBHY, this time a single-seater, was produced as a demonstration aircraft, eventually being sold to the Royal Swedish Air Force in 1925 with a ski undercarriage.

Meanwhile J6583, designated the Siskin Mk III, was flown on 7 May 1923, having undergone prolonged structural tests at Martlesham Heath. Although the aircraft was written off in January 1924, another order for three 'hand-built' Siskin IIIs (J6981-J6983), to meet Specification 14/22, had been signed on 13 October 1922, and the first of these was flown on 22 March 1924. The first two of these Siskins underwent handling and performance trials at Farnborough and Martlesham, before being temporarily registered G-EBJQ and G-EBJS respectively for the 1924 King's Cup race. They were delivered to the RAF in

November that year.

It was now apparent that the Siskin would be introduced into RAF service, although the 1922-23 Air Estimates were insufficient to support a substantial purchase contract. An Instruction to Procced with six further aircraft had been negotiated on 25 January 1923, and Armstrong Whitworth laid down a production bay at its Parkside works at Coventry. All six, J6998-J7003, were flown in January 1924, the first three examples, J7001-J7003, being delivered to No 41 (Fighter) Squadron at Northolt, commanded by Sqn Ldr Gilbert Ware Murlis-Green DSO, MC, on the 25th of that month to begin Service trials. The batch was scheduled for a wide range of other trials, including mounting J6999 on one of HMS *Tiger*'s main armament turrets in October 1926 to investigate the effects of gun blast; it was not flown thereafter. J7000 was converted to become the prototype two-seat trainer with dual controls (the Mark IIIDC) under Specification 33/23, and first flew as such on 13 October 1924. J7002

and J7003 were also converted to DC standard — the former surviving until written off in April 1933, having flown 433 hours.

The first sizeable production order, for 37 Mark IIIs, was placed on 11 August 1923, and the first of these aircraft, J7145, was flown in March 1924. They were delivered to No 41 (Fighter) Squadron in May, and to No 111 (Fighter) Squadron, commanded by Sqn Ldr T F Hazell DSO, MC, DFC*, at Duxford the next month.

The Siskin III proved to be very popular in service, albeit slightly underpowered. There was, however, adequate power to enable formation aerobatics to be indulged in, and formation air drill was always a popular feature at air displays in the mid-1920s. On account of its metal structure, it was not long before it was being suggested that Siskins would be ideal for service overseas. Accordingly J7157 was shipped out to India for Service trials with No 20 (Army Co-operation) Squadron at Kohat in 1925; this aircraft was converted to Mk IIIA standard (see opposite) in 1927 and underwent further Service trials in this configuration with No 5 (General Reconnaissance) Squadron at Quetta. Tropical trials were performed by J7178 at Heliopolis in June 1925 but, apart from a small number of two-seaters with No 4 Flying Training School in Egypt, the Siskin did not see service overseas.

A total of 63 Siskin IIIs was produced,

A Gloster-built Siskin IIIA, J8947, wearing the pennant of No 1 (Fighter) Squadron's CO, Sqn Ldr E D Atkinson, DFC, AFC, at Tangmere. (Photo: J Bartholomew)

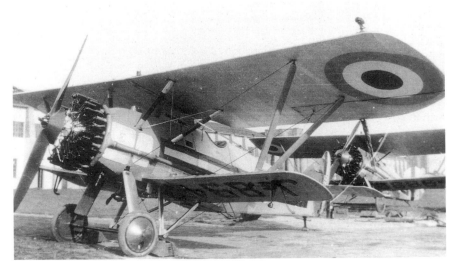

Three Siskin IIIAs of No 43 (Fighter) Squadron, Bristol-built aircraft J8837 ('O'), and J8863 ('B'), and Blackburn-built J8866 ('B'). Just visible are the elastic cords connecting the three aircraft for a tied-together aerobatic demonstration which the Squadron gave later that month, June 1930, at the Hendon Air Display. (Photo: via R C Sturtivant)

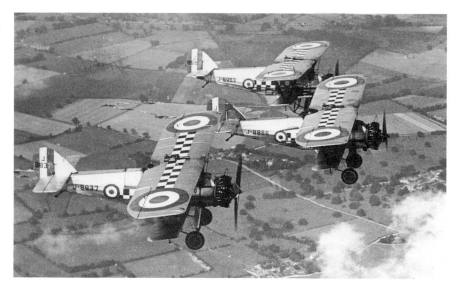

of which six were built as Mk IIIDC two-seaters; a further 31 were converted to Mk IIIDCs from single-seaters. In September 1926 deliveries to the RAF of the Siskin IIIA began, and as the Mark III came to be replaced on Nos 41 and 111 Squadrons, the older aircraft underwent conversion to two-seat trainers and were distributed among Nos 1, 2, 3, 4 and 5 Flying Training Schools, the Armament & Gunnery School, the Central Flying School and the RAF College, Cranwell. A number also equipped No 54 (Fighter) Squadron at Hornchurch, commanded by Sqn Ldr (later Gp Capt) Walter Edward George Bryant MBE during 1930, while it awaited delivery of Bristol Bulldogs (see page 194).

The Siskin IIIA, of which no fewer than 450 were produced, equipped eleven fighter squadrons. Powered initially by 450hp Jaguar IV normally-aspirated engines, and later by Jaguar IVA supercharged engines, the Mark IIIA was readily distinguishable by its modified rudder outline and the deletion of the ventral tailfin. The inclusion of a supercharger had no effect on performance below about 10,000 feet, but it bestowed a much improved speed and climb above that height, compared with the earlier version.

The first Siskin IIIA to be powered by the Jaguar IV, J8428, had flown on 21 October 1925, and spent about eight years undergoing all manner of tests at Farnborough and Martlesham Heath until eventually scrapped. The first order for production Siskin IIIAs was signed in June 1926, and these equipped No 111 Squadron, commanded by Sqn Ldr G W Roberts MC, in September that year. In 1927 Nos 1, 41 and 56 Squadrons followed suit as more and more aircraft were ordered. In August that year the last order for 50 Siskin IIIAs was placed with Armstrong Whitworth before a programme of sub-contracted production was begun, involving Bristol, Blackburn, Glosters and Vickers. One of the aircraft of this batch was J8626 which, having flown with No 56

Squadron between November 1927 and February 1928, was returned to the manufacturers to be fitted with the supercharged Jaguar IVS (first flight on 12 October 1928), and then the 460hp Jaguar VIII. It was displayed at the 1929 Olympia Show with a Townend ring fitted, and spent the next two years as a test bed for various experimental Jaguar and Panther engines, appearing in the New Types Park (as No 4) at the Hendon Air Display on 28 June 1930.

Foreign sales of the Siskin had begun in a promising manner following the demonstration tours by the single-seat Mark II, G-EBHY, in 1924-25. Romania placed an order for 65 Siskins in 1924, and the first was flown in October that year. Seven aircraft were delivered but, following a fatal accident involving one of these machines, the contract was summarily cancelled. Estonia also took delivery of a pair of Siskin two-seaters.

The Siskin IIIs J7758 and J7759 were shipped to Canada in December 1925 for cold weather trials, and the following month both were purchased by the Royal Canadian Air Force; both flew with No 2 Squadron, RCAF, and the latter survived until March 1935 when it

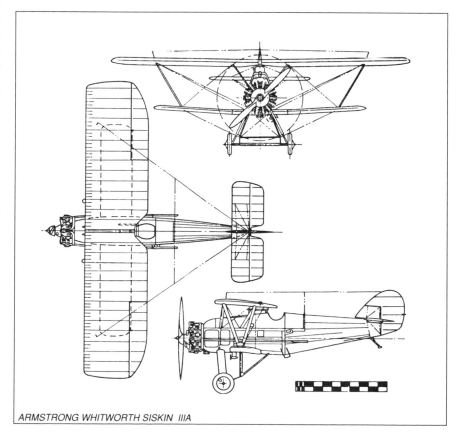

ARMSTRONG WHITWORTH SISKIN IIIA

was struck off charge following an accident. A further Siskin, a Mk IIIDC J9236, underwent trials at the A & AEE on behalf of the RCAF in June 1929, but no further aircraft were supplied to Canada.

In Britain five Siskins appeared on the civil register after the original four, already mentioned. G-EBLL, designated a Mark IV, was flown from scratch into second place in the 1925 King's Cup race by Flt Lt H W G Jones MC (later to command No 19 Squadron with Siskins at Duxford). Two other Siskins also entered the race, both termed Mark Vs; these were wooden single-seaters with parallel interplane struts and no ventral tailfin, but were powered by 385hp Jaguar III engines. G-EBLN retired after damaging its undercarriage during a refuelling stop, but Frank Barnard in G-EBLQ won the race at a speed of 151.43 mph.

Finally, in 1931, two Siskin IIIDCs, G-ABHT and G-ABHU, were built for advanced flying instruction with the Armstrong Whitworth Reserve Flying School at Whitby, being transferred to Air Service Training Ltd at Hamble the same year. G-ABHU survived for many years, but was destroyed in a crash in January 1938.

Type: Single-engine, single-seat, single-bay biplane interceptor fighter.
Manufacturers: Sir W G Armstrong Whitworth Aircraft Ltd, Parkside, Coventry; The Gloster Aircraft Co Ltd, Hucclecote, Gloucester; The Bristol Aeroplane Co Ltd, Filton, Bristol; The Blackburn Aeroplane & Motor Co Ltd, Brough, East Yorkshire; Vickers (Aviation) Ltd, Weybridge, Surrey.
Air Ministry Specifications: Mk III, Spec 14/22; Mk IIIDC, Spec, 33/23; Mk IIIA, Spec 25/25; Mk IIIDC(Stage II), Spec 1/28.
Powerplant: Mk III, one 325hp Armstrong Siddeley Jaguar III 14-cylinder two-row air-cooled radial engine; Mk IIIA, 450hp Jaguar IV; Mk IIIB, 460hp Jaguar IVS; also 460hp Jaguar VIII, and Armstrong Siddeley Panther.
Structure: Fabric-covered box-girder structure with high tensile steel tubular members, and twin steel wing spars.
Dimensions: Mk IIIA. Span, 33ft 2in; length, 25ft 4in; height, 10ft 2in; wing area, 293 sq ft.
Weights: Mk IIIA. Tare, 2,061lb; all-up, 3,012 lb.
Performance: Mk IIIA. Max speed, 156 mph at sea level, 145 mph at 15,000ft; climb to 10,000ft, 7 min 5 sec; service ceiling, 27,500ft.
Armament: Two synchronized 0.303in Vickers machine guns in the upper nose decking with 600 rounds per gun; provision to carry up to four 20lb bombs under the lower wings.
Prototypes: Mk III, one, J6583 (first flown, 7 May 1923); Mk IIIA, one, J8428 (first flown, 21 October 1925).
Production: Mk III (excluding prototype, civil and exported aircraft), 102 (all by Armstrong Whitworth: J6981-J6983, J6998-J7003, J7145-J7818, J7549-J7554 (DC), J7758-J7764, J7820-J7822 and J9190-J9236 (DC)); Mk IIIA/B (excluding prototype), 339 (Armstrong Whitworth, 87: J8048-J8060, J8381-J8404 and J8623-J8672; Gloster, 74: J8933-J8974, J9331-J9352 and J9912-J9921; Blackburn, 42: J8864-J8905; Bristol, 84: J8822-J8863, J9304-J9330 and J9897-J9911; Vickers, 42: J9353-J9379 and J9872-J9876).
Summary of Service: Siskin IIIs served with Nos 41 and 111 (Fighter) Squadrons between February 1924 and March 1927; Siskin IIIAs served with Nos 1, 17, 19, 25, 29, 32, 41, 43, 54, 56 and 111 (Fighter) Squadrons between September 1926 and October 1932. Single- and two-seat Siskin IIIs also served with Nos 1, 2, 3, 4 and 5 Flying Training Schools; Armament & Gunnery School; Central Flying School; RAF College, Cranwell; No 23 Squadron, No 24 (Communications) Squadron, Home Communications Flight and the Duxford Meteorological Flight.

Bristol Type 84 Bloodhound

Failure by the Bristol Badger and Bullfinch to gain acceptance by the Air Ministry to replace the Bristol F.2B Fighter was followed by the temporary departure of Capt Frank Barnwell, his place as Bristol's chief designer being taken by Wilfrid Reid, who put forward a number of project designs during 1921, but these were also rejected largely on account of the Air Ministry's reluctance to accept the relatively untried Cosmos/Bristol Jupiter engine.

In June 1922 a new Specification, 3/22, was issued calling for a two-seat fighter in which a supercharged engine was recommended so as to maintain power up to 10,000 feet. Reid tendered two designs, the Type 78 Fighter C two-bay biplane and the Type 80 Fighter D monoplane. As it was felt that the cantilever monoplane wing would take many months to develop to suit opera-

Bristol Bloodhound prototype, G-EBGG, with lengthened rear fuselage, increased wing stagger and sweepback; the upper wing is flat and dihedral on the lower wing has been increased; in this form it reappeared in 1925 as J7236. (Photo: The Bristol Aeroplane Co Ltd, Neg No 392)

tional strength requirements, Bristol decided to go ahead and build the Fighter C as a private venture. Powered by a 425hp Bristol Jupiter IV, this aircraft became the Type 84 Bloodhound, registered G-EBGG, and first flown at the end of May 1923. In its initial form the Bloodhound possessed equal dihedral and sweepback on upper and lower wings, and a small, unbalanced rudder.

Having re-written Spec 3/22 and come up with 22/22, the Air Ministry placed an order for three Type 84s late in June 1922; the first (J7248) was to be of all-metal construction, and the other two (J7236 and J7237) were to possess wooden wings and tails. As flight trials on G-EBGG continued in the hands of Capt Norman Macmillan, it was found necessary to increase the wing sweepback, dihedral and stagger and, after the return of Barnwell in October, the fuselage was lengthened as well.

G-EBGG was rebuilt with these alterations and re-appeared as J7236, but the all-metal Bloodhound, J7248, was the first to fly in the altered form on 4 February 1925. These two aircraft underwent a number of trials at Martlesham later that year, and J7237 was assigned to the RAE at Farnborough.

Although it had been intended to evaluate the Bloodhound in competition with the Hawker Duiker, Armstrong Whitworth Wolf and de Havilland D.H. 42 Dormouse, no such formal assessment was made as all four aircraft had been designed to different Specifications; only the Bloodhound was considered in the context of a fighter, whereas the other three were intended to fill various reconnaissance rôles.

It soon became evident that none of these aircraft came anywhere near meeting the Bristol Fighter replacement requirements, and the Bloodhound was relegated to becoming an engine test bed. J7236 was accordingly powered by a Jupiter IV with variable timing gear as an alternative means of maintaining power up to 10,000 feet, while J7237's Jupiter IV featured the exhaust-driven supercharger developed by the RAE.

J7236 reverted to G-EBGG and its armament was removed; it was fitted in turn with Jupiter V and VI during 1925 and 1926, and in 1928 was engaged in endurance trials with the geared Jupiter VIII driving a four-blade propeller.

The accompanying data table refers to the Bloodhound J7236 with standard Jupiter IV engine.

Type: Single-engine, two-seat, two-bay biplane reconnaissance fighter.
Manufacturer: The Bristol Aeroplane Co Ltd, Filton, Bristol.
Air Ministry Specifications: 3/22 and 22/22.
Powerplant: One 425hp Bristol Jupiter IV, IV (with variable timing) and IVS; also 450hp Jupiter V; 450hp Jupiter VI; and 485hp Jupiter VIII.
Dimensions: Span, 40ft 2in; length, 26ft 6in; height, 10ft 8in; wing area, 494 sq ft.
Weights: Tare, 2,515lb; all-up, 4,236lb.
Performance: Max speed, 130 mph at sea level, 118 mph at 10,000ft; service ceiling, 22,000ft; endurance, 3 hr.
Armament: Provision made for two synchronized 0.303in Vickers machine guns in nose, and a Lewis gun with Scarff ring on rear cockpit; provision made to carry up to four 20lb bombs.
Prototypes: Three, J7236, J7237 and J7248 (J7236, as G-EBGG, first flown at the end of May 1923). No production.

Bristol Type 76 Jupiter-Fighter

Continuing scepticism by the Air Council with regard to the Bristol Jupiter engine, combined with the availability of a large number of war-surplus Bristol F.2B Fighter airframes still in storage, prompted Wilfrid Reid to design an adaptation of the F.2B to take the Jupiter, a project that had the enthusiastic support of Roy Fedden. It was hoped to interest potential foreign air forces in the two-seat fighter with a relatively inexpensive airframe, yet still possessing a worthwhile performance. At the same time it was hoped that, by doing so, Bristol would be able to demonstrate to the Air Ministry that the nine-cylinder Jupiter was at least as reliable as the fourteen-cylinder Armstrong Siddeley Jaguar which, of roughly similar power, was nevertheless a good deal more troublesome to maintain in service.

Three conversions, designated the Bristol Type 76, were authorised as private ventures, being identified as G-EBGF, G-EBHG and G-EBHH. The

The first Bristol Type 76, G-EBGF, with Capt Norman Macmillan in the cockpit; during the course of installing the Jupiter, the opportunity was taken to introduce an oleo-strutted undercarriage. (Photo: Author's Collection)

Jupiter installation itself proved entirely straightforward although, with a much higher fuel consumption than the Rolls-Royce Eagle, previously fitted, the endurance was reduced to no more than two hours — or a radius of action of little over one hundred miles. Capt Norman Macmillan first flew G-EBGF at the beginning of June 1923, but reported adversely on the pilot's view forward, while the airflow over the rear cockpit proved too boisterous to allow the observer to aim his Lewis gun.

These shortcomings, combined with the aircraft's very short range, ruled out the Type 76 as a realistic fighter.

The second aircraft, G-EBHG, was displayed at the Göteborg International Aero Exhibition in July 1923, and was subsequently purchased by the Swedish government. G-EBHH was subject of an interesting trial as part of the programme aimed at maintaining the Bristol Fighter's performance up to around

10,000ft. Powered by a high compression Jupiter IV, the aircraft took off using alcohol fuel and, on reaching an altitude at which detonation would not occur, the pilot switched over to petrol, which passed through a second carburettor; the alcohol tank was located on the upper wing centre section. However, the two-fuel system was abandoned on account of tank corrosion, the normal engine supercharging being preferred.

Despite the demise of the Jupiter-Fighter, the feasibility of the engine installation was further exploited in a number of dual-control advanced trainers for both the RAF and commercial agencies.

Type: Single-engine, two-seat, two-bay experimental biplane fighter.
Manufacturer: The Bristol Aeroplane Co Ltd, Filton, Bristol.
Powerplant: One 425hp Bristol Jupiter IV nine-cylinder radial engine.
Dimensions: Span, 39ft 3in; length, 25ft 0in; height, 9ft 6in; wing area, 405 sq ft.
Weights: Tare, 2,190lb; all-up, 3,080lb.
Performance: Max speed, 134 mph at sea level; service ceiling, 22,150ft.
Armament: Provision for two synchronized Vickers machine guns and one Lewis gun in the rear cockpit.
Prototypes: Three, G-EBGF, G-EBHG and G-EBHH (G-EBGF first flown by Capt Norman Macmillan in June 1923). No production.

Hawker Woodcock

After the demise of the old Sopwith company following voluntary liquidation, a successor came into being in 1920 with the formation of H G Hawker Engineering Co Ltd in the former Sopwith premises at Kingston-upon-Thames, Surrey. Although Hawker sought survival through the repair of war-surplus Snipes and Camels, it was not long before its design office, under Capt B Thomson, embarked on new aircraft, the first fighter to be built being the Woodcock.

Leaning heavily on the Snipe's configuration, the Woodcock — as it appeared initially — was a two-bay biplane of all-wooden construction, powered by a 358hp Armstrong Siddeley Jaguar II fourteen-cylinder radial engine. Designed to Specification 25/22, the Jaguar Woodcock prototype (J6987) was first flown late in March 1923 but quickly displayed severe wing flutter as well as serious directional control deficiency. Thomson left Hawker before the Wood-

The sole Hawker Woodcock I, J6987, after being re-engined with a Jupiter IV in 1924; this view emphasises the extraordinarily pedestrian appearance of Hawker's first fighter which represented no significant advance over the Sopwith Snipe. (Photo: British Aerospace PLC)

cock was flown, his place as Chief Designer being taken by W G Carter who set about an extensive redesign of the Woodcock, the Mk II, with single-bay wings, 425hp Bristol Jupiter IV radial and revised tail surfaces. This prototype, J6988, was evaluated at Martlesham Heath in August 1923 and found to be greatly improved, compared to the Mk I.

On return to Brooklands in March 1924 minor modifications (including engine cylinder helmets) were incorporated before J6988's appearance at the 1924 Hendon Pageant, wearing New Aircraft No 2, on 28 June. Engine valve-gear icing was cured by the fitting of a large exhaust collector shroud, and in this form the aircraft underwent night fighter trials at Martlesham the following month.

Perseverence with the Woodcock II was rewarded by initial production orders totalling 19 aircraft at the end of 1924, followed by 19 in 1925. A final order for 25 Woodcock IIs was placed in 1926-27.

Production of the aircraft started at Canbury Park Road, Kingston, early in 1925, the first aircraft being flown on 21 April by Fred Raynham before paying a visit to Martlesham for trials with a

Standard Woodcock II night fighter, J8299, of No 17 (Fighter) Squadron at Upavon in April 1928, by which time the Squadron was already beginning to re-equip with Gloster Gamecocks; note the navigation lights and flare brackets on upper and lower wings. (Photo: via R C Sturtivant)

Jupiter III engine. Meanwhile No 3 Squadron at Upavon was taking delivery of Woodcocks, beginning on 12 May.

Clearance for night flying by Woodcocks was delayed for several weeks owing to the need to install equipment such as flare dispensers and navigation lights. The second production aircraft suffered a main spar failure, and this resulted in a lengthy investigation at Farnborough, but by March 1926 No 17 Squadron at Hawkinge was taking delivery of fully-equipped Woodcock night fighters. However, a new spate of accidents, following collapse of the undercarriage oleos during night landings on Hawkinge's poor field surface, led to the need for local strengthening—and in October No 17 Squadron joined No 3 at Upavon.

These two squadrons were the only fighter units to be equipped with Woodcocks in the RAF, being responsible for night defence of the Midlands. The aircraft was popular among its pilots although, with a maximum speed of 143 mph and an armament of twin Vickers guns, it reprcsented no significant advance over the wartime Snipe. On the other hand, its acceptance by the RAF enabled the fledgling Hawker company to survive at a time of much reduced manufacturing contracts.

W G Carter left Hawker in 1925 to join the Gloucestershire Aircraft Company, whereupon his deputy, Sydney Camm, became Chief Designer. Camm it was who undertook a number of innovations in the Woodcock, introducing slotted wings in J7974 (which performed trials at Farnborough and Martlesham during 1926-27).

The original Woodcock I was re-engined with a Jupiter IV early in 1925 before being re-built to full Mark II standard in 1926 and delivered to No 3 Squadron the following year. One of the last Woodcocks built, J8312, was shipped to Aboukir, Egypt, for tropical trials in 1928.

The RAF's Woodcocks were replaced by Gloster Gamecocks on No 17 Squadron in January 1928, and on No 3 in August that year.

The Woodcock II, J7974, underwent trials with wing slots in 1926 at the RAE in an effort to facilitate night landing; it afterwards served with No 3 (Fighter) Squadron, but the improvement was only marginal and was not generally adopted. (Photo: H G Hawker Engineering Co Ltd, Neg No 376W)

Type: Single-engine, single-seat two-bay (Mk I) and single-bay (Mk II) biplane interceptor night fighter.
Manufacturer: H G Hawker Engineering Co Ltd, Kingston and Brooklands, Surrey
Air Ministry Specifications: 25/22, 3/24 and 20/26
Powerplant: Mk I, one 358 hp Armstrong Siddeley Jaguar II fourteen-cylinder air-cooled radial engine. Mk II, one 425hp Bristol Jupiter IV nine-cylinder air-cooled radial engine.
Structure: All-wood fuselage and two-spar wing structure, all fabric-covered.
Dimensions: Mk I. Span, 34ft 8in; length, 25ft 7in; height, 9ft 0in; wing area, 356 sq ft. Mk II. Span, 32ft 6in; length, 26ft 2in; height, 9ft 11in; wing area, 346 sq ft.
Weights: Mk I. Tare 2,083lb; all-up, 3,023lb. Mk II.Tare, 2,014lb; all-up, 2,979lb.
Performance: Mk I. Max speed, 143 mph at sea level; climb, 8.4 min to 10,000ft; range, 260 miles; service ceiling, 20,550ft. Mk II. Max speed, 141 mph at sea level; climb, 8.3 min to 10,000ft; range, 280 miles; service ceiling, 22,500 ft.
Armament: Two synchronized 0.303in Vickers Mk II machine guns on sides of fuselage.
Prototypes: J6987 and J6988 (Mk II, first flown c.July 1923, by F P Raynham).
Production: 63 (excluding two prototypes): J7512-J7517, J7725-J7737, J7783, J7960-J7977 and J8292-J8316.
Summary of Service: Nos. 3 and 17 Squadrons, 1925-28.

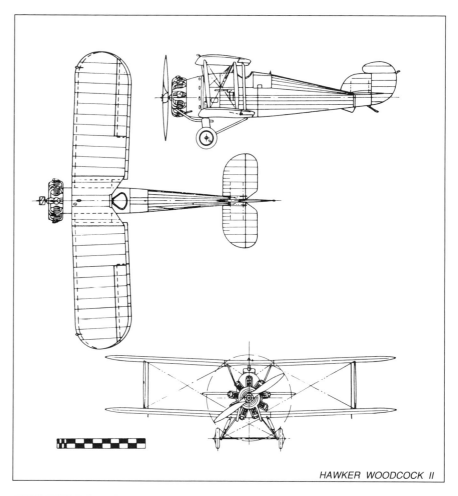

HAWKER WOODCOCK II

Handley Page H.P.21

Two views of the H.P.21, apparently taken at Martlesham Heath in 1923, showing the rudder with what is apparently an out-rigged horn balance, and multiple radius members and V-type fixed struts in the undercarriage. (Photos: A J Jackson Collection)

One of the least known of all British fighter aircraft was flown towards the end of 1923, and was the product of a company more famous for its heavy bombers and airliners. Frederick Handley Page was one of a tiny number of aeronautical engineers who, independent of each other, had discovered that a miniature winglet or slat placed above the leading edge of an aerofoil had the effect of delaying the breakdown of airflow that occurred immediately before the aerofoil 'stalled'. By the end of the War a workable system of retracting the slat had been evolved, and Handley Page applied for world patents.

Among the air forces that became interested in the obvious benefits bestowed by leading-edge slats was the U S Navy which, like all carrier-borne aircraft operators, required suitable research aircraft with which to evaluate such benefits. In 1921 therefore that Service approached Handley Page with an order for three potential fighter aircraft equipped with high lift devices.

Thus was born the H.P.21, an aeroplane that was in numerous respects far ahead of its time. It was an all-wooden, low-wing single-seat monoplane powered by a 230hp Bentley B.R.2 rotary engine, the wings being fitted with full-span, leading-edge retractable slats and trailing-edge flaps, the former being of unusually generous area. The undercarriage employed swing struts reminiscent of the Siddeley Siskin, but with sprung forward members more akin to the Avro 504. The engine was mounted within a clean cowling which constituted a very short nose so that the view from the cockpit, which was located well forward, was excellent. Almost all control rods

and cables were enclosed within the wings and fuselage, the latter being built in two sections, bolted together immediately aft of the cockpit. The cantilever wing was constructed integrally with the forward fuselage. Provision was made for two synchronized 0.300in Marlin machine guns, but these were probably never mounted. The entire aircraft was skinned in wooden ply.

Surviving photographs show the H.P.21 in two differing configurations, and it is not known whether two different aircraft are depicted, or if extensive modification was undertaken on a single

prototype. (American sources suggest that all three aircraft, allotted the numbers A6402-A6404, were delivered, whereas Handley Page records seem to indicate that only one aircraft was produced; no British registration, either military or civil, has been traced.)

In some photographs the H.P.21 is shown with an unbalanced rudder blending smoothly with a triangular fin; elsewhere the aircraft is shown with what appears to be a horn-balanced rudder with a straight trailing edge and much smaller fin. The nose of the aircraft appears to be significantly shorter in

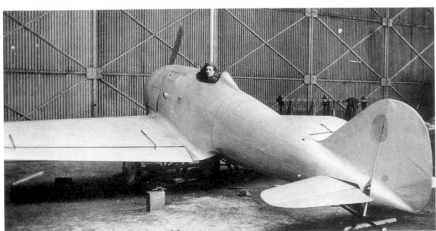

Two views of the H.P.21 with unbalanced rudder and pyramidal struts and single radius members in the undercarriage. (Photos: J M Bruce Collection)

some pictures than in others, and the undercarriage clearly underwent changes, the rear fixed struts being shown as both V-type and pyramidal, while the radius members clearly underwent strengthening at some time.

The H.P.21 was completed in September 1923 and undertook performance and handling trials at Martlesham Heath before being delivered to the USA, where it was designated the HPS-1 (Handley Page Scout). American sources suggest that the aircraft's maximum speed was somewhat less than that quoted in British reports, and it is likely that the former refer to the speed at about 10,000 feet.

A floatplane version was designed, and it is assumed that the float struts would have been attached to the wing spars and lower longerons at the same points as the wheel undercarriage; this would account for the choice of radius strut wheel suspension.

Type: Single-engine, single-seat, cantilever low-wing monoplane naval experimental fighter.
Manufacturer: Handley Page Ltd, Cricklewood, London.
Powerplant: One 230hp Bentley B.R.2 rotary engine driving two-blade propeller.
Dimensions: Span, 29ft 2 in; length, 21ft 5in.
Weights: Tare, 1,410lb; all-up, 1,920lb.
Performance: Max speed, 145 mph at sea level; landing speed, 44 mph; initial rate of climb, 1,800 ft/min; service ceiling, 21,000ft; endurance, 3 hr.
Armament: Provision to mount two synchronized 0.300in Marlin machine guns in the nose.
Prototypes: Three ordered (allotted U S Navy Nos A6402-A6404), but it is not confirmed that all three were built. No production.

Deployment of British Fighter Squadrons — January 1925

Home Bases

No 2 Squadron	Bristol F.2B Fighter*	Manston
No 3 Squadron	Sopwith Snipe	Upavon
No 4 Squadron	Bristol F.2B Fighter*	Farnborough
No 13 Squadron	Bristol F.2B Fighter*	Andover
No 16 Squadron	Bristol F.2B Fighter*	Old Sarum
No 17 Squadron	Sopwith Snipe	Hawkinge
No 19 Squadron	Gloster Grebe	Duxford
No 25 Squadron	Gloster Grebe II	Hawkinge
No 32 Squadron	Gloster Grebe II	Kenley
No 41 Squadron	A.W. Siskin III	Northolt
No 56 Squadron	Gloster Grebe II	Biggin Hill
No 111 Squadron	Gloster Grebe/Snipe	Duxford

Overseas

No 1 Squadron	Sopwith Snipe	Hinaidi, Iraq
No 5 Squadron	Bristol F.2B Fighter*	Dardoni, India

No 6 Squadron	Bristol F.2B Fighter*	Mosul, Iraq
No 14 Squadron	Bristol F.2B Fighter*	Palestine/Iraq
No 20 Squadron	Bristol F.2B Fighter*	Peshawar, India
No 28 Squadron	Bristol F.2B Fighter*	Peshawar, India
No 31 Squadron	Bristol F.2B Fighter*	Ambala, India
No 208 Squadron	Bristol F.2B Fighter*	Ismailia, Egypt

Fleet Air Arm

No 401 Flight	Fairey Flycatcher	Leuchars
No 402 Flight	Fairey Flycatcher	Leuchars
No 403 Flight	Fairey Flycatcher	HMS *Hermes*
No 404 Flight	Fairey Flycatcher	HMS *Furious*
No 405 Flight	Fairey Flycatcher	HMS *Hermes*
No 406 Flight	Fairey Flycatcher	HMS *Furious*

* Bristol F.2B Fighters performed the fighter-reconnaissance rôle

---

Gloucestershire (Gloster) Gamecock

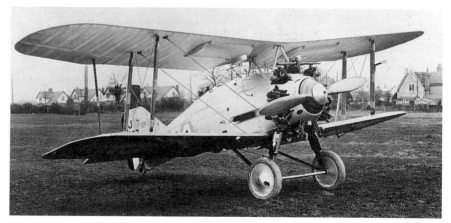

The first Gamecock prototype, J7497, with Jupiter IV engine but retaining the Grebe's tail unit; note the gun troughs in the sides of the fuselage. (Photo: Derek James)

First flown in February 1925, the Gamecock prototype, J7497, was ordered in August 1924 as the Grebe Mark II, powered by a 398hp Bristol Jupiter IV radial. However, with the introduction of the Jaguar IV in the production Grebe II, the new prototype was renamed the Gamecock. Indeed, choice of the lighter, simpler Bristol engine was the *raison d'être* of the Gamecock and no significant advance in performance was forecast. Construction was little changed, the use of H.L.B. wings was retained and, apart from the single-row Jupiter, J7497 was hardly distinguishable from the early Grebe IIs.

Initial handling trials at Martlesham confirmed that none of the Grebe's control crispness had been lost but, by the same token, Glosters were already aware that the Gamecock also retained the earlier aircraft's spinning and wing flutter characteristics, so that an enlarged horn-balanced rudder and bigger fin were quickly substituted. In Septem-

Left: *The third Gamecock prototype, J7757, during the time of its performance trials with No 22 Squadron of the A & AEE at Martlesham Heath in September 1925. This prototype was powered by the 425hp Bristol Jupiter VI engine, and was fitted with parallel-chord ailerons; it was also equipped with wireless.* (Photo: via Derek James)

Below: *Gamecock I, J8409, served with No 23 (Fighter) Squadron during the latter half of 1929; it was lost in a collision with another of the Squadron's Gamecocks, J7903, over Surrey on 7 November that year.* (Photo: RAF Museum, Neg No P008329)

ber 1925 the Air Ministry placed an initial production order for 30 Gamecock Is at a unit price of £2,650 (excluding radio and guns).

Powered by the new 425hp Jupiter VII and prepared to Specification 9/25, the first aircraft were delivered in March 1926 to No 43 (Fighter) Squadron, commanded by Sqn Ldr A F Brooke at Henlow. Two months later Gamecocks joined No 23 (Fighter) Squadron (also at Henlow), commanded by the famous First World War naval airman, Sqn Ldr Raymond Collishaw DSO, OBE, DSC, DFC.

Despite the modifications to the fin and rudder, the Gamecock remained a difficult aeroplane to recover from a spin, there being a tendency for a right-hand spin to flatten soon after entry and, with a short fuselage and engine unusually close to the aircraft's centre of gravity, the spin rate was uncomfortably high. Gamecock J7910, completed early in 1927, was fitted with an additional upper wing centre section, parallel chord ailerons and outboard V-interplane struts; in this configuration Howard Saint dived the aircraft to a speed of 275mph and completed a 22-turn spin, recovery in both instances being made without trouble or appreciable wing flutter.

Opinions were divided among Service pilots as to whether the Gamecock was superior to the Grebe in the air, the later aircraft being distinctly slower, but marginally more manoeuvrable. Nevertheless Gamecock squadrons took the first three places in the fighter races for the annual Sassoon Cup of 1927, and there is no doubt but that the Gamecock's Jupiter engine was much simpler

to maintain than the recalcitrant Jaguar. It is however worth recording that, of the 108 Grebe fighters manufactured for

the RAF, 20 were lost in flying accidents (18.5%) during five years' service, compared with 22 Gamecocks lost out of 91

*Type: Sin*gle-seat, single-engine, single-bay interceptor biplane.
Manufacturer: Gloucestershire/Gloster Aircraft Co Ltd., Cheltenham and Gloucester.
Air Ministry Specification: 18/25 for production Gamecock Mk I.
Powerplant: One 425hp Bristol Jupiter VII nine-cylinder air-cooled radial engine driving two-blade wooden fixed-pitch Watts propeller.
Structure: All-wood construction with fabric covering. Gloster H.L.B. wing sections.
Dimensions (Gamecock I): Span, 29ft 9½in; length, 19ft 8in; height, 9ft 9in; wing area, 264sq ft.
Weights (Gamecock I): Tare, 1,930lb; all-up, 2,742lb.
Performance (Gamecock I): Max speed, 154mph at sea level; climb to 20,000ft, 27 min; service ceiling, 22,100ft; normal range, approx 280 miles.
Armament: Two fixed, synchronised 0.303in Vickers Mk I machine guns firing forward through channels in sides of front fuselage, each with 600 rounds per gun.
*Prototypes: Three Mk I proto*types (J7497, first flown February 1925; J7756 and J7757). Three Mark II prototypes (J7910, converted from Mk I, J8804 and J9248). One two-seat dual control trainer converted from Mk I, J7900.
Production: 90 Mark Is (J7891-J7920, J7959 (cancelled), J8033-J8047, J8069-J8095 and J8405-J8422).
Summary of Service: Gamecocks served with Nos. 3, 17, 23, 32 and 43 (Fighter) Squadrons. Small numbers also served with Nos 2 and 3 FTS, the CFS, the RAF College, Cranwell, and the Home Communications Flight. At least one Gamecock flew with No 19 (Fighter) Squadron in 1929.

built (23.1%) in six years's service. (These figures compare with 80 Siskin III/IIIAs —the other principal RAF fighters between 1924 and 1932 — lost out of 406 aircraft built (19.7%) and during front line service which lasted 8½ years.)

After joining Nos 43 and 23 Squadrons, Gamecocks went on to serve with Nos 3, 17 and 32 Squadrons, the last such aircraft being disposed of by No. 23 Squadron in September 1931 in favour of Siskin IIIAs. One Gamecock, J7900, was converted to a two-seater with dual controls and flew with the Central Flying School from October 1927.

Shortly after the first production contract had been issued in 1925, the Air Ministry decided to investigate the possibility of producing an all-metal Gamecock and, because Glosters were not staffed nor equipped to produce such an aircraft, awarded the contract to Boulton & Paul and ordered a single prototype, J7959. When, however, the Gamecock began to display all the familiar spinning and flutter problems, the metal version was abandoned in preference for a new aircraft not so afflicted.

Meanwhile development had continued with the Gamecock II, a company-sponsored version with added wing centre section and enlarged wing cut-out, parallel-chord ailerons, enlarged rudder, and shallower fuel tanks that projected less from below the top wing. A prototype was built by modifying a Mark I, J7910, and although the Mark II was not adopted for the RAF, this version formed the basis of Gamecocks (known as *Kukkos*) supplied to the Finnish Air Force. Two pattern aircraft were built by Glosters for sale to Finland and 15 others were completed under licence by the National Aircraft Factory in Helsinki. The Gamecock II, J8804,

remained in Britain while another aircraft, G-EBOE — also intended to feature the Mark II changes — was scheduled to be fitted with the Bristol Orion turbo-supercharged radial, but after the engine was abandoned the aircraft was completed as a Mark II with the serial J9248.

Gamecock I, J8047, originally completed for the RAF late in 1926, was returned to Glosters for inclusion of numerous modifications following spin-

ning trials at the RAE, and re-appeared in 1928, known unofficially as the Mark III, with lengthened nose and rear fuselage, wider undercarriage track, enlarged tail surfaces, and parallel-chord ailerons. Later in 1928 it was fitted with a Jupiter VII; in 1934 it was rescued from scrap by a private owner who rebuilt it as G-ADIN. Gamecock I, J8075, was used during 1928 to flight test the Mercury IIA radial before being returned to standard.

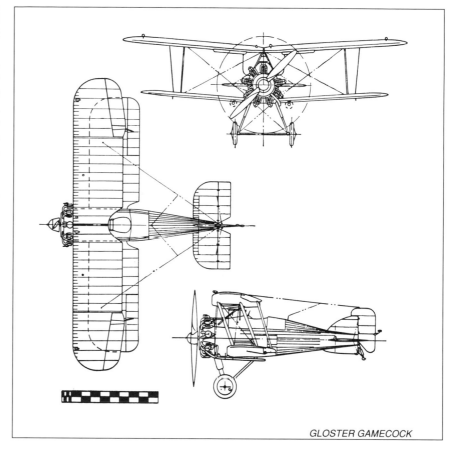

GLOSTER GAMECOCK

Capt Howard Saint demonstrating the Gamecock J7910 at low level. This aircraft had been used for flutter and spinning trials, with an upper wing centre section and parallel-chord ailerons, and dived by Saint at 275 mph. It was eventually re-built as one of the Gamecock II prototypes. (Photo: Author's Collection)

Gloucestershire (Gloster) Gorcock

Spurred by the performance being demonstrated by contemporary racing aircraft, the Air Ministry turned its attention in 1923-24 to the possibility of breaking from the traditional radials in RAF fighters, and encouraged manufacturers to investigate exisitng liquid-cooled in-line engines, at the same time suggesting less dependence on all-wood airframe structures. In effect the choice of engines until 1926 was confined to the Napier Lion twelve-cylinder broad-arrow, and the Rolls-Royce Falcon or Condor V-twelves.

In May 1924 a £24,000 contract was placed with Gloucestershire Aircraft Co Ltd for three prototypes of an experimental single-seat interceptor, of which the first two were to have steel fuselages and wooden wings, and the third to be of all-steel. The choice of this company was largely on account of H P Folland's considerable experience in marrying the Lion engine with his Bamel/Mars I racer and with the excellent series of Gloster racing seaplanes — in spite of the company's predilection for wooden aircraft.

Bearing an obvious resemblance to the successful Gamecock, the new Gorcock, which Howard Saint first flew in 1925, displayed Folland's ingenuity in designing a smooth-contoured nose profile around the awkward broad-arrow Lion, his preference being to mount the radiator under the fuselage — initially as an underslung, circular-section unit and later in a D-shaped fairing, snug up to the fuselage between the undercarriage oleos.

The first Gorcock, J7501, was powered by a geared 450hp Lion IV but, to provide performance comparison, the second composite aircraft, J7502, featured the 525hp Lion VIII direct drive engine. Despite its greater power, however, the performance of the second aircraft differed to no appreciable extent. The all-metal Gorcock Mark II, J7503, reverted to the lighter Lion IV in a slimmer nose cowling, and returned a speed some ten miles per hour faster than J7501. It was not flown by the manufacturers until June 1927 (due mainly to their pre-occupation with Grebe and Gamecock work), by which time the first two Gorcocks were dis-

The second Gorcock, J7502, with direct-drive Napier Lion VIII engine. (Photo: Derek James)

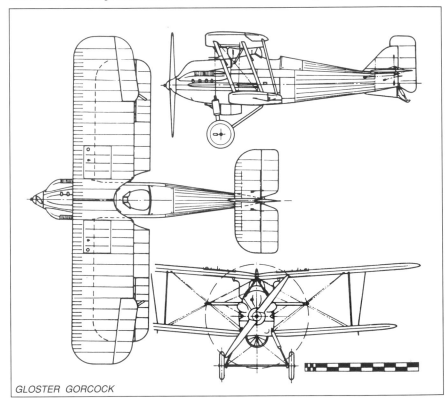

GLOSTER GORCOCK

playing all the Gamecock's wing flutter problems, and additional corrective interplane V-struts were added to provide stiffness to the overhang sections of the upper wings. The original broad-chord ailerons, angled to the wing chord line,

Type: Experimental single-engine, single-seat, single-bay biplane interceptor.
Manufacturer: Gloucestershire Aircraft Co Ltd, Cheltenham and Brockworth
Air Ministry Specification: No formal Specification issued.
Powerplant: One 450hp Napier Lion IV 12-cylinder geared, liquid-cooled broad-arrow engine driving two-blade wooden, fixed-pitch propeller (J7501 and J7503); 525hp Napier Lion VIII direct-drive engine driving two-blade wooden or metal propeller (J7502).
Dimensions: Span (upper), 28ft 6in, (lower), 25ft 0in; length, 26ft 1in; height, 10ft 3in; wing area, 250 sq ft.
Weights: (J7501 and J7502). Tare, 2,364lb; all-up, 3,179lb. (J7503). Tare, 2,422lb; all-up, 3,337lb.
Performance: (J7501 and J7502). Max speed, 164 mph at 5,000ft; climb to 15,000ft, 11 min; service ceiling, 24,000ft. (J7503). Max speed 174 mph at 5,000ft; climb to 15,000ft, 10.5 min; service cciling, 24,000ft.
Armament: Two synchronized 0.303in Vickers machine guns on sides of fuselage; racks for four 20lb bombs under lower wings.
Prototypes: Three; Mark Is, J7501 (first flown by Howard Saint, 1925) and J7502; Mark II, J7503. No production.

were replaced by narrow-chord surfaces hinged parallel to the wing spars. Both Grebe and Gamecock tail units appeared on the Gorcock from time to time.

J7501 was ultimately delivered to the RAE on 16 May 1928, but the aircraft broke up in the air near Aldershot on 4 September the following year; the pilot baled out safely. J7502, also first flown in 1925, paid several visits to Martlesham Heath for handling assessment, and appeared at the 1926 Hendon Display (bearing the New Type No 4). It was delivered to the RAE in 1928 to undertake trials with various types of propeller. It was written off in a landing crash at Farnborough on 27 May 1931. J7503 was delivered for prolonged trials at Martlesham in September 1928, but its ultimate fate is not known.

Though not ordered into production (the Lion was no longer favoured as a fighter engine) the metal Gorcock — armed with twin Vickers guns — returned a top speed identical with that of the Bristol Bulldog, which was to remain in front-line service with the RAF until 1936.

Beardmore W.B.26

Not since the final year of the War had William Beardmore produced a fighter, and in 1925 William Stancliffe Shackleton, the company's newly appointed chief designer, came up with the W.B.26, a somewhat ungainly-looking two-seater intended for Latvia.

Powered by the 360hp Rolls-Royce Eagle IX water-cooled in-line engine, the W.B.26 was an angular single-bay biplane of all-wood construction. The fuselage was of hexagonal section, the box-girder primary structure being provided with triangular-section decking fairings above and below; the box-girder itself was untapered in side elevation from nose to tail.

The upper and lower wings were built in two halves, bolted together on the aircraft's centreline; the parallel-chord upper wing was mounted above the fuselage by two pairs of cabane struts, and the swept-back lower wing was located below the fuselage by means of a central radiator fairing. The Lamblin radiator block itself was situated ahead of the lower wing leading edge between the undercarriage oleo struts; the landing gear was of the split-axle type.

The interplane struts comprised single faired members with upper and lower ends divided to form Vs so as to attach to the front and rear wing spars. All wing

The unmarked Beardmore W.B.26, intended for Latvia. (Photo: A J Jackson Collection)

and tail surfaces were sharply square-ended. Prominent diagonal, parallel struts extended from the upper fuselage longerons to the lower junctions of the interplane struts and the wing spars, these being the primary supporting members carrying the wing structures. All control cables were located within the structure of the aeroplane and, as far as can be discerned, there was no external cable bracing of any sort. The entire aircraft was ply and fabric covered.

Armament comprised a pair of Beardmore-Farquhar machine guns, synchronized by Constantinesco gear, and a similar gun with Scarff ring was provided on the rear cockpit.

Flown by Flt Lt Archibald Norman Kingwill RAFO in 1925, the W.B.26 returned a sea level speed of 145 mph, but its subsequent history is not known, and no British registration, military or civil, was allotted for test purposes.

Type: Single-engine, two-seat, single-bay biplane fighter.
Manufacturer: William Beardmore & Co Ltd, Dalmuir, Dunbartonshire.
Powerplant: One 360hp Rolls-Royce Eagle IX 12-cylinder water-cooled in-line engine.
Structure: All wooden construction with ply and fabric covering.
Dimensions: Span, 37ft 0in.
Weights: Tare, 2,555lb; all-up, 3,980lb.
Performance: Max speed, 145 mph at sea level.
Armament: Two synchronized Beardmore-Farquhar machine guns in nose and a third with a Scarff ring on the rear cockpit.
Prototype: Believed, one only; first flown by Flt Lt A N Kingwill in 1925.

Hawker Hornbill

Although the Napier Lion-powered Gloster Gorcock had not been designed specifically to meet a formal Air Ministry requirement, Specification 24/23 had been written round Henry Folland's proposals, and in 1924 a new version of this Specification appeared as 7/24, calling for a similar fighter to be powered by the direct-drive Rolls-Royce Condor III boosted engine, capable of reaching a speed of 208 mph and a ceiling of 29,000 feet. A single synchronized Vickers Mk II machine gun was to be carried, together with 1,000 rounds of ammunition.

Hitherto such a performance had not been approached by a fighter and W G Carter recognised that, implicit in the Specification, was an attempt by the Air Ministry to break with the traditional wartime fighter formula based on rotary and radial engines. His answer, the Hawker Hornbill, if not radical, was certainly an entirely new design, in no way related to a previous aeroplane.

To begin with, it was small and

Left: *An early configuration of the Hawker Hornbill, J7782, with twin underwing radiators, small fin and very closely-cowled engine. The much smaller wing chord of the lower wing than that of the upper gives a misleading impression of back stagger; there was in fact a four-inch forward stagger.* (Photo: H G Hawker Engineering Co Ltd)

Below: *The Hornbill as it appeared in 1926, wearing the Hendon New Type No 5; the engine cowling is less angular, a centrally mounted Serck radiator has been fitted, and the fin area has been slightly increased. Note the very long gun channel along the side of the front fuselage.* (Photo: H G Hawker Engineering Co Ltd)

compact with single-bay wings with V-type interplane struts, ailerons being fitted to the upper wing only. Much attention was paid to the engine cowling, each bank of cylinders being faired separately in duralumin sheet, with a pronounced cleft between them; indeed, so closely faired were these banks that there was no space to enclose any sort of exhaust branch manifold, so that each cylinder exhaust port (two per cylinder) was fitted with a short stub pipe projecting through the cowling.

Construction was of mixed wood and metal, the front fuselage and engine bearers being of steel tubular members. The primary fuselage structure was a wooden box girder but, unlike most other contemporary fighters, featured oval-section space frames with stringers over the entire circumference of the rear fuselage, resulting in an aerodynamically efficient shape.

As first flown by Fred Raynham, probably early in July 1925, the single Hornbill prototype, J7782, featured twin underwing radiators, but no gun was yet fitted as the Condor III had no provision for gun synchronizing. Flt Lt Paul Ward Spencer ('George') Bulman MC, AFC, who had been appointed Hawker's chief test pilot on 1 July, now took over the Hornbill's flight programme, and at once expressed disappointment at the aircraft's performance, thought to be due to the fine-pitch Watts propeller. This was replaced by a coarser-pitch Fairey Reed metal propeller, but with little improvement. At the Hornbill's preliminary assessment at Martlesham in December, it was found that the engine suffered from over-cooling, and segments of the radiators were blanked off.

In February 1926 J7782 returned to Kingston to be extensively modified to

designs prepared by Hawker's new chief designer, Sydney Camm (who had joined the company two years previously from G H Handasyde). When the Hornbill resumed flying three months later it had been fitted with the Condor IV, now nominally rated at 698hp; a single Serck radiator was located between the undercarriage struts, a longer crankcase cowling incorporated without the cleft between the cylinder banks, and a slightly larger fin fitted.

Bulman now reported a corrected maximum speed of 187 mph, but a ceiling of less than 24,000 feet. After attending the 1926 Hendon Display as New Type No 5 on 2 July (and flown by Howard Saint), the Hornbill underwent full Service evaluation in competition with the Siskin IIIA, and proved significantly faster up to 21,000 feet, however, above that height the Condor's power fell off rapidly so that the Siskin was shown to possess much superior

Type: Single-engine, single-seat, single-bay biplane interceptor fighter.

Manufacturer: H G Hawker Engineering Co Ltd, Kingston-upon-Thames and Brooklands, Surrey.

Air Ministry Specification: 7/24.

Powerplant: One 650hp Rolls-Royce Condor III twelve-cylinder water-cooled in-line engine driving two-blade Watts wooden or Fairey Reed metal propeller; also 698hp Condor IV engine.

Structure: Wooden box-girder fuselage and twin-spar wings; steel tubular engine bearers and sheet duralumin cowling and front fuselage cladding; remainder of aircraft fabric covered.

Dimensions: Span, 31ft 0in; length, 26 ft 7¼in; height, 9ft 8in; wing area, 317.4 sq ft.

Weights: Tare, 2,975lb; all-up, 3,769lb; overload, 3,820lb.

Performance: Max speed, 187 mph at sea level; climb, 6 min 30 sec to 10,000ft; service ceiling, 22,700 ft; range, approx, 200 miles.

Armament: One synchronized 0.303in Vickers machine gun on port side of fuselage with 1,000 rounds of ammunition.

Prototype: One, J7782 (first flown by F P Raynham at Brooklands, c.July 1925). No production.

performance at high altitude.

This alone effectively killed any hope of a production contract for the Hawker fighter. The Hornbill, however, displayed other disagreeable characteristics both in handling and design. Although the single, side-mounted Vickers gun was located with its body in the left side of the cockpit, so cramped was the pilot that it proved impossible to attend to any gun stoppage. While low-speed handling was generally regarded as excellent, as speed increased it was found impossible to maintain height in turns without use of full opposite rudder.

The Hornbill was accordingly reclassified as a purely experimental prototype, but went on to contribute much research data, at one time being fitted with a high-speed upper wing with automatic slats for trials at the RAE. It was ultimately struck off Air Ministry charge in February 1932, having amassed no fewer than 1,080 flying hours; it was last flown on 18 May 1933.

Bulman was to sum up his opinion of the aeroplane: 'The Hornbill was too clever by half. . .the designer almost forgot that the pilot is an important part of the design'. Camm was never to forget that verdict.

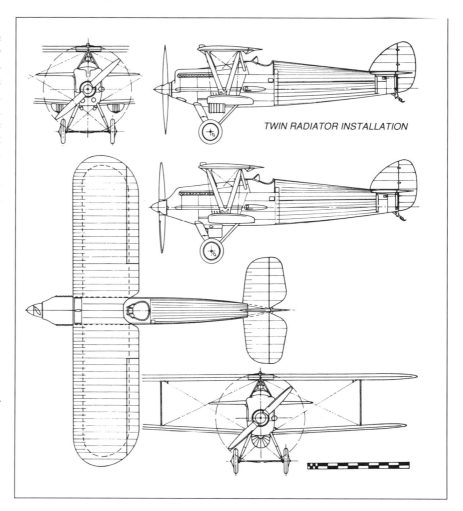

TWIN RADIATOR INSTALLATION

Hawker Heron

At first glance it might be thought that the Hawker Heron was simply another permutation of the wartime fighter formula; indeed, the aircraft itself originated as the third Woodcock prototype. It was, however, for its manufacturer a supremely important landmark as being the first predominantly metal aircraft to emerge from the Kingston factory.

Ever since the beginning of the 1920s it had become increasingly obvious that the Air Ministry was looking to the industry to introduce metal construction in fighter designs, so that late in 1923 the Hawker company began introducing limited metal working in the Canbury Park Road shops. To begin with the company obtained permission to complete the third Woodcock, J6989, with a mainly metal airframe structure. The fuselage box-girder structure was built-up using round steel and aluminium tubes, swaged to rectangular section

With little to show of its Woodcock parentage, the metal Heron, J6989, is pictured on its home airfield at Brooklands; beyond it are the original flight sheds dating from 1910. The Heron was unusual for a private venture fighter in carrying full wireless equipment. (Photo: H G Hawker Engineering Co Ltd, Neg No 14N)

at their extremities and bolted together using fishplates, the box struture being cross-braced with tensioning wires. The staggered, single-bay wings of constant chord, and without sweepback, employed twin light-gauge steel tubular spars without web (not of dumbbell section, as introduced later) to which were attached wooden ribs. Ailerons were fitted to the upper wings only.

Design of the Heron, undertaken as a private venture, was delegated by Carter to Sydney Camm in mid-1924, it being realised that fairly significant changes in structural weight distribution would result in an entirely new aircraft. Power was provided by a 455hp Bristol Jupiter VI engine, and provision was made to mount two Vickers guns in the upper nose decking.

First flown by Raynham in about May 1925, J6989 featured a fine-pitch Watts laminated walnut propeller, and attended the Hendon Display on 27-28 June as New Type No 2. In December the Heron was delivered to Martlesham Heath for Service trials by Nos 15 and 22 Squadrons, also being fitted with a metal Fairey Reed propeller for comparison purposes. Despite being marginally heavier than the standard Woodcock, the Heron (inevitably dubbed the Tincock by the Service pilots), demonstrated a speed some 15 mph higher, and earned favourable comment on its pleasant handling qualities, excellent view from the cockpit and relative ease of maintenance — stemming from its metal construction.

After prolonged trials at Martlesham, the Heron was eventually returned to Brooklands where it was transferred to the civil register as G-EBYC and entered for the 1928 King's Cup race. Unfortunately, however, while being taxied to the starting line, Bulman struck a parked car and severely damaged the starboard wing. Although it was repaired, the company decided not to seek renewal of the certificate of airworthiness, and the Heron was removed from the civil register in January 1930.

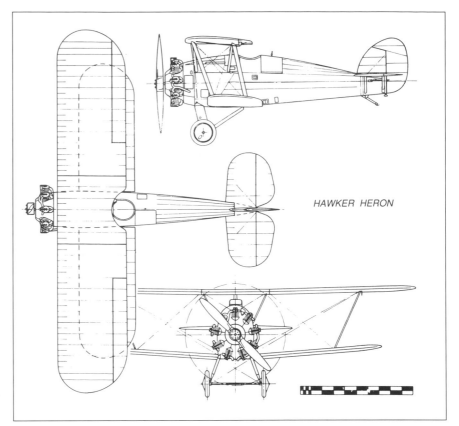

HAWKER HERON

Type: Single-engine, single-seat, single-bay experimental biplane interceptor.

Manufacturer: H G Hawker Engineering Co Ltd, Kingston-upon-Thames and Brooklands, Surrey.

Powerplant: One 455hp Bristol Jupiter VI nine-cylinder air-cooled radial engine driving two-blade Watts or Fairey Reed propeller.

Structure: Predominantly metal tubular structure with wooden wing ribs, covered with sheet duralumin, ply and fabric.

Dimensions: Span: 31ft 10in; length, 22ft 3in; height, 9ft 9in; wing area, 291 sq ft.

Weights: Tare, 2,120lb; all-up, 3,126lb.

Performance: Max speed, 156 mph at 9,800ft; climb to 10,000ft, 5 min 30 sec; service ceiling, 23,300ft; endurance, 3½hr.

Armament: Two synchronized 0.303in Vickers Mk II machine guns in upper nose decking with 600 rounds per gun.

Prototype: One, J6989 (later G-EBYC), first flown by F P Raynham in about May 1925. No production.

The three Hawker-built pattern Danecocks at Brooklands before delivery to Denmark in 1926. The furthest aircraft, 151, used for performance, handling and gun-firing evaluation, is the only example fitted with its Madsen guns; both it and 152, the centre aircraft, are without their spinners. (Photo: H G Hawker Engineering Co Ltd, Neg No 32)

Hawker Danecock

Following the demonstration of a Hawker Woodcock II in Denmark (possibly G-EBMA) in mid-1925, the Danish government placed an order for three pattern aircraft with the Hawker company and negotiated a licence agreement to build a small number of further aircraft. The Danecock (or L.B.II Dankok as it was to be termed at its destination) was to be powered by an Armstrong Siddeley Jaguar engine, and design of the various modifications was undertaken by Sydney Camm. Among these was provision to mount a pair of 7.7mm Madsen machine guns in place of the customary Vickers guns.

Camm also slightly lengthened the rear fuselage to take account of the heavier engine, marginally increased the span of the upper wing and shortened that of the lower. Although the Dan-ecock was slightly heavier than the standard Woodcock II, the airframe alterations resulted in a small improvement in speed.

The first Danecock was flown by Bulman on 15 December 1925 and was followed by the other two within a month, and all were delivered to Denmark in February 1926. Twelve further aircraft were licence-built at the Royal Danish Navy Dockyard during 1927-28 and served with an Army Air Service Squadron as well as No 2 Naval Squadron, remaining in service until 1937. One of the Hawker-built examples established a Scandinavian altitude record of 28,028 feet in January 1927, a record that was to stand for about eight years.

One of the Danish-built Dankoks survived the Second World War and, after restoration, was placed on permanent display in the Copenhagen Museum — its logbook testifying to a flying life of 704 flying hours.

Type: Single-engine, single-seat, single-bay biplane interceptor fighter.
Manufacturers: H G Hawker Engineering Co Ltd, Kingston and Brooklands, Surrey; Danish Royal Navy Dockyard.
Powerplant: One 385hp Armstrong Siddeley Jaguar IV fourteen-cylinder radial engine driving two-blade propeller.
Dimensions: Span, 32ft 7in; length, 26ft 1¼in; height, 10ft 1in; wing area, 340 sq ft.
Weights: Tare, 2,128lb; all-up, 3,045lb.
Performance: Max speed, 145 mph at sea level; climb to 10,000ft, 8 min 15 sec; service ceiling, 22,800ft; endurance, approx 2½ hr.
Armament: Two synchronized 7.7mm Madsen machine guns with 720 rounds per gun.
Production: Three Hawker-built pattern aircraft, Nos 151-153 (No 151 first flown by Flt Lt P W S Bulman on 15 December 1925) and twelve aircraft (Nos 154-165) licence-built in Denmark.

Vickers-Wibault Type 121 (7C.1)

It is certainly arguable that the Vickers Type 121 was not strictly a British fighter, being a direct structural duplication of the French Wibault 7C.1 Scout. The British company had sought to expand its knowledge of the use of metal construction in aircraft in 1922 with its invitation addressed to the Frenchman Michel Wibault to act as a consulting engineer for Vickers. Wibault, whose pioneering work in metal aircraft structures had run closely parallel with that of Claude Dornier and Hugo Junkers of Germany, had evolved a structural form employing fabricated light-alloy components of simple shape (usually of duralumin, a patented aluminium alloy which possessed the strength and hardness of mild steel).

A Wibault wing structure might thus consist of twin mainspars each comprising plain booms and plate webs with closely-pitched plate ribs, over which were laid corrugated light-alloy skins only four-tenths of a millimetre thick, the corrugations lying chordwise. Attachment of the skins to the ribs was by a hand-levered riveting tool. The fuse-

A Vickers-built Type 121 Scout for Chile, generally said to have been the first genuinely all-metal fighter produced in Britain, albeit of French origin. (Photo: Vickers Ltd)

lage structure might typically comprise a box-girder with L-section longerons and struts with T-section diagonal members; 'bowler hat-section' stringers would be riveted to the box girder and the thin alloy corrugated skin riveted to the stringers, whose pitch matched the skin corrugations.

This metal structure, which was neither a monocoque nor stressed skin (in the later accepted sense), was claimed in comparison with wooden structures to enjoy longer life, quicker production, improved durability in extremes of ambient temperature and reduced material wastage, while maintenance in the field was considered to be simplified.

An aircraft which employed this type of structure was the Wibault 7C.1 parasol monoplane, and in 1925 Vickers

Type: Single-engine, single-seat parasol monoplane fighter.
Manufacturer: Vickers (Aviation) Ltd, Weybridge, Surrey.
Powerplant: One 455hp Bristol Jupiter VI nine-cylinder radial engine.
Dimensions: Span, 36ft 1in; length, 23ft 8in; height, 11ft 6in; wing area, 237 sq ft.
Weights: Tare, 1,920lb; all-up, 2,970lb.
Performance: Max speed, 154 mph at sea level, 144 mph at 15,000ft; climb to 10,000ft, 7 min 40 sec; service ceiling, 23,000ft; range, approx 300 miles.
Armament: Two synchronized 0.303in Vickers machine guns in nose.
Production: No prototype. Twenty-six Type 121 Scouts built for Chile (first flight in June 1926 by E R C Scholefield).

ordered a single example for demonstration purposes, proposing to fit a British-made Bristol Jupiter VI, Vickers oleo-pneumatic undercarriage, British instruments and other equipment. This aircraft was delivered from Villacoublay to Weybridge in February 1926.

Among the demonstrations given by this French-built aircraft (F-AHFH) was one before the Chilean Air Mission early that year, resulting in an order for twenty-six Vickers-Wibault Scouts.

The first flight by a Chilean Scout was made from Brooklands by E R C ('Tiny') Scholefield at the end of June, but unfortunately the aircraft failed to recover from a succession of inverted spins and crashed; the pilot baled out and was unhurt. On investigation, it was decided that the aircraft's centre of gravity position was critical with the tailplane incidence rigged at five degrees positive — an excessive angle for a parasol monoplane employing a high-lift wing.

After reduction of the tailplane incidence, flying of the remaining aircraft resumed and no further accidents were suffered from this cause, the Chilean order being completed in 1926.

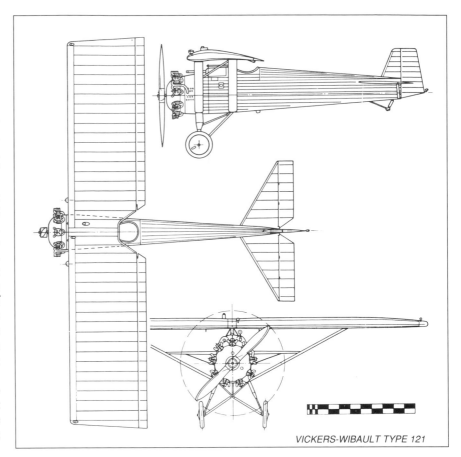

VICKERS-WIBAULT TYPE 121

Westland Wizard

Another company which had been engaged in producing a single-seat parasol monoplane fighter early in 1926 was the Westland Aircraft Works at Yeovil where work had been done on a private venture design by Arthur Davenport, based on his experience with the successful Westland Widgeon light aircraft. However, in the interests of low cost the new fighter, named the Wizard, was constructed entirely of wood.

Powered by a 275hp Rolls-Royce Falcon III in-line engine, salvaged from a Westland Limousine which had suffered an accident the previous September, the Wizard was first flown during the spring of 1926 by Maj Laurence Openshaw. At this time the engine was partly exposed, as little attempt had been made to cowl the upper half. Early flights disclosed poor aileron control, ineffective rudder and over-sensitive elevator, resulting in increased horn balances being added to the ailerons, a glove fairing added over the rudder to

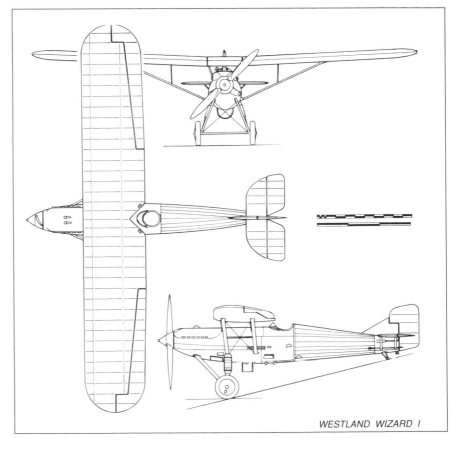

WESTLAND WIZARD I

The Westland Wizard, J9252, in its Mark I configuration, before installation of the supercharged Rolls-Royce F.XIS and fitting of the metal wing; in this form the aircraft underwent evaluation at Martlesham Heath in 1928. (Photo: R C Sturtivant)

increase its area, and the stripping of some fabric from the trailing edge of the elevator. In this form the Wizard paid a short visit to Martlesham Heath in June.

Unfortunately the aircraft was badly damaged in a forced landing following an air lock in the fuel supply shortly after return to Yeovil, and the decision was taken to rebuild it from scratch. In the meantime Openshaw had been at Martlesham where he was able to examine the metal structure of the Hawker Heron, and suggested to Robert Bruce that a similar method of construction in the Wizard would provide valuable experience for the company, at limited cost, in view of the Air Ministry's increasing preference for all-metal fighter aircraft.

Accordingly, the rebuilt Wizard emerged in November 1927 with an all-metal fuselage; sheet aluminium covered the forward half, and fabric to the rear. The primary structure, a wire-tensioned box-girder fabricated with square-section steel longerons and round-section tubular struts, carried oval frames to which were attached light-alloy stringers. The wing remained a fabric-covered wooden structure.

Flown by Louis Paget that month (Openshaw having been killed during an air race earlier in 1927), the Wizard, powered by a beautifully cowled 490hp

Rolls-Royce F.XI, later to be named the Kestrel, demonstrated a maximum speed of 188 mph and, after some further modifications to the ailerons, was delivered to Martlesham Heath in January 1928 bearing the number J9252 and termed the Wizard Mk I.

Being generally well received by the Service pilots at the A & AEE, the Wizard was rewarded with a development contract from the Air Ministry, who now recommended the inclusion of a metal wing. Other alterations included a new wing centresection of considerably reduced thickness (to improve the pilot's forward view), and installation of a supercharged 500hp Rolls-Royce F.XIS engine, and J9252 was re-termed the Wizard Mk II. These changes, however, as well as the need for an enlarged radiator, which retracted into the underside of the centre fuselage, reduced the speed performance somewhat and, although the aircraft continued to fly until the end of 1931, official interest in the Wizard waned.

Type: Single-engine, single-seat parasol monoplane interceptor fighter.
Manufacturer: Westland Aircraft Works, Yeovil, Somerset.
Powerplant: One 275hp Rolls-Royce Falcon III twelve-cylinder water-cooled in-line engine; Mk I, 490hp Rolls-Royce F.XI normally-aspirated engine; Mk II, 500hp Rolls-Royce F.XIS supercharged engine.
Dimensions: Span, 39ft 6in (Mk I), 40ft 0in (Mk II); length, 26ft 10in; height, 9ft 4in; wing area, 238 sq ft (Mk I), 234 sq ft (Mk II).
Weights: Tare, 2,352lb; all-up, 3,320lb.
Performance: Max speed, 188 mph at 10,000ft; initial rate of climb, 2,600 ft/min; service ceiling, 17,500ft.
Armament: Two synchronized 0.303in Vickers Mk II machine guns in sides of fuselage; provision to carry four 20lb bombs under fuselage.
Prototype: One, later numbered J9252; first flown by Maj Laurence Openshaw in spring of 1926. No production.

Avro Type 566 Avenger

Designed by Roy Chadwick as a private venture, the Avro 566 Avenger was an attractive single-seat, single-bay biplane fighter, and was first flown by H J L ('Bert') Hinkler on 26 June 1926. Powered by a 525hp Napier Lion VIII

The private venture Avro 566 Avenger Mk I, G-EBND, powered by the Napier Lion VIII engine in 1926. (Photo: British Aerospace (Manchester) PLC, Neg No A.10/17)

direct-drive engine whose three cylinder banks were individually faired to produce neat cowling contours, the Type 566 featured a semi-monocoque wooden fuselage of oval section; its elm frames and spruce stringers were planked with mahogany, fabric-covered and varnished. The well-staggered wings were built up on two spruce spars with ply ribs and fabric-covered. Ailerons were fitted on the upper wing only. Twin Lamblin radiators were incorporated in the underside of the top wing, and provision was made to mount a synchronized Vickers gun in each side of the fuselage with the gun bodies and cocking handles on either side of the pilot.

Appearing with the Lion-powered Gloster Gorcock and Condor-powered Hawker Hornbill at the 1926 Hendon Display on 3 July, the Avenger carried the civil markings G-EBND. It paid a brief visit to the A & AEE at Martlesham Heath in October for a Service assessment but, by then, the Air Ministry favoured neither the Lion nor Condor

as future fighter engines, and none of these aircraft was ordered into quantity production.

Instead, the Avenger returned to its manufacturer for a sporting life, being entered for the 1927 King's Cup race by Sir Kenneth Crossley; it was, however, scratched when it was allotted an exaggerated handicap speed of 244 mph (its maximum speed being 180 mph).

Thereafter the Type 566 was re-termed the Type 567 Avenger Mk II and fitted with a 533hp Lion IX; revised, equal-span wings with I-type interplane struts, upper and lower ailerons, and a modified undercarriage were also included. Flown by Fg Off J ('Mutt') Summers, it was placed 13th in the 1928 King's Cup race.

Despite further attempts to secure production orders at home and overseas, all was of no avail and G-EBND ended its days as an instructional airframe at Hamble.

The accompanying data table refers to the Type 566 Avenger I.

Type: Single-engine, single-seat, single-bay biplane fighter.
Manufacturer: A V Roe & Co Ltd, Manchester and Hamble, Hampshire.
Powerplant: One 525hp Napier Lion VIII 12-cylinder broad-arrow water-cooled in-line engine.
Structure: All-wooden semi-monocoque fuselage and two-spar fabric-covered wings.
Dimensions: Span, 32ft 0in; length, 25ft 6in; height, 10ft 3in; wing area, 244 sq ft.
Weights: Tare, 2,368lb; all-up, 3,220lb.
Performance: Max speed, 180 mph at sea level; initial rate of climb, 2,100 ft/min; ceiling, 22,000ft.
Armament: Provision to mount two synchronized 0.303in Vickers machine guns in the sides of the fuselage.
Prototype: One, G-EBND, first flown by H J L Hinkler on 26 June 1926.

Gloucestershire (Gloster) Guan

Continuing the programme of investigation into in-line engine development centred on the Napier Lion, D Napier and Sons conferred with Gloster and the Air Ministry late in 1924 to put forward a proposal for a Lion IV geared engine fitted with an exhaust-driven turbo-supercharger which, it was calculated would increase the engine power to that of the geared Lion VIII and maintain that power to over 15,000 feet. Folland suggested at the same time that Gloster should widen the development scope by providing an aeroplane with a wing span greater than that of the Gorcock to achieve a significantly greater ceiling, thereby enabling the supercharged engine to be evaluated at greater heights. He also suggested that the aircraft should feature the same mixed metal and wood composite structure of the third Gorcock prototype.

A contract for three Guan experimental prototypes was raised with Gloucestershire Aircraft early in 1925, the first, J7722, being first flown by Howard Saint in August the following year, and delivered to the RAE the same month.

Powered by a 450hp geared Lion IV with an exhaust-driven turbo-supercharger fitted below the propeller shaft, J7722 certainly possessed improved performance at medium altitude although the maximum speed was disappointing due to continual difficulties with the supercharger. Flying trials continued

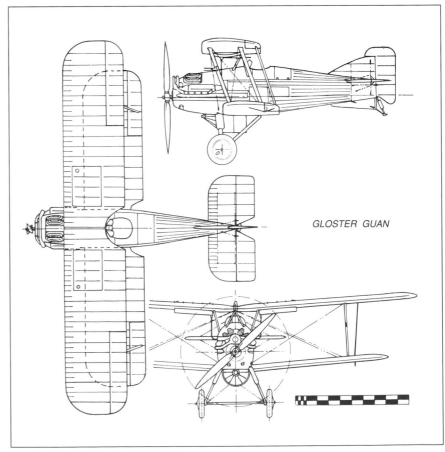

GLOSTER GUAN

The Guan, J7722, powered by a geared Lion IV engine with turbo-supercharger fitted below the propeller shaft. (Photo: via Derek James)

until the end of 1927, and before the aircraft was withdrawn from use, a Hele-Shaw Beecham variable-pitch propeller was fitted to investigate its benefit to climb performance above 15,000 feet.

The second Guan, J7723, flew in March 1927 and fared somewhat better, its direct-drive 525hp Lion VI, with the supercharger above the propeller shaft, giving a top speed of 175 mph at 15,000 feet. Nevertheless Napier was unable to come up with any satisfactory solution to the supercharger problems and this aircraft was grounded on 11 May 1928.

A third Guan, allocated the serial J7724, was to have been powered by the inverted Napier Lioness — also turbo-supercharged — but owing to the apparently insuperable troubles encountered by the other two Guans, the aircraft was cancelled. This effectively brought to an end Gloster's interest in the Lion in fighter aircraft, although Folland persisted with this engine in his beautiful racing seaplanes until 1929, by which time Rolls-Royce had produced the superb Kestrel V-twelve.

Type: Experimental single-engine, single-seat high-altitude interceptor biplane.
Manufacturer: Gloucestershire Aircraft Co Ltd, Cheltenham and Gloucester.
Air Ministry Specification: No formal Specification issued.
Powerplant: One 450hp Napier Lion IV twelve-cylinder liquid-cooled geared broad-arrow in-line engine with external exhaust-driven turbo-supercharger below the propeller shaft (J7722); one 525hp Napier Lion VI direct drive engine with supercharger above the propeller shaft (J7723).
Structure: All-steel fuselage structure and wooden wings, all fabric-covered.
Dimensions: Span, 31ft 10in; length 22ft 0in; height, 10ft 2in; wing area 298 sq ft.
Weights: (J7722). Tare, 2,859lb; all-up, 3,660lb. (J7723). Tare, 2,972lb; all-up, 3,803lb.
Performance: (J7722). Max speed, 155 mph at 16,000ft; climb to 20,000ft, 12 min; service ceiling, 31,000ft. (J7723). Max speed, 175 mph at 15,000ft; climb to 20,000ft, 12.5 min; service ceiling, 31,000ft.
Armament: Provision for two Vickers machine guns on the sides of the fuselage, but not fitted.
Prototypes: Two; J7722 (first flown by Howard Saint, August 1926) and J7723; third prototype, J7724, cancelled. No production.

Westland Westbury

With the removal of a specific continental threat to Britain after the defeat of Germany in 1918, the small but slowly growing RAF fighter defences were obliged to equip and deploy against the bombers of France as being the only force theoretically within range of these Islands, however unlikely that threat might prove to be. Once that policy was adopted, a study of the contemporary bombers flown by the French air force suggested that they could well be capable of mounting shell-firing guns of 20mm calibre or more; such guns, possessing an effective range far greater than the British Vickers and Lewis gun, could therefore render existing RAF interceptor fighters impotent.

Air Ministry Specification 4/24 was therefore drafted in 1924 calling for a big fighter capable of mounting two large-calibre weapons — of an initially undisclosed type — and a number of Lewis

The first Westland Westbury, J7765, during an engine run; this aircraft featured an all-wooden structure, angular nose profile and short engine nacelles. It was ultimately struck off charge following a wing centre section failure in August 1932. (Photo: R C Sturtivant)

guns for the aircraft's own protection from enemy bomber escort fighters. Two manufacturers were contracted to built prototypes, Westland being required to produce two examples of the Westbury (J7765 and J7766) and Bristol a single Bagshot (see page 191).

Work by Arthur Davenport started at

Yeovil on the Westbury early in 1925, a large twin-engine biplane of strictly orthodox configuration, by which time it had been confirmed that the intended primary armament was to be the 1½-pounder, 37mm Coventry Ordnance Works gun, a weapon which, it will be recalled, had been specified for a number of wartime 'gun carriers' and which had undergone a degree of development in the intervening years.

The Westbury's initial design featured two-bay wings of moderate aspect ratio, but after tunnel tests these were changed to higher aspect ratio with three bays. The first example employed wooden construction throughout and was powered by a pair of 450hp Bristol Jupiter VI radial engines in short nacelles mounted on top of the lower wings, the armament being confined to two COW guns. The front weapon was located on a ring mounting with all-round traverse on a nose gunner's cockpit, but the rear weapon, of only limited movement, was situated immediately aft of the upper wing and was remotely fired by the pilot who was provided with a gunsight forward of his windscreen. The undercarriage, of divided-axle type, comprised three pyramidal struts on either side with the wheels mounted at their apices.

J7765 was first flown at Andover by Capt Frank Courtney, specially engaged for the purpose, and ballast was carried in lieu of the guns which may never have been fitted in this aircraft. J7766 was first flown early in 1927 by Laurence Openshaw (shortly before his death in an accident) initially with Jupiter VI engines in lengthened nacelles which extended beyond the wing trailing edges.

In addition to the COW guns, now fitted, a second dorsal cockpit was added, aft of the rear 1½-pounder position, with a Scarff ring mounting for a Lewis gun, and provision was made to carry a second Lewis gun firing aft through a hatch in the floor of the centre fuselage. The shape of the nose was also improved, being now rounded in side elevation. More significantly, this second aircraft was fitted with wings employing duralumin box spars, but retaining spruce ribs.

The new Jupiter VIII engines, with epicyclic reduction gears, were fitted in J7766 in 1928 and this prototype was then delivered to Martlesham Heath for gun-firing trials with the heavy guns, these lasting until 1931. On 17 April that year, during engine starting with a Hucks starter and with the throttle

accidentally wide open, the aeroplane suddenly overrode the chocks and collided with the Hucks vehicle; the Westbury was damaged beyond economic repair and was struck off charge.

No further interest was expressed in these large-calibre guns in big aircraft which possessed little better manœuvra-bility than the target bombers and would therefore have had scant chance of reaching and maintaining an attacking position. Instead, much smaller and more nimble fighters were being examined as likely carriers of the COW gun, and the Westland F.29/27 fighter (see page 232) had already flown.

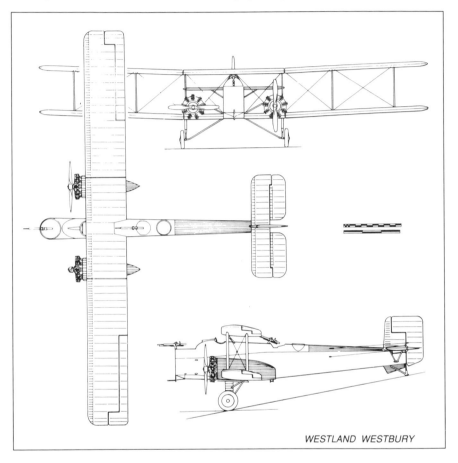

WESTLAND WESTBURY

Type: Twin-engine, three-seat, three-bay biplane fighter (or bomber destroyer).
Manufacturer: Westland Aircraft Works, Yeovil, Somerset.
Powerplant: Two 450hp Bristol Jupiter VI nine-cylinder air-cooled radial engines in J7765; two 480hp Jupiter VIII geared engines later fitted in J7766.
Structure: All-wooden construction in J7765; composite wood-and-metal construction with duralumin wing spars in J7766.
Dimensions: Span, 68ft 0in; length, 43ft 4¾in; height, 13ft 9in; wing area, 875 sq ft.
Weights: Tare, 4,854lb; all-up, 7,877lb.
Performance: Max speed, 125 mph at 5,000ft; climb to 15,000ft, 19 min; service ceiling, 21,000ft.
Armament: One 37mm COW gun on traversing mount in nose gunner's cockpit and one 37mm COW gun with limited movement on midships position aft of wings, each gun with one hundred 1½lb shells. One 0.303in Lewis machine gun with Scarff ring on second midships cockpit and one ventral Lewis gun firing aft through midships hatch in fuselage floor.
Prototypes: Two, J7765 and J7766 (J7765 first flown by Laurence Openshaw at Andover in September 1926). No production.

Vickers Type 123/141 Scouts

It has been shown that the mid-1920s found British designers of fighter aircraft pre-occupied with efforts to advance along two paths, the one leading to all-metal construction, the other — beset by dangerous pitfalls, as was becoming frustratingly all too familar — towards greater speed. Against a background of severely restricting financial limitations, the latter path was further obscured by the Air Ministry's difficult task of selecting the most promising engines for support and recommendation; that is to say, engines giving promise of equal suitability for bombers, transports *and* fighters. And, as already explained, fighters were not of paramount importance in the view of the Air Staff of the day.

Since the War the principal engines available had been the Armstrong Siddeley Jaguar and Bristol Jupiter air-cooled radials, and the Napier Lion and Rolls-Royce Condor water-cooled in-line engines, not forgetting the wartime Rolls-Royce Falcon. By 1925 something of an impasse had been reached as any substantial increase in power forthcoming from these engines was usually accompanied by an unacceptably disproportionate increase in weight, something the designers of heavy aircraft could learn to live with more comfortably than the fighter designers, particularly as they were already struggling to avoid possible weight penalties inherent in all-metal construction.

In 1925 it became known that Rolls-Royce was working on a development of the Falcon that promised something of a breakthrough with regard to power/weight ratio, by casting the cylinder

The Vickers Type 123 Hispano Scout, G-EBNQ, as it appeared at the end of 1926; this view well illustrates the very clean lines of the engine panelling. (Photo: via E B Morgan)

blocks in one, rather than as separate cylinders. At the same time Vickers, one of the companies least vulnerable to financial constriction, had probably gained most confidence and experience in metal construction, and had paid due attention to foreign techniques. A start was therefore made on the design of a new all-metal single-seat interceptor biplane, to be powered by the new Rolls-Royce engine, now designated the F.XI.

By the time the new private venture fighter, the Vickers Type 123, was completed in March 1926, however, the first F.XI was still almost a year away, and it was decided to go ahead with an alternative engine as an interim expedient, and a single 480hp Hispano-Suiza T52 twelve-cylinder water-cooled in-line engine was purchased from France. The entire airframe was of metal, duralumin tubes and plates being employed in the fuselage box-girder structure, wing spars and ribs, while the detachable blades of the propeller were also of forged duralumin; class one stressed members, including engine mounting, wing struts and undercarriage structure were of steel tube.

The upper wing was located close

above the nose decking, in line with the pilot's eye level, and the lower wing passed below and clear of the fuselage, a semi-circular engine radiator being situated below the centre section. The equal-span, sharply staggered wings all carried ailerons, and a pair of fuel tanks were incorporated in the upper wing.

Being of broad-V (90 degrees) configuration, the Hispano engine was carefully faired, with each cylinder bank being separately enclosed in order to achieve a slim nose contour, the oil cooler being located flush in the underside of the cowling. Twin synchronized Vickers guns were fitted in streamlined blisters on the sides of the fuselage alongside the cockpit, without recourse to blast channels.

The Vickers Type 123, registered G-EBNQ as a private venture, was first flown at Brooklands on 9 November 1926; no name was given to the aircraft which was simply referred to as the Hispano Scout, and G-EBNQ returned a maximum speed of 149 mph at 10,000 feet.

In May 1927, with the availability of early flight examples of the Rolls-Royce F.XI engine now in prospect, it was decided to rebuild the Type 123 with this engine, and seek Service assessment as a contender to Air Ministry Specification F.9/26 which had, however called for use of a radial engine. Unfortunately, in cleaning up the airframe, it was decided to move the radiator from its underslung wing position to the nose,

The Type 141 as it first appeared in its rebuilt form during 1927, powered by a Rolls-Royce F.XI; hardly visible in this view is the so-called chin radiator lying flush with the upward curve of the front engine cowling. (Photo: Vickers Ltd, Neg No 3001)

The Vickers Type 141 Scout on a compass base at Brooklands in its final military guise, in the configuration in which it was assessed as a shipborne fighter to Specification N.21/26. For the naval trials aboard HMS Furious in June 1929 the undercarriage rear struts were attached to the front wing spar instead of the rear spar; the lower wing dihedral was also increased from three to five degrees to improve stability. Note the nose cheat lines referred to in the text.
(Photo: Vickers Ltd, Neg No 3268)

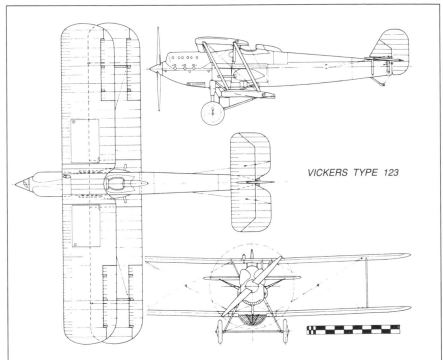

VICKERS TYPE 123

and the resulting bulbous contours cancelled out much of the drag-saving achieved in the Type 123. The result was that the new version, the Type 141, possessed a somewhat pedestrian performance.

Nothing daunted, Vickers decided to re-submit the Type 141 with a super-charged F.XIS engine for evaluation under a new Specification, N.21/26, which called for a fleet fighter without indicating a preferred type of engine. Several modifications were now incorporated, including the fitting of wheel brakes, arrester gear, catapult points and quickly detachable wings. The guns were raised about twelve inches and 'buried' in the sides of the fuselage with channels that extended to the nose. An improved chin radiator was designed but, with the wing set below the fuselage, the design was already compromised by being unable to accommodate a semi-retractable radiator amidships. As if to emphasise the designer's frustration in re-locating the radiator, the aircraft appeared with a prominent cheat line painted on the nose suggestive of the contours which could have been achieved had it been possible to position the radiator elsewhere!

In the event, the Type 141 successfully negotiated the land trials at Martlesham Heath and passed on to its deck trials aboard HMS *Furious* in June 1929. These proved less successful, and the Service pilots, who were more familiar with very different shipborne fighters, such as the small Fairey Flycatcher, were critical of the Type 141's deck handling qualities. As some consolation, Vickers could point to the fact that neither the Hawker Hoopoe nor the Gloster Gnatsnapper, the remaining contestants, were granted production contracts.

G-EBNQ's life reached its final episode as scratch starter in the 1929 King's

Cup race but its pilot, Fg Off J ('Mutt') Summers — who had been appointed Vickers' chief test pilot following the death of Scholefield — was forced to retire before reaching the finishing line.

Type: Single-engine, single-seat, single-bay experimental biplane fighter.
Manufacturer: Vickers (Aviation) Ltd, Weybridge, Surrey.
Air Ministry Specification: Private venture submitted to Specifications F.9/26 and N.21/26.
Powerplant: Type 123: 480hp Hispano-Suiza T52. Type 141: 500hp Rolls-Royce F.XI; 525hp Rolls-Royce F.XIS.
Structure: All-metal construction with fabric covering (duralumin tube and plate components in low stress areas and steel tube in class one stressed components).
Dimensions: Span, 34ft 0in; length, 28ft 6in (Type 123), 27ft 0in (Type 141); height, 9ft 4in; wing area, 378 sq ft.
Weights: Type 123: Tare, 2,278lb; all-up, 3,300lb. Type 141: Tare, 2,650lb; all-up, 3,700lb.
Performance: Type 123: Max speed, 149 mph at 10,000ft; climb to 10,000ft, 6 min 40 sec. Type 141: Max speed, 177 mph at 10,000ft; climb to 10,000ft, 5 min 40 sec; service ceiling, 25,500ft.
Armament: Two synchronized 0.303in Vickers guns on sides of fuselage.
Prototype: One, G-EBNQ (first flown as Type 123 on 9 November 1926), rebuilt as Type 141 and flown in mid-1927. No production.

Boulton & Paul P.31 Bittern

The first Bittern, J7936, in 1927; unarmed, but with small gun blisters on the fuselage sides, the aircraft is shown with mid-set Lynx engines and long oleo struts. (Photo: R C Sturtivant)

Commentators have been less than complimentary regarding John North's radical Bittern single-seat, twin-engine night fighter, designed to Air Ministry Specification 27/24, yet in many respects it was a dozen years ahead of its time in concept and execution. Powered by a pair of 230hp Armstrong Siddeley Lynx seven-cylinder air-cooled radial engines, the Bittern was a shoulder-wing monoplane with parallel-chord wings, all flying surfaces being square-ended. The pilot's cockpit was located in line with the wing leading edge, thereby affording an excellent view for night landing and unrestricted all-round view in the upper hemisphere.

The structure was extremely simple throughout, the box-girder fuselage being fabric-covered without rounded decking or fairings; entry to the cockpit was by means of foot-holes in the fuselage aft of the wing and along a locally-strengthened walkway forward along the top of the fuselage. The first of two prototypes, J7936, was flown in February 1927 with the engines mid-set on the wings, and with crankcase cowlings which left the cylinder heads exposed for cooling. The undercarriage was relatively simple, each unit comprising a single long, vertical oleo-pneumatic strut below the engine nacelle and swing V-struts attached to the lower fuselage longerons, their apices lying at the base of the oleo strut.

The Bitterns's armament was ingenious in that a pair of Lewis guns were mounted in rotating barbettes on the sides of the fuselage below the cockpit; these rotated vertically through 45 degrees in concert with a ring-and-bead gunsight arm forward of the pilot's windscreen, thereby permitting the fighter to attack an enemy from below and astern.

A second prototype, J7937, was flown later in 1927 embodying a number of improvements, principle among which was the inclusion of Handley Page leading-edge wing slats, and remounting the engines in underslung nacelles. The latter enabled shorter undercarriage oleos to be employed, together with a stronger system of radius struts and underwing bracing V-struts to be added. The wings, of uniform thickness from root to tip were also increased in span by about 5ft 6in, while the Lynx engines were encircled by Townend rings, so that the crankcase cowlings were discarded.

Both aircraft underwent periodic trials at Martlesham Heath between 1927 and 1931 and, despite its limited power, the Bittern possessed a speed some 30 mph greater than any European heavy bomber at the time of its first appearance. It has been suggested that North should have chosen to mount more powerful engines, yet to have done so would have demanded a larger and much heavier structure. As it was, the Bittern was little larger than many a single-engine fighter of its day, and was applauded for its general handling qualities.

Both aircraft continued to fly until the early 1930s, by which time the Air Staff had decided that it was unnecessary to develop dedicated night fighters in the foreseeable future, but to ensure that all future Service interceptors were suitable for both day and night operation.

Type: Twin-engine, single-seat, shoulder-wing monoplane night fighter.

Manufacturer: Boulton & Paul Ltd, Norwich, Norfolk.

Air Ministry Specification: 27/24

Powerplant: Two 230hp Armstrong Siddeley Lynx seven-cylinder air-cooled radial engines.

Dimensions: Span (J7936), 41ft 0in; length, 32ft 4in.

Weights: Tare, 3,215lb; all-up, 4,500lb.

Performance: Max speed, 145 mph at sea level; service ceiling, 16,200ft; endurance, 3¾ hr.

Armament: Two 0.303in Lewis machine guns in rotating barbettes on the sides of the front fuselage.

Prototypes: Two, J7936 and J7937 (J7936 first flown in February 1927). No production.

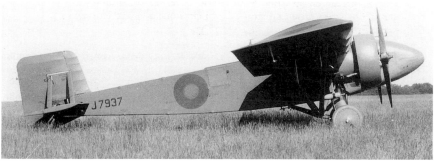

Two views of the second Bittern, J7937, on Mousehold aerodrome, Norwich, in 1931; sometimes referred to as the Mark II, this aircraft displays the wing slats, Lewis guns, Townend rings and the more extensive underwing struts; it is also fitted with Holt flare brackets under the wings. Just visible are racks under the fuselage for landing flares. (Photo: Boulton Paul Ltd, dated 12 October 1931).

Hawker Hawfinch

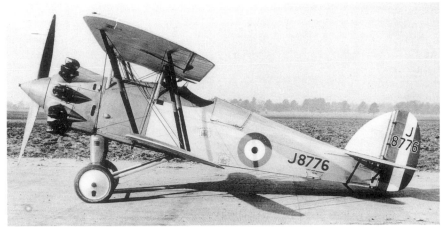

The Hawker Hawfinch, J8776, during its Service trials at Martlesham Heath in March 1928, before going on to the Squadrons. (Photo: Air Ministry Neg No 3244 dated 15 March 1928)

By January 1926 the end of the Sopwith Snipe's service was in sight; Armstrong Whitworth Siskin IIIs, Gloster Grebes and Hawker Woodcocks were in service; and the Gloster Gamecock was expected to join the RAF shortly. Yet none of these fighters possessed a performance much advanced from that of the fighters which had served during the final year of the Great War.

Believing that by 1928 the Siskin III, Grebe and Woodcock would be due for replacement, the Air Ministry issued Specification F.9/26 calling for a single-seat, day-and-night fighter to be powered by an air-cooled radial engine, and showing a significant improvement in speed, climb and ceiling over fighters extant. Implicit in the requirement was therefore an aeroplane capable of a speed of more than 160 mph at 10,000 feet, a ceiling of 24,000 feet or more, and of reaching 10,000 feet in under eight minutes. The structure was to be entirely of metal, and an armament of two machine guns, each with 600 rounds, was mandatory.

In the event, nine companies tendered designs to this Specification, and five prototypes came to be ordered. Sydney Camm produced the Hawker Hawfinch, a two-bay biplane of wholly conventional appearance powered initially by a 455hp Bristol Jupiter VI radial. More important, however, from the manufacturers' viewpoint was that the Hawfinch was the company's first entirely metal structured fighter for, apart from the steel and duralumin box girder employed in the fuselage (previously flown in the Heron), the wings were built up on steel spars and aluminium ribs. The spars consisted of a pair of light gauge steel strips, rolled to octagonal section and connected by a corrugated steel plate web, a design technique patented in 1927 by Roy Chaplin, Camm's assistant designer.

The prototype Hawfinch, J8776, was first flown by P W S Bulman in March 1927, but almost immediately underwent an engine change to the 450hp Jupiter VII. In June it was delivered for preliminary trials and performance assessment by the A & AEE, and initial reaction was very promising, although it should be pointed out that other companies' prototypes were not yet available for competitive evaluation. During July

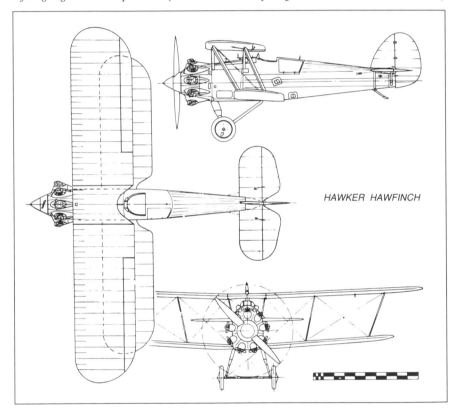

HAWKER HAWFINCH

J8776 flew deck trials aboard HMS *Furious* at the request of the Admiralty.

By the beginning of 1928 it seemed that the ultimate choice was likely to lie between the Hawfinch and the Bristol Bulldog, and it was decided to prepare these prototypes for delivery to Nos 1, 23 and 41 Squadrons for assessment by

Type: Single-engine, single-seat, two-bay biplane interceptor fighter.
Manufacturer: H G Hawker Engineering Co Ltd, Kingston and Brooklands, Surrey.
Air Ministry Specification: F.9/26.
Powerplant: One 455hp Bristol Jupiter VI nine-cylinder air-cooled radial engine; also 450hp Jupiter VII and 400hp Armstrong Siddeley Jaguar V.
Structure: All-metal construction with fabric covering.
Dimensions: Span, 33ft 6in (two-bay wings), 31ft 3in (single-bay wings); length, 23ft 8in (wheels), 25ft 6in (floats); height, 9ft 4in; wing area, 294 sq ft (two-bay wings).
Weights: Jupiter VII. Tare, 1,925lb; all-up, 2,910lb.
Performance: Jupiter VII. Max speed, 171 mph at 9,800 ft; climb to 10,000ft, 7 min 40 sec; service ceiling, 24,000ft.
Armament: Two synchronized 0.303in Vickers Mk II machine guns, each with 600 rounds; provision made to carry four 20lb bombs.
Prototype: One, J8776, first flown by P W S Bulman in March 1927. No production.

operational units, the Hawfinch being flown by these squadrons between May and July that year. By a narrow margin the Bulldog was declared the superior fighter and more popular aeroplane at the beginning of August, the Bristol aircraft being slightly faster; moreover, it proved to be simpler to maintain, and preference was expressed by the RAF for a single-bay biplane.

This was clearly a setback for Hawker, although Camm had repeatedly expressed some reluctance to set much store by the continued official preference for a radial engine. Be that as it may, the Hawfinch now embarked on a long programme of research. Before the year was out, it had been temporarily fitted with single-bay wings and a twin-float undercarriage for trials at the Marine Aircraft Experimental Establishment at Felixstowe, returning to wheels and two-bay wings in 1929; it was then fitted with a Jaguar V fourteen-cylinder radial engine in 1929. It was ultimately struck off charge at Martlesham Heath in 1934.

Armstrong Whitworth A.W.XIV Starling

Another contender to Specification F.9/26 was the Armstrong Whitworth A.W.XIV Starling, originally conceived as a private venture to meet an earlier requirement, set out in 28/24, but considered suitable to tender to the important new Specification. Two prototypes were ordered, J8027 and J8028, the first being flown on 12 May 1927.

The first Starling was a single-bay biplane of all-metal construction with wings of unequal span, and was powered initially by a 385hp Armstrong Siddeley Jaguar VII. It paid a very brief visit to Martlesham to obtain a quick impression of its chances in the context of F.9/26, but met with an uncompromising verdict that it was underpowered and that control at low speed was inadequate.

J8027 was hurriedly returned to the manufacturers who undertook an engine change to a 460hp Jaguar V, although little could be done to improve the control problems for, being in effect a sesquiplane, ailerons could not be fitted to the lower wings. It was flown with the new engine on 6 July and spent much of the remainder of that year undergoing adjustments to engine and airframe. Design figures had suggested that a maximum speed of about 180 mph should be attainable but, as far as can be discovered, the first Starling never exceeded 160 mph at 10,000 feet.

It returned to Martlesham on 15 February 1928 for the official evaluation to decide on the best tender to F.9/26.

The Armstrong Whitworth Starling I, J8027, at Martlesham Heath, probably in 1928, shown here with Jaguar VII engine and Fairey Reed metal propeller. (Photo: via R C Sturtivant)

J8027 was found, however, to have improved little in the intervening months — poor view from the cockpit, heavy controls and difficulty in landing at night were among the comments passed. Indeed the Starling proved to be some fifteen per cent heavier than the Bristol Bulldog with five per cent less power.

After failure to interest the Service as a fighter, J8027 was assigned to research flying, being fitted with Clark YH wings later in 1928. The second Starling, J8028, referred to as the Mark II, had undergone extensive re-design by the time it was first flown on 5 December 1929, being now entered to meet the naval fighter Specification N.21/26. It was powered by the new 525hp Armstrong Siddeley Panther II engine, and the lower wing was even smaller than that of the Mark I. Lengthened undercarriage struts permitted use of a large propeller, and although the aircraft was not successful in securing a production contract under N.21/26, it did participate in deck trials aboard HMS *Furious* in September 1930, and afterwards contributed much useful flight and control data to the benefit of the later A.W.XVI and Scimitar fighters.

Type: Single-engine, single-seat, single-bay biplane interceptor fighter.
Manufacturer: Sir W G Armstrong Whitworth Aircraft Ltd, Parkside, Coventry.
Air Ministry Specifications: 28/24, F.9/26 and N.21/26
Powerplant: One 385hp Armstrong Siddeley Jaguar VII fourteen-cylinder two-row air-cooled radial engine; also 460hp Jaguar V and 525hp Armstrong Siddeley Panther II.
Dimensions: Span, 31ft 4in; length, 25ft 2in; wing area, 246.4 sq ft.
Weights: All-up, 3,095lb.
Performance: Max speed, 160 mph at 10,000ft.
Armament: Two synchronized 0.303in Vickers machine guns in nose.
Prototypes: Two, J8027 and J8028 (J8027 first flown on 12 May 1927). No production.

Gloster Goldfinch

Just as the Hawfinch (see opposite) represented a landmark in the history of Hawker fighter design, so it was with the Gloster Goldfinch, and the fortunes of the two aircraft followed similar paths.

In January 1926 the Gloucestershire Aircraft Company received a contract from the Air Ministry to design and build to Specification 16/25 an all-metal, high-altitude version of the Gamecock, and Henry Folland decided to approach this design in two phases, producing the aircraft initially with metal wings and tail, and a mixed wood and metal fuselage; the aircraft would then be rebuilt with a fuselage similar to that of the Gamecock Mk III, J8047, that is to say slightly lengthened and comprising an all-steel primary structure.

In its initial composite wood-and-metal form, the single Goldfinch prototype, J7940, was first flown in May 1927, powered by a 436hp Bristol Jupiter V, and was delivered to Martlesham Heath for preliminary handling and performance assessment, returning a maximum speed of 160 mph at 10,000 feet. At this time the Goldfinch featured wing spars whose booms were of light-gauge high tensile steel strip rolled to tri-circular section and joined by light-gauge continuous plain steel strip.

J7940 returned to Hucclecote in July to be almost entirely rebuilt with new engine, wings, fuselage and tail. The engine was changed to a supercharged 450hp Jupiter VIIF; the wing spars were replaced by the Gloster lattice girder type — heavy gauge drawn strips of high tensile steel joined by light steel strip lattice with Warren girder steel ribs. The fuselage was built up in two parts, the forward section comprising an unbraced square section box structure employing square-section steel tubes jointed with fishplates; the rear section was a tapering, braced box girder of round tube, given shape with aluminium fairings with spruce formers and stringers. The production Gamecock-type tail was replaced by the taller, triangular fin of the Gamecock III.

This work occupied much of the remainder of 1927. In the meantime Folland had had the opportunity to study Specification F.9/26, and realised that, subject to performance estimates being confirmed, the Goldfinch stood an excellent chance of satisfying the requirement and obtaining a production contract. Indeed, a short visit to the A & AEE in December showed the aircraft to possess a maximum speed of 172 mph at 10,000 feet. J7940 returned to Martlesham in April 1928 for evaluation by No 22 Squadron of the A & AEE, carrying the high hopes of its manufacturers.

In almost every respect the Goldfinch was commended for its handling and performance in the air, but unfortunately failed to meet range requirements, and carried only 500 rounds for each of its two Vickers gun (instead of the required 600), and it was pointed out that to rectify these two deficiencies would certainly reduce the aircraft's speed, climb and ceiling performance, and might adversely affect its handling qualities.

Like the Hawker Hawfinch, therefore, the Goldfinch failed to secure further Air Ministry support, but contributed experience of inestimable value to the continuing development of all-metal fighters in the coming years.

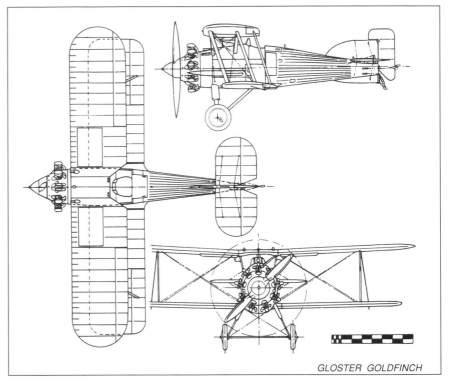

GLOSTER GOLDFINCH

Type: Single-engine, single-seat, single-bay interceptor fighter.
Manufacturer: Gloster Aircraft Co Ltd, Hucclecote, Gloucester.
Air Ministry Specifications: 16/25 and F.9/26.
Powerplant: One 436hp Bristol Jupiter V nine-cylinder air-cooled, normally-aspirated radial engine; later 450hp Bristol Jupiter VIIF supercharged engine.
Structure: All-metal construction (see text).
Dimensions: Span, 30ft 0in; length, 22ft 3in; height, 10ft 6in; wing area, 274.3 sq ft.
Weights: Tare, 2,058lb; all-up, 3,236lb.
Performance: Max speed, 172 mph at 10,000ft, 157.5 mph at 15,000ft; climb to 10,000ft, 7 min 20 sec, to 20,000ft, 16 min; service ceiling, 26,900ft.
Armament: Two synchronized 0.303in Vickers Mk I machine guns, with 500 rounds per gun.
Prototype: One, J7940 (first flown by Howard Saint in May 1927). No production.

The Gloster Goldfinch, J7940, as it was originally flown with a fin similar to that of the production Gamecock; at this stage the fuselage was of composite wood-and-metal construction; note also the curiously asymmetric centre-section strut arrangement. (Photo: Rolls-Royce (Bristol) Ltd.)

The Bristol Type 95 Bagshot, J7767, experimental night fighter prototype, during an engine run at Filton around the time of its first flight in July 1927. The large aerofoil fairings over the wheel axles were intended to contribute lift. (Photo: The Bristol Aeroplane Co Ltd).

Bristol Type 95 Bagshot

Flown for the first time some ten months after the first contender (the Westland Westbury, see page 183) to the Air Ministry's twin-engine night fighter Specification 4/24, the Bristol Type 95 Bagshot must be seen as little short of a failure. Faced with meeting a requirement that called for a maximum speed of 125 mph and a landing speed not exceeding 50 mph, but without the nature of the armament being disclosed for some nine months, Frank Barnwell opted to design an all-metal monoplane with semi-cantilever wings. On being informed, late in 1925, that the aircraft would be required to mount two Coventry Ordnance Works 37mm 1½-pounder guns and not less than two Lewis machine guns, the designer realised that his aircraft would be substantially overweight, with a landing speed of not less than 57 mph.

To his credit, however, Barnwell suggested that little would be gained by persevering with the Bagshot in its existing configuration, only to be told that the Air Ministry was adamant that the aircraft should be completed and flown, if only to compare the relative benefits of a cantilever monoplane with those of a biplane.

The Bagshot, J7767, was accordingly first flown by Cyril Uwins on 15 July 1927, and the maiden flight was accomplished without incident. During subsequent flying, however, as speeds were increased — at weights considerably below those ultimately proposed —

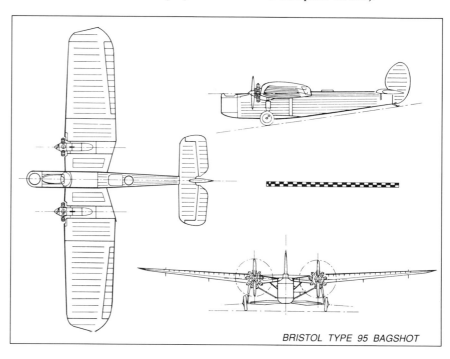

BRISTOL TYPE 95 BAGSHOT

Uwins found the lateral control was quite inadequate owing to aileron reversal, caused by the wings flexing in torsion. Despite considerable difficulty, the aircraft was landed safely, and was summarily grounded until the wing could be subjected to an exhaustive programme of structural testing, and

the results digested.

As the original Specification had been allowed to lapse, the Bagshot was transferred to Air Ministry experimental charge, and resumed flying on 31 July 1931, only to be scrapped shortly afterwards.

Type: Twin-engine, three-seat, shoulder-wing monoplane night fighter.
Manufacturer: The Bristol Aeroplane Co Ltd, Filton, Bristol.
Air Ministry Specification: 4/24.
Powerplant: Two 450hp Bristol Jupiter VI nine-cylinder air-cooled radial engines.
Structure: Steel tubular structure of triangular section built on three longerons; wing of twin steel spar structure with duralumin nose ribs; wide-track undercarriage with aerofoil fairings over half-axles; balanced rudder without tail fin.
Dimensions: Span, 70ft 0in; length, 44ft 11in; height, 9ft 6in; wing area, 840 sq ft.
Weights: Tare, 5,100lb; all-up, 8,195lb.
Performance: Max speed, 125 mph at sea level; landing speed, 58 mph.
Armament: Designed to mount one 37mm COW gun in the nose and amidships, and single Lewis guns in the same positions. (Armament never installed)
Prototype: One, J7767 (first flown by Cyril Uwins at Filton in July 1927). No production.

Bristol Type 101

Encouraged by the undoubted success achieved by the Jupiter engine with growing Air Ministry contracts, Bristol was anxious not only to continue the development of the air-cooled radial but to demonstrate its own improving quality of aircraft thus powered, while both Fedden and Barnwell were well aware that, spurred by the appearance of the Fairey Fox light bomber with a foreign liquid-cooled in-line engine, the British manufacturers of such engines would be staging a powerful come-back to promote their own products. Moreover Bristol was reaching the stage when it would be able to offer its own new radial engine, the long-life version of the Mercury nine-cylinder air-cooled radial.

Barnwell therefore submitted drawings of his Type 101 single-bay biplane two-seat fighter in January 1926, to be powered by the 480hp Mercury, but this was turned down uncompromisingly by the Air Ministry on account of its wooden construction. Thereafter the manufacture and development of the Type 101 went ahead as a private venture, and the single prototype, G-EBOW, was first flown by Cyril Uwins on 8 August 1927, powered temporarily by a Jupiter VI. Later fitted with a Jupiter

The inelegant Bristol Type 101, G-EBOW, in its fighter guise, with front Vickers guns and the Lewis gun Scarff ring fitted. Ailerons are only fitted to the lower wing, but when raced in the 1928 King's Cup race they were transferred to the upper wing.(Photo: The Bristol Aeroplane Co Ltd.)

VIA, it was flown by Uwins into second place in the 1928 King's Cup race at an average speed of 159.9 mph.

Thereafter it was employed as a test bed for the 485hp Mercury II and as a company hack; and it was while being subjected to engine overspeeding tests on 29 November 1929 that the wing centre section failed; the pilot, C R L Shaw, baled out safely.

The Type 101 was the last wooden Bristol fighter to be built.

Type: Single-engine, two-seat, single-bay private venture biplane fighter.
Manufacturer: The Bristol Aeroplane Co Ltd, Filton, Bristol.
Powerplant: One 450hp Bristol Jupiter VI and VIA nine-cylinder radial, and one 485hp Bristol Mercury II nine-cylinder radial engine.
Structure: All-wood box-girder fuselage and two-spar wings.
Dimensions: Span, 33ft 7in; length, 27ft 4in; height, 9ft 6in; wing area, 360 sq ft.
Weights: Tare, 2,100lb; all-up, 3,540lb.
Performance: Equipped as fighter. Max speed, 160 mph at sea level; ceiling, 21,000ft.
Armament: Two synchronized 0.303in Vickers machine guns on the sides of the fuselage, and one Lewis gun with Scarff ring on rear cockpit.
Prototype: One, G-EBOW (first flown by Cyril Uwins at Filton on 8 August 1927). No production.

Bristol Type 105 Bulldog

The ultimate winner of the contest to select the 'standard' RAF day-and-night fighter under the terms of Specification F.9/26 was the Bristol Type 105 Bulldog, a choice frequently reviled in retrospect as having served to perpetuate the age-old formula of radial engined, two-gun biplane. That the Bulldog continued to serve in front-line squadrons until thoroughly outdated in the mid-

The prototype Bristol Bulldog II, J9480, the aircraft that won the all-important evaluation competition to Specification F.9/26 in 1928, seen here with full night flying equipment, armament and wireless. (Photo: Author's collection)

1930s cannot be denied, yet at the time of its selection in the early summer of 1928 it was undoubtedly the best single-seater on offer, taking into consideration its metal construction, reliable engine and its good flying qualities. It is true

that, within two years of its selection for production, the hitherto deadlocked radial engine formula was well and truly superseded by acceptance of the in-line Rolls-Royce Kestrel as a magnificent fighter powerplant. Unfortunately, with

Right: *The first production Bristol Bulldog Mark II, J9567, shown at Martlesham Heath in June 1929. This aircraft spent almost its entire life undergoing trials either at Filton or with the A & AEE; it ended its days, however, with the Air Armament School in 1937.* (Photo: The Bristol Aeroplane Co Ltd, dated 24 June 1929). Below: *Comparison of this production Bulldog with the prototype on the opposite page discloses a number of changes, such as the inclusion of light bomb carriers under the wings, longer fairings behind the engine cylinders and omission of the Aldis gun sight.* (Photo: A J Jackson collection)

the effects of the Depression biting hard on military expenditure, it was necessary to continue purchasing the elderly, but well-tried and less costly Jupiter radial, rather than place very large and expensive orders for the Rolls-Royce engine for, to have kept within the annual Air Estimates, this would have caused a gradual reduction in the number of RAF fighter squadrons.

As will be shown in due course, the departure of Trenchard as Chief of the Air Staff at the end of 1929 heralded a policy of *increasing* Britain's fighter defences. Nevertheless, the fact that the Bulldog continued to serve bestowed a sense of well-established reliability and experience among the RAF line pilots of the day, eventually providing a hard core of excellent squadron and flight commanders in the crucial early months of the Second World War.

After Frank Barnwell finished his work on the unsuccessful Bagshot twin-engine fighter in April 1926, he returned

to his work in single-seat projects developed from the Type 99 Badminton racer which was due to fly shortly. Accordingly, he concentrated on two designs, the Types 105 and 107, both intended to be powered by the new Bristol Mercury engine. Mock-ups of both projects were built, and were examined by Air Ministry officers — who opted for the Type 107, later to become the Bullpup; both were intended to be powered by a geared Mercury III (see page 202).

Realising that production examples of the Mercury might not be available for a further two years, Bristol's board of

directors decided to go ahead and build a prototype of the Type 105 as a private venture, powering it with a Jupiter. Although this was originally designed with wings of equal span, tunnel tests showed advantages in reducing the span of the lower wing, and in this form the Type 105 Bulldog was first flown by Cyril Uwins on 17 May 1927, unregistered on account of its private venture status.

Employing a structure of high-tensile steel strip, rolled to flanged section, as previously used in the Bristol Boarhound general purpose aircraft, the Bulldog featured high-lift upper wings of Bristol IA section, developed by Barnwell and Frise, and lower wings of Clarke YH low-drag section, and reduced chord and span; Frise ailerons were fitted to the upper wing only, being operated by twin control cables which passed through the lower wings and up to anchor points forward and aft of the aileron hinges above. The customary armament of twin synchronized Vickers guns were mounted just below the shoulder line of the fuselage, and a wireless set was located aft of the cockpit.

Barnwell had always regarded Specification F.9/26 as representing the most appropriate requirement for the Bulldog to meet, and the company-owned air-

A pilot boards his night flying-equipped Bulldog IIA, K1676, of No 23 (Fighter) Squadron at Kenley. This was the first RAF squadron to give up the Bulldog (in 1933) in favour of the Hawker Demon two-seat fighter. (Photo: Author's collection)

craft was followed by a prototype, designated the Mark II, J9480, ordered by the Air Ministry in November 1927 and first flown on 21 January 1928. It was subject of a special agreement with the Air Ministry to allow its entry to the F.9/26 competition alongside the Hawker Hawfinch, Armstrong Whitworth Starling, Boulton & Paul Partridge and Gloster Goldfinch, which took place during the spring of 1928 at Martlesham Heath. In the final analysis the Bulldog and Hawfinch were selected to go on to general handling assessment by Nos 1, 17, 23 and 41 Squadrons, and in a narrow decision the Bristol aircraft was declared the winner. The Hawfinch possessed marginally better spinning qualities, but its two-bay wings were regarded as retrograde, and to remedy the Bulldog's shortcomings demanded less airframe modification than the Hawfinch, which would have needed major redesign and prolonged trials. In the event, the Bulldog was modified with a 26-inch longer rear fuselage.

A production Specification, F.17/28, was drawn up and in September 1928 an order for 25 Bulldog IIs, J9567-J9591, powered by 425hp Jupiter VII engines, was placed by the Air Ministry, to which an extra aircraft was added (between J9575 and J9576) as a company-owned demonstrator. The first of these aircraft was flown on 12 April 1929, and twelve subsequent Bulldogs were allocated in June to No 3 (Fighter) Squadron at Kenley, commanded by Sqn Ldr (later Air Cdre) Eric Digby Johnson AFC, replacing Gamecocks. The remainder of the batch was delivered to No 17 (Fighter) Squadron at Upavon, commanded by Sqn Ldr (later Gp Capt) Arthur Rex Arnold DSO, DFC, beginning in October and replacing Siskin IIIAs.

Being designed as a private venture, albeit submitted to an RAF requirement, no limitation existed on the export of Bulldogs. Already five had been delivered to Latvia in September, powered by Gnome-Rhône Jupiter VI engines and armed with 7.7mm Oerlikon machine guns. A Bulldog II was supplied to the USA in October for evaluation, but this machine crashed and was replaced by a second aircraft in February 1930. Two Bulldogs were sold to Siam in January that year, and were followed later in the same month by eight to the Royal Australian Air Force. A second production batch included 23 machines for the RAF (K1079-K1101) delivered between March and June 1930,

the next Squadron to be re-equipped being No 54 at Hornchurch, commanded by Sqn Ldr (later Gp Capt) Walter Edward George Bryant MBE, followed by No 32 (Fighter) Squadron at Kenley in September, commanded by Sqn Ldr Brian Edmund Baker DSO, MC, AFC (later Air Marshal Sir Brian, KBE, CB, DSO, MC, AFC). Three others were sold to Sweden and seven more to Latvia.

Inserted in the above production batch was another company demonstrator, which was registered G-ABBB on 12 June 1930; powered by a Gnome-Rhône

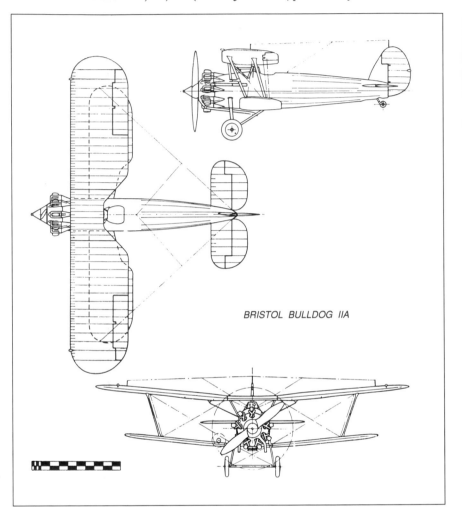

BRISTOL BULLDOG IIA

Type: Single-engine, single-seat, single-bay biplane interceptor fighter.
Manufacturers: The Bristol Aeroplane Co Ltd, Filton, Bristol.
Air Ministry Specifications: F.9/26, F.17/28 and F.11/29.
Powerplant: One 425hp Bristol Jupiter VII nine-cylinder air-cooled radial engine (Bulldog Mk I and II); 440hp Bristol Jupiter VIIF (Bulldog Mk IIA).
Structure: Construction of high-tensile steel strip rolled to flanged section to form Warren girder, the whole aircraft fabric covered.
Dimensions: Span, 33ft 10in; length, 25ft 2in; height, 8ft 9in; wing area, 307 sq ft.
Weights: Mark II. Tare, 2,200lb; all-up, 3,490lb; Mark IIA. Tare, 2,222lb; all-up, 3,660lb.
Performance: Max speed, 174 mph at 10,000ft; service ceiling, 29,300ft.
Armament: Two synchronized 0.303in Vickers Mk I or II machine guns on sides of nose with 600 rounds per gun.
Prototypes: One Mk I (no serial number, first flown by Cyril Uwins on 17 May 1927); one Mk II, J9480; one Mk IIA, J9480 modified. Numerous other *ad hoc* prototypes modified to special standards of preparation.
Production: Total of 346 military Bulldogs produced for the Air Ministry, excluding the Mk II/IIA prototype. Mk II and IIA: J9567-J9591, K1079-K1101, K1603-K1694, K2135-K2234, K2859-K2872, K2946-K2963 and K3504-K3513; TM two-seaters: K3170-K3186, K3923-K3953 and K4566-K4576; K4189 (stainless steel aircraft to 11/31).
Summary of RAF Service: Bulldog fighters served with Nos 3, 17, 19, 23, 29, 32, 41, 54, 56 and 111 (Fighter) Squadrons; Bulldog two-seaters served with the above Squadrons, as well as No 24 (Communications) Squadron; Central Flying School; RAF College, Cranwell; and Nos 3 and 5 Flying Training Schools.

The Bulldog Mk IIIA, R-5, in June 1932, carrying the New Type No 5 for the Hendon Display that year. This aircraft was powered by the 560hp Bristol Mercury IVS2 surrounded by a Townend ring with inner shroud; other airframe refinements included wheelbrakes and fairings and integral navigation lights and made possible a maximum speed of 208 mph. (Photo: A J Jackson Collection)

9ASB (supercharged Jupiter VII), it undertook numerous demonstrations throughout Europe until 1935. During this period it was progressively strengthened and given modified wing spars and ailerons. The same modifications, as well as installation of a Bristol-made Jupiter VII, were incorporated in the original Air Ministry Bulldog J9480 to become the Mark IIA prototype, which was ordered into production, beginning with a batch of 92 aircraft, following by another for 100 (K1603-K1694 and K2135-K2234 respectively).

As well as providing replacements on squadrons previously equipped with Bulldog IIs, the Mk IIAs were delivered to No 111 (Fighter) Squadron at Hornchurch in January 1931, commanded by Sqn Ldr (later Gp Capt) Edward Reginald Openshaw; to No 23 (Fighter) Squadron at Kenley in April, commanded by Sqn Ldr H H Woollett; to No 19 (Fighter) Squadron at Duxford in September, under Sqn Ldr Alfred Clifford Sanderson DFC (later Air Marshal Sir Clifford, KBE, CB, DFC); and to No 41 (Fighter) Squadron at Northolt in October, commanded by Sqn Ldr Stanley Flamank Vincent AFC (later Air Vice-Marshal, CB, DFC, AFC). An aircraft in the second of these batches, K2188, was completed as the Type 124 Bulldog TM two-seat trainer prototype (see below).

The demonstrator G-ABBB went on to become an engine test bed for the Bristol Aquila sleeve-valve radial, carry-ing the Class B registration R-11, after which it was put into storage at Filton in 1936. After the Second World War it was completely restored and given a Jupiter VIIIFP engine; it was flown once more on 22 June 1962 by Godfrey Auty and then presented to the Shuttleworth Trust — only to be destroyed in a crash following an ill-judged low-level loop during an SBAC air display at Farnborough.

Three final production batches, totalling 42 Bulldog IIAs (K2859-K2872, K2946-K2963 and K3504-K3513) were built for attrition replacement and to equip the last two Squadrons to fly the Bulldog, both at North Weald, No 29 Squadron in June 1932 under Sqn Ldr Henry Dunboyne O'Neill (later Air Cdre, CBE, AFC), and No 56 (Fighter) Squadron the following October, commanded by Sqn Ldr G E Wilson.

Completion of a Bulldog two-seater, K2188, referred to above, and its evaluation at the Central Flying School in 1932, had led to the issue of Specification T.12/32 and three production batches, totalling 59 trainers, known as Bulldog TMs. Produced between December 1932 and December 1934, these were distributed among the ten Bulldog fighter squadrons, as well as No 24 (Communications) Squadron, the Central Flying School, the Royal Air Force

Above: *The first Bulldog Mk IVA prototype, K4292, powered by the Bristol Mercury VIS2 engine in a long-chord cowling; this aircraft was submitted for official trials to decide on a four-gun fighter for the RAF under Specification F.7/30, and possessed a maximum speed of 224 mph (probably without armament). The successful contender to this Specification was the Gloster Gladiator. Left: This Bulldog, J9591, was the final aircraft in the first production batch of Mk IIs, but was completed as a Mark III with 485hp Mercury IVA; it ended its days at the RAE, Farnborough, in 1935, having at one time carried the civil letters G-AATR. (Photos: A J Jackson Collection)*

College, Cranwell, and Nos 3 and 5 Flying Training Schools.

Export of Bulldogs continued apace during the early 1930, further aircraft being sold to Sweden (three of these being presented to Finland in 1939). New orders were received from Estonia and Denmark, while two examples of a Bulldog derivative (the JSSF) were licence-built by Nakajima in Tokyo.

Bulldogs used as test beds abounded, and participated in the Bristol Mercury and Aquila development programmes alongside the Type 107 Bullpup. The Bulldog Mk IIIA was a private venture project of which two prototypes were produced; the first, with 'B' clase registration R-5, was powered by a prototype Mercury IVA and first flew on 17 September 1931, being later fitted with a production Mercury IVS2; the second, R-7, took over Mercury development after R-5 crashed at Martlesham on 30 March 1933. In March 1934 R-7 was converted to meet Specification F.7/30 as the Bulldog IVA, although it is not known whether the four machine guns were ever fitted, as called for in the requirement. With a Mercury VIS2 radial, the aircraft achieved a maximum speed of 224 mph at 10,000 feet, but even this was far from matching the winning Gloster Gladiator's 250 mph. A second Bulldog IVA, G-ACJN and later R-8, was used as a test bed for the Bristol Perseus IA sleeve-valve engine.

The last Bulldogs to serve with a first-line RAF squadron were those of No 3 (Fighter) Squadron in June 1937, still at Kenley — although it had taken its Bulldogs to the Sudan for a year in 1935 during the Abyssinian crisis. Less than a year after the last Bulldog left No 3 Squadron, it would be flying the Hawker Hurricane monoplane fighter whose maximum speed of over 300 mph, armament of eight machine guns, enclosed cockpit, landing flaps and retractable undercarriage emphasized the anachronism presented by the Bulldog in its final years.

Blackburn F.1 Turcock

Designed by Maj Frank Arnold Bumpus and B A Duncan, the Blackburn F.1 was, as its designation implied, the company's first fighter project for some eight years, and was an attempt to produce an aircraft equally suitable as a land-based interceptor and a ship-borne fighter; the general terms of reference were fairly superficial interpretations of the Air Ministry Specifications F.9/26 and N.21/26. To achieve this unusual degree of universality in a single aircraft, the design was intended to be offered with three alternative engines, namely the 585hp Bristol Mercury, the 510hp Rolls-Royce Falcon X, and the 446hp Armstrong Siddeley Jaguar VI. This family of designs was named the Blackcock, although individual names would be bestowed as different versions came to be built.

The airframe was of all-metal construction, the fuselage being a built-up structure of steel tubular members; the wing spars were of steel strips, riveted together, with drawn duralumin ribs. The front fuselage covering and wing root fairings were of formed duralumin sheet, the remainder of the airframe being fabric-covered. The unequal-span, swept-back wings were of parallel chord with square tips, and ailerons were fitted to the upper wings only. Provision was made to include two synchronized Vickers guns with 500 rounds per gun

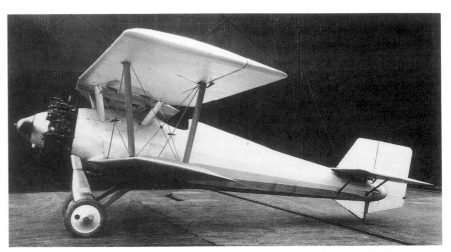

The Turcock in December 1927, before being allotted its civil markings, G-EBVP; the rear fuselage cone, aft of the sternpost, was integral with the rudder. (Photo: A J Jackson Collection)

in the sides of the fuselage.

The Air Ministry indicated no interest in the project, and Blackburn decided to go ahead with a single prototype as a private venture, selecting the Jaguar engine as the most readily available and least costly. The aircraft, without guns, was flown by Flt Lt Arthur George Loton AFC on 14 November 1927, having been purchased by the Turkish government, and therefore named the Turcock. It was allotted the civil registration G-EBVP for test and delivery purposes in January 1928, but was destroyed in a flying accident a month later, on 13 February.

No other aircraft in the Blackcock family was built.

Type: Single-engine, single-seat, single-bay biplane fighter.
Manufacturer: The Blackburn Aeroplane & Motor Co Ltd, Leeds and Brough, Yorkshire.
Powerplant: One 446hp Armstrong Siddeley Jaguar VI fourteen-cylinder air-cooled radial engine.
Structure: Fabric-covered steel and duralumin construction.
Dimensions: Span, 31ft 0in; length, 24ft 4in; height, 8ft 11in.
Weights: Tare, 2,282lb; all-up, 2,726lb.
Performance: Max speed, 176 mph; climb to 10,000ft, 8 min; service ceiling, 27,500ft.
Armament: Two synchronized 0.303in Vickers machine guns in sides of fuselage with 500 rounds per gun.
Prototype: One, G-EBVP (first flown by Flt Lt A G Loton on 14 November 1927). No production.

Avro Type 584 Avocet

Roy Chadwick's first fighter essay in metal stressed-skin construction was the Avro 584 Avocet, designed to Specification 17/25. This was a single-seat, single-bay sesquiplane with, perhaps surprisingly, the relatively low-powered Armstrong Siddeley Lynx IV seven-cylinder supercharged radial engine, rated at only 230hp.

The circular-section fuselage comprised a number of rolled duralumin sheets riveted together tapering in section only at the rear; it was located in the centre of the wing gap by steel centre-section struts anchored to the upper and lower longerons which formed the primary structure of the front fuselage. The interplane struts were of N-type with large single diagonal struts attached to the front spars of the upper and lower wings to provide a Warren truss, thereby obviating any need for wire bracing. Frise-type full-span ailerons were fitted to the upper wing only, which was of broad, parallel chord with square-cut tips; both wings were of uniform thickness from root to tip, the upper wing having generous dihedral, the lower wing being flat. Armament comprised two synchronized Vickers guns in the sides of the fuselage, firing along troughs just above the fuselage centreline.

Though intended for naval assessment, the Avocet's wings did not fold, but were capable of quick detachment; uniquely, however, the tailplane was made to fold vertically upwards for ease of shipboard stowage.

Two prototypes, N209 and N210, were built, the former being flown with wheel undercarriage during December 1927, followed by the latter as a twin-float seaplane in April 1928. The vertical tail surfaces of the two aircraft differed in that N209 possessed a large triangular fin with unbalanced rudder, whereas N210 featured a shortened fin with an enlarged, horn-balanced rudder.

Wheels were also fitted to N210 in June, and both aircraft underwent trials for the Fleet Air Arm at Martlesham in February 1929. The floats were then re-fitted to the second Avocet, and it was delivered to the RAF High Speed Flight at Calshot to provide seaplane experience for the Schneider Trophy pilots.

The second Avro Avocet, N210, with twin floats, shortly before its first flight at Hamble in April 1928 (Photo: British Aerospace (Manchester, Neg No A/10/14)

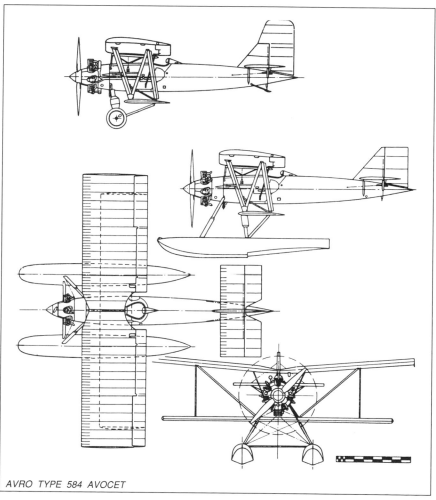

AVRO TYPE 584 AVOCET

Type: Single-engine, single-seat, single-bay sesquiplane land- and seaplane fighter.
Manufacturer: A V Roe & Co Ltd, Manchester, and Hamble, Hampshire.
Air Ministry Specification: 17/25
Powerplant: One 230hp Armstrong Siddeley Lynx IV seven-cylinder radial engine.
Structure: All-metal construction with stressed-skin fuselage.
Dimensions: Span; 29ft 0in; length, 24ft 6in (wheel undercarriage), 27ft 6in (floats); height, 11ft 8⅜in (wheels); wing area, 308 sq ft.
Weights: (Wheel undercarriage) Tare, 1,621lb; all-up, 2,495lb.
Performance: (Wheel undercarriage) Max speed, 133 mph at 10,000ft; ceiling, 23,000ft.
Armament: Two synchronized 0.303in Vickers machine guns in sides of fuselage.
Prototypes: Two, N209 and N210 (N209 first flown in December 1927). No production.

Gloster Gambet

The Gambet was the last wooden fighter produced by the Gloster (formerly Gloucestershire) Aircraft Company. Although Henry Folland had, before 1926, been engaged in preparing designs of experimental metal fighters under contract to the Air Ministry, it had occurred to him that there might be a need to replace the old wooden Sparrowhawk with a wooden aircraft, and had schemed the Gambet when the Fairey Flycatcher was adopted for the Fleet Air Arm.

Therefore, when, early in 1926, the Japanese manufacturer Nakajima Hikoki approached Gloster with a request to acquire the manufacturing rights of the Gamecock with which to replace the Sparrowhawks in service with the Imperial Japanese Navy, Folland was able to produce the Gambet's drawings. In July 1927 Nakajima negotiated to purchase one pattern example from Gloster together with a licence to build the type.

Externally the Gambet closely resembled the Gamecock, but featured wings similar to those of the Guan, with a span of 31ft 10in and swaged steel rod internal bracing. Internal equipment comprised flotation bags, and arrester claws were attached to the wheel axle fairings. Armament was a pair of Vickers guns, each with 600 rounds.

The sole Gloster-built Gambet was first flown by Howard Saint on 12 December 1927 and, although an application was made for the aircraft to undergo RAF evaluation at Martlesham, the Air Ministry expressed no interest in the fighter and it was shipped out to Japan early in 1928, where it won the competition to produce a naval fighter. One hundred and fifty aircraft were built as A1N1s and A1N2s between 1929 and 1932, the first fifty being powered by Nakajima-built Jupiter VIs and the remainder by Nakajima Kotobuki 2 engines.

The Gloster Gambet naval fighter for Japan, shown at Hucclecote in December 1927 before delivery. The fin's straight leading edge and additional wire bracing outboard of the interplane struts readily distinguished the fighter from the Gamecock. (Photo: Whitworth-Gloster, Neg No G6/63)

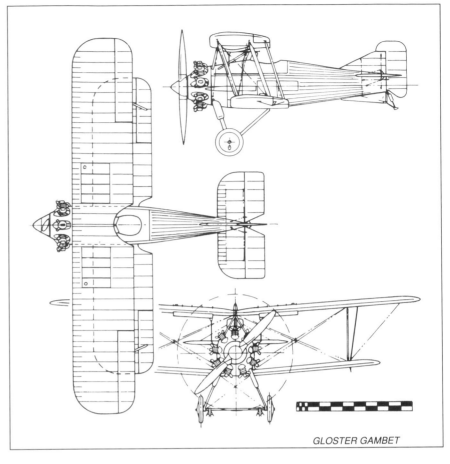

GLOSTER GAMBET

Type: Single-engine, single-seat, single-bay naval biplane fighter.

Manufacturers: The Gloster Aircraft Co Ltd, Hucclecote, Gloucester; Nakajima Hikoki KK, Japan.

Powerplant: One 420hp Bristol Jupiter VI nine-cylinder air-cooled radial engine driving Watts wooden two-blade propeller.

Structure: Fuselage of ash longerons and spruce struts, and wing structure of spruce spars and ribs, the whole airframe fabric-covered.

Dimensions: Span, 31ft 10in; length, 21ft 3½in; height, 10ft 8in; wing area, 284 sq ft.

Weights: Tare, 2,010lb; all-up, 3,075lb.

Performance: Max speed, 152 mph at 5,000ft; climb to 10,000ft, 7 min; service ceiling, 23,200ft.

Armament: Two synchronized 0.303in Vickers machine guns in sides of fuselage with 600 rounds per gun; provision to carry four 20lb bombs under the wings.

Prototype: One, un-numbered (first flown by Howard Saint on 12 December 1927).

Production: 150 aircraft built in Japan for the Imperial Japanese Navy.

Boulton & Paul
P.33 Partridge

The Boulton & Paul Partridge Mk I, J8459, during its trials at Martlesham Heath in the spring of 1928; following some criticism of its handling during these trials, ailerons were added to the lower wing. (Photo: Air Ministry)

John North's Partridge fighter was the last of the four F.9/26 designs ordered by the Air Ministry in prototype form to fly before the beginning of the official trials at Martlesham to decide on the winning tender. Unfortunately the Specification had made clear the Air Ministry's engine preferences and had recommended for use the Armstrong Siddeley Jaguar V, the Rolls-Royce F.X Falcon with evaporative cooling, the turbo-supercharged Bristol Orion or the Bristol Mercury, of which none had achieved successful type-clearance by mid-1927 — the point at which designers had to reach a decision on the type of engine to be installed in their evaluation prototypes.

The Bristol Mercury had probably reached the most advanced development stage when North opted for this engine, only to be informed in September that it would not have completed its 50-hour type clearance in time for the trials. The Air Ministry then made it clear that other engines would be accepted, so that work was hurriedly put in hand to fit a 440hp Jupiter VIIS supercharged engine.

Like the P.31 Bittern twin-engine night fighter, the Partridge's flying surfaces were of parallel chord with square wingtips. As first flown, ailerons were only fitted to the upper wings (but later also fitted to the lower wings), and a variable-incidence tailplane was adjustable through a screw-jack by a handwheel in the cockpit. The primary airframe structure was of steel and light alloy with duralumin sheet panelling on the nose and upper decking rearwards to a point just aft of the cockpit.

The prototype, J8459, was first flown in January 1928, and the next month was delivered to the A & AEE for preliminary handling; in general this proved satisfactory, and the Partridge remained at Martlesham for the official trials. In these it came third behind the Bristol Bulldog and Hawker Hawfinch, and succeeded in attaining or bettering the performance criteria stated in the Specification; it did not, however, progress to

evaluation by the fighter squadrons.

A number of modifications resulted in the aircraft being re-termed the Mark II, but a Mark III version, intended for the Mercury engine, was not proceeded with; nor did attempts by the manufacturers to interest South American countries in the fighter come to fruition.

J8459 was displayed at the Hendon Display on 30 June 1928 as New Type No 2, and in December 1929 it was transferred to the Air Ministry's experimental charge and delivered to the RAE at Farnborough.

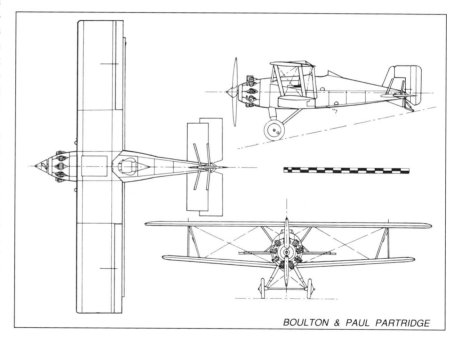

BOULTON & PAUL PARTRIDGE

Type: Single-engine, single-seat, single-bay biplane interceptor fighter.
Manufacturer: Boulton & Paul Ltd, Norwich, Norfolk.
Air Ministry Specification: F.9/26
Powerplant: One 440hp Bristol Jupiter VIIS nine-cylinder supercharged radial engine.
Structure: All-metal construction with fabric covering.
Dimensions: Span, 35ft 0in; length, 23ft 1in; height, 10ft 10in.
Weights: Tare, 2,021lb; all-up, 3,100lb.
Performance: Max speed, 167 mph at 10,000ft; service ceiling, 25,300ft.
Armament: Two synchronized 0.303in Vickers machine guns in sides of fuselage.
Prototype: One, J8459 (first flown in January 1928). No production.

Gloster Gnatsnapper

Passing mention has already been made of the new naval fighter Specification, N.21/26, draft details of which became known to the industry before the end of 1926, but were not finalised until the following May. It called for an all-metal single-seater to be powered by the 450hp Bristol Mercury IIA radial and to possess a maximum speed of not less than 160 mph at 10,000 feet. It was, in short, otherwise little different from F.9/26, while listing additional naval equipment as well as setting out new minimum parameters for the pilot's field of view. Indeed, one or two manufacturers chose, in the interests of time and cost, to attempt the design of aircraft which, with limited alterations, might satisfy either or both Specifications.

Not so Gloster, however, and Folland's first Gnatsnapper design was complete by about September 1927, when the first available flight example of the Mercury was delivered to Hucclecote. This engine proved to be quite unsatisfactory, being unreliable, incapable of producing the promised power, as well as being 160 lb overweight and, rather than persevere with an airframe that was now in effect redundant, a second aircraft, N227, was completed with a 450hp Jupiter VII so as to start flight trials without further delay. Its first flight took place in February 1928.

N227 featured a steel wire-braced structure aft of the cockpit employing round section steel frames with light-alloy formers; forward of this was a square-section primary structure of square-section steel tubular frames and formers to which were riveted ribbed metal sheet panels. The engine bearer frame was hinged to the front members of this structure so that it could be swung to either side for maintenance. The wings featured the now-familiar Gloster lattice steel spars, and ailerons were fitted to the upper wings only.

Further Mercury engines were delivered during 1928 and, although these were flown in N227, it was obvious that there was little point in pursuing this powerplant further and, as the Gnatsnapper had missed participation in the first N.21/26 evaluation (in which no contender had been declared the winner), the Jupiter VII was re-fitted, and with it

The Gnatsnapper Mk I, N227, as originally flown with Jupiter VII engine, ailerons on upper wings only, and side-mounted Vickers machine guns. (Photo: via Derek James)

underwent performance assessment on its own with the A & AEE. Moreover it showed itself able to meet all the main requirements of the original Specification. Meanwhile a new fin and rudder had been designed, and this was to be fitted in 1930 when the Air Ministry announced a new Ship Fighter Competition.

Gloster was instructed to re-design the Gnatsnapper with the Armstrong Siddeley Jaguar VIII geared and super-

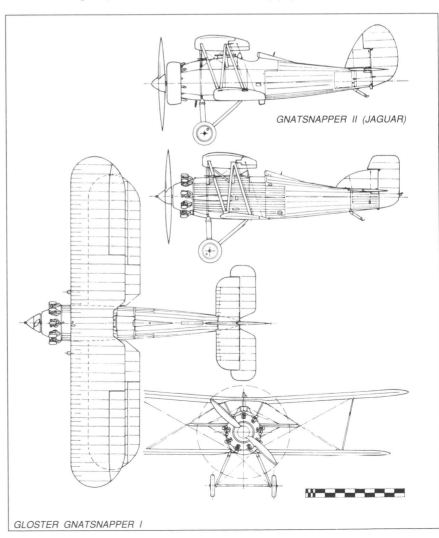

GNATSNAPPER II (JAGUAR)

GLOSTER GNATSNAPPER I

charged engine. In this form, and now designated the Mark II, the Gnatsnapper entered the competition early in 1931, only to be badly damaged in a landing accident before completion of the trials.

This put paid to Gloster's hopes of a production contract, although by that time the Rolls-Royce Kestrel-powered Hawker Norn (Nimrod) had rendered the outcome of the competition superfluous.

N227 was returned to Hucclecote for repair, and to be fitted with a Townend ring. After a series of armament trials, it again underwent extensive alteration, this time to accommodate a 525hp Rolls-Royce Kestrel IIS in-line engine with steam-condensers in the leading edge of two-bay wings. In this guise, as the Gnatsnapper Mk III, N227 was delivered for evaluation at Martlesham in June 1931. Later still, it was used by Rolls-Royce to fly the Goshawk III steam-cooled engine, and ended its days in 1934 as a company hack.

Another Gnatsnapper, N254, had been ordered in May 1929, but was not flown until about March 1930 with a Mercury IIA engine. Evidence suggests that this was almost certainly the Mercury-powered aircraft, N215, which had been discontinued in 1927 on first signs that the Mercury would not be suitable to meet N.21/26. An attempt was made to modify this aircraft to Specification 16/30, but work stopped when the Hawker Nimrod, also prepared to this Specification, returned performance figures quite unattainable by the Mercury-powered Gnatsnapper.

The demise of this aircraft was particularly unfortunate for Gloster, as the company had been called on to do a great deal of work at its own expense and, following the ending of Gamecock production, was forced in 1932 to undertake contracts far removed from aviation in order to survive the ravages of the Depression.

The accompanying data table refers to the Gnatsnapper Mk II, except where stated otherwise.

Type: Single-engine, single-seat, single-bay carrier-borne biplane interceptor.
Manufacturer: The Gloster Aircraft Co Ltd, Hucclecote, Gloucester.
Air Ministry Specifications: N.21/26 and 16/30.
Powerplant: Mk I. One 450hp Bristol Jupiter VII nine-cylinder air-cooled radial engine; also 450hp Bristol Mercury IIA. Mk II. 540hp Armstrong Siddeley Jaguar VIII fourteen-cylinder two-row radial engine. Mk III. 525hp Rolls-Royce Kestrel IIS(S) steam-cooled in-line engine; also 600hp Rolls-Royce Goshawk III.
Structure: Steel and duralumin construction with metal and fabric covering.
Dimensions: Span, 36ft 6in; length, 24ft 7in; height, 10ft 11in; wing area, 360 sq ft.
Weights: Tare, 3,095lb; all-up, 3,804lb.
Performance: Max speed, 177 mph at 15,000ft; climb to 20,000ft, 19 min; service ceiling, 24,500ft; range, 490 miles.
Armament: Two synchronized 0.303in Vickers Mk II machine guns with 600 rounds per gun.
Prototypes: Two known prototypes, N227 and N254; however N215 may have been a third aircraft, or re-numbered to become N254. (N227 was first flown in February 1928). No production.

N227 as the Gnatsnapper Mk II with Jaguar VIII engine in Townend ring, guns moved to the upper decking of the nose, and rounded fin and rudder. (Photo: via Derek James)

Vickers
Type 125 Vireo

As early as 15 December 1925 Vickers submitted outline proposals for an all-metal single-seat shipborne monoplane fighter to meet Air Ministry Specification 17/25, its purpose being to demonstrate the benefits of the Vickers-Wibault system of metal construction in a small fighter with a cantilever wing and to explore the performance potential of low-powered lightweight fighters. From the outset it was proposed to make the wheel undercarriage interchangeable with

The Vireo, N211, during its trials at Martlesham Heath; note the starboard wing-mounted Vickers machine gun. (Photo: Air Ministry)

The Vireo equipped with float undercarriage. On the recommendation of the engine manufacturers, an exhaust ring manifold was fitted at this stage in an attempt to improve the engine performance. Though also flown with a metal propeller, the wooden type, seen here, was found to give a marginally better speed. (Photo: Vickers Ltd)

a twin-float chassis, and a 230hp Armstrong Siddeley Lynx IV supercharged seven-cylinder radial engine was selected for the prototype.

Armament consisted of a pair of the new Vickers Auto RC machine guns in the wings, free-firing outboard of the propeller arc, made possible by the relatively thick cantilever wings; because most of the gun bodies were situated below the barrel line, the muzzles of the guns projected from the wings well above their centreline.

Owing to Vickers' decision to submit many components of the airframe structure for test by the RAE before incorporating them in the prototype, N211, so as to satisfy the Air Ministry's strength requirements, the Vireo (named after the American songbird) was not flown until early in March 1928, and was delivered to Martlesham for handling and performance evaluation the following month. As had been discovered by several other manufacturers, the Lynx failed to produce the anticipated power and the Vireo's performance was disappointing, to say the least.

In July N211 was delivered to Gosport for deck landing trials aboard HM Carrier *Furious* on the 12th. However, although the twin-float chassis was afterwards fitted in place of the wheel undercarriage, no further flight trials were made. Moreover, although Vickers was now firmly committed to metal construction, the Wibault system was no longer considered appropriate in interceptors, largely on account of the drag inherent in the corrugated skinning, and future Vickers fighter designs followed more orthodox structural paths.

The accompanying data table refers to the wheel-equipped Vireo prototype.

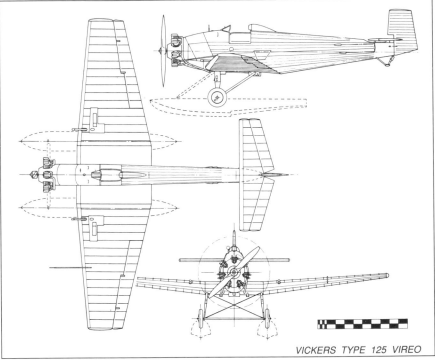

VICKERS TYPE 125 VIREO

Type: Single-engine, single-seat, low-wing monoplane lightweight naval fighter.
Manufacturer: Vickers (Aviation) Ltd, Weybridge, Surrey.
Air Ministry Specification: 17/25.
Powerplant: One 230hp Armstrong Siddeley Lynx IV seven-cylinder air-cooled supercharged radial engine.
Structure: All-metal Vickers-Wibault structure employing fabricated steel and light-alloy components with corrugated light-alloy skin. Wheel or twin-float undercarriage.
Dimensions: Span, 35ft 0in; length, 27ft 8in; height, 11ft 5in; wing area, 214 sq ft.
Weights: Tare, 1,951 lb; all-up, 2,550lb.
Performance: Max speed, 120 mph at 5,000ft; service ceiling, 14,750ft.
Armament: Two free-firing 0.303in Vickers E (Auto RC) machine guns in wings outboard of propeller arc.
Prototype: One, N211 (first flown early in March 1928). No production.

Bristol Type 107 Bullpup

Failure by the Bristol Mercury radial engine to materialise in reliable form in time for the F.9/26 evaluation competition had prompted the Air Ministry to re-write this Specification as F.20/27 in 1927 with a number of up-graded requirements, including a speed of not less than 170 mph and an ability to climb to 10,000 feet in under six minutes.

It will be recalled that Frank Barnwell's Bristol Type 107 Bullpup was still on the ground, awaiting its geared Mercury III engine, when his Jupiter-powered Bulldog had first flown in May 1927. It was still on the ground nine months later, and once again a Jupiter (this time the engine from the Type 101) was fitted for the first flight of the Bullpup which

The Bristol Bullpup, J9051, shortly before its participation in the inconsequential F.20/27 trials, powered by the Mercury IIA engine. Like the Bulldog, the Bullpup was only fitted with ailerons on its upper wing. (Photo: The Bristol Aeroplane Co Ltd, Neg No 814)

was made on 28 April 1928. Troubles continued to dog the Mercury and, once again, the failure of this engine prevented any contender to F.20/27 from being named the outright winner, although the Bullpup performed fairly well with a Mercury IIA engine.

On returning to Filton after the trials, it was tested briefly with a Townend ring, and then fitted with a 440hp Jupiter VIIF; with this engine it appeared as New Type No 2 at the Hendon Display on 28 June 1928. By then the Bullpup had been transferred to Air Ministry experimental charge and leased back to Bristol for engine development.

At about this time it was modified to make provision to mount up to four Lewis machine guns under the lower wings, although the motive for this is uncertain, as it was not until rather later

that Air Ministry Specification F.7/30 was issued calling for the four-gun armament. Certainly the Bullpup was never considered in the context of this requirement.

In June 1931 it was fitted with the 400hp short-stroke version of the Mercury and underwent trials at Martlesham during the early part of 1933. Thereafter

it was flown with a variety of Bristol engines, and performed the 200-hour endurance programme on the 500hp Bristol Aquila sleeve-valve radial during the spring of 1935; it was also flown with the Aquila III and 600hp Perseus IA.

After appearing at the 1935 SBAC Hendon Display the Bullpup was finally scrapped.

Type: Single-engine, single-seat, single-bay experimental biplane interceptor fighter.
Manufacturer: The Bristol Aeroplane Co Ltd, Filton, Bristol.
Air Ministry Specification: F.20/27.
Powerplant: Flown with 450hp Bristol Jupiter VI, 480hp Mercury IIA, 440hp Jupiter VIIF, 400hp Mercury SS, 500hp Aquila I and III, and 600hp Perseus IA radial engines.
Dimensions: Span, 30ft 0in; length, 23ft 6in; height, 9ft 5in; wing area, 230 sq ft.
Weights: Tare, 1,910lb; all-up, 2,850lb.
Performance: Mercury IIA. Max speed, 190 mph at 8,000ft; service ceiling, 30,100ft.
Armament: Two synchronized 0.303in Vickers Mk II machine guns in sides of front fuselage; at one time the Bullpup was modified to make provision for up to four 0.303in Lewis guns under the lower wings.
Prototype: One, J9051 (first flown, 28 April 1928).

Blackburn F.2 Lincock

Although Maj F A Bumpus had proposed a design tender to the F.20/27 Specification with his Blackcock (an all-metal fighter intended to be powered by the 510hp Rolls-Royce Falcon X but which failed to attract a prototype order), he and G E Petty returned to the lightweight fighter concept with the F.2 Lincock, a private venture intended to achieve a relatively efficient yet inexpensive aircraft that might be attractive among nations with smaller air forces

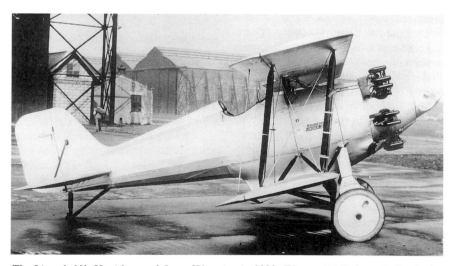

The Lincock Mk II with geared Lynx IV engine in 1928. (Photo: A J Jackson Collection)

and less demanding military responsibilities.

The first Lincock was of all-wood construction with a plywood monocoque fuselage located in mid-gap position. Ailerons were fitted on upper and lower wings to ensure a good rate of roll, and a variable-incidence tailplane could be adjusted in flight. Civil registered as G-EBVO, the Lincock Mk I was unarmed and was probably first flown in late April or early May 1928. In July it was flown by Sqn Ldr (later Gp Capt) Jack Noakes AFC, MM, into 10th place in that year's King's Cup race.

The Lincock quickly attracted the attention of the Canadian government who asked for a demonstration to be staged, insisting that the aircraft should be of all-metal construction. This was agreed, and henceforth all Lincocks featured steel and duralumin fuselage with drawn-steel wing spars and stamped-out duralumin ribs. The space between the fuselage and lower wing was 'filled in' by adding a narrow fairing between the lower N-struts. A 255hp geared Lynx IV engine, driving a Fairey Reed metal propeller was fitted, and provision was allowed for an armament of two Vickers guns in the sides of the fuselage,

though no armament was in fact fitted. This version, the Lincock Mk II, was demonstrated in Canada during May and June 1930, and there were even suggestions that Lincocks might be built in Canada for the RCAF.

The RCAF, however, saw the aircraft, not as a front-line fighter, but more as an advanced trainer for would-be fighter pilots, and, as no funding was available for this additional category of Service aircraft, no order was forthcoming.

The Lincock Mk III was the only version to carry the intended armament, and was powered by the 270hp Lynx Major. A lighter, transverse-axle undercarriage was also fitted. A total of five Mk IIIs was built, namely a company demonstrator registered G-ABFK, and two each for Japan and China — all these being flown in 1930.

It is unlikely that the manufacturers ever considered it likely that the Air Ministry would order the Lincock, as it performed no recognised rôle in the RAF. Yet among the evergreen memories of the inter-War years were the astonishing crazy-flying displays at Chicago in 1930 by that incorrigible RAF pilot, Flt Lt Dick (later Air Marshal Sir Richard) Atcherley.

Type: Single-engine, single-seat, single-bay lightweight biplane fighter.
Manufacturer: The Blackburn Aeroplane & Motor Co Ltd, Leeds and Brough, Yorkshire.
Powerplant: Mk I. One 240hp Armstrong Siddeley Lynx IVC; Mk II. 255hp Lynx IV (geared); Mk III. 270hp Lynx Major.
Structure: Mk I, all-wood; Mk II and III, all-metal.
Dimensions: Span: 22ft 6in; length, 18ft 1½in (Mk I), 19ft 6in (Mk II and III); height, 7ft 10in (Mk II and III); wing area, 170 sq ft.
Weights: Mk II. Tare, 1,244lb; all-up, 2,000lb.
Performance: Mk II. Max speed, 155 mph at sea level; initial rate of climb, 1,450 ft/min; service ceiling, 20,000ft; range, 390 miles.
Armament: Mk III. Two synchronized 0.303in Vickers machine guns in sides of fuselage.
Prototypes: One Mk I, G-EBVO (first flown in late April or early May 1928); one Mk II, G-AALH.
Production: Five Mk IIIs (one demonstrator, two for Japan and two for China).

Hawker F.20/27

By 1928 Sydney Camm had joined the small but growing number of aircraft designers who were convinced that the bulky, air-cooled radial engine had had its day as a fighter powerplant, and had already completed the design of a very fast light bomber (soon to become the Hawker Hart), powered by the new Rolls-Royce F.XI in-line engine.

In submitting his design for a Bristol Mercury-powered fighter to Specification F.20/27, which was never even named, he saw it as no more than a useful exercise to perfect an airframe which could, with relative ease, be adapted to accommodate the Rolls-Royce engine.

Of all-metal construction, employing the familiar wire-braced box structure of tubular steel members and the patented dumb-bell wing spars, the Hawker F.20/27, J9123, was first flown by Flt Lt 'George' Bulman in August 1928 with a Bristol Jupiter VIIF engine, owing to the non-availability of a flight-cleared

The sole Hawker F.20/27 interceptor, J9123, at Brooklands, with Mercury IIA engine during the winter of 1928-29. (Photo: H G Hawker Engineering Co Ltd, Neg No 1902)

Mercury. It featured sharply-staggered wings without sweepback and of unequal span and parallel chord, and ailerons were fitted to the upper wings only — as with every Camm-designed biplane which followed the Danecock. The fuselage was fairly deep at mid-position, thereby providing the pilot with an excellent view from his cockpit.

Before the end of the year J9123 was delivered to Martlesham for tests to decide the best propeller pitch for the

forthcoming F.20/27 evaluation, returning a best speed of 194 mph with the Jupiter engine. After the inconclusive evaluation trials a numnber of Mercury IIA engines were installed, but all had to be returned to Filton for correction of faults. In January 1930, by which time Camm's Kestrel-powered fighter, the Hornet, had flown successfully, J9123 was sent to the RAE on Air Ministry experimental charge, powered by a 485hp Mercury IIIA; five months later it was fitted with a prototype Mercury VI of 520hp, and with this the aircraft demonstrated a maximum speed of 202 mph at 10,000 feet at Martlesham in July.

By then of little more than academic interest, J9123 ended its days at Farnborough when it overturned while landing on 14 January 1931.

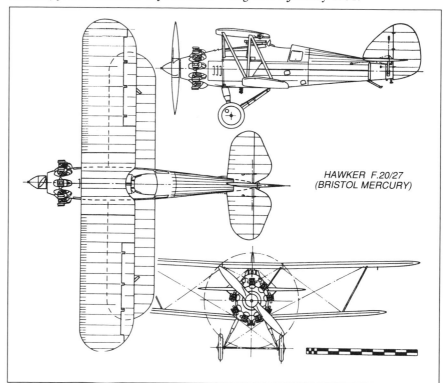

HAWKER F.20/27 (BRISTOL MERCURY)

Type: Single-engine, single-seat, single-bay biplane interceptor.
Manufacturer: H G Hawker Engineering Co Ltd, Kingston and Brooklands, Surrey.
Air Ministry Specification: F.20/27
Powerplant: One 530hp Bristol Jupiter VIIF nine-cylinder radial engine; also 440hp Mercury IIA, 485hp Mercury IIIA and 520hp Mercury VI.
Structure: Steel and duralumin construction throughout, fabric and duralumin covered.
Dimensions: Span, 30ft 0in; length 22ft 9in; height, 9ft 5in; wing area, 228 sq ft.
Weights: Tare, 2,155lb; all-up, 3,150lb.
Performance: Mercury VI. Max speed, 202 mph at 10,000ft; climb to 10,000ft, 5 min 5 sec; service ceiling, 24,800ft; range 360 miles.
Armament: Two synchronized Vickers 0.303in machine guns, each with 600 rounds, semi-buried in upper decking of nose.
Prototype: One, J9123 (first flown by Flt Lt P W S Bulman in August 1928).

Westland F.20/27 Interceptor

If Sydney Camm's design tender to Specification F.20/27 was entirely conventional, no one could regard another aircraft which also flew for the first time in August 1928 as being conceived without imagination as well as a considerable element of technical bravado. For Arthur Davenport at Westland essayed a monoplane design, knowing full well the extent of official prejudice with regard to such a configuration in fighter aircraft.

Be that as it may, despite the importance said to have been attached by the Air Ministry to both the F.9/26 and F.20/27 requirements, it was becoming increasingly unlikely that there would be any outright winner of the latter 'competition' once a successful tender had been found for the former — given the continuing delay in producing a reliable Mercury engine. And it is likely that Westland came to regard the issue of F.20/27 as a useful opportunity to

The Westland F.20/27, J9124, in an early configuration featuring the low aspect ratio vertical tail surfaces. Just visible in the engine crankcase cowling is the channel for the port Vickers gun, the guns themselves being located some six feet further aft. (Photo: Harald Penrose)

advance its own experience in designing and flying an all-metal monoplane fighter, even though it would not possess a cantilever wing.

Structurally the F.20/27's fuselage comprised the company's established box-girder of square-section duralumin tube jointed with flitch plates and tubular rivets, to which formers and stringers were added. Small stub wings were built integrally with the fuselage, to which the

main wing sections were attached. Duplicated wing bracing wires were anchored to the wing spars and to the upper longerons, and below to the apices of the rear undercarriage V-struts.

Westland was fortunate in being supplied with a 'working' example of the Mercury IIA from the outset and, although this was consistently short on power, Louis Paget flew the F.20/27, J9124, for the first time in August 1928, the aircraft becoming known by the company simply as the Interceptor. For the first few flights the aircraft featured a low aspect ratio fin and rudder.

Despite an uneventful first flight, extending the performance and handling limits gave rise to a number of problems, not least of which was the aircraft's inability to complete a loop — instead rolling off the top of its own accord. Wind-tunnel tests disclosed airflow instability around the wing roots which reduced the effect of the tail control surfaces. The opportunity was taken to install a 480hp Mercury IIIA, and eventually entirely new fin and rudder of much increased aspect ratio were fitted. Small leading-edge slats were incorporated in the wing roots, but with only marginal benefit, and ultimately it was discovered that the root flow instability was cured simply by the addition of small trailing-edge root fillets.

In an attempt to gain better performance with the Bristol engines, a Townend ring was added and the Interceptor was eventually accepted for evaluation at Martlesham in May 1929. Meanwhile, however, as Westland's monoplane fighter struggled in vain to match the performance of contemporary biplanes, the Air Ministry had tacitly accepted that the new Rolls-Royce Kestrel in-line engine, and its equally promising derivatives, should feature in future fighter Specifications.

J9124 was transferred to Air Ministry experimental charge and fitted with a 420hp Jupiter VII for delivery to the RAE on 21 August 1931, being last flown at Farnborough on 14 March 1933.

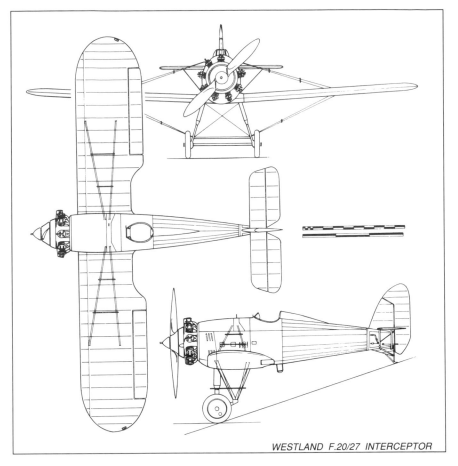

WESTLAND F.20/27 INTERCEPTOR

Type: Single-engine, single-seat, low-wing monoplane fighter.
Manufacturer: Westland Aircraft Works, Yeovil, Somerset.
Air Ministry Specification: F.20/27.
Powerplant: One 440hp Bristol Mercury IIA nine-cylinder air-cooled radial engine; also 480hp Mercury IIIA and 420hp Jupiter VII.
Structure: All-metal construction with duralumin box structure with formers and stringers; externally-braced two-spar wing with fabric covering; fixed oleo-sprung cross-axle undercarriage.
Dimensions: Span, 38ft 0in; length, 25ft 4½in; height, 9ft 8in; wing area, 214 sq ft.
Weights: Tare, 2,350lb; all-up, 3,325lb.
Performance: Max speed, 192 at 10,000ft; landing speed, 59 mph.
Armament: Two synchronized 0.303in Vickers Mk II machine guns in sides of fuselage.
Prototype: One, J9124 (first flown by Louis Paget at Yeovil in August 1928).

Parnall Pipit

Air Ministry Specification N.21/26, issued on 30 September 1926 set out requirements for an all-metal naval interceptor with a maximum speed of not less than 152 mph at 10,000 feet, a service ceiling not less than 23,000 feet and for provision for interchangeable wheel and float undercarriage. The engine was required to be either a 550hp Bristol Mercury radial or a 480hp Rolls-Royce Falcon X in-line.

Harold Bolas opted for the latter

powerplant and produced design drawings for a single-bay biplane with equal-span wings with long Frise-type ailerons on the lower wings only. The fuselage structure was a metal box-girder with duralumin formers and stringers, fabric-covered aft of the sheet metal engine cowling. A mock-up of this, the Parnall Pipit, was inspected by Air Ministry technical staff in February 1927 and in January the following year Parnall received a contract for two prototypes, N232 and N233.

Neither the date of N232's first flight, nor its pilot on that occasion, is known, but evidence indicates that it

took place between 22 June and 23 July 1928. When first flown, the Pipit featured unbalanced rudder and elevators, but shortly afterwards the rudder was slightly increased in area, and later still the entire tail unit underwent redesign to include horn balances on all control surfaces. Hubert Broad delivered N232 to Martlesham for a preliminary handling report on 7 September.

The Service pilots were critical of the Pipit's handling qualities, recording that it was longitudinally unstable, that the directional control was very poor, and that as speed increased beyond about 150 mph the wings flexed to such an

The first Parnall Pipit, N232, almost certainly in the form in which it was first flown; it certainly made its initial flight with a Fairey Reed metal propeller (as shown here), but this had been replaced by a Watts wooden propeller by the time of the aircraft's accident. One of the requirements of Specification N.21/26 was that provision was to be made for an armament of one 0.303in, and one 0.5in machine gun, and that these guns should not employ blast channels; the 0.5in gun was not available for inclusion in any contender, so all featured standard 0.303in Vickers guns, and all employed blast channels — those on the Pipit being of considerable length. (Photo: via J M Bruce)

extent that vibration damping rods had failed in flight.

N232 was written off in a crash landing on 20 September, following structural failure of the port tailplane; the Martlesham pilot, Sqn Ldr Jack Noakes AFC, MM, suffered a broken neck when he was thrown clear as the aircraft somersaulted.

The second Pipit was completed by the end of 1929, powered by a 520hp Rolls-Royce F.XIIS (Kestrel IIS) and with large Frise ailerons on both upper and lower wings. The elevator had been elarged, but the fin considerably reduced in area to accommodate the rudder's horn balance, now introduced.

Shortly after its first flight at about the turn of the year another Martlesham pilot, Sqn Ldr Sydney Leo Gregory Pope DFC, AFC, visited Yate (Parnall's airfield) to undertake handling tests in N233 on 24 February. Once again the Pipit's tail unit failed, this time the fin

and rudder parting company with the aeroplane. Despite baling out from under 1,000 feet, Pope's life was saved by his parachute — despite being a very large man. Following recovery of the aircraft's rudder, it was deduced that the fitting of a heavy tail lamp on the rudder's trailing edge not only countered the effect of the large horn balance but substantially increased the moment of inertia about an unsupported hinge

tube, allowing violent flutter of the rudder to occur, to which a lack of torsional rigidity in the rear fuselage structure contributed.

Not surprisingly, the Pipit was regarded as wholly unacceptable by the Air Ministry, and its rejection all but ended Parnall's long and fruitless endeavours to produce an effective fighter aircraft.

Type: Single-engine, single-seat, single-bay shipborne fighter.
Manufacturer: George Parnall & Co Ltd, Bristol, and Yate, Gloucestershire.
Air Ministry Specification: N.21/26.
Powerplant: N232. One 480hp Rolls-Royce F.XIS (Kestrel IS) twelve-cylinder liquid-cooled in-line engine; N233, one 520hp Rolls-Royce F.XIIS (Kestrel IIS) engine.
Structure: All-metal construction with fabric covering.
Dimensions: Span, 35ft 0in; length, 26ft 0in; height, 10ft 5½in; wing area, 361 sq ft.
Weights: Tare, 3,050lb; all-up, 3,980lb.
Performance: N232. Max speed, 173 mph at 3,000ft; climb to 10,000ft, 7 min 30 sec.
Armament: Provision for two synchronized 0.303in Vickers Mk II machine guns in sides of fuselage, each with 600 rounds; provision to carry four 20lb bombs under the port wing.
Prototypes: Two, N232 and N233 (N232 first flown at Yate in late June or July 1928). No production.

Hawker Hoopoe

A late contender to the naval Specification N.21/26, originally intended to find a replacement for the Fairey Flycatcher, was the Hawker Hoopoe, which first flew at about the same time as the Hawker F.20/27 and which it closely resembled. Indeed the relationship between the two radial engine-powered

The Hoopoe, N237, with its original two-bay wings and Mercury IIA engine. (Photo: Air Ministry [A & AEE] Neg No 1256)

N237 in 1930, fitted with 560hp Panther III engine and modified to the naval equipment standard set out in Specification 16/30. The lengthened tailskid was a requirement for the deck-landing trials. (Photo: British Aerospace, Military Aircraft Ltd, Kingston)

fighters was to be perpetuated when they came to be developed into the Kestrel-engined Hawker Fury and Nimrod fighters.

The Hoopoe was originally a private venture in which Camm intended to demonstrate that there was little reason for a naval fighter, derived from a land-based counterpart, to be significantly compromised by the various accoutrements demanded for shipboard operation. When first flown, the prototype Hoopoe N237 featured two-bay wings as it had been intended to incorporate wing-folding; when it became clear that no aircraft would fully meet the specified requirements of N.21/26, and that folding wings would not be demanded, heavily-staggered, unswept single-bay wings were later substituted on the Hoopoe.

When N237 was delivered to Martlesham late in 1928 for Service handling assessment (still with two-bay wings) the aircraft was powered by a Mercury IIA and, despite its inability to produce its forecast power, met with an encouraging response. Hawker was therefore asked to submit the aircraft, equipped with twin float undercarriage, for water handling trials at the MAEE at Felixstowe. To counter the power shortage the opportunity was taken to substitute a Mercury VIA engine, rated at 520hp. Both Hawker and Armstrong Whitworth floats were flown on the Hoopoe at that time.

No longer constrained by the old N.21/26 requirements, N237 was then fitted with a Jaguar V with Townend ring at the end of 1929 in an attempt to raise the performance. Another visit to Martlesham brought further encouragment and the Hoopoe underwent a further engine change, this time to the 560hp Armstrong Siddeley Panther III with two concentric Townend rings and driving a 10ft 10in diameter Watts propeller. The aircraft was prepared to Specification 16/30 with full naval equipment, including flotation gear, naval wireless, oxygen, twin Vickers guns with 1,060 rounds, provision to carry four 20lb bombs and full night flying lamps and flares; Palmer wheels and

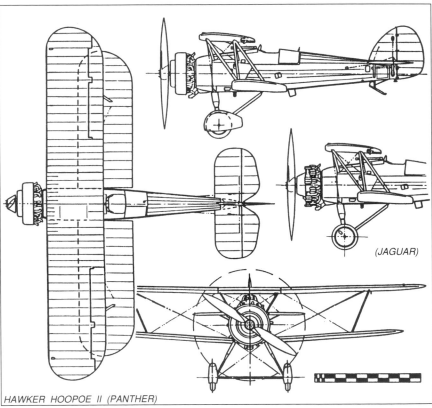

(JAGUAR)

HAWKER HOOPOE II (PANTHER)

wheelbrakes were also fitted, together with wheel spats, and in this configuration N237 underwent a series of success-

ful deck landing trials aboard HM Carrier *Glorious* with No 405 Flight of the Fleet Air Arm. It also recorded a maximum

Type: Single-engine, single-seat, single- and two-bay naval biplane fighter.

Manufacturer: The H G Hawker Engineering Co Ltd, Kingston and Brooklands, Surrey.

Air Ministry Specifications: N.21/26 (later modified to 16/30)

Powerplant: One 450hp Bristol Mercury IIA radial engine; later 520hp Mercury VIA, 400hp Armstrong Siddeley Jaguar V and 560hp Panther III.

Dimensions: Span, 34ft 6in (two-bay wings), 33ft 2in (single-bay); length, 25ft 4in (Mercury), 24ft 6in (Panther); wing area, 306 sq ft (two-bay), 288.5 sq ft (single-bay).

Weights: Panther III. Tare, 2,785lb; all-up, 3,910lb.

Performance: Panther III. Max speed, 196.5 mph at 12,500ft; climb to 10,000ft, 6 min 40 sec; service ceiling, 23,600ft.

Armament: Two synchronized 0.303in Vickers Mk II machine guns with 530 rounds per gun; provision to carry four 20lb bombs.

Prototype: One, N237 (first flown in about August 1928). No production.

speed of 196.5 mph at 12,500 feet in its fully-equipped state.

Sometimes, though unofficially referred to as the Hoopoe Mk II, the Panther III-powered aircraft had been purchased by the Air Ministry and was then placed on experimental charge, being flown by Armstrong Siddeley and the RAE until, in 1932, it was scrapped.

Gloster S.S.18 and S.S.19

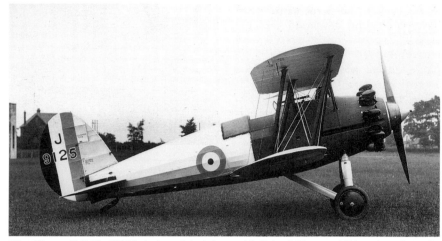

The Gloster S.S.18, J9125, in its original form with Bristol Mercury IIA engine; from this aeroplane stemmed the Gladiator, the RAF's last biplane fighter. (Photo: via Derek James)

When the Fairey Aviation Company acquired American Curtiss D-12 liquid-cooled in-line engines for its Fox light bomber in 1925 — an aircraft which outpaced every in-service RAF interceptor of the day — the Air Ministry had issued Specification F.9/26 for a fighter intended to replace the Gamecock and Siskin three or four years hence. A maximum speed of around 170 mph was implicit, but the requirements made only one concession to technical advance in specifying a predominantly metal structure, but clearly continued to favour an air-cooled radial engine and stuck to the age-old armament formula of twin synchronized Vickers guns. (It should be pointed out that the current high-powered British in-line engines, such as the Napier Lion and Rolls-Royce Condor, were relatively heavy, and that the new Rolls-Royce F.XI, a derivative of the Falcon,

was still an unknown quantity.)

The courage of Roy Fedden's conviction that in his much-maligned Mercury radial engine lay the foundations of an efficient and reliable powerplant was matched by the dogged determination of Henry Folland to persist with his line of biplane fighters which, by the late 1920s, had been given new lease of life by the successful development of a viable form of metal construction by Gloster Aircraft.

F.9/26 attracted no fewer than nine contenders, but in the early evaluation trials none of them succeeded in meeting the requirements (although Barnwell's Bristol Bulldog, undertaken initially as a private venture, was re-submitted for extended competition against the Hawker Hawfinch, and was declared the winner). As already recorded, Gloster's Goldfinch, failed to measure up to the load carrying demands and, when a new Specification, F.20/27, was drafted, Folland embarked on a new design.

The Gloster S.S.18 was a two-bay biplane, initially fitted with a Bristol Mercury IIA, allegedly capable of delivering 450 hp. Wings and fuselage were all-metal structures, fabric-covered except forward of the cockpit which was metal sheet clad. Twin high tensile steel spars and steel ribs were employed in the wings, the fabric being attached by the patent Gloster wired-on method. Two Vickers guns were located in the sides of the front fuselage, each with 600 rounds.

The S.S.18, J9125, was first flown by Howard Saint in January 1929 and returned a top speed of 183 mph at 10,000 ft. By then, however, it was too late to undertake extensive changes to adapt the S.S.18 for an in-line Rolls-Royce Kestrel, and when the Mercury IIA failed to come up to expectations, Folland decided to change over to the well-tried Bristol Jupiter VII. Flight

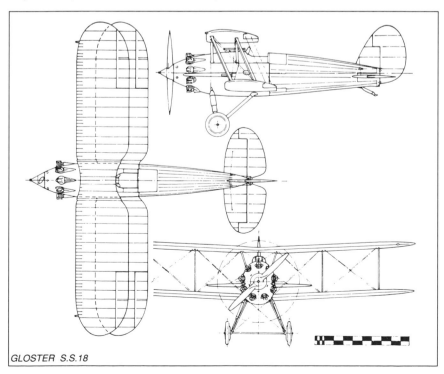

GLOSTER S.S.18

trials with J9125, now designated the S.S.18A, continued until 1930, when further engine changes were made — first to the Armstrong Siddeley Panther III, then to the Panther IIIA. Despite the increased power available from these engines, the two-row radials were much heavier than the Bristol Jupiter and, although they bestowed a maximum speed of 205 mph at around 10,000 ft, Saint experienced handling problems, and Folland decided to return to the Jupiter VIIF, now provided with a Townend ring.

In the meantime, Folland had had a chance to examine the radical new F.7/30 Specification which called for an armament of four machine guns and a top speed of 250 mph. Realising that no amount of cosmetic surgery would coax J9125 up to that speed, Folland now took the bold step of increasing its armament to six guns, leaving the two Vickers where they could be attended to by the pilot in the event of jamming, and mounting drum-fed, but reliable Lewis guns under the top and bottom wings. He argued that, by enabling the guns to be fired in pairs or together, the fighter would possess a much longer duration of fire than those armed with four guns which all exhausted their ammunition together. This argument failed to impress the Air Ministry, particularly as J9125, now re-styled the S.S.19, returned a top speed of only 188 mph at 10,000 ft. Undaunted, Gloster persisted, removing the two Lewis from the top

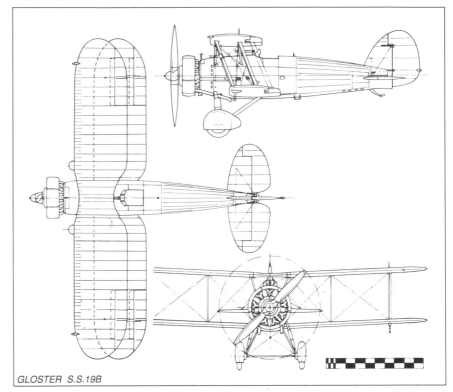

GLOSTER S.S.19B

wing, re-locating the remaining Lewis *inside* the lower wings, fitting wheel spats to the undercarriage and enlarging the fin and rudder; this version, the S.S.19A, possessed a top speed of 204 mph.

The final stage of the saga was approached with the appearance of Bristol's much-improved 570hp Mercury VIS and, thus powered, J9125 (now the S.S.19B) underwent trials with the

A & A E E, whose report, M/572/3, of August 1933 stated that it achieved a speed of 215.5 mph at 16,500 feet. When Bristol announced that the Mercury VIS2 would be available, capable of developing 640 bhp, the Air Ministry stepped in and rewarded Gloster with an initial production order for 24 aircraft in September, to be named the Gauntlet (see page 236).

Although handicapped by its continued use of the Bristol Jupiter VIIF, the two-bay four-gun S.S.19A (seen here with Townend ring, wheel spats and full night flying equipment) had a top speed of 204 mph at 10,000ft — thirty miles an hour faster than the Bristol Bulldog — and reflected Henry Folland's extraordinary attention to design detail. (Photo: Via Derek James)

Type: Single-engine, single-seat, two-bay interceptor biplane.
Manufactuer: Gloster Aircraft Co Ltd, Hucclecote, Gloucester.
Air Ministry Specifications: F.20/27 (S.S.18), F.10/27 and F.7/30 (S.S.19)
Powerplant: S.S.18. 480hp Bristol Mercury IIA, 440hp Jupiter VII and VIIF, Armstrong Siddeley Panther III and IIIA radials; S.S.19. 440hp Bristol Jupiter VIIF, 640hp Mercury VIS and VIS2 radials.
Structure: Fabric-covered all-metal structure with twin steel wing spars.
Dimensions: S.S.18. Span, 32ft 9in; length, 25ft 9in; height, 11ft 10in; wing area, 332 sq ft. S.S.19. Span, 32 ft 9½in; length, 25ft 4in; height, 10ft 2in; wing area, 315 sq ft.
Weights: S.S.18. Tare, 2,195lb; all-up, 3,270lb. S.S.19B. Tare, 2,704lb; all-up, 3,858lb.
Performance: S.S.18. Max speed, 183 mph at 10,000ft; climb to 10,000ft, 13.6 min; service ceiling, 28,000ft. S.S.19B. Max speed, 215 mph at 15,800ft; climb to 20,000ft, 12 min 10 sec; service ceiling, 33,350ft.
Armament: S.S.18. Two 0.303in fixed synchronized Vickers Mk.III machine guns in sides of front fuselage with 600 rounds per gun. S.S.19. As above, plus two Lewis guns under upper wing and two under lower wing, each with a single 97-round drum.
Prototype: One, J9125 (first flown as S.S.18 by Howard Saint in January 1929; as S.S.19 in June 1930). Became Gauntlet prototype.

Saunders-Roe A.10

Henry Knowler had joined Vickers Ltd (Aviation Department) in 1914 at the age of fourteen, and went on to become Chief Designer with S E Saunders Ltd in 1923 (later Saunders-Roe Ltd), a position he was to occupy for the next twenty-nine years. This time span embraced the A.10 biplane fighter and the SR.A/1 twin-jet flying-boat fighter (see page 352). He was one of a number of designers attracted by the surge of fighter Specifications issued during 1926-28 and, as a private venture, designed the A.10 to meet the terms of F.10/27, which called for a 'multi-gun' high-altitude interceptor fighter.

The A.10 was one of the first fighter aircraft to be completed with the new 480hp Rolls-Royce F.XIS supercharged in-line engine (later to become the Kestrel IIS), and was an all-metal, single-bay biplane with dihedral and ailerons on the upper wing only; the rudder was unbalanced. It carried an armament of four synchronized Vickers machine guns — two in the sides of the fuselage and two in the nose decking, with a total of 1,640 rounds of ammunition.

Carrying the SBAC classification number L2 (being an armed aircraft not purchased by the Air Ministry), the A.10 was first flown on 10 January 1929 but experienced cooling problems with the engine whose cooling system included a radiator situated under the

The Saunders-Roe A.10 'multi-gun' fighter prototype. (Photo: via R C Sturtivant)

crankcase. This was provided with roller blind-type shutters which opened and closed between slide-ways in the sides of a chin fairing in the lower part of the nose of the aircraft. The shutters were opened for take-off and low-speed flying, but progressively closed as speed and altitude increased. At the time Knowler designed this system he was unaware that other manufacturers (notably Hawker) were employing a retractable radiator beneath the fuselage, thereby effectively achieving reduced drag as speed increased, not to mention a much slimmer nose cowling.

Further development of the A.10 was pre-empted in 1930 with the issue of Specification F.7/30, also for a 'multi-gun' fighter, but calling for a speed of 250 mph at the same time.

Type: Single-engine, single-seat, single-bay high altitude fighter.
Manufacturer: Saunders-Roe Ltd, East Cowes, Isle of Wight.
Air Ministry Specification: F.10/27.
Powerplant: One 480hp Rolls-Royce F.XIS supercharged twelve-cylinder liquid-cooled in-line engine.
Dimensions: Span, 32ft 0in; length, 24ft 5in.
Weight: All-up, 3,276lb.
Performance: Max speed, 186 mph at 12,500ft; service ceiling, 23,200ft.
Armament: Four synchronized 0.303in Vickers machine guns on sides of fuselage and nose decking with 1,640 rounds of ammunition.
Prototype: One, registered L2 (first flown on 10 January 1929). No production.

Fairey Firefly (Biplanes)

It has been said, with more than a grain of truth, that the Air Ministry never forgave Richard Fairey for introducing the American Curtiss D-12 in-line engine into Britain in 1925, and for having the effrontery to produce the Fox light bomber that was able to show a clean pair of heels to every RAF fighter in sight. That Sir Hugh Trenchard himself had seen fit to direct that the Fox should equip an RAF bomber squadron had not made matters any better. And when

The Fairey Firefly Mk II (F1130) at about the time it was delivered to Martlesham for its Service evaluation in 1929. (Photo: The Fairey Aviation Co Ltd, Neg No R13).

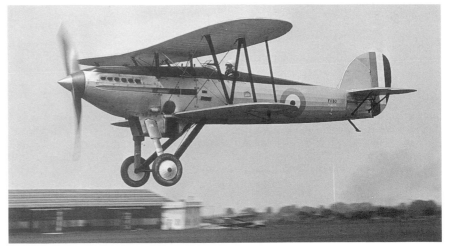

Fairey had produced, as another private venture, a single-seat fighter (which flew on 9 November 1925), also powered by the American engine, the Air Ministry gave it the cold shoulder and even refused to accept it for evaluation, stating that, being primarily of wooden construction, it did not qualify for consideration or Service effort. That aircraft was the Fairey Firefly (in retrospect termed the Firefly Mk I).

However, on the credit side, there is no doubt that the arrival of the Curtiss engine in Britain certainly concentrated minds at the Air Ministry on the obvious benefits of liquid-cooled in-line engines, and hastened support for the emerging Rolls-Royce F.XI engine, so that by 1927 that eminent company could confidently forecast an excellent power/weight ratio and promise early flight-cleared engines.

Undeterred by the implied snub, Fairey set Marcel Lobelle to redesign the Firefly late that year, again without Air Ministry backing, inexplicably retaining the mainly wooden airframe, but including an F.XIS supercharged engine. It was an attractive aircraft with beautifully cowled engine, slim fuselage, and parallel-chord wings with gracefully rounded tips. Ailerons were fitted to both upper and lower wings.

First flown at Hayes on 5 February 1929, the Firefly Mk II quickly demonstrated a sparkling performance and, carrying only its company sequence number (F1130), was authorised to undergo evaluation at Martlesham in May, trials that inevitably developed into an unofficial competition with Sydney Camm's Hawker Hornet proto-

type, which arrived at about the same time. Despite recording a maximum speed of 212 mph (compared with 204 mph by the Hornet), the Firefly was criticised as being much heavier on the controls — and attention naturally centred on the Firefly's wooden airframe. That was the deciding factor that condemned the Firefly to obscurity in Britain.

By the time Lobelle had completed a redesign of the Firefly II with all-metal airframe, it was 1930 before F1130 had been rebuilt (and civil registered as G-ABCN); and Hawker had been

awarded a production contract for its Fury fighter — *née* Hornet.

Now re-designated the Mk IIM, G-ABCN appeared at the 1930 Hendon Display and spent the next two years as a company demonstrator, attending air shows at home and on the continent. These were instrumental in securing for the company an order from the Belgian government for 25 aircraft, followed by licence production of 62 others by the Avions Fairey factory at Gosselies.

Another Firefly II airframe (F1137) was adapted as a naval fighter in 1931, being termed the Mark III; it featured

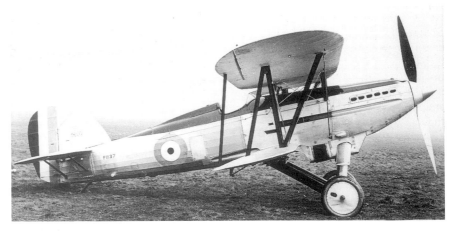

Above: *The Firefly III (F1137) naval fighter prototype. Martlesham reports suggest that the main reason for the Firefly's heavy controls, compared with those of the Hawker Hornet, lay in their being fitted to both upper and lower wings; they certainly failed to impart the same degree of manœuvrability. (Photo: via R C B Ashworth)*

Left: *The Fairey IIIM fitted with twin floats, almost certainly pictured at Calshot, temporary station of the RAF High Speed Flight in 1931. (Photo: via R C B Ashworth)*

enlarged wings and a Kestrel IIS engine, and carried the customary range of naval equipment. Although the company embarked on this as yet another private venture, the aircraft being registered as G-ABFH during manufacture, it was purchased by the Air Ministry before completion, and it emerged as S1592. This Firefly was soon to be strengthened with numerous steel components with a twin-float undercarriage and, as the Mark IIIM, was delivered as a training seaplane to Calshot where the RAF High Speed Flight was preparing for the Schneider Trophy contest. The following year S1592, once more fitted with its wheel undercarriage, was flown by C S Staniland at a number of air displays.

Whether any 'political' stigma attached to the Firefly biplane may never be known. Yet, for all the prejudice — real or imagined — surrounding the Firefly, Fairey's persistence with wooden structures did represent poor judgement, particularly at a time when the Service was divesting itself of the wood-working trades. In other words, no matter how good the Firefly's performance proved to be, the RAF simply did not want it.

The accompanying data table refers to the Firefly Mk II.

Type: Single-engine, single-seat, single-bay biplane interceptor fighter.
Manufacturer: The Fairey Aviation Co Ltd, Hayes, Middlesex.
Powerplant: One 480hp Rolls-Royce F.XI Kestrel I twelve-cylinder liquid-cooled in-line engine.
Dimensions: Span: 31ft 6in; length, 24ft 7¼in; height, 9ft 4¼in; wing area, 236.81 sq ft.
Weights: Tare, 2,387lb; all-up, 3,285lb.
Performance: Max speed, 212 mph at 12,500ft; climb to 10,000ft, 5 min 20 sec; service ceiling, 26,000ft; range, 240 miles.
Armament: Two synchronized 0.303in Vickers machine guns, each with 600 rounds, in the sides of the fuselage.
Prototype: One (company sequence No. F1130; first flown on 5 February 1929). No production for the RAF. (25 aircraft produced for Belgium).

Hawker Hornet and Fury

It is a paradox that the first fighter to join the RAF capable of a level speed of over 200 mph, and arguably the most beautiful fighting biplane ever designed, only served with three squadrons. Yet a paradox also existed in the very fact that Sydney Camm's little masterpiece was ever ordered into production at all, for it first flew at a time when the effects of the Depression were beginning to be reflected in the annual Air Estimates and *after* the RAF's standard fighter for the next six years — the Bristol Bulldog — had been selected and was already in full-scale production. And a fully-equipped Fury cost almost 25 per cent more than a fully-equipped Bulldog.

Genesis of the Fury lay in the logical marriage between the Hawker F.20/27 and the 420hp Rolls-Royce F.XI (Kestrel) in 1928, without ignoring the lessons learned in building the Hart light bomber and the naval Hoopoe prototype. The first opportunity to display Camm's latest creations was the 1929 Olympia Aero Show, at which both the Hart and the Hornet (as the new fighter was then known) were displayed.

The Hornet had been first flown by Bulman in March 1929, but within a month the supercharged 480hp Kestrel IS had been fitted, and almost immediately replaced by one of the first 525hp Kestrel IIS flight engines. On 27 May it paid the first of several visits to the A &

The Hawker Hornet J9682 during one of its visits to Martlesham Heath in 1929. (Photo: Air Ministry (A & AEE), Neg Neg No 1260).

AEE where, as previously recorded, it underwent an unscheduled comparative assessment with the Fairey Firefly II. At once it drew unstinted praise for its outstanding crispness of control, and returned a maximum speed of 204 mph at 13,000 feet, climbing to 10,000 feet in 5 minutes 30 seconds. The only adverse remarks concerned the unsuitable propeller pitch which seemed to be too coarse.

After the Olympia Show the Hornet returned to Brooklands on 30 July for a host of performance checks, as well as several inspections by Air Ministry technical staff members. At about this time Hawker was asked to quote production costs, and informed that future RAF fighters should carry names that 'reflected ferocity'; the name Fury was accepted and, from 1 January 1930, as the property of the Air Ministry, the aircraft carried the number J9682.

Specification 13/30 was written around

Camm's formal design tender and a contract raised for the production of 21 aircraft, the first three aircraft to be completed in advance of the remainder for a substantial trials programme. Meanwhile J9682 underwent its full Service evaluation at Martlesham in February, going on to Farnborough the following month. At the end of March it was delivered to Tangmere for trials with No 1 (Fighter) Squadron. Unfortunately, in mid-April, it suffered the loss of its upper wing following a collision with a Siskin of No 43 Squadron, and crashed near Chichester.

Loss of the prototype was something of a setback both to the manufacturer and to the Air Ministry test establishments until the first three production Furies could be completed (as it was customary at Hawker and elsewhere for the first batch of production aircraft to complete each stage of assembly together in order to achieve a common

Displaying no obvious external differences from the Hornet, this Fury I, K1927, was the second production aircraft and was scheduled for a rigorous trials programme in 1931. (Photo: Author's Collection)

batch as a company-owned demonstrator and general development aircraft. First flown as a standard fighter with Kestrel IIS on 13 April 1932, and civil registered as G-ABSE, it came to be known as the Intermediate Fury and, not only undertook numerous displays at home and in Europe, but was flown with Kestrel VIS with a Rolls-Royce Goshawk supercharger, Kestrel VI, and Goshawk III engines. It was also flown with wheel spats, cantilever undercarriage, internally-sprung wheels and electro-magnetic bomb gear.

Camm was also aware in 1930 of the

state of preparation and to fully equip the first operational unit together). It was therefore not until May 1931 that the first Fury squadron was fully re-equipped, twelve aircraft being taken on charge at Tangmere by No 43 (Fighter) Squadron, commanded by Sqn Ldr Leonard Horatio Slatter OBE, DSC*, DFC (later Air Marshal Sir Leonard, KBE, CB, DSC*, DFC). A second production order for 48 Furies was placed that year, and in February 1932 No 1 (Fighter) Squadron, commanded by Sqn Ldr Charles Basil Slater Spackman DFC (later Air Vice-Marshal, CB, CBE, DFC*) at Tangmere, and No 25 (Fighter) Squadron, commanded by Sqn Ldr W E G Bryant MBE at Hawkinge, took delivery of their new fighters.

It will be noted that these three squadrons were based at the RAF's two fighter stations on the South Coast and, indeed, came to represent the premier fighter squadrons of the RAF. Intense rivalry now existed between them in the various applied flying competitions, for air drill, air gunnery, navigation, and for the coveted Sassoon Trophy for the highest aggregate placing in the other competitions. The latter trophy was to be won outright by No 25 Squadron in 1935 (then commanded by Sqn Ldr William Forster Dickson DSO, OBE, AFC (later Chief of the Air Staff as Marshal of the RAF Sir William, GCB, KBE, DSO, AFC), having performed tied-together aerobatics in three consecutive Hendon Displays, and won the gunnery prize two years running. As further reward, No 25 Squadron was selected as the first to receive the Fury Mk II in November 1936.

It is necessary, however, to return to 1931 to trace the various Fury developments that took place after the placing of the first Mark I production order, and led to the introduction of the Mark II six

years later. Obviously Hawker hoped to receive large production orders as the initial batch entered service, and after the first three Furies had been allocated to test establishments it was decided to add an extra aircraft to the first RAF

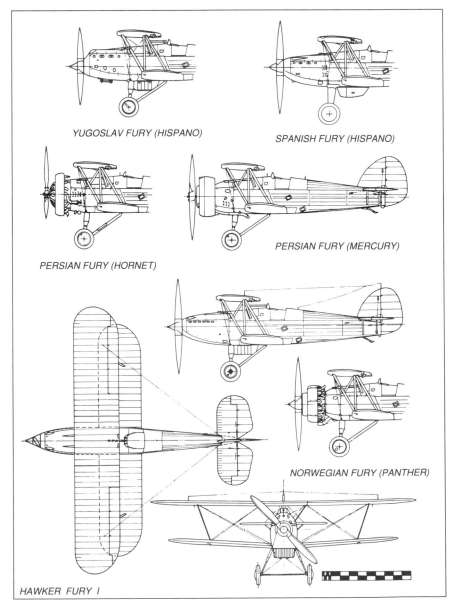

YUGOSLAV FURY (HISPANO)

SPANISH FURY (HISPANO)

PERSIAN FURY (HORNET)

PERSIAN FURY (MERCURY)

NORWEGIAN FURY (PANTHER)

HAWKER FURY I

The Hawker Intermediate Fury, G-ABSE, at Brooklands shortly after its first flight in 1932. The three Hawker test pilots, Bulman, Sayer and Lucas, all flew this aeroplane on sales demonstrations throughout Europe and were successful in attracting useful export orders for the Fury. (Photo: A J Jackson Collection)

Air Staff's determination to embark on a complete modernization and ultimate expansion of the RAF's fighter arm, having discussed future fighter equipment with Sir John Salmond before the retirement of Sir Hugh Trenchard as Chief of the Air Staff on 1 January 1930. With the issue in draft form of Specification F.7/30 that year (about which more is told under later aircraft entries), Camm realised that, if the Fury was to be considered in its context, it would require considerable development and modification, not least in the accommodation of a new engine. In brief, F.7/30 demanded a day-and-night single-seat fighter capable of a 250 mph top speed, a four-gun armament, the ability to reach 10,000 feet in under four minutes and a service ceiling of 30,000 feet. Added to this was the Air Ministry's stipulation that the aircraft should be powered by the Rolls-Royce Goshawk steam-cooled engine, being persuaded

that this was a logical advance on the traditional water cooling system.

The lext logical step was therefore to build an entirely new Fury embodying all the latest results of tunnel tests and trial installations so far undertaken on the standard aircraft, as well as G-ABSE. This aeroplane was variously termed the High-Speed Fury and Super-Fury, K3586, first flown by Bulman at Brooklands on 3 May 1933, placed on Air Ministry experimental charge, and leased back to Hawker. Although the design of K3586 had been considerably influenced by F.7/30, a special Specification, F.14/32, was prepared to be used for general airframe and engine development, as well as enabling it to be evaluated by the Service as an interceptor.

The High-Speed Fury was flown with a wide range of Rolls-Royce engines in the course of over 800 hours' in the air, including the 525hp Kestrel IIS,

600hp Kestrel (Special), 525hp Kestrel IIIS, 600hp Kestrel VIS, 695hp Goshawk III and Goshawk B.41, and the 980hp PV.12 (later named the Merlin); it was variously fitted with swept-back upper wings, swept-forward lower wings, V-type interplane struts and steam-condensers along the entire leading edge of the upper wing. Most of its life was spent with wheel spats of different designs, and when flown by Bulman in 1934 with a Kestrel VIS, swept-back upper and swept-forward lower wings with V-struts, K3586 returned a maximum level speed of 258 mph at 12,500 feet — the fastest yet attained by a British fighter. Unfortunately this could not be regarded as satisfying Specification F.7/30 as only two guns were carried, nor was it achieved with a Goshawk engine.

As the industry began to suspect that the Air Ministry had picked a loser in the Goshawk engine (as a fighter powerplant), Camm suggested offering a less radically altered version of the original Fury as a short term replacement for those fighters already in service (includ-

Successive squadron commanders of RAF fighter squadrons aspired to lead their pilots through aerobatic displays, particularly at the annual Hendon Display. With plenty of power available, the Fury was particularly suitable for formation aerobatics, and No 25 Squadron's speciality was air drill and aerobatics with all nine aircraft attached by elastic cords with streamers, as shown here. (Photo: Author's Collection)

The High Speed Fury, K3586, seen here with a Goshawk steam-cooled engine and steam-condensers along the full length of the upper wing. Although these condensers were slightly heavier than a conventional radiator, the absence of the latter resulted in a significant reduction in drag. In this configuration, it might be said that the Fury represented the zenith of biplane fighter design. (Photo: Author's Collection)

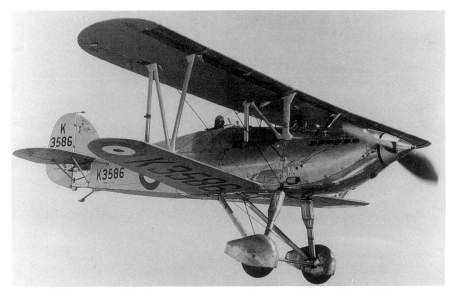

ing the ageing Bulldog), in effect a production version of the Intermediate Fury with Kestrel VI, wheel spats and locally-strengthened airframe. A standard Fury of the original production batch, K1935, was accordingly modified and flown at Martlesham, recording a maximum speed of 228 mph. Owing, however, to the need to include greater fuel tankage to offset the new Kestrel's higher consumption, this speed came to be reduced to 223 mph.

A new Specification, 6/35, was formulated around Camm's proposal and an order for 23 aircraft, Fury Mk IIs, was placed with Hawker in 1935, and was followed by another for 89 (the latter being sub-contracted to General Aircraft Ltd of Hanworth, owing to Hawker factories being stretched to the limit). Following the first deliveries to No 25 (Fighter) Squadron, Fury IIs went on to join Nos 41, 73 and 87 Squadrons in 1937.

Total Fury production for the Royal Air Force amounted to 117 Mk Is and 113 Mk IIs. However, Hawker also conducted a lively export business between 1931 and 1937, supplying 16 Furies to Yugoslavia, 22 to Persia, three to Portugal, three to Spain and one to Norway. These aircraft were delivered with a variety of engines as specified by their customers, including 500hp Hispano-Suiza 12Nb and 720hp Lorraine Petrel Hfrs (Yugoslavia), Armstrong Siddeley Panther IIIA (Norway), 750hp Pratt & Whitney Hornet S2B1G and Bristol Mercury VISP (Persia). The last ten aircraft sold to Yugoslavia in 1936, powered by 745hp Kestrel XVI engines, were four-gun fighters with low-drag radiators and cantilever undercarriage with internally-sprung wheels, and possessed a top speed of 242 mph — the fastest of any production Fury. Some ex-RAF Furies were also supplied to South Africa.

Ironically, the beautiful Hawker Fury was ultimately eclipsed by the Gloster Gladiator, which was eventually declared the successful tender to Specification F.7/30, meeting in all respects the performance demands — yet did so with a radial engine. That engine, moreover, was none other than Roy Fedden's Bristol Mercury.

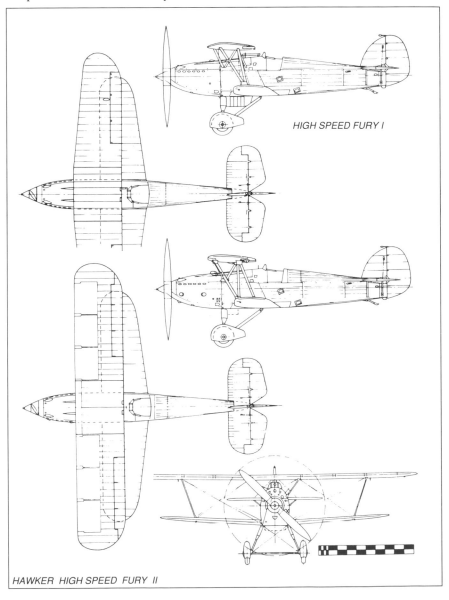

HIGH SPEED FURY I

HAWKER HIGH SPEED FURY II

Type: Single-engine, single-seat, single-bay biplane interceptor.

Manufacturers: H G Hawker Engineering Co Ltd (from 1933 Hawker Aircraft Ltd), Kingston and Brooklands, Surrey; General Aircraft Ltd, Hanworth (Mk II).

Air Ministry Specifications: F.20/27, 13/30, 13/32, F.14/32 and 6/35 (Mk II).

Powerplant: Mk I. One 525hp Rolls-Royce Kestrel IIS 12-cylinder liquid-cooled supercharged in-line engine driving 2-blade Watts wooden propeller. Mk II. 640hp Kestrel VI. For other engines, see text.

Structure: All-metal construction.

Dimensions: Span, 30ft 0in; length, 26ft 8in (Mk I), 26ft 9in (Mk II); height, 10ft 2in; wing area, 252 sq ft.

Weights: Mk I. Tare, 2,623lb; all-up, 3,490lb. Mk II. Tare, 2,734lb; all-up, 3,609lb.

Performance: Mk I. Max speed, 207 mph at 14,000ft; climb to 10,000ft, 4 min 25 sec; service ceiling, 28,000ft; range, 305 miles. Mk II. Max speed, 223 mph at 16,500ft; climb to 10,000ft, 3 min 50 sec; service ceiling, 29,500ft; range, 270 miles.

Armament: Two synchronized 0.303in Vickers Mk III (on Mk I) or V (on Mk II) machine guns in upper nose decking with 600 rounds per gun.

Production for the RAF: 117 Mk Is (K1926-K1946, K2035-K2082, K2874-K2883, K2899-K2903, K3730-K3742 and K5662-K5682); 113 Mk IIs: 24 by Hawker (K7263-K7286) and 89 by General Aircraft (K8218-K8306).

Summary of Service: Fury Mk Is served with Nos 1, 25 and 43 (Fighter) Squadrons, as well as No 3 Flying Training School, Central Flying School, and the Advanced Training Squadron, RAF College, Cranwell; Mk IIs served with Nos 25, 41, 73 and 87 (Fighter) Squadrons, and Nos 2, 3, 5, 6, 7, 8, 9, 10 and 11 Flying Training Schools, No. 1 Air Armament School and No. 2 AACU.

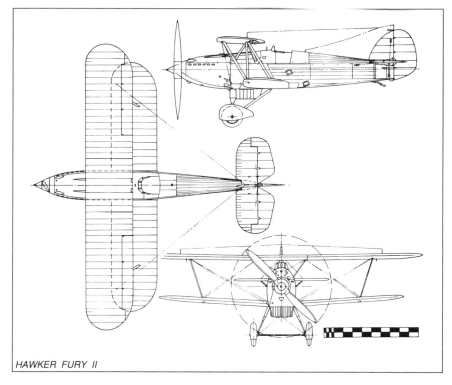

HAWKER FURY II

Fury IIs of No 25 (Fighter) Squadron taxying out at the 1937 Hendon Display. To many who recall those pre-War displays, the Furies were always the highspot. (Photo: Author's Collection)

Short Gurnard

During the early 1920s Short Brothers found themselves without an aerodrome from which to fly their landplanes when the Marine Experimental Establishment moved to Felixstowe and Grain was closed down. Although the company had facilities at Lympne, that aerodrome was too far away to conduct day-to-day testing of landplanes. When, however, a number of Specifications were issued that were suitable for designs to be tendered by the company, Lympne came to be used increasingly from 1927. One such set of requirements was set out in

The Gurnard Mk I prototype, N228, at Martlesham Heath during its competitive evaluation with the Hawker Osprey in the autumn of 1929. (Photo: Air Ministry (A & AEE) Neg No 6144, dated 23 October 1929)

Another view of the Gurnard I, N228, here shown fitted with the twin-float undercarriage during its water-handling trials with the Marine Experimental Establishment at Felixstowe. Like the Hawker Osprey, the Gurnard was fitted with ailerons on the upper wing only, and proved to be fully aerobatic with wheel and float undercarriage alike.(Photo: RAF Museum, Neg No P020468)

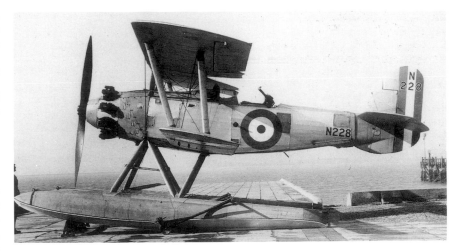

Specification O.22/26, calling for a two-seat carrier-borne naval fighter capable of being converted to a twin-float spotter-reconnaissance seaplane in four hours.

Shorts tendered the Gurnard single-bay biplane, the Mark I being powered by a 525hp Bristol Jupiter X supercharged radial engine, and the Mark II by a 530hp Rolls-Royce F.XIIS (Kestrel IIS) water-cooled supercharged in-line engine; one prototype of each version was ordered in 1927, being numbered N228 and N229 respectively.

N229, equipped as a floatplane, was completed first and was flown by John Lankester Parker on 16 April 1929, but the pilot only just managed to alight safely on the Medway river when it was found that the ailerons were considerably overbalanced. This was quickly corrected and the Gurnard I landplane was flown successfully at Lympne on 8 May. N229 was also converted to a wheel undercarriage and was delivered to Martlesham by Parker on the 12th.

The Jupiter Gurnard was flown both with and without Townend ring, and the two prototypes underwent official evaluation by the A & AEE and the MAEE in the context of O.22/26 in competition with the Hawker Osprey prototype (converted from the Hart). Although the Short aeroplanes fully satisfied the requirements demanded, the Hawker tender was declared the winner, probably on account of the degree of commonality with the RAF's light bomber.

In 1931 the Gurnard II was fitted with an experimental central float amphibian undercarriage with underwing balancing floats and landing wheels which folded down on either side of the central float. In this form Parker first flew N229 on 15 June that year, and nine days later it was displayed at the Hendon Display as New Type No 7. Thereafter it was employed to test various engine cooling systems.

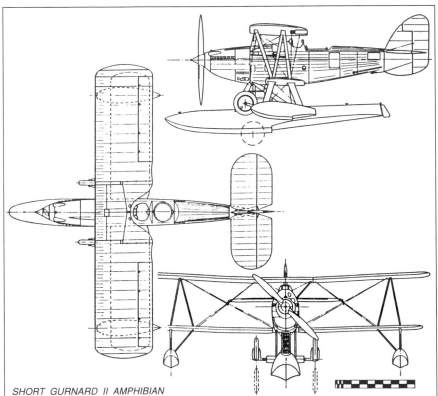

SHORT GURNARD II AMPHIBIAN

Type: Single-engine, two-seat, single-bay biplane, landplane, seaplane and amphibian fighter.

Manufacturer: Short Brothers (Rochester and Bedford) Ltd, Rochester, Kent.

Air Ministry Specification: O.22/26

Powerplant: Mk. I. One 525hp Bristol Jupiter X supercharged radial engine; Mk II. One 530hp Rolls-Royce Kestrel IIS supercharged in-line engine.

Structure: Fuselage of welded steel-tubular box-girder construction with fabric-covered detachable panels. Wing structure of duralumin throughout with corrugated box-spars and tubular lattice ribs.

Dimensions: Mk I landplane. Span, 37ft 0in; length, 28ft 7in; wing area, 429 sq ft. Mk II floatplane. Span, 37ft 0in; length, 31ft 6in; wing area, 429 sq ft.

Weights: Mk I landplane. Tare, 3,086lb; all-up, 4,785lb. Mk II floatplane. Tare, 3,660lb; all-up, 5,194lb. Amphibian. All-up, 5,500lb.

Performance: Mk I landplane. Max speed, 160 mph. Mk II floatplane. Max speed, 162 mph. Amphibian. Max speed, 132 mph.

Armament: One synchronized 0.303in Vickers machine gun in nose decking, offset to port, and provision for one Lewis gun with Scarff ring on rear cockpit.

Prototypes: Two, N228 and N229 (N229 flown first on 16 April 1929 by J L Parker).

Blackburn Nautilus

Apart from the Handley Page H.P.37 project, which was not built, four designs to Specification O.22/26 were submitted and came to be ordered by the Air Ministry, the second of which to fly was Maj Bumpus' Blackburn 2F.1 Nautilus, a somewhat ponderous two-bay biplane whose fuselage was located midway between the upper and lower wings, the space between the fuselage and the lower wing being occupied by a fairing which housed the radiator for the 525hp Rolls-Royce F.XIIMS (Kestrel II) water-cooled in-line engine.

Wing-folding was achieved without the necessity for jury struts (as, for instance, required by the Hawker Osprey), and the Nautilus featured substantial inboard interplane struts, the forward strut on each side being a class one stressed member of high tensile steel, faired with a wooden sheath. Wide-span Frise-type ailerons were fitted on upper and lower wings which featured large trailing-edge cutouts to improve the downward view from the cockpits. Provision was made for single- and twin-float undercarriages as alternatives to wheels.

The exceptionally slim engine cowling lines were to some extent spoiled by the ungainly radiator fairing, and this, as well as thick wings and a plethora of wing, undercarriage and tail struts must have been responsible for the poor speed performance which, nevertheless, was marginally above the minimum demanded.

First flight of the sole Nautilus prototype, N234, was made by T Neville Stack early in May 1929. However he evidently reported unsatisfactory engine cooling and flaws in the aircraft's handling, and flight trials were not begun in earnest until 21 August by Flt Lt A M ('Dasher') Blake, by which time the underfuselage radiator fairing had been modified and a narrower-chord elevator fitted.

The competitive evaluation trials were conducted at Martlesham during October and, together with the Naval Hart (Hawker Osprey prototype) and Fairey Fleetwing, the Nautilus joined No 405 Flight, the Fleet Air Arm's fighter trials unit, at Gosport for carrier trials aboard HMS *Furious* on 1 January 1930. Al-

The Blackburn Nautilus, N234, in Fleet Air Arm insignia after being allotted to Naval communications duties; the rear gun and mounting had been removed to enable a passenger to be carried in more comfort than previously. (Photo: A J Jackson Collection)

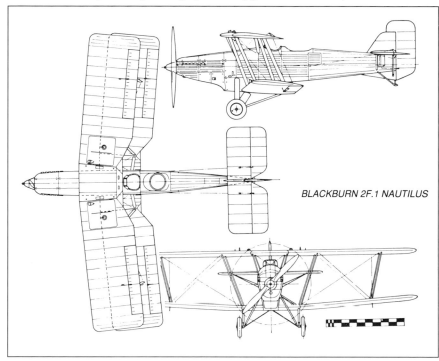

BLACKBURN 2F.1 NAUTILUS

though the Blackburn aeroplane was rejected on several counts (among them poor access to on-board equipment, poor rate of roll and a suspicion of incipient tail flutter above 150 mph), N234 was taken on Air Ministry Service charge, and used for ship-to-shore communications duties aboard HMS *Furious*, and later between Martlesham and other airfields.

Type: Single-engine, two-seat, two-bay biplane interceptor and spotter/reconnaissance aircraft.

Manufacturer: The Blackburn Aeroplane & Motor Co Ltd, Leeds and Brough, Yorkshire.

Air Ministry Specification: O.22/26.

Powerplant: One 525hp Rolls-Royce F.XIIMS supercharged water-cooled in-line engine.

Structure: All-metal (steel and duralumin) structure, mainly fabric-covered.

Dimensions: Span, 37ft 0in; length, 31ft 8in; height, 10ft 10in; wing area, 458 sq ft.

Weights: Tare, 3,223lb; all-up, 4,750lb.

Performance: Max speed, 154 mph at 5,000ft; service ceiling, 18,800ft.

Armament: One synchronized 0.303in Vickers machine gun in port side of fuselage, and provision for one Lewis gun with Scarff ring on rear cockpit.

Prototype: N234 (first flown by T Neville Stack in May 1929).

Fairey Fleetwing

First flown at Northolt on 16 May 1929, Marcel Lobelle's Fairey Fleetwing two-seat fighter/fleet spotter reconnaissance aircraft, designed to O.22/26, was yet another example of Richard Fairey's persistent use of a largely wooden airframe, despite the Air Ministry's insistence on an all-metal structure.

Aerodynamically the Fleetwing, of which a single prototype, N235, was produced, was an exceptionally clean aeroplane, with elegantly styled engine cowling blending with a slim, gracefully tapering fuselage. The single-bay wings carried ailerons top and bottom, and slats were fitted on the upper wing leading edge. If one feature marred the fighter's general appearance it was the unnecessary use of very broad N-type interplane and centre section struts.

This attention to design detail resulted in a top speed of 169 mph at 12,500 feet, and had the prototype, when it appeared for the official trials at Martlesham in October 1929, featured the metal wings — with which it was fitted later — there is no doubt but that the Service would have been more generous in its verdict. Nevertheless it was accepted to go forward to participate in carrier trials aboard HMS

The Fairey Fleetwing, N235. (Photo: Real Photographs Co Ltd., Neg No 2791)

Furious in January 1930 with No 405 (Trials) Flight of the Fleet Air Arm; the ultimate result was, however, inevitable, and the verdict in favour of the Hawker Naval Hart (Osprey) could not be altered by Fairey's promise to modify the Fleetwing with metal wings.

To some observers, the selection of the Hawker entry (see below) was a foregone conclusion, as the Kingston company had been developing the basic design for a year longer than the other prototype manufacturers. To Fairey, however, it seemed no less than a continuation of the seemingly petty prejudice that was said to have existed in the Air Ministry against the company since 1925.

Type: Single-engine, two-seat, single-bay biplane fleet spotter reconnaissance fighter.
Manufacturer: The Fairey Aviation Co Ltd, Hayes, Middlesex.
Air Ministry Specification: O.22/26
Powerplant: One 480hp Rolls-Royce F.XIIMS (Kestrel IIMS) water-cooled in-line engine.
Dimensions: Span, 37ft 0in; length, 29ft 4in; height, 11ft 5in; wing area, 363 sq ft.
Weight: All-up, 4,737lb.
Performance: Max speed, 169 mph at 12,500ft.
Armament: One synchronized 0.303in Vickers machine gun in port side of fuselage and provision for one Lewis gun with Fairey mounting on rear cockpit.
Prototype: One, N235; first flown at Northolt on 16 May 1929. No production.

Hawker Osprey

The development of Sydney Camm's Hawker Hart light bomber is beyond the scope of this work, yet the fact that it came to provide the basis of two fighters, one ordered into production for the Fleet Air Arm and the other for the Royal Air Force, justify a brief summary of the bomber's early fortunes, for the Hart prototype also served as the evaluation aircraft for the purpose of the O.22/26 trials.

Specification 12/26, issued in 1926, had outlined proposals for a light bomber

The Naval Hart, J9052, fully modified to Stage II of Specification O.22/26, with Short F.45 Type I fighter floats, pictured on the slipway at the Marine Aircraft Experimental Establishment, Felixstowe, on 6 January 1931. (Photo: MAEE, Neg No 6888C)

to enter service with the RAF in 1930, and in due course came to be amended in the light of Camm's suggestion to employ the new Rolls-Royce F.XI in-line engine in place of the Falcon X. It was to be an all-metal single-bay biplane with a two-man crew, and capable of carrying a bomb load of up to 520 pounds.

When preliminary design performance figures suggested that the light

bomber would possess a speed of around 180 mph and a ceiling of about 23,000 feet, it was logical for Hawker to look more carefully at Specification O.22/26, issued in draft form towards the end of 1926, to see whether the Hawker design could also be considered in the context of the naval fleet spotter-cum-fighter. Indeed, so closely did the two requirements resemble each other that it seemed that the Air Ministry had used a carbon

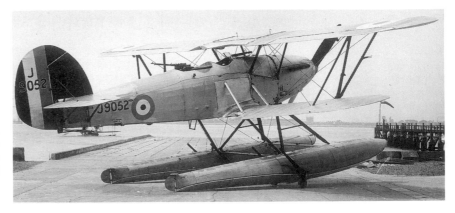

One of the trial Ospreys, S1699, originally a Mark I, but completed as a special Mark III with extensive use of stainless steel; a much lower proportion of the standard Mark III airframe was constructed in this material. (Photo: H G Hawker Engineering Co Ltd, Neg No 31H)

copy of 12/26 to begin setting out the naval requirement, substituting additional equipment and airframe strengthening for the 12/26's bomb load. The inclusion of provision for wing folding seemed to be the main divergence from the light bomber's structural requirements.

Fortunately the Rolls-Royce F.XI engine was supplied on time, enabling the Hart bomber prototype, J9052, to be completed and flown in June 1928, so that before the end of the year it had completed its preliminary trials with No 22 Squadron at the A & AEE, and by May 1929 it had provided the Air Ministry with sufficient information to enable a production order to be placed.

Meanwhile Camm's small staff had completed the drawings necessary to modify J9052 to meet O.22/26, such as strengthening some 46 areas of the airframe to withstand catapult loads, and making provision for wing folding. The latter involved constructing wing stubs integral with the fuselage, to which the lower wings would be hinged, and incorporating attachment points for jury struts to maintain box rigidity during folding.

J9052 was entirely rebuilt with the airframe strengthening and a 525hp Kestrel VI in less than three weeks, and was flown by Bulman in mid-June, and before the end of that month the aircraft had passed through the hands of No 22 Squadron at Martlesham and performed its first deck landing. It joined No 405 Flight on 1 November (more than a month before any other O.22/26 contender) and completed the official deck trials aboard HMS *Furious* early in January 1930.

An Osprey, S1694, on the cruiser HMS Leander's *catapult on 9 September 1933. The photograph illustrates the various jury struts necessary to prevent the aircraft from being damaged by winds while in this exposed position. These include V-struts under the lower wings, the wing-folding V-struts, the stays between the stern extremities of the floats, and the support struts between the lower wingtips and the floats while the wing is in the folded position. (Photo: RAF Station, Mount Batten, Neg Ref.R/224/G)*

Thus far the folding wings had not been mandatory in the official trials, and J9052 returned to Brooklands for their inclusion. In July J9052, having been declared the winning contender under O.22/26, was delivered to Farnborough for catapult trials, successful completion of which was followed by Stage 2 conversion to accommodate a twin-float undercarriage. Wind-tunnel tests had shown that the fitting of these floats would require the fin and rudder to be slightly enlarged and a distinctive new tail outline was introduced forthwith. A visit to the MAEE at Felixstowe in December for water handling trials confirmed that no unforeseen problems existed, the seaplane returning a maximum speed of 146 mph at 4,700 feet with a Kestrel IIMS engine installed and all specified military equipment fitted.

Its experimental responsibilities now completed, J9052 returned to Brooklands with its wheel undercarriage restored and underwent thorough overhaul be-

fore accompanying No 407 Flight of the Fleet Air Arm on a sales tour to the Argentine aboard HMS *Eagle*. On return to Britain the aircraft resumed flying with Hawker until it was wrecked in an accident while taking off with crossed aileron controls on 9 May 1931.

Meanwhile success in the O.22/26 trials had been followed by an order for twenty-eight aircraft, S1677-S1704, of which the first two were regarded as prototypes (some redundant Hart features had been retained in J9052), the name Osprey being formally confirmed.

Specification 19/30 set out the Osprey I's standard of preparation, namely Kestrel IIMS engine and provision for Short F.45 Type I floats. S1677 and S1678 underwent performance comparison trials at the MAEE, recording almost identical figures to those obtained with J9052.

Osprey Is entered service with Nos 404, 407 and 409 Flights of the Fleet Air Arm in November 1932, and with No

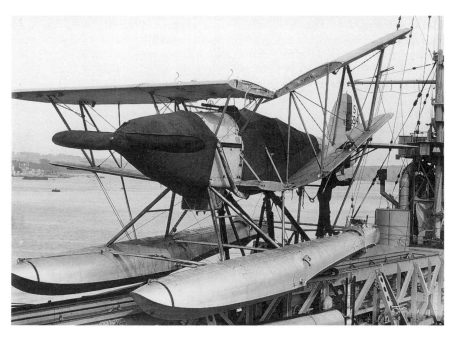

An Osprey III, K3628, of No 801 Squadron, flying from HMS Courageous during the late 1930s. It is carrying full night flying equipment and is fitted with light bomb racks under the wings. (Photo: Author's Collection)

405 Flight the following month, each unit taking delivery of four aircraft. A second order for seventeen aircraft, placed early in 1931, allowed an increase in Flight establishment to six aircraft, but in April 1933 the Fleet Air Arm underwent some re-organization. No 402 Flight (with Nimrods) joined No 404 Flight to form No 800 Squadron under the command of Lt-Cdr Charles James Norman Atkinson, aboard HMS *Courageous*. No 408 (Nimrods) combined with No 409 to form No 802 Squadron under Sqn Ldr Edward Michael Conolly Abel-Smith, embarked in HMS *Glorious*.

The second batch of Ospreys, originally termed Mark IIs, were mostly completed as Mark IIIs with float attachments to accommodate Short F.51 or F.59 Type II floats, and incorporated certain fuselage and wing-fold components manufactured in stainless steel (following tests on three Osprey Is whose airframes were constructed almost entirely in this material in an effort to resist sea water corrosion).

In common with other seaplanes of the time, an Osprey, S1700, underwent trials (as allowed for in O.22/26) with a central float undercarriage and outrigged balancing floats. This aircraft, also largely constructed in stainless steel, remained at Felixstowe for many months before being retired to the RAF College, Cranwell, as a ground instruction airframe.

From mid-1933 until 1935 all Ospreys were delivered as Mark IIIs, these aircraft equipping No 801 Squadron, embarked in HMS *Furious* under the command of Sqn Ldr Sydney Leo Gregory Pope (later Gp Capt, CB, CBE, DFC, AFC), and No 803 Squadron aboard HMS *Eagle*. The latter Squadron, commanded by Sqn Ldr Robert Rule Graham, transferred to HMS *Hermes* while on the China Station, its Ospreys taking

Type: Single-engine, single-seat, single-bay wheel- or float-equipped biplane fleet spotter reconnaissance fighter.

Manufacturer: H G Hawker Engineering Co Ltd (Hawker Aircraft Ltd from 1933), Kingston and Brooklands, Surrey.

Air Ministry Specifications: O.22/26, 19/30 (Osprey Mk I), 10/33 (Osprey Mk III and stainless steel), 26/35 (Osprey Mk IV).

Powerplant: One 525hp Rolls-Royce Kestrel IIMS supercharged twelve-cylinder water-cooled in-line engine; also 600hp Kestrel V (Osprey Mk IV).

Dimensions: Span, 37ft 0in (15ft 7¼in folded); length, 29ft 4in (31ft 10½in as floatplane); height, 10ft 5in (12ft 5in as floatplane); wing area, 339 sq ft.

Weights: Landplane. Tare, 3,405lb; all-up, 4,950lb. Floatplane. All-up, 5,570lb.

Performance: Landplane. Max speed, 168 mph at 5,000ft; climb to 10,000ft, 7 min 40 sec; service ceiling, 23,500ft. Floatplane. Max speed, 146 mph at 4,700ft; climb to 10,000ft, 10min 30 sec; service ceiling, 20,700ft.

Armament: One synchronized 0.303in Vickers Mk II or III machine gun in port side of fuselage with 600 rounds; one Lewis gun with Hawker mounting on rear cockpit with six 97-round magazines; racks for either two 112lb or eight 20lb bombs under wings.

Prototype: One (O.22/26), J9052 (modified Hart prototype, first flown as Osprey by Bulman at Brooklands in June 1929).

Production: Total of 133. (45 Mark Is, S1677-S1704 and K2774-K2790; 62 Mark IIIs, K3615-K3653, K3914-K3920, K3954 and K4322-K4336; 26 Mark IVs, K5742-K5767). Some Mk Is completed or modified as Mk IIIs, and some Mk IIIs modified as Mk IVs.

Summary of Service: Ospreys served with Nos 403, 404, 405, 406, 407, 409, 433, 444 and 445 Flights, and with Nos 701, 711, 712, 713, 714, 715, 716, 718, 750, 755, 757, 758, 759, 800, 801, 802 ans 803 Squadrons.

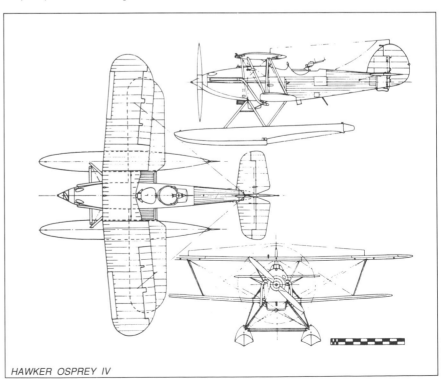

HAWKER OSPREY IV

part in the operations to recapture the vessel *Tungchow*, threatened by mutiny in January 1935.

In addition to these Squadrons, float-equipped Ospreys served aboard ships of the 1st, 2nd, 3rd, 4th, 5th, 6th and 8th Cruiser Squadrons of the Home and Mediterranean Fleets, and on the China, South Africa, American and West Indies Stations, and on ships of the 1st Battle Squadron.

In 1935 a new Specification, 26/35, called for the 600hp Kestrel V engine to be fitted, together with the Vickers Mk III machine gun, and twenty-six Osprey IVs, thus equipped, were produced. These, and about a dozen modified Mark IIIs, equipped Nos 701, 711, 712,

713, 714, 715, 716 and 718 (Catapult) Squadrons from July 1936 onwards.

Ospreys continued to serve with the Fleet, No 802 Squadron being the last operational unit to give up its aircraft in May 1939. Nevertheless the aircraft survived as land-based trainers with naval telegraphist/air gunner training squadrons as well as the Eastleigh pilots' conversion course school until 1942.

Hawker also sold Ospreys abroad,

four being supplied to Sweden with licence-built Mercury engines, and two Kestrel-powered aircraft to Portugal. One aircraft was supplied to Spain; it had been the company-owned demonstrator (G-AEBD) but a purchase order from Spain in 1935 called for a 620hp Hispano-Suiza 12Xbr engine to be fitted in 1936; it subsequently fought with the Republican Air Force during the Spanish Civil War.

The Osprey S1700, fitted with the experimental central float undercarriage with underwing balancing floats, on the slipway at Felixstowe. (Photo: Air Ministry)

Vickers Type 143 (Bolivian Scout)

Early in 1929 the Bolivian government, engaged in war with Paraguay, placed an order for six fighters with Vickers, adapted from the company's Type 141 Scout (see page 186). Because the Bristol Jupiter VIA engine was already in service in other aircraft serving in Bolivia, this engine was specified for the new fighter, requiring fairly extensive re-design of the fuselage. Other specific demands included a stronger undercarriage and underwing hoop skids, on account of the very poor airfield surfaces in use.

The first Type 143 was flown by Fg Off Joseph ('Mutt') Summers on 11 June 1929 at Brooklands, the bulk of the routine flying being taken over by Sqn Ldr Harold James Payn AFC, RAFO, thereafter, and all performance criteria were achieved.

Delivery of the aircraft began in January 1930 and, after re-assembly at Alto La Paz, were test flown by Fg Off Harold William Russell Banting RAFO.

A Bolivian Scout at Brooklands in 1929. A split-axle undercarriage was fitted, and the Jupiter VIA engine drove a Fairey Reed metal propeller. (Photo: Vickers Ltd, Neg No 3354B)

The Scouts proved popular in service with the Bolivian Air Force, then faced with a renewal of the Chaco War with Paraguay. Three surviving Vickers Scouts were flown after the truce broke down in 1932, and are said to have given a good account of themselves until replaced by American Curtiss Hawks.

One Type 143, temporarily fitted with a Jupiter VII, was flown at Martlesham before being returned to standard and delivered to Bolivia.

Type: Single-engine, single-seat, single-bay biplane fighter.
Manufacturer: Vickers (Aviation) Ltd, Weybridge, Surrey.
Powerplant: One 450hp Bristol Jupiter VIA nine-cylinder air-cooled radial engine.
Dimensions: Span, 34ft 0in; length, 27ft 10½in; height, 11ft 3in; wing area, 336 sq ft.
Weights: Tare, 2,246lb; all-up, 3,120lb.
Performance: Max speed, 150 mph at 11,500ft; service ceiling, 20,000ft.
Armament: Two synchronized 0.303in Vickers machine guns in sides of fuselage.
Production: No prototype. Six aircraft delivered to Bolivia, beginning in January 1930. First aircraft flown by J Summers on 11 June 1929.

de Havilland D.H.77

The D.H.77, J9771, in its final form with Napier Rapier II engine, crash pylon, low-pressure tyres and armament removed. (Photo: A J Jackson Collection)

First to fly of the two monoplane prototypes designed to Specification F.20/27 and ordered by the Air Ministry was the D.H.77 (the other being the Vickers Type 151 Jockey, see page 227). Under an arrangement that had existed since 1926, whereby Gloster Aircraft Co Ltd undertook the development of all military de Havilland aircraft, the D.H.77 was designed by W G Carter of Gloster, working in close collaboration with Maj F B Halford who had designed an H-type air-cooled engine in which four banks of cylinders drove a pair of crankshafts, geared together. Under another agreement, signed in 1928, Halford engines of over 404 cu in capacity were built by D Napier & Son at Acton, so that this engine came to be referred to as the Napier H, and later the Rapier.

The D.H.77 itself was an exceptionally ingenious design which, despite its 'Gloster' designer, clearly owed much to de Havilland influence. A metal primary structure with wooden formers and ribs were fabric-covered and this, combined with low installed power/weight ratio of the engine, limited the aircraft's tare weight to 1,655 lb—less than 75 per cent of that of the Vickers Jockey. As would be expected of Britain's leading light aircraft manufacturer, considerable attention was paid to control precision; very large ailerons were

provided, and—unusual at the time—the tailplane was a single all-moving component, providing good spin-recovery characteristics. The semi-cantilever low wing was braced by single broad-chord struts on either side of the fuselage, attached to the wing at the same spar station as the outer rubber-in-compression struts of the fixed, wide-track undercarriage.

The D.H.77, J9771, was first flown by Hubert Broad at de Havilland's Stag Lane aerodrome on 11 July 1929, and in the months following minor adjustments were made in the control surfaces and engine settings, so that on 12 December that year the little interceptor was delivered to No 15 Squadron of the A & AEE at Martlesham Heath for performance evaluation. It appeared at the Hendon Display on 28 June 1930 (as New Type No 3), and in September was

delivered to Glosters to undergo a 100-hour type test of the engine—now termed the Napier Rapier I. Extensive flying trials continued until 1932 when, on 8 December, J9771 was passed to the RAE at Farnborough, and a Rapier II engine with external oil cooler and exhaust manifolds was fitted in 1933; by then the aircraft had also acquired a curved tubular crash pylon over the pilot's windscreen, and enlarged low-pressure tyres on the undercarriage.

The D.H.77 was last flown at the RAE on 1 June 1934, and was withdrawn from use shortly afterwards. Despite its relatively limited power resources, it had proved that by careful attention to design detail excellent performance and handling could be achieved, and it is worth observing that it possessed an almost identical top speed to that of the Hawker Fury I biplane fighter, but on

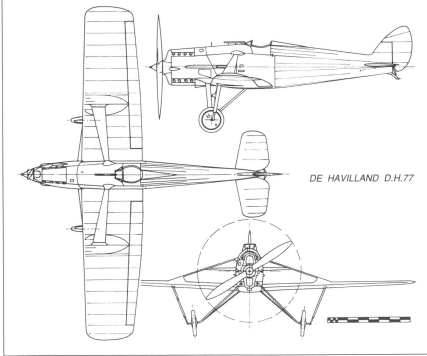

DE HAVILLAND D.H.77

Type: Single-engine, single-seat low-wing monoplane interceptor fighter.

Manufacturers: The de Havilland Aircraft Co Ltd, Stag Lane Aerodrome, Edgware, Middlesex

Air Ministry Specification: F.20/27

Powerplant: One 301hp Napier Halford H (renamed Napier Rapier I); later one 295hp Napier Rapier II; lightweight wooden two-blade propeller.

Structure: Metal primary box girder with wooden secondary frames, all fabric-covered; externally braced low wing with non-retractable undercarriage.

Dimensions: Span, 32ft 2in; length, 24ft 5in; height, 8ft 0in; wing area, 163 sq ft.

Weights: Empty, 1,655lb; loaded, 2,279lb.

Performance: Max speed, 204 mph at 10,000ft; climb to 10,000ft, 4 min 40 sec; service ceiling, 25,900ft.

Armament: Two synchronized 0.303in Vickers Mk II machine guns in sides of front fuselage, with 500 rounds per gun.

Prototype: J9771 (first flown, 11 July 1929, by Hubert Broad at Stag Lane). No production.

less than 60 per cent of the power.

The D.H.77, however, was effectively outdated about six months after it first flew, with the provisional issue of Specification F.7/30 which, in due course, called for fighter armament to be increased to four machine guns, and speeds towards 250 mph. Such demands could never have been met by the lightweight airframe of the D.H.77.

J9771 as it originally appeared, without crash pylon and powered by a Napier Rapier I enigne: (Photo: via R C Sturtivant)

Vickers Type 177

It was while Vickers was engaged in preparing the design of the Bolivian Scout (Type 143), early in 1929, that it became clear that none of the prototype tenders to the naval fighter Specification N.21/26 was likely to be declared the outright winner, and it was decided to add a seventh Scout to the Bolivian batch and, with suitable adaptation, to tender it as a private venture.

To bring it into line with the requirements of N.21/26, the new fighter, the Type 177, was powered by a 540hp Bristol Jupiter XF radial with Townend ring and driving a four-blade propeller. Hydraulic steerable wheel braking was fitted to facilitate on-deck manœuvring, but the split-axle undercarriage of the Bolivian fighter was retained.

The Type 177 (without military number) was first flown by 'Mutt' Summers on 26 November 1929, and the following February it paid a visit to Martlesham for Service assessment — where, incidentally it returned a maximum speed of 190 mph, faster than any of the formally-tendered designs.

The aircraft underwent carrier trials

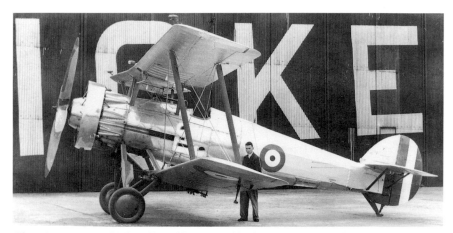

The private venture Vickers Type 177 at Brooklands, complete with full night flying equipment and bomb shackles — mandatory for N.21/26. (Photo: Vickers Ltd, Neg No 4045).

during June aboard HMS *Furious*, by which time the Specification had been allowed to lapse as it seemed almost inevitable that a navalised version (already flying in prototype form) of the Hawker Fury would be adopted for the Fleet Air Arm, and a new Specification had been written around it.

Type: Single-engine, single-seat, single-bay biplane naval interceptor.
Manufacturer: Vickers (Aviation) Ltd, Weybridge, Surrey.
Air Ministry Specification: Private venture design to N.21/26.
Powerplant: One 540hp Bristol Jupiter XF nine-cylinder air-cooled radial engine driving four-blade propeller.
Dimensions: Span, 34ft 3in; length, 27ft 6in; height, 11ft 3in; wing area, 336 sq ft.
Weights: Tare, 2,835lb; all-up, 4,050lb.
Performance: Max speed, 190 mph at 13,120ft; absolute ceiling, 30,000ft.
Armament: Two synchronized 0.303in Vickers machine guns in sides of fuselage.
Prototype: One, un-numbered (first flown by J Summers on 26 November 1929 at Brooklands). No production.

Deployment of British Fighter Squadrons and Flights — January 1930

Home Bases

No 1 Squadron	A.W. Siskin IIIA	Tangmere
No 3 Squadron	Bristol Bulldog IIA	Upavon
No 17 Squadron	Bristol Bulldog IIA	Upavon
No 23 Squadron	Gloster Gamecock	Kenley
No. 25 Squadron	A.W. Siskin IIIA	Hawkinge
No 29 Squadron	A.W. Siskin IIIA	North Weald
No 32 Squadron	A.W. Siskin IIIA	Kenley
No 41 Squadron	A.W. Siskin IIIA	Northolt
No 56 Squadron	A.W. Siskin IIIA	North Weald
No 111 Squadron	A.W. Siskin IIIA	Hornchurch

Overseas

No 6 Squadron	Bristol F.2B Fighter*	Ismailia, Egypt
No 20 Squadron	Bristol F.2B Fighter*	Peshawar, India

No 28 Squadron	Bristol F.2B Fighter*	Ambala, India
No 31 Squadron	Bristol F.2B Fighter*	Quetta, India
No 208 Squadron	Bristol F.2B Fighter*	Heliopolis, Egypt

Fleet Air Arm

No 401 Flight	Fairey Flycatcher	HMS *Argus*
No 402 Flight	Fairey Flycatcher	HMS *Eagle*
No 403 Flight	Fairey Flycatcher	HMS *Hermes*
No 404 Flight	Fairey Flycatcher	HMS *Courageous*
No 405 Flight	Fairey Flycatcher	HMS *Furious*
No 407 Flight	Fairey Flycatcher	HMS *Courageous*
No 408 Flight	Fairey Flycatcher	HMS *Glorious*

* Bristol F.2Bs performed the 'fighter reconnaissance' rôle

4. BIPLANES AT THEIR ZENITH

The year 1930 brought to an end an era in the Royal Air Force, an age sometimes referred to as the Trenchard Era. That much venerated leader had succeeded, not only in securing the survival of the Service — independent of the Royal Navy and Army — but in fostering its traditions, created in less than two decades. By means of the Royal Air Force College at Cranwell and the Apprentice Scheme centred on Henlow, Trenchard had built a Service in which young men could be proud to serve, in which to build for themselves a career no less honourable than in the older Services, and with a chance to see the world.

Nevertheless, for whatever reason, the decade that had followed the Great War had seen the Royal Air Force operationally unbalanced, with the lion's share of the annual defence budget being apportioned to the creation and maintenance of a substantial force of bombers, with little thought allowed for the effective protection of the nation or, more particularly, of the bomber bases themselves.

Trenchard had also been careful to ensure that senior officers, who had displayed a balanced understanding of the principles of air power during the War, assume command and staff appointments, and other positions of great responsibility; such a man, eminent among these, was Sir John Salmond. This officer had learned to fly in 1912, and the same year became an instructor at the Central Flying School; by the end of the War he commanded the RFC and RAF in the Field as a 37-year-old Major General. Much more important, however, was his appointment as Air Officer Commanding-in-Chief, Air Defence of Great Britain from 1925 until 1929.

Salmond had thus been best placed to experience the strengths and weaknesses of the RAF's fighter arm during that period, and had been largely instrumental in securing the issue of imaginative fighter requirements between 1926 and 1929. That the aircraft industry had not always succeeded in meeting these demands was not so much because they were pitched too high by international standards, but rather that development and acquisition of RAF equipment was necessarily considered in the light of tight budgetary restrictions.

It has been shown that, in the all-important sphere of engine development, certain engines had continued to attract Air Ministry favour on account of their suitability of application to the widest possible range of aircraft. Such esoteric considerations as power-weight ratio, drag and fuel consumption carried little weight among the finance committees striving to make ends meet.

Yet Salmond had, with tacit encouragement from Trenchard, sought successfully to encourage those traditional attributes of the fighter pilot — individuality, skill and a certain air of *élan*.

And when Sir John was appointed Chief of the Air Staff on 1 January 1930, in succession to Trenchard, he not only sustained this process but also directed a significant shift in the Service's priorities. Adequately open-ended bomber requirements had been issued since 1927 to keep the established bomber manufacturers busy for several years to come, so that attention could henceforth be paid to the *real* advance of fighter technology — not least by discarding the age-old two-gun biplane powered by a bulky radial engine. It would, nevertheless, be many more years before the venerable biplane fighter disappeared from the RAF. Indeed, such aircraft as the Hawker Fury were, in 1930, on the threshold of their scintillating lives as, year after year, the little fighters captivated the Hendon crowds with their formation aerobatics, trailing smoke and tied together with elastic cords.

Behind the glitter the Royal Air Force had set its sights on technical transformation, and one man, more than any other, was to embark on a professional saga that was to embrace six years of technical development of Britain's air defences, followed by four in command of those defences. This was Hugh Dowding who, as an Air Vice-Marshal in 1930, was to be appointed Air Member for Research and Development on the Air Council, and made responsible for the advancing development of Britain's air defence equipment, be that equipment aircraft, engines, weapons, radio and so on. In the ultimate circumstance both Salmond and Dowding would be the authority to sanction the new aircraft requirements of the RAF, and their staffs would formulate the all-important Specifications.

1930 was not many months old when the first of these important Specifications was drafted. F.7/30 was a masterpiece of shrewd judgement, as much in technical respects as in an understanding of the industry's strengths. After all, it demanded a fine appreciation of the industry's resources to demand, at a stroke, a twenty-five percent increase in the fighter's performance as well as doubling its armament, while advocating the use of a wholly untried engine;

all at a time when the costs of developing such a fighter aircraft would have to be borne by private industry rather than the nation.

It is unquestionably true to say that F.7/30 dominated the fighter scene in Britain for the first half of the coming decade. By insisting that the aircraft must be both day and night fighter, huge production contracts for the successful tender were implicit. It was intended to replace all other fighters in service.

That, in the event, the Specification failed in its ultimate purpose, that of breaking the old design stalemate, was not a disaster for either the RAF or industry: it was finally satisfied, at the eleventh hour, by Henry Folland's radial-powered Gladiator biplane. The

Specification itself was to be compromised in the first place by the failure of the Rolls-Royce Goshawk steam-cooled engine to live up to the Air Ministry's belief that it would represent a suitable fighter powerplant. Overriding both these circumstances was the appearance on the scene of the cantilever-wing monoplane fighter, itself to some extent a beneficiary of all the research that had been pursued in the quest for a successful F.7/30 fighter. Even the magnificent Rolls-Royce Merlin engine would benefit from much of the research conducted into the installation problems posed by the discredited Goshawk.

So the next five years would bring the biplane to its zenith; thereafter it would decline through eclipse to extinction.

Vickers Type 151/171 Jockey

The appearance of the Fairey Fox light bomber in service with No. 12 Squadron during June 1926—with its operating speed of 150 mph at 10,000 feet, emphasized the glaring inadequacy of RAF interceptor fighters in terms of climb and speed performance (Siskin III, 130 mph at 10,000 ft; Grebe, 145 mph; Gamecock, 145 mph; and Woodcock, 140 mph). Although No 12 Squadron remained alone in its use of the Fox in the RAF, the writing was on the wall and prompted the Air Ministry to draft a series of fighter Specifications, beginning with F.9/26 which, as already shown, brought forth the Brstol Bulldog. By 1927, however, it was beginning to dawn on the Service that the traditional fighter design formula—biplanes armed with two rifle-calibre machine guns and powered by bulky radial engines—was nearing the limit of its performance potential. Exactly how to break from this tradition was far from straightforward, bearing in mind the low level of funding for the British armed forces in the mid-1920s, and the chronic lack of suitable aero engines, not to mention the age-old prejudice against monoplanes.

By drafting Specification F.20/27 in relatively general terms—the most important of which was the need for a single-seat interceptor capable of reaching and attacking an enemy aircraft

The Vickers Type 151 at Brooklands either shortly before or after its first flight at Martlesham in April 1930. Note the horn balanced rudder and tail construction. (Photo: R C Sturtivant)

passing overhead at 20,000 feet at 150 mph—it was intended to exploit the ingenuity of the aircraft industry's designers to the full. In due course the requirement crystallized more clearly, and it was intended to evaluate three basic configurations: high- and low-wing monoplanes, and biplanes; although no specific choice of powerplant was stipulated, official preference became obvious by the offer to loan Bristol Mercury and Jupiter engines at Air Ministry expense for those prototypes selected for manufacture.

The Specification was issued to a dozen manufacturers, from whom no fewer than six prototypes emerged, of which three were low-wing monoplanes and three were biplanes. No high-wing monoplane prototypes were ordered, and although the modified Westland Wizard (see page 180) was submitted as a private venture, its performance did not apparently do full justice to the

490 hp Rolls-Royce F.XII engine.

Unquestionably the most promising of the low-wing monoplane prototypes was the Vickers Type 151 (unofficially known as the Jockey). Its design was undertaken by J Bewsher under the direction of Rex Pierson, and employed a developed form of the Wibault structural principles, the all-metal frame being covered by unstressed metal skinning to provide a semi-monocoque structure. The cantilever wing was of rectangular planform and of RAF 34 section, while power was provided initially by an uncowled 480 hp Bristol Mercury IIA nine-cylinder air-cooled radial driving a two-blade propeller. The pilot possessed an excellent field of vision in an open cockpit situated well forward; twin Vickers guns were located in the sides of the front fuselage with their cocking handles accessible to the pilot.

First flight of the Vickers Type 151, J9122 (purchased by the Air Ministry

As the Vickers Type 171, the much modified Jockey J9122 at Martlesham Heath in 1932 with Townend ring, spatted wheels and re-designed tail unit. (Photo: Air Ministry, A & AEE)

	Vickers Type 171	*Boeing XP-936*
Powerplant:	530 hp Bristol Jupiter VIIF	500 hp P & W R-1340-27
Span:	32 ft 6 in	27 ft 11 in
Length:	23 ft 0 in	23 ft 10 in
Height:	8 ft 3 in	10 ft 5 in
Wing area:	150 sq ft	149 sq ft
Tare weight:	2,260 lb	2,271 lb
All-up weight:	3,161 lb	3,012 lb
Max speed:	218 mph at 10,000 ft	234 mph at 7,500 ft
Service Ceiling:	29,100 ft	27,400 ft

for £6,393, excluding engine), was made by E R C ('Tiny') Scholefield at Martlesham Heath, in April 1930, remaining there for intermittent evaluation trials until May 1931. Several minor modifications were incorporated, including the provision of cockpit side doors to enable the pilot to escape in the event of the aircraft overturning on landing. Although the Jockey displayed a number of disagreeable habits (for instance, vibration of the tail unit and a flat spin tendency), it was generally liked by the Service test pilots.

Accordingly, J9122 returned to Weybridge in 1931 for fairly extensive re-design, which included an entirely new rear fuselage, designed by Barnes Wallis, incorporating triangulated tube trusses within the semi-monocoque skin. A Townend ring was fitted round the Mercury engine, and large wheel spats were added to the undercarriage. In February 1932 the Mercury was replaced by a 530 hp Bristol Jupiter VIIF supercharged engine, and the Jockey, now termed the Type 171, embarked on a new series of trials at Martlesham—attending the Hendon Air Display on 25 June that year (wearing New Type No 1).

Unfortunately, during spinning trials at Martlesham on 15 July, the aircraft entered a flat spin and crashed at Woodbridge, Suffolk, and was destroyed. The pilot baled out safely at 5,000 feet. Loss of the Vickers Jockey occurred at a time when it was considered that most of its difficulties had been overcome, although it is difficult to see how it could have overcome the handicap of the untidy radial engine without complete re-design. Moreover a new generation of biplane fighters had emerged in the shape of Camm's Hawker Fury and Nimrod.

Be that as it may, it is perhaps of interest to compare the size, weight and performance of the Vickers Type 171 with that of the American Boeing P-26A monoplane fighter whose prototype (XP-936) had flown on 20 March 1932, and for which exaggerated claims were made at the time:

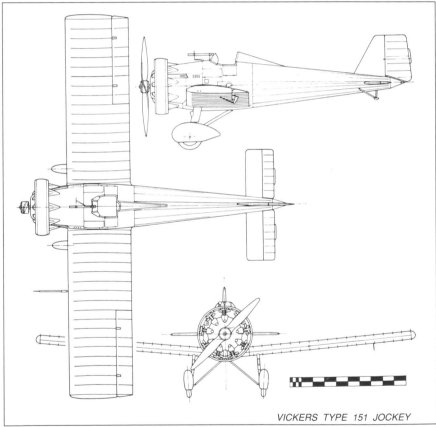

VICKERS TYPE 151 JOCKEY

Type: Single-engine, single-seat low-wing monoplane interceptor

Manufacturer: Vickers (Aviation) Ltd, Weybridge, Surrey

Air Ministry Specification: F.20/27

Powerplant: Type 151. One 480 hp Bristol Mercury IIA nine-cylinder air-cooled radial engine. Two-blade Watts wooden propeller.

Structure: All-metal semi-monocoque with cantilever wing of RAF 34 section; non-retractable undercarriage with tailskid.

Dimensions: Span, 32ft 6in; length, 23ft 0in; height, 8ft 3in; wing area, 150 sq ft.

Weights: Type 151. Tare, 2,180 lb; all-up, 3,080 lb.

Performance: Type 151. Max speed, 207 mph at 9,500ft; climb to 10,000ft, 5 min 35 sec; service ceiling, 27,800ft.

Armament: Two nose-mounted, synchronized 0.303in Vickers Mark III machine guns with 600 rounds per gun.

Prototype: J9122 (first flown, April 1930, by E R C Scholefield). No production.

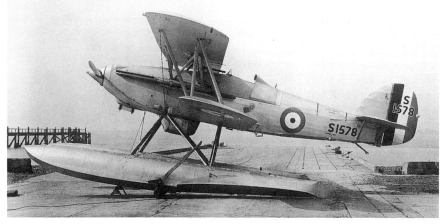

Left: *Though technically the two Nimrod Is, S1577 and S1578, were the first production aircraft, they underwent the full range of prototype trials and evaluations normally performed by prototypes; indeed they spent their lives in the development of equipment installations. S1577 flew with at least four exhaust pipes of different lengths and shapes before the pattern shown was adopted as standard.* (Photo: Air Ministry A & AEE, Neg No 7155 dated 11 January 1932). Below: *S1578, shown at Felixstowe, made over thirty flights to discover the optimum number of elements in the oil cooler under the nose. The aircraft is shown with a trial installation of the pilot's faired headrest.* (Photo: Air Ministry, MAEE)

Hawker Nimrod

There is some evidence to suggest that the idea of Hawker producing a Kestrel-powered naval fighter pre-dated the start of the Hawker Hornet by as much as five months, and that the N.21/26 Hoopoe's design continued alongside a similar aircraft powered by the Rolls-Royce F.XIS, so that, when problems arose with the deliveries of Bristol Mercury radial engines, work restarted in 1929 to modify the 'Kestrel-Hoopoe' project to bring it closer to the Hornet.

Indeed when the naval fighter was first flown, as a private venture in mid-1930, it was scarcely distinguishable from the Hornet, the engine oil cooler element being combined with the radiator fairing and the engine being devoid of long exhaust pipes. Being a private venture, the fighter carried a company number only (H.N.1=Hornet Naval), and was known locally as the Norn.

As Camm's design proposals were being studied at the Air Ministry, a second aircraft, H.N.2, was being produced for structural testing; these dis-

closed the need for stronger undercarriage oleos, and they were incorporated in H.N.1 before it visited Martlesham for preliminary handling tests.

By August the Air Ministry had issued Specification 16/30, written around Camm's proposals, confirming the higher vertical descent velocities during deck landing, and setting out the naval equipment to be included. The 525hp Kestrel IIS (or IIMS) was required in place of H.N.1's Kestrel IMS, as was external oil cooler and increased metal skinning aft of the cockpit (H.N.1 had ply panels in this area).

An initial production order for twelve aircraft, now officially named the Nimrod, was signed early in October, and a late requirement for buoyancy boxes in the upper wing and rear fuselage was added after flotation tests had been performed using H.N.2.

Philip Edward Gerald ('Jerry') Sayer, who had joined Hawker in 1930 as Bulman's assistant pilot, flew the first Nimrod on 14 October 1931; both this and the second aircraft (S1577 and S1578) were then shipped out to Japan where they were flown for demonstration by Flt Lt Philip Gadesden Lucas RAFO. On return to England they were made ready for their official Service trials, S1577 with wheel undercarriage going to Martlesham, and S1578 with twin floats to Felixstowe. Deck landing trials followed as S1577 visited HMS *Eagle* in April 1932. Service clearance

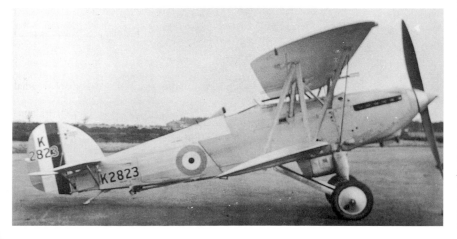

Nimrod K2823 was originally completed as a standard Mark I and was progressively modified with such items as arrester hook, pilot's headrest, Vickers Mk III guns, and improved wheelbrakes, thereby becoming the prototype Mark II. (Photo: Air Ministry, MAEE Felixstowe).

was forthcoming immediately afterwards, and the first six Nimrods joined No 402 Flight of the Fleet Air Arm, embarked in HMS *Courageous* during July. (It was immediately on his return from Japan that Philip Lucas applied for release from the RAF and joined Hawker as its first 'production test pilot').

A second production order, for twenty-six Nimrods, was completed in the late summer and were ready for delivery to Nos 404, 408 and 409 Flights aboard HM Carriers *Courageous* and *Glorious*. In April the following year these Flights, together with Hawker Osprey Flights, combined to form the composite naval fighter squadrons, Nos 800, 801 and 802. These three Squadrons paid frequent visits to the Mediterranean during the next five years, landing ashore at Hal Far, Malta, and at Aboukir, Egypt — particularly during the Abyssinian crisis of 1935.

In November 1938, No 803 Squadron was re-formed at Worthy Down under the command of Sqn Ldr (Lt-Cdr, RN) Brian Harold Maule, using its Nimrods as trainers in preparation for taking on Blackburn Skuas and Rocs.

Early Service experience with Nimrods had prompted the issue of a new Specification, 11/33, calling for a number of modifications, including the addition of a faired headrest above the rear coaming of the cockpit to support the pilot's head during catapulting, and inclusion of a deck arrester hook together with local structural reinforcing.

A Mark I, K2823, was modified as prototype, and was followed by a total of thirty production examples, the Nimrod Mark II. An addendum to this Specification required the preparation of three of these aircraft (K2909-K2911) to be constructed making use of a number of structural components in stainless steel, particularly in the engine bearers and wing centre section. The Mark IIs were powered initially by Kestrel IIS engines but, beginning in 1935, Service aircraft were returned to Brooklands in rotation to be fitted with 608hp Kestrel VFP engines and slightly enlarged tail units to assist recovery from inverted spins with floats fitted.

The last operational Nimrods were retired from No 802 Squadron in May 1939, their place being taken by Sea Gladiators. A small number of Nimrods was exported, namely two to Denmark with Kestrel IIIS engines, one to Japan and one to Portugal.

A Nimrod Mk II, K4620, of No 801 Squadron, Fleet Air Arm. Some pilots evidently preferred to remove the faired headrest; note the arrester hook. (Photo: Author's Collection)

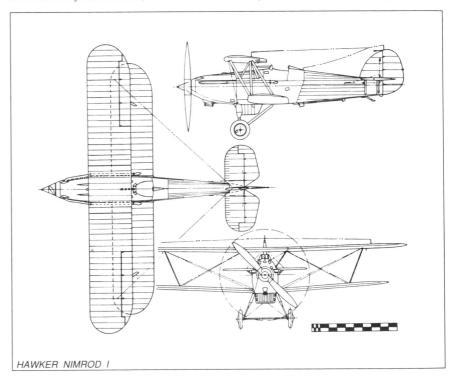

HAWKER NIMROD I

Type: Single-engine, single-seat, single-bay biplane naval fighter.

Manufacturer: H G Hawker Engineering Co Ltd (from 1933 Hawker Aircraft Ltd), Kingston and Brooklands, Surrey.

Air Ministry Specifications: Mk I, 16/30; Mk II, 11/33.

Powerplant: Mk I. One 525hp Rolls-Royce Kestrel IIMS twelve-cylinder liquid-cooled in-line engine driving two-blade Watts wooden propeller. Mk II. 608hp Kestrel VFP.

Dimensions: Span, 33ft 6¾in; length, 26ft 6½in; height, 9ft 10in; wing area, 301 sq ft.

Weights: Mk I landplane. Tare, 2,901lb; all-up, 3,867lb. floatplane, all-up, 4,250lb.

Performance: Max speed, 196 mph at 12,000ft (Mk I landplane), 148.5 mph at 8,800ft (Mk I floatplane); climb to 10,000ft, 6 min 8 sec; service ceiling, 26,900ft.

Armament: Two synchronized 0.303in Vickers Mk III machine guns with 600 rounds per gun in upper nose decking; provision to carry four 20lb bombs.

Prototype: One unregistered prototype (first flown in about June 1930).

Production: Total of 87 aircraft built to Air Ministry order (57 Mk Is: S1577-S1588, S1614-S1639 and K2823-K2841; 30 Mk IIs: K2909-K2914, K2925-K2926, K3654-K3662, K4620-K4629 and K5056-K5058).

Summary of Service: Nimrods served with Nos 402, 404, 408 and 409 Flights, and Nos 759, 780, 781, 800, 801, 802 and 803 Squadrons, Fleet Air Arm, aboard HM Carriers *Courageous*, *Furious* and *Glorious*

Armstrong Whitworth A.W.XVI

John Lloyd's A.W.XVI was a direct development of the Starling, taking advantage of the experience of the Armstrong Siddeley Panther's installation in the second Starling, J8028, which had flown on 5 December 1929. The A.W.XVI had originally been conceived in the context of Specification F.9/26 but, as it was completed much too late to compete in the official trials, it was decided to enter the prototype as a private venture centender for the naval Specification N.21/26, even though, or perhaps because the Service evaluation of all the other aircraft produced to this requirement had failed to sustain a suitable answer.

Considerable trouble was experienced with the AW.XVI's engine installation, and the prototype, S1591 (formerly A-2) was not flown before the Air Ministry decided on the Hawker Nimrod and, although it was purchased by the Service, it was too late.

The AW.XVI was an attractive, compact and robust aeroplane and, despite its lack of balanced rudder in the aircraft's early configuration, handled fairly well. When first submitted for *ad hoc* evaluation at Martlesham early in 1931, it was fitted with a cross-axle undercarriage with wheel spats. It had then been fitted with a full range of naval equipment and returned a top speed of 203 mph at 10,000 feet. The principal cause for concern was the unreliability of the Panther IIIA engine which, although developing its promised power, was prone to overheating, and the so-called 'double-Townend' ring was thought to be the cause.

The inner ring was removed, limited naval equipment was then fitted and further performance trials were undertaken with No 402 Flight of the Fleet Air Arm in 1932, alongside the first production Nimrods. By then S1591's performance had suffered appreciably, and proved markedly inferior to the fully-equipped Nimrod; it was also found to be almost unmanageable on an exposed carrier deck.

Convinced that the naval accoutrements had compromised an otherwise sound fighter, Armstrong Whitworth persevered with the AW.XVI, and produced a second prototype, G-ACCD (as the first aircraft had been civil registered G-ABKF). The more reliable Panther IIA was fitted for a re-submission to the new F.7/30 Specification, but the aircraft was so far removed from the official requirements that it was quickly discarded as a serious contender. In truth, Armstrong Whitworth had simply not been fully aware of the radical advances in fighter design and performance now being espoused by the Air Staff.

The company, nevertheless, exported a small number of AW.XVIs, five being supplied to Hong Kong, and four to China; the British civil register shows that AW.XVIs were also registered as G-ABRH, G-ABRI, G-ABRJ and G-ABZL (in addition to the two prototypes referred to above), but these are generally thought to have covered the export aircraft while on test in Britain; that being so, the total number of AW.XVIs built would have been eleven.

The second AW.XVI, G-ACCD, came to be rebuilt as the prototype A.W.35 Scimitar (see page 248).

Type: Single-engine, single-seat, single-bay biplane interceptor fighter.
Manufacturer: Sir W G Armstrong Whitworth Aircraft Ltd., Coventry.
Air Ministry Specifications: F.9/26, N.21/26 and F.7/30.
Powerplant: One 525hp Armstrong Siddeley Panther IIA fourteen-cylinder air-cooled radial engine; also 500hp Panther IIIA.
Dimensions: Span, 33ft 0in; length, 25ft 6in; wing area, 261.35 sq ft.
Weight: All-up, 4,067lb.
Performance: Max speed, 203 mph at 10,000ft (naval, part-equipped, 183 mph); climb to 10,000ft, 8 min 40 sec; service ceiling, 26,100ft; range, 270 miles.
Armament: Two synchronized 0.303in Vickers Mk II or III machine guns in sides of fuselage with 500 rounds per gun.
Prototypes: Two, A-2 (later S1591 and G-AGKF, first flown in 1930), and G-ACCD.
Production: Probably nine (five for Hong Kong and four for China), but some sources quote thirteen, excluding prototypes.

Right: Two views of the first A.W.XVI prototype. Above: As originally tested by the A & AEE with private venture A-2 marking, Panther IIIA and exhaust collector ring with long pipe. A balanced rudder had by then been fitted. Below: S1591 featured a Panther IIA with large spinner and radial exhaust stubs; the inner Townend ring was removed shortly afterwards. (Photos: Air Ministry, A & AEE)

Westland F.29/27

Continuing Air Ministry interest in the Coventry Ordnance Works' large-calibre, quick-firing gun was manifest in the preparation of Specification F.29/27, issued in draft form to no fewer than seven manufacturers late in 1928. Several of the terms of this Specification were clearly based on F.20/27, not least the definition of the target threat, namely an enemy bomber formation approaching at 20,000 feet and flying at 150 mph. (Such a performance was entirely arbitrary, and was in no way based on current RAF bombers which, when loaded with bombs, could perhaps reach 12,000 feet and a speed of 80 mph!). Implicit in the Specification, which called for a single COW gun to be mounted so as to fire at an elevation of not less than 45 degrees to the horizontal, was an attack from below and behind the target.

Two prototypes were eventually ordered from Westland and Vickers. Arthur Davenport retained the basic configuration of his F.20/27 Interceptor monoplane (see page 205), mounting the 200lb COW gun in the starboard side of the fuselage with the gun body accessible to the pilot. A Westland-designed rotary shell-dispenser, loaded with 39 rounds of the 1½-pound 37mm ammunition, was operated by a handwheel in the cockpit.

Like the Interceptor, the COW-gun fighter was first flown with a small, low aspect-ratio fin and rudder, its uncowled Mercury IIIA driving a wooden four-blade propeller. The maiden flight was undertaken by Louis Paget during December 1930, and the preliminary test programme continued without serious problems. The climb performance proved disappointing and it was decided to reduce weight by substituting a Watts two-blade propeller. The fin and rudder were replaced by surfaces identical to those of the Interceptor.

Service evaluation of the prototype, J9565, by No 15 Squadron at the A & AEE began on 15 April 1931 and continued intermittently until the following year when, fitted with a Mercury IVA, it embarked on performance trials with No 22 Squadron at Martlesham. Climb performance was still considered to be poor, and it was pointed out that, although ingenious, the shell-dispenser was not only too heavy but contained eleven rounds less than the fifty demanded in the Specification.

Trials continued until July 1934, but by then interest in the COW gun had waned, and J9565 was struck off Air Ministry charge on 3 December 1935, ending its days as an instructional airframe (738M) at Henlow.

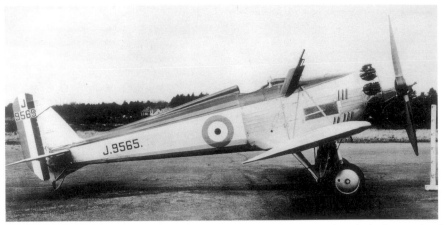

The Westland F.29/27 COW-gun fighter, J9565, at Martlesham Heath with the later style of fin and rudder in 1931. (Photo: via R C Sturtivant)

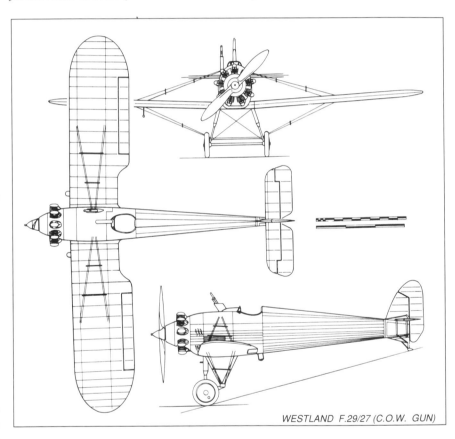

WESTLAND F.29/27 (C.O.W. GUN)

Type: Single-engine, single-seat, low-wing monoplane interceptor fighter.
Manufacturer: Westland Aircraft Works, Yeovil, Somerset.
Air Ministry Specification: F.29/27
Powerplant: One 485hp Bristol Mercury IIIA (later Mercury IVA) nine-cylinder air-cooled geared and supercharged radial engine.
Dimensions: Span, 40ft 10in; length, 29ft 10in; height, 10ft 7in; wing area, 223 sq ft.
Weights: Tare, 2,615lb; all-up, 3,885lb.
Performance: Max speed, 185 mph at 13,000ft; climb to 10,000ft, 7 min; service ceiling, 27,900ft.
Armament: One 37mm 1½-pounder COW gun, firing upwards at 55 degrees to the horizontal with 39 rounds, in the starboard side of the fuselage.
Prototype: One, J9565 (first flown by Louis Paget in December 1930). No production.

Vickers F.29/27

Second of the single-seat fighters armed with the 37mm Coventry Ordnance Works gun ordered as a prototype in response to Specification F.29/27 was the Vickers Type 161 which, despite its resurrection of the ancient Gunbus configuration, emerged as a surprisingly sophisticated design.

Although fitted with a Mercury IIA engine early in its construction, the Type 161, J9566, was completed with a Jupiter VIIF, driving a wooden four-blade pusher propeller when it was first flown by Summers on 21 January 1931. It featured a metal monocoque nacelle close-up under the upper wing with the pilot's cockpit on the port side, the COW gun beside it, angled obliquely upwards to starboard. The staggered, parallel-chord wings of RAF 34 section and with ailerons fitted on the upper wings only were of two-bay, two-spar configuration with duralumin lattice ribs. Single-tube I-type interplane struts were rigged with prominent outward rake to provide slight dihedral on upper and lower wings. The upper and lower steel tail booms converged in side elevation to carry the tail unit, being attached to the mainplanes aft of the inboard interplane struts, and to the tailplane near its tips.

An unusual feature was a tapered sheet-metal tubular fairing aft of the propeller, supported by short struts attached to the four tail booms. When first flown, J9566 was fitted with an unbalanced rudder but, after some yawing instability was experienced, the rudder was enlarged and provided with a horn balance. Small auxiliary fins were later added above and below the junctions of the tail booms with the tailplane.

J9566 was delivered to Martlesham on 3 September 1931, remaining there for performance, handling and armament trials with Nos 15 and 22 Squadrons until the following July. The aircraft does not appear to have posed any serious problems, nor did the gun trials present any unforeseen difficulties.

Nevertheless, speeds of both fighters and bombers were beginning to increase significantly, and it is hard to imagine the relatively slow-firing COW gun being able to cause fatal damage in the fleeting moments of air combat, particularly as J9566 possessed an unremarkable performance.

The single Vickers Type 161, J9566, at about the time of its first flight, before the mounting of the COW gun and modifications to the tail unit; note the robust, split-axle undercarriage and the hooped crash pylon aft of the cockpit. (Photo: Vickers PLC, Neg No 4570A)

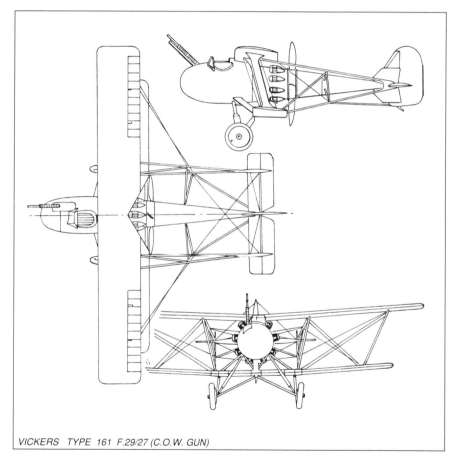

VICKERS TYPE 161 F.29/27 (C.O.W. GUN)

Type: Single pusher engine, single-seat, two-bay biplane interceptor fighter.
Manufacturer: Vickers (Aviation) Ltd, Weybridge, Surrey.
Air Ministry Specification: F.29/27.
Powerplant: One 530hp Bristol Jupiter VIIF nine-cylinder radial air-cooled engine driving four-blade wooden pusher propeller. (Originally fitted with Bristol Mercury IIA engine during manufacture, but replaced for completion.)
Dimensions: Span, 32ft 0in; length, 23ft 6in; height, 12ft 4in; wing area, 270 sq ft.
Weights: Tare, 2,382lb; all-up, 3,350lb.
Performance: Max speed, 185 mph at 10,000ft; climb to 10,000ft, 5 min 50 sec.
Armament: One 1½-pounder 37mm Coventry Ordnance Works gun mounted in starboard side of cockpit nacelle with 50 rounds and angled to fire obliquely upwards.
Prototype: J9566 (first flown at Brooklands by Fg Off J Summers on 21 January 1931). No production.

Hawker Demon

Much has been made of the influence exerted by the introduction of the Rolls-Royce Kestrel engine into Service aircraft from 1928, not least in the Hawker Hart light bomber. In 1930 and 1931 this aeroplane was virtually immune from interception by RAF fighters on account of its high speed; and although it seemed likely that the new Fury fighters would be capable of returning an effective performance superiority when they became operational, they were considered to be expensive and their production was expected to be somewhat limited by cost.

When Camm put forward a design proposal to adapt the Hart itself as a two-seat day-and-night fighter in mid-1930, armed with a pair of front guns in addition to the Scarff-mounted Lewis gun while still retaining the Hart's performance, it was quickly realised that all manner of side benefits, not least cost, would accrue from the large degree of commonality of the two aircraft.

Accordingly, as soon as the first production Hart bomber, J9933, had completed its Service trials at Martlesham Heath, it was leased back to the manufacturers for development as the proposed fighter version. The immediate modifications included the installation of a supercharged 580hp Kestrel IIS engine, and inclusion of the Fury's twin front gun armament. The rear cockpit area of the fuselage was redesigned so that a Scarff No 15 ring was depressed on the forward side by an angle of 15 degrees so, it was said, to obtain some protection for the gunner from slipstream buffet while manning the Lewis gun. (Later J9933 underwent a series of tests to discover whether any of several forms of fixed enclosed canopy could be devised, but all were found to restrict

Early production Demons of No 23 (Fighter) Squadron. (Photo: Author's Collection)

the gunner's field of view and fire; however, see below.)

A preliminary Specification, 15/30, was drafted around Hawker's proposals and a pilot batch of six aircraft was ordered, it being planned to deliver these to a Bulldog squadron for a comparison with the old radial engine fighters. No 23 (Fighter) Squadron, commanded by Sqn Ldr H H Woollett at Kenley, was selected and the Hart Fighters equipped a separate Flight on the Squadron.

It quickly became clear that the Hart Fighter was not only capable of matching the single-seat Bulldog's manoeuvrability, but possessed a significant edge in both climb and speed. It was therefore decided to raise a full production Specification, 6/32, and a production batch of seventeen aircraft was placed, sufficient to enable No 23 Squadron to discard its Bulldogs in favour of

a full complement of two-seaters, now named the Demon.

It has to be said at this point that, while the Demon performed the task to which it was allotted — that of providing a 'defence' against the Hawker Hart during defence exercises — its entire concept in the wider sense was flawed. Sydney Camm is on record as having stated that his proposal 'to set a Hart to catch a Hart' was never intended to be more that a very short term expedient. He was well aware that his new Fury was the answer to any bomber threat extant in Europe in the early 'thirties. Indeed, the Demon came to be perpetuated as a product of financial necessity. Unfortunately, what came also came to be perpetuated, probably owing to the success of the Demon in its very limited context, was that the two-seat interceptor represented an essential item of equipment in the RAF's arsenal, which it most certainly was not.

As it was, 1933 and 1934 brought forth a further 61 production Demons, and these equipped No 41 (Fighter) Squadron, commanded at Northolt in July 1934 by Sqn Ldr John Auguste Boret MC, AFC (a First World War fighter pilot who had destroyed 27 enemy aircraft and who would later

The CO's Demon of No 604 Squadron, the first of the Auxiliary Air Force Squadrons to be equipped with these fighters. (Photo: A J Jackson Collection)

become an Air Vice-Marshal), and No 65 (Fighter) Squadron, commanded by Sqn Ldr Frank Ormond Soden DFC at Hornchurch the following month. Twenty aircraft were shipped out to Egypt at the end of the year where they joined No 29 (Fighter) Squadron in March, then commanded by Sqn Ldr (later Gp Capt) Edward Percy MacKay.

The onset of the Abyssinian crisis in 1935 accelerated the deployment of Demons in the Middle East and, following their issue to No 29 Squadron, No 74 (Fighter) Squadron under Sqn Ldr Henry George Crowe MC (later Air Cdre, CBE, MC) was deployed to Malta in September that year, and the same month No 208 Squadron at Heliopolis received sufficient Demons to equip a Flight, as did No 6 Squadron in Egypt and Palestine during October.

Meanwhile, at home, Specification 8/34 called for a new version of the Demon to be equipped with a novel fairing to protect the gunner, euphemistically referred to as a turret. In fact this comprised no more than four segmented shields which could be rotated up and down to provide the gunner with some protection from the slipstream. The entire Frazer-Nash gun ring mounting, to which the shield was attached, and the gunner's seat, were rotated hydraulically, and the system was generally popular among the gunners. When, however, the gun was traversed to either beam, the 'lobster-claw' shield set up severe airflow instability, resulting in fairly powerful changes in aircraft trim.

A second Turret Demon Specification, 40/34, was raised to cover a change to the more powerful Kestrel V engine, and also the transfer of production of the aircraft to Boulton Paul (Hawker was now filled to capacity with production of Hart and Fury variants, not to mention the possibility of having to make way for production of a fighter that was to become the Hurricane). These new production contracts covered the manufacture of 106 Demons, of which 61 were to be equipped with the Frazer-Nash turret; Hawker itself only produced four turret Demons, of which K4496 (an ex-604 Squadron aircraft) served as a trial installation machine which underwent tests at Martlesham.

The introduction of the Turret Demon followed an announcement in 1934 that squadrons of the Auxiliary Air Force would, in due course, become fighter units, and in June 1935 No 604 Squadron exchanged its Hart bombers for

Demons, although the turret aircraft were not delivered until 1936. Among the Regulars, Nos 23, 29 and 64 Squadrons also flew Turret Demons. No 25, now warned to discard its beloved Furies in preparation to transfer to the night-fighting rôle in 1937, was a late convert to Demons, and received its two-seaters in October that year; these were a hybrid version, possessing the Frazer-Nash gun

mounting without the folding shield.

By the time of the Munich crisis of September 1938, the two-year-old Fighter Command fielded eight Demon squadrons — a larger number at home than at any other time. Unfortunately this apparent dependence upon a two-seat, single-engine interceptor had artificially established within the Command a class of fighter which, when consid-

Type: Single-engine, two-seat, single-bay biplane interceptor fighter.
Manufacturers: The H G Hawker Engineering Co Ltd (Hawker Aircraft Ltd from 1933), Kingston and Brooklands, Surrey; Boulton Paul Aircraft Ltd, Norwich, Norfolk, and Wolverhampton, Staffs.
Air Ministry Specifications: 15/30, 6/32, 1/34 (for Australia), 8/34, 40/34 and 46/36.
Powerplant: One 580hp Rolls-Royce Kestrel IIS twelve-cylinder liquid-cooled supercharged in-line engine driving two-blade Watts wooden propeller. 696hp Kestrel VDR.
Structure: All-metal Hawker construction with fabric and duralumin sheet covering.
Dimensions: Span, 37ft 3in; length, 29ft 7in; height, 10ft 7in; wing area, 347 sq ft.
Weights: Early aircraft. Tare, 3,067lb; all-up, 4,464lb. Turret aircraft. Tare, 3,336lb; all-up, 4,668lb.
Performance: Kestrel IIS. Max speed, 182 mph at 13,000ft; climb to 10,000ft, 7 min 25 sec; service ceiling, 24,500ft. Kestrel VDR. Max speed, 202 mph at 15,000ft; climb to 10,000ft, 6 min 10 sec; service ceiling, 28,850ft.
Armament: Two synchronized Vickers Mk III or V machine guns in sides of fuselage with 600 rounds per gun, and one Lewis gun on Scarff No 15 ring or on Frazer-Nash mounting with folding shields and six 97-round magazine drums.
Prototype: One, J9933 (a converted Hart, first flown as a fighter in March 1931); J9933 was also used as prototype Turret Demon.
Production: Total of 239 for RAF (Hawker, 133: K1950-K1955 (Hart Fighters), K2842-K2858, K2904-K2908, K3764-K3807, K3974-K3985 and K4496-K4544; Boulton Paul, 106: K5683-K5741, K5898-K5907 and K8181-K8217). Also 64 for Australia (18 General Purpose Fighters, 36 army co-operation fighters, and 10 target tugs).
Summary of RAF Service: Demons served with Nos 6, 23, 25, 29, 41, 64, 65, 74, and 208 Squadrons, RAF, and with Nos 600, 601, 604, 607 and 608 Squadrons, Auxiliary Air Force. Also with No 1 Air Armament School, No 9 Bombing and Gunnery School, Nos 6 and 9 Air Observers' Schools, Nos 3 and 14 Flying Training Schools, No 24 E & RFTS, and No 1 Anti-Aircraft Co-operation Unit.

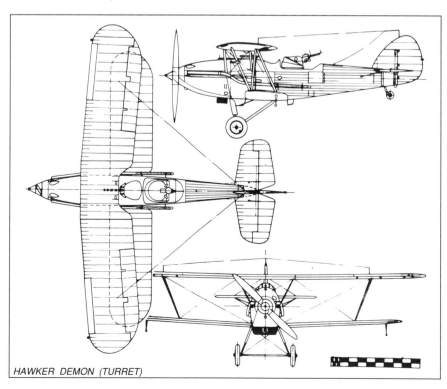

HAWKER DEMON (TURRET)

ered due for retirement, engendered a requirement for a replacement — the Boulton Paul Defiant, as it transpired — which, in the great battle of 1940, was not only found to be technically and tactically flawed but, worse, was wholly superfluous to the needs of Fighter Command.

Above: *Still bearing its No 604 Squadron fin badge, Demon K4496 underwent tests of the Frazer-Nash turret gun at the A & AEE, probably late in 1935.* (Photo: Air Ministry).

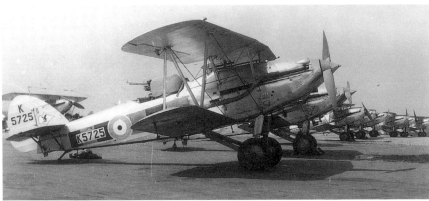

Left: *Turret Demons of No 23 (Fighter) Squadron at Northolt in 1937.* (Photo: A J Jackson Collection)

Gloster Gauntlet

The Gauntlet was born out of the S.S.18B (see page 210) at the time that Hawker Aircraft Ltd finalised its take-over of the Gloster company in 1934, an event brought about as much by the lingering effects of the Depression as by the latter manufacturer's failure to secure any worthwhile production contract for four years. By contrast the Hawker company had inadequate fac-tory facilities in which to accommodate the considerable manufacturing under-takings stemming from the Hart and Fury variants for the RAF, Fleet Air Arm and numerous overseas customers.

It is ironic that the company take-over was completed just as the Gauntlet was

A Gloster Gauntlet II, K7824, of No 66 (Fighter) Squadron, flying from Duxford in 1936. (Photo: via R C Sturtivant)

Gauntlet II, K7810, was one of several aircraft flown as a 'target' by the RAE during secret trials in November 1936 in which Gauntlets of No 32 (Fighter) Squadron were directed by the new coastal radar, then in its infancy. (Photo: Imperial War Museum, Neg No MH3400)

ordered into production and as the initial signs of RAF expansion were being signalled. As preparations were made to put the Gauntlet into production, J9125 (the S.S.19B) continued development trials to assist in the process of agreeing the final production specification, and as late as April 1935 the veteran aeroplane, powered by a Mercury VIS2, achieved a speed of 230 mph at 15,800 feet and at a loaded weight of 3,910lb while at the A & AEE. This compared with 207 mph by the Hawker Fury I, 182 mph by the Hawker Demon and 174 mph by the Bristol Bulldog—the current in-service fighters with the RAF.

Apart from the old J9125, there was no new Gauntlet prototype, and the first production aircraft, K4081, made its maiden flight with P E G Sayer on 17 December 1934. Both this and the second example underwent trials at the A & AEE early in 1935 where they returned the same performance figures as J9125, referred to above, though at a marginally higher all-up weight. The sixth aircraft was delivered to No 19 (Fighter) Squadron at Duxford for preliminary Service trials on 18 February. Indeed, this Squadron, commanded by Sqn Ldr John Reginald Cassidy (later Air Vice-Marshal, CBE) had been selected to become the first to re-equip with Gauntlets, replacing Bulldogs, and in May and June nineteen such aircraft were taken on charge. And it is an interesting statistic that the margin of speed by which the Gauntlet exceeded that of the Bulldog, which it replaced (56 mph) was almost exactly the same as that by which the Hurricane exceeded the speed of the Gladiator — which it replaced some three years later, such was the untrumpeted advance represented by the Gauntlet.

Nevertheless, despite being widely applauded by its Service pilots, the Gauntlet was still firmly cast in a bygone mould — two-bay biplane wings, air-cooled radial, two Vickers guns and open cockpit — and as such did not even approach the requirements of Specification F.7/30, rather to demands being

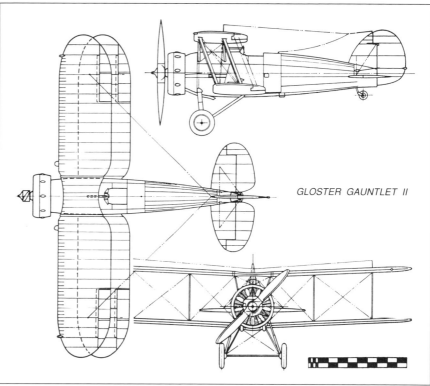

GLOSTER GAUNTLET II

Type: Single-engine, single-seat two-bay biplane interceptor fighter.

Manufacturer: Gloster Aircraft Co Ltd, Hucclecote, Gloucester.

Air Ministry Specification: F.20/27, and 24/33 (for Mark I production).

Powerplant: One 640hp Bristol Mercury VIS2 nine-cylinder air-cooled supercharged radial engine driving 10ft 9in diameter Watts two-blade wooden fixed-pitch propeller.

Structure: All-metal welded steel primary structure, all fabric-covered (Mark Is). Steel and aluminium Warren box girder formed to oval section with fishplate joints and steel wire internal bracing (Mark IIs).

Dimensions: Span, 32ft 9½in; length (Mark I), 26ft 2in, (Mark II), 26ft 5in; height, 10ft 3in; wing area, 315 sq ft.

Weights: Mark I. Tare, 2,755lb; all-up, 3,950lb. Mark II. Tare, 2,770lb; all-up, 3,970lb.

Performance: Mark II. Max speed, 230 mph at 15,800ft; climb to 20,000ft, 9 min; service ceiling, 33,500ft.

Armament: Two fixed synchronized 0.303in Vickers Mk V machine guns in the sides of the front fuselage with 1,200 rounds of ammunition.

Prototype: None (but see Gloster S.S.18/S.S.19).

Production: 24 Mark Is (K4081-K4104); 204 Mark IIs (K5264-K5367 and K7792-K7891)

Summary of Service: Served with Nos 17, 19, 32, 46, 54, 56, 65, 66, 74, 79, 80, 111, 151, 213 and 234 Squadron of the RAF, and Nos 601, 602, 615 and 616 Squadrons, AAF, in Britain; and with Nos 6, 33 and 112 Squadrons in the Middle East. Also served with Met Flights in the UK, Middle East and Africa.

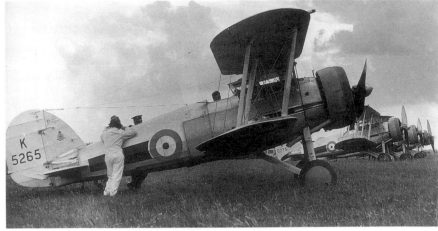

Gauntlet IIs of No 111 (Fighter) Squadron at Northolt during the major air defence exercises of 1937. No 111 Squadron had been one of the first to receive the Mark II version in May 1936 when it replaced the Bristol Bulldog; it would be the first to convert to the new Hurricane monoplane just before Christmas 1937. (Photo: Author's Collection)

made as long ago as 1927. That it achieved the performance it did was powerful testimony to Folland's persistent attention to detail.

Meanwhile, as No 19 Squadron's pilots demonstrated the excellence of their new biplanes (by winning the inter-squadron air firing competitions in 1935 and 1936), Gloster put forward proposals to adopt the patent Hawker form of construction in the Gauntlet. This comprised a metal Warren girder box frame fuselage, formed to oval section, and employing fishplate joints and ball-ended steel tubes, together with wing spars comprising cold-rolled octagonal-section booms connected by a single plate web. It was widely acknowledged that this form of structure was much simpler to build and repair than the Gloster welded structure. Accordingly, in April, the Air Ministry issued an intial order for 104 such aircraft, known as Gauntlet Mark IIs, following it with a further Contract for 100 in September. This version possessed a performance almost identical to that of the Mark I.

Deliveries of the Mark II began in May 1936 to No 56 Squadron at North Weald, and No 111 Squadron at Northolt, Nos 17, 46, 54, 65, 66 and 151 Squadrons also converting to Gauntlets by the end of the year. An interesting series of trials, albeit highly secret at the time, involved aircraft of No 32 Squadron which were directed on to 'target' aircraft by experimental ground radar at Bawdsey Manor on the Suffolk coast, trials which confirmed the enormous potential of a planned chain of coastal radar warning stations.

Delays in the Service introduction of the Hurricane and Spitfire were only partly offset by the appearance of the Gladiator in 1937, and Gauntlets continued to re-equip the fighter squadrons, namely Nos 74, 79, 80 and 213, although three of those re-equipped during 1936, Nos 54, 56 and 65, changed to Gladiators during the summer of 1937. This process continued through-out the following two years; as the Gladiators, Hurricanes and Spitfires appeared in squadron service, the Gauntlets were 'handed on' to newly reformed units to provide operational training until they were ready to take on the new eight-gun monoplane fighters.

By 1939 sufficient surplus Gauntlets had become available to allow the shipment of about 70 aircraft to the Middle East, where they joined No 6 Squadron in Palestine, and Nos 33 and 112 Squadrons in the Western Desert in 1940. All had been removed from front-line service by the time of Italy's entry into the War in June that year. They nevertheless continued to fly with meteorological flights until 1943.

Gauntlets were also exported to Finland early in 1940, and seventeen Mark IIs were built under licence by the *Flyvertroppernes Vaerksteder* at Copenhagen.

Westland Pterodactyl Mark V

The Westland company had first become associated with the work of Capt Geoffrey T R Hill in 1926. Hill, formerly chief test pilot with Handley Page, had been interested in the behaviour of aircraft beyond the point of stall, and had built and flown a tailless glider. After submitting a report on his ideas for a powered version to the Air Ministry, Westland was asked to undertake development of tailless aeroplanes in collaboration with Hill. All such aircraft built were to be named Pterodactyls.

A number of light experimental tailless examples was produced, powered by progressively more powerful engines, beginning with the 34hp Bristol Cherub, and continuing with the 70hp Armstrong Siddeley Genet and the 120hp D.H. Gipsy III, the last being installed in a three-seat cabin monoplane produced to Specification 16/29.

Following the successful demonstration of this aircraft, the Pterodactyl Mk IV, Hill submitted a proposal for a two-seat fighter based on his tailless principles, and in due course Specification F.3/32 was written around this design tender. An armament of two forward-firing synchronized Vickers Mk III guns and a flexibly-mounted Lewis gun was called for, as was use of a 600hp Rolls-Royce Goshawk steam-cooled engine. Such requirements demanded that exceptionally complex design studies be pursued, largely owing to the absence of data relating to safe stressing limits of swept wings, bearing in mind also that the fighter should be fully aerobatic.

The Pterodactyl Mk V, K2770, was completed during the autumn of 1932 as one of the most radical fighter aircraft ever built. Into its exceptionally narrow nacelle, 17ft 4in long, were packed a Goshawk I engine, the pilot and gunner, steam condenser, semi-enclosed fixed tandem-wheel undercarriage, guns and fuel tank. The aircraft was a sesquiplane with very sturdy but diminutive stub wings which carried balancing skids at their tips. The upper wing, of 46ft 8in span, was swept back at about 45 degrees on the leading edge from a point some eight feet from the aircraft's centreline, while the trailing edge was swept back at about 35 degrees along its entire semi-span. The gunner was to be enclosed in an electro-hydraulically controlled turret, but this was probably never fitted. Elevons were fitted at the outer ends of the upper wing, as were Handley Page leading-edge slats. Mounted at the wing tips were oval fins and rudders, which could also act as airbrakes.

Unfortunately, during initial taxying runs undertaken by Harald Penrose, the Pterodactyl's port wing collapsed following failure of the strut between the rear wing spar and the outrigger skid, owing to a stressing miscalculation. The accident resulted in a major re-build of the aircraft which was to delay its first flight until May 1934, when Penrose flew K2770 at Andover.

Although the Pterodactyl itself behaved perfectly satisfactorily in the air, problems with the Goshawk engine were soon encountered, and it was found necessary to fit a larger condenser with a hexagonal air intake. In a second series of modifications, the 615hp Goshawk II engine was installed, the condenser intake again changed, the nose of the nacelle lengthened to enable the rear turret to be balanced (if and when fitted), the engine exhaust system recessed into the sides of the engine cowling, and balancing wheels mounted at the rear of the skids. The main undercarriage was re-positioned, offset to port in order to counter the engine's torque which tended to dig the port balancing wheel into the ground.

It was decided to deliver the Pterodactyl to the RAE to continue its trials during the summer of 1935 but, shortly after take-off at Yeovil, the Goshawk engine seized, and the aircraft was force-landed. Although no damage was suffered by the airframe, there was no spare Goshawk available, and the aircraft was never flown again.

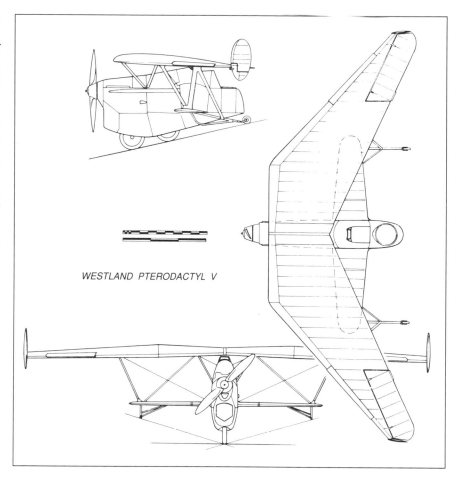

WESTLAND PTERODACTYL V

Type: Single-engine, two-seat tailless sesquiplane experimental fighter.

Manufacturer: Westland Aircraft Works, Yeovil, Somerset.

Air Ministry Specification: F.3/32.

Powerplant: One 600hp Rolls-Royce Goshawk I twelve-cylinder evaporatively-cooled, geared and supercharged in-line engine; also 615hp Goshawk II.

Structure: All-metal construction with fabric-covered wings.

Dimensions: Span, 46ft 8in; length, 20ft 6in; height, 11ft 8in; wing area, 396 sq ft.

Weights: Tare, 3,534lb; all-up, 5,100lb.

Performance: Max speed, 165 mph at 15,000ft; climb to 15,000ft, 12 min 45 sec; service ceiling, 30,000ft.

Armament: Two synchronized 0.303in Vickers Mk III machine guns in sides of nacelle, and one Lewis machine gun on No 19 ring mounting at rear of nacelle.

Prototype: One, K2770 (first flown by Harald Penrose at Andover in May 1934). No production.

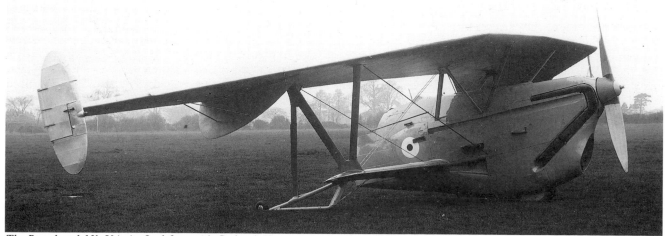

The Pterodactyl Mk V in its final form with Goshawk II, recessed exhaust manifolds and outrigger wheels. (Photo: via R C Sturtivant)

Westland P.V.4 (F.7/30)

The Westland P.V.4, K2891, with the cockpit canopy, added shortly after its first flight. (Photo: Westland Aircraft Ltd.)

Although Air Ministry Specification F.7/30, originally circulated in draft form throughout the aircraft industry late in 1930, underwent constant amendment during the next three years, its basic demands were uncompromising. It required a single-seat, single-engine interceptor capable of being flown by day and night, to be capable of attaining a level speed of 250 mph at 15,000 feet, and to be armed with four forward-firing machine guns. Metal primary structure was mandatory throughout. Implicit in the wording of the Specification was the Air Ministry's preference for the Rolls-Royce Goshawk evaporatively-cooled in-line engine. No preference regarding the aircraft's configuration was expressed, so that manufacturers could submit either biplane or monoplane designs.

By means of the latter omission, the Air Ministry intended to encourage industry to bear the burden of research into radical expedients, so long as the basic requirements were met. In return, the winning manufacturer would be rewarded with very large production contracts.

The result was that more than a dozen design tenders from seven companies had been offered by mid-1931, of which three were accepted for prototype contract, subject to successful preliminary evaluation not later than September 1933. Most of those companies, not fortunate enough to receive prototype orders, opted to go ahead with private venture projects — remembering the past failures by officially-sponsored prototypes to meet Air Ministry requirements.

One of those manufacturers to be awarded a prototype contract was Westland, where Arthur Davenport conceived a biplane of singular appearance and radical approach. (An alternative, high-wing monoplane was also tendered, but rejected.) The Westland P.V.4 featured a gull upper wing, its spars being attached to the fuselage primary structure. The pilot's cockpit was located immediately forward of the wing while the engine, a 600hp Goshawk IIS, was installed amidships, its centre of gravity being unusually close to that of the aircraft and in a position that enabled the

armament to be grouped around the short nose, as well as contributing an excellent field of view for the pilot. The engine drove the propeller by means of a five-foot shaft which passed beneath the cockpit to the reduction gear in the extreme nose. Locating the engine behind the cockpit also relieved the pilot of exhaust glare, an important consideration in night flying. Leading-edge slats

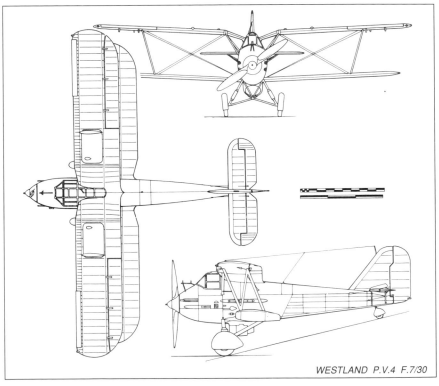

WESTLAND P.V.4 F.7/30

Type: Single-engine, single-seat, single-bay biplane interceptor fighter.

Manufacturer: Westland Aircraft Works, Yeovil, Somerset.

Air Ministry Specification: F.7/30.

Powerplant: One 600hp Rolls-Royce Goshawk IIS twelve-cylinder evaporatively-cooled in-line engine driving two-blade Watts propeller.

Structure: Westland steel and duralumin construction throughout with fabric covering.

Dimensions: Span, 38ft 6in; length, 29ft 6in; height, 10ft 9in; wing area, 370 sq ft.

Weights: Tare, 3,624lb; all-up, 5,170lb.

Performance: Max speed, 185 mph at 15,000ft; climb to 20,000ft, 17 min 30 sec; service ceiling, 26,100ft.

Armament: Four synchronized 0.303in Vickers Mk III machine guns, each with 140 rounds of ammunition in fuselage nose; provision to carry four 20lb bombs under the port wing.

Prototype: One, K2891 (first flown by Harald Penrose at Andover on 23 March 1934). No production.

were fitted to the upper wing.

It transpired that none of the tendered designs were ready for flight by the date stipulated, due largely to delays in the Goshawk's development, and the Service evaluation was therefore postponed until 1934. The Westland P.V.4, K2891, was the first of the purpose-designed F.7/30 biplanes to be flown (Mitchell's Supermarine Type 224 monoplane having flown on 19 February 1934, see page 250). On 23 March 1934 Harald Penrose flew the new fighter at Andover and, from the outset, expressed concern that the engine cooling was unsatisfactory. Temperatures were constantly at or near their maximum limit, and it was found necessary frequently to throttle back to allow the engine to cool. Penrose also reported that severe airstream buffeting in the open cockpit could only be avoided provided the pilot kept his head behind the exact centre of the windscreen; the latter complaint was quickly remedied when Davenport designed an effective canopy which faired neatly into the cleft between the upper wing roots.

When K2891 was delivered to Martlesham in May for competitive evaluation it was found to be inferior to the other contenders in many respects, not least in speed and climb, being capable of attaining no more than 185 mph at 15,000 feet. Despite its ingenious design, the overall drag (generated by the deep, blunt nose, extensive wetted areas, gull-wing configuration, oversize wheel spats, deep steam condenser, etc) ruled out any likelihood of success from the start. Some comfort could, however, be gained at Yeovil from the fact that no other Goshawk-powered contender, officially-sponsored or private venture, biplane or monoplane, was adjudged capable of meeting the F.7/30 requirement.

Bristol Type 123 (F.7/30)

Despite the Air Ministry's implied preference for use of the Goshawk steam-cooled in-line engine (a view, it must be said, shared by several of the industry's aircraft designers) and the justifiably parochial attitude at Bristol towards the engines of other manufacturers, the valuable prize offered for the winning contender for the F.7/30 Specification was sufficient attraction to prompt Frank Barnwell to produce a private venture biplane design employing the Goshawk engine. (Later, when it became all too obvious that this engine would not be suitable for fighters, Bristol also tendered a Mercury-powered monoplane, the Type 133; see page 251).

Barnwell's Type 123 was a relatively small biplane of conventional configuration, employing high-tensile steel Warren box-girder primary structure in the fuselage; the heavily staggered wings were built up on twin spars with high-tensile steel flanges with light alloy sheet webs. The entire upper wing leading edge, a duralumin stressed-skin torsion box, carried slats, divided into two sections on each side; full-span ailerons were fitted. The leading edge of the cantilever lower wing carried steam condensers which were linked to a central condenser mounted in a tunnel fairing in the underside of the front fuselage. The main undercarriage comprised wheels in large trouser fairings, their structure anchored to the front and rear spars of the lower wing; contrary to early hopes, it was found necessary to

The Bristol Type 123 at Filton. (Photo: The Bristol Aeroplane Co Ltd., Neg No T123/11)

add a conventional cross-axle. The mandatory four-gun armament was located in the upper sides of the nose, but only carried 150 rounds per gun.

Barnwell selected as his powerplant the 695hp Goshawk III version and, after some delay in the delivery of this engine as well as the then-familiar cooling problems, Cyril Uwins made the first flight of the prototype (which car-

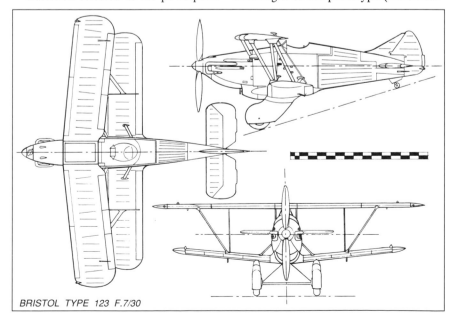

BRISTOL TYPE 123 F.7/30

ried no Service serial number) at Filton on 12 June 1934.

There appears to be no record in this instance of engine cooling problems once the flight programme started. The aircraft itself, however, proved to be laterally unstable and, in attempts to rectify this, the inner slats were fixed in the closed position and the vertical tail surfaces were enlarged. These remedies seem to have restored stability at low speeds but were ineffective as speed increased, giving rise to a belief that wing tip flexing was the cause of the instability.

Accordingly, Uwins recommended that development of the Type 123 be discontinued on the grounds of time and cost.

Type: Single-engine, single-seat, single-bay biplane interceptor fighter.
Manufacturer: The Bristol Aeroplane Co Ltd, Filton, Bristol.
Air Ministry Specification: Private venture to F.7/30.
Powerplant: One 695hp Rolls-Royce Goshawk III twelve-cylinder evaporatively-cooled in-line engine.
Dimensions: Span, 29ft 7in; length, 25ft 2in; height, 9ft 6in; wing area, 248 sq ft.
Weights: Tare, 3,330lb; all-up, 4,737lb.
Performance: Max speed, 235 mph at 14,000ft.
Armament: Four synchronized 0.303in Vickers Mk III machine guns in sides of front fuselage with 150 rounds per gun.
Prototype: One, unregistered (first flown by Cyril Uwins at Filton on 12 June 1934). No production.

Hawker P.V.3 (F.7/30)

There is no doubt that the terms of Specification F.7/30 came as something of a surprise to the Hawker company, although there is evidence that Sydney Camm was well aware early in 1930 that a very demanding requirement was then being formulated at the Air Ministry. Later that year, Hawker was asked to build a special Hart (K1102) incorporating a trial installation of the wing leading edge steam condensers on both upper and lower wings, associated with the new Goshawk engine. Thus the company was to become all too aware of the problems being faced in the course of that engine's development. (The aircraft was required to be fitted with an enclosed cockpit canopy to protect its crew from scalding steam blowing off the condensers when the engine overheated.)

Nevertheless, Camm felt that, as work continued on the standard Fury and the later High-Speed Fury, if any aircraft could meet the demands of F.7/30, an improved version of his aircraft stood as good a chance as any. Design of the company's private tender, the P.V.3, began early in 1932, this being a scaled-up version of the standard Fury I with scaled-down Hart wings. A 695hp Goshawk III was selected initially, with steam condensers on the top wing, and a small retractable condenser under the fuselage. Almost every new component, including the engine installation, underwent flight trials on either the Intermediate Fury G-ABSE or the High-Speed Fury K3586, so that by the time the

The attractive but disappointing Hawker P.V.3; the aircraft is shown fitted with the newly-developed 'ram's horn' exhaust stubs, designed to suppress the engine exhaust glare at night; unfortunately they had a habit of exploding. (Photo: Author's Collection)

P.V.3 was first flown by Bulman on 15 June 1934 scarcely any aspect of the aircraft's handling or performance in the air presented any significant difficulty.

As Hawker was not required to deliver the P.V.3 for evaluation at Martlesham until completion of trials involving the prototypes supported by the Air Ministry (from Westland, Blackburn and Supermarine), it was decided to await delivery of the later liquid-cooled Goshawks. Unfortunately, neither of these arrived at Brooklands until

May 1935, by which time a late-comer, the Gloster Gladiator — also a private venture — had been declared the F.7/30 winner.

Ironically, neither of the 700hp liquid-cooled Goshawks significantly improved the P.V.3's performance, and the eventual Martlesham trials were of no more than academic interest. The highest level speed attained by the aircraft (231 mph at 15,000ft) was with the B.43 engine driving a three-blade Fairey Reed metal propeller.

Type: Single-engine, single-seat, single-bay biplane interceptor fighter.
Manufacturer: Hawker Aircraft Ltd, Kingston and Brooklands, Surrey.
Air Ministry Specification: Private venture to F.7/30.
Powerplant: One 695hp Rolls-Royce Goshawk III twelve-cylinder evaporatively-cooled in-line engine; later 700hp Goshawk B.41 and B.43 liquid-cooled engines.
Dimensions: Span, 34ft 0in; length, 28ft 2in; height, 10ft 5in; wing area, 290.5 sq ft.
Weights: Tare, 3,530lb; all-up, 4,850lb.
Performance: (Goshawk III). Max speed, 224 mph at 14,000ft; climb to 20,000ft, 12 min 5 sec; service ceiling, 29,600ft.
Armament: Four synchronized 0.303in Vickers Mk III machine guns in upper decking and sides of front fuselage with 450 rounds per gun.
Prototype: One, unregistered, but marked IPV-4 (first flown by P W S Bulman at Brooklands on 15 June 1934). No production.

Blackburn F.3 (F.7/30)

The Blackburn F.3, designed by George Edward Petty, was the second biplane selected by the Air Ministry for proto-type manufacture under the terms of Specification F.7/30. Like the Westland P.V.4, it was also of unorthodox configuration, and one that stemmed from an exaggerated interpretation of the night flying demands.

Superficially the aircraft could be regarded as a mid-wing monoplane with a smaller wing added some two feet below the fuselage, to which it was attached by a trunk structure enclosing a large steam condenser. The pilot's cockpit was thus situated above the upper wing, thereby affording the pilot a superlative field of view. The wide-track undercarriage comprised spatted wheels mounted in steel cantilever crutches with oleos and coil-spring shock absorbers anchored to the lower wing front spars, the landing loads being transmitted to the lower fuselage longer-ons by means of twin parallel diagonal struts. The rear fuselage was a semi-monocoque structure with sheet duralu-min covering.

The Goshawk III engine was cleanly cowled and drove a two-blade wooden propeller, and the four synchronized Vickers guns were mounted in the sides of the fuselage, the top pair being situated inboard of the upper wing roots, with the two lower guns mounted to fire through ports directly above the steam condenser fairing.

Taxying of the F.3 began at Brough on 20 July 1934 but the pilot, Flt Lt A M ('Dasher') Blake, immediately re-ported overheating of the engine, sug-gesting that the single condenser was inadequate. Not less important was the discovery that the aircraft was extremely difficult to taxy safely, owing to the very short fuselage and high centre of gravity.

The wheel spats were therefore re-moved and a tailwheel fitted in place of the tailskid but, hardly surprisingly, this was of very little benefit. Furthermore, when an inspection of the rear fuselage disclosed cracks and distortions of the skin resulting from the early taxying

The ill-starred Blackburn F.3, K2892, after initial taxying and removal of the wheel spats. (Photo: A J Jackson Collection)

tests, the Air Ministry withdrew its support on the grounds that the aircraft would be delayed too long to enter the offficial evaluation trials. The project was therefore abandoned without the F.3 ever being flown.

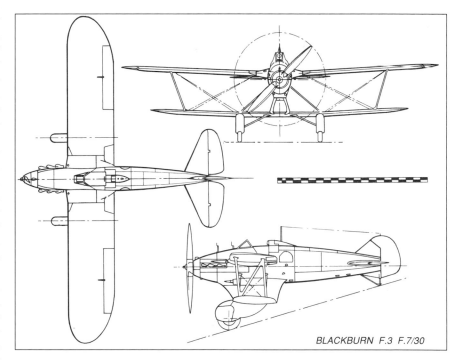

BLACKBURN F.3 F.7/30

Type: Single-engine, single-seat, single-bay biplane interceptor fighter.
Manufacturer: The Blackburn Aeroplane & Motor Co Ltd, Brough, East Yorkshire.
Air Ministry Specification: F.7/30
Powerplant: One 695hp Rolls-Royce Goshawk III twelve-cylinder evaporatively-cooled in-line engine.
Dimensions: Span, 36ft 10¾in; length, 27ft 0in; height, 10ft 0in.
Weights: Tare, 2,500lb; all-up, 3,960lb.
Performance: Estimated max speed, 190 mph at 14,500ft.
Armament: Four synchronized 0.303in Vickers Mk III machine guns in sides of fuselage with 200 rounds per gun.
Prototype: One, K2892 (not flown; taxying trials began on 20 July 1934).

Gloster Gladiator

Pilots and Gloster Gladiator Mk Is of No 54 (Fighter) Squadron await their turn to practice their flying routine at the 1937 Hendon Air Display; this Squadron would fly Spitfires during the Battle of Britain, then just three years ahead. (Photo: *Flight*, Neg No T2999)

The Gloster Gladiator marked the closing of a golden era of biplane fighters with Britain's air forces, an age that spanned a quarter of a century from the earliest years of military aviation until the advent of those saviours of the nation, the immortal Hurricane and Spitfire. Yet the Gladiator itself might never have come to be built had it not been for the steadfast confidence of its manufacturers in the capabilities of Henry Folland, whose talents were synonymous with biplane development throughout that quarter century.

Specification F.7/30, on which so much had been staked by both the Air Ministry and aircraft industry alike — such were the rewards implicit — had brought forth a host of designs, which had ranged from the exotic to the banal, only to suffer as the result of the Air Ministry's stated preference for the Rolls-Royce Goshawk steam-cooled engine. And when it was realised that this engine would demand much lengthier develop-

ment than Rolls-Royce had forecast, it had seemed likely that not only would F.7/30 be abandoned altogether but that entirely new fighter requirements, such as those foreshadowed in Specification F.5/34 for eight-gun monoplane interceptors, might render further biplane fighters superfluous. Certainly no manufacturer had yet succeeded in meeting the overall demands of F.7/30.

When it became clear that the new monoplane interceptors would be unlikely to enter service before 1937 at the earliest, and with in-service two-gun interceptor biplanes capable of speeds no higher than around 230 mph (and remembering that the Bristol Bulldog, whose top speed was no more than 174 mph, still served with ten RAF squadrons in 1933), it occurred to the Gloster Board that there would be a pressing need to introduce an interim fighter into service quickly which — ignoring the demand for a Goshawk engine — could still meet the F.7/30 requirements.

Moreover Gloster, which had failed to secure production contracts since the days of the Gamecock, found itself in a much healthier position in May 1934, once the Company had been purchased and financed by T O M Sopwith at Hawker, especially when this resulted in final acceptance of the Gauntlet for production.

Folland had been authorised to undertake further design development of the S.S.19/Gauntlet as a private venture at the end of 1933 and when, in February 1934, Bristols promised that their Mercury ME.35 radial would be delivering 800bhp within a year, Glosters decided to go ahead with the manufacture of a new prototype, the S.S.37, using where possible Gauntlet components to save time and cost. Most obvious differences were a change to single-bay wings and inclusion of single cantilever undercarriage legs with internally sprung Dowty wheels that had proved so successful on Hawker Furies sold abroad. Construction throughout was similar to that of the S.S.19, and the four-gun armament, demanded by F.7/30, comprised a pair of nose mounted Vickers guns and a Lewis gun under each lower wing. Another innovation was the addition of landing flaps on both upper and lower wings to enable the new fighter to meet the landing speed limitations while operating at night.

The prototype S.S.37, K5200, was first flown by P E G Sayer (recently moved from Hawker to Gloster after the

A Gladiator Mk I, K7985, of No 73 (Fighter) Squadron, flying from Debden in 1937. Note the faired Lewis gun under the starboard lower wing. (Photo: Air Ministry, Neg No H1558)

company had been taken over) on 12 September 1934, powered by a 530hp Mercury IV radial which bestowed a top speed of 236 mph. Soon afterwards a Mercury VIS was fitted and K5200 underwent preliminary Service evaluation under F.7/30 auspices, now disclosing a top speed of 242 mph.

In the meantime Folland submitted proposals for a number of improvements which, apart from the planned adoption of the Mercury IX, included a changeover to the Hawker-style construction, cleaned-up undercarriage and tail unit, and inclusion of a sliding cockpit canopy. Supported by calculations which promised a maximum speed of not less than 252 mph at 14,000ft, this tender was rewarded by an initial production order for 23 aircraft, to be termed the Gladiator I, and Specification F.14/35 was issued. Such was the increasing tempo of the RAF's Expansion Programme that, by September 1935, a further 180 Gladiators had been ordered.

The first production aircraft were delivered during January and February 1937. First Fighter Command Squadron to be equipped with Gladiator Is was No 72, newly re-formed at Tangmere from a flight of No 1 Squadron, commanded by Flt Lt Edward Mortlock Donaldson (later Air Cdre, CB, CBE, DSO, AFC*). Before the end of 1937 Gladiators had also joined Nos 3, 54, 56, 65, 80 and 87 Squadrons; No 54, equipped in June that year at Hornchurch, was the first to receive aircraft armed with Browning machine guns in place of the Vickers and Lewis guns, fitted initially. The following year Nos 25, 85 and 607 (County of Durham) Squadrons converted to Gladiators, but No 85 only flew them for three months before changing to Hurricanes in September. Meanwhile, in the Middle East, No 33 had received Gladiators in February, to be joined by No 80, which shipped out from England in March.

It is worth recording that, at the time of the Munich crisis in September 1938, six Gladiator squadrons were still operational with Fighter Command, compared with two of Hurricanes and no Spitfire squadrons; the balance of its strength comprised Hawker Furies and Demons, and Gloster Gauntlets. By the outbreak of war one year later the transformation to monoplane fighters was almost complete. The Auxiliary Air Force Squadrons, Nos 603, 605, 607 and 615 still flew the biplanes, and Nos. 141, 152 and 263 would all equip temporarily

with Gladiators in October 1939, pending the arrival of Hurricanes and Spitfires.

Meanwhile Glosters had introduced the Gladiator Mark II in response to Specification F.36/37 which specified the use of the shadow factory-produced Mercury VIIIAS engine driving a three-blade metal fixed-pitch Fairey propeller, introduction of provision for desert flying equipment and an improved blind flying panel. A total of 300 Gladiator IIs had been ordered during 1938, of which 38 were to be completed as Sea Gladiators (Interim) and 60 as full-standard Sea Gladiators — see page 246.

It should also be mentioned that Glosters had conducted a flourishing

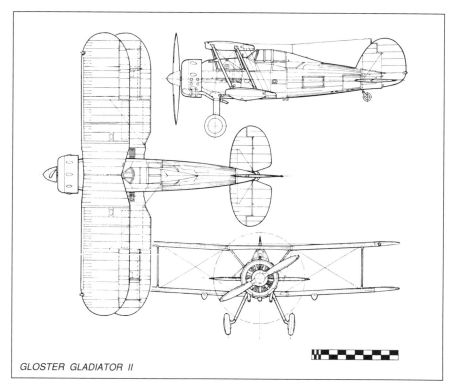

GLOSTER GLADIATOR II

Type: Single-engine, single-seat, single-bay interceptor biplane
Manufacturer: Gloster Aircraft Co Ltd, Brockworth (Hucclecote) Gloucester.
Air Ministry Specifications: F.7/30 (prototype); F.14/35 (Mark I production); F.36/37 (Mark II production).
Powerplant: Prototype, one 530hp Bristol Mercury IV nine-cylinder air-cooled radial engine (later 645hp Mercury VIS); Mark I, one 830hp Mercury IX radial driving two-blade Watts fixed-pitch wooden propeller; Mark II and Sea Gladiator, one 830hp Mercury VIIIAS radial driving three-blade Fairey fixed-pitch metal propeller.
Structure: Mixed metal and wood construction with steel tubular box girder structure in fuselage faired to oval section with wooden formers and stringers. Two-spar, single-bay wings; rear fuselage, tail and wings fabric-covered. Single-strut cantilever fixed undercarriage with internally-sprung wheels.
Dimensions: Span, 32ft 3in; length, 27ft 5in; height (Mk. I), 11ft 9in; (Mark II), 11ft 7in; wing area, 323 sq ft.
Weights: Mark I. Tare, 3,217lb; all-up, 4,594lb. Mark II. Tare, 3,444lb; all-up, 4,864lb.
Performance (Mark II): Max speed, 257 mph at 14,600ft; climb to 10,000ft, 4.5 min; service ceiling, 33,500ft.
Armament: (Late Mark Is, Mark IIs and Sea Gladiators) Two synchronized 0.303in Browning machine guns in fuselage sides with 600 rounds per gun, and two Browning guns under the lower wings, outside the propeller arc, each with 400 rounds.
Prototype: One, K5200 (first flown by P E G Sayer at Brockworth on 12 September 1934)
Production (RAF only): Mark I, 231 aircraft (K6129-K6151, K7892-K8055, L7608-L7623 and L8005-L8032); Mark II, 300 aircraft (N5500-N5549, N5565-N5594, N5620-N5649, N5680-N5729, N5750-N5789, N5810-N5859 and N5875-N5924).
Summary of Service: Served with Nos 3, 25, 54, 56, 65, 72, 73, 80, 85, 87, 141, 152, 247, 263, 521, 603, 605, 607 and 615 Squadrons, RAF, in the UK, and with Nos 6, 14, 33, 80, 94, 112, 117, 123, 127, 237, 261, 267, 274 and 520 Squadrons in the Mediterranean and Middle East. Sea Gladiators served with Nos 759, 760, 767, 769, 770, 771, 775, 776, 778, 787, 791 and 797 Training Squadrons, and Nos 801, 802, 804, 805, 806, 813, 880 and 885 Operational Squadrons of the FAA.

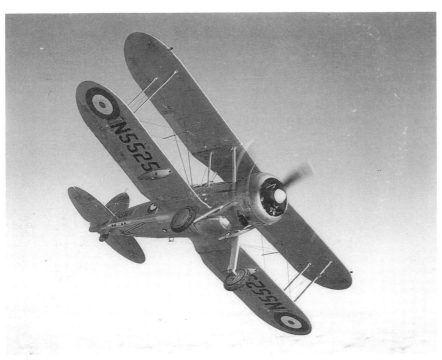

A full-standard Sea Gladiator, N5525, showing the dinghy stowage fairing between the undercarriage struts. (Photo: Via Derek James)

export business in Gladiators before the War, aircraft being sold to Latvia (26), Lithuania (14), China (36), Norway (12), Belgium (22), Eire (4), Sweden (73), Greece (2), Portugal (15) and Egypt (18), some of these aircraft being supplied from RAF stocks. Later, during the War, ex-RAF Gladiators would be supplied to Finland (30), Greece (17), Egypt (27), Iraq (9) and South Africa (11).

The Sea Gladiator

The Sea Gladiators, referred to earlier, were the outcome of an approach in 1937 by the Admiralty to the Air Ministry with a request for the adaptation of a suitable RAF fighter for fleet defence duties, to replace the four-year-old Hawker Nimrod. Replacement of the unsuitable Blackburn Skua by an aircraft based on the Fairey P.4/34 two-

seat light bomber (later to become the Fulmar) was already under consideration, but would not join the Royal Navy until 1940, and so the Gladiator was recommended as a quickly available stopgap. Thirty-eight aircraft (N2265-N2302), completed as RAF Mark IIs, were therefore modified to include V-frame arrester hooks and naval TR.9 radio, these being termed Sea Gladiators (Interim), and issued to naval shore stations for training purposes.

The main order for sixty full-standard Sea Gladiators (N5500-N5549 and N5565-N5574) incorporated the same modifications as those above in addition to provision for a dinghy stowage between the undercarriage legs as well as inclusion of catapult strongpoints.

Sea Gladiators eventually joined Nos. 801, 802, 804, 805, 806, 813, 880 and 885 Squadrons, serving aboard HM Carriers *Courageous, Eagle, Formidable, Furious,*

Glorious and *Illustrious* between 1939 and 1941. Their most memorable wartime action was, however, in defence of Malta in 1940 after a small number of Sea Gladiators, being held in naval storage on the island, was hurriedly assembled and flown by RAF pilots for several weeks after Italy's entry into the War. Many of the Sea Gladiators (Interim) were returned to RAF standard when the definitive Sea Gladiators began delivery; they were then shipped out to Aden where they equipped No 94 Squadron, later taking part in the defence of the British base at Habbaniya before being handed on to the South African Air Force.

Returning to the Gladiators in service with the RAF, No 263 Squadron was still equipped with the biplanes when it was ordered to embark in HM Carrier *Glorious* for Norway when the Germans invaded that country in April 1940. Flying from a frozen lake in central Norway their pilots contrived to provide air cover for British troops but were forced to return home when the lake was bombed and most of the Gladiators were destroyed. Given fresh aircraft, the Squadron returned, this time to defend the northern port of Narvik. Once again, despite inflicting some losses on the *Luftwaffe*, the situation became hopeless owing to the impossibility of supporting an expeditionary force far out of range from home bases and conditions of enemy air superiority.

When Italy entered the War in June 1940 and attacked in Egypt and East Africa, the Gladiators were the most modern RAF fighters in the theatre, and were heavily engaged until the arrival of the first Hurricanes some weeks later. They were then sent to Greece after the Italians attacked that country. Their pilots acquitted themselves well until the Germans joined the invasion and the surviving Gladiators were withdrawn. And it is worth recording that the

The sole surviving flying example of the Gloster Gladiator, restored by Gloster apprentices after the War and later owned by the Shuttleworth Trust, seen here flying over Gloucester. (Photo: A J Jackson Collection)

highest-scoring RAF pilot of the Second World War, Sqn Ldr M T St J Pattle DFC (a South African) achieved fifteen of his forty victories while flying Gladiators over North Africa and Greece.

The last enemy aircraft to fall to an RAF Gladiator was shot down by No 6 Squadron over Libya on 26 September 1941. By then German Messerschmitt Bf 109s had arrived in North Africa and the flow of modern allied fighters to the Middle East was adequate to allow the withdrawal of the old biplanes from front line service. Thereafter they continued to perform a multitude of second-line duties — not least that of weather reconnaissance — until January 1945.

Fairey Fox Mk VII

Although not designed to the terms of Specification F.7/30, Marcel Lobelle's two biplane fighters, the Fox Mark VII and the Fantôme, were certainly influenced by the performance and armament trends implicit in the current Air Ministry requirements.

The Fox fighter, derived from a need to provide the Belgian Air Force with an aircraft that could, as a matter of expediency, follow on from the production of Fox and Firefly aircraft at Fairey's Belgian factory.

Powered by an 860hp Hispano-Suiza 12Ydrs liquid-cooled in-line engine, the Fox Mark VII single-seat fighter was developed from the two-seat Mark V and VI reconnaissance fighters. Dubbed the *Kangourou* on account of its large ventral radiator being re-located further aft, the Fox VII possessed a heavy armament of a 20mm Oerlikon cannon firing through the propeller shaft and four synchronized machine guns in the nose; alternatively, the aircraft could mount six machine guns. Its design also

One of only two Fox Mk VIIs produced, this aircraft carries Belgian tail markings and shows the midships position of the large ventral radiator bath. (Photo: Via R C B Ashworth)

allowed for its conversion to a two-seater within one hour.

Capable of achieving a maximum speed of 232 mph at 12,500 feet, the Fox VII was never seriously considered for evaluation by the RAF owing to a general lack of manoeuvrability and its dependence on a continental engine.

Type: Single-engine, single-seat, single-bay biplane fighter.
Manufacturer: The Fairey Aviation Co Ltd, Hayes, Middlesex.
Powerplant: One 860hp Hispano-Suiza 12Ycrs liquid-cooled in-line engine.
Dimensions: Span, 38ft 0in; length, 29ft 8in.
Weight: All-up, 4,760lb.
Performance: Max speed, 232 mph at 12,500ft; service ceiling, 27,400ft.
Armament: One hub-mounted 20mm cannon and four 7.62mm FN machine guns, or six FN machine guns, in the nose.
Prototypes: Two, unregistered, flown in 1935.

Fairey Fantôme

If Lobelle's Fox VII was something of a makeshift expedient, his attractive Fantôme interceptor represented the climax of biplane fighter design, rivalling the Hawker Fury for grace and aesthetic appearance. With a speed of no less than 270 mph at 13,000 feet and a service ceiling of 36,000 feet, it eclipsed all other British biplane fighters.

With the imminent début of such monoplane fighters as the Hawker Hurricane and Supermarine Spitfire, and the Gloster Gladiator already de-

clared winner of the F.7/30 fighter competition, the Fantôme was not intended for RAF use; instead it was designed to replace the Firefly II fighter in Belgium, and was an entry for the International Fighter Competition to be staged at Evère in July 1935.

Powered by a 925hp Hispano-Suiza 12Ycrs in-line engine, the aircraft was of all-metal construction with fabric-

The attractive Fairey Fantôme, L7045, during its trials at Martlesham Heath in 1938. (Photo: RAF Museum, Neg No 019409)

covered wings, rear fuselage and tail. The fully-enclosed spatted cantilever undercarriage was faired to the lower wing roots and bracketed the very large ventral radiator bath. Armament was either a single hub-mounted 20mm Oerlikon cannon and two 7.62mm FN machine guns, or four machine guns, two of the latter being mounted within the lower wings.

One example was built in Britain and flown in June 1935, being delivered to Evère the following month after being displayed by Chris Staniland at the Hendon SBAC Show on 1 July. Although it was known to meet all the requirements demanded by the Belgian Air Force, the aircraft crashed during the competition at Evère on 17 August, killing the pilot S H G Trower. Three other Fantômes were later delivered to Belgium in kit form (where they were assembled and named the Féroce). In the meantime, however, the Belgian Air Force had changed its requirements and the Fairey fighters were no longer required.

Two of the Fantômes were purchased by the government of the USSR* and the other was returned to Britain where, purchased by the Air Ministry in December 1937 as L7045, it underwent flight tests at Farnborough, and armament trials at Martlesham Heath. The latter gave rise to a number of interesting reports, not least those concerning a comparison of the pneumatic gun cocking system on the Fantôme's wing FN guns with that in use in the Hurricane's Brownings. And the inability to achieve a clean shoot-out with the hub-mounted Oerlikon cannon provided the first indication that this gun, already intended for service with the RAF, would not be suitable on account of its dependence on greased ammunition.

The aircraft was subsequently delivered to the Air Gunnery School at Rollestone in December 1940, and was struck off charge on 19 March 1943.

* It has been suggested elsewhere that these two Fantômes were shipped to Spain and fought with the Republican Air Force during the Civil War. However, as disclosed by Gerald Howson (*Aircraft of the Spanish Civil War, 1936-1939*, Putnam, 1990), they were indeed embarked in a Soviet vessel at Antwerp on 18 August 1936, but were delivered direct to Leningrad. At least one was flown by the test pilot Gen Pyotr Stepanovich in the USSR during 1938.

Type: Single-engine, single-seat, single-bay biplane fighter.
Manufacturer: The Fairey Aviation Co Ltd, Hayes, Middlesex.
Powerplant: One 925hp Hispano-Suiza 12Ycrs twelve-cylinder liquid-cooled in-line engine.
Dimensions: Span, 34ft 6in; length, 27ft 7in; height, 11ft 4in; wing area, 293 sq ft.
Weights: Tare, 2,500lb; all-up, 4,120lb.
Performance: Max speed, 270 mph at 13,000ft; service ceiling, 36,000ft; range, 360 miles.
Armament: Either one hub-mounted 20mm Oerlikon cannon and two 7.62mm FN machine guns, or four FN machine guns.
Prototype: One, registered F-6 (Class B) and G-ADIF (first flown in June 1935 by C S Staniland).
Production: Three aircraft (two purchased by the USSR and one by the Air Ministry as L7045).

Armstrong Whitworth A.W.35 Scimitar

Resigned to the fact that the days of the biplane interceptor fighter were numbered, Armstrong Whitworth persevered with one last development of the company's Starling/A.W.XVI formula, rebuilding the second A.W.XVI, G-ACCD, with a 735hp Panther X engine. The nose decking was lowered, the fin and rudder enlarged and the undercarriage redesigned to have smaller wheel spats and split axle. In this form it was first flown on 29 June 1935. A second conversion of an A.W.XVI airframe was also completed and registered G-ADBL.

Four production Scimitars were produced for Norway and were delivered during 1936. Two of these underwent evaluation with the A & AEE at the end of 1935 (sometimes, incorrectly, said to be evaluation trials in the context of F.7/30 — which had ended almost a year previously). These Norwegian Scimitars returned a speed of no more than 217 mph at 14,000 feet, but handled well in the air.

The first Armstrong Whitworth Scimitar prototype, G-ACCD. (Photo: Via R C Sturtivant)

The Scimitar was the last fighter built by the company. G-ACCD was scrapped in 1936, but G-ADBL survived until disposed of in October 1958.

Type: Single-engine, single-seat, single-bay biplane interceptor fighter.
Manufacturer: Sir W G Armstrong Whitworth Aircraft Ltd, Coventry.
Powerplant: One 735hp Armstrong Siddeley Panther X fourteen-cylinder radial engine; also 624hp Panther IXA and 640hp Panther VII.
Dimensions: Span, 33ft 0in; length, 25ft 0in; height, 12ft 0in; wing area, 261.3 sq ft.
Weights: Tare, 2,956lb; all-up, 4,100lb.
Performance: Max speed, 221 mph at 14,000ft; climb to 10,000ft, 5 min 15 sec.
Armament: Two synchronized 0.303in Vickers Mk V machine guns in the nose decking.
Prototypes: Two, G-ACCD and G-ADBL (G-ACCD flown as A.W.35 on 29 June 1935).
Production: Four aircraft sold to Norway.

Deployment of British Fighter Squadrons — January 1935

Home-Bases

No 1 Squadron	Hawker Fury I	Tangmere		No 54 Squadron	Bristol Bulldog IIA	Hornchurch
No 3 Squadron	Bristol Bulldog IIA	Kenley		No 56 Squadron	Bristol Bulldog IIA	North Weald
No 17 Squadron	Bristol Bulldog IIA	Kenley		No 65 Squadron	Hawker Demon	Hornchurch
No 19 Squadron	Bristol Bulldog IIA	Duxford		No 111 Squadron	Bristol Bulldog IIA	Northolt
No 23 Squadron	Hawker Demon	Biggin Hill				
No 25 Squadron	Hawker Fury I	Hawkinge		*Fleet Air Arm*		
No 29 Squadron	Bristol Bulldog IIA	North Weald		No 801 Squadron	Hawker Nimrod/Osprey	HMS *Courageous*
No 32 Squadron	Bristol Bulldog IIA	Biggin Hill		No 802 Squadron	Hawker Nimrod	HMS *Furious*
No 41 Squadron	Hawker Demon	Northolt		No 803 Squadron	Hawker Osprey	Seletar
No 43 Squadron	Hawker Fury I	Tangmere				(Singapore)

5. THE FIRST GENERATION MONOPLANES

The Specification F.7/30, despite its extravagant demands, did not in itself succeed in breaking the shackles of the biplane fighter formula. That had not been its purpose *per se*, rather, by encouraging engineers and designers to divest themselves of traditional attitudes, to exploit the latent talents that were known to exist — but stifled by prejudice — within the industry. On the other hand Sir John Salmond had been all too conscious that the Air Ministry had frequently made ill-judged decisions in its selction of certain aircraft and engines, and the industry had not only exposed those decisions as faulty but had suffered accordingly. A string of ill-advised recommendations to support aero engines, such as the ABC Dragonfly and the Bristol Mercury (to name only the best remembered), had cost the aircraft manufacturers dearly in failed prototypes. And the latest failure of the Rolls-Royce Goshawk could have been the greatest disaster of all.

The real value of F.7/30 had been to demonstrate dramatically the ultimate limitations of the biplane. The very emergence of the Gladiator as the winning contender, by means of extreme attention to detail rather than any significant excursion into new technology, did *not* act as a spur to other designers but simply as a demonstration of how far a radial-engine biplane was ever likely to go. The subsequent appearance of the sleek Fairey Fantôme, with its in-line engine, merely rammed the lesson home — a lesson that was already being learned, if not yet put into practice.

Of course monoplanes had been produced experimentally, but all were compromised by traditional forms of construction, bulky engines of unspectacular performance and a lack of incentive to engage in fundamental research. The triumphant Schneider Trophy seaplanes had demonstrated that there were men of imagination and skill, particularly in the sphere of engine and fuel technology; monocoque structures had appeared from time to time over the past dozen years, as had cantilever wing structures, retractable undercarriages, landing flaps and variable-pitch propellers. There had been no incentive to undertake the necessary radical approach to combine these innovations so long as the biplane reigned supreme and prejudice against the small, high performance monoplane remained rife.

In 1933 these attitudes changed abruptly. It would be possible to list a score of reasons, political, economic and technical. Britain was emerging from the Depression, and this was manifest in a modest increase in the Air Estimates; and there were ominous signs that Germany was setting course for a return to militarism and a dangerous dictatorship. Yet the Royal Air Force itself, for all its glitter, was stuck on a technical plateau of no great eminence. By 1934 that technical stalemate appeared to have been further compounded by the failure of the Goshawk, with its knock-on effect on so many of the F.7/30 contenders, not least the Supermarine Type 224 monoplane (see over). Indeed no one appeared to have produced a fighter significantly advanced beyond the Hawker Fury, by now already four years old.

Yet, as the result of closer ties between the Air Ministry's research and development directorate and the RAE, A & AEE and other experimental agencies, fostered by Hugh Dowding, a much deeper understanding of the industry's difficulties had been acquired, exposing the reasons why industry had not felt free to exploit its full range of talents.

One of the stultifying influences on fighter design had been in the sphere of gun armament, the so-called 'front gun'. Ever since the old pusher gun carrier had temporarily solved the problem of unrestricted forward fire, the Lewis and Vickers guns had been the staple armament of British fighters (with occasional goodwill gestures towards the exponents of the heavy COW gun). However, the Lewis gun was essentially a rear defence weapon, usually mounted on a rotating cockpit ring and demanding manual replenishment; and the Vickers gun was so notoriously prone to jamming that it had to be located within physical reach of the pilot.

It was therefore decided to stage a competitive evaluation of all the leading aircraft guns from abroad, with a view to obtaining a licence to manufacture the winning weapon in Britain. This was to result in the Air Ministry successfully negotiating to produce the American Colt, adapted for 0.303in ammunition and named the Browning, for this gun was shown to have a stoppage rate of less than one-sixtieth of that of the Vickers Mk III.

Even before this gun evaluation was announced, let alone staged, a new Specification, F.5/34, was drafted in fairly general terms, calling for a monoplane fighter to be armed with no fewer than eight front machine guns, at least some of which would *have* to be mounted out of the pilot's reach.

And while most designers were scratching their heads, trying to decide how best to meet this requirement, Sydney Camm at Hawker, and Reginald Mitchell at Supermarine were discussing specific monoplane projects with the Directorate of Technical Development at the Air Ministry, designs which initially took no account of F.5/34 but were essays in new aircraft configuration and advanced performance. Fairly quickly it dawned on these designers that there was little in the radical nature of their proposals that would prevent them from satisfying, indeed surpassing the requirements of F.5/34.

However, whereas Camm proposed to remain with the well-tried metal box-girder primary structure — not only in the interests of rapid introduction into service and production, but because

Hawker was only staffed and equipped for that type of construction — Mitchell opted to advance to full metal monocoque. In the event both proposals were accepted, each on its individual merits, and each company was provided with its own Specification.

Both designers opted for the same make of engine, an engine that was, in the next ten years, to be built in greater numbers than any other; this was the Rolls-Royce Merlin, then just beginning its flight trials as the P.V.12. Decisions taken at that time, with regard to aircraft and engines, can be seen in long retrospect as having been entirely fundamental for the survival of Britain in the war that would break out half a decade later.

It would be wrong to suggest that the Hurricane and Spitfire came to dominate the activities of the aircraft industry, although they certainly concentrated the minds of their respective parent companies. The apparently in-

exorable re-armament of Nazi Germany spurred Britain to an accelerating expansion of her armed forces. All categories of aircraft in the RAF demanded modernization, not least its bomber force and training organization. And while the Hurricane and Spitfire were regarded solely as metropolitan day interceptors, other fighters, the night interceptors and fleet fighters, were all due to be retired and replaced. Yet despite a doubling of the manufacturing capacity of the industry in little over four years, there was a limit to what could be undertaken, so that aircraft such as the Demon two-seater and the Sea Gladiator would not finally disappear from the squadrons for some years yet.

So profound was the effect produced by the appearance of Hurricanes and Spitfires in squadron service in 1938, that only one year later almost every biplane had disappeared from the front line, and those that remained were already anachronisms.

Supermarine Type 224 (F.7/30)

Ironically the best known aircraft submitted to Specification F.7/30 was Reginald Mitchell's Type 224 monoplane, an aircraft which certainly turned many heads when it first appeared at the 1934 Hendon Display, yet fared no better than any of the other Goshawk-powered prototypes. The public's interest lay in the fact that the designer had produced the superb seaplanes which won the Schneider Trophy outright for Britain three years previously.

The original Type 224 design proposal had been submitted to the Air Ministry on 20 February 1932, and finally emerged as an officially spon-

The Supermarine Type 224, K2890, as it appeared for its Service evaluation at Martlesham Heath in 1934 with RAF rudder markings. (Photo: Via R C Sturtivant)

sored prototype, K2890, after constant changes for its first flight in the hands of 'Mutt' Summers almost exactly two years later on 19 February 1934. It was a low gull-wing monoplane employing steam condensers for its 600hp Goshawk II engine along the leading edge of

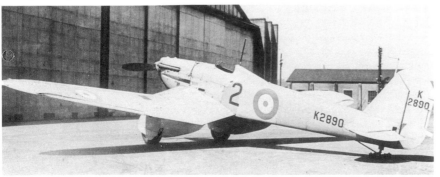

the wings outboard of the wing crank. The wing itself was constructed about a single light-alloy spar, the condensers occupying the entire wing surface forward of this spar; aft, the wings were fabric-covered. The rear fuselage was of semi-monocoque form with longitudinal light-alloy stringers and frames covered by flush-riveted panels. The wide-track cantilever undercarriage was enclosed in large trousers, and the main oleo struts were attached to the wing spar at the outboard ends of the anhedralled centre section. Two of the Vickers guns were located in the wing roots,

K2890 wearing the New Type No 2 for the 1934 Hendon Air Display. (Photo: E B Morgan)

and the other two in the sides of the fuselage with long blast channels.

Known unofficially by the manufacturers as the Spitfire (a name that did not impress Mitchell), the Type 224 was submitted for its official evaluation at Martlesham after appearing at Hendon on 30 June, wearing the New Type number 2. Despite early design estimates, the all-up weight had risen by some 700 pounds, and K2890 returned a maximum speed of 228 mph at 15,000 feet — about 12 mph down on earlier estimates. Its landing speed, at 60 mph, was 10 mph higher than the maximum allowed for in the Specification.

No one was less surprised by this disappointing performance than Mitchell himself, who was already discussing with the Air Ministry extensive alterations to the prototype, including straight (uncranked) wings, retractable undercarriage and an enclosed cockpit. The Goshawk engine was retained on the assumption that the cooling problems would soon be overcome.

These alterations were accepted by the Air Ministry at a cost of around £3,000, but no progress in implementing them was made and, in any case, an entirely new design — albeit deriving lessons from the Type 224 — was being discussed, and further work on K2890 was suspended in favour of this new, infinitely more distinguished Spitfire.

In mid-1935 K2890 was delivered to Farnborough for use as a 'hack' until it was flown to Martlesham in 1937 and subsequently moved to Orfordness as a gunnery target.

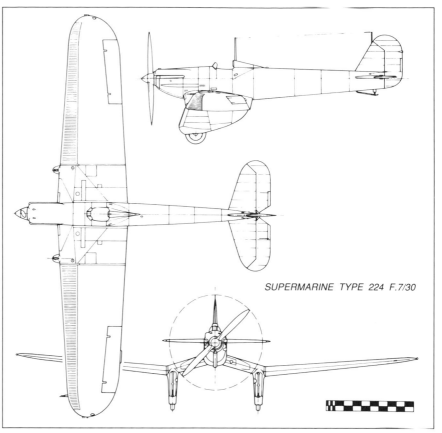

SUPERMARINE TYPE 224 F.7/30

Type: Single-engine, single-seat, low gull-wing monoplane fighter.
Manufacturer: Supermarine Aviation Works (Vickers) Ltd, Southampton, Hampshire.
Air Ministry Specification: F.7/30.
Powerplant: One 600hp Rolls-Royce Goshawk II twelve-cylinder evaporatively-cooled in-line engine.
Dimensions: Span, 45ft 10in; length, 29ft 5¼in; height, 11ft 11in; wing area, 295 sq ft.
Weights: Tare, 3,422lb; all-up, 4,743lb.
Performance: Max speed, 228 mph at 15,000ft; climb to 15,000ft, 9 min 30 sec; absolute ceiling, 38,800ft.
Armament: Four synchronized 0.303in Vickers Mk III machine guns, of which two were mounted in the wing roots and two in the sides of the fuselage.
Prototype: One, K2890 (first flown by J Summers on 19 February 1934).

Bristol Type 133 (F.7/30)

Convinced that Specification F.7/30 was intended to set the aircraft industry on the path of monoplane development, and that it would fail to be fully satisfied by an aircraft powered by the Goshawk engine, Roy Fedden suggested in February 1932 that Barnwell should, as quickly as possible, prepare the design

of a monoplane with the new Bristol Mercury VIS2 radial, as a private venture insurance against failure of the Type 123 (see page 241).

Making extensive use of Alclad sheet, recently invented in America, the prototype Type 133 fighter was, like the Supermarine Type 224, a low gull-wing

Taxying the Bristol 133 in its final configuration, with sliding cockpit canopy, split flaps, and short ailerons. (Photo: The Bristol Aeroplane Co Ltd, Neg No T133/32)

monoplane with a cantilever wing, but with an undercarriage that retracted rearwards into underwing fairings situated at the wing crank.

When first flown by Uwins on 8 June 1934 — only fourteen months, be it noted, after the start of the design — the Bristol prototype featured an open cockpit, but within two months this had been provided with a sliding canopy and faired headrest. Split flaps and short-span ailerons replaced the long-span, drooping ailerons originally fitted. A low-drag circular exhaust collector ring was incorporated in the leading edge of a long-chord cowling enclosing the 640hp Mercury VIS2 engine.

Manufacturer's handling and performance trials were completed at Filton by the end of February 1935, and on 8 March Uwins performed the necessary spinning and diving trials before the aircraft was due to be delivered to Martlesham for Service evaluation. However, before the scheduled departure, the company pilot Flt Lt Thomas Wight Campbell RAFO took off for a final half-hour's handling flight. On reaching 14,000 feet he put the fighter into a spin, but overlooked the fact that he had not retracted the undercarriage. A flat spin developed, from which the aircraft would not recover, and the pilot was forced to bale out; the new fighter crashed and was destroyed.

No time remained in which a replacement could be prepared, and the project had to be abandoned. By then, however, Barnwell was already examining a new Specification, F.5/34, which called for an eight-gun monoplane fighter (see page 264).

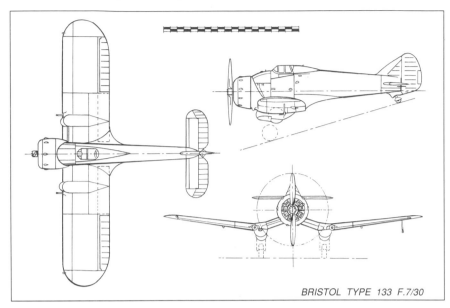

BRISTOL TYPE 133 F.7/30

Type: Single-engine, single-seat, low gull-wing monoplane fighter.
Manufacturer: The Bristol Aeroplane Co Ltd, Filton, Bristol.
Air Ministry Specification: Private venture to F.7/30.
Powerplant: One 640hp Bristol Mercury VIS2 nine-cylinder radial engine.
Dimensions: Span, 39ft 9in; length, 28ft 0in; height, 9ft 9in; wing area, 247 sq ft.
Weights: Tare, 3,322lb; all-up, 4,738lb.
Performance: Max speed, 260 mph at 15,000ft.
Armament: Two synchronized 0.303in Vickers Mk III machine guns in the front fuselage and two free-firing Lewis guns in the wings immediately outboard of the undercarriage fairings.
Prototype: One, R-10 (Class B), first flown by Cyril Uwins on 8 June 1934. No production.

Hawker Hurricane I

In long retrospect it may be seen that there was an inevitability in the emergence of Sydney Camm's Hurricane. That this fighter should have evolved in the way it did was logical, for the Hawker designer had not been notable for radical adventure as perhaps had Mitchell at Supermarine, and Pierson and Wallis at Vickers. His sound and successful biplane fighters, the Fury, Demon and Nimrod were the best in

their respective categories in service with the Royal Air Force, yet had failed to shift away from the two-gun biplane formula. Nor was Hawker Aircraft equipped to transfer to metal monocoque construction, and while Camm's Hart family filled the factories of the British aircraft industry with orders stretching away for several years to come there was, in 1933, little to recommend immediate and costly investment in a change to new plant.

Yet change was in the air. Almost every other major aircraft manufacturer had produced a monoplane project (and as long ago as 1925 Camm himself had schemed a Jupiter-powered monoplane interceptor). Air Ministry Specification F.7/30 had only partly succeeded in encouraging aircraft designers to break with the old biplane formula; Mitchell had produced a nondescript monoplane but, predictably perhaps, Camm had gone no further than to produce a

The Hawker Hurricane prototype, K5083, seen at Brooklands before its first flight in November 1935; it is fitted with the small convergent/divergent radiator, single canopy stiffener, wheel-door D-flaps and tailplane strut; radio and armament have not yet been installed. (Photo: Hawker Aircraft Ltd, Neg No 54A dated 6 November 1935)

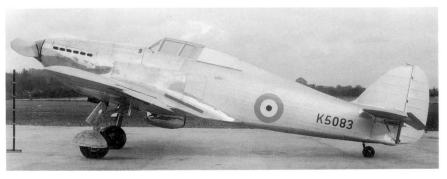

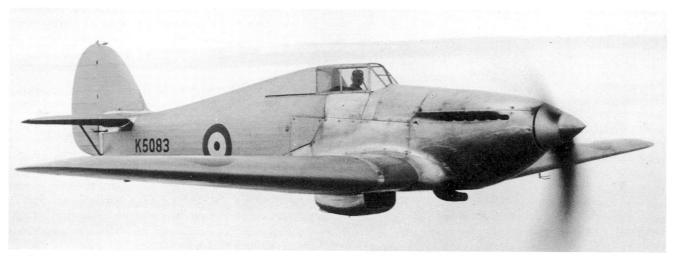

Flt Lt P W S ('George') Bulman flying the Hurricane prototype in December 1935 in its original form. (Photo: Cyril Peckham)

limited re-working of the Fury biplane.

Realising that F.7/30 was heading for nothing more exceptional than a compromise, Camm took soundings at the Air Ministry to try to discover how this failure was being viewed by the Service, and at the same time instructed his senior design staff to examine the possibility of evolving a monoplane from the Fury. Two fundamental pointers to the future path were soon in evidence.

In the first place the constant demand for greater speed exposed a growing weakness in the traditional interceptor fighter's armament. Two or four Vickers machine guns, because of their inherent unreliability, had usually been mounted in the fuselage so as to be within reach of the pilot, and therefore had to be synchronized to fire through the propeller. It was being pointed out that such meagre armament was quite inadequate to inflict fatal damage in the fleeting bursts possible in a dogfight at speeds approaching 300 miles per hour — now being seriously considered.

Secondly, the Air Ministry was beginning to express doubts as to the suitability of the steam-cooled Rolls-Royce Goshawk engine for fighter air-craft, despite having previously strongly supported this engine in the context of F.7/30. And Rolls-Royce itself had been working on a new V-twelve liquid-cooled in-line engine at its own expense. Known then as the PV.12, this engine was less radical in its power output (as several engines were already developing about 1,000 horse power) than its power-weight ratio and, at an installed weight of around 1,200 pounds, suggested that it would be ideal for a fighter aircraft.

While Camm and his design staff were now obliged to discard any pretence at extending the 'Fury Monoplane' concept, a new Air Ministry Specification, F.5/34, had been drafted, calling for an interceptor monoplane to be armed with a wing-mounted battery of eight machine guns. The Air Ministry was now also calling for fighter aircraft to be capable of speeds *in excess* of 300 mph.

During the first nine months of 1934 a new Hawker design was schemed up. The Goshawk of the 'Fury Monoplane' was replaced by the new PV.12, and an entirely new wing was designed, incorporating an immensely strong centre-section into which the landing gear retracted. By anchoring the undercarriage at the outboard extremities of this centresection so as to fold inwards into the thickest part of the wing, the undercarriage was of wide track and very strong. A large radiator for engine cooling was located under the fuselage directly below the cockpit. The structure was traditionally 'Hawker', the fuselage comprising the familiar Warren box girder fabricated in steel tube, with wooden frames and stringers. Aft of the cockpit the entire aircraft was fabric-covered. The wings, with Hawker dumbbell spars and Warren bracing, ribs and frames, were also fabric-covered. And, as a sign of the times, the cockpit was enclosed by a sliding canopy.

This scheme was submitted to the Air Ministry although, pending a decision on the type of machine gun preferred by the Service, the Hawker project featured four Vickers guns mounted in the fuselage and wing roots. Top speed was calculated to be about 315 mph. Stemming from this tender, a new Specification was prepared relating specifically to Hawker's ideas, and covering the manufacture of a single prototype. Early in 1935 this Specification, F.36/34, was amended to include a battery of eight American Colt (Browning) 0.303in machine guns in the wings.

The prototype F.36/34 — the first fighter capable of more than 300 mph to be ordered for the RAF — made its

The first production Hurricane I, L1547; compare with the photograph opposite; this aeroplane fought in the Battle of Britain but was shot down while serving with a Czechoslovak squadron. (Photo: Hawker Aircraft Ltd, Neg No 198K dated October 1937).

Formerly a standard Hurricane I of No 56 Squadron, this aircraft was returned to Hawker for repairs and was subsequently employed by the company, civil registered as G-AFKX, for a wide variety of trial installations, including numerous versions of the Merlin engine and the Rotol constant-speed propeller, as seen here at Brooklands shortly before the War. (Photo: Author's Collection)

maiden flight in the hands of Flt Lt P W S Bulman at Brooklands on 6 November 1935. Only four months later the aircraft, K5083, now named the Hurricane, paid the first of several visits to Martlesham Heath for preliminary Service evaluation, where it was flown by Sergeant Sammy Wroath (later Gp Capt, CBE, AFC *), the pilot charged with seeing the new fighter through its various trials during the next few years.

The eight-gun armament was first installed in K5083 in July 1936, by which time the external bracing struts beneath the tailplane had been discarded as superfluous, as had the hinged D-doors on the lower edge of the undercarriage fairings.

Early in 1937 occurred a temporary setback when it was decided to change over to the Mark II version of the Merlin (as the PV.12 had been named); the angled rocker-box flanges of the later engine required an entirely new nose profile to be designed. This delayed production of the Hurricane by almost three months and it was not until 12 October that year that the first production aircraft, L1547, was flown by Philip Lucas, Bulman's assistant test pilot.

Nevertheless the first four aircraft had been delivered to No 111 (Fighter) Squadron (commanded by Sqn Ldr John Woodburn Gillan) at Northolt

before Christmas. Benefitting from familiar manufacturing techniques, production of the Hurricane accelerated quickly, and Nos 3 (Sqn Ldr Hugh Lewis Pingo Lester) and 56 (Sqn Ldr Charles Leslie Lea-Cox) Squadrons re-equipped during the first six months of 1938. In the meantime, extended spinning trials and wind tunnel tests had shown that, in the deep-stalled condition, spin recovery was unnecessarily slow owing to a breakdown of airflow over the whole of the underside of the rear fuselage with a result that a ventral spine fairing was added to restore the effectiveness of the lower half of the rudder; this modification was introduced from the 61st Hurricane onwards. By the end of 1938 ten Hurricane squadrons had received their new aircraft, of which five had been declared fully operational.

All aircraft delivered thus far had been powered by the Merlin II driving the standard two-blade fixed-pitch Watts wooden propeller, but already tests had been made on the 16th production aircraft, L1562, with the D.H.-Hamilton two-pitch three-blade metal propeller which was found to give improved take-off and climb. However, an even better design had been developed by Rotol Ltd (from the old Hele-Shaw-Beecham experiments) employing a

constant-speed unit on the front of the engine which supplied hydraulic power to the propeller pitch-change gear to ensure constant speed during the climb. In order to permit the use of either D.H. or Rotol propeller, a further change introduced the Merlin III with universal propeller shaft. Rotol-equipped Hurricanes were beginning to reach the RAF at the end of 1939—although most were still fitted with the D.H. pattern.

The other major change to occur during 1939 was the introduction of metal-clad wings to the Hurricane, the first set being flown by Lucas with L1877 on 28 April. The inevitability of war following the Munich crisis was widely recognised, and with it the likelihood of hostilities with Italy in the Middle East. Accordingly a Hurricane, L1669, was prepared for tropical trials with the addition of a Vokes Multi-Vee sand filter under the Hurricane's nose, on the carburettor air intake, and shipped out to Khartoum during the summer.

Another important trial installation involved the mounting of a pair of Oerlikon 20mm cannon under the wings of L1750 and first flown by Lucas on 24 May 1939. This gun was to be widely used on ships of the Royal Navy but, owing to the need to grease the ammunition, it was found to be unsuitable for aircraft and was quickly discarded, the alternative British Hispano Mark I gun being generally adopted. (Nevertheless L1750 remained at Martlesham Heath after the A & AEE moved to Boscombe Down on the outbreak of war — and was to fly in combat during the Battle of Britain.)

Evidence that the Hurricane could withstand severe battle damage and survive was provided by this aircraft during the Battle of Britain. Plt Off Anthony John Jamieson Truran of No 615 Squadron was attacked by Messerschmitts off Dungeness but, despite cannon hits in the rear fuselage, made his way back to his base at Kenley and landed safely. (Photo: Author's Collection)

By the outbreak of war in September a total of 497 Hurricanes had been completed, out of 1,500 then on order. Fifteen squadrons of the RAF and Auxiliary Air Force had been re-equipped with the eight-gun fighters, and the early redundant aircraft with Merlin IIs and fabric wings were being passed to training units. Yet, despite the importance attached to creating new Hurricane squadrons in Fighter Command, Hawker had also undertaken a number of export orders, with Mark Is being supplied to Yugoslavia (12), Canada (20), Belgium (20), Romania (12), Turkey (15) and South Africa (3). Gloster Aircraft Co Ltd at Brockworth was already well advanced with a Hurricane production line, and plans were in hand to build the aircraft in Canada.

Four Hurricane Squadrons (Nos 1, 79, 85 and 87) were flown to France as part of the Air Component and Advanced Air Striking Force to provide cover for the BEF and as escort for RAF light bombers. And it was to the guns of a Hurricane flown by Plt Off Peter Mould of No 1 Squadron that the first German aircraft, a Dornier Do 17P, fell in France on 30 October. At home, on 29 November, a Heinkel He 111H was shot down off Newcastle by the CO of No 111 (Fighter) Squadron, Sqn Ldr H. Broadhurst (later Air Chief Marshal Sir Harry, GCB, KBE, DSO*, DFC*, AFC).

The Hurricane I was involved in the short and disastrous Norwegian campaign during the spring of 1940 when, in its closing stages No 46 (Fighter) Squadron (Sqn Ldr K B B Cross, later Air Chief Marshal Sir Kenneth, KCB, CBE, DSO, DFC) sailed in HM Carrier *Glorious* to the northern port of Narvik. The Squadron was almost entirely lost on the voyage home when the carrier was sunk by enemy warships; the Hurricanes had been involved in the air defence of the Narvik area while operating from Bardufoss. Stemming from this evidence of Britain's inability to provide adequate support for a detachment of land-based short-range fighters was a proposal to fit floats to a Hurricane to enable it to operate from Norwegian fjords but, although a pair of Blackburn Roc floats was delivered to Hawker, the quick end of the campaign early in June caused the whole scheme to be abandoned.

The Hurricane will forever be synonymous with the Battle of Britain. Although rather slower than the Spitfire, the Hurricane equipped no fewer than 29 squadrons of Fighter Command

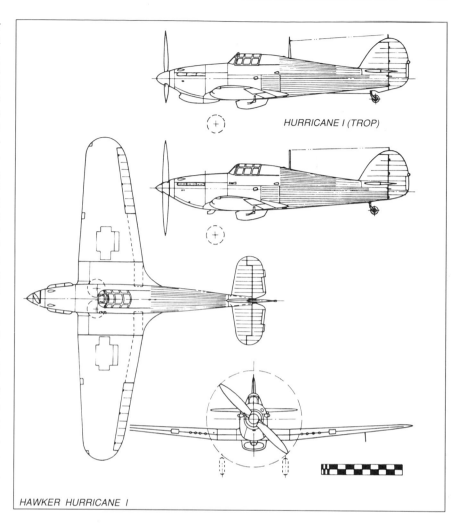

HURRICANE I (TROP)

HAWKER HURRICANE I

Type: Single-engine, single-seat low-wing monoplane interceptor fighter.

Manufacturers: Hawker Aircraft Ltd, Kingston-upon-Thames, Brooklands and Langley; Gloster Aircraft Co Ltd, Brockworth; Canadian Car & Foundry Corporation, Montreal.

Air Ministry Specifications: Prototype, F.36/34; production, 15/36P

Powerplant: One 1,030hp Rolls-Royce Merlin II or III twelve-cylinder, liquid-cooled supercharged in-line engine driving two-blade wooden fixed-pitch Watts propeller, or three-blade metal two-pitch D.H.-Hamilton propeller, or three-blade metal constant-speed Rotol propeller.

Structure: Fuselage of Warren girder box fabricated in steel tube with wooden secondary frames and stringers, fabric-covered aft of the cockpit; twin-spar wings with Warren inter-spar structure (fabric-covered on early aircraft, metal-clad later). Wide-track, inwards retracting undercarriage; all but very early aircraft had fixed tailwheel.

Dimensions: Span, 40 ft 0 in; length, 31 ft 4 in; height, 12 ft 11½ in; wing area, 258 sq ft.

Weights (Merlin III, Rotol propeller): Tare, 4,982 lb; all-up, 6,447 lb.

Performance (Merlin III, Rotol propeller): 324 mph at 17,800 ft; rate of climb at sea level, 2,200 ft/min; time to 20,000 ft, 8.1 min; absolute ceiling, 35,400 ft; normal range, 470 miles.

Armament: Eight wing-mounted 0.303in Browning machine guns with 2,660 rounds of ammunition.

Prototype: One, K5083 (first flown, 6 November 1935, by Flt Lt PWS Bulman at Brooklands).

Production: 1,994 by Hawker Aircraft Ltd; 1,850 by Gloster Aircraft Co Ltd.; 380 by Canadian Car & Foundry Corporation. (Total, 4,224 Mark Is)

Summary of Service: Served with Nos 1, 3, 6, 17, 29, 30, 32, 33, 43, 46, 56, 71, 79, 80, 85, 87, 94, 95, 96, 98, 111, 116, 121, 123, 126, 127, 128, 145, 151, 173, 182, 185, 193, 195, 208, 213, 225, 229, 232, 237, 238, 239, 242, 245, 247, 249, 250, 253, 255, 256, 257, 258, 260, 261, 263, 273, 274, 286, 288, 289, 302 (Polish), 303 (Polish), 306 (Polish), 308 (Polish), 310 (Czech), 312 (Czech), 315 (Polish), 316 (Polish), 317 (Polish), 318 (Polish), 331 (Norwegian), 335 (Greek), 401 (Canadian), 402 (Canadian), 450 (Australian), 488 (New Zealand), 516, 527, 534, 680 and 691 Squadrons, RAF; Nos 605, 607, 610 and 615 Squadrons, AAF; Nos. 748, 760, 803 and 806 Squadrons, Fleet Air Arm.

Left: *An early Hurricane I, with a tropical filter under the nose, shipped out to West Africa on the long reinforcement route to the Middle East. It was allocated to No 1 Squadron of the South African Air Force and is seen about to take off from Agordat in Eritrea during the East African campaign in February 1941 against the Italians.* (Photo: South African Air Force)

Right: *Another very early tropical Hurricane I, this time a Tac R Mark I, almost certainly of No 208 Squadron. Retaining its eight wing guns, this version featured a vertical or oblique camera in the fuselage just aft of the cockpit for tactical reconnaissance in the Western Desert. The 'sand and spaghetti' style of camouflage on the nose and wing leading edges was unusual on British aircraft, and was copied from the Italians.*

Below: *The Hillson bi-mono slip-wing Hurricane at Boscombe Down during experiments to enable fighters to operate out of very small airfields; the upper wing would have been jettisoned after take-off. The tests were discontinued in September 1943.* (Photo: Author's Collection)

at the beginning of the Battle in July — a figure which grew to 33 during the next four months. The great majority of the Hawker fighters were by then late standard Mark Is with either D.H. or Rotol propellers, and with metal-clad wings. Moreover, such was the relative ease with which new pilots could be trained on the Hurricane, it was this fighter that was to be flown by the Canadian, Polish and Czech squadrons which were formed in Fighter Command during 1940. Indeed it was a Czech pilot who topped the scores of enemy aircraft destroyed by RAF pilots in the great Battle; Sergeant Josef Frantisek of No 303 (Polish) Squadron de-

stroyed seventeen German aircraft in just one month before being killed in an accident.

Hurricanes outnumbered all other RAF fighters together during the Battle of Britain by about five to three, and accounted for more enemy aircraft than those by all other defences combined by roughly the same ratio. Halfway through the Battle the Mark I began to be joined by the Mark II with Merlin XX engine (see page 293) and, in addition, Hurricanes were beginning to be employed in the night fighting rôle. A couple of experimental cannon-armed Mark Is, one with two guns (L1760, already mentioned) and the other (P2640) with

four guns, were flown on a small number of combat sorties during the Battle.

After the Battle of Britain was over, accelerating production enabled the Mark II to re-equip most of the front-line squadrons while the Mark Is were often relegated to training duties. However, beginning in June 1940 with Italy's entry into the War, Hurricanes began delivery to the Mediterranean and North Africa. An early trickle soon became a steady flow and in due course Hurricanes were being embarked in carriers for delivery to Malta, then coming under increasing attack by the Italians. By the end of 1940 Hurricane Is equipped three Squadrons (Nos 33, 73 and 274) in the Western Desert. By then most aircraft were being fitted with the cumbersome Vokes tropical air filter under the nose, a necessary modification which, however, reduced the Hurricane I's top speed to about 310 mph.

Hurricane Is continued to serve in the combat rôle during the first six months of 1941 in the Mediterranean and were present in the latter stages of the Greek campaign in which No 33 (Fighter) Squadron was led for a short time before his death in action by Sqn Ldr M T St J Pattle DFC, the South African who (flying Gladiators as well as Hurricanes) shot down more enemy aircraft than any other RAF pilot in the Second World War.

Numerous trials involved Hurricane Is before and early in the War, including slotted wings on L1696, and numerous tests with non-standard Merlins. The most important development programme in the Mark I's later life was its evolution as a ship-borne catapult fighter, aircraft being fitted with spools to enable the Hurricane to be catapulted from the fo'c'sles of merchant ships to provide protection of convoys from German anti-shipping raiders. This series of trials, towards the end of 1940, led in turn to the introduction of the Sea Hurricane (see page 296).

It was a Hurricane I that was to be employed in one of the most unusual experiments. Messrs Hill & Son Ltd had been engaged in bi-monoplane trials with a light aircraft before acquiring a redundant Hurricane, 321 (built in Britain as L1884 before the War, shipped to Canada for service with the Royal Canadian Air Force, but then returned to the UK), to which was fitted a jettisonable upper wing. The purpose of the scheme, proposed by Hills, was to enable the Hurricane to operate out of very small airfields by using the extra lift of the top wing, which was then to be jettisoned. Trials were undertaken at Boscombe Down but the scheme was abandoned in September 1943.

The Hurricane I was renowned for its viceless flying qualities, capacity to withstand extensive battle damage, steadiness as a gun platform, ease and speed of refuelling and re-arming, and its agility in combat. Its sturdy, wide-track undercarriage recommended it for operations from relatively poor airfield surfaces and this, combined with its ease of maintenance and repair, resulted in the Hurricane serving both in the Middle and Far East about two years before the first Spitfires arrived. The Hurricane it was therefore that fought at times and in theatres under greatest threat, and suffered heavy casualties accordingly. Yet, on account of this weight of responsibility, Hurricane pilots destroyed more enemy aircraft — German, Italian and Japanese — than any other Allied fighter during the Second World War, and by a substantial margin.

Supermarine Spitfire (Merlin versions)

Pre-eminent among British fighters, the classic Spitfire owed its existence to the foresight of the Air Ministry, the provision of a superlative engine and the technical brilliance of the Supermarine design team led by Reginald Mitchell. Yet while the Spitfire and Hawker Hurricane — both high-speed low-wing monoplanes with enclosed cockpit and retractable undercarriage — were conceived at roughly the same time, their respective designers interpreted the Air Ministry's requirements in entirely different fashions. On the one hand, Camm at Hawker Aircraft was constrained by his company's lack of experience in and facilities for the production of an all-metal monocoque aircraft, and therefore evolved an aircraft whose structure was directly related to the long-established family of biplanes which had been supplied in very large numbers to the RAF since 1930. This composite wood and metal structure ensured a rapid build-up in the production rate to such a degree that the Hurricane had become RAF Fighter Command's standard interceptor fighter by the outbreak of the Second World War. By the same token the Hurricane possessed less ultimate development potential than the Spitfire, and the margin in performance by which the Spitfire led the Hurricane from the start inevitably widened as

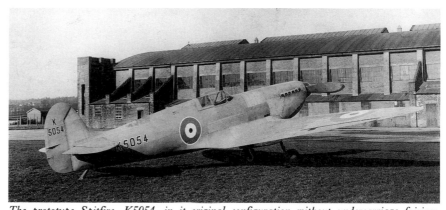

The prototype Spitfire, K5054, in it original configuration without undercarriage fairings, radio or armament at about the time of its first flight. (Photo: Author's Collection)

the War years passed.

It is often suggested that Mitchell developed the Spitfire from his successful Schneider Trophy racing seaplanes; nothing could be further from the truth. Certainly the sleek racers had proved the superiority of monoplanes over biplanes, and no doubt their success provided the spur and inspiration for the development of a high performance monoplane interceptor, yet scarcely any common feature — either structural or visual — can be detected in the designs. Moreover, whereas the seaplane racers featured wings heavily braced with external wires, the military aircraft demanded a far more robust cantilever wing.

Mitchell's first monoplane fighter essay, the ungainly Supermarine Type 224 with inverted gull wing and non-retractable, trousered undercarriage, had proved disappointing to say the least, but the shortcomings of this design had stemmed largely from the preference expressed for an unsuitable engine, as already explained. Once freed of the need to employ this entirely unsuitable powerplant, the designers were free to cast further afield for a better engine, and it was early in 1934 that Rolls-Royce issued preliminary design and performance details of a new derivative of the familiar Kestrel family — the PV.12 (later to become the famous Rolls-Royce Merlin).

It may be said that the Supermarine 224 constituted the Spitfire's starting point. Adapting the general design to feature a retractable undercarriage itself eliminated the need for the cranked wing, and Mitchell evolved and substituted a much smaller cantilever, elliptical wing whose span was reduced by some nine feet. The cockpit was moved aft by about two feet so as to allow space for two fuel tanks, located immediately forward of a fireproof bulkhead. Now provided with a sliding canopy, the

cockpit superstructure was faired into the top line of the rear fuselage. The coolant radiator was located under the starboard wing root, while the oil cooler occupied a similar position under the port wing.

Like that of the Hurricane, initial evolution of the Supermarine fighter was undertaken as a private venture, that is, until Mitchell was able to forecast the fighter's likely performance, and this awaited clarification of the Air Ministry's armament requirements. Hitherto the only requirement extant was for the four Vickers guns demanded by F.7/30, but already pressure was growing for replacement of these old weapons. All manner of guns were evaluated by the Service establishments before the American 30-calibre Colt was declared the most suitable, and negotiations were concluded to produce the gun in large numbers in Britain, under the name Browning, and adapted to fire British 0.303in ammunition. The light weight, compactness and reliability of the Browning encouraged the Air Ministry to call for a battery of eight such guns to be mounted in the wings of the Hurricane and Spitfire (the battery being first mentioned in Specification F.5/34), and by the end of 1934 Specification F.37/34 had been prepared around Mitchell's proposed fighter, now termed the Supermarine Type 300.

First flight of the Spitfire prototype, K5054, took place on 5 March 1936 at Eastleigh airport, the pilot being Capt J ('Mutt') Summers. When first flown, K5054 carried no armament and the undercarriage panels were omitted, short individual engine exhaust stubs were fitted and the aircraft had a tailskid. Mitchell's inspired choice of a thin elliptical wing did, however, give rise to difficulties in locating the wing gun battery, not least on account of the outward-retracting undercarriage. Unlike the Hurricane, which possessed a much thicker wing — allowing the guns to be grouped in a single bay—the Spitfire's guns were individually located

Above: First Fighter Command Squadron to be equipped with Spitfires was No 19 at Duxford. This photograph shows aircraft still fitted with two-blade wooden propellers but bulged canopies have replaced the early flat-topped hoods. (Photo: Author's Collection)

Right: No 19 (Fighter) Squadron in action in 1940, based on the Duxford satellite airfield at Fowlmere. The aircraft shown has evidently been in action with the gun patches blown away, but unlike the Hurricane, the ammunition tanks had to be replenished from underneath the wings. (Photo: Author's Collection)

Spitfire Mk VBs of No 243 Squadron. This version was the standard equipment of RAF Fighter Command in 1941. (Photo: Temple Press Ltd.)

in widely spaced bays; this not only resulted in the inconvenience of re-arming from below the wing, but also required more time to effect gun har-monization in the field.

The Spitfire prototype was first dis-played to the public at the Hendon Display of 27 June 1936, and six days later Vickers-Armstrongs received the first Air Ministry contract for 310 pro-duction aircraft, it being intended that these aircraft should all be in service by March 1939.

Mitchell only lived to see the first Spitfire fly for, on 11 June 1937 he died, his place as Chief Designer being taken the following year by his former chief draughtsman, Joseph Smith. The Spit-fire in the meantime had run into production problems. The Merlin I (formerly referred to as the Merlin F) had been destined for both the Hurri-cane and Spitfire, but this version was discarded during 1937 as a fighter en-gine — and was then confined to the Fairey Battle light bomber — and the Merlin II (or Merlin G) allocated to the eight-gun fighters. Because this engine featured angled rocker box flanges, new cowling contours had to be drawn and fresh jigs made up — thereby delaying both Hurricane and Spitfire production by several months.

The first Spitfire production line was established in the Woolston factory at Southampton but, in 1937, as new Spit-fire contracts were being negotiated, the first plans were laid for a new factory to be built at Castle Bromwich — specifi-

cally for the production of Spitfires.

The first production Spitfire Is began leaving the Woolston factory in June 1938 and the first Service squadron delivery was made to No 19, com-manded by Sqn Ldr Henry Iliffe Cozens at Duxford in August that year. Early aircraft differed from the prototype in being fitted with fixed tailwheel and triple exhaust manifolds; they featured two-blade, fixed pitch, wooden propel-lers and retained the flat topped cockpit canopy of the prototype. Production was slow to accelerate, largely due to the time taken to master the monocoque manufacturing techniques, but by the end of 1938 No 66 Squadron, also at Duxford, had received its first Spitfires. Neither of these squadron was declared operational until 1939, a year which saw Nos 41, 54, 65, 72, 74, 602, 609 and 611 Squadrons re-equipped before the out-break of war. As the production rate picked up, the early aircraft were passed on to Nos 6 and 7 Operational Training Units, new aircraft being delivered with domed cockpit canopies and D.H. vari-able-pitch three-blade propellers.

The Spitfire squadrons were not sent to France during 1939-40, largely on account of the relative lack of mainte-nance facilities for the fighters' mono-coque construction, and because it was felt that the Spitfire's narrow track undercarriage was unsuitable for the poor surface conditions of French air-fields. It was not, as often averred, on account of Air Marshal Dowding wish-ing to husband his Spitfire squadrons

for home defence. In any case the Spitfire still displayed a number of serious problems, not least that of gun icing and misting of the windscreen following descent from high altitude. Consequently Spitfires were not widely used in combat until the War was eight months old when, in May 1940, they went into action over the BEF during the Dunkirk evacuation. Nos 602 and 603 Squadrons had, however, destroyed a pair of He 111 bombers over the Firth of Forth on 16 October 1939 — the first enemy aircraft to fall to RAF fighters over Britain during the Second World War.

By the beginning of the Battle of Britain 19 Spitfire squadrons were listed in Fighter Command's order of battle, although four of these were not yet fully operational, the total number of Spit-fires on strength being 292, of which 199 were combat-ready. The number of Spitfire squadrons actually dropped by one during the first two months of the Battle, while those of Hurricanes in-creased from 29 to 31, but thereafter, as deliveries from Castle Bromwich accel-erated, the Supermarine fighter began to assume a dominant place in Fighter Command. The Mark IB version had been introduced with No. 19 Squadron during the Battle of Britain with an armament of two 20 mm cannon and four Brownings, but the cannon instal-lation was deemed to be unsatisfactory and this version was withdrawn in September. A total of 1,566 Spitfire Is was produced before the Mark II appeared, powered by the 1,175 hp Merlin XII engine; 750 Mark IIAs were produced, having the standard eight Browning armament, and 170 Mark IIB were built with two 20 mm Hispano cannon and four Brownings. Mark IIC was the designation given to Mark IIAs serving with air-sea rescue squadrons. Unarmed photographic reconnaissance versions, designated types A, B, C, D, E and F, were converted from Mark Is, but the production version, the type G — of which 229 were built — entered service as the PR Mark IV.

By 1941 RAF Fighter Command had gone over to the offensive, with sweeps over the French Channel coast and further afield. The Type 349 Spitfire Mark V, powered by the 1,440 hp Merlin 45, first entered servivce with No 92 Squadron, commanded by Sqn Ldr James Rankin at Biggin Hill in February 1941. Thereafter Mark V Spitfires served with no fewer than 117 squadrons of the RAF at home and overseas, gaining the reputation as the most pleasant to fly of all Spitfires. Certainly the Mark V dominated Fighter Command squadrons in Northern Europe during 1941-42, participating in countless 'Rhubarb', 'Circus' and 'Rodeo' operations over enemy-occupied territory. Three principal sub-variants were produced; the Mark VA retained the old eight Browning gun armament, the VB with two cannon and four Brownings, and the VC with 'universal' wing capable of being adapted to mount either armament or four Hispano cannon. The Mark V was also the first fighter-bomber version of the Spitfire, being adapted to carry either a single 500 lb bomb under the fuselage or two 250 lb bombs under the wings. Later, many Spitfire Vs had their wings clipped from 36 ft 10 in to 32 ft 2 in to improve their manœuvrability at low altitude.

When first introduced into service the Spitfire V's main enemy fighter adversary was the Messerschmitt Bf 109E, and against this it displayed a definite superiority. The Bf 109F was introduced in 1941, and thereafter the two fighters were more closely matched. The first Spitfire fighters to be sent overseas did not reach the Mediterranean theatre until March 1942 when 15 Mark VBs were embarked in HM Carrier *Eagle* to reinforce Malta—then being heavily attacked by the *Luftwaffe*. Spitfires destined to fight over the Western Desert (from August 1942 onwards) were fitted with cumbersome tropical

air filters under the nose — essential equipment to protect the Merlin engine from the effects of dust and sand, but which reduced the fighter's top speed from 374 mph at 13,000 feet to around 330 mph.

The appearance over Northern Europe of the German Focke-Wulf Fw 190A before the end of 1941 had a profound effect on RAF Fighter Command, and Spitfires were being lost several weeks before it was firmly estab-

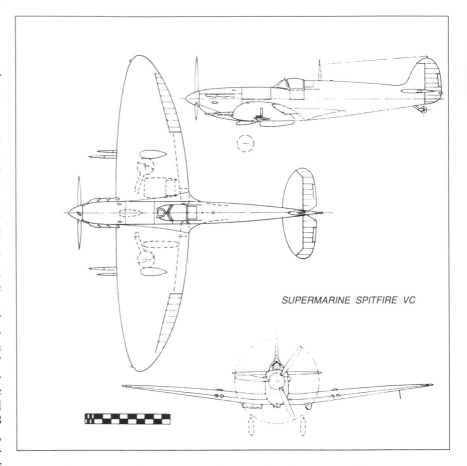

SUPERMARINE SPITFIRE VC

Type: Single-seat, single-engine low-wing monoplane interceptor fighter
Manufacturers: Supermarine Division of Vickers-Armstrongs Ltd, Woolston, Southampton; and Westland Aircraft Ltd., Yeovil, Somerset
Air Ministry Specification: F.37/34 and, as amended, F.16/36 (for production)
Powerplant: One 1,030hp Rolls-Royce Merlin II driving two-blade wooden fixed-pitch propeller (first 74 aircraft) and Merlin III two-stage supercharged twelve-cylinder liquid cooled in-line engine driving metal D.H. variable-pitch three-blade propeller.
Structure: All-metal monocoque with cantilever wings; outward retracting undercarriage, and fixed tailwheel. Fabric-covered control surfaces.
Dimensions: Span, 36ft 10in; length, 29ft 11in; height, 11ft 8in; wing area, 242 sq ft.
Weights: Tare, 4,341lb; all-up (normal loaded), 5,784lb
Performance (Mark IA): Max speed, 364 mph at 19,000ft; climb to 15,000 ft, 6 min 10 sec; range, 390 miles; service ceiling, 32,000ft.
Armament (Mark IA): Eight wing-mounted 0.303in Browning machine guns with up to 500 rounds per gun.
Prototype: K5054 (first flown, 5 March 1936, by J Summers)
Production: A total of 17,582 Merlin-powered Spitfire fighters were built as follows: Mk I, 1,566; Mk II, 920; Mk V, 6,479; Mk VI, 100; Mk VII, 140; Mk VIII, 1,658; Mk IX, 5,665; Mk XVI, 1,054.
Service Summary: Merlin-powered Spitfires served with Nos 1, 6, 19, 28, 32, 33, 41, 43, 54, 56, 63, 64, 65, 66, 67, 71, 72, 73, 74, 80, 81, 87, 91, 92, 93, 94, 111, 118, 122, 123, 124, 126, 127, 129, 130, 131, 132, 133, 136, 145, 152, 153, 154, 155, 164, 165, 167, 183, 184, 185, 186, 208, 213, 222, 225, 229, 232, 234, 237, 238, 241, 242, 243, 249, 253, 256, 257, 266, 274, 275, 276, 277, 278, 279, 287, 288, 290, 302, 303, 306, 308, 310, 312, 313, 315, 316, 317, 318, 322, 326, 327, 328, 329, 331, 332, 335, 336, 340, 341, 345, 349, 350, 352, 401, 402, 403, 411, 412, 416, 417, 421, 441, 442, 443, 451, 452, 453, 457, 485, 501, 504, 518, 520, 521, 527, 541, 543, 544, 567, 577, 595, 601, 602, 603, 607, 609, 610, 611, 615, 616, 680, 695 and 1435 Squadrons.

Like the Hurricane, the Spitfire was equipped with a bulky tropical air filter when serving in the Middle East. A Spitfire V (Trop) is shown here in inappropriate surroundings during performance trials with the filter at Boscombe Down. (Photo: Air Ministry, Neg No 10,748C)

lished that the *Luftwaffe* had indeed introduced a fighter that was markedly superior to the Spitfire V in most respects. To remedy this, a new version was hurriedly introduced with the 1,660 hp Merlin 61 with two-speed two-stage supercharger and driving a four-blade propeller. This powerplant was already scheduled for the Spitfire VIII, but as this version was still many months away, the Mark IX was introduced as a stop-gap, the first examples being delivered to No 81 Squadron, commanded by Sqn Ldr R Berry at Hornchurch in May 1942. By the end of that year Spitfire IXs were also serving with Nos 64, 72, 122, 133 (Eagle), 306 (Polish), 315 (Polish), 331 (Norwegian), 332 (Norwegian), 340 (French), 401 (Canadian), 402 (Canadian) and 611 (AuxAF) Squadrons, and ultimately served with 90 squadrons of the RAF. The first major operation in which the Spitfire IX participated was that in support of the landings at Dieppe on 19 August 1942 when a Wing of three Spitfire IX squadrons participated in high altitude patrols; unfortunately, owing to confused orders, the Spitfire pilots attacked a Wing of Typhoons in error, shooting down two.

Despite its interim nature, the Mark IX proved an efficient medium and high altitude interceptor with a maximum speed of just over 400 mph, and remained in service until after the end of the War, equipping five squadrons of the 2nd Tactical Air Force in Germany after VE-Day, as well as 22 squadrons of the Balkan and Desert Air Forces. The Mark IX was produced in high, medium and low altitude versions with extended, standard and clipped wings, as well as with four-cannon, and mixed cannon and Browning gun armament. A total of 5,665 Mark IXs was built, and some

A Spitfire LF Mk V (FR), EP688, reconnaissance fighter carrying the markings of No 40 Squadron, South African Air Force, serving in the Central Mediterranean towards the end of the War; the large reconnaissance camera port is aft of the cockpit. (Photo: A J Jackson Collection)

were converted from Mark Vs.

The Spitfire Mark VI, of which 100 examples were built, was the first Spitfire designed specifically for high altitude interception (of the Ju 86P high altitude aircraft which had begun appearing over Britain in 1942). Powered by a 1,415hp Merlin 47 or 49 driving a four-blade propeller, the Mark VI was equipped with a pressurized cockpit and featured wing tips extended to give a span of 40ft 2in. This version ultimately equipped Nos 124, 129, 234, 310 (Czech), 313 (Czech), 519, 602 (AuxAF), 616 (AuxAF) and 680 Squadrons.

The extended wings were also fitted to the Type 351 Spitfire Mark VII, another dedicated high altitude fighter but now powered by the two-speed two-stage supercharged Merlin 61. Fitted with a retractable tailwheel, the Mark VII equipped seven RAF squadrons—including two photo-reconnaissance Squadron, Nos 519 and 542 — and a total of 140 was produced. This version also introduced a new rudder of increased area (pointed at the top), a measure found to be necessary owing to the increased length of nose required to house the longer Merlin 61 engine.

The Type 359 Spitfire Mark VIII had been intended from the outset as the definitive Merlin-powered version, and was designed to take the Merlin 61; it also featured the enlarged rudder and retractable tailwheel. Most important however was the inclusion of an integral tropical air filter, identifiable by a longer carburettor air intake under the nose. Thus equipped this version served extensively in the Mediterranean and Far Eastern theatres; Mark VIIIs first joined No 92 Squadron under Sqn Ldr P H Humphreys DFC at Pachino in Sicily in July 1943, complementing the Squadron's Mark IXs; 17 other squadrons in the Mediterranean were similarly re-equipped. They also equipped 14 squadrons in India, Burma and Ceylon, beginning with No 81 *en route* to Alipore, India, in November 1943. Performance of the Mark VIII proved little different from that of the Mark IX, although optional use of a special ventral slipper fuel tank increased the Mark VIII's range to more than 650 miles.

The only other Merlin-powered Spitfire fighter was the Mark XVI, introduced into the production lines at Winchester, Swindon and Castle Bromwich alongside the Marks VIII and IX. This variant introduced the Packard-built Merlin 266 (equivalent to the British-built Merlin 66), and was produced with the same wing and armament option as the earlier Marks, most

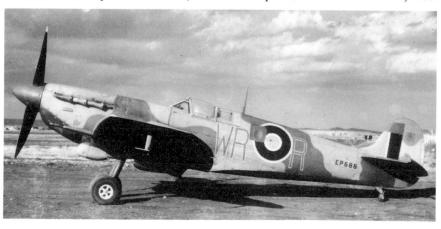

— but not all — incorporating the enlarged rudder. Late production Mark XVIs had a re-designed rear fuselage, cut down to feature a sliding, tear-drop canopy. By carrying overload external fuel tanks (adding 90 gallons of fuel), the Mark XVI possessed a maximum range of 980 miles. Alternatively it was capable of carrying two 500lb bombs under the wings, or six 3in rocket projectiles with 60lb warheads. Total production of the Mark XVI reached 1,054, and these aircraft served with 44 RAF squadrons from 1944. In due course Spitfire XVIs were supplied to post-War Royal Auxiliary Air Force Squadrons, Nos 501, 601, 603, 604, 609, 612 and 614, and served for several years; the last survivors were disposed of by No 612 Squadron at Dyce, Aberdeen, in July 1951.

The Marks X, XI and XIII were all photo-reconnaissance variants, the first two being unarmed and the third, a low-level reconnaissance fighter, which retained four of the Browning guns for self-protection. Of the three Marks, the Mark XI gave most service; 471 examples were built, and these served with thirteen squadrons; being unarmed, it was also the fastest Merlin-powered Spitfire, possessing a top speed of 422 mph and a maximum range of about 2,000 miles.

Total production of all Merlin Spitfires reached 18,298, and it is not surprising to record that many aircraft were set aside for experimental work, the majority being concerned with evaluating new engine installations. Among the early projects was the Type 323 Speed Spitfire which was completed early in 1939 and intended to raise the World Air Speed Record, then held by Germany at 379.4 mph with a special Bf 109 prototype. Flush riveting was employed throughout; a modified wing planform with a span reduced to 33 ft 8 in was incorporated, as was a specially-rated 2,160 hp Merlin III driving a four-blade propeller. The aircraft, K9834 (re-numbered N.17) was expected to achieve 410 mph and was exhibited at the Brussels Aero Show in July that year. However, after Germany had again raised the World record, this time to no less than 469.22 mph in the Me 209V1 on 26 April 1939 (a record for piston-engined aircraft that stood for more than 30

years), the Speed Spitfire — which, it was expected would reach no more than 410 mph — was abandoned.

Spitfires also joined the towed-fighter experiments, undertaken by Flight Refuelling Ltd at Staverton, Glos, during the mid-War years, these being intended to examine the feasibility of towing fighters behind bomber aircraft (Wellingtons, Halifaxes and Lancasters) to reinforce the RAF in North Africa. However, by the time the various snags had been overcome (such as icing-up of the Merlin, preventing the engine from being started before landing), reinforcements were flowing to the Middle East by more conventional means.

Spitfires were never considered pleasant aeroplanes to fly at night, due largely to their narrow-track undercarriage and poor forward vision, and so — unlike the Hurricane — never had to undergo the numerous and prolonged night fighter trials of its contemporary.

Used primarily for ground attack, the Spitfire LF Mk XVI was a development of the Mk IX powered by the Packard-built Rolls-Royce Merlin 266; it featured the cut-down rear fuselage and increased fuel tankage. It served with 44 squadrons of the RAF. (Photo: A J Jackson Collection)

Vickers Type 279 Venom (F.5/34)

Among the major manufacturers, Vickers (Aviation) Ltd was one of the few that did not seriously consider tendering a design to Specification F.7/30, being fairly heavily committed in other spheres. When, however, Specification F.5/34

Although the Vickers Venom seemed outwardly to be a neat and compact aeroplane, its structure, wingform and powerplant were scarcely comparable to the more sophisticated Spitfire. (Photo: Vickers Ltd., Neg No 4928)

was issued in 1934, calling for a fighter to be armed with eight machine guns, a maximum speed of 275 mph at 15,000

feet and a service ceiling of 33,000 feet, it was decided to extend the seven year old Vickers Jockey formula (see page

227) as a private venture by providing it with a new powerplant, enclosed cockpit and inwards-retracting undercarriage. The relatively new 625hp Bristol Aquila sleeve-valve radial engine was selected, and the Wibault sysyem of metal wing construction was finally discarded as being unsuitable owing to the wing space required by the machine guns; the latter expedient enabled smooth sheet duralumin to be used. Like the Jockey, the wing was of uniform thickness from root to tip, employing RAF 34 section. The fuselage was a monocoque structure but, unusually, was of polygonal rather than circular cross-section.

The most singular feature of the Type 279 Venom was, however, the engine mounting which, being enclosed in a long-chord cowling, was hinged to rotate sideways to provide access to the engine ancillaries; this demanded that all drives, controls and fuel lines had to be flexible and, although ingenious, was found to be unsatisfactory.

The prototype, as a private venture marked PVO-10, was first flown by 'Mutt' Summers at Brooklands on 17 June 1936 with full armament installed (before the eight-gun armament had yet been fitted in either the Hurricane or Spitfire prototypes). Having flown the Spitfire some three months earlier, Summers was in a good position to express his opinions on the relative merits of the Venom and, in view of the promise held by the Supermarine and Hawker fighters, these were bound to be less than sanguine. Although the Vickers aeroplane was rather smaller than the other prototypes, its bulky radial engine of lower power was unable to bestow a worthwhile performance.

Constant trouble with the Aquila engine and its ancillary systems prevented it from undergoing full Service trials, although Fg Off Jeffrey Kindersley Quill AFC, RAFO, who had recently joined Vickers, continued to perform the manufacturers' trials for some months. The Venom was, nevertheless, scrapped in 1939.

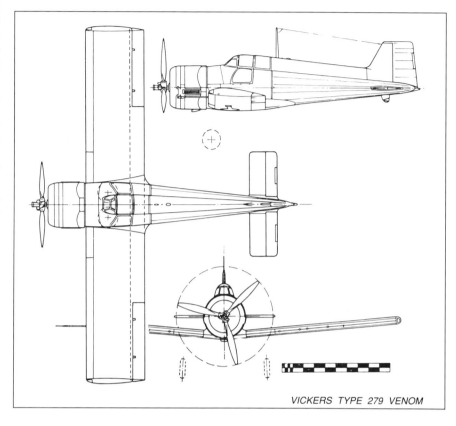

VICKERS TYPE 279 VENOM

Type: Single-engine, single-seat low-wing monoplane interceptor fighter.
Manufacturer: Vickers (Aviation) Ltd, Weybridge, Surrey.
Air Ministry Specification: Private venture to F.5/34.
Powerplant: One 625hp Bristol Aquila sleeve-valve air-cooled radial engine.
Dimensions: Span, 32ft 9in; length, 24ft 2in; height, 10ft 9in; wing area, 146 sq ft.
Weight: All-up, 4,156lb.
Performance: Max speed, 312 mph at 16,125ft; service ceiling, 32,000ft.
Armament: Eight 0.303in Browning machine guns in wings with 300 rounds per gun.
Prototype: One, PVO-10 (first flown by J Summers at Brooklands on 17 June 1936). No production.

Gloster F.5/34

One of the attractions of Specification F.5/34 was that no preference was expressed by the Air Ministry for a particular powerplant (such had been the poor official track record of backing losers over so many years). This allowed Henry Folland a free hand to further

Even though the F.5/34 was fated for obscurity, being grounded in 1941, Folland's real legacy lay in his immortal Gladiator, still in the front line that year. (Photo: Imperial War Museum, Neg No MH5187)

exploit the Bristol Mercury radial that had brought him such success with his Gladiator, tendered to F.7/30. Indeed, his tender to F.5/34 emerged as not only

the most attractive of the various designs submitted but the most efficient in terms of speed and climb.

Unlike the Vickers Venom, two proto-

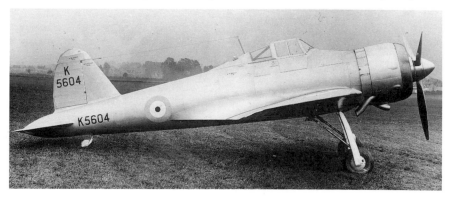

types of the Gloster design (which remained un-named), K5604 and K8089, were ordered, and the first, unarmed, example was flown by P E G Sayer in December 1937.

The Gloster F.5/34's fuselage was of all-metal monocoque construction with strongpoints incorporated for attachment of engine, wings and tail unit. The wing was a single structure extending from tip to tip, with stressed skin covering and continuous light alloy spars and steel ribs and duralumin struts. The cockpit, with sliding canopy, afforded the pilot an excellent field of view, and the undercarriage retracted rearwards, leaving more than half the wheels exposed so as to take much of the aircraft's weight in the event of a forced landing with the undercarriage raised. The 840hp Mercury IX supercharged engine, with controllable cooling gills on its long-chord cowling, drove a two-pitch three-blade D.H. metal propeller.

The second example, K8089, was flown in March 1938 with full armament fitted; the eight Browing machine guns were mounted to fire outboard of the propeller arc and were provided with a total of 2,600 rounds.

However, although the Gloster fighter came close to meeting all the requirements of F.5/34, it was inevitable that no production orders would be forthcoming, as both the Hurricane and Spitfire had already been ordered into large-scale production, having satisfied far more demanding specifications and, after a long period of experimental

flying, both K5604 and K8089 were relegated to become ground instruction airframes in May 1941.

Indeed, for a man who had excelled in biplane design for almost a quarter century, it was a bitter pill for Folland that Sydney Camm appeared to have assumed a pre-eminent status in the

Hawker Siddeley Group as the most influential designer of fighters, and the fact that the Gloster F.5/34 had been pre-empted long before it first flew was evidently the final humiliation for Folland, and it was the last of his designs for Gloster to fly.

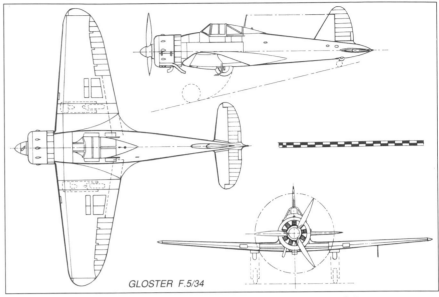

GLOSTER F.5/34

Type: Single-engine, single-seat, low-wing monoplane interceptor fighter.
Manufacturer: Gloster Aircraft Co Ltd, Hucclecote, Gloucester.
Air Ministry Specification: F.5/34
Powerplant: One 840hp Bristol Mercury IX nine-cylinder supercharged radial engine driving three-blade D.H. two-pitch metal propeller.
Dimensions: Span, 38ft 2in; length, 32ft 0in; height, 10ft 2in; wing area, 230 sq ft.
Weights: Tare, 4,190lb; all-up, 5,400lb.
Performance: Max speed, 316 mph at 16,000ft; climb to 20,000ft, 11 min 0 sec; service ceiling, 32,500ft.
Armament: Eight 0.303in Browning machine guns in wings with total of 2,600 rounds.
Prototype: Two, K5604 (unarmed) and K8089 (armed). K5604 first flown by P E G Sayer in December 1937. No production.

Bristol Type 146 (F.5/34)

The loss of Bristol's Type 133 fighter prototype before it could be evaluated by the Service establishments (see page 252) had been a considerable blow to the company, and served to emphasise the risks borne by manufacturers with so much depending on a single prototype,

With the benefit of two years' later development, the Bristol Type 146 featured a much more advanced cockpit enclosure than either the Hurricane or the Spitfire and made its first flight with a two-pitch three-blade propeller. (Photo: The Bristol Aeroplane Co Ltd, Neg No T.146/21).

and it is worth reflecting on the consequences for Britain had disaster overtaken either the Hurricane or Spitfire prototype during the early months of their trials programmes.

Fortunately Bristol was at work on at least two other promising aircraft pro-

jects and felt able to support a design tender to Specification F.5/34, and in 1935 received a contract worth £11,500 to produce one prototype of its Type 146 single-seat fighter — taking the precaution of manufacturing components for a second example.

By the following year both the Hurricane and Spitfire had flown, and seemed likely to set the standard for future RAF fighters and, with the Blenheim light bomber on its way towards largescale production, work on the Type 146 continued at low priority. As a result the prototype, K5119, was not flown by Uwins until 11 February 1938.

Originally intended to be powered by the 835hp Bristol Perseus sleeve-valve radial, K5119 was completed with a Mercury IX as the proposed engine was not ready in time. The aircraft was of all-metal construction with monocoque fuselage, avoiding double curvature skinning as it tapered aft to the tail. The high aspect ratio wing incorporated straight taper from root to tip, the undercarriage retracting inwards in the centre section. The outer wing sections, with moderate dihedral, accommodated the mandatory battery of eight Browning machine guns. Only the control surfaces were fabric covered.

K5119 was duly delivered to Martlesham in April 1938 for its Service assessment but, although it came fairly close to the specified requirements, neither it nor any of the other contenders was ordered into production. Later in the year, after landing at Filton the Type 146 was involved in a taxying accident and was too badly damaged to

warrant repair and was scrapped shortly afterwards. Thus passed into history the

last Bristol single-engine, single-seat fighter ever to be built.

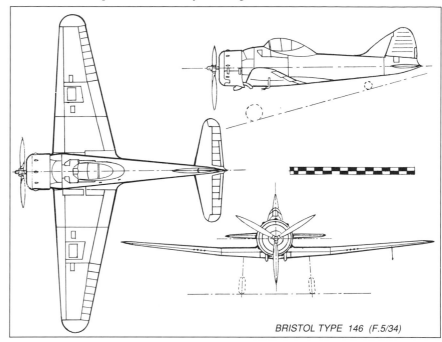

BRISTOL TYPE 146 (F.5/34)

Type: Single-engine, single-seat low-wing monoplane interceptor fighter.
Manufacturer: The Bristol Aeroplane Co Ltd, Filton, Bristol.
Air Ministry Specification: F.5/34.
Powerplant: One 840hp Bristol Mercury IX nine-cylinder supercharged radial engine.
Dimensions: Span, 39ft 0in; length, 27ft 0in; height, 10ft 4in; wing area, 220 sq ft.
Weights: Tare, 3,282lb; all-up, 4,600lb.
Performance: Max speed, 287 mph at 16,000ft; ceiling, 38,100ft.
Armament: Eight 0.303in Browning machine guns in outer wings.
Prototype: One, K5119, flown by Cyril Uwins at Filton on 11 February 1938. No production.

Martin-Baker M.B.2 (F.5/34)

As the Bristol company was engaged in producing what would be its last single-engine interceptor fighter, another company, scarcely known outside the aircraft industry, was hard at work on its first — with only a fraction of the resources. Formed by James Martin (later Sir James, CBE) in 1929, the tiny company of Martin Aircraft Works produced its first aeroplane (later termed the M.B.1) during the next five years; this was a two-seat cabin monoplane powered by a 160 hp Napier Javelin six-cylinder air-cooled engine. In 1934 Captain Valentine Baker joined Martin to form Martin-Baker Aircraft Co Ltd at Higher Denham, Middlesex, and work started the following year on the M.B.2, a single-seat interceptor which was

The Martin-Baker M.B.2, P9594, after being fitted with a conventional fin and rudder. (Photo: Martin-Baker Aircraft Ltd.)

designed and built as a private venture to Air Ministry Specification F.5/34, the first to specify an armament of eight wing-mounted machine guns.

Underlying the design philosophy was simplicity of construction, the fuselage structure comprising steel tubes pinned to the longerons, the whole being

faired with fabricated light alloy hoops and stiffened by closely-spaced light gauge stringers. The wing was built up on a single spar fabricated with three large-diameter thin-gauge booms webbed by small-diameter tubes to provide strength in the vertical and longitudinal planes; the spar was bolted directly to the fuselage primary structure. Wing and fuselage forward of the cockpit were covered with duralumin sheet and provided with numerous access panels; the rear fuselage was fabric covered, as were the control surfaces. In the interests of simplicity and weight-saving, a non-retractable 'trousered' undercarriage was employed, the port fairing including the engine oil cooler. Powered by a 1,000hp Napier Dagger III H-type air-cooled in-line engine driving a 10ft 6in diameter two-blade wooden propeller, the M.B.2 possessed a top speed of 305 mph at 9,250 feet.

When first flown on 3 August 1938 by Captain Baker at Harwell, Oxfordshire, no orthodox tail fin was fitted, the rudder being in effect an extension of the rear fuselage and of the same depth. It was immediately discovered that the aircraft was directionally unstable, and a small, interim fin was fitted. When, on 10 November the M.B.2, P9594, was delivered to Martlesham Heath for Service assessment the initial report stated that the aircraft still lacked directional control and stability, and the aircraft was quickly fitted with a conventional fin and rudder. While this went a long way to correcting the deficiency, it became clear in December 1938 that the entire F.5/34 concept had been rendered superfluous by Specifications F.36/34 and F.37/34 which had produced the Hurricane and Spitfire—both already coming into squadron service.

Apart from its lightweight, simplified structure, the M.B.2 demonstrated a number of ingenious features, and the gun installation in particular was commended by the A & AEE. The four guns on each side were located in a single wing bay and were accessible by means of a single hinged panel. Martin had, moreover, designed a system wherein

the ammunition tanks were located alongside each gun, the belts being guided through a 90-degree 'swan-neck' channel to each breech. This system permitted very fast re-arming times, all eight guns being capable of removal by two men in three minutes (the equivalent times for the Hurricane and Spitfire were 60 and 70 minutes respectively).

While simplicity of structure consti-

tuted a fundamental advantage, it was however essential in order to facilitate widespread sub-contracting of component manufacture — such was the very limited manufacturing capacity at Martin-Baker. Nevertheless the largescale production of Hurricanes and Spitfires rendered further effort on the M.B.2 unnecessary.

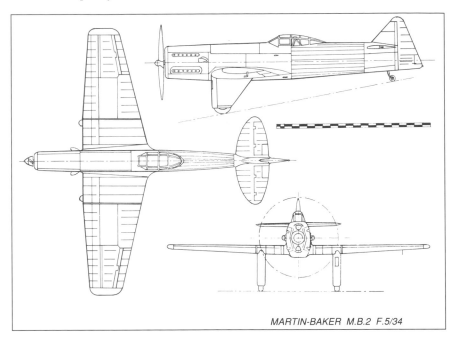

MARTIN-BAKER M.B.2 F.5/34

Type: Single-seat, single engine low-wing monoplane interceptor fighter.
Manufacturer: Martin-Baker Aircraft Co. Ltd, Higher Denham, Middlesex.
Air Ministry Specification: Private venture to F.5/34
Powerplant: One 1,000hp Napier Dagger III sixteen-cylinder H-type air-cooled in-line engine driving 10 ft 6 in diameter two-blade wooden fixed-pitch propeller.
Structure: Fuselage of steel tubular primary structure with hooped frames and light-alloy stringers, fabric-covered aft of cockpit. Single-spar wing structure, duralumin-covered. Non-retractable undercarriage in large fairings.
Dimensions: Span, 34ft 0in; length (final configuration), 34ft 9in; wing area, 212 sq ft.
Weight: All-up, 5,537lb.
Performance: Max speed, 305 mph at 9,250ft; initial rate of climb, 2,200 ft/min; service ceiling, 29,000ft.
Armament: Eight 0.303in Browning machine guns in wings with 300 rounds per gun.
Prototype: One, P9594, first flown on 3 August 1938 by Capt V Baker. No production.

Blackburn B-24 Skua

The Skua was unique among British naval aeroplanes as being both a fleet fighter and a dive-bomber. Designed by George Edward Petty to Specification O.27/34 as a replacement for the Hawker Osprey (in its carrier-borne rôle) and the Nimrod fighter, two prototypes, K5178 and K5179, of the Blackburn B-24 two-

The Skua prototype, K5178, with short nose and flat wingtips. (Photo: Author's collection)

seat, low-wing monoplane were ordered in April 1935, the first of which was flown by Flt Lt A M Blake, the company's chief test pilot, on 9 February 1937; it later appeared in the New Types Park (as No 8) at the 1937 Hendon Display on 26 June, being named the Skua on 17 August.

Powered by an 840hp Bristol Mercury IX (as fitted in the Gloster Gladiator) driving a two-pitch, three-blade D.H. propeller, K5178 was of all-metal construction with flush-riveted Alclad sheet covering, the fuselage incorporating two buoyancy compartments, one forward and the other aft. A long transparent superstructure enclosed both cockpits, the pilot being situated above the wing leading edge and the observer/gunner, armed with a Lewis Mk IIIE gun over the trailing edge. The wings, which could be folded manually to lie aft alongside the rear fuselage, accommodated the four Browning Mk II machine guns and were fitted with modified Zap flaps which served both to reduce the landing speed and as dive brakes. The undercarriage, hinged to the front wing spar at the outer extremities of the fixed centre section, was retracted hydraulically outwards into cells provided in the outer wing sections. To assist dive recovery the elevators were located at the extreme tail to provide the greatest control moment, but for positive spin recovery the fin and rudder were placed three feet further forward to avoid blanking the latter. For dive bombing operations the Skua could carry a single 500lb semi-armour-piercing bomb, partly recessed into the fuselage belly on a swinging ejector crutch.

The second Skua prototype was flown on 4 May 1938 by Flt Lt Henry Bailey RAFO (who had succeeded 'Dasher' Blake). This aircraft featured a nose lengthened by 2ft 4¾in, and up-swept wingtips; a retractable, hydraulically-damped, V-type arrester hook was fitted under the rear fuselage.

Owing to the urgent need to introduce the Skua into service, a production contract for 190 aircraft to Specification 25/36P had been placed in July 1936. However, owing to the distasteful associations in the public's mind with the German dive-bomber as a terror weapon in the Spanish Civil War, emphasis was

Skua IIs of No 803 Squadron, FAA, the most illustrious of the Skua Squadrons, carrying the ship codes of HMS Ark Royal in 1939. (Photo: Cdr R N Everett, RN)

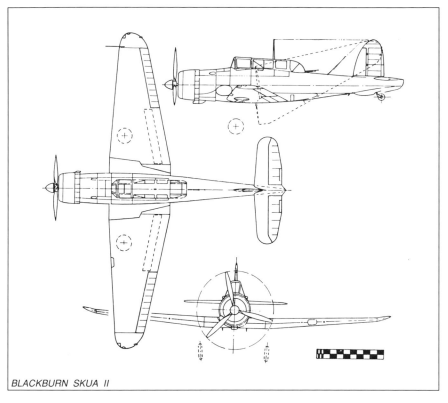

BLACKBURN SKUA II

Type: Single-engine, two-seat, low-wing monoplane naval fighter/dive bomber.
Manufacturer: Blackburn Aircraft Ltd, Brough, East Yorkshire.
Air Ministry Specification: O.27/34 (prototypes) and 25/36P (production).
Powerplant: Prototypes. One 840hp Bristol Mercury IX nine-cylinder air-cooled poppet-valve radial engine. Production Mk II. 890hp Bristol Perseus XII nine-cylinder sleeve-valve radial engine.
Structure: All-metal construction covered with Alclad sheet; folding wings with outwards retracting undercarriage.
Dimensions: Span, 46ft 2in (folded, 15ft 6in); length (Mk II), 35ft 7in; height, 12ft 6in; wing area, 319 sq ft.
Weights: As fighter. Tare, 5,496lb; all-up, 8,124lb.
Performance: As fighter. Max speed, 225 mph at 6,500ft; service ceiling, 20,200ft; range, 435 miles.
Armament: Four 0.303in Browning Mk II machine guns in the outer wings and one Lewis Mk IIIE gun in the rear cockpit.
Prototypes: Two, K5178 (first flown by Flt Lt A M Blake on 9 February 1937) and K5179.
Production: 190 Mk IIs: L2867-L3056.
Summary of Service: Skuas served with Nos 800, 801, 803 and 806 Fleet Fighter Squadrons of the Fleet Air Arm, and with the following second-line Squadrons, Nos 757, 758, 759, 760, 767, 769, 770, 771, 772, 774, 776, 778, 779, 780, 782, 787, 788, 789, 791, 792, 794 and 797. Skuas also served with the following RAF units: No 418 Flight, the Ferry Pilots Pool and No 2 Anti-Aircraft Co-operation Unit.

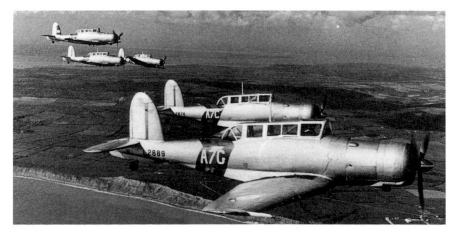

widely placed on the Skua's rôle as a naval fighter rather than as a dive bomber. The first production aircraft, L2867, designated the Mark II and powered by an 890hp Bristol Perseus XII sleeve-valve engine, was flown by Flt Lt Hugh Joseph Wilson RAFO on 28 August 1938, and early subsequent aircraft successfully completed the heavy programme of Service trials. Between October that year and March 1940 all 190 aircraft were delivered to the Service.

First deliveries were made to No 800 Squadron in October 1938, commanded by Lt-Cdr Brian Harold Maule Kendall RN aboard HMS *Courageous* in home waters, followed two months later by No 803 Squadron at Hatston. In March 1939 No 801 Squadron, under Lt-Cdr Charles Alfred Kingsley-Rowe RN, gave up its Ospreys in favour of the Skua II, before embarking in *Courageous*; and in February 1940 the last operational Skua

squadron, No 806, which formed at Donibristle on 1 March that year under Lt-Cdr Charles Leo Glandore Evans DSC, RN, took charge of a mixed complement of Blackburn Skuas and Rocs.

Although inferior to current fighters in performance, the Skua filled an important place in the naval inventory during the early months of the Second World War, and chalked up at least two memorable 'firsts'. In the first month, on 25 September 1939, the Skua, crewed by Lt Bruce Straton McEwen RN and Petty Officer B M Seymour of No 803 Squadron, launched from HMS *Ark Royal* and shot down a Dornier Do 18 flying-boat over the North Sea, the first German aircraft to fall to a British fighter's guns in the War.

No 803 Squadron was again in the news during the Norwegian campaign of April 1940 when, on the 10th, nine aircraft led by Lt William Paulet Lucy RN, accompanied by six from No 800, led

by Capt Richard Thomas Partridge RM, took off from Hatston, Orkney, and, at extreme range, dive bombed and sank the German light cruiser *Königsberg* in Bergen harbour, the first enemy surface warship to be sunk in the War by a British aircraft.

Design of the Skua broke new ground and thereby caused it to be later entering service than had been intended; as a result the Fairey Fulmar (see page 287) was hurriedly ordered as an interim measure, and this dedicated fighter — that is to say one that was not compromised by a secondary dive bombing rôle — began to assume the deck fighter duties with the fleet in 1940.

Nevertheless the Skua served with naval second line squadrons from 1939 until September 1944 in a host of rôles, including deck training, target towing and armament training, as well as on numerous fleet requirements squadrons.

Boulton Paul P.82 Defiant

Introduced to replace the Hawker Demon two-seat turret fighter in Fighter Command, the Boulton Paul Defiant was designed by J D North to Specification F.9/35 in competition with the Hawker Hotspur, the Bristol Type 147 and the Armstrong Whitworth A.W.34, of which the two last-named failed to attract Air Ministry interest. The trouble with the Specification lay not so much in the constantly changing requirements but in conflicting views as to whether the two-seat interceptor had any real place at all in the fighter defence system, for it should be recalled that the Demon had only been introduced with one purpose in mind — that of intercepting its related light bomber version, the Hart. Such an aircraft posed no strategic threat to Britain, and the manner in which Boulton Paul (and Hawker) interpreted the requirement brought forth aeroplanes which were hopelessly inept, being quite useless in combat with nimble enemy single-seaters and, lamentably, possessing no forward-firing fixed guns. Even the manner in which the Defiant was expected to engage enemy bombers required complex cross-over manœuvres in order to enable the gunner to bring his

The Defiant prototype, K8310, after being fitted with its dorsal turret. (Photo: Author's collection)

turret-mounted guns to bear.

Flt Lt Cecil Feather RAFO flew the prototype Defiant K8310 on 11 August 1937 at Wolverhampton, but without the turret, returning a maximum speed of 302 mph. Soon afterwards a Boulton Paul A Mk IID turret with four Browning machine guns was installed, together with fairings forward and aft of the turret, which retracted into the fuselage to permit greater freedom of gun rotation. Power was provided by a 1,030hp Rolls-Royce Merlin III — the same engine as was fitted in the Hurricane, which was no less than 32 per cent lighter than the Defiant. Moreover, the turret was electro-hydraulically rotated so that, in the event of a failure in the

system, such as a blown fuse — by no means infrequent — the aircraft was defenceless; at a surprisingly late stage, it was also discovered that the gunner was faced with an almost impossible task in abandoning the aircraft in the event of an emergency.

Production Defiants, built to Specification F.5/37, began equipping No 264 (Fighter) Squadron, commanded by Sqn Ldr Stephen Haistwell Hardy, at Martlesham Heath in December 1939 (the A & AEE having moved to Boscombe Down). This squadron became engaged in the heavy air fighting over Dunkirk in the following spring, and achieved a fair degree of success in this its baptism of fire, for it transpired that German fighter

Defiants of No 264 (Fighter) Squadron in 1940, probably at Kirton-in-Lindsey; after having enjoyed considerable success over Dunkirk, this squadrons suffered heavily at the end of August 1940, losses which included the Squadron Commander. (Photo: Author's collection)

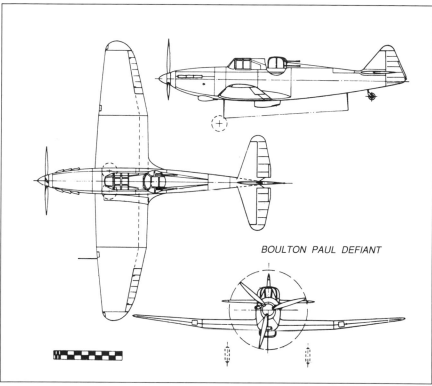

BOULTON PAUL DEFIANT

pilots misidentified the Defiants as Hurricanes and fell victims of the dorsal guns.

By the time a second Squadron, No 141, commanded by Sqn Ldr William Arthur Richardson, had been declared operational early in the Battle of Britain, the Germans had learned their lesson. On 19 July nine Defiants were attacked by a number of Messerschmitt Bf 109Es off Folkestone, and lost six of their number and almost all their crews. After a further disastrous spell in action at the end of August, the Defiant was summarily removed from daylight fighter operations.

Discredited as a day interceptor, the Defiant was immediately transferred to night operations for, within a fortnight of that final *débâcle*, the German Blitz broke over Britain, merging with the final stage of the Battle of Britain. After a slow start the aircraft began to demonstrate a useful capability of adapting to night interception tactics although, being at this time without the benefit of airborne radar, success against enemy night bombers depended in the last resort upon the pilot's night vision. By the end of the German's first night bombing campaign in May 1941, Defiant night fighters equipped Nos 96, 141, 151, 255, 256, 264 and 307 (Polish) Squadrons.

In due course the Defiant Mk II, with 1,260hp Merlin XX engine, was introduced, as was the Defiant NF Mk IA equipped with pilot-interpreted airborne radar (AI Mk IV and VI).

Other duties undertaken by Defiants included electronic countermeasures, as

Type: Single-engine, two-seat low-wing monoplane day and night turret fighter.
Manufacturer: Boulton Paul Aircraft Ltd, Wolverhampton, Staffordshire.
Air Ministry Specifications: F.9/35 (prototype) and F.5/37 (production).
Powerplant: Mk I. One 1,030hp Rolls-Royce Merlin III twelve-cylinder liquid-cooled in-line engine. Mk II. 1,260hp Merlin XX.
Dimensions: Span: 39ft 4in; length, 35ft 4in; height, 12ft 2in; wing area, 250 sq ft.
Weights: Tare, 6,282lb; all-up, 8,424lb.
Performance: Mk II. Max speed, 313 mph at 16,500ft; service ceiling, 30,350ft; range, 465 miles.
Armament: Four 0.303in Browning machine guns in electro-hydraulically operated dorsal turret
Prototype: One, K8310. First flown by Flt Lt Cecil Feather on 11 August 1937.
Production: Total of 1,060: 713 Mk I fighters, 207 Mk II fighters and 140 Mk III target tugs.
Summary of Service: Defiant day fighters served with Nos 141 and 264 Squadrons, and as night fighters with Nos 85, 96, 125, 141, 151, 153, 255, 256, 264 and 307 (Polish) Squadrons. They also flew with four air-sea rescue squadrons, with seven target-towing squadrons and No. 515 Countermeasures Squadron. The Defiant also underwent Service trials with No 2 Squadron in the army co-operation rôle.

No 515 Squadron began operating 'Moonshine' patrols, intended to disrupt German coastal radar in the path of

Allied bombing attacks during 1942. Relegated to target-towing duties, the Defiant TT Mk III served with seven anti-aircraft co-operation squadrons, and other aircraft — sometimes stripped of their turrets — became engaged in air-sea rescue work. The Defiant was withdrawn from the night fighting rôle in July 1942 when No 151 Squadron re-equipped with Mosquitos. The last Defiant was retired from target-towing with No 691 Squadron in April 1945.

A Defiant NF Mk II, AA370, undergoing trials at the A & AEE, Boscombe Down, in August 1941, equipped with AI Mk IV radar; note the 'broad arrow' aerials projecting forward of the wing. (Photo: A J Jackson Collection)

Hawker Hotspur

When Specification F.9/35 was originally issued, the Hawker Hurricane prototype had not flown, let alone been ordered into production, so that Sydney Camm's Hotspur turret fighter design tender was originally considered to be an insurance against any unforeseen difficulty in meeting the Hurricane's own requirements. When the Hurricane so clearly demonstrated its fulfilment of the Specification demands, the Hotspur tender was modified to emphasise the use of numerous components and jigs common to both aircraft.

A single prototype, K8309, was ordered on 10 December 1935, and when it became clear that the Hawker factories would be fully extended to meet Hurricane production demands, a new Specification, 17/36P, was issued calling for Hotspur production to be undertaken by A V Roe & Co Ltd, another member company of the recently established Hawker Siddeley Group, together with a second prototype, K8621.

Such was the enormous pressure on the Hawker company, however, to get Hurricane production underway, with all that entailed in preparing new drawings and jigs, that work on the Hotspur advanced very slowly, and it was not until 14 June 1938 that Philip Lucas first flew K8309. By then the Defiant had been flying for almost a year and an initial production order was in hand.

The Hotspur never received its scheduled Boulton Paul power-operated turret, being fitted instead with a wooden

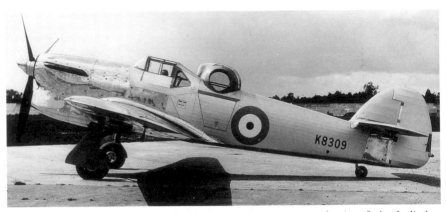

The Hawker Hotspur K8309. Though of fairly attractive appearance, the aircraft clearly displays its dependence on traditional manufacturing techniques, with much of the airframe structure fabric-covered. Such familiar techniques were justified in the Hurricane whose speed of production was of paramount importance. (Photo: Hawker Aircraft Ltd, Neg No HO/64H)

mock-up. Compared with the Defiant, the Hotspur was somewhat smaller and lighter and, when fitted with a similar Merlin, proved to be faster by about a dozen miles an hour. Like the Hawker Henley light bomber, also closely related to the Hurricane, the Hotspur employed a chin radiator; it did, however, feature provision for a single forward-firing Vickers gun.

With the cancellation of the proposed Avro production of the Hotspur, together with the second prototype, all development work was halted; the rear cockpit of K8309 was faired over and the aircraft was delivered to the RAE, being finally written off after a forced landing at Yateley Common, Hampshire, on 12 February 1942.

Type: Single-engine, two-seat low-wing monoplane turret fighter.
Manufacturer: Hawker Aircraft Ltd, Kingston and Brooklands, Surrey.
Air Ministry Specifications: F.9/35 (Prototype) and 17/36P (production by A V Roe & Co).
Powerplant: One 1,025hp Rolls-Royce Merlin II twelve-cylinder liquid-cooled in-line engine.
Dimensions: Span, 47ft 10¼in; length, 36ft 1½in; height, 14ft 4in; wing area, 342 sq ft.
Weights: Tare, 5,800lb; all-up, 7,650lb.
Performance: Max speed, 316 mph at 15,800ft; climb to 15,000ft, approx 10min 30 sec; service ceiling, 28,100ft.
Armament: Provision for four Browning machine guns in power-operated dorsal turret, and single synchronized Vickers gun on starboard side of fuselage.
Prototype: One, K8309. First flown by P G Lucas on 14 June 1938. (Second prototype, K8621, cancelled). No production.

Blackburn Roc

Following the issue of Specification F.9/35, the Air Ministry turned its attention to a more specialized replacement than the Skua for the Hawker Osprey which, since 1933, had been performing the nebulous rôle of reconnaissance fighter with the Royal Navy in both land- and seaplane guises. At the outset it was thought likely that the successful contender for F.9/35 contracts would be adaptable as a fleet fighter and indeed Boulton Paul put forward a navalised derivative of the Defiant to meet the new Specification, O.30/35. This, however, failed to meet the wing-folding dimensions without extensive redesign with the result that Blackburn's proposal for an aircraft based on the Skua two-seat fighter dive bomber was accepted. On the face of it, this seemed a logical and relatively straightforward expedient, but in the event the design alterations were more extensive than originally anticipated, and the Skua's 890 hp Perseus XII engine — retained in the new fighter, the Roc — proved severely under-powered. Even with the Skua's four wing-mounted Browning machine guns omitted, the big power-operated Boulton Paul four-gun turret amidships raised the Roc's tare weight to over 6,000 lb, compared to the Skua's 5,496 lb.

An order for 136 Blackburn Rocs was awarded to Blackburn on 28 April 1937 (but later transferred to Boulton Paul on sub-contract) and the first aircraft, L3057 which served as a prototype, was flown by Flt Lt Hugh Joseph Wilson RAFO, Blackburn's test pilot, on 23 December 1938. A second Specification, 20/37, calling for a floatplane variant had been prepared, and the second and third examples, flown late in 1939 with twin floats, underwent tests at the MAEE at Helensburgh; these proved unsatisfactory and the floatplane version was discontinued.

In the meantime Roc production with wheel undercarriage had got underway and No 803 Squadron, Fleet Air Arm, commanded by Lt-Cdr Dennis Royle Farquharson Cambell RN at Worthy Down, was the first to receive the turret fighter in April 1939, followed the next month by No 800 Squadron, also at Worthy Down, where they joined Skuas. A total of five operational squadrons took delivery of Rocs but, although the

The first Blackburn Roc prototype, L3057. (Photo: A J Jackson Collection)

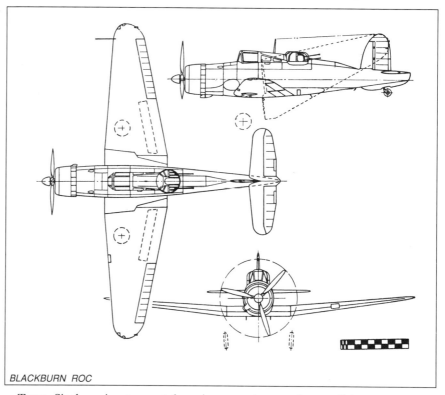

BLACKBURN ROC

Type: Single-engine, two-seat, low-wing monoplane naval turret fighter
Design Origin: Blackburn Aircraft Ltd, Brough, East Yorkshire. *Manufacturer:* Boulton Paul Aircraft Ltd, Wolverhampton, Staffordshire.
Air Ministry Specifications: O.30/35 (landplane); 20/37 (floatplane).
Powerplant: One 890hp Bristol Perseus XII nine-cylinder air-cooled sleeve-valve radial engine driving three-blade de Havilland propeller.
Structure: All-metal monocoque with two-spar folding wings; retractable mainwheels and fixed tailwheel; modified Zap flaps. Fabric-covered control surfaces.
Dimensions: Span, 46ft 0in (15ft 6in folded); length, 35ft 7in (39ft 4in floatplane); height, 12ft 1in; wing area, 310 sq ft.
Weights: Landplane. Tare, 6,124lb; all-up, 7,950lb. Floatplane. Tare, 7,987lb; all-up, 8,670lb.
Performance: Landplane. Max speed, 223 mph at 10,000ft; initial climb, 1,500 ft/min; service ceiling, 18,000ft; max range, 810 miles. Floatplane. Max speed, 193 mph at 10,000ft; service ceiling, 14,600ft.
Armament: Four 0.303in Browning machine guns in midships Boulton Paul Type A Mk II hydraulically-operated turret; provision to carry one 250lb bomb.
Prototypes: Three, L3057 (landplane, first flown 23 December 1938 by Flt Lt H J Wilson); L3058 and L3059 (floatplanes).
Production and Summary of Service: L3060-L3192 (133 aircraft). Served with naval fighter squadrons, Nos 800, 801, 803, 805 and 806; and Nos 725, 758, 759, 760, 765, 769, 770, 771, 772, 773, 774, 775, 776, 777, 778, 782, 787, 789, 791, 792, 793 and 794 Training Squadrons; also No 2 AACU, RAF.

aircraft were equipped for deck operation, none was ever flown from a carrier.

Like the RAF's Defiant, the Roc proved a failure — largely on account of its dismal performance which would prevent it ever gaining a combat position from which it could bring its turret guns to bear on an enemy. Quite simply it fell victim of the same flawed concept that produced the Defiant — also devoid of forward-firing guns.

Rocs were finally discarded as operational equipment in June 1940, and thereafter joined a total of 22 Fleet Air Arm Training Squadrons, as well as No. 2 Anti-Aircraft Co-operation Unit at Gosport. Later a number of Rocs served at target tugs with Air Gunnery Schools.

The second Roc floatplane prototype, L3059. (Photo: Air Ministry RTP Neg No 10254C)

Bristol Type 142M Blenheim Fighters

RAF Coastal Command flew Blenheim fighters on offensive operations from 1940; this Mk IF belonged to No 248 Squadron at North Coates. (Photo: The Bristol Aeroplane Co Ltd.)

The Blenheim twin-engine light bomber occupied an exceptionally important place in the Royal Air Force's inventory in the first two years immediately before the Second World War and, like so many of those aircraft whose Service life spanned many years, owed its origins to privately-funded enterprise.

Those origins lay in a proposal early in 1934 by Lord Rothermere, proprietor of the *Daily Mail*, to purchase a twin-engine aircraft from Bristol that would be 'the fastest commercial aircraft in Europe' for his personal use. Barnwell and Fedden proposed a low-wing monoplane, powered by 500hp Bristol Aquila I sleeve-valve radials and this aircraft, the Type 142 (named *Britain First*), was first flown at Filton on 12 April 1935. When delivered to Martlesham for airworthiness trials, it returned a maximum speed with full load of 307 mph — and this was five months before the Hawker Hurricane prototype was first flown!

Lord Rothermere presented '*Britain First*' to the Air Council, who promptly ordered a military prototype, termed the Bristol Type 142M, having prepared Specification B.28/35, and followed this with a contract for 150 production aircraft. The prototype Type 142M, K7033 — now a mid-wing monoplane powered by Mercury radial engines — was first flown on 25 June 1936, and production Blenheim bombers began delivery to the first RAF Squadron, No 114 at Wyton, in March 1937. By the end of that year four further light bomber squadrons were flying the new aircraft.

By mid-1938, with more than 600 Blenheim Is already delivered or on order, the Air Ministry had decided to introduce the aircraft into service as a night fighter, being attracted by its relatively long range and endurance, and by the ease with which it could be flown and landed at night. Moreover, since 1936, work had been progressing on airborne radar, although no such equipment had yet passed the 'breadboard' stage, let alone been installed in an aircraft. Yet it seemed that an aircraft such as the Blenheim might ultimately be suitable with which to introduce this most secret equipment into service.

Little modification was required to match the Blenheim to the rôle of night fighter, and consisted principally of adding a self-contained tray with four Browning machine guns and their ammunition tanks under the fuselage, the bomb doors being made inoperable. These gun packs were manufactured by the Southern Railway's Ashford works in Kent. The guns were fired in the customary manner by a trigger button on the pilot's control column. The Blenheim bomber's dorsal turret, mounting a Vickers 'K' gas-operated machine gun was retained.

Termed Blenheim Mk IFs, the fighter version was cleared for operational use late in October 1938, and in December the first examples were collected from Filton by No 25 (Fighter) Squadron, commanded by Sqn Ldr Donald Malcolm Fleming. Before the month was out, Nos 23, 29 and 64 Squadrons had also taken delivery of their new aircraft, and in the following month three Auxiliary Squadrons, Nos 600, 601 and 604, converted to the night fighting rôle with Blenheim IFs.

Night fighter training began in earnest during the spring of 1939, with Bomber Command putting up Whitleys as targets, but progress was slow, and success depended largely on the ground searchlights being able to expose the 'target' raiders in their beams. More often than not the Blenheim crews were themselves blinded by the probing lights. Nevertheless results were sufficiently promising to encourage further deliveries to fighter squadrons, and during the first four months of the War Nos 92, 141, 145, 219, 222, 229, 234, 242, 248 and 254 Squadrons were equipped with Blenheim fighters.

Meanwhile No 25 Squadron, now based at Northolt, had detached a flight of aircraft (among them N6193 and N6194) to Martlesham in August for trials with the first airborne radar (AI Mk III). These aircraft were the later version of the Blenheim, the Mk IV with lengthened nose, and performed trials both by day and night, their crews trying to locate 'targets' over the Thames Estuary on their rudimentary cathode ray displays. These were the first experiments in the world involving the use of airborne radar. By November the Blenheims were flying operational patrols over the North Sea, but were frustrated owing to the absence of German aircraft.

Meanwhile, on 26 November, the other aircraft of No 25 Squadron attempted a long-range daylight attack on the German seaplane base at Borkum, but failed to locate their target. Two days later, in company with six Blenheim fighters of No 601 Squadron, No 25 made a successful attack on this target by strafing enemy minelaying seaplanes, the first occasion that RAF fighters were in action over German territory during the War.

By the beginning of the Battle of Britain, Blenheim IFs and IVFs equipped no more than eight squadrons of Fighter and Coastal Commands, some of those mentioned above having converted to Hurricanes, Spitfires and Defiants. Nevertheless these twin-engine aircraft represented the backbone of the nation's night fighter defences. More important, their operations, if not claiming much success against enemy aircraft, served to provide vital training and experience for pilots who would soon be flying the new Beaufighter, the RAF's first purpose-designed twin-engine night fighter.

It was appropriate that it should have

Another No 248 Squadron Blenheim, this time a Mk IVF, N6239/WR-L at North Coates in about April 1940. The gun tray beneath the fuselage is clearly visible, as is the characteristic shape of the Blenheim's lengthened nose. (Photo: The Bristol Aeroplane Co Ltd, Neg No T149/167)

been a Blenheim fighter that achieved the world's first combat victory using airborne radar when, on the night of 22/23 July 1940, an aircraft of the Fighter Interception Unit, flying from Tang-

mere and crewed by Fg Off Glynn Ashfield, Plt Off Geoffrey Morris and Sgt Reginald Leyland, intercepted and shot down a Dornier Do 17Z into the English Channel off Brighton.

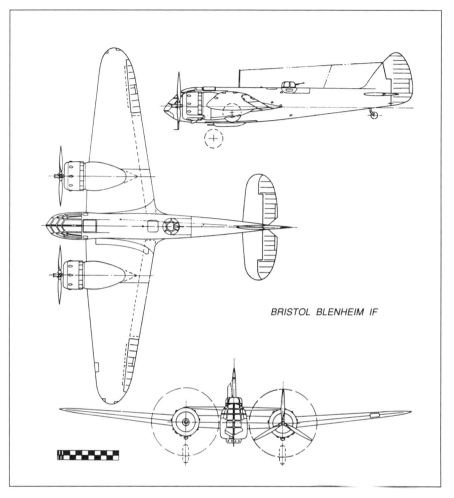

BRISTOL BLENHEIM IF

Type: Twin-engine, three-crew, mid-wing monoplane night fighter.
Manufacturers: The Bristol Aeroplane Co Ltd, Filton, Bristol; A V Roe & Co Ltd, Manchester.
Powerplant: Mk IF. Two 840hp Bristol Mercury VIII nine-cylinder air-cooled radials. Mk IVF. Two 920hp Mercury XV.
Dimensions: Span, 56ft 4in; length (Mk IF), 39ft 9in; height, 12ft 10in; wing area, 469 sq ft.
Weights: Tare, 8,025lb; all-up, 11,975lb.
Performance: Max speed (Mk IF), 282 mph at 13,600 ft, (Mk IVF) 292 mph at 13,100ft; service ceiling, 31,400ft; normal range, 1,050 miles.
Production: Approx 320 aircraft (Mk IFs and IVFs) converted.
Summary of RAF Service: Blenheim IFs served with Nos 23, 25, 29, 30, 64, 68, 92, 141, 145, 219, 222, 229, 234, 235, 242, 248, 254, 600, 601 and 604 Squadrons; Mk IVFs served with Nos 25, 27, 235, 236 and 248 Squadrons.

Westland P.9 Whirlwind

The first Whirlwind prototype, L6844, without radio or guns installed, an unbalanced rudder and pitot head mounted on the leading edge of the fin. (Photo: Westland Aircraft Ltd.)

Neither the Hurricane nor the Spitfire prototypes had flown when Specification F.37/35 was first circulated in draft form among British aircraft manufacturers in October 1935, calling for a single-seat interceptor fighter armed with four 20mm cannon and capable of a speed of 'over' 320 mph at 15,000 feet. In due course half a dozen designs were tendered (including four-cannon versions of the Hurricane and Spitfire), but the most promising, albeit most radical proposal emanated from the design staff headed by William Edward Willoughby Petter, newly appointed Technical Director at Westland Aircraft Ltd., Yeovil. The P.9 design was of a small twin-engine, low-wing, all-metal monocoque monoplane powered by a pair of 885hp Rolls-Royce Peregrine I supercharged engines in underslung nacelles with radiators in the wing centre section leading edge. As originally conceived the proposed Oerlikon cannon were to be mounted as a horizontal battery in the nose and the aircraft featured twin fins and rudders. The latter feature was discarded at an early stage in favour of a single vertical tail surface with high-set tailplane. Extensive use was made of elektron castings and the high aspect ratio wing incorporated large Handley Page leading-edge slats and a wide-span, single piece Fowler trailing-edge flap which extended outboard of the engine nacelles and across the underside of the fuselage.

The Westland P.9 was an exceptionally clean aircraft, this effect being heightened by the use of a single-piece sliding 'tear-drop' cockpit canopy — one of the first to appear on a British fighter and a feature that bestowed excellent field of vision for the pilot.

As originally conceived the F.37/35 fighter requirement was intended to provide a 'day and night bomber destroyer', its heavy cannon armament being central to this rôle. When it was first flown by Harald Penrose on 11 October 1938 at Yeovil, the prototype L6844 carried ballast in lieu of armament and soon proved to be faster than the Spitfire I below 10,000 feet and, with Frise ailerons, lighter on the controls. It was however somewhat tricky during take-off and landing as, in the nose-up attitude at low airspeed, the wing tended to blank the elevators.

The generally good performance and handling characteristics were confirmed when L6844 visited the RAE, Farnborough, during January 1939, and before the end of that month a production order for 140 aircraft was issued, followed seven months later by a second contract for another 200. By the end of 1938, however, the urgency lent by the Munich crisis for increased and uninterrupted production of Merlin engines caused the proposed delivery rate of Peregrines to be severely reduced. Furthermore early tests with the Oerlikon cannon — which required 'greased' ammunition — resulted in a switch to the Hispano Mark I and a redesign of the P.9, now named the Whirlwind. The second prototype, L6845, was thus delayed and only flew at about the time that the first production aircraft began to appear in May 1940. (By then use of the wing slats had been discontinued, and were fixed in the closed position.)

By the time the Whirlwind was ready for RAF Fighter Command the terms of its Specification had been overtaken by events. The rôle of night fighter had been assumed by the Bristol Blenheim IF, and airborne interception (AI) radar had appeared in service — the operation of which demanded a second crew member in such night fighters. Moreover the Whirlwind was proving a difficult aeroplane to operate at night — as demonstrated when two aircraft, P6966 and P6967, were delivered for operational trials with No 25 Squadron.

It was accordingly decided to confine the Whirlwind's operations to daylight interception, and subsequent deliveries were made to No 263 Squadron, previously equipped with Gloster Gladiators and now re-formed at Drem under Sqn

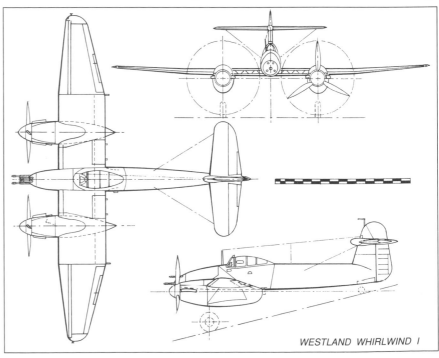

WESTLAND WHIRLWIND I

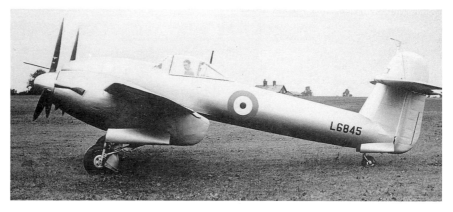

The second Whirlwind prototype, L6845, showing the addition of a small 'acorn' fairing at the
junction of tailplane and fin, and the production-type pitot head, now mounted high above
the tail fin. (Photo: Westland Aircraft Ltd.)

WESTLAND WHIRLWIND   275

Ldr Henry Eeles after severe losses in
Norway. Owing to slow delivery of
engines only eight Whirlwinds had
reached No 263 Squadron by October
1940, by which time production orders
had been cut back to only 114 aircraft.

Operating from Exeter and St Eval,
No 263 engaged in offensive fighter
operations and convoy escort over the
Channel early in 1941. A second Squadron, No 137, began receiving Whirlwinds in September that year, and shortly
afterwards the aircraft was adapted as a
fighter-bomber to carry either a 250 or
500lb bomb under each wing outboard
of the engines. In this rôle the Whirlwind was very successful in offensive
sweeps over France and the Channel
coast, but production of the aircraft had
run out in January 1942 and no further
Whirlwind squadrons were formed.
Nevertheless it was not until June 1943
that No 137 was re-equipped with
Hurricane IV fighter-bombers, while
No 263 Squadron did not receive Typhoons until December that year.

*The fourth production Whirlwind I, P6969, of
No 263 (Fighter) Squadron, before the aircraft
was modified to carry bombs under the wings.
Note the very large 'acorn' fairing on the fin,
adopted as standard on production aircraft. This
photograph was almost certainly taken in
1940. (Photo: Real Photographs Co Ltd.)*

Type: Twin-engine single-seat low-wing monoplane fighter (later fighter-bomber).
Air Ministry Specification: F.37/35
Manufacturer: Westland Aircraft Ltd., Yeovil, Somerset.
Powerplant: Two 885hp Rolls-Royce Peregrine I twelve-cylinder liquid-cooled super-
charged in-line engine.
Structure: All-metal monocoque low-wing monoplane with stressed skin; Frise ailerons
and Fowler trailing-edge flaps. Tailwheel undercarriage with mainwheels retracting
rearwards into engine nacelles; retractable tailwheel.
Dimensions: Span, 45ft 0in; length, 32ft 3in; height, 10ft 6in; wing area, 250 sq ft.
Weights: Tare, 8,310lb; all-up (fighter), 10,356lb; (fighter-bomber), 11,388lb.
Performance: Max speed, 360 mph at 15,000ft (without bombs); 270 mph at 15,000ft (with
two 500lb bombs); climb to 15,000ft, 5 min 45 sec.
Armament: Four 20mm Hispano Mk I cannon in nose with 60 rounds per gun; Mk III
universal bomb carriers under wings for two 500lb bombs.
Prototypes: L6844 and L6845 (L6844 first flown by Harald Penrose, 11 October 1938).
Production: 114 aircraft (P6966-P7015; P7035-P7064; P7089-P7122)
Service Summary: No. 25 Squadron (two aircraft only); Nos. 137 and 263 Squadrons.

Deployment of British Fighter Squadrons — January 1940

Home Bases

No 3 Squadron	Hawker Hurricane I	Hawkinge
No 17 Squadron	Hawker Hurricane I	Debden
No 19 Squadron	Supermarine Spitfire I	Duxford
No 23 Squadron	Bristol Blenheim IF	Northolt
No 25 Squadron	Bristol Blenheim IF	Northolt
No 29 Squadron	Bristol Blenheim IF	Debden
No 32 Squadron	Hawker Hurricane I	Gravesend
No 41 Squadron	Supermarine Spitfire I	Catterick
No 43 Squadron	Hawker Hurricane I	Acklington
No 46 Squadron	Hawker Hurricane I	Digby
No 54 Squadron	Supermarine Spitfire I	Hornchurch
No 64 Squadron	Bristol Blenheim IF	Church Fenton
No 65 Squadron	Supermarine Spitfire I	Northolt
No 66 Squadron	Supermarine Spitfire I	Duxford
No 72 Squadron	Supermarine Spitfire I	Drem
No 74 Squadron	Supermarine Spitfire I	Hornchurch
No 79 Squadron	Hawker Hurricane I	Manston
No 92 Squadron	Bristol Blenheim IF	Croydon
No 111 Squadron	Hawker Hurricane I	Drem
No 141 Squadron	Bristol Blenheim IF	Grangemouth
No 145 Squadron	Bristol Blenheim IF	Croydon
No 151 Squadron	Hawker Hurricane I	North Weald
No 152 Squadron	Gloster Gladiator II	Acklington
No 213 Squadron	Hawker Hurricane I	Wittering
No 219 Squadron	Bristol Blenheim IF	Catterick
No 222 Squadron	Bristol Blenheim IF	Duxford
No 229 Squadron	Bristol Blenheim IF	Digby
No 234 Squadron	Bristol Blenheim IF	Leconfield
No 236 Squadron	Bristol Blenheim IF	Martlesham
No 242 Squadron	Hawker Hurricane I	Church Fenton
No 245 Squadron	Bristol Blenheim IF	Leconfield
No 248 Squadron	Bristol Blenheim IF	Hendon
No 254 Squadron	Bristol Blenheim IF	Sutton Bridge
No 263 Squadron	Gloster Gladiator II	Filton
No 264 Squadron	Boulton Paul Defiant I	Martlesham
No 266 Squadron*	Supermarine Spitfire I	Sutton Bridge
No 501 Squadron	Hawker Hurricane I	Tangmere
No 504 Squadron	Hawker Hurricane I	Debden

No 600 Squadron	Bristol Blenheim IF	Manston
No 601 Squadron	Bristol Blenheim IF	Tangmere
No 602 Squadron	Supermarine Spitfire I	Drem
No 603 Squadron	Supermarine Spitfire I	Prestwick
No 604 Squadron	Bristol Blenheim IF	Northolt
No 605 Squadron	Hawker Hurricane I	Tangmere
No 609 Squadron	Supermarine Spitfire I	Drem
No 610 Squadron	Supermarine Spitfire I	Wittering
No 611 Squadron	Supermarine Spitfire I	Digby
No 616 Squadron	Supermarine Spitfire I	Leconfield

France

No 1 Squadron	Hawker Hurricane I	Vassincourt
No 73 Squadron	Hawker Hurricane I	Rouvres
No 85 Squadron	Hawker Hurricane I	Lille
No 87 Squadron	Hawker Hurricane I	Lille
No 607 Squadron	Gloster Gladiator II	Vitry-en-Artois
No 615 Squadron	Gloster Gladiator II	Vitry-en-Artois

Middle East

No 6 Squadron	Gloster Gauntlet	Ramleh, Palestine
No 30 Squadron	Bristol Blenheim IF	Ismailia, Egypt
No 33 Squadron	Gloster Gladiator II	Mersa Matruh, Egypt
No 80 Squadron	Gloster Gladiator II	Amriya, Egypt
No 94 Squadron	Gloster Gladiator II	Sheikh Othman, Egypt
No 112 Squadron	Gloster Gladiator II	Helwan, Egypt

Fleet Air Arm

No 800 Squadron	Blackburn Skua	HMS *Ark Royal*
No 801 Squadron	Blackburn Skua	Donibristle
No 802 Squadron	Gloster Sea Gladiator	Aboukir, Egypt
No 803 Squadron	Blackburn Skua	Wick
No 804 Squadron	Gloster Sea Gladiator	Hatston

*   One Flight only

6. THE MONOPLANE SUPREME

By the end of 1936 the Air Ministry had completed its immediate preparations to equip the Royal Air Force and Fleet Air Arm with a modern array of monoplane interceptors, and the foremost of these — the Hurricane and Spitfire prototypes — had flown and had already demonstrated their potential excellence. Other variations on the monoplane theme had been defined in Specification form, and these would materialise in due course as the Skua, Defiant, Roc and Whirlwind.

The rapid and successful development of the Rolls-Royce Merlin engine, and the promise already being shown under test conditions by the installation of multiple machine gun batteries in the Hurricane and Spitfire, encouraged the Air Ministry and the aircraft industry to discuss the feasibility of even more powerfully-armed fighters. Into these discussions were injected preliminary details of a range of new engines, albeit originally conceived as providing power for a new generation of heavy bombers

— but now seen as potentially applicable to a new generation of interceptor fighters.

From D Napier & Sons came provisional information of a new 24-cylinder liquid-cooled sleeve-valve H-type supercharged engine, later to be named the Sabre, from which a power output of 2,000 horse power was confidently predicted. With slightly less power, the new Rolls-Royce Vulture comprised in effect two Peregrine engines, one erect and one inverted, mated to a single crankcase and driving a pair of shafts geared together to drive a single propeller; this engine was expected to develop about 1,800 hp, albeit at a weight significantly less than that of the Napier Sabre. Bristol Engines had extended their promising Hercules fourteen-cylinder sleeve-valve two-row radial engine to produce a 53.6 litre engine which was expected to develop about 2,500 hp (compared with about 1,500 hp from the 38.7 litre Hercules); this was to emerge as the Bristol Centaurus.

There is no doubt but that each of these engine manufacturers possessed considerable acumen in their respective fields — Napier in twin-shaft H-type engines, Rolls-Royce in liquid-cooled supercharged Vee-twelve engines, and Bristol in sleeve-valve air-cooled radials. Unfortunately there was scarcely any interchange of research information between companies (on peacetime commercial grounds, particularly in view of the huge production contracts at large); for instance, Bristol carefully protected its experience in manufacturing dimpled sleeve-valve barrels with the result that Napier persevered with smooth-barrelled sleeves, in turn leading to lubrication problems with the Sabre. Indeed there was very little interchange of research data on cooling and lubrication of these powerful engines, resulting in much tedious and lengthy duplication of system development.

Assuming, correctly as it transpired, that the progressive development of the Merlin would permit the Hurricane and Spitfire to remain effective in service for some years to come, the Air Ministry set about formulating requirements for the 'heavy fighter' in a number of widely differing Specifications. They may be summarised in three categories:

1) The heavily-armed, high-speed interceptor,
2) The heavily-armed bomber destroyer, and
3) The heavily-armed long-range escort fighter.

These categories soon became blurred as aircraft designers discovered that an aircraft suited primarily to one rôle possessed performance characteristics that bestowed quite adequate capabilities in another. A further complication arose in the night fighting rôle when it was discovered that, first, the Spitfire was quite unsuitable for night fighting and, second, that the single-seat interceptor was unable to combat night raiders efficiently without use of airborne radar which, it transpired, demanded a second crew member to operate.

It was the Germans who, in their successive *blitzkrieg* campaigns early in the Second World War, demonstrated the manner by which single- and two-seat fighters could be adapted to carry bombs so as to provide ground support in the land battle. The absence of close support for the Army by the RAF in the early stages in the War brought forth a torrent of criticism on the heads of the Air Force, and it was not long before Hurricanes were being fitted to carry 250lb bombs under their wings. In due course the term 'fighter-bomber' came to be applied to any fighter — be it a Hurricane or Mosquito — whose task was to support the ground forces, and still be capable of defending itself in air combat.

The great majority of the 1937 Specifications failed to produce satisfactory operational aircraft. The most successful — yet the most demanding — was F.18/37 which came into being following a long period of discussions with Sydney Camm at Hawker. Constrained by the knowledge that all three of the new engines, described above, would demand lengthy development and that any of them might fail to meet operational requirements for power and reliability, Camm undertook to produce alternative designs to accommodate either Sabre or Vulture (and even to investigate the possibility of using the Centaurus—in spite of his dislike of radial engines). Implicit in Hawker's determination to succeed in the F.18/37 Specification was a decision to abandon its traditional use of wood in its secondary structures and move towards monocoque construction—a move that would coincide with the opening of a large new factory at Langley, Buckinghamshire. In the event Hawker built only a small number of F.18/37 aircraft — the Typhoon — its main production being switched to Gloster. Mainstream production of the Hurricane persisted at Langley until 1944.

If Hawker regarded the Typhoon as a 'second generation Hurricane', Supermarine persisted with the Merlin-engine Spitfire for ten years but, from 1942, embarked on a 'second generation Spitfire' by adopting the new Rolls-Royce Griffon engine in 1942, and a year later introducing a new wing planform. It has been averred that the Griffon-Spitfire Mark XIV was as different from the Merlin Spitfire I as the Typhoon was from the Hurricane I.

Two outstanding fighters, both with two engines, were unpremeditated in original Air Ministry Specifications. They were the Bristol Beaufighter and the de Havilland Mosquito. The former, carrying an exceptionally heavy gun armament, was the RAF's first purpose-designed monoplane night fighter and the first to be designed from the outset to accommodate airborne interception (AI) radar. The latter, the incomparable Mosquito, was a logical follow-on from the brilliantly successful unarmed, high-speed two-seat bomber. Between them, these two two-seat, twin-engine aircraft shouldered the major share of the RAF's wartime night fighting responsibilities in all their tactical variations.

The Fleet Air Arm had progressed less quickly in its programme to re-equip with monoplane fighters. As if to acknowledge the makeshift nature of the Skua as a fighter, the Air Ministry sought another expedient, this time adapting the Fairey P.4/34 — a light bomber that had failed to impress the RAF — for the fleet fighter rôle. The resulting Fulmar did not however fly in prototype form until January 1940 and entered service alongside Sea Gladiators in June that year. Due largely to its size and weight, this eight-gun two-seat fighter possessed a poor performance, but nevertheless remained in operational service until 1943.

To overcome the glaring absence of a dedicated single-seat monoplane fleet fighter, the British government ordered large numbers of the American Grumman Wildcat, re-naming it the Martlet in the Fleet Air Arm, and the first of these joined the Navy in September 1940. Subsequent variants remained in service until the end of the European War. If the Martlet was at least a true naval fighter, it was paradoxical that the Royal Navy's best shipborne interceptor during the first three years of the War was yet another adaptation of an RAF fighter, the Hurricane, and for four years this provided the backbone of the Navy's fighter defences the world over, ultimately carrying a four-cannon armament. As will be told, the Sea Hurricane performed an extraordinary range of fighter duties at sea, ultimately giving pride of place to the Seafire and various American naval fighters.

Returning to the RAF's wartime fighters, the Hurricane I and Spitfire I together held centre stage throughout the Battle of Britain before improved versions began delivery to Fighter Command, first with the Hurricane II and then with the superb Spitfire V— and it was the latter that effectively became Fighter Command's standard fighter over the English Channel and Northern France throughout 1941 and 1942, armed with two cannon and four machine guns. The Hurricane II, on the other hand, now armed with either twelve machine guns or four cannon, proved its value as a night intruder and as a fighter-bomber, being progressively adapted to carry a pair of bombs, 60lb rocket projectiles and 40mm anti-tank guns. The Hurricane it was that was to become the RAF's standard fighter in overseas theatres, beginning in North Africa and the Middle East and later in the Far East until joined much later by the Spitfire.

After the Rolls-Royce Vulture engine was discontinued in 1941 (and cancellation of the Vulture-powered Hawker Tornado at the same time), emphasis switched to the Typhoon — itself beset by problems stemming largely from the lack of development in the hard days of 1940. The appearance of improved German fighters over France and Britain in 1941 and 1942, notably the Messerschmitt Bf 109F and the Focke-Wulf Fw 190A, focussed attention on the need for an RAF fighter capable of a speed of over 400 mph. Work was accordingly stepped up to introduce the Typhoon into service quickly with the result that it reached its first squadron in the late summer of 1941. However, although it proved capable of matching the German fighters at heights below 10,000 feet, its performance fell off rapidly at greater altitude, due largely to its thick wing. Fortunately Rolls-Royce was working on a new two-speed, two-stage super-charged version of the Merlin and, as an interim measure this engine was married to the Spitfire V to produce the Mark IX. Both Typhoon and Spitfire IX became operational with Fighter Command in 1942; as recorded in the previous chapter the Spitfire IX, despite its makeshift origins, remained in widespread service until the end of the War.

In due course the Typhoon, disappointing as an interceptor, followed the Hurricane into the fighter-bomber rôle, winning its spurs in the cross-Channel attacks in the campaign leading to the Normandy landings of 1944, and afterwards during the Allied advance through Northern Europe. As already mentioned, continuing development of the Spitfire centred on the introduction of the Rolls-Royce Griffon engine (of 36.7 litres capacity, compared to the Merlin's 27 litres), and the Spitfire XII entered service with this engine in 1943 to counter low-flying Fw 190 raiders over Southern England. This was followed by the Mark XIV the following year, a truly remarkable fighter with a top speed of 448 mph at 26,000 feet and an armament of two cannon and four machine guns. Its Griffon 65 drove a Rotol five-blade propeller, and the aircraft featured an entirely new wing and tail.

Meanwhile Sydney Camm had been working on an improved derivative of the Typhoon, being concerned principally to discard the inefficient thick wing in favour of an elliptical planform of much reduced thickness/chord. And so was born the Tempest, to become what was arguably the best British single engine fighter of the War. Retaining the powerful Sabre engine — which had by 1943 overcome its early troubles — the Tempest V, with a speed of about 430 mph and an armament of four 20 mm cannon, entered service in 1944 in time to lead the defences against the V 1 flying bombs; in the fighter-bomber rôle the Tempest could carry two 1,000 lb bombs or a load of 60lb rocket projectiles. It could also be dived at over 500 mph without undue trouble from compressibility with the result that it destroyed more Messerschmitt Me 262 jet fighters than any other Allied aircraft.

In other areas of piston-engine fighter design, British designers had come up with such aircraft as the Fairey Firefly, a Griffon-powered two-seat replacement for the Fulmar fleet fighter, and this showed considerable promise despite poor performance in its early versions. Westlands had extended their Whirl-wind formula to produce the Welkin high altitude fighter—an intended reply to German high-flying bombers. Stemming from the successful use of the Beaufighter in the anti-shipping strike rôle while carrying bombs and rockets in addition to its heavy gun armament, a new operational category came into being, the torpedo fighter. Both the Beaufighter and the Sea Mosquito were adapted to become torpedo carriers, and were followed by single-engine, single-seat designs such as the Blackburn Firebrand and, shortly after the War, the Westland Wyvern; both had started life as naval fighters.

Yet pride of place in the arena of single-seat piston engine fighter design must surely go to Martin-Baker, the tiny company which had produced the radical M.B.2 in reply to Specification F.5/34 just before the War (and referred to in the previous chapter). James Martin followed this with a Sabre-powered fighter, armed with no fewer than six 20 mm cannon. Unfortunately the 415-mph prototype crashed following failure of its engine and before it could be fully assessed by the RAF. Undeterred, Martin went ahead with a new aeroplane to be powered by a 2,340 hp Griffon driving contra-rotating propellers, and the prototype was flown in May 1944. As the result of meticulous attention to design detail, the M.B.5 was extraordinarily compact and aerodynamically 'clean' and earned unstinted praise from the RAF. Alas, despite superb flying qualities, four cannon armament and a top speed of 460 mph, the M.B.5 never progressed beyond the prototype stage. The end of the War was in sight and already the new jet fighters—the Gloster Meteor and de Havilland Vampire, not to mention the German Me 262— were uncompromisingly indicating the path to the future.

Gloster F.9/37

It has been shown that between 1933 and 1936 the Air Ministry and industry alike came finally to accept the monoplane as the only means at their disposal by which to advance aircraft performance materially, and had done so spectacularly with such aeroplanes as the Hurricane, Spitfire and Whirlwind fighters. A new chapter opened in 1937 as the engine manufacturers introduced a host of new engines, and the Air Ministry, capitalising on their increased power, began to step up their demands for further improvement in performance and armament.

One of the first of the new Specifications was F.9/37 which called for a very

The Bristol Taurus-powered Gloster F.9/37 prototype, L7999, with constant-speed Rotol propellers on Brockworth airfield. The provision of two pitot heads was for trial purposes only. (Photo: via Derek James)

heavy fixed armament, to which Gloster submitted an extremely promising tender with a twin-engine low-wing monoplane. Origins of the design dated back to 1934 when Folland had prepared drawings of a two-seat turret fighter to Specification F.5/33, intended to replace the Hawker Demon (and also tendered to by Armstrong Whitworth with the A.W.34, and Bristol with the Type 140). Nothing came of this requirement, but in 1935 Gloster resurrected the design to meet a new Specification, F.34/35, calling for a twin-engine, two-seat turret fighter, mounting four guns in the dorsal turret and fixed guns in the nose. Gloster's tender had been accepted and a prototype was ordered (as K8625), but this was cancelled when the Defiant was ordered — despite its lack of front guns.

On taking up his appointment as Gloster's chief designer, W G Carter straightway turned to Folland's F.34/35 design, discarded the dorsal turret and increased the fixed armament to no fewer than six 20mm cannon. (It is worth remarking here that, during the next fifteen years, successive designers put forward aircraft designs with six-cannon armament and, although one or two were ultimately flown, none ever entered service).

In contrast to the earlier design, Carter's F.9/37 was a single-seater of metal stressed-skin throughout, save for fabric-covered control surfaces. The wing shape remained unaltered, but two alternative types of engine were envisaged. The first prototype, L7999, featured a pair of 1,000hp Bristol Taurus T-S(a) fourteen-cylinder sleeve-valve radial engines driving three-blade Rotol constant-speed propellers, while the second aircraft, L8002, was powered by two 885hp Rolls-Royce Peregrine V-12s. Although both aircraft were fitted with two cannon in the nose, there appears to be no evidence that the other four guns were ever fitted.

L7999 was first flown by P E G Sayer at Hucclecote on 3 April 1939. From the outset the aircraft gave an excellent impression, being reported on very favourably after a short time with the A & AEE in July, returning a maximum speed of 360 mph at 15,000ft, the fastest

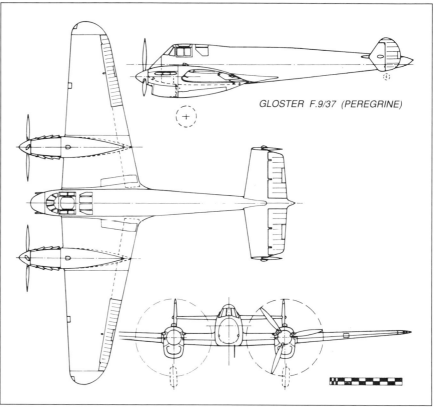

GLOSTER F.9/37 (PEREGRINE)

Type: Twin-engine, single-seat low-wing monoplane interceptor fighter.
Manufacturer: Gloster Aircraft Co Ltd, Hucclecote, Gloucester.
Air Ministry Specification: F.9/37
Powerplant: L7999. Two 1,000hp Bristol Taurus T-S(a) fourteen-cylinder sleeve-valve two-row air-cooled radial engines; also 900hp Taurus T-S(a) III engines. L8002. Two 885hp Rolls-Royce Peregrine twelve-cylinder liquid-cooled in-line engines.
Structure: Metal stressed-skin construction with fabric-covered control surfaces.
Dimensions: Span, 50ft 0½in; length, 37ft 0½in; height, 11ft 7in; wing area, 386 sq ft.
Weights: L7999. Tare, 8,828lb; all-up, 11,615lb. L8002. Tare, 9,222lb; all-up, 12,108lb.
Performance: L7999. Max speed, 360 mph at 15,000ft; climb to 28,000ft, 19 min 36 sec; service ceiling, 30,000ft. L8002. Max speed, 330 mph at 15,000ft; climb to 25,000ft, 19 min; service ceiling, 28,700ft.
Armament: Provision for six 20mm British Hispano Mk I cannon mounted in fuselage to fire forward.
Prototypes: Two, L7999 and L8002 (L7999 first flown by P E G Sayer on 3 April 1939).

level speed yet attained by a British military aircraft. Unfortunately it was badly damaged in a landing accident on 27 July only partway through the trials, and was not repaired until April 1940, then fitted with 900hp Taurus T-S(a) III engines, which reduced the maxi-

mum speed to 332 mph.

The second prototype, L8002, had been flown by Sayer on 22 February 1940, returning a performance roughly the same as the re-built L7999. By mid-1940, however, the Bristol Beaufighter had been ordered into production and,

The second Gloster F.9/37, L8002, powered by Rolls-Royce Peregrine in-line engines with D.H. two-pitch propellers; two of the 20mm cannon are visible in the nose. The pilot's good field of view from the cockpit is readily apparent. (Photo: via Derek James)

although L8002 continued flying until struck off charge in May 1942, development of the F.9/37 was discontinued. Nor did it fare any better when Gloster tendered the design to a new day-and-night fighter requirement, F.18/40. It was, nevertheless, an exceptionally prom-

ising aeroplane, with viceless flying qualities; it suffered none of the directional stability problems experienced by

the Beaufighter — probably on account of the more effective twin tail control surfaces.

Bristol Type 156 Beaufighter

Following the death of Frank Barnwell (killed in a flying accident on 2 August 1938) Roy Fedden and Leslie Frise submitted a private venture fighter development of the Bristol Beaufort torpedo-bomber, itself a development of the Blenheim. Owing to the speed with which the latter had been required to join the RAF, no time had been available to plan for ease of production, with convenient breakdown into sub-assemblies for sub-contracting purposes. This deficiency was rectified in the Beaufort, and the ready availability of major components encouraged Frise to evolve the Type 156 two-seat, twin-engine long-range fighter using the wings, tail and undercarriage of the torpedo-bomber, an attractive proposal in the interests for speed and ease of production.

Having been involved under the leadership of Barnwell in designs tendered to all manner of fighter Specifications, among them F.37/35, F.11/37 and F.18/37 — all calling for heavy gun armament — Frise proposed mounting four 20mm

The unarmed Beaufighter prototype, R2052, probably at Filton before its first flight on 17 July 1939, powered by Hercules I engines. (Photo: The Bristol Aeroplane Co, Neg No T156/8)

cannon under the nose of his Type 156, and selected the new Hercules sleeve-valve radials in place of the Beaufort's Taurus, now seen to be unsuitable as a fighter engine.

Despite the absence of an official Specification, the Air Ministry reacted with enthusiasm to Frise's proposals, although some scepticism was voiced at the high weight estimate of 16,000lb. Detail design began on 16 November 1938, and four prototypes together with a batch of seven further pre-production examples and 139 full production aircraft were ordered. (This was the first instance of the Air Ministry agreeing to set aside a number of development

aircraft in advance of full production, and was unquestionably the major single factor that enabled the new fighter to reach the RAF in less than two years from the start of the design.)

The prototype, R2052, was first flown on 17 July 1939, by which time the initial production batch had been extended by a further 150 aircraft to feature the Rolls-Royce Merlin XX, and a formal Specification, F.17/39, was raised to cover the production standard of preparation. The new Rolls-Royce Griffon engine was specified in the event of meeting production delays with the Hercules, but in the event the prototypes R2052 and R2053 were flown with Hercules Is, followed by Hercules III. In any case, owing to the onset of the Battle of Britain, work on the Griffon itself was slowed considerably in the interests of increasing Merlin production.

Flight trials of the four prototypes

The fourth Beaufighter prototype, R2055, at Tangmere before the German raid of 16 August 1940 in which it was slightly damaged. Note the black and white undersurfaces in vogue at the time. (Photo: Author's collection)

An early Beaufighter IC, R2153, of No 252 Squadron at Chivenor, Devon, in December 1940, the first Coastal Command squadron to receive Beaufighters. Only the nose cannon are fitted in this aircraft. (Photo: Imperial War Museum, Neg No CH2736)

went ahead with few problems although, even at this early stage, longitudinal and directional instability came in for criticism, and a slight increase in fin area was made. The first Beaufighter to be armed with the four cannon was R2054, and all four prototypes had been delivered by April 1940 to the A & AEE for Service trials, although R2055, with Hercules IIs, was initially set aside for armament trials.

Meanwhile, wide-ranging discussions on the operational rôle of the Beaufighter had been in train at the Air Ministry for more than a year and, although the aircraft had been judged initially in the context of long-range offensive and bomber escort duties, the need for defensive night fighters was accepted as overriding all others. By early 1939 the stage was being set for the new airborne interception radar to be taken aloft for the first time and, as already stated (see page 273), the first flight trials were undertaken using Blenheims, beginning in August 1939. Thus from an early stage in the Beaufighter's design it was anticipated that the AI radar would be an integral item of operational equipment. All the prototypes were accordingly ballasted to take account of the radar's weight.

Thus, when the Beaufighter underwent its early Service trials at Boscombe Down, the all-up weight had increased to 21,500lb and, on the limited power available from the Hercules III, the fully equipped aircraft possessed a speed of no more than 309 mph at 15,000 feet, instead of the estimated 335 mph. Moreover the directional control at low speed was still giving cause for anxiety,

A standard Beaufighter Mk IF, V8322, complete with AI Mk IV radar; the four light coloured patches on the leading edge of the starboard wing indicate that the full machine gun armament is fitted. (Photo: The Bristol Aeroplane Co Ltd., Neg No T156/276)

and the acceleration to safety speed on take-off was unacceptably low.

Production deliveries of Beaufighters began in July 1940, and the fourth prototype R2055 arrived at the Fighter Interception Unit, commanded by Wg Cdr George Philip Chamberlain (later Air Vice-Marshal, CB, OBE) at Tangmere on 12 August — only to suffer minor damage in the German daylight attack on the airfield four days later. By the end of the month the aircraft was given provisional clearance to join operational squadrons. The first two Beaufighter Is (both pre-production aircraft, without radar) were delivered on 2 September to No 25 (Fighter) Squadron at North Weald, commanded by Sqn Ldr Wilfred William Loxton (later Wg Cdr, AFC) and No 604 Squadron at Middle Wallop under Sqn Ldr Michael Frederick Anderson (later Wg Cdr, DFC).

Apprehension at the handling problems at low speeds prompted Fighter Command to introduce the Beaufighter to the squadrons slowly at first, and although Nos 25 and 604 Squadrons each received three aircraft during September, only six aircraft were distributed among the other squadrons for limited conversion by their most experienced crews. The first aircraft to be lost was R2067 of No 25 Squadron, destroyed in a night accident at Biggin Hill on 15 September, though without loss of life.

By the end of the year more than 100

Beaufighter IFs had been delivered to the RAF, including Nos 25, 29, 219, 600 and 604 Squadrons. The 'F' in the aircraft's designation had been introduced to denote Fighter Command and differentiate from 'C' for Coastal Command: six Beaufighter Is had also joined No 252 Squadron as long-range coastal patrol fighters, these being replaced by Mk ICs in March 1941, this version being fitted with additional radio and navigation equipment.

The Beaufighters with the FIU undertook crew training with the new AI Mk IV radar, now being introduced. No 29 Squadron reported two crews fully operational on 17 September, and No 25 Squadron flew the first operational sorties on 10 October; the first enemy aircraft destroyed at night by a Beaufighter was a Junkers Ju 88A shot down by No 604 Squadron on 19 November. Thereafter successes mounted steadily during the German night *Blitz* of 1940-41.

Late in 1940 work had begun to prepare Beaufighter Is for service in the Mediterranean and Middle East, and tropicalised Mark ICs, with additional fuel tanks in the fuselage, began delivery to No 252 Squadron in April 1941, flying out to Malta via Gibraltar at the beginning of May.

The first fifty Beaufighter Is had been delivered to the RAF armed only with the four 20mm British Hispano Mk I cannon in the nose, but thereafter aircraft were armed with six additional Browning machine guns, two in the port wing and four in the starboard. Aircraft equipped with AI Mk IV radar could be distinguished by the characteristic 'broad arrow' aerial on the nose and dipoles on the outer wings.

Left: *A standard Beaufighter IIF night fighter powered by Rolls-Royce Merlin XX in-line engines.* (Photo: The Bristol Aeroplane Co Ltd, Neg No T156/160)

Below: *One of more than a hundred ex-RAF Beaufighter IIFs served with the Fleet Air Arm. Stripped of its night fighter paint scheme, this aircraft, T3099, flew with No 789 Squadron, a Fleet Requirements Unit at Wingfield during 1944-45.* (Photo: Lt Cdr W T E White)

A new version of the night fighter was the Beaufighter Mk II, powered by 1,250hp Rolls-Royce Merlin XX in-line engines, three aircraft, R2058, R2061 and R2062, of the original pre-production batch being intended as prototypes — although R2062 was destroyed in an air raid on Filton on 13 October 1940. First flight by a production Mark IIF was made on 22 March 1941, and before the end of that year equipped Nos 307 (Polish), 406 (Canadian), 409 (Canadian) and 456 (Australian) Squadrons, all based in Britain.

1941 brought to the fore an increasing number of night fighter Beaufighter pilots of considerable skill, the first of whom was undoubtedly Sqn Ldr (later Gp Capt) John Cunningham, who had opened his score before the end of 1940, and assumed command of No 604 Squadron in August 1941. Cunningham (and his radar operator Sgt, later Gp Capt, Cecil Frederick Rawnsley DSO, DFC, DFM*) became not only highly skilled in night fighting but contributed immeasurably to the evolution of night interception tactics. Cunningham (who retired from the Service as a Group Captain with three DSOs and two DFCs after the War to become de Havilland's chief test pilot) ultimately destroyed twenty enemy aircraft at night, of which fourteen were Heinkel He 111s. Another Beaufighter pilot, Fg Off (later Gp Capt) John Randall Daniel Braham achieved an even higher score; he flew

with No 29 Squadron during 1940 and 1941, his radar operator being Sgt (later Wg Cdr, DSO, DFC*, DFM) William James Gregory, and assumed command of No 141 Squadron flying Beaufighters from January 1942. By the time Braham was shot down over Norway in June 1944 and taken prisoner, he had destroyed 29 enemy aircraft — not all of them at night — and was awarded three DSOs, three DFCs and the AFC, the most decorated

member of the British forces.

It was the Beaufighter IIF which introduced a partial remedy for the Beaufighter's directional stability at low speeds with the fitting of a tailplane featuring fifteen degrees of dihedral, a modification included in all subsequent versions from mid-1941. Before going on to record the next major production variant, the Beaufighter VI, it is necessary to mention the Mark III, the so-

Above: *Although the Beaufighter Mk IV was not built as such, the Mark II T3177 was modified with Rolls-Royce Griffon engines, driving four-blade Rotol propellers. Unfortunately no performance figures appear to have survived.* (Photo: The Bristol Aeroplane Co Ltd, Neg No T156/603)

Left: *The Beaufighter V, R2274, with Boulton Paul four-gun turret. This aeroplane underwent trials with several operational squadrons but was generally unpopular.* (Photo: The Bristol Aeroplane Co Ltd, Neg No T156/401)

called 'sports' variant (Type 158) with slimmer fuselage, which was not built. The Mark IV had been intended to fly before the end of 1940 with Rolls-Royce Griffon engines, but had been shelved owing to the priority accorded to Merlin production; as it was, an example was produced by modifying a Beaufighter II, T3177, with Griffon IIBs and this was delivered to Rolls-Royce as an engine test bed.

The Beaufighter Mk V was an attempt to provide a more flexible battery of guns for night engagement of enemy aircraft by introducing a power-operated Boulton Paul four-gun turret immediately aft of the pilot's cockpit; two Mark IIs, R2274 and R2306, were thus modified, and the former underwent brief trials with Nos 25, 29, 406 and 600 Squadrons in April and May 1942, but were not considered successful. Another experiment involved the fitting of twin fins and rudders on R2268 in a further attempt to improve stability during relatively low speeds, but these tended to make the controls heavy and sluggish as speed increased and this experiment was also short-lived.

The Beaufighter VI introduced the 1,650hp Hercules VI and XVI engines, and appeared in both 'F' and 'C' variants, of which a total of 1,832 was produced, serving with night fighter and anti-shipping squadrons of the RAF in the United Kingdom, Mediterranean and the Far East. Following trials in March 1941 with a Mark I, X8065,

carrying an 18-inch torpedo, many Mark VICs were adapted to carry this and the American 22½-inch weapon, and in November 1942 began delivery to No 254 Squadron, one of the components of the first Beaufighter Strike Wings. This Wing's other two Squadrons were No 143 with gun-armed Beaufighters, and

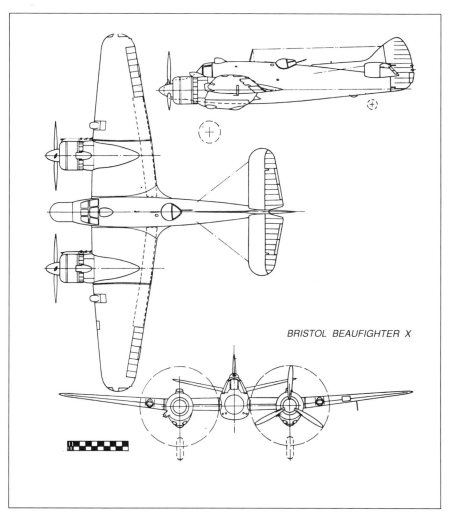

BRISTOL BEAUFIGHTER X

Type: Twin-engine, two/three-crew, mid-wing monoplane night and strike fighter.

Manufacturers: The Bristol Aeroplane Co Ltd, Filton and Whitchurch, Bristol; The Fairey Aviation Co Ltd, Stockport, Cheshire; MAP Shadow Factory, Old Mixon, Weston-super-Mare, Somerset; Rootes Securities Ltd, Blyth Bridge, Staffordshire; Beaufort Division, DAP, Fishermen's Bend, Victoria, Australia.

Air Ministry Specification: F.17/39

Powerplant: Mk I. Two 1,000hp Bristol Hercules III, X or XI fourteen-cylinder sleeve-valve two-row air-cooled radial engines. Mk II. Two 1,250hp Rolls-Royce Merlin XX twelve-cylinder liquid-cooled in-line engines. Mk VI. 1,600hp Hercules VI or XVI. Mk X and XIC. 1,735hp Hercules XVII. Mk 21. Hercules XVIII.

Dimensions: Span, 57ft 10in; length, 41ft 4in (or 42ft 9in, Mk II); height, 15ft 10in; wing area, 503 sq ft.

Weights: Mk VI. Tare, 14,900lb; all-up, 21,000lb. Mk X. Tare, 15,600lb; all-up, 25,400lb.

Performance: Max speed, 330 mph at 15,000ft; service ceiling, 29,000ft; normal range, 1,500 miles; max range, 1,750 miles.

Armament: Standard. Four 20mm British Hispano Mk I or II cannon in underside of front fuselage, four 0.303in Browning guns in starboard wing, and two in port wing. Specialist versions had provision for up to four 500lb bombs, a 1,760lb 18in torpedo or up to eight 60lb rocket projectiles.

Prototypes: Four Mk I prototypes, R2052-R2055 (R2052 first flown 17 July 1939); three Mk II prototypes, R2058, R2061 and R2062.

Summary of Production: Total of 5,563 in Britain (300 between R2052 and R2479; 300 between T3009 and T3447; 500 between T4623 and T5352; 600 between V8131 and X8269; 18, BT286-BT303; 300 between EL145 and EL534; 555 between JL421 and JM417; 500 between KV896 and KW673; 480 between LX779 and LZ544; 100 between MM838 and MM948; 150 between ND139 and ND322; 500 between NE193 and NE832; 500 between NT888 and NV632; 500 between RD130 and RD867; and 10, SR910-SR919; comprising 913 Mk Is, 450 Mk IIs, 1,832 Mk VIs, 2,205 Mk Xs and 163 Mk XICs).

Summary of RAF Service: Beaufighters served on Nos 25, 29, 46, 68, 89, 96, 108, 125, 141, 153, 176, 219, 255, 256, 307 (Polish), 406 (Canadian), 409 (Canadian), 410 (Canadian), 456 (Australian), 488 (New Zealand), 600 and 604 Squadrons as night fighters/intruders; as fighter-bombers with Nos 27, 84, 177, 211, 217 and 272 Squadrons; as coastal anti-shipping fighters and strike aircraft with Nos 22, 39, 42, 45, 47, 143, 144, 227, 235, 236, 248, 252, 254 and 603 Squadrons; as RCM aircraft with No 515 Squadron; as reconnaissance aircraft with Nos 69, 680 and 684 Squadrons; and as target tugs with Nos 5, 17, 20, 34, 285, 287, 288, 577 and 695 Squadrons. Beaufighters (principally Mk IIs) also served with Nos 721, 726, 728, 733, 736, 762, 770, 772, 775, 779, 781, 788, 789, 797 and 798 Squadrons of the Fleet Air Arm.

Left: *Beaufighter R2268, fitted with twin fins and rudders in an attempt to cure the directional control deficiencies.* (Photo: The Bristol Aeroplane Co Ltd, Neg No T156/167).

Below: *A standard Beaufighter VIC torpedo strike fighter, EL223/G. Note the dihedral tailplane and retention of the cannon armament.* (Photo: The Bristol Aeroplane Co Ltd, Neg No T156/385)

No 236 with aircraft equipped to carry a pair of 500lb bombs. Another anti-shipping version of the Beaufighter VIC was the so-called 'flak-Beau', armed with up to eight 60lb rocket projectiles under the wings, often employed to quell enemy guns while other Beaufighters attacked with guns, bombs and torpedoes. Most Coastal Command Mk VICs were also armed with a single Vickers K or Browning gun in the dorsal hatch. AI Mk VIII and ASV radar was also being introduced by 1942, and this was enclosed by a 'thimble radome' on the nose of Mark IIFs and VICs.

The Mark X Beaufighter, of which 2,205 were produced by a number of factories, introduced the 1,735hp Hercules XVII which incorporated a cropped, single-speed supercharger impeller, bestowing a maximum speed of 336 mph at 500 feet. Mark Xs, which could carry the torpedo, and Mark XICs, which could not, eventually equipped 23 squadrons in Northern Europe, the Middle and Far East. After the War many Mark Xs were converted for use as target tugs, and as such equipped a further eight

squadrons.

The Beaufighter remained in service until 1950, service that had included operations in South-East Asia during the last three years of the War. It was flown in a wide variety of rôles that included night and day interception, intruder, bomber-support, coastal patrol and anti-shipping strike and torpedo fighter, photo and tactical photo

reconnaissance, radio countermeasures and target towing. It also served in a number of Fleet Air Arm squadrons. No 45 Squadron, serving in Malaya, was the last to retire its Beaufighters in February 1950. 364 examples (the Marks VIII and 21) were produced at Fishermen's Bend in Australia; and ex-RAF aircraft were exported to Turkey, the Dominican Republic and Portugal.

The last Beaufighter built, SR919. This Mark X for Coastal Command features torpedo crutches, underwing rails for rocket projectiles, ASV anti-shipping radar, camera fairing over the cockpit, and dihedral tailplane. (Photo: The Bristol Aeroplane Co Ltd, Neg No T156/547)

Hawker Tornado

The obvious success that attended the early Service trials of the Hurricane and Spitfire during 1936, and the raising of substantial production orders for these radical interceptors, did little to side-

The first Tornado, P5219, as originally flown with ventral radiator and small fin and rudder. (Photo: Author's collection)

Left: *The second Tornado , P5224, shown at Boscombe Down in October 1941, with the 'chin' radiator installation, improved canopy and enlarged fin and rudder.* (Photo: Sydney Camm collection)

Below: *The sole Avro-built production Tornado I, P7936, employed as a propeller test bed; it is shown with a six-blade Rotol contraprop at Staverton, Gloucester, probably in 1944.* (Photo: Author's collection)

track the constant process of seeking further advances in fighter performance and armament. For several years three of Britain's leading engine manufacturers — Rolls-Royce, Bristol and Napier — had been pursuing the development of engines of greatly increased power, namely those that would ultimately become known as the Vulture, Sabre and Centaurus respectively. That is not to say that these big new engines were foreseen as being exclusive to fighters, and already the Vulture had been specified in a heavy bomber requirement which would eventually bring forth the Avro Manchester and Handley Page Halifax (although the design of the latter was soon to be changed to accommodate Merlins).

The Rolls-Royce Vulture 24-cylinder liquid-cooled X-type in-line engine was, in effect a pair of 12-cylinder Peregrine engines (developed from the Kestrel) combincd, onc crect and the other inverted; by employing a common crankcase it was anticipated that twice the power of a Peregrine at much less than twice the weight would be achieved. It was, nevertheless, a very big engine to be considered for a single-engine, single-seat interceptor. Yet this was the engine favoured by George Carter in his proposal to meet Specification F.11/37 for a dual-rôle single-seat fighter for defence and ground support. Although this Specification was abandoned, another, F.18/37, was issued in draft form in the late summer of 1937 and attracted the attention of Sydney Camm at Hawker. He believed the new Rolls-Royce engine could be matched to an aircraft no bigger than the Hurricane. A top speed of 400 mph at 20,000 feet was specified.

Moreover, as an insurance against failure of the Vulture, Camm went to work on a parallel design to be powered by the Napier Sabre. The two aircraft were to emerge as the Tornado and Typhoon respectively, and it was in-

tended that production would be undertaken at Hawker's proposed new factory at Langley in Buckinghamshire which was to be equipped for metal monocoque manufacture.

The original armament requirements called for either six 20mm Oerlikon cannon or twelve rifle-calibre Browning machine guns to be mounted in the wings, each wing to incorporate a single gun bay for ease of re-arming. The Oerlikon gun came to be refused by the RAF in favour of the 20mm Hispano, and the number of cannon required reduced to four. Nevertheless both of Camm's fighters perpetuated the very thick wing originally designed for the six cannon — to the detriment of their performance above 20,000 feet.

Manufacture of the first Tornado prototype, P5219, led the Typhoon by several months, and was first flown by Philip Lucas on 6 October 1939. Before the end of the year it had been flown up to a TAS of 370 mph. For these early flights P5219 featured a large ventral radiator fairing in a position similar to that on the Hurricane, the oil cooler being located in the centre of the engine coolant radiator matrix. Oil cooling problems were to dog the Vulture for many months and, in response to suggestions by Rolls-Royce (and Napiers

for their Sabre engine) a new 'chin' radiator was incorporated in all the F.18/37 prototypes from early 1940 onwards.

From the outset Lucas had reported that the Tornado suffered from a lack of directional stability and control, and this was further aggravated by the inclusion of the new chin radiator, particularly during take-off and landing. When the first Typhoon prototype crashed in May 1940, and P5219 was grounded pending modifications to its radiator fairing, enlarged fins and rudders were fitted to all the F.18/37 aircraft and the directional stability problems were eased considerably.

In July P5219 visited Rolls-Royce for improvements to be made to the oil system, after which it returned to Langley where, on the 27th, Dick Reynell recorded a maximum TAS of 396.5 mph at 20,500 feet, and a climb to 20,000 feet in 6.6 minutes at an all-up weight of 10,225lb with twelve Browning guns fitted. (At the time this was the best known climb performance of any interceptor at its full operational weight.)

Summer 1940, with the Battle of Britain being fought out in the skies over Southern England, was a hectic time for the fighter industry. Top priority was afforded to the manufacture and repair

Type: Single-engine, single-seat low-wing monoplane interceptor fighter.

Manufacturers: Hawker Aircraft Ltd, Kingston, Surrey, and Langley, Bucks; A V Roe & Co Ltd, Woodford, Cheshire.

Air Ministry Specification: F.18/37

Powerplant: One 1,760hp Rolls-Royce Vulture II 24-cylinder liquid-cooled two-stage supercharged X-type in-line engine driving 14ft-diameter three-blade D.H. propeller; later 1,980hp Vulture V driving 13ft 3in-diameter three-blade Rotol propeller. Also one 2,210hp Bristol Centaurus CE.4S 18-cylinder air-cooled sleeve-valve radial engine (in HG641).

Structure: All-metal monocoque construction. Fabric-covered rudder. Inwards retracting mainwheels and forward-retracting tailwheel.

Dimensions: Span, 41ft 11in; length (Vulture), 32ft 10in; height (Rotol propeller), 14ft 8in; wing area, 283 sq ft.

Weights: Tare, 8,377lb; all-up (max), 10,668lb.

Performance: Max speed, 396.5 mph at 20,500ft; climb, 6.6 min to 20,000ft; service ceiling, 32,800ft. [Note, R7936 achieved 402 mph at 21,800ft]

Armament: Twelve 0.303in Browning machine guns in wings; alternative provision for four 20mm Hispano cannon.

Prototypes: Three; P5219 (first flown by Philip Lucas, 6 October 1939, at Langley) and P5224; HG641 (built from production components). One production aircraft, R7936.

of Hurricanes and Spitfires with a result that work on the second Tornado prototype, P5224, was delayed, and the aircraft was not flown until 5 December that year. In the meantime a production order for 200 Tornados (to be built by A V Roe & Co) had been received, but this plan was already seen to be at risk owing to doubts being expressed as to the future of the Vulture engine. RAF Bomber Command had announced in August 1940 that the British heavy bomber force would re-equip entirely with four-engine aircraft at the earliest possible opportunity, thereby implying that the twin-Vulture Manchester would come to be regarded as no more than a stopgap.

Lubrication and cooling problems were still being experienced with the Vulture engine and — with the emphasis now being placed on Merlin production — the big engine suffered a cutback in its development. Final cancellation of the Tornado production order was notified in June 1941, so that P5219 and P5224 remained the only Hawker-built examples completed. At Avro, however, production plans had already reached an advanced stage and the first aircraft from the line, R7936, was completed and flown on 31 August, thereafter being employed as an engine and propeller test bed (in due course being

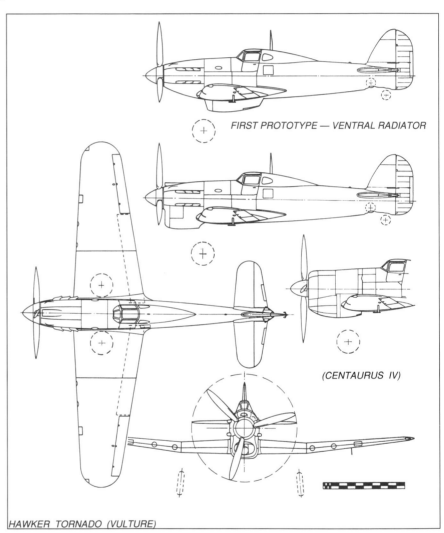

FIRST PROTOTYPE — VENTRAL RADIATOR

(CENTAURUS IV)

HAWKER TORNADO (VULTURE)

Although this modified installation of the Centaurus radial in the Tornado test bed, HG641, was generally regarded as 'a great improvement', one need only compare it with the contemporary installation of the BMW 801 radial engine in the Focke-Wulf Fw 190A to understand why so many British fighter designers were at pains to avoid radials wherever possible. (Photo: Author's collection)

flown with Rotol and D.H. contraprops). It is perhaps worth recording that this Tornado, powered by the much improved Vulture V engine, experienced scarcely any trouble, records suggesting that the engine came to be regarded as efficient and reliable. R7936 was not struck off charge until 1946.

One other Tornado, HG641, was completed from Avro-built components. This was fitted with a 2,210hp Bristol Centaurus CE.4S on the recommendation of Camm who, despite his long-standing dislike of radials in single-engine interceptor fighters, had authorized project work to proceed as long ago as 1939 to investigate the use of the big Bristol engine in the F.18/37 design. Only when the first German Focke-Wulf Fw 190A was captured intact did British designers fully appreciate what could be achieved by careful attention to detail when matching a bulky air-cooled radial to a small fighter. As will be shown in due course, the experience gained with the Centaurus in the Tornado HG641, combined with the knowledge gained from the Germans' use of the BMW 801 in the Fw 190, led directly to the development of the Tempest Mark II and ultimately to the Hawker Fury monoplane and Sea Fury fighters.

Fairey Fulmar

The second production Fairey Fulmar I, N1855, in contract paint scheme; this aircraft underwent Service trials and features an anti-spin parachute. (Photo: A J Jackson collection)

Compromised from the outset as a naval interceptor fighter by the Admiralty's insistence on a two-man crew, the Fulmar was conceived as a long-endurance carrier-borne fleet defence fighter, capable of maintaining patrols against unescorted enemy bombers and maritime reconnaissance aircraft. High speed and manœuvrability were not therefore deemed essential. The shifting fortunes of war were to render this idea flawed.

Bearing this in mind, the Fairey Aviation Co submitted a navalised version of its P.4/34 light bomber (designed by Marcel Lobelle and itself a smaller and lighter derivative of the Battle light bomber) to Specification O.8/38, thereby avoiding lengthy development. Maximum speed called for was 250 mph at 20,000 feet, together with a four-hour patrol endurance. On the strength of assurances that this aircraft would satisfy O.8/38, Fairey was awarded an order for 127 production machines in mid-1938, soon to be increased to 250. An early requirement was for the aircraft, named the Fulmar, to be capable of adaptation to operate with a twin-float undercarriage, but this was quickly abandoned.

Although the Rolls-Royce Merlin II had been fitted in the second P.4/34 for evaluation as a fleet fighter, Fairey's confidence of meeting the performance demands had been based on the use of a Merlin developed to produce 1,100hp. As it was, the first Fulmar to fly (N1854) made its first flight on 4 January 1940 at Ringway with a Merlin III uprated to 1,080hp, and in this form — even with reduced load — a maximum speed of no more than 230 mph was all that it could manage, a deficiency that was attributed to an untidy engine installation.

Within three months the Merlin VIII had become available and, by dint of much tidying up of cowling and radiator, this engine bestowed a top speed of 255 mph. Such was the paramount need for fighters at this stage of the War that production of the Fulmar I quickly accelerated, and it first entered service with the naval trials unit, No 778 Squadron of the Fleet Air Arm at Lee-on-Solent, in May 1940. One of the most telling criticisms expressed by the Service was the lack of a rear cockpit gun, especially in view of the Fulmar's pedestrian speed performance.

The following month it joined No 806 Squadron at Worthy Down, commanded by Lt-Cdr C L G Evans DSC, RN, aboard HMS *Illustrious*, while ashore Fulmar Is equipped No 808 Squadron at Worthy Down in July. By the year's end a total of 159 aircraft had emerged from Fairey's new Heaton Chapel factory at Stockport, and these had joined a total of seven squadrons of the FAA. Some Fulmar pilots had also flown dockyard defence patrols during the Battle of Britain.

The aircraft was of conventional all-metal monocoque construction with manually-folding wings and an armament of eight wing-mounted Browning machine guns. The pilot was afforded a good view from the cockpit, being located almost directly over the wing leading edge; the navigator was situated some eight feet further aft under a long

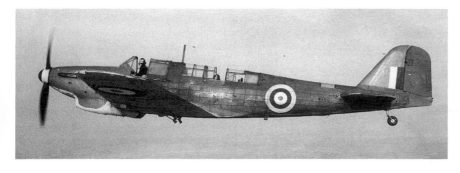

In-flight view of a Fulmar I, probably serving with a Fleet Requirements Squadron. Despite a poor performance, these aircraft earned themselves a reputation for reliability, and achieved remarkably good results in combat during the mid-War years. (Photo: A J Jackson Collection)

glazed canopy. Early in 1941 trials started with the 1,300hp Merlin 30 and with this powerplant the Fulmar Mark II entered service later that year. The maximum speed had been increased to only some 270 mph, the aircraft becoming encumbered by tropical equipment and additional radio. Trials were also undertaken with the Fulmar as a night fighter, equipped with AI Mark VI airborne radar, following night attacks by Italian bombers against the Mediterranean Fleet. AI Mk VI proved disappointing and later in the War a small number of Fulmar NF IIs with improved AI Mk IV served with the FAA.

Equipped with HF radio, Fulmar Is and IIs were shipped to India after Japan's entry into the War and, during 1942, flew long-endurance fleet reconnaissance patrols over the Indian Ocean. This in itself represented a valuable contribution during the early Japanese operations in the theatre, but the Fulmar proved no match for the enemy carrier-borne fighters

Despite its mediocre capabilities, the Fulmar performed a vital rôle, bridging the gap between the Sea Gladiator biplane and more modern naval fighters such as the Sea Hurricane and Seafire, apart from being the Royal Navy's first eight-gun fighter. Fulmars also participated in early operations as catapult fighters aboard merchant ships during 1940-41, and also played a vital part in defending the famous Malta convoys. A total of 602 Fulmar Is and IIs was produced by February 1943, when production ran out and Seafires were beginning to appear in substantial numbers; the following month, moreover, the first Fairey Firefly was delivered to the FAA.

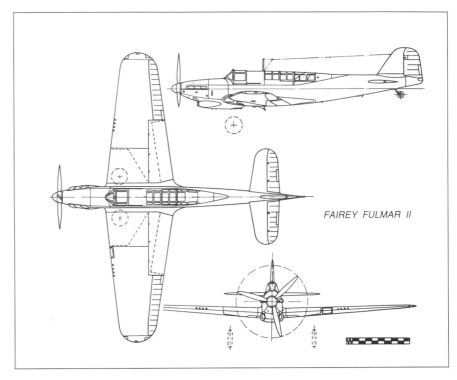

FAIREY FULMAR II

Type: Single-engine, two-seat shipborne naval interceptor monoplane.
Manufacturer: Fairey Aviation Co Ltd, Heaton Chapel, Stockport, Cheshire.
Air Ministry Specification (Naval): O.8/38
Powerplant: Mark I, one 1,080hp Rolls-Royce Merlin VIII twelve-cylinder liquid-cooled supercharged in-line engine driving three-blade Rotol propeller. Mark II, one 1,300hp Merlin 30 engine.
Dimensions: Span, 46ft 4¼in; length, 40 ft 2in; height, 14ft 0in; wing area, 342 sq ft.
Weights (Mark I): Tare, 8,720lb; all-up, 10,700lb.
Performance (Mark I): Max speed, 255 mph at 9,000 ft; climb to 10,000ft, 13.4 min; max endurance, 4¼ hours; max range, approx 740 miles.
Armament: Eight 0.303in Browning guns in the wings.
Prototypes: Two, N1854 (first flown by Duncan Menzies, 4 January 1940) and N1855.
Production: 250 Mark Is and 350 Mark IIs.
Summary of Service: Fulmars served with a total of 53 squadrons of the FAA between May 1940 and February 1946 (comprising the operational Squadron Nos 800, 803, 804, 805, 806, 807, 808, 809, 815, 822, 827, 835, 879, 881, 884, 886, 887, 889, 893 and 897, and the training and Fleet Requirement Squadrons Nos 700, 726, 731, 733, 739, 740, 748, 756, 757, 759, 760, 761, 762, 766, 767, 768, 769, 772, 775, 778, 779, 780, 781, 782, 784, 787, 788, 789, 790, 793, 794, 795, 798).

Hawker Typhoon

Second of Sydney Camm's design essays to Specification F.18/37 (see also the Hawker Tornado, page 284), the Napier Sabre-powered Typhoon suffered all the frustrations and delays that afflicted its erstwhile partner but, owing to perseverance with the big and power-

The first prototype Typhoon, P5212, which flew with a 'chin' radiator from the outset, and which was saved from destruction by Philip Lucas when the primary structure failed. (Photo: Air Ministry, RTP Neg No 10280C)

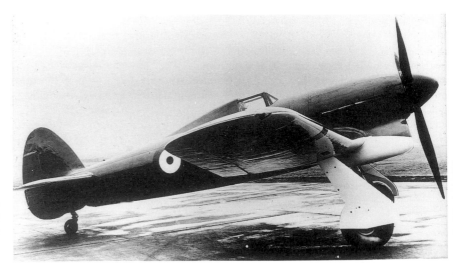

The second Typhoon prototype, P5216, with four-cannon armament, enlarged fin and rudder and the much criticised cockpit enclosure with 'car doors', but no provision for rear view. (Photo: Author's collection)

ful 24-cylinder sleeve-valve H-type engine, it survived to join RAF Fighter Command. Ironically, however, it failed to meet the Service's demands for a high performance interceptor, only to excel as an exceptionally potent ground-support fighter.

While George Carter at Gloster tendered to F.18/37 the design of a radical twin-boom aircraft powered by a Sabre located at the rear of the cockpit nacelle and driving a pusher propeller, Camm had opted for an entirely conventional approach to his design tenders. Bearing in mind the great urgency for fighter aircraft at the end of the 1930s, this was a logical policy, and Hawker was rewarded with an order for two prototypes of both Tornado and Typhoon. The Sabre engine represented a bold advance by Napier who possessed scarcely any experience in the manufacture of sleeve valves, while the cooling and lubrication of this immensely complex engine were to pose daunting problems for many months before satisfactory solutions could be evolved.

Only readily distinguishable from the Tornado by its single row of exhaust ports on each side of the nose, the first Typhoon prototype, P5212, was flown by Philip Lucas at Langley on 24 February 1940 and, being still fitted with the same small fin and rudder as the Tornado P5219, displayed the familiar lack of directional control, particularly as this aircraft featured the 'chin radiator from the outset.

P5212 suffered a serious accident on 9 May when the primary structure immediately aft of the cockpit failed, causing the metal skin to buckle and begin to disintegrate, and the aircraft would certainly have been destroyed had not Lucas remained at the controls to make a forced landing, also ensuring that vital vibration records were saved for examination. Progress in ironing out problems with the engine and airframe were, like the Tornado, delayed by reduced

priorities during the Battle of Britain, and of course, with P5212 grounded for repairs, no Typhoon was available for development flying until the second prototype, P5216, first flew on 3 May 1941. This was the first F.18/37 to be armed with the scheduled armament of four Hispano cannon (this version being termed the Typhoon Mark IB).

In the meantime, however, the Typhoon had been ordered into production, fifteen development aircraft being built by Hawker at Langley, and 500 by Gloster Aircraft Co at Brockworth. The Gloster assembly line had reached an advanced state by the time P5216 flew, and the first production aircraft, R7576, a Typhoon IA with twelve Browning machine guns, was flown by Michael Daunt on 27 May. The first Langley-built development aircraft, R8198 — also a Mark IA — was not flown until 26 November that year! By that time the Browning gun-armed Mark IA had been discarded in favour of the cannon-armed Mark IB.

The air war over Northern Europe was undergoing a profound change in the spring and summer of 1941. The Spitfire VB, which was superior to the Messerschmitt Bf 109E early in 1941, met its match in the improved Bf 109F,

an unexpected turn of events in the light of RAF Fighter Command's decision to adopt the Spitfire V as its standard single-seat fighter for the foreseeable future. There was thus an increasing urgency to introduce the Typhoon into service as soon as possible, with its 400 mph top speed and heavy cannon armament.

Accordingly the first operational Typhoons were delivered to Duxford on 11 September, it being intended to equip No 56 Squadron, then commanded by Sqn Ldr Prosser Hanks DSO, DFC, AFC, by the end of the year. However it became immediately clear that much development work still needed to be done before the fighter could be committed to operations; engine failures were still commonplace; carbon monoxide seepage into the cockpit was found to be due to the breakdown of trunk seals in the front bulkhead; and pilots complained that there was wholly inadequate rearward vision from the cockpit.

Solution of these problems became all the more vital when, in the autumn of 1941, the *Luftwaffe* introduced the Focke-Wulf Fw 190A into service in France. At once casualties among the Spitfire Vs began to increase sharply. Unfortunately a new spate of Typhoon accidents

A Typhoon IB, JP853/SA-K, of No 486 (New Zealand) Squadron; it features the interim canopy which retained the 'car doors', but allowed some measure of rear view. (Photo: Sydney Camm collection)

A late production Hawker Typhoon IB showing the final standard of preparation, including Napier Sabre IIB, four-blade propeller, single-piece sliding canopy, faired cannon barrels and whip aerial. (Photo: Hawker Aircraft Ltd, Neg No TYG/11)

now occurred, caused by the entire tail unit breaking away from the fuselage at the rear transport joint, in most instances resulting in the death of the pilot. At once the Service suspected that the fault lay in a weakness of the joint and demanded that it be strengthened. It was not until a Typhoon, flown by Hawker pilot Kenneth Seth-Smith, who was killed, crashed near Windsor and allowed a complete tail unit — which had parted company in flight — to be minutely examined. This disclosed that a small bracket, supporting the elevator mass balance, had failed, resulting in instantaneous and violent elevator flutter, in turn imposing massive loads on the rear fuselage joint and causing it to fail. The remedy was simple, inexpensive and wholly effective.

By mid-1942 other refinements had been incorporated in the Typhoon, including an entirely new cockpit enclosure which, by reducing the depth of the rear fuselage, now consisted of a fully transparent superstructure located on top of the fuselage; the original 'car doors' were retained. However, shortly afterwards, this superstructure was superseded by a sliding single-piece canopy which enabled the side doors to be eliminated. Other minor improvements included the addition of fairings over the cannon barrels to reduce drag, and the replacement of the radio mast by a low-drag whip aerial.

One shortcoming of the Typhoon

Upper left: *The single experimental Typhoon NF IB, R7881, with AI Mk IV, much of whose associated equipment was mounted in the underwing tanks.* (Photo: Author's collection). Lower left: *One of the three 'Desert Typhoons', DN323, which were shipped to North Africa for tropical trials in 1943 with No 451 (Australian) Squadron in the Western Desert.* (Photo: Hawker Aircraft Ltd, Neg No DTG36)

could not be overcome. Owing to the six-cannon design legacy (see Hawker Tornado), the Typhoon retained a massively thick wing which severely restricted performance above 20,000 feet and, as this was by now the altitude at which most air-to-air combat occurred, the days of the Typhoon as an interceptor were clearly numbered.

It was Sqn Ldr R P Beamont DSO, DFC, commanding No 609 Squadron, who, during a series of offensive sorties, had demonstrated the Typhoon's effectiveness as a ground attack fighter, and now recommended that henceforth this should be the aircraft's principal rôle, an idea that took root.

By the end of 1942 a dozen Typhoon squadrons had been equipped (Nos 1, 56, 181, 182, 183, 195, 197, 198, 245, 257, 266 and 609) and, while some of these continued to operate in the low level interception rôle as being an effective means to counter the hit-and-run attacks over Southern England by Fw 190A fighter-bombers, the other squadrons began offensive operations against coastal targets in France and the Low Countries.

In due course Typhoons equipped 30 squadrons, the majority of these being flown on offensive operations in Wings of three or four squadrons apiece. From 1943 onwards considerable work was done by Hawker at Langley and the A & A E E at Boscombe Down to clear the aircraft to carry external stores which included up to sixteen three-inch rocket projectiles, two 1,000lb bombs, drop tanks, supply canisters, smoke screen dispensers, and combinations of these loads.

In the constant attacks flown over Northern France, preparatory for the Normandy landings, the Typhoons were particularly prominent, with numerous 'set-piece' assaults on enemy radar sites, airfields, gun emplacements, road and rail targets and German troop and armour concentrations. They supported the D-Day landings themselves in considerable strength and continued to provide support for the Allied armies in their advance through Northern Europe, often

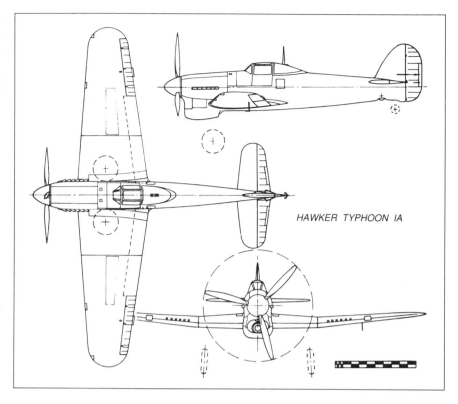

HAWKER TYPHOON IA

Type: Single-engine, single-seat low-wing monoplane interceptor and ground attack fighter.

Manufacturers: Hawker Aircraft Ltd, Kingston, Surrey, and Langley, Bucks (prototypes and 15 production aircraft); Gloster Aircraft Co Ltd, Brockworth, Glos (remaining production aircraft).

Powerplant: One 2,100-2,200hp Napier Sabre II, IIA or IIB twenty-four cylinder sleeve-valve side-canted H-type liquid-cooled two-stage supercharged in-line engine driving three-or four-blade D.H. variable-pitch propeller.

Structure: All-metal monocoque construction with fabric-covered rudder; inwards-retracting mainwheels and forward-retracting tailwheel.

Dimensions: Span, 41ft 7in; length, 31ft 11in; height, 15ft 3½in; wing area, 279 sq ft.

Weights: Tarc, 8,800lb; all-up, 13,250lb (with two 1,000lb bombs).

Performance: Max speed, 422 mph at 12,500ft; climb to 12,500ft, 3.2 min; normal range, 980 miles; service ceiling, 31,800ft.

Armament: Mark IA, twelve wing-mounted 0.303in Browning machine guns. Mark IB, four 20mm Hispano Mk. I cannon with 140 rounds per gun.

Prototypes: Two, P5212 (first flown, 24 February 1940, by Philip Lucas at Langley) and P5216.

Production: Fifteen aircraft (R8198-R8200 and R8220-R8231) built by Hawker. 3,315 aircraft (in R, DN, EJ-EK, JP-JR, MM-MP, PD, RB and SW serial ranges) built by Gloster.

Summary of Service: Served with Nos, 1, 3, 4, 56, 137, 164, 168, 174, 175, 181, 182, 183, 184, 186, 193, 195, 197, 198, 245, 247, 257, 263, 266, 268, 438, 439, 440, 485, 486 and 609 Squadrons. Trials in Western Desert with No 451 (Australian) Squadron.

The engine manufacturer D Napier & Son Ltd used this Typhoon IB, R8694, in an extended trials programme to develop an annular radiator for the Sabre engine; note the fan at the front of the radiator cowling. (Photo: Author's collection)

operating from hastily prepared landing strips close behind the front line. Their most famous achievement was the destruction of enemy armour — using salvoes of rockets — at Falaise, as enemy troops fought to escape a huge encircling movement.

A temporary setback occurred on 1 January 1945 when the *Luftwaffe* staged heavy surprise attacks on Allied airfields in Holland and Belgium, catching many of the Typhoons on the ground. Among the 300-odd Allied aircraft destroyed, no fewer than 162 were Typhoons — all of which were replaced from reserves within a few days, such was the enormous strength of the Allied air forces.

During the Allied advance in Northern Europe a small number of Typhoons was modified for armed reconnaissance, with forward-facing, oblique and vertical cameras in the wing centre section. Termed TacR, FR and PR Mark IBs, these aircraft served with Nos 4 and 268 Squadrons.

Three Typhoons, R8891, DN323 and EJ906, had been shipped to North Africa in April 1943 for trials with No 451 (Australian) Squadron in preparation for service in support of Allied operations in the Central Mediterranean when it seemed likely that RAF Spitfire Vs would be opposed by Fw 190s. The arrival of later Spitfires, however, overcame the threat, and no further Typhoons were shipped out.

The Typhoon finally disappeared from operational service in September 1945, the majority of squadrons being disbanded while others re-equipped with Hawker Tempest IIs and Vs. Total production had amounted to 3,330 aircraft, all but fifteen having been produced by Gloster. Just as the Hurricane had been the RAF's first fighter capable of more than 300 mph in level flight, so the Typhoon was the first in service to exceed 400.

Miles M.20

It was no secret within the aircraft industry at the time of the Munich Crisis of September 1938 that it would be touch and go whether production of the Hurricane and Spitfire would accelerate sufficiently quickly to allow all Fighter Command day interceptor squadrons to be fully re-equipped by the time a European war — becoming increasingly inevitable — started. That inevitability focussed attention on the supply of strategic materials which could become critical in the event that Britain suffered a sea blockade and isolation from her sources of minerals.

It has already been shown that the tiny company of Martin-Baker was engaged in preparing an all-wooden fighter (the M.B.2, see page 265) as a demonstration of what could be achieved without dominant use of steel and light alloys, or on the Rolls-Royce Merlin. Another company, not hitherto successful in producing a single-seat fighter, was Miles Aircraft Ltd of Woodley, Reading, and before the end of 1938 Frederick George Miles, formerly Chief Designer of Phillips and Powis Aircraft (Reading) Ltd, submitted the design of a wooden aircraft, the M.20, powered by a Rolls-Royce Peregrine engine and owing much of its configuration to the successful Miles Master advanced trainer. This was not accepted, largely because production of the Peregrine was reserved for the Westland Whirlwind and was, in any case, being reduced so as not to compromise delivery of the all-important Merlin engine.

The Miles M.20/2, AX834. The outsize spinner was a component of the Merlin XX 'power egg', but was changed in the M.20/4. (Photo: Real Photographs Co Ltd.)

Not to be discouraged, Miles persisted with his contention that a fighter aircraft *could* be produced, not only in wood, but employing numerous components common to an aircraft already in production. After Lord Beaverbrook became Minister of Aircraft Production in May 1940, this proposal won qualified approval, Specification F.19/40 was raised and a single prototype was ordered from Miles.

Re-design of the M.20 was undertaken by Walter G Capley, who produced a low-wing monoplane design, the M.20/2, but eliminated the Master's cranked wing; moreover power was to be provided by a 1,260hp Rolls-Royce Merlin XX, adapted from the Beaufighter Mk II installation; the undercarriage was non-retractable with large wheel spats. The very thick wings of NACA230 section carried eight Browning machine guns, but were so designed as to enable four further guns to be fitted if required.

Construction was of spruce and plywood throughout, except at the wing tips and wing root fairings, which were of light alloy. Unique at the time was the single-piece moulded Perspex cockpit canopy which slid fore and aft for access to the cockpit without interrupting the fuselage structure and bestowed a field of view superior to any in-service fighter at the time.

First flight of the M.20/2, carrying Class B registration U9, was made by Major Thomas ('Tommy') Rose DFC, Miles' Chief Test Pilot, on 15 September 1940, only 65 days after design of the aircraft had started. Despite its cumbersome undercarriage, the M.20/2 returned a maximum speed of 333 mph at 20,400 feet (faster than the Hurricane I) but, owing to its high wing loading, touched down at 80 mph. Given the serial number AX834 shortly afterwards, the M.20/2 suffered an accident at Woodley when landing on snow and was badly damaged; the pilot, Flt Lt Hugh Vincent Kennedy RAFO, was unhurt.

In the meantime Miles had submitted the design of a fighter-bomber version, the M.20/3, capable of carrying a pair of 250lb bombs under the wings, but this was not accepted. Instead, work had gone ahead as a private venture to produce a naval fighter version and this, the M.20/4, with Class B registration U-0228, was flown early in April 1941. (P Jarrett has suggested that this aircraft was AX834 rebuilt, cf *Aeroplane Monthly*, January 1992.)

The motivation behind this project had been the threat posed by German long-range shipping raiders, and provision of an eight-gun fighter capable of being catapulted from merchant ships to intercept the enemy bombers. Fitted with a less cumbersome undercarriage, the M.20/4 would normally have it removed once it had been mounted on its catapult for, in the event of being launched at sea, it would invariably be ditched at the end of its sortie.

The prototype was submitted to Specification N.1/41 (written around Frederick Miles' proposals) and, taken on charge by the Air Ministry as DR616, was delivered to the A & AEE at Boscombe Down on 18 April 1941, where it met with mixed reactions. Despite some improvements (including the lighter undercarriage and a better shaped spinner) the maximum speed was still 333 mph. Catapult spools were incorporated under the centre fuselage.

By then, however, the Hurricane I had proved suitable for catapult conversion and, being readily available in large numbers, had already entered service as the Sea Hurricane Mk IA, and development of the Miles M.20/4 was suspended. After a brief visit to the RAE, it was returned to Woodley on 19 March 1942 and scrapped in 1943.

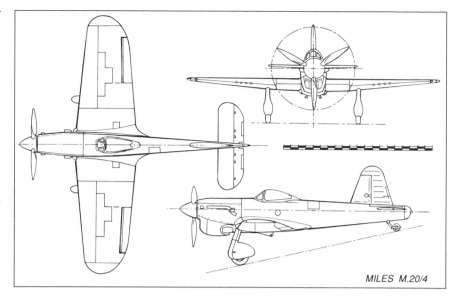

Type: Single-engine, single-seat, low-wing monoplane interceptor fighter.
Manufacturer: Miles Aircraft Ltd, Woodley, Reading, Berkshire.
Air Ministry Specifications: F.19/40 (for M.20/2) and N.1/41 (for M.20/4)
Powerplant: One 1,260hp Rolls-Royce Merlin XX twelve-cylinder liquid-cooled supercharged in-line engine driving three-blade Rotol propeller.
Structure: Spruce and ply semi-monocoque construction with two-spar wings of wooden construction, and ply and fabric covering. Non-retractable undercarriage.
Dimensions: M.20/4. Span, 34ft 7in; length, 30ft 8in; height, 12ft 6in; wing area, 234 sq ft.
Weights: M.20/4. Tare, 5,908lb; all-up, 8,000lb.
Performance: M.20/4. Max speed, 333 mph at 20,400ft; climb to 20,000ft, 9 min 36 sec; service ceiling, approx 32,800ft; range, 920 miles.
Armament: Eight 0.303in Browning Mk II machine guns in wings with 600 round per gun.
Prototypes: One M.20/2 (Class B, U9, later AX834; first flown by Flt Lt T Rose DFC at Woodley on 15 September 1940); one M.20/4 (Class B, U-O228, later DR616; first flown, April 1941). No production.

The Miles M.20/4, DR616, showing the pointed spinner, the lighter undercarriage fairings and the catapult spool fairings under the centre fuselage; note the closely-spaced machine gun ports in the wings. (Photo: RAF Museum, Neg No P004004)

Hawker Hurricane II, IV and Sea Hurricane

The Battle of Britain was at its height in September 1940 when a new version of the Hawker Hurricane, the Mark II with Merlin XX engine, was beginning to reach the RAF. At the same time a sinister threat was developing at sea — the beginning of operations by German Focke-Wulf Fw 200s and Heinkel He 111s against deep-sea merchant shipping approaching British ports from distant countries. As the older Hurricanes came to be replaced by the new Mark IIs, many Mark Is underwent modification as Sea Hurricanes to meet this threat at sea (see page 296).

Development of the Merlin had gone ahead at Rolls-Royce unchecked since it had first flown in test beds in 1934, and by 1938 versions running on 100-octane fuel were under test. The Merlin XX was intended for delivery to the airframe manufacturers as a 'power egg', that is a self-contained unit with Rotol constant-speed propeller, CSU, exhaust system and cowlings assembled. This arrangement was not suitable for the Hurricane principally owing to the existing fuselage contours, but it was found possible to mount the new engine with little alteration to the engine bearers and cowlings.

The first Merlin XX-powered Hurricane had been flown as a prototype, P3269, at Langley (the new Hurricane factory) by Philip Lucas GM on 11 June 1940, even before the Battle of Britain opened. With a maximum speed of 342 mph at 20,000 feet, the Mark IIA Series 1, with an armament of eight Browning machine guns, began delivery to Fighter Command in October, and by April 1941 had reached eighteen squadrons. The Mark IIA Series 2 had quickly replaced the Series 1 in production, featuring a slightly improved engine mounting.

The Hurricane Mk IIB, with armament increased to twelve Browning guns in the wings, began joining the Squadrons in February 1942, first reaching No 56 Squadron, commanded by Sqn Ldr Edgar Norman Ryder DFC (later Gp Capt, CBE, DFC*) at North Weald.

By this time, however, Fighter Command had gone over to the offensive, flying an increasing number of sweeps along the French and Belgian coasts, either seeking targets of opportunity or escorting light raids by Blenheim bombers. To counter these, the *Luftwaffe* introduced the Messerschmitt Bf 109F, a fighter much superior to the Hurricane, and although the Mark IIs continued to participate in the offensive operations they were used increasingly as night intruders, either in the fighter rôle or as fighter-bombers, equipped initially to carry a pair of 250lb bombs under the wings. Later the load was increased to cater for 500lb bombs but, thus weighed down, they seldom operated without a Spitfire escort by day. In due course Hurricane IIAs and IIBs equipped a total of 79 squadrons.

By the late summer of 1941 Fighter Command Hurricanes were almost exclusively employed as night fighters, either in the intruder rôle or for home defence. A number of aircraft equipped the Turbinlite Squadrons, together with American Douglas Boston and Havoc twin-engine aircraft equipped with AI radar and a searchlight in the nose. The Hurricane accompanied the larger aircraft whose purpose was to locate and illuminate enemy raiders, so that the single-seater could close in and deliver the *coup de grâce*. Despite being operational for twenty months between May 1941 and January 1943, the ten Turbinlite Squadrons (Nos 530-539) only succeeded in destroying a single enemy raider when, on 30 April 1942, Flt Lt Charles Vivian Winn of No 538 Squadron shot down a Heinkel He 111.

The most effective Hurricane II night fighter was the Mark IIC, armed with four 20mm Hispano cannon, first delivered to No 3 Squadron at Martlesham Heath in April 1941, commanded by Sqn Ldr Russell Faulkner Aitken (later Gp Capt CBE, AFC), initially for daylight offensive sweeps but, from August that year, for night defence, based at Hunsdon. Possessing a maximum speed of 328 mph at 20,000 feet, the four-cannon Mark IIC ultimately equipped a total of 80 squadrons.

Hurricane IIs began arriving in the Mediterranean and North Africa in the spring of 1941, and soon became the RAF's standard fighter and fighter-bomber in the Western Desert. With the entry into the War by Japan at the end of that year, many Hurricane IIAs and IIBs, originally destined for the Middle East, were diverted on to Burma and Malaya, a small number arriving at Singapore in time to participate in the last weeks' fighting before the base fell to the Japanese. Thereafter increasing numbers of Mark IIs arrived in India to cover the retreat by British and Commonwealth forces northwards through Burma. Hurricanes serving in the tropical and sub-tropical theatres were obliged to carry Vokes air filters over their carburettor air intakes — cumbersome fairings under the nose that reduced the fighters' speed by around eight per cent in any particular configuration.

It was in North Africa that the next sub-variant of the Mark II, the IID, made its mark on the conduct of operations when this version, armed with a pair of 40mm Vickers anti-tank guns under the wings joined No 6 Squadron in the Western Desert in April 1942, commanded by Wg Cdr Roger Cave Porteous DSO. These aircraft were first committed to action during the Battle of Bir Hakim, and later in the Battle of El

Above: *An early standard production Hurricane IIC, BP352, seen at Langley in 1941; apart from very minor changes of internal equipment, this four-cannon version of the aircraft remained externally unaltered until it went out of production in September 1944.* (Photo: Author's Collection)

Right: *One of the relatively small number of Hurricane IIDs with 40mm anti-tank guns retained for service in Britain; note the absence of tropical filter under the nose.* (Photo: Sydney Camm Collection)

Alamein, being found to be very effective against all but the thickest-skinned enemy tanks. Though also widely used against the Japanese in Burma, in Britain the Mk IID only served with Nos 164 and 184 Squadrons.

By 1943, with purpose-designed, radar-equipped night fighters in widespread service, the Hurricane was firmly established as a ground attack fighter, armed with four 20mm cannon or 500lb bombs. To this armament was now added the three-inch rocket projectile, of which the Hurricane could carry eight, each fitted with a 60lb warhead, under the wings.

The next Hurricane was the Mark IV which introduced the 1,620hp Merlin 24, 27 or 32 engines together with a 'low-attack universal wing', fitted with two Browning machine guns for sighting purposes and to which could be attached combinations of rockets, 40mm guns, bombs, smoke-screen tanks, and long-range or ferry fuel tanks. This version was introduced in 1944 and came to be used almost exclusively in the Mediterranean theatre and Burma.

Hurricanes continued in production until September 1944, and served with RAF front line squadrons until December 1946, when No 6 Squadron gave up its Mark IVs in Cyprus to re-equip with Vampires. Hawker factories are said to have built a total of some 10,030 examples, and Gloster had contributed 2,750 Mark Is and IIs between October 1939 and March 1942, while the Austin Motor Company had built 300 Mark IIs. To these were added 1,451 aircraft, built in Canada by the Canadian Car & Foundry Corporation, Montreal (designated the Marks X, XI and XII) and mostly powered by Packard-built 1,300hp Merlin 28 and 29 engines. Notwithstanding these production figures, widely quoted elsewhere, they do not tally with the number of aircraft received by the Services, and are complicated by fairly large numbers of aircraft which were completed as one version, only to be converted to another before delivery. The correct total figure is now generally believed to have been about 14,670.

Hurricanes were exported to Belgium, Egypt, Eire, Finland, India, Iran, Poland, Portugal, Romania, South Africa and Turkey, and no fewer than 2,952 were supplied to the Soviet Union during the War — although some of these were lost *en route*.

The Hurricane was employed in numerous experiments. The Mark V was a version intended as a purpose-designed ground attack version powered by a ground-boosted Merlin to give maximum performance below 5,000 feet; one prototype (NL255) was newly built, and two Mk IVs, KX405 and KZ193, were converted. A Hurricane was employed to test the installation of a jetti-

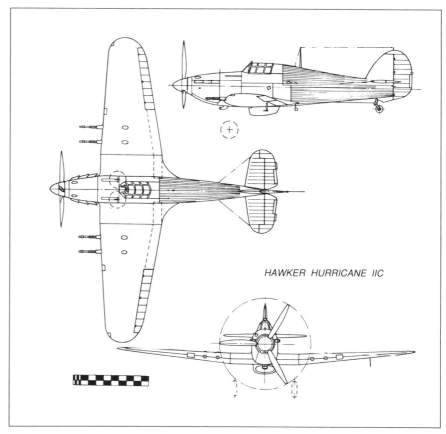

HAWKER HURRICANE IIC

Type: Single-engine, single-seat, low-wing monoplane fighter.

Manufacturers: Hawker Aircraft Ltd, Kingston and Brooklands, Surrey, and Langley, Buckinghamshire; Gloster Aircraft Co Ltd, Hucclecote, Gloucester; The Austin Motor Co Ltd, Longbridge, Birmingham. The Canadian Car & Foundry Corporation, Montreal, Canada.

Powerplant: One 1,260hp Rolls-Royce Merlin XX twelve-cylinder liquid-cooled in-line supercharged engine driving three-blade Rotol constant-speed propeller.

Dimensions: Span, 40ft 0in; length, 32ft 2¼in; height, 13ft 6in; wing area, 258 sq ft.

Weights: Tare, 5,467lb; all-up, 7,544lb (with drop tanks, 8,044lb)

Performance: Max speed, 328 mph at 20,000ft; time to 20,000ft, 7 min 42 sec; service ceiling, 32,400ft; normal range, 460 miles; max range, 1,086 miles.

Armament: Four 20mm British Hispano Mk II cannon in wings with 364 rounds. Provision to carry two 250lb or two 500lb bombs, eight 3-inch rocket projectiles, two combat (44 gallon) drop tanks or two 90 gallon ferry tanks.

Summary of production: The following total production figures for the Mark II and IV have been widely quoted, but are known to be slightly inaccurate owing to an unknown number of conversions undertaken by the manufacturers. Hawker: Mk IIA, 418; Mk IIB, 1,718; Mk IIC, 4,711; Mk IID, 296; Mk IV, 524. Gloster: Mk IIA, 33; Mk IIB, 867. Austin: Mk IIB, 244; Mk IIC, 56. Total Hurricane production was approximately 14,670 (plus or minus up to 13 aircraft).

Summary of RAF and Fleet Air Arm Service: Hurricane IIs served with Nos 1, 3, 5, 6, 11, 17, 20, 28, 30, 32, 33, 34, 42, 43, 46, 56, 60, 63, 67, 69, 71, 73, 74, 79, 80, 81, 87, 94, 96, 111, 113, 116, 121, 123, 126, 127, 128, 133, 134, 135, 136, 146, 151, 164, 174, 175, 176, 184, 185, 193, 208, 213, 225, 229, 232, 237, 238, 239, 241, 242, 247, 249, 250, 253, 256, 257, 258, 261, 273, 274, 279, 284, 285, 286, 287, 288, 289, 291, 302, 303, 306, 309, 310, 312, 316, 317, 318, 331, 335, 336, 351, 352, 400, 401, 402, 417, 451, 504, 516, 518, 520, 521, 527, 530, 531, 532, 533, 534, 535, 536, 537, 538, 539, 577, 587, 595, 598, 601, 605, 607, 615, 631, 667, 679, 680, 681, 691 and 695 Squadrons, RAF; Hurricane IVs served with Nos 6, 20, 42, 63, 137, 164, 184, 186, 279, 286, 287, 309, 351, 439, 567, 577, 587, 595, 598, 639, 650 and 679 Squadrons, RAF. Sea Hurricanes served with Nos 700, 702, 731, 748, 759, 760, 761, 762, 766, 768, 769, 774, 776, 778, 779, 781, 787, 788, 789, 791, 792, 794, 795, 800, 801, 802, 804, 813, 824, 825, 880, 882, 883, 885, 891, 895 and 897 Squadrons, Fleet Air Arm.

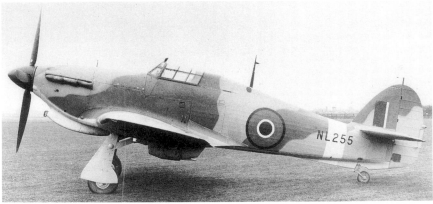

Left: The sole newly-built Hurricane Mk V prototype, NL255, intended as a specialised ground attack version for the Far East; its specially-rated Merlin drove a four-blade Rotol propeller, and it was fitted with additional armour plate around pilot and engine. (Photo: Hawker Aircraft Ltd, Neg No H5G-3)

Below: A Hurricane II, Z3687, at the RAE, Farnborough, in September 1948 fitted with an experimental Armstrong Whitworth-designed laminar-flow wing. (Photo: Author's Collection)

sonable upper wing as a means of enabling the aircraft to operate out of very small airfields, or alternatively to carry extra fuel for very long range flights. Hurricanes were towed behind bombers in trials to examine the feasibility of delivering them to North Africa over flight stages far beyond the Hurricane's maximum range. A two-seat Hurricane was developed and delivered to Iran for training purposes. Photographic reconnaissance Hurricanes were developed by the RAF in the Middle East and flown by the PRUs in the Mediterranean and over Burma. And among the projects examined, but not built, were Hurricanes to be powered by the Napier Dagger, Rolls-Royce Griffon and Bristol Hercules as alternatives to the Merlin lest the supplies of this engine were threatened.

The Hawker Hurricane was never at any time during the Second World War the fastest fighter in the RAF. It was, however, frequently the best British fighter available, arriving in many theatres months, even years before the first Spitfire. This accounts for the remarkable statistic, that of all enemy aircraft — German, Italian and Japanese — claimed shot down by Royal Air Force, Royal Navy and Commonwealth fighter pilots, 55 per cent fell to the pilots of Hurricanes, compared with 33 per cent to Spitfire pilots and 12 per cent to the pilots of other fighters.

The Sea Hurricane

The first suggestion that the Hurricane should be used as a naval fighter was made in April 1940, and a pair of Blackburn Roc floats was delivered to Hawker, it being intended that a seaplane version should be available to operate from fjords during the Norwegian campaign, then being fought following the German invasion. This project was discontinued when the cam-

paign ended, and no such Hurricane was completed.

Later that year, with the onset of German maritime operations against British shipping in the Atlantic, it was proposed that redundant Hurricane Is should be catapult mounted on the fo'c's'les of merchant ships and launched against approaching enemy raiders. Being unable to land back aboard his parent ship, the pilot would most likely have to ditch in the hope of being rescued.

Conversion of 35 eight-gun Sea Hurricane Mk IAs (confined to the provision of catapult spools) began in November 1940, and the first were delivered to the Royal Navy two months later for service aboard HMS *Ariguani*, *Maplin*, *Patia* and *Springbank* (known as Fighter Catapult Ships), while merchant ships, termed Catapult Aircraft Merchantmen were fitted out. Such was the urgency to protect British shipping, as enemy anti-shipping operations were stepped up during the spring of 1941, that Churchill himself was moved to demand greater priority for the scheme and, by mid-1941, a further 214 Sea Hurricane IA conversions had been ordered, the greater share of this work being done by General Aircraft Ltd of Hanworth. These Hurricanes were carried aboard ships on the North Atlantic routes, and those sailing to and from

Gibraltar. Later they played a conspicuous, though extremely hazardous part in the defence of the North Cape convoys which sailed between Iceland and the North Russian Ports.

While the CAM-ships were originally intended as no more than a short-term expedient, a longer-term plan involved the extensive conversion of merchant ships to embody a flight deck, known as escort carriers, to supplement the relatively small number of fleet carriers available for convoy escort. For operation from such decks, the Sea Hurricane Mk IB was produced, incorporating an arrester hook under the rear fuselage; again the conversion involved eight-Browning gun ex-RAF Mark Is. Again the Sea Hurricane pilots gave an excellent account of themselves, particularly on the North Cape and Malta convoys.

The Mark IC introduced the four-cannon armament but, on account of retaining the Merlin III, it was capable of a speed of no more than 290 mph. This was remedied in 1943 with the appearance of the Sea Hurricane Mk IIC, a Merlin XX-powered deck fighter with arrester hook, catapult spools, naval radio and four-cannon armament; this version equipped naval fighter squadrons aboard fleet and escort carriers in every wartime theatre from the North Atlantic to the South Pacific.

Canadian production also included Sea Hurricanes, namely Sea Hurricane Xs and XIIAs, armed respectively with eight and twelve machine guns. Mk XIIAs of No 800 Squadron, embarked in HMS *Biter*, supported the Allied landings in North Africa in November 1942 as part of Operation Torch.

Sea Hurricanes served with no fewer than 38 Squadrons of the Fleet Air Arm. The table of data on page 295 refers to the Hawker Hurricane Mk IIC.

Above: *The Sea Hurricane IC was intended primarily as bomber destroyer in circumstances when no enemy escort fighters were present; the Merlin III engine was therefore considered acceptable even when offset by the four-cannon armament.* (Photo: Sydney Camm Collection)

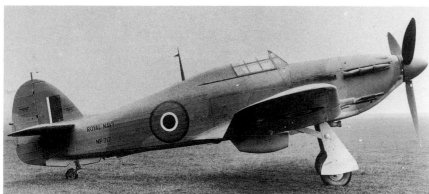

Left: *The Sea Hurricane IIC was only distinguishable from the RAF's Hurricane IIC by the addition of the arrester hook, although many of the naval fighters were painted white overall in service.* (Photo: Sydney Camm Collection)

de Havilland Mosquito and Sea Mosquito

The de Havilland Mosquito was one of aviation's truly outstanding aeroplanes of all time simply because it performed with unqualified success all the tasks for which it was originally designed (as well as many others) and was available for service at exactly the right time. That it was constructed almost entirely of wood — a non-strategic material — and could therefore call upon widely available manufacturing skills, was an obvious bonus for a nation at war and so largely dependant upon imported metal ores from overseas. Moreover, the performance of this remarkable aeroplane placed it in a class of its own. A measure of the recognition of this pre-eminence may be judged by the fact that Mosquitos served with no fewer than 86 squadrons of the

RAF (40 of them fighter squadrons) and 20 of the Fleet Air Arm.

Origins of the aircraft lay in the long experience in manufacturing wooden aircraft possessed by the de Havilland company, which approached the Air Ministry in 1938 with a proposal for an unarmed wooden bomber powered by a pair of Rolls-Royce Merlins and capable of reaching Berlin with a bombload of four 250lb bombs. Despite coming at a time of international crisis, this proposal was turned down, presumably on the grounds that an unarmed wooden aircraft was unimaginable in skies likely to be dominated by very fast single-engine interceptors. Fortunately, resulting from representations by Air Marshal Sir

Wilfrid Freeman, KCB, DSO, MC, Air Member for Development and Production on the Air Council, this decision was reversed, and on 29 December 1939 detail design of the proposed aircraft was sanctioned, and on 1 March 1940 a Contract was raised for 50 aircraft (W4050-W4099) to be designed and built to Specification B.1/40. From the outset it was a fundamental requirement that the aircraft should be equally suitable for service in fighter, bomber and reconnaissance duties.

Design was under the direction of Ronald Eric Bishop (later CBE), and the first prototype was flown by Geoffrey de Havilland, Jnr, on 25 November 1940, straightway impressing observers with

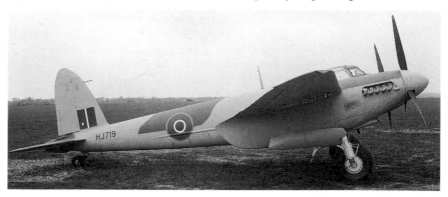

A Mosquito FB VI, HJ719, with bomb shackles under the wings. (Photo: Air Ministry, RTP dated May 1943)

A Mosquito NF XIII, MM512, of No 409 (Canadian) Squadron on a captured airfield in the Low Countries late in 1944 or early 1945. Note the flat, single-piece windscreen, a feature of all Mosquito fighters. (Photo: RAF Museum, Neg No P021630)

its astonishing speed and agility. This aircraft, W4050, the light bomber prototype, was following into the air on 15 May 1941 at Salisbury Hall, Herts, by W4052, the night fighter prototype, designed to Specification F.21/40. The Mosquito — for such it was now named — was an all-wooden, cantilever, mid-wing monoplane with curvilinear tapering fuselage constructed of cedar ply laminations separated by a layer of balsa wood. The single-piece wing, also of bonded ply and balsa sandwich stressed-skin construction, was built up around the engine radiators (in the centre section leading edges) and ten fuel tanks together containing 539 gallons.

The two Merlin 21 engine nacelles were low slung to allow the mainwheels to be housed within them, and the two-man crew was situated, side-by-side, in a cockpit located well forward in the nose of the fuselage. The armament of four 20mm Hispano cannon was mounted in the underside of the fuselage directly below the cockpit, and was supplemented by four 0.303in Browning machine guns in the extreme nose. The tail surfaces were of elliptical outline, for years characteristic of de Havilland designs. Unlike the bomber and photo-reconnaissance versions, the Mosquito fighters (and fighter-bombers) featured optically-flat bullet-proof windscreens, and entry to the cockpit was through a hatch low down on the starboard side of the nose.

The first production night fighter, the NF Mk II, which accounted for 21 of the original order for 50 aircraft, began delivery in January 1942 to No 157 Squadron under the command of Wg Cdr Richard Gordon Slade at Castle Camps, followed by No 23 Squadron at Middle Wallop under Wg Cdr Bertie Rex O'Brien Hoare DFC* shortly after. The latter Squadron pioneered long-range night intruder operations by Mosquitos over Northern Europe during the autumn of that year before moving to Malta whence, in the first three months, it destroyed seventeen enemy aircraft at night.

Among a number of trial installations made on the NF II prototype was the fitting of a dummy Bristol B XI four-gun power-operated dorsal turret in the rear of the cockpit. Later, the same aircraft was equipped with a pneumatically-operated, segmented airbrake, arranged radially around the centre fuselage, in an attempt to provide rapid deceleration in the final stages of a stern chase without causing a change in trim as the pilot sought to bring his guns to bear. Neither installation was adopted in service.

The Mosquito NF II was equipped initially with AI Mk IV radar, characterized by the broad-arrow aerial on the nose, but this was later replaced by AI Mk V. The next fighter, or rather fighter-bomber version was the Mosquito FB Mk VI, the most widely-used of all Mosquitos. Dispensing with the nose radar altogether, this version appeared initially in Series 1 form, capable of carrying two 250lb bombs in the rear of the bomb bay (the front half being occupied by the cannon bodies), and two more under the wings. As short-finned 500lb bombs became available, these could replace the lighter weapons, and the Mk VI Series 2 was accordingly strengthened to accommodate the heavier bombs in the fuselage and under the wings. The prototype Mosquito VI, HJ662 (a converted Mk II), was first flown in February 1943, and was followed by operational service, starting with No 418 (Canadian) Squadron in May that year, flying from Ford under the command of Wg Cdr J H Little DFC.

Throughout the remainder of the War Mosquito VIs equipped numerous squadrons of Fighter and Coastal Command and, after the Normandy landings, the Second Tactical Air Force.

MP469 was one of a small number of Mosquito XV high-altitude fighters; this view illustrates the extended wings and the under-fuselage gun pack. (Photo: via R C Sturtivant)

Among them were Nos 143, 235 and 248 Squadrons of Coastal Command's Banff Strike Wing whose task was to attack enemy shipping off the Norwegian coast, the Mosquitos' gun armament being supplemented by the mounting of up to sixteen 60lb rockets under their wings in addition to the pair of 500lb bombs carried internally. Another armament variation appeared on a Mark VI derivative, Coastal Command's Mosquito FB Mk XVIII, armed with a single 57mm Molins gun in the nose; this version, of which about 30 examples were produced, served with No 248 Squadron on anti-shipping operations over the English Channel and in the Bay of Biscay during 1944; the Squadron succeeded in sinking a German submarine off the French coast on 25 March that year. At the end of the War the surviving aircraft were handed on to No 254 Squadron. Mosquito VIs also undertook countless night intruder operations and, being without radar, flew 'cat's eye' sorties over enemy railways and airfields during the final two years of the War.

The next dedicated Mosquito night fighter was the Mark XII, which first flew in March 1943 and differed in a number of important respects from the NF II (of which 97 were converted to the new version), most important of which was the installation of AI Mk VIII, the first operational British centimetric airborne radar; this equipment employed a scanner and hemispherical radome in the nose, necessitating re-

moval of the four Browning guns; henceforth all Mosquito night fighters were armed solely with the four Hispano cannon. The NF XIII was similar but was newly built, a total of 270 being produced. Between them these two versions equipped ten squadrons, but this British radar, though an improvement on earlier sets, was not considered satisfactory, and the aircraft were fairly quickly succeeded by the Mosquito NF XVII, equipped with the excellent American AI Mk X centimetric radar (which continued in service for eight years with the RAF). The Mark XVII again comprised 100 converted NF IIs, and 220 similar NF XIXs were newly built. The Mark X radar was characterized by a much enlarged nose radome whose extra drag was largely offset by installation of 1,635hp Merlin 25s.

Before going on to record the various Mosquito night fighters which entered service at the end of the War, one other fighter variant should be referred to. This was the high altitude F XV. The appearance in British skies of high flying Junkers Ju 86P reconnaissance aircraft in the summer of 1942 prompted the hurried conversion of the prototype Mosquito B XVI bomber, MP469, a version which was powered by 1,680hp Merlin 72/73 engines, one of which drove a cabin blower for a pressurized cockpit. To increase the aircraft's ceiling, the wing span was increased to 62ft 6in, lighter landing wheels were fitted and almost all armour protection was

removed. AI Mk VIII, considered satisfactory at high altitudes, was installed in the nose, and a gun pack containing four Browning machine guns — the sole armament — was added under the fuselage. Based on this prototype, four Mark IV bombers were similarly converted and the five aircraft delivered to No. 85 Squadron in March 1943, equipping one flight until August. With all-up weight reduced to 17,600lb, these fighters possessed a top speed of 412 mph and a service ceiling of 43,500 ft.

Returning to the night fighters, the NF XXX, with AI Mk X, equipped 21 squadrons and was the last to enter operational service before the end of the War. It was the first of three night fighter versions to be equipped with pressurized cockpits, being powered by either Merlin 72/73s, 76/77s or 113/114s, the second engine in each instance driving the cabin blower. First squadron to fly the NF XXX, in July 1944, was No 219, commanded by Wg Cdr Archibald Douglas McNeill Boyd DSO, DFC, at Bradwell Bay. By the end of the War nine squadrons had been re-equipped, about half of them flying bomber support duties over Germany. The last NF 30 was withdrawn from service with No 39 Squadron in mid-1952 at Fayid, Egypt.

The Mosquito NF 36 was similar to the NF 30, but introduced the 1,690hp Merlin 113/114 engines while retaining American AI Mk X radar. A total of 266 was built, equipping nine peacetime squadrons — starting with No 85 Squadron in January 1946 at West Malling. Last Fighter Command NF 36s were withdrawn in March 1953, again from No 39 Squadron, although aircraft serving on radio and radar countermeasures duties with No 199 (Bomber) Squadron remained in service until March 1954.

The last Mosquito night fighter variant to be produced was the NF 38, which made its maiden flight in November 1947. Similar with respect to engines

Above: *Just visible in this view of Mosquito FB XVIII, MM424, is the barrel of its 57mm Molins gun in the nose; used for anti-shipping strikes, these aircraft only equipped Nos 248 and 254 Squadrons.* (Photo: Air Ministry, dated February 1944)

Right: *Mosquito NF 36, RL125/ZK-G, of No 25 (Fighter) Squadron at its post-War station, West Malling; the two horizontal bars on the fin represented a muted return to the pre-War squadron insignia.* (Photo: RAF Museum, Neg No P019018)

to the NF 36, the new aircraft reverted to British radar, this time to AI Mk IX, resulting in the cockpit being moved forward by five inches. A total of one hundred was built, of which 54 were exported to Yugoslavia. The aircraft did not enter full squadron service with the RAF, although a small number was distributed among one or two fighter squadrons on a trial basis.

When, however, the last NF 36s were withdrawn from service with Fighter Command in 1953, the day fighter squadrons were fully equipped with jet aircraft, and the Mosquito had become an operational anachronism. The first Vampire and Meteor night fighters had been in service more than eighteen months, and the Venom NF 2 was almost ready to start taking their place.

Sea Mosquitos

Mosquitos served with the Royal Navy from November 1944 onwards for about six years, though it must be said that most of the aircraft were employed for trials and training with the 700-series Squadrons, using a heterogeneous collection of T Mk IIIs, FB VIs, B XVIs, PR XVIs, B 25s and B 34s; all were strictly land-based and not equipped for deck landing.

Towards the end of 1943, following the success of the torpedo-carrying Beaufighter, the Admiralty began discussions on the feasibility of a deck-landing torpedo fighter-reconnaissance adaptation of the Mosquito, and Specification N.15/44 was issued the following year. A Mosquito VI was fitted with a deck arrester hook under the rear fuselage and, on 25 March that year, Lt-Cdr E M Brown MBE, DSC, made a landing on HMS *Indefatigable* — the first time that a British operational twin-engine aircraft landed on a carrier. Further conversions were made, but continuing trials indicated that the Mosquito was not a 'natural' naval aircraft, and it was clear that extensive modifications would be needed. The first true Sea Mosquito prototype, LR387, a converted FB Mk VI, featured a small thimble radome in the nose, strengthened rear fuselage and arrester hook, Merlin 25s driving large four-blade propellers, and folding wings. The customary four-cannon armament was retained.

Meanwhile, as a production order for 50 Sea Mosquito TR Mk 33s was placed,

training got underway on Mosquito T IIIs and FB VIs with Nos 703, 751, 762, 771, 787 and 790 Squadrons. To cater for future deck operation, the undercarriage of the TR 33 was changed from the 14th production aircraft onwards to feature long-travel Lockheed oleo legs in place of the standard Mosquito's

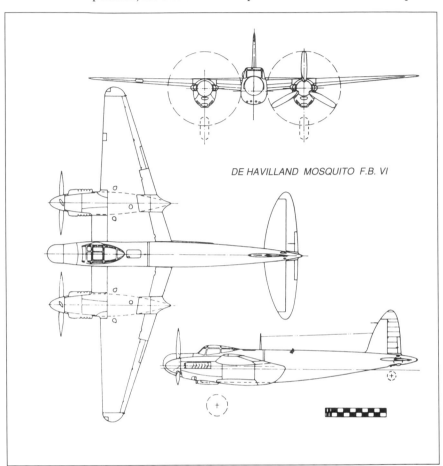

DE HAVILLAND MOSQUITO F.B. VI

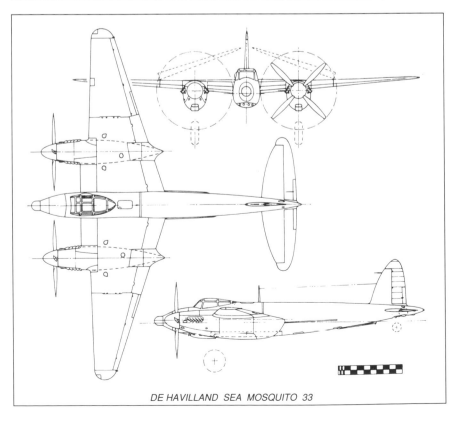

DE HAVILLAND SEA MOSQUITO 33

A de Havilland Sea Mosquito TR 33, TW256/ 593 of No 771 Squadron, Fleet Air Arm, complete with nose ASV radar, arrester hook and flat windscreen. This Squadron was a Fleet Requirements Unit which flew its Mosquitos from Lee-on-Solent during the late 1940s. (Photo: via R C Sturtivant)

rubber-in-compression type. All aircraft had provision to mount a naval 18in torpedo under the fuselage, and various rocket loads and drop tanks could be carried under the wings. As on all Mosquito fighters, the Sea Mosquitos featured flat, single-piece windscreens, but also included slightly enlarged elevators to provide better longtiudinal control for deck landing.

TR 33s first joined No 787 (Trials) Squadron in March 1946 at West Raynham, commanded by Cdr R A Kilroy DSC RN. Seven other training and trials squadrons received small numbers of TR 33s, and in April the first of twelve aircraft reached No 811 Squadron at Ford, commanded by Lt-Cdr S M P Walsh, DSO, DSC*, RNVR.

This, however, was the sum total of the TR 33's Service life, and the aircraft never flew operationally from a deck, the principal reason given being the aircraft's difficult take-off and landing characteristics, the Mosquito always being known for its powerful tendency to swing (a tendency overcome in the Sea Hornet with its handed propellers).

A second Sea Mosquito variant was the TR 37, which carried British ASV radar in a much enlarged nose. The prototype, TW240 (a converted TR 33) was followed by fourteen production aircraft, and these were distributed between No 703 Squadron at Lee-on-Solent and No 771 at Ford, beginning in December 1948. None reached an op-

Type: Twin-engine, two-crew, mid-wing monoplane day and night fighter, intruder and fighter bomber; also naval torpedo/reconnaissance fighter.

Manufacturers: de Havilland Aircraft Ltd, Hatfield, Herts; Leavesden, Herts; Hawarden, Cheshire. Airspeed Ltd, Christchurch, Hants; Standard Motor Co Ltd. de Havilland Aircraft Pty Ltd, Bankstown, Sydney, NSW, Australia. de Havilland Aircraft of Canada Ltd, Downsview, Toronto.

Air Ministry Specifications: F.21/40 for night fighter prototype; N.15/44 for Sea Mosquito prototype.

Powerplant: Two 1,460hp Rolls-Royce Merlin 21 or 23 V-twelve cylinder liquid-cooled supercharged in-line engine driving three-blade DH variable-pitch propellers (NF II, FB VI, NF XII, NF XIII and NF XVII); 1,635hp Merlin 25s (FB VI, FB XVIII, TR 33 and TR 37); 1,705hp Merlin 66s (TR 33); 1,680hp Merlin 72/73s (F XV and NF 30); 1,710hp Merlin 76/77s (F XV and NF 30); 1,690hp Merlin 113/114s (NF 30, NF 36 and NF 38).

Structure: All-wood cantilever monoplane employing cedar ply laminations sandwiching layer of balsa. Retractable tailwheel undercarriage with mainwheels retracting rearwards into underslung engine nacelles. Engine radiators located in wing centre section leading edge.

Dimensions: Span (all versions execpt F XV), 54ft 2in; length (all versions except F XV, NF 30, NF 36, TR 37 and NF 38), 40ft 6in; (F XV, NF 30, NF 36 and TR 37), 44ft 6in; (NF 38) 41ft 2in; height (all versions), 12ft 6in; wing area (all versions except F XV), 454 sq ft; (F XV) 479 sq ft.

Weights: Tarc (NF II), 13,431lb; (FB VI), 14,344lb; (NF XII), 13,696lb; (F XV), 13,746lb; (NF XVII), 13,224lb; (NF 30), 13,400lb; (TR 33) 14,850lb; (NF 38), 16,000lb. All-up (NF II), 18,547lb; (FB VI), 22,258lb; (NF XII), 19,700lb; (F XV), 17,600lb; (NF XVII), 19,200lb; (NF 30), 21,600lb; (TR 33), 23,850lb; (NF 38), 21,400lb.

Performance: Max speed, (NF II), 382 mph; (FB VI) 378 mph; (NF XII), 370 mph; (F XV), 412 mph; (NF 30), 407 mph; (TR 33), 376 mph; (NF 38), 404 mph. Climb to 15,000ft (NF II), 7.2 min; (FB VI), 7 min; (F XV), 6.1 min; (NF 30, NF 36 and NF 38), 7.5 min. Service ceiling (NF II), 36,000ft; (FB VI), 33,000ft; (NF XII), 36,000ft; (F XV), 43,500ft; (NF 30), 38,000ft; (TR 33), 30,100ft; (NF 38) 36,000ft.

Armament: (NF II) Four 20mm Hispano cannon and four 0.303in Browning machine guns; (F XV), four 0.303in Browning machine guns; (all other night fighters), four 20mm Hispano cannon; (FB VI), four 20mm Hispano cannon, four 0.303in Browning machine guns, up to four 500lb bombs, or two 500lb bombs and up to sixteen 60lb, 3in rocket projectiles; (TR 33 and TR 37), four 20mm Hispano cannon, one 18in naval torpedo and underwing rocket projectiles.

Prototypes: (NF II), W4052; (FB VI), HJ662; (F XV), MP469; (FB XVIII), HJ732; (TR 33), LR387.

Production: (NF II), 466; (FB VI), 2,718 approx; (NF XIII), 270; (NF XIX), 220; (NF 30), 350 approx; (TR 33), 50; (NF 36), 266; (TR 37), 14; (NF 38) 100. Australian production, 178 FB 40s; Canadian production, 3 FB 21s, 1 FB 24 and 338 FB 26s. Total night fighter, fighter-bomber and naval aircraft, approx 4,954.

Summary of RAF and RN Service: Mosquito night fighters served with Nos 23, 25, 27, 29, 39, 46, 68, 85, 89, 96, 108, 125, 141, 143, 151, 157, 169, 176, 199, 219, 239, 255, 256, 264, 307, 333, 500, 502, 504, 515, 600, 604, 605, 608, 609, 616, 681 and 684 Squadrons of the RAF and RAuxAF; fighter bombers served with Nos 4, 8, 11, 14, 18, 21, 22, 23, 25, 27, 29, 36, 39, 45, 47, 55, 69, 82, 84, 89, 107, 110, 114, 141, 143, 151, 157, 162, 169, 211, 235, 239, 248, 249, 256, 264, 268, 305, 307, 333, 515, 540, 605, 618, 681 and 684; Sea Mosquitos served with Nos 700, 703, 704, 721, 728, 733, 739, 751, 762, 770, 771, 772, 773, 777, 778, 780, 787, 790, 797 and 811 Squadrons of the Fleet Air Arm.

erational squadron. It is believed that the last Sea Mosquitos were withdrawn from service in about June 1953.

It may be that, had the War continued longer, much greater design effort would have been available to better suit the Sea Mosquito for naval operations; as it was, the aircraft was generally considered unpopular, particularly when encumbered by a torpedo.

The first Sea Mosquito with folding wings was the converted Mark VI, LR387, seen here with four-blade propellers, ASV radar and carrying a torpedo. (Photo: British Aerospace (Hatfield), Neg No 1922/I)

Fairey Firefly

Designed by Herbert Eugene Chaplin, the Fairey Firefly was the outcome of Specification N.5/40 which laid down requirements for a two-seat fleet reconnaissance fighter to replace the Fulmar — itself only intended as a stopgap replacement for the Blackburn Skua. In essence these requirements (amalgamating the former Specifications N.8/39 and N.9/39) initially required a maximum speed of 320 mph at 15,000 feet and a service ceiling of 30,000 feet; a patrol endurance of four hours, folding wings, an armament of four 20mm cannon and full deck operating equipment were mandatory. Choice of the new Rolls-Royce Griffon was logical as this was expected to be developing close to 2,000 hp by the time full production was underway. In fact that figure was not reached in production engines for another four years.

The Firefly was superficially of the same configuration as the Fulmar, but featured wings with elliptical trailing edges, incorporating large Fairey-

The first Firefly prototype, Z1826, with mock-up cannon fairings; the reason for the absence of the pilot's canopy is not known. (Photo: Air Ministry RTP Neg No 11003B, dated May 1942).

Youngman flaps which bestowed good low-speed and cruise range properties. Steel and duralumin construction was employed throughout. The four cannon were located in the wings outboard of the wing fold, and the wing folding was effected manually. No rear defensive armament was carried and the observer's cockpit was located immediately aft of the wing trailing edge. The Griffon

engine drove a three-blade Rotol constant-speed propeller and featured a prominent 'chin' radiator.

An order for 200 aircraft (between Z1826 and Z2126) was placed 'off the drawing board' in 1940, the first four examples being specified as prototypes. Unfortunately, development of the Griffon engine was severely set back by demands for Merlin engine production during 1940 and 1941 and, by the time the first Firefly prototype, Z1826, was flown by Chris Staniland on 22 December 1941, the Griffon IIB was only rated at 1,730hp, resulting in a performance somewhat below the figure demanded.

Further engine delays, caused by conflicting demands on the Griffon for RAF fighters, resulted in production of

Early full-standard production Firefly F Mk I, Z1956. (Photo: Ministry of Aircraft Production RTP Neg No 12593C, dated February 1944)

the Firefly getting off to a slow start. Nevertheless the other three prototypes and the first twenty or so production aircraft were flying by the end of 1942, and these came to be employed for development of new versions of the Firefly. Z1875/G, for example, was converted to the prototype of a night fighter version (the NF Mk II), and Z1846 became the prototype FR Mk I reconnaissance fighter with ASH radar in a pod carried under the front fuselage.

By 1943 deliveries of the Griffon IIB enabled production of the Firefly to be accelerated, and an order was placed for 200 aircraft with General Aircraft Ltd under sub-contract — though the last 68 of these were later cancelled. No fewer than 380 Firefly Mk Is had been built by the summer of that year, many of them awaiting engines, and it was decided to begin delivery to the Fleet Air Arm. Twelve aircraft were flown to Yeovilton in September where they formed the initial equipment of No 1770 Squadron, commanded by Lt-Cdr I P Godfrey RNVR.

Training on the Fireflies with No 1770 Squadron continued for four months, and in January 1944 the original aircraft were replaced by Firefly Is powered by 1,990hp Griffon XII engines, and similar aircraft equipped No 1771 Squadron on 1 February at Yeovilton, commanded by Lt-Cdr H M Ellis DFC, DSC, RN.

No 1770 Squadron, embarked in HMS *Indefatigable*, was first in action when, in May, it undertook strikes against shore defences protecting the German battleship *Tirpitz* in its Norwegian fjord. By the end of 1944 three Firefly squadrons were fully operational, of which No 1772, equipped with new long-range fuel tanks in its aircraft, embarked for the Far East to fly strikes against the Japanese mainland.

Two variants of the basic Mark I had been developed and were now in production, the FR Mk I and the NF Mk I, whose prototypes are referred to above. The early night fighters featured large section fairings on the wing leading edges containing the aerials and associated equipment for the AI radar, but this was soon moved to an underslung pod beneath the nose, in the same manner as the ASH equipment of the FR Mk I. These two derivatives began delivery to the Fleet Air Arm early in 1944.

To train Firefly crews, No 766 Squadron at Inskip had received Firefly Is in October 1943, so that by the following

summer a steady flow of replacement crews was reaching the growing number of squadrons. By the end of the War against Japan, five Firefly squadrons were in the Pacific, with No 1790 on its way, and two others at home. Indeed the tempo of deliveries to newly-equipped squadrons accelerated in the twelve months following the War, and Firefly Is eventually equipped a total of 21 operational, and 47 second-line squadrons. 931 F, FR and NF Mk I Fireflies

were built, of which about 300 — previously in store for many months — were converted to trainers.

A new version, the FR Mk 4, powered by the 2,100hp Griffon 74 engine driving a four-blade Rotol propeller, began delivery to the Fleet Air Arm in July 1946, the first operational Squadron, No 825 with Canadian personnel serving aboard HMCS *Warrior*, receiving its first aircraft in August 1948. The Mark 4 differed externally from the

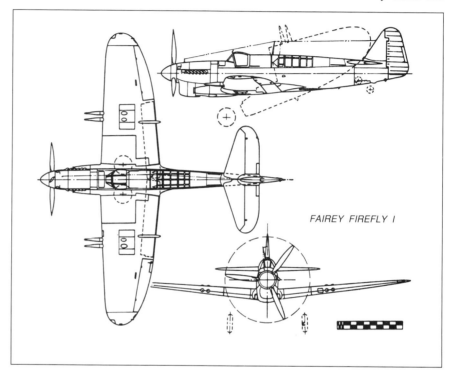

FAIREY FIREFLY I

Type: Single-engine, two-seat, low-wing monoplane naval reconnaissance and ground attack fighter.

Manufacturers: The Fairey Aviation Co Ltd, Stockport, Cheshire; General Aircraft Ltd.

Air Ministry Specification: N.5/40

Powerplant: Mk I. One 1,730hp Rolls-Royce Griffon IIB twelve-cylinder liquid-cooled supercharged in-line engine driving three-blade Rotol propeller; also 1,990hp Griffon XII. Mk IV (4). One 2,100hp Griffon 74 engine driving four-blade Rotol propeller.

Dimensions: Span, 44ft 6in (Mk 4, 41ft 2in); length, 27ft 7¼in (Mk 4, 27ft 11in); height, 14ft 4in; wing area, Mk 4, 330 sq ft.

Weights: Mk I. Tare, 9,460lb; all-up, 14,040lb. Mk 4: Tare, 9,674lb; all-up, 16,096lb.

Performance: Mk I. Max speed, 316 mph at 13,600ft. Mk 4. Max speed, 386 mph at 14,000ft; service ceiling, 28,400ft; max range, 1,300 miles.

Armament: Four 20mm Hispano Mk II or V cannon in wings, and provision to carry two 1,000lb bombs or up to eight three-inch rocket projectiles.

Prototypes: Mk I, four, Z1826-Z1829 (Z1826 first flown by C S Staniland on 22 December 1941); FR Mk I, Z1846; F Mk II, Z1831/G; NF Mk II, Z1875; F Mk III, Z1855; FR Mk IV, Z1835 and Z2118.

Production: Total, 1,703. Mk I, 931 (Fairey, 799: Batches between Z1830-Z2126, DT926-DV150, PP391-PP600 and TW677-TW679; General Aircraft, 132: between DK414-DK667); Mk 4, 120 (Fairey, batches between TW687-TW754 and VG957-VH144). 652 other versions built comprising AS Mk 5, 6 and 7, T Mk 7 and U Mk 8).

Summary of Service with Fleet Air Arm: Firefly F and FR Mk Is served with Nos 700, 703, 706, 719, 730, 731, 736, 737, 741, 744, 748, 759, 764, 766, 767, 768, 771, 772, 778, 780, 781, 782, 783, 787, 790, 795, 796, 798, 799, 805, 812, 814, 816, 822, 824, 825, 826, 827, 837, 860, 861, 1770, 1771, 1772, 1790, 1791, 1830 and 1841 Squadrons; Firefly NF Mk Is served with Nos 732, 746, 784, 792, 794, 805, 812, 816, 827, 1790, 1791 and 1792 Squadrons; Firefly NF Mk IIs served with Nos 746 and 772 Squadrons; Firefly FR Mk 4s served with Nos 703, 727, 736, 767, 778, 781, 782, 787, 799, 810, 812, 814, 816, 825 and 1840 Squadrons.

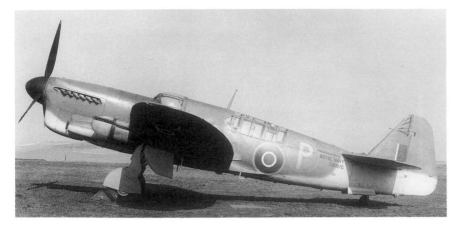

Left: *The second production Firefly Mk I, Z1831/G, modified as the prototype Mark II with large radome extending forward from the inner wing leading edge, pictured at Boscombe Down.* (Photo: Air Ministry RTP, Neg No 11324C, dated March 1943)

Below: *Preserved Firefly AS Mk 5, WB271, painted in Korean War colours and carrying the markings of No 812 Squadron, Fleet Air Arm, as embarked in HMS Glory in about August 1951. Note the square wingtips and enlarged fin. Aircraft of this type were employed on ground attack sorties.* (Photo: Author's Collection)

Mark I in featuring radiator and oil cooler in the inboard wing leading edge and slimmed nose cowling; the wings were square tipped and the fin area increased. The Mark 5, first delivered to No 812 Squadron in July 1948, was externally similar but carried different internal equipment. Later production examples of the Mark I and Mark 4 onwards featured mechanically-folding wings.

The other principal operational rôle performed by Fireflies was anti-submarine duty and would normally be outside the scope of this work, except that, in numerous instances, the aircraft (being cannon-armed, and capable of mounting rockets and bombs) were employed as ground attack fighters.

The involvement of the Royal Navy in the Korean War took Firefly AS and FR 5s into action, the aircraft of Nos 810 and 825 Squadrons aboard HMS *Ocean*, and those of No 812 in HMS *Glory*, flying many hundreds of strike sorties using guns, rockets and bombs.

Total Firefly production amounted to 1,703, of which 931 were Mark Is and 120 FR Mk 4s. The remainder were Mks 5, 6 and 7 anti-submarine aircraft, a few trainers and un-manned target aircraft.

The Firefly was a sound, reliable and fairly popular aeroplane, its drawback being that it always seemed to arrive in a war theatre when already obsolescent. There is no doubt that it was a big aeroplane to aspire to high performance on a single engine, and it might be said that it was the last in that tradition of naval fighters whose design was inevitably compromised by extravagant demands for maritime impedimenta.

Blackburn B-37 Firebrand

If the Fairey Firefly suffered serious delays before introduction into service, the frustrations that afflicted the Blackburn Firebrand were somewhat worse, so much so that although its original Specification was issued at much the same time as the Firefly's N.5/40, it did not reach an operational squadron until the penultimate day of the Second World War, and never fired its guns in anger.

In 1939, Specifications N.8/39 and N.9/39 called for two-seat naval fighters with, respectively, four fixed cannon and a four-gun turret. These were re-written the next year, following experience with the Roc and Defiant turret fighters, to re-appear as N.5/40, for which the Firefly was ordered, and N.8/40, now demanding a single-seater. This was again re-written as N.11/40

The first B-37 Firebrand prototype, DD804, with Napier Sabre III engine. Though fully navalised, the aircraft did not carry the four-cannon armament. Note the large radiator fairings on the wing leading edge. (Photo: A J Jackson Collection)

One of the small number of Firebrand TF Mk IIIs with Centaurus IX engine. DK411 was one of the aircraft delivered to the Fleet Air Arm for Squadron trials in the summer of 1945. (Photo: A J Jackson Collection).

and both Hawker and Blackburn tendered designs. The former was the Hawker P1009 proposal — a navalised version of the Typhoon, which was not accepted — and the latter was the Blackburn B-37, an entirely new design by G E Petty.

The B-37 was a low-wing monoplane of all-metal semi-monocoque construction, powered by the 2,305hp Napier Sabre III driving a three-blade DH variable-pitch propeller. The wings comprised an immensely strong two-spar centre section, into which the main undercarriage retracted inwards; the engine's radiators and oil cooler were enclosed in fairings forward of the wing root leading edge. Combined Fowler and subsidiary flaps occupied almost the entire trailing edge inboard of the Frise ailerons. The outer wings folded aft to reduced the aircraft's width to 13ft 6in for stowage, the four 20mm Hispano guns being located in these folding wing sections. The tail unit followed the configuration of Petty's Skua, the fin and rudder being set well forward to avoid blanking the elevator which, on early aircraft, was mass-balanced and inset.

Despite all the difficulties that beset the Napier Sabre in its early development stages, the Blackburn B-37 was accepted, and three prototypes were ordered, together with 50 production aircraft, the name Firebrand being allocated on 11 July 1941. The first, unarmed, prototype DD804 made its maiden flight on 27 February 1942, being delivered to Boscombe Down in June for performance assessment trials, which attracted minor criticism with regard to directional control at low speeds. The second, armed, prototype DD810 was flown in July, and the third, DD815, in May 1943.

In the meantime, however, the future of the Firebrand had been placed in doubt following a decision to allocate all available Sabre engines to the Hawker Typhoon. Moreover, the Seafire had been adopted as the main fighter equipment of the Fleet Air Arm; therefore much of the Firebrand's *raison d'être* had evaporated. Nevertheless, the Ministry of Aircraft Production and the Directorate of Technical Development, mindful of the Firebrand's considerable load-carrying potential, and aware that both RAF Coastal Command and the Fleet Air Arm were voicing support for the concept of high performance torpedo strike aircraft, instructed Blackburn to redesign the Firebrand as a carrier-borne torpedo-fighter.

Work was already well advanced on the first 23 production Sabre III-powered Firebrands, and the first nine (DK363-DK371) were therefore completed as F Mk I fighters, without torpedo-carrying provision; the next two airframes were set aside for development of a Bristol Centaurus-powered torpedo fighter (later to become prototypes of the Firebrand TF Mk III), and the remaining dozen aircraft were modified to carry the 1,850lb 18-inch torpedo, while retaining the Sabre III engine.

On 3 October 1943, Specification S.8/43 was issued around the Firebrand, redesigned to accommodate the 2,400hp Centaurus VII eighteen-cylinder sleeve-valve radial engine driving a four-blade Rotol propeller. This was far from straightforward for the Sabre installation had bestowed exceptionally slim fuselage contours; adaptation to

Above: *EK603 was the third Firebrand TF Mk IV, and was fitted with the enlarged fin with horn-balanced rudder. (Photo: Air Ministry RTP Neg No 13763B, dated May 1945).*

Right: *A Firebrand TF 5A at Brough in 1947, showing the wing spoilers outboard of the cannon, introduced to limit the speed during dive attacks. (Photo: Air Ministry, RTP Neg No. 16298B, dated October 1947)*

cater for the big radial therefore called for complete remodelling of the nose (without reducing the pilot's field of view while landing) and elimination of the wing root radiators — and all this entailed with respect to the aircraft's c.g. The Type Number B-45 was bestowed on the Firebrand TF Mk III, the first prototype, DK372 — referred to above — being first flown on 21 December 1943. This also featured a cut-down rear fuselage allowing a superimposed cockpit enclosure, later changed to a single-piece Perspex sliding tear-drop canopy which greatly improved the pilot's rearward field of view.

The first of 27 production Firebrand TF Mk IIIs, DK386, was flown by Sqn Ldr James Richard Tobin in November 1944. Most of the aircraft were allotted to experimental development, armament and handling trials, but the last eight were delivered to the Fleet Air Arm at Anthorn. Several of these were passed to No 778 Squadron (which had conducted Service trials with the third Mk I prototype, DD815) at Arbroath under the command of Lt-Cdr E M Britton, and the others to Nos 700, 703 and 708 Squadrons. All these Service aircraft were powered by Centaurus IXs with vibration dampers in the engine mountings.

Continued criticism of the Firebrand's poor directional control at low speed prompted Blackburn to design a much larger fin and rudder, and these featured in the Mark IV, of which 102 examples were ordered in 1944. This version also included provision to mount a pair of 2,000-pound bombs, or up to sixteen three-inch rocket projectiles under the wings as alternatives to the torpedo. To limit the speed to 350 mph in diving attacks, retractable spoilers were added to the upper and lower wing leading edge surfaces. The first Firebrand IVs to reach an operational Squadron were delivered to No 813, commanded by Lt-Cdr K Lee-White RN at Ford on 1 September 1945.

The final versions were the Firebrand TF Mk V and 5A, the former introducing horn-balanced elevator and lengthened aileron tabs, and the latter hydraulically-boosted aileron controls to improve the rate of roll. When heavily laden with full fuel and external weap-

ons, Firebrands were fitted with rocket-assisted take-off gear to enable them to operate from carrier decks (in the absence of catapults).

No 813 was the last operational Squadron to dispose of its Firebrands, doing so in August 1953, thereafter changing to Westland Wyvern S Mk 4s.

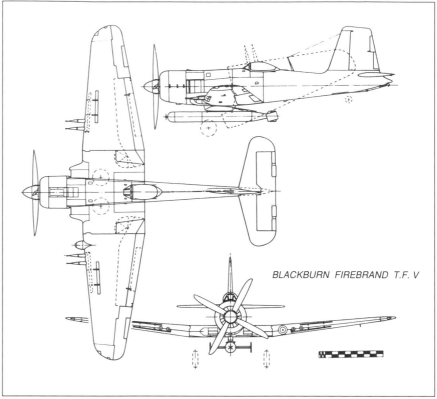

BLACKBURN FIREBRAND T.F. V

Type: Single-engine, single-seat, low-wing monoplane naval fighter and torpedo strike fighter.

Manufacturer: Blackburn Aircraft Co Ltd, Brough, East Yorkshire.

Air Ministry Specifications: N.11/40 for Mks I and II; S.8/43 for TF Mk III.

Powerplant: Mk I and II. One 2,305hp Napier Sabre III 24-cylinder sleeve-valve liquid-cooled in-line engine driving three-blade DH variable-pitch propeller. Mk III. One 2,400hp Bristol Centaurus VII eighteen-cylinder sleeve-valve air-cooled radial engine driving four-blade constant-speed Rotol propeller; also 2,520hp Centaurus IX. Mark IV, V and 5A. Centaurus IX; also Centaurus 57.

Dimensions: Span, 51ft 3½in (Mk I, 50ft 0in); span folded, 13ft 6in (Mk IV and V, 16ft 10in); length, 38ft 2in (Mk III, 37ft 7in; Mk IV and 5, 38ft 9in); wing area, 383 sq ft (Mk I, 369 sq ft).

Weights: Mk I. Tare, 11,100lb; all-up, 13,643lb. Mk V. Tare, 11,835lb; all-up, 17,500lb.

Performance: Mk I. Max speed, 353 mph; service ceiling, 32,500ft; range 805 miles. Mk V. Max speed, 340 mph; service ceiling, 28,500 ft; range 745 miles.

Armament: Mk I. Four 20mm Hispano cannon in wings with 800 rounds. Mk V. Four 20mm Hispano cannon and either one 1,850lb 18-inch torpedo, two 2,000lb bombs or up to sixteen 3-inch 60lb rocket projectiles.

Prototypes: Mk I, three, DD804, DD810 and DD815 (DD804 first flown 27 February 1942); Mk II, DD815 (rebuilt as NV636); Mk III, DK372 and DK373.

Summary of Production: Total, 220. Mk I, 9: DK363-DK371; Mk II, 12: DK374-DK385; Mk III, 27: DK386-DK412; Mk IV, 102: batches between EK601-EK470; Mk V and 5A, 70: batches between EK741-EK850. Some Mk IVs were converted to Mk Vs.

Summary of Service with Fleet Air Arm: Firebrand F.1 underwent Service trials with No 778 Squadron, February 1943; Firebrand TF Is underwent various trials with No 764 Squadron, September 1944; Firebrand TF II underwent trials with Nos 700, 703, 708 and 778 Squadrons from August 1945. Firebrand TF IVs served with Nos 703, 736, 738, 778 and 813 Squadrons. Firebrand TF V and 5As served with Nos 703, 759, 767, 787, 799, 813 and 827 Squadrons, and aboard HM Carriers *Illustrious*, *Implacable* and *Eagle*, 1947-53.

Supermarine Spitfire (Griffon versions)

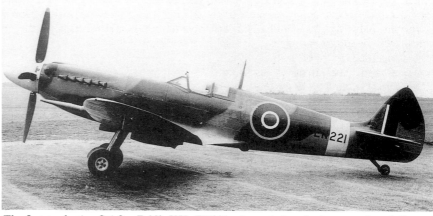

The first production Spitfire F Mk XII, EN221; the majority of subsequent aircraft featured clipped wings for low level interception of the Focke-Wulf Fw 190A over Southern England. (Photo: Vickers Armstrong, Neg No E948)

For some years thought to be impossible to mount in the Spitfire on account of its size, the Rolls-Royce Griffon was first intended to replace the Merlin XX, experimentally applied in the Spitfire III, N3295 (which eventually became the prototype Mark VIII). Instead, two new prototypes, DP845 and DP851, were built to Specification F.4/40 and provisionally termed Spitfire Mk IVs. By the time DP845 flew in 1941, however, this designation had been issued to cover a photo reconnaissance version, and the aircraft became the Mark XX, it being intended that the Griffon-powered Spitfires would carry mark numbers in the '20 range'.

Installation of the Griffon in the Spitfire was facilitated by the relocation of the camshaft and supercharger gear drives at the front of the engine, so that the overall engine length was not much different from that of the Merlin; the overall length of the aircraft was, nevertheless, increased by some two feet owing to the bigger spinner and the enlarged rudder to compensate. The greater depth of the engine resulted in fairings over the cylinder blocks breaking the outline of the upper nose contours — a feature that immediately identified the new Spitfires as being Griffon-powered. Another feature of the Griffon was the reversal of the propeller rotation and, such was the increase in torque on take-off, it was common practice to wind on full left rudder trim before opening the throttle to help counter the powerful tendency to swing to the right.

DP845, fitted in turn with Griffon IIB, IV and VI engines, ultimately became the prototype of the Spitfire F Mk XII, a version intended for low level operations with clipped wings and an armament of six 20mm cannon; however, DP845 only ever appeared with a mock-up of the six cannon armament.

When German Focke-Wulf Fw 190A fighter-bombers began their low level hit-and-run attacks over Southern

England in 1942, the Spitfire XII was quickly ordered into production as it was considered that the early single-stage supercharged Griffon engines would bestow their best performance at low altitude, while the airframe had been strengthened for ground attack operations. The first aircraft joined No 41 (Fighter) Squadron, commanded by Sqn Ldr T F Neil DFC*, AFC, at High Ercall in February 1943, moving to Hawkinge two months later. No 91 Squadron, under Sqn Ldr R R Harries DFC, received Spitfire XIIs in April, also at Hawkinge — shooting down five Fw 190s in a dogfight over the Channel on 25 May. Later both squadrons went over to the offensive, flying sweeps over Northern France once the enemy raids over the South Coast had diminished.

Thus far the Griffon had only been single-stage supercharged, but with the introduction of the Mark 61 engine, with two-stage supercharger, the Spitfire underwent a number of airframe modifications to cater for the increased engine length and power. While six standard Mark VIII airframes (JF316-JF321) were delivered to Rolls-Royce for trial installations of the Griffon 61,

driving the new Rotol five-blade propeller, and of the Griffon 85 driving Rotol contraprops, Joseph Smith's design staff at Supermarine was at work adapting the aircraft for the new engine, among the modifications required being a pair of enlarged radiator and oil cooler fairings under the wings, replacing the asymmetric fairings common to all previous Spitfires.

An order was received on 14 August 1943 to convert a further number of Spitfire VIIIs, already in production, to incorporate the 2,050hp Griffon 65 two-stage supercharged engine which, being equipped with an intercooler, required the nose of the aircraft to be further lengthened, in turn necessitating further enlarging of the fin and rudder.

The new version, the Spitfire F XIV, was first flown in 1943, and joined No 610 Squadron in December that year, the Squadron becoming involved in the defence against the German V 1 flying bombs which began falling in Southern England in June 1944. By the end of that year Spitfire XIVs equipped six squadrons, Nos 2, 41, 91, 130, 322 (Dutch) and 610; those flown by the first-named Squadron were a tactical reconnaissance

A Spitfire FR Mk XIV, MX259, displaying the large camera port in the side of the fuselage and the deep radiators, characteristic of Griffon Spitfires after the Mark XII. (Photo: A J Jackson Collection)

The second Castle Bromwich-built Spitfire F Mk 21, LA188, without armament fitted while on test at the RAE, Farnborough; the photograph illustrates the newly-introduced wing with broad-chord tips. (Photo: Royal Aerospace Establishment, Farnborough)

variant, the FR XIV with clipped wings, a rear fuselage fuel tank and an oblique camera mounted aft of the cockpit. Late production Mark XIVs featured cut-down rear fuselages with single-piece tear-drop cockpit canopy. The Mk XIVE possessed a 'universal armament wing' and was armed with a pair of 20mm cannon, two 0.50in machine guns and two 500lb bombs.

A total of 957 Spitfire XIVs was built, and eventually equipped 25 squadrons, some of which received their aircraft in the Far East. On the re-forming of the Royal Auxiliary Air Force in May 1946 the Spitfire XIV was temporarily selected as its standard day fighter, joining Nos 600, 602, 607, 610, 611, 612, 613 and 615 Squadrons. It was one of the fastest Allied fighters of the War, and was the first RAF fighter to destroy an enemy jet fighter in air combat (on 5 October 1944).

The Spitfire XVIII did not see squadron service during the War, but joined Nos 11 and 208 Squadrons in 1946. It was produced in fighter and reconnaissance fighter versions, and was the final variant to employ the classic Spitfire wing, originally evolved by Reginald Mitchell more than a dozen years before. The cut-down rear fuselage with tear-drop canopy was standard on all Mk XVIIIs, which ultimately equipped six peacetime fighter squadrons.

Joseph Smith's long-awaited strengthened wing, built up on six torsion boxes aft of the high-tensile steel spar booms

Type: Single-engine, single-seat, low-wing monoplane fighter, fighter-bomber and reconnaissance fighter.

Manufacturers: Supermarine Division of Vickers-Armstrong Ltd, Southampton, Swindon, Winchester and Castle Bromwich.

Air Ministry Specification: F.4/40 for Griffon Spitfire prototypes.

Powerplant: F Mk XII. One 1,735hp Rolls-Royce Griffon IIB, III and IV twelve-cylinder liquid-cooled single-stage supercharged in-line engine driving four-blade Rotol propeller. F Mk XVI. 2,050hp Griffon 65 two-stage supercharged engine driving five-blade Rotol propeller. F Mk XVIII. 2,050hp Griffon 65 or 2,340hp Griffon 67. F Mk 21, 22 and 24. 2,050hp Griffon 65 or Griffon 85 driving six-blade Rotol contraprop.

Dimensions: F Mk XIVE. Span, 36ft 10in; length, 31ft 10½in; height, 11ft 8¾in; wing area, 242 sq ft. F Mk 21. Span, 36ft 11in; length, 32ft 8in; height, 11ft 9¾in; wing area, 243.6 sq ft.

Weights: F Mk XIVE. Tare, 6,376lb; all-up, 8,475lb. F Mk 21. Tare, 6,923lb; all-up, 9,182lb.

Performance: F Mk XIVE. Max speed, 439 mph at 24,500ft; climb to 20,000ft, 7 min; service ceiling, 43,000ft; normal range, 465 miles. F Mk 21. Max speed, 450 mph at 19,000ft; climb to 20,000ft, 8 min; service ceiling, 43,000ft; normal range, 580 miles.

Armament: F Mk XIVE. Two 20mm Hispano Mk I cannon and two 0.50in Browning machine guns in wings. F Mk 21. Four 20mm Hispano Mk 5 cannon.

Prototypes: Mk XII, DP845; Mk XIV, JF316-JF321 (converted Mk VIIIs); F 21, JF319 (converted F XIV); F 22, PK312.

Production: (Griffon-powered fighters). Total, 1,836. Mk XII, 100; Mk XIV, 957; Mk XVIII, 300; Mk 21, 120; Mk 22, 278; Mk 24, 81.

Summary of Service: Spitfire F Mk XIIs served with Nos 41, 91 and 595 Squadrons; Spitfire F Mk XIVs (14s) served with Nos 2, 11, 16, 17, 20, 26, 28, 41, 91, 130, 132, 136, 152, 268, 273, 322, 350, 600, 602, 607, 610, 611, 612, 613 and 615 Squadrons; Spitfire F Mk XVIIIs (18s) served with Nos 11, 28, 32, 60, 81 and 208 Squadrons; Spitfire F Mk 21s served with Nos 1, 41, 91, 122, 595, 600, 602 and 615 Squadrons; Spitfire F Mk 22s served with Nos 73, 502, 504, 600, 602, 603, 607, 608, 610, 611, 613, 614 and 615 Squadrons; Spitfire F Mk 24s served with No 80 Squadron.

and with metal-covered ailerons, appeared on the Spitfire F Mk 21. The wing itself was of modified elliptical planform, and of fractionally greater span, the tips being of broader chord than hitherto. The undercarriage was strengthened to cater for the greater all-up weight and to allow for the provision of 18-gallon fuel tanks in the wing

leading edges inboard of the guns. Production aircraft were preceded by a modified Mark XIV, JF319. Standard powerplant was the Griffon 61 driving a five-blade Rotol propeller, although a few aircraft had Griffon 85 engines driving Rotol contraprops.

Spitfire F 21s entered service with No 91 Squadron in April 1945 at Ludham, commanded by Sqn Ldr I J P Marshall, and went on to equip six further fighter squadrons during the next two years.

A total of 120 Spitfire F 21s were followed by 278 F 22s with cut-down rear fuselage and tear-drop canopy, while the ultimate Spitfire was the F Mk 24 which incorporated two 33-gallon fuel tanks in the rear fuselage, Hispano Mk 5 cannon, provision to fit zero-length rocket launchers under the wings, and an entirely new, enlarged elliptical fin and rudder (as fitted on the Spiteful, see page 322). Production amounted to only 81 Mark 24s, and they equipped but one Squadron, No 80, being delivered to Germany in January 1948.

The last Spitfire F 24, VN496, left the South Marston factory on 20 February 1948, bringing the total Spitfire production to 20,351 in little over ten years.

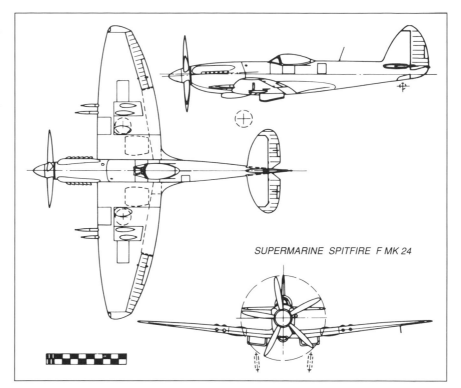

SUPERMARINE SPITFIRE F MK 24

The greater part of the Spitfire's final period of service was with the Royal Auxiliary Air Force. PK596/RAT-L was an F Mk 22 which served with No 613 (City of Manchester) Squadron, flying from Ringway in the late 1940s before the Squadron converted to Vampires in 1951. (Photo: Leslie Hunt)

Supermarine Seafire

Just as the *Luftwaffe* had failed to undertake development of aircraft designed to attack naval vessels at sea prior to the Second World War, so the Fleet Air Arm's very limited fighter interception capabilities were considered to be adequate so long as Germany remained without aircraft carriers and her aircraft were confined to bases within her own frontiers. After the German invasion of Norway and France, and Italy's entry into the War, the problem of sea defence and protection of shipping became acute for the Fleet Air Arm, and it has been explained how the hurried development of the Sea Hurricane, both as a catapult and a deck-operating interceptor fighter, went far towards blunting enemy air attacks on ships at sea. When it also became clear that the War would likely be won by the Allies only after largescale amphibious landings had been made on continental Europe and elsewhere was it clear that aircraft, such as the Hurricane, would be wholly outclassed by enemy land-based fighters.

The Sea Hurricane, however, during 1941-42 possessed a performance adequate to meet the threat of unescorted bombers, without necessarily possessing the armament with which to destroy them, and it was the ready availability of redundant Hurricanes that recommended their use as makeshift naval fighters in the first place. In 1942 the Spitfire followed suit, although the conversion process was more complex.

Like the Hurricane, the Spitfire came in for abortive experimental development as a twin-float seaplane fighter in 1940, although in this instance the proposal was revived in 1942 with the completion of a small number of float-equipped Spitfire VBs and a Mark IX. By the following year interest in the

Left: *A late Westland-built Seafire F XV, SW847, shown carrying a 50-gallon ventral drop tank; note the 'sting-type' arrester hook whose fairing merges into the lower curve of the rudder.* (Photo: Vickers-Armstrong Ltd, Neg No E2807)

Below: *A Westland-built Seafire F XVII of No 800 Squadron from HMS Triumph fitted with the special underwing long-range fuel tanks; note also the extended 'sting-type' arrester hook below the rudder.* (Photo: Peter Cook)

project had completely vanished.

The first naval Spitfire deliveries to the Fleet Air Arm were made for training purposes and comprised a number of 'hooked' Spitfires, of which the first example was a converted Spitfire VB, AB205, first flown on 7 January 1942. A total of 60 Naval Spitfire conversions was undertaken (not all with arrester hooks), and these were officially 'loaned' to the Royal Navy, and all but one (a Spitfire VIII) involved former Spitfire VBs.

Fully navalized Seafires (with naval radio, arrester hook, slinging points and nose ballast to correct the c.g.) were produced by conversion of Spitfire VBs by Air Service Training Ltd of Hamble, beginning in February 1942 with Spitfire BL676. Designated Seafire Mk IBs, a total of 166 such aircraft underwent conversion by AST and at Supermarine's South Marston factory, delivery of these continuing until July 1943. They eventually equipped a total of sixteen training squadrons and, for training purposes, ten operational squadrons of the Fleet Air Arm. Initial deck landing trials were performed by BL676 aboard HMS *Illustrious* in May 1942.

The next version, the Seafire Mk IIC, was produced by converting Spitfire VCs but in addition to the modifications included in the Mk IB was the inclusion of catapult spools, and strengthened

fuselage and undercarriage. A prototype, AD371, was followed by 372 further conversions. All retained their tropical filters and were therefore some 25 mph slower than the Seafire IBs. Deliveries to operational squadrons began in September 1942 as No 885 Squadron, commanded by Lt-Cdr Rodney Harold Power Carver DSC, RN, received its aircraft at Machrihanish and embarked in HMS *Formidable* the following month. In November the Seafires were in action when they provided cover for the North African landings. However, most Seafire IIC deliveries were made in 1943.

After a total of 538 Seafire IB and IIC conversions had been set in train (all of them receiving new serial numbers, a matter that has in the past led to confusion when arriving at the total

Spitfire/Seafire production figures), the next Seafires were newly built. A total of 1,250 Seafire IIIs was to be produced by Westland Aircraft Ltd and Cunliffe Owen Aircraft Ltd.

The Supermarine Type 358 Seafire III had no direct RAF counterpart, being powered by a Merlin 55 (or 55M, with cropped supercharger impeller) with automatic boost control and driving a four-blade propeller. It was moreover equipped with folding wings, following a trial installation on the first completed Seafire IIC, MA270, in November 1942. Wing folding was manual, requiring a team of five men, the wings being folded upwards and the tip outwards so as to limit the folded aircraft height. The majority of aircraft were designated LF Mk IIIs with the Merlin 55M engine rated to deliver 1,585hp at below 3,000 feet, and Cunliffe Owen produced 129 examples, termed FR Mk III, equipped with a pair of F24 cameras.

First deliveries of the Mark III were made on 27 November 1943 to No 894

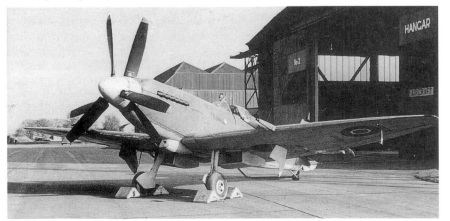

An unidentified Seafire F 45 with Griffon 85 driving six-blade Rotol contraprops; one of the great benefits of these propellers was the relative lack of torque during take-off and landing, much appreciated during carrier operations. (Photo: via R C Sturtivant)

Squadron at Henstridge, commanded by Lt-Cdr F R A Turnbull DSC, RN, and embarked with No 887 Squadron (also with Seafire IIIs) in HMS *Indefatigable* the following May to provide cover for air attacks on the German battleship *Tirpitz* in Norway. Seafire IIIs were also equipped to carry ground attack stores which included either a single 500lb bomb under the fuselage or a pair of 250-pounders under the wings, underwing rockets, drop tanks or 250lb depth charges.

Rolls-Royce Griffon-powered Seafires began with the F Mk XV, of which six prototypes were ordered, followed by 384 production aircraft (again built by Westland and Cunliffe Owen). Designed to Specification N.4/43, the Mark XV was powered by the 1,750hp Griffon VI driving a four-blade Rotol propeller. Although a few early aircraft retained the earlier A-frame arrester hook under the rear fuselage, a new 'sting-type' hook, hinged to the base of the fuselage stern post, was introduced and featured on all subsequent Seafires. Lake the RAF's Griffon Spitfires, the Seafire XV also incorporated the increased rudder area, as well as introducing a retractable tailwheel.

With a top speed of 392 mph, the Seafire XV was too late to see combat service during the War, and, owing to problems of positively engaging the supercharger clutch during take-off, did not embark in carriers with Squadrons until the trouble was cured in 1947, Just before production of this version ended, some aircraft were produced with the cut-down rear fuselage with tear-drop sliding cockpit canopy.

The latter improvement was standardized in the next Seafire, the F.XVII, whose prototype was one of the Mk XV prototypes modified, NS493.

The most important modification that characterized the Mk XVII was the introduction of a 24-volt electrical system in place of the traditional 12-volt installation, as well as an undercarriage with increased travel to withstand high sink rate during deck landing. Seafire XVIIs first joined Nos 809 and 887 Squadrons at Nutts Corner in November 1945.

The last three Seafire versions, the F 45, 46 and 47, were equivalent in most respects to the RAF's Spitfire F 21, 22 and 24, and were produced to Specification N.7/44, incorporating Joseph Smith's strengthened wing. Powered by the Griffon 61, the Seafire 45 had a

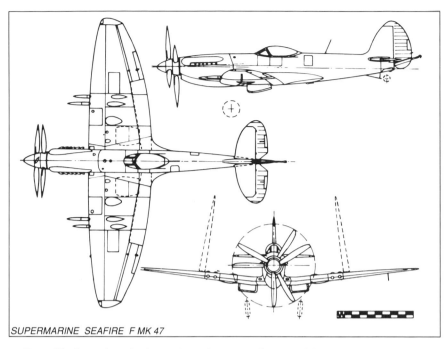

SUPERMARINE SEAFIRE F MK 47

Type: Single-engine, single-seat low-wing monoplane naval interceptor fighter.

Manufacturers: Supermarine Division of Vickers-Armstrongs Ltd, South Marston, Wiltshire; Westland Aircraft Ltd, Yeovil, Somerset; Cunliffe Owen Aircraft Ltd, Eastleigh.

Air Ministry Specification: N.4/43 for Seafire XV/XVII; N.7/44 for Seafire F45/46/47.

Powerplant: F IB and F IIC. 1,440hp Rolls-Royce Merlin 45 driving three-blade propeller; F III. 1,470hp Mcrlin 55 or 1,585hp Merlin 55M driving four-blade propeller; F XV and XVII. 1,750hp Rolls-Royce Griffon VI driving four-blade Rotol propeller; F 45. 2,050hp Griffon 61 or 65 driving five-blade Rotol propeller; F 46 and 47. 2,340hp Griffon 85, 87 or 88 driving five-blade or six-blade contraprops.

Dimensions: F III. Span, 36ft 10in; length, 30ft 2½in; height, 11ft 5½in; wing area, 242 sq ft. F.47. Span, 36ft 11in; length, 34ft 6in; height, 12ft 6in; wing area, 243.6 sq ft.

Weights: F III. Tare, 5,317lb; all-up, 7,232lb. F 47. Tare, 7,625lb; all-up, 10,200lb.

Performance: F III. Max speed, 359 mph at 25,000ft; climb to 20,000ft, 8 min 5 sec; service ceiling, 36,000ft; normal range, 465 miles. F 47. Max speed, 452 mph at 20,500ft; climb to 20,000ft, 4 min 50 sec; service ceiling, 43,100ft; normal range, 405 miles.

Armament: F III. Two 20mm Hispano Mk II cannon and four 0.303in Browning machine guns, and provision to carry up to 500lb of bombs or four three-inch rocket projectiles. F 47. Four 20mm Hispano Mk 5 cannon and up to 1,000lb of bombs.

Prototypes: One 'hooked Spitfire' prototype, AB205; one Seafire IB, BL676; one Seafire IIC, AD371; six Seafire XVs, NS487, NS490, NS493, PK240, PK 243 and PK245; one Seafire XVII, NS493 (Mk XV converted); one Seafire 45, TM379; one Seafire 47, TM383.

Production: 60 converted 'Naval Spitfires'; 166 converted Seafire IB (between MB328-MB375 and NX879-PA129); 372 converted Seafire IIV (between MA970-MB327, LR631-LR764 and EN686-EN759). Newly built: 1,250 Seafire III (between LR765-LR881, NF418-NF665, NM984-NN330, NN333-NN641, PP921-PR334, PX913-PX962, RX156-RX353 and SP136-SP197); 390 Seafire XV (between PR338-PR506, SR446-SR645 and SW781-SW921); 233 Seafire XVII (between SP323-SP355 and SW781-SX389); 51 Seafire 45 (between LA428-LA499); 24 Seafire 46 (LA541-LA564); 92 Seafire 47 (PS944-PS957, between VP427-VP495 and VR961-VR972).

Summary of Service: Seafire IBs served with Nos 700, 708, 715, 719, 731, 736, 748, 759, 761, 768, 778, 779, 781, 787, 790, 798, 801, 807, 809, 816, 842, 879, 885, 887, 894 and 897 Squadrons; Seafire IICs served with Nos 700, 708, 718, 719, 728, 731, 748, 757, 761, 768, 770, 775, 776, 778, 787, 790, 794, 798, 799, 801, 833, 834, 842, 879, 880, 884, 885, 886, 887, 889, 894, 895, 897 and 899 Squadrons; Seafire IIIs served with 700, 706, 708, 709, 715, 718, 721, 728, 733, 736, 740, 744, 748, 757, 759, 760, 761, 766, 767, 768, 771, 772, 778, 781, 782, 787, 790, 794, 799, 801, 802, 803, 805, 806, 807, 808, 809, 879, 880, 883, 885, 886, 887, 889, 894, 899 and 1832 Squadrons; Seafire XVs served with Nos 700, 701, 706, 709, 715, 718, 721, 728, 733, 736, 737, 751, 759, 761, 766, 767, 768, 771, 773, 777, 778, 780, 781, 787, 790, 791, 799, 800, 801, 802, 803, 804, 805, 806, 809, 883, 1831, 1832 and 1833 Squadrons; Seafire XVIIs served with Nos 701, 703, 727, 728, 736, 746, 759, 761, 764, 766, 778, 781, 782, 787, 799, 800, 805, 807, 809, 879, 1830, 1831, 1832 and 1833 Squadrons; Seafire 45s served with Nos 700, 703, 709, 771, 777, 778, 780 and 787 Squadrons; Seafire 46s served with Nos 736, 738, 767, 771, 777, 778, 781, 787 and 1832 Squadrons; and Seafire 47s served with Nos 759, 777, 778, 800, 804 and 1833 Squadrons.

maximum speed of 442 mph — some 50 mph faster than the Mk XV — and, during diving trials, recorded a speed of Mach 0.88. Relatively few examples featured the cut-down rear fuselage, but at least three were powered by the Griffon 85 engine driving Rotol contra-props. Sea trials were performed by five F 45s aboard HMS *Pretoria Castle*, and the fighter joined eight second-line units, beginning with No 703 Squadron, which was the naval component of the Air-Sea Warfare Development Unit, in December 1945, commanded by Lt-Cdr J H Dundas DSC.

The Seafire F 46 standardized the cut-down rear fuselage and featured the improved elliptical fin and rudder of the final Spitfires. Griffon 87 (with contra-prop) and 88 engines were also standard. The Seafire F 47 introduced a new wing fold-line, this being located outboard of the four Hispano Mk 5 cannon; by shortening the length of wing that folded, there was no need for the former tip fold. The majority of the 92 F 47s built featured contraprops, and extensive trials were flown to clear the carriage of exter-nal stores so that the aircraft was even-tually cleared for combat flying with a ventral 90-gallon drop tank, two under-wing 500-lb bombs and wing slipper tanks.

Seafire F 47s were still serving with No 800 Squadron aboard HMS *Triumph* when, late in 1949, the carrier was ordered to the Far East, and the aircraft flew strikes against terrorist forces in the jungle. The squadron also operated in Korean waters during the first six months of that war, before returning to Britain to disband in November 1950.

Martin-Baker M.B.3

Said to have been taken on the occasion of the M.B.3's first flight on 31 August 1942, this photograph shows well the very wide-track undercarriage and the exceptionally clean engine cowling lines. (Photo: Martin-Baker Aircraft Co Ltd, Neg No 27804)

After the failure of Specification F.5/34 to bring forth any interceptor that would represent a worthwhile advance on the Hurricane and Spitfire eight-gun fight-ers, and with the future of aircraft such as the Hawker Tornado and Typhoon still in the balance, the Air Ministry issued Specification F.18/39, calling for a single-seat fighter capable of a top speed of not less than 400 mph at 15,000 feet, and with an armament of two 20mm cannon or eight machine-guns. With a world war seeming inevitable at the time the Specification was being drafted, emphasis was placed on the fighter's ability to operate anywhere in the world, and be capable of being turned round very rapidly between sorties, thereby spotlighting ease of accessibility to engine, guns and systems (fuel, oil, hydraulics, electrics, pneu-matics, oxygen, etc.)

Attracted by the challenge, particu-larly with regard to high speed and the ease of servicing, James Martin set about the design of another extraordinary fighter, powered by the yet-untried Napier Sabre engine. Emphasis was laid on simplicity and compactness, the steel tubular structure being extensively covered by detachable metal panels. The low-set, low aspect ratio wings housed no fewer than six 20mm Hispano Mk II cannon with 200 rounds per gun, and an inwards-retracting undercarriage of very wide track.

Renouncing the need for a large 'chin' radiator (as on the Hawker Typhoon), Martin achieved remarkably slim nose contours by moving the coolant and oil radiators to the undersides of the wings, adopting a very long, low-profile radia-tor for the engine coolant on the star-board side.

Before completion, the prototype M.B.3, R2492, was fitted with the six cannon, but these were removed before flight trials started. The aircraft was first flown by Capt Valentine Henry Baker at Wing, Buckinghamshire, on 31 August 1942, and at once confirmed an out-standing performance, returning a maximum speed of 415 mph at 20,000 feet while carrying ballast in lieu of guns and ammunition. According to surviv-ing records, the M.B.3 handled well, displaying a high rate of roll as well as

Possessing lines almost suggestive of a racing aircraft, the M.B.3 was provided with numer-ous detachable panels for access to the aircraft systems and structure, the fuselage capable of being stripped of its covering from engine to sternpost. (Photo: Martin-Baker Aircraft Co Ltd, Neg No 27806)

crisp controls. The landing speed was on the high side, the aircraft touching down at around 88 mph with full flap, but directional control was perfectly adequate at low speeds.

Disaster struck on 12 September when the Sabre II engine failed in the air, and R2492 struck a haystack as Capt Baker attempted to force land and was destroyed, killing the pilot. For such a small company as Martin-Baker Ltd, this was an enormous blow, not least to James Martin, a friend of long standing of Capt Baker, and further development of the M.B.3 was halted forthwith.

Another fighter, the M.B.4 (in effect an aircraft similar to the M.B.3 but powered by a Rolls-Royce Griffon) was, at the time of the M.B.3's loss, under consideration, and a photograph, taken in the factory as the M.B.3 neared completion, shows a second aircraft partly completed, and it has been suggested that this was possibly the M.B.4, although this has not been confirmed. In any case, James Martin now turned his attention to another, even more advanced design essay but this, the M.B.5, was still eighteen months away.

It has also been stated that the M.B.3 had been modified with a cut-down rear fuselage and fitted with a single-piece tear-drop cockpit canopy when it crashed. This is incorrect as clearly no time existed between the date of R2492's first flight and that of its loss for such a major

alteration to the airframe to be made. Indeed the photographs purporting to show the tear-drop canopy *in situ* are all known to have been 'doctored'. That

such a change was clearly intended is confirmed on surviving design drawings which include the cut-down rear fuselage and new canopy.

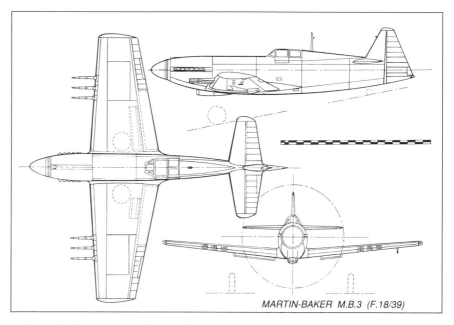

MARTIN-BAKER M.B.3 (F.18/39)

Type: Single-engine, single-seat, low-wing monoplane interceptor.
Manufacturer: Martin-Baker Aircraft Co Ltd, Higher Denham, Middlesex.
Air Ministry Specification: F.18/39.
Powerplant: One 2,020hp Napier Sabre II twenty-four cylinder liqiuid-cooled in-line engine driving three-blade de Havilland propeller.
Dimensions: Span, 35ft 0in; length, 35ft 4in.
Weight: All-up, 11,497lb.
Performance: Max speed, 415 mph at 20,000ft; service ceiling, 37,500ft; range, approx 420 miles.
Armament: Six 20mm Hispano Mk II cannon with 200 rounds per gun in the wings.
Prototype: One, R2492 (first flown by Capt V H Baker on 31 August 1942). No production.

Hawker Tempest

From the early days of the Typhoon's design Sydney Camm had been aware that the aircraft's high altitude performance would be compromised by its very thick wing (a thickness/chord ratio of about 18 per cent), a relic of an original intention to make provision for an armament of six cannon. In 1940, therefore, his project staff evolved a new wing with a root t/c ratio of 14.5, decreasing to 10 at the tip; by adopting an elliptical

planform , the wing was also considerably thinner at semi-span.

In March 1941 Camm put forward a proposal to the DTD for a new fighter

employing this wing, together with a developed version of the Sabre engine, then known as the Napier EC.107C, which was expected to produce about

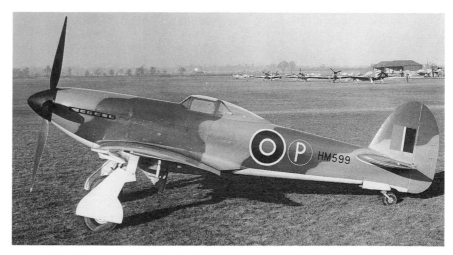

The prototype Tempest Mk I, HM599, fastest of all versions, showing the retention of the Typhoon's cockpit canopy, 'car-type' door and tail unit. (Photo: Author's Collection)

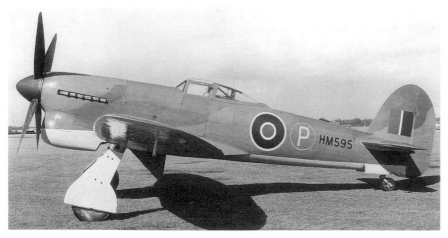

The Tempest V prototype, HM595, showing the longer nose, and the Typhoon-style fin and rudder originally fitted. This version became one of the RAF's outstanding fighters of the Second World War. (Photo: Air Ministry, RTP Neg No 10,983C, dated September 1942).

2,400hp. Specification F.10/41 was raised, calling for a maximum speed of 430 mph at 20,000 feet and an armament of four 20mm Hispano cannon. Two prototypes (HM595 and HM599), referred to initially as Typhoon IIs, were ordered. When Camm pointed to the ridiculous situation that had arisen after the crash of the first Typhoon, leaving no prototype available on which to continue development, the order was increased by a further four prototypes (LA602, LA607, LA610 and LA614). The name was also changed to Tempest.

Camm had also proposed discarding the chin radiator of the Typhoon, changing instead to wing root radiators, and the DTD suggested that HM595 should retain the chin-type, and mount the wing root type on HM599. Design figures suggested that the Tempest with the new radiators would possess a speed of around 450 mph at 22,000 feet and, on the strength of this, 400 production aircraft were ordered, to be known as the Tempest F Mk I and powered by the new Sabre IV engine.

Delays with the first Sabre IV prompted Hawker to go ahead with the 'conventional' Tempest prototype, if only to confirm the benefits of the new wing, and HM595 was first flown by Philip Lucas at Langley on 2 September

1942. Powered by a standard Sabre II, in a slightly lengthened nose, driving a four-blade de Havilland Hydromatic propeller, the aircraft returned a maximum speed of 430 mph at 20,300 feet on 2 October. HM595 was termed the Tempest Mk V, the Mark II being proposed as being powered by a Bristol Centaurus (see page 315), and the Marks III and IV by the Rolls-Royce Griffon; the last two projects did not come to fruition.

The lengthened nose of the Tempest V prototype, resulting from the insertion of a new fuel tank forward of the cockpit, gave rise to directional control problems, which were soon resolved by introducing an enlarged fin. This was not found necessary when Lucas first flew the Tempest I HM599 on 24 February 1943, owing to the absence of the chin radiator. When Bill Humble carried out the initial performance checks with HM599 on 4 June that year, he recorded a maximum speed of 460 mph TAS at 24,000 feet and, after fitting a thinner tailplane, this was increased to 472 mph in September. Unfortunately difficulty was being experienced in achieving adequate reliability with the Sabre IV, and this engine never succeeded in reaching the 50-hour standard.

Thus, with a pressing demand for a fighter with a speed of 430 mph being expressed by the RAF in 1943 — with which to match German fighters, such as the Messerschmitt Bf 109G, above 20,000 feet — the MAP changed the order for 400 Tempest Is to a similar number of Tempest Vs. (The first 300 Tempest Is were already beginning production, and it was deemed simpler to start Tempest V production from scratch; this accounts for aircraft with JN serial numbers being completed before those with EJ, for the latter had to be altered to Mk V wing jigs.)

The first production Tempest V, JN729, was flown by Humble on 21 June 1943 (by which time the prototype had been flown with a Sabre IV with chin radiator and had achieved a speed of 459 mph at 24,900 feet, fully loaded). Production tests on early Tempest F Mk Vs at Boscombe Down confirmed a maximum speed at full load of 434 mph at 22,800 feet, and a climb to 20,000 feet in 6 minutes 36 seconds. By the end of the year eighteen Tempest Vs had been delivered to the RAF, exactly meeting the terms of the contract.

The first Squadron to receive Tempest Vs was No 486 (New Zealand) Squadron, commanded by the 25-year-old Sqn Ldr James Henry Iremonger DFC, at Beaulieu in Hampshire in January 1944 but, owing to the pressing need to keep up attacks with the Squadron's Typhoons on German flying bomb sites, being built along the French coast, there was no time to train on the Tempests, with the result that the new aircraft were handed over to No 3 Squadron (Sqn Ldr A S Dredge DFC) at Manston in February. (No 486 Squadron eventually converted to Tempests in March).

The Tempest V was introduced into service primarily as a fighter, intended to keep the skies clear over the ground

An early production Tempest V Series 1 with the long-barrelled Hispano Mk I cannon and the extended dorsal fin. The aircraft shown carries the code letters of No 486 (New Zealand) Squadron, the first to receive Tempest Vs in January 1944. (Photo: Sydney Camm Collection).

The first prototype Tempest II, LA602, at Brooklands with finely cowled Centaurus IV engine. While this photograph illustrates the Typhoon-style tail still fitted, the aircraft features the later, single-piece sliding canopy. Note the grouped exhaust pipes on the side of the fuselage. (Photo: Author's Collection)

forces when the long-awaited invasion of Europe was launched. And to this end the first Tempest Wing, No 150, began formation under the command of Wg Cdr Roland Prosper Beamont DSO, DFC* (who had previously been seconded to Hawker Aircraft as a test pilot during the Tempest's development). However, in anticipation of the flying bomb assault on Southern England, the three Squadrons of this Wing (Nos 3, 56 and 486) moved to Newchurch in April and May. Not only were the Tempests of the Newchurch Wing to become the cornerstone of the fighter defences during the flying bomb attacks (destroying some 638 of the weapons), but went over to the offensive with sweeps over France and the Low Countries.

By the end of 1944 seven Tempest squadrons had converted to the new fighters (Nos 3, 33, 56, 80, 222, 274 and 486), many of the aircraft now carrying wing drop tanks to enable them to penetrate deep into Germany from their new bases in the Netherlands and Belgium with the 2nd Tactical Air Force. With their speed of around 450 mph and armed with four Hispano cannon, they were the fastest and hardest-hitting Allied fighters in the field, and began to take a toll of German Messerschmitt Me 262 jet fighters (the first falling to Plt Off R W Cole of No 3 Squadron), and by the end of hostilities had destroyed about 20 of these aircraft.

Tempest Vs continued to serve until December 1948 when No 16 Squadron at Wunstorf in Germany gave up its aircraft in favour of Vampire Vs.

Tempest II and VI

It will be recalled that the Bristol Centaurus had originally been proposed as an alternative powerplant for the Tempest when additional prototypes were allocated, and accordingly LA602 and LA607 were set aside for this engine. This proposal had been made by Camm's staff as a result of experience being gained in 1942 with the Centaurus Tornado (see page 287), rather than for any liking of radial engines in fighters by

the great designer himself; and certainly British designers were slower than their German counterparts in arriving at a truly efficient installation in a single-engine fighter. By the time work went ahead with the prototype Tempest LA602 early in 1943, a captured Focke-Wulf Fw 190 had been thoroughly examined, and the Hawker installation was similar in many respects, not least in the exhaust system.

LA602 was first flown by Philip Lucas at Brooklands on 28 June 1943, powered by a 2,400hp Centaurus IV sleeve-valve radial engine, and within a couple of months was returning a maximum speed of 432 mph. More significant was its rate of roll at 88 degrees per second (compared with 54 degrees by

the Typhoon and 66 by the Spitfire IX). The same difficulties with directional control as on the Tempest V were experienced, and the enlarged fin was fitted to the production Mark II which, powered by the Centaurus V, achieved a maximum speed of 448 mph TAS at 19,100 feet.

Owing to heavy Hurricane and Tempest V production commitments at Langley, all production of Tempest IIs was intended to be undertaken by the Bristol Aeroplane Company's shadow factory at Old Mixon, Weston-super-Mare, and a production line was established there during 1944 but, when Hurricane production ran out in September that year, Hawker also made preparations to build the Tempest II. In

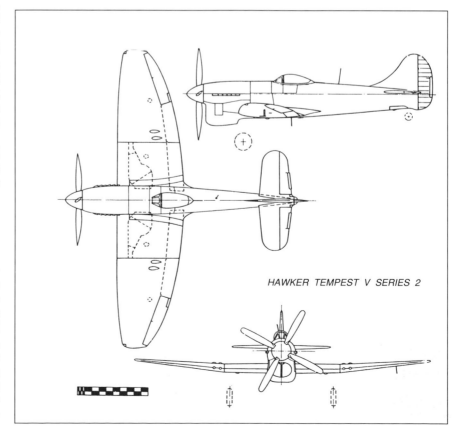

HAWKER TEMPEST V SERIES 2

due course, orders totalling 1,530 aircraft were placed with the two companies.

However, with the sudden ending of the Pacific War, the orders were cut back severely, Bristol only completing 50 aircraft, and Hawkers 402. The first 150 Tempest F IIs were built as pure fighters, simply mounting the customary four Hispano guns, but the remaining aircraft were cleared at a maximum all-up weight of 13,900 pounds, enabling them to carry up to sixteen three-inch rocket projectiles, two 1,000lb bombs or two 90 gallon drop tanks as the FB Mk II.

Powered by 2,520hp Centaurus V engines, production Tempest F IIs were just starting delivery to the RAF when the Pacific War ended in September 1945. It had been planned to send a Tempest Wing to the Far East (under the command of Wg Cdr R P Beamont), but this plan was now abandoned. Instead, three home-based Squadrons were re-equipped, beginning with No 183, commanded by Sqn Ldr J R Cullen DFC at Chilbolton, followed by Nos 54 and 247 Squadrons.

Problems with the Centaurus engines dogged the early Tempest IIs, but improvements in their lubrication brought about better serviceability, and during 1946 Nos 16 and 33 Squadrons in Germany were issued with fighter-bomber Mark IIs, while in India Nos 5, 20, 30 and 152 also re-equipped with FB IIs. Those based in India were brought to operational status during the period of communal unrest during the British withdrawal from the sub-continent the following year. The last Tempest IIs with an operational squadron were those of No 33 which had moved to Malaya in 1949, where they flew ground attack operations against the Communist guerrilla forces during the Emergency. No 33 Squadron exchanged its Tempests for de Havilland Hornets in June 1951.

A total of 114 RAF-surplus Tempest F and FB IIs was supplied to the air forces of India and Pakistan between 1947 and 1951.

The Tempest F Mk VI was a Sabre V-powered version of the Mark V, but was specifically developed for deployment in the Middle East immediately after the War. A tropicalized and enlarged radiator occupied the chin position, while the oil coolers were moved to the wing roots. Aileron spring tabs were fitted, and a change made to the Rotol four-blade propeller.

The original Tempest V prototype, HM595, was modified to Mark VI standard and first flown by Humble in this form on 9 May 1944, and production examples were flying before the end of the following year. The production order with Hawker was for 300 aircraft, but this was later reduced to 142. Performance trials at Boscombe Down revealed a maximum speed of 462 mph at 19,800 feet, and exhaustive trials were flown to clear the carriage of a wide range of ground attack stores.

Owing to the gradual run-down of the RAF's deployment in the Middle East that followed the end of the War, it was not until December 1946 that the first Squadron received its Tempest VIs, No 249 Squadron, commanded by Sqn Ldr C K Gray DFC, at Habbaniya in Iraq being followed the same month by No 6 Squadron at Nicosia in Cyprus.

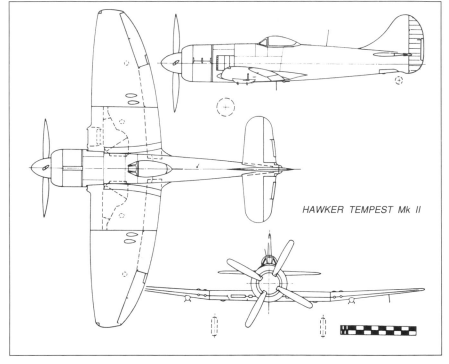

HAWKER TEMPEST Mk II

Type: Single-engine, single-seat low-wing monoplane interceptor and ground attack fighter.

Manufacturers: Hawker Aircraft Ltd, Langley, Buckinghamshire (Mks I, II, V and VI); The Bristol Aeroplane Co Ltd, Old Mixon, Weston-super-Mare, Somerset.

Air Ministry Specification: F.10/41.

Powerplant: Mk I. One 2,350hp Napier Sabre IV twenty-four cylinder sleeve-valve liquid-cooled in-line engine driving four-blade DH Hydromatic propeller. Mk II. 2,520hp Bristol Centaurus V 18-cylinder sleeve-valve air-cooled radial engine driving four-blade Rotol constant-speed propeller. Mk V. 2,180hp Sabre II with DH propeller. Mk VI. 2,300hp Sabre V with Rotol propeller.

Dimensions: Span, 41ft 0in; length, 33ft 8in (Mk II, 34ft 5in); height, 16ft 1in; wing area, 302 sq ft.

Weights: Mk II. Tare, 8,915lb; all-up, 13,600lb. Mk V. Tare, 8,990lb; all-up, 12,820lb. Mk VI. Tare, 9,150lb; all-up, 13,900lb.

Performance: Mk II. Max speed, 448 mph at 19,100ft; climb to 15,000ft, 4 min 30 sec; service ceiling, 37,000ft; normal range, 800 miles; max range, 1,640 miles. Mk V. Max speed, 434 mph at 22,800ft; climb to 15,000ft, 5 min; service ceiling, 36,000ft; normal range, 740 miles. (Mk I, max speed, 472 mph at 24,000ft)

Armament: All versions armed with four 20mm Hispano cannon (Mk 5 cannon on late production Mk Vs, and on Mks II and VI). Provision for external stores up to 2,200lb.

Prototypes: Mk I, one, HM599; Mk II, two, LA602 and LA607; Mk V, one, HM595; Mk VI, one (HM595 converted).

Production: Total, 1,394. Mark IIs, 452 (Hawker, 402: Between MW735-MW856 and PR525-PR921; Bristol, 50: Between MW374-MW435). Mark Vs, 800, all by Hawker (between EJ504-EJ896, JN729-JN877, NV639-NV793, NV917-NV996 and SN102-SN355). Mark VIs, 142, all by Hawker (between NV997-NX288).

Summary of Service: Tempest IIs served with Nos 5, 16, 20, 26, 30, 33, 54, 152, 183 and 247 Squadrons; Tempest Vs served with Nos 3, 16, 33, 56, 80, 174, 222, 274, 287, 349, 486 and 501 Squadrons; Tempest VIs served with Nos 6, 8, 39, 213 and 249 Squadrons.

A late-production tropicalized Tempest F Mk 6 (written thus after 1948 when Arabic numerals replaced Roman), NX201; hardly visible are the wing-root oil coolers, and the short Hispano Mk 5 cannon barrels are buried in the wings. Many Tempest 5s and 6s were converted to target tugs when they became redundant at the end of the 1940s. (Photo: Author's Collection).

The Tempest VI's service was, as intended, confined to the tropics, and equipped five squadrons which were based at one time or another in Egypt, Sudan, Cyprus, Iraq, Somaliland, Aden and Kenya. No 249 Squadron was also the last to give up its Tempest VIs in March 1950 while based at Deversoir in Egypt, having then started to receive Vampire 5s.

Apart from its fine fighting record during the final year of the War in Europe, the Tempest's prominent place in the RAF's history is also owed to its service during the transition to jet-powered fighters, a position it shared with equal distinction with the de Havilland Hornet and Supermarine Spitfire.

The engine manufacturer Napier used this Tempest V, NV768, for trial installations in its quest to develop an alternative to the cumbersome chin radiator; the aircraft is shown at Luton fitted with an annular radiator and a massive ducted spinner. A Rotol propeller, with short, broad-chord blades was specially produced for this aeroplane. (Photo: D Napier & Son Ltd, Neg No 1830)

Westland P.14 Welkin

Although considerable research had been conducted on pressure cabins for high flying aircraft during the 1930s, it was not until the issue of Specification F.4/40 in July 1940 that a formal attempt was made to encourage the aircraft industry to produce a very high flying fighter, and then in the belief that Germany was engaged in developing high-altitude bombers. The Specification, issued to Fairey, General Aircraft, Hawker, Vickers-Armstrongs and Westland, called for a two-seat aircraft capable of a top speed of 450 mph, an operating ceiling of 45,000 feet, equipped with airborne interception radar and armed with six Hispano cannon.

Being otherwise pre-occupied, neither Fairey nor Vickers tendered designs, and General Aircraft's likely candidate, the GAL.46 design, had been changed to a medium-altitude interceptor. Hawker, who submitted the P1004 — a much enlarged Typhoon derivative

The first Welkin prototype, DG558/G, as originally flown with short engine nacelles and tall fin and horn-balanced rudder. (Photo: via R C B Ashworth)

with six cannon — soon withdrew on the grounds of design saturation on the Typhoon and Tempest. This left two design proposals by Westland, one a twin-Merlin project in which the engines were mounted in tandem in the fuselage, driving counter-rotating propellers through a single reduction gearbox. Edward Petter's other proposal was the Westland P.14 of fairly conventional twin-engine layout that was clearly derived from the Whirlwind.

As originally schemed, the P.14 was a low-wing monoplane with a span of 60 feet, powered by two Merlin XXs and armed with a pair of cannon in the wing roots and four in the nose. However, after discussions early in 1941 the Specification was substantially relaxed. The AI radar was discarded, and with it went the need for a second crew member; the top speed requirement was reduced to 400 mph, and the mandatory six cannon armament was reduced to four. These changes were embodied in Specification F.7/41, issued in April that year, and prepared largely around Westland's suggestions. The P.14 was changed to feature mid-set wings and the armament was confined to the four nose-mounted cannon. The pressure cabin was attached to the front wing spar of the centre section and pressurized by air from a blower driven by the starboard engine. Two-speed, two-stage supercharged Rolls-Royce Merlin 61 engines were installed in low-slung nacelles, their radiators being incorporated in the forward section of the wings inboard of the nacelles. The wings, of very high aspect ratio, spanned no less than 70 feet.

Two prototypes (DG558/G and DG562/G) of the aircraft, named the Welkin, were ordered and the first was flown by Harald Penrose on 1 November 1942. As flown initially, DG558/G featured a tall fin and horn-balanced rudder, and engine nacelles which extended only just aft of the wing trailing-edge, but tunnel tests suggested the necessity to lengthen the engine nacelles and shorten the fin and rudder, and this in turn resulted in a change to a mass-balanced rudder.

DG558/G survived two forced landings, both attributable to powerplant malfunctioning, before the second prototype was flown in March 1943. Meanwhile production was getting underway with an initial order for 100 aircraft, of which the first fifty were fitted with Mosquito VI-type three-blade D.H. propellers; aircraft thereafter would switch to four-blade Rotol fully-feathering propellers.

When the first prototype paid a visit to the A & AEE at Boscombe Down, a top speed of about 380 mph at 29,000 feet was confirmed, and soon afterwards the second aircraft climbed to 44,000 feet. Unfortunately there then followed a spate of accidents — more often than not with little damage — involving engine fires and propeller failures.

The German high-altitude bomber threat failed to materialise and, in view of continuing flight problems, not least a relatively low diving speed limit which would have prevented the Welkin from following an enemy bomber whose pilot chose to escape by diving away, the Westland fighter was never issued to a fighter squadron, although 75 production examples were completed, as well as 25 further airframes.

A two-seat, high-altitude night fighter version was developed to Specification F.9/43 and this, powered by Merlin 76 and 77 engines, was equipped with AI Mark VIII radar. This, the Welkin NF

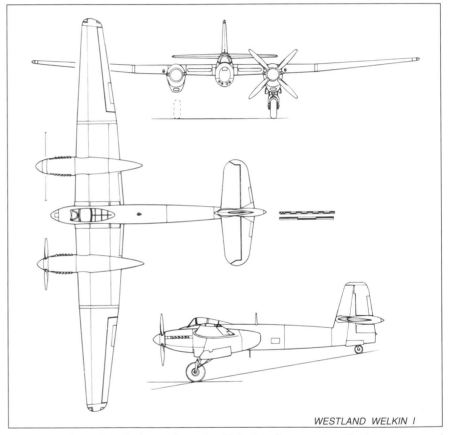

WESTLAND WELKIN I

Type: Twin-engine, single-seat low-wing high-altitude monoplane day interceptor, and two-seat high-altitude night fighter.

Manufacturer: Westland Aircraft Ltd, Yeovil, Somerset.

Air Ministry Specifications: F.4/40. F.7/41 for Mk I; F.9/43 for Mk II.

Powerplant: Prototype and early Mk Is: Two 1,530hp Rolls-Royce Merlin 61 two-stage, two-speed supercharged in-line engines driving three-blade DH variable-pitch propellers. Remaining aircraft: 1,630hp Merlin 72/73 or 76/77 engines driving four-blade Rotol fully-feathering propellers.

Dimensions: Span, 70ft 0in; length, 41ft 6in (Mk II, 44ft 1in); height, 15ft 3in; wing area, 460 sq ft.

Weights: Mk I. Tare, 11,974lb; all-up, 19,775lb. Mk II. Tare, 13,580lb; all-up, 21,892lb.

Performance: Mk I. Max speed, 387 mph at 26,000ft; climb to 40,000ft, 20 min; service ceiling, 44,000ft. Mk II. Max speed, 346 mph at 20,000ft; service ceiling, 40,000ft.

Armament: Both versions. Four 20mm Hispano Mk II cannon with total of 566 rounds in the front fuselage.

Prototypes: Mk I, two, DG558/G and DG562/G (DG558/G first flown by H Penrose on 1 November 1942). Mk II, one, PF370 (later changed to WE997).

Production: 100 Mark Is. 67 delivered to No 5 Maintenance Unit, contractors and trials establishments: DX278-DX295, DX308-DX349 and DX364-DX370. 33 not fitted with engines, and not taken on RAF charge: DX371-DX389 and DX407-DX420. No RAF service.

Mk II, PF370, was converted from the 83rd production F Mk I airframe DX386, having been taken out of store at No 5 Maintenance Unit. Its first flight was made with Penrose at the controls on 23 October 1944, but its performance was disappointing, returning a maximum speed of no more than 346 mph at 20,000 feet. Plans to alter the contract for the second one hundred Welkins as NF IIs came to naught, and the second prototype was not built. PF370 went on

The sole Welkin II prototype two-seat night fighter, PF370, showing the shortened vertical tail surfaces and lengthened engine nacelles adopted on all production aircraft. The night fighter featured a large nose radome for the AI equipment; the aircraft was later re-serialled WE997. (Photo: MAP Photo Neg No 131210C, dated October 1944)

to undertake a number of trials programmes associated with pressure cabin development, and carried the markings P.17 and WE997 after the War.

Welkins underwent a host of Service and other trials, no fewer than five examples visiting Boscombe Down from time to time; DX286 was flown by the Air Fighting Development Unit, and

DX289 by the Fighter Interception Unit. One of the last in flying condition was DX330, tested by Rotol Ltd at Staverton with a new cabin blower during the summer of 1947.

For all its difficulties, it is perhaps ironic that the Welkin seldom encountered any serious problem with its pressurizing system or pressure cabin.

Vickers Type 432 (F.7/41)

As already recorded, issue of Specification F.4/40 in July 1940 had failed to attract a design tender from Vickers. However, after the requirements for a high-altitude fighter had been relaxed and re-written into Specification F.7/41, Vickers decided to submit a design proposal, the Type 432, employing the fruits, not only of the company's fund of experience in metal structures but that achieved in developing the high-altitude Wellington Mark V bomber, which featured a successful pressure cabin and which had first flown in September 1940.

The Type 432 was a mid-wing monoplane, powered by two 1,565hp Merlin 61 two-speed, two-stage supercharged engines, the wing being a unique structure developed by Vickers. This was, in effect, a spanwise torsion box of oval section with heavy gauge skins, thickened locally to accommodate steel spar booms for which no web was necessary; leading and trailing edge skins were flush-riveted to the torsion box to provide the necessary wing plan form (in this instance elliptical leading and trailing edges) and aerofoil section. The fuselage comprised alloy skins flush-riveted to closely-spaced circular frames,

anchored to the cigar-shaped pressure vessel in the nose which constituted the pilot's cockpit; a hemispherical perspex dome was provided as a canopy. The tail unit, although of course an all-metal structure, was strangely similar to that of the de Havilland Mosquito, and this gave rise to the popular name, the

'tin Mossie' for the Type 432.

Unlike the Welkin, the Type 432 retained its provision for an armament of six 20mm Hispano cannon, these to be carried in a large ventral fairing (though in fact they were never fitted). No provision is believed to have been made for AI radar as there were never

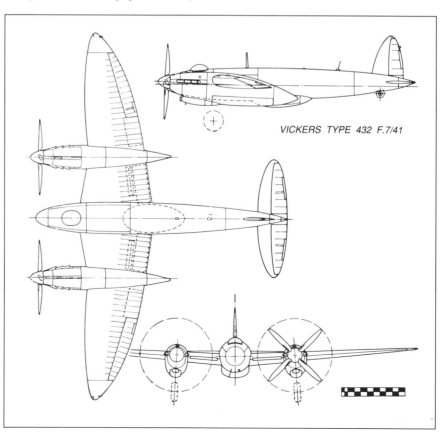

VICKERS TYPE 432 F.7/41

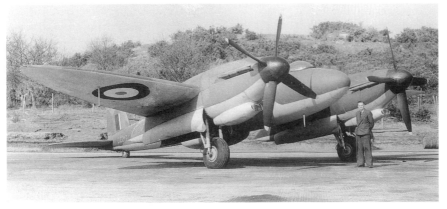

The Vickers Type 432, DZ217. The difficulties experienced with the Merlin 61 engines in this aircraft are something of a mystery as the same powerplant was, by the end of 1942, being flown in Spitfire IXs on operations without significant trouble, and at heights well above 30,000 feet. (Photo: Vickers plc, Neg No 5088)

any plans to accommodate a second crew member.

Two prototypes, DZ217 and DZ223, were ordered, and the first — built at Foxwarren, near Weybridge — was flown by Flt Lt Douglas Webster ('Tommy') Lucke RAFO at Farnborough on 24 December 1942. Criticism of the handling characteristics were voiced by Lucke and other pilots, resulting in a change of ailerons and of tailplane incidence, but these alerations only went some way towards curing the problems. The second prototype was not completed, being cancelled on 1 May 1943. The highest speed ever attained by DZ217 was 380 mph at 20,000 feet on 14 May, and high altitudes were not attempted owing to the pressure cabin never being completed.

The main problem encountered by the Type 432, however, was said to have been the failure of the aircraft's Merlin 61s to function reliably above 23,000 feet. The reason for this was never discovered as DZ217 only completed 28 flights before the programme was halted at the end of 1943, when it was clear that the German high altitude bombing threat would not materialize.

The accompanying performance figures are design estimates.

Type: Twin-engine, single-seat mid-wing monoplane high-altitude interceptor fighter.
Manufacturer: Vickers-Armstrongs Ltd, Weybridge, Surrey.
Air Ministry Specification: F.7/41.
Powerplant: Two 1,565hp Rolls-Royce Merlin 61 twelve-cylinder, two-speed, two-stage supercharged, liquid-cooled, in-line engines driving four-blade propellers.
Dimensions: Span, 56ft 10½in; length, 40ft 7½in; height, 13ft 9in; wing area, 441 sq ft.
Weights: Tare, 16,373lb; all-up, 20,168lb.
Performance: Max speed, 435 mph at 28,000ft; service ceiling, 37,000ft; range, 1,500 miles.
Armament: Provision to mount six 20mm Hispano Mk II cannon in ventral fairing.
Prototypes: Two, DZ217 and DZ223 (DZ217 first flown by Flt Lt D W Lucke RAFO on 24 December 1942 at Farnborough; DZ223 not completed). No production.

Martin-Baker M.B.5

Following the loss of the Martin-Baker M.B.3 on 12 September 1942, and the abandoning of the M.B.4 project, James Martin determined to persist with a fighter based on the original Specification F.18/39, continuing to employ the Martin-Baker steel tubular primary structure to which large detachable panels were fixed. The new aircraft, the M.B.5, carried the serial number R2496, very close numerically to that of the ill-fated M.B.3 — suggesting that Martin had intended building a second M.B.3, or that it had been scheduled for the M.B.4.

However, twenty-one months were to elapse before the M.B.5 was ready for flight. The M.B.3's wing plan form was retained, but the armament was reduced from six to four 20mm Hispano cannon, with Martin's patented flat belt-feed mechanism. A 2,340hp Rolls-Royce Griffon 83 engine, with two-speed, two-stage supercharger, was enclosed in an exceptionally slim fuselage nose, made

Looking every inch a thoroughbred, the Martin-Baker M.B.5 displays its very wide-track undercarriage and short-span wings; the excellent view from the cockpit is also apparent from this photograph. (Photo: Martin-Baker Aircraft Co Ltd., Neg No. 17551)

possible by locating the interchanger, coolant and oil radiators well aft in a laminar-flow duct beneath the fuselage aft of the cockpit. The engine itself, mounted on a pair of molybdenum-steel tapered cantilever booms, drove six-blade de Havilland contra-rotating propellers (though a change was later made to Rotol propellers).

The wings of low aspect and thick-

ness/chord ratios employed a D-type torsion box whose main member was a laminated steel spar of considerable strength; split trailing edge flaps, a very sturdy, wide-track inwards-retracting undercarriage and wheel brakes were all operated pneumatically. Particular attention was paid to the cockpit layout, allied to ease of accessibility, each instrument console hinging outwards to

Take-off view of the M.B.5. The lines of fastners on the fuselage disclose the extent of detachable panels, in effect from the spinner to the stern post. (Photo: Martin-Baker Aircraft Co Ltd., Neg No 17552).

provide access for servicing from inside the cockpit; a clear-view single-piece sliding canopy over the cockpit could be jettisoned in an emergency.

First flight by R2496 was undertaken by Capt Leslie Bryan Greensted, Rotol's chief test pilot, on 23 May 1944 at Harwell, Berkshire, and the aircraft quickly established an impeccable reputation for its crisp and positive controls, possessing a very rapid rate of roll at 94 degrees per second.

The M.B.5 clearly represented the peak of piston-engine fighter design, being applauded on every count when it was delivered to Boscombe Down for assessment. And it is a little-remembered fact that in 1945 plans were laid to attack the world's speed record, the engine being re-rated to produce 2,480hp at low altitude with Rotol contraprops. A speed of 484 mph was recorded over a measured course near Gloucester while the aircraft was flying from Rotol's airfield at Staverton. The plans came to nothing, however, as the Air Ministry was determined to leave the field clear for the Gloster Meteor's speed record attempt — which was vindicated by the dramatic success of the jet fighter in September that year at a speed of 606 mph.

The M.B.5 was, of course, pre-empted by the arrival of the turbojet-powered fighter for, even had it been ordered into production for the RAF, that production would have demanded a sub-contracted assembly line to be set up on another manufacturer's premises — a time consuming process, even in wartime. With the arrival in service of the Gloster Meteor, even before the M.B.5 first flew, James Martin's masterpiece would have been an anachronism.

Although Martin's mind turned to other spheres of aviation, in particular becoming the world's leading producer of ejector seats, he made one final essay in aircraft design, the M.B.6, a delta-wing, tailless single-seat fighter with a single turbojet, but this reached no further than the drawing board.

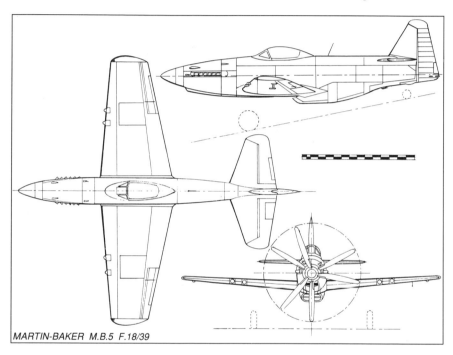

MARTIN-BAKER M.B.5 F.18/39

Type: Single-engine, single-seat low-wing monoplane experimental interceptor fighter.
Manufacturer: Martin-Baker Aircraft Co Ltd, Higher Denham, Middlesex.
Air Ministry Specification: F.18/39.
Powerplant: One 2,340hp Rolls-Royce Griffon 83 twelve-cylinder, two-speed, two-stage supercharged, liquid-cooled, in-line engine, driving six-blade de Havilland contra-rotating propellers.
Dimensions: Span, 35ft 0in; length, 37ft 9in; height, 15ft 0in; wing area, 262 sq ft.
Weights: Tare, 9,233lb; all-up, 11,500lb.
Performance: Max speed, 460 mph at 20,000ft; service ceiling, 36,900 ft.
Armament: Four 20mm Hispano Mk II cannon in wings.
Prototype: One, R2496; first flown by Capt L B Greensted at Harwell on 23 May 1944. No production.

Supermarine Spiteful and Seafang

As early as 1940 it was commonplace for aircraft in combat to dive at speeds around 450 mph TAS, their pilots acutely aware that their controls were becoming much less effective; indeed it often required considerable muscular effort to recover from such dives. The phenomenon of aileron reversal became identified as the research establishments studied the problems associated with the onset of compressibility as the aircraft approached the local speed of sound.

In the course of diving trials at Langley during 1942-43, the Hawker test pilots were frequently diving Typhoons at over 500 mph, while on 12 December 1942 Philip Lucas reached 575 mph (Mach 0.76) at 20,000 feet in a full-

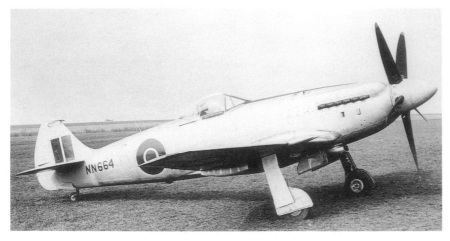

Left: *The first Spiteful prototype to be built as such from scratch, NN664, featuring the same fin and rudder as on the Spitfire F XIV; this was shortly changed to the production type.* (Photo: via R C B Ashworth)

Below: *The third Spiteful prototype, NN667, with production-type tail unit and the lengthened carburettor air intake duct, extended forward to the front of the engine cowling.* (Photo: Vickers Armstrongs Ltd, Neg No E2797)

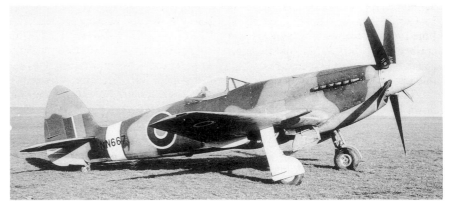

throttle dive from 27,000 feet in the prototype Tempest V. Thereafter tests were flown on production aircraft, often firing their guns in dives at around 550 mph 'to see if the wings came off'.

At Farnborough, diving trials with Spitfire PR Mk XIs during the late summer of 1943 produced some remarkable figures. Sqn Ldr James Richard Tobin recorded Mach 0.92 between 25,000 and 30,000 feet (a figure later amended to about 0.90, but still a speed of around 650 mph TAS); of course no Spitfire would have retained its wings had it fired its guns at this speed.

While American aerodynamicists were evolving a new series of high-speed aerofoil sections, Supermarine, in collaboration with the National Physical Laboratory, was designing a new wing section, intended to maintain laminar flow over the wing as far aft as possible, it being intended to fit this to a derivative of the Spitfire. This aircraft, designed to Specification F.1/43, was the Supermarine Type 371 Spiteful, and it was an expressed requirement that it should feature a laminar-flow wing. Maximum wing thickness was to be at 42 per cent of the chord (compared with about 25 per cent on the early Spitfires, and straight leading and trailing edges replaced the characteristic elliptical plan form of Mitchell's classic aeroplane, the wing area being reduced from 248.5 sq ft of the Spitfire F 21's 'new wing' to 210 sq ft of the laminar flow wing.

Three prototype Spitefuls, NN660, NN664 and NN667, had been ordered on 6 February 1943 and, on June that

Above: *A standard production Spiteful F XIV, RB517. This version possessed a maximum speed of 483 mph at 21,000 feet, a speed that had already been eclipsed by British Meteor jet fighters coming into service.* (Photo: Ministry of Supply, RTP Neg No 14408C, dated March 1946)

Right: *The sole Spiteful F XVI, RB518, powered by the Griffon 101 with three-speed supercharger; this was the aircraft that achieved a level speed of 494 mph at a boost of 25lb and little thought for the engine's welfare!* (Photo: Vickers-Armstrongs Ltd, Neg No 3930)

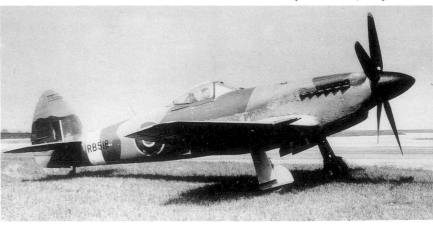

What might be considered the last in the Spitfire family was the Supermarine Seafang F Mk 32, of which the second prototype, VB895, is shown here, completed with Rotol contraprop, folding wing and sting-type arrester hook. (Photo: Ministry of Supply, RTP Neg No 14852B)

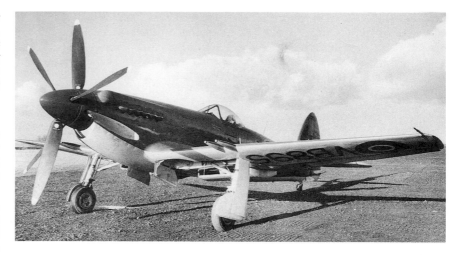

year, 60 Spitfires, ordered previously, were required to be completed as Spitefuls, but these were later cancelled; instead, 21 production Spitefuls were ordered, of which 17 were completed.

The first Spiteful prototype, NN660, was a converted Spitfire XIV, to which the laminar-flow wing, with Spiteful undercarriage, was fitted, and flown by Lt-Cdr Jeffrey Kindersley Quill on 30 June 1944. Unfortunately this aeroplane crashed on 13 September, and its pilot, Frank Furlong, was killed; no reason for this loss was officially established.

The second aircraft, NN664, was flown by Quill on 8 January 1945, and problems encountered with NN660 were the subject of prolonged investigation. This was the first true Spiteful prototype, having been built to the full Specification F.1/43 standard, even though its still featured the Spitfire XIV's vertical tail surfaces. The handling characteristics that were giving rise to concern included aileron snatch, wing-drop immediately before the stall, and a powerful flick in a high g stall. In the course of flight tests using tufted wings, it was discovered that a breakdown of the airflow occurred forward of the ailerons before the wing itself stalled, thereby rendering the ailerons useless at the stall.

It quickly became obvious that considerable work remained to be done, not only on the laminar-flow wing, but in most other areas of the airframe. However, the substitution of the Spitfire XIV's tail unit by the improved Spitfire F 21's tail, resulted in some improvements in directional stability and control.

However, faced with many months of delay before the modifications could be designed into production Spitefuls, and then with no guarantee they would be wholly effective, production was cut back to just those aircraft whose manufacture had begun. In the end only 17 aircraft were completed, the first production Spiteful F XIV, RB515, being flown in April 1945. Most of the production aircraft were F XIVs, but several, powered by Griffon 89 or 90 engines driving Rotol contraprops, became the Mk XV, and the single F XVI, RB518 — with a three-speed Griffon 101 driving a five-blade Rotol — achieved a level speed of 494 mph with 25lb boost, believed to have been the fastest level speed ever achieved by a British piston-engine aircraft.

Supermarine Seafang

Origins of a naval fighter with the laminar-flow wing lay in a private venture scheme of October 1943 to modify the Seafire XV accordingly; however, this aroused no enthusiasm at the MAP, and the aircraft was not produced. Instead the Navy preferred to persist with the planned Seafire under Specification N.7/44. Despite the loss of the first Spiteful prototype, this attitude began to change at the end of 1944, and Specification N.5/45 was issued calling for a naval fighter with laminar-flow, folding wings.

Named the Seafang, the first prototype was RB520, a converted Spiteful, and featured a sting-type hook, but the wings remained fixed. The first purpose-built prototype Seafang was VB895, powered by a Griffon 89 with Rotol contraprop, folding wings and sting-hook, this being representative of the Seafang F Mk 32; the F 31 was powered by a Griffon with five-blade Rotol.

150 production aircraft were ordered, but this contract was soon cut back, and only ten F 31s and six F 32s were finally completed. The prototype VB895 was taken on charge briefly by No 778 Squadron (Lt-Cdr R H P Carver DSC, RN), the Naval Trials Unit at Ford, in May 1947, but by then the Royal Navy's first jet fighter, the Supermarine Attacker, had been flying in prototype form for ten months, and further interest in the Seafang quickly evaporated.

The Spiteful and Seafang programme must be seen as a failure in that the two

---

Type: Single-engine, single-seat, low-wing monoplane interceptor (Spiteful) and naval fighter (Seafang).

Manufacturer: Supermarine Division of Vickers-Armstrongs Ltd.

Air Ministry Specifications: F.1/43 (Spiteful) and N.5/45 (Seafang).

Powerplant: Spiteful F XIV. One Rolls-Royce Griffon 69 with five-blade Rotol propeller. F XV. Griffon 89 or 90 with six-blade Rotol contraprop. F XVI. Griffon 101 (3-speed supercharged) with five-blade Rotol propeller. Seafang F 31. Griffon 69 with five-blade Rotol propeller. F 32. Griffon 89 with six-blade Rotol contraprop.

Dimensions: Span, 35ft 0in; length, 32 ft 11in (Seafang F 32, 34ft 1in); height, 13ft 5in (Seafang F 32, 12ft 6½in); wing area, 210 sq ft.

Weights: Spiteful F XIV. Tare, 7,350lb; all-up, 9,950lb; Seafang F 32. Tare, 8,000lb; all-up, 10,450lb.

Performance: Spiteful F XIV. Max speed, 483 mph at 21,000ft; service ceiling, 42,000ft; range, 564 miles. Seafang F 32. Max speed, 475 mph at 21,000ft; service ceiling, 41,000ft; range, 393 miles.

Armament: Four 20mm Hispano Mk V cannon in wings with total of 624 rounds; provision to carry two 1,000lb bombs or four rocket projectiles.

Prototypes: Spiteful, three, NN660, NN664 and NN667 (NN660 first flown on 30 June 1944 by J K Quill). Seafang, three, RB520 (converted from Spiteful), and two scratch-built, VB893 and VB895.

Production: Spiteful. Total of 17 (RB515-RB525, RB527-RB531 and RB535). Seafang. Total of 10 Mk 31s (VG471-VG480) and 6 Mk 32s (VG481, VG482, VG486 and VG488-VG49).

fighters, as such, failed to materialise in time to be of value to the two Services. That is not to say that they represented wasted time and money. They demonstrated graphically that to push an aeroplane ever closer towards transonic speeds demanded examination of the aerodynamics of every component of the airframe, indeed the shape of the aircraft as a whole — not simply the wing itself. New parameters had to be established and their compilation would occupy another dozen years. The research work conducted on the Spiteful was but a step towards the completion of that work.

de Havilland test pilot Pat Fillingham flying an early production Hornet F I, PX217. (Photo: A J Jackson Collection)

de Havilland Hornet and Sea Hornet

The de Havilland Mosquito was just beginning to make its mark as a fighter and bomber in service during 1942 when its manufacturers decided to pursue as a private venture the idea of a long-range single-seat development of that magnificent aeroplane, that would be well suited for operations over the vast areas involving air operations in the Pacific theatre. To this end, de Havilland and Rolls-Royce worked in close harmony to develop a version of the Merlin with the lowest possible frontal area in their efforts to reduce to a minimum the drag of a twin engine fighter.

A mock-up of the D.H.103 was shown to officials of the Ministry of Aircraft Production in January 1943, and in due course Specification F.12/43 was prepared around de Havilland's proposals, the project gaining official sanction with an order for two prototypes.

Athough resembling the Mosquito in general outline, the D.H.103 was an entirely new design, its construction employing wood-to-metal bonding for the first time with the new Redux adhesive. The balsa sandwich construction was used only in the manufacture of the exceptionally slim fuselage, while the two-spar wings, of laminar-flow concept, comprised a metal and wood internal structure covered by a stressed double birch ply upper skin, and a reinforced Alclad lower skin. Wing-root radiators were incorporated for the two 2,070hp Merlin engines, which were handed in order to reduce swing on take-off and landing, the starboard engine being a Merlin 130, and that on the port side a Merlin 131. The standard fighter armament of four 20mm Hispano cannon was located under the fuselage nose, directly below the cockpit which afforded the pilot a superlative field of view.

Geoffrey de Havilland Jnr flew the first prototype, RR915, now named the Hornet, on 28 July 1944 at Hatfield, and showed the aircraft to meet the most sanguine demands, recording a maximum speed of 485 mph at 22,000 feet. When the aircraft was delivered to Boscombe Down for Service assessment, a rate of roll was measured at 72 degrees per second — the highest yet recorded by a twin-engine aircraft. The second prototype, RR919, was completed with a modified fuel system to allow a pair of 200 gallon drop tanks to be carried and, with these fitted, the

A late production Hornet F 3, PX396, with the wide-span tailplane. (Photo: British Aerospace plc (Hatfield), Neg No 3260H)

Left: *A pair of Hornet F 3s, PX293/QV-A and PX332/QV-D, of No 19 (Fighter) Squadron bearing a mixture of post-War Fighter Command's markings and colour schemes.* (Photo: A J Jackson Collection)

Below: *A Hornet F 4, WF977/B of No 80 (Fighter) Squadron, based at Kai Tak, Hong Kong, in the early 1950s; it is shown carrying the 200 gallon underwing tanks and rocket rails outboard.* (Photo: A J Jackson Collection)

aircraft possessed a range of 2,500 miles at 330 mph when flying at 30,000 feet.

Experimental flying of the two prototypes was undertaken by Geoffrey Haig Pike, and production testing by William Patrick Ingram Fillingham and, after production got underway at Hatfield late in 1944, deliveries began to the RAF in February 1945. A total of 179 aircraft had been ordered, but the final 34 of these were cancelled. The first 60 were completed as F Mk Is.

Hornet F Mk Is equipped four home-based squadrons of Fighter Command, beginning with No 64 (Fighter) Squadron at Horsham St Faith, Norfolk, in May 1946, being followed by Nos 65 and 19 the same year, and No 41 Squadron in June 1948. They were immensely popular in service, being a delight to fly, and almost viceless.

The Mark II was intended to perform the other proposed Hornet rôle, that of photo reconnaissance, and three early Mark Is, PX216, PX220 and PX249, were converted as prototypes with cameras in the rear fuselage. 23 production examples were ordered before it was decided that the current reconnaissance versions of the Mosquito would suffice until a jet-powered aircraft became available, and only five Hornet PR Mk IIs were completed; these were scrapped.

The main production version was the Hornet F Mk 3, of which 123 were built. This variant was specifically tailored for service in the Far East, particularly in the ground attack rôle. In the event the aircraft equipped four home-based squadrons before being deployed to South East Asia. The Mark 3 featured a wider tailplane with enlarged elevator horn balance, and the underwing drop tanks could be removed to be replaced by a pair of 1,000lb bombs; four three-inch rocket projectiles could be carried in addition to the drop tanks. A dorsal fin fairing was added (and retrospectively fitted to most Mark Is) to improve stability at high speeds as well as to reduce the one-engine-out critical speed on take-off. The internal fuel capacity was raised from 360 gallons to 540, thereby increasing the range to 3,000 miles. Most Mark 3s were powered by 2,030hp Merlin 133/134 engines.

As an indication of what could be achieved by the Hornet, a fully-equipped Mark 3 was flown from Gibraltar to Bovingdon by Gp Capt Anthony Courtenay Power Carver at a speed of 435.87 mph on 19 September 1949, landing with fifteen minutes' fuel remaining, and establishing a new point-to-point record.

The Hornet F 3 served on the same four home-based RAF squadrons as the F 1s, first replacing them on No 64 in

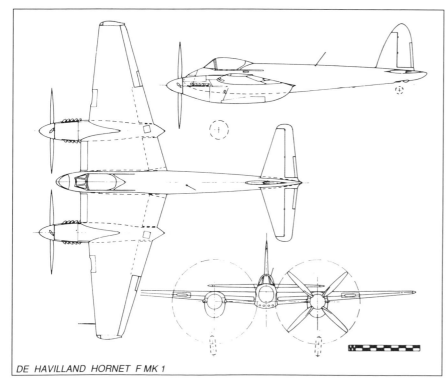

DE HAVILLAND HORNET F MK 1

The fourth production Sea Hornet F 20, TT189. The position of the wing-fold line was immediately outboard of the flaps, seen here fully lowered. The picture gives an indication of the pilot's excellent field of view. (Photo: Ministry of Supply, RTP Neg No 14921B)

March 1948. They went on to serve in Malaya, joining the Bristol Brigands of No 45 Squadron at Tengah, Singapore, in January 1951, and replacing Tempest F 2s on No 33 Squadron at Kuala Lumpur later that year. These two Squadrons flew hundreds of sorties against the Communist guerrilla forces operating in the Malayan jungle, usually attacking with three-inch rocket projectiles.

A final fighter version for the RAF was the Hornet F 4, in which the upper fuselage fuel tank was reduced in size to make space for a vertical F 52 camera. 12 examples were built and supplied to No 80 Squadron, in company with F 3s, based at Kai Tak, Hong Kong, between December 1951 and May 1955, commanded for most of that time by Sqn Ldr Eric Wilmot Tremlett DFC.

Production of the Hornet was switched from Hatfield to Chester late in 1948.

de Havilland Sea Hornet

The idea of the Hornet being operated by the Fleet Air Arm was integral with the original private venture undertaken in 1942, and motivated the inclusion of handed engines in the first place, for the absence of swing on take-off was of paramount importance in a twin-engine deck-operating aeroplane.

Three early production Hornet F Is, PX212, PX214 and PX219, were set aside for preparation to Specification N.5/44, and responsibility for the Sea Hornet's detail design was entrusted to Heston Aircraft Co Ltd, that company designing Lockheed hydraulic power-folding wings, a steel V-frame arrester hook and accelerator pick-up points with local strengthening of the airframe. Airdraulic main undercarriage oleos were supplied by de Havilland to cater for the higher rate of descent

during carrier deck landing.

The first Sea Hornet prototype, PX212, with arrester hook but with fixed wings, was flown on 19 April 1945, and the first with folding wings, PX219, began deck trials aboard HM Light Fleet Carrier *Theseus* on 10 August that year. The first production Sea Hornet F XX, TT186, flew at Hatfield on 13 August 1946, and in July the following year accompanied other early aircraft on Service trials with No 703 Squadron, commanded by Lt-Cdr J C N Shrubsole DSC, RN, at Thorney Island. A sub-variant was the Sea Hornet FR Mk I which carried a camera in the rear fuselage, a window for this camera being incorporated in the port side of the rear fuselage of all F Is to cater for this optional equipment. Armament included four 20mm Hispano cannon in the nose and provision for either two 1,000lb bombs or up to sixteen 60lb three-inch rockets under the wings. Operating, however, at high take-off and landing weights during carrier trials disclosed a weakness in the torque link in the undercarriage, necessitating replacement of the main oleo legs, and this delayed the final deck clearance trials until 1948, and it was not until 27 January 1949 that No 801 Squadron, commanded by Lt-Cdr D H Richards RN, was able to embark in HMS *Implacable* with fully operational Sea Hornets for service with the 1st Carrier Air Group, Home Fleet.

Towards the end of the War it had been suggested that a night fighter version of the Hornet could perform an important rôle with the Fleet Air Arm, not only performing the night interception task, but as a night air strike navigation aircraft. Specification N.21/45 was raised for a two-seater, and two prototypes were converted by Heston, the first, PX230 (an ex-Hornet F I) without folding wings, and the other, PX239 (formerly a Sea Hornet F XX), fully modified with folding wings, ASH scanner in a nose radome and flame-damping exhaust shrouds. The radar-navigator's heated cockpit was located over the wing trailing edge. The extended fin was also introduced at this stage to the Sea Hornet.

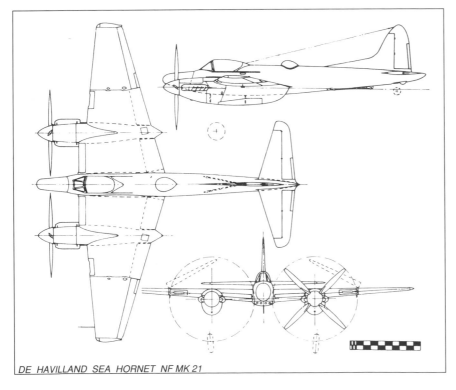

DE HAVILLAND SEA HORNET NF MK 21

Production of the Sea Hornet NF Mk 21 totalled 78, many of the later aircraft being produced at Chester. The final version of the aircraft was the single-seat photo-reconnaissance Mk 22, of which 43 examples were produced, serving with two operational, one reserve and five second-line squadrons.

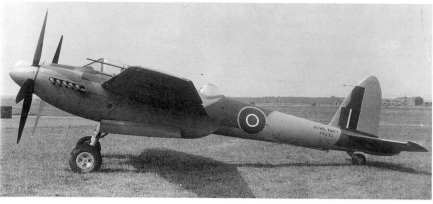

The first Sea Hornet NF 21 prototype, PX230, showing the blister canopy over the navigator/ radar operator's compartment. (Photo: Ministry of Supply Neg No 14554F)

Type: Twin-engine, single-seat low/mid-wing monoplane long-range fighter, ground attack aircraft and naval fighter, and two-seat naval night fighter.

Manufacturer: The de Havilland Aircraft Co Ltd, Hatfield, Hertfordshire, and Hawarden, Chester.

Air Ministry Specifications: F.12/43 (Hornet); N.5/44 (Sea Hornet F 20) and N.21/45 (Sea Hornet NF 21).

Powerplant: Early aircraft. Two 2,070hp Rolls-Royce Merlin 130/131 twelve-cylinder supercharged liquid-cooled in-line engines driving four-blade handed propellers. Later aircraft. 2,030hp Merlin 133/134 engines.

Dimensions: Span, 45ft 0in; length, 36ft 8in (F 20, 36ft 9in; NF 21, 37ft 10in); height, 14ft 2in (Sea Hornets, 13ft 0in); wing area, 361 sq ft.

Weights: F I. Tare, 12,502lb; all-up, 17,700lb. F 20. Tare, 13,300lb; all-up, 18,530lb. NF 21. Tare, 14,250lb; all-up, 19,530lb.

Performance: F.1. Max speed, 472 mph at 22,000ft; service ceiling, 37,500ft; range, 2,500 miles. F 20. Max speed, 467 mph at 22,000ft; service ceiling, 35,000ft; range, 1,500 miles. NF 21. Max speed, 430 mph at 22,000ft; service ceiling, 36,500ft; range, 1,500 miles.

Armament: Four 20mm Hispano cannon in nose; provision to carry two 1,000lb bombs or up to sixteen three-inch rocket projectiles.

Prototypes: Hornet, two, RR915 and RR919 (RR915 first flown by G de Havilland Jnr at Hatfield on 28 July 1944). Sea Hornet, three, PX212, PX214 and PX219.

Production: Hornet, total 195. F I, 60 (between PX210-PX288); F 3, 123 (between PX289-PX398, WB870-WB912 and WF954-WF967); F 4, 12 (WF968-WF979). Sea Hornet, total 190. F 20, 112 (between TT186-TT248, VR836-VR893 and VZ707-VZ717). NF 21, 78 (between VV430-VV431 and VZ671-VZ698)

Summary of Service: Hornet fighters served with Nos 19, 33, 41, 45, 64, 65 and 80 Squadrons, RAF. Sea Hornets served with Nos 703, 728, 736, 738, 739, 759, 771, 778, 787, 792, 801, 806, 809 and 1833 Squadrons of the Fleet Air Arm, and aboard HMS *Implacable*, *Indomitable*, *Vengeance* and *Eagle*.

Hawker Fury and Sea Fury

Although the Typhoon II, later to be named the Tempest, seemed likely to rectify the obvious shortcomings of the F.18/37 designs, compromised from the outset by their thick wings, Camm expressed anxiety at the steep rise in the weight of his single-seat fighters, with the Tempest prototype tipping the scales at almost 11,000 pounds on its first flight (about 20 per cent higher than the Typhoon on its maiden flight, in spite of using a similar engine).

Shortly after the Tempest flew in September 1942, Hawker therefore began investigating the feasibility of replacing the aircraft's wing centre-section with a much shorter structure, so that the landing wheels, when retracted, almost met on the centreline of the aircraft. These deliberations coincided with the successful evolution of an efficient radial

The first Hawker F.2/43 Fury prototype, NX798, with Bristol Centaurus engine and Rotol four-blade propeller. (Sydney Camm Collection)

engine installation (which would materialise as the Tempest Mark II) so that Camm now felt confident that a new fighter could be produced which might meet the requirements of Specification F.6/42, which had attracted design tenders from English Electric, Folland and Westland, but without success.

Hawker tendered the new design, termed the Tempest Light Fighter (Centaurus) and this attracted some interest at the Air Ministry, although it did not quite meet the speed and climb requirements. In January 1943, however, following discussions with the DTD, a new Specification, F.2/43, was drafted around Camm's proposals and two prototypes, NX798 and NX802, were ordered by the MAP for the Air Ministry. It was also agreed that the third Tempest II prototype, LA610, then just beginning manufacture, should be completed as an additional prototype of the new fighter. In April that year another Specification, N.7/43 for a naval interceptor fighter, was issued, and Camm expressed confidence that this was capable of being met by his F.2/43 design, if powered by the proposed up-rated Centaurus XII engine.

By December 1943 the situation regarding the choice of engines had become complicated by the offers of new engines by Napier, whose Sabre IV had failed to achieve the 50-hour test, by Rolls-Royce with the new family of two-stage, two-speed supercharged Griffons, and by Bristol with the up-rated Centaurus XXII. Six prototypes were now on order, of which four were to be naval fighters. Production contracts totalled 400 aircraft, of which half were for the RAF, and the remainder to N.22/43 (which superseded N.7/43) for the Royal Navy. Boulton Paul would produce one hundred of the naval fighters.

The first F.2/43 to be flown was NX798, which Lucas flew on 1 September 1944, the same month that the RAF aircraft were named the Fury, and those for the Navy, Sea Furies. NX798 was powered by the Centaurus XII on a rigid

mounting, though this engine was scheduled to be changed after development of a dynafocal mounting at Filton. LA610 was the next Fury to fly, on 27 November, powered by a Rolls-Royce Griffon 85 driving six-blade contraprops but, owing to the large annular radiator, its top speed was about ten miles per hour down on the Spiteful with similar powerplant.

The third Fury, NX802 with Centaurus XV was flown on 25 July 1945, after further delay with the dynafocal mounting. Meanwhile LA610 was re-designed to accommodate the Napier Sabre VII with wing root radiators, this becoming the fastest Hawker piston engine-powered fighter, with a speed of about 485 mph. A fourth Fury, VP207, was completed from stock components in 1947, and was also powered by a Sabre VII.

With the ending of the War in September 1945, and the inevitable widespread introduction of jet fighters, there was no place for the Fury in post-War RAF plans as it was felt that existing propeller-driven fighters — the Spitfire, Hornet and Tempest — would suffice in the short term. The Fleet Air Arm, on the other hand, faced with possible long-term trouble with the Seafang, and equipped with obsolescent Fireflies, persisted with the N.22/43 Sea Fury, and by so doing effectively provided the

financial basis on which Hawker Aircraft Ltd survived in the lean post-War years.

Hawker Sea Furies

Two N.7/43 prototypes, SR661 and SR666, had been ordered from Hawker in 1943, together with one from Boulton Paul Aircraft Ltd, VB857, the latter being delivered to Hawker for assembly after the Boulton Paul Sea Fury production contract was cancelled at the end of the War.

SR661 was first flown on 21 February 1945, powered by a Centaurus XII with four-blade Rotol propeller, but was only 'semi-navalised' with a sting-type arrester hook, but with fixed wings. SR666, fully navalised with hydraulically-operated, upwards-folding wings, and arrester hook, was flown on 12 October that year, powered by a Centaurus XV with five-blade Rotol. The Boulton Paul machine, VB857, was flown on 31 January 1946.

The initial production version of the Sea Fury, the Mark X, was an interceptor fighter, without provision for external weapons. Fifty examples were produced during 1946, differing from the prototypes in having enlarged fin and rudder as early deck trials in 1945 had disclosed inadequate directional control during deck landing. Early production Mark Xs were fitted with Rotol four-blade propellers, but these gave way to five-bladers in due course, the engine reduction gearing being increased.

The first Service deliveries were made to No 778 Squadron in February 1947 at Tangmere under the command of Lt-Cdr R H P Carver DSC, RN, for Service trials by the Intensive Trials Development Flight. The first operational Squadron with Sea Fury Xs was No 803, serving with the Royal Canadian Navy, stationed at Eglinton, Co Londonderry,

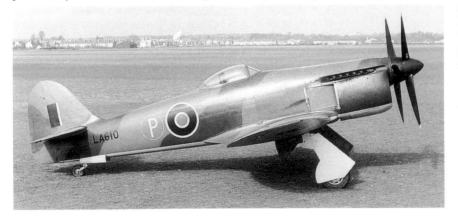

Above: *The Griffon-powered Fury, LA610, was disappointing and efforts were made to improve performance by cropping the propeller blades by up to about six inches, but with no appreciable effect.* (Photo: Author's Collection)

Right: *The fastest propeller-driven Hawker aeroplanes were the Sabre VII-powered Furies, of which LA610, shown here, reached a speed of about 485 mph TAS — by 1945 of academic interest only.* (Photo: Ministry of Supply RTP Neg No 14528C)

The first Sea Fury prototype, SR661, with short sting-type arrester hook and fixed wings. The original four-blade propeller has been replaced by a five blader. (Photo: Hawker Aircraft Ltd, Neg No SFG8)

and commanded by Lt-Cdr H J G Bird RCN.

By the time No 803 Squadron received its Sea Fury F Xs a new variant had begun production and this, the FB Mark 11 fighter-bomber, was the definitive version. Early deck trials had disclosed a weakness in the arrester hook, the hook sometimes breaking away on engaging the deck cables. The hook was lengthened and strengthened, this modification being introduced in the Mk 11 (and retrospectively in earlier aircraft), while the new fighter-bombers were flown in an intensive programme to clear the carriage of stores, including two 1,000lb bombs, depth charges, drop tanks, napalm tanks and rocket projectiles to complement its four-cannon armament.

Large production orders continued to be placed for the Mark 11, following on from the remaining 50 (the second half of the original 100 ordered during the War). 35 were ordered in 1946, 147 in 1947, 135 in 1948, and 248 between 1949 and 1951.

Sea Fury FB 11s were first delivered to No 803 Squadron in February 1948, still at Eglinton, and these embarked in HMCS *Magnificent* on 8 May that year. In April No 802 (Lt-Cdr M Hordern DSC, RN) became the first Fleet Air Arm Squadron to receive FB 11s, at Lee-on-Solent, embarking in HMS *Vengeance* on 18 August.

By the beginning of the Korean War in June 1950 the Sea Fury was in service as the Fleet Air Arm's standard shipborne fighter-bomber, serving with eight operational and nine second-line squadrons. Six Squadrons served in Korean waters (Nos 801, 802, 804, 805, 807 and 808), the first to arrive being No 807, commanded by Lt-Cdr B Bevan RN; flying from HMS *Theseus*, this Squadron flew 800 sorties in six months — being later awarded the 1950 Boyd Trophy for its achievement.

Sea Furies undertook hundreds of ground attack sorties during the Korean War, at first being capable of defending themselves against enemy propeller-driven fighters but, with the appearance of Communist-flown MiG-15 jets, the Sea Furies often operated under top

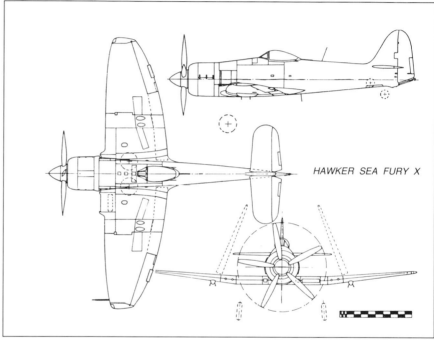

HAWKER SEA FURY X

Type: Single-engine, single-seat low-wing monoplane interceptor and naval fighter and fighter-bomber.

Manufacturer: Hawker Aircraft Ltd, Kingston-upon-Thames, Surrey, and Langley, Buckinghamshire.

Air Ministry Specifications: Fury. F.2/43. Sea Fury: N.7/43 and N.22/43.

Powerplant: Fury. One 2,480hp Bristol Centaurus XII and XV eighteen-cylinder, sleeve-valve, radial engine; also Rolls-Royce Griffon 85 with contraprops, and 2,500hp Napier Sabre VII. Sea Fury. 2,480hp Bristol Centaurus XII, XV, XVIII and 22.

Dimensions: Sea Fury. Span, 38ft 4¾in (16ft 1in folded); length, 34ft 3in (Mk X), 34ft 8in (Mk 11); wing area, 280 sq ft.

Weights: Mark 11. Tare, 9,240lb; all-up, 12,500lb.

Performance: Mk 11. Max speed, 460 mph at 18,000ft; time to 30,000ft, 10 min 48 sec; service ceiling, 35,800ft; normal range, 700 miles.

Armament: Mk 11. Four 20-mm Hispano Mk 5 cannon in outer wings; provision to carry two 1,000lb bombs, two 90 gallon drop tanks or up to sixteen three-inch 60lb rockets.

Prototypes: Fury, four, NX798, NX802, LA610 and VP 207 (NX798 first flown by P G Lucas on 1 September 1944). Sea Fury, three, SR661, SR666 and VB857. No production of Fury.

Production: Sea Fury F Mk X, 50 (between TF895-TF955). FB Mk 11, 615 (between TF956-TG129, VR918-VR952, VW224-VW718, VX608-VX764, WE673-WE806, WF590-WF627, WG564-WG630, WH581-WH623, WJ221-WJ301, WM472-WM495, WN474-WN487 and WZ627-WZ656). 22 aircraft licence-built in Holland.

Summary of Fleet Air Arm Service: Sea Fury F Xs served with Nos 700, 703, 736, 738, 778, 781, 787, 799, 802, 803, 805 and 807 Squadrons. FB 11s served with Nos 700, 703, 723, 724, 725, 736, 738, 739, 744, 751, 767, 773, 778, 781, 782, 787, 799, 801, 802, 803, 804, 805, 806, 807, 808, 810, 811, 850, 870, 871, 883, 898, 1831, 1832 and 1834 Squadrons.

Left: A composite formation of a Sea Fury F 10 and two FB 11s of No 805 Squadron flying from St Merryn, Cornwall, late in 1948; the nearest aircraft, TF925, is the Mark 10. (Photo: Sydney Camm Collection)

Below: A Sea Fury FB 11, VX667, of No 738 Squadron at Culdrose, Cornwall, in the early 1950s. This Squadron was part of the Naval Air Fighter School, and provided armament training to newly-qualified naval pilots. The aircraft shown here is fitted with rocket-assisted take-off gear under the fuselage, and not being engaged in deck flying has discarded its arrester hook. (Photo: Author's Collection)

cover provided by American F-80s. Occasionally the enemy fighters attacked the Fleet Air Arm aircraft, and the first MiG-15 destroyed by a Sea Fury fell to the guns of Lt Peter Carmichael RN on No 802 Squadron, launched from HMS *Ocean* on 9 August 1952.

Sea Furies continued to serve with the Fleet Air Arm until the mid-1950s, eventually equipping a total of fifteen operational squadrons and seventeen at second line, in addition to three Royal Naval Volunteer Reserve Squadrons, Nos 1831, 1832 and 1834.

A total of 615 Mark 11s was built, and 22 were licence-built in the Netherlands. Export orders were brisk with 45 Furies supplied to Iraq, 93 to Pakistan, 12 to Egypt, 18 (ex-Fleet Air Arm aircraft) to Burma, and 15 to Cuba.

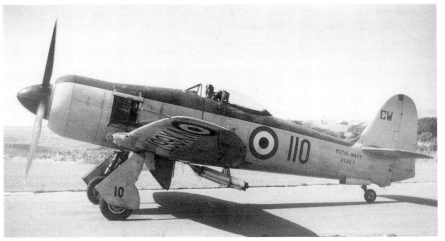

Numerous aircraft were delivered to the navies of Canada and Australia. These figures do not include numbers of two-seat trainers, of which the Fleet Air Arm also ordered a total of 60, termed the Sea Fury T Mk 20.

Blackburn B-48

The Blackburn B-48 was designed under the direction of G E Petty in 1944 to requirements set out in Specification S.28/43 for a replacement of the Firebrand torpedo fighter. Emphasis in the Specification, finalized and issued on 26 February 1944, was laid on increased pilot's field of view and an improved wing design. It is arguable whether this was strictly classifiable as a fighter, being primarily intended as a torpedo strike aircraft without any integral gun armament, although the design included

The first B-48, RT651, pictured during the winter of 1946-47, before its first flight. (Photo: Ministry of Supply RTP Neg No 14948D, dated February 1947)

wing strongpoints to which a pair of external 0.5in Browning machine guns could be attached.

Powered by a 2,475hp Bristol Centaurus 59, driving a Rotol five-blade propeller and with a Coffman cartridge starter system, the B-48 — known locally as the Firecrest (and YA.1 under SBAC nomenclature) — was a low, inverted-gull wing monoplane with

pronounced sweepback on the leading edge only. This served the double purpose of enabling a short, inwards-retracting undercarriage to be employed, and affording the pilot with an excellent field of view, particularly for deck landing. The tail unit was reminiscent of the Firebrand, with fin and rudder set forward of the elevator. A sting-type arrester hook was located under the

extreme tail, aft of the tailwheel.

Four high-lift Fowler flaps were located under the wings which incorporated a double fold, the outer wing sections (including the ailerons) folding up and inwards before the centre portion of each wing folded upward to the vertical position.

Two prototypes, RT651 and RT656, were ordered, and RT651 was first flown on 1 April 1947; the second of these aircraft was not completed, but a third example, VF172, was produced with power-boosted ailerons, and this was retained by the manufacturers for research purposes.

In truth, the Blackburn aircraft was pre-empted by the relatively swift acceptance of the propeller turbine as a likely powerplant for strike and torpedo

fighters and, although Blackburn pursued projects intended for such engines as the Armstrong Siddeley Python and

Rolls-Royce Clyde, the lead had already been snatched by the Westland Wyvern, a true strike fighter.

Type: Single-engine, single-seat, low inverted-gull wing monoplane torpedo strike aircraft.
Manufacturer: Blackburn and General Aircraft Ltd, Leeds and Brough, Yorkshire.
Air Ministry Specification: S.28/43.
Powerplant: One 2,475hp Bristol Centaurus 59 eighteen-cylinder, sleeve-valve, air-cooled radial engine driving Rotol five-blade propeller.
Dimensions: Span, 44ft 11½in (18ft 0in, folded); length, 39ft 3½in; height, 14ft 6in; wing area, 361.5 sq ft.
Weights: Tare, 10,513lb; all-up, 15,280lb.
Performance: Max speed, 380 mph at 19,000ft; service ceiling, 31,600ft; range, 900 miles (750 miles with torpedo).
Armament: Two 250-lb bombs or up to sixteen three-inch rocket projectiles and one torpedo; two 0.50in Browning machine guns could be carried in external pods in place of wing stores.
Prototypes: Two ordered, RT651 and RT656 (RT651 first flown on 1 April 1947; RT656 not completed); one additional prototype, VF172, retained by manufacturers. No production.

Westland W.34 and W.35 Wyvern

It is appropriate that the final aircraft to be included in this section should have been conceived as a piston engine-powered fighter which went on to give operational, indeed combat service with the Royal Navy as a propjet-powered strike fighter, for the Westland W.34 Wyvern's conception occurred in 1943 when the idea of harnessing the turbojet to propellers had hardly been mooted. It was also to be Westland Aircraft's last fixed-wing aeroplane to be built before the company turned its attention to rotorcraft.

The mid-War years brought increasing interest in fighter aircraft capable of delivering torpedoes, following the successful adaptation of the Beaufighter as an anti-shipping strike aircraft, and among the Specifications raised to express such ideas were S.6/43, S.11/43 and S.28/43, the last-named producing the Blackburn B-48, described above. At Westland, Dennis Edkins, assistant designer to Edward Petter, had schemed project designs to the first two requirements, labelled P 9, featuring the new horizontally-opposed flat-H sleeve-valve Rolls-Royce Eagle engine, mounted amidships in the fuselage aft of the cockpit, the contra-rotating propellers being driven through co-axial shafts.

This configuration met with a cool

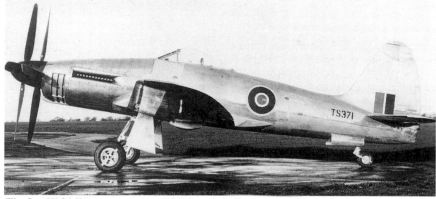

The first W.34 Wyvern prototype, TS371, with Rolls-Royce Eagle piston-engine; note the short fin and rudder. (Photo: via R C B Ashworth)

reception from the Westland pilots, and Edkins revised the design to mount the engine in the nose in the orthodox manner, and the project now received the Westland design number W.34. The aircraft featured a low-set wing with straight leading, and elliptical trailing edge, and the generously proportioned inboard sections, without dihedral, accommodated the undercarriage, a pair of 30-gallon fuel tanks, three-position Youngman-type flaps, two of the four 20mm Hispano cannon proposed, and the two low-profile engine radiators immediately aft of the undercarriage cells. Both the vertical and horizontal tail surfaces followed the wing planform with elliptical trailing edges, and a sting arrester hook was incorporated under the extreme rear of the fuselage.

The deep fuselage was dictated by affording the pilot with a good view over the very big engine and the wing leading

edge, and allowed two fuel tanks, one of 95 and the other of 173 gallon capacities, to be located forward and aft of the cockpit. The rear fuselage was an all-metal monocoque structure.

Specification N.11/44 was raised to cover the W 34 design, and six prototypes were ordered. In the meantime Westland had been studying early proposals for the development of propeller-turbines, and in August suggested this type of engine should be considered as an alternative powerplant for the W.34. The MAP, however, decided that all six prototypes should proceed with the Eagle, as planned, together with twenty pre-production aircraft under consideration. At this point the Air Ministry, aware of the need for long-range escort fighters in the Far East, stepped in with a request that two of the prototypes should be set aside for the RAF, and Specification F.13/44 was accordingly

Below: *One of the two Python-powered Wyvern TF 2 prototypes (probably VP109 as it is without arrester hook), showing the Fowler flaps extended and the final, tall fin, adopted on the production Wyvern S 4.* (Photo: Author's Collection)

prepared to cover these aircraft. (This proposal lapsed when both the Hornet and Tempest II demonstrated exceptionally good long-range capabilities.)

By late 1944 Frederick John William Wingfield Digby had been appointed Westland's chief designer, and it thus fell to him to manage the W.34's detail design and, although this went ahead fairly smoothly, development of the new Eagle engine was far from rapid. It was, after all, a very large and complex engine which broke new ground in many respects and, as the Westland W.34 would take the engine into the air for the first time, no flight experience could be gained during its development. It was not until 7 February 1945 that an instruction to proceed with manufacturing jigs was received and, following a number of bench running failures, the first W.34, TS371 — now named the Wyvern TF Mk I — was flown by Harald Penrose on 16 December 1946 from Boscombe Down's long runway. TS371 and TS375, were completed without folding wings, ejector seat, arrester hook and armament, the latter aircraft being flown on 10 September 1947.

Numerous problems were encountered, stemming largely from the enormous overhang of the engine and propeller installation, and this led to flexing of the long shaft to the front propeller and a difficulty in maintaining lubrication to the pitch-change bear-

ings. On 15 October TS375 suffered failure of these bearings, and, without being able to feather the eight blades, crashed; the pilot, Peter Garner, was killed.

The remaining four prototypes flew during 1948, completed to full Service equipment standard; TS378 was fitted with six-blade de Havilland contraprops; TS380 was used for external stores clearance and initial deck landing trials; TS384 was employed on gun firing and other armament trials; and TS387 flew full Service handling and performance assessment trials.

The original order for twenty pre-production Wyvern TF Is had been reduced to ten, VR131-VR140, but according to Mr Derek James (*Westland Aircraft since 1915*, Putnam, page 304), only seven of these may have been completed. As far as can be discovered, no Eagle-powered Wyvern

reached a Fleet Air Arm unit.

Instead, interest had by now centred firmly on the introduction of the propeller-turbine in the forms of the 4,000shp (plus 1,550lb thrust) Rolls-Royce Clyde and the 3,560shp (plus 1,100lb thrust) Armstrong Siddeley Python engines, and three prototypes had been under construction for some months, designed to Specification N.12/45, VP109 and VP113 with Python, and VP120 with the Clyde.

Demanding less airframe modification than the Python, the Clyde Wyvern TF Mk 2 (the W.35) was the first completed and, flown once again by Penrose, made its maiden flight at Boscombe Down on 18 January 1949 — an exceptionally brief flight when a fuel leak on to the hot exhaust pipe filled the cockpit with dense smoke immediately after take-off; only the pilot's great skill enabled him to land the aircraft safely. Once again Penrose had flown a new engine without the benefit of any previous test bed experience.

The second Wyvern TF Mk 2 prototype, VP113, in Service paint scheme and featuring most of the equipment and modifications thus far deemed necessary. In order to accommodate the undercarriage in the wing a system was introduced to shorten the main oleo struts during retraction. This picture gives a good impression of the great length of the turboprop engine. (Photo: via R C B Ashworth)

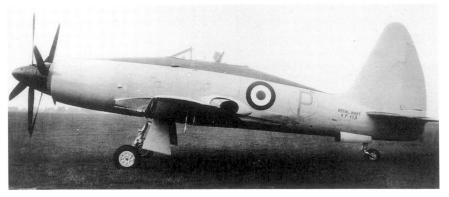

Unfortunately development of the Clyde was brought to a swift end, owing to Rolls-Royce's heavy commitment to another propjet engine, the Dart, now urgently required for the Viscount airliner, so that development of the Wyvern was now confined to the Python, a less compact engine which involved extensive design alterations owing to its bifurcated jet pipes which exhausted on both sides of the fuselage. (VP120 was later allocated to D Napier & Son Ltd at Luton for development of a project, the Wyvern IA, intended to feature the Napier Nomad compound engine, but neither this nor a proposed Wyvern 5E with the Double-Eland turboprop, came to fruition.)

A pre-production batch of twenty Wyvern TF 2s had been started when the Clyde was discontinued, and five aircraft were completed with the Python engine. Another aircraft, the Wyvern T Mk 3, VZ739, two-seat trainer, ordered to Specification T.12/48, was also built, but did not survive beyond the prototype stage.

The definitive Wyvern was the Python-powered S Mk 4, whose gestation period was longer than even the original Eagle-powered Mark I, for it should be emphasized that the principal rôle for which the aircraft was intended was that of a naval fighter, its ability to deliver a torpedo being a secondary function. Thus the inclusion of the very long Python engine imposed unusually severe combat stressing problems, not to mention the now familiar flexing tendencies of the front propeller shaft. A taller fin and rudder were necessitated to offset the much increased nose length, and in order to improve the deceleration (not an embarrassment with a piston engine), particularly in combat manœuvres, small wing-mounted airbrakes were added, in turn necessitating the use of small boundary layer fences to avoid aileron snatching when selecting the airbrakes.

The last nine pre-production TF Mk 2s were in most respects similar to the Wyvern S 4, and apart from final clearance of external stores, differed in only one significant respect; this was the adoption of a dihedral tailplane with winglets at semi-span to avoid rudder locking in sustained sideslip at low speeds.

A qualified Service release was granted in December 1952, and delivery of the first production Wyvern S 4s began early the following year. In May 1953

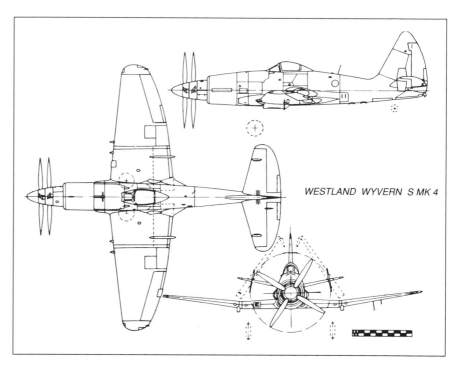

WESTLAND WYVERN S MK 4

Type: Single-engine, single-seat, low-wing monoplane naval fighter and torpedo-strike fighter.

Manufacturer: Westland Aircraft Ltd, Yeovil, Somerset.

Air Ministry Specifications: Mark I. N.11/44 (prototypes); 17/46P (pre-production). Mark 2. N.12/45 (prototypes); 21/48P (pre-production).

Powerplant: TF Mk I. One 2,690hp Rolls-Royce Eagle 22 twenty-four cylinder, flat-H horizontally-opposed, sleeve-valve, liquid-cooled, supercharged and geared in-line engine driving eight-blade Rotol or six-blade de Havilland contraprops. TF Mk 2. One 4,000shp (plus 1,550lb thrust) Rolls-Royce Clyde RCl.1 axial-flow turboprop or 3,560shp (plus 1,100lb thrust) Armstrong Siddeley Python ASP3 axial-flow turboprops. S Mk 4. 3,670shp (plus 1,180lb thrust) Python 3 with eight-blade Rotol contraprops.

Dimensions: Span, 44ft 0in (20ft 0in folded); length 42ft 3in; height, 15ft 9in (18ft 2in folded); wing area, 355 sq ft.

Weights: TF Mk I. Tare, 15,443lb; all-up (with torpedo), 21,879lb; S Mk 4. Tare, 15,600lb; all-up (with torpedo), 24,550lb.

Performance: TF Mk I. Max speed, 456 mph at 23,000ft; service ceiling, 32,100ft; max range, 1,186 miles. S Mk 4. Max speed, 383 mph at sea level; service ceiling, 28,000ft; max range, 910 miles.

Armament: Four 20mm Hispano Mk 5 cannon with 200 rounds per gun; one 2,500lb torpedo, or three 1,000lb bombs, or up to sixteen 90lb rocket projectiles.

Prototypes: TF Mk I, six, TS371, TS375, TS378, TS380, TS384 and TS387 (TS371 first flown by Harald Penrose on 16 December 1946 at Boscombe Down). TF Mk 2, three, VP109, VP113 and VP120.

Production: Total of 87 S Mk 4s (between VZ745-VX799, WL876-WL888 and WN324-WN336). In addition nine TF Mk 2s (VW870, VW873 and VW880-VW886) were converted to S 4s.

Summary of Service: Wyvern S Mk 4s served with Nos 700, 703, 764, 787, 813, 827, 830 and 831 Squadrons, Fleet Air Arm.

No 813 Squadron, commanded by Lt-Cdr C E Price, AFC, RN at Ford, was equipped with twelve aircraft, but were unable to embark in HMS *Albion* until September 1954 for service in the Mediterranean. The Wyvern's prolonged teething troubles were still not over as it was found that fuel starvation during high g catapult launching was causing flame-outs, and it was as a result of such a failure that Lt B O Macfarlane survived a unique escape; his Wyvern

VZ783 fell in the sea immediately after a catapult launch and was cut in half as *Albion*'s bows ran down the aircraft, and the pilot ejected while underwater in his Martin-Baker Mk 1B seat. No 827 Squadron re-equipped in 1954, and Nos 830 and 831 at the end of 1955.

No 830 Squadron, under the command of Lt-Cdr C V Howard RN, embarked in HMS *Eagle* in April 1956 for exercises in the Mediterranean, and was in that theatre when the Suez Crisis occurred in November. Called in at short notice to support the Allied operations, No 830 flew 82 strike and reconnaissance sorties against Egyptian airfields and other targets in the Canal Zone, losing two aircraft whose pilots ejected over the sea and were rescued safely.

The last Wyverns were withdrawn from operational service with the Fleet Air Arm when No 813 Squadron was disbanded at Ford in April 1958.

The first production Wyvern S Mk 4, VZ745, serving with No 813 Squadron aboard HMS Eagle, probably early in 1958. The aircraft includes the cut-back annular engine intake lips (giving the impression of a lengthened spinner), underwing drop tanks and rocket rails, and the dihedral tailplane with finlets. (Photo: Via R C B Ashworth)

Deployment of British Fighter Squadrons — January 1945

(Including Fighter Squadrons of the Commonwealth Air Forces and of Free Europeans serving with the Royal Air Force)

Home Based

No 1 Squadron	Supermarine Spitfire IX	Lympne
No 19 Squadron	(North American Mustang III/IV)	Andrews Field
No 23 Squadron	D.H. Mosquito VI	Little Snoring
No 25 Squadron	D.H. Mosquito NF 30	Castle Camps
No 26 Squadron	Supermarine Spitfire V	Exeter
No 29 Squadron	D.H. Mosquito NF 30	Hunsdon
No 33 Squadron	Hawker Tempest V	Predannack
No 63 Squadron	Supermarine Spitfire VC	North Weald
No 64 Squadron	(North American Mustang III)	Bentwaters
No 65 Squadron	(North American Mustang III)	Andrews Field
No 68 Squadron	D.H. Mosquito NF XVII	Coltishall
No 85 Squadron	D.H. Mosquito NF 30	Swannington
No 91 Squadron	Supermarine Spitfire IXB	Manston
No 118 Squadron	Supermarine Spitfire IX	Castletown
No 122 Squadron	(North American Mustang III)	Andrews Field
No 124 Squadron	Supermarine Spitfire IX	Manston
No 125 Squadron	D.H. Mosquito NF XVII	Coltishall
No 126 Squadron	(North American Mustang III)	Bentwaters
No 129 Squadron	(North American Mustang III)	Bentwaters
No 141 Squadron	D.H. Mosquito VI	West Raynham
No 144 Squadron	D.H. Mosquito II/VI	Banff
No 151 Squadron	D.H. Mosquito NF 30	Hunsdon
No 154 Squadron	Supermarine Spitfire VIII	Biggin Hill
No 157 Squadron	D.H. Mosquito XIX	Swannington
No 165 Squadron	Supermarine Spitfire IX	Bentwaters
No 169 Squadron	D.H. Mosquito VI/XIX	Great Massingham
No 222 Squadron	Hawker Tempest V	Predannack
No 229 Squadron	(1)Supermarine Spitfire XVI	Coltishall
No 234 Squadron	(North American Mustang III)	Bentwaters
No 235 Squadron	D.H. Mosquito VI	Banff
No 236 Squadron	(2)Bristol Beaufighter X	North Coates
No 239 Squadron	D.H. Mosquito NF 30	West Raynham

No 245 Squadron	Hawker Typhoon IB	Warmwell
No 248 Squadron	D.H. Mosquito VI/XVIII	Banff
No 254 Squadron	(2)Bristol Beaufighter X	North Coates
No 303 Squadron	Supermarine Spitfire IX	Coltishall
No 306 Squadron	(North American Mustang III)	Andrews Field
No 307 Squadron	D.H. Mosquito NF XII	Church Fenton
No 309 Squadron	(North American Mustang III)	Andrews Field
No 312 Squadron	Supermarine Spitfire IX	Bradwell Bay
No 313 Squadron	Supermarine Spitfire IX	Bradwell Bay
No 315 Squadron	(North American Mustang III)	Peterhead
No 316 Squadron	(North American Mustang III)	Andrews Field
No 333 Squadron	D.H. Mosquito VI	Banff
No 340 Squadron	Supermarine Spitfire IX	Turnhouse
No 403 Squadron	Supermarine Spitfire XVI	Warmwell
No 406 Squadron	D.H. Mosquito NF 30	Manston
No 441 Squadron	Supermarine Spitfire IX	Skaebrae
No 451 Squadron	Supermarine Spitfire IX/XVI	Hawkinge
No 453 Squadron	Supermarine Spitfire XVI	Matlaske
No 456 Squadron	D.H. Mosquito NF 30	Church Fenton
No 504 Squadron	Supermarine Spitfire IX	Manston
No 514 Squadron	D.H. Mosquito VI	Little Snoring
No 602 Squadron	Supermarine Spitfire XVI	Matlaske
No 603 Squadron	Supermarine Spitfire XVI	Coltishall
No 605 Squadron	D.H. Mosquito VI	Hartford Bridge
No 611 Squadron	(North American Mustang IV)	Hawkinge
No 616 Squadron	Gloster Meteor I/III	Manston

The Netherlands

No 2 Squadron	Supermarine Spitfire XIV	Gilze-Rijen
No 3 Squadron	Hawker Tempest V	Volkel
No 56 Squadron	Hawker Tempest V	Volkel
No 66 Squadron	Supermarine Spitfire XVI	Woensdrecht
No 80 Squadron	Hawker Tempest V	Volkel
No 127 Squadron	Supermarine Spitfire XVI	Woensdrecht

No 137 Squadron	Hawker Typhoon IB	Eindhoven
No 168 Squadron	Hawker Typhoon IB	Eindhoven
No 174 Squadron	Hawker Typhoon IB	Volkel
No 175 Squadron	Hawker Typhoon IB	Volkel
No 181 Squadron	Hawker Typhoon IB	Eindhoven
No 182 Squadron	Hawker Typhoon IB	Eindhoven
No 184 Squadron	Hawker Typhoon IB	Volkel
No 247 Squadron	Hawker Typhoon IB	Eindhoven
No 268 Squadron (3)(North American		
	Mustang II)	Gilze-Rijen
No 274 Squadron	Hawker Tempest V	Volkel
No 322 Squadron	Supermarine Spitfire XVI	Woensdrecht
No 331 Squadron	Supermarine Spitfire IX	Woensdrecht
No 332 Squadron	Supermarine Spitfire IX	Woensdrecht
No 401 Squadron	Supermarine Spitfire IX	Heesch
No 402 Squadron	Supermarine Spitfire XIV	Heesch
No 411 Squadron	Supermarine Spitfire IX	Heesch
No 412 Squadron	Supermarine Spitfire IX	Heesch
No 438 Squadron	Hawker Typhoon IB	Eindhoven
No 439 Squadron	Hawker Typhoon IB	Eindhoven
No 440 Squadron	Hawker Typhoon IB	Eindhoven
No 442 Squadron	Supermarine Spitfire IX	Heesch
No 485 Squadron	Supermarine Spitfire IX	Gilze-Rijen
No 486 Squadron	Hawker Tempest V	Volkel

Belgium

No 41 Squadron	Supermarine Spitfire XIV	Ophoven
No 74 Squadron	Supermarine Spitfire IX	Deurne
No 130 Squadron	Supermarine Spitfire XIV	Ophoven
No 164 Squadron	Hawker Typhoon IB	Chièvres
No 183 Squadron	Hawker Typhoon IB	Chièvres
No 193 Squadron	Hawker Typhoon IB	Deurne
No 197 Squadron	Hawker Typhoon IB	Deurne
No 198 Squadron	Hawker Typhoon IB	Chièvres
No 257 Squadron	Hawker Typhoon IB	Deurne
No 263 Squadron	Hawker Typhoon IB	Deurne
No 266 Squadron	Hawker Typhoon IB	Deurne
No 302 Squadron	Supermarine Spitfire IX	St Denis Westrem
No 308 Squadron	Supermarine Spitfire IX	St Denis Westrem
No 317 Squadron	Supermarine Spitfire IX	St Denis Westrem
No 329 Squadron	Supermarine Spitfire IX	Deurne
No 341 Squadron	Supermarine Spitfire IX	Deurne
No 345 Squadron	Supermarine Spitfire IX	Deurne
No 349 Squadron	Supermarine Spitfire IX	Maldeghem
No 350 Squadron	Supermarine Spitfire XIV	Ophoven
No 416 Squadron	Supermarine Spitfire XVI	Evère
No 421 Squadron	Supermarine Spitfire XVI	Evère
No 443 Squadron	Supermarine	
	Spitfire IX/XVI	Evère
No 609 Squadron	Hawker Typhoon IB	Chièvres
No 610 Squadron	Supermarine Spitfire XIV	Ophoven

France

No 219 Squadron	D.H. Mosquito NF 30	Amiens/Glissy
No 264 Squadron	D.H. Mosquito NF XIII	Lille
No 305 Squadron	D.H. Mosquito VI	Cambrai
No 326 Squadron	Supermarine Spitfire IX	Luxeuil
No 327 Squadron	Supermarine Spitfire IX	Nancy
No 328 Squadron	Supermarine Spitfire VIII	Dijon
No 488 Squadron	D.H. Mosquito NF 30	Amiens/Glissy
No 604 Squadron	D.H. Mosquito NF XIII	Lille
No 613 Squadron	D.H. Mosquito VI	Cambrai

Mediterranean and Egypt

No 6 Squadron	Hawker Hurricane IV	Canne, Italy
No 32 Squadron	Supermarine Spitfire IX	Salonika, Greece
No 39 Squadron	Bristol Beaufighter X	Hassani, Greece
No 43 Squadron	Supermarine Spitfire IX	Rimini, Italy
No 72 Squadron	Supermarine Spitfire IX	Rimini, Italy

No 73 Squadron	Supermarine Spitfire IX	Canne, Italy
No 87 Squadron	Supermarine Spitfire IX	Pontedera, Italy
No 92 Squadron	Supermarine Spitfire VIII	Bellaria, Italy
No 93 Squadron	Supermarine Spitfire IX	Rimini, Italy
No 94 Squadron	Supermarine Spitfire V	Hassani, Greece
No 111 Squadron	Supermarine Spitfire IX	Rimini, Italy
No 112 Squadron	(North American	
	Mustang III)	Fano, Italy
No 145 Squadron	Supermarine	
	Spitfire VIII/IX	Bellaria, Italy
No 185 Squadron	Supermarine Spitfire IX	Pontedera, Italy
No 208 Squadron	Supermarine Spitfire IX	Peretola, Italy
No 213 Squadron	(North American	
	Mustang III)	Biferno, Italy
No 225 Squadron	Supermarine	
	Spitfire VC/IX	Peretola, Italy
No 237 Squadron	Supermarine Spitfire IX	Falconara, Italy
No 241 Squadron	Supermarine	
	Spitfire VIII/IX	Bellaria, Italy
No 249 Squadron	(North American	
	Mustang III)	Biferno, Italy
No 250 Squadron	(Curtiss Kittyhawk IV)	Fano, Italy
No 252 Squadron	Bristol Beaufighter X	Mersa Matruh, Egypt
No 253 Squadron	Supermarine	
	Spitfire VIII/IX	Canne, Italy
No 255 Squadron	D.H. Mosquito XIX	Foggia, Italy
No 256 Squadron	D.H. Mosquito	
	NF XII/XIII	Foggia, Italy
No 260 Squadron	(North American	
	Mustang III)	Cervia, Italy
No 272 Squadron	Bristol Beaufighter X/XI	Foggia, Italy
No 318 Squadron	Supermarine Spitfire V	Forli, Italy
No 335 Squadron	Supermarine Spitfire V	Hassani, Greece
No 336 Squadron	Supermarine Spitfire V	Hassani, Greece
No 351 Squadron	Hawker Hurricane IV	Canne, Italy
No 352 Squadron	Supermarine Spitfire V	Canne, Italy
No 417 Squadron	Supermarine Spitfire VIII	Bellaria, Italy
No 450 Squadron	(Curtiss Kittyhawk IV)	Fano, Italy
No 600 Squadron	Bristol Beaufighter VI	Cesenatico, Italy
No 601 Squadron	Supermarine Spitfire IX	Bellaria, Italy
No 1435 Squadron	Supermarine Spitfire IX	Grottaglie, Italy

South-East Asia and Australia

No 5 Squadron	(Republic	
	Thunderbolt II)	Nazir, India
No 11 Squadron	Hawker Hurricane IIC	Tamu, Burma
No 17 Squadron	Supermarine Spitfire VIII	Taukkyan, Burma
No 20 Squadron	Hawker Hurricane IV	Sapan, India
No 27 Squadron	Bristol Beaufighter X	Chiringa, India
No 28 Squadron	Hawker Hurricane IIC	Tamu, Burma
No. 30 Squadron	(Republic	
	Thunderbolt I/II)	Jumchar, India
No 34 Squadron	Hawker Hurricane IIC	Yazagyo, Burma
No 42 Squadron	Hawker Hurricane IV	Kangla, India
No 45 Squadron	D.H. Mosquito VI	Kumbhirgram, India
No 54 Squadron	Supermarine Spitfire VIII	Darwin, Australia
No 60 Squadron	Hawker Hurricane IIC	Taukkyan, Burma
No 67 Squadron	Supermarine Spitfire VIII	Maunghama, Burma
No 79 Squadron	(Republic	
	Thunderbolt II)	Wangjing, India
No 81 Squadron	Supermarine Spitfire VIII	Ratmalana, Ceylon
No 82 Squadron	D.H. Mosquito VI	Kumbhirgram, India
No 89 Squadron	Bristol Beaufighter VI	Baigachi, India
No 113 Squadron	Hawker Hurricane IIC	Yazagyo, Burma
No 123 Squadron	(Republic	
	Thunderbolt II)	Nazir, India

No 132 Squadron Supermarine Spitfire VIII Vavuniya, Ceylon
No 134 Squadron (Republic
                 Thunderbolt II)   Ratnap, Burma
No 135 Squadron (Republic
                 Thunderbolt I)   Jumchar, India
No 136 Squadron Supermarine Spitfire VIII Minneriya, Ceylon
No 146 Squadron (Republic
                 Thunderbolt I)   Wangjing, India
No 152 Squadron Supermarine Spitfire VIII Tamu, Burma
No 155 Squadron Supermarine Spitfire VIII Tulihal, India
No 176 Squadron Bristol Beaufighter VI   Minneriya, Ceylon
No 177 Squadron Bristol Beaufighter X   Chiringa, India
No 211 Squadron Bristol Beaufighter X   Chiringa, India
No 258 Squadron (Republic
                 Thunderbolt I/II) Ratnap, Burma
No 261 Squadron (Republic
                 Thunderbolt I/II) Wangjing, India
No 548 Squadron Supermarine Spitfire VIII Darwin, Australia
No 549 Squadron Supermarine Spitfire VIII Darwin, Australia
No 607 Squadron Supermarine Spitfire VIII Tulihal, India
No 615 Squadron Supermarine Spitfire VIII Baigachi, India

Fleet Air Arm
No 800 Squadron (Grumman Hellcat II)   Long Kesh
No 801 Squadron Supermarine Seafire III   Grimsetter
No 804 Squadron (Grumman Hellcat II)   HMS *Ameer*
No 807 Squadron Supermarine Seafire III   Dekheila, Egypt
No 808 Squadron (Grumman Hellcat I)   Ballyhalbert
No 809 Squadron Supermarine Seafire III   Dekheila, Egypt
No 879 Squadron Supermarine Seafire III   Dekheila, Egypt
No 880 Squadron Supermarine Seafire III   Skaebrae
No 881 Squadron (Grumman Wildcat VI)   HMS *Trumpeter*
No 882 Squadron (Grumman Wildcat V/VI)   Long Kesh

No 885 Squadron (Grumman Hellcat I/II)   HMS *Ruler*
No 887 Squadron Supermarine Seafire III HMS *Indefatigable*
No 894 Squadron Supermarine Seafire III HMS *Indefatigable*
No 896 Squadron (Grumman Hellcat II)   Wingfield
No 898 Squadron (Grumman Hellcat II)   Wingfield
No 899 Squadron Supermarine Seafire III Long Kesh
No 1770 Squadron Fairey Firefly I   HMS *Indefatigable*
No 1771 Squadron Fairey Firefly I   Hatston
No 1772 Squadron Fairey Firefly I   Burscough
No 1790 Squadron Fairey Firefly I   Burscough
No 1830 Squadron (Vought Corsair II)   HMS *Illustrious*
No 1833 Squadron (Vought Corsair II)   HMS *Illustrious*
No 1834 Squadron (Vought Corsair II)   HMS *Victorious*
No 1835 Squadron (Vought Corsair IV)   Brunswick, USA
No 1836 Squadron (Vought Corsair II)   HMS *Victorious*
No 1839 Squadron (Grumman Hellcat II)   HMS *Indomitable*
No 1840 Squadron (Grumman Hellcat II)   HMS *Speaker*
No 1841 Squadron (Vought Corsair II)   Dekheila, Egypt
No 1842 Squadron (Vought Corsair II)   HMS *Formidable*
No 1843 Squadron (Vought Corsair II)   Eglinton
No 1844 Squadron (Grumman Hellcat I)   HMS *Indomitable*
No 1845 Squadron (Vought Corsair IV)   HMS *Slinger*
No 1846 Squadron (Vought Corsair III)   Ballyhalbert
No 1850 Squadron (Vought Corsair IV)   Ayr
No 1851 Squadron (Vought Corsair IV)   HMS *Thane*

Notes: (1) Squadron disbanded, 10 January 1945
       (2) Performing torpedo-strike fighter rôle
       (3) Performing fighter-reconnaissance rôle

(United States-built fighter aircraft are shown in brackets)

7. THE DAWN OF THE JET AGE

The Royal Air Force was second only to the *Luftwaffe* in introducing jet fighters into combat service, yet the inclusion of just one Gloster Meteor squadron in the above deployment table conceals the extent of research that had been conducted in Britain to produce a viable turbojet powerplant. And that research, spearheaded by the pioneering work done during the 1930s by Flt Lt F Whittle (later Air Cdre Sir Frank, KBE, CB, FRS) was carried forward by a growing number of manufacturers during the War years so that, by 1945, more than half a dozen companies were contributing in no mean fashion to Britain's world leadership in gas-turbine technology, a leadership that was to remain scarcely challenged for a further quarter century.

Nor were the aircraft designers slow to recognise the enormous potential of this new form of propulsion, which presented all manner of opportunities to dispense with weighty, drag-producing components of the traditional aeroplane.

Elimination of the propeller permitted shorter and lighter undercarriages, allowed the engine to be placed almost anywhere other than the inconvenient nose location — in turn making possible undreamed-of fields of pilot vision — and so on.

It was perhaps appropriate that George Carter, who had been able to witness Whittle's early engine on test, was given the task of designing from scratch Britain's first turbojet-powered research aeroplane, the Gloster E.28/39, and thereafter to embark on the Meteor. Another gifted engineer, Maj Frank Bernard Halford, designer of the D.H.4 during the First World War, took up the challenge and ultimately produced the engines which first took the Meteor into the air; and it was the long-standing association that had existed between Halford and Geoffrey de Havilland that resulted in the development of and powerplant for Britain's second fighter, the Vampire.

Notwithstanding this flying start, Britain was, at the end of the War, obliged to reduce her expenditure on her armed forces and their equipment, though perhaps somewhat less drastically than after the Armistice of 1918. Manpower of the three Services quickly diminished as hundreds of thousands of soldiers, sailors and airmen returned to civilian lives and, as a natural consequence, the RAF's squadrons simply disappeared until, by the end of 1946, the number of fighter squadrons had been reduced to a quarter of the late-wartime strength. Huge numbers of aircraft were flown to maintenance units for scrapping (and American Mustangs and Thunderbolts, supplied under the Lend-Lease Act, were returned to the USA).

Four types of existing propeller-driven fighters were selected to remain in service with Fighter Command for the time being, namely the Spitfire, Tempest, Hornet and Mosquito, while the Meteor and Vampire continued to be delivered to those squadrons selected to survive the post-War cut-backs.

The Meteor proved to be a sound design by the standards of the day, with a limited development potential; the Vampire was equally sound, though of more modest pretensions, and proved an ideal mount for the Royal Auxiliary Air Force.

In short, owing to the pervading atmosphere of post-War austerity, the RAF had to 'make do' with its existing equipment, a task made more palatable by the trumpeting that accompanied the seizure of the world speed record (twice in two years) by the Meteor. But, as is so often the case, the speed record propaganda was a two-edged sword, serving to persuade Westminster politicians no less than the Treasury, that the Meteor was a world beater in a much wider sense. In other words, with no other war on the horizon, the Meteor and the Vampire could soldier on in service, at least until Britain's economy was strong enough to support the luxury of new military aeroplanes.

Unfortunately this state of affairs was presented at just the moment that the fastest fighters in service were beginning to encounter the phenomena, known then as compressibility effects, as their level speeds approached that of the speed of sound. And it was the research needed to examine these effects, and the research aircraft to provide the data, that were to be denied the essential support by the Treasury under Clement Attlee's socialist government. Such esoteric subjects as the investigation of high speed flight, in all probability extremely costly to investigate, had no chance of attracting the slightest sympathy among a society struggling to find its feet in a war-weary nation.

Instead, the aircraft industry — itself shrinking as the shadow factories discontinued aircraft production and contracts were cancelled — was required to undertake the necessary research at its own expense and risk. This at least offered the possibility of obtaining manufacturing contracts in the longer term, as individual companies gained the necessary technical knowledge through their own research efforts. The industry was thus spared a repetition of the swingeing tax burden of excess war profits that had almost destoyed it in 1919 and 1920. Those companies that could afford to retain their large design and research staffs to conduct this research were those that survived, and to support those staffs the companies had already to be producing aircraft in quantity.

Unfortunately British engineers had not been given adequate opportunities at the end of the War to examine the fruits of German technical progress, American and Russian authorities being diligent in removing vast quantities of records so that they could be analysed in great detail at their own research establishments. Inducements, very attractive to citizens of war-torn Germany, were offered to selected aircraft design staff members to enter the USA to continue their work. Scarcely anything of this nature was undertaken by Britain, other than to assemble examples of captured enemy aircraft, such as the Messerschmitt Me 262, Arado Ar 234 and Heinkel He 162, and, on account of a lack of the necessary specialist support services, relatively little experimental flying was done, and examination of airframes and engines was cursory to say the least. It is said that the development of the North American F-86 Sabre, the world's first successful transonic fighter, in little over two years after the War, benefitted immeasurably from a highly detailed and programmed examination of the Me 262's wing.

Sadly, while companies like Rolls-Royce, Armstrong Siddeley and de Havilland advanced fairly rapidly in engine technology, Britain had to feel her way cautiously in aircraft design, first with rocket-propelled models, and shortly afterwards by means of relatively inexpensive prototypes of strictly limited application.

While de Havilland followed its own path towards the radical Comet jet airliner, with the diminutive D.H. 108 Swallow tailless research aircraft (in which Geoffrey de Havilland Jnr was to lose his life), Supermarine and Hawker each progressed through a succession of relatively orthodox research prototypes. And just as these companies succeeded in reaching production of their Swift and Hunter transonic fighters, America flew her first 'Century' fighter, the supersonic North American F-100 Super Sabre.

The folly of neglecting defence research was brought home to the British government when the Soviet Union's sabre-rattling brought about the blockade of Berlin in June 1948, and the parlous state of Britain's air force became all too obvious, without a single jet fighter capable of providing any sort of deterrent to this manifestation of what would soon be understood as the Cold War. Ironically the same government had sanctioned the supply of new Rolls-Royce Tay jet engines to Russia only the previous year, and adaptations of these same engines were to power the Soviet Union's first successful transonic jet fighter, the MiG-15.

And while the United States deployed modern jet fighters to Korea, after a fighting war broke out in that country in 1950, the only British fighters to be deployed were Gloster Meteors of the Royal Australian Air Force. Needless to say, the Communist air forces opposing the United Nations, were equipped with MiG-15s.

The lean years of 1946-53 for RAF Fighter Command were so nearly disastrous for Britain's aircraft industry. Fortunately the financially powerful Hawker Siddeley Group was able to distribute its contracts among its component companies with the founder member, Hawker Aircraft Ltd, able to sub-contract both the Sea Hawk and Hunter as its own production of the Sea Fury eventually ran out. Supermarine had produced the Attacker to fill the gap left by the failed Spiteful, and this aircraft formed the basis of a family of research prototypes which in turn led to the Swift and Scimitar fighters.

Thus, having concentrated on the development of their successful wartime propeller-driven fighters, Vickers and Hawker were relatively late into the jet fighter field. Gloster, on the other hand, kept hard at work on Meteor development (including a night fighter variant, whose production was taken over by Armstrong Whitworth at Coventry), produced an experimental single-engine jet fighter, but this failed to impress as presenting little significant advance over the Meteor. The company did, however, produce prototypes of the big Javelin all-weather fighter, and this, as a contemporary of the Hawker Hunter, put Gloster on a fairly firm footing as production of the Meteor ran out.

De Havilland, soon to be absorbed into the Hawker Siddeley Group, had its hands full with Vampire production, not to mention its development of the Comet jet airliner. After development of two-seat night fighter and trainer versions of the Vampire, de Havilland introduced an improved wing for the Venom, a very useful fighter and fighter bomber considering its outdated basic technology. Moreover, another contemporary of the

Hunter and Javelin was the D.H. 110 Sea Vixen which, after a tragic accident which cost the lives of John Derry and his flight observer Tony Richards, went on to serve as a naval all-weather fighter of some potency.

In the field of fighter armament, the cannon remained the basis of Service requirements for ten years after the War, and the 30mm Aden gun was introduced in the Hunter and its contemporaries, but even as the first Hunters were coming off the production lines

the first trial installations were being attempted of air-to-air guided missiles such as the Fairey Fireflash beam-rider and de Havilland Firestreak infra-red seeker.

The creation of NATO in 1949, apart from leading to the establishment of permanent RAF bases in Germany, with their attendant RAF fighter and light bomber squadrons, generated a ready market for British fighters among the European partners, as well as a consortium of manufacturers of those aircraft

in the Low Countries.

Yet the truth remains that the sharp edge of the Western Allies' sword was provided by America whose aircraft industry had experienced little reduction since the end of the Second World War, and the arrival in Europe of F-100s, and later the F-101 and F-104, forced the RAF to employ its Hunters almost exclusively in the ground attack and fighter reconnaissance rôles — until the arrival in service of its first Mach 2 fighter, the English Electric Lightning.

Gloster Meteor

During the first 40 years of British military aviation — the era of multiple independent aircraft manufacturers — the fighter scene was dominated by half a dozen companies, namely Bristol, Fairey, Gloster, Hawker, Sopwith and Supermarine, while a host of smaller firms contributed numerous interesting, and often useful prototypes which played their part in advancing technology. Survival among the major companies, however, was frequently precarious, and all too often a period of profitable enterprise would be followed by fallow years owing simply to the company's inability to support continuing originality of thought among its project designers and research departments.

When viewed overall this was probably healthy for a competitive industry, even if it was painful for individual manufacturers. The Gloster Aircraft Company suffered lean years in the early 1930s before capturing healthy production orders for its Gauntlet and Gladiator biplane fighters which lasted until 1938. After they were exhausted the labour force was heavily committed to undertake sub-contracted production orders for the Hawker Henley, Hurricane and Typhoon, and the Armstrong Whitworth Albermarle. Only towards the end of the War was the company once again able to engage in production of an in-house aircraft, the Gloster Meteor. And this classic, first generation jet fighter, bought survival for the company's infrastructure throughout the lean post-War years.

The company's veteran Chief Designer, Henry Folland, who, perhaps naturally, felt that Gloster's design

efforts were being overshadowed by Sydney Camm's influence, left in 1937 when it had become obvious that his long line of biplane interceptors could go no further, his place being taken by Wilfred George Carter. (It will be recalled that Carter had himself left the H G Hawker Engineering Company in the mid-1920s.) Carter's early responsibilities as Chief Designer lay in development of the Gloster F.9/37 twin-engine fighter and of a radical twin-boom pusher fighter to Specification F.18/37 powered by a single Napier Sabre. The former progressed no further than the prototype stage, and the latter was abandoned without being built owing to uncertainty of the Sabre's future. It was profoundly ironic that the successful

tender to F.18/37, was Sydney Camm's Hawker Typhoon, powered by the Sabre engine, and that Gloster was to be that fighter's principal manufacturer.

Although Carter's F.18/37 essay was abandoned, it was to have an important influence on events at Gloster. The twin-boom pusher layout appeared to be appropriate to the use of a gas turbine powerplant, and it was in this context that Carter became aware of the work being done by Flt Lt Frank Whittle in the field of jet propulsion, and a growing empathy existed between the two men. (It is worth remarking here that, although Carter persisted no further with a twin-boom jet aircraft, this was exactly the configuration adopted by de Havilland for that company's first jet fighter

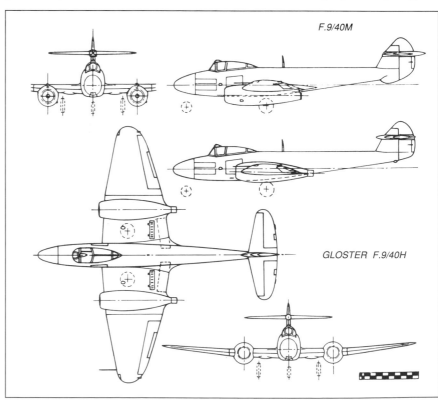

F.9/40M

GLOSTER F.9/40H

The first Gloster F.9/40 prototype, DG202/ G, powered by de Havilland-Halford H1 engines, during deck-handling trials aboard HMS Pretoria Castle *in August 1945.* (Photo: via Derek James)

design that was to become the Vampire.)

Having been present at the bench running of Whittle's first successful gas turbine at Lutterworth, Carter agreed to begin preliminary work on an aircraft in which the engine could be flown. Specification E.28/39 was duly issued by the Air Ministry to Gloster on 3 February 1940, and this small single-engine research prototype, W4041, was eventually flown by P E G Sayer at Cranwell on 15 May 1941. The series of trials with this historic aircraft, together with a similar example (W4046) were outstandingly successful and were vindication of a dozen years of pioneering work by Whittle, and half a dozen of his engines, as well as the Rover W.2B turbojet were flown. Although the E.28/39 was in no sense a fighter prototype, the original Specification had required representative space and weight allowances to be made for armament.

Some months before manufacture of W4041 had even started, Carter was giving thought to the configuration of a turbojet-powered fighter aircraft and, with very low thrust being anticipated from the early Whittle engines — the first flights of the E.28/39 were achieved with only 860lb thrust — he opted for a twin-engine design with, as in the E.28/39, a nosewheel undercarriage. The same line of reasoning had been taken by the Germans (unbeknown to anyone in Britain), who had flown their first jet research aircraft, the single-engine Heinkel He 176 on 27 August 1939, and whose first purpose-designed jet fighters were the twin-engine He 280 and Messerschmitt Me 262.

At the height of the Battle of Britain, in August 1940, Carter submitted to the Air Ministry his initial design proposals for his new fighter, and three months later Specification F.9/40, drafted around these proposals, was issued to Gloster (see Appendix, page 433). Although this requirement also called for an armament of six 20mm Hispano cannon, Carter pointed to the lack of power then ex-

pected to be available from the Whittle engines and managed to gain acceptance of an armament reduced to four cannon. A partial mock-up of the aircraft was inspected in February 1941, and shortly afterwards Gloster received an order for twelve F.9/40 prototypes; this was later reduced to eight (DG202—DG209), and in June the initial production requirement for 250 aircraft was notified to the company.

Manufacture of the prototypes advanced very slowly, and the first, DG202/G, underwent ground running of its Rover-built W.2B engines on 29 June 1942, by which time the name Meteor had been selected for the new fighter. Continuing delays with W.2B flight engines prompted the MAP to press for accelerated development of the de Havilland-Halford H.1 and Metropolitan Vickers F.2 engines. The fundamental differences between these engines lay in their compressor type. The W.2B employed a two-sided centrifugal compressor with reverse gas flow through the radially-distributed individual combustion cans. The H.1 engine featured a single-sided centrifugal compressor providing straight-through gas flow in the combustion cans; and the Metrovick F.2 employed an annular intake to a multi-stage axial-flow compressor and straight-through gas flow.

Accordingly, the first flight by a Meteor prototype was made by Michael Daunt, Gloster's Chief Test Pilot (died July 1991) in DG206/G on 5 March 1943, powered by H.1 engines at

Cranwell. The other F.9/40s, apart from DG202/G with W.2B/23 Wellands, were powered by a variety of engines: DG203/G, W.2/500s and W.2/700s; DG204/G, Metrovick F.2s; DG205/G, W.2B/23 Wellands; DG207/G, H.1B Goblins; DG208/G, W.2B/23 Wellands; and DG209/G, W.2B/37 Derwents, see below. (DG207/G became the sole prototype of the proposed Meteor Mark II, which was not pursued further.)

Despite early delays and problems with the W.2B engines, its development and production was taken over by Rolls-Royce — the name Welland becoming the first of a long line of river names bestowed by the company on its jet engines — and was selected to power the production Meteor F 1, the prototype of which, EE210/G, was flown by Daunt on 12 January 1944; this aircraft was shipped to the United States for evaluation, in exchange for an American Bell XP-59A Airacomet jet fighter.

Twenty production Meteor F 1s (EE210—EE229) were built, of which twelve were delivered to No. 616 (South Yorkshire) Squadron, starting on 12 July 1944. They were soon in action against the German V 1 flying bombs, the first being destroyed by Fg Off Dean on 4 August; in this action Dean's cannon jammed and the pilot caused the bomb to crash by using his wingtip to upset the weapon's autopilot. In general, however, the Meteor was not considered successful against the flying bombs as its speed and acceleration were signifi-

A production Meteor F III with the short engine nacelles enclosing the new Rolls-Royce Derwent I turbojets of 2,000lb thrust. (Photo: Rolls-Royce Ltd, Neg No A/273)

Left: *A production Gloster Meteor F IV, EE592, showing the lengthened engine nacelles and short-span wings in November 1946, two months after a similar aircraft had established a new World Speed Record at almost 616 mph.* (Photo: Author's Collection)

Below: *The first production Meteor F 8, VZ438, with angular tail surfaces and the original small diameter engine intakes.* (Photo: Author's Collection)

cantly inferior to the Tempest V and Spitfire XIV.

Several of the other Meteor Is were used for experimental purposes, the most important of which was EE227/G, fitted with a pair of Rolls-Royce RB.50 Trent turboprops driving five-blade Rotol propellers; flown by Eric Greenwood on 20 September 1945, this was the world's first turboprop-powered aircraft.

The Meteor III was the first major production version, of which a total of 210 examples was built. The first fifteen aircraft were powered by 2,000lb-thrust Welland engines, but almost all the remainder were fitted with the new 'straight-through' 2,000lb-thrust Rolls-Royce W.2B/37 Derwent I turbojets. Following trials with the Meteor I, EE211/G, lengthened nacelles were incorporated in the final fifteen Meteor IIIs. This version ultimately served with Nos 1, 56, 63, 66, 74, 91, 92, 124, 222, 234, 245, 257, 263, 266, 500, 504 and 616 Squadrons, remaining with Fighter Command from January 1945 until October 1951.

The lengthened engine nacelles, referred to above, were found to increase the Meteor III's top speed by some 60 mph, and in 1945 Rolls-Royce came up with a much improved version of the Derwent, the Mark 5, producing 3,500lb thrust, and this engine was introduced in the Meteor F IV. 535 examples were produced for the RAF, beginning with EE517; of these, 46 were built by Armstrong Whitworth. The Mark IV was strengthened throughout and featured a pressurized cockpit. Service aircraft were intended to be cleared to Mach 0.85, but in practice the maximum speed was in the region of Mach 0.81 at 30,000 ft, at which directional instability (caused by airflow breakdown round the rudder) rendered the aircraft difficult to control.

Two Meteor F IIIs, EE454 and EE455, were completed to early Mark IV standard with Derwent 5s for an attack on the World Speed Record, and on 7 November 1945 Gp Capt Hugh Joseph Wilson (later CB, AFC**) of the RAF High Speed Flight, established a new record at 606.38 mph in EE454. Shortly afterwards Gloster introduced wings reduced in span to 37ft 2in on the Meteor IV, a modification that increased the rate of roll to more than 80 degrees/second. Three such aircraft, EE548, EE549 and EE550, were delivered to the High Speed Flight in 1946, and on 7 September that year, flown by Gp Capt Edward Mortlock Donaldson (later Air Cdre, CB, CBE, DSO, AFC*), EE549 raised the speed record to 615.78 mph.

By 1946 RAF Fighter Command was committed to become an all-jet force, and at the end of that year eight squadrons were flying the Meteor F III (the first F IV joined No 92 Squadron in January 1947). Vampire Is equipped three other squadrons. However, postWar austerity and Service cut-backs deprived the aircraft industry of financial support to pursue the necessary research into transonic and supersonic flight and — perhaps influenced by the exaggerated potential implied by the Meteors' speeds records — the Air Ministry realised that the RAF would have to make do with the Meteor and Vampire for the foreseeable future. Meanwhile both the USA and the Soviet Union were already well advanced with the development of

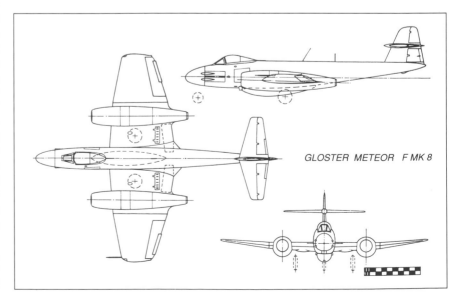

GLOSTER METEOR F MK 8

their first transonic fighters.

Production of the Meteor F IV — written as F 4 from 1948 — lasted until April 1950. In the meantime, however, the two-seat Meteor T 7 trainer had flown in March 1948 and had at once displayed noticeably improved directional control. As the aircraft differed primarily in having a nose lengthened by 27 inches to accommodate the instructor's cockpit, it was decided to lengthen the nose of the single-seaters in due course by inserting an extra fuselage bay containing a 95gal fuel tank between the ammunition bay and the main fuselage fuel tank, this modification being first flown in RA382.

Meteor F 4s were exported to Argentina, Belgium, Denmark, Egypt and the Netherlands, while others underwent extensive trials with new turbojets. Reheat systems were flown in Derwent-powered RA435 and VT196; RA490 was flown with Metrovick Beryl axial-flow turbojets and later with specially-modified Rolls-Royce Nenes for trials with a jet-deflection system; RA491 flew with Rolls-Royce Avon axial-flow engines, and later with French SNECMA Atar turbojets. Several Mark 4s were experimentally fitted with nose probes for flight refuelling trials with No 245 Squadron at Horsham St Faith, Norfolk.

RA418 flew with a trial installation of reconnaissance cameras in the nose and, although this was not successful owing

to persistent icing up of the camera ports, it led to the development of a new version, the Meteor FR Mark 5. The prototype, VT347, featured forward facing and oblique cameras in the nose and a vertical camera in the rear fuselage. Unfortunately this aircraft broke up in the air during its first flight on 15 June 1949, killing its pilot, Rodney Dryland. This version was not proceeded with.

The next fighter version was the Meteor F 8, an aircraft that was to become Fighter Command's standard interceptor between 1950 and 1954— the years that saw the introduction of the American 'century-series' of supersonic fighters. The prototype, VT150, was first flown by Jan Zurakowski on 12 October 1948 and featured an entirely new tail unit (similar to that being developed on the Gloster E.1/44) with straight-tapered fin, rudder, tailplane and elevator. Production aircraft also included the additional fuselage bay flown in RA382, referred to above, a Martin-Baker ejection seat, lengthened cartridge ejector fairings and provision for a large ventral fuel tank. Derwent 8 engines were standard, and the primary structure was further strengthened by the inclusion of high tensile steel components. Early Meteor 8s possessed small-diameter engine intakes, but later these were enlarged.

The improvements represented by the Meteor F 8 were not manifest so

much in improved performance (now 550 mph TAS at 36,000 feet, Mach 0.83) as by more precise control and improved steadiness as a gun platform. No fewer than 1,090 Mark 8s were produced on MoS contracts for the RAF between September 1949 and April 1954, first joining No 1 Squadron, commanded by Maj D F Smith USAF, at Tangmere in December 1949. They subsequently served with 21 squadrons of the RAF and 10 of the RAuxAF. Others were exported to Australia, Belgium, Brazil, Denmark, Egypt, Israel, the Netherlands and Syria, and substantial licence production was undertaken in Belgium and the Netherlands.

Although RAF fighters were not directly involved in the Korean War, 89 ex-RAF Meteor 8s were supplied to the Royal Australian Air Force whose No 77 Squadron was thus equipped and fought for 30 months between February 1951 and July 1953, losing 48 of their number, many of them to the Communist MiG-15s. Three of the enemy jets were claimed destroyed by the Meteor pilots.

Not surprisingly Meteor 8s were extensively employed for trial installations. Engine test beds included VZ517 with Armstrong Siddeley Screamer rocket under the fuselage, and WA820 powered by Armstrong Siddeley Sapphire Sa.2 turbojets (the latter aircraft establishing a new World time-to-height record on 31 August 1951, attaining 12,000m in 3min 9½sec). WA982 was

Right: The Meteor F 8, WH505/A, of Sqn Ldr S Kirtley, CO of No 611 (West Lancashire) Squadron, Royal Auxiliary Air Force, awaiting take-off at Hooton Park. (Photo: A J Jackson Collection)

Below: WK935, a Meteor 8 with additional cockpit for a prone pilot in the extreme nose for trials at the RAE. Note the additional fin area needed to compensate for the much lengthened nose. (Photo: Sir W G Armstrong Whitworth Aircraft Ltd, Neg No NF369)

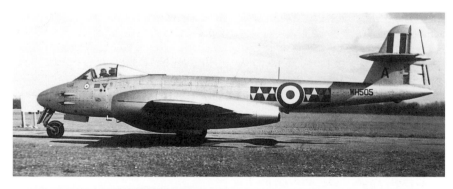

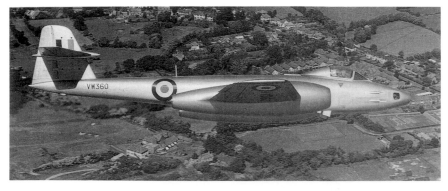

The prototype Meteor FR Mk 9, VW360, showing the lateral camera ports in the nose. This aircraft was later converted to F Mk 8 standard and employed for trials with the American six-inch HVAR weapon. (Photo: via Derek James)

fitted with a pair of Rolls-Royce Soar lightweight turbojets on the wingtips. Several aircraft were equipped with nose probes for the continuing in-flight refuelling trials; WK660 featured an armament of two 30mm Aden guns; WH483 was fitted with spring-tabbed ailerons (leading to a general modification which resulted in the Meteor 8 being cleared for service with underwing rocket projectiles); and WA775 was fitted with nose radar for use with D.H. Firestreak AAMs. The most interesting trials involved the extension of the nose on WK935 to accommodate a second cockpit for a prone pilot; this was first flown on 10 February 1954 and was subsequently tested at the RAE in the context of a Bristol rocket-powered interceptor which, however, was cancelled.

After acceptance of the spring tabs for rocket-armed Meteors, Gloster undertook a fully-modified ground attack fighter version as a private venture. This aircraft, G-AMCJ, featured provision for wingtip fuel tanks and a strengthened airframe capable of sustaining a load of up to four 1,000lb bombs and 24 rocket projectiles under the wings; provision was also made for a rocket-assisted take-off installation on the rear fuselage. This aircraft failed to gain Air Ministry favour.

The prototype fighter-reconnaissance Metoer FR Mk 9 was first flown on 23 March 1950 by Zurakowski and was followed by 125 production aircraft, all built by Gloster. No 208 Squadron, in the Middle East, was the first to receive FR 9s; indeed the majority of these aircraft served overseas. The full gun armament was retained and provision was made for forward-facing and oblique photography with nose-mounted F 24 cameras, heating of which was achieved by tapping hot air from the starboard engine. Ex-RAF Meteor FR 9s were exported to Ecuador (12), Israel (7) and Syria (2).

A Meteor FR 9, VZ608, was modified for flight trials of the Rolls-Royce RB 108 jet-lift turbojet, this engine being mounted vertically in the fuselage, replacing the main fuel tank. Fuel for very short endurance test flights was carried in underwing tanks, the trials being conducted in conjunction with Shorts in preparation for that company's S.C. 1 V/STOL research aircraft.

Final single-seat operational version of the Meteor was the photo-reconnaissance PR Mk 10, first flown on 29 March 1950. With all armament removed and reversion to the long-span wings, the PR 10 retained the FR 8's nose camera installation and possessed additional mountings for two vertical F 52 cameras in the rear fuselage. Fifty-nine PR 10s were produced and served with Nos 2, 13, 81 and 541 Squadrons between December 1950 and July 1961.

Meteor Night Fighters

Failure of Specification F.44/46 to produce a new high performance night fighter (due largely to a lack of experience in supersonic design in Britain) resulted in Gloster being asked to produce an interim night fighter derivative of the two-seat Meteor T 7 trainer.

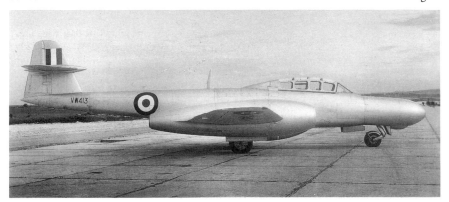

Above: *The aerodynamic prototype of the Meteor NF 11 night fighter, VW413; it was in fact the fourth production Meteor T 7 two-seat trainer, extensively modified with lengthened nose and F 8 tail unit. (Photo: Author's Collection)*

Right: *A standard production Meteor NF 11, WD597, in normal operational trim, with twin 20mm Hispano cannon in each wing, ventral and wing drop tanks and radar altimeter aerials under the rear fuselage. Ejection seats could not be fitted under the heavy-framed cockpit canopy. (Photo: via Derek James)*

Owing, however, to that company's preoccupation with the Meteor F 8 and the Javelin, it was agreed that design and development of the night fighter should be transferred to Sir W G Armstrong Whitworth Aircraft Ltd at Coventry.

The new aircraft, termed the Meteor NF Mk 11, featured the familiar AI Mk X radar in a nose lengthened by no less than five feet over that of the Mk 7, while the four cannon armament was moved to the outer wings, which in turn reverted to the long span; the tail unit was the same as on the Mk 8.

An aerodynamic test aircraft for the new night fighter was provided by modifying the fourth production T 7, VW413, and the prototype NF 11, WA546, was first flown by Eric Franklin on 31 May 1950. First Squadron to receive the Meteor night fighter was No 29 at Tangmere in August 1951, commanded by Sqn Ldr H E Borlien DSO, DFC, and which thereby became only the world's second jet night fighter squadron (after No 25 with Vampire NF 10s).

Although these early jet night fighters were strictly subsonic, they did nevertheless represent a substantial advance over the veteran Mosquito NF 36 which had entered service in January 1946. Mark 11s also equipped Nos 5, 11, 68, 87, 96, 125, 141, 151, 256, 264 and 527 Squadrons. In practice exercises NF 11s were able to cope easily with Lancaster and Lincoln targets, and only when Canberra and Valiant jet bombers became widespread in service did the night defences temporarily lose the initiative.

This was to some extent offset by a change to the American APS-21 radar in the NF Mk 12 which first entered service with No 25 Squadron, commanded by Sqn Ldr J Cameron-Cox, at West Malling in March 1954. The NF 12's new radar required the aircraft's nose to be further lengthened by seventeen inches to 49ft 11in, a slight deficiency in tail fin area being satisfied by adding small fillets above and below the tailplane bullet fairing. Total production of NF 12s was one hundred, and these served with nine squadrons.

The NF 13 pre-dated the NF 12 by a few months and was a tropicalized version of the NF 11. It was introduced to replace the ageing Mosquito NF 36s in service in the Middle East, joining Nos 39 and 219 Squadrons at Kabrit and Fayid in Egypt in March and April 1953 respectively. Only forty were produced, being distinguished by a pair of conditioning air intakes just forward of

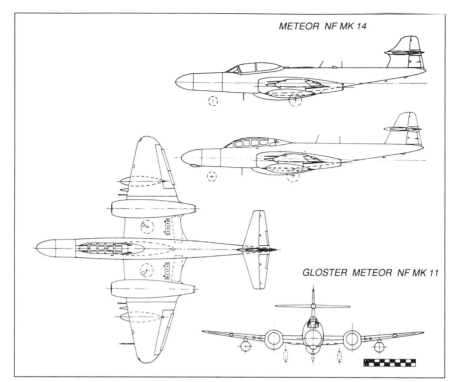

METEOR NF MK 14

GLOSTER METEOR NF MK 11

Type: Twin-engine single-seat low-wing monoplane day interceptor fighter (Mk I, III, 4 and 8); twin-engine two-seat low-wing night fighter (NF11, 12, 13 and 14).

Manufacturers: Gloster Aircraft Co Ltd, Hucclecote, Glos (Mks I to 8); Sir W G Armstrong Whitworth Aircraft Ltd, Baginton, Coventry (Mks 4, 8 and 11 to 14)

Air Ministry Specification: F.9/40 for prototype and early fighters.

Powerplant: See text for F.9/40 prototypes. F I: 1,700lb-thrust Rolls-Royce W.2B/23C Welland turbojets; F III: 2,000lb-thrust Rolls-Royce Welland or 2,000lb-thrust Rolls-Royce Derwent I turbojets. F 4: 3,500lb-thrust Rolls-Royce Derwent 5 turbojets. F 8-NF 14: 3,500lb-thrust Rolls-Royce Derwent 8 or 3,800lb-thrust Derwent 9 turbojets.

Structure: All-metal stressed-skin construction; twin wingspar structure with banjo frame sections for engine mountings. Nosewheel undercarriage.

Dimensions: Mks I and III: Span, 43ft 0in; length, 41ft 3in; height, 13ft 0in; wing area, 374 sq ft. Mk 4: Span, long wings, 43ft 0in; short wings, 37ft 2in; length, 41ft 0in; height, 13ft 0in; wing area, 374 or 350 sq ft. Mk 8: Span, 37ft 2in; length, 44ft 7in, height, 13ft 0in; wing area, 350 sq ft. NF Mk 11: Span, 43ft 0in; length, 48ft 6in; height, 13ft 11in; wing area, 374 sq ft; NF Mk 14: span, 43ft 0in; length, 51ft 4in; wing area, 374 sq ft.

Weights: Mk I: Tare, 8,140lb; all-up, 13,795lb. Mk III: Tare, 10,519lb; all-up, 13,920lb. Mk 4: Tare, 11,217lb; all-up, 14,545lb (short wings). Mk 8: Tare, 10,684lb; all-up, 15,700lb. NF Mk 11: Tare, 12,019lb; all-up, 20,035lb (ventral and wing tanks). NF Mk 14: Tare, 12,620lb; all-up, 21,200lb (ventral and wing tanks).

Performance: Mks I and III: Max speed, 415 mph at 10,000ft; climb to 30,000ft, 15 min; service ceiling, 40,000ft. Mk 4: Max speed, 580 mph at 10,000ft; climb to 30,000ft, 6 min; service ceiling, 44,500ft. Mk 8: Max speed, 598 mph at 10,000ft; climb to 30,000ft, 6.5 min; service ceiling, 43,000ft. NF Mk 11: Max speed, 554 mph at 10,000ft; climb to 30,000ft, 11.2 min; service ceiling, 40,000ft. NF Mk 14: Max speed, 578 mph at 10,000ft; climb to 30,000ft, 13.2 min; service ceiling, 40,000ft.

Armament: All single-seat fighters armed with four 20mm Hispano Mk 5 cannon in nose with 780 rounds of ammunition; night fighters armed with 20mm Hispano Mk 5 cannon in outer wings with 640 rounds. Provision on Mk 8 to carry up to sixteen 3in rocket projectiles under outer wings.

Prototypes: F.9/40, eight (see text; DG206/G first flown by Michael Daunt on 5 March 1943); Mk III, EE230; Mk IV, EE360; Mk 8, VT150; NF Mk 11, WA546; NF Mk 12, WS950; NF Mk 13, WM308; NF Mk 14, WM261.

Summary of Production: 20 Mk Is; 210 Mk IIIs; 658 Mk 4s (including 123 for export); 1,183 Mk 8s (including 93 for export, but excluding 300 licence-built in Holland and 30 assembled in Belgium); 335 NF Mk 11s; 100 NF Mk 12s; 40 NF Mk 13s; 100 NF Mk 14s.

Summary of RAF Service: Single-seat Meteor fighters served with Nos 1, 19, 34, 41, 43, 54, 56, 63, 64, 65, 66, 72, 74, 85, 91, 92, 111, 124, 222, 234, 245, 247, 257, 263, 266, 500, 504, 600, 601, 604, 609, 610, 611, 615 and 616 Squadrons; two-seat night fighters served with Nos 5, 11, 25, 29, 33, 39, 46, 60, 64, 68, 72, 85, 87, 96, 125, 141, 151, 152, 153, 219 and 264 Squadrons.

the ventral fuel tank, and by DME aerials on the outer wings.

Final Meteor night fighter variant was the NF 14, powered by Derwent 9s with large diameter intakes. The nose was still further extended to give an overall length of 51ft 4in, and the aircraft featured a two-piece blown cockpit canopy in place of the heavily framed enclosure of the previous

versions; spring-tabbed ailerons and an autostabilizer were also fitted as standard. The prototype flew on 23 October 1953, and the first of one hundred production aircraft joined

No 25 Squadron in April 1954.

The last Meteor night fighter in squadron service was withdrawn from No 60 Squadron at Tengah, Singapore, in September 1961.

Formation photo of Meteor NF 14, WS724/P of No 72 (Fighter) Squadron, taking off from Church Fenton in the late 1950s. Photo: via Derek James)

de Havilland Vampire and Sea Vampire

While the main interest centred on the development of Britain's first jet fighter, the Gloster Meteor, another aeroplane was taking shape on drawing boards at de Havilland, designed to Specification E.6/41. It will be recalled that one of the types of turbojet scheduled to fly in the F.9/40 Meteor prototypes was the H.1, a 'straight-through' gas turbine with single-sided centrifugal compressor designed by Maj Frank Halford, an engineer of considerable talent and long experience. And it was the H.1's relia-

bility and availability that resulted in the Meteor being first flown with a pair of these engines, whose manufacture was taken over by the de Havilland company under the name Goblin.

The low power of all the early jet engines resulted in de Havilland's design being fairly small, with a central nacelle accommodating the cockpit and engine, the tail unit being carried on two small-section booms which terminated in the tail fins, with the tailplane located between them. The front of the nacelle, containing the cockpit with the four cannon armament mounted in the underside, was of balsa and ply construction — as in the Mosquito — but the remainder of the airframe was of steel and light alloy. With no propeller, the aircraft

possessed a very short nosewheel undercarriage, the aircraft's overall height being less than nine feet.

De Havilland's design tender had been accepted by the Air Ministry in April 1942, and detail work started the following month on two prototypes (and later a third), which carried the unofficial name 'Spidercrab'. By the time the first of these, LZ548/G, was complete, the Goblin engine was developing 2,700lb thrust and, on 20 September 1943, was first flown by Geoffrey de Havilland Jnr; during the next eight weeks the aircraft achieved a speed of around 480 mph at 22,000 feet. Some pitching instability was experienced at low speed and, at high speed, the aircraft tended to snake, suggesting that airflow turbulence was occurring high on the tail fins, and it was decided to shorten the vertical tail surfaces by about fifteen inches. The third prototype, MP838/G, was the first to carry the four cannon armament.

On 13 May 1944 a production order was placed for 120 aircraft, named the Vampire, to be built at the Preston factory of the English Electric Co Ltd. Apart from the first 40 aircraft, which retained the Goblin I engine, they were to be powered by the improved Goblin II, which developed 3,100lb thrust, and

Above: *The first E.6/41 Vampire prototype, LZ548/G, at about the time of its first flight, with the tall fins and rudders.* (Photo: A J J Jackson Collection)

Right: *LZ548/G, at Hatfield after some rather crude surgery to its empennage.* (Photo: Air Ministry)

Vampire F Mk Is of No 247 (Fighter) Squadron, the first to equip with the new fighter in 1946. Formation flying in this aircraft was somewhat tedious owing the lack of power reserves and the slow throttle response. (Photo: A J Jackson Collection)

would incorporate the square-cut tail fins, pending further investigation of airflow behaviour at the junctions of tail boom, fin and tailplane.

The first production example, TG274/G, made its maiden flight at Samlesbury on 20 April 1945 and was quickly followed by about a score of aircraft which were allocated for test and evaluation purposes at Boscombe Down, Farnborough and the various Service establishments. Various improvements were added on the production line at Preston; cockpit pressurization was introduced from TG336, and single-piece cockpit canopies from TG386 in January 1946.

Vampire F Is were first delivered to No 247 (Fighter) Squadron at Chilbolton in March 1946, replacing Tempest F IIs, and to this Squadron fell the task of establishing combat handling with a fighter that was as yet unquestionably somewhat underpowered. Yet it is seldom remembered that the Vampire was the first production fighter to exceed 500 mph in level flight among the air forces of the Western Allies. Nevertheless, being short of thrust, the Vampire's throttle response was slow on account of the risk of flame-out, and it demanded much more careful anticipation of speed loss on the landing approach than the former piston-engine

fighters. That said, the Vampire was a delightful little aeroplane to fly with crisp flying controls and a superb view from the cockpit.

The F Mk 1 went on to equip Nos 54 and 130 Squadrons at Odiham in October that year, and eventually joined eight squadrons of RAF Fighter Command in the United Kingdom. In April 1948 they replaced Tempest 5s on No 3 (Fighter) Squadron under Sqn Ldr Colin Hamilton Macfie DFC with the Second Tactical Air Force at Wunstorf in Germany, and became the first jet fighters of the peacetime Royal Auxiliary Air Force when Vampire Is were issued to No 605 (County of Warwick) Squadron at Honiley on 3 July 1948, replacing Mosquito 30 night fighters.

The Royal Swedish Air Force had placed an order for 70 Vampire Is, the first of which were delivered early in 1946; with the designation J28, they gave excellent service and, after being superseded, ten were re-sold to the Dominican Republic in 1955-56 where

they served as fighter-bombers.

As already mentioned, early Vampire Is came in for a wide range of trials, of which one was of particular significance. TG278, was set aside as a test bed for the new 4,400lb-thrust de Havilland Ghost 2/2 turbojet, then planned to power the Comet airliner and a future version of the Vampire (the Mark 8, which emerged as the Venom). For high-altitude trials, TG278 was fitted with wings extended to 48ft span and, on 8 May 1947, Gp Capt John Cunningham, the company's chief test pilot since the death of Geoffrey de Havilland Jnr the previous September, established a new World altitude record at 59,446 feet.

Two early Vampire Is, TG276 and TG280, and a special prototype, TX807, were modified to Specification F.11/45 with 4,500lb-thrust Rolls-Royce Nene I turbojets, to become the Vampire II. As the Rolls-Royce engines featured double-sided impellers, additional air intakes were incorporated on the nacelle immediately aft of the cockpit canopy. Airflow

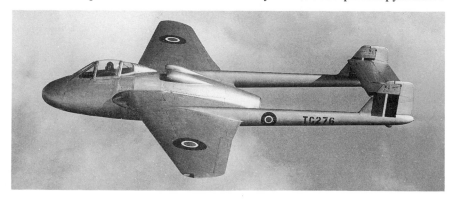

The first Nene-Vampire, TG276, with the dorsal intakes; airflow instability aft of the cockpit canopy caused them to be discarded. (Photo: A J Jackson Collection)

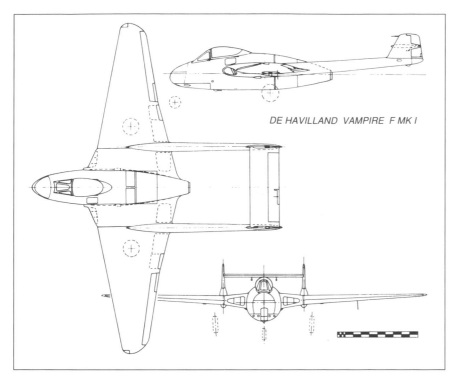

DE HAVILLAND VAMPIRE F MK I

problems were encountered with these intakes and Boulton Paul was contracted to rebuild the engine bay of TX807 to enable the wing root ducts to supply air into a plenum chamber from which both sides of the engine's impeller would be supplied. This aircraft was then shipped to Australia where it served as a prototype Vampire Mark 30 for the Royal Australian Air Force, the fastest of all Vampires with a top speed of 570 mph.

Earlier reference above to the death of Geoffrey de Havilland prompts mention of a Vampire-related programme of trials. Vampire I front nacelle sections, from TG283 and TG306, were used in the manufacture of two experimental high-speed aircraft, the D.H.108, fitted with swept wings but no horizontal tail surfaces to investigate the high speed characteristics of the these wings in preparation for the Comet airliner and the D.H.110 transonic fighter. Powered by specially prepared Goblin engines, the first of these experimental aeroplanes was soon reaching level speeds

over 600 mph at low altitude but, on 27 September 1946, TG283 broke up in the air over the Thames Estuary, killing de Havilland. It later became clear that the pilot had probably reached a speed of about Mach 0.90 in a dive from 10,000 feet and that the aircraft's structure was simply not stressed to withstand the loads imposed by compressibility at these high speeds. A third D.H.108, VW120, was built, but this featured a nose section different from that of the Vampire. The second aircraft, TG306, was to become the first British aeroplane to exceed the speed of sound when, on

9 September 1948, John Derry carried out a dive between 40,000 and 30,000ft. All three D.H.108s were to be lost in accidents involving the death of their pilots.

Returning to the Vampire proper, the F Mk III, developed to Specification F.3/47 and also powered by the Goblin 2, introduced the ability to carry 100-gallon wing drop tanks. Flight trials with these tanks on the Mark I, TG275, had demonstrated a deterioration of the Vampire's longitudinal stability, and this was remedied by increasing the tailplane chord by 4½ inches and reducing that of the elevator by 1½ inches. Fin and rudder shapes were more rounded and long acorn fairings incorporated at the junction of the fin and tailplane. Tare weight of this version increased by about 800 pounds, and all-up weight by around 1,500, resulting in a slight reduction in the maximum speed to 531 mph (some 50 miles per hour less than the current Meteor 4).

Vampire F 3s first joined No 54 Squadron at Odiham in April 1948 and in July six aircraft, led by the squadron commander, Sqn Ldr (later Gp Capt) Robert Wardlow Oxspring DFC** AFC, made the first-ever crossing of the Atlantic by jet fighters, flying to Goose Bay via Iceland and Greenland for a goodwill tour of Canada and the United States.

This version served with twelve RAF squadrons, including No 73 based in Malta and No 32 in Cyprus. Tropical trials were conducted with VG703 at Singapore and Khartoum late in 1949, while export versions were supplied to

Above: *A Vampire F 3, VF335, which was to many pilots the most pleasant version to fly. The vertical tail surfaces were much more in keeping with a de Havilland design.* (Photo: The de Havilland Aircraft Co Ltd)

Left: *As part of de Havilland Engines' research into re-heat systems, VV451 featured afterburning in a much-lengthened engine tailpipe, necessitating under-tail bumpers to avoid damage while landing.* (Photo: The de Havilland Aircraft Co Ltd, Neg No 4273B dated 5 September 1949)

de Havilland Vampire FB Mk 9s of No 73 (Fighter) Squadron over Valletta harbour, Malta, in 1954.

Norway and 83 aircraft equipped four squadrons of the Royal Canadian Air Force.

The Vampire IV was intended as being the Rolls-Royce Nene-powered variant but, as previously explained, TX807 was already serving as a prototype in Australia, and 80 Nene-powered Vampire Mark 30s were built by de Havilland Aircraft Pty Ltd, Sydney, the first being flown by Brian Walker on 29 June 1948.

The main production variant of the Vampire was the Mk 5 fighter-bomber, of which 473 were produced for the RAF. This ground-attack aircraft introduced a strengthened airframe with a wing span reduced to 38 feet with square-cut wingtips. Wing strongpoints were included to allow bombs or rockets to be carried, and a longer-stroke undercarriage fitted to cater for increased landing weights. Vampire FB 5s served at home and in Germany, Malta, Egypt, Iraq, the Persian Gulf, Hong Kong and Singapore, equipping no fewer than 40 squadrons, including eleven of the Royal Auxiliary Air Force. It was also flown on operations against communist guerrilla forces in the Malayan jungle, replacing Spitfires on No 60 Squadron at Tengah in December 1950.

Apart from its widespread use in the RAF, this fighter-bomber attracted considerable attention among foreign air forces, and eventually served with those of Australia (as FB 31s), Ceylon, Egypt, Finland, India, Iraq, Italy, Jordan, Lebanon, New Zealand, Norway, Rhodesia, South Africa, Sweden (as J 28Bs), Switzerland and Venezuela. They were also licence-built in Switzerland and Italy, while 67 British-manufactured FB 5s were assembled in France before 433 examples were built by SNCA du SE at Marignane from 1950 under the designation SE.535 *Mistral*.

Among the numerous Mark 5s used

for experimental purposes was VV454, flown by de Havilland and the RAE with a re-heat system and an extended engine tailpipe.

The final single-seat Vampire fighter for the RAF was the FB Mk 9, a tropicalized version of the Mark 5, and of which 297 were produced and equipped 21 RAF and RAuxAF squadrons, including No 8 at Aden and No 45 in Malaya. Fifty of these aircraft were produced by The Fairey Aviation Co Ltd at Ringway, Manchester. The sole external distinguishing feature was a lengthened wing fillet forward of the starboard wing root which enclosed part of the cockpit conditioning equipment.

One other operational version of the Vampire was flown RAF Fighter Command, the two-seat Mark 10 night fighter. This, the D.H. 113, had been specifically designed to meet export orders, and featured an entirely new nacelle accommodating pilot and navigator/radar operator side-by-side under a canopy similar to that of the Mosquito, except that entry to the cockpit was through this canopy. Ejection seats were not

fitted and AI Mk 10 centimetric radar was enclosed in a large nose radome. Two prototypes were produced (G-5-2 and G-5-5), and the first was flown by G H Pike on 28 August 1949.

Egypt ordered twelve aircraft and these were put into production at Hatfield in 1949. However, when the export of military equipment to Egypt was banned in 1950, the aircraft were taken over by the Ministry of Supply for the RAF as the Vampire NF Mk 10, and production extended to enable the aircraft to serve as interim equipment pending the arrival in service of the Meteor night fighters.

The Vampire NF 10 was first delivered to No 25 (Fighter) Squadron, commanded by Sqn Ldr R W Leggett, at West Malling in June 1951, thereby becoming the first jet night fighter squadron among Western air forces. Powered by up-rated 3,350lb-thrust Goblin 3 engines, the Vampire 10 had a surprisingly good performance, bearing in mind that it was almost 1,000lb heavier all-up than the Vampire FB 9, yet could attain 538 mph below 10,000

The first de Havilland D.H. 113 Vampire night fighter prototype, G-5-2, at Hatfield. Produced as an aerodynamic test vehicle for the large nacelle and a demonstration aircraft, it was unarmed and carried no radar. Note the Mosquito fighter-style flat windscreen. (Photo: The Havilland Aircraft Co Ltd, Neg No 4272A dated 4 September 1949)

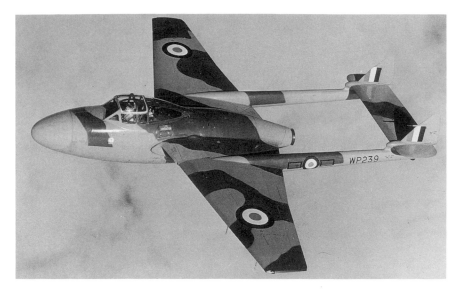

Vampire NF 10, WP239 of No 25 (Fighter) Squadron, being flown by the author from West Malling in 1951. Note the extended tailplane outboard of the fins and rudders, found necessary to compensate for the increased nacelle mass forward of the wing's centre of pressure. Although shown here in the 'clean' condition, the Vampire night fighters were usually flown with the 100-gallon underwing drop tanks. (Photo: Air Ministry)

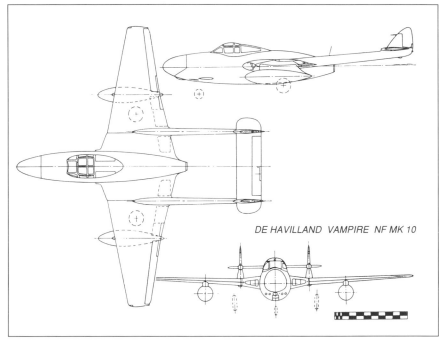

DE HAVILLAND VAMPIRE NF MK 10

on the Vampire, even if only to obtain an aircraft as quickly as possible on which to examine the problems posed in such aircraft as slow throttle response during deck operation. As plans were put in hand to examine the suitability of the Supermarine Attacker (see opposite), by the end of the War still considered as an experimental aircraft, modifications were undertaken to equip the second Vampire prototype, LZ551, with an arrester hook, long-travel undercarriage oleos and enlarged landing flaps.

Deck landing trials by the Service Trials Unit (No 778 Squadron) with LZ551, now termed the Sea Vampire Mark X, began aboard HMS *Ocean* on 3 December 1945, flown by Lt-Cdr (later Cdr) Eric Melrose Brown OBE, DSC, AFC — the first-ever occasion on which a pure-jet aircraft operated from a carrier.

A second 'hooked Vampire', TG426, was followed by two fully-navalised Sea Vampire prototypes, VF315 and TG328, and by 18 production Sea Vampire F Mk 20s with squared wing tips, strengthened undercarriage, re-stressed airframe for accelerated deck launching, and enlarged airbrakes and flaps. The A-frame arrester hook was located above the engine tailpipe, rotating downwards through the jet efflux for engagement.

The Vampire Mk 21 was an experimental version, of which a small number was modified (including TG286, VG701 and VT802) with strengthened underfuselage for landing trials on a rubberized landing surface with undercarriage

feet. No 25 Squadron was joined in Fighter Command by Nos 23 and 151 Squadrons, which received Vampire NF 10s in September, the former at Coltishall and the latter at Leuchars. In all cases they replaced Mosquito night fighters.

Sea Vampires

During the War years the Royal Navy was concerned to obtain the best possible performance by developing existing propeller-driven fighters, in particular the Griffon-Seafires, and later the Seafang. Once the Meteor and Vampire had proved their potential superiority over the existing piston-engine fighters it was clearly only a matter of time before it would be necessary to introduce jet-powered naval fighters.

No doubt concerned to ensure that such fighters should be as small as possible, for reasons of deck and lift sizes, attention from the outset centred

The first fully-navalized Sea Vampire prototype, VF315. The temporary nature of the Vampire's service with the Fleet Air Arm was suggested by the fact that no attempt was ever made to fit folding wings. (Photo: Ministry of Supply RTP Neg No 14,719B)

retracted. These tests were performed on a dummy rubber 'deck' at Farnborough and at sea aboard HMS *Warrior* early in 1949 to examine the feasibility of naval aircraft dispensing with the conventional wheel undercarriage. For his work in this programme, Lt-Cdr Brown was awarded the King's Commendation and the Boyd Trophy in 1949.

The only Sea Vampire fighter to fly with an operational Fleet Air Arm squadron was the F 20 prototype, VF315, which joined No 806 Squadron's unique aerobatic team that also included a pair of Sea Hornets and two Sea Furies, giving displays in Canada and the United States during the summer of 1948.

The other Sea Vampires to join the Fleet Air Arm were two-seat trainers, the T Mk 22.

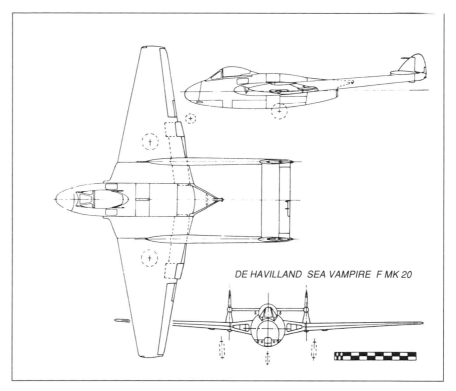

DE HAVILLAND SEA VAMPIRE F MK 20

Type: Single-engine, single-seat twin-boom mid-wing monoplane interceptor fighter and fighter bomber.

Manufacturers: The de Havilland Aircraft Co Ltd, Hatfield, Hertfordshire; Hawarden, Cheshire; and Christchurch, Hampshire. The English Electric Co Ltd, Preston, Lancashire. The Fairey Aviation Co Ltd, Ringway, Manchester.

Air Ministry Specifications: E.6/41 (prototypes and Mk I); F.11/45 (Mk II); F.3/47 (Mark 3).

Powerplant: Prototypes: One 2,700lb thrust de Havilland Goblin I turbojet. Mks I, 3 and 5. Goblin 2. Mks 9 and 10. Goblin 3.

Dimensions: Mks I and 3. Span, 40ft 0in; length, 30ft 9in; height, 8ft 10in; wing area, 266 sq ft. Mks 5 and 9. Span, 38ft 0in; length, 30ft 9in; height, 8ft 10in; wing area, 261 sq ft. Mk 10. Span, 38ft 0in; length, 34ft 7in; height, 8ft 7in; wing area, 261 sq ft.

Weights: Tare: 6,372lb (Mk I); 7,134lb (Mk 3); 7,253lb (Mk 5); 7,238lb (Mk 9); 6,984lb (Mk 10); 7,623lb (Mk 20). All-up: 10,480lb (Mk I); 11,970lb (Mk 3); 12,360lb (Mk 5); 12,390lb (Mk 9); 13,100lb (Mk 10); 12,660lb (Mk 20).

Performance: Mk I. Max speed, 540 mph; range, 730 miles. Mk 5. Max speed, 535 mph; service ceiling, 40,000ft; max range, 1,170 miles. Mk 10. Max speed, 538 mph at 5,000ft; max range, 1,220 miles. Mk 20. Max speed, 526 mph at 20,000ft; service ceiling, 43,500ft.

Armament: Four 20mm Hispano Mk 5 cannon. Mks 5 and 9 had provision to carry two 1,000lb bombs or three-inch rocket projectiles.

Prototypes: Original prototypes, three, LZ548/G, LZ551/G and MP838/G (LZ548/G first flown by Geoffrey de Havilland Jnr at Hatfield on 20 September 1943). Sea Vampire prototypes, two, VF315 and TG328.

Production: Total of 1,158 Vampire fighters produced in UK for the RAF and Fleet Air Arm. Mks I and 3, 291 (between TG274-TG448, VF265-VF283, VF300-VF348, VG692-VG703, VT793-VT874 and VV187-VV213); Mk 5, 473 (between VV214-VV232, VX461-VX476, VZ808-VZ877, WA101-WA460, WE830-WE849, WF578-WF586 and WG793-WG847); Mk 9, 297 (between WG848-WG931, WL493-WL616, WP990-WR269 and WX200-WX260); Mk 10, 78 (between WM659-WM733, WP232-WP256 and WV689-WV691); Mk 20, 19 (between VV136-VV165).

Summary of Service: Vampire F Is served with Nos 3, 20, 54, 72, 130, 247, 501, 595, 605, 608 and 631 Squadrons, RAF and RAuxAF; Vampire F 3s served with Nos. 5, 20, 32, 54, 72, 73, 247, 601, 602, 604, 608 and 614 Squadrons, RAF and RAuxAF; Vampire FB 5s served with Nos 3, 4, 5, 6, 11, 14, 16, 25, 26, 28, 32, 54, 60, 67, 71, 72, 73, 93, 94, 112, 118, 145, 185, 213, 234, 247, 249, 266, 501, 502, 602, 603, 605, 607, 608, 609, 612, 613 and 614 Squadrons, RAF and RAuxAF; Vampire FB 9s served with Nos 6, 8, 20, 26, 28, 32, 45, 60, 73, 93, 185, 213, 234, 249, 501, 502, 602, 607, 608, 613 and 614 Squadrons, RAF and RAuxAF; Vampire NF 10s served with Nos 23, 25 and 151 Squadrons, RAF; Sea Vampire X served with No 778 Squadron, FAA; Sea Vampire F 20s served with Nos 700, 702, 703, 728, 759, 764, 771, 787 and 806 Squadrons, FAA; Sea Vampire 21s served with Nos 703 and 771 Squadrons, FAA.

Supermarine Attacker

The first Supermarine E.10/44 prototype, TS409 (Photo: Ministry of Supply Neg No 14665C)

Early in 1944 Specification E.1/44 was drafted, setting down speculative design parameters for an experimental single-engine fighter to be powered by a turbojet of about 4,000lb-thrust, which

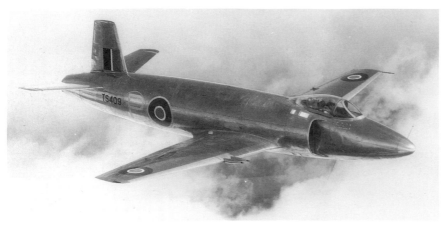

The E.10/44 prototype TS409 after installation of the Hispano cannon in the wings. (Photo: via R C Sturtivant)

Rolls-Royce was invited to design and develop. As Joseph Smith was working on a laminar flow wing for the Supermarine Spiteful, that company was asked to prepare a proposal to meet E.1/44, and this was duly tendered to the DTD in the summer of that year.

In the meantime Smith had expressed his preference for a smaller engine, and the Rolls-Royce design was accordingly scaled down, but was still expected to produce well over 3,000lb-thrust; this was the RB.41, later to become the Nene, one of the most successful of the centrifugal-flow turbojets originally pioneered by Frank Whittle. The preliminary Supermarine design was given the Type number 392, and was provisionally referred to as the 'Spiteful replacement'. Its wings were of similar planform to those of the Spiteful, the Griffon's wing radiators being replaced by fuel tanks, but the four-cannon armament remaining unchanged. After some early difficulties, the Rolls-Royce RB.41 turbojet was beginning to show considerable promise during bench-

running, and was soon to be uprated to 4,500lb-thrust.

Three prototypes, TS409, TS413 and TS416, were ordered on 5 August, and members of the DTD inspected a part mock-up before producing a new draft Specification, E.10/44, along the lines proposed by Supermarine.

Much depended on research data from the Spiteful prototypes, and the loss of the prototype NN660 on 13 September that year was a considerable setback, particularly when it was realised that the laminar-flow wing research had a long way to go before it could be confidently applied to an aircraft as advanced as the E.10/44 design. In particular, the behaviour of the wing continued to give rise to anxiety at low speeds, the very regime in which the turbojet possessed its least comfortable throttle response. Nevertheless the Ministry of Aircraft Production was determined to push ahead with the E.10/44, confident that the laminar-flow wing's problems would be resolved as more Spitefuls joined the flight test

programme, and on 7 July 1945 ordered 24 pre-production aircraft, of which six were to be to Specification E.10/44 and the remainder to a new naval fighter Specification, E.1/45.

The delays in the wing research, compounded by swingeing reductions in research funding, further delayed the first flight of TS409, and the Admiralty temporarily withdrew from the E.1/45 programme, ordering instead eighteen Sea Vampire F 20s as an interim measure. TS409 was eventually flown at Chilbolton by Jeffrey Quill on 27 July 1946, being immediately transferred to Boscombe Down where flight trials continued for some months.

In its initial form TS409 was flown with a Nene restricted to 12,000 rpm, giving a thrust of 4,300lb, which bestowed a maximum speed of 542 mph at sea level (Mach 0.70), but shortly afterwards the engine limitations were raised so as to give a thrust of 5,000lb, increasing the aircraft's speed to 580 mph (Mach 0.75).

The second aircraft, TS413, was modified to Specification E.1/45 before completion, and the name Attacker was approved at the time of its first flight on 17 June 1947 with Michael John Lithgow at the controls. This aircraft differed in numerous respects from TS409, featuring a smaller fin, enlarged tailplane,

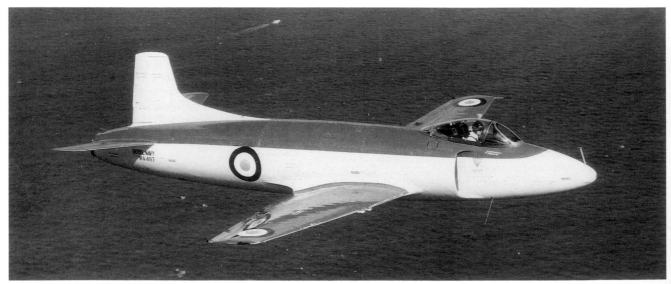

A Supermarine Attacker F Mk 1, WA497, under test before delivery to the Fleet Air Arm in 1950, showing the extended dorsal fin which had been introduced to avoid rudder-locking during side-slip at low speeds. (Photo: Vickers-Armstrongs Ltd)

Supermarine Attacker FB Mk 2, WP292/143 of No 890 Squadron, at a shore station in 1952 but carrying HMS Eagle's fin code. Note the metal-framed cockpit canopy, introduced in this version. (Photo: via R C Sturtivant).

a Martin-Baker ejection seat, increased fuel capacity, undercarriage oleos with increased travel, and modified engine air intakes with bypass bleeds. Deck landing trials by TS413 began aboard HMS *Illustrious* on 28 October 1947, Lithgow performing the first landing, followed by Lt-Cdr E M Brown of the RAE.

TS413 was, however, lost in an accident in June 1948 while undergoing trials with a 270 gallon ventral fuel tank, the pilot, Lt T J A Joyce-King RN of the A & AEE being killed. In the meantime, the RAF had lost interest in the E.10/44 project, opting for transonic fighters which were expected to result from other Specifications being discussed with Supermarine and Hawker. TS409 was therefore modified to Supermarine Type 498 Naval Standard with the intention of undergoing full naval trials, and a production order for 60 aircraft (beginning WA469) was placed in August. In its new guise TS409 was first flown on 5 March 1949.

It had been deduced that the loss of TS413 had probably been caused by rudder lock-over, sometimes experienced in a sideslip while carrying the large ventral fuel tank. This was found to be cured by adding a long dorsal fin on all production Attackers, the first of which was flown by Lithgow on 5 May 1950. These aircraft featured folding wings, the outer four feet of each wing, including the outboard half of the ailerons, folding upwards to a near-vertical position. (This prompts mention of an instance of involuntary wing folding. On 23 May 1950 the Supermarine pilot, Leslie R Colquhoun, was flying WA469 to test the airbrakes during high-speed runs over the South Marston airfield, when he experienced a sudden nose-down pitch as the starboard wingtip folded upwards. Able to use only rudder — due to the ailerons jamming — Colquhoun made a wide circuit, touching down at about 200 knots, and just pulling up before reaching the end of the runway with a burst tyre. The pilot was awarded the George Medal for his tenacity in remaining with the aircraft and skill in saving the aircraft in daunting circumstances.)

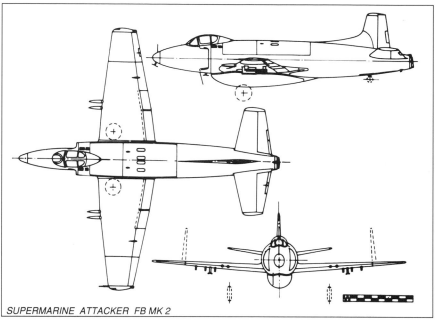

SUPERMARINE ATTACKER FB MK 2

Type: Single-engine, single-seat low-wing monoplane naval fighter and fighter-bomber.

Manufacturer: Supermarine Division of Vickers-Armstrongs Ltd, Winchester and Swindon.

Air Ministry Specifications: E.1/44 and E.10/44 (prototypes); E.1/45 (for naval prototypes).

Powerplant: Prototypes and Mk 1. One 5,000lb-thrust Rolls-Royce Nene 1 and 3 centrifugal-flow turbojet. Mk 2. 5,000lb-thrust Nene 102.

Dimensions: Span, 36ft 11in (28ft 11in folded); length, 37ft 1in; height, 9ft 6½in; wing area, 227.2 sq ft.

Weights: Tare, 8,426lb; all-up, 12,211lb.

Performance: F Mk 1. Max speed, 590 mph at sea level (Mach 0.77); climb to 30,000ft, 6 min 36 sec; service ceiling, 45,000ft.

Armament: Four 20mm Hispano Mk 5 cannon in wings with total of 624 rounds; provision on fighter-bombers to carry two 1,000lb bombs or up to four 300lb rocket projectiles.

Prototypes: Three, TS409, TS413 and TS416 (TS409 first flown on 27 July 1946 by J K Quill; TS413 first flown as naval aircraft on 17 June 1947 by M J Lithgow).

Production: Total of 145. F 1s, 52 (between WA469-WA527); FB 1s, 8 (WA528-WA535); FB 2s, 85 (between WK319-WK342, WP275-WP304, WT851 and WZ273-WZ302). Note: WT851 was a replacement aircraft, ordered separately, to replace WA477, a Mark 1, lost on test before delivery to the Fleet Air Arm.

Summary of Service with Fleet Air Arm: Attacker F 1s served with Nos 702, 703, 736, 767, 787, 800, 803 and 890 Squadrons; Attacker FB 1s served with Nos 703, 767, 787, 800 and 890 Squadrons; Attacker FB 2s served with Nos 700, 703, 718, 736, 767, 787, 800, 803 and 890 Squadrons, and Nos 1831, 1832 and 1833 Squadrons, RNVR.

After 52 Attacker F 1s had been completed, production switched to a fighter-bomber version, capable of carrying a 1,000lb bomb under each wing and up to eight three-inch rocket projectiles. Mark 1 fighters first joined No 800 Squadron of the Fleet Air Arm, commanded by Lt-Cdr G C Baldwin DSC* RN, at Ford on 17 August 1951, but embarked with eight FB 1s in HMS *Eagle* on 4 March the following year. No 803 Squadron, commanded by Lt-Cdr T D

Handley RN, also at Ford, received eight Attacker F 1s in November 1951, also joining HMS *Eagle* in 1952.

Only eight FB 1s were produced before the Nene 102-powered FB 2 was introduced. First flown on 25 April, deliveries began in July 1952 to No 890 Squadron but, after a short spell in *Eagle* that autumn, this squadron was disbanded in order to increase the establishment to twelve aircraft on the other two squadrons. The most important feature of the new Nene was an acceleration control unit on the throttle to prevent flaming out if the pilot opened up too quickly, especially if he received

a wave-off while landing. Cartridge starting, for many years a requirement for naval aircraft, gave place to an electric starter with high energy igniter unit. The Attacker FB 2 also included a metal-framed cockpit canopy.

85 Attacker Mk 2s were produced and, apart from the operational squadrons just mentioned, equipped six second-line squadrons. In 1955, when Attackers had been replaced on the operational units by Hawker Sea Hawks, the Supermarine fighters began distribution among the RNVR squadrons, starting with No 1831 in May, commanded by Lt-Cdr P L V Rougier RNVR

at Stretton, Cheshire. All three of these Attacker squadrons were to be disbanded on 10 March 1957 as part of the defence cuts announced that year.

Attackers never fired their guns in anger with the Royal Navy, yet they gave the Fleet Air Arm good service as being its first pure-jet fighter to attain operational status during the transition from propeller-driven aircraft. It had been hoped that it might attract considerable export business but, in the event, only 36 examples were supplied to Pakistan, these being delivered between 1951 and 1953.

Geoffrey Tyson taking off in the first prototype of the Saunders-Roe SR.A/1, TG263, possibly on its maiden flight. It is interesting to note that the wingtip floats have already been retracted. (Photo: A J Jackson Collection)

Saunders-Roe SR.A/1

Towards the end of 1943, with no end in sight of the Pacific War against Japan and with the prospect of a long series of island-hopping operations, the Air Ministry began discussing with the DTD the possibility of developing a small jet-powered flying-boat fighter capable of operating from sheltered coastal waters and, in due course, Specification E.6/44 was drafted and sent to Henry Knowler, the veteran chief designer and a director of Saunders-Roe Ltd at East Cowes in the Isle of Wight.

Three prototypes of a twin-engine

TG263 on beaching gear in its ultimate form with acorn fairing on the tail fin and carrying the G-12-1 markings. This view gives an excellent impression of the aircraft's size. (Photo: A J Jackson Collection)

aircraft were ordered and their manufacture began early in 1946, the new fighter being designated the SR.A/1. Although the War had ended, there remained sufficient interest in their potential and the project escaped cancellation, the first prototype, TG263, being flown by Flt Lt Geoffrey Arthur Virley Tyson OBE at Cowes in July 1947.

The aircraft, a hefty, shoulder-wing

aircraft spanning 46 feet with a boat hull 50 feet long, was powered by a pair of 3,300lb-thrust Metropolitan-Vickers F.2/4A Beryl MVB.1 axial-flow turbojets faired into the flanks of the hull amidships; they were provided with air from a central intake in the bows by ducts which passed either side of the cockpit, and exhausted through short tailpipes immediately aft of the wing

trailing edge. Balancing floats under the wingtips retracted inwards, the floats themselves rotating about their own axes during retraction so as to present smooth fairings under the wings. The four 20mm Hispano Mk 5 cannon armament was located in the upper decking of the bow section of the nose. The tailplane was set high on the fin as much to avoid water spray as for aerodynamic considerations, and, after a number of flights an acorn fairing was added at the intersection of tailplane and fin.

TG263 (also flown as G-12-1) was followed by TG267 with 3,500lb-thrust Beryls, and TG271 with 3,850lb-thrust Beryl MVB.2s, the third of these aeroplanes recording a maximum speed of 516 mph.

Inevitably the SR.A/1s remained strictly experimental and, despite their good turn of speed and manœuvrability from fairly modest power, their development was ended before the end of the 1950s.

Type: Twin-engine, single-seat shoulder-wing monoplane flying-boat experimental fighter.
Manufacturer: Saunders-Roe Ltd, East Cowes, Isle of Wight.
Air Ministry Specification: E.6/44.
Powerplant: Two 3,300lb-thrust Metrovick F.2/4A Beryl MVB.1 axial-flow turbojets; also 3,500lb-thrust Beryl MVB.1 and 3,850lb-thrust Beryl MVB.2.
Dimensions: Span, 46ft 0in; length, 50ft 0in.
Weights: Tare, 11,262lb; all-up, 16,255lb.
Performance: Max speed, 516 mph at 20,000ft.
Armament: Four 20mm Hispano Mk 5 cannon in upper decking of bows.
Prototypes: Three, TG263, TG267 and TG271 (TG263 first flown by G A V Tyson on 16 July 1947 at Cowes). No production.

Hawker P1040 and Sea Hawk

In some respects the development of the Hawker Sea Hawk and that of the Supermarine Attacker followed very similar patterns. Their manufacturers had both been wholly occupied with the progressive advance of pre-eminent propeller-driven fighters during the War, and neither had therefore succeeded in producing jet aircraft until half a dozen years after the first British jet fighter had flown. And when they eventually began work in earnest on their first jet fighters, ostensibly for the RAF, both found themselves producing the aircraft for the Royal Navy. What perhaps seems less logical is that the Sea Hawk, developed along a less advanced technological path, superseded the Attacker.

Unlike Supermarine, who had opted to develop a true laminar-flow wing,

The Hawker P1040, VP401, in the form in which it was first flown with single concave exhaust exit fairings and curved single-piece windscreen. (Photo: Ministry of Supply, Neg No 16274)

believing this to be the answer to the problems of near-sonic compressibility, Hawker had persisted with relatively conventional aerofoils of progressively lower thickness/chord ratio but which possessed less semblance of laminar-flow qualities, for the aerofoil contours favoured Hawker's established wing-construction.

When Hawker received details of the proposed Rolls-Royce RB.41 turbojet (scheduled for the Supermarine E.10/44, see page 350), the company's project staff, in November 1944, proposed incorporating this engine amidships in the basic Fury design, moving the cockpit to the nose, this project being termed the P1035. The following month this scheme was developed further, bifurcating the engine jetpipes so as to exhaust on each side of the fuselage immediately aft of the wing trailing edge. This proposal, the P1040, attracted general approval from the Air Staff, and Hawker was encouraged to begin detail design, securing patents on the split tailpipe, and collaborating with Rolls-Royce in such areas as a wing-root air intake design.

Gradually any remaining resemblance with the Fury disappeared, the former elliptical wings, shown in tunnel tests to be unsuitable at high subsonic speeds, giving place to mid-set, straight-tapered wings with a thickness/chord ratio of

The first N.7/46 prototype, VP413, probably at Farnborough, showing the starboard 'pen-nib' fairing aft of the engine jetpipe and orthodox flat windscreen. The folded wings give a good indication of the wing section. (Photo: Hawker Aircraft Ltd)

The second N.7/46, VP422, being flown by Sqn Ldr T S Wade DFC, AFC, Hawker's Chief Test Pilot; this was representative of the Sea Hawk F 1 with lengthened arrester hook (just visible aft of the elevator), and provision for 100 gallon drop tanks and RATOG. (Photo: Cyril Peckham, Hawker Aircraft Ltd Neg No H158)

0.095; thickened wing roots incorporated engine intakes and jetpipe fairings. The cockpit was situated in the extreme nose, and a nosewheel undercarriage adopted, the mainwheel units being mounted at the outer edges of the stub wings so as to retract inwards with the wheels housed below the engine compartment in the fuselage.

With the ending of the War, and the absence of any further evidence of Air Staff interest, in October 1945 the Hawker Board decided to undertake the manufacture of a P1040 prototype as a private venture. However, the successful bid to establish a new World speed record by the Meteor explained the Air Ministry's disinterest in the Hawker fighter, being confident that the Gloster aircraft would retain its world superiority for

some years to come.

The Admiralty, on the other hand, perhaps frustrated by the continuing delays with the laminar-flow wing, recognised in the P1040 the basis of an efficient fleet support fighter, and Hawker again submitted the design, now modified to include folding wings and arrester hook. A naval Specification, N.7/46, was quickly written around Sydney Camm's proposals, and two naval prototypes, VP413 and VP422, were ordered. Hawker was also asked to proceed with its own prototype, VP401, for aerodynamic confirmation and without any military equipment being fitted.

VP401 was first flown at Boscombe Down on 2 September 1947, powered by a Rolls-Royce Nene I which, at that time, was limited by engine speed to

4,500lb-thrust, but this was replaced early the next year by a 5,000lb-thrust Nene 102 which bestowed a maximum speed of 570 mph TAS at sea level.

The only significant alteration found to be necessary at this stage was to the fairings aft of the jetpipes, which were changed to a 'pen nib' shape so as to maintain airflow stability along the rear fuselage. The frameless, curved windscreen was also criticised on account of vision distortion, and was replaced by a conventional flat, armoured screen.

The first true N.7/46 prototype, VP413, with armament, folding wings, hook and catapult spools, was flown on 3 September 1948. As part of a year-long series of Service trials, VP413 underwent deck landing trials aboard HMS *Illustrious*, as a result of which a much lengthened arrester hook was fitted on the second N.7/46 aircraft, VP422, which flew on 17 October 1949. This prototype also included provision for a pair of 100 gallon drop tanks as well as rocket-assisted take-off gear.

A preliminary production order for 35 aircraft, now named the Sea Hawk F Mk 1, was signed with Hawker Aircraft on 22 November 1949, the first of these, WF143, being flown on 14 November 1951. This order, however, was the full extent of Hawker Aircraft Ltd's participation in the Sea Hawk programme. One of the first steps taken by Churchill's Conservative administration, which came to office in 1951, was to introduce measures to speed up the production and introduction into service of a number of key military aircraft whose development had been severely delayed by the ponderous administrative pro-

Above: *The first Hawker-built production Sea Hawk F Mk 1, WF143, at Dunsfold, Hawker's newly acquired airfield in November 1951; note the absence of 'acorn' tail fairing, introduced shortly after.* (Photo: Ministry of Supply Neg No 21928C)

Right: *Sea Hawk F Mk 1, WM905/172 of No 806 Squadron, the first to equip with the Hawker fighter.* (Photo: Author's Collection)

A Sea Hawk FGA Mk 4 fitted experimentally with in-flight refuelling probes on the phenolic-asbestos underwing tanks; the system was not adopted in Service Sea Hawks. (Photo: Sir W G Armstrong Whitworth Aircraft Ltd.)

cesses of the past six years. There is no doubt that what rankled in the minds of the Air Staff was that the RAF, which had been so far ahead of the USAF in fighters only six years previously, was now about four years behind. . .

Two of the aircraft types on the Government's 'super priority' list were the Hawker Hunter and Sea Hawk, and, in view of continuing production of the Sea Fury (as well as the closure of the Hawker factory and airfield at Langley after the War, owing to its proximity to London's Heathrow airport), it was decided to switch all future development and production of the Sea Hawk to Sir W G Armstrong Whitworth Aircraft Ltd at Baginton, Coventry, then also engaged in the development of another Hawker Siddeley Group aircraft, the Gloster Meteor night fighter.

Ironically, this move probably delayed production of the Sea Hawk and, although a further contract for 60 F Mk 1s was placed immediately with Armstrong Whitworth, the first of these was not flown until 1953. Powered by Nene RN4 (Mark 101) engines, the F Mk 1s first equipped No 806 Squadron in March that year at Brawdy, Pembrokeshire, then commanded by Lt-Cdr P C S Chilton RN, this squadron embarking in HMS *Eagle* the following February for

a spell in the Mediterranean. No 804 Squadron, commanded by the renowned Lt-Cdr E M Brown OBE, DSC, AFC, RN, followed suit in November 1953 at Lossiemouth. By that time, Sea Hawk F 1s had reached the Naval Air Fighting Development Unit (No 787 Squadron) of the Central Fighter Establishment at West Raynham in Norfolk, commanded by another distinguished former naval test pilot, Lt-Cdr S G Orr, DSC, AFC, RN.

Although the Sea Hawk appears to have been free of the 'snaking' phenomenon that had affected several other early jet aircraft, the onset of compressibility had been manifest in tail buffeting, and this was alleviated by the addition of an 'acorn' fairing at the junction of the tailplane and fin (starting partway through the Hawker-built production batch). Nevertheless the Sea Hawk was a popular aeroplane among naval pilots, the more so when power-assisted ailerons were introduced in the F Mk 2 to eliminate control oscillation. Only 40 Sea Hawk F 2s were built, equipping Nos 802 and 807 Squadrons aboard HMS *Eagle* and *Bulwark* respectively.

Provision had been made to carry the 100 gallon drop tanks on the Marks 1 and 2, but in the Mark 3 fighter-bomber,

first flown on 13 March 1954, 500lb bombs or mines could be substituted, and henceforth the ground attack rôle became the Sea Hawk's primary duty with the Fleet Air Arm. A total of 116 Mark 3s was built, being flown by eight operational squadrons before being joined, and eventually replaced by the FGA Mk 4, which was capable of carrying either four 500lb bombs or up to sixteen rocket projectiles.

By 1955 the performance of the Sea Hawk was beginning to be regarded as somewhat pedestrian, and an attempt was made to improve the aircraft's speed performance with the introduction of the uprated 5,200lb-thrust Nene 103; the retrospective substitution of this engine in the Marks 3 and 4 resulted in the F Mk 5 and FGA Mk 6 respectively. In addition, a production order for 86 newly-built Mark 6s, completed in 1956, brought the total Sea Hawk production for the Fleet Air Arm to 434 — by far the largest number of a single type of jet fighter ever produced for the Royal Navy.

By the time of the Suez crisis, towards the end of 1956, Sea Hawk FGA 6s had equipped Nos 800, 801, 803, 804, 806, 810, 895, 897, 898 and 899 Squadrons.

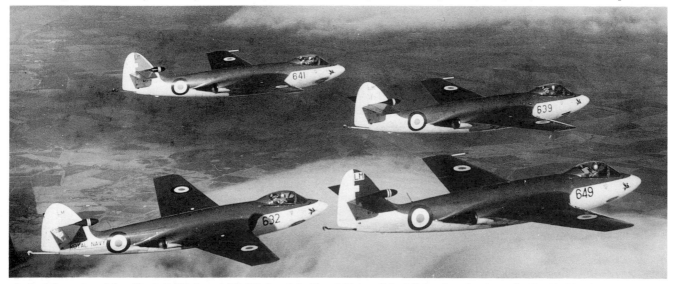

A mixed formation of Sea Hawk F Mk 1s and FB Mk 3s of the Naval Fighter School flying from Lossiemouth, identified by the Pegasus device on the nose of the aircraft; it is said that the rank of the pilots was denoted by the rings on the tail 'acorn' fairing. (Photo: Author's Collection)

Of these, No 800 in HMS *Albion*, Nos 804 and 810 in HMS *Bulwark*, and Nos 897 and 899 in HMS *Eagle* flew their Sea Hawks in action against Egyptian military installations and airfields, as well as providing air cover over British and French ground forces advancing south along the Canal, losing two aircraft to ground fire.

The Sea Hawk remained in service with the operational squadrons until 1960, No 806 being disbanded in December that year. Apart from providing the main fighter strength of the Royal Navy for six years, the Sea Hawk underwent countless trials to examine other possible rôles, including that of reconnaissance fighter, with an F 94 camera in an otherwise standard underwing drop tank; another aircraft was used for flight refuelling trials; and a Mark 6 was flown with two 100 gallon drop tanks, two 500lb bombs and ten 60lb rockets under the wings —the top-weight configuration, though probably not flown on operations. At one time it was intended to introduce powered elevators in production Sea Hawk, and a trial installation was made on an FGA 4, WV825, being distinguishable by a row of vortex generators along the tailplane.

Fairly large exports of Sea Hawks had been forthcoming, 32 Mk 50s (similar to the FGA Mk 6) were produced for the Royal Netherlands Navy during 1957-58, and 64 Mark 100s and 101s with EKCO Type 34 search radar were built for the West German Navy between 1957 and 1959. And even after the production line at Baginton had been dismantled, India ordered 36 aircraft in 1959 (some of which were ex-Royal Navy Sea Hawks), and these were joined later by 28 ex-German Navy aircraft.

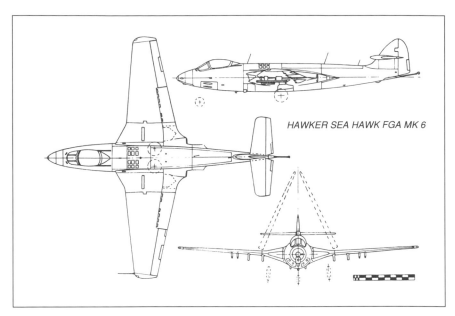

HAWKER SEA HAWK FGA MK 6

Type: Single-engine, single-seat, mid-wing monoplane naval fighter, fighter-bomber and ground-attack fighter.

Manufacturers: Hawker Aircraft Ltd., Kingston-upon-Thames and Dunsfold, Surrey; Sir W G Armstrong Whitworth Aircraft Ltd, Baginton, Coventry.

Air Ministry Specification: N.7/46

Powerplant: One 5,000lb-thrust Rolls-Royce Nene 101 and 102; 5,200lb-thrust Nene 103.

Dimensions: Span, 39ft 0in (13ft 3in folded); length, 39ft 8in; height, 8ft 8in (16ft 9in folded); wing area, 278 sq ft.

Weights: Tare, 9,190lb; max all-up, 15,225lb.

Performance: Mark 6. Max speed, 554 mph TAS at 36,000ft (Mach 0.84); climb to 35,000ft, 11 min 50 sec; service ceiling, 44,500ft.

Armament: Mark 6. Four 20mm Hispano Mk 5 cannon in nose, and provision for two 100 gal drop tanks, two 500lb bombs and up to ten 60lb three-inch rocket projectiles.

Prototypes: One, P1040, VP401. Two, N.7/46, VP413 and VP422. VP401 first flown 2 September 1947 at Boscombe Down. VP413 first flown 3 September 1948.

Production for Fleet Air Arm: Total, 434 Sea Hawks for the Fleet Air Arm. 95 F Mk 1s (between WF143-WF235 and WM901-WM905); 40 F Mk 2s (WF240-WF279); 116 FB Mk 3s (between WF280-WF303 and WM906-WN119); 97 FGA Mk 4s (between WV792-WV922 and XE327-XE338); and 86 FGA Mk 6s (between XE339-XE490).

Summary of Service with Fleet Air Arm: Sea Hawk F 1s served with Nos 700,736, 738, 764, 767, 787, 802, 804, 806 and 807 Squadrons, FAA, and No 1832 RNVR Squadron; F 2s served with Nos 700, 736, 738, 764, 767, 802 and 807 Squadrons; FB 3s served with Nos 700, 703, 736, 738, 764, 767, 787, 800, 802, 803, 806, 807, 811, 895 and 897 Squadrons; FGA 4s served with Nos 700, 736, 738, 764, 787, 800, 801, 802, 804, 806, 807, 810, 811, 895 and 898 Squadrons; FB 5s served with Nos 700, 736, 802 and 806 Squadrons; and FGA 6s served with Nos 700, 736, 738, 764, 781, 800, 801, 803, 804, 806, 810, 895, 897, 898 and 899 Squadrons.

Gloster E.1/44

Uncertainty regarding the future of the Gloster F.9/40 (Meteor), owing to the delays in delivery of suitable engines with which to start its flight programme in 1942, prompted George Carter to seek an alternative requirement for which he might tender a design as insurance against failure of his twin engine fighter to materialise. As de Havilland had already succeeded in obtaining a development and prototype contract under Specification E.6/41, Carter turned to

another single-jet requirement, E.5/42, for which the 2,300lb-thrust Halford H1 engine seemed the most promising.

This design, the Gloster GA.1, went ahead in 1943, and was accepted with the raising of a contract for three prototypes, SM801, SM805 and SM809. However, while work was underway on two of these aircraft, E.5/42 was withdrawn, re-written and re-issued in 1944 as E.1/44, calling for the use of an engine with a thrust of more than 3,000 pounds; this engine (as related on page 350) became the Rolls-Royce RB.41, and later the Nene. Work had progressed too far on SM801 and SM805 to

accommodate the much larger RB.41 and these aircraft were therefore abandoned.

As preliminary details of the Rolls-Royce engine were provided by its makers, the GA.1 design was altered accordingly and manufacture of SM809 started in Gloster's experimental shops at Bentham towards the end of 1944 as the GA.2. The aircraft was a small mid-wing metal monoplane with stressed-skin structure, the fuselage being built in five separate assemblies to facilitate sub-contract manufacture. The cockpit was located well forward in the nose but, unlike the Meteor, the four-cannon ar-

The second Gloster E.1/44 prototype, TX145. An anti-spin parachute is housed in the fairing aft of the rudder. (Photo: via Derek James)

mament was placed underneath so as to fire either side of the nosewheel unit. The rear fuselage was of semi-monocoque construction and, like the Supermarine E.1/44 (later the E.10/44), the engine, with lateral intake ducts and mounted amidships, exhausted through a very long tailpipe which extended to the extreme rear of the fuselage. The tailfin was placed on top of the rear fuselage, its upper section being of wooden construction. Fuel was carried in five tanks in the centre fuselage.

A very wide-track undercarriage retracted inwards into the wings which carried wide-span landing flaps under the trailing edge and small airbrakes on the upper and lower surfaces at semi-span.

By the end of 1945, when tunnel tests confirmed the general configuration seemed satisfactory, three further prototypes, TX145, TX148 and TX150, were ordered, and shortly afterwards a production Specification, 24/46P, was issued (for which the Gloster designation GA.4 was allotted). SM809 was completed early in 1947; however, while being transferred to Boscombe Down for its initial flight, the vehicle on which it was being carried crashed and the aircraft was damaged beyond economic repair.

The second E.1/44, TX145, was flown by Sqn Ldr W A Waterton AFC*, Gloster's recently-appointed Chief Test Pilot, on 8 March 1948, and proved capable of achieving its design speed of 620 mph with the 5,000lb-thrust Rolls-Royce Nene II engine. The aircraft, however, possessed slow acceleration and displayed a number of disagreeable handling characteristics, not least being a lack of pitch control at speeds well above the stall, as well as the familiar 'snaking' at high speeds. A number of minor adjustments had a marginal effect only, and it was decided

to adapt the tail unit then being designed for the Meteor F 8, and fit this to the second aircraft, TX148, which was flown in 1949.

The new tail unit proved to remedy most of the handling ills of the E.1/44, but had no appreciable effect on the performance. It was recognised that the

limiting Mach 0.80 represented no advance on the Meteor and that further effort to improve the design would be too costly, particularly as transonic fighters were already on the horizon. Work on the fourth E.1/44 (the GA.3) was therefore halted and the project came to an end late in 1949.

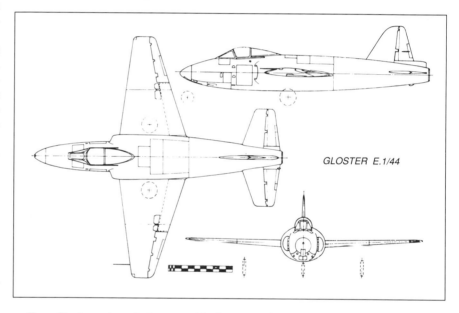

GLOSTER E.1/44

Type: Single-engine, single-seat, mid-wing monoplane experimental fighter.
Manufacturer: Gloster Aircraft Co Ltd, Hucclecote, Gloucester.
Air Ministry Specifications: E.1/44 for prototypes. (24/26P for proposed production).
Powerplant: One 5,000lb-thrust Rolls-Royce Nene II centrifugal-flow turbojet.
Dimensions: Span, 36ft 0in; length, 38ft 0in; height, 11ft 8in; wing area, 254 sq ft.
Weights: Tare, 8,260lb; all-up, 11,470lb.
Performance: Max speed, 620 mph at sea level; climb to 40,000ft, 12 min 30 sec; service ceiling, 44,000ft; range, 410 miles.
Armament: Four 20mm Hispano cannon in nose with 720 rounds.
Prototypes: Four, SM809, TX145, TX148 and TX150 (SM809 destroyed before flight; TX145 first flown by Sqn Ldr W A Waterton on 9 March 1948; and TX150 not completed). No production.

Hawker P1052

Several weeks after the end of the Pacific War, when the future of the P1040 appeared in doubt, Hawker submitted

several schemes to the DTD by which to advance its performance well beyond that of the Meteor, in an attempt to rekindle interest in the Air Ministry. One of these proposals was the P1047, which employed the fuselage and tail of the P1040 but was fitted with swept-

back wings and powered by a rocket motor. No such rocket powerplant then existed in Britain, but the opportunity to fly a research aircraft with a swept wing appealed to the Royal Aircraft Establishment. When the Admiralty confirmed its interest in the P1040, and Specifica-

The first Hawker P1052, VX272, as originally flown, with pressure-plotting swept wing prepared to E.38/46. (Photo: Author's Collection)

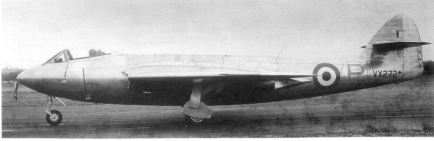

tion N.7/46 was prepared, thereby raising Hawker's hopes of a production contract, a new Specification was prepared in conjunction with the DTD and the Admiralty for a research aircraft fitted with a swept wing which, if found satisfactory, might form the basis of a naval fighter to replace the Sea Hawk in due course. The idea of using a rocket motor was shelved until a suitable design could be developed.

Specification E.38/46 was drafted and issued to Hawker on 16 January 1947, and a project design, the P1052, submitted two months later, resulting in a contract for two flying prototypes, VX272 and VX279, as well as a structural test specimen. As originally suggested, the fuselage remained virtually unchanged from that of the P1040, although the stub wing chord was enlarged to allow for a wing of lower aspect ratio. The wing, which would be the first pressure-plotting, high-speed swept wing to be made available for tests by the RAE, was to be of 10 per cent thickness/chord with quarter-chord sweepback of 35 degrees, and the P1052 was expected to provide essential flight data at speeds up to at least Mach 0.86. Indeed, in 1947, the Air Staff began seriously to consider asking that the P1052 be put into production, alongside the Sea Hawk, replacing the Meteor which now seemed irrevocably confined to a maximum of Mach 0.81. However, as the Air Staff soon began thinking in terms of transonic speeds, the idea was soon dropped.

VX272 was first flown on 19 November 1948 from Boscombe Down's long runway by Sqn Ldr 'Wimpey' Wade, and VX 279 followed on 13 April 1949. Before being committed to research by the RAE, however, VX272 underwent assessment by the A & AEE on behalf of the Australian government, following a proposal to introduce it into service as a fighter with the RAAF.

In July 1949 the Ministry of Supply asked Sydney Camm to examine the possibility of installing an Armstrong Siddeley Snarler rocket motor in the P1052, and Hawker accordingly produced a project design (the P1078, which was expected to achieve Mach 0.90). However, the RAE now expressed

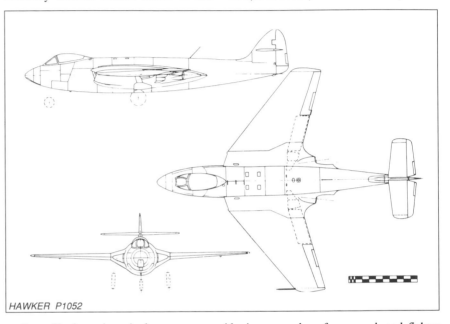

HAWKER P1052

Type: Single-engine, single-seat, swept mid-wing monoplane for research and fighter assessment.

Manufacturer: Hawker Aircraft Ltd, Kingston-upon-Thames, Surrey.

Air Ministry Specification: E.38/46

Powerplant: One 5,000lb-thrust Rolls-Royce Nene 102 centrifugal-flow turbojet.

Dimensions: Span, 31ft 6in; length (straight tailplane), 39ft 7in, (swept tailplane, 40ft 3in); height, 10ft 6in; wing area, 258 sq ft.

Weights: Tare, 9,450lb; all-up, 13,488lb.

Performance: Max speed, 670 mph at sea level (Mach 0.87 at 36,000ft); climb to 35,000ft, 9 min 30 sec; service ceiling, 45,500ft.

Prototypes: Two, VX272 and VX279 (VX272 first flown by Sqn Ldr T S Wade at Boscombe Down on 19 November 1948). No production.

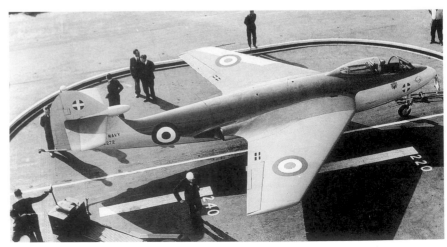

The P1052, VX272, resplendent in Fleet Air Arm colours, aboard HMS *Eagle in May 1952 for carrier trials; note the Sea Hawk-type sting-hook and tail 'acorn'.* (Photo: Author's Collection)

the view that, with tunnel data now available, the basic P1052's tail configuration was not suitable for this speed; and in any case work was already underway on the P1072 with rocket (see below).

For this reason, and confirmed by structural tests on the third P1052, VX272 was returned to Kingston for strengthening of the wing spars, while VX279 underwent further modification to the tail (becoming the P1081, see page 367).

On return to flying, however, VX272 suffered two accidents which delayed its flight programme until 1952 when, equipped to naval standard of preparation (fitted with tail 'acorn', long sting-type hook and Sea Hawk long-stroke undercarriage), the aircraft underwent its long-awaited deck trials aboard HMS *Eagle*. Following these, VX272 was fitted with a fully-swept, variable incidence tailplane, achieving Mach 0.87 during tests at the RAE which lasted until 1953 when it was struck off charge following another accident.

Hawker P1072

Brief reference should be made here to another development of the Hawker P1040, for it may be recalled that as early as October 1945 Hawker suggested a rocket-powered derivative as a means of keeping the Air Ministry interested in the P1040, as the manufacturers were about to undertake the construction of a prototype as a private venture.

The rocket installation was shelved as, at that time, no such powerplant existed in Britain. At the end of 1947, however, Armstrong Siddeley Motors Ltd began work on a 2,000 pound-thrust liquid-fuel rocket motor, it being intended that this would be used as a secondary source of power in a conventionally-powered turbojet aircraft to provide brief bursts of increased speed, for instance during combat. At first it was planned that Hawker Aircraft Ltd should build an additional P1040 prototype, but this proved unnecessary as VP401 itself would become available for modification by the time the rocket motor, named the Snarler, was ready for flight. The aircraft was returned to Kingston in September 1949 for the installation to be made under the project designation P1072.

The Rolls-Royce Nene installation remained virtually unaltered, although the turbojet's fuel capacity was drastically reduced to no more than 175 gallons. The Snarler rocket motor itself was installed in VP401's extreme tail. 75

The Hawker P1072, VP401, with tail-mounted Snarler rocket motor; the fairing running along the underside of the fuselage is the liquid oxygen transfer pipe.(Photo: Author's Collection)

gallons of liquid oxygen was carried in a spherical tank located between the pilot's cockpit and the Nene engine, and 120 gallons of water-methanol was contained in a tank aft of the rear turbojet fuel tank. This fuel was adequate for just 2 minutes 45 seconds of rocket power. A separate pneumatic system operated the rocket fuel supply jacks and valves, the liquid oxygen passing through a long transfer pipe under the fuselage.

Installation of the Snarler was completed at Kingston during the latter half of 1950, and on 16 November VP401 was flown north to Bitteswell under turbojet power only. Four days later, while on a flight from that airfield, the Snarler was started and all the rocket fuel was expended successfully.

Such were the strides being made with afterburners on turbojets, however, that interest in rocket-powered aircraft waxed and waned during the 1950s. The P1072, first British high-performance rocket-powered aeroplane, only made a dozen flights under the power of the Snarler before it was damaged by a minor explosion in the tail, and, although VP401 was fully repaired by February 1951, it never again made a rocket-powered flight. (Its other claim of interest was that it was the only twin-engine aeroplane ever completed by Hawker Aircraft Ltd.)

Type: Twin-engine, single-seat mid-wing monoplane jet/rocket research aircraft.
Manufacturer: Hawker Aircraft Ltd, Kingston-upon-Thames, Surrey.
Powerplant: One 5,000lb-thrust Rolls-Royce Nene 102 centrifugal-flow turbojet and one 2,000lb-thrust Armstrong Siddeley Snarler ASSn.1 liquid-fuel rocket.
Dimensions: Span, 36ft 6in; length, 37ft 7in; height, 8ft 9in; wing area, 256 sq ft.
Weights: Tare, 11,050lb; all-up, 14,050lb.
Performance: Max speed, 630 mph at sea level (Mach 0.82); climb to 35,000ft, 10 min 30 sec; service ceiling, 44,500ft; endurance of rocket power, 2 min 45 sec.
Prototype: VP401 (modified P1040); first flown on rocket power on 20 November 1950.

de Havilland Venom and Sea Venom

The extraordinarily ill-conceived decision by the British Government to bring about the cancellation of the Miles M.52 supersonic research aircraft programme in 1946 forced on the British aircraft industry all manner of alternative expedients in attempts to claw its way forward through the difficult transonic speed regime, a process that would occupy more than ten years, costing tens of millions of pounds in duplicated research and unwanted production, not to mention the many lives lost as pilots faced the hazards of exploring the countless deficiencies of engines and airframes.

After the death of Geoffrey de Havilland Jnr, when his D.H .108 broke

The first D.H. 112 Venom fighter-bomber prototype, VV612, at Hatfield with the new wingtip fuel tanks; the tail unit is unchanged from that of the Vampire 5. (Photo: Ministry of Supply).

up in the air on 28 September 1946, it became all too clear that merely sweeping back the relatively thick wings of bygone fighters was not the answer to successful transition to supersonic speed. Therefore, when the need arose to advance the Vampire's performance, not only was much greater engine power required to overcome the sharp increase in drag as aircraft speeds approached the speed of sound, but thinner aerofoils must be developed with the object of maintaining laminar flow over a much greater area of the wing.

Much of the design preparation for such a fighter was undertaken (as briefly mentioned on page 345) on the Vampire 8, intended for the de Havilland Ghost engine. When it emerged that a new wing would be required for this aircraft, an entirely new designation was allotted as the D.H. 112 Venom. In this the wing root chord remained little changed, but the wing leading edge was swept back 17 degrees. However, as there was no taper on the trailing edge, it was not, as claimed at the time, a 'swept wing' (a statement characteristic of the attempts to persuade the gullible into believing that British fighter design was still matching that of the United States). True, the wing thickness/chord was reduced from 14 to 10 per cent, but this, together with the Ghost's 40 per cent greater power, merely raised the Venom's critical Mach number from the Vam-

pire's 0.74 to 0.83; it was still a thoroughly subsonic aeroplane. And despite Dunlop's efforts to produce a single-disc wheel brake and the use of thinner, high pressure tyres on the mainwheels, the undercarriage could not be accommodated inside the wings without prominent bulged fairings on their upper surfaces.

The increased fuel consumption of the Ghost engine, whose greater size incidentally demanded little alteration to the nacelle, resulted in provision being made to carry four drop tanks, two in the customary underwing location and two outboard on the wingtips, thus demanding a much stronger wing structure. Thus, when the prototype Venom was completed, its tare weight had increased to 9,000 pounds, compared with 7,250 of the Vampire 5. All too soon the aircraft was to encounter the familiar problems associated with increasing compressibility effects, all manner of aerodynamic 'fixes' being necessary to overcome them.

Having said this, the Venom was to give yeoman service, and over 1,000 examples were to be produced for the Royal Air Force and the Fleet Air Arm. The first prototype, VV612, which had been taken from the English Electric company's production line of Vampire 5s and delivered to Hatfield for modification, was flown there on 2 September 1949, and made its debut at the SBAC

Display a few days later, but without external fuel tanks. The second prototype, VV613, was flown on 23 July 1950, and together these two aircraft underwent prolonged trials as production (originally intended to be undertaken by the Bristol Aeroplane Co Ltd at Filton, but abandoned) got underway in the de Havilland factory at Chester, and by the Fairey Aviation Co Ltd at Ringway, Manchester. During flight trials it was found necessary to introduce a large wing fence at semi-span to avoid tip stall at high angles of attack and, in order to clear the carriage of the wingtip fuel tanks, small fixed leading-edge slats were added immediately inboard of the tanks, also to prevent tip stall. Spring-tabbed control surfaces were also introduced.

The first production Venom FB Mk 1, WE254, capable of carrying two 1,000lb bombs or eight three-inch rocket projectiles in place of the underwing drop tanks, was flown in June 1951, and at about this time it was announced that the aircraft would become the standard NATO fighter bomber in Europe, alongside the American Republic F-84 Thunderjet.

After CA Release, which was not gained until mid-1952, the first RAF deliveries were made to No 11 Squadron at Wunstorf in Germany in August that year, under the command of Sqn Ldr D H Seaton DFC, AFC*. Re-equipping with the Venom was a long drawn-out process, generally due to the run-down condition of the British aircraft industry, and did not gain momentum until 1954 when seven squadrons, namely Nos 6 and 73 at Habbaniya, Iraq, No 32 in Egypt, and Nos 16, 94, 98 and 145 in Germany, discarded their Vampire 5s. In all, Venom FB 1s served with fifteen squadrons, the last to receive its aircraft being No 28 at Sek Kong, Hong Kong, in February 1956. A total of 373 aircraft of this type was built for the RAF.

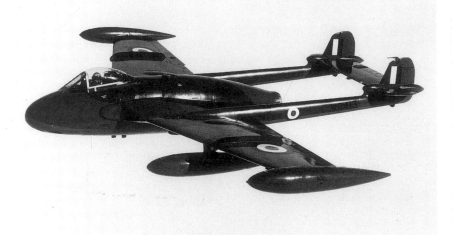

WR413 was a full-standard Venom FB Mk 4 with tail bullet fairings fore and aft of the fins and rudders, wingtip and underwing fuel tanks and cartridge ejector chutes under the nacelle. (Photo: A J Jackson Collection)

The private venture Venom night fighter prototype, carrying the SBAC markings G-5-3.
(Photo: A J Jackson Collection)

An improved fighter-bomber version introduced hydraulically-boosted ailerons with artificial spring-feel, bestowing a respectable rate of roll; the entire tail unit was improved by adding bullet fairings aft of the power-assisted rudders, and the tailplane was extended outboard of the fins. The prototype FB Mk 4, of which 150 production examples were built, was a converted FB 1, and first flew on 29 December 1953, serving with eleven squadrons, of which several were flown in action during the Suez Crisis of 1956.

Just as the Vampire had been pressed into service as an interim night fighter, so the Venom also appeared as a two-seater in this rôle with the home-based night/all-weather force. Having obtained no encouragement from the Air Ministry — owing to a persistent lack of Treasury support — to pursue this version, even though de Havilland had proposed it as early as 1948, the company again embarked on a prototype as a private venture, and this, carrying SBAC Class B registration G-5-3, was first flown on 22 August 1950. Like the Vampire NF 10, the Venom two-seater featured a greatly enlarged nacelle with the two-man crew seated side-by-side,

and still without ejection seats. Design of the new aircraft was directed by William Alban Tamblin, de Havilland's chief designer at Christchurch, retaining the single-seater's tail assembly but with enlarged rudders. Designated the NF Mk 2, the first of ninety aircraft, WL804, was flown at Hatfield on 4 March 1952, and this night fighter, still equipped with the wartime AI Mk X radar, entered service with No 23 Squadron at Coltishall, Norfolk, in September 1953. Plagued by structural failures and a dismal serviceability rate — resulting in a short, precautionary grounding and a limitation imposed at 523 mph and 10,000ft altitude following canopy failures — further Mark 2s were withheld from the squadrons until 1955 when Nos 33, 219 and 253 re-equipped. Some of these aircraft introduced an improved

clear-view canopy and extended dorsal fins, being unofficially known as NF Mk 2As.

The NF Mk 3 was a much improved night fighter, powered by a slightly uprated Ghost Mk 104, with AI Mark 21 radar (in reality the American Westinghouse AN/APS-57) in a stronger radome, short-span tailplane and hydraulically-boosted ailerons. The Mark 3, of which 129 were produced, served with Nos 23, 89, 125, 141 and 151 Squadrons, all of which were thus equipped during 1955, was an altogether better aircraft, and remained in service until replaced by the Gloster Javelin at the end of the decade.

Venoms were also supplied to the Royal New Zealand Air Force, FB 1s serving with No 14 Squadron RNZAF at Tengah, Singapore, and being flown in action against the communist guerrillas in the Malayan jungle. Export versions were designated the FB Mk 50, NF Mk 51, NF Mk 52 and FB Mk 54. FB 50s were supplied to Iraq and Switzerland (the latter also licence-building a further 250 such aircraft); NF 51s, supplied to Sweden, were powered by Swedish-built Ghost engines, and served with *Flygvapnet* designated the J33; and Venezuela ordered 22 Venom FB 54s. A plan for Fiat to licence-build Venoms was, however, dropped although Fiat-built Ghost engines were supplied to Switzerland and France.

Sea Venoms

The Royal Navy declined to consider the Venom for ground attack duties, being adequately equipped with Attackers and Sea Hawks. In the night/all-weather fighter rôle, however, there threatened a gap in the Fleet Air Arm's inventory in the mid-1950s until the arrival in service of the swept-wing Sea Vixen.

The prototype Venom Mk 2 G-5-3

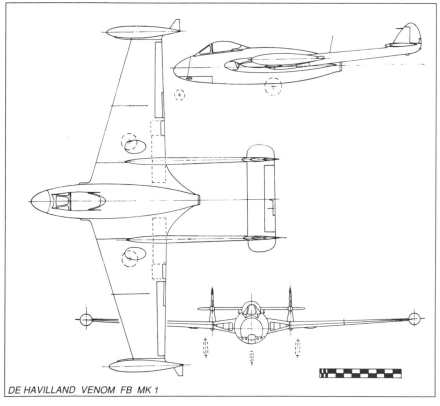

DE HAVILLAND VENOM FB MK 1

A Sea Venom FAW Mk 20, WM512/263, of the All-Weather Fleet Requirements Unit, flying from Brawdy in about 1955; the aircraft is carrying wingtip drop tanks with finlets, introduced partway through the Venom's service. (Photo: A J Jackson Collection)

(as WP227) was evaluated by naval pilots in 1950 and this led to the issue of Specification N.107, which called for a replacement of the Sea Hornet NF 21. Termed the Sea Venom NF Mk 20, the prototype WK385 was flown on 19 April 1951, and WP227 undertook the initial deck trials from HMS *Illustrious* on 9 July that year. A fully navalised prototype, WK376, with folding wings was produced at Hatfield, and production aircraft were completed in 1953, the first F(AW) Mk 20, WM500, being flown at Christchurch on 27 March. These featured the improved clear-view canopy and tail unit, but were still equipped with manual ailerons. They were followed by the F(AW) Mk 21, powered by Ghost 104 engines and fitted with AI Mark 21 radar, boosted ailerons, powered rudders and Maxaret non-skid wheelbrakes; 39 examples of this version were also supplied to the Royal Australian Navy as the F(AW) Mk 53, and went on to serve with that Service's No 808 Squadron.

The F(AW) Mk 22 was powered by the 5,300lb-thrust Ghost 105 engine and was equipped with AI Mk 22 radar; more important was the long-overdue inclusion of Martin-Baker Mk 4A ejection seats, the canopy being bulged on the port side so as to allow clearance for the pilot's helmet.

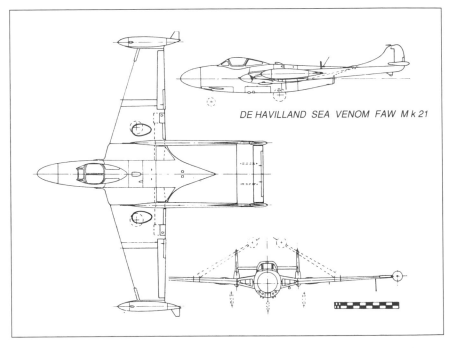

DE HAVILLAND SEA VENOM FAW Mk 21

Owing to early delays in the development of the Sea Vixen, which was not ready for service until 1960 — almost five years behind schedule — Sea Venoms remained in service much longer than originally intended, the last front line F(AW) Mk 22s being discarded by No 891 Squadron in July 1961. In the

WW200/VL/735, a Sea Venom F(AW) Mk 21 of No 766 Squadron based at RNAS Yeovilton in the late 1950s. This unit served as an All-Weather Fighter Pool. (Photo: R C Sturtivant)

Royal Australian Navy they continued to serve with No 816 Squadron until August 1967!

In the evening of their naval lives, many Sea Venom F(AW) 22s were armed with de Havilland Firestreak infrared-guided air-to-air missiles carried on the wing pylons, and these first served with No 893 Squadron in January 1959 at Yeovilton and soon afterwards aboard HMS *Victorious* under the command of Lt-Cdr E V H Manuel RN.

Perhaps the most remarkable feat of adaptation and production was that undertaken in France by the *Société Nationale de Constructions Aéronautiques du Sud-Est* which, in collaboration with de Havilland, established a design office to enable licence-production to be undertaken of Sea Venoms for the *Aéronavale* under the name Aquilon (Sea Eagle). These aircraft were all fitted with Fiat-built Ghost 48 engines. After assembling four Hatfield Mark 20s (which became Aquilon 20s) which first flew on 20 February 1952, production continued with 75 Aquilon 202s with Martin-Baker N4 ejection seats, Hispano 404 guns and American AN/APQ-65 radar, 40 single-seat Aquilon 203s with AN/APQ-94 radar and Nord 5103 command-guided missiles, and, finally, 15 Aquilon 204 trainers.

Type: Single-engine mid-wing monoplane, single-seat fighter-bomber and two-seat night/all-weather fighter.

Manufacturers: de Havilland Aircraft Co Ltd., Hatfield, Hertfordshaire; Chester, Cheshire and Christchurch, Hampshire; Fairey Aviation Co Ltd, Ringway, Manchester.

Air Ministry Specification: No Specification for RAF Venom; N.107 for naval night/all-weather fighter.

Powerplant: One 4,850lb-thrust de Havilland Ghost 103 centrifugal-flow turbojet (FB Mks 1 and 4, NF Mk 2 and F(AW) Mk 20); 4,950lb-thrust Ghost 104 (NF Mk 3 and F(AW) Mk 21); 5,300lb-thrust Ghost 105 (F(AW) Mk 22).

Dimensions: FB Mk 4. Span, 41 ft 8in; length, 31ft 10in; height, 6ft 2in; wing area, 279.75 sq ft. F(AW) Mk 22. Span, 42ft 11in; length, 36ft 7in; height, 8ft 6¼in; wing area, 279.75 sq ft.

Weights: FB Mk 4. Tare, 9,202lb; all-up, 15,310lb. F(AW) Mk 22. All-up, 15,800lb.

Performance: FB Mk 4. Max speed, 640 mph at sea level (Mach 0.83); service ceiling, 48,000ft; max range, 1,075 miles. F(AW) Mk 22. Max speed, 575 mph at sea level (Mach 0.75); service ceiling, 40,000ft; range, 705 miles.

Armament: Four 20mm Hispano Mk 5 cannon each with 150 rounds; provision to carry two 1,000lb bombs and eight three-inch 60lb rocket projectiles.

Prototypes: FB Mk 1, two, VV612 and VV613 (converted Vampire 5s; VV612 first flown at Hatfield on 2 September 1949); FB Mk 4, one, WE381; NF Mk 2, one, G-5-3; NF Mk 3, one, WV928; Sea Venom F(AW) 20, three, WK376, WK379 and WK385.

Production: Total of 887 for the RAF and Fleet Air Arm: FB Mk 1, 373; NF Mk 2, 90; NF Mk 3, 129; F(AW) Mk 20, 50; F(AW) Mk 21, 206; F(AW) Mk 22, 39.

Summary of Service: Venom FB Mk 1s served with Nos 5, 6, 8, 11, 14, 16, 28, 32, 45, 60, 73, 94, 98, 145 and 266 Squadrons; NF Mk 2 served with Nos 23, 33, 219 and 253 Squadrons; NF Mk 3s served with Nos 23, 89, 125, 141 and 151 Squadrons; FB Mk 4s served with Nos 5, 6, 8, 11, 28, 60, 94, 142, 208, 249 and 266 Squadrons of the RAF. Sea Venom F(AW) Mk 20s served with Nos 700, 766, 808, 809, 890 and 891 Squadrons; F(AW) Mk 21s served with Nos 700, 736, 738, 750, 766, 787, 809, 891, 892, 893 and 894 Squadrons; F(AW) Mk 22s served with Nos 750, 891, 893 and 894 Squadrons, Fleet Air Arm.

Supermarine Type 510 and Swift

The efforts of Hawker to produce an aircraft to meet the research Specification E.38/46 have been recorded under the P1052 (see page 357, *et seq*), and while those efforts ultimately led to the creation of the Hunter, parallel work being done by Joseph Smith at Supermarine gave effect to the Swift.

The Supermarine project design, the Type 510, tendered to E.38/46, was also successful in attracting an order for two prototypes, VV106 and VV119, from the Ministry of Supply. Built at Hursley Park experimental department, these two aircraft were powered by Rolls-Royce Nene 2 engines and were to be, in effect, Attackers fitted with wings swept back on their leading edges by 40 degrees and, unlike the Hawker P1052, incorporated all-swept tail surfaces from the start. And when VV106 was first flown by M J Lithgow on 29 December 1948, it was still the first British jet-powered aircraft to fly with sweepback on wings and tailplane. (The North American XP-86, be it noted, had flown on 1 October 1947, had exceeded Mach 1.0 in a dive on 26 April 1948, and had done so with a 35-degree sweepback on a wing of root thickness/chord of 11 per cent).

Early flights inspired confidence that the Type 510 represented the basis of an exceptionally fine fighter. Lithgow reported achieving speeds of around 630 mph at 10,000 feet, although at its limiting Mach 0.93 the port wing could only be held up by full right aileron. Moreover it was discovered that the swept wing introduced longitudinal instability before the stall (as on the P1052) so that, without more power available from the Nene, the aircraft could do little more than fly straight and level at 40,000 feet. The aircraft showed none of the familiar signs of snaking, and

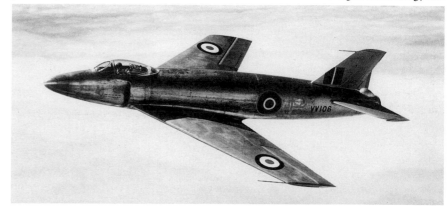

An early view of the Type 510, VV106; the bulged fairing over the extreme rear fuselage housed an anti-spin parachute for trials purposes. (Photo: Vickers-Armstrongs Ltd.)

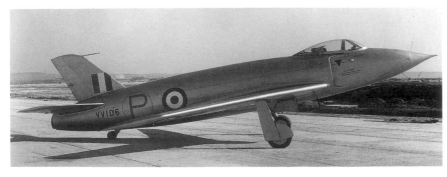

The Type 510, VV106, after being fitted with the lengthened, pointed nose section. (Photo: Author's Collection)

its positive aileron control bestowed an excellent rate of roll at low altitude. On the other hand the aircraft's retention of the Attacker's tailwheel undercarriage attracted criticism from Service pilots at Boscombe Down.

Because the Admiralty regarded the research Specification E.38/46 as representing the basis of an Attacker replacement, VV106 underwent limited modification for deck operating trials, incorporating an A-frame arrester hook under the rear fuselage and including attachments points for assisted take-off rockets. Being thus cleared at a take-off weight of 12,790 pounds, VV106 became the first swept-wing aircraft in the world to land on and take-off from an aircraft carrier when, on 8 November 1950, Lt J Elliot RN landed on HMS *Illustrious* (pre-empting the navalized P1052 by four months owing to its accidents, and beating the American FJ-2 Fury by over two years).

After completion of its carrier trials, VV106 was returned to Supermarine for a new series of modifications to improve the longitudinal stability. It had been suggested that in order to retain full control at high Mach numbers a variable-incidence tailplane would probably be essential. This, however, was not possible in VV106, as it stood, as the tailplane attachment was anchored to a banjo frame which was part of the structure supporting the engine tailpipe. There was therefore no alternative but to rotate the entire rear fuselage, tailplane and tailpipe to achieve changes in the tailplane's incidence. With a conventional variable-incidence tailplane, flown later on VV119, the modification was considered to be a great improvement.

The second E.38/46, VV119, had been first flown by Lithgow on 27 March 1950 as the Type 528 with tailwheel undercarriage and lengthened nose, fitted with an instrumentation probe. Soon after this flight the aircraft was returned to the works to be given a nosewheel undercarriage (although it retained the twin tailwheels to act as landing 'bumpers'). In this form VV119 was flown as the Type 535, but also differed in numerous other respects;

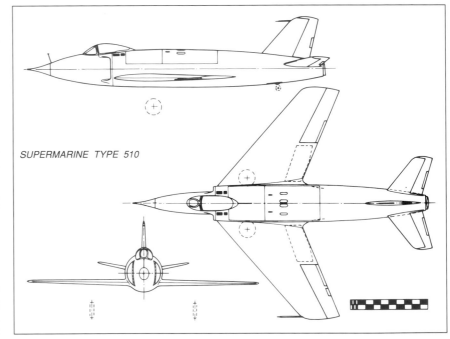

SUPERMARINE TYPE 510

The Supermarine Type 535, VV119, after acquiring the nosewheel undercarriage; just visible below the wing are the twin tailwheels, also retained. (Photo: Vickers-Armstrongs Ltd.)

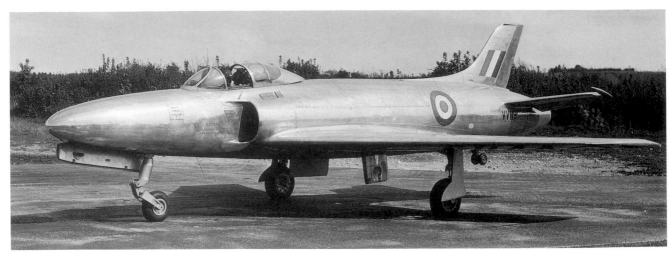

Intended to meet Operational Requirement OR.228, Specification F.105 was raised to cover two Type 541 Swift prototypes, of which WJ960, shown here, was the first. It was powered by a 7,500lb-thrust Avon RA1. (Photo: Ministry of Supply, Neg No 22632, dated April 1952)

these included a rear fuselage of increased diameter to accommodate a larger tailpipe with afterburner, improved engine air intakes, provision for four guns in the wings (demanding shorter ailerons), a steel-framed cockpit canopy, a lengthened nose to introduce radar ranging, a fuel capacity increased to 400 gallons and, perhaps most significant, a revision of the wing shape by reducing the sweepback of the trailing edges of the inboard section — thereby giving a kinked planform.

VV119 was first flown in this form on 23 August 1950, and the re-heat was 'lit' for the first time on 1 September, the only such use of an afterburner on the Nene engine. A performance check, made at this time, disclosed that the Type 535 possessed a maximum level speed of Mach 0.88 at 35,000 feet, somewhat below its critical Mach number. In November that year Supermarine received a contract for 100 production aircraft with Rolls-Royce AJ.65 Avon axial-flow turbojets, to be named the Swift, as well as two prototypes, WJ960 and WJ965, designed to meet Specification F.105. This contract was raised as an insurance by the Air Ministry against failure of the Hawker Hunter, whose prototype was still nine months away. (VV119 was subsequently flown for the film *Sound Barrier*, and in 1955 was fitted with dummy Firestreak AAMs to test their effect on handling, before the aircraft was grounded.)

The first Supermarine Type 541 Swift prototype, WJ960, was flown by Lithgow at Boscombe Down on 1 August 1951, the benefits of the 7,500lb-thrust Avon being immediately apparent. As the armament, consisting of a pair of 30mm Aden guns, was to be moved to the fuselage, a return to the longer span ailerons of the Type 510 was possible. Unfortunately a couple of forced landings caused the start of the full flight programme to be delayed until February 1953, the second aircraft having flown on 18 July 1952.

WJ965, however, was also to be grounded shortly after the SBAC Display of September 1952 when the prototype de Havilland D.H. 110 (Sea Vixen

prototype) flown by John Derry broke up in the air, an accident thought to have been caused by catastrophic elevator flutter induced by spring-tabs on the tail control surfaces.

After replacing the Swift's spring tabs by rigidly-geared tabs, the two Type 541 prototypes resumed flying, and on 26 February 1953 WJ965 exceeded the speed of sound in a dive over the airfield at Chilbolton.

The first Swift F 1s, WK194 and

WK195, were produced at Hursley Park, and were followed by the first true production aircraft, WK196, which flew in March 1953 with fully-boosted controls. However, while the first eighteen examples were still being assembled, the Specification was altered, increasing the armament to four 30mm Aden guns (following the successful installation of this number of guns in the Hunter).

The new armament was included in the next seventeen Swifts, the F Mk 2.

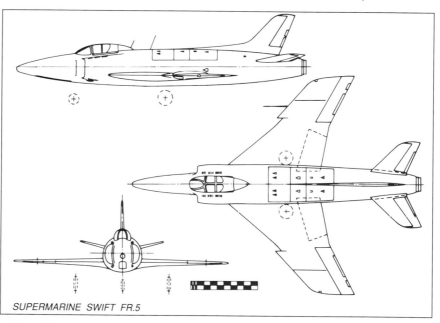

SUPERMARINE SWIFT FR.5

Type: Single-engine, single-seat, low-wing interceptor fighter.

Manufacturer: The Supermarine Division of Vickers-Armstrongs Ltd.

Air Ministry Specifications: E.38/46 (for Type 510 prototypes) and F.105 (for Swift F 1).

Powerplant: Type 510. One 5,000lb-thrust Rolls-Royce Nene 102 centrifugal-flow turbojet (also with re-heat). Type 541 Swift. 7,500lb-thrust Rolls-Royce Avon RA 1 axial-flow turbojet (9,000lb-thrust with re-heat).

Dimensions: Span, 32ft 4¼in; length, 41ft 6in; height, 13ft 6in; wing area, 306.2 sq ft.

Weights: Tare, 11,892lb; all-up, 15,800lb.

Performance: Max speed, 660 mph at sea level; climb to 40,000ft, 5 min 10 sec; service ceiling, 45,500ft.

Armament: Two 30mm Aden guns in lower fuselage below engine intakes.

Prototypes: Type 510, VV106 and Type 535, VV119; two Type 541, WJ960 and WJ965; two Mk 7s, XF774 and XF780.

Production: F Mk 1, 18 (between WK194-WK213); F Mk 2, 17 (WK199 and between WK214-WK246); F Mk 3, 25 (WK247-WK271); F Mk 4, six (WK198, WK272, WK273, WK275, WK279 and WK308); F Mk 5, 94 (between WK274-WK315, WM583-WM656, WN124-WN127, WV949-WN952 and XD903-XD976); Mk 7, 12 (XF113-XF124).

Summary of Service: Swift F 1s and F 2s served with No 56 Squadron; Swift FR 5s served with Nos 2 and 79 Squadrons; Swift Mk 7s served with Guided Weapon Development Squadron, Valley.

The second Type 541 Swift prototype, WJ965, showing the kinked leading and trailing edges of the wing. (Photo: E B Morgan)

However, to accommodate the additional ammunition for the guns, the inboard wing leading edges had to be extended forward, and this straightway gave rise to the phenomenon known as 'pitch-up', an uncontrollable manœuvre which occurred if g was applied at above Mach 0.85, causing the nose to rear up, and the aircraft to flick on to its back. Various remedies were tried, ranging from the addition of wing fences to the introduction of a toothed wing extension of the wing leading-edge outboard, all resulting in partial cure. On the Swift, however, the final remedy proved to be no less sophisticated than the addition of considerable ballast in the nose, and this, not surprisingly, had the effect of severely reducing the high altitude performance of the fighter.

In the meantime, Swift F 1s, with considerable operating restrictions, were delivered to No 56 (Fighter) Squadron at Waterbeach on 13 February 1954, the provisional CA Release being conditional on gun firing being limited to 30,000 feet, the speed limited to Mach 0.85 and altitude to 40,000 feet; these limitations were relaxed on 30 August with the Mark 1's replacement by the Mark 2s. However, the aircraft were summarily grounded shortly afterwards following the loss of two aircraft which appeared to pitch up uncontrollably during take-off.

Only the eighteen Swift F 1s were built, followed by seventeen F 2s. The next version, the F 3 equipped with re-heat, had aleady been built, but it was not flown by an RAF squadron; instead, all but one were delivered to Schools of Technical Training for use as ground instruction machines.

The F Mk 4, termed the Supermarine Type 546, was expected to be trouble-free, the first example (converted from a Mk 1, WK198) having been flown on 2 May 1953. It was equipped with re-heat and included the long-awaited variable-incidence tailplane and the toothed wing leading-edge which, together, appeared to bring the pitch-up

under control. However, a number of engine failures (not suffered by the Hunter with the same engine) disclosed that the Avons in the Swifts featured compressor blades of a different design; after their replacement no further engine failures were reported. Thus encouraged, Supermarine sent Lithgow and Swift Mk 4 WK198 to Tripoli in Libya for an attempt on the World Absolute Speed Record, and on 26 September they established a new record at 735.7 mph, thereby exceeding Neville Duke's record of 727 mph, set up in the Hunter 3 only three weeks earlier in a much lower ambient temperature.

The Swift F 4 was abandoned after only six had been built, principally because the re-heat could not be lit at high altitude, and was therefore largely superfluous in a would-be interceptor fighter. Production by Short Bros of 146 F 4s had been ordered, but all were cancelled.

Instead, the remaining 35 aircraft were completed as Type 549 Swift FR Mk 5s, which were similar to the F 4 but featured a lengthened nose housing a forward-facing and two oblique reconnaissance cameras. The re-heat was retained as the fighter reconniassance sortie profile was invariably well below 20,000 feet. A follow-up order for 59 further FR 5s was placed early in 1955, and in March 1956 they began equipping No 2 (Fighter Reconnaissance) Squadron at Geilenkirchen in Germany, followed by No 79 Squadron in June the

same year at Laarbruch. These aircraft, the first in the RAF with re-heat, remained in service until replaced by the Hunter FR Mk 10.

The Type 550 Swift PR Mk 6 was not pursued owing to its high altitude problems, but the Type 552 Swift was employed to test fire the Fairey Fireflash beam-riding AAM. A Swift Mk 4, WK279, was converted as an aerodynamic prototype, and successfully fired three unarmed rounds in October 1955. Two new-build Mark 7 prototypes, XF774 and XF780, were followed by twelve production aircraft, equipped with the beaming radar, which were delivered to the Guided Weapon Development Squadron at RAF Valley, Anglesey, for wepon firing over the Aberporth range between December 1956 and July 1957, consitituting the first RAF fighters to fire air-to-air missiles.

It is perhaps all too facile to regard the Swift as a total failure, yet it should be remembered that, for all the effort that had gone into it, the basic design had been evolved around the more corpulent Nene engine and, in the context of being an 'insurance' against failure of the Hunter, there would have been little time to evolve a slimmer aircraft — as the Hunter itself was — tailored to the Avon. The Swift was an impressive aircraft, for all its faults, and in some respects its wing was more advanced aerodynamically than that of the Hunter.

The data table, on the previous page, refers to the Swift F Mk 1 except where stated otherwise.

A Swift FR Mk 5, XD904, of the type which finally gave useful service as a reconnaissance fighter with Nos 2 and 79 Squadrons of the RAF in Germany in the late 1950s. (Photo: Vickers-Armstrongs Ltd).

Hawker P1081

The Hawker P1081, VX279, being flown by Sqn Ldr T S Wade, after being fitted with wing fences and a slightly taller rudder. (Photo: Sydney Camm Collection)

It might, perhaps, be thought a logical step in the evolution of the Hawker Hunter to replace the Sea Hawk-type tail unit of the swept-wing P1052 with an all-swept tail. The decision to do so, however, had more to do with the continuing interest by the Australian government in introducing a development of the P1052 into service with the RAAF, than a belief that such an aircraft would have much relevance to the Hunter which, after all, possessed an entirely new wing and fuselage.

Although it had been intended to introduce a Rolls-Royce Tay engine — a more powerful derivative of the Nene — the future of this turbojet was in doubt, and it was decided to retain the Nene, but employ an Attacker-type engine tailpipe, exhausting through the tail.

The second P1052, VX279, was the only aircraft now available for the conversion, and this was first flown by Sqn Ldr T S ('Wimpey') Wade DFC, AFC, Hawker's chief test pilot, on 19 June 1950. Four days later the aircraft was displayed at the Brussels Air Show, and soon afterwards at the RAF Display at Farnborough.

During the course of flight trials the P1081 achieved a speed of 685 mph TAS at sea level, but in a dive from 40,000 feet Wade reported the onset of snaking at Mach 0.89, with the port wing dropping sharply during recovery.

A new tailplane, of eighteen inches greater span was fitted, as well as wing fences to counter tip stall, and these were stated to improve the handling considerably.

Although Australian interest evaporated in November (as negotiations got underway to build the F-86 Sabre in that country), Hawker decided to continue flying the P1081, and introduced further modifications, including an electrically-actuated variable-incidence tailplane and a slightly larger rudder. These alterations were still under test when, on 3 April 1951, VX279 crashed near the Farnborough airfield after Wade appeared to lose control in the landing circuit and ejected. He was unfortunately killed when his ejection seat (not a Martin-Baker type) failed.

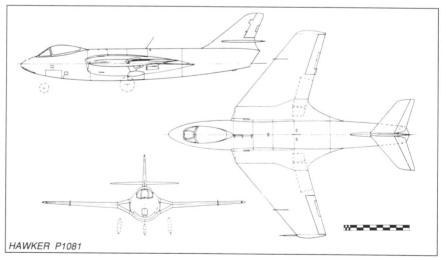

HAWKER P1081

Type: Single-engine, single-seat, swept mid-wing monoplane fighter research aircraft.
Manufacturer: Hawker Aircraft Ltd, Kingston-upon-Thames, Surrey.
Powerplant: One 5,000lb-thrust Rolls-Royce Nene RN2 (Mk 102) centrifugal-flow turbojet.
Dimensions: Span, 31ft 6in; length, 37ft 4in; height, 13ft 3in; wing area, 258 sq ft.
Weights: Tare, 11,200lb; all-up, 14,480lb.
Performance: Max speed, 685 mph at sea level; Mach 0.89 at 36,000ft; climb to 35,000ft, 9 min 12 sec; service ceiling, 45,600ft.
Prototype: One, VX279 (modified P1052, first flown by Sqn Ldr T S Wade on 19 June 1950). No production.

Hawker Hunter

The speed with which the Gloster Meteor was rendered obsolescent in the years following the Second World War came as a shock to the Royal Air Force and an acute embarrassment to the British government. No replacement was in sight and it was all too clear that any advance in aerodynamic research to enable fighter aircraft to approach and exceed the speed of sound would be very costly — at a time when funding for defence was anathema for a government struggling to finance the creation of a new Welfare State. Nor were significant production contracts for other types of aircraft commonplace in the aircraft industry from which private companies could support this research.

Hawker Aircraft Ltd was perhaps in a better position than most manufacturers in this respect, possessing a substantial production order for Sea Furies and with continuing interest in what showed promise to become a new naval jet interceptor. As has been shown, the Hawker P1040 was useful as a basis for new research with the development of the swept-wing P1052, and later the 'all-swept' P1081.

Unfortunately the Air Ministry became sidetracked in 1946 by an attempt to increase the weight of fighter armament at the expense of performance, and two Specifications (F.43/46 and F.44/46), issued that year called for day and

Upper: *Sqn Ldr Neville Duke in the first Hunter prototype, WB188, immediately before its first flight on 20 July 1951 at Boscombe Down.* Lower: *The same pilot in the third, Sapphire-powered prototype, WB202, at Dunsfold.* (Photos: Hawker Aircraft Ltd.)

night fighters to be armed with the 57 mm Molins gun. Such demands were quickly seen to be retrogressive and in 1947 Sydney Camm entered discussions with both the Air Ministry and the Ministry of Supply to prepare a day fighter Specification embodying the new 6,000 lb thrust Rolls-Royce AJ.65 axial-flow turbojet and an armament of either two or four 20 mm Hispano cannon. In

due course Specification F.3/48 was issued calling for a single-seat interceptor to be armed with either four Hispano cannon or two of the new 30 mm Aden guns. A level speed capability of Mach 0.90 (620 mph at 36,000 feet or 724 mph at sea level) was demanded and power was to be provided by either the AJ.65 Avon or Armstrong Siddeley Sapphire axial-flow turbojets.

Hawker's tender was to be the P1067, which at first featured an annular engine air intake in the extreme nose and an unswept tailplane mounted on top of a swept fin and rudder. However, progress was being made with a radar ranging gunsight which prevented the use of a nose intake so that reversion to wing-root intakes (Sea Hawk fashion) was adopted. Tunnel tests also suggested that the aircraft might be susceptible to Dutch rolling and a swept tailplane was

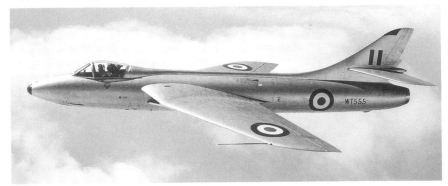

Above: *Duke airborne in the first Hawker-built production Hunter F 1, WT555, yet without the cartridge case tanks under the nose and the ventral airbrake.* (Photo: Author's Collection.

Right: *The first Sapphire-powered Hunter F 2, WN888, at Baginton, also without the early Service modifications.* (Photo: Sir W G Armstrong Whitworth Aircraft Ltd, Neg No A423.)

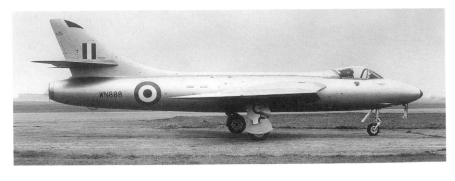

One of the Hunter 1s used for basic aerodynamic research was WT571 with bulged fairings on the sides of the rear fuselage to test the effects of the 'area rule'; the speed benefit was very marginal at subsonic speeds. (Photo: Author's Collection)

incorporated about three feet lower on the fin. Elimination of the engine intake ducts from the front fuselage allowed an armament of four 30 mm Aden guns to be accommodated — the heaviest gun armament yet to be fitted in a British fighter — the weapons being housed in an ingenious detachable pack to facilitate quick re-arming.

When manufacture of the first, unarmed F.3/48 prototype, WB188, was completed, it appeared as a surpassingly beautiful aeroplane with slender fuselage and gracefully swept wings. Painted pale green overall, it was first flown on 20 July 1951 at Boscombe Down by Sqn Ldr Neville Frederick Duke DSO, OBE, DFC**, AFC (Hawker's newly appointed Chief Test Pilot after the death of Sqn Ldr Wade). Already a production order for 198 aircraft (in addition to two prototypes) had been signed with Hawker on 14 March that year and the name Hunter was selected. The second prototype, WB195, fully armed with Aden guns and almost representative of the production version, was flown by Duke on 5 May 1952. A third prototype, WB202, powered by an Armstrong Siddeley Sapphire engine flew at Dunsfold on 30 November that year.

Production was already underway and the first Hunter F Mk 1, WT555, was flown by Frank Murphy on 16 May 1953. Performance and handling evaluation of the prototypes at the A & AEE had shown that use of the landing flaps as speed brakes imposed a severe pitching moment and after a number of alternative airbrakes had been tested (including 'clam-shell' brakes on the sides of the rear fuselage) the most effective was found to be a large hydraulically-operated flap under the rear fuse-

lage. Deliveries of the Hunter 1s were delayed while these airbrakes were incorporated.

The Hunter F 1s, powered by 7,500 lb thrust RA.7 Avons, were first delivered to the Central Fighter Establishment at West Raynham in July 1954, and in the same month started delivery to No 43 (Fighter) Squadron, commanded by Sqn Ldr R Lelong at Leuchars. Almost immediately the new fighters ran into serious trouble during high altitude gun firing trials, it being found that severe engine compressor surging occurred when the guns were fired at high altitude, this being due to local pressure disturbance around the engine intakes; the surging was frequently followed by flame-out. Limitations were at once

imposed on Hunter gun firing until Rolls-Royce could produce a remedy. A total of 139 Mk 1 Hunters was built at a unit cost of £172,000 each.

Meanwhile the Hunter F 2, of which 45 were produced powered by the Sapphire engine, was also issued to the Service, No 257 Squadron receiving its first aircraft in July, and No 263 Squadron the following month. The Sapphire was, however, found to be immune to surging, and the Hunter 2 was cleared for gun firing up to 47,500 feet.

The next problem reflected a shortcoming in the original Specification and, although the Hunter fully met the one hour's endurance requirement, on real-life operational sorties the fuel reserves were found to be quite inadequate, and

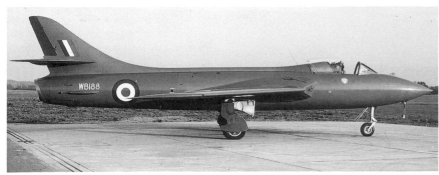

Above: *Owing to the very short endurance of the Hunter F 1, underwing drop tanks were introduced on the F 4; this Mk 1, WT569, was employed to fly trial installations of the tanks, those shown here not being fitted with tail fins.* (Photo: Hawker Aircraft Ltd, Neg No H2518)

Left: *Painted bright red, the original Hunter prototype, WB188, with lateral airbrakes and re-heated Avon, established a new World Speed Record, flown by Neville Duke in September 1953.* (Photo: Author's Collection).

Left: *Hunter 4, XF310, was modified to incorporate AI Mk 20 radar and a pair of Fairey Fireflash (Blue Jay) beam-riding air-to-air missiles which were test-fired over the Aberporth range.* (Photo: Hawker Aircraft Ltd.)

Below: *A private venture trial installation of five cameras in the nose of Hunter 4 WT780 led to the drafting of an official fighter reconnaissance Specification and ultimately to the Hunter FR Mark 10.* (Photo: Hawker Aircraft Ltd, Neg No HG.10/56)

several aircraft were lost simply through running out of fuel.

The upshot of these early setbacks was the immediate switch to improved Hunters, the Marks 4 and 5. The former was powered by surge-resistant Avon 115s (RA.14), fuel capacity was increased from 337 to 414 gallons and the aircraft was equipped with a 'full flying tail' to alleviate stick loads during high-g manœuvres. The airframe improvements were also included in the Sapphire-powered Mark 5. Modifications were included in the fuel system to permit carriage of two, and later four 100-gallon drop tanks under the wings.

These improvements transformed the Hunter, and many pilots considered the Mark 4 to be the most pleasant of all versions to fly. A total of 365 Hunter 4s was produced for the RAF, and these equipped 22 Squadrons, many of them serving in Germany. 105 Mark 5s equipped seven RAF squadrons, and some were involved in the air operations during the Suez crisis of 1956.

Perhaps not surprisingly the Hunter had attracted widespread interest among air forces overseas, anxious to acquire replacement of their first generation jet fighters. The first customer for the Mk 4 was Sweden with an order for 120 aircraft, termed Mk 50s, of which the first 25 were built by Hawker at Kingston and the remainder by Hawker Aircraft (Blackpool) Ltd. Thirty Mk 51s were purchased by Denmark and 16 ex-RAF Mk 4s were sold to Peru as Mk 52s. Dutch and Belgian companies negoti-

ated substantial licence production undertakings, Fokker-Aviolanda of Amsterdam producing 96 Mk 4s for the *Koninklijke Luchtmacht*, and Avions Fairey of Brussels a further 112 for the *Belgische Luchmacht* during 1955-56.

Before leaving the early generation of Hunters it is worth recording that the original prototype, WB188, had been fitted with an afterburning Avon RA.7R engine during 1953 as part of the development programme for the supersonic 'thin-wing' P1083 (which, in the event, was cancelled). On 7 September that year WB188 (now unofficially termed the Hunter 3), flown by Duke over the sea off Rustington, Sussex, established a new World Absolute Air Speed Record at 727.63 mph. At the time WB188 was also fitted with side-mounted airbrakes as part of the current trials, already mentioned. Other trials included investigation of AAMs on the Hunter (Fairey

Fireflash on Mk 4, XF410, and D.H. Firestreak on the Sapphire prototype WB202), 'area rule' on the Mk 1, WT571, and blown flaps on the Mk 1, WT656. Hunter 4, WT780, was employed on a wide range of trials which included the fitting of a ram-air turbine in the rear fuselage, a dummy drag parachute tail fairing, and ultimately modification as a private venture fighter reconnaissance version, the FR Mk 4.

Cancellation of the supersonic P1083 with its re-heat Avon in 1953 caused attention to be transferred to the use of the new 200-series 'dry' Avon, delivering 10,500 lb thrust. However, so long as the Hunter retained the thick wing there was no question of achieving supersonic speed in level flight (although all versions were transonic in a dive). Nevertheless, the proposed English Electric Lightning — with its Mach 2 performance — was scheduled for service in 1958, so that emphasis was henceforth laid on the Hunter's rôle as a ground attack fighter. Powered by the big Avon, the aircraft would become a potent, heavy load carrying ground support

Hunter F 5, WN979/ E of No 56 (Fighter) Squadron at Waterbeach during the mid-1950s. Although cleared to carry external stores, this version was used almost exclusively as a home-based interceptor fighter. (Photo: Author's Collection)

After the P1099 Hunter 6 prototype had completed its handling and performance trials, it was allocated to Rolls-Royce for trial installation of a thrust reversal system, characterized by the large lateral exhaust apertures in the rear of the fuselage; the aircraft is shown taking off at Farnborough. (Photo: Rolls-Royce Ltd)

aircraft. Time would show that, in any case, supersonic performance in this rôle was superfluous.

The prototype Avon 200-powered Hunter, the P1099 XF833, soon to be termed the Mark 6, was first flown by Duke at Dunsfold on 22 January 1954, and was followed two years later by the first of 415 production examples for the RAF. Manufacture of these aircraft (at a contracted unit price of £217,660) was divided between Hawker at Kingston and Sir W G Armstrong Whitworth Aircraft Ltd at Coventry, and was completed in 1957, the year in which a Defence White Paper was published stating that the forthcoming Lightning would be the last manned interceptor fighter to enter service with the RAF — resulting in the cancellation of a further planned 150 Hunters 6s.

The intention to switch the Hunter to the punishing ground attack rôle in 1955 meant that a prolonged series of searching trials to enable the aircraft to carry a wide range of external stores had to be undertaken, both by Hawker and the A & AEE—including 1,000lb and practice bombs, 60lb rocket projectiles, multiple rocket batteries, napalm bombs, and drop tanks. Gun firing trials were performed at all altitudes, disclosing the need to fit gun blast deflectors on the Aden cannon, while to overcome the pitch-up tendency wing leading-edge 'saw tooth' extensions were found to cure the problem; the latter were applied retrospectively to all Hunters in service and production, for which a modification centre was set up at Horsham St Faith in 1955.

Having thus set in train the replacement of all Sabre, Venom and Meteor day fighters in Europe with either Hunter 4s or 6s, it was now the turn of elderly aircraft in the Mediterranean, Middle and Far East, and preparatory for the Hunter 6's operation in the these theatres two late production examples, XK149 and XK150, underwent tropical trials at Aden in 1958; these showed that in order to operate from 'hot and high' airfields the Hunter required uprated cockpit conditioning and a landing parachute. The latter had already been developed for the Hunter two-seat trainer and so it was with no difficulty that a drag chute was installed in a fairing over the engine tailpipe.

Gradually almost all Hunter 6s un-

A fully modified Hunter F Mk 6, XF389, complete with gun blast deflectors, ammunition link chutes, cartridge collector tanks, and toothed wing leading edge extensions, and carrying two 100 gallon drop tanks and 24 three-inch rockets. (Photo: Sydney Camm Collection)

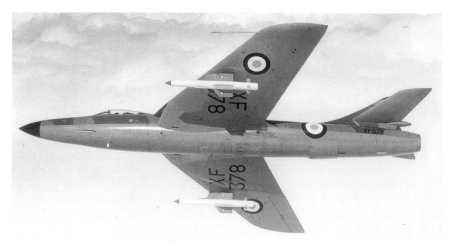

The P1109B Hunter XF378, equipped with nose radar and de Havilland Firestreak infrared-guided AAMs and two Aden gun armament. (Photo: Hawker Aircraft Ltd, Neg No AH.12/57)

derwent these modifications, thereafter being termed the F 6 (Interim Mark 9) during 1958-59, but one further requirement remained to be satisfied, the ability of Hunters to fly long-stage reinforcement flights to the Middle and Far East from home bases. This resulted in the development of 230 gallon ferry tanks, and their carriage on the inboard wing pylons. The full-standard Hunter FGA (fighter, ground attack) Mark 9 was characterised by gun blast deflectors, wing leading-edge extensions, ammunition case collector fairings, lengthened ammunition link ejector chutes, strut-strengthened inboard wing pylons stressed to carry 230-gallon drop tanks under combat loads, store ejector guns on the outboard pylons, and tail parachutes; increased on-board oxygen supply was also provided to cater for long-distance flights.

By January 1960 fourteen squadrons had received Hunter 6s, and No 8 Squadron at Aden Hunter FGA 9s; all the Hunter 6 squadrons were based either in Britain or Germany. During the next five years almost all the Mark 6 units re-equipped with FGA 9s.

Two further single-seat Hunter variants were produced, although one of these, the Fleet Air Arm's Hunter GA Mk 11, a modified Mark 4 with airfield arrester hook fitted and with guns removed, was a training aircraft of which 40 examples were converted. The Mark 10, however, was a derivative of the Mark 6/9 and stemmed largely from Hawker's private venture FR Mk 4, WT780. Experience with this aircraft had encouraged the issue of Specification FR.164 in 1957, calling for a fan of three nose-mounted reconnaissance cameras. Hawker set about converting a Mark 6, XF429, to become the prototype FR Mk 10; this was to be followed by 33 production examples (all con-

verted from Mark 6s or 9s) which equipped Nos 2 and 4 (Fighter Reconnaissance) Squadrons at Gütersloh. Nos 2, 20, 28 and 208 Squadrons in the Middle and Far East each received two or three FR 10s apiece in addition to their Mark 9s.

It should also be mentioned here that

the 'missing' Marks of Hunter, namely the Mark 7, 8 and 12 were all two-seat training versions and are therefore outside the scope of this work.

The big Avon engine-powered Hunters performed a number of trials quite unconnected with the clearance of ground attack weapons, beginning with the prototype Mark 6, XF833, which was delivered to Rolls-Royce Ltd for experiments with a thrust reversal scheme for reduced landing run; shutters were located in the engine's tailpipe which, when closed, deflected the exhaust gases laterally and slightly forward through louvres in the sides of the rear fuselage.

Type: Single-engine, single-seat mid swept-wing interceptor (Marks 1,2,4 and 5), ground attack fighter (Marks 6 and 9), and reconnaissance fighter (Mark 10).

Manufacturers: Hawker Aircraft Ltd, Kingston-upon-Thames, Surrey; Hawker Aircraft (Blackpool) Ltd, Blackpool, Lancashire; Sir W G Armstrong Whitworth Aircraft Ltd, Coventry, Warwickshire.

Air Ministry Specifications: F.3/48 (as progressively amended) and FR.164 D (Mark 10).

Powerplant. Mks 1, 4 and 11. One 7,500lb thrust Rolls-Royce Avon RA.7/21 axial-flow turbojet. Mks 2 and 5. 8,000lb thrust Armstrong Siddeley Sapphire 101 turbojet. Mks 6, 9 and 10. 10,000lb thrust Rolls-Royce Avon RA.28 turbojet.

Structure: Mid-wing, all-swept, all-metal monocoque monoplane with nosewheel undercarriage; engine located amidships with fixed-geometry air intakes in wing roots and exhausting through extreme tail.

Dimensions. Span, 33ft 8in; length (all single-seat versions except Mk 10), 45ft 10½in; length (Mk 10), 46ft 10in; height, 13ft 2in; wing area (with leading-edge extensions), 349 sq ft.

Weights. Tare, (Mk 1), 12,128lb; (Mk 2), 11,973lb; (Mk 4), 12,543lb; (Mk 9), 13,010lb; (Mk 10), 13,100lb. Max all-up, (Mks 1 and 2), 16,200lb; (Mk 4), 17,100lb; (Mk 9), 18,000lb; (Mk 10), 18,090lb.

Performance. (Avon RA.21 engines): Max speed, Mach 0.94 at 36,000ft; climb to 45,000ft, 9 min 50 sec; service ceiling, 50,000ft. (Avon RA.28 engines): Max speed, Mach 0.95 at 36,000ft; climb to 45,000ft, 7 min 30 sec; service ceiling, 51,500ft.

Armament: All single-seaters (excluding Mk 11 fighter-trainer) carried four 30mm Aden guns in nose with 137-150 rpg. External weapons on Mks 6 and 9 included two 1,000lb iron bombs or 230 gallon drop tanks on inboard wing pylons, and two 100 gallon drop tanks or rocket batteries on outboard pylons. Alternatively British 3in, French T-10, Swedish Bofors, American 5in HVARs or Swiss Hispano rockets on outboard strongpoints.

Prototypes: Two Mk 1, WB188 and WB195 (WB188 first flown on 20 July 1951 by Sqn Ldr N F Duke at Boscombe Down; WB195, 5 May 1952); Mk 2, WB202 (30 November 1952); Mk 6 prototype, XF833 (22 January 1954).

Production: Total built in UK, 139 Mk 1s (between WT555-WT700 and WW599-WW645); 45 Mk 2s (between WN888-WN953); 365 Mk 4s (between WT701-WT811, WV253-WV412, WW589-WW591, WW646-WW665, XE657-XE718, XF289-XF999, XG341 and XG342); 105 Mk 5s (between WN954-WP194); and 415 Mk 6s (between WW592-WW598, XE526-XE656, XF373-XF527, XG127-XG298, XJ632-XJ718 and XK136-XK224).

Summary of RAF Service: Mark 1s served with Nos 43, 54, 222 and 247 Squadrons; Mark 2s with Nos 257 and 263 Squadrons; Mark 4s with Nos 3, 4, 14, 20, 26, 43, 54, 66, 67, 71, 74, 92, 93, 98, 111, 112, 118, 130, 222, 234, 245 and 257 Squadrons; Mark 5s with Nos 1, 34, 41, 56, 208, 257 and 263 Squadrons; Mark 6s with Nos 1, 4, 19, 20, 26, 43, 54, 56, 63, 65, 66, 74, 92, 93, 111, 208, 247 and 263 Squadrons; Mark 9s with Nos 1, 8, 20, 28, 43, 45, 54, 58 and 208 Squadrons; and Mark 10s with Nos 2, 4, 8 and 79 Squadrons. Mark 11s served with Nos 738 and 764 Training Squadrons of the Fleet Air Arm.

Hunter FGA Mk 9s of No 1 (Fighter) Squadron, fully equipped for tropical reinforcement, with 230 gallon drop tanks on combat-stressed inboard wing pylons, three rocket rails and outboard pylon on each wing and landing parachutes. (Photo: Hawker Siddeley Aviation Ltd.)

Three aircraft, WW594, WW598 and XF378, joined a programme to equip the Hunter with Firestreak AAMs and AI Mk 20; known as the P1109, these Hunters continued with trials until 1957 when, with the publication of the Defence White Paper (already referred to), all work on the Hunter as an interceptor stopped. The AI 20 radar had necessitated a lengthened nose of fine profile, and one of the P1109s, WW598, was flown in the Middle East under the aegis of the RAE, undertaking high-speed flights at very low level in high ambient temperatures to investigate the effects of severe gust loading on the aircraft and to provide data for the forthcoming Blackburn Buccaneer and BAC TSR.2 strike aircraft.

Another Hunter project was the all-weather two-seat fighter (P1114 with Avon and P1115 with Sapphire). Nei-

ther came to be built, but Hunter 6, XG131, was flown with slim, fixed wing-tip fuel tanks — proposed for the all-weather fighter so as to free the underwing store pylons for AAMs. Another trial installation associated with the P1114/P1115 was that of very large lateral 'clam shell' airbrakes on the sides of the rear fuselage — the all-weather fighter demanding increased deceleration during operations. Like the P1109, development of the two-seat fighter was also halted.

Overseas interest in the Avon 200-series Hunter was widespread, particularly when surplus RAF, Dutch and Belgian Mk 6s were re-purchased by Hawker during the 1960s and offered for re-sale after considerable refurbishing.

Such was the highly lucrative business generated by these aircraft (many of which had flown 3,000 hours) that Hawker undertook the task — previously considered to be uneconomic — of converting veteran Hunter 4s to accommodate the larger engine.

Although Peru, Sweden and Denmark did not express interest in following their Mark 4s with orders for the Mark 6, it was perhaps natural that the licence production lines in the Netherlands and Belgium should change over to the new version, and Fokker-Aviolanda produced 93 examples between 1956 and 1958; Belgium built 144 Mark 6s during the same period.

The first new customer was India, which country was quick to take advantage of accelerated deliveries following cancellation of the RAF's final Mark 6s and placed an initial order for 160 Mark 56s, and followed this with an order for 36 Mk 56As in 1965—at the same time bringing all aircraft up to FGA Mk 9 standard; other Indian orders totalled seventeen aircraft. Many of these aircraft were flown in action during the Indo-Pakistani wars of 1965 and 1971, and remained in operational service into the 1980s.

Switzerland placed an order for 100 Hunter 6s, restyled the Mark 58, in 1958, following this with orders for 52 Mk 58As; some of these were re-worked ex-RAF Mark 4s, brought up to the latest FGA Mk 9 standard, and it has been suggested that Hunters may continue in service with the Swiss *Flugwaffe* until the turn of the century.

Following the completion of the last newly-built Hunter 6 (an Indian Mark 56 on 5 October 1960), export of single-seaters continued for a further fourteen years, comprising refurbished and modified aircraft declared surplus by the RAF and other air forces and re-purchased by Hawker. Twelve FGA Mk 9s were sold to Rhodesia; four Mk 57s to Kuwait; 24 Mk 59s, eighteen Mk 59As and four Mk 59Bs to Iraq; four Mk 60s

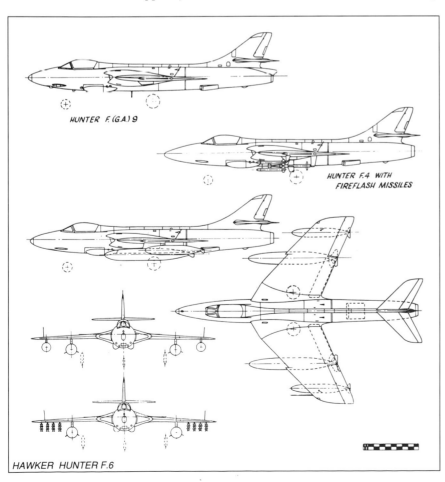

HUNTER F.(G.A.) 9

HUNTER F.4 WITH FIREFLASH MISSILES

HAWKER HUNTER F.6

A total of 33 Hunters were converted to Fighter Reconnaissance Mark 10s, replacing Swift FR 5s on Nos 2, 4 and 79 Squadrons; many were later sold abroad. (Photo: Hawker Aircraft Ltd, Neg No HG11/60)

to Saudi Arabia; four Mk 70s to Lebanon; 28 Mk 71s and FR Mk 71As to Chile; two Mk 73s, thirteen Mk 73As and three Mk 73Bs to Jordan; twelve FGA Mk 74s, four FR Mk 74As and 22 FR Mk 74Bs to Singapore; seven FGA Mk 76s and three FR Mk 76As to Abu Dhabi; three FGA Mk 78s to Qatar; and four FGA Mk 80s to Kenya. Many of the Hunters delivered to the Arab nations were subsequently transferred to second states, particularly to Jordan whose air force suffered heavily in wars with Israel. (Again, the 'missing' Mark numbers were applied to two-seat Hunter trainers.)

Among British fighters, that the Hunter was a classic aircraft cannot be denied. It was never a world leader among interceptors, having paid the penalty imposed by the lack of Treasury research funding during 1945-48, during which period the American aircraft industry gained technological leadership — which has never been disputed since. Yet the Hunter soon became a viceless aircraft, a 'pilot's aeroplane' and one that was quickly acclaimed by those who flew it. It also possessed an extraordinary fatigue life, ensuring many years' service under the most rigorous operational conditions. Like the Hurricane earlier, it was a 'go anywhere, do anything' fighter, robust and inexpensive by the standards of its day, and one that suited the demands of many nations seeking protection from predatory neighbours.

It also ensured the survival of Hawker as a military aircraft constructor when extinction faced the British aircraft industry.

Deployment of British Fighter Squadrons — January 1950

Home Bases

Squadron	Aircraft	Base
No 1 Squadron	Gloster Meteor F 4	Tangmere
No 17 Squadron	Supermarine Spitfire LF 16E	Chivenor
No 19 Squadron	D.H. Hornet F 3	Church Fenton
No 20 Squadron	D.H. Vampire F 3	Valley
No 23 Squadron	D.H. Mosquito NF 36	Church Fenton
No 25 Squadron	D.H. Mosquito NF 36	West Malling
No 29 Squadron	D.H. Mosquito NF 36	West Malling
No 41 Squadron	D.H. Hornet F 3	Church Fenton
No 43 Squadron	Gloster Meteor F 4	Tangmere
No 54 Squadron	D.H. Vampire FB 5	Stradishall
No 56 Squadron	Gloster Meteor F 4	Thorney Island
No 63 Squadron	Gloster Meteor F 4	Thorney Island
No 64 Squadron	D.H. Hornet F 3	Linton-on-Ouse
No 65 Squadron	D.H. Hornet F 3	Linton-on-Ouse
No 66 Squadron	Gloster Meteor F 4	Linton-on-Ouse
No 72 Squadron	D.H. Vampire FB 5	Odiham
No 74 Squadron	Gloster Meteor F 4	Horsham St Faith
No 85 Squadron	D.H. Mosquito NF 36	West Malling
No 92 Squadron	Gloster Meteor F 4	Linton-on-Ouse
No 141 Squadron	D.H. Mosquito NF 36	Church Fenton
No 222 Squadron	Gloster Meteor F 4	Thorney Island
No 245 Squadron	Gloster Meteor F 4	Horsham St Faith
No 247 Squadron	D.H. Vampire FB 5	Odiham
No 257 Squadron	Gloster Meteor F 4	Horsham St Faith
No 263 Squadron	Gloster Meteor F 4	Horsham St Faith
No 264 Squadron	D.H. Mosquito NF 36	Coltishall
No 500 Squadron	Gloster Meteor F 3	West Malling
No 501 Squadron	D.H. Vampire F 1	Filton
No 502 Squadron	Supermarine Spitfire F 22	Aldergrove
No 504 Squadron	Gloster Meteor F 4	Wymeswold
No 600 Squadron	Supermarine Spitfire F 21	Biggin Hill
No 601 Squadron	D.H. Vampire F 3	North Weald
No 602 Squadron	Supermarine Spitfire F 22	Abbotsinch
No 603 Squadron	Supermarine Spitfire F 22	Turnhouse
No 604 Squadron	D.H. Vampire F 3	North Weald
No 605 Squadron	D.H. Vampire F 1	Honiley
No 607 Squadron	Supermarine Spitfire F 22	Ouston
No 608 Squadron	D.H. Vampire F 3	Thornaby
No 609 Squadron	Supermarine Spitfire LF 16E	Yeadon
No 610 Squadron	Supermarine Spitfire F 22	Hooton Park
No 611 Squadron	Supermarine Spitfire F 22	Hooton Park
No 612 Squadron	Supermarine Spitfire F 14	Dyce
No 613 Squadron	Supermarine Spitfire F 22	Ringway
No 614 Squadron	Supermarine Spitfire F 22	Llandow
No 615 Squadron	Supermarine Spitfire F 21/22	Biggin Hill
No 616 Squadron	Gloster Meteor F 3	Finningley

Germany

Squadron	Aircraft	Base
No 2 Squadron	Supermarine Spitfire FR 19	Wunstorf
No 3 Squadron	D.H. Vampire FB 5	Gütersloh
No 4 Squadron	D.H. Mosquito FB 6	Celle
No 11 Squadron	D.H. Mosquito FB 6	Celle
No 16 Squadron	D.H. Vampire FB 5	Gütersloh
No 26 Squadron	D.H. Vampire FB 5	Wunstorf

Mediterranean and Middle East

Squadron	Aircraft	Base
No 6 Squadron	D.H. Vampire FB 5	Habbaniya, Iraq
No 32 Squadron	D.H. Vampire F 3	Nicosia, Cyprus
No 39 Squadron	D.H. Mosquito NF 30/36	Fayid, Egypt
No 73 Squadron	D.H. Vampire F 3	Ta Kali, Malta
No 208 Squadron	Supermarine Spitfire FR 18	Fayid, Egypt
No 213 Squadron	D.H. Vampire FB 5	Deversoir, Egypt
No 249 Squadron	Hawker Tempest F 6	Deversoir, Egypt

Far East

Squadron	Aircraft	Base
No 28 Squadron	Supermarine Spitfire FR 18	Hong Kong
No 33 Squadron	Hawker Tempest F 2	Changi, Singapore

No 60 Squadron	Supermarine	Kuala Lumpur,
	Spitfire FR 18	Malaya
No 80 Squadron	Supermarine Spitfire F 24	Hong Kong

Fleet Air Arm

No 800 Squadron	Supermarine Seafire F 47	Sembawang,
		Singapore
No 801 Squadron	D.H. Sea Hornet F 20	Lee-on-Solent
No 802 Squadron	Hawker Sea Fury FB 11	Culdrose
No 803 Squadron	Hawker Sea Fury FB 11	Dartmouth,
		Canada
No 804 Squadron	Hawker Sea Fury FB 11	HMS *Glory*
No 805 Squadron	Hawker Sea Fury FB 11	Nowra, Australia
No 807 Squadron	Hawker Sea Fury FB 11	St Merryn

No 809 Squadron	D.H. Sea Hornet	
	F 20/NF 21	Culdrose
No 810 Squadron	Fairey Firefly FR 4	Eglinton
No 812 Squadron	Fairey Firefly NF 1/FR 4	HMS *Glory*
No 813 Squadron	Blackburn	
	Firebrand TF 5	Lee-on-Solent
No 814 Squadron	Fairey Firefly 5	Culdrose
No 816 Squadron	Fairey Firefly FR 4/5	Nowra, Australia
No 825 Squadron	Fairey Firefly 5	Dartmouth,
		Canada
No 826 Squadron	Fairey Firefly FR 1	Dartmouth,
		Canada
No 827 Squadron	Fairey Firefly FR 1	Sembawang,
		Singapore

Supermarine Types 508, 525 and 529

The Supermarine Type 508, VX133, during the winter of 1951-52. (Photo: Vickers Ltd.)

The last family of jet fighters designed, built and flown by the famous Supermarine company was born soon after the end of the Second World War, and ultimatcly attained operational status a dozen years later as the Scimitar twin-engine naval fighter. Such a long gestation would inevitably have deleterious consequences for an aircraft at the best of times, but in the environment of post-War British aviation austerity it proved almost fatal.

The original design was conceived as the Supermarine Type 508, a practical attempt to bring reality to the naval preoccupation with the idea of eliminating the undercarriage from deck-operating fighters, launching them by catapult and landing them on a rubberized deck, using a reinforced under-fuselage. However unorthodox this idea may have seemed, it was expected to bestow a number of important benefits on fighter design, not least the omission of a weighty airframe component, and all the structural and aerodynamic liabilities this imposed. (The trials involving

Vampires landing wheels-up on rubberized decks have been referred to on pages 348-349.)

The elimination of the undercarriage enabled the Type 508's wing to be designed from the outset without the necessity to provide retraction cells, and the thickness/chord was therefore no more than seven per cent. Thc engines were located side-by-side in the fuselage with lateral intakes immediately aft of the cockpit, and exhausting through very short tailpipes aft of the wing. By 1948 choice of engine had settled on Rolls-Royce AJ.65 Avon axial-flow turbojets, then expected to deliver about 6,500lb-thrust. Swept wings were considered, but discarded owing to the lack of knowledge at the time, yet a butterfly tail form was selected so as to clear the jet effluxes.

In 1948 the Admiralty became disenchanted with the undercarriageless idea (even though the Vampire trials went ahead the following year), but Supermarine was convinced that the side-by-side engine arrangement was an important aspect of future twin-engine jet aircraft design, providing as it did thc prospect of 'clean' wings. The company therefore decided to persevere with the fundamental design, now providing a nosewheel undercarriage, with mainwheels retracting inwards into the lower fuselage. The wing thickness/chord was increased to nine per cent (this also having more beneficial properties for conventional deck landing). The main wing spars were angled down at the fuselage, to pass beneath the engines thereby providing anchorage for the retracted undercarriage, as well as allowing access to the engine bay from above.

These alterations were incorporated in design proposals labelled the Type 508 and submitted to the DTD in 1948 to Specification N.9/47, and three proto-

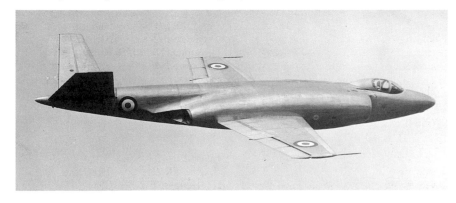

The Type 508 was, by the standards of its time, a very large aeroplane for a potential shipboard fighter, being almost twice as long as a Seafire, and over twice its weight, yet British fleet carriers had not increased in size. (Photo: E B Morgan)

The second N.9/47 prototype, the Type 529, VX136, showing the modified intake fairings and the long fences forward of the tail surfaces. (Photo: Vickers-Armstrongs Ltd)

types, VX133, VX136 and VX138, were ordered from Supermarine. The first flight of VX133 was made by Mike Lithgow at Boscombe Down on 31 August 1951, and carrier trials were performed aboard HMS *Eagle* in May the following year, VX133 being fitted at that time with an A-frame arrester hook under the rear fuselage.

The original design tender had included the possibility of including a variable-incidence tailplane, and it was intended to fit this on the V-form tail of the second aircraft. However, not only were there mechanical difficulties but tunnel tests suggested that under some conditions of flight it could well result in uncontrollable pitch-up. This aircraft, termed the Type 529, therefore retained the butterfly tail and acquired long strakes forward of the tailplanes to delay airflow separation over the surface roots at low speeds. Entry airflow in the engine intake ducts was improved by including longer lip extensions at the junction with the fuselage, although boundary layer problems in the intakes do not appear to have been overcome until the appearance of the third aircraft, VX138. The Type 529 was to be lost in an accident while flying from Boscombe

Down on 5 July 1955.

In the event, VX138 underwent major design changes, Supermarine having gained sanction to fit a swept wing to this aircraft in 1950, and the designation was changed to the Type 525. At that time concensus opinion was that landing speeds of swept-wing aircraft were becoming unacceptably high, due largely to the sharp increase in wing loading. To reduce the loss of boundary layer energy at large landing flap angles, it was proposed to tap high pressure air from the compressors of the Avon engines and discharge it from slots in the wings immediately forward of the flap hingeline (research flying being done at

this time on a blown-flap Hunter). Thus an aircraft's landing approach and stalling speed was quite substantially reduced with a reduced angle of attack, thereby improving the pilot's forward angle of vision during deck landing. The Type 525 also dispensed with the V-form tail unit, acquiring a single, sharply-swept, high aspect ratio fin and rudder. The A-frame arrester hook was replaced by a sting hook.

Inclusion of flap-blowing in the Type 525 had been motivated by a new naval fighter's draft Specification, N.113D, issued at the end of 1950 which, subject to a reduction in the landing speed, seemed likely to be satisfied by the Supermarine design. Three new prototypes were ordered at that time, and these would eventually appear as the first true Scimitar prototypes (see page 395).

Type: Twin-engine, single-seat, mid-wing monoplane naval fighter/research aircraft.
Manufacturer: Supermarine Division of Vickers-Armstrongs Ltd.
Air Ministry Specification: N.9/47
Powerplant: Two 6,500lb-thrust Rolls-Royce AJ.65 Avon RA.3 axial-flow turbojets.
Dimensions: Span, 41ft 0in (Type 525, 38ft 6in); length, 50ft 0in (Type 525, 55ft 0in).
Performance: Max speed (Type 525), 670 mph at sea level; service ceiling, 42,600ft.
Prototypes: Type 508, VX133 (first flown by M J Lithgow on 31 August 1951); Type 529, VX136; and Type 525, VX138.

The Type 525, VX138, equipped with blown flaps, variable-incidence tailplane and sting-type arrester hook. (Photo: via R C Sturtivant)

Gloster Javelin

The Air Ministry's policies on future night fighter requirements, formulated in 1946, became hopelessly confused by conflicting opinions being expressed on the nature of future armament and the rate of engine power increase. Moreover

there was the growing realisation that the recent War had blurred the demarcation between the day interceptor fighter, the night fighter and a fighter capable of operating in bad weather, day or night. That War had brought to an advanced state a bomber's ability to attack through total overcast, while the single-seat day interceptor, without airborne radar, was powerless to intercept

it, particularly if its own airfield was unable to operate on account of bad weather. The realisation began to dawn on the Royal Air Force (and no less on the United States Air Force) that a need existed for the fighter force to become an 'all-weather' fighting arm.

In the matter of armament, the days of the short-range, small-calibre gun were numbered, and the armament research departments and establishments began to examine various guns, existing or under development, not previously considered in the context of interceptor fighters, including the Molins 57mm, the Rolls-Royce and Vickers 40mm, the Aden 30mm and a 4.5-inch recoilless gun being developed at Fort Halstead. In the event, pending the introduction of guided missiles, the choice settled on the Aden gun, with an open mind on the recoilless weapon.

After two Specifications, F.43/46 (for a single-seater) and F.44/46 (a two-seater), had brought forth more than fifty proposals — many of them imaginative, but few realistic — from almost every manufacturer extant, it was realised that there were still far too many imponderables in the design of high subsonic fighters, and the operational requirements, OR.228 and OR.227 respectively, were held in abeyance pending lengthy discussions with industry and the research establishments. It should be remembered that scarcely any government finance was being made available to support high-speed research. (As an interim measure, however, the Meteor was recommended for development as a night fighter under OR.227/F.44/46.)

The Gloster Aircraft Company had tendered several delta-wing project schemes to Specification F.44/46, among them the two-seat, twin-engine P238 with a delta tailplane and an armament of four 30mm Aden guns, and this became the subject of discussions between the Ministry of Supply, the DTD and George Carter, at which it was proposed to replace the 30mm guns with four 4.5-inch Halstead recoilless guns (each of which weighed 1,810 pounds) in the wings. Airborne radar, employing a 42-inch scanner, was to be installed in the nose, and, to ensure full control over a very large speed range, a variable-incidence tailplane was considered essential. The engines suggested at this time were Rolls-Royce AJ.65s, two of

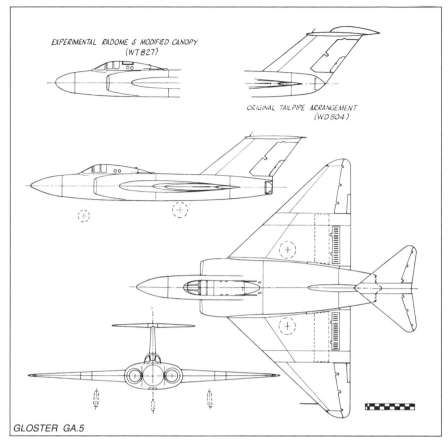

EXPERIMENTAL RADOME & MODIFIED CANOPY
(WT 827)

ORIGINAL TAILPIPE ARRANGEMENT
(WD 804)

GLOSTER GA.5

which would deliver a thrust of 13,000 pounds, considered adequate to bestow a Mach 0.90 performance on an aircraft estimated to weight about 25,000lb all-up.

These alterations were incorporated in a new project design, the P272, and submitted to a new all-weather fighter Specification, F.4/48, although in view of preference beginning to shift towards the 30mm Aden guns, these weapons were offered as an alternative to the recoilless weapons. The new Armstrong Siddeley Sapphire 2, with an expected thrust of 9,000 pounds, replaced the AJ.65s.

Meanwhile a considerable amount of work on delta wings was underway at the RAE, Farnborough, and among other manufacturers, among them Boulton Paul who designed and built its own

P.111 research aircraft to Specification E.27/46 with a very thin delta wing, but this flew too late to provide useful advance information during the Gloster F.4/48's design. A V Roe also produced four delta-wing Type 707s in preparation for that company's own Vulcan heavy bomber but, apart from enabling Gloster's pilot, Sqn Ldr W A Waterton, to gain experience in flying delta-wing aircraft, were also too late to influence Gloster's design.

In March 1948 the DTD notified Gloster that the P272 design had been accepted in broad principle, and in July four prototypes were ordered at a cost-plus contract price of £1,950,000. In the meantime orthodox power-boosted ailerons had been decided on to replace all-moving wingtip segments, previously proposed, and an electrically actuated tailplane with powered elevators were adopted. Bench-running of the Sapphire showed the most suitable version

The Gloster GA.5, WD804, as originally flown by Bill Waterton showing the tiny 'portholes' allowed for the occupant of the rear cockpit and the troublesome fairings around the engine tailpipes. The large fairing above the tailplane housed the anti-spin parachute. (Photo: Russell Adams, Neg No 557/51)

XA557 was the fourteenth production JavelinF(AW) Mk 1, and was used for engine trials by Armstrong Siddeley Motors Ltd. Being fitted with guns in the wings, the Javelin suffered none of the engine surge problems experienced by aircraft, such as the Hunter, whose guns were located forward of the engine air intakes. (Photo: Russell Adams, Neg No P154/55)

would be the Sa.3 of 7,500lb-thrust and, despite a new estimate of the aircraft's all-up weight at 29,200 lb, this engine was decided upon for the prototypes.

That year the 59-year-old George Carter stepped down as Gloster's Chief Designer, his place being taken by Richard W Walker, and on 13 April the following year the company received an Instruction to Proceed with the manufacture of the four prototypes, However, under pressure from the Treasury to effect defence economies, the Ministry of Supply ordered the cancellation of the last two aircraft. The absurdity of this false economy with such a radical and complex aircraft was not appreciated by the Ministry until March 1951 when three further prototypes and a structural test specimen were ordered.

The unarmed first and second prototype Gloster GA.5s, WD804 and WD808, were manufactured at Hucclecote and assembled at Bentham, the major sub-assemblies then being moved to Moreton Valence for final assembly and installations of engines and systems. WD804 was first flown by Sqn Ldr Waterton on 26 November 1951. Specification F.4/48 had called for a prototype maximum speed of 605 mph at 40,000 feet (Mach 0.92) and a service ceiling of not less than 45,000 feet; the time from engine starting to the aircraft reaching 45,000 feet was to be not more than ten minutes but, on account of down-rated engines and an unforeseen weight increase of about 700 pounds,

none of these criteria were realised with WD804.

During the early flight programme Waterton experienced rudder buffeting, caused by interference between the jet effluxes and the airflow round the rear fuselage, causing the latter to impinge on the base of the rudder, this being rectified by modifying the jetpipe fairings. Unfortunately, on 29 June 1952, during its 99th flight, WD804 suffered the loss of both elevators following violent flutter; nevertheless Waterton managed to put the aircraft down on the long runway at Boscombe Down where, despite the undercarriage collapsing, the important autopilot records were recovered intact. For his courage in remaining with the aircraft Waterton was awarded the George Medal.

The second prototype, WD808, was flown on 21 August that year, but already the decision had been taken to order the GA.5 into production with a contract for 40 F(AW) Javelin Mark 1s — Fighter, All-Weather — being signed on 14 July.

By the time the first of these was flown, on 22 July 1954 by Wg Cdr R F Martin DFC* AFC, a great deal of development flying had been undertaken to prepare for the Service versions. The third prototype, WT827, was armed with four 30mm Aden guns in the wings, as well as the British AI Mark 17 radar in the nose, and several radomes were flown to decide the best dielectric and aerodynamic properties. And fol-

lowing some criticism of the Javelin's endurance, WT827 was flown with a pair of 250 gallon ventral tanks, mounted side-by-side, to increase the total fuel carried to 1,265 gallons.

High-altitude manœuvrability had been criticised since the early flights with tip stalling limiting manœuvres at high angles of attack; while the Javelin displayed no significant pitch-up tendencies, it was decided to increase the chord of the wingtips by reducing the sweepback on the outer wing sections, thereby giving a kinked as distinct from a toothed wing planform. The new wing was flown on WD808 on 28 May 1953, and was reported successful in reducing tip stall. This aircraft was to be lost, however, only about a fortnight later when the pilot experienced super stall while testing the effect of using flap at medium altitude; the aircraft crashed and the pilot ejected too low down to survive. It was deduced that, under certain conditions, particularly with the c.g. well aft, the use of the very large flaps would exaggerate the angle of attack, entirely blanking the elevators, leaving the pilot with no control to recover. Moreover the Javelin was found to lose about 240 feet/second in a spin.

Such was the amount of testing and clearance flying still to be done when the first production Mark 1s flew that twelve of them were allocated to development work. This first production version was also equipped with AI Mark 17 radar, and retained the 8,000lb-thrust Sapphire Sa.6 engines of the third and fourth prototypes. Work undertaken by the production Mark 1s included the early Firestreak trials on XA547, a trial installation by de Havilland of the Gyron Junior turbojet in XA552, while XA560 was the first Javelin tested with Sap-

XD158 was the prototype Javelin Mark 2, first flown on 31 October 1955 with the aerodynamic shape of the American AI Mk 22, introduced in this version, which also first featured the all-flying tail. (Photo: Gloster Aircraft Co Ltd, Neg No P66/56)

The Javelin F(AW) Mk 4, XA631, was a trials aircraft and was without AI radar, being fitted with a plain metal nose cone. Note the 'pen nib' fairing aft of the jetpipes, the definitive shape for those aircraft without reheat. (Photo: Gloster Aircraft Co Ltd, Neg No P28A/56)

phire Sa.7s equipped with reheat.

The Javelin F(AW) Mk 2 differed from the Mark 1 principally in its American AN/APQ-43 radar (AI Mark 22), and this version, of which 30 were built, introduced the all-flying tail. Again, the first to receive this Javelin was No 46 Squadron, who passed on its Mark 1s to No 87 Squadron at Bruggen in Germany, commanded by Wg Cdr G C Lamb AFC. Mark 2s also equipped Nos 85 and 89 Squadrons, but owing to the relatively small numbers of Javelins yet being produced up to that time it was a matter of each new squadron being equipped with 'second-hand' aeroplanes.

The Javelin Mark 3 was a two-seat trainer which equipped No 228 Operational Conversion Unit, and the next fighter variant was the F(AW) Mark 4, which reverted to the British AI Mk 17 radar. Eighteen of this version were produced by Gloster, but the remaining 32 were built by Sir W G Armstrong Whitworth Aircraft Ltd at Coventry in order to speed the production and introduction of later variants. The first 40 Mark 4s were fitted with variable-incidence tailplanes with power-boosted elevators, and thereafter an all-moving tailplane was standard.

No 141 Squadron was the first operational Javelin unit based in Eastern Sector, Fighter Command, when they took delivery of Mark 4s in February 1957 at Horsham St Faith, Norfolk (before moving back to its permanent

station at Coltishall in May). And it was with No 141 Squadron — one of the RAF's oldest established night fighter units — that the Javelin took its place on the RAF's instant readiness rosta, for which a section of fighters took their turn at two minutes' Standby, 'plugged-into' the operations centre on an operational readiness platform (ORP) at the end of the runway — a procedure codenamed Fabulous. This was the operation to provide instant reaction to a possible threat, conceived when the Iron Curtain came down in 1948, that had dictated the stringent starting and climbing requirement in Specification F.4/48.

Among the Javelin 4s used for experimental purposes was XA629, flown with Kuchemann bodies, large streamlined fairings extending aft from the wing trailing-edge as a means of delaying and reducing airflow separation at high subsonic speeds so as to extend the buffet boundary. Much the same effect was provided by vortex generators which energised the boundary layer over parts of the wing and fuselage, and these were in fact introduced on the Javelin from the Mark 4. Three Javelins, XA720, XA721 and XA723 were sent to Canada for winterization trials.

Mention has already been made of the early Javelins' lack of sortie endurance without external fuel tanks, and this was

to be remedied with the introduction of the F(AW) Mark 5, of which 64 examples were built, and which had provision to carry an additional 125 gallons in each wing. The aircraft could also carry four Firestreak AAMs on underwing pylons, although the aircraft was not operational with these weapons. Gloster built the first 20 Mark 5s, and Armstrong Whitworth 44.

Again equipped with AI Mark 17, Javelin 5s were first issued to No 151 Squadron in mid-1957 at Leuchars, replacing Venom NF 3s, and went on to serve with Nos 41 and 72, also in the United Kingdom, and Nos 5, 11 and 87 in Germany.

All 33 examples of the Javelin F(AW) Mark 6, with AI Mk 22, were built by Gloster, and served with Nos 29, 46 and 89 Squadrons (the last being renumbered No 85 on 30 November 1958 at Stradishall, Suffolk).

The Javelin F(AW) Mark 7 was the principal Service version, being in numerous respects an advanced derivative of all those that had preceded it. In the first place it introduced the 11,000lb-thrust Sapphire Sa.7 engines which bestowed a maximum sea level speed of 709 mph and Mach 0.92. It maximum design all-up weight had been increased to 40,270 pounds, which resulted when carrying 900 gallons of fuel externally — four 100 gallon underwing drop tanks

A standard production Javelin F(AW) Mk 5, XA656. This version introduced increased fuel capacity and provision to carry pylons for the Firestreak missiles, although operational weapons were not used by Javelin 5 Squadrons. (Photo: Gloster Aircraft Co Ltd, Neg No P/5/57)

and the two 250 gallon ventral tanks. The aircraft was operational with Firestreak AAMs which were carried on special underwing pylons, while two of the Aden guns were omitted. 85 were built by Gloster and 57 by Armstrong Whitworth.

The Mark 7's controls had also been further developed, and included fully-powered, hydraulically-operated rudder with yaw stabilizer. The pilot's controls included three-channel electro-hydraulically operating autopilot with pitch autostabilizer coupled to automatic landing approach and altitude control. The rear fuselage contours had been revised and lengthened to reduce base drag, while to improve aileron control these surfaces featured thickened trailing edges, and two rows each of thirteen vortex generators were added at approximately 10 and 80 per cent of the wing chord.

The first production Javelin Mk 7, XH704, had been flown on 9 November 1956 by Wg Cdr Martin, but CA Release was not obtained until January 1958 owing to the considerable pre-service development work to be completed, for which no fewer than 24 production aircraft were allocated. Deliveries to the RAF began on 30 May that year.

Among the squadrons to fly the Mark 7 was No 25 (Fighter) Squadron, this famous night fighter unit, commanded by Wg Cdr K H H Cook DFC at Waterbeach, disposing of its Meteor NF 14s in March 1959, and straightway applying the Squadron 'bars' to the fins of its Firestreak missiles. The other Squadrons to fly Javelin 7s were Nos 23, 33 and 64.

While the Javelin 7 was equipped with AI Mk 17, the Mark 8 featured the American AI Mk 22 but, perhaps more significantly, it was powered by Sapphire Sa.7R engines with limited re-heat which, when lit above 20,000 feet, increased the thrust from 11,000 to 12,300lb. This version also featured the new flying control equipment of the Mark 7. Forty-seven F(AW) Mk 8s were built as such from new, and the first were delivered to No 41 Squadron in November 1959, followed by No 85 in March the following year.

The Mark 8 was the last production Javelin but, such was the advance represented by this version that it was decided the upgrade the last 76 Mark 7s (which had yet to leave the factory) up to Mark 8 standard, while retaining their British radar, and as such they were designated the F(AW) Mark 9. Some aircraft were

The Javelin had provision for standard store-carrying wing pylons; this aircraft, a Mark 7, XH758, underwent trials with Microcell unguided rocket battery pods, shown here inboard of a Firestreak infrared-seeking missile. (Photo: Gloster Aircraft Co Ltd, Neg No P294/57)

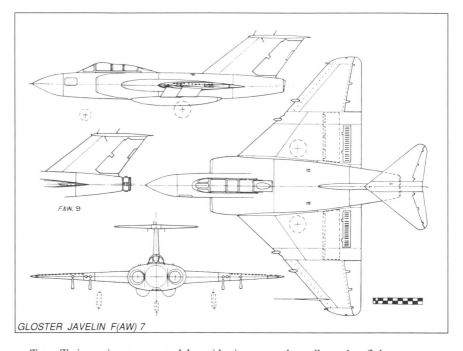

Type: Twin-engine, two-seat, delta mid-wing monoplane all-weather fighter.

Manufacturers: Gloster Aircraft Co Ltd, Hucclecote, Gloucester; Sir W G Armstrong Whitworth Aircraft Ltd, Baginton, Coventry.

Air Ministry Specification: F.4/48

Powerplant: Prototype, Marks 1, 2, 4 and 6. Two 8,000lb-thrust Armstrong Siddeley Sapphire Sa.6 axial-flow turbojets. Mark 7. 11,000lb-thrust Sapphire Sa.7. Marks 8 and 9. 11,000lb-thrust Sapphire Sa.7R (12,300lb-thrust with reheat lit above 20,000ft.)

Dimensions: Span (all versions), 52ft 0in; length (Mks 1-8), 56ft 3in, (Mk 9), 56ft 9in; wing area (all versions), 927 sq ft.

Weights: Max overload. (Mk 1), 36,690lb; (Mk 2), 37,200lb; (Mk 4), 37,480lb; (Mk 5), 39,370lb; (Mk 6), 40,600lb; (Mk 7), 40,270lb; (Mk 8), 42,510lb; (Mk 9), 43,165lb.

Performance: (Mk 9) Max speed, 702 mph at sea level (Mach 0.92 at 36,000ft); climb to 50,000ft, 9 min 15 sec; service ceiling, 52,000ft.

Armament: Four 30mm Aden guns on Mks 1-6; two 30mm Aden guns and four de Havilland Firestreak AAMs on Mks 7-9.

Prototypes: Total of six, WD804, WD808, WT827, WT830 and WT836 (WD804 first flown by Sqn Ldr W A Waterton on 26 November 1951); XD158 was F(AW) Mk 2 prototype. Modified production aircraft used as prototypes for other fighter Marks.

Production: Total, 406 Mk 1, 40 (between XA544-XA628); Mk 2, 30 (between XA768-XA814); Mk 4, 50 (between XA629-XA767); Mk 5, 64 (XA641-XA719 and XH687-XH692); Mk 6, 33 (between XA815-XA836 and XH693-XH703); Mk 7, 142 (between XH704-XH965); Mk 8, 47 (between XH966-XJ165). Note: 76 Mk 7s were upgraded to Mk 8 standard and designated F(AW) Mk 9s.

Summary of Service: Javelin Mk 1s served with Nos 46 and 87 Squadrons; Mk 2s with Nos 46, 85 and 89 Squadrons; Mk 4s with Nos 3, 11, 41, 72, 87 and 151 Squadrons; Mk 5s with Nos 5, 11, 41, 72, 87 and 151 Squadrons; Mk 6s with Nos 29, 46, 85 and 89 Squadrons; Mk 7s with Nos 23, 25, 33 and 64 Squadrons; Mk 8s with Nos 41 and 85 Squadrons; and Mk 9s with Nos 5, 11, 23, 25, 29, 33, 60 and 64 Squadrons.

Left: *Javelin F(AW) Mk 8, XH970, one of the aircraft of the original production batch. Note the much larger radome that characterized the American AI Mk 22 radar, also the all-flying tail and ventral tanks.* (Photo: Derek James)

Below: *XH881/M, a Javelin F(AW) Mk 9 of No 25 (Fighter) Squadron, complete with operational Firestreak missiles and ventral fuel tanks.* (Photo: No 25 (Fighter) Squadron)

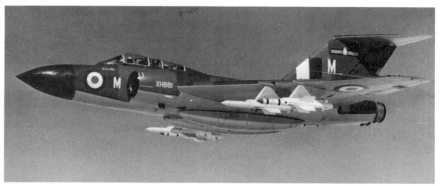

also modified to make provision for in-flight refuelling with a 20 feet-long probe on the starboard shoulder of the front fuselage.

It was perhaps appropriate that the first squadron to fly this, the last Gloster fighter, should be No 25 (Fighter) Squadron, as having gained such acclaim with Gloster Grebes in the mid-1920s; its new aircraft were delivered in December 1959. No 23 Squadron also flew Javelin 9s, and in October 1960 four of its aircraft made the flight from Britain to Singapore nonstop, being refuelled in flight from Vickers Valiant tankers. Other Squadrons with Mark 9s were Nos 5, 11, 29, 33, 60 and 64, the last such aircraft in front-line service being retired by No 60 Squadron at Tengah, Singapore, on 30 April 1968, when that Squadron was disbanded.

de Havilland
D.H. 110 Sea Vixen

One of the design tenders put forward for the aborted Specification F.44/46 was a twin-engine development of the Vampire twin-boom configuration, termed the D.H. 110. As already explained, the RAF's armament proposals in this Specification proved impractical and the requirement was allowed to lapse. While de Havilland continued to work on the D.H. 110, the proposed Ghost-powered Vampire 8 evolved into the Venom, and later into the D.H. 116, which itself was a 'swept-wing Venom' mated to what would eventually become AI Mk 17 radar. It soon became clear that such was the bulk of the radar that

a much larger aircraft would be required if the fighter was to retain any worthwhile performance. So attention centred once more on the D.H. 110 which, in 1948, was being prepared for tender to Specification F.4/48, the requirement that was eventually met by the Gloster Javelin.

The Admiralty was not long in realising that the Javelin would not be suitable for deck operation; the high nose-up landing attitude of the big delta promised to create all manner of problems for naval pilots, while the enormous wing would involve complex and costly wing folding problems. On the other hand the Royal Navy considered that the de Havilland tender represented a worthwhile starting point for a potent fleet fighter, even though it seemed likely to be the largest and heaviest aircraft ever to operate from a British aircraft carrier. It was hoped that by the time it was ready for its carrier trials, decks and aircraft lifts would be somewhat larger. (HMS *Victorious* was to be rebuilt in the

The first, ill-fated, F.4/48 D.H. 110 prototype, WG236, showing the original plain swept wings; note the blunt nose radome and the offset pilot's canopy with windows for the navigator's station. (Photo: A J Jackson Collection)

Echelon formation of early production Sea Vixen F(AW) Mk 1s of No 766 Squadron, flying from Yeovilton. (Author's Collection)

mid-1950s with full angled deck to enable the new generation of twin-engine high performance aircraft to operate from what was a relatively small fleet carrier.)

A new Specification, N.131T, was prepared around de Havilland proposals, and the company was asked to tender its latest ideas. Design work immediately centred on the task of accommodating the AI Mk 17 radar, expected to be ready for installation by about 1954. Like the Javelin, the D.H. 110 was conceived as an all-weather fighter with a two-man crew; the pilot's cockpit, however, was situated on the port side of the nacelle, with the navigator's compartment at a lower level, to starboard with a small window. The 50ft span wings, of ten per cent thickness/chord, were swept back 40 degrees on the quarter-chord, and carried the deep, elliptical section tail booms which, at their rear, curved upwards into integral

twin swept fins; between these was carried a variable-incidence tailplane, situated high so as to be clear of the jet effluxes.

The wings, which employed machined skins with three spars, were attached to stub roots which enclosed wing leading edge intakes to the twin Rolls-Royce AJ.65 axial-flow turbojets which exhausted well forward of and below the tailplane. The mainwheel units of the wide-track tricycle undercarriage retracted inwards into the inboard sections of the wings.

Being somewhat less radical than its Javelin cousin, the first prototype D.H. 110, WG236, was first flown by Gp Capt John Cunningham CBE, DSO** DFC* at Hatfield on 26 September 1951, and first exceeded the speed of sound in a shallow dive on 9 April 1952. As the geometric details of the definitive AI Mk 17 scanner were not yet known, the nose radome shape was somewhat specula-

tive, being relatively blunt on this prototype and the second aircraft, WG240, which flew on 25 July the same year.

Tragedy was to strike when WG236 appeared at the 1952 SBAC Flying Display at Farnborough on 6 September. The aircraft heralded its arrival with the characteristic sonic boom, flew fast and low over the airfield and completed a fairly tight decelerating circuit before lining up to start a reverse turn. The aircraft was seen to pitch up violently and disintegrate, scattering wreckage over a very large area, killing 28 members of the public; the pilot, John Derry, and his flight observer, Tony Richards, were killed instantly.

The cause of the accident was not immediately apparent as comprehensive, accident-immune flight recorders were not then available, and many contributory factors had to be considered, as the aircraft had earlier given rise to handling difficulties during a dive recovery at supersonic speed, yet it appeared that the aircraft had not previously displayed any of the familiar pitching-up and was not thought to be executing any manoeuvre that might have induced pitch-up. It was eventually

Late production Sea Vixen F(AW) Mk 1, XN696, of No 899 Headquarters Squadron, carrying two Firestreaks under each wing as well as drop tanks; it is also fitted with an in-flight refuelling probe. (Photo: A J Jackson Collection)

established that disintegration had followed structural failure of the wing (possibly weakened earlier), almost certainly resulting from violent tail flutter.

The remaining D.H. 110 prototype was grounded pending the investigation and for modifications to be made. When next flown in June 1954, WB240 displayed the alterations then being applied to several other transonic aircraft, such as a saw-tooth cambered wing leading-edge extensions outboard of the wing fences, and all-moving tailplane, as well as reduced tail fin area.

Although these modifications transformed the handling of the D.H. 110, considerable further design work needed to be done to meet the naval Specification, and this was completed under the leadership of W A Tamblin when production of the aircraft was switched to de Havilland's Christchurch plant. A third prototype D.H. 110, XF828, now named the Sea Vixen, was built to an updated Specification, having been ordered with two pre-production development aircraft and 76 production examples, in February 1955. XF828, enigmatically referred to as the Sea Vixen Mark 20X, featured non-folding wings, arrester hook, hydraulically-steerable nosewheel, and all provision for gun armament removed (thereby becoming the first British naval fighter since early in the Kaiser's War not to carry integral guns). It was first flown by Lt J Elliot RN at Christchurch on 20 June 1955. Non-arrested, touch-and-go landings by WG240 had been performed on HMS *Albion* the previous September, and the first fully-arrested landings were made by XF828 on HMS *Ark Royal* on 5 April 1956.

By the time the Sea Vixen was ready for full Service trials it was already slightly heavier than the Scimitar, and underwent a comprehensive store clearance programme to enable it to undertake dual interceptor/strike rôles with combinations of Firestreak AAMs, Microcell air-to-air rocket batteries, 500 or 1,000lb bombs and other weapons. In the interceptor rôle the aircraft could carry four Firestreak AAMs, two underwing drop tanks and 28 air-to-air folding-fin unguided two-inch rockets in a pair of retractable fuselage packs. These weapons were aimed by a Ferranti attack sight. For the low-level strike rôle the Sea Vixen was equipped with a LABS system.

The first pre-production Sea Vixen F(AW) Mk 1, XJ474, was flown on 20

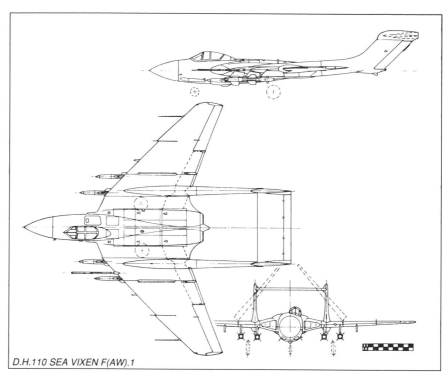

D.H.110 SEA VIXEN F(AW).1

Type: Twin-engine, two-seat, swept mid-wing monoplane all-weather naval interceptor/strike fighter.

Manufacturer: de Havilland Aircraft Co Ltd, Hatfield, Hertfordshire, and Christchurch, Hampshire.

Air Ministry Specifications: F.4/48 (D.H. 110); N.131T (Sea Vixen).

Powerplant: D.H. 110. Two 7,500lb-thrust Rolls-Royce AJ.65 Avon Ra.7 axial-flow turbojets. Sea Vixen. 10,000lb-thrust Rolls-Royce Avon Mk 208 turbojets.

Dimensions: Span 50ft 0in; length, 53ft 6½in (50ft 2½in, nose folded); height, 10ft 9in (22ft 3in, wings folded); wing area, 648 sq ft.

Weight: Max all-up, 41,575lb.

Performance: Sea Vixen F(AW) Mk 2. Max speed, 690 mph (Mach 0.90); climb to 10,000ft, 1 min 30 sec; service ceiling, 48,200ft.

Armament: Up to four Firestreak AAMs (F(AW) Mk 1) or four Red Top AAMs (F(AW) Mk 2); provision to carry up to four Microcell rocket batteries under wings or up to four 1,000lb bombs, and twin retractable batteries in fuselage for 2in unguided AAMs.

Prototypes: D.H. 110, two, WG236 and WG240. Sea Vixen, one, XF828 (WG236 first flown by Gp Capt J Cunningham at Hatfield, 26 September 1951; XF828 first flown by Lt J Elliot RN at Christchurch on 20 June 1955).

Production: Sea Vixen F(AW) Mk 1, 119 (between XJ474-XJ611, XN647-XN710 and XP918). F(AW) Mk 2, 29 (between XP919-XP959 and XS576-XS590).

Summary of Service: Sea Vixen F(AW) Mk 1s served with Nos 700Y, 766B, 890, 892, 893 and 899 Squadrons; F(AW) Mk 2s served with Nos 766, 890, 892, 893 and 899 Squadrons, Fleet Air Arm.

March 1957 and, with XJ475, underwent handling and performance assessment at Boscombe Down and Farnborough, making landings at sea on HM Carriers *Ark Royal* and *Centaur*.

Early production Sea Vixens joined No 700Y Squadron in November 1958, commanded by Cdr M H J Petrie RN at Yeovilton, this component of No 700 Squadron being established specially to conduct the Sea Vixen's intensive flying trials. The first operational Fleet Air Arm Squadron with the aircraft was No 892 at Yeovilton in July 1959 under Cdr Petrie, who joined from No 700Y Squad-

ron. The Squadron embarked in HMS *Victorious* during October, before its 'B' Flight broke away to form an element of No 766 Squadron (the naval all-weather training unit) to carry out trials and training with the Firestreak AAMs. During their six years' service with No 892 Squadron the Sea Vixens served most of their time operating from HMS *Hermes* (commissioned in 1959) in the Mediterranean and the Far East.

No 890 Squadron (Lt-Cdr W R Hart AFC, RN) received Sea Vixen F(AW) 1s at Yeovilton in February 1960, and was followed by Nos 893 and 899 Squadrons

Left: *One of a number of Sea Vixen Mark 1s, XN684, converted to Mark 2 standard with the tail booms extended forward of the wings. The aircraft is carrying what appears to be a recording camera pod under the starboard wing.* (Photo: A J Jackson Collection)

Below: *A converted Sea Vixen F(AW) Mk 2, XN653, of No 892 Squadron at Yeovilton, but carrying the fin code of* HMS Hermes. (Photo: via R C B Ashworth)

during the next twelve months, the latter being designated the Sea Vixen Headquarters Squadron, serving mostly at Yeovilton, but occasionally embarking in HM Carriers *Centaur* and *Hermes*.

A total of 119 Sea Vixen Mark 1s was built before a much enhanced version, the F(AW) Mark 2, entered production. Powered by a pair of 10,000lb-thrust Rolls-Royce Avon 208 turbojets, the aircraft differed fundamentally in a switch to Red Top AAMs which possessed a greatly increased target acquisition arc, thereby increasing the interception envelope.

The aircraft also underwent some airframe changes, notably the extension of the tail booms forward of the wing leading edges to accommodate more internal fuel, while in-flight refuelling was made possible by the 'buddy' system whereby one Sea Vixen, carrying underwing tanker packs with hose and drogue (developed by Flight Refuelling Ltd), could refuel another to extend its range. Provision was made in all Sea Vixens to mount a nine-feet refuelling probe in the leading edge of the port wing. (In May 1961 a Sea Vixen remained airborne for eight hours by use of this system.) Martin-Baker Mk 4D or 4DS ejection seats were fitted in Sea Vixens.

F(AW) Mark 2s first entered service with No 899 Headquarters Squadron in February 1964 under Lt-Cdr J A Sanderson RN, and subsequently replaced the Mark 1s on Nos 890, 892 and 893 Squadrons. The last Sea Vixens were retired from operational service on 26 January 1971 when No 899 Squadron was disbanded.

By then, however, the entire operational rôle of the Fleet Air Arm had come under scrutiny, with plans being laid to eliminate the fixed-wing element altogether. The American Mach 2 McDonnell Douglas F-4 Phantom had been introduced into service with a single operational squadron but, having been adapted for use of British engines — which proved unsuitable — most Phantoms purchased by Britain were now being delivered to the RAF instead. Without a naval fighter then under development, it was being said that no alternative existed to the termination of the Fleet Air Arm's air combat rôle. Fortunately these plans were held in abeyance until the outcome of a radical new project could be examined, and the single naval Phantom squadron remained in being until 1978 when the extraordinary Sea Harrier was introduced in its place.

Deployment of British Fighter Squadrons — January 1960

Home Bases

No 1 Squadron	Hawker Hunter F 6	Stradishall
No 19 Squadron	Hawker Hunter F 6	Leconfield
No 23 Squadron	Gloster Javelin F(AW) 7	Coltishall
No 25 Squadron	Gloster Javelin F(AW) 9	Waterbeach
No 29 Squadron	Gloster Javelin F(AW) 6	Leuchars
No 33 Squadron	Gloster Javelin F(AW) 7	Middleton St George
No 41 Squadron	Gloster Javelin F(AW) 5/8	Wattisham
No 43 Squadron	Hawker Hunter F 6	Leuchars
No 46 Squadron	Gloster Javelin F(AW) 2/6	Waterbeach
No 54 Squadron	Hawker Hunter F 6	Stradishall
No 56 Squadron	Hawker Hunter F 6	Wattisham
No 64 Squadron	Gloster Javelin F(AW) 7	Duxford
No 65 Squadron	Hawker Hunter F 6	Duxford
No 66 Squadron	Hawker Hunter F 6	Acklington
No 72 Squadron	Gloster Javelin F(AW) 4/5	Leconfield
No 74 Squadron	Hawker Hunter F 6	Coltishall
No 85 Squadron	Gloster Javelin F(AW) 2/6	West Malling
No 92 Squadron	Hawker Hunter F 6	Middleton St George
No 111 Squadron	Hawker Hunter F 6	Wattisham
No 151 Squadron	Gloster Javelin F(AW) 5	Leuchars

Germany

No 2 Squadron	Supermarine Swift FR 5	Jever
No 3 Squadron	Gloster Javelin F(AW) 4	Geilenkirchen
No 4 Squadron	Hawker Hunter F 6	Jever
No 5 Squadron	Gloster Javelin F(AW) 5	Laarbruch
No 11 Squadron	Gloster Javelin F(AW) 4	Geilenkirchen
No 14 Squadron	Hawker Hunter F 4	Gütersloh
No 20 Squadron	Hawker Hunter F 6	Gütersloh
No 26 Squadron	Hawker Hunter F 6	Gütersloh
No 79 Squadron	Supermarine Swift FR 5	Gütersloh
No 87 Squadron	Gloster Javelin F(AW) 4/5	Bruggen
No 93 Squadron	Hawker Hunter F 6	Jever

Africa and the Middle East

No 8 Squadron	Hawker Hunter FGA 9	Khormaksar, Aden
No 208 Squadron	D.H. Venom FB 4	Eastleigh, Kenya

Far East

No 28 Squadron	D.H. Venom FB 4	Kai Tak, Hong Kong
No 60 Squadron	AW Meteor NF 14	Tengah, Singapore

Fleet Air Arm

No 800 Squadron	Supermarine Scimitar F 1	Lossiemouth
No 801 Squadron	Hawker Sea Hawk FGA 6	HMS *Centaur*
No 803 Squadron	Supermarine Scimitar F 1	Lossiemouth
No 807 Squadron	Supermarine Scimitar F 1	Lossiemouth
No 831 Squadron	D.H. Sea Venom 21/22ECM	Culdrose
No 891 Squadron	D.H. Sea Venom F(AW) 22	Seletar, Singapore
No 892 Squadron	D.H. Sea Vixen F(AW) 1	Yeovilton
No 893 Squadron	D.H. Sea Venom F(AW) 22	Yeovilton
No 894 Squadron	D.H. Sea Venom F(AW) 22	Yeovilton

8. TECHNOLOGY FOR THE COLD WAR

As Britain disengaged from Imperial administration of her worldwide empire in the 1950s, the permanent distant deployment of armed forces was replaced by treaty agreements that involved military reinforcement from home at short notice at times of threat. This eventually led to the closure of numerous RAF bases 'East of Suez' between 1960 and 1975. During this period aircraft, such as the Hunter, were held in readiness at home and in Cyprus for any call to mount a 'presence' in areas that might come under local threat.

Air defence of the British Isles, following the 1957 Defence White Paper, rested largely on a dwindling generation of subsonic all-weather jet fighters, and also on a growing presence of American supersonic fighters, deployed for the defence of USAF bases in Britain. And it was not until mid-1960 that the first RAF squadron re-equipped with the supersonic English Electric Lightning which had already undergone ten years of design development and six of flight trials. It was an impressive aeroplane, of highly individualistic concept and configuration — certainly matching some of its American contemporaries, even though it suffered early limitations.

Unfortunately a change in British air defence policy in 1956, which caused the cancellation of a large Javelin-replacement (designed to OR.329) together with its large, long-range Red Dean and Red Hebe air-to-air missiles, on account of high cost and a mistaken belief that the Russian threat was confined to ballistic missiles.

The subsequent cancellation of production contracts, which left several manufacturers without adequate work to sustain expensive design and research staffs, tended to support the British government's contention that if the surviving indigenous aircraft projects and programmes were to remain economically viable and competitive with American, European and Russian aircraft, widespread rationalisation within the aircraft industry was essential. This led to the creation of three major manufacturing Groups, of which the Hawker Siddeley Group was already in existence, comprising Hawker Aircraft Ltd, Gloster Aircraft Co Ltd, A V Roe & Co Ltd, and Sir W G Armstrong Whitworth Aircraft Ltd, and which Folland Aircraft Ltd, de Havilland Aircraft Ltd and Blackburn & General Aircraft Ltd now joined. The British Aircraft Corporation came into being with the amalgamation of Vickers-Armstrongs Ltd, Bristol Aeroplane Co Ltd, Hunting Percival Aircraft Ltd and English Electric Co Ltd. The third Group was formed by the amalgamation of the engine manufacturers Rolls-Royce Ltd, Bristol Siddeley Engines Ltd (itself only recently formed by the merging of Bristol Engine Co Ltd and Armstrong Siddeley Motors Ltd), and de Havilland Engine Co Ltd. Several companies declined to 'rationalise', preferring to remain independent. Handley Page Ltd (a bomber and airliner manufacturer) was eventually obliged to close, while Westland Aircraft Ltd, having completed its last Wyvern strike fighter, survived to become Britain's largest manufacturer of helicopters.

Fortunately this division of British aircraft manufacturers into two very large groups gave neither a monopoly in any category of military aircraft which, in theory at any rate, permitted a degree of aircraft choice and competition between companies. Nevertheless, competition between companies was fatally compromised when the cost of modern technology became all too apparent with the issue of Operational Requirement (OR) 339. Indeed it was the enormity of this highly imaginative but economically suicidal programme that was employed by the Conservative government to browbeat the industry into the rationalisation referred to above.

While OR.339, which brought about the ill-fated TSR.2 project, does not lie within the scope of this work, it served to illustrate the folly (only seen as such in retrospect) of attempting to undertake a massive project with only the prospect of parochial customer interest.

The Hawker Siddeley Group had submitted design tenders to OR.339, with elaborate proposals from Hawker, A V Roe and Gloster *inter alia*. However, whereas BAC had intended to 'go it alone' with the TSR.2, both BAC and HSA were busy entering into collaborative agreements with overseas manufacturers as being politically logical expedients to attract foreign investment, as well as encouraging foreign customers.

This was nowhere more evident than in the affairs of Hawker Aircraft Ltd, which had suffered a series of setbacks in the mid-1950s. To begin with the company's 'thin-wing' Hunter, the P1083, had been cancelled in 1954; this was followed by cancellation of OR.329 for which the company had tendered the P1103, and then the 1957 Defence White Paper had brought about cancellation of a year's production of Hunters. Finally the Hawker P1121 strike/air superiority fighter had been forced into oblivion by the issue of OR.339.

By extraordinary good fortune, however, Sydney Camm's design staff had already started along a path leading in a

different direction following the news that Bristol Siddeley was examining the proposal to adapt a turbojet to provide thrust vectoring. After a period of close consultation between the two companies, Bristol Siddeley obtained financial support for the Pegasus engine from the Mutual Weapons Development Programme, funded by the United States, while Hawker went ahead with its design of the P1127 vertical take-off research aircraft as a private venture (no government finance being yet available owing to prior claims for the TSR.2).

As will be shown in this section, the P1127 put Hawker back on the map, first with remarkable demonstrations of its extraordinary flight envelop and later as the Harrier, truly a front-line, though relatively small component of RAF Strike Command. A supersonic version came close to realisation when the P1154 was declared the winner of a NATO design competition — only to be defeated by politics. Both the Royal Air Force and the Royal Navy expressed their support for the project, and Ministry of Defence Specifications (SR.250D and P) were raised to cover the manufacture of prototypes. This supersonic strike and naval fighter came to nothing and the same socialist government that cancelled the TSR.2, brought work to an end on the P1154 early in 1965.

While the subsonic Harrier (and much later the Sea Harrier) entered service — and have continued to serve ever since — the vacuum threatened by the Healey cancellations in the mid-1960s were to be filled, first by the purchase of American Phantoms and sometime afterwards by the Anglo-French Jaguar. Meanwhile the Lightning Marks 2, 3 and 6 remained in service with nine RAF fighter squadrons as Javelins served out their final years with a pair of all-weather fighter squadrons.

The McDonnell Douglas F-4 Phantom was unquestionably an impressive fighter but, in 1966, represented 14-year-old technology. Nevertheless, equipped with long-range AAMs and possessing genuine Mach 2-plus performance, it should have constituted a potent weapon with both the RAF and Fleet Air Arm except that, in order to alleviate unemployment in Britain, the British government insisted that Rolls-Royce Spey turbofans be fitted instead of the American engines, an unfortunate choice as the Speys proved generally unsuitable for the fighter aircraft. Nev-

ertheless, RAF Phantoms remained in service until the 1980s.

A rather more satisfactory aircraft that stemmed from Anglo-French project collaboration was the SEPECAT-British Aerospace Jaguar, which originated in a French design of the mid-1960s and which was successfully adapted to RAF needs and entered service in the early 1970s as a strike fighter, serving with eight RAF squadrons, three of which are still flying them at the time of writing.

Perhaps the most impressive outcome of a military aircraft project as a genuine international work-sharing programme is the Panavia Tornado. This was also conceived towards the end of the 1960s by a continental European consortium as a Lockheed F-104 Starfighter replacement, of which Britain was not a member. As several nations exercised their options to withdraw from the programme on the grounds of high costs, Britain joined the consortium, hoping to influence the design to such an extent that it could be regarded as a Canberra bomber replacement. In due course, as well as adopting the aircraft as an exceptionally potent strike bomber, Britain also adopted a unilateral design adaptation as a missile-armed interceptor fighter.

Today the Tornado F 3 equips seven Royal Air Force fighter squadrons, all tasked with home defence in the traditional sense, and, despite early problems with its radar, is now an impressive component of Britain's air defences.

While the full implications for Western defence forces have yet to become resolved, following the break-up of the Soviet Union, the long-term future of Britain's air defences cannot yet be determined. Advanced technology fighters are being pursued both unilaterally and through international collaboration by half a dozen European countries, Britain among them. Yet there is bound to be some opposition to the cost of pursuing these very costly projects as the risk of a European conflict apparently recedes. Nevertheless, the history of the twentieth century provides plenty of hard-won lessons on the folly of allowing air defences to become run down in a belief that the danger of conflict has gone for good. An air defence system can be dismantled in weeks; to build one takes years. The short-term saving is relatively small and the ultimate cost is enormous.

The first P.1B prototype, XA847, which first flew on 4 April 1957 powered by Rolls-Royce Avons with limited afterburning. It exceeded the speed of sound on its first flight and became the first British aeroplane to reach Mach 2, doing so on 25 November 1958. Note the original small type of ventral fuel tank fairing. (Photo: British Aerospace (Preston) plc, Neg No AW/OP20)

English Electric Lightning

Reference has already been made to the cancellation of the Miles M.52 super-sonic research aircraft in 1946; some sources stated that this was on account of the programme's high cost, while others pointed to the unjustifiable risk to the pilot. Whatever the reason, the cancellation left the British aircraft industry without the immediate prospect of any manned research aeroplane in which level sustained flight at super-sonic speed could be investigated. Clearly such a glaring deficiency would quickly result in Britain being left far behind in military aircraft technology, a situation which passed from the realm of specu-lation into reality when, on 1 October 1947, the American transonic XP-86 fighter prototype made its first flight. A fortnight later the rocket-powered Bell X-1, flown by 'Chuck' Yeager, exceeded the speed of sound in level flight. It required little eloquence to convince the British Ministry of Supply that steps must be taken to restore a continuing research programme to attain level supersonic flight.

It was at this time that the English Electric Company, a relative newcomer to the aircraft industry, was beginning construction of the prototype of Brit-ain's first jet bomber (which would in time become the Canberra), and its

brilliant designer had recently had time to engage in discussions with the MoS on the looming crisis in supersonic research. W E W Petter, whose former design appointment with Westland had brought much original expression in such designs as the Lysander, Whirl-wind and Welkin aircraft, had moved to English Electric in 1944 where he soon become engaged in the B.3/45 (Can-berra) design, being obliged to confine his efforts to what was a strictly ortho-dox high subsonic aircraft. Logically such an aircraft, if accepted for service, warranted progress towards develop-ment of supersonic interceptors.

Following these discussions, two experimental research Specifications were prepared in collaboration with the RAE to investigate the properties of highly-swept wings. The first, ER.100, defined the need for a low-speed research air-craft in which to examine the aerody-namic and handling properties of a highly-swept wing, particularly at and

close to the stall. Detail design and manufacture of the prototype was under-taken by Short Brothers and Harland Ltd as the Short S.B.5, and this aircraft was to be flown on 2 December 1952.

The other Specification, ER.103, was prepared around Petter's proposals and reached English Electric in May 1947, calling for investigation of a supersonic research aircraft capable of attaining a speed of Mach 1.5 at 36,000 feet. In the event no prototype to ER.103 was or-dered, the end product being a series of wind tunnel aircraft models with wings swept back at 50 and 60 degrees on their leading edge, and with their tailplanes located at various heights between the base of the rear fuselage and the top of the fin. The latter became a bone of contention between the RAE, who fa-voured the high position, on account of assumed positive control at high and medium speeds, and Petter (*inter alia*) who pointed to the likelihood of control loss at high angles of attack resulting

The original English Electric P.1, WG760, prepares to take off at Warton; the aircraft featured a plain ovoid nose air intake without any centrebody. Note the position of the all-moving tailplane. (Photo: British Aerospace (Preston) plc, Neg No AW/SG866)

Afterburners lit on Lightning F 1, XM145, of No 74 (Fighter) Squadron at Coltishall in 1960; without external fuel these early Lightnings had an endurance of about 40 minutes' sortie time. (Photo: British Aerospace (Preston) plc, Neg No AW/CN48)

from blanking by the wing and wing flaps.

Within two years Petter had reached a promising configuration of a genuine supersonic, twin-engine aircraft, locating the engines one above the other in the centre fuselage with a nose intake and ducts passing below the cockpit. In order to avoid the concentration of too much engine weight aft, the lower engine was to be located well forward of the upper.

In keeping with his expressed preference, the all-moving tailplane was to be located at the base of the rear fuselage. Without the benefit of afterburning, then only starting the development stage with engine manufacturers, Petter suggested using the most powerful axial-flow turbojet then available, the 7,000lb-thrust Armstrong Siddeley Sapphire.

In order to achieve the lowest possible drag, the wing was swept back 60 degrees on the leading edge but, with the aileron trailing edges at right angles to the line of flight, this resulted in a semi-delta planform except that the inboard trailing edges, with the landing flaps, was swept back almost parallel to the leading edge. This arrangement allowed what was at the time an exceptionally low thickness/chord of only 5 per cent, yet was sufficiently thick to accommodate wing fuel tanks as well as moderately wide-track undercarriage which retracted outwards. Despite its thin section, the wing structure was immensely strong (and undeniably heavy), and was built up on two spars and three sub-spars, the ribs being aligned at right angles to the wing's leading edge; the front main spar passed through the

fuselage above the lower engine and below the intake duct to the upper engine. (The latter aroused much criticism owing to the difficulty of removing the lower engine, but was accepted in the interests of developing a supersonic aircraft).

Although this design was strictly a research essay when it reached the DTD in 1949, there seemed no reason why it should not form the basis of an interceptor fighter and, with this in mind, Specification F.23/49 was drawn up around Petter's proposals, but with the rider that consideration should be given to the application of armament, and that handling and performance should be assessed with a possible interceptor rôle in mind. Two flight prototypes were ordered (WG760 and WG763) together with a structural test specimen. As such it represented the first potential fighter design to be drafted after the beginning of the Cold War — generally considered to have started with the Russian blockade of Berlin and the subsequent Berlin Airlift.

Without waiting for flight trials of the Short S.B.5, detail design of the first F.23/49, the P.1, went ahead as Petter himself left English Electric to join Folland Aircraft Ltd in 1950. The 60-degree swept wing was adopted despite tunnel tests suggesting that a straight, uncambered leading edge terminating in

Line-up of Firestreak-armed Lightning F Mk 1As of No. 56 (Fighter) Squadron at Wattisham. RAF fighter squadrons in the 1960s flew their aircraft devoid of camouflage, and were permitted to adopt distinctive colour schemes, badges and fin flashes. (Photo: A J Jackson Collection)

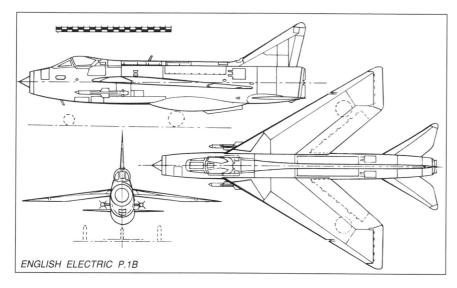

ENGLISH ELECTRIC P.1B

an almost pointed wingtip would almost certainly result in tip stalling. Before completion of WG760, Wg Cdr Roland Prosper Beamont DSO*, DFC* (appointed to the OBE in 1953 following his early flight testing of the Canberra as English Electric's Chief Test Pilot) was able to experience low-speed handling of a highly-swept aircraft when he flew the Short S.B.5 on a number of occasions during the summer of 1953.

Powered by a pair of 7,500lb-thrust Sapphire turbojets, WG760 was first flown at Boscombe Down by Beamont on 4 August 1954, and proved satisfactory, apart from some buffet experienced when the airbrakes were extended. On the second flight the following day the speed was increased to Mach 0.98, and on 11 August WG760 was allowed to accelerate to Mach 1.01, the first occasion a British aircraft exceeded the speed of sound in level flight.

It should again be emphasized that, at this stage in the programme, WG760 was regarded solely as a supersonic research aircraft, little thought having yet been given in the design to its underlying possible potential as an interceptor. Air-to-air guided missiles were under development (among them Blue Jay, Blue Sky, Red Dean and Red Hebe), and it was not yet established to what extent such missiles would supplement or replace the traditional gun armament.

In the course of his flight trials in WG760, therefore, Beamont was pre-occupied with the aircraft's handling throughout the expanding flight envelope, though with particular concern for the lower end of the speed bracket and in respect of the effect of the wing and landing flaps on the tailplane. There had been no evidence of snaking at high subsonic speeds and, although wingtip stall was apparent, this was to be cured by an extraordinarily simple remedy (discovered in the USA) of introducing a notch in the outer wing leading edge close to the tip, found to energize the boundary layer and maintain streamwise airflow over the wing and aileron.

Beamont did, however, express his concern for the P.1's chronic lack of flight endurance which, under test conditions, was effectively 35 minutes, allowing just 50 gallons of fuel for each engine for landing — scarcely sufficient for a single overshoot. With the existing engines, capable of attaining Mach 1.28, this was considered just acceptable, though uncomfortably restricting. However, in the context of possible consideration as a fighter, and with limited afterburning on the horizon, such a very short endurance would be wholly unacceptable. (The RAF was at this time particularly sensitive about shortage of fuel in its fighters, almost an entire formation of Hunter F 1s having being lost at West Raynham owing to fuel shortage.)

By the end of the first nine months of flying, the P.1 had been flown by a number of other pilots, and all had expressed satisfaction with the aircraft's handling properties. The second prototype, the P.1A WG763, was first flown on 18 July 1955, and introduced an armament of two 30mm Aden guns in the upper shoulders of the nose, as well as foot-operated wheel brakes. By then the 10,000lb-thrust Avon 200-series turbojets were available and these engines, with primitive, four-stage afterburning, increased the aircraft's flight envelope to Mach 1.52, and it was now that directional instability was encountered, resulting in progressive enlargement of the fin.

It was during this period (1954-56) that all manner of cancellations were being imposed by the Conservative government on the RAF and aircraft industry, and many of these had a direct bearing on the future of the English Electric F.23/49. Both the thin-wing Hunter and thin-wing Javelin supersonic fighter projects were cancelled as probably offering little scope for performance potential above Mach 1.2, and, with the cancellation of the big all-weather aircraft requirement in OR.329 as well as both of Britain's long-range AAMs, Red Dean and Red Hebe, the way was being paved for the eventual total dependence on surface-to-air missiles for defence of the United Kingdom, as well as the creation of the deterrent V-force of jet-powered heavy bombers. Until these defences could be brought to operational status, the air defences would be confined to the Javelin all-weather fighter and the English Electric aircraft. Three fighter prototypes had been ordered in 1954, to

The third production Lightning Mk 1A, XM171. This version was distinguishable by the addition of the UHF aerial under the nose. (Photo: British Aerospace (Preston) plc, Neg No AW/FA 212)

XN723 was the first Lightning F 2 to be flown, seen here during a test flight from Warton in mid-1961 without the customary ventral fairing. This version was the first to be powered by Avon 200-series engines with fully-variable afterburning, but the last to include the Aden gun armament in the fuselage nose. (Photo: British Aerospace (Preston) plc, Neg No AW/FA 218)

become the P.1B, and 20 pre-production aircraft, then named the Lightning, were ordered late in 1956.

The first P.1B prototype, XA847, was flown on 4 April 1957, powered by a pair of Avon 201 engines which, with four-stage afterburning, were wet-rated at 14,430lb-thrust. By now a ventral fairing had been introduced to accommodate 250 gallons of additional fuel, this fairing conforming to the 'area rule', and this would in due course be progressively developed and enlarged to incorporate an extra pair of Aden guns and a further increased fuel capacity. For the first time the hitherto American concept of a 'weapons system' was being mooted in Britain, the weapon-carrying fighter being the armed element of a defence system that embraced long-range radar reporting approaching targets, control of intercepting fighters, and short-range, last-resort, point-defence, surface-to-air guided missiles.

The P.1B XA847 first attained Mach 2 in level flight on 25 November 1958 as

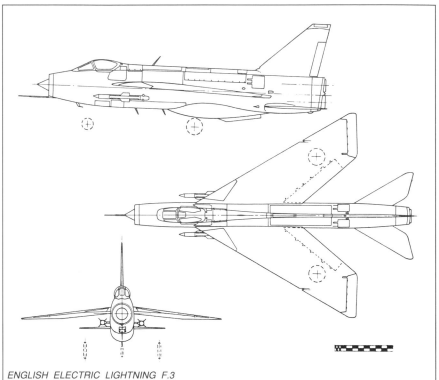

ENGLISH ELECTRIC LIGHTNING F.3

Third production Lightning F Mk 6, the definitive version for the RAF. Note the enlarged, angular fin and huge ventral pack. Just visible on the wing's cambered leading edge is the 'notch', introduced to alleviate tip stall. (Photo: British Aerospace (Preston) plc, Neg No AW/FA 320).

the other pre-production aircraft joined the flight programme, introducing the Ferranti AI-23 radar in a conical centre-body located within a circular nose intake which replaced the P.1s' ovoid intakes. Pylon mountings for a pair of Firestreak infrared-seeking AAMs were introduced low on the sides of the nose. In October 1958 the Ministry of Supply raised a contract for 20 full production standard Lightning F Mk 1 fighters, and twelve of these provided the initial complement of No 74 (Fighter) Squadron, commanded by Sqn Ldr J F G Howe at Coltishall, the first deliveries being made in June 1960.

These initial deliveries of Lightning 1s to No 74 Squadron were intended to provide preliminary experience in integrating the supersonic interceptor into Fighter Command's key Eastern Sector defence structure, and it was accepted that difficulties might arise owing to the new aircraft's still-limited endurance, which would prove quite inadequate should the necessity arise to reinforce overseas RAF Commands. The next version, the F 1A, of which 28 examples were ordered, therefore introduced provision to mount a long in-flight refuelling probe under the port wing root. UHF, by now necessary on reinforcement flights, was also included.

The first Lightning F 1A, XM164, was flown on 16 August 1960 and this variant was quickly delivered to the Wattisham 'reinforcement Wing', formerly equipped with long-range Hunter F 6s, the first aircraft arriving on No 56 (Fighter) Squadron in January 1961, followed by No 111 (Fighter) Squadron in April.

Progressive development continued at the manufacturers and produced the F Mark 2, of which 44 examples were ordered, the first of which, XN723, flew on 11 July 1961. This was an important, though interim, variant as it featured fully-variable afterburning Rolls-Royce Avon 210 engines, as well as autopilot, liquid oxygen system, and a steerable nosewheel. A second Lightning Wing, at Leconfield, was equipped with this version, No 19 re-equipping in November 1962, and No 92 in April 1963, in both instances Hunter 6s being replaced.

Much later, 31 Mark 2s underwent extensive modification, being provided with an enlarged, angular fin, and a kinked and cambered wing leading edge, terminating in a broad-chord tip, the wing-notch being retained. This ver-

sion, termed the F Mark 2A, entered service in 1968.

Following the initial delivery of the Lightning F 2, the F 3 made provision for the 'advanced Firestreak' or Red Top AAMs whose target infrared seeker possessed all-aspect acquisition, operating in conjunction with the aircraft's advanced Ferranti AI-23B Airpass fire-control radar system as well as an improved master gyro with OR.946 instrumentation. The Aden cannon were deleted and additional fuel was carried in a pair of jettisonable over-wing fuel tanks. A total of 62 Lightning F 3s was built, commencing with XP693 which first flew on 16 June 1962, and equipped Nos 23, 29, 56, 74 and 111 Squadrons, the last three giving up their earlier Lightnings. On Nos 23 and 29 Squadrons the Lightning F 3s replaced the Javelin.

The last production version of the Lightning fighter for the RAF (and thus the last wholly indigenous RAF fighter) was the F Mark 6, whose prototype, XP697 — originally referred to as the Mark 3A — first flew on 17 April 1964. This was essentially a Mark 3 with the outer sections of the wings extended forward to incorporate leading-edge camber, resulting in a broad-chord tip (as on the Mark 2A, referred to above). A much enlarged ventral pack included

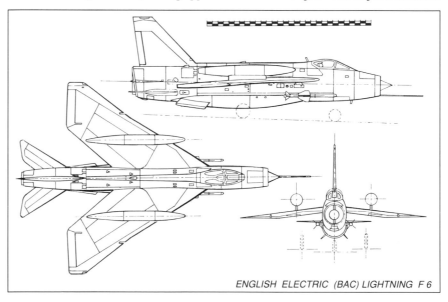

ENGLISH ELECTRIC (BAC) LIGHTNING F 6

Type: Twin-engine, single-seat, swept mid-wing supersonic day and night all-weather interceptor fighter.

Manufacturer: The English Electric Co Ltd, Preston, Lancashire; later British Aircraft Corporation (Preston) Ltd.

Air Ministry Specification: F.23/49

Powerplant: P.1. Two 7,500lb-thrust Armstrong Siddeley Sapphire ASSa.2 axial-flow turbojets. Lightning F 1. Two 14,430lb wet-thrust Rolls-Royce Avon 201 axial-flow turbojets with four-stage afterburning. Lightning F 2. 14,430lb wet-thrust Avon 210 turbojets with variable afterburning. Lightning F 6. 16,360lb wet-thrust Avon 301 turbojets with variable afterburning.

Dimensions: Span, 34ft 10in; length, 55ft 3in; height, 19ft 7in; wing area, 380.1 sq ft (Mk 1), 458.5 sq ft (Mk 6).

Weights: F Mk 6. Tare, 28,041lb; all-up, 42,000lb.

Performance: F Mk 6. Max speed, 847 mph at sea level (Mach 1.10); 1,320 mph at 36,000ft (Mach 2.0); climb to 40,000ft, 2 min 30 sec; service ceiling, 55,000ft.

Armament: F Mk 6. Two Red Top short-range infrared-seeking AAMs in conjunction with Ferranti Airpass AI Mk 23B or S airborne radar. Provision to mount two 30mm Aden guns in ventral pack and retractable fuselage packs with 48 two-inch unguided folding-fin AAMs.

Prototypes: P.1,one, WG760; P.1A, one, WG763; P.1B, three, XA847, XA853 and XA856.

Production: Total (fighters for RAF), 236. Pre-production Lightnings, 20 (XG307-XG313 and XG325-XG337); F 1, 20 (from XM134); F 1A, 28 (from XM164); F 2, 44 (from XN723); F 3, 62 (from XP693); and F 6, 62 (from XR752). (Note. 31 Mark 2s were converted to Mark 2As.)

Summary of Service: Lightning F 1s served with Nos 56, 74 and 111 (Fighter) Squadrons; F 2s and F 2A served with Nos 19 and 92 (Fighter) Squadrons; F 3s served with Nos 23, 29, 56, 74 and 111 (Fighter) Squadrons; and F 6s served with Nos 5, 11, 23, 56 and 74 (Fighter) Squadrons.

a fuel tank containing 610 gallons of fuel, the forward section making provision for a pair of 30mm Aden guns, each with 120 rounds, to replace the guns removed from the nose of earlier Lightnings. Two 16,300lb-thrust Avon Mk 301-C engines with variable afterburning enabled the aircraft to achieve supersonic speed at any height from sea level, and the aircraft could be flown hands-off and rolled at Mach 1.8 without autostabilization. Updated Ferranti Airpass AI-23S fire control radar was included, and the pilot was provided with a Martin-Baker Type BS4.C Mk 2 ejection seat, capable of being operated down to 104 mph on the ground. The Red Top missiles and overwing tanks were retained from the F Mk 3.

Lightning F 6s first reached No 5 (Fighter) Squadron at Binbrook in October 1965, followed by No 74 in 1966, Nos 11 and 23 in 1967, and No 56 in September 1971. The last two Lightning Squadrons of the RAF, Nos 5 and 11, disposed of their aircraft towards the end of the 1980s in favour of the Panavia Tornado F 3 — forty years after the original requirement had been formulated.

Lightnings were also exported to Saudi Arabia and Kuwait. 34 Mark 53 fighters, equivalent to the RAF's Mark 6 but with added ground attack capability, and 6 T Mark 55 two-seat trainers, similar to the RAF's T Mark 5, were supplied to Saudi Arabia, with 12 F 53s and 2 T 55s going to Kuwait. Although these aircraft gave good service in the harsh desert conditions of the Gulf, the nature of their servicing requirements proved generally beyond the capabilities of those nations' facilities, with the result that there was considerable dependence on back-up facilities provided by both British Aerospace and the Royal Air Force. The first Saudi Lightning flew on 1 December 1966, and three years later F 53s were flown in action against ground targets in the Yemen.

Folland Midge

The company of Folland Aircraft Ltd originated as British Marine Aircraft Ltd in August 1935, but assumed the name from Henry Folland when that distinguished aircraft designer left Gloster in 1937 to form his own company at BMA's premises at Hamble in Hampshire. Following the development of a family of engine test-beds, which gave useful service during the Second World War, the Folland company turned to sub-contracted manufacture of aircraft components, such as wings for de Havilland Vampires and Venoms.

As mentioned on page 388, the 38-year-old 'Teddy' Petter, who had established the basic design of the English Electric P.1, left that company and joined Folland in 1950 as managing director and chief engineer. Within a

The attractive little Midge fighter prototype, G–39-1. The entire cockpit canopy, including the integral windscreen, hinged upwards, and the pilot was provided with a lightweight ejection seat of Folland's own design. (Photo: A J Jackson Collection)

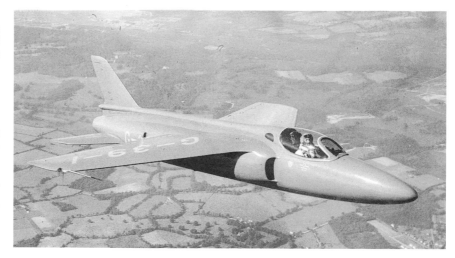

year he was at work on the design of yet another innovative project which constituted the very antithesis of the F.23/49, conceived with his former employer.

Deprecating the unchecked spiral of rising costs of military aircraft, and frustrated by the pervading aura of post-War austerity, not to mention a Treasury parsimonious where military research was concerned, Petter determined to examine the potential of a lightweight turbojet-powered fighter, bearing in mind a new series of lightweight axial-flow engines being proposed by the Bristol Engine Company. In pursuit of the optimum low-cost, low-complexity aircraft, Petter studied all manner of configurations, but the path led inexorably back through such mundane obstacles as development timescale and the cost of aerodynamic research, and logic determined resort to an orthodox, if diminutive aircraft whose principal design parameters lay firmly within an established aerodynamic state-of-the-art.

Preliminary drawings were prepared in 1951 of a small swept-wing fighter, intended to be powered by the 3,750lb-thrust Bristol BE.22 Saturn engine, and this attracted some interest at the Air Ministry until Bristol decided to discontinue the Saturn in favour of a new design which promised to offer a somewhat improved thrust/weight ratio (and would appear as the Orpheus two years later). Nevertheless, determined to demonstrate the validity of his lightweight fighter concept, Petter decided to proceed with a smaller feasibility prototype as a private venture, the Fo 139, to be powered by the 1,640lb-thrust Armstrong Siddeley Viper 'long life' axial-

flow turbojet which, with an overall diameter of only 24 inches was expected to weigh little more than 500 pounds.

The single Folland Fo 139 Midge prototype, which carried the Class 'B' registration markings G-39-1, was first flown at Boscombe Down on 11 August 1954 by Sqn Ldr E A Tennant DFC and, despite its very low-powered engine, demonstrated a remarkable performance, possessing a maximum speed of 600 mph at sea level and a service ceiling of 38,000 feet. Its shoulder wing was swept back 40 degrees on the quarter-chord and featured a thickness/chord ratio of 8 per cent. Moreover, during the course of 220 flights in less than a year, much of which time it spent undergoing evaluation by the A & AEE, it was dived at supersonic speed. Thereafter it attracted considerable interest abroad, being flown by evaluation pilots of the United States Air Force, Royal Canadian Navy, Royal New Zealand Air Force, Indian

Air Force and Royal Jordanian Air Force. Unfortunately the Midge was destroyed in a fatal accident at Chilbolton on 26 September 1955, while being flown by a Swiss pilot.

Although the Air Ministry had displayed scant interest in the Midge, the little aircraft fully vindicated Petter's ideas by careful attention to a very clean design and, following Bristol's announcement in November 1953 that the more powerful Orpheus was to go into production, he returned to the slightly larger Saturn-powered project to develop it around the new Bristol engine.

It is not too fanciful to point to the Folland Midge as the seed which gave life to a whole new concept of light fighters and dual-rôle fighter/trainers which gained increasing favour among the world's smaller air forces during the next thirty years, and found expression in the Hawker Siddeley (British Aerospace) Hawk in the 1970s.

Type: Single-engine, single-seat, swept shoulder-wing, lightweight fighter prototype.
Manufacturer: Folland Aircraft Ltd, Hamble, Hampshire.
Powerplant: One, 1,640lb-thrust Armstrong Siddeley Viper ASV.5 (Mk 101) axial-flow lightweight turbojet engine.
Dimensions: Span, 20ft 8in; length, 28ft 9in; height, 9ft 3in; wing area, 125 sq ft.
Weight: All-up, 4,500lb.
Performance: Max speed, 600 mph at sea level (Mach 0.85 at altitude); service ceiling, 38,000ft.
Armament: None fitted, but ballast provision for two 20mm Hispano cannon.
Prototype: One, G-39-1 (first flown at Boscombe Down on 11 August 1954).

Folland Gnat

While the Folland Gnat two-seat trainer remains a colourful memory in many minds as the agile mount of the RAF's famous Red Arrows formation aerobatic

team that gained such popularity during the 1960s and 1970s, it is less often remembered that the Gnat originated as a single-seat fighter, the brainchild of W E W Petter in his early years as chief engineer with Folland Aircraft Ltd.

As told above, Petter returned to his original plans for a lightweight fighter

in 1953 when Bristol Engines announced its intention to put the Orpheus engine into production. This engine, itself a private venture, first ran on 17 December 1954 at an initial thrust of 3,285 pounds, and successfully completed its 150-hour type test during the following spring at a thrust/weight ratio

of 4.4lb-thrust/lb weight.

The general configuration of the Fo 141 Gnat followed that of the Midge although, in effect, the airframe was scaled up by approximately ten per cent, as much to provide the necessary structure and strength to accommodate the larger engine as to permit the installation of 30mm guns and external stores.

The private venture prototype, G-39-2, was first flown on 18 July 1955, again by Tennant at Boscombe Down, this also being the first flight by the Bristol Orpheus BOr.1 engine, temporarily rated at 3,285lb-thrust. In August, however, a re-rated BOr.1 of 4,000lb-thrust was fitted in time for the Gnat's appearance at the SBAC Farnborough display the following month. The aircraft was most favourably received by the A & AEE pilots, with the result that six development aircraft were ordered by the Ministry of Supply, these being powered by 4,520lb-thrust Orpheus BOr.2 (Mark 701) engines.

The first of these MoS aircraft, XK724, was flown on 26 May 1956, this and the following four aircraft being prepared for a very wide-ranging series of trials, including the clearance of underwing stores for the ground attack rôle and the investigation of possible gun firing problems. In respect of the latter, both the Hunter and Swift had experienced

engine surge in their early Avons during gun firing at high altitude, and it was considered possible that the Gnat, whose Aden guns were located in the outer walls of the engine intakes, might suffer the same ills. No such problem with the Orpheus was encountered, and a number of overseas air forces began to express interest in this highly competent low-cost fighter.

It is very doubtful that the Air Ministry was ever seriously interested in adopting the Gnat as a fighter for the Royal Air Force, although there was a powerful but short-lived lobby which, as a means of preventing the demise of the Royal Auxiliary Air Force flying squadrons, advocated equipping them with Gnat fighters; the suggestion was peremptorily brushed aside as the politicians were fixed in their resolve to be seen to be reducing defence costs.

When, however, the need arose to operate RAF ground support fighters in the Arabian peninsula at the end of the 1950s as part of the process of the British withdrawal of military involvement 'east of Suez', the RAF staged a tropical evaluation of the Hunter and Gnat at Aden, operating from 'hot and high' airfields with ground attack weapons. The Gnat was not successful in matching the Hunter's airfield performance and weapon-carrying abilities.

Although Folland fought a losing battle to have the Gnat single-seater adopted by the RAF, the Finnish Air Force took delivery of 13 aircraft during 1958-59, and these aircraft remained in service until 1972. The largest customer was, however, the Indian Air Force (which had acquired the last MoS aircraft, XK768, for evaluation), and 25 completed Gnat fighters were exported, together with 15 kits. Thereafter licence production was established by Hindustan Aeronautics Ltd at Bangalore, where 175 Gnat single-seaters were produced from 1958 onwards, ultimately equipping eight squadrons of the Indian Air Force.

In Britain, interest at Folland centred on the possibility of evolving a two-seat derivative for the RAF's all-through jet training system, and, following a company investigation into the extent of alterations to the Gnat design needed to accommodate instructor and student pilots in tandem, the Air Ministry evaluated the comparative merits of the proposed Gnat advanced trainer against a further development of the Hunter two-seater (hitherto ordered as an operational trainer), and decided in favour of the Gnat. There was, nevertheless, a penalty to be paid. Folland had steadfastly resisted the acceptance of rationalisation, and had preferred to remain independent of the large manufacturing Groups then being proposed in the context of OR.329 and OR.339, and had accordingly suffered the implied stigma as an 'also ran'. As the price of acceptance as becoming part of a substantial, financially sound organisation, Folland opted to join the Hawker Siddeley Group to safeguard a production contract for Gnat trainers.

Manufacture of Gnat T Mk 1s amounted to 14 pre-production aircraft, followed by three orders for 30, 20 and 41 aircraft, placed in 1960, 1961 and 1962 respectively. These served with No 4 Flying Training School at RAF Valley, and with the Central Flying School between 1965 and 1979, during which period they were flown by the Red Arrows aerobatic team, being finally retired at the end of the 1979 display season.

Type: Single-engine, single-seat, shoulder swept-wing fighter and ground attack aircraft.
Manufacturer: Folland Aircraft Ltd, Hamble, Hampshire.
Powerplant: One 4,250lb-thrust Bristol Orpheus BOr.2 Mark 701 axial-flow turbojet.
Dimensions: Span, 22ft 2in; length, 29ft 9in; height, 8ft 10in.
Weights: All-up, 6,575lb (interceptor), 8,765lb (ground attack fighter).
Performance: Max speed, 745 mph at 36,000ft (Mach 0.98); climb to 45,000ft, 5min; service ceiling, 50,000ft; range (with underwing fuel tanks), 980 miles.
Armament: Two 30mm Aden guns each with 115 rounds, mounted in sides of fuselage beneath wing roots; provision to carry two 500lb bombs or twelve three-inch rocket projectiles under the wings.
Prototypes: One, G-39-2 (first flown by Sqn Ldr E A Tennant at Boscombe Down on 18 July 1955); six development aircraft for MoS, XK724, XK739–XK741, XK767 and XK768 (XK768 supplied to India for evaluation). Two further trials aircraft, XN122 and XN326. Subsequent production (105 aircraft) of two-seat trainers started with XP500.

Supermarine Scimitar

Supermarine's efforts to evolve a successful transonic twin-engine naval fighter were rewarded by the issue of a new draft Specification, N.113D, at the end of 1950 and, in order to meet the stringent landing speed limitations of this Specification, a flap-blowing system had been incorporated in Supermarine's Type 525 (see page 376).

Two prototypes, based on the Type 525, were ordered in 1951, WT854 and WT859, and a third, WW134, was added later. The first of these was flown by Mike Lithgow at Boscombe Down on 19 January 1956, by which time naval operational requirements had undergone wide-ranging re-appraisal. To begin with, the de Havilland D.H. 110 Sea Vixen was well on its way towards a production order and operational status as an all-weather naval fighter, with a performance not significantly different from that of the Supermarine Type 525. With the confirmed development of Soviet strategic nuclear weapons, and their inevitable tactical use, a need had been expressed for a naval low-level strike aircraft, possessing fighter-like performance, and it was to meet this

The first Supermarine Type 544 Scimitar prototype, WT854, identified by the long nose instrumentation boom. (Photo: Ministry of Supply ATP Neg No 28366B)

requirement (not initially written up in a formal Specification), that fundamental changes had been made in the new Supermarine prototypes, now termed the Scimitar. Added to this, the pitch-up phenomenon was pre-empted by the design of an entirely new wing with streamwise wingtips, cambered wing leading-edge extensions with saw-tooth and fences. To meet the previous demands of air combat, the design had included power-assisted aileron controls which imparted an exceptionally high rate of roll, but had been found to be over-sensitive, and now duplicated hydraulic jacks with differential gearing were introduced to provide a finer degree of accuracy. At high subsonic speeds precision pitch control had been adversely affected by shock-induced airflow separation over the wing, causing

increased downwash over the single-piece tailplane, a situation considerably alleviated by introducing marked anhedral on the tailplane. The opportunity was also taken to incorporate a slight waisting of the fuselage (in plan) over the wings to achieve partial conformity to the area rule to alleviate drag rise at transonic speed by smoothing the increase in overall cross-section area of the aircraft.

The Scimitar's new rôle would involve punishing stresses at low level with exposure to severe gusting. Unfortunately such manœuvres as rolling pull-outs would generate considerable inertia forces, potentially dangerous to the structure of an aircraft with a long fuselage and short wings, as on the Scimitar. Accordingly, advanced manufacturing techniques were employed in the aircraft's wings, including chemically-etched skins and high-tensile steel spars. To overcome panel damage by cracking, resulting from accoustic resonance, to which

The third Scimitar prototype, WW134, at almost production standard of preparation during the full carrier trials in November 1957. Note the under-tail bumper in the lowered position, on which the aircraft rested before being launched by catapult. (Photo: via R C B Ashworth)

The first production Supermarine Scimitar F Mk 1, XD212, was retained by the manufacturers for some months to undergo a handling and performance flight programme; the stained gun ports indicate the position of the 30mm Aden guns. (Photo: via E B Morgan)

the Type 525 had been prone (with its two powerful Avons exhausting along each side of the rear fuselage), heat shields were manufactured in titanium sheet, and panel thickness increased and secured by synthetic bonding. Eric Morgan states in his book (*Supermarine Aircraft since 1914*, page 304) that a fatigue life of 1,000 hours was claimed for production Scimitars but, even by the standards of the day, this was by no means outstanding, though certainly an achievement in view of the severe stresses.

Despite being declared a low-level strike aircraft, the Scimitar was not exclusively employed in this rôle, and throughout its Service life retained its original armament of four 30mm Aden guns and fighter designation.

As an angled deck carrier was not immediately available, WT854 underwent simulated deck landing trials on a dummy deck at the RAE, Bedford, but in April 1956 made its first deck landing aboard HMS *Ark Royal*, followed by full deck trials in November 1957 with WW134, by which time a production order for 100 aircraft had been placed with Supermarine to Specification N.113P.

Pending the completion of production Scimitars, the three prototypes were employed in a number of handling clearance trials: WT854 flew a flight programme to investigate the possibility of inertia coupling, as well as development trials with wing fences and external stores (confined at this stage to a pair of drop tanks and two 1,000lb bombs); WT859 was employed to develop the flap-blowing system with supercircula-

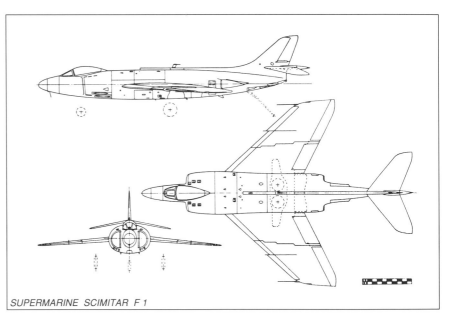

SUPERMARINE SCIMITAR F 1

Type: Twin-engine, single-seat, swept mid-wing naval strike fighter.

Manufacturer: Supermarine Division of Vickers-Armstrongs Ltd, South Marston, Wiltshire.

Air Ministry Specifications: N.113D and N.113P

Powerplant: Two 11,250lb-thrust Rolls-Royce Avon RA.24 or RA.28 axial-flow turbojets.

Dimensions: Span, 37ft 2in (20ft 6½in folded); length, 55ft 3in; height, 17ft 4in; wing area, 484.9 sq ft.

Weights: Tare, 23,962lb; all-up, 34,200lb.

Performance: Max speed, 747 mph at sea level (Mach 0.97); 570 mph at 30,000ft; service ceiling, 46,000ft; range, 1,422 miles.

Armament: Four 30mm Aden guns in lower fuselage, aft of engine air intakes; provision to carry one tactical nuclear weapon, up to four 1,000lb bombs, four AIM-9 Sidewinder AAMs, or four Martin Bullpup ASMs.

Prototypes: Three Type 544 prototypes, WT854, WT859 and WW134 (WT854 first flown by M J Lithgow at Boscombe Down on 19 January 1956).

Production: Total, 76 (XD212-XD250, XD264-XD282 and XD316-XD333). 24 aircraft cancelled.

Summary of Service: Scimitar F 1s served with Nos 700, 700X, 736, 764B, 800, 803, 804 and 807 Squadrons, and aboard HM Carriers *Ark Royal*, *Centaur*, *Eagle*, *Hermes* and *Victorious*. Also served with Airwork Fleet Requirements Unit, Hurn, and at RNAS Arbroath and Hal Far, Malta.

Scimitar F 1s with the Airwork Fleet Requirements Unit at Hurn in the late-1960s. This civilian-staffed unit performed for the Fleet Air Arm much the same task as Maintenance Units for the Royal Air Force. (Photo: A J Jackson Collection)

tion, and WW134, powered by production examples of the 11,250lb-thrust Rolls-Royce Avon RA.24s (Mk 202) turbojets, was prepared for the full deck trials, already referred to.

As production Scimitars neared completion, it was decided that the first twenty aircraft would be set aside to complete Service trials and other weapons programmes. The former were conducted by the Scimitar Intensive Flying Trials Unit (No 700X Squadron), which came into being on 27 August 1957 under the command of Cdr T G Innes AFC, RN, at Ford, the first six aircraft being delivered that month. XD216, XD218 and XD229 were used to extend the range of weapons carried, these including a dummy Target Marker Bomb (TMB, a euphemism for Britain's early tactical nuclear weapon), four 1,000lb iron bombs, four AIM-9 Sidewinder AAMs or four Martin Bullpup ASMs. It was intended that the Scimitar would, if called on to do so, deliver the TMB by the straight toss, offset toss or over-the-shoulder delivery, the aircraft being equipped with LABS (Low Altitude Bombing System).

The intensive flying trials were completed by the end of May 1958, and No 700X Squadron was disbanded. The first operational Scimitar Squadron was No 803 (re-formed around ex-No 700X personnel), commanded by Cdr J D Russell RN at Lossiemouth in June that year. In September it embarked in HMS *Victorious* for four-months' duty in the Mediterranean. During the next six years this squadron paid three visits to the Far East, as well as spending many months in the Mediterranean.

No 807 Squadron (Lt-Cdr W A Tofts RN) received Scimitar F 1s in October 1958, also at Lossiemouth, and embarked in HMS *Ark Royal* early in 1960 to take over duty in the Mediterranean from No 803. These Squadrons were followed by Nos 800 and 804, but it was No 803 that was the first and last operational Squadron to fly Scimitars,

being disbanded on 1 October 1966.

The Scimitar came to be regarded as an interim naval strike aircraft, yet was an aircraft of fairly impressive qualities, bearing in mind the limitations imposed upon it by operation from relatively small fleet carriers (at least by comparison with the much larger American ships), and by the one-man crew. Even before the first Scimitar reached an operational squadron in June 1958, the first dedicated twin-engine, low-level naval nuclear strike aircraft, the Blackburn Buccaneer, had flown.

An all-weather two-seat Scimitar development, the Supermarine Type 556, had been put in hand in 1954, equipped with Ferranti Airpass AI Mk 23 radar, but this was abandoned the following year when the de Havilland Sea Vixen captured the production contracts.

Supermarine Type 545

It is with bitter irony that one recalls that it was a socialist administration that, immediately following the Second World War, called a virtual halt to government support for research into flight at supersonic speeds, thereby placing the onus upon private industry to bear the costs of meeting this very demanding challenge if Britain was to have the slightest chance of maintaining technological

parity with the United States. Yet it was Churchill's Conservative government which, having afforded absolute priority for fighters such as the subsonic Sea Hawk, and the transonic Hunter and Swift fighters, then ordered discontinuation of Britain's first generation of

supersonic fighters — even though some of them were approaching completion, with a high proportion of the development costs already met.

An example of this wanton and financially illogical butchery of young and potentially important projects was pro-

The almost-completed Supermarine Type 545 prototype, XA181, at the College of Aeronautics, Cranfield, Bedfordshire, where the aircraft was delivered after its cancellation in 1954. (Photo: via E B Morgan)

vided by the Supermarine Type 545, an entirely realistic supersonic derivative of the Swift that was proposed by the company in February 1951, and accepted by the Ministry of Supply two months later. Air Ministry Specification F.105D2 was raised and two prototypes, XA181 and XA186, were ordered.

The aircraft was of low-wing configuration, the compound-swept wing employing 60, 50 and 30 degrees of sweepback with thickness/chord reducing from 8 to 6 per cent towards the tip. A fully area-ruled fuselage accommodated an afterburning Rolls-Royce Avon RA.14R turbojet, delivering 14,500lb thrust with afterburner lit.

A major divergence from the Swift's design was the use of a nose intake, with split ducts passing either side of the cockpit, resulting in a wide fuselage which in turn permitted better shaping of the wing junction with reduced low-speed drag losses that had been present of the previous design. The second prototype was to have featured a more powerful engine with a chin intake surmounted by a conical nose radome for radar ranging gun sighting equipment. Increased wing strength was achieved by use of thicker skins over closely-spaced spanwise spar webs.

The prototype, XA181, was more than 80 per cent complete when Ministry support was withdrawn in 1954 (together with that for the Hawker P1083) on the pretext of the ending of the Korean War — a conflict in which the Royal Air Force had been so inade-quately equipped as to be unable to contribute any fighter aircraft at all. One cannot help but be struck by the more than superficial similarity between the Supermarine Type 545 and the North American F-100 Super Sabre (with an almost identical performance) which entered service with the USAF in September that year. Six more years were to elapse before the RAF's first supersonic fighter, the Lightning, was ready for service.

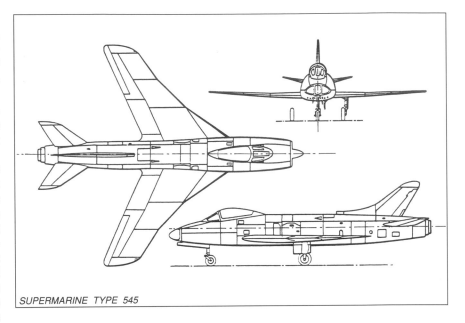

SUPERMARINE TYPE 545

Type: Single-engine, single-seat, compound-swept low-wing interceptor fighter.
Manufacturer: Supermarine Division of Vickers-Armstrongs Ltd, Hursley Park, Hampshire.
Air Ministry Specification: F.105D2
Powerplant: One 9,500lb-thrust (14,500lb with afterburner lit) Rolls-Royce Avon RA.14R axial-flow turbojet.
Dimensions: Span, 39ft 0in; length, 47ft 0in.
Weight: All-up, 20,147lb.
Performance: Max speed, 858 mph at 36,000ft (Mach 1.3); service ceiling, 53,000ft.
Armament: Four 30mm Aden guns in underside of front fuselage.
Prototypes: Two, XA181 and XA186 (the former was more than 80 per cent complete when both aircraft were cancelled.

The F.155T Designs

At about the time the first generation supersonic fighters suffered cancellation in 1954, referred to above, the Air Ministry's Operational Requirements department was formulating the general terms of an extraordinary new fighter requirement, OR.329. Broadly, these expressed the need of a fighter capable of intercepting a target flying at Mach 2.0 at 60,000 feet. It was assumed that to do so the fighter would be a two-seat aircraft, armed with air-to-air missiles, long-range intercept radar, and a maximum speed in excess of Mach 2.0.

On 15 January 1955 the Ministry of Supply issued Specification F.155T calling for a fighter capable of climbing to 60,000 feet in not more than four minutes, of sustaining a Mach 2.0 speed at that altitude, then accelerating to Mach 2.3 and climbing to 92,000 feet. It was required to carry either four Red Top short-range AAMs, or two Vickers

Mock-up of the Hawker P1121 strike/air superiority fighter which was a short-lived private venture project directly developed from the P1103, designed to F.155T. With a 32,000lb-thrust Gyron engine it was expected to possess a maximum speed of Mach 2.3 (Photo: Author's Collection)

Red Dean or Red Hebe semi-active homing long-range AAMs. By implication this would demand the use of mixed powerplant — almost certainly a very powerful turbojet with re-heat (the de Havilland Gyron, Bristol Olympus and Rolls-Royce Conway, all of more than 20,000lb dry-thrust, were then being developed) and rocket motors to accelerate the fighter into its high-altitude climb. The aircraft was said to constitute the 'fighting element' of an integrated weapons system that would embrace the long-range Type 80 ground radar network, then coming into service.

It is said that more than a dozen design tenders were prepared by five aircraft manufacturers, several of whom were invited to prepare mock-ups for inspection by Ministry technical staffs. Two such designs are illustrated here to indicate the widely differing interpretations of the Specification, these being the designs that attracted the greatest interest.

The Supermarine Type 559 adopted a canard layout, with a massive fuselage, 67ft 10⅞in long and 6ft 4in wide, accommodating a pair of 26,000lb-thrust de Havilland Gyron PS.26/1 turbojets with 1,000 degrees K afterburning, one above the other at the rear. The 41ft 5in-span wing of 5 per cent thickness/chord was modestly swept back 37 degrees on its leading edge and carried endplate fins and rudders, and the foreplane was of semi-delta planform. A very large engine intake was located beneath the nose with variable-geometry ramp, and the ducts were divided laterally to supply air to the upper and lower engines which were positioned above and below the wing spar carry-through members. The tandem mainwheel units retracted forwards into the lower sides of the fuselage amidships. Situated on either side of the rear fuselage were two de Havilland Spectre Junior rocket motors for high altitude climbing boost. It is unlikely that this aircraft would have weighed less than 80,000lb all-up as provision was made to carry 1,960 gallons of fuel — and this was just for the turbojet engines!

The Hawker P1103 was rather more orthodox, though also large for an interceptor. It employed a wing of low aspect ratio, swept back 42 degrees on the leading edge, and was powered by a single de Havilland Gyron, also with

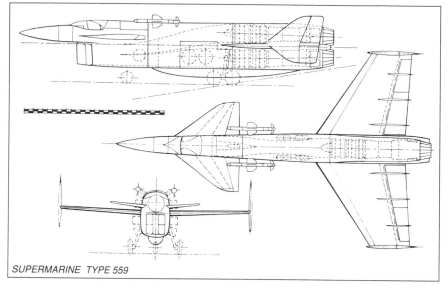

SUPERMARINE TYPE 559

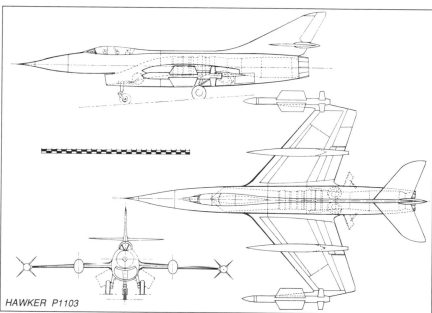

HAWKER P1103

1,000 degrees K afterburning. Two unspecified rocket motors were mounted in long streamlined fairings on the wings at semi-span, and Vickers Red Hebe semi-active homing missiles were mounted on special shoes, raked forward at each wingtip. The P1103 also featured a large under-nose engine air intake with central vertical, variable geometry ramp or wedge.

It is difficult to speculate whether any of the designs tendered would have held any promise of entering service within a financially sustainable development timescale, but then the whole F.155T project was doomed once the British government made clear its determination to abandon a manned fighter defence system. By 1957 OR.329 had been

withdrawn but, by then, word was reaching the aircraft industry that a new Requirement (OR.339) was being prepared for an advanced low-level strike aircraft. As such this project is beyond the scope of this work, save to say that it achieved notoriety as the ill-fated TSR.2. It is also worth mentioning that several manufacturers, believing that the considerable design work undertaken in the context of F.155T/OR.329, might be adaptable in a design tender to OR.339. Thus it was that Hawker persevered for two years with its P.1103, ultimately producing the P1121 strike fighter project. However, if only for a short time, the word 'fighter' had become anathema throughout Whitehall.

Avro Type 720

During the early 1950s there existed a strain of interest that lay in the use of liquid-fuelled rocket engines as a means of enabling fighters to achieve high supersonic speeds at high altitude. Unfortunately such powerplants have voracious appetites for fuel and, not breathing air as does a turbojet, its fuel has to provide the oxygen. The *Luftwaffe* had pioneered the high performance rocket-powered interceptor during the Second World War and, despite the extreme hazards attending the handling of hydrogen peroxide compound and hydrazine hydrate in methyl alcohol, achieved an astonishing performance with the Messerschmitt Me 163 interceptor. This little fighter was powered solely by a rocket motor which, with relatively little fuel at its disposal, had a running time of little over two minutes — sufficient to climb to 40,000 feet and begin a dive towards its target before becoming a glider with a very high wing loading!

Following British examination of German rocket engines in the years immediately after the War, and a continuing investigation of the most suitable fuel combinations, a tentative Specification F.124T, was issued in about 1951 for a rocket-powered interceptor, but this only served to discover which manufacturers were prepared to

consider entering a field that was generally felt to be of minority interest. In 1952 two new Specifications, F.137D and F.138D, were issued, calling for mixed-power, supersonic interceptor fighters; that is, aircraft powered by a light, relatively low-thrust turbojet for cruising flight, and a liquid-fuelled rocket engine for bursts of very high speed at high altitude.

With Avro's experience in small delta-wing aircraft, gained from a family of aerodynamic research aeroplanes (the Avro 707s, produced in preparation for the big Vulcan bomber), this company embarked on a design intended to meet Specification F.137D, under the design leadership of Stuart Duncan Davies, Avro's Chief Designer.

Apart from the overall concept of mixed powerplant, this design, the Avro Type 720, was of exceptionally advanced concept, the aircraft being expected to achieve a speed of Mach 2 at a height of 40,000 feet and above. Its structure was wholly radical in that 85 per cent of it consisted of metal honeycomb sandwich, the fuselage comprising a monocoque cylindrical shell of one-inch thick honeycomb; the near perfect delta wings dispensed with conventional spars, being formed with a structure of light shear webs set spanwise, overlaid by strips of half-inch thick metal honeycomb sandwich. A thickness/chord of 3 per cent was attained in the wings and fin; there was no tailplane, tailerons being featured on the wings instead.

The rocket unit was an 8,000lb-thrust Armstrong Siddeley ASSc.1 Screamer which employed liquid-oxygen as its oxidizer, and a 1,750lb-thrust Armstrong Siddeley Viper turbojet as the cruise powerplant, its small intake being situated beneath the nose. The tricycle undercarriage featured mainwheels which retracted inwards into the wing roots, and a pair of Firestreak AAMs would have been carried on underwing pylons.

The prototype, XD696, was 95 per cent complete in 1956, but doubts had by then been fairly widely expressed as to the wisdom of employing liquid oxygen as a fuel component and, when work stopped on the Screamer for this reason, the Avro 720 became an obvious target for cancellation in the defence cost reductions of that period, and this highly imaginative project was abandoned.

Type: Composite rocket/turbojet-powered, single-seat, mid-set delta-wing research fighter prototype.
Manufacturer: A V Roe & Co Ltd, Middleton, Manchester.
Air Ministry Specification: F.137D
Powerplant: One 8,000lb-thrust Armstrong Siddeley Screamer ASSc.1 liquid-fuel rocket engine, and one 1,750lb-thrust Armstrong Siddeley Viper ASV.8 (Mk 102) axial-flow turbojet.
Dimensions: Span, 27ft 3½in; length, 42ft 2¾in.; wing area, approximately 166 sq ft (gross).
Weights: Tare, 7,812lb; all-up, 17,575lb.
Performance (design figures): Max speed, 1,320 mph (Mach 2.0) at 40,000ft; time to 40,000ft, approximately 1 min 50 sec; service ceiling, approximately 60,000ft.
Armament: Provision to carry two Firestreak AAMs under wings.
Prototype: One, XD696 (not flown).

Above and right: *Two views of the almost-complete Avro 720, XD696. Once doubts came to be expressed about the safety aspects of the choice of fuels for the Screamer rocket, the entire project was doomed, and the fact that the aircraft subsequently suffered cancellation on the grounds of national economy was entirely academic.* (Photos: British Aerospace (Manchester) plc, Neg Nos A10/36 and A10/37)

Saunders-Roe S.R.53 and SR.177

One of the small number of companies that had expressed some interest in the preliminary Specification F.124D (see opposite) for a rocket-powered interceptor was Saunders-Roe Ltd, who opted to prepare the design of a mixed-power fighter to Specification F.138D. Unlike the Avro Type 720, however, the Saunders-Roe S.R.53, designed by Maurice Joseph Brennan, was of orthodox construction and employed a fin-mounted tailplane; both wing and tailplane were of delta planform, provision being made to mount Firestreak AAMs on the wingtips.

An Armstrong Siddeley Viper low-thrust cruise engine was located in the upper part of the fuselage amidships, with small intakes set into the shoulders of the fuselage immediately aft of the cockpit canopy. Unlike the Avro Type 720, the S.R.53 featured a conventional optically-flat windscreen with curved quarterlights.

The principal difference, however, lay in the choice of rocket, and Brennan's design incorporated the de Havilland Spectre variably-throttleable engine which was fuelled with aviation kerosene and concentrated hydrogen peroxide as the oxidant. Apart from being somewhat less hazardous during ground handling, the use of a relatively inert fuel that was also common to the turbojet resulted in simpler tank arrangement, all of which could be housed in the deep fuselage beneath the Viper engine.

This design was regarded with little more than polite interest by the RAF which, in 1954, finally opted for turbojet afterburning in preference to rockets for power-boosting, and it was the Admiralty that caused a new order to be raised for a development of the S.R.53. This was to be powered by an 8,000lb-thrust de Havilland Gyron Junior with nose intake, in place of the Viper, and a Spectre 5A rocket engine. This aircraft, the SR.177, of which six prototypes were ordered, was required to have a much strengthened airframe, arrester hook, catapult points and an undercarriage stressed for deck landing. (It was

The first Saunders-Roe S.R.53 prototype, XD145, at Boscombe Down. It is interesting to recall that aircraft designers were somewhat cautious in placing tailplanes at the top of the fin, believing that at the high nose-up landing approach angles pitch control could deteriorate in the turbulence behind the wings and landing flaps, yet aircraft such as the Gloster Javelin and S.R.53 do not appear to have suffered unduly in this respect. (Photo: A J Jackson Collection)

the last requirement that posed the biggest design alteration as the low-profile, high-pressure mainwheel tyres of the SR.53 could only just be accommodated within the very thin wing, whereas the lower-pressure tyres and longer-travel undercarriage of the SR.177 would be required to retract into the fuselage.) Provision for in-flight refuelling with jet fuel was to be made.

The first S.R.53 was flown at Boscombe Down on 16 May 1957 by Sqn Ldr J S Booth and soon demonstrated a remarkable performance, achieving a climb to 50,000 feet in 2 minutes and reaching Mach 1.33 in level flight at that height; it was expected ultimately to attain Mach 2.2 at high altitude. The second prototype S.R.53, XD151, was flown but crashed on 5 June 1958 while taking off at Boscombe Down, and Sqn Ldr Booth lost his life.

Ministry of Supply support was withdrawn for both the S.R.53 and SR.177 as a stated consequence of the 1957 Defence White Paper. Saunders-Roe, however, decided to continue with the

project on the strength of interest being shown by the West German government, and the first SR.177 prototype was nearing completion when this interest disappeared, and all work on the project was abandoned in 1958.

One is perhaps left wondering how serious the Air Ministry and Admiralty ever were in introducing a rocket-powered fighter into service, even for point defence in the British Isles, bearing in mind the time and cost of training pilots in an entirely new concept of fighter handling, and of installing the extensive facilities for highly volatile fuel storage at operational airfields, for it should be remembered that the defence cost cutting that continued into the early 1960s were imposed pregressively less in the context of the 1957 Defence White Paper, and increasingly to satisfy the rapidly mounting cost of the TSR.2 strike aircraft on which so many professional reputations were being staked.

The accompanying data table refers to the S.R.53, except where stated.

Type: Composite rocket/turbojet-powered, single-seat, mid-set delta-wing research fighter prototype.

Manufacturer: Saunders-Roe Ltd, East Cowes, Isle of Wight, Hampshire.

Air Ministry Specifications: F.138D and SR.177.

Powerplant: One 8,000lb-thrust de Havilland Spectre liquid-fuel rocket engine and one 1,750lb-thrust Armstrong Siddeley Viper ASV.8 (Mk 102) axial-flow turbojet.

Dimensions: Span, 25ft 1½in; length, 45ft 0in; height, 10ft 10in; wing area, 274 sq ft. Weights: Tare, 7,400lb; all-up, 18,400lb.

Performance: Design figures. Max speed, Mach 2.2 at 45,000ft. Achieved figures. Max speed, Mach 1.33; initial rate of climb, 52,800 ft/min.

Armament: Provision to mount two Firestreak AAMs on wing tips.

Prototypes: Two, XD145 and XD151 (XD145 first flown by Sqn Ldr J S Booth at Boscombe Down on 16 May 1957). No production.

Short S.C.1

During the dozen years following the end of the Second World War several Western nations pursued attempts to produce fixed-wing aircraft capable of vertical take-off. It was generally recognised that such aircraft would be able to operate without dependence on vulnerable airfield runways. It was seen that this freedom of action would be a valuable asset in allowing considerable flexibility of operation — particularly in the tactical sphere of air power. Fundamental to the concept of vertical take-off is that the vertical component of engine thrust exceeds the weight of the aircraft, and in view of the limited power available from turbojets of the mid-1950s attention tended to focus on the use of multiple jet-lift engines — small turbojets installed in groups whose purpose was simply to lift the aircraft vertically into the air before a 'cruise' engine or engines accelerated the aircraft into horizontal wing-borne flight.

It was Dr A A Griffiths, Chief Scientist at Rolls-Royce Ltd, who conceived the jet-lift principle in the context of a supersonic airliner, and initiated the design of a small lightweight lift turbojet, the RB.108. The Rolls-Royce Thrust Measuring Rig (the 'Flying Bedstead') went some way towards proving the feasibility of the concept in 1953, and the following year the Ministry of Supply issued Specification ER.143 for a research aeroplane employing the jet-lift principle. In August 1954 Short Brothers & Harland Ltd was awarded a contract to produce two prototypes, XG900 and XG905, of the S.C.1.

The S.C.1 was a small single-seat delta aircraft with fixed tricycle undercarriage; four Rolls-Royce RB.108 lift engines were to be mounted vertically in pairs in the centre fuselage and a fifth engine in the tail to provide forward thrust in cruising flight. After engine tests and taxying trials had been completed, XG900 was first flown conventionally at Boscombe Down on 2 April

In no sense a fighter aircraft, the S.C.1 is included in this work to illustrate the basis of thought being pursued by elements of the aircraft industry by which fighter aircraft might achieve vertical take-off. XG905 is shown here in free hover, equipped with an early form of autostabilizer. (Photo: Short Brothers and Harland Ltd, Neg No AC5-3723)

The Short S.C.1 XG905 being flown by J R Green, at Sydenham, with an improved autostabilizer shortly before the fatal accident in which Green lost his life on 2 October 1963. (Photo: Short Brother and Harland Ltd, Neg No AC5-3878-1)

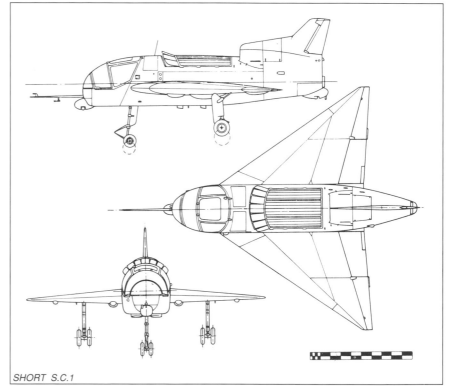

SHORT S.C.1

1957 by Tom Brooke-Smith, only the tail-mounted cruise engine being installed. XG905, fitted with all five engines and flown by Brooke-Smith, achieved the first tethered hovering flight over a special platform on 23 May 1958, and the first untethered hovering flight on 25 October that year.

Considerable development of the two prototypes followed as widespread interest was being shown in the multi-jet-lift principle, not least in the field of fighter aircraft. XG905 was badly damaged in a fatal accident on 2 October 1961 when an RAE pilot, J R Green was killed, following failure of the autostabilizer. By then, however, an alternative to the lift-jet engine — the vectored thrust concept — was being demonstrated by the Hawker P1127 (see below), and the Short S.C.1 came to be employed increasingly in the development of the three-channel autostabilizer and blind-landing systems.

Nevertheless, experience gained with the S.C.1 prompted Shorts to embark on a series of flat risers — notably the PD.45, PD.49 and PD.56 strike fighters — but these remained stillborn following acceptance of the BAC TSR.2 strike aircraft.

Type: Single-seat five-engine VTO delta-wing research aircraft
Specification: ER.143
Manufacturer: Short Brothers & Harland Ltd, Sydenham, Belfast
Powerplant: Four 2,000lb-thrust Rolls-Royce RB.108 lift engines mounted vertically in centre fuselage and one RB.108 in the tail, exhausting rearwards.
Structure: Two-spar delta wing, tailless aircraft with fixed tricycle undercarriage.
Dimensions: Span, 23ft 6in; length, 29ft 10in; wing area, 141.9 sq ft.
Weights: Tare, 6,000lb; all-up (VTO), 7,700lb; (STO), 8,050lb.
Performance: Max speed, 246 mph; range, 150 miles.
Armament: None.
Prototypes: XG900 (first flown, 2 April 1957 — conventional take-off); XG905 (first tethered hover, 23 May 1958; first free hover, 25 October 1958). No production.

Hawker P1127

Publication of the 1957 Defence White Paper (which forecast the imminent assumption of air interceptor duties by ground-to-air guided missiles in the RAF) had an immediate and profound effect on British fighter manufacturers, not least Hawker Aircraft Ltd. This company had for two years been engaged in producing the large, supersonic interceptor, the P1103. Although this project continued to be pursued for a further year — developed into the P1121 strike aircraft — Hawker turned its attention to the vertical take-off and landing (V/STOL) concept. It was during 1957 that Dr Stanley Hooker, Technical Director at Bristol Engines, discussed with Sir Sydney Camm a proposal to vector the thrust of a turbojet both vertically and horizontally by means of rotatable enhaust nozzles. This idea eliminated the need to include separate lift engines which would otherwise become redundant in all regimes of flight other than take-off and landing.

Before the end of the year Ralph Hooper, a senior project engineer at Kingston, had schemed a design, the P1127, in which a Bristol Siddeley

Roll-out picture of the first P1127, XP831, showing the large temporary bell-mouth intake fairings intended to alleviate hot-gas recirculation while hovering. (Photo: Author's Collection)

BS.53 turbojet exhausted through four nozzles; these could be directed vertically downwards for vertical take-off and rearwards for conventional horizontal flight. Owing, however, to official pre-occupation with other projects — not least OR.339, later to become the TSR.2 — the Ministry of Supply was unwilling to provide financial support for the Hawker/Bristol project, and the

P1127 went ahead for two years as a private venture, although Bristol obtained assistance through the American-sponsored Mutual Weapons Development Programme.

Although the P1127 itself was at no time conceived as a fighter, Hawker was at pains to point out that an aircraft of its size and configuration could be developed to perform a very wide range of

XP831 on its first tethered hovering flight over the special grid at Dunsfold on 21 October 1960, and stripped of all extraneous weight, including paint. However, the pilot, 'Bill' Bedford carried extra weight as he was nursing a broken leg encased in a big plaster cast. Fuel for just two minutes' hovering was carried. (Photo: Hawker Aircraft Ltd)

XP980 taking off vertically from the grass at Dunsfold in 1964. (Photo: Hawker Aircraft Ltd, Neg No 66/64)

tactical rôles — pointing, for instance, to the extraordinary rate of climb bestowed by the power/weight ratio of the aircraft. The P1127 was a relatively small aeroplane, its single-piece wing being mounted across the top of the fuselage over the engine bay and incorporating integral fuel tanks. The Bristol Pegasus vectored-thrust engine employed large air intakes on the sides of the fuselage immediately behind the cockpit and featured twin rotatable nozzles discharging 'cold' air from the compressor and two hot exhaust rotatable nozzles at the rear end of the engine turbine. Conventional flying controls — ailerons, elevators and rudder — operated during normal horizontal flight, but below wing-borne airspeeds, and while hovering, reaction controls using pressurized air bled from the engine compressor provided stability and control in all three axes, with valves located at wing tips, nose and tail. A 'zero-track' tricycle undercarriage, comprised nosewheel, twin-wheel main landing unit and wing-tip outrigger wheels.

The first prototype, XP831, flown by A W ('Bill') Bedford, lifted from a special gridded platform at Dunsfold, Surrey, on 21 October 1960, albeit restrained by ground tethers. At this stage the Pegasus 2 engine was developing an installed thrust of about 10,600 lb, and XP831 weighed slightly over 10,200lb all-up, a weight only achieved by omitting such extraneous equipment as radio, nose pitot boom and undercarriage doors, and by reducing the fuel carried to that sufficient for just two minutes' hovering flight. On 19 November XP831 successfully hovered with the tethers removed.

On 22 June the Ministry of Aviation had concluded a contract with Hawker Aircraft Ltd to cover the manufacture and preliminary testing of the two prototype P1127s, and on 2 November signed a contract for a further four aircraft,

XP972, XP976, XP980 and XP984.

The second prototype, XP836, was first flown on 7 July 1961. This aeroplane was destined to extend the flight envelope at both high and low speeds,

and at the upper end achieved 538 knots, 40,000 feet, Mach 1.02 and 6g; at the lower end it decelerated to 95 knots in part jet, part wing-borne flight. As XP831 had previously accelerated to 95 knots from a vertical take-off, clearance was given to undertake full transition from vertical take-off to horizontal wing-borne flight, and this transition was achieved by both prototypes on 12 September, flown by Bedford and Hugh Merewether, Hawker's chief experimental test pilot. XP836 was to be lost in an accident on 14 December when a 'cold' nozzle was lost in flight; the aircraft

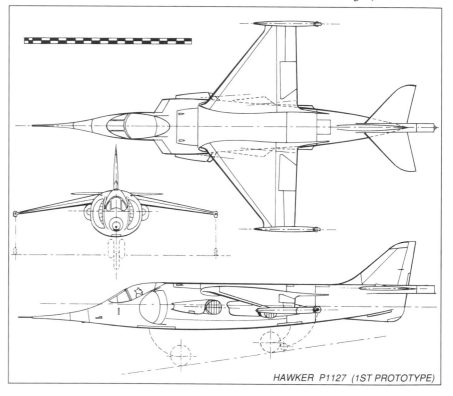

HAWKER P1127 (1ST PROTOTYPE)

Type: Single-engine, single-seat, shoulder-wing, vectored-thrust V/STOL research aircraft.

Ministry of Supply Specification: ER.204D

Manufacturer: Hawker Aircraft Ltd., Kingston-upon-Thames and Dunsfold, Surrey.

Powerplant: One 11,000lb-thrust Bristol Siddeley BS.53 Pegasus 2 vectored-thrust turbojet; later 13,500lb-thrust Pegasus 3 and 15,500lb-thrust Pegasus 5 turbofan.

Structure: Two-spar single-piece shoulder wing with chemically-milled skin and monocoque fuselage; retractable zero-track tricycle undercarriage with wingtip outrigger wheel units.

Dimensions: (XP831) Span, 24ft 4in; length, 49ft 0in; height, 10ft 3in. (XP984) Span, 22ft 11in; length, 44ft 5in; height, 10ft 2in.

Weights: (XP831) Tare, 9,150lb; all-up, 10,950lb (later 11,540lb). (XP984) Tare, 10,440lb; all-up, 12,810lb (later 14,300lb).

Performance (Pegasus 5): Max speed, approx 720 mph (Mach 0.97 at 36,000ft); initial rate of climb, 21,900 ft/min; service ceiling, 49,800feet.

Armament: None.

Prototypes: Six. XP831 (first untethered hover, 19 November 1960, A W Bedford); XP836 (first flight, 7 July 1961); XP972 (first flight, 5 April 1962); XP976 (first flight, 12 July 1962); XP980 (first flight, May 1963); XP984 (first flight, October 1963).

XP980 prepares for a short take-off at Dunsfold in 1963; note the inflated intake lips and the nozzles angled slightly aft. (Photo: Hawker Aircraft Ltd, Neg No 80/63)

became uncontrollable as it approached to land at Yeovilton, and Bedford ejected successfully at only 200 feet.

The third prototype, XP972, made its first flight on 5 April 1962, followed by XP976 on 12 July. The latter introduced inflatable lips on the engine air intakes, an expedient to reduce hot air re-circulation while the aircraft hovered near the ground; it also featured a fin-mounted pitot head. XP972 was severely damaged in an accident on 30 October when the Pegasus failed following a main bearing seizure in a high-g turn; Merewether attempted a force landing at Tangmere, but the undercarriage collapsed and a titanium fire followed. The pilot escaped unhurt but the aircraft was not repaired.

Meanwhile XP831 continued its test programme and, in February 1963, both Bedford and Merewether flew carrier trials aboard HM Carrier *Ark Royal*. By then the Pegasus was delivering about 13,000 lb thrust so that vertical and short take-offs were being made from grass surfaces, as well as paved runways. An unfortunate accident occurred in-

volving XP831 during the Paris Air Show on 16 June while Bedford was demonstrating low level hovering; a tiny fragment of debris fouled a nozzel actuating motor causing the aircraft to lose height rapidly and crash. The pilot was unhurt, and the aircraft was repaired.

XP980 had made its maiden flight in May 1963, introducing an anhedral tailplane and streamwise wingtips; this prototype continued flying for many years on all manner of trials. The final P1127 prototype, XP984, was first flown in October 1963 and this appeared with an entirely new swept wing with leading edge extensions and steel cold nozzles; it was damaged in a force landing at Thorney Island on 19 March 1965; it

was, however, repaired and continued flying until finally destroyed in a landing accident at the RAE, Bedford, on 31 October 1975.

By the time XP984 first flew, the entire vectored-thrust principle had been successfully proved and, such was the interest generated in the RAF and the USA, Hawker had already received an order for nine further aircraft to undergo Service evaluation under 'field' conditions. This was to become the Hawker Siddeley Kestrel.

The historic P1127 prototype, XP831, survived to be preserved for posterity and came to be displayed in the Sir Sydney Camm Memorial Hall at the RAF Museum, Hendon.

The P1127s, XP831, XP976 and XP980, flown in 1963 by Bill Bedford, Hugh Merewether and Duncan Simpson; XP976 (leading) features the streamwise wingtips and flat tailplane, and all are equipped with inflatable intake lips. (Photo: Hawker Aircraft Ltd Neg No 115/63)

Hawker Siddeley Kestrel

As the manufacturers' trials with the Hawker P1127 prototypes continued during 1962-63, and the power output of the Pegasus vectored-thrust engine steadily increased, so the operating envelope of this remarkable aircraft attracted the attention of air forces at home and overseas — in particular the US Army, US Marine Corps and the German *Luftwaffe*, not forgetting of course the Royal Air Force and the Royal Navy. From the outset it was appreciated that an aircraft such as the P1127 would be invaluable as a battlefield close support weapon, capable as it appeared to be of being operated from confined pads or strips close to the ground combat zone. In the context of a naval amphibious force, such as the US Marines, the P1127 seemed likely to be the ideal ground attack aircraft, able to operate from small vessels during amphibious assaults and from small beachhead strips.

In Britain the Air Staff had prepared a Requirement, GOR 345, whose terms were clearly written around the expected capabilities of the P1127; these terms came to be progressively increased

The first Hawker Siddeley Kestrel, XS688, early in its flight trials and still fitted with the short-span tailplane and inflatable bag-type engine intake lips. (Photo: Author's Collection)

to a point at which it was clear that an entirely new design would be required, demanding much increased research and finance and, in the context of the P1127, the Requirement was withdrawn. Nevertheless it was recognised that the first step was to acquire an aircraft, akin to the P1127, for Service evaluation, and in 1962 a contract was raised with Hawker Siddeley for nine P1127s, suitably

equipped for limited operation from sites remote from established airfields. These aircraft were in effect closely similar to the final P1127 prototype, XP984, with swept wing, streamwise wingtips and fin-mounted pitot head. Rubberised, inflatable engine intake lips were to be retained and the aircraft marked with a special tri-national emblem denoting Britain, the USA and

Very tight formation by Kestrels being flown by pilots of the tripartite evaluation squadron based at West Raynham; note that all aircraft are now fitted with fixed metal intake lips as well as the lengthened tailplanes. (Photo: Hawker Siddeley Aviation Ltd.)

Germany. Pegasus 5 turbofans, now producing 18,000 lb thrust were installed and military equipment was confined to a nose camera—although space was provided for a Doppler navigator. Provision was also made to carry underwing stores, these normally being employed for drop tanks, although obviously adaptable for AAMs.

The first of the new aircraft, XS688, was flown on 7 March 1964, and was followed during the next twelve months by the remainder of the batch. During flight trials with XS688 it was decided to extend the tailplane span to 14 feet, and this modification was incorporated in all aircraft — now named Kestrel. Meanwhile ten pilots (four RAF, two *Luftwaffe*, two US Army, one US Air Force and one US Navy) began training at Dunsfold, commencing on the P1127 prototypes. In due course it was decided to dispense with the inflatable in-take lips and fixed metal lips were substituted.

A tri-national evaluation squadron was formed under the joint command of Wg Cdr D McL Scrimgeour, RAF, and Oberst Gerhard Barkhorn, *Luftwaffe*, at the Central Fighter Establishment, West Raynham, Norfolk, early in 1965. By the end of March the Kestrels were being delivered to the new Squadron. In the meantime A W Bedford had given a convincing demonstration of night flying in the Kestrel, performing conventional and vertical take-offs and landings. After a preliminary assessment of the Kestrels operating from the paved runways at West Raynham, the Squadron moved to a number of semi-prepared sites in the Norfolk countryside for operation from steel pads set down in clearings in woods and other confined spaces.

During the summer of 1965 the Kestrels flew a total of 930 sorties, amounting to about 600 flying hours. Despite the loss of one aircraft (XS696) in a take-off accident, considerable field operating experience and data was gained. The tri-partite Squadron was disbanded towards the end of 1965 and the remaining eight Kestrels were returned to Dunsfold for inspection and overhaul.

Kestrel XS695 of the tri-partite evaluation squadron operating at a dispersed site at Buckenham Tofts in Norfolk. The aircraft flew from time to time with underwing drop tanks, hence the wing pylon shown here. (Photo: Hawker Siddeley Aviation Ltd.)

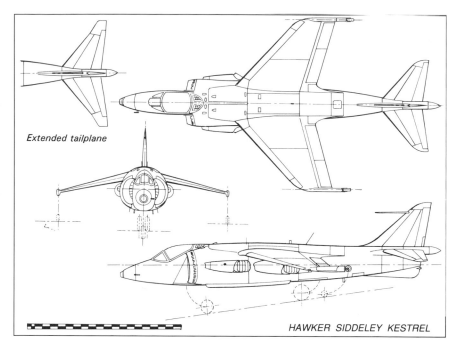

Extended tailplane

HAWKER SIDDELEY KESTREL

Six of them (XS688-XS692 and XS694) were then shipped to the USA for further evaluation by the USAF, US Navy and US Marine Corps, including shipboard trials.

In Britain XS693 was fitted with a 19,000lb-thrust Pegasus 6 in 1967, but crashed during trials at Filton on 21 September that year; Sqn Ldr H Rigg escaped safely. XS695 underwent further trials at the A & AEE and the RAE. However, the entire V/STOL concept had by then gained recognition by the RAF as a viable operational procedure with the issue to Hawker Siddeley of a production contract for a Pegasus 6-powered derivative. This was to become the Harrier — an aircraft that was likely to remain in front-line service for more than thirty years.

Type: Single-engine, single-seat V/STOL Service evaluation ground support reconnaissance fighter.

Manufacturer: Hawker Siddeley Aviation Ltd., Kingston-upon-Thames and Dunsfold, Surrey.

Ministry of Aviation Specification: GOR 345, as amended (later withdrawn).

Powerplant: One 18,000lb-thrust Bristol Siddeley Pegasus 5 vectored-thrust turbofan.

Structure: As for Hawker P.1127 (but fuselage lengthened by nine inches). Martin-Baker 6HA zero-zero ejection seat.

Dimensions: Span, 22ft 11in; length, 42ft 6in; height, 10ft 9in.

Weights: Tare, 9,800lb; all-up (VTO), 14,500lb; (STO), 17,500lb.

Performance: Max speed, 710 mph at sea level (Mach 0.92); 635 mph at 36,000ft (Mach 0.96); initial rate of climb, approx 30,000 ft/min at sea level; service ceiling, approx 55,000ft.

Armament: No fixed armament; provision for underwing stores.

Production: Nine aircraft (XS688-XS696; first flight by XS688, 7 March 1964).

Hawker Siddeley P1150 and P1154

The approach by Bristol Siddeley to the Mutual Weapons Development Programme in Paris in 1958-59 to solicit funds to support development of the vectored-thrust engine had the effect of drawing the attention of NATO to the progress of the Hawker P1127 in the light of a need to find an ultimate successor for the Fiat G.91 close-support aircraft — then scheduled for service with NATO air forces in Europe. The ability of the P1127 to operate from forward dispersed sites opened up new vistas of tactical deployment, and when the French company Avions Marcel Dassault put forward proposals for an alternative scheme by which the supersonic Mirage fighter might be equipped with separate lift engines (in the manner of the Short S.C.1) to achieve V/STOL operation, the NATO authorities began formulating a requirement for a high performance close support V/STOL aircraft intended ultimately to supersede the Fiat G.91.

NATO Basic Military Requirement 3 (NBMR 3) was issued in 1960 — at a time when the first P1127 had yet to begin initial hovering trials — calling for Mach 2 performance at 50,000 feet. It was quickly seen that the P1127 could never approach this performance, and work started under Ralph Hooper at Kingston on a single-seat supersonic derivative powered by a new version of the Pegasus, the BS.53/6 with 1,200 degrees K plenum chamber burning (to be redesignated the BS.100). Work on this project, the P1150, continued in 1961, but new issues of NBMR 3 showed that the performance being demanded was being progressively increased beyond that expected from the P1150, and Hooper switched to a new design, initially referred to as the P1150/3 and then changed to P1154. Powered by a scaled-down BS.100/9 developing 33,000 lb thrust with PCB, this design was submitted to the NBMR 3 competitive evaluation by NATO in 1962 and was ultimately declared the winner on technical and tactical grounds. The French entry, the Rolls-Royce/Dassault/Sud

Mirage IIIV (with eight Rolls-Royce RB.162 lift engines) was, however, favoured politically owing to the international manufacturing collaboration and, in a stalemate situation, the NATO requirement was withdrawn.

Meanwhile the British Air Ministry and Admiralty, which had remained aloof from the NBMR 3 fiasco, had issued their own Requirement — euphemistically referred to as a Joint RAF/RN Operational Requirement (quantified as Specification SR.250D and P) so as to dispel political and financial ramifications. In fact the demands of the two Services were entirely different, the RAF's need being for a single-seat V/STOL aircraft with emphasis on ability to deliver a nuclear strike weapon at low altitude while the Royal Navy required a two-seat interceptor fighter armed with air-to-air missiles. Indeed the two designs differed considerably; the RAF P1154 featured a single Pegasus 6 with PCB and the naval version — with different wing and undercarriage configuration — employed two Spey engines modified with vectored thrust and PCB.

Manufacture of a prototype started in 1963, at a time when financial constraints were already apparent (as cost escalation of the TSR.2 began to worry the Treasury), and early in 1964 the

Admiralty withdrew its interest in the P1154. Then, following the election of a socialist government later that year, all work on the RAF version was also halted on 2 January 1965.

In due course, the British government, having cancelled the three major indigenous projects destined for the armed forces, was forced to look overseas to fill the gaps and, after having abandoned an order for the American General Dynamics F-111 and been forced to make enormous cancellation payments as a result, opted for the 12-year-old McDonnell Douglas F-4 with which to equip the Fleet Air Arm. Such a course might have been justifiable on the grounds of relatively low cost, but the insistence that the aircraft should be powered by Rolls-Royce Speys (on the grounds of alleviating unemployment in the British aircraft industry) proved ill-advised, unexpectedly costly and technically unsound. And the irony of that situation was that the P1154, built entirely with British labour, could have done almost everything the F-4 could do but, with its V/STOL capability could have operated from much smaller carriers and less sophisticated shore-based assets. It would be another dozen years before the Royal Navy received a P1127-derivative — in the shape of the Sea Harrier.

Type: RAF. Single-engine, single-seat, swept shoulder-wing V/STOL supersonic strike aircraft. RN. Single- or twin-engine two-seat V/STOL shipborne V/STOL supersonic naval interceptor fighter.

Manufacturer: Hawker Siddeley Aviation Ltd., Kingston-upon-Thames, Surrey.

Ministry of Defence Specification: SR.250D and P.

Powerplant: RAF. One 33,000lb-thrust Bristol Siddeley BS.100/Pegasus vectored-thrust turbofan with 1,200 degrees K PCB. RN. Either one BS.100 with PCB, or two 14,000lb-thrust Rolls-Royce Spey turbofans with vectored-thrust adaptation and PCB.

Structure: Mixed steel and light alloy construction with titanium components in high temperature areas; chemically-milled skins. RAF aircraft with zero-track tricycle undercarriage with wingtip balancing wheels. RN aircraft with tricycle undercarriage and main units retracting into wing trailing-edge pods.

Dimensions: RAF. Span, 24ft 0in; length, 49ft 5in. RN. Span, 36ft 0in (folded, 22ft 0in); length, 58ft 6in; wing area, 350 sq ft.

Performance: RAF. Max speed, Mach 2.0 at altitude; Mach 1.3 at sea level. RN. Max speed, Mach 2.3 at altitude; climb, approx 30,000 ft/min at sea level.

Armament: RAF. One 2,000lb tactical strike nuclear weapon. RN. Air-to-air missiles.

Prototype: Construction of one prototype commenced, but not completed.

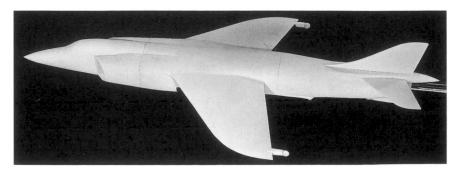

High-speed wind-tunnel model of the Hawker Siddeley P1154 (RAF version). (Photo: Author's Collection)

Deployment of British Fighter Squadrons — January 1965

Home Bases

No 1 Squadron	Hawker Hunter FGA 9	West Raynham
No 19 Squadron	English Electric Lightning F 2	Leconfield
No 23 Squadron	English Electric Lightning F 3	Leuchars
No 54 Squadron	Hawker Hunter FGA 9	West Raynham
No 56 Squadron	English Electric Lightning F 1A	Wattisham
No 64 Squadron	Gloster Javelin F(AW) 9	Binbrook
No 74 Squadron	English Electric Lightning F 3	Leuchars
No 92 Squadron	English Electric Lightning F 2	Leconfield
No 111 Squadron	English Electric Lightning F 1/3	Wattisham

Germany

No 2 Squadron	Hawker Hunter FR 10	Gütersloh
No 4 Squadron	Hawker Hunter FR 10	Gütersloh

No 5 Squadron	Gloster Javelin F(AW) 9	Laarbruch
No 11 Squadron	Gloster Javelin F(AW) 9	Geilenkirchen

Middle and Far East

No 8 Squadron	Hawker Hunter FGA 9	Khormaksar, Aden
No 20 Squadron	Hawker Hunter FGA 9	Tengah, Singapore
No 28 Squadron	Hawker Hunter FGA 9	Kai Tak, Hong Kong
No 29 Squadron	Gloster Javelin F(AW) 9	Akrotiri, Cyprus
No 43 Squadron	Hawker Hunter FGA 9	Khormaksar, Aden
No 60 Squadron	Gloster Javelin F(AW) 9	Tengah, Singapore
No 208 Squadron	Hawker Hunter FGA 9	Muharraq, Bahrain

Fleet Air Arm

No 803 Squadron	Supermarine Scimitar F 1	HMS *Ark Royal*
No 890 Squadron	D.H. Sea Vixen F(AW)1	HMS *Ark Royal*
No 892 Squadron	D.H. Sea Vixen F(AW)1	Yeovilton
No 893 Squadron	D.H. Sea Vixen F(AW)1	HMS *Victorious*
No 899 Squadron	D.H. Sea Vixen F(AW)2	HMS *Eagle*

Hawker Siddeley (BAe) Harrier

It was announced that, at the time of its cancellation, the cost of the P1154's development programme which, including a development batch of aircraft, was expected to be incurred during the period 1965-68, would have amounted to not less than £500m. Bearing in mind that the RAF's P1154 was to have been a strike aircraft, it is difficult to see how the Service could have justified ordering both it and the TSR.2, even given the fact that the Hawker aircraft possessed V/STOL capabilities. Without pursuing this matter in any length, it also has to be asked whether the British aircraft industry could have engaged in the *production* of the TSR.2 and the *development* of the P1154 simultaneously, as well as persevering with the Concorde supersonic airliner, which had escaped the socialist axe. All three ventures were colossal by the standards of their day.

That said, the other, much less costly alternative then being pursued by Hawker offered the RAF a rather more tactically flexible, if slightly less radical aircraft, the greater proportion of whose development had already been paid for, and whose operational concept had been evaluated, and not found wanting. This was of course the transonic Kestrel; still

Last of the Development Batch Harrier GR Mk 1s, XV281; these were distinguishable by the larger number of pressure relief doors on the engine intakes. (Photo: Author's Collection)

handicapped by relatively low power, this aircraft had carried no armament, and could not take-off vertically if burdened by external fuel tanks, instead 'resorting to' the short take-off manœuvre.

With the prospect of thrust from the Bristol Siddeley Pegasus vectored-thrust turbofan increasing well beyond the 15,000 pounds, available in 1964, Camm was able to offer an aircraft that could realistically be regarded as a ground support fighter, capable of lifting combinations of gun pods, bombs, rocket-launchers and/or extra fuel after a very short take-off (of the order of 200 yards). This was seen as an attractive alternative to the P1154, bearing in mind the very limited runways that might be available close to the front line in the event of a

ground conflict occurring in Europe. In other words, the V/STOL aircraft was now seen, not so much as an offensive strike weapon but as an important tactical support asset, ideal for deployment in Europe. After all, much of the tripartite evaluation of the Kestrel had been undertaken in the environment of dispersed sites, away from extensive, fixed airfield facilities that could expect to be targeted in the opening hours of any conflict with the Soviet Union.

The Ministry of Defence accordingly prepared a new requirement early in 1965, GOR.356, and Specifications were drawn up as SR.255D, P and P2; shortly afterwards Specifications T.259D and P were also issued for a two-seat conversion trainer, capable also of performing the operational rôle along-

A Harrier GR Mk 3 of No 3 Squadron operating out of a wood during an exercise in Germany during the early 1970s; note the Aden gun pods being carried under the fuselage amidships. (Photo: Author's Collection)

side the single-seater.

By the end of 1965 Hawker Siddeley Aviation Ltd had received an order for six development aircraft, XV276–XV281, to be powered by 19,000lb-thrust Pegasus 6 (Mk 101) turbofans, together with an instruction to proceed with long-lead items and materials for a production run of 60 aircraft.

What came to be referred to as the development batch (DB) aircraft, now named the Harrier, were taking shape at Kingston when, on 12 March 1966, the great Hawker designer died. Sydney Camm was a powerful advocate of uncomplicated aircraft design, being unconvinced, for example, that the P1127 should ever have to depend on a three-channel autostabilizer, preferring that the aircraft should always be entirely capable of being flown without dependence on 'extraneous systems that could go wrong'. It is also said that he regarded the pilot as the starting point of all his designs, rather than a 'system' to be accommodated at a later stage. For many years he was regarded as being conservative in his approach to design, preferring to develop established concepts rather than to attempt the radical. The successful outcome of the P1127 development, in which he became wholly absorbed, was ample testimony to his own brilliance, never forgetting his support for his design lieutenants. He was always, first and foremost, a designer of fighter aircraft.

The first DB Harrier, XV276, was flown by Bill Bedford at Dunsfold on 31 August 1966, and was followed by the other five aircraft during the next eleven months, these being employed on a wide range of trials to clear the carriage of weapons, including a number of British and foreign unguided AAMs in battery launchers, iron bombs, cluster bombs, practice bombs and Aden gun pods; the last were to be mounted side-by-side as strake fairings under the fuselage, thereby providing extra VTO lift in take-off by containing the ground-reflected jets. The DB Harriers were to be seen with the RAE, the A & AEE, and Bristol Siddeley, as well as at Dunsfold over the next ten years as they undertook all manner of handling trials in the various regimes of flight that became attainable as products of the new source of propulsion.

The initial order for sixty production Harrier GR Mark 1s was duly placed, and the first, XV738, also powered by the Pegasus 101, was flown on 12 December 1967; five further aircraft were completed in 1968, and these joined the DB Harriers at Dunsfold and Boscombe Down. As pilots of the United States Marine Corps (which had expressed an early interest in the aircraft following tri-Service trials with some of the Kestrels in the USA) flew a brief assessment trial of production Harriers at Dunsfold, RAF pilots underwent a conversion course under instruction from Hawker test pilots. The first Harrier (XV746) to be delivered to an RAF squadron was taken on charge by No 1 (Fighter) Squadron at Wittering on 18 April 1969 and, by early the following year this had been followed by eleven others. This station was designated as the sole base of RAF Harriers in the United Kingdom, and has remained so ever since.

Various modifications had by 1970 been cleared in the Harrier GR 1, including the use of detachable wingtip extensions, which provided additional lift when taking off with overload ferry tanks. And it was in aircraft fitted with these 'bolt-on' wingtip extensions that two pilots of No 1 Squadron participated in the unique inter-city Transatlantic Air Race of 1969, flying non-stop from an open space outside St Pancras Station in London to downtown New York and return; also employing

Three Harrier GR Mk 3s of No 3 Squadron during an armament practice detachment to Cyprus in 1976; each has a practice bomb carrier under the fuselage in addition to underwing drop tanks. (Photo: Hawker Siddeley Aviation Ltd, Neg No 763608)

During the campaign to repossess the Falkland Islands in 1982 the Harrier GR 3s of No 1 (Fighter) Squadron were adapted to carry AIM-9 Sidewinder AAMs for self-defence, as shown by this aircraft, landing on a carrier at sea. (Photo: British Aerospace (Kingston) Ltd)

plug-in air-refuelling probes, the Harriers were refuelled in flight several times in each direction.

As No 1 Squadron continued to work up, the Harrier Conversion Unit at Wittering was established (soon to become No 233 OCU) to provide pilots for new Harrier squadrons, all of which were to be based in Germany. The first, No 4, received Harrier GR 1s in April 1970 at Wittering, before moving to Wildenrath in June, the pilots being selected from No 1 Squadron and the Conversion Unit. No 20 Squadron was re-formed at Wildenrath on 1 December and received its Harriers a few days later. The third Squadron, No 3, also at Wildenrath, converted to the aircraft in January 1972.

By the time No 3 Squadron received its aircraft the Pegasus Mk 103 had been developed, with thrust increased to 21,500lb by introducing a re-bladed fan to increase the mass-flow. This engine was installed in existing Harrier 1s, such aircraft being termed Mark 1As. This version first entered service with No 3 Squadron, and aircraft on the other units were retrospectively modified during the next twelve months.

The Harrier's introduction into squadron service passed fairly smoothly, although during the first three years the accident rate was high, and this inevitably prompted questions about the aircraft's inherent operational safety. An analysis of these accidents, however, indicated that fewer then half were directly attributable to any mechanical defect — usually loss of power while in thrust-borne flight. A fairly common phenomenon was the bird-strike or bird-ingestion (usually in the vicinity of the base airfield) which frequently resulted in engine failure or loss of power. Another cause of accidents was pilot-induced pitch-up or pitch-down during take-off or landing transition, the result of an instinctive pilot reaction — a reaction that would be normal in a conventional aircraft.

Fortunately the Harrier was equipped with an exceptionally efficient Martin-Baker seat, capable of ejecting the pilot

from an aircraft in low hover to a safe distance from any explosion that might occur when the aircraft impacted.

Meanwhile the Harrier had entered production at Kingston and Dunsfold for the US Marine Corps, a total of 102 AV-8A Harrier Mark 50s being built between 1970 and 1975. Production of RAF Harrier 1s and 1As amounted to 78, of which 40 Mark 1s were converted to Mk 1As.

The two-seat Harrier T Mk 2 had also entered service, twelve production examples following two DB aircraft. These were flown principally at the OCU, but single aircraft were taken on charge by the operational squadrons. The T Mk2A was fitted with the Pegasus 103 in the same manner as in the GR Mk 1A.

By 1972 No 1 Squadron had established a routine programme of detachments to Cyprus for armament practice camps as means of providing pilots with experience in gun and rocket firing as well as delivery of bombs. In due course, all four squadrons flew these detachments in rotation. Furthermore, as part

of Britain's treaty obligations, Harriers were also flown on detachment to Belize in the former colony British Honduras in Central America.

The Harrier GR 3 represented the first significant advance on the original operational requirement, remaining in front line service for fourteen years. It introduced the Laser Ranging and Marked Target Seeking system (LRMTS), integrated with the Ferranti 541 inertial navigation-attack system, the laser equipment being accommodated in a lengthened nose; this system provided the pilot with laser-pulse-derived range to a ground target as well as a target-search facility by seeking infra-red (IR) radiation from a coded IR designator laser operated by a Forward Air Controller on the ground. The Mark 3 also introduced a radar warning receiver (RWR) system which displayed a warning in the cockpit when the aircraft was being illuminated on host-ile radar; the RWR antennae were located in a fairing on the leading edge of the aircraft's fin and at the rear of

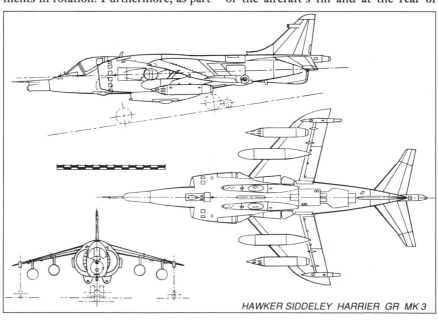

HAWKER SIDDELEY HARRIER GR MK 3

Painted in an all-black scheme with white cheat-lines, the Harrier Mark 5, ZD402, was flown by Rolls-Royce (Bristol) Ltd for test purposes and was powered by a 23,800lb-thrust Pegasus 11-61 turbofan; it was first flown on 9 June 1989. (Photo: British Aerospace plc. Neg No 8904028)

the tail reaction control fairing.

Two production orders for new Harrier GR 3s, one for twelve aircraft placed in 1974 and the other for 24 in 1978, were placed, while the surviving Mark 1s and 1As were returned to Kingston to undergo the necessary modifications to bring them up to the new standard (18 Mark 1s and 37 Mark 1As being thus converted).

No 20 Squadron gave up its Harriers in February 1977 and moved to Bruggen to re-equip with SEPECAT Jaguars, but the other three Harrier squadrons continued in service; and it was No 1 Squadron that was committed to combat during the Falkland Islands repossession in 1982, although the Sea Harrier (see page 418) with the Fleet Air Arm consituted the main air combat element during that extraordinary campaign.

After undergoing modifications to enable the Harrier GR 3s to arm with self-defence AIM-9 Sidewinder AAMs, pilots of No 1 Squadron, commanded by Wg Cdr P T Squire DFC, AFC, were quickly trained to operate from carrier decks — including the ski ramps recently introduced to the Royal Navy's carriers — four aircraft were flown from Wittering to Ascension Island, and thence to the naval task force in the South Atlantic on 8 May. Six further Harriers were launched from the merchantman

Atlantic Conveyor and landed on HM Carrier *Hermes* on 18 May. Immediately before and during the crucial landings on the Falkland Islands themselves, the GR 3s were flown against the opposing ground forces and airstrips, using cluster bombs. In the fierce air operations which followed, and lasted until the final Argentine surrender, three Harriers were lost to surface-to-air missiles, but none in air combat. In the final stages of the decisive battle, Harriers armed with laser-guided bombs attacked gun emplacements with great precision.

The Harrier II

Despite some pressure in America to transfer production of the AV-8A Harrier Mark 50 to the United States, it was decided on the grounds of cost to continue production of this version at Kingston. Nevertheless, following the signing of a Memorandum of Understanding (in effect a work-sharing arrangement) between Hawker Siddeley Aviation Ltd and McDonnell Douglas Corporation of Saint Louis, the Ameri-

can company embarked on an extensive re-design of the basic Harrier, first of all as a supersonic aircraft with an advanced Pegasus engine and then (after failure by the Americans to gain financial support for the development of this engine) as a subsonic attack aircraft with considerably increased load-carrying and range capabilities. This latter proposal involved the development of a supercritical wing, allied with lift improvement devices (LIDs) including underfuselage cross-dam and enlarged gun pod strakes. Extensive use was to be made of an advanced heat-resistant resin, Bismaleimide (BMI), which is stronger than titanium up to 450 degrees Fahrenheit, yet is almost seven times lighter. It also possesses a fatigue life far in excess of conventional materials. The new composite material was to be employed throughout the wing as well as in numerous other components.

While the British Air Staff agonised for several years on the manner in which the RAF's Harrier could be significantly advanced at a cost that reflected the relatively small British demand, British

A Harrier GR 5 of No 233 OCU photographed in 1989 at Wittering in maximum load condition, with gun pods, underwing drop tanks, AIM-9 Sidewinder missiles and four 500lb bombs. (Photo: British Aerospace (Kingston) plc, Neg No 8901186)

Aerospace (which had combined all major component companies into one state-owned conglomerate, including Hawker Siddeley Aviation) was instructed to make limited improvements in the Harrier within an absurdly low budget.

When, however, McDonnell Douglas demonstrated the considerable advance of their AV-8B Harrier II, the British government entered into a further agreement with the American company by which a single basic design would be shared by each country, 40 per cent of the airframe and 60 per cent of the engine work would be completed in Britain, and vice versa in the United States. In view of the relatively large number of AV-8Bs ordered for the United States Marine Corps (over 300), this was clearly highly advantageous to the Kingston and Dunsfold factories, not to mention the obvious benefit to Rolls-Royce (Bristol), as the initial RAF order for what was to become the Harrier GR Mark 5 was for no more than 60 aircraft.

The RAF order, signed in August 1982, was for two DB aircraft, ZD318 and ZD319, and production aircraft between ZD320 and ZD412. Powered by the new 21,750lb-thrust Pegasus 11 (Mark 105) turbofan, and with substantially the same airframe as the AV-8B with its extensive use of composite materials, the Harrier introduced a gun armament of two 25mm cannon in underfuselage strake fairings, as well as no fewer than eight underwing and one underfuselage store pylons, capable of carrying, as a typical STO load, two 190 gallon drop tanks, two AIM-9 AAMs and four 500lb bombs, or seven 582lb Hunting BL755 cluster bombs and two AAMs.

The first DB Harrier GR 5, ZD318, was flown at Dunsfold by Mike Snelling on 30 April 1985, and the first Service aircraft, ZD323, was delivered to RAF Wittering on 5 May 1987. Before the order for all sixty GR 5s had been completed, development of specialized operational equipment for the Royal Air Force had reached the point where it could be introduced into the Harrier, and the last 19 aircraft (between ZD430 and ZD470) were completed as GR 5As,

incorporating General Electric forward-looking infra-red sensors (FLIR) on the nose. The first GR 5A was flown in 1989

and, on 17 March that year No 3 Squadron, commanded by Wg Cdr Peter Moulins, began converting to Mark 5s,

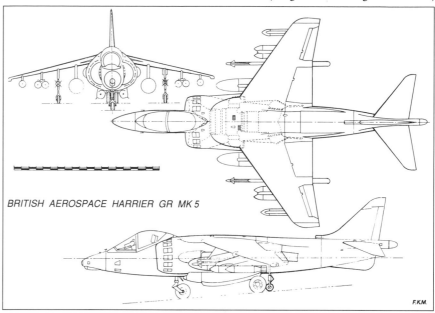

BRITISH AEROSPACE HARRIER GR MK 5

F.K.M.

Type: Single thrust-vectoring engine, single-seat, shoulder-wing V/STOL ground support fighter.

Manufacturer: Hawker Siddeley Aviation Ltd (later British Aerospace (Kingston) plc), Kingston-upon-Thames and Dunsfold, Surrey.

Ministry of Defence Specification: SR.255D, P and P2 for Harrier GR Mk 1

Powerplant: GR Mk 1. One 19,000lb-thrust Rolls-Royce (Bristol) Pegasus 6 (Mk 101) vectored-thrust turbofan. GR Mk 1A and GR Mk 3. 21,500lb-thrust Pegasus Mk 103. GR Mk 5, GR Mk 5A and GR Mk 7. 21,750lb-thrust Pegasus 11 (Mk 105).

Dimensions: GR Mk 3. Span, 25ft 2in; length, 46ft 10in; height, 11ft 11in; wing area, 201 sq ft. GR Mk 5. Span, 30ft 4in; length, 46ft 4in; height, 11ft 7½in; wing area, 237.7 sq ft.

Weights: GR Mk 3. Tare, 13,535lb; max all-up (STO), 25,200lb. GR Mk 5. Tare, 13,086lb; max all-up (STO), 31,000lb.

Performance: GR Mk 3. Max speed, 740 mph at sea level; max level speed, Mach 0.98 at altitude; max speed in dive, Mach 1.3 at altitude; service ceiling, 51,200ft; initial rate of climb, 22,500 ft/min; maximum unrefuelled range, 2,340 miles. GR Mk 5. Max speed, 647 mph at sea level; max level speed, Mach 0.91 at altitude; max unrefuelled range, 2,440 miles.

Armament: GR Mk 5. Provision for two 25mm ROF (Aden) cannon in underfuselage fairings, each with 100 rounds; one underfuselage and eight underwing pylons/fairings capable of carrying stores of up to 9,200lb (typically two 190 gallon fuel tanks, two AIM-9 Sidewinder AAMs, and four 500lb bombs, or sixteen Mark 82 bombs and two AIM-9 AAMs).

Prototypes: (DB aircraft). GR Mk 1, six (XV276-XV281); GR Mk 5, two (ZD318 and ZD319).

Production: (For RAF). Total, 208. GR Mk 1, 78 (between XV738-XV810, XW630 and XW763-XW924); GR Mk 3 (new build), 36 (XZ128-XZ139 and between XZ963-XZ999); GR Mk 5, 41 (between ZD320-ZD412); GR Mk 5A, 19 (between ZD430-ZD470); GR Mk 7, 34.

Summary of Service: All versions of the Harrier served with Nos 1, 3 and 4 Squadrons; Harrier GR Mk 1s and 1As also served with No 20 Squadron.

An early production British Aerospace Harrier GR Mark 7 at Dunsfold, showing the revised nose profile enclosing the sensors for the GEC FLIR equipment. (Photo: British Aerospace (Kingston) plc, Neg No D1119204)

Fine flying view of Harrier GR Mk 7, ZD438, in 1990. This was one of the aircraft converted from GR 5 standard before delivery to the Service. (Photo: British Aerospace (Military Aircraft) Ltd, Kingston, Neg No 900249)

being declared operational by the end of the year.

Further equipment advances resulted in a change to the Harrier GR Mark 7, ultimately scheduled to feature Computing Devices ACCS-2500, head-up display (HUD), General Electric Digital Colour Map Unit (DCMU), and night-goggle compatible instruments, in addition to the GEC FLIR. Not all this equipment had been cleared for operational use by the time the GR 7 first flew in 1989, but it was decided to go ahead with conversion of No 4 Squadron to Mark 7s in Germany early in 1990.

A production order for 34 new Harrier GR 7s was placed, and it was intended to convert all former GR 5s and GR 5As to this standard, No 1 Squadron at Wittering being the last of the three Harrier units to receive Mark 7s.

Harriers have been exported to Spain, eleven AV-8S (Harrier Mark 55s, equivalent to the USMC AV-8A) being built in Britain between 1976 and 1980. In accordance with a curiously convoluted political circumstance, the first six aircraft were shipped from Britain to the USA and thence to Spain, where they served with the Naval Air Arm under

the name Matador at Rota, embarking from time to time in the carrier PH-01 *Dédalo* with *Escuadrilla* 008. In 1987-88 Spain took delivery of twelve EAV-8B Matadors, for occasional deployment aboard the Spanish ski-deck carrier *Principe de Asturias*.

The 'missing' Harrier marks, the T 4, T 6, T 8 and T 10 were all assigned to two-seat training versions, the last being the RAF version of the US Marine Corps' TAV-8B and with British equipment; these will ultimately be employed to train RAF pilots for the Harrier GR Mark 7.

British Aerospace Hawk 200 Series

Originally schemed as a private venture in the project office of Hawker Aircraft Ltd as the P1182 in the mid-1960s, the Hawk was submitted to the Ministry of Defence in response to an RAF Requirement for a basic and advanced jet trainer, and came to be selected in October 1971

First flight of the Hawk 200, XG200, was made on 19 May 1986. This aircraft was to be lost in a fatal accident at Dunsfold on 2 July that year, the pilot, Jim Hawkins losing his life. The second aircraft, ZH200, seen here in primer finish, was first flown by Chris Roberts on 24 April 1987. (Photo: British Aerospace (Kingston) plc)

to replace the Folland Gnat in preference to a design tendered by the British Aircraft Corporation. In March the following year it was stated that the new aircraft would be powered by a Rolls-Royce Turboméca Adour turbofan (without afterburning), and an order for 176 aircraft was signed, there being no

requirement for a prototype trainer.

The first example, XX154, was flown on 21 August 1974 and was set aside for development and acceptance trials. From the outset the aircraft had been conceived as a dual-rôle trainer/ground support light fighter, and represented an attempt to break into the growing mar-

The second prototype Hawk 200-Series flying during 1987 in demonstration configuration with seven bombs and two nose-mounted cannon. In the anti-shipping strike rôle the aircraft can carry up to three Sea Eagle sea-skimming ASMs. (Photo: British Aerospace (Kingston), Neg No 8704091)

ket for low-cost, lightweight fighters capable, in normal circumstances, of being used as an all-through trainer.

As the Hawk T Mk 1 trainers were being delivered to the RAF, equipping the Tactical Weapons Units (TWUs) at Brawdy and Chivenor, and No 4 Flying Training School at Valley, the Kingston design office completed modifications to enable additional equipment to be included in a potential export version, the Mark 50-series, with a slightly more powerful version of the Adour engine. This attracted orders from Finland, Kenya and Indonesia, the Mark 51 also being built under licence by Valmet in Finland. A further enhanced version, the Mark 60-series, capable of carrying ground attack stores on four wing strong points as well as an underfuselage 30mm gun pod, was ordered for the air forces of Zimbabwe, Dubai, Abu Dhabi, Kuwait, Saudi Arabia and Switzerland.

Following a fairly recent custom in the Royal Air Force of declaring advanced training units as 'shadow' front line squadrons, staffed by their instructors in an emergency, Nos 1 and 2 TWUs were nominated as Nos 63, 79, 151 and 234 Squadrons, their operational rôle being that of local point defence. In order to provide limited close combat armament, the outboard wing pylons were modified to enable AIM-9 Sidewinder AAMs to be carried; 72 Hawks were thus modified and re-termed T Mark 1As.

A more elaborate re-design of the Hawk began in 1982 with the Series 100 which, although still a two-seater, made provision for combat-capable equipment, including a head-up display-weapon aiming computer, a Singer Kearfott inertial navigator, air data sensor package, passive warning radar, full-colour multi-purpose CRT display in each cockpit, ECM pod, and an up-dated weapons management system. Although there is no known requirement for such an aircraft in the RAF, the Series 100 attracted attention among the smaller air forces, and in 1989 six aircraft were ordered for the Royal Brunei Armed Forces; more recently, ten Series 100 were ordered by Malaysia for delivery beginning in 1993.

On 20 June 1984 British Aerospace announced a single-seat version of the Hawk, the Series 200, which would feature provision for a much wider range of combat equipment and weapons than the 100 Series, enabling the aircraft to undertake a considerable variety of operational tasks, namely airspace denial, close air support, battlefield interdiction, long-range photo reconnaissance, anti-shipping strike, and day-and-night and all-weather interception. A private venture prototype, XG200, was flown by Mike Snelling on 19 May 1986, and work is currently in hand to meet a substantial order for the aircraft as part of the *Al Yamamah 2* re-equipment programme for the Royal Saudi Air Force.

The accompanying data table refers to the single-seat Hawk 200-Series.

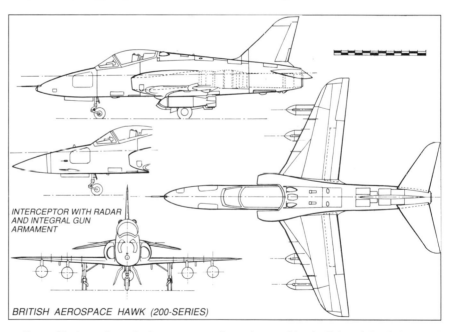

INTERCEPTOR WITH RADAR AND INTEGRAL GUN ARMAMENT

BRITISH AEROSPACE HAWK (200-SERIES)

Type: Single-engine, single-seat, swept low-wing multi-rôle lightweight fighter and ground support aircraft.

Manufacturer: British Aerospace (Military Aircraft) Ltd, Warton, Preston, Lancashire.

Powerplant: One 5,845lb-thrust Rolls-Royce Turboméca Adour turbofan, without afterburning.

Dimensions: Span, 30ft 9¾in; length, 37ft 4in; height, 13ft 8in; wing area, 179.64 sq ft.

Weights: Tare, 9,100lb; max take-off, 20,065lb.

Performance: Max speed, 645 mph at sea level (Mach 0.87); never-exceed speed, Mach 1.2 at altitude; initial rate of climb, 11,510 ft/min; service ceiling, 44,600ft; range on internal fuel, 550 miles; max ferry range, 2,250 miles.

Armament: Either one or two 25mm or 27mm guns mounted internally, and up to approximately 8,000lb of external ordnance, including AAMs, ASMs, bombs, rockets, ECM stores or fuel tanks.

Prototypes: Two single-seaters, XG200 (first flown by Mike Snelling on 19 May 1986 at Dunsfold), and ZH200. Production continues of overseas orders.

SEPECAT Jaguar

Unusual landing view of the first British Jaguar single-seat prototype XW560 at Warton. Although featuring gun blisters on the fuselage, this aircraft was unarmed. (Photo: British Aerospace (Warton), Neg No AWFA 517)

It was only three months after the Government's cancellation of Britain's advanced aircraft projects that, on 17 May 1965, the Ministry of Defence signed a Memorandum of Understanding with the French Defence Ministry to collaborate in the development and production of a supersonic light strike-fighter/trainer. A joint management committee was set up to safeguard the interests of each nation, and a complementary industrial management organisation, *Société Européenne de Production de l'Avion Ecole de Combat et Appui Tactique* (SEPECAT) was established at the same time.

While the British Aircraft Corporation represented the British airframe manufacturing interests, the French were represented by the companies of Avions Marcel Dassault and Breguet Aviation. And it happened that the Breguet Br 121 project seemed to come fairly close to matching the joint requirement and formed the basis of the aircraft, the Jaguar, selected for joint manufacture.

Under the terms of the agreement, eight prototypes were ordered, of which five were to be built to French requirements, and three to British. These were distributed between five distinct versions, namely the Jaguar Type A (French single-seat tactical support fighter, two prototypes), Type B (British two-seat operational trainer, one prototype), Type E (French two-seat advanced trainer, two prototypes), Type M (French naval attack fighter, one prototype), and Type S (British tactical support fighter, two prototypes). It was agreed that the total initial production would amount to 400 aircraft of all types, equally divided between each nation, and that each nation would contribute equally to the total cost, said to have amounted to slightly over £1.7bn by 1973. It was

planned to introduce the French aircraft into service in 1972, and the British in 1973.

The Jaguar was of fairly conventional construction for its day, being predominantly of aluminium with sandwich panels, and honeycomb panels in the cockpit area. In areas of high temperatures, such as the engine bay, use was made of titanium. The wings, set at shoulder position, were swept back at 40 degrees on the quarter-chord, and were built on a two-spar torsion box whose skins were machined from solid aluminium alloy. Without conventional ailerons, lateral control was by two-section spoilers and, at low speeds, functioned in association with differential all-moving tailplanes. Full-span, double-slotted trailing-edge flaps and leading-edge slats were fitted, the latter being capable of being operable in combat manœuvres. The entire wing, tail unit and fuselage aft of the main undercarriage wheel bays were of British manufacture, each nation building its own engines.

British orders totalled 165 Type S (Jaguar GR Mark 1s) and 38 Type M (Jaguar T Mark 2s), these figures excluding the prototypes. The first British prototype single-seater, XW560, was flown on 12 October 1969; the second, XW563, on 12 June 1970. The first British production aircraft were com-

pleted in 1972, these being employed in further development programmes and store clearance trials.

The first RAF Strike Command Squadron to receive Jaguar GR 1s was No 54 at Lossiemouth in March 1974, where they replaced American Phantoms, this squadron assuming the ground attack and tactical reconnaissance rôle. Next was No 6 Squadron, also at Lossiemouth, which received Jaguars in October that year, also replacing Phantoms.

By now the production and delivery programme was running about a year behind schedule, and it was to fall further behind as only three Squadrons, Nos 14, 17 and 31 — all based at Bruggen in Germany — converted to Jaguars in 1975, in each case replacing the Phantom which, with its unsuitable Spey engines, was proving thoroughly disappointing in RAF service. Only three further RAF Squadrons flew Jaguars, No 2 at Laarbruch, No 20 at Bruggen and No 41 at Coningsby, receiving their aircraft in 1976 and 1977. Training of Jaguar crews on the T Mark 2 two-seat trainer was undertaken by No 226 Operational Conversion Unit, which moved to Lossiemouth in 1974 for the purpose.

The Jaguar proved to be an exceptionally efficient and useful aircraft in service, and its Mach 1.6 performance was perfectly adequate for its operational rôles. Originally conceived as a Hunter replacement, it became regarded more as a successor to the Canberra and

The Jaguar prototype, XW563, flying with a pair of underwing drop tanks and two 1,000lb bombs on a centreline store pylon. In time the Jaguar would become an exceptionally heavy load-carrying fighter. (Photo: British Aerospace (Warton) Neg No AWFA 586)

Formation picture of representative Jaguars from the five German-based RAF Squadrons; the nearest aircraft is a reconnaissance fighter of No 2 Squadron based at Laarbruch, with strike/attack fighters from Nos 14, 17, 20 and 31 Squadrons based at Bruggen formating in that order. All aircraft are fitted with RWR aerial fairings on their fins. (Photo: via British Aerospace (Warton), Neg No 182525)

Phantom and, as a single-seater with its digital inertial system, head-up display, optically-projected moving map and LRMTS, it was an infinitely more cost-effective aircraft than most of its European contemporaries; it was, moreover, a true all-weather ground support fighter with a genuine tactical nuclear strike capability.

As the first Jaguars were entering service with the RAF in 1974, a new version was being developed for sale to air forces other than those of Britain and France. This differed principally in the engines which were progressivley up-rated in the Adour 800-series to produce 8,400lb-thrust with afterburners lit. (These engines were later introduced into RAF aircraft, which were then termed GR Mk 1As). Also introduced were over-wing mountings for SRAAMs, such as Matra Magic or AIM-9P Side-winders, for self-defence. India was the largest customer for the Jaguar International, with orders for 35 single-seaters and five trainers, and licensed to produce over one hundred further aircraft. Other orders were received from Ecuador, Oman and Nigeria. Total production of Jaguars amounted to 573 aircraft.

Among Jaguar trials aircraft in Britain, one is of particular note. XX765 was allocated by the Ministry of Defence for a fly-by-wire control development pro-

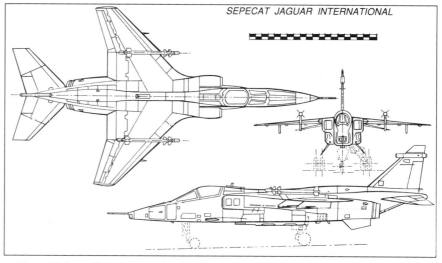

SEPECAT JAGUAR INTERNATIONAL

Type: Twin-engine, single-seat, shoulder-mounted swept-wing ground support fighter.

Manufacturer: SEPECAT, comprising British Aircraft Corporation Ltd, Warton, Preston, Lancashire, and Avions Marcel Dassault — Breguet Aviation, France.

Powerplant: Two 8,040lb-thrust (afterburner lit) Rolls-Royce Turboméca Adour tur-bofans.

Dimensions: Span, 28ft 6in; length, 55ft 2½in; height, 16ft 0½in; wing area, 260.28 sq ft.

Weights: Tare, 15,432lb; max take-off, 34,612lb.

Performance: Max speed, 1,056 mph at 36,000ft (Mach 1.6); service ceiling, 44,600ft; low-level radius of action on internal fuel, 334 miles; hi-lo-hi radius on internal fuel, 530 miles.

Armament: Two 30mm Aden guns mounted internally and up to 10,500lb of external stores; typical load comprised two 1,000lb iron bombs, two 264 gallon drop tanks, four Hunting BL755 cluster bombs and two over-wing AIM-9P Sidewinder SRAAMs.

Prototypes (British): Three; single-seaters, XW560 and XW563; two-seater, XW566. XW560 first flown on 12 October 1969.

Summary of Production for RAF: Total, 203. GR Mark 1s and 1As, 165 (XX108-XX122, XX719-XX768, XX817-XX827, XX955-XX974, XZ101-XZ120, XZ365-XZ378 and XZ381-XZ400). Also 38 T Mark 2s.

Summary of RAF Service: SEPECAT Jaguar GR 1s and GR 1As served with Nos 2, 6, 14, 17, 20, 31, 41 and 54 Squadrons, and with No 226 OCU.

Left: *The distinctively painted ACT Jaguar, XX765, which was employed in the development of a fly-by-wire control system.* (Photo: British Aerospace (Warton), Neg No CN35800)

Below: *The Jaguar International carrying six underwing Hunting BL755 cluster bombs and Magic Matra SRAAMs on their over-wing mountings. An Aérospatiale AM39 (Exocet-type) anti-shipping weapon lies beneath the fuselage.* (Photo: British Aerospace (Warton)

gramme (ACT, or Active Control Technology), as it was considered this would be a feature of any future major development of the Jaguar. This was not to be, however, and the fund of knowledge provided by XX765 set British Aerospace firmly in the forefront of aircraft instability technology. All modern high performance aircraft are designed to be fundamentally unstable and, with 600 pounds of ballasted weight added in the rear fuselage and large forward wing-root extensions, the ACT Jaguar possessed a pitch instability of ten per cent. In order that the aircraft could be flown in this condition it was provided with a fast computer to translate pilot demands into stress-manageable outputs to the controls. This system is central to the control management technology in the new BAe EAP and EFA aircraft (see page 427).

By the early 1990s three RAF Squadrons still flew Jaguars, all based at Coltishall in Norfolk, Nos 6 and 54 operating in the tactical fighter strike rôle, and No 41 in the fighter reconnaissance rôle. The remaining Jaguars were serving with No 226 OCU at Lossiemouth, and one aircraft was flying with the Strike Attack Operational Evaluation Unit (SAOEU) at Boscombe Down.

The RAF Jaguars constituted a major element of the RAF's involvement in Operation Desert Storm which broke over Iraq on 17 January 1991. Flying offensive combat sorties from the first day, the Jaguars were tasked to operate ground attacks against Iraqi positions near the Kuwaiti border; on Day 10 they made a highly successful attack on a Silkworm anti-shipping missile battery in Kuwait, and on Day 13 used American CBU-87 cluster bombs in a similar attack, two days later switching their sights to Iraqi artillery positions inland. On Day 18 the Jaguars dropped 1,000lb air-burst bombs over gun batteries on an Iraqi-held island in the Gulf. The same weapons were used against the Iraqi Republican Guard as it began to withdraw from the area north of Kuwait. No RAF Jaguar was lost to enemy action in the entire Gulf War.

British Aerospace Sea Harrier

In February 1963 the Hawker test pilots Bill Bedford and Hugh Merewether performed the first deck operations by a jet V/STOL aircraft from an aircraft carrier at sea, when they flew trials aboard HMS *Ark Royal* off Portland in the first P1127, XP831. This was at a time when the Admiralty was expressing interest in a naval version of the supersonic P1154 V/STOL fighter for which it had formulated a Requirement.

Although it was the Admiralty itself that withdrew its Requirement later that year — as much as anything on the grounds of high cost — there is little

An early production Sea Harrier FRS Mark 1 with No 700A Squadron during type carrier trials aboard HMS Hermes late in 1979. Photo: British Aerospace (Military Aircraft) Ltd, Neg No. 795561)

A Sea Harrier FRS 1 of No 899 Squadron, the Harrier Headquarters Unit, in 1988. (Photo: British Aerospace (Military Aircraft) Ltd, Neg No 8804360)

doubt but that there remained a continuing determination to acquire jet V/STOL aircraft for the Royal Navy in due course, when the political climate in Britain was more favourable towards the matter of defence.

At that time the Royal Navy possessed the fleet carriers, HMS *Ark Royal*, *Eagle* and *Hermes*, and two commando carriers, HMS *Bulwark* and *Albion*, the two latter ships normally embarking small complements of helicopters. And when, in 1966, the socialist government cancelled the Navy's large fleet carrier, CVA-01, the Admiralty's attention turned towards the possibility of operating a naval Harrier from the Commando carriers. Accordingly, one of the RAF's early production Harriers, XV758, underwent trials aboard HMS *Bulwark* in September 1969 in support of a proposal to employ Harriers in the rôle of air support for amphibious landing operations alongside the commando carriers' helicopter complements.

At about this time, warned that the Royal Navy's fixed-wing air arm's days were numbered, and would cease to exist when the remaining fleet carriers were de-commissioned, the Admiralty began planning a new class of ship, the Anti-submarine Cruiser (a delicate euphemism employed so as to avoid the attention of predatory politicians bent on scuttling anything that might be mistaken for an aircraft carrier).

Little could be done in the early 1970s to order a naval version of the Harrier until the new ships were nearing completion, although as early as 1972 Hawker Siddeley Aviation effectively completed the design of a Harrier for the Fleet Air Arm.

It was during that year that a Royal Naval engineering officer, Lt-Cdr D R Taylor MBE, RN, evolved a proposal for what was later generally known as the ski-ramp deck, from which a V/STOL

aircraft with thrust-vectoring, such as the Harrier, might be launched on an upwards trajectory. Depending on ramp-angle and wind conditions, the aircraft would make its take-off run with the engine nozzles directed aft and down by about 45 degrees, thereby obtaining both forward accelerating thrust and a substantial component of vertical lift. As the aircraft left the ramp it would be accelerating along a curving trajectory, but with the wing-lift deficiency progressively diminishing as the aircraft accelerated towards full wing-borne flight. Using this technique the aircraft would, for any given load, require reduced deck length for take-off.

After some scepticism had been voiced by the Admiralty, no doubt alarmed by the concept of anything but a flat deck, Hawker Siddeley — also working on a similar concept — confirmed the validity of Lt-Cdr Taylor's proposal and, late in 1976, secured a contract to design a variable-angle test ramp at the RAE, Bedford, this being built by British Steel (Redpath Dorman Long) and made ready for trials by Harriers in August 1977.

In the meantime the first Anti-submarine Cruiser, HMS *Invincible*, 19,810 tons (now re-classified as a Through-Deck Cruiser), had been launched in May that year, and in September the Admiralty decided to complete the ship with a seven-degree ramp at the forward end of the deck — the ship's classification being changed once more, this time to Command Cruiser, to avoid the slightest political connotation with an aircraft carrier.

By now Hawker Siddeley had been awarded a contract for the Sea Harrier, three development batch and 31 production aircraft having been ordered in 1975. The aircraft were designed to an Admiralty Requirement which required them, when employed in the air interception rôle against long-range maritime

patrol and ship-based fighters, to possess a radius of action of 400 nautical miles at altitude and be armed with AAMs. In the reconnaissance rôle the Sea Harrier was required to have a sea-search capability of 20,000 square miles in one hour, and in the surface attack rôle against ship and shore targets to possess a minimum sortie radius of action of 250 miles at low level, while armed with an AShM.

Not surprisingly the Sea Harrier differed from the RAF's Harrier in respect of equipment. It carried Ferranti Blue Fox radar, developed from Seaspray helicopter radar but modified for use in both the air-to-air and air-to-surface modes. Other systems included a larger Smiths Industries head-up display with a 20,000-word digital computer, and a Ferranti self-aligning attitude reference platform. Also included was a radar warning receiver system similar to that of the Harrier GR 3. Airframe deviations from the Harrier were limited by cost considerations, being generally confined to the nose to accommodate the Blue Fox radar; the cockpit was raised by some eleven inches to improve angle of vision for deck landing, and a new Martin-Baker Type 10 zero-zero rocket ejection seat was fitted, with an initiation-deployment sequence reduced to 1.5 seconds. The Pegasus engine was little changed, its thrust rating remaining at 21,500lb, but with all major casings now in aluminium instead of magnesium-zirconium, and all ferrous components coated with sacrificial aluminium paint to better withstand salt water corrosion. This version of the Pegasus was accordingly changed to Mark 104. The weight penalty of all these design alterations was no more than 100 pounds.

The first Sea Harrier to fly was in fact the first production example owing to its lower instrumentation standard than that of the three development batch aircraft. XZ450 was flown by John Farley at Dunsfold on 20 August 1978 in time to appear at that year's SBAC Display at Farnborough; it was followed by the first DB aircraft, XZ438, flown by Mike Snelling on 30 December.

The three DB Sea Harriers, in company with the first three production

aircraft were delivered to the Sea Harrier Trials Unit, No 700A Squadron, commanded by Lt-Cdr Nigel David Ward RN, and underwent type operational trials aboard HMS *Hermes* in the Irish Sea between 24 October and 8 November 1979.

On 31 March 1980 No 700A Squadron disbanded, effectively becoming No 899 Squadron the same day at Yeovilton, and under the same CO. This was to be the Sea Harrier Headquarters and Training Squadron, and remains so to this day. Sea Harrier FRS Mark 1s were delivered simultaneously to their first operational Squadron, No 800, commanded by Lt-Cdr T J H Gedge RN, also at Yeovilton; in May the Squadron embarked in HMS *Invincible*. Lt-Cdr Ward, AFC, RN, was given command of No 801 Squadron when it received Sea Harriers in January 1981, first flying them to HMS *Invincible* in May that year.

Perseverance with, and faith in the Sea Harrier was wholly vindicated in 1982 when, following the illegal seizure of the Falkland Islands by Argentine armed forces, a naval task force was dispatched to the South Atlantic on 5 April to recover the islands. Indeed, had

it not been possible to deploy Sea Harriers, no such operation could have been contemplated. Moreover, the two carriers available to operate these aircraft were themselves scheduled for disposal: HMS *Hermes* was due to be scrapped, according to a 1981 Defence Review, and HMS *Invincible* was scheduled to be sold to Australia two years hence. As it was, the tiny force of twenty Sea Harriers would face an enemy shore-based air force with ten times that number of aircraft, many of them modern fighters. All three Sea Harrier Squadrons were to be involved in Operation Corporate, No 800 Squadron now commanded by Lt-Cdr Andrew Donaldson Auld, No 801 by Lt-Cdr Ward, and No 899 by Lt-Cdr Neil Wynell Thomas. All would win the Distinguished Service Cross.

The Task Force arrived in the vicinity of the Falkland Islands at the end of April and at dawn on 1 May Lt-Cdr Auld with nine Sea Harriers attacked the airport at Port Stanley with bombs and guns, returning to HMS *Hermes* without loss or significant damage. Later in the day, in action against the Argentine air force, the Sea Harriers destroyed a

Mirage, a Skyhawk and a Canberra, again without loss. Four days later a Sea Harrier (XZ450 — the first production aircraft) was lost to ground fire over the isalnds. As reinforcements from home reached the task force (including Harrier GR 1s of No 1 (Fighter) Squadron, RAF, and eight further Sea Harriers), the naval fighters were usually tasked with providing a fighter screen to limit the extent of interference by Argentine mainland-based aircraft.

During the main landings in San Carlos Bay on 21 May, the Sea Harriers had the difficult task of maintaining the fighter screen as not only were the enemy attacks stepped up but the carriers were obliged to stand further away from the islands. Nevertheless at least seven of the attackers were destroyed, including two by Lt-Cdr Auld. By the end of the campaign, Sea Harriers had destroyed about fifteen enemy aircraft for the loss of six of their own number (including two thought to have collided during a patrol). Like the RAF Harriers, not one Sea Harrier was lost in air combat. The senior Sea Harrier pilot, Lt-Cdr Nigel Ward RN, destroyed three enemy aircraft.

As if to applaud the naval pilots' achievement, as well as to confirm the correctness of the Sea Harrier concept, an order for 14 additional FRS Mark 1s was raised, not simply to make good the losses suffered during Operation Corporate but to raise the aircraft establishment of the Sea Harrier squadrons.

Sea Harrier FRS Mk 2

The Falkland Islands campaign confirmed a fundamental tactical weakness which had been apparent for several years but which, owing to financial

Top and above. *Two views of the first development Sea Harrier FRS Mk 2, ZA195, photographed in 1989 carrying four air-to-air missiles and a pair of drop tanks; the fuselage-mounted missiles are fitted in place of the gun pods.* (Photo: British Aerospace Neg No 8901413)

restrictions, could not immediately be remedied. This was the Sea Harriers' inability to target more than one opponent simultaneously, particularly during Operation Corporate when the enemy attacking forces approached the fighter screen in relatively large numbers from different directions and at different heights.

Although the budgetary limitations were scarcely improved after the South Atlantic operations, it was decided to undertake a 'mid-life' update (MLU) of existing Sea Harrier FRS 1s by replacing the Blue Fox radar with the advanced multi-mode pulse-doppler Blue Vixen radar in conjunction with AIM-120 AMRAAMs (advanced medium-range air-to-air missiles) and the new BAe Sea Eagle sea-skimming anti-ship missile (AShM). This weapons system is expected to meet the requirement for a look-down/shoot-down capability and beyond-visual range (BVR) multiple engagement capability at least until the end of the century. Two development conversions were ordered in 1985, and the first Sea Harrier FRS Mark 2, ZA195, was flown on 19 September 1988; the second, XZ497, followed on 8 March 1989. In addition to the conversion of an estimated 29 former FRS Mk 1s, an Instruction to Proceed with 'about' ten to sixteen newly-built FRS Mk 2s was received at Kingston on 6 March 1990 at a cost of over £100m.

The Sea Harrier FRS Mk 2 is likely to enter Fleet Air Arm service during 1993, hot weather trials were scheduled for early summer 1992 and the missile-firing programe early in 1993.

The accompanying data table refers to the Sea Harrier FRS Mk 2, except where otherwise stated.

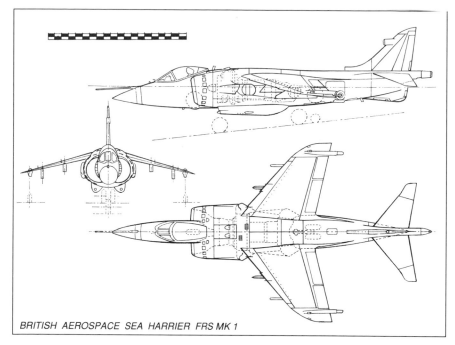

BRITISH AEROSPACE SEA HARRIER FRS MK 1

Type: Single thrust-vectoring engine, single-seat, shoulder swept-wing, carrier-borne multi-rôle V/STOL naval fighter.

Manufacturer: British Aerospace (Military Aircraft) Ltd, Dunsfold, Surrey, and Brough, East Yorkshire.

Powerplant: One 21,500lb-thrust Rolls-Royce Bristol Pegasus Mk 104 vectored-thrust turbofan.

Dimensions: Span, 27ft 3in; length, 46ft 3in; height, 12ft 2in.

Weights: Tare, 14,620lb; max take-off, 26,500lb.

Performance: Max speed, 720 mph at sea level (Mach 0.94); 627 mph at 36,000ft (Mach 0.95); service ceiling, approx 45,000ft; radius of action at low level on internal fuel, 230 miles; 480 miles at 36,000ft.

Armament: Three fuselage store stations (centreline store and two 25mm or 30mm Aden gun-strake pods) and four underwing store stations capable of carrying free-fall, retarded or cluster bombs, Matra rocket batteries, AIM-9L or AIM-120 AAMs, Sea Eagle AShMs or Alarm ARMs.

Prototypes: Three development batch FRS Mark 1s, XZ438-XZ440 (first aircraft to fly was the production aircraft, XZ450 (see below), first flown by J F Farley on 20 August 1978). Two FRS Mark 2s, ZA195 and XZ497 (both converted from FRS Mk 1s; ZA195 first flown on 19 September 1988).

Production: FRS Mark 1s, 45 (XZ450-XZ460, XZ491-XZ500, ZA174-ZA177, ZA190-ZA195, ZD578-ZD582 and ZD607-ZD615). Total of Estimated 29 FRS Mk 1s to be converted to FRS Mk 2s (depending on prior attrition), commencing XZ497. Approx 10—16 new-build aircraft. Scheduled to enter operational service in 1993.

Deployment of British Fighter Squadrons — January 1980

* No 1 TWU ** No 2 TWU

Home Based					
No 1 Squadron	BAe Harrier GR 3	Wittering, Northants	No 111 Squadron	(McDonnell Douglas Phantom FGR 2)	Leuchars, Fife
No 5 Squadron	BAe Lightning F 6	Binbrook, Lincolnshire	No 151 Squadron**	BAe Hawk T 1	Chivenor, Devon
No 6 Squadron	BAe Jaguar GR 1	Coltishall, Norfolk	No 234 Squadron*	BAe Hawk T 1	Brawdy, Pembrokeshire
No 11 Squadron	BAe Lightning F 6	Binbrook, Lincolnshire			
No 23 Squadron	(McDonnell Douglas Phantom FGR 2)	Wattisham, Suffolk	*Germany*		
			No 2 Squadron	BAe Jaguar G .1	Laarbruch
No 29 Squadron	(McDonnell Douglas Phantom FGR 2)	Coningsby, Lincolnshire	No 3 Squadron	BAe Harrier GR 3	Gütersloh
No 41 Squadron	BAe Jaguar GR 1	Coltishall, Norfolk	No 4 Squadron	BAe Harrier GR 3	Gütersloh
No 43 Squadron	(McDonnell Douglas Phantom FG 1)	Leuchars, Fife	No 14 Squadron	BAe Jaguar GR 1	Bruggen
			No 17 Squadron	BAe Jaguar GR 1	Bruggen
No 54 Squadron	BAe Jaguar GR 1	Coltishall, Norfolk	No 19 Squadron	(McDonnell Douglas Phantom FGR 2)	Gütersloh
No 56 Squadron	(McDonnell Douglas Phantom FGR 2)	Wattisham, Suffolk	No 20 Squadron	BAe Jaguar GR 1	Bruggen
No 63 Squadron**	BAe Hawk T 1	Chivenor, Devon	No 31 Squadron	BAe Jaguar GR 1	Bruggen
No 64 Squadron (No 228 OCU)	(McDonnell Douglas Phantom FGR 2)	Coningsby, Lincolnshire	No 92 Squadron	(McDonnell Douglas Phantom FGR 2)	Wildenrath
			Fleet Air Arm		
No 79 Squadron*	BAe Hawk T 1	Brawdy, Pembrokeshire	No 700A Squadron	BAe Sea Harrier FRS 1	Yeovilton, Somerset

Panavia/BAe Tornado F 2 and F 3

Roll-out view of the first Panavia/ BAe Tornado F 2 prototype, ZA254; no nose radar was fitted in this aircraft. (Photo: British Aerospace (Warton), Neg No AW13416)

The origins of the tri-national Tornado lay in the late 1960s with a requirement by a number of NATO nations (of which Britain was not originally one) which espoused a need to replace the American F-104G Starfighter missile-armed Mach 2 interceptor. It was their avowed intent that the new aircraft should be the joint production of a consortium of European manufacturers and that the fighter should be capable of long-loiter endurance — and, by implication, the economic cruise loiter suggested the use of variable-geometry wing (or 'swing-wing') configuration.

The implications quickly showed that financial contribution by the smaller European partners would be considerable in relation to strictly parochial benefits, and one by one these nations opted out of the project until only Germany and Italy remained. Britain, on the other hand, had not flown the F-104 and had had no such replacement need; it did, however, have a pressing requirement for a low-level strike bomber — a rôle that had been left unfilled following cancellation of the BAC TSR.2. In the short term the rump of the V-force, that is to say Vulcan bombers, assumed the low-level semi-strategic bombing rôle, while the British Aircraft Corporation had entered a bi-lateral agreement with France to join in a programme to purchase and produce jointly the SEPECAT Jaguar supersonic strike aircraft, but in the longer term this would be inadequate to accommodate the approaching generation of sophisticated weaponry, delivery, navigation and ECM systems. When French plans to pursue variable geometry — at least in conjunction with Britain — were halted the British government approached Germany and Italy with a view

to joining the so-called Starfighter Replacement project, and went further by succeeding in arguing that Europe's primary need was for the same strike aircraft as that required by the RAF. The proposed aircraft thus came known as the Multi-Rôle Combat Aircraft (MRCA) and later the Panavia Tornado.

A work-sharing agreement was negotiated, Britain contributing the overall work management of the variable-geometry wings. Germany would build the centre-fuselage, Britain the front fuselage and tail unit, and Italy the wings outboard of the axis of rotation; prime contractor for the powerplant would be Rolls-Royce working through an Anglo-German company, Turbo-Union. Aircraft for the RAF, *Luftwaffe* and *Aeronautica Militare Italiana* would undergo final assembly at factories in their respective countries, and each country would develop its own operational systems according to its specific requirements. Despite considerable scepticism that potential political domination of the project could only result in administrative chaos, the very advanced aircraft went ahead extraordinarily smoothly and in due course came to fruition, the nine prototypes (four British, three German and two Italian) being first flown

between August 1974 and February 1977. Two of the British prototypes were 'two-stick' trainers.

Production contracts were signed, beginning in July 1976, and by January 1984 a total of 651 strike bombers (of which 218 were for the RAF) had been ordered. These were designated Tornado GR Mark 1s in RAF Strike Command.

As long ago as the early 1970s it had been recognised that the RAF's metropolitan fighter force was approaching obsolescence, depending as it did largely upon 1950s-technology English Electric Lightnings. In an effort to bolster the defences at minimum cost, American McDonnell Douglas F-4 Phantoms (of equally ancient technology) had been purchased for both the RAF and the Fleet Air Arm, the British government insisting that they be powered by adapted Rolls-Royce Spey turbofans; unfortunately the engine did not prove satisfactory, and the RAF's F-4K was disappointing. Several other American fighters were evaluated by British pilots, including the Grumman F-14 Tomcat, McDonnell Douglas F-15 Eagle and the General Dynamics F-16 Fighting Falcon but none proved to meet the RAF's fighter requirement in the context of NATO strategy and tactics.

The fighter requirement, when issued in 1976, called for an ability to engage Soviet Sukhoi Su-24 Fencer-'A'

The second Tornado fighter prototype, ZA267, after acquiring a 14-inch rear fuselage extension to accommodate the RB.199 Mark 104 engines, thus becoming in effect the F Mark 3 prototype. The fin fairing on this aircraft carried a test recording camera. (Photo: British Aerospace (Warton), Neg No AW59966)

and Tupolev Tu-22M Backfire-'B' supersonic strike aircraft at any height from sea level up to 50,000 feet, and engage multiple targets simultaneously. To do so, the fighter must carry multiple medium-range radar-guided AAMs, a radar with track-while-scan and lookdown/shoot-down capabilities and long-range CAP ability. With regard to performance the Tornado appeared to meet or exceed all the necessary prerequisites — particularly with its in-flight refuelling system.

Three prototypes of the Air Defence Variant (ADV), ZA254, ZA267 and ZA283, were ordered with the first batch of interdiction strike (IDS) Tornados, and the first was flown on 27 October 1979 by David Eagles with Roy Kenward. Supply of the major airframe components was shared by the same British, German and Italian manufacturers, assembly of all fighters being undertaken at Warton, Lancashire, by British Aerospace.

The basis of the Tornado fighter's operation is as the weapon component of the Joint Tactical Information Distribution System (JTIDS), a secure, spread spectrum, ECM-resistant data link which provides access to target data over a very wide area, gathered by AEW aircraft, ground radars and other on-CAP interceptors. The Tornado carries electronic displays on which this data can be shown, individual targets being annotated so as to indicate to the pilot those within attack range.

The Tornado's AI Mark 24, the Marconi Foxhunter radar employs microwave techniques, digital circuitry and data handling technology to provide and store data optimized for long-range interception; its detection range is more than 100 miles. At the heart of the avionics is a 128K main computer with which are integrated the Foxhunter radar, threat-warning receivers, the data link, a missile management system, two inertial navigators, defensive aids, and air-data computer, TACAN and approach aids.

The engines remain the same basic Rolls-Royce RB.199s, initially delivering 8,000 lb thrust dry, and 16,000 lb with reheat. This three-spool turbofan is associated in the Tornado fighter with a Digital Engine Control Unit which provides optimized engine power management and fuel efficiency during long-loiter sorties.

Normal armament of the Tornado fighter comprises four BAe Avionics Skyflash medium-range air-to-air missiles (MRAAMs) mounted semi-recessed into the aircraft's belly. For close-in combat four AIM-9L SRAAMS are carried on lateral mountings attached to the inboard underwing tank pylons. The weapons system is also compatible with the later Hughes AIM-120A active-radar AMRAAM and BBG AIM-132 ASRAAM for medium- and short-range action respectively.

Trouble was encountered in the early development of the Foxhunter radar and early aircraft flew with ballast in lieu of the radar while development continued. More serious was the failure of the Nimrod AEW aircraft to meet operational requirements, with the result that

A Tornado F 2 of No 229 OCU in 1987 mounting four Skyflash and two Sidewinder AAMs. (Photo: British Aerospace, Neg No 8701340)

The first production Tornado F 3, ZE154, with the RB.199 Mk 104 turbofans. The dark area on the tailplane is protected from blast effects of the wing missiles when fired with the wings fully swept. (Photo: British Aerospace, Neg No FH835)

the British AEW programme was cancelled; in its place the American Boeing Sentry aircraft was ordered, causing a six year delay in the full implementation of the JTIDS.

Nevertheless production orders for the Tornado fighter, designated the F Mark 2, had been placed on 5 August 1981, the fourth production batch including a total of 18 such aircraft for the RAF. While these aircraft were beginning to pass along the assembly line at Warton, however, a new version of the RB.199 turbofan was introduced, the Mark 104, which featured extended reheat tailpipes to provide additional burning space as well as an increase in thrust by about ten per cent for combat and take-off power demands. The new variant of the Tornado became the F Mark 3, and earlier aircraft were retrospectively upgraded to the improved standard. The first production Tornado F 2, ZD899, made its maiden flight on 12 April 1984 — the first six examples being 'two-stick' trainers. All but two of this initial batch of Tornado F 2s were delivered to No 229 OCU, the Tornado fighter Operational Conversion Unit at Coningsby. By January 1984 orders for a total of 162 F 2s and F 3s had been placed at a cost of £2.92bn (a unit cost of about £18m per aircraft).

While No. 229 OCU assumed 'shadow' operational status (as No 65 (Fighter) Squadron), No 29 (Fighter) Squadron began receiving its first Tornado F 3s, also at Coningsby, early in 1987. Later that year this squadron performed the first two successful firings of Skyflash AAMs in conjunction with Foxhunter radar operating in the look down/shoot down mode, the Tornado 3s flying at 10,000 feet and shooting down targets at 250 feet. No 29 Squadron was declared to NATO (ie, became operational) on 1 November, and No 5 (Fighter) Squadron began converting, being declared to NATO on 1 May 1988.

Next it was Leeming's turn as its first F 3s arrived on 1 July, this time for No 11 (Fighter) Squadron. This squadron

underwent specialist conversion training in the Maritime Air Defence Rôle, being declared to NATO in this rôle on 1 November the same year. Leuchars

was to be the third Tornado fighter base, Nos 43 and 111 (Fighter) Squadrons achieving their operational status during 1989. Last of the six F 3 Squadrons, originally planned, was No 25 (Fighter) Squadron which became operational at Leeming late in 1990, under the memorable command of Wg

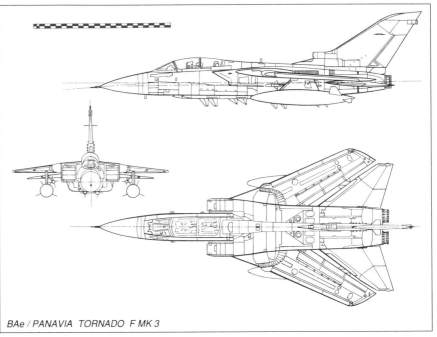

BAe / PANAVIA TORNADO F MK 3

Type: Twin-engine, two-seat, variable-geometry air defence fighter

Manufacturers (Prime Contractors): British Aerospace (Military Aircraft Division), Warton, Lancashire, England; Messerschmitt-Bölkow-Blohm GmbH, Munich, Germany; Societa per Azion Aeritalia, Turin, Italy. All fighters assembled at Warton.

Air Staff Requirement: Not known

Powerplant: Two 9,000lb dry thrust (17,000lb with reheat) Turbo Union (Rolls-Royce) RB.199-34R Mark 104/105 three-spool reheated bypass turbofans with axial-flow three-stage compressor and three-stage turbine.

Structure: All-metal monocoque fuselage with variable-geometry wings hinged on extremities of elektron beam-welded torque box (which serves as an integral fuel tank). Engines mounted side-by-side with titanium firewall in rear fuselage. Nosewheel undercarriage. Rudder and much of all-moving tailerons constructed of metal honeycomb. Full-span leading-edge slats, full-span double-slotted Fowler flaps and spoilers/lift-dumpers on wings. Spade-type airbrakes on rear fuselage shoulders.

Dimensions: Span (wings forward, 25 degrees sweep), 45ft 7¼in; (fully swept, 68 degrees), 28 ft 2½in; length, 59ft 3⅞in; height, 18ft 8½in; wing area, 322.9 sq ft.

Weights (approx): Tare, 31.970lb; normal all-up, 50,700lb; max take-off, 56,000lb.

Performance (approx): Max speed, 920 mph at sea level (Mach 1.2); 1,450 mph at 40,000ft (Mach 2.20); climb to 30,000ft, 1.2 min. tactical radius of action (with 2hr CAP loiter), up to 450 miles; max unrefuelled range, 2,650 miles.

Armament: Normal, one 27mm Aden gun in nose, four Skyflash MRAAMs under fuselage and four AIM-9L SRAAMs on sides of two underwing tank pylons.

Prototypes, Production and Summary of RAF Service: Three prototypes, ZA254 (first flown 27 October 1979 by David Eagles and Roy Kenward at Warton), ZA267 and ZA283. Total of 165 production aircraft (including 18 F Mark 2s). First production aircraft (F 2) flown, 5 March 1984. Serving with Nos 5, 11, 25, 29, 43 and 111 (Fighter) Squadrons, and No 229 OCU.

Tornado F 3, ZE288/ BI, of No 29 (Fighter) Squadron. The colour finish of these aircraft was termed Barley Grey, after the originator of the shade. (Photo: Flt Lt T Paxton, via British Aerospace)

Cdr A M Martin (see Frontispiece).

Considerable efforts to gain export orders for the Tornado bore first fruit in 1986 when Saudi Arabia ordered 48 Tornado strike aircraft and 24 fighters, while eight further fighters were ordered for the Sultan of Oman's Air Force; these orders were together worth some £1½bn.

If these substantial orders reflected unease among the Gulf states, with the Iran-Iraq War more than six years old, this was to be fully vindicated in August 1990 when Iraqi forces seized the small state of Kuwait. Failure to respond to UN demands for a withdrawal by Iraq prompted the despatch of a huge multinational military force to Saudi Arabia — including Tornado strike and fighter aircraft of the RAF.

In a short but devastating war, which began in January 1991, the RAF Tornado GR 1s undertook the vital, but supremely hazardous task of destroying

Iraqi airfield runways from very low level, as well as bridges and other key military installations, while the F 3s flew CAP sorties in support, or over the northern Gulf area. No enemy aircraft, however, fell to the British fighters, for the Iraqi Air Force seldom ventured into the skies, other than to seek safety by landing in neighbouring Iran to escape what amounted to Allied air supremacy. No Tornado fighter was lost in action.

It seems likely that the Tornado F 3 (or derivatives) will remain in RAF service for most of the 1990s and, that being so, it is almost inevitable that new weapons and avionics will be added as part of a 'mid-life' updating programme. The redundant F 2s, placed in storage on the arrival of the F 3 and possessing little flying time, will probably undergo the necessary modification to bring them up to F 3 standard.

Fine in-flight study of ZE339/ CE, a Tornado F 3 of No 5 (Fighter) Squadron with wings in the intermediate swept position. (Photo: Flt Lt T Paxton, via British Aerospace)

Deployment of British Fighter and Ground Support Squadrons — January 1991

Excluding 'Operation Desert Storm' deployments to the Arabian Peninsula and associated detachments

Home-based

Squadron	Aircraft	Base
No 1 Squadron	BAe Harrier GR 5	Wittering, Northants
No 5 Squadron	Panavia Tornado F 3	Coningsby, Lincs
No 6 Squadron	BAe Jaguar GR 1A	Coltishall, Norfolk
No 11 Squadron	Panavia Tornado F 3	Leeming, Yorkshire
No 23 Squadron	Panavia Tornado F 3	Leeming, Yorkshire
No 25 Squadron	Panavia Tornado F 3	Leeming, Yorkshire
No 29 Squadron	Panavia Tornado F 3	Coningsby, Lincs
No 41 Squadron	BAe Jaguar GR 1A	Coltishall, Norfolk
No 43 Squadron	Panavia Tornado F 3	Leuchars, Fife
No 54 Squadron	BAe Jaguar GR 1A	Coltishall, Norfolk
No 56 Squadron	(McDonnell Douglas Phantom F-4J(UK)	Wattisham, Suffolk
No 63 Squadron (No 2 TWU)	BAe Hawk T 1A	Chivenor, Devon
No 65 Squadron (No 229 OCU)	Panavia Tornado F 3	Coningsby, Lincs
No 74 Squadron	(McDonnell Douglas Phantom F-4J(UK)	Wattisham, Suffolk
No 79 Squadron (No 1 TWU)	BAe Hawk T 1A	Brawdy, Pembroke
No 111 Squadron	Panavia Tornado F 3	Leuchars, Fife

Squadron	Aircraft	Base
No 151 Squadron (No 2 TWU)	BAe Hawk T 1A	Chivenor, Devon
No 234 Squadron (No 1 TWU)	BAe Hawk T 1A	Brawdy, Pembroke

Overseas Stations

Squadron	Aircraft	Base
No 3 Squadron	BAe Harrier GR 5	Gütersloh, Germany
No 4 Squadron	BAe Harrier GR 5/7	Gütersloh, Germany
No 19 Squadron	(McDonnell Douglas Phantom FGR 2	Wildenrath, Germany
No 92 Squadron	(McDonnell Douglas Phantom FGR 2	Wildenrath, Germany
No 1435 Flight	(McDonnell Douglas Phantom F-4J(UK)	Mount Pleasant Falkland Islands
No 1417 Flight	BAe Harrier GR 3	Honduras

Fleet Air Arm

Squadron	Aircraft	Base
No 800 Squadron	BAe Sea Harrier FRS 1	Yeovilton, Somerset
No 801 Squadron	BAe Sea Harrier FRS 1	Yeovilton, Somerset
No 899 Squadron	BAe Sea Harrier FRS 1	Yeovilton, Somerset

British Aerospace EAP and EFA

The EAP demonstrator, ZF534, at Warton. (Photo: British Aerospace, Neg No AWOP1599)

It will have been evident from this work that, in the past thirty years, Britain by herself has produced no more than three different fighter designs that have attained full operational status — the Lightning, the Harrier/Sea Harrier and the Tornado 2/3. This state of affairs stemmed from the infamous 1957 Defence White Paper, and was compounded by the government cancellation of advanced projects of 1964 and 1965. While Britain opted to develop the Tornado fighters on her own to meet a short-term need to replace the remaining Lightnings and Phantoms in service, there existed a longer-term requirement by NATO nations to develop an advanced, dedicated fighter capable of entering service by the turn of the century which would match the future state-of-the-art being achieved by the Soviet Union and the USA, without being beholden to the latter nation. More recent events in the Soviet Union, and the so-called 'peace dividend', have shown the wisdom of that requirement.

While much was being discussed along these lines on an international basis, the collective NATO staffs were formulating a development requirement programme for an advanced fighter in the context of ESR-D (European Staff Requirement—D), capable of gaining and sustaining air superiority, both in close combat and beyond visual range. The implications were that the aircraft must be not only agile, and possess STOL airfield performance, but capable of mounting medium-range AAMs, and able to operate in all weathers from short runways.

Meanwhile British Aerospace, MBB and Aeritalia, as component partners of Panavia, as well as Dassault-Breguet of France, had since 1979 been investigating separately the design feasibility of agile fighters, and then sat down together to attempt to agree on a common broad approach to a true European design. This unfortunately failed to materialise owing principally, but not exclusively to the French requirement, which was not negotiable, for a marginally smaller aircraft capable of deck operation. At the same time Dornier, in collaboration with Northrop, prepared an independent proposal.

In 1982 the three Panavia companies agreed on a joint proposal, stemming largely from the BAe P.110 and MBB's TKF90 projects (which were very similar in concept), known then as the Agile Combat Aircraft (ACA), to be powered by a new engine, the XG-40 to be produced by the Turbo-Union partnership. Lip-service had been paid to an agreement for work-sharing between the three national partners, with at least one prototype being built in each country. Unfortunately, shortly afterwards, the governments in Bonn and Rome decided to withdraw from the programme, leaving British Aerospace with the option of following suit or going ahead on its own. And it is to the considerable credit of the British industry that not only did British Aerospace persevere, but countless sub-contractors agreed to contribute components to the proposed British prototype.

In fact, of course, the BAe aeroplane could no longer be regarded as a prototype, but instead became an advanced technology demonstrator. Moreover it is worth remarking that the aircraft, ZF534, was flown by David Eagles on 8 August

ZF534 airborne with four Skyflash missiles and two ASRAAMs. (Photo: British Aerospace (Warton), Neg No AWCN44534)

1986 — only three months beyond the schedule agreed at a time when all three nations were planning to contribute a share in manufacture.

In configuration the EAP (Experimental Aircraft Programme) demonstrator is a canard, low-wing modified delta with compound-swept wing leading edge for high lift; the all-moving foreplane augments both pitch damping and manoeuvrability. In conjunction, the wing and foreplane provide an optimum overall aircraft instability to ensure maximum manoeuvrability while at the same time retaining the necessary pitch control. The wing carries full-span trailing-edge flaperons in four sections for roll and pitch control, and leading-edge flaps operate in conjunction with those at the trailing edge to optimise wing camber for the greatest possible manoeuvrability. The outer pair of flaperons are locked at high supersonic speeds.

The large 'chin' engine air intakes employ hinged lips to obviate the need for auxiliary intakes, and exactly match intake performance with engine requirements. A central vertical splitter plate divides the ducts to the two rear-mounted engines. To minimise supersonic wave drag, the fuselage is area-ruled.

In ZF534 power is provided by a pair of RB.199 Mark 104D turbofans, but without thrust reversal buckets. The aircraft's structure is far advanced beyond anything that has been achieved elsewhere in Europe, and at least matches in most respects that which has been produced in the USA; in some it is superior. Carbon-fibre reinforced plastics (CFRP) are widely used throughout, together with aluminium/lithium alloys. An interesting feature of the wing is that it has been designed aeroelastically so that, as the structure deforms under aerodynamic stresses, it does so in such a way as to impose minimum drag, this being achieved by very carefully reducing the number of CFRP laminates in the wing skin progressively towards the tip.

The aims of the EAP aircraft are primarily to demonstrate that a highly unstable aeroplane can achieve considerable agility by use of a full-authority fly-by-wire system employing canards, with a computer that is adequately flexible to allow 'control law optimisation'. All capabilities of modern performance and handling are demonstrated, including flight manoeuvres at high angles of attack at moderate speeds. In other

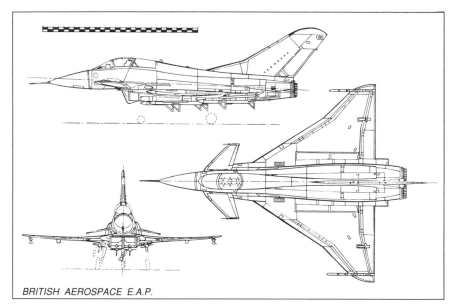

BRITISH AEROSPACE E.A.P.

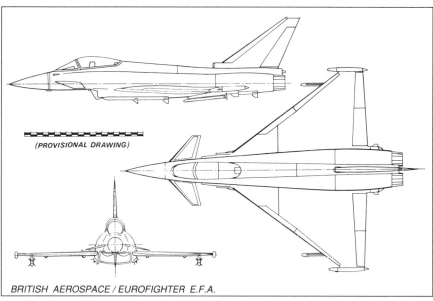

(PROVISIONAL DRAWING)

BRITISH AEROSPACE / EUROFIGHTER E.F.A.

Type: Twin-engine, single-seat semi-delta canard advanced-technology demonstrator (EAP) and high-performance, agile and STOL-capable fighter (EFA).

Manufacturers: EAP. British Aerospace (Military Aircraft) Ltd, Warton, Preston, Lancashire. EFA. Manufacturers' Management Company (currently termed Eurofighter) comprising: British Aerospace (Military Aircraft) Ltd, Warton, Preston, Lancashire, England; Messerschmitt-Bölkow-Blohm GmbH, Munich, Germany; Società Aerospaziale Italiana pA (Aeritalia), Turin, Italy; Construcciones Aeronauticas SA (CASA), Madrid, Spain.

Specification: EFA. European Staff Requirement—D (ESR-D).

Powerplant: EAP. Two 17,000lb-thrust (with reheat lit) Turbo-Union RB.199 Mk 104D turbofans. EFA. Two 20,200lb-thrust (with reheat lit) 'Eurojet' EJ200 turbofans.

Dimensions: EAP. Span, 38ft 7⅓in; length, 58ft 1½in (but varies with different instrumentation booms); height, 18ft 1¼in; wing area, 520 sq ft. EFP (provisional). Span, 34ft 5½in; length, 47ft 6¾in; wing area, 538.19 sq ft.

Weights: EAP. Tare, 22,050lb; all-up, 32,000lb. EFP (provisional). Tare, 21,500lb; all-up, 37,500lb.

Performance: EAP. Max speed 'in advance of Mach 2 at altitude'. EFA. Max speed 'greater than Mach 1.8' at altitude; combat radius, 290-350 miles.

Armament: EFA. Normal, four AMRAAMs and two ASRAAMs. One 27mm cannon. In ground strike rôle all current ASMs can be carried on total of seven storepoints. Provision for in-flight refuelling.

Prototypes: EAP, one demonstrator, ZF534 (first flown by David Eagles on 8 August 1986). EFA, six development batch aircraft ordered (probably as two British, two German, one Italian and one Spanish).

Pointer to the fighter's future? The EAP ZF534 shows off the configuration of the forthcoming EFA. (Photo: British Aerospace, Neg No CN44537)

respects ZF534 has been prepared to investigate and demonstrate optimum low-drag weapon (missile) installations, low radar and infra-red signatures, and not least to demonstrate the extensive use of advanced materials and manufacturing techniques that would be applicable in the event of a production run being ordered.

As stated above, ZF534 was flown in August 1986, and during its maiden flight was accelerated in level flight to supersonic speed, Eagles reaching Mach 1.1 at 30,000 feet, and performing general handling manœuvres, including Dutch rolls. Within a week the aircraft had flown nine times.

Not surprisingly, British Aerospace kept up the flight programme tempo for, early in 1987, ESR-D was issued in its definitive form, and it was important that the success with which the EAP aircraft had demonstrated the feasibility of the proposed fighter in its finite form (known unimaginatively as the EFA, or European Fighter Aircraft) should be appreciated not only by the European Staff but by the Panavia partners, and the Spanish manufacturer, CASA, which would join the new consortium.

The new management company would operate in the same manner as, and in parallel with that of Panavia, being provisionally termed Eurofighter, as would a new powerplant company, known as Eurojet. On 23 November 1988 the

two main Development contracts were signed with these industrially-owned management companies, calling for seven development aircraft (the modern euphemism for prototypes), and a number of non-flying structures for test purposes, the development programme being costed at £5.5bn.

It is anticipated that the first EFA example will be flying in 1992. The first two aircraft will be powered by RB.199 turbofans, but thereafter the new EJ200 will be installed. This possesses such state-of-the-art features as wide-chord aerofoils, single-crystal turbine blades, convergent-divergent exhaust nozzle, and integral blade/disc assemblies. Thrust with afterburning will be of the order of 20,200 pounds.

The EAP has continued to provide design, performance and handling data for the EFA during the past five years, among the new features flown by the former being a large centreline dorsal airbrake in place of the twin rear brakes originally flown. As also demonstrated by the EAP, normal armament is expected to comprise four AMRAAMs and two ASRAAMs (but up to ten missiles when required). A single 27mm cannon will be mounted internally.

Production was to be undertaken according to the workshare agreed, with Britain and Germany each contributing 33 per cent, Italy 21 per cent and Spain 13 per cent. Britain's share of the airframe

would comprise manufacture of the entire nose and canards and much of the starboard mainplane. Production figures are still obviously highly speculative, but a working figure of 765 aircraft is the current aim.

In mid-1992, however, the German government announced its intention to withdraw from the EFA programme, stating that the cost burden incurred by the re-unification with the former East German state precluded further participation in expensive defence programmes. Such a unilateral withdrawal obviously increased the cost shares to be borne by Great Britain, Italy and Spain, not to mention the threat of widespread unemployment in the event of outright cancellation on this account. At the time this work went to press, efforts were being made, principally by Britain, to persuade the German government to reconsider its withdrawal, perhaps opting to pursue a reduced-cost version of the EFA by seeking a less sophisticated weapons system, avionics and armament. Such economies may well find favour with Spain and Italy, leaving Britain free to develop her own systems. Various other alternatives were mooted in Britain, it even being suggested that the Royal Air Force should re-equip with the American F-16 (an aircraft of 20-year-old technology, and one that the RAF evaluated and refused in the late-1970s).

APPENDIX. AIR MINISTRY SPECIFICATIONS

Frequent references are made in this work to 'Air Ministry Specifications' as being the administrative instruments by which the Services made known the design, performance and timescale parameter for future requirements. These documents have seldom constituted arbitrary 'wishful thinking', but have stemmed from logical reasoning based on the opinions distilled from a continuing process of knowledge acquired by specialist Service departments (not excluding military Intelligence), the research establishments and professional staffs in industry.

The manner by which 'Air Ministry Specifications' came to be prepared and issued has changed little in essence down the years although, as would be expected with the unremitting growth in the complexity of military aircraft and international conflict, the ultimate Requirement document increased from a single sheet of foolscap paper in 1915 to many hundreds of pages in numerous folders for aircraft such as the P1154 and TSR.2 of the 1960s.

Broadly speaking, the Specifications have come into being in two ways. On the one hand the Service itself, through a natural state of inevitable obsolescence in existing equipment, expresses a requirement for this equipment to be replaced. To do this the Specification must reflect the areas in which advances are required, be they in performance, heavier armament, greater strength, reduced vulnerability, improved access for servicing, or simply reflect the changing operational 'states of the art' prevailing. Sometimes these requirements have been overstated and have been impossible to satisfy and have resulted in compromise. On the other hand, instances of considerable ingenuity within the aircraft industry have resulted in the terms of the Specification being surpassed, thereby rendering the new requirement itself redundant. In many cases this had led to the original Specification being allowed to lapse or to be withdrawn, so that a replacement may be 'written around a manufacturer's tender' — to paraphrase

references which have appeared from time to time in this work. And this process, let it be said, has through private initiative and venture resulted in a galaxy of outstanding British aircraft down the years: names like Fury, Gladiator, Hurricane, Spitfire, Beaufighter and Mosquito, to name but a few.

Two Specifications are reproduced below as examples of fighter requirements being issued at the end of the biplane age and the beginning of the turbojet era.

F.18/37 was issued in 1937 to half a dozen likely manufacturers in a bid to attract design tenders for a replacement of the Hurricane and Spitfire, neither of which had then even entered service with the RAF. The successful aircraft design — if such it may be termed — was the Hawker Typhoon, an aircraft which failed to come up to expectations as an interceptor (and was overtaken by events) but which sired a family of excellent fighters and fighter-bombers eight years later and which were among the last piston-engine combat aircraft to serve with the Royal Air Force.

The other Specification proved to be elemental both in concept and outcome, for it set down the parameters for the first British jet-powered fighter, and one that established briefly for Britain world leadership in fighter design at the end of the Second World War. The Specification was speculative in the extreme and stemmed from the growing awareness in the Air Ministry of the real advances being achieved by British engineers in jet engine technology, led by Frank Whittle, and the likely development of a realistic jet-powered combat aeroplane by the one designer who expressed the degree of confidence in his ability to achieve this goal. That such an aeroplane came into being within a matter of two years from the issue of the Specification, and went on to serve long into obsolescence is both a tribute to British technological genius and a condemnation of ill-advised political interference that can frustrate that genius when dogma stifles logic.

SPECIFICATION F.18/37
High Speed Single Seat Fighter

I. GENERAL
1.   This Specification and the Appendix 'B' attached thereto detail particular requirements. Relevant general requirements are given in Specification DTD.1028 and it is essential that these shall be as completely fulfilled as the particular requirements of this Specification, except where they are obviously inapplicable to an aeroplane of this type.

II. OPERATIONAL REQUIREMENTS
2.   The main operational requirements are specified in Appendix 'B' to this Specification as amended by the errata issued with this Specification.
3.   Provision shall be made to fit alternative wings and/ or nose portions, carrying combinations of guns and ammunition other than those specified in the Appendix 'B': (eg. eight Browning guns each with 1,000 rounds of ammuntion). These alternatives, if required, will form the basis of a separate contract (or contracts).

4.   Provision is to be made for disposing of empty cartridges and links in such a way as to ensure that there is no danger of their jamming any mechanism or striking any part of the aircraft.
5.   Both the pilot's seat and the rudder bar shall be adjustable in flight, the former 4 inches vertically and the latter 3 inches horizontally.
6.   The height of the cockpit cover must be such as will give ample head room for all pilots and the gun sight must be so positioned in relation to the seat that tall pilots will not have to crouch in order to use it.
7.   The pilot's seat must be capable of taking a seat-type parachute.

III. DESIGN REQUIREMENTS
Mock-up
8.   The mock-up of the aeroplane shall be ready for

preliminary inspection within four months from the date of receipt of order.

Engine Installation

9.   The aeroplane shall be fitted with a British engine which shall have passed 100 hours service type test before delivery of the aeroplane and for which fuel to DTD.230, or a higher octane number, would be suitable. The contractor is to inform the Air Ministry of his selection directly it has been made.

(Note: Further requirements in connection with the engine installation will be found detailed in the Appendix 'B' and Specification DTD.1028)

Exhaust System

10.   A flame damping device shall be incorporated to reduce the illumination caused by exhaust flames to a minimum.

Fuel System

11.   The total fuel capacity shall be sufficient for the endurance called for in the Appendix 'B'.

Oil System

12.   The net capacity of the oil tank(s) shall be sufficient for an endurance, calculated at the maximum rates of consumption, or 2 hours more than that for which fuel is provided.

Fire Extinguisher

13.   The 'Graviner' or other approved type of extinguisher shall be fitted for hand and automatic operation at the engine position(s). It shall be removable for use as a hand extinguisher.

Camouflage Finish

14.   The aeroplane shall be 'camouflaged' if required, as instructions given by the DTD (RDA).

Controls

15.   The range of movement of the elevator, aileron and rudder control surfaces, and also the movement of any trimming devices associated with them, are to be limited by stops so that in no circumstances will the control surface jam or foul parts of the aeroplane. The stops to limit the range of movement of the elevator are to be adjustable on the prototype aeroplane. The range of movement is to be ascertained during the Contractor's stability trials and the stops are then to be locked so as to restrict the movement to that actually needed. These stops will be required to be fixed on the production aircraft at the positions thus determined.

Tail Parachute.

16.   Provision shall be made for fitting a tail parachute, for use during flight trials.

Undercarriage.

17.   The undercarriage wheel brake system shall be suitable for use under all Service conditions; eg, landing downhill on a sloping aerodrome should not cause overheating of the brake drums.

18.   If the undercarriage is made to retract precautions shall be taken to ensure that there is no change in compass deviation with the undercarriage in the 'up' or 'down' position.

Tail Wheel.

19.   The tail wheel and tyre shall be of the size approved for use at a load of 1.1 times the maximum possible tail wheel reaction when the aeroplane is at rest on the ground and fully loaded. The tyre pressure under such conditions should be not greater than 40 lb/sq in.

Anti-Icing Precautions.

20.   The aeroplane shall be designed so that an approved form of de-icing equipment can be readily fitted, but if the equipment is required its provision will be made the subject of separate contract instructions.

21.   An induction system freezing indicator shall be fitted with its indicating instrument on the pilot's instrument board.

Maintenance.

22.   The documents described in contracts circular letter No 22 shall be supplied.

Loads for Strength Requirements and Flight Trials.

23.   The total load to be carried by the aeroplane, for the purpose of the flight trials and to be assumed in the strength investigation shall comprise:-

    (i) The Military load specified hereunder, together with such removable non-standard parts as it will be necessary for the Contractor to supply and fit in order that this military load may be carried;

    (ii) The fuel, oil and (if necessary) cooling liquid for the specified endurance, plus the necessary allowances;

    (iii) The 'tare weight items' shown in column 10 of Appendix 'A'.

Military Load

Weights of Removable Standard Service Items only.

12 Browning guns	252.0 lb.
6,000 rounds of ammunition	375.0 lb.
Forced landing flares	36.0 lb.
First aid outfit	3.0 lb.
Oxygen	14.5 lb.
T.R. (X14 type)	63.0 lb.
Crews (pilot and parachute)	200.0 lb.
Total	943.5 lb.

Note: Ref. Appendix 'B' para. 11 (iii). The weight of the blind approach equipment will be approximately 50 lb.

Structural Strength.

24.   The strength of the aeroplane when flying at 1.1 times its all-up weight in the fullyloaded condition shall be not less than is defined by the ultimate factors stated hereunder:

    (1) Factor throughout the structure with the centre of pressure in its most forward position in normal flight   ..   10.0

(2) Factor through the structure with the centre of pressure in its most backward position in normal flight   ..   7.5

(3) Factor throughout the structure in a dive (i) to an assumed terminal velocity of 450 mph IAS with the aeroplane in the attitude corresponding to maximum tail load   2.0

or (ii) to the terminal velocity assuming the airscrew drag to be zero, if this speed is less than that quoted in (i) the aeroplane to be assumed in the attitude corresponding to maximum tail load   ..   2.0

(4) Factor for the wing structure at the angle of incidence corresponding to an inverted stall   5.0

(5) Factor under a down gust, normal to the flight path of 25 feet per second (indicated) when the aeroplane is flying (engine on) at normal top speed   ..   2.0

(6) Factor under a down gust, normal to the flight path of 25 feet per second (indicated) in an accelerated dive at 1.5 times maximum level speed with the aeroplane in the true terminal velocity attitude   ..   2.0

(7) (i) Factor throughout the structure when diving at constant IAS with flaps down along a flight path at 70 degrees to the horizontal and with zero airscrew drag   ..   2.0

(ii) Factor under up and down gusts of 25 feet per second normal to the flight path in the dive of (i) above   ..   1.5

Note: Item 7 is only applicable if provision is made for the use of flaps, or other spoilers in the dive.

25.   The design requirements of AP970, any corrigenda thereto and all current ADMs applicable to TV class aeroplanes are to be satisfied at 1.1 times the all-up weight in the fully loaded condition at the factors given for 'other than experimental aeroplanes'. The altitude referred to in paragraph on ADM.345 is to be taken as 15,000 feet. All gust cases are to be taken as 25 ft/sec *indicated* airspeed.

26.   The aeroplane at 1.1 times its all-up weight in the fully loaded condition shall be able to withstand an impact with the ground at a vertical velocity of 10 feet per second, and at this velocity the impact load on the undercarriage is not to exceed three times the weight of the aeroplane so loaded. Compliance with this requirement shall be demonstrated by means of approved dropping tests and for this purpose a representative shock absorber for the main undercarriage and for the nose or tail unit, each complete with wheel or tyre, are to be made available to DTD for test at Air Ministry expense unless the type has been previously tested to the satisfaction of the DTD. The required test is not expected to render the component unserviceable. The ulitmate factor for the undercarriage when subject to this impact load shall be not less than 1.33 and for

the remainder of the structure not less than 1.5. This difference between factors is always to be maintained whatever modifications may be made eventually in the design of the aeroplane.

27.   The ultimate factors at the weight previously stated when the aeroplane is at rest on the ground shall not be less than the following:-

For the undercarriage 4.0
For the remainder of the aeroplane   ..   4.5

28.   At the weight stated above the undercarriage is to comply with the special requirements given in the latest issue of ADM.371.

29.   For the stressing assumptions to be made in connection with three-wheeled undercarriages reference shall be made to Airworthiness Department, RAE.

30.   The ultimate factor for control surfaces and systems under tail-to-wing loads in accordance with AP.970 (May 1935 edition), chapter 3, paragraph 24, shall be 2.

IV. FLIGHT TESTS
31.   Prior to the delivery of the aircraft it shall have been certified to the DTD by the Contractor that:

(i) the aircraft has been subjected by the Contractor's pilot to the following tests:

1. General flying trials in accordance with Aircraft Design Memorandum No 291.
2. Diving tests in accordance with Aircraft Design Memorandum No 292.
3. Control and stability tests in accordance with Aircraft Design Memorandum No 293.
4. Spinning tests in accordance with Aircraft Design Memorandum No 294.
5. Acrobatic (*sic*) flying tests in accordance with Aircraft Design Memorandum No 295.

(ii)   The above mentioned tests have shown that the aircraft is safe to be flown by Royal Air Force pilots.

V. SPINNING TEST MODEL
32.   Immediatcly after the Mock-up Conference the design will be considered by the DTD from the point of view of spinning, and such features as are agreed to be necessary shall be incorporated in the design.

33.   In order that a model or models of the complete aeroplane may be constructed for test on its spinning characteristics and in conjunction with paragraph 32, the Contractor is to supply to the Chief Superintendent, Royal Aircraft Establisment (B.A. Dept) drawings in duplicate showing:

(1)   its general arrangement in front elevation, side elevation and plan;
(2)   its wing sections;
(3)   the distribution of its mass relative to each of the three principal axes;

(4)   the position of its centre of gravity.

The drawings shall be forwarded sufficiently early to enable the model to be made and tested at the RAE before the construction of the aeroplane is so far advanced that alteration to the fuselage and tail unit would be difficult. The Contractor shall forward with the above mentioned drawings a completed Aerodynamic Data Sheet, a proforma of which will be supplied to him by the DTD (RDA3) at or about the time when the contract is placed.

VI. CENTRE OF GRAVITY

34.   (Reference DTD.1028, paragraph 8).

The calculated co-ordinate normal to the datum line may be accepted, provided that the error in the calculated value of the co-ordinate parallel to the datum line is not greater than 2% of the mean chord when compared with its measured value.

APPENDIX 'B'

AIR STAFF REQUIREMENT FOR A HIGH SPEED SINGLE SEATER FIGHTER AIRCRAFT
Specification F.18/37

INTRODUCTION
1.   The Air Staff requires a high speed single seater fighter capable of operating in any part of the world, as a replacement for the Spitfire and Hurricane. The outstanding requirement is to obtain the greatest possible superiority over the contemporary bomber.

Density of fire from forward firing unsynchronized machine guns is required and the armament demanded in paragraph 6 is considered to be the minimum with which a satisfactory density can be obtained.

2.   There may be advantages to be obtained from a twin engine design, such as simplification of armament installation by mounting a proportion of the guns in the nose of the aeroplane, and elimination of torque; such a design would be acceptable provided the performance was superior to that which could be obtained from a single engine aeroplane.

3.   For reasons of economy, it is necessary to limit the all-up weight of aircraft built to this specification to 12,000lb.

4.   While the primary duty of this fighter is offensive action against enemy aircraft it would be a desirable feature when employed in conjunction with Army forces, if it were capable of attacking ground targets with machine gun fire. In order to obtain a suitable angle of attack for this purpose, without excessive increase in speed, it would probably be necessary to adopt some drag producing device such as spoiler flaps. This should be investigated and included in the design if it is possible without involving an appreciable loss in speed or increase in landing distance.

PERFORMANCE
5.   (a) *Speed.* The speed at 15,000 feet must not be less than 400 mph, and it is essential that the engine selected should be equipped with a two-speed supercharger so that speeds at altitudes below 15,000 feet may be as high as possible.

(b) *Endurance.* The normal fuel load is to be sufficient to provide 15 minutes' flying at maximum engine speed for take-off conditions (for climb, etc), plus 2 hours at the most economical cruising air speed at 15,000 feet (for patrol), plus 15 minutes at maximum engine speed for level flight at 15,000 feet (for attack). The permanent tankage is to be sufficient for this load plus 30%.

(c) *Service Ceiling.* The service ceiling is to be not less than 35,000 feet.

(d) *Take Off.* When taking off with the normal operational load, the aircraft must be capable of crossing a 50 foot obstacle within 600 yards.

(e) *Landing.* The aircraft must come to rest within 600 yards after crossing a 50 foot obstacle in conditions of still air.

Every opportunity presented by recent developments, such as the tricycle undercarriage, should be exploited in order to minimise the limitation on high speed imposed by this landing requirement.

ARMAMENT
6.   The armament required is not less than twelve Browning guns set to fire along the line of flight.

AMMUNITION
7.   Provision is to be made for 500 rounds of ammunition for each gun.

ARMOUR
8.   Protection for the pilot against armour piercing 0.303in ammunition at a range of 200 yards is required to cover a forward cone with an angle of 20 degrees to the thrust line of the aircraft. Armour for this protection must be designed so that plates damaged in action can be easily changed. Protection afforded by an engine may be considered as armour.

VIEW
9.   The pilot's view must be the best that can be obtained, consistent with high performance, and the view over the forward half of the upper hemisphere to an angle of not less that 5 degrees forwards and downwards over the nose must be unobstructed with the seat adjusted to the gun sighting position. For station keeping a backward view in the upper hemisphere, to an angle of 45 degrees on either quarter is desirable.

MANŒUVRABILITY
10.   Ease of sighting is the essential consideration for manœuvrability; the aeroplane must be a steady gun platform capable of being sighted and held on to its target up to maximum speed without difficulty.

EQUIPMENT
11.   The following equipment is to be incorporated in the aircraft:

(i)   R/T
(ii)   Full night flying equipment, including wing landing lamps.

(iii) Provision for the installation of blind approach equipment.

(iv) Station keeping lights.

(v) Two emergency landing flares, carried in two separate tubes and operated by the pilot.

(vi) Oxygen for the pilot sufficient for 3 hours.

SPECIAL FEATURES

12. (i) For refuelling, re-arming and 'turning round' the aeroplane, speed is of the utmost importance. The guns must be so mounted that access to them on the ground, which, in the case of wing guns should be from above, is quick and easy. Guns and ammunition boxes must be removable by means of quick release attachments.

(ii) *Gun heating.* Provision is to be made for heating the guns, preferably by using surplus heat from the engine. It is desirable that the temperature of the guns should not fall below zero degrees Centigrade. The heating should be controllable so that overheating under tropical conditions can be avoided.

(iii) Cockpit heating. Comfort of the pilot is important; the cockpit must be warm, draughtproof and weatherproof. Some method of articifial heating is required.

(iv) To obtain the R/T range required, it is essential that everything possible should be done to reduce noise within the cockpit to a minimum. Particular attention must therefore be paid to elimination of engine noise and sound proofing of the cockpit.

(v) Engine cooling must be satisfactory for tropical conditions; the cooling additional to that necessary for European conditions may be provided by an attachable system.

(vi) External electrical engine starting under the control of the pilot is required as the normal method of starting, but in addition a small accumulator is to be installed within the aeroplane for quick starting in an emergency. The capacity of this accumulator should be sufficient to provide a minimum of six starts under the lowest temperature conditions likely to be experienced in Europe.

(vii) Class 1.A protective treatment is required.

(viii) The tyre pressures are to be not more than 35 lb/sq in at maximum loading.

(ix) Careful consideration is to be given to providing adequate facilities for escape of the pilot by parachute during flight and in the event of the aeroplane overturning on the ground

---

SPECIFICATION F.9/40
Twin Engine Single Seat Fighter (Whittle Engine)

I. GENERAL

1. This Specification is issued to cover the design and construction of a twin-engine single-seat fighter to develop the application of jet propulsion to a Service aeroplane.

2. This Specification details particular requirements and relative general requirements are given in Specification No DTD 1028 (Issue 11), and these requirements shall be complied with where possible. The following clauses are specifically excepted:

15, 16(a), 16(b), 17, 18(f), 19(b), 19(c), 19(d) and 20.

II. OPERATIONAL REQUIREMENTS

3. The operational requirements are detailed in the Appendix B to this Specification.

III. DESIGN REQUIREMENTS

4. In this design it is considered of great importance that the structure should be kept as simple as possible, to reduce cost and facilitate manufacture.

Engine Installation.
5. The aircraft shall be designed to accommodate two Whittle Type W.2B Jet Propulsion Engines. The installation of the engines, controls, oil and fuel systems and connections to the cockpit heating system and any other ancillary equipment shall be carried out to the satisfaction of Power Jets Ltd.

Exhaust Jets.
6. The Contractor is to be responsible for the general design and construction of the exhaust jets and is to work in close contact with the engine Contractor. Attention is to be given to the effect of the high temperature of the jet on the surrounding structure.

Engine Instruments.
7. The following engine instruments are required:
Tachometer
Oil pressure gauge or indicator
Fuel pressure gauge
Fuel contents gauge.

8. Engine Protection. The engines are to be suitably protected against the ingress of solid bodies to the blower.

9. Engine Cooling. Provision shall be made for the satisfactory operation of the engine under temperate (English Summer) conditions.

10. Engine Starting. A reliable method of starting the engines shall be provided. The system of starting shall not be

dependent on external source of any kind.

11.   Engine Auxiliaries. Each engine will be fitted with a fuel pump, oil pump and tachometer drive. In addition a drive shall be provided on one engine for a 500 watt generator.

12.   *Power Supplies.*

The following systems of power supply shall be adopted:

(a)   Flaps, undercarriage and brakes. Hydraulic actuation by means of hand operated pump.

(b)   Cannon firing. Actuation from high pressure bottle.

(c)   Instrument panel. 'Reversed' instruments to be used, operated by compressed air supply bled from the engine.

Fuel System.

13.   The fuel tank capacity of 250 gallons shall be provided. The fuel system shall be such that the engines will not be starved of fuel if the aeroplane is inverted for 10 seconds.

14.   Consideration shall be given to the effect of boiling of the fuel owing to rapid climb to high altitude. If possible, some means should be incorporated to prevent the boiling of fuel, but otherwise the arrangement of the system and the fuel pump shall be such that an adequate supply of fuel to the engine shall be maintained, when air bubbles are forming in the tank or the fuel is actually boiling.

Pilot's Attitude.

15.   Two alternative positions shall be provided for the rudder pedals or alternatively vertically adjustable rudder pedals shall be provided in order that the pilot may take up the crouched attitude for air fighting. In such an attitude he must be able to use his gun sight effectively.

Miscellaneous Requirements.

16.   Protective Treatment. Class IA protective treatment is required with the proviso that such special protective treatment is as necessitated by the hot gases from the propelling jets is incorporated.

17.   Camouflage. The aircraft shall be camouflaged at A.D.1160 using the 'S' type finish.

18.   Fire Extinguisher. A Graviner or other approved type of fire extinguisher shall be installed in each engine bay. The extinguisher shall be suitable for automatic action by heat, by shock in any direction, or manual operation under the control of the pilot.

19.   Mock-up. The mock-up of the aeroplane shall be ready for preliminary inspection within three months from the date of receipt of the order.

20.   Tail parachute. A tail parachute is to be incorporated in the aircraft, and a spare parachute (ground equipment) is to be provided.

21.   Maintenance. The documents described in Contract circular letter No 22 shall be supplied.

22.   Anti-icing. Ice guards shall be provided in front of the air intake ducts.

IV. EQUIPMENT

Loads for Strength Requirements and Flight Trials

23.   The total load to be carried by the aeroplane for the purpose of flight trials and to be assumed in the strength investigation shall comprise:

(i)   The military load specified hereunder or equivalent weight in ballast together with such removable non-standard parts as it will be necessary for the Contractor to supply and fit in order that this military load may be carried.

(ii)   The fuel specified in paragraph 13 together with the appropriate quantity of oil for the endurance, plus the necessary allowances.

(iii)   The 'Tare weight items' shown in column 10 of the Appendix 'A'.

MILITARY LOAD

Weights of Removable Standard Service Items and Crew only

4	20mm Guns and Accessories	436.0 lb
600	Rounds of Ammunition	360.0 lb
	Gun sight	5.0 lb
	Camera Gun G.45	7.0 lb
1	Flare (Forced landing)	18.0 lb
6	Cartridges for Recognition Device	2.0 lb
2	Oxygen cylinders (for 3 hours)	29.0 lb
	First Ait Outfit	3.0 lb
	Signals TR.1133	79.5 lb
	Signals R.3003	24.0 lb
1	Crew	200.0 lb
		1,163.5 lb

24.   For the purpose of performance and endurance trials the aircraft shall be equipped with the following instruments:

(i)   Fuel flowmeter.

(ii)   Exhaust jet pyrometers and static pressure gauges.

(iii)   Engine compartment thermometers and pressure gauges.

(iv)   Compressor delivery thermometer and pressure gauges.

(v)   External air thermometer.

(vi)   Air temperature thermometers Mark II in such gun bays as are required by the A & AEE.

V. STRUCTURAL STRENGTH

In Flight.

25.   The strength of the aircraft when flying at 1.1 times its maximum all-up weight shall not be less than the following standards:

(i)   The structure shall have an ultimate factor of not less than 2 under any normal acceleration between 0 and +5g inclusive for the full range of speed up to 500 mph IAS. This case shall be complied with without reference to compressibility effects.

(ii)   The structure shall have an ultimate factor of not less than 2 under any normal acceleration between 0 and +5g at a true speed of 600 mph at 30,000ft. In this case the effects of compressibility as agreed with the RAE shall be included.

(iii)   The strength requirements for the fin and rudder shall be in accordance with ADM.367 (Issue III), but the maximum indicated airspeed at 13,000ft may be taken as the design speed.

(iv)   The gust requirements of AP.970, Chapter II paragraph 9 shall be satisfied at 500 mph IAS.

(v)   The requirements of AP. 970 and current ADMs.

Landing and Take-off.
26.   The design requirements for the tricycle undercarriage shall be subject to agreement with the Aircraft Development Department, RAE. The vertical velocity of descent for energy absorption shall be 12 ft/sec, and the weight to be assumed for shock absorption and strength calculations shall be 1.1 times the all-up weight.

27.   Compliance with the requirements agreed with the Aircraft Development Department shall be demonstrated by means of approved drop tests. For this purpose the Contractor is required to supply a shock absorber unit complete with wheel and tyre from both the nose and main undercarriage. These tests will be the subject of an extra to contract or, if made at the RAE will be at the Air Ministry expense. The components are not expected to be damaged in the tests and if serviceable will be available for subsequent incorporation in the aircraft.

28.   Consideration should be given to the design of the wheel brakes to ensure that a short ground run may be achieved without causing heating to an extent which would damage the tube or cover.

VI. WIND TUNNEL TESTS

29.   General. The Contractor will be required to supply a complete model of the aircraft to the RAE for wind tunnel tests. The intake ducts are to be included in the model. The construction of the model shall be the subject of discussion between the Contractor and the RAE.

30.   Spinning. In order that a model or models of the complete aeroplane may, if required, be constructed for test of its spinning characteristics, the contractor is to supply to the Chief Superintendent, RAE, (BA.Dept) drawings (in duplicate) showing:

1.   Its general arrangement in front elevation, side elevation and plan;
2.   Its wing sections;
3.   The distribution of its mass relative to each of the three principal axes;
4.   The position of its centre of gravity.

The drawings shall be forwarded sufficiently early to enable the model to be made and tested at the RAE before the construction of the aeroplane is so far advanced that alteration to the fuselage and tail unit would be difficult. The Contractor shall forward with the above mentioned drawings a completed Aerodynamic Data Sheet, a pro-forma of which will be supplied to him by the DTD (RDT.1) at or about the time the contract is placed.

VII. FLIGHT TESTS

31.   Prior to the delivery of the aircraft it shall have been certified to the DTD by the Contractor that:

(i)   The aeroplane has been subjected by the Company's pilot to the general flying tests in accordance with Aircraft Design Memorandum No 291 at its maximum all-up weight together with such additional tests as are deemed necessary by the DTD.

(ii)   The conditions for the spinning tests shall be as follows (these requirements replacing those under ADM.294 Issue I):

(a)   It is undesirable that spinning should result from the tests of ADM.293 and in addition the following tests shall be made with loading C, E and G of ADM.291. The aeroplane shall be trimmed to glide at 1.2 times the stalling speed and shall then be stalled, the control column pulled right back and full rudder applied.

(b)   If the aeroplane does not spin in any of the tests of ADM.291, nor in the test of (a) above, no further attempts at spinning are required.

(c)   If the aeroplane does spin in any of these tests, its ability to recover shall be checked after two turns with full rudder held in the direction of the spin before recovery is attempted. This is to be checked for each condition of load and direction of spin. Any method of recovery is acceptable and sufficient tests are to be made to determine the best use of controls and the best setting of fore and aft trim for recovery.

(iii)   The above mentioned tests have shown that the aeroplane is safe to be flown by RAF pilots.

APPENDIX 'B' TO SPECIFICATION F.9/40

Operational Requirements

1.   The DTD requires the development of a single-seat fighter utilising the Whittle system of jet propulsion. The salient advantage of this system of propulsion is the possibility of speeds particularly at high altitudes which it would not be possible to obtain by the orthodox arrangement of engine and airscrew.

2.   To make full use of the possibilities available a small aeroplane is essential. It is vital for the success of the project that every item of Service equipment which is not absolutely essential shall be eliminated.

PERFORMANCE

3.   *Speed.* The maximum speed at 30,000 feet shall be not less than 430 mph.

4.   *Take-off.* When taking off from a grass surface with full fuel and military load the aircraft shall be capable of crossing a 50ft screen within a distance of 600 yards in still air.

5.   *Landing.* The aircraft shall be capable of coming to rest in not more than 700 yards after crossing a 50ft screen in still air conditions, with full fuel and military load.

ARMAMENT

6.   Guns. Provision shall be made for six 20mm cannon guns each with 120 rounds. Only four will, however, be fitted normally and when four guns are fitted provision for 150 rounds per gun is required.

HARMONISATION OF GUNS

7.   (i)   The datum line for the gun mounting shall lie parallel to the line of flight of the aircraft when travelling at a true speed of 400 mph at 30,000 ft, a tolerance of $\frac{1}{4}$ degree being permitted on the position of the datum line.

        (ii)   Adjustment exclusive of manufacturing tolerances shall be provided for each gun to allow a movement of $\frac{1}{2}$ degree in all directions around the datum line.

8.   Sights. The installation of a GM.2 reflector gun sight is required, and provision for the prismatic gun sight as an alternative item.

9.   Camera Gun. The installation of G.42b or G.45 cine gun, as alternative, is required at the same time as the cannon guns, and the cine gun must be capable of being aligned over the same ranges of adjustment as the guns.

PROTECTION

10.   *Pilot.* Protection is required for the pilot against 0.303in armour piercing ammunition fired from ahead or astern at 200 yards range, from any angle up to 20 degrees from the aircraft's centre line. A bullet proof windscreen is to be included in the pilot's protection.

11.   *Ammunition.* Protection is required for the ammunition against fire from ahead in the same conditions as for the pilot.

12.   *Fuel Tanks.* The fuel tanks shall be protected by an approved form of self sealing covering.

HEATING AND VENTILATION

13.   Adequate heating and ventilation is required in the cabin and every precaution should be taken to exclude draughts. Wood or plastics should be considered for use where control points come into contact with the pilot's hands and feet.

ANGLE OF GLIDE

14.   In a normal approach for landing, the axis of the fuselage should not be at a large angle to the flight path.

EQUIPMENT

15.   *Flying.* Full night flying equipment. Station keeping lights.

16.   *Navigation.* Suitable stowage for maps.

17.   *Signals.*   (i)   TR.1133
               (ii)   R.3003
               (iii)   Provision for R.1124/1125.

18.   *Pyrotechnics.* Automatic recognition device and six cartridges.

19.   *Crew Equipment.*
               (i)   Oxygen for the pilot for an endurance of 3 hours at 30,000 ft.
               (ii)   First aid outfit.

20.   *Aircraft Equipment*
               (i)   Holding down points for picketing.
               (ii)   A rapid system of starting the turbines other than the use of external batteries.

SPECIAL FEATURES

21.   *Gun Heating.* Provision is to be made for heating of the guns. It is desirable that the temperature of the gun should not fall below zero degrees Centigrade.

GLOSSARY OF ABBREVIATIONS AND ACRONYMS

AACU	Anti-Aircraft Co-operation Unit
A&AEE	Aeroplane & Armament Experimental Establishment
AAM	Air-to-Air Missile
AB	Air Board (at Air Ministry)
ACA	Agile Combat Aircraft
ACT	Active Control Technology
AD	Air Department (at Admiralty)
ADGB	Air Defence of Great Britain
A.E.	Armoured (or Armed) Experimental
AES	Aeroplane Experimental Station
AEW	Airborne Early Warning
AFC	Air Force Cross; Australian Flying Corps
AFDU	Air Fighting Development Unit
AI	Airborne Interception (radar)
AID	Aircraft Inspection Department
AM	Albert Medal
AMRAAM	Advanced Medium Range Air-to-Air Missile
AOC	Air Officer Commanding
AOCinC	Air Officer Commanding-in-Chief
APC	Armament Practice Camp
ASM	Air-to-Surface Missile
AShM	Air-to-Ship Missile
ASR	Air Staff Requirement
AST	Air Staff Target
ATS	Armament Training Station
AWA	Sir W.G. Armstrong Whitworth Aircraft Co Ltd
BAC	British Aircraft Corporation
BAe	British Aerospace
BAT	British Aerial Transport Co Ltd
B.E.	Blériot Experimental
BHP	Beardmore-Halford-Pullinger
B.S.	Blériot Scout
BVR	Beyond Visual Range
CA	Controller (Air)
CAS	Chief of the Air Staff
CFE	Central Fighter Establishment
CFRP	Carbon-Fibre Reinforced Plastics
CFS	Central Flying School
CGM	Conspicuous Gallantry Medal
COW	Coventry Ordnance Works
DB	Development Batch
DC	Dual Control
DCMU	Digital Colour Map Unit
DECU	Digital Engine Control Unit
DFC	Distinguished Flying Cross
DFM	Distinguished Flying Medal
D.H.	de Havilland Aircraft Co Ltd
D of R	Directorate of Research
DSC	Distinguished Service Cross
DSM	Distinguished Service Medal
DSO	Distinguished Service Order
DTD	Directorate of Technical Development
EAP	Experimental Aircraft Programme
ECM	Electronic Countermeasures
EFA	European Fighter Aircraft
E.F.B.	Experimental Fighting Biplane
ESR	European Staff Requirement
FA	Fighting Area
FAA	Fleet Air Arm
F(AW)	Fighter (All Weather)
FB	Fighting Biplane; Fighter Bomber
F.E.	Farman Experimental
FGA	Fighter Ground Attack
FLIR	Forward Looking Infrared
FR	Fighter Reconnaissance
FRS	Fighter Reconnaissance Strike
FTS	Flying Training School
GC	George Cross
GM	George Medal
GOR	General Operational Requirement
GR	General Reconnaissance
HD	Home Defence
HMA	His Majesty's Airship
HOTAS	Hands on Throttle and Stick
HP	Handley Page Ltd.
HUD	Head-up Display
HSA	Hawker Siddeley Aviation Ltd
IA	Inland Area
IDS	Interdiction Strike
IR	Infra red
ITDF	Intensive Trials Development Flight
JTIDS	Joint Tactical Information Distribution System
LABS	Low Altitude Bombing System
LIDS	Lift Improvement Devices
LRMTS	Laser Ranging and Marked Target Seeker
L.R.T.Tr.	(Probably) Long-Range Tractor Triplane
MAEE	Marine Aircraft Experimental Establishment
MAP	Ministry of Aircraft Production
MC	Military Cross
MLU	Mid-Life Update
MM	Military Medal
MoD	Ministry of Defence
MoS	Ministry of Supply
MRCA	Multi-Rôle Combat Aircraft
MU	Maintenance Unit
NBMR	NATO Basic Military Requirement
N.E.	Night Experimental
NF	Night Fighter
NFF	Night Fighter Flight
OCU	Operational Conversion Unit
OR	Operational Requirement
PCB	Plenum Chamber Burning
PV	Private Venture; Port Victoria
QRA	Quick Reaction Alert
RAAF	Royal Australian Air Force
RAE	Royal Aircraft (or Aerospace) Establishment
RAF	Royal Aircraft Factory (pre-April 1918); Royal Air Force (post-April 1918)
RAN	Royal Australian Navy
RCAF	Royal Canadian Air Force
RCN	Royal Canadian Navy
RDF	Radio Direction Finding
R.E.	Reconnaissance Experimental
RFC	Royal Flying Corps
RNAS	Royal Naval Air Service
RNZAF	Royal New Zealand Air Force
RWR	Radar Warning Receiver
SAAF	South African Air Force
SAOEU	Strike Attack Operational Evaluation Unit
SBAC	Society of British Aircraft (Aerospace) Constructors
SD	Special Duties
S.E.	Scout Experimental
SF	Station Flight
SOC	Struck Off Charge
SRAAM	Short-Range Air-to-Air Missile
SSA	Single-Seat Armoured
STOVL	Short Take-off and Vertical Landing
TF	Torpedo Fighter
TI	Trial Installation
TTA	Twin-Tractor Aircraft
TWU	Tactical Weapons Unit
VC	Victoria Cross
V/STOL	Vertical/Short Take-Off and Landing
VT	Vectored Thrust

INDEX

Principal aircraft entries are shown as bold numerals. In the interests of space the RAF
Stations listed on Pages 141 and 334–336 have been omitted from this Index.